——THE——
COMPLETE WORKS OF
WILLIAM SHAKESPEARE
—— VOLUME I ——

A NOTE TO THE READER

For each work in this set the editors have provided supplementary material that will help the reader better understand the work as both a play to be performed and a literary work.

In his general Foreword, Joseph Papp brings Shakespeare alive as he has for the audiences at his productions. The reader is also acquainted with the theater in which the plays were originally performed.

More detailed information precedes the text of each work: an Introduction places the work in context and discusses its structure and action, and performance notes give a director's view of the problems presented by the characters and themes of each work as interpreted in previous productions.

Each work is followed by a brief record of what is known about the original publication and performance and an attempt to date them; textual departures from the copy text; and an extensive essay on Shakespeare's sources. There are also suggestions for further reading on each work.

THE COMPLETE WORKS OF WILLIAM SHAKESPEARE

VOLUME I

LOVE'S LABOR'S LOST

THE COMEDY OF ERRORS

THE TWO GENTLEMEN OF VERONA

HENRY VI

PART ONE
PART TWO
PART THREE

RICHARD III

BANTAM BOOKS
Toronto · New York · London · Sydney · Auckland

THIS EDITION CREATED BY
QUALITY PAPERBACK BOOK CLUB

A Bantam Book / published by arrangement
with Scott, Foresman and Company

PRINTING HISTORY

Scott, Foresman edition published/January 1980
Bantam edition, with newly edited text and substantially
revised, edited, and amplified notes, introductions, and
other materials, published/February 1988
Valuable advice on staging matters has been
provided by Richard Hosley.
Collations checked by Eric Rasmussen.
Additional editorial assistance by Claire McEachern

Cover and display type designed by Charlotte Staub.

Bantam Books are published by Bantam Books,
a division of Bantam Doubleday Dell Publishing Group, Inc.
Its trademark, consisting of the words "Bantam Books"
and the portrayal of a rooster, is Registered in U.S. Patent
and Trademark Office and in other countries. Marca Registrada.
Bantam Books, 666 Fifth Avenue, New York, NY 10103.
Printed in the United States of America.

BOMC offers recordings and compact discs, cassettes
and records. For information and catalog write to
BOMR, Camp Hill, PA 17012.

Foreword

It's hard to imagine, but Shakespeare wrote all of his plays with a quill pen, a goose feather whose hard end had to be sharpened frequently. How many times did he scrape the dull end to a point with his knife, dip it into the inkwell, and bring up, dripping wet, those wonderful words and ideas that are known all over the world?

In the age of word processors, typewriters, and ballpoint pens, we have almost forgotten the meaning of the word "blot." Yet when I went to school, in the 1930s, my classmates and I knew all too well what an inkblot from the metal-tipped pens we used would do to a nice clean page of a test paper, and we groaned whenever a splotch fell across the sheet. Most of us finished the school day with ink-stained fingers; those who were less careful also went home with ink-stained shirts, which were almost impossible to get clean.

When I think about how long it took me to write the simplest composition with a metal-tipped pen and ink, I can only marvel at how many plays Shakespeare scratched out with his goose-feather quill pen, year after year. Imagine him walking down one of the narrow cobblestoned streets of London, or perhaps drinking a pint of beer in his local alehouse. Suddenly his mind catches fire with an idea, or a sentence, or a previously elusive phrase. He is burning with impatience to write it down—but because he doesn't have a ballpoint pen or even a pencil in his pocket, he has to keep the idea in his head until he can get to his quill and parchment.

He rushes back to his lodgings on Silver Street, ignoring the vendors hawking brooms, the coaches clattering by, the piteous wails of beggars and prisoners. Bounding up the stairs, he snatches his quill and starts to write furiously, not even bothering to light a candle against the dusk. "To be, or not to be," he scrawls, "that is the—." But the quill point has gone dull, the letters have fattened out illegibly, and in the middle of writing one of the most famous passages in the history of dramatic literature, Shakespeare has to stop to sharpen his pen.

Taking a deep breath, he lights a candle now that it's dark, sits down, and begins again. By the time the candle has burned out and the noisy apprentices of his French Huguenot landlord have quieted down, Shakespeare has finished Act 3 of *Hamlet* with scarcely a blot.

Early the next morning, he hurries through the fog of a London summer morning to the rooms of his colleague Richard Burbage, the actor for whom the role of Hamlet is being written. He finds Burbage asleep and snoring loudly, sprawled across his straw mattress. Not only had the actor performed in *Henry V* the previous afternoon, but he had then gone out carousing all night with some friends who had come to the performance.

Shakespeare shakes his friend awake, until, bleary-eyed, Burbage sits up in his bed. "Dammit, Will," he grumbles, "can't you let an honest man sleep?" But the playwright, his eyes shining and the words tumbling out of his mouth, says, "Shut up and listen—tell me what you think of *this*!"

He begins to read to the still half-asleep Burbage, pacing around the room as he speaks. ". . . Whether 'tis nobler in the mind to suffer the slings and arrows of outrageous fortune—"

Burbage interrupts, suddenly wide awake, "That's excellent, very good, 'the slings and arrows of outrageous fortune,' yes, I think it will work quite well. . . ." He takes the parchment from Shakespeare and murmurs the lines to himself, slowly at first but with growing excitement.

The sun is just coming up, and the words of one of Shakespeare's most famous soliloquies are being uttered for the first time by the first actor ever to bring Hamlet to life. It must have been an exhilarating moment.

Shakespeare wrote most of his plays to be performed live by the actor Richard Burbage and the rest of the Lord Chamberlain's men (later the King's men). Today, however, our first encounter with the plays is usually in the form of the printed word. And there is no question that reading Shakespeare for the first time isn't easy. His plays aren't comic books or magazines or the dime-store detective novels I read when I was young. A lot of his sentences are complex. Many of his words are no longer used in our everyday speech. His profound thoughts are often condensed into poetry, which is not as straightforward as prose.

Yet when you hear the words spoken aloud, a lot of the language may strike you as unexpectedly modern. For Shakespeare's plays, like any dramatic work, weren't really meant to be read; they were meant to be spoken, seen, and performed. It's amazing how lines that are so troublesome in print can flow so naturally and easily when spoken.

I think it was precisely this music that first fascinated me. When I was growing up, Shakespeare was a stranger to me. I had no particular interest in him, for I was from a different cultural tradition. It never occurred to me that his plays might be more than just something to "get through" in school, like science or math or the physical education requirement we had to fulfill. My passions then were movies, radio, and vaudeville—certainly not Elizabethan drama.

I was, however, fascinated by words and language. Because I grew up in a home where Yiddish was spoken, and English was only a second language, I was acutely sensitive to the musical sounds of different languages and had an ear for lilt and cadence and rhythm in the spoken word. And so I loved reciting poems and speeches even as a very young child. In first grade I learned lots of short nature verses— "Who has seen the wind?," one of them began. My first foray into drama was playing the role of Scrooge in Charles Dickens's *A Christmas Carol* when I was eight years old. I liked summoning all the scorn and coldness I possessed and putting them into the words, "Bah, humbug!"

From there I moved on to longer and more famous poems and other works by writers of the 1930s. Then, in junior high school, I made my first acquaintance with Shakespeare through his play *Julius Caesar*. Our teacher, Miss McKay, assigned the class a passage to memorize from the opening scene of the play, the one that begins "Wherefore rejoice? What conquest brings he home?" The passage seemed so wonderfully theatrical and alive to me, and the experience of memorizing and reciting it was so much fun, that I went on to memorize another speech from the play on my own.

I chose Mark Antony's address to the crowd in Act 3,

scene 2, which struck me then as incredibly high drama. Even today, when I speak the words, I feel the same thrill I did that first time. There is the strong and athletic Antony descending from the raised pulpit where he has been speaking, right into the midst of a crowded Roman square. Holding the torn and bloody cloak of the murdered Julius Caesar in his hand, he begins to speak to the people of Rome:

> If you have tears, prepare to shed them now.
> You all do know this mantle. I remember
> The first time ever Caesar put it on;
> 'Twas on a summer's evening in his tent,
> That day he overcame the Nervii.
> Look, in this place ran Cassius' dagger through.
> See what a rent the envious Casca made.
> Through this the well-belovèd Brutus stabbed,
> And as he plucked his cursèd steel away,
> Mark how the blood of Caesar followed it,
> As rushing out of doors to be resolved
> If Brutus so unkindly knocked or no;
> For Brutus, as you know, was Caesar's angel.
> Judge, O you gods, how dearly Caesar loved him!
> This was the most unkindest cut of all . . .

I'm not sure now that I even knew Shakespeare had written a lot of other plays, or that he was considered "timeless," "universal," or "classic"—but I knew a good speech when I heard one, and I found the splendid rhythms of Antony's rhetoric as exciting as anything I'd ever come across.

Fifty years later, I still feel that way. Hearing good actors speak Shakespeare gracefully and naturally is a wonderful experience, unlike any other I know. There's a satisfying fullness to the spoken word that the printed page just can't convey. This is why seeing the plays of Shakespeare performed live in a theater is the best way to appreciate them. If you can't do that, listening to sound recordings or watching film versions of the plays is the next best thing.

But if you do start with the printed word, use the play as a script. Be an actor yourself and say the lines out loud. Don't worry too much at first about words you don't immediately understand. Look them up in the footnotes or a dictionary, but don't spend too much time on this. It is more profitable (and fun) to get the sense of a passage and sing it out. Speak naturally, almost as if you were talking to a friend, but be sure to enunciate the words properly. You'll be surprised at how much you understand simply by speaking the speech "trippingly on the tongue," as Hamlet advises the Players.

You might start, as I once did, with a speech from *Julius Caesar*, in which the tribune (city official) Marullus scolds the commoners for transferring their loyalties so quickly from the defeated and murdered general Pompey to the newly victorious Julius Caesar:

> Wherefore rejoice? What conquest brings he home?
> What tributaries follow him to Rome
> To grace in captive bonds his chariot wheels?
> You blocks, you stones, you worse than senseless
>   things!
> O you hard hearts, you cruel men of Rome,
> Knew you not Pompey? Many a time and oft
> Have you climbed up to walls and battlements,
> To towers and windows, yea, to chimney tops,
> Your infants in your arms, and there have sat
> The livelong day, with patient expectation,
> To see great Pompey pass the streets of Rome.

With the exception of one or two words like "wherefore" (which means "why," not "where"), "tributaries" (which means "captives"), and "patient expectation" (which means patient waiting), the meaning and emotions of this speech can be easily understood.

From here you can go on to dialogues or other more challenging scenes. Although you may stumble over unaccustomed phrases or unfamiliar words at first, and even fall flat when you're crossing some particularly rocky passages, pick yourself up and stay with it. Remember that it takes time to feel at home with anything new. Soon you'll come to recognize Shakespeare's unique sense of humor and way of saying things as easily as you recognize a friend's laughter.

And then it will just be a matter of choosing which one of Shakespeare's plays you want to tackle next. As a true fan of his, you'll find that you're constantly learning from his plays. It's a journey of discovery that you can continue for the rest of your life. For no matter how many times you read or see a particular play, there will always be something new there that you won't have noticed before.

Why do so many thousands of people get hooked on Shakespeare and develop a habit that lasts a lifetime? What can he really say to us today, in a world filled with inventions and problems he never could have imagined? And how do you get past his special language and difficult sentence structure to understand him?

The best way to answer these questions is to go see a live production. You might not know much about Shakespeare, or much about the theater, but when you watch actors performing one of his plays on the stage, it will soon become clear to you why people get so excited about a playwright who lived hundreds of years ago.

For the story—what's happening in the play—is the most accessible part of Shakespeare. In *A Midsummer Night's Dream*, for example, you can immediately understand the situation: a girl is chasing a guy who's chasing a girl who's chasing another guy. No wonder *A Midsummer Night's Dream* is one of the most popular of Shakespeare's plays: it's about one of the world's most popular pastimes— falling in love.

But the course of true love never did run smooth, as the young suitor Lysander says. Often in Shakespeare's comedies the girl whom the guy loves doesn't love him back, or she loves him but he loves someone else. In *The Two Gentlemen of Verona*, Julia loves Proteus, Proteus loves Sylvia, and Sylvia loves Valentine, who is Proteus's best friend. In the end, of course, true love prevails, but not without lots of complications along the way.

For in all of his plays—comedies, histories, and tragedies—Shakespeare is showing you human nature. His characters act and react in the most extraordinary ways—and sometimes in the most incomprehensible ways. People are always trying to find motivations for what a character does. They ask, "Why does Iago want to destroy Othello?"

The answer, to me, is very simple—because that's the way Iago is. That's just his nature. Shakespeare doesn't explain his characters; he sets them in motion—and away they go. He doesn't worry about whether they're likable or not. He's interested in interesting people, and his most fascinating characters are those who are unpredictable. If you lean back in your chair early on in one of his plays, thinking you've figured out what Iago or Shylock (in *The Merchant of Venice*) is up to, don't be too sure—because that great judge of human nature, Shakespeare, will surprise you every time.

He is just as wily in the way he structures a play. In *Macbeth*, a comic scene is suddenly introduced just after the bloodiest and most treacherous slaughter imaginable, of a guest and king by his host and subject, when in comes a drunk porter who has to go to the bathroom. Shakespeare is tickling your emotions by bringing a stand-up comic on-stage right on the heels of a savage murder.

It has taken me thirty years to understand even some of these things, and so I'm not suggesting that Shakespeare is immediately understandable. I've gotten to know him not through theory but through practice, the practice of the *living* Shakespeare—the playwright of the theater.

Of course the plays are a great achievement of dramatic literature, and they should be studied and analyzed in schools and universities. But you must always remember, when reading all the words *about* the playwright and his plays, that *Shakespeare's* words came first and that in the end there is nothing greater than a single actor on the stage speaking the lines of Shakespeare.

Everything important that I know about Shakespeare comes from the practical business of producing and directing his plays in the theater. The task of classifying, criticizing, and editing Shakespeare's printed works I happily leave to others. For me, his plays really do live on the stage, not on the page. That is what he wrote them for and that is how they are best appreciated.

Although Shakespeare lived and wrote hundreds of years ago, his name rolls off my tongue as if he were my brother. As a producer and director, I feel that there is a professional relationship between us that spans the centuries. As a human being, I feel that Shakespeare has enriched my understanding of life immeasurably. I hope you'll let him do the same for you.

Joseph Papp

Joseph Papp gratefully acknowledges the help of Elizabeth Kirkland in preparing this Foreword.

The Playhouse

This early copy of a drawing by Johannes de Witt of the Swan Theatre in London (c. 1596), made by his friend Arend van Buchell, is the only surviving contemporary sketch of the interior of a public theater in the 1590s.

From other contemporary evidence, including the stage directions and dialogue of Elizabethan plays, we can surmise that the various public theaters where Shakespeare's plays were produced (the Theatre, the Curtain, the Globe) resembled the Swan in many important particulars, though there must have been some variations as well. The public playhouses were essentially round, or polygonal, and open to the sky, forming an acting arena approximately 70 feet in diameter; they did not have a large curtain with which to open and close a scene, such as we see today in opera and some traditional theater. A platform measuring approximately 43 feet across and 27 feet deep, referred to in the de Witt drawing as the *proscaenium*, projected into the yard, *planities sive arena*. The roof, *tectum*, above the stage and supported by two pillars, could contain machinery for ascents and descents, as were required in several of Shakespeare's late plays. Above this roof was a hut, shown in the drawing with a flag flying atop it and a trumpeter at its door announcing the performance of a play. The underside of the stage roof, called the heavens, was usually richly decorated with symbolic figures of the sun, the moon, and the constellations. The platform stage stood at a height of 5½ feet or so above the yard, providing room under the stage for underworldly effects. A trapdoor, which is not visible in this drawing, gave access to the space below.

The structure at the back of the platform (labeled *mimorum aedes*), known as the tiring-house because it was the actors' attiring (dressing) space, featured at least two doors, as shown here. Some theaters seem to have also had a discovery space, or curtained recessed alcove, perhaps between the two doors—in which Falstaff could have hidden from the sheriff (*1 Henry IV*, 2.4) or Polonius could have eavesdropped on Hamlet and his mother (*Hamlet*, 3.4). This discovery space probably gave the actors a means of access to and from the tiring-house. Curtains may also have been hung in front of the stage doors on occasion. The de Witt drawing shows a gallery above the doors that extends across the back and evidently contains spectators. On occasions when action "above" demanded the use of this space, as when Juliet appears at her "window" (*Romeo and Juliet*, 2.2 and 3.5), the gallery seems to have been used by the actors, but large scenes there were impractical.

The three-tiered auditorium is perhaps best described by Thomas Platter, a visitor to London in 1599 who saw on that occasion Shakespeare's *Julius Caesar* performed at the Globe:

The playhouses are so constructed that they play on a raised platform, so that everyone has a good view. There are different galleries and places [*orchestra, sedilia, porticus*], however, where the seating is better and more comfortable and therefore more expensive. For whoever cares to stand below only pays one English penny, but if he wishes to sit, he enters by another door [*ingressus*] and pays another penny, while if he desires to sit in the most comfortable seats, which are cushioned, where he not only sees everything well but can also be seen, then he pays yet another English penny at another door. And during the performance food and drink are carried round the audience, so that for what one cares to pay one may also have refreshment.

Scenery was not used, though the theater building itself was handsome enough to invoke a feeling of order and hierarchy that lent itself to the splendor and pageantry onstage. Portable properties, such as thrones, stools, tables, and beds, could be carried or thrust on as needed. In the scene pictured here by de Witt, a lady on a bench, attended perhaps by her waiting-gentlewoman, receives the address of a male figure. If Shakespeare had written *Twelfth Night* by 1596 for performance at the Swan, we could imagine Malvolio appearing like this as he bows before the Countess Olivia and her gentlewoman, Maria.

Love's Labor's Lost, with Rae Allen (seated l.) as Rosaline, Tom Aldredge (c.) as Boyet, and Jane White as the Princess of France, directed by Gerald Freedman in 1965.

LOVE'S
LABOR'S LOST

LOVE'S LABOR'S LOST

Introductory Material
Foreword by Joseph Papp
Introduction
Love's Labor's Lost in
Performance

THE PLAY

Supplementary Material
Date and Text
Textual Notes
Shakespeare's Sources
Further Reading

Foreword

What I like most about *Love's Labor's Lost* is how much Shakespeare refers to his own art; the play sometimes seems to be just one big display of language. It's fascinating to watch Shakespeare exploring the very tools he uses as a playwright—word order, rhetorical devices, word combinations, foreign vocabulary, and much more. It's as if he wanted to see how high he could fly with his language just for the sheer fun of it. The pompous Spanish word-broker Don Armado expresses this well with his triumphant cry, "Devise, wit; write, pen; for I am for whole volumes in folio."

Shakespeare is very clever about his linguistic showing-off, however, and goes about it backhandedly, by making fun of it. And in mocking all the high-falutin' rhetoric and language, he is also showing what he can do with it. For example, the exchanges between the young ladies and the young men who are wooing them are sharp-tongued, pun-filled, and quick-witted. And yet the young men are nearly done in by their excesses in language, which one of them lists as "Taffeta phrases, silken terms precise, / Three-piled hyperboles, spruce affectation, / Figures pedantical."

But of all the characters in *Love's Labor's Lost*, the ones who use language in the most spectacularly affected way are the schoolteacher Holofernes and his sidekick, Sir Nathaniel the curate. These two, with the constable Dull for contrast, engage in conversations laden with actual Latin phrases and Latin-derived English words. They are obviously impressed with themselves and their educated use of the Latin tongue as they casually throw around literary references and use smart-sounding tags such as *"Satis quod sufficit"* instead of the plainer "Enough is enough."

Even if Shakespeare's audience didn't understand all the Latin words these characters were bandying about the stage (and you can be sure that modern audiences understand even fewer), they would still have found Holofernes and company hilariously funny, and even have warmed to them. For they are completely ridiculous figures. The low-life characters Mote and Costard make fun of them in whispered asides; Mote says, "They have been at a great feast of languages and stolen the scraps," and Costard whispers back, "O, they have lived long on the alms basket of words."

Throughout the play, Shakespeare shows himself perfectly capable of using the resources of Elizabethan language to their fullest. And yet he manages to keep it all in perspective, to let the lifeblood of humanity run through the play in the laughable but somehow endearing characters of the schoolteacher and his cronies. Shakespeare never loses sight of that human element, even in such a highly stylized play as *Love's Labor's Lost*.

Joseph Papp

Joseph Papp gratefully acknowledges the help of Elizabeth Kirkland in preparing this Foreword.

Introduction

In much the same way that *The Comedy of Errors* is Shakespeare's apprenticeship to Plautus and neoclassical comedy, *Love's Labor's Lost* is his apprenticeship to John Lyly's courtly drama of the 1580s, to the court masque, and to conventions of Petrarchan lyric poetry. The play is word conscious and stylistically mannered to an extent that is unusual even for the pun-loving Shakespeare. The humor abounds in the pert repartee for which juvenile actors were especially fitted, and an extraordinarily high percentage of roles are assigned to boys: four women and a diminutive page (Mote) among seventeen named roles. The social setting is patrician and the entertainments aristocratic. In some ways, little seems to happen in *Love's Labor's Lost*. Fast-moving plot is replaced by a structure that includes a series of debates on courtly topics reminiscent of John Lyly: love versus honor, the flesh versus the spirit, pleasure versus instruction, art versus nature. The songs and sonnets composed by the courtiers for the ladies (4.3.23–116) gracefully caricature the excesses of the Petrarchan love convention (named for the influential Italian sonneteer, Francesco Petrarch): the lovers are "sick to death" with unrequited passion, they catalogue the charms of their proud mistresses, they express their exquisitely tortured emotions through elaborate poetical metaphors, and so on. Stage movements are often masquelike; characters group themselves and then pair off two by two as in a formal dance. Actual masques and pageants, presented by the courtiers or devised for their amusement, are essential ingredients of the spectacle.

Yet beneath the brightly polished surfaces of this sophisticated comedy, we often catch glimpses of a candor and a simplicity that offset the tinsel and glitter. The wits ultimately disclaim (with some qualification) their wittiness, and the ladies confess they have tried too zealously to put down the men; both sides disavow the extreme postures they have striven so to maintain. The clowns, though deflated by mocking laughter for their naiveté and pomposity, deflate the courtiers in turn for lack of compassion. From this interplay among various forms of courtly wit, Petrarchism, pedantry, and rustic speech emerges a recommended style that is witty but not irresponsibly so, courtly yet sincere, polished and yet free of affectation or empty verbal ornament. This new harmony is aptly expressed by Berowne and Rosaline, whose witty quest for self-understanding in love foreshadows that of Benedick and Beatrice in *Much Ado about Nothing*. The perfect expression of the true style is found in the song at the end of the play; taking the form of a medieval literary debate between Spring and Winter, it beautifully fuses the natural and the artificial into a concordant vision transcending the mundane.

Like *The Comedy of Errors, Love's Labor's Lost* may either be a very early play or just an early play. It was published in quarto in 1598 "as it was presented before Her Highness this last Christmas" (1597). The text also purports to be "newly corrected and augmented," though we know of no earlier published version. Perhaps a play that was already several years old may have seemed in need of stylistic revision. Acts 4 and 5 do in fact contain two long duplicatory passages, suggesting that a certain amount of rewriting did take place. The revisions alter the meaning only slightly, however, and give little support to the widely held notion that Shakespeare must have reworked the ending of his play. The unresolved ending, in which no marriages take place and in which the Princess's territorial claims to Aquitaine are left unsettled, should be regarded not as unfinished but as highly imaginative and indeed indispensable. The title after all assures us that "love's labors" will be lost and the Princess affirms the principle of "form confounded."

Equally inconclusive are theories that the play was a topical satire written for a special audience, or that it was a comparatively late play of Shakespeare's "lyric" period, 1594–1595. Topical hypotheses arise from the quest for Shakespeare's sources. Since the plot of *Love's Labor's Lost* is derived from no known literary source, may it have been drawn instead from the Elizabethan contemporary scene, poking fun at the pretentiousness of literary figures and intellectuals, such as John Florio, Thomas Nashe, Gabriel Harvey, Sir Walter Ralegh, and George Chapman? Or should we seek topical meaning in the undoubted currency of such names as Navarre (Henry of Navarre, King Henry IV of France), Berowne (Biron, Henry IV's general), Dumaine (De Mayenne, brother of the Catholic Guise), and others? From the point of view of dating the play, however, such names would have been distastefully controversial in a courtly comedy after 1589. That date saw the beginning in France of a bitter civil conflict between the Catholic Guise and Protestant Navarre, continuing until Henry abjured Protestantism in 1593 and assumed the French throne. In the 1580s, on the other hand, the tiny kingdom of Navarre would have seemed charmingly appropriate as a setting for Shakespeare's play. Such an early date, although by no means certain, would also help explain the Lylyan tone of the comedy and its early techniques of versification: the high percentage of rhymed lines in couplets and quatrains, the end-stopped blank verse, the use of various sonnet forms and of seven-stress (septenary) couplets, and the like. Possibly, then, the play was first written in about 1588–1589 for a boys' company, and revised for Shakespeare's company in about 1596–1597.

The world of *Love's Labor's Lost*, as compared with that of most of Shakespeare's comedies, is not only uneventful but is remarkably unthreatened by danger or evil. The characters are menaced by nothing worse than themselves and stand to lose nothing more serious than their dignity. In such an artificial world, however, the preservation of one's self-esteem assumes undue importance. Using the criteria of wit and self-awareness, Mote and Boyet, as manipulators and controllers of point of view, show us how to laugh at folly in love and pomposity in language. They present to us variations on a theme of courtly behavior, creating in effect a scale of manners ranging from the most aristocratic (the King and the Princess, Berowne and Rosaline) to the most absurdly pretentious (Armado, Holofernes). Nearly all the characters are mocked, but those at the lower end of the scale are especially vulnerable because they are grossly unself-aware and hence unteachable.

The King and his companions deserve to be mocked because of their transparent lack of self-knowledge, their affectation, and the futility of their vows against love. As Berowne concedes from the start, such defiance of love is at odds with a fundamental natural rhythm that ultimately cannot be thwarted—a rhythm that provides a counterpoint and corrective to the frequently artificial rhythms of courtly life. This natural rhythm asserts itself throughout the play until it becomes starkly insistent in the death of the Princess's royal father and in the resulting twelve-month delay of all marriages.

Hypocritical defiance of love is doomed to comic failure and satirical punishment. The basic devices used to expose this hypocrisy are misdirected love letters and overheard speech, both devices of unmasking. Appropriately the young ladies administer their most amusing comeuppance to the men by seeing through their Muscovite masks. The code governing this merry conflict is one of "mock for mock," and "sport by sport o'erthrown" (5.2.140, 153). In a prevailing legal metaphor, the young men are guilty of perjury, of forswearing their written oaths, and must be punished accordingly. Love is metaphorically a war, a siege, a battle of the sexes in which the women come off virtually unscathed. The language of love is that of parry and thrust (with occasional bawdy overtones). The men naturally are chagrined to be put down by the ladies but are on their way to a cure: they laugh at their own pretentiousness and, even if hyperbolically, vow to cast aside all "affectation" and "maggot ostentation" in favor of "russet yeas and honest kersey noes" (ll. 403–416). At the same time Berowne's renunciation of artful language is cast in the form of a perfect fourteen-line sonnet; Shakespeare is having it both ways.

The clownish types are generally more victimized by their affectations. The fantastical Don Armado, as lover of Jaquenetta the country wench, apes the courtly conventions of the aristocrats to whose company he aspires. Enervated by base passion, penning wretched love letters, and worshiping a dairymaid as though she were an unapproachable goddess, he is a caricature of the Petrarchan lover. Generally, however, the affectations of the comic characters have to do with language rather than love. Armado himself is known as a phrase-maker, a "plume of feathers," a "weathercock": "Did you ever hear better?" (4.1.94–95). His letter to Jaquenetta, read aloud for the Princess's amusement, is an exquisite spoof of John Lyly's exaggeratedly mannered style called Euphuism: "Shall I command thy love? I may. Shall I enforce thy love? I could.

Shall I entreat thy love? I will. What shalt thou exchange for rags? Robes. For tittles? Titles. For thyself? Me" (ll. 80–83). Here we see the repeated antitheses, the balanced structure (reflected also in the structure of the play), and the alliterative effects that so intoxicated literary sophisticates of the 1580s. In a similar spirit, other comic types are distinguished by their verbal habits: Constable Dull by his malapropisms (anticipating Dogberry and Elbow), Holofernes by his Latinisms, his philological definitions, and his varied epithets, Nathaniel by his deference to Holofernes as a fellow bookman, Costard by his amiable but unlettered confusion over such grandiose terms as "remuneration" and "guerdon" (3.1.167–171). The word-conscious humor of the play gives us parodies of excruciatingly bad verse (as in Holofernes's "extemporal epitaph on the death of the deer," 4.2.49–61), teeth-grating puns ("enfranchise," "en-Frances," 3.1.118–119), and the longest Latin word in existence (*"honorificabilitudinitatibus,"* 5.1.41).

A little of this sort of thing goes a long way, and occasional scenes of verbal sparring are as tedious as anything Shakespeare ever wrote. He tries to have it both ways, reveling in linguistic self-consciousness while laughing at its excesses. Yet the self-possessed characters do at least come to a realization that verbal overkill, like Petrarchan posturing, must be cast aside in favor of decorum and frankness in speech. There will always be "style," but it must be an appropriate style. The comic characters at their best help emphasize this same point. Costard especially is blessed with a pragmatic folk wisdom and simplicity that enable him to stand up unflinchingly to the ladies and gentlemen. He does not hesitate to tell the Princess that she is the "thickest and the tallest" of the ladies, for "truth is truth" (4.1.48). His forebearing description of Nathaniel as "a little o'erparted" (5.2.580–581) in the role of Alexander serves as a gentle rebuke to the wits, whose caustic observations on "The Nine Worthies" have gotten out of hand. Even Holofernes justly chides, before retiring in confusion as Judas Maccabaeus, that "This is not generous, not gentle, not humble" (l. 626).

Above all, however, it is the play's unexpected ending that introduces an invaluable new insight on the courtiers' brittle war of wits. The death of the Princess's father brings everyone back to reality, to sober responsibility, to an awareness that marriage requires thoughtful decision. Devouring Time has entered the never-never land of Navarre's park. The song at the end, appropriately cast in the form of a dialogue or debate, gives us the two voices of Spring and Winter, love and death, carnival and Lent, to remind us that human happiness and self-understanding are complex and perishable. And the song reminds us as well, in its "living art," of that subtle power of the imagination which transforms time, love, and death into artistic creation.

Love's Labor's Lost
in Performance

Love's Labor's Lost disappeared from the stage from the early seventeenth century until the nineteenth and did not enjoy any real theatrical currency until recently. It did well, however, in Shakespeare's lifetime. The first quarto of 1598 describes the play as having been "presented before Her Highness this last Christmas," probably in 1597, and Robert Tofte (*Alba*, 1598) reports of *Love's Labor's Lost* that "I once did see a play / Ycleped so," i.e., by that name. It was played before the Queen at "my Lord of Southampton's" in 1604, and, according to the title page of a second quarto in 1631, was "acted by His Majesty's servants at the Blackfriars and at the Globe." These references seemingly all point to revivals some years after the play had been originally written and performed. Yet despite this evidence of durability, the play suffered virtually total neglect for the next two hundred years. A single uninspired and anonymous adaptation, *The Students*, was published in 1762 but was probably never acted. It added to the low comedy, especially the rivalry of Don Armado and Costard for Jaquenetta, and improbably gave to Berowne some comic business as a letter carrier disguised in Costard's coat.

Charles James Mathews and his wife, Madame Vestris (Lucia Elizabeth Mathews), were the first to try a revival, at the beginning of their management of the Theatre Royal, Covent Garden, in 1839, but they unwisely decided to close the shilling gallery on this occasion and so had a riot on their hands instead of a successful performance. Madame Vestris played Rosaline, and Louisa Cranstoun Nisbett played the Princess of France. The text cut out a great deal of the wordplay between Don Armado and Mote, along with some of the material involving Costard and Jaquenetta, and gave prominence instead to the poetical raptures of the young lovers. Expensive and gorgeous sets required omission, transposition, and the running together of scenes. The opening spectacle gave "a reach of the country as far as the eyes can carry," according to *John Bull*'s admiring review of October 7, while another panorama proved to be a "gem," "a little rustic background with a pool in front." Madame Vestris had to endure a number of jests on the application of the play's title—*Love's Labor's Lost*—to her theatrical failure.

Apart from this disappointment, the record in the later nineteenth century is meager. Samuel Phelps took the part of Don Armado in a sparkling revival at Sadler's Wells in 1857 set in wooded landscapes and with the luxurious costumes of a late medieval court. Augustin Daly produced *Love's Labor's Lost* in New York in 1874 and then again in 1891 with Ada Rehan as the Princess of France. The Shakespeare Memorial Theatre at Stratford-upon-Avon first staged the play on Shakespeare's birthday in 1885 and again in 1907 with Frank Benson directing and starring as Berowne.

Twentieth-century productions thus had no entrenched tradition against which to rebel. Nor did *Love's Labor's Lost* lend itself to iconoclastic and revisionist interpretation, as did *Troilus and Cressida,* for example, or *Coriolanus,* or even *A Midsummer Night's Dream.* Little attempt has been made to discover the dark side of *Love's Labor's Lost.* Instead, the play has been rediscovered as a delightful romp, one that does well in Edwardian dress with the ladies in flowing dresses and the men in wing collars. The old-fashioned and slightly silly atmosphere of the play encourages any sort of period setting the audience can feel nostalgic about. Navarre is a never-never land, a dream of youth. Tyrone Guthrie saw it as such in his decorative production at the Westminster Theatre in 1932 and again in 1936 at the Old Vic. Ten years later, Peter Brook made his debut as a director at Stratford-upon-Avon with a bright and playful version of the play set in the world of Watteau or Fragonard. In 1949 Hugh Hunt's production at the Old Vic was given a beautiful lakeside setting and costumes modeled on miniatures by Nicholas Hilliard and Isaac Oliver. In 1956 Peter Hall directed a frothy *Love's Labor's Lost* at Stratford-upon-Avon with characters in gorgeous Elizabethan costumes and a palace setting dominated by a spiral staircase. Michael Kahn, in 1968 at Stratford, Connecticut, provided a hippy court of Navarre echoing with music of the sitar. More elegantly, at London's National Theatre that same year, Laurence Olivier staged the play in sumptuous Renaissance dress and with luminous sets reminiscent of medieval illuminated manuscripts.

Productions in recent years have continued to emphasize the play's dazzling wit and exuberance, but have also engaged in somewhat more challenging explorations of the complexities of the text and in critiques of earlier stage productions. In 1978 at Stratford-upon-Avon, John Barton used an autumnal set by Ralph Koltai to balance the intoxicating verbal display. The following year at Stratford, Ontario, Robin Phillips and Urjo Kareda set the play in the fashionable world of Europe's social and intellectual aristocracy in the years before the First World War. As the characters were bid to leave the stage, an ominous rumbling could be heard, an indication of the war that would follow *la belle époque*. In 1984 at Stratford-upon-Avon, Barry Kyle emphasized and provocatively focused the play's physical and verbal energies by a Chekhovian setting and a melancholy musical score.

Clearly *Love's Labor's Lost*, so daunting in the study, can be one of Shakespeare's most vital comedies onstage. A character in George Bernard Shaw's *Misalliance* observes, presumably with a jest at the expense of Shaw's own reputation for wordiness, "Yes, it reads well, but it doesn't act well." *Love's Labor's Lost* is just the opposite: it may not always read well, but it can work delightfully in the theater. The wordplay, so apt to seem tedious as one reads, becomes charmingly adolescent and zany in performance. The play revels in disguises, in masques, in misdirected letters. It choreographs its big scenes with an eye to stage picture in a way that must have been especially attractive on the scenery-free Elizabethan stage, as when the King and his fellow students successively eavesdrop on one another's love letters (4.3) or when they come dressed as Muscovites to woo their ladies one by one in a patterned dance (5.2). *Love's Labor's Lost* contains what is probably Shakespeare's first play within a play, the performance onstage of "The Nine Worthies." Theatrical self-reflexivity encourages Shakespeare's audience to reflect on levels of illusion and on the issue of what constitutes good dramatic art.

Love's Labor's Lost's insistence on its own artifice helps to keep that artifice from cloying the appetite. The play is a confection, one that rewards good acting and never seems to grow old.

—LOVE'S—
LABOR'S LOST

[*Dramatis Personae*

FERDINAND, *King of Navarre*
BEROWNE,
LONGAVILLE, } *lords attending the King*
DUMAINE,

THE PRINCESS OF FRANCE
ROSALINE,
MARIA, } *ladies attending the Princess*
KATHARINE,
BOYET, *a French lord attending the Princess*
MARCADE, *a French gentleman acting as messenger*
Two French LORDS

DON ADRIANO DE ARMADO, *a Spanish braggart*
MOTE, *his page*
NATHANIEL, *a curate*
HOLOFERNES, *a schoolmaster, called a pedant*
DULL, *a constable*
COSTARD, *a rustic, also referred to as a clown*
JAQUENETTA, *a dairymaid*
A FORESTER

Lords and Attendants; Attendants disguised as blackamoors

SCENE: *Navarre*]

1.1

Enter Ferdinand, King of Navarre, Berowne, Longaville, and Dumaine.

KING

Let fame, that all hunt after in their lives,
Live registered upon our brazen tombs,   2
And then grace us in the disgrace of death,   3
When, spite of cormorant devouring Time,   4
Th' endeavor of this present breath may buy   5
That honor which shall bate his scythe's keen edge   6
And make us heirs of all eternity.
Therefore, brave conquerors—for so you are,
That war against your own affections   9
And the huge army of the world's desires—
Our late edict shall strongly stand in force: 11
Navarre shall be the wonder of the world;
Our court shall be a little academe,   13
Still and contemplative in living art.   14
You three, Berowne, Dumaine, and Longaville,
Have sworn for three years' term to live with me
My fellow scholars, and to keep those statutes
That are recorded in this schedule here.   18
                 [*He shows a document.*]
Your oaths are passed; and now subscribe your names,   19
That his own hand may strike his honor down   20
That violates the smallest branch herein.   21
If you are armed to do as sworn to do,   22
Subscribe to your deep oaths, and keep it too.

1.1. Location: The King of Navarre's park. (The locale remains the same throughout the play, sometimes immediately outside the gates of Navarre's court.)
2 registered recorded. **brazen** brass **3 grace** honor. **the disgrace of death** (1) the taking away of the grace of life by death (2) the overthrowing of death by proper fame **4 spite of** despite. **cormorant** ravenous, rapacious. (The cormorant is a large, voracious seabird.) **5 breath** breathing time, i.e., life itself; also, speech **6 bate** abate, blunt **9 affections** emotions, passions **11 late** recent **13 academe** academy. (From the name of the grove near Athens where Plato and his followers gathered.) **14 Still** constant. **living art** (1) the art of living (an idea probably derived from the *ars vivendi* of the Roman Stoics) (2) infusing learning (*art*) with vitality **18 schedule** document **19 passed** pledged **20 hand** (1) armed hand of a warrior (2) handwriting **21 branch** i.e., clause **22 armed** i.e., prepared (with a play on the military sense, as in *hand*, l. 20)

LONGAVILLE [*Signing*]
   I am resolved. 'Tis but a three years' fast.
   The mind shall banquet, though the body pine.   25
   Fat paunches have lean pates, and dainty bits   26
   Make rich the ribs but bankrupt quite the wits.

DUMAINE [*Signing*]
   My loving lord, Dumaine is mortified.   28
   The grosser manner of these world's delights
   He throws upon the gross world's baser slaves.   30
   To love, to wealth, to pomp, I pine and die,
   With all these living in philosophy.   32

BEROWNE
   I can but say their protestation over.   33
   So much, dear liege, I have already sworn,   34
   That is, to live and study here three years.
   But there are other strict observances:
   As, not to see a woman in that term,
   Which I hope well is not enrollèd there;   38
   And one day in a week to touch no food,   39
   And but one meal on every day besides,   40
   The which I hope is not enrollèd there;
   And then to sleep but three hours in the night,
   And not be seen to wink of all the day—   43
   When I was wont to think no harm all night,   44
   And make a dark night too of half the day—
   Which I hope well is not enrollèd there.
   O, these are barren tasks, too hard to keep,
   Not to see ladies, study, fast, not sleep!

KING
   Your oath is passed to pass away from these.

BEROWNE
   Let me say no, my liege, an if you please.   50

25 pine languish, waste away **26 pates** heads. **dainty bits** delicate morsels **28 mortified** i.e., dead to worldly desire **30 throws upon** leaves to. **baser slaves** i.e., slaves to passion and pleasure **32 With . . . philosophy** i.e., the pleasure afforded by these (love, wealth, pomp) I find in philosophy (or, perhaps, living with these companions in our commitment to philosophy) **33 over** again **34 liege** lord **38 well** fervently. **enrollèd** written. **there** i.e., on the document detailing the oaths **39 in a** of each **40 but** only. **on** in **43 wink of all** close the eyes at any time in **44 wont** accustomed. **think no harm** i.e., think it no harm to sleep soundly **50 an if** if

I only swore to study with Your Grace
And stay here in your court for three years' space.   52

LONGAVILLE
You swore to that, Berowne, and to the rest.

BEROWNE
By yea and nay, sir, then I swore in jest.   54
What is the end of study, let me know?   55

KING
Why, that to know which else we should not know.

BEROWNE
Things hid and barred, you mean, from common sense?   57

KING
Ay, that is study's godlike recompense.   58

BEROWNE
Come on, then, I will swear to study so   59
To know the thing I am forbid to know,
As thus: to study where I well may dine,
    When I to feast expressly am forbid;
Or study where to meet some mistress fine,
    When mistresses from common sense are hid;
Or, having sworn too hard-a-keeping oath,   65
Study to break it and not break my troth.   66
If study's gain be thus and this be so,
Study knows that which yet it doth not know.
Swear me to this, and I will ne'er say no.

KING
These be the stops that hinder study quite,   70
And train our intellects to vain delight.   71

BEROWNE
Why, all delights are vain, but that most vain
Which, with pain purchased, doth inherit pain: 73

---

52 space time   **54 By . . . nay** earnestly. (A meaning derived from Matthew 5:33–37; Berowne is using a pious equivocation frequently invoked
by those not having a proper answer.)   **55 end** goal   **57 common sense**
ordinary observation or intelligence   **58 recompense** compensation,
payment   **59 Come on** (with a quibble on *common*, l. 57)   **65 too
. . . oath** an oath too hard to keep   **66 troth** faith   **70 stops** obstacles
71 train lure, entice.   **vain** (1) foolish (2) overly proud   **73 pain** labor,
effort (with pun on "suffering").   **purchased** acquired.   **inherit** take
possession of

As, painfully to pore upon a book   74
   To seek the light of truth, while truth the while   75
Doth falsely blind the eyesight of his look.   76
   Light seeking light doth light of light beguile;   77
So, ere you find where light in darkness lies,
Your light grows dark by losing of your eyes.   79
Study me how to please the eye indeed   80
   By fixing it upon a fairer eye,   81
Who dazzling so, that eye shall be his heed   82
   And give him light that it was blinded by.   83
Study is like the heaven's glorious sun,
   That will not be deep searched with saucy looks.   85
Small have continual plodders ever won   86
   Save base authority from others' books.   87
These earthly godfathers of heaven's lights,   88
   That give a name to every fixèd star,
Have no more profit of their shining nights   90
   Than those that walk and wot not what they are.   91
Too much to know is to know naught but fame;   92
And every godfather can give a name.   93

KING
How well he's read, to reason against reading!

DUMAINE
Proceeded well, to stop all good proceeding!   95

LONGAVILLE
He weeds the corn and still lets grow the weeding.   96

74 painfully laboriously. **upon** over   **75 the while** at that same time
76 falsely treacherously. **his look** its power to see; or, the looker's
vision   **77 Light . . . beguile** i.e., searching for truth by excessive study
paradoxically takes from the eyes their ability to see at all, just as
staring at a bright light causes blindness   **79 eyes** sight   **80 Study me**
let me study   **81 fairer** i.e., of a fair lady   **82 Who dazzling so** i.e., the
man who has fixed his eye on a fair lady being thus dazzled.   **heed**
(1) protection, guard (2) object of attention   **83 it** i.e., his own eye
85 deep searched scrutinized.   **saucy** presumptuous, insolent
86 Small little   **87 Save** except.   **base** commonplace, lower   **88 earthly
godfathers** astronomers (who name stars just as godparents pronounce
the name of the child at a christening)   **90 shining** i.e., starlit   **91 wot**
know   **92 fame** report, secondhand information   **93 every . . . name** i.e.,
anyone, acting as godparent, can do as much as astronomers   **95 Proceeded** advanced (in the academic sense of taking a degree)   **96 He . . .
weeding** he pulls out the wheat and allows the weeds to grow

BEROWNE
   The spring is near when green geese are a-breeding.   97
DUMAINE
   How follows that?
BEROWNE   Fit in his place and time.   98
DUMAINE
   In reason nothing.
BEROWNE   Something then in rhyme.   99
KING
   Berowne is like an envious sneaping frost   100
     That bites the firstborn infants of the spring.   101
BEROWNE
   Well, say I am. Why should proud summer boast   102
     Before the birds have any cause to sing?
   Why should I joy in an abortive birth?   104
   At Christmas I no more desire a rose
   Than wish a snow in May's newfangled shows,   106
   But like of each thing that in season grows.   107
   So you, to study now it is too late,   108
   Climb o'er the house to unlock the little gate.   109
KING
   Well, sit you out. Go home, Berowne. Adieu.   110
BEROWNE
   No, my good lord, I have sworn to stay with you.
   And though I have for barbarism spoke more   112
     Than for that angel knowledge you can say,
   Yet, confident, I'll keep what I have sworn   114
     And bide the penance of each three years' day.   115

---

97 green geese i.e., young geese born the previous autumn and sold at green-goose fair, a season of merriment, held on Whitmonday; here, young simpletons **98 Fit in his** appropriate to its **99 In reason nothing** i.e., it doesn't follow at all logically. **rhyme** (Berowne, answering Dumaine, plays upon the proverbial phrase "neither rhyme nor reason.") **100 envious** malignant, malicious. **sneaping** biting, nipping **101 infants** buds **102 proud** glorious **104 abortive** monstrous, unnatural **106 May's . . . shows** i.e., the display of spring flowers **107 like of** approve of. **season** i.e., its proper season **108 too late** i.e., too late in our lives to be students **109 Climb . . . gate** i.e., you begin at the wrong end **110 sit you out** don't take part **112 for barbarism** on the side of ignorance **114 confident** confidently **115 bide** endure. **each . . . day** every day of the three years

Give me the paper. Let me read the same,
And to the strictest decrees I'll write my name.
                                        [*He takes the paper.*]
KING
How well this yielding rescues thee from shame!
BEROWNE [*Reads*] "Item, That no woman shall come
within a mile of my court—" Hath this been pro-
claimed?
LONGAVILLE   Four days ago.
BEROWNE   Let's see the penalty—"on pain of losing
her tongue." Who devised this penalty?
LONGAVILLE
Marry, that did I.
BEROWNE   Sweet lord, and why?   125
LONGAVILLE
To fright them hence with that dread penalty.
BEROWNE
A dangerous law against gentility!   127
[*He reads.*] "Item, If any man be seen to talk with a
woman within the term of three years, he shall endure
such public shame as the rest of the court can possibly
devise."
This article, my liege, yourself must break,
     For well you know here comes in embassy   133
The French King's daughter with yourself to speak—
     A maid of grace and complete majesty—   135
About surrender up of Aquitaine
     To her decrepit, sick, and bedrid father.   137
Therefore this article is made in vain,
     Or vainly comes th' admirèd Princess hither.
KING
What say you, lords? Why, this was quite forgot.
BEROWNE
So study evermore is overshot.   141
While it doth study to have what it would,   142
It doth forget to do the thing it should,

---

125 Marry (A mild oath, derived from "by the Virgin Mary.")   **127 gentility** civilized custom   **133 in embassy** as an ambassador   **135 complete** perfect   **137 bedrid** bedridden   **141 overshot** wide of the mark by
shooting over the target, mistaken   **142 would** desires

And when it hath the thing it hunteth most,
'Tis won as towns with fire—so won, so lost.   145

KING
We must of force dispense with this decree.   146
She must lie here on mere necessity.   147

BEROWNE
Necessity will make us all forsworn   148
  Three thousand times within this three years' space;
For every man with his affects is born,   150
  Not by might mastered, but by special grace.   151
If I break faith, this word shall speak for me: 152
I am forsworn on "mere necessity."
So to the laws at large I write my name.   [*He signs.*]   154
  And he that breaks them in the least degree
Stands in attainder of eternal shame.   156
  Suggestions are to other as to me;   157
But I believe, although I seem so loath,   158
I am the last that will last keep his oath.   159
But is there no quick recreation granted?   160

KING
Ay, that there is. Our court, you know, is haunted   161
  With a refinèd traveler of Spain,   162
A man in all the world's new fashion planted,   163
  That hath a mint of phrases in his brain;   164
One who the music of his own vain tongue   165
  Doth ravish like enchanting harmony;
A man of compliments, whom right and wrong   167

---

145 with fire by being burned down (continuing the metaphor of siege in *overshot*, l. 141)   **146 of force** necessarily   **147 lie** lodge. **on mere** out of absolute   **148 forsworn** guilty of breaking an oath, perjured **150 affects** natural passions   **151 might** i.e., his own strength. **special grace** divine intervention   **152 word** motto   **154 at large** as a whole, in general   **156 in attainder** under penalty, accused   **157 Suggestions . . . me** temptations affect me as much as they do any other   **158 loath** reluctant   **159 I . . . oath** I that speak last will be the last to break my oath (but with an equivocal meaning also of being the last person to keep his oath to the last)   **160 quick** lively   **161–162 haunted With** frequented by   **163 planted** established, involved   **164 mint** place or source of invention   **165 who** whom   **167 compliments** those formal manners that go to complete a gentleman (with a sense also of *complements*, the quarto spelling, "sometimes that fills up, completes, or makes perfect")

Have chose as umpire of their mutiny.   168
This child of fancy, that Armado hight,   169
    For interim to our studies shall relate   170
In high-borne words the worth of many a knight   171
    From tawny Spain, lost in the world's debate.   172
How you delight, my lords, I know not, I,   173
But I protest I love to hear him lie,
And I will use him for my minstrelsy.

BEROWNE
Armado is a most illustrious wight,   176
A man of fire-new words, fashion's own knight.   177

LONGAVILLE
Costard the swain and he shall be our sport;   178
And so to study three years is but short.

    Enter [Dull,] a constable, with Costard with a
    letter.

DULL Which is the Duke's own person?   180
BEROWNE This, fellow. What wouldst?   181
DULL I myself reprehend his own person, for I am His   182
Grace's farborough. But I would see his own person in   183
flesh and blood.
BEROWNE This is he.
DULL Señor Arm—Arm—commends you. There's vil-   186
lainy abroad. This letter will tell you more.
                    [He gives the letter to the King.]
COSTARD Sir, the contempts thereof are as touching me.   188
KING A letter from the magnificent Armado.   189

---

168 mutiny discord   **169 child of fancy** fantastic or grotesque creature. **hight** is called. (An archaic, affected term.)   **170 interim** inter-
lude   **171 high-borne** borne on high, elegantly lofty. (Or perhaps
highborn, patrician, born of high rank.)   **172 tawny** sunburned. **debate**
warfare   **173 How you delight** what delights you   **176 wight** person
177 fire-new newly coined   **178 Costard** (The name means a large apple;
the term is frequently applied humorously or derisively to the head.)
swain rustic young fellow   **180 Duke's** i.e., King's   **181 fellow** (Customary form of address to a servant.)   **182 reprehend** (Malapropism for
represent.)   **183 farborough** (Malapropism for *tharborough* or *third-
borough,* a petty constable.)   **186 commends you** sends you his greetings   **188 contempts** (Malapropism for *contents.*)   **189 magnificent
Armado** boastful or grandiose Armado (with an allusion to the great
Armada of Spain)

BEROWNE   How low soever the matter, I hope in God   190
for high words.   191

LONGAVILLE   A high hope for a low heaven. God grant   192
us patience!

BEROWNE   To hear, or forbear hearing?   194

LONGAVILLE   To hear meekly, sir, and to laugh moderately, or to forbear both.

BEROWNE   Well, sir, be it as the style shall give us cause   197
to climb in the merriness.

COSTARD   The matter is to me, sir, as concerning Jaque-   199
netta. The matter of it is, I was taken with the manner.   200

BEROWNE   In what manner?

COSTARD   In manner and form following, sir—all those   202
three: I was seen with her in the manor house, sitting   203
with her upon the form, and taken following her into   204
the park; which, put together, is "in manner and form
following." Now, sir, for the manner—it is the manner
of a man to speak to a woman. For the form—in some
form.

BEROWNE   For the "following," sir?

COSTARD   As it shall follow in my correction; and God   210
defend the right!   211

KING   Will you hear this letter with attention?

BEROWNE   As we would hear an oracle.

COSTARD   Such is the simplicity of man to hearken after   214
the flesh.

KING [*Reads*]   "Great deputy, the welkin's vicegerent,   216
and sole dominator of Navarre, my soul's earth's god,   217
and body's fostering patron—"   218

---

190 How low soever however debased   **191 high** lofty, exalted   **192 low
heaven** i.e., small blessing   **194 forbear** refuse   **197 be it** so be it.
style (with a pun on *stile*, giving point to *climb* in the next line)   **199 is
to** applies to   **200 with the manner** with the stolen goods. (An Anglo-
French law term *mainoure*, from *manoeuvre*.)   **202 In manner and form**
(A familiar empty cliché of the time.)   **202–203 those three** i.e., manner
and form following. (Costard proceeds to illustrate each term as it
applies to his case.)   **204 form** bench   **210 correction** punishment
210–211 God defend the right (Prayer before mortal combat.)   **214 simplicity** (The quarto's *sinplicity* may be a malapropism, and has an ironic
fitness, but the joke would be hard to hear in the theater.)   **216 welkin's
vicegerent** heaven's deputy. (A pompous phrase, as most in the letter
are.)   **217 dominator** ruler   **218 fostering** nurturing

COSTARD Not a word of Costard yet.

KING [*Reads*] "So it is—"

COSTARD It may be so, but if he say it is so, he is, in
telling true, but so.   222

KING Peace!

COSTARD Be to me and every man that dares not fight.

KING No words!

COSTARD Of other men's secrets, I beseech you.

KING [*Reads*] "So it is, besieged with sable-colored   227
melancholy, I did commend the black oppressing hu-   228
mor to the most wholesome physic of thy health-   229
giving air, and, as I am a gentleman, betook myself to
walk. The time when? About the sixth hour, when
beasts most graze, birds best peck, and men sit down
to that nourishment which is called supper. So much
for the time when. Now for the ground which—which,
I mean, I walked upon. It is yclept thy park. Then for 235
the place where—where, I mean, I did encounter that
obscene and most preposterous event that draweth   237
from my snow-white pen the ebon-colored ink which   238
here thou viewest, beholdest, surveyest, or seest. But
to the place where. It standeth north-northeast and by
east from the west corner of thy curious-knotted gar- 241
den. There did I see that low-spirited swain, that base 242
minnow of thy mirth—"   243

COSTARD Me?

KING [*Reads*] "that unlettered, small-knowing soul—" 245

COSTARD Me?

KING [*Reads*] "that shallow vassal—"   247

COSTARD Still me?

KING [*Reads*] "which, as I remember, hight Cos-   249
tard—"

COSTARD O! Me.

---

222 but so i.e., not saying much   **227 sable-colored** i.e., black
228–229 black oppressing humor black bile or melancholy   **229 physic**
medicine   **235 yclept** called. (Archaic usage.)   **237 obscene** disgusting
238 snow-white pen i.e., white goose quill.   **ebon-colored** i.e., black (like
ebony)   **241 curious-knotted** delicately or intricately designed
242 low-spirited ignoble   **243 minnow** contemptible little creature
245 unlettered illiterate   **247 vassal** base slave   **249 hight** is called.
(Archaic usage.)

KING [*Reads*] "sorted and consorted, contrary to thy es- 252
tablished proclaimed edict and continent canon, 253
with, with—O, with—but with this I passion to say 254
wherewith—"

COSTARD With a wench.

KING [*Reads*] "with a child of our grandmother Eve, a
female; or, for thy more sweet understanding, a
woman. Him I, as my ever-esteemed duty pricks me 259
on, have sent to thee, to receive the meed of punish- 260
ment, by thy sweet Grace's officer, Anthony Dull, a
man of good repute, carriage, bearing, and estima- 262
tion." 263

DULL Me, an 't shall please you. I am Anthony Dull. 264

KING [*Reads*] "For Jaquenetta—so is the weaker vessel 265
called which I apprehended with the aforesaid swain
—I keep her as a vessel of thy law's fury, and shall at 267
the least of thy sweet notice bring her to trial. Thine, 268
in all compliments of devoted and heartburning heat
of duty,   Don Adriano de Armado."

BEROWNE This is not so well as I looked for, but the best
that ever I heard.

KING Ay, the best for the worst.—But, sirrah, what say 273
you to this?

COSTARD Sir, I confess the wench.

KING Did you hear the proclamation?

COSTARD I do confess much of the hearing it, but little
of the marking of it.

KING It was proclaimed a year's imprisonment to be
taken with a wench.

COSTARD I was taken with none, sir. I was taken with
a damsel.

KING Well, it was proclaimed "damsel."

COSTARD This was no damsel neither, sir. She was a
virgin.

---

252 sorted and consorted associated   **253 continent canon** restraint
enforced by law   **254 passion** grieve   **259 pricks** spurs   **260 meed**
reward   **262–263 estimation** reputation   **264 an 't** if it   **265 weaker
vessel** i.e., woman. (See 1 Peter 3:7.)   **267–268 at . . . notice** i.e., at your
first hint   **268 bring her to trial** (with perhaps a bawdy double meaning
of testing her mettle as a woman)   **273 best . . . worst** i.e., best example
of the worst.   **sirrah** (Ordinary form of address to inferiors.)

KING   It is so varied too, for it was proclaimed "virgin." 286
COSTARD   If it were, I deny her virginity. I was taken
   with a maid.
KING   This "maid" will not serve your turn, sir.   289
COSTARD   This maid will serve my turn, sir.
KING   Sir, I will pronounce your sentence: you shall fast
   a week with bran and water.
COSTARD   I had rather pray a month with mutton and 293
   porridge.   294
KING
And Don Armado shall be your keeper.
My Lord Berowne, see him delivered o'er.   296
And go we, lords, to put in practice that
Which each to other hath so strongly sworn.
       [*Exeunt the King, Longaville, and Dumaine.*]
BEROWNE
I'll lay my head to any good man's hat,   299
These oaths and laws will prove an idle scorn.   300
Sirrah, come on.
COSTARD   I suffer for the truth, sir; for true it is, I was
   taken with Jaquenetta, and Jaquenetta is a true girl; 303
   and therefore welcome the sour cup of prosperity! 304
   Affliction may one day smile again, and till then, sit 305
   thee down, sorrow!   *Exeunt.* 306

❖

1.2   *Enter Armado and Mote, his page.*

ARMADO   Boy, what sign is it when a man of great spirit 1
   grows melancholy?

---

286 so varied alternatively phrased (in typical legal jargon)   **289 serve
your turn** i.e., get you out of your difficulty. (But Costard, in the next
line, interprets the phrase in a ribald sense.)   **293–294 mutton and
porridge** mutton broth (with a pun on *mutton*, whore)   **296 delivered
o'er** handed over   **299 lay** wager.   **good man's** i.e., yeoman's   **300 idle
scorn** worthless object of mockery   **303 true** honest   **304 prosperity**
(Malapropism for *austerity?*)   **305 Affliction** (Costard mixes this up with
prosperity.)   **305–306 sit thee down** i.e., stay, settle down with me

1.2. Location: The same. Navarre's park.
s.d. Mote (The word in the first quarto is *Moth,* pronounced identically
with *mote* and meaning "dust speck." The sense of "moth" or tiny
winged creature may also be present. There may possibly be a play also
on *mot,* French for "word.")   **1 sign is it** is it a sign of

MOTE   A great sign, sir, that he will look sad.

ARMADO   Why, sadness is one and the selfsame thing,
dear imp.   5

MOTE   No, no, O Lord, sir, no.

ARMADO   How canst thou part sadness and melancholy,   7
my tender juvenal?   8

MOTE   By a familiar demonstration of the working, my   9
tough señor.   10

ARMADO   Why "tough señor"? Why "tough señor"?

MOTE   Why "tender juvenal"? Why "tender juvenal"?

ARMADO   I spoke it, tender juvenal, as a congruent epi-   13
theton appertaining to thy young days, which we may   14
nominate "tender."   15

MOTE   And I, tough señor, as an appertinent title to   16
your old time, which we may name "tough."

ARMADO   Pretty and apt.

MOTE   How mean you, sir? I pretty and my saying apt?
Or I apt and my saying pretty?

ARMADO   Thou pretty, because little.   21

MOTE   Little pretty, because little. Wherefore apt?

ARMADO   And therefore apt, because quick.   23

MOTE   Speak you this in my praise, master?

ARMADO   In thy condign praise.   25

MOTE   I will praise an eel with the same praise.

ARMADO   What, that an eel is ingenious?

MOTE   That an eel is quick.   28

ARMADO   I do say thou art quick in answers. Thou   29
heat'st my blood.   30

MOTE   I am answered, sir.

ARMADO   I love not to be crossed.   32

MOTE [*Aside*]   He speaks the mere contrary; crosses love   33
not him.

---

5 imp young shoot, child   **7 part** distinguish between   **8 juvenal** youth;
satirist (after Juvenal, the Roman satirist)   **9 familiar** plain, easily
understood.   **working** operation (of these emotions)   **10 señor** sir (with
pun on *senior*)   **13–14 congruent epitheton** appropriate epithet
14 appertaining belonging   **15 nominate** call   **16 appertinent** appropriate   **21 Thou . . . little** (Armado refers to the commonplace "little things
are pretty.")   **23 quick** quick-witted   **25 condign** worthily deserved
28 quick alive   **29–30 Thou . . . blood** you make me angry   **32 crossed**
thwarted, opposed   **33 mere** absolute.   **crosses** coins. (So called because many of them were impressed with crosses.)

ARMADO I have promised to study three years with the
Duke.   36
MOTE You may do it in an hour, sir.
ARMADO Impossible.
MOTE How many is one thrice told?   39
ARMADO I am ill at reckoning; it fitteth the spirit of a 40
tapster.   41
MOTE You are a gentleman and a gamester, sir.   42
ARMADO I confess both. They are both the varnish of a 43
complete man.   44
MOTE Then I am sure you know how much the gross
sum of deuce-ace amounts to.   46
ARMADO It doth amount to one more than two.
MOTE Which the base vulgar do call three.   48
ARMADO True.
MOTE Why, sir, is this such a piece of study? Now here 50
is three studied ere ye'll thrice wink; and how easy it
is to put "years" to the word "three," and study three
years in two words, the dancing horse will tell you.   53
ARMADO A most fine figure!   54
MOTE [Aside] To prove you a cipher.   55
ARMADO I will hereupon confess I am in love; and as it
is base for a soldier to love, so am I in love with a base
wench. If drawing my sword against the humor of af- 58
fection would deliver me from the reprobate thought   59
of it, I would take Desire prisoner and ransom him to
any French courtier for a new-devised curtsy. I think   61
scorn to sigh; methinks I should outswear Cupid.   62
Comfort me, boy. What great men have been in love?
MOTE Hercules, master.

36 Duke i.e., King   39 told counted   40 ill at reckoning no good at
arithmetic   41 tapster bartender   42 gamester gambler   43 varnish
finish, ornament   44 complete accomplished   46 deuce-ace (A throw of
two and one in dice.)   48 vulgar common people   50 piece master-
piece   53 dancing horse (Probably a reference to a famous trained
horse brought to London in 1591, named Morocco, that could count by
tapping with its hoof.)   54 figure rhetorical flourish   55 cipher zero.
(Mote takes Armado's figure in l. 54 to mean "numeral.")   58–59 humor
of affection inclination to passion   59 deliver me save me.   reprobate
depraved, degrading   61 new-devised curtsy newfangled manner of
bowing; any new fashion   61–62 think scorn disdain   62 outswear
overcome by swearing, or, swear to do without

ARMADO Most sweet Hercules! More authority, dear
   boy, name more; and, sweet my child, let them be
   men of good repute and carriage.   67
MOTE Samson, master; he was a man of good carriage,
   great carriage, for he carried the town gates on his
   back like a porter; and he was in love.
ARMADO O well-knit Samson! Strong-jointed Samson!   71
   I do excel thee in my rapier as much as thou didst me   72
   in carrying gates. I am in love too. Who was Samson's
   love, my dear Mote?
MOTE A woman, master.
ARMADO Of what complexion?   76
MOTE Of all the four, or the three, or the two, or one of
   the four.
ARMADO Tell me precisely of what complexion.
MOTE Of the seawater green, sir.
ARMADO Is that one of the four complexions?
MOTE As I have read, sir; and the best of them too.
ARMADO Green indeed is the color of lovers; but to   83
   have a love of that color, methinks Samson had small
   reason for it. He surely affected her for her wit.   85
MOTE It was so, sir, for she had a green wit.   86
ARMADO My love is most immaculate white and red.
MOTE Most maculate thoughts, master, are masked un-   88
   der such colors.   89
ARMADO Define, define, well-educated infant.   90
MOTE My father's wit and my mother's tongue assist
   me!
ARMADO Sweet invocation of a child, most pretty and
   pathetical!   94

---

67 carriage bearing (with pun on "ability to carry" in the following
speech; see Judges 16:3 for the account of Samson's deed)   **71 well-knit**
well-proportioned   **72 in my rapier** in my swordsmanship. (The rapier
replaced the old-fashioned long sword in the 1590s.)   **76 complexion**
skin color; also temperament. (The four complexions were sanguine,
choleric, phlegmatic, and melancholic, and were supposedly determined
by the relative proportions of the four humors.)   **83 Green** (A reference
to lovers' "greensickness," an anemic condition of puberty.)   **85 affected**
loved.   **wit** intelligence   **86 green** immature (with a punning reference perhaps to the seven green withes with which Samson was bound,
Judges 16:7–9)   **88 maculate** stained, polluted   **89 colors** (with a pun on
"pretexts")   **90 Define** explain   **94 pathetical** moving

MOTE

> If she be made of white and red,   95
>> Her faults will ne'er be known,   96
> For blushing cheeks by faults are bred,   97
>> And fears by pale white shown.   98
> Then if she fear or be to blame,
>> By this you shall not know,   100
> For still her cheeks possess the same   101
>> Which native she doth owe.   102

A dangerous rhyme, master, against the reason of 103 white and red.   104

ARMADO   Is there not a ballad, boy, of the King and the 105 Beggar?   106

MOTE   The world was very guilty of such a ballad some three ages since, but I think now 'tis not to be found; 108 or if it were, it would neither serve for the writing nor 109 the tune.   110

ARMADO   I will have that subject newly writ o'er, that I may example my digression by some mighty prece- 112 dent. Boy, I do love that country girl that I took in the park with the rational hind Costard. She deserves 114 well.

MOTE [*Aside*]   To be whipped; and yet a better love than 116 my master.

ARMADO   Sing, boy. My spirit grows heavy in love.

---

95 be made of i.e., has a complexion that is. (With a play on *maid*. Mote also hints that the red and white are cosmetic.)   **96 Her . . . known** i.e., she will never be betrayed by blushes or pallor, since the red and white (perhaps cosmetic) will mask those effects   **97 by faults are bred** are caused by an awareness of being at fault   **98 fears** i.e., fears of detection   **100 this** i.e., her complexion or coloring (which is perhaps produced by cosmetics)   **101–102 For . . . owe** i.e., for her cheeks are always (and therefore suspiciously) colored with the red and white of her natural coloration   **103–104 A dangerous . . . red** i.e., a warning in rhyme against trusting in white and red complexions. (The sentence plays on the contrast of *rhyme* and *reason*.)   **105–106 ballad . . . Beggar** ballad of King Cophetua and the beggar maid. (Cf. 4.1.66–67.)
108 since ago   **109–110 it would . . . tune** i.e., both the lyrics and the tune would seem out of date.   **serve** suffice   **112 example** give an example of.   **digression** lapse, waywardness   **114 rational** capable of reason. (Said patronizingly.)   **hind** rustic or clown   **116 To . . . love** i.e., she deserves to be whipped, as prostitutes are whipped, and yet even at that she deserves a better lover

MOTE *[Aside]*   And that's great marvel, loving a light wench. 119
ARMADO   I say, sing.
MOTE   Forbear till this company be past.   121

> Enter *[Costard the] clown, [Dull the] constable,*
> *and [Jaquenetta, a] wench.*

DULL   Sir, the Duke's pleasure is that you keep Costard
safe, and you must suffer him to take no delight nor 123
no penance, but 'a must fast three days a week. For 124
this damsel, I must keep her at the park. She is allowed 125
for the deywoman. Fare you well.   126
ARMADO *[Aside]*   I do betray myself with blushing.—Maid!
JAQUENETTA   Man?
ARMADO   I will visit thee at the lodge.
JAQUENETTA   That's hereby.   130
ARMADO   I know where it is situate.   131
JAQUENETTA   Lord, how wise you are!
ARMADO   I will tell thee wonders.
JAQUENETTA   With that face?   134
ARMADO   I love thee.
JAQUENETTA   So I heard you say.
ARMADO   And so farewell.
JAQUENETTA   Fair weather after you!
DULL   Come, Jaquenetta, away!
                      Exeunt [Dull and Jaquenetta].
ARMADO   Villain, thou shalt fast for thy offenses ere 140
thou be pardoned.
COSTARD   Well, sir, I hope when I do it I shall do it on a 142
full stomach.   143
ARMADO   Thou shalt be heavily punished.
COSTARD   I am more bound to you than your fellows, 145
for they are but lightly rewarded.   146
ARMADO *[To Mote]*   Take away this villain. Shut him up.

---

119 light wanton (with a play on the opposite of *heavy,* l. 118)   **121 Forbear** hold off   **123 suffer** allow   **124 penance** (Malapropism for *pleas-
ance,* i.e., joy.)   **'a** he   **125–126 allowed . . . deywoman** approved or
assigned to serve as dairymaid   **130 hereby** close by   **131 situate**
located   **134 With that face** i.e., you don't mean it? (Slang, like most
of Jaquenetta's expressions.)   **140 Villain** (1) servant (2) rascal
142–143 on . . . stomach (with a pun on *full-stomached,* with good
courage)   **145 bound** obliged.   **fellows** servants   **146 but lightly** only
slightly

MOTE Come, you transgressing slave, away!

COSTARD Let me not be pent up, sir. I will fast, being
loose.

MOTE No, sir, that were fast and loose. Thou shalt to 151
prison.

COSTARD Well, if ever I do see the merry days of deso- 153
lation that I have seen, some shall see.   154

MOTE What shall some see?

COSTARD Nay, nothing, Master Mote, but what they
look upon. It is not for prisoners to be too silent in
their words, and therefore I will say nothing. I thank
God I have as little patience as another man, and 159
therefore I can be quiet.   *Exit [with Mote]*.

ARMADO I do affect the very ground, which is base, 161
where her shoe, which is baser, guided by her foot,
which is basest, doth tread. I shall be forsworn, which 163
is a great argument of falsehood, if I love. And how 164
can that be true love which is falsely attempted? Love
is a familiar; Love is a devil. There is no evil angel but 166
Love. Yet was Samson so tempted, and he had an excellent strength; yet was Solomon so seduced, and he
had a very good wit. Cupid's butt shaft is too hard for 169
Hercules' club, and therefore too much odds for a 170
Spaniard's rapier. The first and second cause will not 171
serve my turn; the passado he respects not, the duello 172
he regards not. His disgrace is to be called boy, but his
glory is to subdue men. Adieu, valor! Rust, rapier! Be
still, drum! For your manager is in love; yea, he loveth. 175

---

151 fast and loose a cheating trick.   **Thou shalt** you will go
153–154 desolation (Malapropism for *consolation?*)   **154 some shall see**
(Costard seems to imply that some who have wronged him will see how
he can revenge, although he refuses to say so when Mote queries his
meaning.)   **159 patience** (Costard means the opposite of what he
says.)   **161 affect** love   **163 be forsworn** break my oath   **164 argument**
proof   **166 familiar** attendant evil spirit   **169 butt shaft** unbarbed
arrow, used in archery practice   **170 too much odds** at too great an
advantage   **171 first . . . cause** (An allusion to certain situations that
necessitated a duel according to the code of honor. Armado complains
that Cupid will not follow this code of honor.)   **172 passado** forward
thrust with the sword, one foot being advanced at the same time.
duello established code of duelists   **175 manager** skilled practitioner

Assist me, some extemporal god of rhyme, for I am 176
sure I shall turn sonnet. Devise, wit; write, pen; for I 177
am for whole volumes in folio.   *Exit.* 178

❖

176 extemporal . . . rhyme god of impromptu poetry   **177 sonnet** i.e.,
sonneteer   **178 am for** am destined to produce.   **folio** large format

2.1   *Enter the Princess of France, with three*
attending Ladies [Rosaline, Maria, Katharine]
and three Lords [one being Boyet].

BOYET
Now, madam, summon up your dearest spirits.   1
Consider who the King your father sends,
To whom he sends, and what's his embassy: 3
Yourself, held precious in the world's esteem,
To parley with the sole inheritor   5
Of all perfections that a man may owe,   6
Matchless Navarre; the plea of no less weight   7
Than Aquitaine, a dowry for a queen.
Be now as prodigal of all dear grace
As Nature was in making graces dear   10
When she did starve the general world beside   11
And prodigally gave them all to you.   12
PRINCESS
Good Lord Boyet, my beauty, though but mean,   13
Needs not the painted flourish of your praise.   14
Beauty is bought by judgment of the eye,
Not uttered by base sale of chapmen's tongues.   16
I am less proud to hear you tell my worth   17
Than you much willing to be counted wise
In spending your wit in the praise of mine.
But now to task the tasker. Good Boyet,   20
You are not ignorant all-telling fame   21
Doth noise abroad Navarre hath made a vow: 22
Till painful study shall outwear three years,   23
No woman may approach his silent court.
Therefore to 's seemeth it a needful course,   25

2.1. **Location: The same. Outside the gates of Navarre's court.**
1 dearest spirits best wits   **3 embassy** message   **5 parley** meet, speak
6 owe own   **7 the plea of** that which is claimed is of   **10 dear** bearing a
high price (playing on *dear*, "beloved," of the previous line)   **11 starve**
i.e., withhold graces from.   **beside** i.e., excepting yourself   **12 prod-**
igally extravagantly, too generously   **13 mean** average, moderate
14 flourish adornment   **16 uttered** (1) spoken (2) offered for sale.
chapmen's merchants'   **17 tell** (1) speak of (2) reckon   **20 task**
(1) chastise (2) lay a task upon   **21 ignorant** unaware that.   **fame** rumor   **22 noise** spread the news   **23 painful** strenuous   **25 to 's** to us.
(The royal "we.")   **needful** necessary

Before we enter his forbidden gates,
To know his pleasure; and in that behalf,   27
Bold of your worthiness, we single you   28
As our best-moving fair solicitor.   29
Tell him the daughter of the King of France,
On serious business craving quick dispatch,
Importunes personal conference with His Grace.   32
Haste, signify so much, while we attend,   33
Like humble-visaged suitors, his high will.

BOYET
Proud of employment, willingly I go.

PRINCESS
All pride is willing pride, and yours is so. *Exit Boyet.*   36
Who are the votaries, my loving lords,   37
That are vow-fellows with this virtuous duke?   38

A LORD
Lord Longaville is one.

PRINCESS   Know you the man?

MARIA
I know him, madam. At a marriage feast,
Between Lord Perigord and the beauteous heir   41
Of Jaques Falconbridge, solemnized
In Normandy, saw I this Longaville.
A man of sovereign parts he is esteemed,   44
Well fitted in arts, glorious in arms.   45
Nothing becomes him ill that he would well.   46
The only soil of his fair virtue's gloss—   47
If virtue's gloss will stain with any soil—   48
Is a sharp wit matched with too blunt a will,   49
Whose edge hath power to cut, whose will still wills   50
It should none spare that come within his power.   51

27 **in that behalf** for that purpose   28 **Bold of** confident of.   **single**
choose   29 **best-moving** most eloquent.   **fair** just   32 **Importunes** requests   33 **Haste . . . attend** hurry, speak exactly this, while we await
36 **pride** (The Princess wittily interprets Boyet's *Proud* in l. 35 as "vain"
rather than, as he intended, "honored.")   37 **votaries** those who have taken
vows   38 **vow-fellows** individuals bound by the same vow   41 **beauteous**
beautiful   44 **sovereign parts** excellent qualities   45 **fitted** furnished.   **in
arts** with learning   46 **becomes him ill** is unbecoming in him.   **would well**
wants to do well   47 **soil . . . gloss** blot on the appearance of his general
excellence   48 **gloss** fair appearance.   **soil** blemish   49 **too . . . will** i.e., an
insensitivity to the feelings of others   50 **Whose** i.e., the wit's.   **still** continually   51 **his** its

PRINCESS
　Some merry mocking lord, belike—is 't so?   52
MARIA
　They say so most that most his humors know.
PRINCESS
　Such short-lived wits do wither as they grow.
　Who are the rest?
KATHARINE
　The young Dumaine, a well-accomplished youth,
　Of all that virtue love for virtue loved;   57
　Most power to do most harm, least knowing ill,   58
　For he hath wit to make an ill shape good,   59
　And shape to win grace though he had no wit.   60
　I saw him at the Duke Alençon's once,
　And much too little of that good I saw   62
　Is my report to his great worthiness.   63
ROSALINE
　Another of these students at that time
　Was there with him, if I have heard a truth.
　Berowne they call him; but a merrier man,   66
　Within the limit of becoming mirth,   67
　I never spent an hour's talk withal.   68
　His eye begets occasion for his wit,   69
　For every object that the one doth catch
　The other turns to a mirth-moving jest,
　Which his fair tongue, conceit's expositor,   72
　Delivers in such apt and gracious words
　That agèd ears play truant at his tales   74
　And younger hearings are quite ravishèd,
　So sweet and voluble is his discourse.   76

52 belike most likely   **57 Of . . . loved** esteemed for his virtue by all
who love virtue   **58 Most . . . ill** i.e., Dumaine, as a talented and graceful person, has the utmost power of doing the greatest harm by the ill
employment of those qualities, yet he is ignorant of ill   **59–60 For
. . . no wit** he has intelligence enough to compensate for a poor physique, if he had one, and conversely a physique shapely enough to
compensate for lack of intelligence   **62 little** short, inadequate   **63 to**
compared with   **66 Berowne** (The name suggests *brown* to Rosaline, as
in the expression "brown study," the opposite of being merry.)   **67 becoming** suitable   **68 withal** with   **69 begets occasion** creates opportunities   **72 conceit's expositor** imagination's interpreter   **74 play truant**
i.e., neglect important business   **76 voluble** fluent

PRINCESS
God bless my ladies! Are they all in love,
That every one her own hath garnishèd
With such bedecking ornaments of praise?
A LORD
Here comes Boyet.

Enter Boyet.

PRINCESS   Now, what admittance, lord?   80
BOYET
Navarre had notice of your fair approach,
And he and his competitors in oath   82
Were all addressed to meet you, gentle lady,   83
Before I came. Marry, thus much I have learned:
He rather means to lodge you in the field,
Like one that comes here to besiege his court,
Than seek a dispensation for his oath
To let you enter his unpeopled house.   88

*Enter [King of] Navarre, Longaville, Dumaine,
and Berowne.*

Here comes Navarre.
KING   Fair Princess, welcome to the court of Navarre.
PRINCESS   "Fair" I give you back again, and "welcome"
I have not yet. The roof of this court is too high to be 92
yours, and welcome to the wide fields too base to be
mine.
KING
You shall be welcome, madam, to my court.
PRINCESS
I will be welcome, then. Conduct me thither.
KING
Hear me, dear lady: I have sworn an oath.
PRINCESS
Our Lady help my lord! He'll be forsworn.
KING
Not for the world, fair madam, by my will.   99

---

80 admittance reception **82 competitors** associates **83 addressed**
prepared **88 unpeopled** inadequately staffed with servants **92 The
roof of this court** i.e., the sky **99 by my will** willingly. (A common mild
oath.)

PRINCESS
Why, will shall break it—will and nothing else.   100
KING
Your ladyship is ignorant what it is.
PRINCESS
Were my lord so, his ignorance were wise,
Where now his knowledge must prove ignorance.
I hear Your Grace hath sworn out housekeeping.   104
'Tis deadly sin to keep that oath, my lord,
And sin to break it.
But pardon me, I am too sudden-bold;
To teach a teacher ill beseemeth me.
Vouchsafe to read the purpose of my coming,   109
And suddenly resolve me in my suit.   110
                    [*She gives him a paper.*]
KING
Madam, I will, if suddenly I may.
PRINCESS
You will the sooner that I were away,   112
For you'll prove perjured if you make me stay.
                    [*The King reads silently.*]
BEROWNE [*To Rosaline*]
Did not I dance with you in Brabant once?   114
ROSALINE
Did not I dance with you in Brabant once?
BEROWNE
I know you did.
ROSALINE   How needless was it then
To ask the question?
BEROWNE   You must not be so quick.   117
ROSALINE
'Tis long of you, that spur me with such questions.   118
BEROWNE
Your wit's too hot. It speeds too fast; 'twill tire.   119
ROSALINE
Not till it leave the rider in the mire.   120

100 will desire   **104 sworn out housekeeping** renounced hospitality
109 Vouchsafe deign, agree   **110 suddenly resolve** quickly answer
112 that . . . away to procure my departure   **114 Brabant** a province in
central Belgium   **117 quick** sharp   **118 long of** on account of.   **spur**
goad   **119 hot** ardent, eager   **120 mire** mud

BEROWNE
What time o' day? 121
ROSALINE
The hour that fools should ask.
BEROWNE
Now fair befall your mask! 123
ROSALINE
Fair fall the face it covers! 124
BEROWNE
And send you many lovers!
ROSALINE
Amen, so you be none.
BEROWNE
Nay, then will I be gone. *[He stands aside.]*
KING
Madam, your father here doth intimate 128
The payment of a hundred thousand crowns, 129
Being but the one half of an entire sum
Disbursèd by my father in his wars. 131
But say that he or we—as neither have— 132
Received that sum, yet there remains unpaid
A hundred thousand more, in surety of the which 134
One part of Aquitaine is bound to us,
Although not valued to the money's worth. 136
If then the King your father will restore
But that one half which is unsatisfied,
We will give up our right in Aquitaine
And hold fair friendship with His Majesty.
But that, it seems, he little purposeth, 141
For here he doth demand to have repaid 142
A hundred thousand crowns, and not demands, 143
On payment of a hundred thousand crowns,
To have his title live in Aquitaine— 145

---

121 time o' day time is it   **123 fair befall** good luck to   **124 fall** befall
128 intimate refer to, discuss, imply   **129 The payment** i.e., that he has
already paid   **131 his** i.e., the King of France's   **132 he** i.e., my father
134 in surety as a guarantee   **136 valued** equal in value   **141 little
purposeth** scarcely intends   **142 demand . . . repaid** insists he has
already repaid   **143 and not demands** i.e., instead of proposing or
stipulating   **145 To have . . . Aquitaine** i.e., to regain his title to Aquitaine by paying the 100,000 crowns that are owed to Navarre

Which we much rather had depart withal,   146
And have the money by our father lent,
Than Aquitaine, so gelded as it is.   148
Dear Princess, were not his requests so far
From reason's yielding, your fair self should make
A yielding 'gainst some reason in my breast,   151
And go well satisfied to France again.

PRINCESS
You do the King my father too much wrong,
And wrong the reputation of your name,
In so unseeming to confess receipt   155
Of that which hath so faithfully been paid.

KING
I do protest I never heard of it;
And, if you prove it, I'll repay it back
Or yield up Aquitaine.

PRINCESS   We arrest your word.   159
Boyet, you can produce acquittances   160
For such a sum from special officers
Of Charles, his father.

KING   Satisfy me so.   162

BOYET
So please Your Grace, the packet is not come
Where that and other specialties are bound.   164
Tomorrow you shall have a sight of them.

KING
It shall suffice me; at which interview
All liberal reason I will yield unto.   167
Meantime, receive such welcome at my hand
As honor, without breach of honor, may
Make tender of to thy true worthiness.   170
You may not come, fair Princess, within my gates,
But here without you shall be so received   172
As you shall deem yourself lodged in my heart,   173

---

146 depart withal part with   **148 gelded** emasculated, weakened in
value   **151 A yielding . . . breast** i.e., a willingness on my part to compromise, despite the fact that right is on my side   **155 unseeming** being
apparently unwilling   **159 arrest** take as security   **160 acquittances**
receipts for payment of a debt   **162 Satisfy me so** prove to me that this
is true   **164 specialties** warrants, special documents   **167 liberal**
gentlemanlike   **170 Make tender of** offer   **172 without** outside
173 As that

Though so denied fair harbor in my house.
Your own good thoughts excuse me, and farewell.
Tomorrow shall we visit you again.

PRINCESS
Sweet health and fair desires consort Your Grace!   177

KING
Thy own wish wish I thee in every place.
                    Exit [with Longaville and Dumaine].

BEROWNE [*To Rosaline*] Lady, I will commend you to
mine own heart.

ROSALINE   Pray you, do my commendations. I would be
glad to see it.

BEROWNE   I would you heard it groan.

ROSALINE   Is the fool sick?   184

BEROWNE   Sick at the heart.

ROSALINE
Alack, let it blood.   186

BEROWNE
Would that do it good?

ROSALINE
My physic says "ay."   188

BEROWNE
Will you prick 't with your eye?   189

ROSALINE
Non point, with my knife.   190

BEROWNE
Now, God save thy life!

ROSALINE
And yours from long living!

BEROWNE
I cannot stay thanksgiving.   *Exit.* 193

          Enter Dumaine.

DUMAINE [*To Boyet*]
Sir, I pray you, a word. What lady is that same?

---

177 consort attend **184 the fool** (A term of endearment or gentle
raillery.) **186 let it blood** bleed it. (A reference to the medical practice
of drawing blood.) **188 physic** medical knowledge **189 Will . . . eye**
i.e., will you stab me through the heart with your glance, smiting me as
with Cupid's arrow. (With wordplay on *eye* and *ay* in l. 188.) **190 Non
point** (1) not at all (2) it is dull **193 stay thanksgiving** stay long enough
to thank you properly

BOYET
The heir of Alençon, Katharine her name.

DUMAINE
A gallant lady. Monsieur, fare you well.   *Exit.*

          [*Enter Longaville.*]

LONGAVILLE
I beseech you a word. What is she in the white?   197

BOYET
A woman sometimes, an you saw her in the light.   198

LONGAVILLE
Perchance light in the light. I desire her name.   199

BOYET
She hath but one for herself; to desire that were a shame.

LONGAVILLE
Pray you, sir, whose daughter?

BOYET
Her mother's, I have heard.

LONGAVILLE
God's blessing on your beard!   203

BOYET
Good sir, be not offended.
She is an heir of Falconbridge.

LONGAVILLE
Nay, my choler is ended.   206
She is a most sweet lady.

BOYET
Not unlike, sir. That may be.   *Exit Longaville.* 208

          Enter Berowne.

BEROWNE
What's her name in the cap?

BOYET
Rosaline, by good hap.   210

BEROWNE
Is she wedded or no?

BOYET
To her will, sir, or so.   212

197 What who   **198 an** if   **199 light in the light** wanton when her
conduct is known or brought to light   **203 God's . . . beard** (Here,
mildly insulting.)   **206 choler** anger   **208 unlike** unlikely   **210 hap**
fortune   **212 or so** or something of that kind

BEROWNE
  O, you are welcome, sir. Adieu.
BOYET
  Farewell to me, sir, and welcome to you.   214

                                     Exit Berowne.

MARIA
  That last is Berowne, the merry madcap lord.
  Not a word with him but a jest.
BOYET   And every jest but a word. 216
PRINCESS
  It was well done of you to take him at his word.   217
BOYET
  I was as willing to grapple as he was to board.   218
KATHARINE
  Two hot sheeps, marry.
BOYET   And wherefore not ships?   219
  No sheep, sweet lamb, unless we feed on your lips.
KATHARINE
  You sheep, and I pasture. Shall that finish the jest?   221
BOYET
  So you grant pasture for me.   [*Offering to kiss her.*]
KATHARINE   Not so, gentle beast.   222
  My lips are no common, though several they be.   223
BOYET
  Belonging to whom?
KATHARINE   To my fortunes and me.
PRINCESS
  Good wits will be jangling; but, gentles, agree.   225
  This civil war of wits were much better used
  On Navarre and his bookmen, for here 'tis abused.   227
BOYET
  If my observation, which very seldom lies,

---

214 Farewell . . . you i.e., you bid me "farewell" and I will say "you're
welcome to go"   **216 Not . . . jest** everything he says is a joke
217 take . . . word i.e., vie with him in wordplay (with a pun on "take
him literally")   **218 grapple, board** (Tactics of sea warfare, here applied
to wordplay, with bawdy overtones.)   **219 sheeps, ships** (Pronounced
nearly alike by Elizabethans.)   **221 pasture** (with a play on *pastor,*
shepherd)   **222 So** provided   **223 common** common land for pasturing
(with a bawdy suggestion of "available to all men").   **several** private
enclosed land (with a pun on "more than one" and "parted")   **225 jangling** quarreling.   **gentles** gentlefolk   **227 bookmen** scholars.   **abused**
misapplied

By the heart's still rhetoric disclosèd with eyes,   229
Deceive me not now, Navarre is infected.

PRINCESS   With what?

BOYET

With that which we lovers entitle "affected."   232

PRINCESS   Your reason?

BOYET

Why, all his behaviors did make their retire   234
To the court of his eye, peeping thorough desire.   235
His heart, like an agate, with your print impressed,   236
Proud with his form, in his eye pride expressed.   237
His tongue, all impatient to speak and not see,   238
Did stumble with haste in his eyesight to be;   239
All senses to that sense did make their repair,   240
To feel only looking on fairest of fair.   241
Methought all his senses were locked in his eye,
As jewels in crystal for some prince to buy,   243
Who, tend'ring their own worth from where they were
    glassed,   244
Did point you to buy them, along as you passed.   245
His face's own margent did quote such amazes   246
That all eyes saw his eyes enchanted with gazes.
I'll give you Aquitaine and all that is his,   248
An you give him for my sake but one loving kiss.   249

PRINCESS

Come to our pavilion. Boyet is disposed.   250

---

229 **still** silent   232 **affected** being in love   234 **behaviors** actions.
make their retire withdraw, retire. (Navarre was dumbstruck, unable to
do anything except gaze at the Princess.)   235 **thorough** through
236 **agate** (An allusion to small figures cut in agate stones.)   **print
impressed** image engraved   237 **Proud . . . expressed** proud of the form
(of the Princess) imprinted on it, expressed that pride through the look
in his eye   238 **to speak . . . see** at being able to speak only and not to
see   239 **in his . . . be** to take part in his seeing   240 **that sense** i.e., the
eyesight. **make their repair** go   241 **To . . . looking** to express themselves solely through looking   243 **in crystal** enclosed within crystal
glass   244 **Who, tend'ring** which, offering. **glassed** encased in the
glass (crystal) of his eyes   245 **point** appoint, direct, invite   246 **His
. . . amazes** i.e., his expression of amazement offered such a visible
commentary on what his eyes saw. (*Margents* or margins of books often
bore commentary on the text proper.)   248 **I'll give you** i.e., I warrant
you can have   249 **An** if   250 **disposed** inclined (to be merry)

BOYET
But to speak that in words which his eye hath disclosed. 251
I only have made a mouth of his eye,
By adding a tongue which I know will not lie.

ROSALINE
Thou art an old lovemonger and speakest skillfully.

MARIA
He is Cupid's grandfather, and learns news of him.

KATHARINE
Then was Venus like her mother, for her father is but
    grim.   256

BOYET
Do you hear, my mad wenches?

MARIA   No.

BOYET   What, then, do you see? 257

KATHARINE
Ay, our way to be gone.

BOYET   You are too hard for me.   258

                                                      Exeunt omnes.

❖

251 But merely.   **his** i.e., the King's   **256 Then . . . grim** i.e., Boyet isn't
nearly handsome enough to have given Venus her beauty   **257 Do you
hear** i.e., won't you listen to me. (But the ladies parry Boyet's *hear*
and *see* to their own witty purposes.)   **mad** high-spirited   **258 our . . .
gone** the way out of here.   **hard** sharp, difficult to outwit   **s.d. omnes**
all

3.1   *Enter [Armado the] braggart and [Mote,] his boy.*

ARMADO   Warble, child. Make passionate my sense of ¹
hearing.

MOTE [*Singing*]   Concolinel. ³

ARMADO   Sweet air! Go, tenderness of years. [*He gives* ⁴
a key.] Take this key, give enlargement to the swain, ⁵
bring him festinately hither. I must employ him in a ⁶
letter to my love.

MOTE   Master, will you win your love with a French
brawl?
⁹

ARMADO   How meanest thou? Brawling in French? ¹⁰

MOTE   No, my complete master, but to jig off a tune at ¹¹
the tongue's end, canary to it with your feet, humor it ¹²
with turning up your eyelids, sigh a note and sing a
note, sometimes through the throat as if you swallowed
love with singing love, sometimes through the nose as
if you snuffed up love by smelling love, with your hat
penthouse-like o'er the shop of your eyes, with your ¹⁷
arms crossed on your thin-belly doublet like a rabbit ¹⁸
on a spit, or your hands in your pocket like a man after ¹⁹
the old painting, and keep not too long in one tune, ²⁰
but a snip and away. These are compliments, these are ²¹
humors, these betray nice wenches that would be ²²

3.1. Location: Navarre's park.
1 passionate impassioned, responsive   **3 Concolinel** (Unidentified;
perhaps the name or refrain of a song.)   **4 air** song   **5 enlargement**
release from confinement   **6 festinately** quickly   **9 brawl** a French
dance figure   **10 Brawling** quarreling   **11 complete** accomplished.
jig . . . tune sing a jiglike tune   **12 canary** dance. (From the name of a
lively dance; cf. *jig*.)   **17 penthouse-like** like the projecting second story
of a house built out to shelter the shop on the ground floor   **18 arms**
crossed (Betokening melancholy; cf. 4.3.131.)   **thin-belly doublet**
(1) man's jacket over his thin belly, thin because of lovesickness (2) a
jacket thinly padded in the waist   **19 after** in the style of   **20 old**
painting (If Mote refers here to a specific painting, it remains unidentified, but he may merely mean "some old painting.")   **21 a snip and**
away a snippet or scrap of one song and then on to another.   **compli-**
ments gentlemanly accomplishments. (Or perhaps *complements*, those
things that complete or make perfect.)   **22 humors** moods.   **nice** coy

betrayed without these, and make them men of note— 23
do you note?—men that most are affected to these. 24

ARMADO   How hast thou purchased this experience?

MOTE   By my penny of observation.

ARMADO   But O, but O— 27

MOTE   "The hobbyhorse is forgot." 28

ARMADO   Call'st thou my love "hobbyhorse"?

MOTE   No, master, the hobbyhorse is but a colt, and 30
your love perhaps a hackney. But have you forgot your 31
love?

ARMADO   Almost I had.

MOTE   Negligent student, learn her by heart.

ARMADO   By heart and in heart, boy.

MOTE   And out of heart, master. All those three I will
prove. 37

ARMADO   What wilt thou prove? 38

MOTE   A man, if I live; and this "by," "in," and "without,"
upon the instant: "by" heart you love her because your
heart cannot come by her; "in" heart you love her be- 41
cause your heart is in love with her; and "out" of heart
you love her, being out of heart that you cannot en- 43
joy her.

ARMADO   I am all these three.

MOTE   And three times as much more—[Aside] and yet
nothing at all.

ARMADO   Fetch hither the swain. He must carry me a 48
letter.

MOTE [Aside]   A message well sympathized—a horse to 50
be ambassador for an ass.

ARMADO   Ha, ha! What sayest thou?

MOTE   Marry, sir, you must send the ass upon the
horse, for he is very slow-gaited. But I go.

ARMADO   The way is but short. Away!

23 note (1) distinction (2) musical notation   24 affected inclined,
drawn   27–28 But O . . . forgot (Probably the refrain of a popular song;
it turns up again in *Hamlet*, 3.2.133. The hobbyhorse was the figure of a
horse made of light material and fastened over the torso and head of a
morris dancer.)   30–31 hobbyhorse, colt, hackney (Slang terms for
prostitutes or wanton persons.)   37 prove demonstrate   38 prove turn
out to be   41 come by possess   43 out of heart discouraged, depressed   48 me for me   50 sympathized matched

MOTE   As swift as lead, sir.

ARMADO   The meaning, pretty ingenious?
Is not lead a metal heavy, dull, and slow?

MOTE
Minime, honest master; or rather, master, no.   59

ARMADO
I say lead is slow.

MOTE   You are too swift, sir, to say so.
Is that lead slow which is fired from a gun?

ARMADO   Sweet smoke of rhetoric!
He reputes me a cannon, and the bullet, that's he.
I shoot thee at the swain.

MOTE   Thump, then, and I flee.   64

                                              [*Exit.*]

ARMADO
A most acute juvenal, voluble and free of grace!   65
By thy favor, sweet welkin, I must sigh in thy face.   66
Most rude melancholy, valor gives thee place.   67
My herald is returned.

          Enter [*Mote the*] *page and* [*Costard the*] *clown.*

MOTE
A wonder, master! Here's a costard broken in a shin.   69

ARMADO
Some enigma, some riddle. Come, thy *l'envoi*. Begin.   70

COSTARD   No egma, no riddle, no *l'envoi*, no salve in   71
the mail, sir. O, sir, plantain, a plain plantain. No   72
l'envoi, no *l'envoi*, no salve, sir, but a plantain!

ARMADO   By virtue, thou enforcest laughter; thy silly

---

59 Minime not at all   **64 Thump** (Representing the sound of cannon.)
65 voluble quick-witted   **66 favor** good will, permission.   **welkin** sky
67 gives thee place gives way to you   **69 costard . . . shin** an apple or a
head with a bruised shin. (An *enigma*, as Armado points out, since
apples and heads don't have shins.)   **70 l'envoi** i.e., postscript or com-
mendatory statement to the reader attached to a composition; here, an
explanation   **71 egma** (Costard's attempt at *enigma;* he evidently mistakes this strange name, along with *riddle* and *l'envoi*, as a kind of salve
for his hurt shin.)   **salve** (With a play seemingly on *salve*, meaning
"hail!" Armado points out in his next speech that Costard has mistaken
salve, a salutation, for *l'envoi*, a farewell.)   **72 mail** pouch, bag (suggesting the bag of a mountebank or seller of cures).   **plantain** an old-
fashioned herbal remedy (which Costard prefers to the strange-sounding
egma, etc.)

thought, my spleen; the heaving of my lungs provokes 75
me to ridiculous smiling. O, pardon me, my stars! 76
Doth the inconsiderate take "salve" for *l'envoi*, and the 77
word *l'envoi* for a salve?

MOTE
Do the wise think them other? Is not *l'envoi* a salve?

ARMADO
No, page, it is an epilogue or discourse to make plain
Some obscure precedence that hath tofore been sain. 81
I will example it: 82
          The fox, the ape, and the humble-bee 83
          Were still at odds, being but three. 84
There's the moral. Now the *l'envoi*. 85

MOTE
I will add the *l'envoi*. Say the moral again.

ARMADO
          The fox, the ape, and the humble-bee
          Were still at odds, being but three.

MOTE
          Until the goose came out of door
          And stayed the odds by adding four. 90
Now will I begin your moral, and do you follow with
my *l'envoi*.
          The fox, the ape, and the humble-bee
          Were still at odds, being but three.

ARMADO
          Until the goose came out of door,
          Staying the odds by adding four.

MOTE   A good *l'envoi*, ending in the goose. Would you 97
desire more?

---

75 spleen (The seat of emotions and passions; held to be the organ that
controlled excessive mirth or anger.)   **76 ridiculous** scornful (but with
unintended meaning of "absurd")   **77 inconsiderate** mindless fellow.
salve (Here used in the Latin sense of "hail.")   **81 precedence** preceding
discourse.   **tofore** previously.   **sain** said   **82 example** give an example
of   **83 humble-bee** bumblebee   **84 still** continually.   **at odds** (1) at
enmity (2) an odd number, i.e., three   **85 moral** riddle or allegory
90 stayed the odds (1) stopped the enmity (2) changed odd to even.   **four**
a fourth   **97 l'envoi ... goose** (Mote's joke is based on the fact that
l'envoi ends with the same sound as the French word for goose, *oie*.
Armado has made himself the goose by playing Mote's game.)

COSTARD

   The boy hath sold him a bargain—a goose, that's flat. 99

   Sir, your pennyworth is good, an your goose be fat. 100

   To sell a bargain well is as cunning as fast and loose. 101

   Let me see: a fat *l'envoi*—ay, that's a fat goose.

ARMADO

   Come hither, come hither. How did this argument begin? 103

MOTE

   By saying that a costard was broken in a shin. 104

   Then called you for the *l'envoi*.

COSTARD   True, and I for a plantain. Thus came your
argument in; then the boy's fat *l'envoi*, the goose that
you bought; and he ended the market. 108

ARMADO   But tell me, how was there a costard broken 109
in a shin?

MOTE   I will tell you sensibly. 111

COSTARD   Thou hast no feeling of it, Mote. I will speak
that *l'envoi:*

   I Costard, running out, that was safely within,

   Fell over the threshold and broke my shin.

ARMADO   We will talk no more of this matter.

COSTARD   Till there be more matter in the shin. 117

ARMADO   Sirrah Costard, I will enfranchise thee. 118

COSTARD   O, marry me to one Frances! I smell some
l'envoi, some goose, in this. 120

ARMADO   By my sweet soul, I mean setting thee at liberty, enfreedoming thy person. Thou wert immured, 122
restrained, captivated, bound.

COSTARD   True, true, and now you will be my purgation 124
and let me loose.

99 sold . . . goose i.e., outwitted him. **flat** certain **100 your . . . good**
i.e., you got your money's worth. **an** if **101 fast and loose** a cheating
trick. (See 1.2.151.) **103 argument** discussion **104 broken in a shin**
with a broken shin **108 and . . . market** (Costard refers to the proverbial
expression "Three women and a goose make a market.") **109 how** in
what sense **111 sensibly** feelingly. (But Costard protests that Mote
cannot personally know what it *feels* like.) **117 matter** pus (playing on
matter, business, in l. 116) **118 enfranchise** release from confinement.
(Costard hears this as *en-Frances*, "provide with a Frances.") **120 goose**
(Slang for "prostitute.") **122 immured** imprisoned **124 be my purgation** purge me of guilt (with pun on the sense of giving a purgative so
that Costard's bowels will be *let loose*)

ARMADO   I give thee thy liberty, set thee from durance, 126
and in lieu thereof impose on thee nothing but this:
Bear this significant [*Giving a letter*] to the country 128
maid Jaquenetta. There is remuneration. [*Giving* 129
money.] For the best ward of mine honor is rewarding 130
my dependents. Mote, follow.   [*Exit.*]

MOTE
Like the sequel, I. Seigneur Costard, adieu.   *Exit.* 132

COSTARD
My sweet ounce of man's flesh, my incony Jew!   133
Now will I look to his remuneration. [*He looks at his
money*.] Remuneration! O, that's the Latin word for
three farthings. Three farthings—remuneration. 136
"What's the price of this inkle?"—"One penny."— 137
"No, I'll give you a remuneration." Why, it carries it. 138
Remuneration! Why, it is a fairer name than French 139
crown. I will never buy and sell out of this word.   140

        Enter Berowne.

BEROWNE   My good knave Costard, exceedingly well 141
met.   142
COSTARD   Pray you, sir, how much carnation ribbon 143
may a man buy for a remuneration?
BEROWNE   What is a remuneration?
COSTARD   Marry, sir, halfpenny farthing.   146
BEROWNE   Why then, three farthing worth of silk.
COSTARD   I thank your worship. God be wi' you!

                            [*He starts to leave.*]
BEROWNE   Stay, slave, I must employ thee.
As thou wilt win my favor, good my knave,
Do one thing for me that I shall entreat.

---

126 set release.   **durance** imprisonment   **128 significant** sign, token
129 remuneration payment   **130 ward** guard   **132 the sequel** that which
follows; *l'envoi*   **133 incony** fine, rare, delicate.   **Jew** (Here a term of
playful insult, possibly suggested by *juvenile*.)   **136 farthings** silver coins
worth a quarter of a penny   **137 inkle** a kind of linen tape   **138 carries
it** wins the day   **139–140 French crown** (1) a coin (2) a bald head, the
result of syphilis or "the French disease"   **140 out of** i.e., without using   **141–142 exceedingly well met** i.e., how fortunate to see you just
now   **143 carnation** flesh-colored   **146 halfpenny farthing** i.e., three
farthings (a *halfpenny*, worth two farthings, plus one farthing)

COSTARD   When would you have it done, sir?

BEROWNE   This afternoon.

COSTARD   Well, I will do it, sir. Fare you well.

BEROWNE   Thou knowest not what it is.

COSTARD   I shall know, sir, when I have done it.

BEROWNE   Why, villain, thou must know first.

COSTARD   I will come to your worship tomorrow
morning.

BEROWNE   It must be done this afternoon. Hark, slave,
it is but this:
The Princess comes to hunt here in the park,
And in her train there is a gentle lady;
When tongues speak sweetly, then they name her name,
And Rosaline they call her. Ask for her,
And to her white hand see thou do commend   166
This sealed-up counsel. There's thy guerdon; go.   167
          [*Giving him a letter and a shilling.*]

COSTARD   Gardon, O sweet gardon! Better than remu-   168
neration, a 'levenpence farthing better. Most sweet   169
gardon! I will do it, sir, in print. Gardon! Remunera-   170
tion!   *Exit.*

BEROWNE
And I forsooth in love! I that have been Love's whip,
A very beadle to a humorous sigh,   173
A critic, nay, a night-watch constable,
A domineering pedant o'er the boy,   175
Than whom no mortal so magnificent!
This wimpled, whining, purblind, wayward boy,   177
This Senior Junior, giant dwarf, Dan Cupid,   178
Regent of love rhymes, lord of folded arms,   179
Th' anointed sovereign of sighs and groans,
Liege of all loiterers and malcontents,

---

166 commend entrust   **167 counsel** private or secret communication.
guerdon reward   **s.d. shilling** a silver coin worth twelve pence
168 Gardon (Costard anglicizes the French *guerdon*.)   **168–169 Better . . .
better** (Costard delights that the shilling he has been given is worth
eleven pence and a farthing more than the three farthings he had.)
170 in print i.e., most exactly   **173 beadle** parish officer responsible for
whipping minor offenders.   **humorous** moody   **175 pedant** schoolmaster   **177 wimpled** blindfolded.   **purblind** wholly blind   **178 Dan** don,
sir. (From the Latin *dominus*.)   **179 Regent** ruler.   **folded arms** (Betokening melancholy; see 3.1.18.)

Dread prince of plackets, king of codpieces,   182
Sole imperator and great general   183
Of trotting paritors—O my little heart!   184
And I to be a corporal of his field,   185
And wear his colors like a tumbler's hoop!   186
What? I love, I sue, I seek a wife?
A woman, that is like a German clock,
Still a-repairing, ever out of frame,   189
And never going aright, being a watch,
But being watched that it may still go right?   191
Nay, to be perjured, which is worst of all;
And, among three, to love the worst of all—
A whitely wanton with a velvet brow,   194
With two pitch-balls stuck in her face for eyes;   195
Ay, and, by heaven, one that will do the deed   196
Though Argus were her eunuch and her guard.   197
And I to sigh for her, to watch for her,   198
To pray for her! Go to, it is a plague
That Cupid will impose for my neglect
Of his almighty dreadful little might.
Well, I will love, write, sigh, pray, sue, groan.
Some men must love milady, and some Joan.   [*Exit.*]   203

❖

182 **plackets** slits in petticoats (referring bawdily to women).   **codpieces**
flaps or pouches concealing the opening in the front of men's breeches
(referring bawdily to men)   183 **imperator** absolute ruler   184 **paritors**
apparitors, summoners of ecclesiastical courts (who could make a profit
by spying out sexual offenders)   185 **corporal of his field** his field officer   186 **tumbler's hoop** (Such hoops were usually brightly decorated
with silks and ribbons.)   189 **Still** always.   **a-repairing** needing repair.
frame order   191 **But being watched** unless it is watched carefully (like
a wandering wife)   194 **whitely** pale of complexion (considered beautiful; but cf. 4.3.250–273, where the lords joke about the darkness of
Rosaline's features).   **velvet** i.e., soft-skinned   195 **pitch-balls** balls made
of pitch, a lustrously black substance created by distilling tar   196 **do
the deed** engage in sex   197 **Argus** a fabulous monster with a hundred
eyes, some of which were always awake. (Juno gave Argus custody over
Io, of whom Jove was enamored.)   **eunuch** i.e., guard in a seraglio
198 **watch** lose sleep, stay awake   203 **milady, Joan** (Opposite types on
the social scale, one a lady of quality and one a peasant woman.)

4.1   *Enter the Princess, a Forester, her Ladies, and*
her Lords, [Boyet and others].

PRINCESS
　Was that the King that spurred his horse so hard
　Against the steep uprising of the hill?
BOYET
　I know not, but I think it was not he.
PRINCESS
　Whoe'er 'a was, 'a showed a mounting mind.　　　　　4
　Well, lords, today we shall have our dispatch;　　　　5
　On Saturday we will return to France.
　Then, Forester, my friend, where is the bush
　That we must stand and play the murderer in?
FORESTER
　Hereby, upon the edge of yonder coppice,　　　　　　9
　A stand where you may make the fairest shoot.　　　　10
PRINCESS
　I thank my beauty, I am fair that shoot,
　And thereupon thou speak'st "the fairest shoot."
FORESTER
　Pardon me, madam, for I meant not so.
PRINCESS
　What, what? First praise me, and again say no?　　　14
　O short-lived pride! Not fair? Alack for woe!
FORESTER
　Yes, madam, fair.
PRINCESS　　　　　　　　　　Nay, never paint me now.　　16
　Where fair is not, praise cannot mend the brow.　　　17
　Here, good my glass, take this for telling true.　　　18
　　　　　　　　　　　　　　　　　[*She gives him money.*]
　Fair payment for foul words is more than due.

4.1. Location: Navarre's park. A hunter's station at the edge of a coppice.
4 'a he.　**mounting** (1) rising (2) aspiring　**5 dispatch** settlement
9 coppice grove of trees　**10 stand** hunter's station, toward which the
game is driven.　**fairest** most favorable. (The Princess chooses to play
on the word in a compliment to herself.)　**14 again** i.e., then　**16 paint**
flatter　**17 fair** beauty.　**brow** forehead, i.e., face　**18 good my glass** my
true mirror (i.e., a counselor who will not flatter. The Princess amuses
herself with Renaissance commonplaces about the value of honest
counselors to a true prince, much to the discomfort of the Forester.)

FORESTER

Nothing but fair is that which you inherit.   20

PRINCESS

See, see, my beauty will be saved by merit!   21
O heresy in fair, fit for these days!   22
A giving hand, though foul, shall have fair praise.
But come, the bow. [*She takes the bow.*] Now mercy goes
   to kill,   24
And shooting well is then accounted ill.   25
Thus will I save my credit in the shoot: 26
Not wounding, pity would not let me do 't;   27
If wounding, then it was to show my skill,
That more for praise than purpose meant to kill.   29
And out of question so it is sometimes,   30
Glory grows guilty of detested crimes,   31
When for fame's sake, for praise, an outward part,   32
We bend to that the working of the heart;   33
As I for praise alone now seek to spill
The poor deer's blood that my heart means no ill.   35

BOYET

Do not curst wives hold that self-sovereignty   36
Only for praise' sake when they strive to be
Lords o'er their lords?

PRINCESS

Only for praise; and praise we may afford
To any lady that subdues a lord.

    Enter [*Costard the*] *clown* [*with a letter*].

---

20 inherit possess   **21 my . . . merit** i.e., my beauty is complimented
again in return for my giving a gratuity. (To be *saved by merit* was,
however, a heresy according to orthodox Anglican doctrine, which
taught salvation by faith rather than by merit or good works.)   **22 in
fair** regarding beauty.   **these days** i.e., these times of religious controversy   **24 mercy** i.e., the Princess, who as a royal woman is an emblem
of mercy   **25 then** i.e., when a merciful person like the Princess goes
hunting   **26 credit** reputation   **27 Not . . . do 't** i.e., I can claim, if I
miss, that pity restrained me   **29 That . . . kill** i.e., I shot to earn praise
for my skill rather than for the sake of killing   **30 out of question**
undoubtedly.   **sometimes** sometimes (that)   **31 Glory . . . crimes** i.e., an
excessive desire for glory prompts us to commit detestable crimes
32 an outward part a superficial thing   **33 bend** force, adapt.   **that** i.e.,
fame   **35 The poor . . . ill** the blood of the poor deer that means me no
harm   **36 curst** shrewish.   **hold** maintain

BOYET
Here comes a member of the commonwealth.   41

COSTARD   God-i-good-e'en all! Pray you, which is the   42
head lady?

PRINCESS   Thou shalt know her, fellow, by the rest that
have no heads.

COSTARD   Which is the greatest lady, the highest?

PRINCESS   The thickest and the tallest.   47

COSTARD
The thickest and the tallest! It is so; truth is truth.
An your waist, mistress, were as slender as my wit,   49
One o' these maids' girdles for your waist should be fit.
Are not you the chief woman? You are the thickest here.

PRINCESS   What's your will, sir? What's your will?

COSTARD   I have a letter from Monsieur Berowne to one
Lady Rosaline.

PRINCESS
O, thy letter, thy letter! He's a good friend of mine.
Stand aside, good bearer. Boyet, you can carve;   56
Break up this capon.   [*The letter is given to Boyet.*]

BOYET   I am bound to serve.   57
This letter is mistook; it importeth none here.   58
It is writ to Jaquenetta.

PRINCESS   We will read it, I swear.
Break the neck of the wax, and everyone give ear.   60

BOYET (*Reads*) "By heaven, that thou art fair is most
infallible; true that thou art beauteous; truth itself that   62
thou art lovely. More fairer than fair, beautiful than
beauteous, truer than truth itself, have commiseration   64
on thy heroical vassal! The magnanimous and most   65
illustrate King Cophetua set eye upon the pernicious   66

41 commonwealth ordinary citizenry   **42 God-i-good-e'en** God give you
good evening   **47 The thickest and the tallest** (The Princess quips that
greatest could be defined this way. Costard undiplomatically observes that
the terms could indeed be applied to her.)   **49 An** if   **56 carve** (1) cut up,
i.e., open (2) make courtly gestures   **57 Break up** cut up (a technical term
in carving), i.e., open.   **capon** (Like the French *poulet, capon* designates
figuratively a love letter.)   **bound** obliged   **58 mistook** mis-taken, misdirected.   **importeth** concerns   **60 wax** seal   **62 infallible** certain, incontro-
vertible   **64 commiseration** pity   **65 vassal** humble servant   **66 illustrate**
illustrious

and indubitate beggar Zenelophon; and he it was that 67
might rightly say, *"Veni, vidi, vici"*; which to annotha- 68
nize in the vulgar—O base and obscure vulgar!—vi- 69
delicet, "He came, saw, and overcame." He came, one; 70
saw, two; overcame, three. Who came? The King.
Why did he come? To see. Why did he see? To overcome. To whom came he? To the beggar. What saw
he? The beggar. Who overcame he? The beggar. The
conclusion is victory. On whose side? The King's. The
captive is enriched. On whose side? The beggar's. The
catastrophe is a nuptial. On whose side? The King's— 77
no, on both in one, or one in both. I am the King, for 78
so stands the comparison; thou the beggar, for so wit- 79
nesseth thy lowliness. Shall I command thy love? I 80
may. Shall I enforce thy love? I could. Shall I entreat
thy love? I will. What shalt thou exchange for rags?
Robes. For tittles? Titles. For thyself? Me. Thus, ex- 83
pecting thy reply, I profane my lips on thy foot, my 84
eyes on thy picture, and my heart on thy every part.
    Thine, in the dearest design of industry, 86
                      Don Adriano de Armado.
Thus dost thou hear the Nemean lion roar 88
    'Gainst thee, thou lamb, that standest as his prey.
Submissive fall his princely feet before, 90
    And he from forage will incline to play. 91
But if thou strive, poor soul, what art thou then? 92
Food for his rage, repasture for his den." 93

PRINCESS
What plume of feathers is he that indited this letter? 94

---

67 indubitate undoubted.   **Zenelophon** Penelophon, the beggar maid in
the ballad about King Cophetua. (See 1.2.105–106.)   **68 Veni, vidi, vici** I
came, I saw, I overcame. (The words are Julius Caesar's terse account of
his victory over King Pharnaces.)   **68–69 annothanize** annotate (pseudo-
Latin), or, anatomize, explain, interpret   **69 vulgar** vernacular
69–70 videlicet namely   **77 catastrophe** conclusion   **78–79 for . . .
comparison** according to this analogy   **80 lowliness** low social standing   **83 tittles** insignificant specks or dots   **84 profane** desecrate
86 dearest . . . industry most excellent pattern of zealous gallantry
88 Nemean lion lion slain by Hercules in the first of his twelve labors
90 Submissive fall if you fall submissively   **91 forage** raging, raven-
ing.   **incline** turn, shift   **92 strive** resist   **93 repasture** food
94 What . . . feathers what kind of bird, dandy.   **indited** wrote

What vane? What weathercock? Did you ever hear
    better? 95
BOYET
I am much deceived but I remember the style. 96
PRINCESS
Else your memory is bad, going o'er it erewhile. 97
BOYET
This Armado is a Spaniard that keeps here in court, 98
A phantasime, a Monarcho, and one that makes sport 99
To the Prince and his bookmates.
PRINCESS   Thou fellow, a word. 100
Who gave thee this letter?
COSTARD   I told you—my lord.
PRINCESS
To whom shouldst thou give it?
COSTARD   From my lord to my lady.
PRINCESS
From which lord to which lady?
COSTARD
From my lord Berowne, a good master of mine,
To a lady of France that he called Rosaline.
PRINCESS
Thou hast mistaken his letter. Come, lords, away. 106
[*To Rosaline.*] Here, sweet, put up this; 'twill be thine
    another day.   [*Exeunt Princess and attendants.*] 107
BOYET
Who is the shooter? Who is the shooter?
ROSALINE   Shall I teach you to know? 108
BOYET
Ay, my continent of beauty.
ROSALINE   Why, she that bears the bow. 109

---

95 vane weathervane (with play on *vain*)   **96 but** unless   **97 Else** otherwise.   **going o'er it** (1) reading it over (2) climbing over a *stile*, playing on *style*.   **erewhile** just now   **98 keeps** lives, dwells   **99 phantasime** one who entertains fantastic notions.   **Monarcho** (The nickname of an eccentric Italian at the Elizabethan court who fancied himself the emperor of the world; hence, anyone who displays absurd pretensions.)   **100 To** for.   **bookmates** fellow scholars   **106 mistaken** incorrectly delivered   **107 up** away.   **'twill be thine** i.e., it will be your turn.   **s.d. attendants** (Perhaps the Forester exits here.)   **108 shooter** archer. (With a pun on *suitor*. Boyet may be asking who is to shoot, now that the Princess has left. Perhaps Rosaline has been given the bow.) **109 continent of** container of all

Finely put off!   110

BOYET
My lady goes to kill horns, but if thou marry,   111
Hang me by the neck if horns that year miscarry.   112
Fine!y put on!   113

ROSALINE
Well, then, I am the shooter.

BOYET   And who is your deer?   114

ROSALINE
If we choose by the horns, yourself come not near.   115
Finely put on, indeed!

MARIA
You still wrangle with her, Boyet, and she strikes at the
  brow.   117

BOYET
But she herself is hit lower. Have I hit her now?   118

ROSALINE   Shall I come upon thee with an old saying   119
that was a man when King Pepin of France was a little   120
boy, as touching the hit it?   121

BOYET   So I may answer thee with one as old, that was   122
a woman when Queen Guinevere of Britain was a little   123
wench, as touching the hit it.

ROSALINE
"Thou canst not hit it, hit it, hit it,
Thou canst not hit it, my good man."

---

110 put off answered evasively   **111 horns** i.e., deer   **112 horns** i.e.,
cuckold's horns. (Boyet saucily suggests that if Rosaline marries, cuckold's horns will not be in short supply.)   **miscarry** do not appear
113 put on urged, applied   **114 deer** (with pun on *dear;* Rosaline is the
natural target of all this double-entendre about the huntress who is
hunting for a husband, since Berowne is known to have written her a
love letter)   **115 If . . . near** (Rosaline retorts to Boyet acerbically by
intimating that he couldn't possibly be her choice.)   **117 she . . . brow**
i.e., she takes good aim at you (with pun on the idea that she has also
put Boyet down with a joke about cuckoldry)   **118 hit lower** i.e., in the
heart, or, more bawdily, in the genital region.   **hit her** scored on her in
this game of wit, described her situation aright   **119 come upon thee**
answer or hit back (continuing the metaphor of hunting and marksman-
ship)   **120 was a man** i.e., was already old.   **King Pepin** Carolingian
king (died 768)   **121 as . . . hit it** concerning a catch or round, to be
sung dancing. (The song itself is obviously bawdy.)   **122 So** as long as,
or similarly   **123 Guinevere** King Arthur's unfaithful queen

BOYET
　"An I cannot, cannot, cannot,   127
　An I cannot, another can."

Exit [Rosaline].

COSTARD
　By my troth, most pleasant. How both did fit it!   129

MARIA
　A mark marvelous well shot, for they both did hit it.   130

BOYET
　A mark! O, mark but that mark! "A mark," says my
　　lady!
　Let the mark have a prick in 't to mete at, if it may be.   132

MARIA
　Wide o' the bow hand! I' faith, your hand is out.   133

COSTARD
　Indeed, 'a must shoot nearer, or he'll ne'er hit the clout.   134

BOYET
　An if my hand be out, then belike your hand is in.   135

COSTARD
　Then will she get the upshoot by cleaving the pin.   136

MARIA
　Come, come, you talk greasily; your lips grow foul.   137

COSTARD
　She's too hard for you at pricks, sir. Challenge her to
　　bowl.   138

BOYET
　I fear too much rubbing. Good night, my good owl.   139

[Exeunt Boyet, Maria, and Katharine.]

127 An if   **129 troth** faith.   **fit it** fit the lyrics to the tune. (*Fit it* often has a bawdy meaning as well.)   **130 mark** target   **132 prick** spot in the center of the target, the bull's-eye (with sexual double meaning, as throughout this passage. *Mark* here suggests "pudendum.")   **mete at** measure with the eye, aim at   **133 Wide . . . hand** wide of the mark on the left side, too far to the left.   **out** inaccurate, out of practice   **134 clout** mark at the center of the target (continuing the bawdry)   **135 An if . . . is in** i.e., if I'm out of practice (sexually as well as at shooting), no doubt you're in practice. **belike** most likely   **136 upshoot** leading or best shot.   **cleaving the pin** splitting exactly the small nail holding the clout in place (with sexual suggestion, as Maria observes in the next line)   **137 greasily** indecently (referring to sexual double entendre in *cleaving, hit it, prick, your hand is in,* etc.)   **138 pricks** informal or illegal archery (with sexual pun) **139 rubbing** grazing or striking together of the bowling balls (with sexual pun).   **owl** (Maria is so addressed because the owl is a bird of night and because to "take owl" is to take offense; also with a bawdy hint at *'ole,* rhyming with *bowl.*)

COSTARD

By my soul, a swain, a most simple clown!   140
Lord, Lord, how the ladies and I have put him down!
O' my troth, most sweet jests, most incony vulgar wit!   142
When it comes so smoothly off, so obscenely, as it were,
    so fit.   143
Armado o' th' one side—O, a most dainty man!   144
To see him walk before a lady and to bear her fan!
To see him kiss his hand, and how most sweetly 'a will
    swear!
And his page o' t'other side, that handful of wit!
Ah, heavens, it is a most pathetical nit! *Shout within.*   148
Sola, sola!   *Exit* [*Costard, running*].   149

❖

4.2   *Enter Dull, Holofernes the pedant, and
          Nathaniel.*

NATHANIEL   Very reverend sport, truly, and done in the   1
testimony of a good conscience.   2
HOLOFERNES   The deer was, as you know, *sanguis*, in   3
blood, ripe as the pomewater, who now hangeth like   4
a jewel in the ear of *caelo*, the sky, the welkin, the   5
heaven, and anon falleth like a crab on the face of *terra*, 6
the soil, the land, the earth.
NATHANIEL   Truly, Master Holofernes, the epithets are
sweetly varied, like a scholar at the least. But, sir, I   9
assure ye it was a buck of the first head.   10
HOLOFERNES   Sir Nathaniel, *haud credo*.   11

---

140 swain peasant   **142 incony** fine, rare   **143 obscenely** (Perhaps a
malapropism for *seemly,* with unintended appropriateness to the preceding passage.)   **fit** suitable   **144 dainty** refined, elegant   **148 it** he.
pathetical nit i.e., touching little fellow. (A *nit* is the egg of a small
insect.)   **149 Sola** (A hunting cry.)

4.2. Location: Navarre's park.
1 reverend worthy of respect   **1–2 in the testimony** with the warrant
3–4 in blood in prime condition   **4 pomewater** a kind of apple.   **who
now** which at one moment   **5 welkin** sky   **6 anon** at the next moment.   **crab** crab apple   **9 at the least** to say the least   **10 of . . . head**
in its fifth year, hence with newly full antlers   **11 Sir** (Term of address
for ordinary clergymen.)   **haud credo** I cannot believe it

DULL 'Twas not a *haud credo*, 'twas a pricket. 12

HOLOFERNES Most barbarous intimation! Yet a kind of 13
insinuation, as it were, *in via*, in way, of explication; 14
facere, as it were, replication, or rather, *ostentare*, to 15
show, as it were, his inclination, after his undressed,
unpolished, uneducated, unpruned, untrained, or
rather, unlettered, or, ratherest, unconfirmed fashion, 18
to insert again my *haud credo* for a deer. 19

DULL I said the deer was not a *haud credo*, 'twas a
pricket.

HOLOFERNES Twice-sod simplicity, *bis coctus!* 22
O thou monster Ignorance, how deformed dost thou
look!

NATHANIEL
Sir, he hath never fed of the dainties that are bred in a
book. 24
He hath not eat paper, as it were; he hath not drunk 25
ink. His intellect is not replenished. He is only an ani-
mal, only sensible in the duller parts; 27
And such barren plants are set before us that we
thankful should be—
Which we of taste and feeling are—for those parts that
do fructify in us more than he. 29
For as it would ill become me to be vain, indiscreet, or a
fool,
So were there a patch set on learning, to see him in a
school. 31
But *omne bene*, say I, being of an old father's mind: 32
Many can brook the weather that love not the wind. 33

---

12 haud credo (Dull mistakes the Latin for something like "old gray
doe.") **pricket** buck in its second year **13 intimation** intrusion **14 insinuation** hint, suggestion, beginning **15 facere** to make. **replication**
explanation **18 unconfirmed** inexperienced **19 insert again** substitute,
interpret. (Holofernes's point is that Dull unwittingly makes sense by
interpreting *haud credo* as a doe rather than a buck.) **22 Twice-sod**
twice sodden or cooked, boiled. **bis coctus,** twice cooked. (Holofernes
is incensed at Dull's twice insisting on his error.) **24 of** on. **dainties**
delicacies **25 eat** eaten. (Pronounced "et.") **27 sensible** capable of
perception **29 Which we** we who. **fructify** grow fruitful. **he** in him
31 were . . . learning (1) it would be setting a fool or dolt to learn (2) it
would be a disgrace to learning itself **32 omne bene** all is well. **being
of** in agreement with. **an old father's mind** opinion of a Church Father,
one of the teachers of the early Christian church **33 brook** put up with
(i.e., one must endure what one cannot change)

DULL
  You two are bookmen. Can you tell me by your wit
  What was a month old at Cain's birth that's not five
  ● weeks old as yet?
HOLOFERNES
  Dictynna, goodman Dull, Dictynna, goodman Dull.   36
DULL What is Dictima?
NATHANIEL A title to Phoebe, to Luna, to the moon.   38
HOLOFERNES
  The moon was a month old when Adam was no more,   39
  And raught not to five weeks when he came to fivescore. 40
  Th' allusion holds in the exchange.   41
DULL 'Tis true indeed. The collusion holds in the ex-   42
  change.
HOLOFERNES God comfort thy capacity! I say, th' allu-   44
  sion holds in the exchange.
DULL And I say the pollution holds in the exchange,   46
  for the moon is never but a month old; and I say be-
  sides that 'twas a pricket that the Princess killed.
HOLOFERNES Sir Nathaniel, will you hear an extemporal   49
  epitaph on the death of the deer? And to humor the
  ignorant, call I the deer the Princess killed a pricket.
NATHANIEL Perge, good Master Holofernes, perge, so it   52
  shall please you to abrogate scurrility.   53
HOLOFERNES I will something affect the letter, for it ar- 54
  gues facility.   55
  The preyful Princess pierced and pricked a pretty
    pleasing pricket;   56
  Some say a sore, but not a sore till now made sore with
    shooting.   57

36, 38 Dictynna, Phoebe, Luna (Classical names for the moon. The first
is uncommon and is appropriate to the pedant. It occurs in Golding's
translation of Ovid, a book that Shakespeare knew.)   **39 more** older
40 raught reached, attained   **41 Th' allusion . . . exchange** i.e., the
riddle is still valid even if Cain's name (see l. 35) is substituted for
Adam's   **42 collusion** conspiracy. (Dull's error for *allusion*.)   **44 comfort** have pity on   **46 pollution** (Another error for *allusion*, with perhaps
unintended relevance to the linguistic *pollution* of Holofernes's Latin.)
49 extemporal impromptu   **52 Perge** proceed   **53 abrogate** refrain
from.   **scurrility** bawdry   **54 something . . . letter** somewhat make use
of alliteration   **54–55 argues** demonstrates   **56 preyful** intent upon
prey   **57 sore** deer in its fourth year.   **made sore** wounded

The dogs did yell. Put "l" to "sore," then sorel jumps
  from thicket,   58
Or pricket sore, or else sorel. The people fall a-hooting.   59
If sore be sore, then "l" to "sore" makes fifty sores o'
  sorel.   60
Of one sore I an hundred make by adding but one more l.

NATHANIEL A rare talent!

DULL [*Aside*] If a talent be a claw, look how he claws   63
him with a talent.

HOLOFERNES This is a gift that I have, simple, simple; a
foolish extravagant spirit, full of forms, figures,
shapes, objects, ideas, apprehensions, motions, revo-   67
lutions. These are begot in the ventricle of memory,   68
nourished in the womb of *pia mater*, and delivered   69
upon the mellowing of occasion. But the gift is good   70
in those in whom it is acute, and I am thankful for it.

NATHANIEL Sir, I praise the Lord for you, and so may
my parishioners, for their sons are well tutored by you,
and their daughters profit very greatly under you. You 74
are a good member of the commonwealth.

HOLOFERNES *Mehercle*, if their sons be ingenious, they 76
shall want no instruction; if their daughters be capa-   77
ble, I will put it to them. But *vir sapit qui pauca loqui-* 78
tur. A soul feminine saluteth us.   79

Enter Jaquenetta and [*Costard*] *the clown.*

JAQUENETTA God give you good morrow, Master Person. 80
HOLOFERNES Master Person, *quasi* pierce-one. And if one 81

---

58 sorel deer in its third year   **59 Or** either   **60 "l."** Roman numeral
fifty   **63 talent** i.e., talon.   **claws** (1) scratches (2) flatters   **67 motions**
impulses   **67–68 revolutions** turns of thought   **68 ventricle of memory**
one of the three sections of the brain, believed to contain the memory
69 pia mater the membrane surrounding the brain; the brain itself
69–70 delivered . . . occasion born when the moment is propitious
74 under you under your instruction. (With unintended sexual double
meaning.)   **76 Mehercle** by Hercules.   **ingenious** clever   **77 want** lack
77–78 capable (1) apt as pupils (2) able to bear children (an unconscious
sexual pun that goes back to *under you* in l. 74)   **78 put it to them**
(with unintended sexual meaning)   **78–79 vir . . . loquitur** he is a wise
man who speaks little   **80 Person** (Normally pronounced *parson* in
Elizabethan English, but here pronounced *person*, in rustic speech,
thereby eliciting a pedantic witticism from Holofernes.)   **81 quasi** that
is, as if

should be pierced, which is the one?   82

COSTARD Marry, Master Schoolmaster, he that is
likeliest to a hogshead.   84

HOLOFERNES Of piercing a hogshead! A good luster of   85
conceit in a turf of earth; fire enough for a flint, pearl 86
enough for a swine. 'Tis pretty, it is well.

JAQUENETTA Good Master Person, be so good as read
me this letter. It was given me by Costard, and sent
me from Don Armado. I beseech you, read it.

> [*She hands the letter to Nathaniel.*]

HOLOFERNES *"Fauste, precor gelida quando pecus omne* 91
sub umbra ruminat," and so forth. Ah, good old Man- 92
tuan! I may speak of thee as the traveler doth of Venice:
      Venezia, Venezia,   94
      Chi non te vede, chi non ti prezia.   95
Old Mantuan, old Mantuan! Who understandeth thee
not, loves thee not. [*He sings.*] Ut, re, sol, la, mi, fa. [*To* 97
Nathaniel, who is examining the letter.] Under pardon, 98
sir, what are the contents? Or rather, as Horace says in
his—What, my soul, verses?

NATHANIEL Ay, sir, and very learned.

HOLOFERNES Let me hear a staff, a stanza, a verse. *Lege,* 102
domine.   103

NATHANIEL [*Reads*]
"If love make me forsworn, how shall I swear to love? 104
Ah, never faith could hold, if not to beauty vowed!

---

82 pierced (Pronounced "persed"; playing on *pers-one,* pierce one. This is
sometimes taken as an allusion to Nashe's *Pierce Penniless, His Supplication
to the Devil,* a fantastic satire in which the author, in the character of Pierce,
comments on the vices of the times; also to Harvey's answer, *Pierce's Su-
pererogation,* in which Pierce is referred to as "the hogshead of wit";
cf. l. 85.) **84 likeliest** most like. **hogshead** barrel **85 piercing a hogshead**
broaching a barrel, i.e., getting drunk **85–86 luster of conceit** spark of
fancy **91–92 Fauste . . . ruminat** (The first line of the first eclogue of the
Italian Renaissance poet Mantuan. It was a well-known text in the schools.
The passage means "Faustus, I beg, while all the cattle chew their cud in the
cool shade.") **94–95 Venezia . . . prezia** Venice, Venice, only he who sees you
not loves you not **97 Ut** (Equivalent to the modern *do.* If Holofernes intends
to sing the scale, *do, re, mi, fa, sol, la,* he displays his ignorance, but he may
be singing a fragment of a melody.) **98 Under pardon** i.e., excuse me
102 staff stanza **102–103 Lege, domine** read, master **104–117 If . . . tongue**
(These lines were printed with minor changes in *The Passionate Pilgrim,*
1599, a collection of poems by various authors but attributed to Shakespeare.
Two others of the volume are from this play, that read by Longaville,
4.3.56–69, and that by Dumaine, 4.3.97–116.)

Though to myself forsworn, to thee I'll faithful prove;
  Those thoughts to me were oaks, to thee like osiers
    bowed.   107
Study his bias leaves and makes his book thine eyes,   108
  Where all those pleasures live that art would
    comprehend.
If knowledge be the mark, to know thee shall suffice;   110
  Well learnèd is that tongue that well can thee
    commend,
All ignorant that soul that sees thee without wonder;
  Which is to me some praise that I thy parts admire.
Thy eye Jove's lightning bears, thy voice his dreadful
    thunder,
  Which, not to anger bent, is music and sweet fire.   115
Celestial as thou art, O, pardon love this wrong,   116
That sings heaven's praise with such an earthly
    tongue."   117

HOLOFERNES You find not the apostrophus, and so miss   118
the accent. Let me supervise the canzonet. [*He takes*   119
the letter.] Here are only numbers ratified, but, for the   120
elegancy, facility, and golden cadence of poesy—*caret.*   121
Ovidius Naso was the man. And why indeed   122
"Naso," but for smelling out the odoriferous flowers
of fancy, the jerks of invention? *Imitari* is nothing. So 124
doth the hound his master, the ape his keeper, the
tired horse his rider. But, damosella virgin, was this   126
directed to you?

JAQUENETTA Ay, sir, from one Monsieur Berowne, one
of the strange queen's lords.   129

---

107 to me were i.e., seemed to me as firm as. **osiers** willows
108 Study . . . leaves i.e., the student leaves his true inclination
110 mark target **115 bent** turned, directed **116 pardon . . . wrong**
excuse this failure in my loving **118 find** heed. **apostrophus** apostro-
phes, marks of elision used to indicate omitted vowels and shortened
pronunciation of a word **119 supervise** glance over, peruse. **canzonet**
i.e., poem **120 only numbers ratified,** i.e., merely language made
metrical **121 caret** it is lacking **122 Ovidius Naso** (The Roman poet
Ovid, born in 43 B.C.; *Naso,* his surname, is derived from *nasus,* nose.)
124 fancy imagination. **jerks of invention** strokes of imagination.
Imitari to imitate **126 tired** attired, harnessed, in full tackle. **damosella** i.e., damsel **129 strange** foreign. (Jaquenetta seems mistakenly to
believe that Berowne is attached to the Princess's retinue; or this may
be a matter on which Shakespeare changed his mind as he revised.)

HOLOFERNES   I will overglance the superscript: "To the 130
snow-white hand of the most beauteous Lady Rosaline." I will look again on the intellect of the letter for 132
the nomination of the party writing to the person writ- 133
ten unto: "Your ladyship's in all desired employment, 134
Berowne." Sir Nathaniel, this Berowne is one of the
votaries with the King, and here he hath framed a let- 136
ter to a sequent of the stranger queen's, which acci- 137
dentally, or by the way of progression, hath miscar- 138
ried.—Trip and go, my sweet; deliver this paper into 139
the royal hand of the King. It may concern much. 140
[*He gives her the letter.*] Stay not thy compliment. I for- 141
give thy duty. Adieu. 142

JAQUENETTA   Good Costard, go with me.—Sir, God save
your life!

COSTARD   Have with thee, my girl. 145

                          Exit [*with Jaquenetta*].

NATHANIEL   Sir, you have done this in the fear of God,
very religiously; and as a certain Father saith— 147

HOLOFERNES   Sir, tell not me of the Father; I do fear col- 148
orable colors. But to return to the verses: did they 149
please you, Sir Nathaniel?

NATHANIEL   Marvelous well for the pen. 151

HOLOFERNES   I do dine today at the father's of a certain
pupil of mine, where, if before repast it shall please 153
you to gratify the table with a grace, I will, on my priv- 154
ilege I have with the parents of the foresaid child or
pupil, undertake your *ben venuto;* where I will prove 156
those verses to be very unlearned, neither savoring of
poetry, wit, nor invention. I beseech your society. 158

---

130 superscript address   **132 intellect** meaning, import, contents
133 nomination name   **134 all desired employment** any service you
require of me   **136 votaries** those who have taken a vow   **137 sequent**
follower, attendant   **138 by ... progression** in process of delivery
139 Trip and go move nimbly and swiftly. (A phrase from a popular
song.)   **140 concern much** be of importance   **141 Stay ... compliment**
i.e., don't stand on ceremony   **141–142 forgive thy duty** set aside the
requirement of a curtsy   **145 Have with thee** I'll go with you
147 Father Church Father   **148–149 colorable colors** plausible pretexts   **151 pen** penmanship, or style   **153 repast** the meal   **154 gratify**
(1) delight (2) grace.   **the table** i.e., those at the table   **156 ben venuto**
welcome   **158 society** company

NATHANIEL And thank you too; for society, saith the
text, is the happiness of life.

HOLOFERNES And certes the text most infallibly con- 161
cludes it. [*To Dull.*] Sir, I do invite you too. You shall
not say me nay. *Pauca verba.* Away! The gentles are at 163
their game, and we will to our recreation.   *Exeunt.* 164

❖

4.3   *Enter Berowne, with a paper in his hand,*
alone.

BEROWNE The King, he is hunting the deer; I am cours- 1
ing myself. They have pitched a toil; I am toiling in a 2
pitch—pitch that defiles. Defile! A foul word. Well, 3
set thee down, sorrow! For so they say the fool said, 4
and so say I—and I the fool. Well proved, wit! By the
Lord, this love is as mad as Ajax. It kills sheep; it kills 6
me, I a sheep. Well proved again o' my side! I will not
love; if I do, hang me. I' faith, I will not. O, but her
eye! By this light, but for her eye I would not love her.
Yes, for her two eyes. Well, I do nothing in the world
but lie, and lie in my throat. By heaven, I do love, and 11
it hath taught me to rhyme and to be melancholy; and
here is part of my rhyme, and here my melancholy.
Well, she hath one o' my sonnets already. The clown
bore it, the fool sent it, and the lady hath it—sweet
clown, sweeter fool, sweetest lady! By the world, I
would not care a pin if the other three were in. Here 17

---

161 certes surely   **163 Pauca verba** few words.   **gentles** gentlefolk
164 game i.e., hunting

4.3. Location: Navarre's park.
1–2 coursing pursuing   **2 pitched a toil** set a snare   **2–3 toiling . . .**
pitch i.e., struggling with being in love. (*Pitch* means "a fixed opinion,"
with a quibbling reference to Rosaline's eyes, which he has earlier,
3.1.195, called *two pitch-balls*.)   **3 defiles** corrupts. (See Ecclesiasticus
13:1: "Whoso toucheth pitch shall be defiled withal.")   **4 set thee down**
i.e., stay, settle down with me. (See 1.1.305–306.)   **6 mad as Ajax** (An
allusion to the story of Ajax, who, maddened by his failure in a contest
for Achilles' armor, attacked a flock of sheep, supposing them to be
those who had denied him the prize.)   **11 in my throat** i.e., utterly
17 in involved (i.e., in love)

comes one with a paper. God give him grace to groan!   18
                                        He stands aside.

    The King entereth [with a paper].

KING   Ay me!
BEROWNE   [*Aside*] Shot, by heaven! Proceed, sweet
Cupid. Thou hast thumped him with thy bird-bolt un-   21
der the left pap. In faith, secrets!   22
KING [*Reads*]
    "So sweet a kiss the golden sun gives not
        To those fresh morning drops upon the rose
    As thy eyebeams when their fresh rays have smote   25
        The night of dew that on my cheeks down flows.   26
    Nor shines the silver moon one half so bright
        Through the transparent bosom of the deep   28
    As doth thy face, through tears of mine, give light;
        Thou shin'st in every tear that I do weep.
    No drop but as a coach doth carry thee;
        So ridest thou triumphing in my woe.
    Do but behold the tears that swell in me,
        And they thy glory through my grief will show.
    But do not love thyself; then thou wilt keep
    My tears for glasses, and still make me weep.   36
    O queen of queens! How far dost thou excel,
    No thought can think nor tongue of mortal tell."
How shall she know my griefs? I'll drop the paper.
Sweet leaves, shade folly. Who is he comes here?   40

    *Enter Longaville [with papers]. The King steps
    aside.*

What, Longaville, and reading! Listen, ear.
BEROWNE [*Aside*]
    Now, in thy likeness, one more fool appear!   42
LONGAVILLE   Ay me, I am forsworn!

---

18 God . . . groan i.e., may God grant that he be moved to groan for
love   **s.d. He stands aside** (Possibly Berowne hides in a tree or some
elevated place; see 4.3.75, 161.)   **21 bird-bolt** blunt arrow for shooting
birds   **22 left pap** left breast (where the heart is located).   **In faith,
secrets** i.e., in truth, we will now hear a confession of love   **25 smote**
struck   **26 night of dew** tears that flow nightly   **28 deep** i.e., night
36 glasses mirrors   **40 shade** conceal   **42 thy** i.e., the King's

BEROWNE [*Aside*]
　Why, he comes in like a perjure, wearing papers.　　44
KING [*Aside*]
　In love, I hope. Sweet fellowship in shame!
BEROWNE [*Aside*]
　One drunkard loves another of the name.
LONGAVILLE
　Am I the first that have been perjured so?
BEROWNE [*Aside*]
　I could put thee in comfort: not by two that I know.
　Thou makest the triumviry, the corner-cap of society,　49
　The shape of Love's Tyburn, that hangs up simplicity.　50
LONGAVILLE
　I fear these stubborn lines lack power to move.　　51
　[*Reading.*] "O sweet Maria, empress of my love!"—
　These numbers will I tear, and write in prose.　　53
　　　　　　　　　　　　　　[*He tears the paper.*]
BEROWNE [*Aside*]
　O, rhymes are guards on wanton Cupid's hose.　　54
　Disfigure not his shop.
LONGAVILLE [*Taking another paper*]　This same shall go.　55
　(*He reads the sonnet.*)
　"Did not the heavenly rhetoric of thine eye,　　56
　　'Gainst whom the world cannot hold argument,　57
　Persuade my heart to this false perjury?
　　Vows for thee broke deserve not punishment.
　A woman I forswore, but I will prove,
　　Thou being a goddess, I forswore not thee.
　My vow was earthly, thou a heavenly love.
　　Thy grace being gained cures all disgrace in me.　63
　Vows are but breath, and breath a vapor is.

44 perjure perjurer.　**wearing papers** (An allusion to the custom of
attaching to a convicted perjurer's breast the papers involved in and
setting forth his offense—in this case, the poem, which is an open
indication of Longaville's having forsworn his oath of celibacy.)　**49 triumviry** triumvirate.　**corner-cap** three-cornered cap.　**society** fellowship　**50 Tyburn** a place of public execution in London (with reference
here to the triangular structure of the gallows)　**51 stubborn** rough,
harsh　**53 numbers** verses　**54 guards** trim, decorative embroideries.
hose breeches　**55 shop** (Slang for "codpiece," a baggy pouch at the fly
of a man's hose.)　**56–69 Did . . . paradise** (See note on 4.2.104–117.)
57 whom i.e., which　**63 grace** favor

Then thou, fair sun, which on my earth dost shine,
Exhal'st this vapor vow; in thee it is.   66
If broken, then, it is no fault of mine.
If by me broke, what fool is not so wise
To lose an oath to win a paradise?"   69

BEROWNE [*Aside*]
This is the liver vein, which makes flesh a deity,   70
A green goose a goddess. Pure, pure idolatry.   71
God amend us, God amend! We are much out o' the way.   72

     Enter Dumaine [with a paper].

LONGAVILLE
By whom shall I send this?—Company! Stay.
                            [He steps aside.]

BEROWNE [*Aside*]
All hid, all hid—an old infant play.   74
Like a demigod here sit I in the sky,   75
And wretched fools' secrets heedfully o'ereye.   76
More sacks to the mill! O heavens, I have my wish!   77
Dumaine transformed! Four woodcocks in a dish!   78

DUMAINE   O most divine Kate!

BEROWNE [*Aside*]   O most profane coxcomb!

DUMAINE
By heaven, the wonder in a mortal eye!   81

BEROWNE [*Aside*]
By earth, she is not, Corporal. There you lie.   82

DUMAINE
Her amber hairs for foul hath amber quoted.   83

---

66 Exhal'st draws up. (It was thought that the sun drew up vapors from the earth, thereby producing meteors, will-o'-the-wisps, etc.) **69 To** as to   **70 liver vein** i.e., the vein or style of a lover (since the liver was assumed to be the seat of the passions) **71 green goose** gosling, i.e., a young girl, a strumpet **72 amend** improve.   **much . . . way** far gone **74 infant play** child's game of hide and seek (but with a suggestion also of a medieval religious play, in which God appears above) **75 in the sky** (Berowne speaks as though he were looking down on the others from some elevated position, possibly the gallery above the stage; see also 4.3.161.) **76 heedfully** attentively.   **o'ereye** observe **77 More . . . mill** (A proverbial expression, "there's more to come.") **78 woodcocks** (Birds noted for stupidity.) **81 mortal** human **82 Corporal** i.e., field officer for Cupid. (See 3.1.185.) **83 quoted** designated. (Dumaine hyperbolically insists that her amber hair makes real amber seem foul, ugly, by comparison.)

BEROWNE [*Aside*]
An amber-colored raven was well noted.   84
DUMAINE
As upright as the cedar.
BEROWNE [*Aside*]   Stoop, I say!   85
Her shoulder is with child.
DUMAINE   As fair as day.   86
BEROWNE [*Aside*]
Ay, as some days; but then no sun must shine.
DUMAINE   O, that I had my wish!
LONGAVILLE [*Aside*]   And I had mine!
KING [*Aside*]
And I mine too, good Lord!
BEROWNE [*Aside*]
Amen, so I had mine. Is not that a good word?   90
DUMAINE
I would forget her, but a fever she   91
Reigns in my blood and will remembered be.
BEROWNE [*Aside*]
A fever in your blood! Why, then incision   93
Would let her out in saucers. Sweet misprision!   94
DUMAINE
Once more I'll read the ode that I have writ.
BEROWNE [*Aside*]
Once more I'll mark how love can vary wit.   96
DUMAINE (*Reads his sonnet*)
          "On a day—alack the day!—   97
          Love, whose month is ever May,
          Spied a blossom passing fair
          Playing in the wanton air.   100
          Through the velvet leaves the wind,
          All unseen, can passage find;   102
          That the lover, sick to death,   103

84 **An . . . noted** i.e. (ironically), Dumaine has aptly described a black
fowl (with pun on *foul*) as amber-colored   85 **Stoop** (1) stooped, stunted
(2) Dumaine should avoid such lofty comparisons   86 **is with child** i.e.,
is swollen, unshapely   90 **Is . . . word** (1) is that not kind of me (2) is not
amen known to be a good word   91 **a** i.e., as a   93 **incision** letting
blood   94 **in saucers** (1) by the bowlful (2) into bowls to catch the
blood.   **misprision** (1) mistake (2) being released from confinement (of
the veins)   96 **vary wit** inspire intellectual or artistic variety
97–116 **On . . . love** (See note on 4.2.104–117.)   100 **wanton** frolicsome
102 **can** began to   103 **That** so that

Wished himself the heaven's breath.
'Air,' quoth he, 'thy cheeks may blow;
Air, would I might triumph so!
But, alack, my hand is sworn
Ne'er to pluck thee from thy thorn;
Vow, alack, for youth unmeet,   109
Youth so apt to pluck a sweet!
Do not call it sin in me,
That I am forsworn for thee—
Thou for whom Jove would swear
Juno but an Ethiop were,   114
And deny himself for Jove,   115
Turning mortal for thy love.' "   116
This will I send, and something else more plain,
That shall express my true love's fasting pain.   118
O, would the King, Berowne, and Longaville
Were lovers too! Ill, to example ill,   120
Would from my forehead wipe a perjured note,   121
For none offend where all alike do dote.   122

LONGAVILLE [*Advancing*]
Dumaine, thy love is far from charity,   123
That in love's grief desir'st society.   124
You may look pale, but I should blush, I know,
To be o'erheard and taken napping so.

KING [*Advancing*]
Come, sir, you blush! As his, your case is such;
You chide at him, offending twice as much.
You do not love Maria! Longaville
Did never sonnet for her sake compile,
Nor never lay his wreathèd arms athwart   131
His loving bosom to keep down his heart!
I have been closely shrouded in this bush
And marked you both, and for you both did blush.
I heard your guilty rhymes, observed your fashion,

---

109 unmeet inappropriate **114 Ethiop** Ethiopian, black African. (Used here as an example of ugliness.) **115 for Jove** to be Jove **116 for** i.e., to be **118 fasting** hungering **120 example** serve as an example for **121 note** mark, document. (See 4.3.44.) **122 dote** love dotingly **123 charity** Christian love **124 That . . . society** you who, in your suffering from love, uncharitably desire others to suffer also. (Proverbial: "Misery loves company.") **131 lay . . . athwart** i.e., fold his arms in the conventional sign of melancholy; cf. 3.1.18

Saw sighs reek from you, noted well your passion.
"Ay me!" says one. "O Jove!" the other cries;
One, her hairs were gold, crystal the other's eyes.
[*To Longaville.*] You would for paradise break faith and
   troth;   139
[*To Dumaine.*] And Jove, for your love, would infringe an
   oath.   140
What will Berowne say when that he shall hear   141
Faith infringèd, which such zeal did swear?
How will he scorn! How will he spend his wit!
How will he triumph, leap, and laugh at it!
For all the wealth that ever I did see
I would not have him know so much by me.   146
BEROWNE [*Advancing*]
Now step I forth to whip hypocrisy.
Ah, good my liege, I pray thee, pardon me.
Good heart, what grace hast thou, thus to reprove   149
These worms for loving, that art most in love?
Your eyes do make no coaches; in your tears   151
There is no certain princess that appears;   152
You'll not be perjured, 'tis a hateful thing—
Tush, none but minstrels like of sonneting!   154
But are you not ashamed? Nay, are you not,
All three of you, to be thus much o'ershot?   156
[*To Dumaine.*] You found his mote; [*To Longaville*] the
   King your mote did see;   157
But I a beam do find in each of three.   158
O, what a scene of foolery have I seen,
Of sighs, of groans, of sorrow, and of teen!   160
O me, with what strict patience have I sat,
To see a king transformèd to a gnat!   162
To see great Hercules whipping a gig,   163
And profound Solomon to tune a jig,   164

139 **troth** loyalty   140 **infringe** break   141 **when that** when   146 **by** about   149 **reprove** rebuke, condemn   151 **Your . . . coaches** (Alluding to the King's sonnet, 4.3.31–32.)   152 **certain** particular   154 **like** approve   156 **o'ershot** wide of the mark, shooting beyond it; i.e., in error   157, 158 **mote, beam** i.e., small speck, large defect. (See Matthew 7:3–5, Luke 6:41–42.)   160 **teen** affliction, grief   162 **a gnat** i.e., a tiny creature (with a play perhaps on *mote*)   163 **whipping a gig** spinning a top   164 **tune** play

And Nestor play at pushpin with the boys,   165
And critic Timon laugh at idle toys!   166
Where lies thy grief, O, tell me, good Dumaine?
And, gentle Longaville, where lies thy pain?
And where my liege's? All about the breast.
A caudle, ho!
KING   Too bitter is thy jest.   170
Are we betrayed thus to thy overview?   171
BEROWNE
Not you by me, but I betrayed to you.
I that am honest, I that hold it sin
To break the vow I am engagèd in,   174
I am betrayed by keeping company
With men like you, men of inconstancy.
When shall you see me write a thing in rhyme?
Or groan for Joan? Or spend a minute's time
In pruning me? When shall you hear that I   179
Will praise a hand, a foot, a face, an eye,
A gait, a state, a brow, a breast, a waist,   181
A leg, a limb—   [*He starts to leave.*]
KING   Soft! Whither away so fast?
A true man or a thief, that gallops so?   183
BEROWNE
I post from love. Good lover, let me go.   184

        Enter Jaquenetta [*with a letter*] *and* [*Costard the*]
        clown.

JAQUENETTA
God bless the King!
KING   What present hast thou there?   185
COSTARD
Some certain treason.
KING   What makes treason here?   186

---

165 Nestor wise old Greek chieftain in the Trojan War.   **pushpin** a
child's game   **166 critic** critical, censorious.   **Timon** a fifth-century
Athenian notorious for his misanthropy.   **laugh . . . toys** take delight in
mindless entertainments   **170 caudle** warm drink given to sick people
171 overview inspection   **174 engagèd in** sworn to   **179 pruning me**
preening, i.e., trimming, dressing up myself   **181 state** attitude, bearing   **183 true** honest   **184 post** hasten   **185 present** i.e., writing
186 makes treason has treason to do

COSTARD
  Nay, it makes nothing, sir.
KING   If it mar nothing neither,   187
  The treason and you go in peace away together.
JAQUENETTA
  I beseech Your Grace, let this letter be read.
  Our parson misdoubts it; 'twas treason, he said.   190
                    [*She gives the letter.*]
KING Berowne, read it over.
                    He [*Berowne*] *reads the letter* [*silently*].
  [*To Jaquenetta.*] Where hadst thou it?
JAQUENETTA Of Costard.
KING [*To Costard*] Where hadst thou it?
COSTARD Of Dun Adramadio, Dun Adramadio.
                    [*Berowne tears the letter.*]
KING
  How now, what is in you? Why dost thou tear it?
BEROWNE
  A toy, my liege, a toy. Your Grace needs not fear it.
LONGAVILLE
  It did move him to passion, and therefore let's hear it.
DUMAINE [*Gathering up the pieces*]
  It is Berowne's writing, and here is his name.
BEROWNE [*To Costard*]
  Ah, you whoreson loggerhead! You were born to do me
    shame.—   200
  Guilty, my lord, guilty! I confess, I confess.
KING What?
BEROWNE
  That you three fools lacked me fool to make up the mess. 203
  He, he, and you—and you, my liege!—and I,
  Are pickpurses in love, and we deserve to die.   205
  O, dismiss this audience, and I shall tell you more.
DUMAINE
  Now the number is even.
BEROWNE   True, true, we are four.

187 makes . . . mar ("To make and mar" is a proverbial phrase meaning
to do and undo.)   **190 misdoubts** suspects   **200 whoreson loggerhead**
i.e., infernal blockhead   **203 mess** group of four at table   **205 pickpurses** pickpockets (i.e., cheaters)

Will these turtles be gone?

KING   Hence, sirs. Away!   208

COSTARD

Walk aside the true folk, and let the traitors stay.   209

              [Exeunt Costard and Jaquenetta.]

BEROWNE

Sweet lords, sweet lovers, O, let us embrace!
  As true we are as flesh and blood can be.
The sea will ebb and flow, heaven show his face;
  Young blood doth not obey an old decree.
We cannot cross the cause why we were born;   214
Therefore of all hands must we be forsworn.   215

KING

What, did these rent lines show some love of thine?   216

BEROWNE

Did they, quoth you? Who sees the heavenly Rosaline,
That, like a rude and savage man of Ind   218
  At the first opening of the gorgeous east,   219
Bows not his vassal head and, strucken blind,
  Kisses the base ground with obedient breast?
What peremptory eagle-sighted eye   222
  Dares look upon the heaven of her brow
That is not blinded by her majesty?

KING

What zeal, what fury hath inspired thee now?   225
My love, her mistress, is a gracious moon,   226
  She an attending star, scarce seen a light.   227

BEROWNE

My eyes are then no eyes, nor I Berowne.
  O, but for my love, day would turn to night!
Of all complexions the culled sovereignty   230
  Do meet as at a fair in her fair cheek,

---

208 turtles turtledoves, lovers.   **sirs** (An acceptable form of address for
both women and men.)   **209 Walk . . . folk** i.e., those who tell the truth
are sent away for their efforts. (Costard's wry comment need not be
offered as an aside.)   **214 cross . . . born** i.e., continue to defy love
215 of all hands inevitably, in every way, on every side   **216 rent lines**
torn verses   **218 rude** ignorant.   **Ind** India   **219 opening** i.e., dawning   **222 peremptory** bold.   **eagle-sighted** (The eagle was believed to be
the only bird able to look directly at the sun.)   **225 zeal** ardent desire
226 gracious (1) exquisite (2) godly   **227 She** i.e., Rosaline.   **scarce . . .
light** a light scarcely to be seen   **230 the culled sovereignty** those
chosen as most worthy

Where several worthies make one dignity,   232
   Where nothing wants that want itself doth seek.   233
Lend me the flourish of all gentle tongues—   234
   Fie, painted rhetoric! O, she needs it not.   235
To things of sale a seller's praise belongs;   236
   She passes praise, then praise too short doth blot.   237
A withered hermit, fivescore winters worn,
   Might shake off fifty, looking in her eye.
Beauty doth varnish age, as if newborn,   240
   And gives the crutch the cradle's infancy.
O, 'tis the sun that maketh all things shine!

KING
By heaven, thy love is black as ebony.

BEROWNE
Is ebony like her? O wood divine!
   A wife of such wood were felicity.   245
O, who can give an oath? Where is a book,   246
   That I may swear Beauty doth beauty lack
If that she learn not of her eye to look?   248
   No face is fair that is not full so black.

KING
O paradox! Black is the badge of hell,
   The hue of dungeons and the school of night;   251
And beauty's crest becomes the heavens well.   252

BEROWNE
   Devils soonest tempt, resembling spirits of light.   253
O, if in black my lady's brows be decked,   254
   It mourns that painting and usurping hair   255

---

232 worthies excellences.   **dignity** i.e., supreme example of beauty
233 wants is lacking.   **want** desire   **234 flourish** adornment, eloquence.
gentle noble   **235 painted** artificial   **236 of sale** for sale   **237 passes**
surpasses.   **then praise . . . blot** i.e., any praise of her is inadequate and
hence must detract   **240 varnish** embellish   **245 were** would be
246 book i.e., Bible   **248 If . . . look** unless Beauty herself learns from
Rosaline's eyes how beauty should truly appear   **251 school** master,
model (?)   **252 And . . . well** (ironically) and yet you assert that your dark-
eyed beauty is suitable to adorn heaven. (Or, perhaps *beauty's crest* refers
to the sun, and the line means, "and only the sun, i.e., a fair beauty, is
suitable to grace the heavens.")   **253 Devils . . . light** (Berowne suggests
that Rosaline's dark beauty is better than that of fair-seeming devils.)
spirits of light angels   **254 decked** adorned   **255 It mourns that** i.e., it is
as though she is in mourning for the fact that.   **painting** cosmetics.
usurping i.e., false

Should ravish doters with a false aspect;   256
  And therefore is she born to make black fair.
Her favor turns the fashion of the days,   258
  For native blood is counted painting now;   259
And therefore red, that would avoid dispraise,   260
  Paints itself black to imitate her brow.

DUMAINE
To look like her are chimney sweepers black.

LONGAVILLE
  And since her time are colliers counted bright.   263

KING
  And Ethiops of their sweet complexion crack.   264

DUMAINE
Dark needs no candles now, for dark is light.

BEROWNE
Your mistresses dare never come in rain,   266
  For fear their colors should be washed away.   267

KING
'Twere good yours did; for, sir, to tell you plain,
  I'll find a fairer face not washed today.   269

BEROWNE
I'll prove her fair, or talk till doomsday here.

KING
  No devil will fright thee then so much as she.   271

DUMAINE
I never knew man hold vile stuff so dear.   272

LONGAVILLE [*Showing his shoe*]
  Look, here's thy love; my foot and her face see.

BEROWNE
O, if the streets were pavèd with thine eyes,   274
  Her feet were much too dainty for such tread!   275

---

256 false aspect misleading appearance **258 favor** face. **turns** alters, inverts **259 native . . . now** i.e., a natural ruddy complexion is accounted cosmetic now (since rouge is so often used and so successfully deceptive) **260 dispraise** disparagement, censure **263 colliers** coal miners **264 of . . . crack** boast to have attractive complexions **266 come in** walk in, be exposed to **267 colors** makeup **269 I'll . . . today** i.e., many unwashed faces are cleaner and fairer than hers **271 then** i.e., on doomsday **272 hold . . . dear** value worthless things so highly **274–275 O . . . tread** i.e., she walks so lightly that she would not even injure a street paved with your eyes

DUMAINE

O vile! Then, as she goes, what upward lies   276
  The street should see as she walked overhead.

KING

But what of this? Are we not all in love?

BEROWNE

Nothing so sure, and thereby all forsworn.

KING

Then leave this chat, and, good Berowne, now prove
  Our loving lawful and our faith not torn.   281

DUMAINE

Ay, marry, there, some flattery for this evil.   282

LONGAVILLE

O, some authority how to proceed,
  Some tricks, some quillets, how to cheat the devil.   284

DUMAINE

Some salve for perjury.

BEROWNE   O, 'tis more than need.
Have at you, then, affection's men-at-arms.   286
Consider what you first did swear unto:
To fast, to study, and to see no woman—
Flat treason 'gainst the kingly state of youth.   289
Say, can you fast? Your stomachs are too young,
And abstinence engenders maladies.   291
O, we have made a vow to study, lords,
And in that vow we have forsworn our books.
For when would you, my liege, or you, or you,
In leaden contemplation have found out   295
Such fiery numbers as the prompting eyes   296
Of beauty's tutors have enriched you with?
Other slow arts entirely keep the brain,   298
And therefore, finding barren practicers,
Scarce show a harvest of their heavy toil;

276 what upward lies (Dumaine bawdily suggests that a street paved
with his eyes would be able to look up constantly under her dress.)
281 torn broken **282 some . . . evil** i.e., give us some plausible way to
put a good face on this difficulty **284 quillets** verbal niceties, subtle
distinctions **286 Have at you** I come at you, i.e., here it is. **affection's**
love's **289 state** (1) condition (2) majesty **291 maladies** (The quarto
here supplies twenty-two lines that appear to be a first start for
ll. 292–339; seemingly they were meant to be canceled. See Textual
Notes.) **295 leaden** sluggish, dull **296 numbers** verses **298 arts**
branches of knowledge. **keep** dwell within

But love, first learnèd in a lady's eyes,
Lives not alone immurèd in the brain,   302
But with the motion of all elements   303
Courses as swift as thought in every power,   304
And gives to every power a double power
Above their functions and their offices.   306
It adds a precious seeing to the eye:
A lover's eyes will gaze an eagle blind.   308
A lover's ear will hear the lowest sound,
When the suspicious head of theft is stopped.   310
Love's feeling is more soft and sensible   311
Than are the tender horns of cockled snails.   312
Love's tongue proves dainty Bacchus gross in taste.   313
For valor, is not Love a Hercules,
Still climbing trees in the Hesperides?   315
Subtle as Sphinx, as sweet and musical   316
As bright Apollo's lute strung with his hair.   317
And when Love speaks, the voice of all the gods
Make heaven drowsy with the harmony.
Never durst poet touch a pen to write   320
Until his ink were tempered with Love's sighs.   321
O, then his lines would ravish savage ears
And plant in tyrants mild humility.
From women's eyes this doctrine I derive:
They sparkle still the right Promethean fire;   325
They are the books, the arts, the academes,
That show, contain, and nourish all the world;
Else none at all in aught proves excellent.   328
Then fools you were these women to forswear,   329

302 **immurèd** walled up, imprisoned   303 **elements** i.e., earth, air, fire,
and water   304 **Courses** runs.   **power** faculty, natural capacity
306 **Above . . . offices** above and beyond their ordinary functions
308 **gaze** stare   310 **When . . . stopped** when even the most cautiously
alert thief (or one alert to the danger of being robbed) hears nothing
311 **sensible** sensitive   312 **cockled** having a shell   313 **Bacchus**
god of wine and revelry   315 **Hesperides** where the golden apples
grew (the gaining of which was the eleventh of Hercules' twelve labors)   316 **Sphinx** a mythological creature of ancient Thebes who
destroyed all passersby who could not solve her riddle   317 **Apollo's
lute** (Apollo was the Greek god of music, poetry, and prophecy.)
320 **durst** dares   321 **tempered** blended, modified   325 **sparkle** throw
out, emit.   **right** true.   **Promethean fire** divine fire. (From the legend
that Prometheus stole fire from heaven and gave it to mankind.)
328 **Else** otherwise.   **aught** anything   329 **forswear** renounce

Or, keeping what is sworn, you will prove fools.
For wisdom's sake, a word that all men love,
Or for love's sake, a word that loves all men,   332
Or for men's sake, the authors of these women,
Or women's sake, by whom we men are men,
Let us once lose our oaths to find ourselves,   335
Or else we lose ourselves to keep our oaths.
It is religion to be thus forsworn,   337
For charity itself fulfills the law,   338
And who can sever love from charity?

KING
Saint Cupid, then! And, soldiers, to the field!

BEROWNE
Advance your standards, and upon them, lords;   341
Pell-mell, down with them! But be first advised   342
In conflict that you get the sun of them.   343

LONGAVILLE
Now to plain dealing. Lay these glozes by.   344
Shall we resolve to woo these girls of France?

KING
And win them too. Therefore let us devise
Some entertainment for them in their tents.

BEROWNE
First, from the park let us conduct them thither;
Then homeward every man attach the hand   349
Of his fair mistress. In the afternoon
We will with some strange pastime solace them,   351
Such as the shortness of the time can shape,
For revels, dances, masques, and merry hours
Forerun fair Love, strewing her way with flowers.   354

---

332 loves is lovable to, inspires with love   **335 once** for once, one
time.   **lose** break   **337 religion** i.e., in keeping with the tenets of our
religion   **338 For . . . law** (From Romans 13:8: "for he that loveth another hath fulfilled the law.")   **341 Advance** raise.   **standards** flags
serving as a military emblem. (The military metaphor is not only amorous but bawdy.)   **342 Pell-mell** without keeping ranks, in hand-to-hand
combat.   **be first advised** take care first of all   **343 get . . . them** i.e.,
take field position so that the sun is in their eyes (with a play on the
idea of "begetting a son")   **344 glozes** sophistries   **349 attach** seize
351 strange novel, fresh.   **solace** entertain   **354 Forerun** come before,
prepare the way for

KING
    Away, away! No time shall be omitted
    That will betime and may by us be fitted.   356
BEROWNE
    Allons! Allons! Sowed cockle reaped no corn,   357
      And justice always whirls in equal measure.   358
    Light wenches may prove plagues to men forsworn;   359
      If so, our copper buys no better treasure.   *[Exeunt.]*   360

❖

---

356 betime happen.   **fitted** used (i.e., we'll take advantage of every
minute)   **357 Allons** come on, let's go.   **cockle** a weed.   **corn** wheat
(i.e., we won't get results without well-planned efforts)   **358 measure**
proportion (again suggesting that reward comes only from effort)
359 Light frivolous   **360 copper** coin of little value (i.e., as beggars and
as men forsworn, we cannot afford to be choosers)

5.1 *Enter [Holofernes] the pedant, [Nathaniel] the
curate, and Dull [the constable].*

HOLOFERNES *Satis quod sufficit.* 1
NATHANIEL I praise God for you, sir. Your reasons at 2
dinner have been sharp and sententious, pleasant
without scurrility, witty without affection, audacious 4
without impudency, learned without opinion, and 5
strange without heresy. I did converse this quondam 6
day with a companion of the King's who is intituled, 7
nominated, or called Don Adriano de Armado.
HOLOFERNES *Novi hominem tanquam te.* His humor is 9
lofty, his discourse peremptory, his tongue filed, his 10
eye ambitious, his gait majestical, and his general behavior vain, ridiculous, and thrasonical. He is too 12
picked, too spruce, too affected, too odd, as it were, 13
too peregrinate, as I may call it. 14
NATHANIEL A most singular and choice epithet. 15
Draw out his table book.
HOLOFERNES He draweth out the thread of his verbosity
finer than the staple of his argument. I abhor such fa- 17
natical phantasimes, such insociable and point-devise 18
companions, such rackers of orthography, as to speak 19
"dout," fine, when he should say "doubt"; "det" 20
when he should pronounce "debt"—d, e, b, t, not
d, e, t. He clepeth a calf "cauf," half "hauf"; neighbor 22
vocatur "nebor"; neigh abbreviated "ne." This is 23

5.1. Location: Navarre's park.
1 **Satis quod sufficit** enough is as good as a feast **2 reasons** discus-
sions, discourses **4 affection** affectation **5 opinion** arrogance, dogma-
tism **6 strange** novel, new. **this quondam** the other **7 intituled**
entitled, designated **9 Novi . . . te** I know the man as well as I know
you **10 peremptory** positive, overbearing. **filed** polished **12 thrasonical** boastful. (From Thraso, a braggart soldier in Terence's play
Eunuchus.) **13 picked** fastidious. **spruce** dapper, elegant **14 peregrinate** having the manner of one who has traveled **15 singular** unique
s.d. table book notebook **17 staple** fiber, thread. **argument** subject
matter **18 phantasimes** persons who entertain fantastic notions.
insociable unsociable, unpleasant **18–19 point-devise companions**
extremely precise fellows **19 rackers of orthography** torturers of
spelling. (Holofernes's tirade reflects a conscious attempt of some
Renaissance educators to bring the English spelling and pronunciation
of certain borrowed words more nearly to their Latin originals.)
20 fine mincingly, too thinly **22 clepeth** calls **23 vocatur** is called

abhominable—which he would call "abominable." 24
It insinuateth me of insanie. *Ne intelligis, domine?* To 25
make frantic, lunatic.

NATHANIEL   *Laus Deo, bone intelligo.* 27

HOLOFERNES   *Bone? Bone* for *bene.* Priscian a little 28
scratched; 'twill serve. 29

    *Enter [Armado the] braggart, [Mote, his] boy, [and
    Costard].*

NATHANIEL   *Videsne quis venit?* 30

HOLOFERNES   *Video, et gaudeo.* 31

ARMADO [*To Mote*]   Chirrah! 32

HOLOFERNES   *Quare* "chirrah," not "sirrah"? 33

ARMADO   Men of peace, well encountered.

HOLOFERNES   Most military sir, salutation.

MOTE [*Aside to Costard*]   They have been at a great feast
of languages and stolen the scraps.

COSTARD [*To Mote*]   O, they have lived long on the alms 38
basket of words. I marvel thy master hath not eaten 39
thee for a word, for thou art not so long by the head as 40
honorificabilitudinitatibus. Thou art easier swallowed 41
than a flapdragon. 42

MOTE [*To Costard*]   Peace! The peal begins. 43

---

24 abhominable . . . abominable (This is pedantic to the point of being
simply wrong, since the supposed derivation of *abhominable* from *ab
homine*, away from mankind, inhuman, is a false one, but it is a derivation that Shakespeare seems elsewhere to have accepted.)   **25 It . . .
insanie** (1) to me it savors of insanity (2) it drives me mad.   **Ne intelligis, domine** do you understand me, sir   **27 Laus . . . intelligo** praise be
to God, I understand well   **28 Bone for bene** i.e., the Latin should be
bene, "well"   **28–29 Priscian . . . scratched** i.e., your Latin is a little
faulty. (Priscian was a grammarian of the fifth or sixth century whose
textbooks were considered standard.)   **30 Videsne quis venit** do you see
who comes   **31 Video, et gaudeo** I see and I rejoice. (This trivial Latin
dialogue is after the manner of schoolboys' exercises.)   **32 Chirrah**
(Possibly a corruption of the Greek *chaere,* "hail," or merely a dialectal
pronunciation of *sirrah,* a term of address for a social inferior.)
33 Quare why   **38–39 alms basket** a basket used to gather scraps for
the poor   **40 for a word** (Mote's name puns on the French *mot,*
"word.")   **long . . . head** i.e., tall   **41 honorificabilitudinitatibus** (Reput-
edly the longest word in existence. It is the dative plural of a Latin word
meaning something like "honorableness.")   **42 flapdragon** the raisin or
plum in burning brandy to be snapped with the mouth in the game of
snapdragon   **43 peal** i.e., clatter of tongues, like a peal of bells

ARMADO [*To Holofernes*] Monsieur, are you not
  lettered?   45
MOTE Yes, yes, he teaches boys the hornbook. What   46
  is a, b, spelled backward, with the horn on his head?
HOLOFERNES Ba, *pueritia*, with a horn added.   48
MOTE Ba, most silly sheep with a horn. You hear his
  learning.
HOLOFERNES *Quis, quis*, thou consonant?   51
MOTE The last of the five vowels, if you repeat them; or
  the fifth, if I.
HOLOFERNES I will repeat them: a, e, i—
MOTE The sheep. The other two concludes it—o, u.   55
ARMADO Now, by the salt wave of the Mediterraneum,
  a sweet touch, a quick venue of wit! Snip, snap, quick   57
  and home. It rejoiceth my intellect. True wit!
MOTE Offered by a child to an old man—which is
  wit-old.   60
HOLOFERNES What is the figure? What is the figure?   61
MOTE Horns.
HOLOFERNES Thou disputes like an infant. Go whip   63
  thy gig.   64
MOTE Lend me your horn to make one, and I will whip
  about your infamy *manu cita*—a gig of a cuckold's   66
  horn.
COSTARD An I had but one penny in the world, thou   68
  shouldst have it to buy gingerbread. Hold, there is the
  very remuneration I had of thy master, thou halfpenny   70
  purse of wit, thou pigeon egg of discretion. [*He gives*   71
  money.] O, an the heavens were so pleased that thou

---

45 lettered i.e., educated. (Mote replies as though *lettered* meant "able
to teach boys their letters.") **46 hornbook** printed sheets of paper,
covered by a protective thin layer of horn; used for teaching children
their alphabet. (The *horn* sets up a joke on the sheep's or cuckold's
horn.) **48 pueritia** childishness, child **51 Quis** who, what. **consonant**
i.e., nonentity, since the consonants cannot be sounded without also
sounding the vowels **55 The sheep** i.e., Holofernes, by saying "i," that
is, "I," has labeled himself the sheep. **concludes it** (1) completes the
list of the five vowels (2) proves my point. **o, u** i.e., O you **57 venue**
sally, thrust. (A fencing term, continued in *quick and home*, to the
quick.) **wit** intellect **60 wit-old** mentally feeble (with a pun on *wittol*,
a contented cuckold) **61 figure** metaphor, figure of speech **63 Thou**
disputes you reason **64 gig** top **66 manu cita** with ready hand **68 An**
if **70–71 halfpenny purse** a tiny purse, just large enough to hold a
halfpenny **71 pigeon egg** i.e., tiny object

wert but my bastard, what a joyful father wouldst thou
make me! Go to, thou hast it *ad dunghill*, at the fingers' ends, as they say.

HOLOFERNES   O, I smell false Latin! "Dunghill" for *"un-*   76
guem."   77

ARMADO   Arts-man, preambulate. We will be singuled   78
from the barbarous. Do you not educate youth at the
charge-house on the top of the mountain?   80

HOLOFERNES   Or *mons*, the hill.

ARMADO   At your sweet pleasure, for the mountain.

HOLOFERNES   I do, *sans* question.   83

ARMADO   Sir, it is the King's most sweet pleasure and
affection to congratulate the Princess at her pavilion   85
in the posteriors of this day, which the rude multitude   86
call the afternoon.

HOLOFERNES   The posterior of the day, most generous   88
sir, is liable, congruent, and measurable for the after-   89
noon. The word is well culled, chose, sweet, and apt,   90
I do assure you, sir, I do assure.

ARMADO   Sir, the King is a noble gentleman, and my
familiar, I do assure ye, very good friend. For what is   93
inward between us, let it pass. I do beseech thee, re-   94
member thy courtesy; I beseech thee, apparel thy   95
head. And among other importunate and most serious   96
designs, and of great import indeed, too—but let that
pass; for I must tell thee, it will please His Grace, by
the world, sometimes to lean upon my poor shoulder
and with his royal finger thus dally with my excre-   100
ment, with my mustachio; but, sweet heart, let that   101
pass. By the world, I recount no fable! Some certain
special honors it pleaseth his greatness to impart to
Armado, a soldier, a man of travel, that hath seen the
world; but let that pass. The very all of all is—but,   105

76–77 unguem i.e., *ad unguem*, to the fingernail, i.e., perfectly   **78 Arts-
man** scholar.   **preambulate** walk (with me).   **singuled** set apart, distinguished   **80 charge-house** some kind of school   **83 sans** without
85 congratulate greet   **86 in the posteriors** at the end.   **rude** ignorant
88 generous cultivated, wellborn   **89 liable** apt.   **measurable** fitted
90 culled selected   **93 familiar** intimate acquaintance   **94 inward**
private.   **let it pass** never mind about that   **95 thy courtesy** i.e., that
you've removed your hat   **96 importunate** urgent   **100–101 excrement**
outgrowth (of hair)   **105 very all of all** sum of everything

sweet heart, I do implore secrecy—that the King
would have me present the Princess, sweet chuck, 107
with some delightful ostentation, or show, or pageant, 108
or antic, or firework. Now, understanding that the 109
curate and your sweet self are good at such eruptions
and sudden breaking out of mirth, as it were, I have
acquainted you withal, to the end to crave your assis- 112
tance.

HOLOFERNES   Sir, you shall present before her the Nine 114
Worthies. Sir Nathaniel, as concerning some enter- 115
tainment of time, some show in the posterior of this
day, to be rendered by our assistance, the King's command, and this most gallant, illustrate, and learned
gentleman, before the Princess—I say none so fit as to
present the Nine Worthies.   120

NATHANIEL   Where will you find men worthy enough
to present them?

HOLOFERNES   Joshua, yourself; myself; and this gallant 123
gentleman, Judas Maccabaeus; this swain, because of
his great limb or joint, shall pass Pompey the Great; 125
the page, Hercules—

ARMADO   Pardon, sir, error. He is not quantity enough
for that Worthy's thumb. He is not so big as the end of
his club.

HOLOFERNES   Shall I have audience? He shall present 130
Hercules in minority. His enter and exit shall be stran- 131

107 **chuck** chick. (A term of endearment.)   108 **ostentation** display
109 **antic** a pageant or entertainment using fantastic costumes   112 **withal**
with this   114–115 **Nine Worthies** (A conventional subject familiar to
Shakespeare's audience in poems, pageants, and tapestries. The nine were
three pagans, Hector of Troy, Alexander the Great, and Julius Caesar; three
Jews, Joshua, David, and Judas Maccabaeus; and three Christians, Arthur,
Charlemagne, and Godfrey of Bouillon. The list varied, but Shakespeare
makes an unusual departure when he introduces Pompey and Hercules.)
120 **present** represent   123 **myself** (Holofernes does not here assign a part
to himself (see however l. 139), nor does he assign Nathaniel to Alexander
or Armado to Hercules as in the actual production. Perhaps changes occur
later. This present passage may represent an unrevised draft.)   125 **pass**
represent   130 **audience** a hearing   131 **in minority** as a child.   **enter**
entrance   131–132 **strangling a snake** (According to legend, Hercules as an
infant displayed his great strength by strangling two serpents sent by the
envious Juno to destroy him in his cradle.)

gling a snake; and I will have an apology for that pur- 132
pose.

MOTE   An excellent device! So if any of the audience
hiss, you may cry, "Well done, Hercules! Now thou
crushest the snake!" That is the way to make an offense gracious, though few have the grace to do it.

ARMADO   For the rest of the Worthies?

HOLOFERNES   I will play three myself.

MOTE   Thrice-worthy gentleman!

ARMADO   Shall I tell you a thing?

HOLOFERNES   We attend.   142

ARMADO   We will have, if this fadge not, an antic. I be- 143
seech you, follow.

HOLOFERNES   *Via*, goodman Dull! Thou hast spoken no 145
word all this while.

DULL   Nor understood none neither, sir.

HOLOFERNES   *Allons!* We will employ thee.   148

DULL

I'll make one in a dance, or so; or I will play   149
On the tabor to the Worthies, and let them dance the hay. 150

HOLOFERNES

Most dull, honest Dull! To our sport, away!

                                                    Exeunt.

❖

5.2   *Enter the ladies [the Princess, Katharine,*
Rosaline, and Maria].

PRINCESS

Sweet hearts, we shall be rich ere we depart,
If fairings come thus plentifully in.   2
A lady walled about with diamonds!   3

---

132 apology explanatory prologue   **142 attend** listen   **143 fadge** fit,
be suitable   **145 Via** onward! (A cry of encouragement to troops.)
148 Allons let's go   **149 make one** take part   **150 tabor** small drum.
hay country dance

5.2. Location: Navarre's park. Near the ladies' tents.
2 fairings complimentary gifts   **3 A lady . . . diamonds** (The Princess
has evidently received a brooch with a diamond-studded frame enclosing a portrait of a lady.)

Look you what I have from the loving King.

[*She shows a jewel.*]

ROSALINE
Madam, came nothing else along with that?

PRINCESS
Nothing but this? Yes, as much love in rhyme
As would be crammed up in a sheet of paper,
Writ o' both sides the leaf, margent and all,   8
That he was fain to seal on Cupid's name.   9

ROSALINE
That was the way to make his godhead wax,   10
For he hath been five thousand year a boy.   11

KATHARINE
Ay, and a shrewd unhappy gallows too.   12

ROSALINE
You'll ne'er be friends with him. 'A killed your sister.   13

KATHARINE
He made her melancholy, sad, and heavy,   14
And so she died. Had she been light, like you,   15
Of such a merry, nimble, stirring spirit,
She might ha' been a grandam ere she died.   17
And so may you, for a light heart lives long.

ROSALINE
What's your dark meaning, mouse, of this light word?   19

KATHARINE
A light condition in a beauty dark.   20

ROSALINE
We need more light to find your meaning out.

8 **margent** margin   9 **That . . . name** so that he was obliged to append
Cupid's name by sealing a slip of paper to the letter itself, or, for lack of
room, place the seal on top of Cupid's name. (Probably the Princess
shows her letter, as do the other ladies in turn when they show their
love tokens.)   10 **godhead** divinity.   **wax** increase (with pun on the *wax*
of the seal)   11 **he hath . . . boy** i.e., Cupid has remained young ever
since the world began   12 **shrewd unhappy gallows** wicked mischievous
knave, deserving to be hanged   13 **'A killed your sister** (A mocking hint
of a story, not developed here, of a young woman who dies for love.)   **'A**
he   14 **heavy** depressed   15 **light** (1) cheerful (2) unchaste   17 **grandam**
grandmother   19 **dark** hidden.   **mouse** (A term of endearment.)   **light
word** frivolous speech   20 **light condition** wanton temperament

KATHARINE
You'll mar the light by taking it in snuff;   22
Therefore I'll darkly end the argument.   23
ROSALINE
Look what you do, you do it still i' the dark.   24
KATHARINE
So do not you, for you are a light wench.
ROSALINE
Indeed I weigh not you, and therefore light.   26
KATHARINE
You weigh me not? O, that's you care not for me.   27
ROSALINE
Great reason, for past cure is still past care.   28
PRINCESS
Well bandied both! A set of wit well played.   29
But, Rosaline, you have a favor too.   30
Who sent it? And what is it?
ROSALINE   I would you knew.   31
An if my face were but as fair as yours,   32
My favor were as great. Be witness this.   33
              [*She shows a love token.*]
Nay, I have verses too, I thank Berowne;
The numbers true, and, were the numbering too,   35
I were the fairest goddess on the ground.   36
I am compared to twenty thousand fairs.   37
O, he hath drawn my picture in his letter!
PRINCESS   Anything like?
ROSALINE
Much in the letters, nothing in the praise.   40

---

22 taking . . . snuff (1) trimming the burning candlewick (2) taking
offense   **23 darkly** obscurely   **24 Look what** whatever.   **do it . . . i' the
dark** (with obvious sexual meaning)   **26 weigh not you** don't weigh as
much as you   **27 weigh** regard seriously.   **that's** that means   **28 Great
reason** with good reason.   **past cure . . . care** (Proverbial: What can't be
helped shouldn't be worried about. Rosaline implies that Katharine is
incurable, and puns on *care*, have fondness, in l. 27.)   **29 Well bandied
both** i.e., both of you have wittily traded insults. (A tennis term.)
30 favor love token   **31 would** wish   **32 An if** if   **33 favor** personal
appearance (playing on *favor*, love token, in l. 30).   **Be witness this** let
this be witness   **35 numbers** meter.   **numbering** reckoning   **36 were**
would be   **37 fairs** fair women   **40 letters** lettering.   **praise** i.e., contents, what he says of me

PRINCESS
Beauteous as ink—a good conclusion.   41
KATHARINE
Fair as a text B in a copybook.   42
ROSALINE
'Ware pencils, ho! Let me not die your debtor,   43
My red dominical, my golden letter.   44
O, that your face were not so full of O's!   45
KATHARINE
A pox of that jest! And I beshrew all shrows.   46
PRINCESS
But, Katharine, what was sent to you from fair
    Dumaine?
KATHARINE
Madam, this glove.   [*She shows a glove.*]
PRINCESS   Did he not send you twain?   48
KATHARINE
Yes, madam, and moreover
Some thousand verses of a faithful lover,
A huge translation of hypocrisy,   51
Vilely compiled, profound simplicity.   52
MARIA [*Showing a letter and a pearl necklace*]
This, and these pearls, to me sent Longaville.
The letter is too long by half a mile.
PRINCESS
I think no less. Dost thou not wish in heart   55
The chain were longer and the letter short?
MARIA
Ay, or I would these hands might never part.   57

41 ink (Referring to Rosaline's dark complexion.)   **42 a text B** (Perhaps
a heavily ornamented capital B, boldly dark like Rosaline's complexion.)   **43 'Ware pencils** i.e., be wary of bringing painting into the argument, or be wary of this sketching of portraits. (*Pencils* are fine-tipped
brushes.)   **Let . . . debtor** let me repay your insult   **44 red dominical**
red lettering used in calendars to mark Sundays and holy days. (From
dies dominica, the Lord's day; here, a jesting reference to Katharine's
fair complexion.)   **45 O's** i.e., smallpox scars (to which Katharine
replies in the next line with her curse, "A pox")   **46 of** on.   **beshrew all
shrows** i.e., wish a plague on all shrews, scolds. (The quarto/Folio
spelling of *Shrowes* makes plain the rhyme with *O's*.)   **48 twain** two
51 translation communication, metaphor   **52 simplicity** stupidity
55 in heart truthfully   **57 would** wish. (Perhaps Maria demonstrates
what she means by wrapping the pearls around her hands, making
them prisoner in her *chain*.)

PRINCESS
We are wise girls to mock our lovers so.
ROSALINE
They are worse fools to purchase mocking so.   59
That same Berowne I'll torture ere I go.
O, that I knew he were but in by th' week!   61
How I would make him fawn, and beg, and seek,
And wait the season, and observe the times,   63
And spend his prodigal wits in bootless rhymes,   64
And shape his service wholly to my hests,   65
And make him proud to make me proud that jests!   66
So pair-taunt-like would I o'ersway his state   67
That he should be my fool and I his fate.
PRINCESS
None are so surely caught when they are catched   69
As wit turned fool. Folly in wisdom hatched
Hath wisdom's warrant and the help of school   71
And wit's own grace to grace a learnèd fool.
ROSALINE
The blood of youth burns not with such excess
As gravity's revolt to wantonness.   74
MARIA
Folly in fools bears not so strong a note   75
As fool'ry in the wise when wit doth dote,   76
Since all the power thereof it doth apply   77
To prove, by wit, worth in simplicity.   78

        Enter Boyet.

PRINCESS
Here comes Boyet, and mirth is in his face.
BOYET
O, I am stabbed with laughter! Where's Her Grace?
PRINCESS
Thy news, Boyet?

59 purchase earn, invite   **61 in . . . week** i.e., caught, trapped permanently   **63 And wait . . . times** i.e., wait until it suits me, follow my
schedule   **64 bootless** fruitless   **65 hests** behests   **66 And . . . jests** and
make him take satisfaction in glorifying me, the one who mocks him
67 pair-taunt-like like one holding a winning hand (pair-taunt) in the
card game of "post and pair" (with a pun on *taunt*)   **69 surely** securely   **71 warrant** guarantee   **74 As gravity's revolt** as when a wise
man turns   **75 note** stigma, notoriety   **76 dote** grow foolish   **77 thereof**
i.e., of wit   **78 simplicity** foolishness

BOYET   Prepare, madam, prepare!
Arm, wenches, arm! Encounters mounted are   82
Against your peace. Love doth approach disguised,
Armèd in arguments. You'll be surprised.   84
Muster your wits, stand in your own defense,
Or hide your heads like cowards and fly hence.

PRINCESS
Saint Denis to Saint Cupid! What are they   87
That charge their breath against us? Say, scout, say.   88

BOYET
Under the cool shade of a sycamore
I thought to close mine eyes some half an hour,
When, lo, to interrupt my purposed rest,
Toward that shade I might behold addressed   92
The King and his companions. Warily
I stole into a neighbor thicket by
And overheard what you shall overhear—   95
That, by and by, disguised they will be here.
Their herald is a pretty knavish page
That well by heart hath conned his embassage.   98
Action and accent did they teach him there: 99
"Thus must thou speak," and "thus thy body bear."
And ever and anon they made a doubt   101
Presence majestical would put him out;   102
"For," quoth the King, "an angel shalt thou see;
Yet fear not thou, but speak audaciously."   104
The boy replied, "An angel is not evil;
I should have feared her had she been a devil."
With that, all laughed and clapped him on the shoulder,
Making the bold wag by their praises bolder.   108
One rubbed his elbow thus, and fleered, and swore   109
A better speech was never spoke before.

---

82 Encounters mounted are assailants are readied, set in position
84 surprised overcome by surprise attack   **87 Saint Denis** patron saint
of France.   **to** against   **88 charge their breath** aim their words. To
charge is to attack at full gallop or to level as in aiming a weapon.
92 might could.   **addressed** approaching   **95 overhear** hear over
again   **98 conned** memorized.   **embassage** message   **99 Action** gesture   **101 ever and anon** every now and then.   **made a doubt** expressed
a fear (that)   **102 put him out** leave him confused and tonguetied
104 audaciously boldly   **108 wag** young man   **109 rubbed his elbow** (in
a gesture of satisfaction, like rubbing the hands).   **fleered** grinned

Another, with his finger and his thumb,   111
Cried, "*Via!* We will do 't, come what will come."   112
The third he capered and cried, "All goes well!"   113
The fourth turned on the toe and down he fell.   114
With that, they all did tumble on the ground
With such a zealous laughter, so profound,
That in this spleen ridiculous appears,   117
To check their folly, passion's solemn tears.

PRINCESS
But what, but what? Come they to visit us?

BOYET
They do, they do, and are appareled thus,
Like Muscovites or Russians, as I guess.   121
Their purpose is to parle, to court, and dance;   122
And everyone his love suit will advance
Unto his several mistress, which they'll know   124
By favors several which they did bestow.

PRINCESS
And will they so? The gallants shall be tasked;   126
For, ladies, we will every one be masked,
And not a man of them shall have the grace,
Despite of suit, to see a lady's face.   129
Hold, Rosaline, this favor thou shalt wear,
And then the King will court thee for his dear.
Hold, take thou this, my sweet, and give me thine.   132
So shall Berowne take me for Rosaline.   133
          [*The Princess and Rosaline exchange favors.*]
And change you favors too. So shall your loves   134
Woo contrary, deceived by these removes.   135
          [*Katharine and Maria exchange favors.*]

ROSALINE
Come on, then, wear the favors most in sight.   136

---

111 with . . . thumb i.e., snapping his fingers   **112 Via** onward
113 capered skipped, danced   **114 turned on the toe** pirouetted
117 spleen ridiculous ludicrous fit of laughter   **121 Muscovites or
Russians** (Costumes not uncommon in court masquerades.)   **guess** (The
unrhymed word suggests a missing line.)   **122 parle** parley   **124 several**
respective, particular.   **which** whom   **126 tasked** tried, tested   **129 suit**
petition, entreaty (with a play on "suit of clothes")   **132–133 Hold . . .
Rosaline** (Possibly Shakespeare intended this couplet to replace
ll. 130–131.)   **134 change** exchange   **135 removes** exchanges   **136 most
in sight** conspicuously

KATHARINE
　But in this changing what is your intent?
PRINCESS
　The effect of my intent is to cross theirs.   138
　They do it but in mockery merriment,   139
　And mock for mock is only my intent.
　Their several counsels they unbosom shall   141
　To loves mistook, and so be mocked withal   142
　Upon the next occasion that we meet,
　With visages displayed, to talk and greet.   144
ROSALINE
　But shall we dance, if they desire us to 't?
PRINCESS
　No, to the death we will not move a foot,   146
　Nor to their penned speech render we no grace,   147
　But while 'tis spoke each turn away her face.
BOYET
　Why, that contempt will kill the speaker's heart,
　And quite divorce his memory from his part.
PRINCESS
　Therefore I do it; and I make no doubt
　The rest will ne'er come in, if he be out.   152
　There's no such sport as sport by sport o'erthrown,
　To make theirs ours, and ours none but our own.   154
　So shall we stay, mocking intended game,
　And they, well mocked, depart away with shame.
　　　　　　　　　　　　　　　Sound trumpet [*within*].
BOYET
　The trumpet sounds. Be masked; the maskers come.   157
　　　　　　　　　　　　　　　[*The ladies mask.*]

　Enter blackamoors with music; [*Mote*] *the boy,*
　with a speech, and [*the King, Berowne, and*] *the*
　rest of the lords disguised [*as Russians, and*
　visored].

138 **cross** thwart　139 **mockery** mocking　141 **counsels** private intentions, secret purposes.　**unbosom shall** will disclose　142 **withal** with
this　144 **visages** faces　146 **to the death** (as in "fight to the death")
147 **penned speech** speech composed and written out with care.　**grace**
favor　152 **out** confused, having forgotten his lines　154 **theirs** i.e., their
sport　157 **s.d. blackamoors** i.e., attendants in blackface

MOTE
All hail, the richest beauties on the earth!

BOYET
Beauties no richer than rich taffeta.   159

MOTE
A holy parcel of the fairest dames   160
                    The ladies turn their backs to him
That ever turned their—backs—to mortal views!

BEROWNE [*Prompting Mote*]   "Their eyes," villain, "their
eyes."

MOTE
That ever turned their eyes to mortal views!
Out—

BOYET   True; out indeed.   166

MOTE
Out of your favors, heavenly spirits, vouchsafe   167
Not to behold—

BEROWNE [*To Mote*]   "Once to behold," rogue.

MOTE
Once to behold with your sun-beamèd eyes—
With your sun-beamèd eyes—

BOYET
They will not answer to that epithet.
You were best call it "daughter-beamèd eyes."   173

MOTE
They do not mark me, and that brings me out.   174

BEROWNE
Is this your perfectness? Begone, you rogue!   175
                                            [*Exit Mote.*]

ROSALINE [*Speaking as the Princess*]
What would these strangers? Know their minds, Boyet.   176
If they do speak our language, 'tis our will
That some plain man recount their purposes.   178
Know what they would.

BOYET   What would you with the Princess?

---

159 **taffeta** i.e., their masks of taffeta cloth   **160 parcel** company
166 out i.e., having forgotten his lines   **167 vouchsafe** deign, agree
173 daughter-beamèd (substituting *daughter* for *sun*, i.e., son)
174 mark pay attention to   **175 Is . . . perfectness** is this your idea of a
perfectly memorized speech   **176 What . . . minds** what do these
strangers want? Learn their intentions. (Rosaline, masquerading as the
Princess, presides.)   **178 plain** plainspoken

BEROWNE

Nothing but peace and gentle visitation.   180

ROSALINE What would they, say they?

BOYET

Nothing but peace and gentle visitation.

ROSALINE

Why, that they have, and bid them so be gone.

BOYET

She says you have it, and you may be gone.

KING

Say to her we have measured many miles   185

To tread a measure with her on this grass.   186

BOYET

They say that they have measured many a mile

To tread a measure with you on this grass.

ROSALINE

It is not so. Ask them how many inches

Is in one mile. If they have measured many,   190

The measure then of one is easily told.

BOYET

If to come hither you have measured miles,

And many miles, the Princess bids you tell

How many inches doth fill up one mile.

BEROWNE

Tell her we measure them by weary steps.

BOYET

She hears herself.

ROSALINE   How many weary steps,

Of many weary miles you have o'ergone,

Are numbered in the travel of one mile?

BEROWNE

We number nothing that we spend for you.

Our duty is so rich, so infinite,

That we may do it still without account.   201

Vouchsafe to show the sunshine of your face,

That we, like savages, may worship it.

---

180 visitation visit   **185 measured** traversed, paced   **186 tread a measure** perform a dance   **190 measured** (1) traversed (2) taken the measurement of   **201 account** reckoning

ROSALINE
My face is but a moon, and clouded too.   204

KING
Blessed are clouds, to do as such clouds do!
Vouchsafe, bright moon, and these thy stars, to shine,
Those clouds removed, upon our watery eyne.   207

ROSALINE
O vain petitioner! Beg a greater matter;
Thou now requests but moonshine in the water.   209

KING
Then in our measure do but vouchsafe one change.   210
Thou bidd'st me beg; this begging is not strange.   211

ROSALINE
Play, music, then! Nay, you must do it soon.
Not yet? No dance! Thus change I like the moon.
                                        [*Music plays.*]

KING
Will you not dance? How come you thus estranged?   214

ROSALINE
You took the moon at full, but now she's changed.

KING
Yet still she is the moon, and I the man.   216
The music plays; vouchsafe some motion to it.   217

ROSALINE
Our ears vouchsafe it.

KING   But your legs should do it. 218

ROSALINE
Since you are strangers and come here by chance,   219

---

204 a moon (Earlier, at 4.3.226–227, the King described the Princess as
a moon surrounded by her attending stars—as he does again at ll.
206–207. But Rosaline, acting the part of the Princess, hints at change-
ability and reflected beauty more appropriate to Rosaline herself; see
3.1.194.) **clouded** i.e., masked   **207 clouds** i.e., the mask.   **eyne** eyes
209 moonshine . . . water (Proverbial expression meaning "nothing at
all.")   **210 vouchsafe** permit.   **change** a round in dancing (with a play
on the idea of the moon's changing)   **211 strange** odd (with a quibble
on "foreign")   **214 How . . . estranged** why are you disaffected
216 man i.e., man in the moon. (This unrhymed word suggests a missing
line.)   **217 vouchsafe some motion** i.e., deign to dance   **218 Our . . . it**
i.e., I deign to hear your *motion* or proposal. (Rosaline pretends not to
understand an invitation to dance.)   **219 strangers** foreigners

We'll not be nice. Take hands. We will not dance.   220
                              [*She offers her hand.*]

KING
Why take we hands, then?

ROSALINE   Only to part friends.
Curtsy, sweethearts, and so the measure ends.

KING
More measure of this measure! Be not nice.   223

ROSALINE
We can afford no more at such a price.

KING
Price you yourselves. What buys your company?   225

ROSALINE
Your absence only.

KING   That can never be.

ROSALINE
Then cannot we be bought. And so, adieu—
Twice to your visor, and half once to you.   228

KING
If you deny to dance, let's hold more chat.   229

ROSALINE
In private, then.

KING   I am best pleased with that.
                              [*They converse apart.*]

BEROWNE
White-handed mistress, one sweet word with thee.

PRINCESS [*Speaking as Rosaline*]
Honey, and milk, and sugar—there is three.

BEROWNE
Nay then, two treys, an if you grow so nice,   233
Metheglin, wort, and malmsey. Well run, dice!   234
There's half a dozen sweets.

---

220 nice coy   **223 More measure** i.e., (we wish) more quantity; we wish
the kiss that should follow the curtsying   **225 Price you yourselves** set
your own price on yourselves   **228 Twice . . . you** (Rosaline evidently
curtsies, twice to the visor and the face behind it, then a perfunctory
curtsy to her partner; but the line is obscure.)   **229 deny** refuse
233 treys threes.   **nice** subtle   **234 Metheglin** a spiced drink made from
herbs and honey.   **wort,** sweet unfermented beer.   **malmsey** a strong
sweet wine

PRINCESS   Seventh sweet, adieu.
Since you can cog, I'll play no more with you.   236
BEROWNE
One word in secret.
PRINCESS   Let it not be sweet.
BEROWNE
Thou grievest my gall.
PRINCESS   Gall! Bitter.
BEROWNE   Therefore meet.   238
                              [*They converse apart.*]

DUMAINE
Will you vouchsafe with me to change a word?   239
MARIA [*Speaking as Katharine*]
Name it.
DUMAINE   Fair lady—
MARIA   Say you so? Fair lord!   240
Take that for your "fair lady."
DUMAINE   Please it you,
As much in private, and I'll bid adieu.
                              [*They converse apart.*]

KATHARINE [*Speaking as Maria*]
What, was your vizard made without a tongue?   243
LONGAVILLE
I know the reason, lady, why you ask.
KATHARINE
O, for your reason! Quickly, sir, I long.
LONGAVILLE
You have a double tongue within your mask,   246
And would afford my speechless vizard half.   247

---

236 cog cheat   **238 Thou . . . gall** i.e., you cause me pain by irritating
my sore. Gall is bile, a bitter secretion of the liver. (The Princess deliberately misinterprets Berowne's use of *gall*.)   **meet** fitting (with perhaps a
play on "have a meeting")   **239 vouchsafe . . . word** deign to speak with
me. (*Change* means "exchange.")   **240 Say . . . lord** (Maria mischie-
vously takes Dumaine's request for *a word* literally, and so cuts off his
reply at "Fair lady.")   **243 vizard** mask.   **tongue** (A leather projection
held in the mouth to keep the mask on the face. Katharine asks
Longaville why he is "holding his tongue," remaining silent.)   **246 a
double tongue** i.e., (1) both the leather tongue of the mask and your own
tongue (2) enough duplicity of speech for two   **247 And . . . half** i.e., you
talk enough for the two of us

KATHARINE
  "Veal," quoth the Dutchman. Is not "veal" a calf?   248
LONGAVILLE
  A calf, fair lady!
KATHARINE   No, a fair lord calf.
LONGAVILLE
  Let's part the word.
KATHARINE   No, I'll not be your half.   250
  Take all and wean it; it may prove an ox.   251
LONGAVILLE
  Look how you butt yourself in these sharp mocks!   252
  Will you give horns, chaste lady? Do not so.
KATHARINE
  Then die a calf, before your horns do grow.
LONGAVILLE
  One word in private with you, ere I die.
KATHARINE
  Bleat softly then. The butcher hears you cry.
                          [They converse apart.]
BOYET
  The tongues of mocking wenches are as keen
    As is the razor's edge invisible,
  Cutting a smaller hair than may be seen;
    Above the sense of sense, so sensible   260
  Seemeth their conference. Their conceits have wings   261
  Fleeter than arrows, bullets, wind, thought, swifter
    things.
ROSALINE
  Not one word more, my maids. Break off, break off!
        [The ladies break away from the gentlemen.]

---

248 Veal i.e., as a Dutchman would pronounce "well" (with a possible pun on *veil*, mask, as well as *veal*, calf; also, in ll. 245 and 248, Katharine punningly pronounces Longaville's name—*long veal*—and implies that he is a calf or dunce) **250 Let's part the word** i.e., let's reach a compromise. (But Katharine wittily insists on the literal meaning; he must take all the word *calf* to himself.) **your half** (1) sharer with you of two halves (2) your partner in marriage **251 wean** i.e., raise. **ox** (A type of stupidity.) **252 butt** injure (with play on *give horns* in the next line, meaning both to butt with horns and make a cuckold)
260 the sense of the reach of. **sensible** quick-witted **261 conference** conversation. **conceits** fancies

BEROWNE
  By heaven, all dry-beaten with pure scoff!   264
KING
  Farewell, mad wenches. You have simple wits.
                  Exeunt [King, lords, and blackamoors.
                          The ladies unmask.]
PRINCESS
  Twenty adieus, my frozen Muscovits.
  Are these the breed of wits so wondered at?
BOYET
  Tapers they are, with your sweet breaths puffed out.   268
ROSALINE
  Well-liking wits they have; gross, gross; fat, fat.   269
PRINCESS
  O poverty in wit, kingly-poor flout!   270
  Will they not, think you, hang themselves tonight?
  Or ever but in vizards show their faces?
  This pert Berowne was out of countenance quite.   273
ROSALINE
  They were all in lamentable cases!   274
  The King was weeping-ripe for a good word.   275
PRINCESS
  Berowne did swear himself out of all suit.   276
MARIA
  Dumaine was at my service, and his sword.
  "*Non point,*" quoth I. My servant straight was mute.   278
KATHARINE
  Lord Longaville said I came o'er his heart;

---

264 dry-beaten beaten soundly without blood drawn.   **scoff** mockery
268 Tapers candles.   **puffed out** (1) blown out, extinguished (2) puffed
up   **269 Well-liking** in good condition, plump (with a pun on *liking,*
"like-king")   **270 poverty in wit** (The jibe applies to the young men and
to Rosaline for her feeble witticism.)   **kingly-poor flout** poor mockery
of a king (with a possible play on *kingly* as the syllabically reversed
form of *liking,* "ly-king")   **273 out of countenance** flustered, embar-
rassed (with a play on the literal meaning, "without a face," i.e.,
masked)   **274 cases** (1) situations (2) masks   **275 weeping-ripe** ready to
weep.   **good** kind   **276 out of all suit** excessively and to no avail (with a
play on the idea of "costume")   **278 Non point** not at all (quibbling also
on the *point* of his sword. See note on 2.1.190.)   **straight** immediately

And trow you what he called me?

PRINCESS   Qualm, perhaps.   280

KATHARINE
Yes, in good faith.

PRINCESS   Go, sickness as thou art!

ROSALINE
Well, better wits have worn plain statute-caps.   282
But will you hear? The King is my love sworn.

PRINCESS
And quick Berowne hath plighted faith to me.   284

KATHARINE
And Longaville was for my service born.

MARIA
Dumaine is mine, as sure as bark on tree.   286

BOYET
Madam, and pretty mistresses, give ear: 287
Immediately they will again be here
In their own shapes, for it can never be   289
They will digest this harsh indignity.   290

PRINCESS
Will they return?

BOYET   They will, they will, God knows,
And leap for joy, though they are lame with blows.
Therefore change favors, and when they repair,   293
Blow like sweet roses in this summer air.   294

PRINCESS
How "blow"? How "blow"? Speak to be understood.

BOYET
Fair ladies masked are roses in their bud;
Dismasked, their damask sweet commixture shown,   297
Are angels vailing clouds, or roses blown.   298

---

280 trow you would you believe. **Qualm** i.e., heartburn (with a play
perhaps on *came*, l. 279, as suggested by Elizabethan pronunciation)
282 better . . . statute-caps i.e., one could find better wits even among
London apprentices (who were required by statute to wear identifiable
caps) **284 plighted faith** pledged his love **286 sure** firmly united
287 give ear listen **289 In their own shapes** i.e., having put off their
disguises **290 digest** stomach, put up with **293 change favors** exchange love tokens (giving them back to their original owners). **repair**
return **294 Blow** bloom. (But the Princess wonders if *blow* might mean
to give *blows*, as in l. 292.) **297 damask** mingling red and white.
commixture mingling of complexion **298 Are** i.e., they, the fair ladies,
are. **vailing** letting fall, shedding. **blown** blooming, fully opened

PRINCESS
Avaunt, perplexity!—What shall we do   299
If they return in their own shapes to woo?
ROSALINE
Good madam, if by me you'll be advised,
Let's mock them still, as well known as disguised.   302
Let us complain to them what fools were here,
Disguised like Muscovites, in shapeless gear;   304
And wonder what they were, and to what end
Their shallow shows and prologue vilely penned,
And their rough carriage so ridiculous,   307
Should be presented at our tent to us.
BOYET
Ladies, withdraw. The gallants are at hand.
PRINCESS
Whip to our tents, as roes run o'er land.   310
          Exeunt [Princess, Rosaline, Katharine, and Maria].

          Enter the King and the rest [Berowne, Longaville,
          and Dumaine, in their proper dress].

KING
Fair sir, God save you! Where's the Princess?
BOYET
Gone to her tent. Please it Your Majesty
Command me any service to her thither?   313
KING
That she vouchsafe me audience for one word.   314
BOYET
I will, and so will she, I know, my lord.   *Exit.*
BEROWNE
This fellow pecks up wit as pigeons peas,
And utters it again when God doth please.   317
He is wit's peddler, and retails his wares
At wakes and wassails, meetings, markets, fairs;   319

---

299 Avaunt, perplexity i.e., away, riddler   **302 as . . . disguised** in their
familiar appearances just as previously in their disguises   **304 shapeless gear** unshapely apparel   **307 rough carriage** awkward bearing
310 Whip move quickly.   **roes** roe deer (with a pun on a *rose* sending
out runners)   **313 Command . . . thither** do you wish me to take any
message to her there   **314 vouchsafe** grant   **317 utters** (1) speaks
(2) sells.   **when . . . please** i.e., when the moment is propitious
319 wakes and wassails festivals and revels

And we that sell by gross, the Lord doth know,   320
Have not the grace to grace it with such show.
This gallant pins the wenches on his sleeve.   322
Had he been Adam, he had tempted Eve.   323
'A can carve too, and lisp. Why, this is he   324
That kissed his hand away in courtesy.
This is the ape of form, Monsieur the Nice,   326
That, when he plays at tables, chides the dice   327
In honorable terms. Nay, he can sing   328
A mean most meanly; and in ushering   329
Mend him who can. The ladies call him sweet.   330
The stairs, as he treads on them, kiss his feet.
This is the flower that smiles on everyone,
To show his teeth as white as whale's bone;
And consciences that will not die in debt
Pay him the due of "honey-tongued Boyet."

KING
A blister on his sweet tongue, with my heart,
That put Armado's page out of his part!   337

> *Enter the ladies [wearing their original favors,
> with Boyet].*

BEROWNE
See where it comes! Behavior, what wert thou   338
Till this madman showed thee? And what art thou now?   339
KING
All hail, sweet madam, and fair time of day!
PRINCESS
"Fair" in "all hail" is foul, as I conceive.   341

---

320 by gross wholesale (i.e., as the source for the wit that Boyet retails)   **322 pins . . . sleeve** i.e., flaunts his acquaintance with ladies as
one might wear a love token (?)   **323 had** would have   **324 'A** he. **carve**
i.e., woo with courtesy and affability.   **lisp** (A courtly affectation.)
326 ape of form imitator of courtly manners.   **Nice** fastidious
327 tables backgammon   **328 In honorable terms** in polite language
329 mean middle-ranged voice (alto or tenor).   **meanly** moderately
well.   **ushering** serving in the role of gentleman-usher   **330 Mend . . .
can** i.e., let anyone who can improve on him try to do so   **337 put . . .
part** made Armado's page forget his lines   **338 it** i.e., Boyet. **Behavior**
i.e., elegant manners   **339 madman** madcap.   **showed thee** i.e., showed
just how elegant manners could be   **341 all hail** (The Princess deliberately misconstrues the King to have referred to a hailstorm, foul
weather.)   **conceive** understand the matter

KING
  Construe my speeches better, if you may.   342
PRINCESS
  Then wish me better. I will give you leave.   343
KING
  We came to visit you, and purpose now   344
    To lead you to our court. Vouchsafe it, then.
PRINCESS
  This field shall hold me, and so hold your vow.   346
    Nor God nor I delights in perjured men.   347
KING
  Rebuke me not for that which you provoke.
    The virtue of your eye must break my oath.   349
PRINCESS
  You nickname virtue. "Vice," you should have spoke,   350
    For virtue's office never breaks men's troth.   351
  Now by my maiden honor, yet as pure
    As the unsullied lily, I protest,
  A world of torments though I should endure,
    I would not yield to be your house's guest,
  So much I hate a breaking cause to be   356
  Of heavenly oaths, vowed with integrity.
KING
  O, you have lived in desolation here,
    Unseen, unvisited, much to our shame.
PRINCESS
  Not so, my lord. It is not so, I swear.
    We have had pastimes here and pleasant game:
  A mess of Russians left us but of late.   362
KING
  How, madam? Russians?
PRINCESS   Ay, in truth, my lord.
  Trim gallants, full of courtship and of state.   364
ROSALINE
  Madam, speak true.—It is not so, my lord.

---

342 Construe interpret   **343 Then . . . leave** i.e., in that case you must greet me better. I will give you permission to try again.   **344 purpose** intend   **346 so hold** so uphold   **347 Nor** neither   **349 virtue** power. (But the Princess, in the next line, insists on interpreting the word as "moral goodness," the opposite of "vice.")   **350 nickname** misname, mention in error   **351 office** action.   **troth** faith   **356 breaking cause** i.e., cause of breaking   **362 mess** foursome   **364 courtship** courtliness

My lady, to the manner of the days,   366
In courtesy gives undeserving praise.
We four indeed confronted were with four
In Russian habit. Here they stayed an hour
And talked apace; and in that hour, my lord,   370
They did not bless us with one happy word.   371
I dare not call them fools; but this I think,
When they are thirsty, fools would fain have drink.   373

BEROWNE
This jest is dry to me. Gentle sweet,   374
Your wits makes wise things foolish. When we greet,   375
With eyes' best seeing, heaven's fiery eye,   376
By light we lose light. Your capacity   377
Is of that nature that to your huge store   378
Wise things seem foolish and rich things but poor.

ROSALINE
This proves you wise and rich, for in my eye—

BEROWNE
I am a fool, and full of poverty.

ROSALINE
But that you take what doth to you belong,   382
It were a fault to snatch words from my tongue.   383

BEROWNE
O, I am yours, and all that I possess!

ROSALINE
All the fool mine?

BEROWNE   I cannot give you less.

ROSALINE
Which of the vizards was it that you wore?   386

BEROWNE
Where? When? What vizard? Why demand you this?   387

---

366 to the manner of the days in the fashion of the time   **370 talked apace** spoke rapidly, i.e., chattered   **371 happy** felicitous   **373 When . . . drink** i.e., they are fools   **374 dry** stupid, dull (playing on *thirsty* in l. 373)   **375 foolish** i.e., seem foolish by comparison.   **greet** regard, look at   **376 With . . . seeing** with our eyes' sharpest acuity. (Or, *With eyes best seeing*, with our clear-seeing eyes.)   **heaven's fiery eye** i.e., the sun   **377 By . . . light** i.e., the sun's powerful light blinds us   **378 to** compared to   **382–383 But . . . tongue** i.e., you took the words right out of my mouth   **386 vizards** masks   **387 demand** inquire

ROSALINE
There, then, that vizard, that superfluous case   388
That hid the worse and showed the better face.
KING [*Aside to his lords*]
We were descried. They'll mock us now downright.   390
DUMAINE [*Aside to the lords*]
Let us confess and turn it to a jest.
PRINCESS
Amazed, my lord? Why looks Your Highness sad?   392
ROSALINE
Help, hold his brows! He'll swoon! Why look you pale? 393
Seasick, I think, coming from Muscovy.
BEROWNE
Thus pour the stars down plagues for perjury.
  Can any face of brass hold longer out?   396
Here stand I, lady. Dart thy skill at me.   397
  Bruise me with scorn, confound me with a flout,   398
Thrust thy sharp wit quite through my ignorance,
  Cut me to pieces with thy keen conceit,
And I will wish thee nevermore to dance,   401
  Nor nevermore in Russian habit wait.   402
O, never will I trust to speeches penned,
  Nor to the motion of a schoolboy's tongue,
Nor never come in vizard to my friend,   405
  Nor woo in rhyme, like a blind harper's song!   406
Taffeta phrases, silken terms precise,
  Three-piled hyperboles, spruce affectation,   408
Figures pedantical—these summer flies   409
  Have blown me full of maggot ostentation.   410
I do forswear them, and I here protest
  By this white glove—how white the hand, God
    knows!—

---

388 case covering, mask   **390 descried** discovered   **392 Amazed** bewildered   **393 brows** forehead   **396 face of brass** brazen manner
397 Dart thy skill shoot your verbal dexterity   **398 confound** destroy.
flout jeer, insult   **401 wish** entreat   **402 habit** dress.   **wait** be in attendance   **405 friend** sweetheart   **406 harper's** minstrel's   **408 Three-
piled** deep-piled, as in costly velvet.   **spruce** fashionable   **409 Figures**
figures of speech   **410 blown** filled with maggot eggs, made foul.
ostentation pretension, vanity

Henceforth my wooing mind shall be expressed
   In russet yeas and honest kersey noes.   414
And, to begin, wench—so God help me, law!—   415
My love to thee is sound, *sans* crack or flaw.   416

ROSALINE
Sans "sans," I pray you.

BEROWNE   Yet I have a trick   417
   Of the old rage. Bear with me, I am sick;   418
I'll leave it by degrees. Soft, let us see:
Write "Lord have mercy on us" on those three.   420
They are infected; in their hearts it lies;
They have the plague, and caught it of your eyes.   422
These lords are visited; you are not free,   423
For the Lord's tokens on you do I see.   424

PRINCESS
No, they are free that gave these tokens to us.

BEROWNE
Our states are forfeit. Seek not to undo us.   426

ROSALINE
It is not so, for how can this be true,
That you stand forfeit, being those that sue?   428

BEROWNE
Peace! For I will not have to do with you.   429

ROSALINE
Nor shall not, if I do as I intend.

BEROWNE [*To the other lords*]
Speak for yourselves. My wit is at an end.

KING
Teach us, sweet madam, for our rude transgression
Some fair excuse.

---

414 russet simple homespun, russet brown in color. **kersey** plain
woolen cloth **415 law** la **416 sans** without. (But, as Rosaline points
out in the next line, he is still using French expressions.) **417 Yet**
still. **trick** trace **418 rage** fever **420 Lord . . . us** (Sign posted on
houses containing the infectious plague within.) **those three** i.e., his
companions **422 of** from **423 visited** infested by the plague. **free** free
of infection. (But the Princess also quibbles on the meaning "generous
with gifts.") **424 the Lord's tokens** (1) plague sores as visible signs of
infection (2) the love tokens given by the lords, *the lords' tokens*
426 states estates; status as bachelors. **undo** absolve us from forfeiture
(of ourselves) by declaring us *free* (l. 425) **428 being . . . sue** being the
plaintiffs, not the defendants (i.e., how can you bring legal action
against yourselves?) **429 have** have anything

PRINCESS   The fairest is confession.
Were not you here but even now disguised?   434
KING
  Madam, I was.
PRINCESS   And were you well advised?   435
KING
  I was, fair madam.
PRINCESS   When you then were here,
What did you whisper in your lady's ear?
KING
  That more than all the world I did respect her.   438
PRINCESS
  When she shall challenge this, you will reject her.   439
KING
  Upon mine honor, no.
PRINCESS   Peace, peace! Forbear.
Your oath once broke, you force not to forswear.   441
KING
  Despise me when I break this oath of mine.
PRINCESS
  I will, and therefore keep it. Rosaline,
What did the Russian whisper in your ear?
ROSALINE
  Madam, he swore that he did hold me dear   445
As precious eyesight, and did value me
Above this world, adding thereto moreover
That he would wed me or else die my lover.
PRINCESS
  God give thee joy of him! The noble lord
Most honorably doth uphold his word.
KING
  What mean you, madam? By my life, my troth,   451
I never swore this lady such an oath.
ROSALINE
  By heaven, you did! And to confirm it plain,
You gave me this. But take it, sir, again.
              [*She offers him the Princess's favor.*]

---

434 but even now a short while ago   **435 well advised** in your right
mind   **438 respect** value, regard   **439 challenge** lay claim to   **441 force
not** have no hesitation   **445 dear** as valuable   **451 troth** faith

KING

My faith and this the Princess I did give.
I knew her by this jewel on her sleeve.

PRINCESS

Pardon me, sir. This jewel did she wear,
And Lord Berowne, I thank him, is my dear.
[*To Berowne.*] What, will you have me, or your pearl
again?   [*She offers Rosaline's favor.*]

BEROWNE

Neither of either. I remit both twain.   460
I see the trick on 't: here was a consent,   461
Knowing aforehand of our merriment,
To dash it like a Christmas comedy.   463
Some carry-tale, some please-man, some slight zany,   464
Some mumble-news, some trencher-knight, some Dick,   465
That smiles his cheek in years, and knows the trick   466
To make milady laugh when she's disposed,   467
Told our intents before; which once disclosed,
The ladies did change favors, and then we,
Following the signs, wooed but the sign of she.   470
Now, to our perjury to add more terror,
We are again forsworn, in will and error.
Much upon this 'tis. [*To Boyet.*] And might not you   473
Forestall our sport, to make us thus untrue?
Do not you know my lady's foot by the squier,   475
    And laugh upon the apple of her eye?   476
And stand between her back, sir, and the fire,   477
    Holding a trencher, jesting merrily?   478

---

460 either the two. **remit both twain** give up both of them   **461 on 't**
of it.   **consent** agreement, plot   **463 dash** spoil   **464 carry-tale** gossip-
monger, tale-bearer.   **please-man** sycophant.   **slight zany** insignificant
clown   **465 mumble-news** prattler, gossip.   **trencher-knight** i.e., parasite, one who feeds at his master's trencher or wooden dish.   **Dick** (As
in "Tom, Dick, and Harry.")   **466 smiles . . . years** i.e., smiles flat-
teringly so hard that he wrinkles his face   **467 disposed** i.e., disposed to
be merry   **470 the sign of she** the outward appearance of one's sweetheart   **473 Much . . . 'tis** i.e., it must have happened much this way
475 Do . . . squier i.e., don't you know how to suit her fancy. (*Squier*,
rhyming with *fire* in l. 477, means square, carpenter's rule; Boyet
should know the length of her foot.)   **476 And . . . eye** i.e., and know
how to keep her eye amused, wittily catch her eye. (*Apple* means pupil.)   **477 And . . . fire** i.e., and shield her from too much heat
478 trencher wooden dish (with which to offer her refreshment)

You put our page out. Go, you are allowed;   479
Die when you will, a smock shall be your shroud.   480
You leer upon me, do you? There's an eye
Wounds like a leaden sword.
BOYET   Full merrily   482
Hath this brave manage, this career, been run.   483
BEROWNE
Lo, he is tilting straight! Peace, I have done.   484

    Enter [Costard the] clown.

Welcome, pure wit! Thou part'st a fair fray.   485
COSTARD
O Lord, sir, they would know
Whether the three Worthies shall come in or no.
BEROWNE
What, are there but three?
COSTARD   No, sir; but it is vara fine,   488
For every one pursents three.
BEROWNE   And three times thrice is nine.
COSTARD
Not so, sir, under correction, sir, I hope it is not so.   490
You cannot beg us, sir, I can assure you, sir; we know
  what we know.   491
I hope, sir, three times thrice, sir—
BEROWNE   Is not nine?
COSTARD   Under correction, sir, we know whereuntil it   493
  doth amount.
BEROWNE   By Jove, I always took three threes for nine.
COSTARD   O Lord, sir, it were pity you should get your   496
  living by reckoning, sir.   497
BEROWNE   How much is it?
COSTARD   O Lord, sir, the parties themselves, the actors,
  sir, will show whereuntil it doth amount. For mine

479 allowed treated like an allowed fool, allowed to make jests
480 smock woman's undergarment (since Boyet is constantly in wom-
en's company)   **482 leaden sword** a mock weapon (no more threatening
than Boyet's gaze)   **483 brave manage** fine maneuver on horseback.
(Said sardonically.)   **career** running gallop   **484 tilting straight** sparring
with words immediately   **485 Thou . . . fray** you interrupt a fine battle   **488 vara** very   **490 under** subject to   **491 beg us** prove us fools
493 whereuntil to what   **496 it were pity** it would be too bad if.   **get**
make   **497 reckoning** arithmetic

own part, I am, as they say, but to parfect one man in   501
one poor man—Pompion the Great, sir.   502

BEROWNE   Art thou one of the Worthies?

COSTARD   It pleased them to think me worthy of Pompey the Great. For mine own part, I know not the
degree of the Worthy, but I am to stand for him.   506

BEROWNE   Go bid them prepare.

COSTARD
We will turn it finely off, sir. We will take some care.
                                                        Exit.

KING
Berowne, they will shame us. Let them not approach.

BEROWNE
We are shame-proof, my lord; and 'tis some policy   510
To have one show worse than the King's and his
    company.

KING   I say they shall not come.

PRINCESS
Nay, my good lord, let me o'errule you now.
That sport best pleases that doth least know how,
Where zeal strives to content, and the contents   515
Dies in the zeal of that which it presents.   516
Their form confounded makes most form in mirth,   517
When great things laboring perish in their birth.   518

BEROWNE
A right description of our sport, my lord.   519

        Enter [Armado the] braggart.

ARMADO [*To the King*] Anointed, I implore so much   520
expense of thy royal sweet breath as will utter a brace 521
of words.   [*He converses apart with the King and
                            delivers him a paper.*]

PRINCESS   Doth this man serve God?

501 parfect (He means *perform, present.*)   **502 Pompion** pumpkin.
(Malapropism for *Pompey.*)   **506 degree** rank.   **stand for** represent,
play   **510 some policy** a shrewd stratagem   **515–516 and the . . .
presents** and the (feeble) substance of what they perform is overwhelmed by the zeal of the presentation   **517 Their . . . mirth** i.e., the
artistic chaos of their performance has its own reward in mirth
518 laboring striving to be born   **519 right** apt.   **our sport** i.e., our
appearance as Muscovites   **520 Anointed** i.e., King   **521 brace** pair

BEROWNE   Why ask you?

PRINCESS   'A speaks not like a man of God his making.   525

ARMADO   That is all one, my fair sweet honey monarch, for, I protest, the schoolmaster is exceeding fantastical, too too vain, too too vain; but we will put it,
as they say, to *fortuna de la guerra*. I wish you the   529
peace of mind, most royal couplement!   *Exit.*   530

KING   Here is like to be a good presence of Worthies.   531
He presents Hector of Troy, the swain Pompey the
Great, the parish curate Alexander, Armado's page
Hercules, the pedant Judas Maccabaeus;
And if these four Worthies in their first show thrive,
These four will change habits and present the other five.

BEROWNE
There is five in the first show.

KING
You are deceived. 'Tis not so.

BEROWNE
The pedant, the braggart, the hedge-priest, the fool, and
the boy.   539
Abate throw at novum, and the whole world again   540
Cannot pick out five such, take each one in his vein. 541

KING
The ship is under sail, and here she comes amain.   542

         Enter [Costard, as] Pompey.

COSTARD
"I Pompey am—"

BOYET   You lie; you are not he.

COSTARD
"I Pompey am—"

BOYET   With leopard's head on knee.   544

---

525 God his God's   **529 fortuna . . . guerra** the fortune of war
530 couplement couple   **531 presence** assembly   **539 hedge-priest**
illiterate, rural priest   **540 Abate** barring, setting aside.   **throw at
novum** a lucky throw of the dice in a game of *novum* or nines, having
five and nine as its principal throws (joking on the business of offering
nine characters with just five actors)   **541 take . . . vein** i.e., each one
is such a fantastical type   **542 amain** suddenly   **544 leopard's** (referring to his coat of arms, customarily on the shield rather than on the
knee; perhaps Costard is holding his shield upside down or awkwardly
low)

BEROWNE
Well said, old mocker. I must needs be friends with thee. 545
COSTARD
"I Pompey am, Pompey surnamed the Big—"
DUMAINE   "The Great."
COSTARD
It is "Great," sir.—"Pompey surnamed the Great,
That oft in field, with targe and shield, did make my foe
to sweat.   549
And traveling along this coast, I here am come by
chance,
And lay my arms before the legs of this sweet lass of
France."   [*He lays down his weapons.*]
If your ladyship would say, "Thanks, Pompey," I had
done.
PRINCESS   Great thanks, great Pompey.
COSTARD   'Tis not so much worth; but I hope I was per- 555
fect. I made a little fault in "Great."   556
BEROWNE   My hat to a halfpenny, Pompey proves the 557
best Worthy.   [*Costard stands aside.*] 558

Enter [Nathaniel the] curate, for Alexander.

NATHANIEL
"When in the world I lived, I was the world's
commander;
By east, west, north, and south, I spread my conquering
might.
My scutcheon plain declares that I am Alisander—"   561
BOYET
Your nose says no, you are not; for it stands too right. 562
BEROWNE [*To Boyet*]
Your nose smells "no" in this, most tender-smelling
knight.   563

---

545 needs necessarily   **549 targe** shield   **555–556 perfect** accurate in
memorizing   **557 My hat to** I'll wager my hat against   **558 s.d. for** as.
(Also at 583 s.d.)   **561 scutcheon** coat of arms   **562 right** straight.
(Alexander was supposed to have had a wry neck that twisted his head
to one side.)   **563 Your . . . this** i.e., your nose smells out the impostor
because Nathaniel does not smell as sweet as Alexander. (Berowne may
be jibing again at Boyet's fastidiousness, as in ll. 464–482. Alexander
was reputed to have a bodily odor of "marvelous good savor" according
to North's translation of Plutarch.)   **tender-smelling** sensitive to smells

PRINCESS
   The conquerer is dismayed. Proceed, good Alexander.
NATHANIEL
   "When in the world I lived, I was the world's
     commander—"
BOYET
   Most true; 'tis right. You were so, Alisander.
BEROWNE [*To Costard*] Pompey the Great—
COSTARD Your servant, and Costard.
BEROWNE Take away the conqueror; take away Alis-
ander.
COSTARD [*To Nathaniel*] O, sir, you have overthrown
Alisander the conqueror! You will be scraped out of   572
the painted cloth for this. Your lion, that holds his   573
poleax sitting on a closestool, will be given to Ajax;   574
he will be the ninth Worthy. A conqueror, and afeard
to speak? Run away for shame, Alisander. [*Exit
Nathaniel.*] There, an 't shall please you, a foolish mild   577
man, an honest man, look you, and soon dashed. He   578
is a marvelous good neighbor, faith, and a very good
bowler. But, for Alisander—alas, you see how 'tis—a
little o'erparted. But there are Worthies a-coming will   581
speak their mind in some other sort.   582
PRINCESS Stand aside, good Pompey.

     *Enter [Holofernes the] pedant, for Judas, and
     [Mote] the boy, for Hercules.*

HOLOFERNES [*As presenter*]
   "Great Hercules is presented by this imp,   584
   Whose club killed Cerberus, that three-headed *canus;*   585
   And when he was a babe, a child, a shrimp,

572–573 You will . . . this (An allusion to the frequent representation of
the Nine Worthies painted on an arras or tapestry.) **573–574 Your
lion . . . closestool** (A Renaissance memorial emblem of Alexander
described a lion sitting in a chair, holding a battle-ax. A *closestool* is a
seat in a privy.) **574 Ajax** legendary Greek chieftain at the Trojan War
who coveted the slain Achilles' armor (with a pun on *jakes*, privy)
577 an 't if it **578 dashed** rattled, daunted **581 o'erparted** having a
part too difficult **582 sort** manner **584 presented** played, represented. **imp** child **585 Cerberus** three-headed dog at the entrance to
Hades, the capturing of which was one of Hercules' twelve labors.
canus i.e., *canis*, dog (in Latin. *Canus* is needed for the rhyme.)

Thus did he strangle serpents in his *manus*.   587
Quoniam he seemeth in minority,   588
Ergo I come with this apology."   589
[*To Mote*.] Keep some state in thy exit, and vanish.   590

Exit Boy.

[*As Judas*.] "Judas I am—"
DUMAINE   A Judas!   592
HOLOFERNES   Not Iscariot, sir.
"Judas I am, yclept Maccabaeus."   594
DUMAINE   Judas Maccabaeus clipped is plain Judas.   595
BEROWNE   A kissing traitor. How art thou proved Judas?   596
HOLOFERNES   "Judas I am—"
DUMAINE   The more shame for you, Judas.
HOLOFERNES   What mean you, sir?
BOYET   To make Judas hang himself.
HOLOFERNES   Begin, sir. You are my elder.   601
BEROWNE   Well followed. Judas was hanged on an elder.   602
HOLOFERNES   I will not be put out of countenance.   603
BEROWNE   Because thou hast no face.
HOLOFERNES [*Pointing to his face*]   What is this?
BOYET   A citternhead.   606
DUMAINE   The head of a bodkin.   607
BEROWNE   A death's face in a ring.   608
LONGAVILLE   The face of an old Roman coin, scarce   609
seen.   610
BOYET   The pommel of Caesar's falchion.   611

---

587 manus hands   **588 Quoniam** since   **589 Ergo** therefore   **590 state**
dignity   **592 A Judas** i.e., a traitor. (The lords deliberately confuse the
military hero Judas Maccabaeus with Judas Iscariot, who betrayed
Christ.)   **594 yclept** called   **595 clipped** (1) shortened (2) embraced (as
Berowne uses it in l. 596; with a play also on *yclept*)   **596 kissing** (A
reference to Judas' kiss of Jesus by which he betrayed his master;
with a pun on *clipped*, embraced or kissed, in the preceding line.)
601 You . . . elder i.e., you are my senior and so should take precedence.
(But Berowne answers with a pun on *elder*, elder tree, traditionally the
tree on which Judas hanged himself.)   **603 put out of countenance**
disconcerted. (But Berowne in the next line takes *countenance* in its
literal sense, "face.")   **606 citternhead** head of a cithern or guitar (often
grotesquely carved)   **607 bodkin** a long, jeweled pin for a lady's hair, or
a small dagger (similarly carved)   **608 A death's . . . ring** i.e., a death's-
head ring worn as a *memento mori*   **609–610 scarce seen** worn almost
smooth   **611 falchion** curved sword. (The *pommel* or rounded knob on
the hilt would be carved.)

DUMAINE   The carved-bone face on a flask.   612
BEROWNE   Saint George's half-cheek in a brooch.   613
DUMAINE   Ay, and in a brooch of lead.   614
BEROWNE   Ay, and worn in the cap of a tooth drawer.   615
  And now forward, for we have put thee in counte-   616
  nance.   617
HOLOFERNES   You have put me out of countenance.
BEROWNE   False. We have given thee faces.
HOLOFERNES   But you have outfaced them all.   620
BEROWNE
  An thou wert a lion, we would do so.   621
BOYET
  Therefore, as he is an ass, let him go.
  And so adieu, sweet Jude! Nay, why dost thou stay?
DUMAINE   For the latter end of his name.
BEROWNE
  For the ass to the Jude? Give it him. Jud-as, away!   625
HOLOFERNES
  This is not generous, not gentle, not humble.   626
BOYET
  A light for Monsieur Judas! It grows dark; he may
    stumble.   [*Exit Holofernes.*]
PRINCESS
  Alas, poor Maccabaeus, how hath he been baited!   628

  Enter [Armado the] braggart [as Hector].

BEROWNE   Hide thy head, Achilles! Here comes Hector   629
  in arms.
DUMAINE   Though my mocks come home by me, I will   631
  now be merry.

---

612 flask i.e., horn powder flask   **613 half-cheek** profile   **614 of lead**
i.e., of inferior quality   **615 tooth drawer** (Tooth extractors were not
highly regarded; a brooch worn by such people in the cap might be of
an inferior sort.)   **616–617 we . . . countenance** i.e., we've drawn your
portrait. (But Holofernes replies with a quibble meaning "you have
made me forget my lines.")   **620 outfaced** i.e., mocked them, put them
down (playing on *faces* in l. 619)   **621 An** if.   **lion** (One of Aesop's fables
tells of an ass that wears a lion's skin until he is betrayed by his bray.)
625 Jud-as (Jude's *latter end* turns out to be his *ass*.)   **626 gentle** courteous   **628 baited** set upon, attacked   **629 Achilles, Hector** (They were
great antagonists in the Trojan War.)   **631 by me** to me, to my discomfiture (causing me to pay for this later)

KING Hector was but a Trojan in respect of this.   633
BOYET But is this Hector?
KING I think Hector was not so clean-timbered.   635
LONGAVILLE His leg is too big for Hector's.
DUMAINE More calf, certain.   637
BOYET No, he is best endued in the small.   638
BEROWNE This cannot be Hector.
DUMAINE He's a god or a painter, for he makes faces.
ARMADO
   "The armipotent Mars, of lances the almighty,   641
     Gave Hector a gift—"
DUMAINE A gilt nutmeg.   643
BEROWNE A lemon.
LONGAVILLE Stuck with cloves.
DUMAINE No, cloven.   646
ARMADO Peace!—
   "The armipotent Mars, of lances the almighty,
     Gave Hector a gift, the heir of Ilion;   649
   A man so breathed, that certain he would fight, yea   650
     From morn till night, out of his pavilion.   651
   I am that flower—"
DUMAINE That mint.
LONGAVILLE That columbine.
ARMADO Sweet Lord Longaville, rein thy tongue.   655
LONGAVILLE I must rather give it the rein, for it runs   656
   against Hector.
DUMAINE Ay, and Hector's a greyhound.   658
ARMADO The sweet warman is dead and rotten. Sweet
   chucks, beat not the bones of the buried. When he
   breathed, he was a man. But I will forward with my   661

---

633 a Trojan i.e., (1) a resident of Troy (2) a jolly companion, a rois-
terer. **in respect of** in comparison with **635 clean-timbered** clean-
limbed, well built **637 calf** (1) lower part of leg (2) dolt **638 best . . .
small** well endowed in the part of the leg below the calf **641 armipotent** powerful in arms **643 gilt** glazed with egg yolk, saffron, etc.
646 cloven (Dumaine's witticism plays on the contrast between a *lemon
stuck with cloves* to serve as a confection in a drink and a *leman* or
lover who is *cloven* in the act of love.) **649 Ilion** Troy **650 so breathed**
i.e., in good condition, valiant **651 pavilion** tent or camp to which the
combatant retired when not engaged in fight **655 rein** restrain, control **656 give it the rein** allow it to run freely **658 a greyhound** i.e.,
famed for his speed as a runner **661 forward** go forward, continue

device. [*To the Princess*.] Sweet royalty, bestow on me 662
the sense of hearing.

> *Berowne steps forth [to whisper to Costard,*
> *and then resumes his place].*

PRINCESS
Speak, brave Hector. We are much delighted.

ARMADO   I do adore thy sweet Grace's slipper.

BOYET   Loves her by the foot.

DUMAINE   He may not by the yard. 667

ARMADO
"This Hector far surmounted Hannibal—"

COSTARD   The party is gone. Fellow Hector, she is gone! 669
She is two months on her way. 670

ARMADO   What meanest thou?

COSTARD   Faith, unless you play the honest Trojan, the 672
poor wench is cast away. She's quick; the child brags 673
in her belly already. 'Tis yours.

ARMADO   Dost thou infamonize me among potentates? 675
Thou shalt die.

COSTARD   Then shall Hector be whipped for Jaquenetta
that is quick by him and hanged for Pompey that is
dead by him.

DUMAINE   Most rare Pompey!

BOYET   Renowned Pompey!

BEROWNE   Greater than "Great"! Great, great, great Pompey! Pompey the Huge!

DUMAINE   Hector trembles.

BEROWNE   Pompey is moved. More Ates, more Ates! 685
Stir them on, stir them on!

DUMAINE   Hector will challenge him.

BEROWNE   Ay, if 'a have no more man's blood in his
belly than will sup a flea.

ARMADO   By the North Pole, I do challenge thee.

---

662 device dramatic contrivance   **667 yard** (Dumaine puns on the slang
sense, "penis.")   **669 The party is gone** i.e., Jaquenetta is ruined in
reputation. (Costard may have received this news from Berowne when
Berowne whispers to him. Or, if *The party is gone* is part of Armado's
speech, as the quarto and the Folio seem to indicate, it may mean "The
man is dead.")   **670 on her way** i.e., pregnant   **672 the honest Trojan**
i.e., the good-hearted fellow (as at l. 633)   **673 quick** pregnant   **675 infamonize** slander   **685 Ates** i.e., incitements to mischief. (Ate was the
goddess of discord.)

COSTARD   I will not fight with a pole, like a northern 691
man. I'll slash; I'll do it by the sword. I bepray you, let 692
me borrow my arms again.

DUMAINE   Room for the incensed Worthies!

COSTARD   I'll do it in my shirt. [*He takes off his doublet.*]

DUMAINE   Most resolute Pompey!

MOTE   Master, let me take you a buttonhole lower. Do 697
you not see Pompey is uncasing for the combat? What 698
mean you? You will lose your reputation.

ARMADO   Gentlemen and soldiers, pardon me. I will not
combat in my shirt. 701

DUMAINE   You may not deny it. Pompey hath made the
challenge.

ARMADO   Sweet bloods, I both may and will. 704

BEROWNE   What reason have you for 't?

ARMADO   The naked truth of it is, I have no shirt. I go 706
woolward for penance. 707

BOYET   True, and it was enjoined him in Rome for want 708
of linen; since when, I'll be sworn, he wore none but 709
a dishclout of Jaquenetta's, and that 'a wears next his 710
heart for a favor.

Enter a messenger, Monsieur Marcade.

MARCADE   God save you, madam!

PRINCESS   Welcome, Marcade,
But that thou interruptest our merriment.

MARCADE
I am sorry, madam, for the news I bring
Is heavy in my tongue. The King your father—

PRINCESS
Dead, for my life!

MARCADE   Even so. My tale is told.

BEROWNE
Worthies, away! The scene begins to cloud.

691–692 a northern man a boorish ruffian from the north (for whom the
stave or *pole* was a traditional weapon)   **697 take . . . lower** (1) help
remove your doublet (2) "take you down a peg," humiliate you
698 uncasing undressing   **701 combat** duel, fight   **704 bloods** men of .
mettle   **706–707 go woolward for penance** i.e., with woolen clothing
next to the skin and no linen underwear. (Armado's lame excuse is
that he does so to punish the flesh.)   **708 enjoined** required of
708–709 want of linen lack of a clean shirt, etc. (Boyet sees through the
excuse.)   **710 dishclout** dishcloth

ARMADO   For mine own part, I breathe free breath. I   719
have seen the day of wrong through the little hole of   720
discretion, and I will right myself like a soldier.   721

Exeunt Worthies.

KING   How fares Your Majesty?

PRINCESS
Boyet, prepare. I will away tonight.

KING
Madam, not so. I do beseech you, stay.

PRINCESS
Prepare, I say. I thank you, gracious lords,
For all your fair endeavors, and entreat,
Out of a new-sad soul, that you vouchsafe   727
In your rich wisdom to excuse or hide   728
The liberal opposition of our spirits,   729
If overboldly we have borne ourselves
In the converse of breath; your gentleness   731
Was guilty of it. Farewell, worthy lord!   732
A heavy heart bears not a humble tongue.   733
Excuse me so, coming too short of thanks   734
For my great suit so easily obtained.   735

KING
The extreme parts of time extremely forms   736
All causes to the purpose of his speed,   737
And often at his very loose decides   738
That which long process could not arbitrate.
And though the mourning brow of progeny   740
Forbid the smiling courtesy of love   741
The holy suit which fain it would convince,   742

719–721 I have . . . discretion i.e., I now perceive my true situation, my
wrong. (From the proverb "One may see day at a little hole.")
721 right myself i.e., make honorable amends, do the right thing
727 vouchsafe permit   **728 hide** overlook   **729 liberal opposition** too-
free antagonism   **731 converse of breath** conversation.   **gentleness**
courtesy   **732 guilty of** responsible for   **733 humble** i.e., suited to polite
civilities   **734 so** therefore   **735 suit** i.e., the mission on which she
came (which the King evidently has granted)   **736–737 The . . . speed**
i.e., a few last moments demand quick decisions   **737, 738 his** i.e.,
time's   **738 loose** release, discharge. (An archery term.)   **740 progeny**
i.e., the child of the dead king, the Princess   **741 Forbid** deny to
742 The . . . convince the love suit it would like to present.   **convince**
give proof of

Yet since love's argument was first on foot,
Let not the cloud of sorrow jostle it
From what it purposed, since to wail friends lost
Is not by much so wholesome-profitable
As to rejoice at friends but newly found.

PRINCESS
I understand you not. My griefs are double.   748

BEROWNE
Honest plain words best pierce the ear of grief,
And by these badges understand the King.   750
For your fair sakes have we neglected time,
Played foul play with our oaths. Your beauty, ladies,
Hath much deformed us, fashioning our humors
Even to the opposèd end of our intents;   754
And what in us hath seemed ridiculous—
As love is full of unbefitting strains,   756
All wanton as a child, skipping and vain,   757
Formed by the eye and therefore, like the eye,
Full of strange shapes, of habits, and of forms,
Varying in subjects as the eye doth roll
To every varied object in his glance;
Which parti-coated presence of loose love   762
Put on by us, if, in your heavenly eyes,
Have misbecomed our oaths and gravities,   764
Those heavenly eyes, that look into these faults,
Suggested us to make. Therefore, ladies,   766
Our love being yours, the error that love makes   767
Is likewise yours. We to ourselves prove false   768
By being once false forever to be true   769
To those that make us both—fair ladies, you.   770
And even that falsehood, in itself a sin,
Thus purifies itself and turns to grace.

---

748 double i.e., because of my father's death, and because I don't
understand you   **750 badges** signs, i.e., my honest plain words
754 opposèd opposite   **756 strains** impulses   **757 wanton** frivolous.
vain foolish   **762 parti-coated presence** jesting or foolish appearance.
loose unrestrained   **764 misbecomed** been unbecoming to   **766 Suggested us to make** tempted us to commit all these follies of love
767 Our love being yours i.e., since the love we offer you is now yours
768–770 We . . . you i.e., we are false to our vows one time, abandoning
the studies we vowed to pursue, in order to be true forever to you, fair
ladies, who make us both false and true: false to our former vow but
true to you

PRINCESS
We have received your letters full of love,
Your favors, the ambassadors of love,
And in our maiden council rated them   775
At courtship, pleasant jest, and courtesy,   776
As bombast and as lining to the time.   777
But more devout than this in our respects   778
Have we not been, and therefore met your loves   779
In their own fashion, like a merriment.

DUMAINE
Our letters, madam, showed much more than jest.

LONGAVILLE
So did our looks.

ROSALINE   We did not quote them so.   782

KING
Now, at the latest minute of the hour,
Grant us your loves.

PRINCESS   A time, methinks, too short
To make a world-without-end bargain in.
No, no, my lord, Your Grace is perjured much,
Full of dear guiltiness, and therefore this: 787
If for my love—as there is no such cause—   788
You will do aught, this shall you do for me: 789
Your oath I will not trust, but go with speed
To some forlorn and naked hermitage,   791
Remote from all the pleasures of the world;
There stay until the twelve celestial signs   793
Have brought about the annual reckoning.
If this austere insociable life
Change not your offer made in heat of blood;
If frosts and fasts, hard lodging, and thin weeds   797
Nip not the gaudy blossoms of your love,
But that it bear this trial, and last love;   799

---

775 rated evaluated **776 At** as merely **777 bombast** (1) a loosely made
fabric used for padding or stuffing garments, for *lining* (2) puffed-up
rhetoric, fit only to fill up the time **778 devout** serious. **respects**
considerations **779 met** responded to **782 quote** interpret **787 dear**
grievous and precious **788 as . . . cause** i.e., though I can't see why it
should inspire you in that way **789 aught** anything **791 naked** austere **793 twelve celestial signs** signs of the zodiac (encompassing one
year) **797 hard lodging** uncomfortable accommodations. **weeds**
garments **799 last** remain, continue as

Then, at the expiration of the year,
Come challenge me, challenge me by these deserts,   801
And, by this virgin palm now kissing thine,

                    [*Giving him her hand*]

I will be thine; and till that instant shut
My woeful self up in a mourning house,
Raining the tears of lamentation
For the remembrance of my father's death.
If this thou do deny, let our hands part,
Neither entitled in the other's heart.   808

KING
If this, or more than this, I would deny,
    To flatter up these powers of mine with rest,   810
The sudden hand of death close up mine eye!
    Hence hermit then—my heart is in thy breast.   812

                    [*They converse apart.*]

DUMAINE
But what to me, my love? But what to me?
A wife?

KATHARINE   A beard, fair health, and honesty.
With threefold love I wish you all these three.

DUMAINE
O, shall I say, "I thank you, gentle wife?"

KATHARINE
Not so, my lord. A twelvemonth and a day
I'll mark no words that smooth-faced wooers say.
Come when the King doth to my lady come;
Then, if I have much love, I'll give you some.

DUMAINE
I'll serve thee true and faithfully till then.

KATHARINE
Yet swear not, lest ye be forsworn again.

                    [*They converse apart.*]

LONGAVILLE
What says Maria?

MARIA   At the twelvemonth's end
I'll change my black gown for a faithful friend.   824

---

801 challenge claim. **deserts** meritorious actions **808 entitled in**
having a claim to **810 flatter up** pamper **812 Hence hermit then** i.e.,
then off I go to be a hermit **824 friend** sweetheart

LONGAVILLE
    I'll stay with patience, but the time is long.   825
MARIA
    The liker you; few taller are so young.   826
                        [*They converse apart.*]
BEROWNE
    Studies my lady? Mistress, look on me.   827
    Behold the window of my heart, mine eye,
    What humble suit attends thy answer there.   829
    Impose some service on me for thy love.
ROSALINE
    Oft have I heard of you, my Lord Berowne,
    Before I saw you; and the world's large tongue   832
    Proclaims you for a man replete with mocks,
    Full of comparisons and wounding flouts,   834
    Which you on all estates will execute   835
    That lie within the mercy of your wit.
    To weed this wormwood from your fruitful brain,   837
    And therewithal to win me, if you please,
    Without the which I am not to be won,
    You shall this twelvemonth term from day to day
    Visit the speechless sick and still converse   841
    With groaning wretches, and your task shall be
    With all the fierce endeavor of your wit
    To enforce the painèd impotent to smile.   844
BEROWNE
    To move wild laughter in the throat of death?
    It cannot be. It is impossible.
    Mirth cannot move a soul in agony.
ROSALINE
    Why, that's the way to choke a gibing spirit,   848
    Whose influence is begot of that loose grace   849

825 stay wait   **826 liker** more like. (Maria deliberately takes Longaville's *long* in the sense of "tall.")   **827 Studies my lady** i.e., are you in
a brown study   **829 attends** awaits   **832 the world's large tongue** i.e.,
universal report   **834 comparisons** sardonic similes.   **flouts** jeers,
insults   **835 all estates** all classes of people   **837 weed** i.e., remove.
wormwood (A bitter-tasting herb, hence "bitterness.")   **841 still converse** constantly associate   **844 the painèd impotent** helpless suffer-
ers   **848 gibing** mocking, scornful   **849 loose grace** carelessly given
approval. (Rosaline is saying that Berowne's mocking manner has been
nurtured by the fact that others have laughed shallowly and too easily
at his foolish raillery.)

Which shallow laughing hearers give to fools.
A jest's prosperity lies in the ear
Of him that hears it, never in the tongue
Of him that makes it. Then if sickly ears,
Deafed with the clamors of their own dear groans,   854
Will hear your idle scorns, continue then,
And I will have you and that fault withal;   856
But if they will not, throw away that spirit,
And I shall find you empty of that fault,
Right joyful of your reformation.

BEROWNE
A twelvemonth? Well, befall what will befall,
I'll jest a twelvemonth in an hospital.

PRINCESS [*To the King*]
Ay, sweet my lord, and so I take my leave.

KING
No, madam, we will bring you on your way.   863

BEROWNE
Our wooing doth not end like an old play;
Jack hath not Jill. These ladies' courtesy
Might well have made our sport a comedy.

KING
Come, sir, it wants a twelvemonth and a day,   867
And then 'twill end.

BEROWNE   That's too long for a play.

      Enter [Armado the] braggart.

ARMADO [*To the King*]   Sweet Majesty, vouchsafe me—   869
PRINCESS   Was not that Hector?
DUMAINE   The worthy knight of Troy.
ARMADO   I will kiss thy royal finger, and take leave. I
am a votary; I have vowed to Jaquenetta to hold the   873
plow for her sweet love three year. But, most es-   874
teemed greatness, will you hear the dialogue that the   875
two learned men have compiled in praise of the owl   876
and the cuckoo? It should have followed in the end of
our show.

---

854 dear heartfelt   **856 withal** in addition   **863 bring** accompany
867 wants lacks   **869 vouchsafe** permit   **873–874 hold the plow** i.e.,
labor at farming   **875 dialogue** debate   **875–876 the two learned men**
i.e., Holofernes and Nathaniel

KING   Call them forth quickly. We will do so.
ARMADO   Holla! Approach.

> *Enter all [Holofernes, Nathaniel, Mote, Costard,*
> *Jaquenetta, and others. They stand in two*
> *groups.]*

This side is Hiems, Winter, this Ver, the Spring; the
one maintained by the owl, th' other by the cuckoo.   882
Ver, begin.

The Song

SPRING [*Sings*]
          When daisies pied and violets blue,   884
                And lady-smocks all silver-white,   885
          And cuckoo-buds of yellow hue   886
                Do paint the meadows with delight,
          The cuckoo then, on every tree,
          Mocks married men; for thus sings he:
                          Cuckoo!
          Cuckoo, cuckoo! O word of fear,
          Unpleasing to a married ear!   892

          When shepherds pipe on oaten straws,
                And merry larks are plowmen's clocks,   894
          When turtles tread, and rooks and daws,   895
                And maidens bleach their summer smocks,
          The cuckoo then, on every tree,
          Mocks married men; for thus sings he:
                          Cuckoo!
          Cuckoo, cuckoo! O word of fear,
          Unpleasing to a married ear!

WINTER [*Sings*]
          When icicles hang by the wall,

---

882 maintained defended, championed   **884 pied** particolored
885 lady-smocks cuckooflowers   **886 cuckoo-buds of yellow** butter-
cups (?)   **892 Unpleasing** i.e., because the cuckoo suggests cuckoldry
894 clocks (i.e., because plowmen "rise with the lark")   **895 turtles
tread** turtledoves mate.   **rooks and daws** black birds related to the crow

And Dick the shepherd blows his nail,   903
And Tom bears logs into the hall,
   And milk comes frozen home in pail,
When blood is nipped, and ways be foul,   906
Then nightly sings the staring owl:
Tu-whit, tu-whoo! A merry note,
While greasy Joan doth keel the pot.   909

When all aloud the wind doth blow,
   And coughing drowns the parson's saw,   911
And birds sit brooding in the snow,
   And Marian's nose looks red and raw,
When roasted crabs hiss in the bowl,   914
Then nightly sings the staring owl:
Tu-whit, tu-whoo! A merry note,
While greasy Joan doth keel the pot.

ARMADO The words of Mercury are harsh after the   918
songs of Apollo. You that way; we this way.   919

Exeunt.

---

903 blows his nail blows on his fingernails (i.e., to keep warm, and
waiting patiently with nothing to do) **906 nipped** chilled. **ways** path-
ways **909 keel** skim and stir, cool to prevent boiling **911 saw** maxim,
moral observation **914 crabs** crab apples **918 Mercury** messenger of
the gods and associated with eloquence or sophistry in antithesis to
Apollo as the god of music **919 You . . . this way** (Armado may be
directing those who have presented Winter to exit in one direction and
those having presented Spring in another; and he may also be referring
to the audience.)

Date and Text

Love's Labor's Lost first appeared in a quarto dated 1598, without entry in the Stationer's Register, the official record book of the London Company of Stationers (booksellers and printers). Its title page reads:

> *A* PLEASANT Conceited Comedie CALLED, Loues labors lost. As it vvas presented before her Highnes this last Christmas. Newly corrected and augmented *By W. Shakespere.* Imprinted at London by *W. W.* [William White] for *Cutbert Burby.* 1598.

Because the phrase "newly corrected and augmented" also appears on the title page of the good quarto of *Romeo and Juliet*, issued in 1599 to correct a pirated quarto of 1597, many scholars suspect that *Love's Labor's Lost* may similarly have appeared in a bad quarto that is now lost. Such a circumstance would explain why the existing quarto of *Love's Labor's Lost* was not registered: if the play had already been published, even in a pirated version, relicensing would have been unnecessary. (The *Romeo and Juliet* good quarto was not registered for this reason.) But it is also possible that the 1599 quarto is simply reprinting an earlier lost good quarto.

The text shows clear signs of revision. Two long passages (see textual notes at 4.3.291 and 5.2.812) give duplicatory readings of the same speeches, suggesting the printer mistakenly copied both the canceled version in his copy and the revision. Speech headings are unusually confused, sometimes referring to characters by their personal names (Navarre, Armado, Holofernes) and at other times by their generic titles (King, Braggart, Pedant). Some of these errors, notably the long uncanceled passages, suggest that the printer (perhaps new and relatively inexperienced) was copying from Shakespeare's working draft, or foul papers. Whether Shakespeare wrote this draft on one occasion or whether he revised an earlier version is, however, a matter on which scholars disagree. The First Folio text was set from the quarto, and thus gives us little additional information as to when or in what stages the play was written, though the Folio may also have had occasional reference to a playhouse manuscript.

Francis Meres refers to the play in October of 1598 in his *Palladis Tamia: Wit's Treasury* (a slender volume on contemporary literature and art; valuable because it lists most of Shakespeare's plays that existed at that time). The performance before Queen Elizabeth "last Christmas" was probably in late 1597. Robert Tofte tells us in his *Alba* (1598) that "*Love's Labour Lost*, I once did see a play / Ycleped so." His phrasing suggests a performance seen some time in the past, although he could mean that he saw it only once. Apart from these allusions, dating of the play must rely on its presumed internal allusions to contemporary events. Unfortunately, the play has attracted a lot of highly speculative topical hypotheses. One such describes a "School of Night" to which Sir Walter Ralegh, Matthew Roydon, George Chapman, and others are supposed to have belonged. No objective evidence exists to prove the existence of such a school. Ralegh was tried for atheism but acquitted. Other topical hypotheses are discussed briefly in the Introduction to the play. Some allusions to the historical King of Navarre and to his supporters, the Duc de Biron and the Duc de Longueville, are undeniable. These allusions are not very helpful in dating, however, since even by 1588–1589 these persons were the chief figures in a bloody religious civil war in France and hence inappropriate subjects for light comedy. The influence of John Lyly and the children's drama also argues for an early date. If, on the other hand, the Muscovite masque in 5.2 contains a reference to the Gray's Inn (one of the Inns of Court, where young men studied law) revels of 1594, as several scholars have urged, some portions of the play may be from after that date. The hypothesis that Shakespeare revived an old play of his shortly before publication in 1598, although not universally accepted, offers at least a plausible explanation of the phrase "newly corrected and augmented" on the title page.

Textual Notes

These textual notes are not a historical collation, either of the early quarto and the early folios or of more recent editions; they are simply a record of departures in this edition from the copy text. The readings adopted in this edition appears in boldface, followed by the rejected reading from the copy text, i.e., the quarto of 1598. Only major alterations in punctuation are noted. Changes in lineation are not indicated, nor are some minor and obvious typographical errors.

Abbreviations used:
F the First Folio
Q the quarto of 1598
s.d. stage direction
s.p. speech prefix

Copy text: the quarto of 1598.

1.1. s.p. [and elsewhere] King Ferdinand **18 schedule** sedule **24 three** thee **31 pomp** pome **62 feast** fast **104 an** any **123 losing** loosing **127 s.p. Berowne** [at l. 132 (Ber.) in Q] **130 public** publibue **possibly** possible **165 One** On **168 umpire** vmpier **180 s.p. [and elsewhere] Dull** Constab **188 s.p. [and elsewhere, except for ll. 219 and 221] Costard** Clowne **188 contempts** Contempls **216 welkin's** welkis **245 s.p. King** [not in Q; also at ll. 247, 252] **254 with, with** Which with **264 s.p. Dull** Antho **273 worst** wost **286 s.p. King** Ber

1.2. 3 s.p. [and elsewhere] Mote Boy **4 Why,** Why? **97 blushing** blush-in **126 deywoman** Day womand **128 s.p. Jaquenetta** Maide [and elsewhere Maid, Ma] **139 s.p. Dull** Clo **172 duello** [F] Duella

2.1. 13 s.p. [and elsewhere] Princess Queene **32 Importunes** Importuous **34 visaged** visage **36 s.d. Exit Boyet** [at l. 35 in Q] **39 s.p. A lord** Lor [also at l. 80] **Lord Longaville** Longauill **40 s.p. Maria** 1. Lady **44 parts** peerelsse **53 s.p. Maria** Lad **56 s.p. Katharine** 2. Lad **61 Alençon's** Alansoes **64 s.p. Rosaline** 3. Lad **88 unpeopled** vnpeeled **90 s.p. [and elsewhere] King** Nauar **115–126 s.p. Rosaline** Kather **130 half of an** halfe of, of an **142 demand** pemaund **144 On** One **180 mine own** my none **190 Non** No **195 Katharine** Rosalin **210 Rosaline** Katherin **221 s.p. Katharine** La [also at l. 224] **254 s.p. Rosaline** Lad **255 s.p. Maria** Lad. 2 **256 s.p. Katharine** Lad. 3 **257 s.p. Maria** Lad **258 s.p. Katharine** Lad

3.1. 1 s.p. [and elsewhere] Armado Bra **14 as if** if **15 through the nose** through: nose **18 thin-belly** thinbellies **26 penny** penne **65 voluble** volable **69 s.p. [and elsewhere] Mote** Pag **72 the mail** thee male **plain** pline **133 ounce** ouce **136 remuneration** remuration **138 carries it.** carries it **141 My** [preceded by "O" in Q; also ll. 145, 147, 149, 153, 155, 172] **178 Junior** Lunios **188 clock** Cloake **202 sue** shue

4.1. 3 s.p. Boyet Forr **6 On** Ore **49 mistress** [F] Mistrs **70–71 saw . . . saw** See . . . see **71 overcame** couercame **75 King's** King **87 Adriano** Adriana **Armado** Armatho **128 s.d. Exit** [at l. 126 in Q] **130 hit it** hit **134 ne'er**

neare   **136 pin** is in   **144 o' th' one** ath toothen   **148 is a** is   **s.d. Shout**
Shoot   **149 s.d. Exit** Exeunt

4.2. 3 s.p. [and elsewhere] Holofernes Ped   **8 s.p. [and elsewhere] Nathaniel**
Curat. Nath   **14–15 explication; facere,** explication facere: **29 of taste** taste
30 indiscreet indistreell   **36 Dictynna . . . Dictynna** Dictisima . . . dictisima
51 ignorant ignorault   **call I** cald   **53 scurrility** squirilitie   **65 s.p. Holo-**
fernes Nath [the subsequent speech prefixes in this scene of Holofernes and
Nathaniel are reversed in Q through l. 147, except that the speech at l. 104 is
correctly assigned to Nathaniel, and at ll. 118–120 to Pedan]   **69 pia mater**
primater   **71 in whom** whom   **72 s.p. Nathaniel** Holo   **76 ingenious** inge-
nous   **78 sapit** sapis   **81 s.p. Holofernes** Nath [also at ll. 85, 91]   **pierce-one**
Person   **88 Person** Parson   **91 Fauste** Facile   **pecus** pecas   **omne** omnia
94–95 Venezia . . . prezia vemchie, vencha, que non te vnde, que non te
perreche   **101 s.p. Nathaniel** Hol   **102 s.p. Holofernes** Nath   **stanza** stauze
104 s.p. Nathaniel [missing in Q]   **118 apostrophus** apostraphas   **119 can-**
zonet cangenet   **120 Here** [the rest of this speech is assigned to Nath in Q]
130 s.p. Holofernes Nath   **133 writing** written   **135 Sir Nathaniel** Ped. Sir
Holofernes   **143 s.p. Jaquenetta** Mayd   **146 s.p. Nathaniel** Holo
148 s.p. Holofernes Ped   **156 ben** bien

4.3. 12 melancholy mallicholie [also in l. 13]   **35 wilt** will   **45 s.p. King**
Long   **71 idolatry** ydotarie   **83 quoted** coted   **89 And I** And   **95 ode** Odo
104 Wished Wish   **108 thorn** throne   **151 coaches; in your tears** couches in
your teares.   **157 mote . . . mote** Moth . . . Moth   **176 like you** like   **179 me?**
When mee when   **244 wood** word   **255 and usurping** vsurping   **256 doters**
dooters   **279 Nothing** O nothing   **291 And . . . maladies** [Q follows with
twenty-three lines that appear to be a first draft of the lines following:

> And where that you haue vowd to studie (Lordes)
> In that each of you haue forsworne bis Booke.
> Can you still dreame and poare and thereon looke.
> For when would you my Lord, or you, or you,
> Haue found the ground of Studies excellence,
> Without the beautie of a womans face?
> From womens eyes this doctrine I deriue,
> They are the Ground, the Bookes, the Achadems,
> From whence doth spring the true *Promethean* fire.
> Why vniuersall plodding poysons vp
> The nimble spirites in the arteries,
> As motion and long during action tyres
> The sinnowy vigour of the trauayler.
> Now for not looking on a womans face,
> You haue in that forsworne the vse of eyes:
> And studie too, the causer of your vow.
> For where is any Authour in the worlde,
> Teaches such beautie as a womas eye:
> Learning is but an adiunct to our selfe,
> And where we are, our Learning likewise is.
> Then when our selues we see in Ladies eyes,
> With our selues.
> Do we not likewise see our learning there?]

313 dainty Bacchus . . . taste. daintie, *Bachus* . . . taste,   **316 Subtle** Subtit
333 authors authour   **335 Let** Lets   **lose** loose [also in l. 336]   **341 stan-**

dards standars   **356 betime** be time   **357 Allons! Allons!** Alone alone
359 forsworn forsorne

5.1. 1 quod quid   **9 hominem** hominum   **24 abominable** abbominable
25 insanie infamie   **27 bone** bene   **28 Bone . . . bene** Bome boon for
boon   **38 lived** lyud   **56 wave** wane   **57 venue** vene we   **66 manu** vnum
73 wert wart   **74 dunghill** dungil   **76 Dunghill** dunghel   **96 importunate**
importunt   **101 mustachio** mustachie   **106 secrecy** secretie   **109 antic**
antique [also at l. 143]   **115 Nathaniel** Holofernes   **117 rendered** rended
assistance assistants   **148 Allons** Alone

5.2. 13 ne'er neare   **17 ha' been a** a bin   **22 You'll** Yole   **28 cure . . . care**
care . . . cure   **43 pencils, ho!** pensalls, how?   **46 s.p. Katharine** Quee
47 s.p. Princess [not in Q]   **53 s.p. [and elsewhere] Maria** Marg   **53 pearls**
Pearle   **65 hests** deuice   **67 pair-taunt-like** perttaunt like   **74 wantonness**
wantons be   **80 stabbed** stable   **89 sycamore** Siccamore   **93 companions.**
Warily companious warely,   **96 they** thy   **122 parle** parlee   **123 love suit**
Loue-feat   **134 too** two   **148 her** his   **152 ne'er** ere   **159 s.p. Boyet** Berow
160 s.d. The . . . him [after l. 161 in Q]   **164 ever** euen   **176 strangers**
stranges   **179 Princess** Princes   **217 The . . . it** [assigned in Q to Rosa]
232 s.p. [and elsewhere] Princess Quee   **243 s.p. Katharine** Maria [also at
ll. 245, 248, 249, 250, 254, 256]   **265 s.d. Exeunt** Exe   **269 have; gross** haue
grosse   **280 perhaps** perhapt   **298 vailing** varling   **300 woo** woe   **310 run**
runs   **342 Construe** Consture   **353 unsullied** vnsallied   **375–377 foolish.**
When . . . eye, . . . light. foolish when . . . eie: . . . light,   **406 song** songue
408 affectation affection   **464 zany** saine   **479 allowed** aloude   **483 manage**
nuage   **485** [Q supplies a s.p. here, "Ber."]   **501 they** thy   **514 least** best
529 de la guerra delaguar   **543 s.p. Boyet** Bero   **554 s.p. Princess** Lady
563 this his   **582** [Q has "Exit Curat."]   **591 Judas** Pede. Iudas   **596 proved**
proud   **643 gilt** gift   **669 The . . . gone** [Q prints as a s.d. or as part of
Armado's speech]   **686 on, stir** or, stir   **699 lose** loose   **746 wholesome**
holdsome   **759 strange** straying   **764 gravities,** grauities.   **774 the ambas-**
sadors embassadours   **778 this in our** this our   **803 instant** instance
808 entitled intiled   **812 hermit** herrite   **812 Hence . . . breast** [Q follows
with six lines that appear to be a first draft of the lines following:

> *Berow.*   And what to me my Loue? and what to me?
> *Rosal.*   You must be purged to, your sinnes are rackt.
> You are attaint with faultes and periurie:
> Therefore if you my fauour meane to get,
> A tweluemonth shall you spende and neuer rest,
> But seeke the weery beddes of people sicke.]

814 A wife [assigned to Kath. in Q]   **884 s.p. Spring** [not in Q]   **885–886** [the
second and third lines of the song are transposed in Q]   **906 foul** full
918 s.p. Armado [not in Q]   **918–919 The . . . Apollo** [printed in larger type
in Q without s.p.; F adds s.p. "Brag." and "You that way: we this way," thus
incorporating the ending into the text]

Shakespeare's Sources

No main source exists for *Love's Labor's Lost*. For his conception of an "academy" of aristocratic scholars, Shakespeare may have drawn on Pierre de la Primaudaye's *L'Académie française* (1577), translated into English in 1586, in which the ideals of scholarly withdrawal are discussed. A brief selection follows. The notion was, however, commonplace. Certain historical facts about Henry of Navarre may well have provided Shakespeare with a model for the play's action, especially the visit of Catherine de' Medici with her daughter and the famous *l'escadron volant* (flying squadron) to Henry's court in 1578, and a similar visit in 1586 (see the following selection from *The History of the Civil Wars of France*). Published accounts of these visits were not available when Shakespeare wrote his play, but he may well have heard the gossip. John Lyly's plays provided Shakespeare a literary model for the saucy boyish wit of Mote, Boyet, and others; and Armado and Mote are often thought to resemble Sir Tophas and the page Epiton in Lyly's *Endymion*. Traditions of the *commedia dell'arte* provided Shakespeare with stock comic models, especially those of the *dottore* or pedant (Holofernes), his parasite (Nathaniel, the curate), the *capitano* or braggart soldier (Armado), and the rustic servant (Costard). All of these types are individualized and rendered in English terms, however. Many literary quarrels in England in the 1590s have been adduced as possible sources for Shakespeare's play, especially the controversy between Thomas Nashe and Gabriel Harvey, but the evidence remains inconclusive.

The French Academy
By Pierre de la Primaudaye
Translated by T. Bowes

[In his dedication to King Henry III, the author praises the King's grandfather, Francis I, as having presided over a court where many learned persons of every nation came "that they might reap profit and instruction." Henry III's court is now another such place of learned assembly.]

Yours, sir, being compassed about[1] with those who in your presence daily discourse of and hear discoursed many grave and goodly matters, seemeth to be a school erected to teach men that are born to virtue. And for myself, having so good hap[2] during the assembly of your estates at Blois as to be made partaker of the fruit gathered thereof, it came in my mind to offer unto Your Majesty a dish of divers fruits which I gathered in a platonical garden or orchard, otherwise called an academy, where I was not long since with certain young gentlemen of Anjou, my companions, discoursing together of the institution[3] of good manners and of the means how all estates and conditions[4] may live well and happily.

[The four gentlemen of Anjou to whom the author refers have been given hospitable entertainment in a nobleman's home and provided with a learned mentor to direct them in the mastering of Latin, Greek, and other subjects.]

Who[5] behaved himself so well in his charge[6] that, not greatly staying himself[7] in the long degrees of learning which, being ordinary and usual in our French colleges, are often more tedious (besides loss of time) than profitable to youth, after he had indifferently[8] taught his scholars the Latin tongue and some smackering of the Greek, he propounded for the chief part and portion of their studies the moral philosophy of ancient sages and wise men, together with the understanding and searching out of histories, which are the light of life; therein following the intent and will both of him that set him on work[9] and also of the parents of this nobility,[10] who desired to see their children not great orators, subtle logicians, learned lawyers, or curi-

---

1 **compassed about** surrounded   2 **hap** fortune   3 **institution** regulation, establishment   4 **conditions** social ranks   5 **Who** i.e., the learned mentor   6 **behaved . . . charge** carried out his responsibilities so well   7 **staying himself** i.e., lingering   8 **indifferently** to a moderate degree   9 **him that . . . work** i.e., the nobleman who is sponsoring the academy   10 **this nobility** i.e., these four noble young men from Anjou

ous[11] mathematicians, but only sufficiently taught in the doctrine of good living, following the traces and steps of virtue by the knowledge of things past from the first ages until this present, that they might refer all to the glory of the divine majesty and to the profit and utility as well of themselves as of their country.

And yet in the meanwhile these noble and toward[12] youths were not deprived of other exercises meet[13] for them, which, as the divine Plato saith, are very profitable for this age and help much to quicken the spirits of young men and to make their bodies, which are weak by nature, more strong and apt to sustain travail:[14] as, namely, to ride horses, to run at the ring,[15] to fight at barriers,[16] to apply themselves to all kind of weapons, and to follow the chase of beasts, all which exercises this wise and ancient knight did intermingle with their earnest studies by way of recreation, himself standing them in stead of a master. For in such exercises he was as fully furnished[17] as is to be wished in a man of valor and activity, insomuch that he was more expert than many of our time who make no other profession.

Now this school having been continued for the space of six or seven years, to the great profit of this nobility of Anjou, the four fathers on a day[18] took their journey to visit the good old man and to see their children. And after the usual welcome which is between kinfolks and friends, they discoursed together of the corruption which then was in all estates[19] of France, whereupon they foresaw (as they said) some great storm at hand if everyone did not put to[20] his helping hand for the correction and reformation of them, but chiefly the secular power authorized of God for this purpose. They alleged[21] for witness of their saying many examples of ancient estates, commonwealths, and kingdoms which were fallen from the height of glory and excellency

---

11 curious ingenious   **12 toward** eager (to learn)   **13 meet** fit, suitable   **14 travail** labor   **15 run at the ring** i.e., ride toward a metal ring suspended from a post and try to carry it off on the point of one's lance   **16 fight at barriers** i.e., joust, ride toward one's opponent down the center of the lists or tournament ground with a low barrier between the contestants, their lances reaching across it   **17 furnished** accomplished, skilled   **18 on a day** one day   **19 estates** social ranks   **20 put to** i.e., lend   **21 alleged** cited

into a general subversion and overthrow by reason of vices reigning in them unpunished.

[The fathers express a wish to hear their sons discourse on these weighty matters of corruption and reform, in the vernacular rather than in Latin, to see if the sons have profited well from their instruction. Two hours are devoted to such discussion in the morning and two more hours in the afternoon, following dinner. The young men spend much of the remaining time studying diligently in order to do well in talk, and the parents are so pleased that soon six to eight hours a day are being spent in their deliberations.]

In this commendable manner of passing their time they continued certain days. But the sudden and sorrowful news of the last frantic return of France into civil war brake up their happy assembly, to the end that[22] these noble youths, betaking themselves to the service due to their prince[23] and to the welfare and safety of their country, might make trial of their first feats of arms, wherein they wanted[24] neither readiness nor valor of heart, which, being naturally in them, was also increased by the knowledge of philosophy.

[Following the civil war, in which the young men make good account of themselves, they all assemble again at the nobleman's house and make plans for a renewed academy.]

As it was devised by them, the execution thereof followed, so that, all these good old men being assembled together, taking up their first order[25] and conferring anew of the same matters, daily met[26] in a walking place covered over in the midst with a goodly green arbor, allotting for this exercise[27] from eight to ten in the morning and from two to four in the afternoon. Thus they continued this exercise for the space of three whole weeks, which make eighteen days' works, besides the three Sabbath days set apart by them that they might rest and cease from their studies and attend

---

22 to the end that with the result that   **23 prince** king   **24 wanted** lacked   **25 order** order of business   **26 daily met** i.e., daily they met   **27 exercise** i.e., discourse

the better to the chief point of that holy day's institution, which is to the contemplation and consideration of the works of God, of his law, and of his praises. During which time it was my good hap to be one of the company when they began their discourses, at which I so greatly wondered[28] that I thought them worthy to be published abroad,[29] as well to enrich our French tongue with an infinite number of grave sentences[30] and speeches worthy to be remembered, being drawn out of the fountain of Greek and Latin arts and disciplines through the incredible labor of these youths, lovers of virtue, as also to awake and stir up by their example all the nobility with a jealousy and emulation of glory gotten by the same virtue. For only virtue is able to guide and conduct gentlemen to honor.

[The rest of *The French Academy* is a series of disputations on such topics as "Of Man," "Of the Body and Soul," "Of Prudence," "Of the People and of Their Obedience Due to the Magistrate and the Law," "Of Seditions," "Of Peace and of War," and so on, purportedly representing the fruits of the deliberations at this gentlemanly academy.]

Text based on *The French Academy, Wherein is Discoursed the Institution of Manners. . . . by Peter de la Primaudaye. . . . Imprinted at London by Edmund Bollifant for G. Bishop and Ralph Newbery. 1586.* (The original French version by La Primaudaye bears a date on the dedication of 1577.)

The History of the Civil Wars of France
By Enrico Caterino Davila
Translated from the Italian

BOOK 8

[The following account of the visit of Catherine de' Medici to Henry of Navarre in 1586 is here given in an English translation that is considerably too late for Shakespeare to

28 wondered marveled   **29 published abroad** made known publicly
30 grave sentences wise sayings

have consulted, but he may well have been familiar with the incident.]

The Queen Mother (the place of interview with the King of Navarre being appointed) was come to Cognac, attended by Ludovico Gonzaga, Duke of Nevers . . . by the Maréchal de Retz, the Sieurs d'Abin and de Rambouillet, by the Abbot Guadagni, Secretary Pinart, Monsieur de Lansac, and divers other personages who for quality and wisdom were of great esteem.

On the other side, the King of Navarre was come to Jarnac, with the Viscount de Turenne, the Sieur de la Force and Monguidon, the Baron de Salignac, and many other lords of his party; but with so great strength, having with him eight hundred horse and few less than two thousand foot[1] as, at the first notice of them, put the Queen Mother into very great suspicion, there not wanting[2] those who doubted,[3] and who spread abroad a report, that he was come with an intention to take her and carry her away by force to Rochelle.[4] But after it was known that the King of Navarre was come in that manner for his own security, as one who by reason of his own weakness and the usage he had received at other times was in doubt of being deceived, and that the ingenuity of his nature and the absurdity of that business had taken away all jealousies, they met at last upon the eighteenth of October at St. Bris, equally distant from the places whence they came, there being on the Queen's part, besides her ordinary court, only the Captain of her guard with fifty horse, and on the King of Navarre's Captain Lomelle with as many. The gates were guarded by two companies of foot, one of the one party and the other of the other, and in the field the cavalry of both sides in two several squadrons, the King of Navarre's commanded by the Count de la Vall and Monsieur de la Noue, and the Queen Mother's by the Sieur de Malicorne and other gentlemen of the country.

Their public discourses passed in complaints on both

---

1 eight hundred . . . foot 800 horsemen and almost 2,000 foot soldiers
2 wanting lacking   **3 doubted** feared   **4 Rochelle** La Rochelle, the citadel of the Protestant reformers

ruined and suppressed. That to attain so great a good nothing else was required from the King of Navarre but only his conversion to the Catholic religion and his return to court; for, as concerning the excommunication of Rome and the Pope's declaration of his incapacity to succeed in the crown, as soon as he should be a real Catholic, the persecution[13] of the Guises being taken away and the League destroyed, the revocation of it would without difficulty be obtained.

[Navarre, reluctant to convert to Catholicism and mistrustful of the promises made him, declines to accept the negotiating terms, resolving instead "to follow the fortunes of the Huguenots and not to trust the court."]

Text based on *The History of the Civil Wars of France. Written in Italian by H. C. Davila. Translated out of the original* [by Sir Charles Cottrell and William Aylesbury]. *The second impression. . . . Printed by T. N. for Henry Herringman.* [London,] *1678.*

13 persecution i.e., harassment of Navarre and his party

sides—the King[5] lamenting that the King of Navarre'[s] [ob]stinacy not to change his religion[6] and to keep so far f[rom] court put the King upon a necessity of making war, and [on] the other side the King of Navarre complained that wh[ile] he stood still obedient to the King's commands and m[ost] observant of the edicts, he,[7] to satisfy the lords of Guis[e8] and other enemies to quietness, had broke the peace. Bu[t] being come to secret conference, the Queen laid open th[e] conditions which the King propounded of the divorce o[f] Queen Margaret and of the marriage with the Princess of Lorraine,[9] who was there present and, being of an age already marriageable, showed tokens of most noble education and discreet modesty. To this match, the Queen told him that a manifest[10] should be added to declare him[11] first prince of the blood and lawful successor to the crown, and alleged that from thence would necessarily result the disuniting of the Duke of Lorraine, father to the Princess, from the League,[12] and from the lords of Guise, who, losing so principal a foundation, either would become quiet of their own accord or, if they did not submit themselves freely to the King's will, they might with help of the German army, which was upon the point of entering the confines, be easily

5 the King Henry III, corrupt and effeminate son of Catherine de' Medici, the Queen Mother. Henry III's brothers included King Francis II and King Charles IX, who had ruled before him. Henry of Navarre, son of the Queen of Navarre, was married to Henry III's younger sister Marguerite de Valois and was hence a son-in-law of Catherine de' Medici; he came to the French throne in 1589 as the Protestant Henry IV upon the murder of Henry III. Catherine represents Henry III's position in these present negotiations with Henry of Navarre. **6 not to change his religion** i.e., to remain a Protestant recusant **7 he** i.e., Henry III **8 the lords of Guise** Henry, Duke of Guise, and his brother, Louis, the Cardinal, were powerful figures at the French court and leaders of a war against Henry of Navarre in 1585 and following; they formed a league in 1587 to depose the weak Henry III and were murdered at Henry III's instigation in 1588. **9 Princess of Lorraine** (This marriage proposal, one in which Catherine is suggesting that her own daughter, Marguerite de Valois [called *Margaret* in the text] be divorced by the King of Navarre, is offered as a way of weakening the Guises and their league by winning away from them the allegiance of the Duke of Lorraine. Marguerite, known as *La Reine Margot*, was banished from court in 1583 for immorality and eventually was officially separated from Henry of Navarre in 1599.) **10 manifest** public proclamation **11 him** i.e., Henry of Navarre **12 the League** i.e., the Catholic League of the Guises

Further Reading

Barber, C. L. "The Folly of Wit and Masquerade in *Love's Labour's Lost*." *Shakespeare's Festive Comedy*. Princeton, N.J.: Princeton Univ. Press, 1959. In his influential account of the relation of social custom to dramatic structure in Shakespeare's comedies, Barber explores the influence of aristocratic entertainments and folk games upon *Love's Labor's Lost*. The play examines the social implications of these activities, but, with the postponed marriages, finally demands that the men "separate their affections from the occasion to see whether or not their feelings are more than courtly sport."

Calderwood, James L. "*Love's Labour's Lost*: A Dalliance with Language." *Shakespearean Metadrama*. Minneapolis: Univ. of Minnesota Press, 1971. In addition to its moral and emotional concerns, Calderwood argues, the play reveals itself to be about the power of language and dramatic art itself. In the opposition between the men's love of verbal wit and the women's desire for truthful expression, the play locates its concern with language "as a medium of social exchange" both for the characters in the play and for its author and audience.

Carroll, William C. *The Great Feast of Language in "Love's Labour's Lost."* Princeton, N.J.: Princeton Univ. Press, 1976. Carroll's book-length study considers *Love's Labor's Lost* as a sophisticated and self-conscious play debating "the right use of rhetoric, poetry, and the imagination." Exploring the play's preoccupation with language and style, Carroll discovers the recurrence of "obvious dualisms" such as Art and Nature, and finds that the final songs represent a "dialectical blend" of opposites that have at last been reconciled.

Frye, Northrop. "Shakespeare's Experimental Comedy." In *Stratford Papers on Shakespeare 1961*, ed. B. W. Jackson. Toronto: W. J. Gage, 1962. *Love's Labor's Lost* seems to Frye unusual and experimental. In addition to the play's topicality and insistent verbal sophistication, it lacks both the "green world" and the comic conclusion that normally mark Shakespeare's comedies. It does, however, follow the traditional comic pattern in exposing humorous and rigidly antisocial behavior as it rebukes the unnatural vows and "excessive" wit of the courtiers.

Greene, Thomas M. "*Love's Labour's Lost:* The Grace of Society." *Shakespeare Quarterly* 22 (1971): 315–328. Rpt. in *The Vulnerable Text.* New York: Columbia Univ. Press, 1986. Greene considers *Love's Labor's Lost* a serious comedy about social form and feelings. Focusing on various meanings of the word "grace," he traces in the play a movement toward a way of life that is truly gracious, lived "with poise, taste, decorum, and charity." The women constitute a "spirited and witty center of social judgment," leading the men to move beyond their initial immaturity, affectation, and arrogance.

Hawkes, Terence. "*Love's Labour's Lost:* Rhyme Against Reason." *Shakespeare's Talking Animals.* London: Edward Arnold, 1973; Totowa, N.J.: Rowman and Littlefield, 1974. Hawkes argues that *Love's Labor's Lost* explores the social implications of the conflict between the spoken and written word. Berowne's renunciation of the latter encapsulates the play's argument: access to reality is achieved by an involvement with others through the reciprocal world of speech, not the sterile and alienating world of books. Similarly, the play itself, written for the theater and not the printed page, reflects the greater importance Shakespeare assigns to the oral tradition than to a written one.

Hibbard, G. R. "Making a Virtue of Virtuosity: *Love's Labour's Lost* and *Richard II.*" *The Making of Shakespeare's Dramatic Poetry.* Toronto: Univ. of Toronto Press, 1981. Hibbard suggests that linguistic virtuosity, the theme of this transitional work, enabled Shakespeare to work out the artistic conflict of his early creative years between the demands of the poet and the demands of the dramatist. Berowne's reluctant farewell to verbal excess mirrors Shakespeare's own; and Marcade's appearance (like *Love's Labor's Lost* itself) marks a shift from dramatic poetry to poetic drama.

Hoy, Cyrus. "*Love's Labour's Lost* and the Nature of Comedy." *Shakespeare Quarterly* 13 (1962): 31–40. Shakespearean comedy, according to Hoy, explores "the infirmity of human purpose," tracing a movement from artificial and unrealistic desire to a recognition of what is natural. In *Love's Labor's Lost,* this pattern is realized in the "undeceiving of the self-deceived." The play's artificial language comments upon an artificial view of life that is exposed and transcended by the play's end.

Hunter, G. K. "Poem and Context in *Love's Labour's Lost.*" In *Shakespeare's Styles,* ed. Philip Edwards, Inga-Stina Ewbank, and G. K. Hunter. Cambridge and New York: Cambridge Univ. Press, 1980. Hunter explores the implications of the play's "elaborate rhetoric." He claims that emotional authenticity is readily subordinated to eloquence by the play's characters, for whom speech is more a mode of disguise than a means of expression. The penances ordered by the women at the end seek "the abolition of style in order to assert the primacy of experience."

Johnson, Samuel. *"Love's Labour's Lost." Johnson on Shakespeare,* ed. Arthur Sherbo. *The Yale Edition of the Works of Samuel Johnson,* vol. 7. New Haven, Conn.: Yale Univ. Press, 1968. Johnson praises the play's "many speeches of genius" and the certain marks of Shakespeare's authorship. He allows, however, "that there are many passages mean, childish, and vulgar; and some which ought not to have been exhibited, as we are told they were, to a maiden queen."

Leggatt, Alexander. *"Love's Labour's Lost." Shakespeare's Comedy of Love.* New York: Barnes and Noble, 1974. *Love's Labor's Lost* explores the problem of expressing love, primarily through a "critical, comic testing" of the conventions of both love and language. The play, Leggatt argues, shows these conventions to be "comically vulnerable" to misuse and misunderstanding. The inescapable reality of Jaquenetta's pregnancy and the King of France's death declare the inadequacy of the reliance on wit to master the "instability of life."

Montrose, Louis A. " 'Sport by Sport O'erthrown': *Love's Labour's Lost* and the Politics of Play." *Texas Studies in Language and Literature* 18 (1977): 528–552. Montrose focuses on the characters' self-conscious verbal display and their use of costume and disguise as evidence of the efforts to "construct, explore, manipulate, and protect their reality." The play is structured around the deceptions of these courtly games and ultimately reveals the self-deceptions that determine them.

Richmond, Hugh M. "Shakespeare's Navarre." *Huntington Library Quarterly* 42 (1979): 193–216. For Richmond, *Love's Labor's Lost* is a "crucial document for the study of the transposition of life into art." Shakespeare bases his play, he argues, on well-known contemporary French political figures. Navarre's academy reflects Henri IV's court at Nérac, which was inhabited by nobles named Biron (Berowne), Longueville (Longaville), and d'Aumont (Dumaine).

Roesen, Bobbyann. *"Love's Labour's Lost." Shakespeare Quarterly* 4 (1953): 411–426. Rpt. (under the name Anne Barton) in *Essays in Shakespearean Criticism*, ed. James L. Calderwood and Harold E. Toliver. Englewood Cliffs, N.J.: Prentice-Hall, 1970. With Marcade's announcement of the death of the King of France, Roesen argues, reality powerfully confronts the world of the play, destroying the artifice of Navarre's academy. At the end, the characters stand outside the artificial scheme, "a little lost in the sudden glare of actuality." Only through the acceptance of the reality of death, she says, can life and love in their fullest sense be realized.

Wilders, John. "The Unresolved Conflicts of *Love's Labour's Lost.*" *Essays in Criticism* 27 (1977): 20–33. *Love's Labor's Lost*, for Wilders, is Shakespeare's "most elaborately symmetrical play," and yet also his most inconclusive. Neat antitheses are established between characters, actions, and themes; however, instead of the usual reconciliations of comedy, "irresolution" becomes "one of the characteristic effects" of the play, articulating unresolved conflicts within human nature.

Yates, Frances A. *A Study of "Love's Labour's Lost."* London: Cambridge Univ. Press, 1936. Yates studies the relationship of the 1598 quarto edition of the play and the Folio text, but is primarily interested in the play's topical references. She finds that the discussion of Holofernes and Costard in scene 2 of Act 4 satirizes a contemporary literary controversy between Thomas Nashe and Gabriel Harvey, and that Navarre's academy reflects Sir Walter Ralegh and his intellectual circle.

From the 1967 New York Shakespeare Festival production of *The Comedy of Errors*, with (l. to r.) Julienne Marie as Adriana, Jonathan Reynolds as Solinus, Ralph Drischell as Egeon, and Joseph Bova as Antipholus of Ephesus, directed by Gerald Freedman at the Delacorte Theater in Central Park.

THE COMEDY OF ERRORS

THE COMEDY OF ERRORS

Introductory Material
Foreword by Joseph Papp
Introduction
The Comedy of Errors
in Performance

THE PLAY

Supplementary Material
Date and Text
Textual Notes
Shakespeare's Sources
Further Reading

Foreword

The Comedy of Errors is a play of lighthearted fun, non-stop farce, and comical confusion, a wonderful play for young actors to perform. It's also one of Shakespeare's early plays, without the strength and consistency of his later work. And yet occasionally he begins to show his muscle. When he comes up with an idea that catches his fancy, the result is predictably unique. There's one such passage here, in Act 3, scene 2, and it's a favorite of mine.

Dromio of Syracuse is describing the fat kitchen maid to his master, Antipholus. His description is a great example of how Shakespeare can bring a character to life in just a few lines; Dromio paints a vivid picture of this fat, greasy kitchen wench with a mere handful of words.

> She's the kitchen wench, and all grease, and I know not what use to put her to but to make a lamp of her and run from her by her own light. I warrant, her rags and the tallow in them will burn a Poland winter. If she lives till doomsday, she'll burn a week longer than the whole world.

Dromio's description also has topical interest, for he draws parallels between the parts of this poor girl's body and various countries. "She is spherical, like a globe," he confides to his master, "I could find out countries in her." And then he goes into a little geographical routine, making local jokes about England's neighboring countries—Scotland, Ireland, France, Spain, and the Netherlands—that Shakespeare's audience must have loved, since those countries were part of their daily frame of reference. Antipholus asks, "In what part of her body stands Ireland?" and Dromio retorts, "Marry, sir, in her buttocks. I found it out by the bogs." "Where Scotland?" the master continues; "I found it by the barrenness, hard in the palm of the hand," the servant replies. And on they go, bringing to life with words alone a Falstaff-sized female who never comes onstage. Such is the power of Shakespeare's language.

JOSEPH PAPP

JOSEPH PAPP GRATEFULLY ACKNOWLEDGES THE HELP OF ELIZABETH KIRKLAND IN PREPARING THIS FOREWORD.

Introduction

The Comedy of Errors is a superb illustration of Shakespeare's apprenticeship in comedy. It is more imitative of classical comedy, especially that of the Roman playwright Plautus, than is Shakespeare's mature work. Its verbal humor, including the scatological jokes about breaking wind, the bawdy jests about cuckold's horns, and the overly ingenious choplogic banter (as in 2.2) is at times adolescent. The play abounds in the farcical slapstick humor so endearing to children of all ages. It is perhaps the most uncomplicatedly funny of all Shakespeare's plays. Yet the softening touches of Shakespeare's maturity are unmistakably present as well. Shakespeare frames his farce of mistaken identity with old Egeon's tragicomic story of separation, threatened death, and eventual reunion. He adds characters to his main source, Plautus' *Menaechmi*, in order to enhance the love interest and to reconcile Plautus with English moral conventions. He touches upon themes of illusion, madness, and Saturnalian inversion that are to figure prominently in *A Midsummer Night's Dream* and in *Twelfth Night*, a later comedy of mistaken identity. In these respects, *The Comedy of Errors* is both a fascinating prelude to Shakespeare's later development and a rich achievement in its own right. Onstage, it has not attracted the greatest Shakespearean actors, since it offers no complex or dominating roles, but it has seldom failed to delight audiences.

We cannot be sure precisely how early the play was written. A performance took place on December 28, 1594, at Gray's Inn (one of the Inns of Court, where young men studied law), before an unruly assembly of lawyers, law students, and their guests. This was probably not the first performance, however. Topical allusions offer hints of an earlier date. When Dromio of Syracuse speaks of France as "armed and reverted, making war against her heir" (3.2.123–124), Dromio clearly refers to the Catholic League's opposition to Henry of Navarre, who was the heir apparent to the French throne until 1593, when he became king. Another allusion, to Spain's sending "whole armadoes of carracks" (ll. 135–136), would possibly have lost its comic point soon after the Invincible Armada of 1588. The play's style, characterization, and imitative construction are all consistent with a date between 1589 and 1593.

Whatever the exact date, Shakespeare's youthful fascination with Plautus is manifest. Shakespeare's command of Latin, though sneered at by fellow playwright Ben Jonson, was undoubtedly good enough to have let him read Plautus with pleasure. He must have been drilled in Latin for years as a student in the town of Stratford-upon-Avon, and, if biographer John Aubrey is right, went on to teach Latin as a country schoolmaster before becoming an actor. Indeed, the influence not only of Plautus but of Ovid and Seneca (together with touches of Horace, Catullus, et al.) is a prominent feature of Shakespeare's early work, dramatic and nondramatic. Shakespeare may have consulted Plautus both in the original and in a contemporary translation, as was frequently his custom with non-English sources. From Renaissance Latin editions of Plautus he apparently took the odd designation "Antipholis Sereptus" (i.e., "surreptus," snatched away), which appears in the Folio text in a stage direction at 2.1.0 to indicate the twin who was separated from his father. On the other hand, a translation by "W. W." (? William Warner), published in 1595 (which appears in modernized form later in this volume), was registered in 1594 and might have been available earlier to Shakespeare in manuscript.

Plautus had much to offer Shakespeare and his fellow dramatists, especially in the way of tightly organized and complex plot construction. Native English drama of the sixteenth century tended to be episodic and panoramic in its design. Shakespeare's apprenticeship in neoclassical form can be seen in his precise observation of the unities of time and place—those unities which he openly disregarded in most of his later plays. At the play's beginning, Egeon is informed that he has until sundown to raise his ransom money, and the play then moves toward that time with periodic observations that it is now noon, now 2 o'clock, and so on. (At one point time even seems to go backward, but that is part of the illusion of madness.) The action is restricted to the city of Ephesus; events that have happened elsewhere, at an earlier time (such as the separation of the Antipholus family), are told to us by persons in the play, such as old Egeon. Although Shakespeare's company did not employ the sort of painted scenery drawn in perspective used by continental Renaissance neoclassicists, with fixed locations for houses facing on a street, the original production of this play may possibly have used one stage "house" or door to represent the dwelling (called the Phoenix) of Antipholus of Ephesus throughout the drama. The entire play can be staged as if all the action occurs in the vicinity of this single "house," with the house of the Courtesan and the Abbey near at hand. Never again does Shakespeare approximate so nearly the conditions of the neoclassical stage.

These unities of time and place are mechanical matters, but they do also harmonize with a more essential unity of action. The story moves, as though in perfect accord with neoclassical five-act theory, from exposition and complication to climax, anagnorisis (discovery), and peripeteia (reversal of fortune). The brilliance of the plotting is decidedly Plautine. Shakespeare pushes to its limit the interweaving of comic misunderstandings only to unravel all these seemingly tightly woven knots with ease. Yet the imitation of Plautus, even in matters of construction, is by no means slavish, for Shakespeare borrows both from Plautus' comedy on the mistaken identity of twins (*Menaechmi*) and from Plautus' better-known comedy (*Amphitruo*), in which a husband and his servant are excluded from their own house while a disguised visitor usurps the master's role within. Such ingenious adaptations and rearrangements were common among neoclassical dramatists like Ariosto; and although Shakespeare seems not to have used any of the sixteenth-century analogues to this play, he does indicate an acquaintance with neoclassical comedy and an ability to compete with the best that Europe had to offer in this vein. Such versatility is noteworthy in a young dramatist who would reveal himself in time to be far less a neoclassicist than a native English writer. Moreover, even if his self-imposed neoclassical training was only an apprenticeship, it was to prove invaluable to Shakespeare. Despite his later tendency toward "romantic" plotting—toward the depiction of multiple actions extending over widely separated spaces and extended periods of time—Shakespeare's greatest comedies continue to point toward the same gratifying resolution of dramatic conflict in a single and well-structured denouement.

For all its Plautine skill of design, however, *The Comedy of Errors* is quite far removed from *the Menaechmi* in tone and spirit. Gone are the cynicism, the satirical hardness, and the amoral tone of the Roman original. The characters, though still recognizable as types, are humanized. The familiar Plautine parasite is excluded entirely. The usual clever servant becomes the Dromio Twins. Plautus' quack Doctor, Medicus, is hilariously transmuted into Dr. Pinch, a pedantic schoolmaster. The Courtesan's role is no longer prominent. Instead Shakespeare creates Luciana, the virtuous sister of Adriana, who pleads the cause of forbearance in marriage and who eventually becomes the bride of Antipholus of Syracuse. *The Comedy of Errors* does not end, as do most of Shakespeare's later comedies, with a parade of couples to the altar, but the marriage of Antipholus and Luciana is an important gesture in that direction. Besides, we are told of yet another marriage still to come—that of Dromio of Ephesus to Luce, the fat kitchen wench. This below-stairs parody of wedded affection is thoroughly English in character and recalls a similar mirroring of courtship among the comic servants in Henry Medwall's *Fulgens and Lucrece* (c. 1497). The motif is not sufficiently stressed to threaten the unity of the main plot, but the potentiality for a second parallel plot is unmistakable.

An even more significant contrast to Plautine farce is to be found in the romantic saga of old Egeon and his long-lost wife, the Abbess. Their story is one not of mistaken identity (though that contributes to the denouement) but of painful separation, wandering, and reunion. Indeed, the note struck at the beginning of the play might seem tragic, were we not already attuned to the conventional romantic expectation that separated members of a family are likely to be restored to one another again. Egeon, threatened with immediate execution, unfolds to us a narrative of wedded bliss interrupted by the malignancy of Fortune. In contrast to the tightly controlled unity of time in the farcical action, the romantic narrative extends (by recollection) over many years of error and suffering. Egeon's tragicomic story of testing and of patient endurance is very much like that of

Apollonius of Tyre, a popular tale used by Shakespeare in his late romance *Pericles* (c. 1606–1608). The conventions of this sort of romance, ultimately Greek in origin, stress improbability: identical twins who can be told apart only by birthmarks, a storm at sea splitting a vessel in half and neatly dividing the family, and so on. The sea is emblematic of unpredictable Fortune, taking away with one hand and restoring with the other. The wife who is lost at sea, like her counterpart in *Apollonius* or *Pericles,* takes to a life of cloistered devotion, suggesting a pattern of symbolic death, healing, and ultimate rebirth. The ending of *The Comedy of Errors* has just a hint of death restored mysteriously to life: "After so long grief, such nativity!" (5.1.407).

Egeon's story of endurance counterpoints the farce in yet another way. His arraignment before the Duke of Ephesus introduces into the play a potentially tragic world of law, punishment, and death. Egeon's date with the executioner is not illusory. His predicament is the result of the bitter "mortal and intestine jars" (1.1.11) between two cities caught in a frenzy of economic reprisals. The law cannot be merciful, even though the unfairness of Egeon's plight is manifest to everyone, including the Duke. These potentially tragic factors must not be overstressed, for the first scene is brief and we are reassured by the play's hilarious tone (and by our surmising that Egeon is the father of the Antipholus twins) that all will be well. Still, Shakespeare's addition of this romance plot suggests his restlessness with pure farce. As in his later comedies, which are virtually all threatened by catastrophes, the denouement of *The Comedy of Errors* is deepened into something approaching miraculous recovery. Moreover, the backdrop of a near-tragic world of genuine suffering heightens our appreciation of comic unreality in the self-contained world of Plautine farce and stresses the illusory nature of the dilemmas arising out of purely mistaken identity. Such delusions are all the more comic because they are the delusions that supposedly sane people suffer: contentiousness and jealousy in marriage, concern for a respectable appearance in the eyes of one's neighbors, and the suspicion that one is always being cheated in money matters. These are the chimeras which, by being made to look so plausible and yet so patently insane, are farcically exploited in Shakespeare's comic device: the inversion of madness and sanity, dreaming and waking, illusion and reality.

What happens when the actions of one twin are mistaken for those of the other? The situation is of course amusing in itself, but it also serves as a test of the other characters, to discover what mad hypotheses they will construct. Adriana, faced with her husband's seeming refusal to come home to dinner, launches into a jealous tirade against husbands who neglect their wives for courtesans. The illusory situation, in other words, brings out her latent fears. We understand better now why she acts shrewishly: she fears rejection and the fading of her beauty, and imagines that her fading looks may be the cause of her husband's neglect. Actually, even as she speaks, her dutiful husband is busy making arrangements for a chain he plans to give her; but, when he is subsequently locked out of his own house and jumps to the conclusion that Adriana is being faithless, he resolves in his fury to bestow the chain on a courtesan in order to "spite my wife." He would actually do so, were he not saved from this destructively revengeful impulse by the beneficently comic action of the farcical plot: through mistaken identity, the chain is delivered into the hands of his twin. Once again, illusion has prompted a character to assume the worst, to reveal his suspicions of a plot against him. And so it goes when Antipholus of Ephesus is arrested for nonpayment for the chain (he assumes that all merchants are thieves) or is denied his bail money by the servant he thinks he sent to fetch it (he assumes that all servants are thieves). We laugh at the endless capacity of the human mind for distortions of this self-punishing sort.

The metaphor used most often to convey this sense of bewilderment, even confusion about one's own identity, is that of metamorphosis. All have drunk of Circe's cup (5.1.271) and have been transformed into animals—most of them into asses. All have hearkened to the mermaid's song, and are enchanted. Ephesus, they conclude, must be haunted by sorcerers, witches, goblins, and spirits (4.3.11 ff.). In such a mad world the characters assume a license to embark on Saturnalian holiday. The experience of transformation thus leads to various forms of release from ordinary social behavior, but the experience is also disturbing, and continually reminds the characters of exorcism, hell, and devils. The characters can explain their inverted world only by assuming that all men are lunatic, all honest women whores, and all true men thieves. "Do you know me, sir? . . . Am I myself?" "Am I in earth, in heaven, or in hell? / Sleeping or waking, mad or well advised?" (3.2.73–74, 2.2.211–212). It is both reassuring and hilariously anticlimactic that these questionings can finally be dispelled by the most mundane of explanations: there are two Antipholuses and two Dromios.

This playfulness about illusion should not be overemphasized, for the play expends most of its energies in farce. The Dromios, with their incessant drubbings, are often the center of interest in performance, and rightly so. Shakespeare employs no behind-the-scenes manipulator of illusion, such as Puck in *A Midsummer Night's Dream* or the Duke in *Measure for Measure*. His interest in the metaphor of the world as a stage is discernible only as the foreshadowing of greatness to come. Nevertheless, Shakespeare's alterations of Plautus amply reveal the philosophic and idealistic direction that his subsequent comedy is to take.

The Comedy of Errors
in Performance

The Comedy of Errors was performed at Gray's Inn, one of
the Inns of Court, on December 28, 1594. It appeared at the
court of King James I on December 28, 1604. Almost certainly it was acted in public as well, at the Theatre or a similar playhouse. How different were the playing methods
called for in these various locales? At Gray's Inn, it has
been suggested, Shakespeare's company may have used
fixed locations throughout to represent the three houses of
Antipholus of Ephesus, the Courtesan, and the Abbess. If
so, this is the only time Shakespeare adopted such a staging
plan for the entirety of a play. Such uniqueness urges caution in accepting the hypothesis, though it is true that *The
Comedy of Errors* is an early play with an unusually direct
indebtedness to the classical drama and especially to
Plautus' *Menaechmi*. Like its source, *The Comedy of Errors*
preserves the unities of place (Ephesus) and time (one day).

The arguments in favor of fixed locations are as follows.
The play requires only an open place, called a "street" or a
"mart," as is often the case in classical and neoclassical
drama, together with three houses or doors facing onto it.
The houses have names, as if they were labeled: Antipholus
of Ephesus's house is the Phoenix, the Courtesan's is the
Porpentine, and the Abbess's place of residence is the Priory. The use of stage houses with doors was common in
performances at court and at the Inns of Court; there, audiences familiar with neoclassical staging would understand
the use of a conventionalized facade in arcades, each com-
partment of which could be used to represent a house. The
dialogue and stage directions of Shakespeare's play refer to
the three houses as though they are recognizable locations:
Antipholus and Dromio of Ephesus enter *"from the Courtesan's"* at 4.1.13, Antipholus and Dromio of Syracuse exit
"to the priory" at 5.1.37, and a servant exits *"to the Abbess"* at 5.1.282. Dromio of Syracuse's entrance *"from the
bay"* (4.1.85) could suggest that one side entrance is understood to lead to the bay, while the other side leads to the

town, though with only one such stage direction we cannot be at all sure that the convention was rigorously followed throughout the play.

Against the hypothesis of fixed location is the consideration that Shakespeare's actors would have been hampered in arranging their many exits and entrances not specifically to or from the Phoenix, Porpentine, or Priory. The Priory doorway, not employed until Act 5, would have been unavailable to them for most of the action. The play begins with the Duke of Ephesus and others in a location (the Duke's palace? some public place?) that makes no use of the three supposed houses. Quite possibly, even if doorways were marked by placards for a segment of action, the labels could be shifted, letting the middle door for instance represent the Phoenix in Act 2, scene 1, and the Porpentine in Act 4, scene 1; with rearrangements of this sort, three doorways would suffice. Public theaters such as the Swan, of which a drawing survives, do not seem to have provided the number of doorways called for by neoclassical staging plans. Certainly Shakespeare never limited his acting company this way in any other play.

Moreover, the first scene of Act 3 calls for staging effects that seem especially suited to a public theater. Throughout this scene, the theater facade represents the house of Antipholus of Ephesus, into which Antipholus of Syracuse, Adriana, and Luciana have exited at the end of Act 2, scene 2, in order to dine "above" (l. 206). (The word "above" may or may not refer to a gallery or upper acting area.) Dromio of Syracuse is posted at the door as porter, and need not exit at all as Act 2 draws to a close; certainly the sense of location remains continuous as Antipholus of Ephesus and his friends arrive at his door, intending to dine, only to find themselves locked out. Dromio of Syracuse, at the door, may be visible to the audience as he refuses entrance to the irate houseowner and his guests, though they presumably cannot see him. When the maid Luce and then Adriana enter to see what the fuss is about at the door, they probably enter above, in the gallery looking down on the stage, where they can be seen and heard by the audience while presumably invisible to the group at the door. To be sure, this scene must have been staged in some

way at Gray's Inn and at court, as well as in the public theater. We are left finally with conflicting indications of mise-
en-scène in a play flexibly designed for performance
wherever opportunity provided. Still, that very condition of
flexibility must have dictated that the play not be staged in
too rigorously neoclassical a mode.

However it was originally staged, *The Comedy of Errors*
has been the victim ever since of directors who regard it as
too inconsequential to survive without adaptation and embellishment. A revival of sorts in 1716, the first recorded
since the early seventeenth century, took the form of a farce
called *Every Body Mistaken*. The Theatre Royal, Covent Garden, staged in 1734 a comedy in two acts from Plautus and
Shakespeare called *See If You Like It, or, 'Tis All A Mistake*.
Although something resembling Shakespeare's own *The
Comedy of Errors* was performed five times in 1741 at the
Theatre Royal, Drury Lane, with Charles Macklin as Dromio of Syracuse, it was in "improved" versions that the
play was generally seen. Thomas Hull was responsible for
an adaptation called *The Twins* that was performed again
and again at Covent Garden in the late eighteenth century.
Hull added songs, intensified the love interest, and elaborated the recognition scene in Act 5, trimming the wordplay
meanwhile to make room for the improvements. Adriana
was provided with a cousin, Hermia, who sang a plaintive
song about the love of "forsaken Julia" and her faithless
Lysander. W. Woods's *The Twins, or Which Is Which?* (1780,
at the Theatre Royal in Edinburgh) reduced the play to a
three-act farce, lest Shakespeare's "similiarity of character, and quick succession of mistakes" should "pall upon
an audience." John Philip Kemble retained and further extended the Hull version in 1808 and used this script for
many years. All of these adaptations aimed at reducing or
concealing the improbability of incident and the occasionally vulgar wit-combat that eighteenth-century taste evidently found indecorous.

Frederic Reynolds carried the idea of musical elaboration to its logical conclusion by turning the play into an
opera (Covent Garden, 1819). With lyrics from various
Shakespeare plays and sonnets set to the music of Thomas
Arne, Mozart, and others, this production sought to repair

the deficiencies of a short play. In the process, it restored to the theater a number of songs from *Twelfth Night, As You Like It, Love's Labor's Lost, The Merchant of Venice, Measure for Measure, The Tempest, A Midsummer Night's Dream, Othello,* and *King Lear* that had long been neglected in the performance of those plays. Reynolds added characters with such names as Cerimon and Ctesiphon, and provided a climactic scene of drunkenness in the handsomely furnished house of Balthasar with a spirited rendition of the chorus from *Antony and Cleopatra,* "Come, thou monarch of the vine." The scenery evidently made quite a hit: the last scene of Act 3 offered the viewer "a river surrounded by mountains" with snow-covered tops, in front of which Balthasar, Cerimon and others were seen in hunting costume, crossing a rustic bridge and pausing to sing "When icicles hang by the wall" from *Love's Labor's Lost.*

Samuel Phelps brought back something much closer to Shakespeare's play at the Sadler's Wells Theatre in 1855 and at the Princess's Theater in 1864, the year of Shakespeare's tercentenary. Phelps's Dromios at the Princess's, the Irish brothers Charles and Harry Webb, with the help of their family resemblance were able to solve the visual problem of representing identical twins, and the performance without intermission followed all of Shakespeare's scenes in order, though with some cutting. The American actors J. S. Clarke and Harry Paulton were famous as the Dromios in an 1883 production at London's Strand and Opera Comique theaters. In 1895 William Poel with his Elizabethan Stage Society performed the play at Gray's Inn, approximating the conditions of its original staging and delighting George Bernard Shaw: "I am now beginning to cling to [Poel] as the saviour of theatrical art." Frank Benson played Antipholus of Syracuse in his own production at Stratford-upon-Avon and at London's Coronet Theatre in 1905.

Since then the play has enjoyed a number of successful productions, usually swift-paced and aiming at hilarity, as in the joyous slapstick of Andrew Leigh's version at the Old Vic in 1927, and in Theodore Komisarjevsky's fantastic farce at Stratford-upon-Avon in 1938 with the Antipholus brothers dressed as toreadors in plumed Napoleonic hats and with officers outfitted in tunics and pink bowlers. At the Old Vic, April 23, 1957, Walter Hudd produced a double bill of *Titus Andronicus* and *The Comedy of Errors* in cut versions edited by John Barton. Both plays were performed in sixteenth-century costume and were presented as the offerings of Elizabethan traveling players at a country inn. In 1962 Clifford Williams's production at Stratford-upon-Avon was energetically played in the manner of the *commedia dell'arte*, while Jean Gascon's 1963 production at Stratford, Ontario, was, as one reviewer called it, a "Punchinello pantomime affair," with five Punchinellos enthusiastically directing the action onstage. *The Boys from Syracuse*, a musical-comedy version of 1938 (subsequently filmed), still draws large audiences when it is revived (as at Stratford, Ontario, in 1986); even today, the hoary device of musically updating, popularizing, and vulgarizing Shakespeare's play seems irresistible. *A New Comedy of Errors, or Too Many Twins* (1940), another musical adaptation put together out of parts of Plautus, Shakespeare, and Molière, was staged in modern dress at London's Mercury Theatre.

The play has been done as Victorian musical comedy (Arts Theatre, Cambridge, England, 1951), as Brechtian folk opera (Arts Theatre, London, 1956), and as a two-ring circus (Delacorte Theater, New York, 1967). It has been set in the American West at the end of the nineteenth century (Stratford, Ontario, 1975); in a provincial Italian town in the 1930s, with the Duke "a broad-bellied Mafioso in a white suit," as the *New York Post* noted (New York, Delacorte Theater, 1975); and in a modern Greek seaside resort (Stratford-upon-Avon, 1976). It has been propped up with a carnival midway complete with ferris wheel and roller coaster (Ashland, Oregon, 1976) and with circus acts such as tumblers and tightrope walkers, as in Robert Woodruff's production at the Goodman Theater in Chicago in 1983 (and brilliantly revived in 1987 at New York's Vivian Beaumont Theater) designed around The Flying Karamazov Brothers' spectacular juggling. The Adriana of this last production, Sophie Hayden, an expert baton twirler, ended her speeches on duty in marriage by spinning her baton far above her head and then casually catching it behind her back.

Perhaps the many transformations of *The Comedy of*

Errors onstage attest to the play's own interest in transformation. Still, it is good to learn from occasional "straight" performances that the script works marvelously when Shakespeare's inventive humor is allowed to speak for itself.

THE
COMEDY OF
ERRORS

1.1 *Enter the Duke of Ephesus, with [Egeon] the merchant of Syracuse, Jailer, and other attendants.*

EGEON

Proceed, Solinus, to procure my fall,
And by the doom of death end woes and all.   2

DUKE

Merchant of Syracusa, plead no more.   3
I am not partial to infringe our laws.   4
The enmity and discord which of late
Sprung from the rancorous outrage of your duke   6
To merchants, our well-dealing countrymen,
Who, wanting guilders to redeem their lives,   8
Have sealed his rigorous statutes with their bloods,   9
Excludes all pity from our threatening looks.
For since the mortal and intestine jars   11
Twixt thy seditious countrymen and us,
It hath in solemn synods been decreed,   13
Both by the Syracusians and ourselves,
To admit no traffic to our adverse towns.   15
Nay, more, if any born at Ephesus   16
Be seen at any Syracusian marts and fairs;
Again, if any Syracusian born
Come to the bay of Ephesus, he dies,
His goods confiscate to the Duke's dispose,   20
Unless a thousand marks be levièd   21
To quit the penalty and to ransom him.   22

1.1. Location: Some editors argue that the play was staged according to classical practice with three visible doors backstage representing three "houses"—that of Antipholus of Ephesus (in the center), that of the Courtesan, and the Priory—with the stage itself representing a market-place or open area. More probably, the stage may have been open and unlocalized. The present scene may be at the Duke's court.
2 doom judgment **3 Syracusa** Syracuse, in Sicily **4 partial** predis-posed, biased **6 outrage** violence **8 wanting** lacking. **guilders** money; the guilder was a Dutch coin worth about 1 shilling 8 pence. **redeem** ransom **9 sealed** ratified. **bloods** i.e., lives. (The grim analogy is to red sealing wax.) **11 mortal** deadly. **intestine** (The usual meaning, "civil" or "internal," may be used here with *mortal* as an intensifier.) **jars** quarrels **13 synods** assemblies **15 adverse** hostile **16 Ephesus** a port on the Aegean coast of modern Turkey **20 confiscate** confiscated.
dispose disposal **21 marks** money worth 13 shillings 4 pence **22 quit** pay

Thy substance, valued at the highest rate,   23
Cannot amount unto a hundred marks;
Therefore by law thou art condemned to die.

EGEON
Yet this my comfort: when your words are done,
My woes end likewise with the evening sun.

DUKE
Well, Syracusian, say in brief the cause
Why thou departedst from thy native home
And for what cause thou cam'st to Ephesus.

EGEON
A heavier task could not have been imposed
Than I to speak my griefs unspeakable.
Yet, that the world may witness that my end
Was wrought by nature, not by vile offense,   34
I'll utter what my sorrow gives me leave.   35
In Syracusa was I born, and wed
Unto a woman, happy but for me,
And by me, had not our hap been bad.   38
With her I lived in joy; our wealth increased
By prosperous voyages I often made
To Epidamium, till my factor's death   41
And the great care of goods at random left   42
Drew me from kind embracements of my spouse;
From whom my absence was not six months old
Before herself, almost at fainting under
The pleasing punishment that women bear,
Had made provision for her following me
And soon and safe arrivèd where I was.
There had she not been long but she became
A joyful mother of two goodly sons,
And, which was strange, the one so like the other
As could not be distinguished but by names.   52
That very hour and in the selfsame inn
A mean woman was deliverèd   54
Of such a burden, male twins, both alike.
Those, for their parents were exceeding poor,

23 **Thy substance** the sum total of your wealth   34 **by nature** i.e., by
natural affection, here, a father's love   35 **gives me leave** allows me
38 **hap** fortune   41 **Epidamium** i.e., Epidamnus (Epidamnum in Plautus'
Menaechmi), a port on the coast of modern Albania.   **factor's** agent's
42 **care of** anxiety about   52 **As** that they   54 **mean** of low birth

I bought and brought up to attend my sons.
My wife, not meanly proud of two such boys,   58
Made daily motions for our home return;   59
Unwilling I agreed. Alas, too soon
We came aboard.
A league from Epidamium had we sailed   62
Before the always-wind-obeying deep
Gave any tragic instance of our harm.   64
But longer did we not retain much hope;
For what obscurèd light the heavens did grant
Did but convey unto our fearful minds
A doubtful warrant of immediate death,   68
Which, though myself would gladly have embraced,
Yet the incessant weepings of my wife,
Weeping before for what she saw must come,
And piteous plainings of the pretty babes,   72
That mourned for fashion, ignorant what to fear,   73
Forced me to seek delays for them and me.   74
And this it was, for other means was none:
The sailors sought for safety by our boat
And left the ship, then sinking-ripe, to us.   77
My wife, more careful for the latter-born,   78
Had fastened him unto a small spare mast,
Such as seafaring men provide for storms;
To him one of the other twins was bound,
Whilst I had been like heedful of the other.
The children thus disposed, my wife and I,
Fixing our eyes on whom our care was fixed,   84
Fastened ourselves at either end the mast
And, floating straight, obedient to the stream,   86
Was carried towards Corinth, as we thought.
At length the sun, gazing upon the earth,
Dispersed those vapors that offended us;   89
And by the benefit of his wishèd light
The seas waxed calm, and we discoverèd

58 not meanly to no small degree   **59 motions** proposals   **62 league** a
measure of distance, about three miles   **64 instance** proof, sign
68 doubtful dreadful   **72 plainings** wailings   **73 for fashion** in imitation   **74 seek delays** i.e., from death   **77 sinking-ripe** ready to sink
78 careful anxious.   **latter-born** (Cf. l. 124, however, from which we
learn that the younger or "latter-born" was saved with the father.)
84 whom him on whom   **86 straight** at once   **89 vapors** clouds.
offended troubled

Two ships from far, making amain to us,   92
Of Corinth that, of Epidaurus this.   93
But ere they came—O, let me say no more!
Gather the sequel by that went before.   95

DUKE

Nay, forward, old man. Do not break off so,
For we may pity, though not pardon thee.

EGEON

O, had the gods done so, I had not now   98
Worthily termed them merciless to us!   99
For, ere the ships could meet by twice five leagues,
We were encountered by a mighty rock,
Which being violently borne upon,
Our helpful ship was splitted in the midst;   103
So that, in this unjust divorce of us,
Fortune had left to both of us alike
What to delight in, what to sorrow for.   106
Her part, poor soul, seeming as burdenèd   107
With lesser weight, but not with lesser woe,
Was carried with more speed before the wind,
And in our sight they three were taken up
By fishermen of Corinth, as we thought.
At length, another ship had seized on us
And, knowing whom it was their hap to save,
Gave healthful welcome to their shipwrecked guests   114
And would have reft the fishers of their prey   115
Had not their bark been very slow of sail;
And therefore homeward did they bend their course.
Thus have you heard me severed from my bliss,
That by misfortunes was my life prolonged
To tell sad stories of my own mishaps.

DUKE

And, for the sake of them thou sorrowest for,
Do me the favor to dilate at full   122
What hath befall'n of them and thee till now.

92 **making amain** proceeding at full speed   93 **Epidaurus** a Greek town
southwest of Athens and Corinth; or possibly Dubrovnik, on the Adriatic
coast   95 **that** that which   98 **had ... so** i.e., had the gods shown pity
99 **Worthily** justly   103 **helpful ship** i.e., the mast   106 **What** something   107 **as** as if   114 **healthful** saving   115 **reft** bereft   122 **dilate at
full** relate at length

And live; if no, then thou art doomed to die.
Jailer, take him to thy custody.

JAILER   I will, my lord.

EGEON
Hopeless and helpless doth Egeon wend,
But to procrastinate his lifeless end.   *Exeunt.* 158

❖

1.2   *Enter Antipholus [of Syracuse], [First]*
Merchant, and Dromio [of Syracuse].

FIRST MERCHANT
Therefore give out you are of Epidamium,   1
Lest that your goods too soon be confiscate.
This very day a Syracusian merchant
Is apprehended for arrival here
And, not being able to buy out his life,
According to the statute of the town
Dies ere the weary sun set in the west.
There is your money that I had to keep.   8
                              [He gives money.]

S. ANTIPHOLUS *[Giving the money to S. Dromio]*
Go bear it to the Centaur, where we host,   9
And stay there, Dromio, till I come to thee.
Within this hour it will be dinnertime.   11
Till that, I'll view the manners of the town,
Peruse the traders, gaze upon the buildings,
And then return and sleep within mine inn,
For with long travel I am stiff and weary.
Get thee away.

S. DROMIO
Many a man would take you at your word
And go indeed, having so good a means.   18
                              Exit Dromio [of Syracuse].

S. ANTIPHOLUS
A trusty villain, sir, that very oft,   19

---

158 procrastinate postpone

1.2. Location: The street.
1 give out say   **8 keep** safeguard   **9 Centaur** the name of an inn, identifi
by its sign over the door.   **host** lodge   **11 dinnertime** i.e., noon   **18 mea**
(1) opportunity (2) money   **19 villain** servant. (Said good-humoredly.)

EGEON

My youngest boy, and yet my eldest care,
At eighteen years became inquisitive
After his brother and importuned me
That his attendant—so his case was like,   127
Reft of his brother, but retained his name—   128
Might bear him company in the quest of him,
Whom whilst I labored of a love to see   130
I hazarded the loss of whom I loved.
Five summers have I spent in farthest Greece,
Roaming clean through the bounds of Asia,   133
And, coasting homeward, came to Ephesus—   134
Hopeless to find, yet loath to leave unsought   135
Or that or any place that harbors men.   136
But here must end the story of my life,
And happy were I in my timely death   138
Could all my travels warrant me they live.   139

DUKE

Hapless Egeon, whom the fates have marked
To bear the extremity of dire mishap!
Now trust me, were it not against our laws,
Against my crown, my oath, my dignity,
Which princes, would they, may not disannul,   144
My soul should sue as advocate for thee.
But though thou art adjudgèd to the death,   146
And passèd sentence may not be recalled
But to our honor's great disparagement,   148
Yet will I favor thee in what I can.
Therefore, merchant, I'll limit thee this day   150
To seek thy life by beneficial help.
Try all the friends thou hast in Ephesus;
Beg thou, or borrow, to make up the sum,

127 so . . . like in a similar situation   128 Reft . . . name (Evidently
Egeon, presuming that the lost son and servant are dead, has given
their names to the surviving twin brothers.)   130 labored of a love i.e.,
longed greatly   133 clean entirely   134 coasting traveling along the
coast   135 Hopeless despairing   136 Or either   138 timely speedy;
opportune   139 travels "travails," or hardships, as well as travels.
warrant assure   144 would they even if they wished.   disannul annul,
cancel   146 the death i.e., death by judicial sentence   148 But except
150 limit allow, appoint

When I am dull with care and melancholy,
Lightens my humor with his merry jests.   21
What, will you walk with me about the town
And then go to my inn and dine with me?

FIRST MERCHANT
I am invited, sir, to certain merchants,
Of whom I hope to make much benefit;
I crave your pardon. Soon at five o'clock,   26
Please you, I'll meet with you upon the mart
And afterward consort you till bedtime;   28
My present business calls me from you now.

S. ANTIPHOLUS
Farewell till then. I will go lose myself   30
And wander up and down to view the city.

FIRST MERCHANT
Sir, I commend you to your own content.   *Exit.*

S. ANTIPHOLUS
He that commends me to mine own content
Commends me to the thing I cannot get.
I to the world am like a drop of water   35
That in the ocean seeks another drop,
Who, falling there to find his fellow forth,   37
Unseen, inquisitive, confounds himself;   38
So I, to find a mother and a brother,
In quest of them, unhappy, lose myself.   40

        Enter Dromio of Ephesus.

Here comes the almanac of my true date.   41
What now? How chance thou art returned so soon?   42

E. DROMIO
Returned so soon! Rather approached too late:
The capon burns, the pig falls from the spit,
The clock hath strucken twelve upon the bell;
My mistress made it one upon my cheek.   46
She is so hot because the meat is cold;   47

21 **humor** mood, disposition   26 **Soon at** about   28 **consort** accompany   30 **lose myself** roam freely   35 **to** in relation to   37 **forth** out   38 **confounds himself** mingles indistinguishably   40 **unhappy** unlucky   41 **almanac . . . date** (i.e., being born in the same hour, Dromio serves as an almanac by which Antipholus can see his age)   42 **How chance** how comes it   46 **made it one** i.e., struck (as a clock would strike one o'clock)   47 **hot** angry

The meat is cold because you come not home;
You come not home because you have no stomach;   49
You have no stomach, having broke your fast.
But we that know what 'tis to fast and pray
Are penitent for your default today.   52

S. ANTIPHOLUS
Stop in your wind, sir. Tell me this, I pray: 53
Where have you left the money that I gave you?

E. DROMIO
O—sixpence that I had o' Wednesday last
To pay the saddler for my mistress' crupper?   56
The saddler had it, sir; I kept it not.

S. ANTIPHOLUS
I am not in a sportive humor now.
Tell me, and dally not, where is the money?
We being strangers here, how dar'st thou trust
So great a charge from thine own custody?   61

E. DROMIO
I pray you, jest, sir, as you sit at dinner.
I from my mistress come to you in post;   63
If I return, I shall be post indeed,   64
For she will scour your fault upon my pate.   65
Methinks your maw, like mine, should be your clock   66
And strike you home without a messenger.

S. ANTIPHOLUS
Come, Dromio, come, these jests are out of season;
Reserve them till a merrier hour than this.
Where is the gold I gave in charge to thee?

E. DROMIO
To me, sir? Why, you gave no gold to me.

S. ANTIPHOLUS
Come on, sir knave, have done your foolishness,
And tell me how thou hast disposed thy charge.

E. DROMIO
My charge was but to fetch you from the mart

---

49 stomach appetite   **52 penitent** doing penance (i.e., suffering hunger).   **default** fault   **53 wind** i.e., words   **56 crupper** leather strap on a saddle that is passed under the horse's tail in order to keep the saddle from riding forward   **61 charge** responsibility.   **from** out of   **63 post** haste   **64 post** doorpost of a tavern used for keeping reckonings   **65 scour** beat (with a pun on the idea of keeping score)   **66 maw** stomach. (Applied usually to animals.)

Home to your house, the Phoenix, sir, to dinner;   75
My mistress and her sister stays for you.

S. ANTIPHOLUS
Now, as I am a Christian, answer me
In what safe place you have bestowed my money,   78
Or I shall break that merry sconce of yours   79
That stands on tricks when I am undisposed.   80
Where is the thousand marks thou hadst of me?

E. DROMIO
I have some marks of yours upon my pate,
Some of my mistress' marks upon my shoulders,
But not a thousand marks between you both.
If I should pay your worship those again,
Perchance you will not bear them patiently.

S. ANTIPHOLUS
Thy mistress' marks? What mistress, slave, hast thou?

E. DROMIO
Your worship's wife, my mistress at the Phoenix,
She that doth fast till you come home to dinner
And prays that you will hie you home to dinner.   90

S. ANTIPHOLUS
What, wilt thou flout me thus unto my face,
Being forbid? There, take you that, sir knave.
                    [*He beats Dromio of Ephesus.*]

E. DROMIO
What mean you, sir? For God's sake, hold your hands!
Nay, an you will not, sir, I'll take my heels.   94
                    Exit Dromio of Ephesus.

S. ANTIPHOLUS
Upon my life, by some device or other
The villain is o'erraught of all my money.   96
They say this town is full of cozenage,   97
As nimble jugglers that deceive the eye,
Dark-working sorcerers that change the mind,
Soul-killing witches that deform the body,
Disguisèd cheaters, prating mountebanks,   101

---

75 the Phoenix the sign of Antipholus of Ephesus' shop. (He lives and carries on his business in the same dwelling.)   **78 bestowed** deposited
79 sconce head   **80 stands on** insists on, engages in   **90 hie** hasten
94 an if.   **take my heels** take to my heels   **96 o'erraught** cheated
97 cozenage cheating   **101 mountebanks** charlatans

And many suchlike liberties of sin.   102
If it prove so, I will be gone the sooner.
I'll to the Centaur to go seek this slave;
I greatly fear my money is not safe.   *Exit.*

❖

---

102 liberties of sin persons allowed improper freedom to sin

2.1   *Enter Adriana, wife to Antipholus of Ephesus,*
with Luciana, her sister.

ADRIANA
Neither my husband nor the slave returned,
That in such haste I sent to seek his master?
Sure, Luciana, it is two o'clock.

LUCIANA
Perhaps some merchant hath invited him,
And from the mart he's somewhere gone to dinner.
Good sister, let us dine and never fret.
A man is master of his liberty;
Time is their master, and when they see time   8
They'll go or come. If so, be patient, sister.

ADRIANA
Why should their liberty than ours be more?

LUCIANA
Because their business still lies out o' door.   11

ADRIANA
Look when I serve him so, he takes it ill.   12

LUCIANA
O, know he is the bridle of your will.

ADRIANA
There's none but asses will be bridled so.

LUCIANA
Why, headstrong liberty is lashed with woe.   15
There's nothing situate under heaven's eye
But hath his bound, in earth, in sea, in sky.   17
The beasts, the fishes, and the wingèd fowls
Are their males' subjects and at their controls.
Man, more divine, the master of all these,
Lord of the wide world and wild watery seas,
Endued with intellectual sense and souls,   22
Of more preeminence than fish and fowls,
Are masters to their females, and their lords.
Then let your will attend on their accords.   25

ADRIANA
This servitude makes you to keep unwed.

2.1. Location: The house of Antipholus of Ephesus.
8 Time time alone.   **see time** see fit   **11 still** always   **12 Look when**
whenever   **15 lashed** scourged, castigated; also, bound   **17 his** its
22 intellectual sense reason   **25 accords** consent

LUCIANA
Not this, but troubles of the marriage bed.
ADRIANA
But, were you wedded, you would bear some sway.
LUCIANA
Ere I learn love, I'll practice to obey.
ADRIANA
How if your husband start some other where?   30
LUCIANA
Till he come home again, I would forbear.
ADRIANA
Patience unmoved! No marvel though she pause;
They can be meek that have no other cause.   33
A wretched soul, bruised with adversity,
We bid be quiet when we hear it cry;
But were we burdened with like weight of pain,
As much or more we should ourselves complain.
So thou, that hast no unkind mate to grieve thee,
With urging helpless patience would relieve me;   39
But if thou live to see like right bereft,   40
This fool-begged patience in thee will be left.   41
LUCIANA
Well, I will marry one day, but to try.   42
Here comes your man; now is your husband nigh.
        Enter Dromio of Ephesus.
ADRIANA
Say, is your tardy master now at hand?
E. DROMIO   Nay, he's at two hands with me, and that   45
my two ears can witness.
ADRIANA
Say, didst thou speak with him? Know'st thou his mind?
E. DROMIO
Ay, ay, he told his mind upon mine ear.   48
Beshrew his hand, I scarce could understand it.   49

---

30 start . . . where i.e., goes off elsewhere, after other women   **33 other cause** cause to be otherwise   **39 helpless** unavailing, unprofitable
40 see . . . bereft see your rights similarly taken away   **41 This . . . left** you will abandon this foolishly urged patience   **42 but to try** i.e., just to put it to the test   **45 at two hands** (alluding to the beating he received at 1.2.92)   **48 told** (punning on *tolled*)   **49 Beshrew** bad luck to.
understand (with pun on "stand under"; also in l. 53)

LUCIANA
  Spake he so doubtfully thou couldst not feel his meaning?
E. DROMIO Nay, he struck so plainly I could too well
  feel his blows, and withal so doubtfully that I could
  scarce understand them.
ADRIANA
  But say, I prithee, is he coming home?
  It seems he hath great care to please his wife.
E. DROMIO
  Why, mistress, sure my master is horn-mad.   56
ADRIANA
  Horn-mad, thou villain?
E. DROMIO   I mean not cuckold-mad,
  But sure he is stark mad.
  When I desired him to come home to dinner,
  He asked me for a thousand marks in gold.
  "'Tis dinnertime," quoth I. "My gold!" quoth he.
  "Your meat doth burn," quoth I. "My gold!" quoth he.
  "Will you come?" quoth I. "My gold!" quoth he.
  "Where is the thousand marks I gave thee, villain?"
  "The pig," quoth I, "is burned." "My gold!" quoth he.
  "My mistress, sir," quoth I. "Hang up thy mistress!
  I know not thy mistress; out on thy mistress!"
LUCIANA Quoth who?
E. DROMIO Quoth my master.
  "I know," quoth he, "no house, no wife, no mistress."
  So that my errand, due unto my tongue,   71
  I thank him, I bare home upon my shoulders;   72
  For, in conclusion, he did beat me there.
ADRIANA
  Go back again, thou slave, and fetch him home.
E. DROMIO
  Go back again, and be new beaten home?
  For God's sake, send some other messenger.
ADRIANA
  Back, slave, or I will break thy pate across.

56 horn-mad mad as a horned beast (with a quibble on the sense of rage
at being made a cuckold) **71 due ... tongue** which I should have
delivered by my tongue **72 I bare ... shoulders** I took in the form of a
beating

E. DROMIO
And he will bless that cross with other beating.   78
Between you I shall have a holy head.   79

ADRIANA
Hence, prating peasant! Fetch thy master home.

E. DROMIO
Am I so round with you as you with me,   81
That like a football you do spurn me thus?
You spurn me hence, and he will spurn me hither.
If I last in this service, you must case me in leather.
                                                                [Exit.]

LUCIANA
Fie, how impatience loureth in your face!   85

ADRIANA
His company must do his minions grace,   86
Whilst I at home starve for a merry look.
Hath homely age th' alluring beauty took
From my poor cheek? Then he hath wasted it.   89
Are my discourses dull? Barren my wit?   90
If voluble and sharp discourse be marred,   91
Unkindness blunts it more than marble hard.   92
Do their gay vestments his affections bait?   93
That's not my fault; he's master of my state.   94
What ruins are in me that can be found
By him not ruined? Then is he the ground   96
Of my defeatures. My decayèd fair   97
A sunny look of his would soon repair.
But, too unruly deer, he breaks the pale   99
And feeds from home; poor I am but his stale.   100

78 he . . . cross i.e., he will add further devotion in the form of a beating. (There is a pun on "to bless," to wound, from the French *blesser*. *Cross* is a quibble on *across* in the previous line.)   **79 holy** (punning on the sense "full of holes")   **81 round** plain-spoken (with pun on the sense of "spherical")   **85 loureth** frowns, scowls   **86 minions** paramours, darlings.   **grace** honor, favor   **89 wasted** (1) squandered (2) laid waste to, ruined   **90 discourses** conversations   **91 voluble** fluent, agile   **91-92 sharp . . . hard** (*Sharp discourse* is imagined as a knife that is blunted by his unkindness even more than it would be by hard marble.)   **93 affections** passions.   **bait** entice   **94 state** outward estate, condition, i.e., clothes   **96 ground** cause   **97 defeatures** disfigurements.   **decayèd fair** impaired or perished beauty   **99 pale** enclosure   **100 from** away from.   **stale** rejected lover who has become a laughingstock (with a pun on *stale*, tiresomely lacking in freshness; she is stale to him, he dear [*deer*] to her)

LUCIANA
   Self-harming jealousy! Fie, beat it hence!
ADRIANA
   Unfeeling fools can with such wrongs dispense.   102
   I know his eye doth homage otherwhere,
   Or else what lets it but he would be here?   104
   Sister, you know he promised me a chain;
   Would that alone, alone he would detain,   106
   So he would keep fair quarter with his bed!   107
   I see the jewel best enamelèd   108
   Will lose his beauty; yet the gold bides still   109
   That others touch, and often touching will   110
   Wear gold; and no man that hath a name   111
   By falsehood and corruption doth it shame.   112
   Since that my beauty cannot please his eye,
   I'll weep what's left away, and weeping die.
LUCIANA
   How many fond fools serve mad jealousy!   115

                                     Exeunt.

❖

2.2   *Enter Antipholus of Syracuse.*

S. ANTIPHOLUS
   The gold I gave to Dromio is laid up
   Safe at the Centaur, and the heedful slave
   Is wandered forth in care to seek me out
   By computation and mine host's report.   4
   I could not speak with Dromio since at first
   I sent him from the mart. See, here he comes.

102 dispense pardon, condone by dispensation   **104 lets** hinders
106 Would . . . detain would that he would withhold only that token of
his affection (?)   **107 So . . . bed** provided he would remain faithful to
his marriage bed   **108–112 I see . . . shame** (A difficult passage, evidently corrupt. Adriana seemingly compares her beauty to that of a
well-enameled jewel that tarnishes in time through neglect, whereas
some beauty, like gold, is often touched and hence retains its luster
through use; this latter kind of beauty is not shamed through falsehood
and corruption by men of *name* or reputation like Antipholus of Ephesus, as Adriana feels she is being shamed.)   **115 fond** doting

2.2. Location: The street before Antipholus of Ephesus' house.
4 computation estimation, reckoning

Enter Dromio of Syracuse.

How now, sir, is your merry humor altered?
As you love strokes, so jest with me again.   8
You know no Centaur? You received no gold?
Your mistress sent to have me home to dinner?
My house was at the Phoenix? Wast thou mad,
That thus so madly thou didst answer me?

S. DROMIO
What answer, sir? When spake I such a word?

S. ANTIPHOLUS
Even now, even here, not half an hour since.

S. DROMIO
I did not see you since you sent me hence,
Home to the Centaur, with the gold you gave me.

S. ANTIPHOLUS
Villain, thou didst deny the gold's receipt
And toldst me of a mistress and a dinner,
For which I hope thou felt'st I was displeased.

S. DROMIO
I am glad to see you in this merry vein.
What means this jest? I pray you, master, tell me.

S. ANTIPHOLUS
Yea, dost thou jeer and flout me in the teeth?   22
Think'st thou I jest? Hold, take thou that, and that.

                              Beats Dromio.

S. DROMIO
Hold, sir, for God's sake! Now your jest is earnest.   24
Upon what bargain do you give it me?

S. ANTIPHOLUS
Because that I familiarly sometimes
Do use you for my fool and chat with you,
Your sauciness will jest upon my love   28
And make a common of my serious hours.   29
When the sun shines let foolish gnats make sport,
But creep in crannies when he hides his beams.
If you will jest with me, know my aspect   32
And fashion your demeanor to my looks,

---

8 strokes blows   **22 in the teeth** to my face   **24 earnest** serious (with a
pun on the financial sense: money paid as an installment to secure a
bargain)   **28 jest upon** trifle with   **29 common** public playground
32 aspect look, expression; also, astrological favor or disfavor of a planet

Or I will beat this method in your sconce.   34

S. DROMIO "Sconce" call you it? So you would leave battering, I had rather have it a head. An you use these 36
blows long, I must get a sconce for my head and in- 37
sconce it too, or else I shall seek my wit in my shoul- 38
ders. But I pray, sir, why am I beaten?   39

S. ANTIPHOLUS Dost thou not know?

S. DROMIO Nothing, sir, but that I am beaten.

S. ANTIPHOLUS Shall I tell you why?

S. DROMIO Ay, sir, and wherefore; for they say every
why hath a wherefore.

S. ANTIPHOLUS Why, first—for flouting me; and then,
wherefore—for urging it the second time to me.

S. DROMIO
Was there ever any man thus beaten out of season, 47
When in the why and the wherefore is neither rhyme nor
    reason?
Well, sir, I thank you.

S. ANTIPHOLUS Thank me, sir, for what?

S. DROMIO Marry, sir, for this something that you gave 51
me for nothing.

S. ANTIPHOLUS I'll make you amends next, to give you
nothing for something. But say, sir, is it dinnertime?

S. DROMIO No, sir, I think the meat wants that I have. 55

S. ANTIPHOLUS In good time, sir, what's that?   56

S. DROMIO Basting.   57

S. ANTIPHOLUS Well, sir, then 'twill be dry.

S. DROMIO If it be, sir, I pray you, eat none of it.

S. ANTIPHOLUS Your reason?

S. DROMIO Lest it make you choleric and purchase me 61
another dry basting.   62

S. ANTIPHOLUS Well, sir, learn to jest in good time.
There's a time for all things.

---

34 sconce head (with pun on the meaning "fort" in l. 35 and "helmet"
or "protective covering" in l. 37; the *battering*, ll. 35–36, is both a beating and assault by a battering ram) **36 An** if **37–38 insconce** shelter
within a sconce or fortification **38–39 I shall . . . shoulders** i.e., my
head will be beaten into my shoulders **47 out of season** inappropri-
ately **51 Marry** i.e., truly. (A shortened form of the oath "by the Virgin
Mary.") **55 wants that** lacks that which **56 In good time** indeed
57 Basting (1) moistening with butter or drippings during cooking (2)
beating **61 choleric** (Hot or dry food was thought to produce or aggra-
vate the choleric or irascible humor.) **62 dry basting** hard beating

S. DROMIO   I durst have denied that before you were so
choleric.

S. ANTIPHOLUS   By what rule, sir?

S. DROMIO   Marry, sir, by a rule as plain as the plain
bald pate of Father Time himself.

S. ANTIPHOLUS   Let's hear it.

S. DROMIO   There's no time for a man to recover his hair
that grows bald by nature.

S. ANTIPHOLUS   May he not do it by fine and recovery?   73

S. DROMIO   Yes, to pay a fine for a periwig and recover
the lost hair of another man.

S. ANTIPHOLUS   Why is Time such a niggard of hair,
being, as it is, so plentiful an excrement?   77

S. DROMIO   Because it is a blessing that he bestows on
beasts, and what he hath scanted men in hair he hath
given them in wit.

S. ANTIPHOLUS   Why, but there's many a man hath more
hair than wit.

S. DROMIO   Not a man of those but he hath the wit to   83
lose his hair.   84

S. ANTIPHOLUS   Why, thou didst conclude hairy men
plain dealers without wit.

S. DROMIO   The plainer dealer, the sooner lost. Yet he   87
loseth it in a kind of jollity.   88

S. ANTIPHOLUS   For what reason?

S. DROMIO   For two, and sound ones too.

S. ANTIPHOLUS   Nay, not sound, I pray you.   91

S. DROMIO   Sure ones then.

S. ANTIPHOLUS   Nay, not sure, in a thing falsing.   93

S. DROMIO   Certain ones then.

S. ANTIPHOLUS   Name them.

S. DROMIO   The one, to save the money that he spends
in tiring; the other, that at dinner they should not drop   97
in his porridge.

---

73 fine and recovery a legal procedure for converting an entailed estate,
one in which the property is limited to specified heirs, into a fee simple,
one in which the owner has unqualified ownership   **77 excrement**
outgrowth (of hair)   **83–84 he . . . hair** (A reference to the venereal
diseases in which loss of hair was a symptom.)   **87 dealer** i.e., dealer
with women   **88 a kind of jollity** i.e., sexual pleasure   **91 not sound**
invalid (with a pun on "venereally diseased")   **93 falsing** deceptive
(continuing the joke on venereal disease)   **97 tiring** dressing the hair

S. ANTIPHOLUS You would all this time have proved
there is no time for all things.

S. DROMIO Marry, and did, sir; namely, e'en no time to
recover hair lost by nature.

S. ANTIPHOLUS But your reason was not substantial
why there is no time to recover.

S. DROMIO Thus I mend it: Time himself is bald and
therefore to the world's end will have bald followers.

S. ANTIPHOLUS I knew 'twould be a bald conclusion. 107
But soft, who wafts us yonder?   108

Enter Adriana [beckoning them], and Luciana.

ADRIANA
Ay, ay, Antipholus, look strange and frown.   109
Some other mistress hath thy sweet aspects;
I am not Adriana, nor thy wife.
The time was once when thou unurged wouldst vow
That never words were music to thine ear,
That never object pleasing in thine eye,
That never touch well welcome to thy hand,
That never meat sweet-savored in thy taste,
Unless I spake, or looked, or touched, or carved to thee.
How comes it now, my husband, O, how comes it
That thou art then estrangèd from thyself?   119
Thyself I call it, being strange to me,
That, undividable, incorporate,
Am better than thy dear self's better part.
Ah, do not tear away thyself from me!
For know, my love, as easy mayst thou fall   124
A drop of water in the breaking gulf,
And take unmingled thence that drop again
Without addition or diminishing,
As take from me thyself and not me too.   128
How dearly would it touch thee to the quick,   129
Shouldst thou but hear I were licentious

---

107 bald i.e., senseless, stupid   **108 soft** gently, wait a minute.
wafts beckons   **109 strange** estranged, distant   **119 then** therefore.
estrangèd from thyself (1) behaving unlike yourself (2) estranged from
me, your other half   **124 fall** let fall   **128 and not me too** i.e., even when
we are separated we are indivisible   **129 the quick** the most sensitive or
vulnerable part

And that this body, consecrate to thee,   131
By ruffian lust should be contaminate!   132
Wouldst thou not spit at me, and spurn at me,
And hurl the name of husband in my face,
And tear the stained skin off my harlot brow,
And from my false hand cut the wedding ring,
And break it with a deep-divorcing vow?
I know thou canst, and therefore see thou do it.   138
I am possessed with an adulterate blot;
My blood is mingled with the crime of lust;
For if we two be one and thou play false,
I do digest the poison of thy flesh,
Being strumpeted by thy contagion.   143
Keep then fair league and truce with thy true bed,   144
I live distained, thou undishonorèd.   145

S. ANTIPHOLUS
Plead you to me, fair dame? I know you not.
In Ephesus I am but two hours old,
As strange unto your town as to your talk,
Who, every word by all my wit being scanned,
Wants wit in all one word to understand.   150

LUCIANA
Fie, brother, how the world is changed with you!
When were you wont to use my sister thus?   152
She sent for you by Dromio home to dinner.

S. ANTIPHOLUS   By Dromio?
S. DROMIO   By me?

ADRIANA
By thee; and this thou didst return from him:
That he did buffet thee and in his blows
Denied my house for his, me for his wife.

S. ANTIPHOLUS
Did you converse, sir, with this gentlewoman?
What is the course and drift of your compact?   160

S. DROMIO
I, sir? I never saw her till this time.

---

131 **consecrate** consecrated   132 **contaminate** contaminated   138 **see** (I)
imagine; or, go ahead (since you know you have the right) if you hear I
am unfaithful   143 **strumpeted** made a strumpet   144 **Keep . . . truce**
i.e., if you keep faithful covenant   145 **distained** unstained (by contagion)   150 **Wants . . . understand** i.e., lacks the ability to understand
even one word of what has been said   152 **use** treat   160 **compact** plot

S. ANTIPHOLUS
Villain, thou liest, for even her very words
Didst thou deliver to me on the mart.

S. DROMIO
I never spake with her in all my life.

S. ANTIPHOLUS
How can she thus then call us by our names,
Unless it be by inspiration?

ADRIANA
How ill agrees it with your gravity
To counterfeit thus grossly with your slave,   168
Abetting him to thwart me in my mood!   169
Be it my wrong you are from me exempt,   170
But wrong not that wrong with a more contempt.   171
Come, I will fasten on this sleeve of thine.
                              [*She clings to him.*]
Thou art an elm, my husband, I a vine,
Whose weakness, married to thy stronger state,
Makes me with thy strength to communicate.   175
If aught possess thee from me, it is dross,   176
Usurping ivy, brier, or idle moss,   177
Who, all for want of pruning, with intrusion   178
Infect thy sap and live on thy confusion.   179

S. ANTIPHOLUS [*Aside*]
To me she speaks; she moves me for her theme.   180
What, was I married to her in my dream?
Or sleep I now and think I hear all this?
What error drives our eyes and ears amiss?
Until I know this sure uncertainty,   184
I'll entertain the offered fallacy.   185

LUCIANA
Dromio, go bid the servants spread for dinner.   186

S. DROMIO
O, for my beads! I cross me for a sinner.   187
                              [*He crosses himself.*]

---

168 grossly obviously   **169 Abetting** helping.   **mood** anger   **170 exempt**
separated   **171 more** greater   **175 with . . . communicate** share in your
strength   **176 If . . . dross** if anything usurps my possession of you, it is
an impure substance   **177 idle** unprofitable   **178 Who** which.   **want**
lack.   **intrusion** forced entry   **179 confusion** ruin   **180 moves . . .**
theme appeals to me as her subject of discourse   **184 sure uncertainty**
(to be) undoubted illusion   **185 entertain** accept.   **fallacy** delusive
notion, error   **186 spread** set the table   **187 beads** rosary beads

This is the fairy land. O spite of spites,
We talk with goblins, elves, and sprites!   189
If we obey them not, this will ensue:
They'll suck our breath or pinch us black and blue.   191
LUCIANA
Why prat'st thou to thyself and answer'st not?   192
Dromio, thou drone, thou snail, thou slug, thou sot!   193
S. DROMIO
I am transformèd, master, am not I?
S. ANTIPHOLUS
I think thou art in mind, and so am I.
S. DROMIO
Nay, master, both in mind and in my shape.
S. ANTIPHOLUS
Thou hast thine own form.
S. DROMIO   No, I am an ape.   197
LUCIANA
If thou art changed to aught, 'tis to an ass.
S. DROMIO
'Tis true; she rides me and I long for grass.   199
'Tis so, I am an ass; else it could never be
But I should know her as well as she knows me.
ADRIANA
Come, come, no longer will I be a fool,
To put the finger in the eye and weep,
Whilst man and master laughs my woes to scorn.
Come, sir, to dinner.—Dromio, keep the gate.—
Husband, I'll dine above with you today   206
And shrive you of a thousand idle pranks.—   207
Sirrah, if any ask you for your master,   208
Say he dines forth, and let no creature enter.—   209
Come, sister.—Dromio, play the porter well.
S. ANTIPHOLUS [Aside]
Am I in earth, in heaven, or in hell?
Sleeping or waking, mad or well-advised?   212

189 sprites spirits   191 suck our breath (This piece of folklore was perhaps connected with the old idea that the breath of man was his soul.)
192 prat'st thou do you chatter   193 sot fool   197 ape i.e., counterfeit
199 for grass for freedom (as a horse put out to pasture)   206 above i.e.,
on the second floor, above Antipholus' shop   207 shrive hear confession
and give absolution   208 Sirrah (Customary form of address to servants.)   209 forth away from home   212 well-advised in my right mind

Known unto these, and to myself disguised?
I'll say as they say, and persever so,
And in this mist at all adventures go.   215
S. DROMIO
Master, shall I be porter at the gate?
ADRIANA
Ay, and let none enter, lest I break your pate.
LUCIANA
Come, come, Antipholus, we dine too late.
                    [*Exeunt. Dromio of Syracuse remains as
                        porter, visible to the audience but not
                            to those approaching the door.*]

215 at all adventures whatever may happen

3.1   *Enter Antipholus of Ephesus, his man Dromio,*
Angelo the goldsmith, and Balthasar the
merchant.

E. ANTIPHOLUS
  Good Signor Angelo, you must excuse us all;
  My wife is shrewish when I keep not hours.   2
  Say that I lingered with you at your shop
  To see the making of her carcanet   4
  And that tomorrow you will bring it home.
  But here's a villain that would face me down   6
  He met me on the mart, and that I beat him
  And charged him with a thousand marks in gold,   8
  And that I did deny my wife and house.   9
  Thou drunkard, thou, what didst thou mean by this?
E. DROMIO
  Say what you will, sir, but I know what I know.
  That you beat me at the mart, I have your hand to show;   12
  If the skin were parchment and the blows you gave were
    ink,
  Your own handwriting would tell you what I think.
E. ANTIPHOLUS
  I think thou art an ass.
E. DROMIO   Marry, so it doth appear
  By the wrongs I suffer and the blows I bear.
  I should kick, being kicked, and being at that pass,   17
  You would keep from my heels and beware of an ass.
E. ANTIPHOLUS
  You're sad, Signor Balthasar. Pray God our cheer   19
  May answer my good will and your good welcome here.   20
BALTHASAR
  I hold your dainties cheap, sir, and your welcome dear.   21

**3.1. Location: Before the house of Antipholus of Ephesus. The scene is
continuous with the previous.**
2 keep not hours am not punctual   **4 carcanet** necklace (the *chain* of
2.1.105 and l. 115 below)   **6 face me down** maintain to my face that
8 charged entrusted.   **with** i.e., with possession of   **9 deny** disown
12 hand i.e., handiwork on my body (with a pun on "handwriting")
17 at that pass in that situation   **19 sad** serious.   **cheer** entertainment   **20 answer** agree with, match   **21 dainties** delicacies.   **cheap** of
minor importance.   **dear** of primary importance

E. ANTIPHOLUS
O Signor Balthasar, either at flesh or fish,
A table full of welcome makes scarce one dainty dish.   23
BALTHASAR
Good meat, sir, is common; that every churl affords.   24
E. ANTIPHOLUS
And welcome more common, for that's nothing but
  words.
BALTHASAR
Small cheer and great welcome makes a merry feast.
E. ANTIPHOLUS
Ay, to a niggardly host and more sparing guest.   27
But though my cates be mean, take them in good part;   28
Better cheer may you have, but not with better heart.

  [*They approach the door of Antipholus of
  Ephesus' house.*]

But, soft! My door is locked. Go bid them let us in.
E. DROMIO
Maud, Bridget, Marian, Cicely, Gillian, Ginn!
S. DROMIO [*Speaking from the other side of the door*]
Mome, malt-horse, capon, coxcomb, idiot, patch!   32
Either get thee from the door or sit down at the hatch.   33
Dost thou conjure for wenches, that thou call'st for such
  store,   34
When one is one too many? Go get thee from the door.
E. DROMIO
What patch is made our porter? My master stays in the
  street.   36
S. DROMIO
Let him walk from whence he came, lest he catch cold
  on 's feet.   37

23 **makes scarce** scarcely equals   24 **churl** one of mean station
27 **sparing** frugal   28 **cates** provisions, dainties.   **mean** plain, simple
32 **s.d. Speaking . . . door** (Dromio of Syracuse has remained onstage
since the end of the previous scene, visible to the audience but not to
those at the door. Alternatively, he could exit at the end of 2.2 and speak
now *"within,"* or enter at this point, but neither solution seems satis-
factory. Compare the entrances of Luce and Adriana at ll. 47 and 60.)
32 **Mome** dolt, blockhead.   **malt-horse** brewer's horse; stupid person.
patch fool, clown   33 **hatch** a half-door that can be kept closed while
the upper half is opened   34 **conjure for** summon by magic.   **store**
quantity (of wenches)   36 **stays** waits   37 **on 's** in his

E. ANTIPHOLUS
Who talks within there? Ho, open the door!
S. DROMIO
Right, sir, I'll tell you when, an you'll tell me wherefore. 39
E. ANTIPHOLUS
Wherefore? For my dinner. I have not dined today.
S. DROMIO
Nor today here you must not; come again when you may.
E. ANTIPHOLUS
What art thou that keep'st me out from the house I owe? 42
S. DROMIO
The porter for this time, sir, and my name is Dromio. 43
E. DROMIO
O villain! Thou hast stol'n both mine office and my
    name.
The one ne'er got me credit, the other mickle blame. 45
If thou hadst been Dromio today in my place,
Thou wouldst have changed thy face for a name or thy
    name for an ass.   47

> *Enter Luce [above, concealed from Antipholus of
> Ephesus and his companions].*

LUCE
What a coil is there, Dromio? Who are those at the gate? 48
E. DROMIO
Let my master in, Luce.
LUCE   Faith, no, he comes too late,
And so tell your master.
E. DROMIO   O Lord, I must laugh!
Have at you with a proverb: Shall I set in my staff? 51
LUCE
Have at you with another: that's—When, can you tell? 52

---

39 an if. **wherefore** why **42 owe** own **43 for this time** at this moment, for the time being **45 mickle** much **47 thy face for a name** i.e.,
to escape blame (?) (Though perhaps this should read *thy office for an
aim,* i.e., for a blow, as various editors have suggested.) **s.d. Enter
Luce [above]** (Here and at l. 60, Luce and then Adriana may enter above
in such a way that the audience understands them not to be visible to
those who are calling at the door.) **48 coil** noise, disturbance **51 Have
. . . staff** let me come at you with a proverb: Shall I take up my abode
here? (With a bawdy double meaning.) **52 When . . . tell** i.e., never.
(Another proverbial expression, used derisively to turn aside a
question.)

S. DROMIO
If thy name be called Luce, Luce, thou hast answered
   him well.

E. ANTIPHOLUS
Do you hear, you minion? You'll let us in, I hope?   54

LUCE
I thought to have asked you.

S. DROMIO   And you said no.

E. DROMIO
So, come help. Well struck! There was blow for blow.

E. ANTIPHOLUS
Thou baggage, let me in.

LUCE   Can you tell for whose sake?   57

E. DROMIO
Master, knock the door hard.

LUCE   Let him knock till it ache.

E. ANTIPHOLUS
You'll cry for this, minion, if I beat the door down.
                                        [*He knocks.*]

LUCE
What needs all that, and a pair of stocks in the town?   60

>   *Enter Adriana [above, concealed, like Luce and*
>   *Dromio of Syracuse, from those at the door].*

ADRIANA
Who is that at the door that keeps all this noise?   61

S. DROMIO
By my troth, your town is troubled with unruly boys.

E. ANTIPHOLUS
Are you there, wife? You might have come before.

ADRIANA
Your wife, sir knave? Go get you from the door.
                                        [*Exit with Luce.*]

E. DROMIO
If you went in pain, master, this "knave" would go sore.   65

---

54 minion hussy.   **hope** (A line following with an answering rhyme may
be missing; perhaps it would have cleared up the present obscurity of
ll. 55 and 56.)   **57 baggage** good-for-nothing   **60 What . . . town** i.e., why
do we need to put up with this disturbance, when the town provides
stocks for punishment?   **61 keeps** keeps up   **65 If . . . sore** i.e., yourself
and this "knave" she mentions are the same person.   **went** i.e., were

ANGELO
Here is neither cheer, sir, nor welcome. We would fain
  have either.
BALTHASAR
In debating which was best, we shall part with neither. 67
E. DROMIO
They stand at the door, master. Bid them welcome
  hither.
E. ANTIPHOLUS
There is something in the wind, that we cannot get in. 69
E. DROMIO
You would say so, master, if your garments were thin.
Your cake there is warm within; you stand here in the
  cold.
It would make a man mad as a buck to be so bought and
  sold.   72
E. ANTIPHOLUS
Go fetch me something. I'll break ope the gate.
S. DROMIO
Break any breaking here, and I'll break your knave's
  pate.
E. DROMIO
A man may break a word with you, sir, and words are but
  wind,   75
Ay, and break it in your face, so he break it not behind. 76
S. DROMIO
It seems thou want'st breaking. Out upon thee, hind!   77
E. DROMIO
Here's too much "Out upon thee!" I pray thee, let me in.
S. DROMIO
Ay, when fowls have no feathers and fish have no fin. 79
                                                   [*Exit.*]
E. ANTIPHOLUS
Well, I'll break in. Go borrow me a crow.   80

---

67 debating discussing.   **part** depart   **69 something . . . wind** something strange going on. (Dromio of Ephesus, in l. 70, takes the phrase
literally.)   **72 as a buck** i.e., as a male deer in rutting season. (Cf. *horn-
mad,* 2.1.57.)   **bought and sold** i.e., betrayed, ill-treated   **75 break a
word** exchange words   **76 behind** i.e., in farting   **77 thou . . . breaking**
you need to be beaten.   **hind** slave   **79 s.d. Exit** (If Dromio of Syracuse
has been visible to the audience, he probably leaves at this point.)
80 crow crowbar (introducing a quibble by Dromio of Ephesus)

E. DROMIO

A crow without feather? Master, mean you so?
For a fish without a fin, there's a fowl without a
   feather.—
If a crow help us in, sirrah, we'll pluck a crow together.   83

E. ANTIPHOLUS

Go, get thee gone; fetch me an iron crow.

BALTHASAR

Have patience, sir. O, let it not be so!
Herein you war against your reputation
And draw within the compass of suspect   87
Th' unviolated honor of your wife.
Once this—your long experience of her wisdom,   89
Her sober virtue, years, and modesty,   90
Plead on her part some cause to you unknown;
And doubt not, sir, but she will well excuse   92
Why at this time the doors are made against you.   93
Be ruled by me. Depart in patience,
And let us to the Tiger all to dinner,
And about evening come yourself alone
To know the reason of this strange restraint.
If by strong hand you offer to break in   98
Now in the stirring passage of the day,   99
A vulgar comment will be made of it,   100
And that supposèd by the common rout   101
Against your yet ungallèd estimation,   102
That may with foul intrusion enter in
And dwell upon your grave when you are dead;
For slander lives upon succession,   105
Forever housed where it gets possession.

E. ANTIPHOLUS

You have prevailed. I will depart in quiet
And, in despite of mirth, mean to be merry.   108
I know a wench of excellent discourse,
Pretty and witty, wild and yet, too, gentle.

83 pluck . . . together pick a bone together, settle accounts   **87 draw . . . suspect** bring under suspicion   **89 Once this** to be brief, in short **90 virtue** merit, general excellence   **92 excuse** justify   **93 made** fastened   **98 offer** venture   **99 stirring passage** bustle   **100 vulgar** public   **101 And . . . rout** and it will be presumed true by everyone   **102 yet . . . estimation** still unsullied reputation   **105 slander . . . succession** i.e., one slander grows out of another; or, slander passes from one generation to the next   **108 in . . . mirth** despite my not feeling mirthful

There will we dine. This woman that I mean,
My wife—but, I protest, without desert—   112
Hath oftentimes upbraided me withal.
To her will we to dinner. [*To Angelo.*] Get you home
And fetch the chain; by this I know 'tis made.   115
Bring it, I pray you, to the Porpentine,   116
For there's the house. That chain will I bestow—
Be it for nothing but to spite my wife—
Upon mine hostess there. Good sir, make haste.
Since mine own doors refuse to entertain me,
I'll knock elsewhere, to see if they'll disdain me.

ANGELO
I'll meet you at that place some hour hence.

E. ANTIPHOLUS
Do so. This jest shall cost me some expense.   *Exeunt.*

❖

3.2   *Enter Luciana with Antipholus of Syracuse.*

LUCIANA
And may it be that you have quite forgot   1
  A husband's office? Shall, Antipholus,   2
Even in the spring of love, thy love springs rot?   3
  Shall love, in building, grow so ruinous?
If you did wed my sister for her wealth,
  Then for her wealth's sake use her with more
    kindness;
Or if you like elsewhere, do it by stealth;
  Muffle your false love with some show of blindness.   8
Let not my sister read it in your eye;
  Be not thy tongue thy own shame's orator;
Look sweet, speak fair, become disloyalty;   11
  Apparel vice like virtue's harbinger.   12
Bear a fair presence, though your heart be tainted;

112 desert my deserving it   **115 this** this time   **116 Porpentine** Porcupine. (Here, the name of an inn.)

3.2. Location: Antipholus of Ephesus' house, changing to the street by the time of Angelo's entrance at l. 163.
1 may can   **2 office** duty   **3 love springs** tender shoots of love   **8 Muffle** hide.   **show of blindness** deceptive appearance   **11 fair** courteously.   **become disloyalty** carry off your infidelity gracefully   **12 harbinger** messenger

Teach sin the carriage of a holy saint;   14
Be secret-false. What need she be acquainted?
   What simple thief brags of his own attaint?   16
'Tis double wrong to truant with your bed   17
   And let her read it in thy looks at board;   18
Shame hath a bastard fame, well managèd;   19
   Ill deeds is doubled with an evil word.
Alas, poor women! Make us but believe,
   Being compact of credit, that you love us;   22
Though others have the arm, show us the sleeve;
   We in your motion turn, and you may move us.   24
Then, gentle brother, get you in again.
   Comfort my sister, cheer her, call her wife.
'Tis holy sport to be a little vain,   27
   When the sweet breath of flattery conquers strife.

S. ANTIPHOLUS
Sweet mistress—what your name is else, I know not,   29
   Nor by what wonder you do hit of mine—   30
Less in your knowledge and your grace you show not
   Than our earth's wonder, more than earth divine.   32
Teach me, dear creature, how to think and speak;
   Lay open to my earthy-gross conceit,   34
Smothered in errors, feeble, shallow, weak,
   The folded meaning of your words' deceit.   36
Against my soul's pure truth why labor you   37
   To make it wander in an unknown field?
Are you a god? Would you create me new?
   Transform me, then, and to your power I'll yield.
But if that I am I, then well I know
   Your weeping sister is no wife of mine,
Nor to her bed no homage do I owe.
   Far more, far more to you do I decline.   44

---

14 carriage demeanor   **16 simple** simple-minded.   **attaint** stain, dishonor; or possibly, conviction of crime   **17 truant with** be faithless to   **18 board** table   **19 bastard fame** sham reputation   **22 Being ... credit** i.e., since we are made so that we are quick to believe   **24 We ... turn** we are governed by your motion, orbit (referring to the motion of the heavenly spheres)   **27 vain** false   **29 what ... else** what other name you may have   **30 wonder** miracle.   **hit of** hit upon, guess   **32 earth's wonder** (Perhaps a reference to Queen Elizabeth.)   **34 earthy-gross conceit** understanding gross as earth   **36 folded** concealed   **37 Against ... you** why are you working to oppose my soul's knowledge of the simple truth   **44 decline** incline

O, train me not, sweet mermaid, with thy note,   45
    To drown me in thy sister's flood of tears!
Sing, siren, for thyself and I will dote.
    Spread o'er the silver waves thy golden hairs,
And as a bed I'll take them and there lie   49
    And in that glorious supposition think
He gains by death that hath such means to die.
    Let Love, being light, be drownèd if she sink!   52

LUCIANA
What, are you mad, that you do reason so?   53

S. ANTIPHOLUS
Not mad, but mated—how, I do not know.   54

LUCIANA
It is a fault that springeth from your eye.

S. ANTIPHOLUS
For gazing on your beams, fair sun, being by.   56

LUCIANA
Gaze where you should, and that will clear your sight.

S. ANTIPHOLUS
As good to wink, sweet love, as look on night.   58

LUCIANA
Why call you me "love"? Call my sister so.

S. ANTIPHOLUS
Thy sister's sister.

LUCIANA   That's my sister.

S. ANTIPHOLUS   No,
It is thyself, mine own self's better part,
Mine eye's clear eye, my dear heart's dearer heart,
My food, my fortune, and my sweet hope's aim,
My sole earth's heaven, and my heaven's claim.   64

LUCIANA
All this my sister is, or else should be.

S. ANTIPHOLUS
Call thyself sister, sweet, for I am thee.

45 train entice. **mermaid** siren (in classical myth, one of a group of
nymphs who lured sailors to destruction with their sweet singing).
note song **49 take** use **52 light** buoyant (with a pun on the sense of
"wanton," perhaps carrying forward a common sexual pun in which *to
die*, l. 51, is to have sexual climax. The idea in l. 52 is that Love cannot
possibly sink.) **53 reason** talk, argue **54 mated** amazed, confounded
(with quibble on the sense of "matched with a wife") **56 by** near
58 wink close the eyes **64 My sole . . . claim** my sole heaven on earth
and my claim on heaven hereafter

Thee will I love and with thee lead my life;
Thou hast no husband yet, nor I no wife.
Give me thy hand.

LUCIANA O, soft, sir! Hold you still.
I'll fetch my sister, to get her good will. *Exit.*

Enter Dromio of Syracuse, [running].

S. ANTIPHOLUS Why, how now, Dromio, where runn'st
thou so fast?

S. DROMIO Do you know me, sir? Am I Dromio? Am I
your man? Am I myself?

S. ANTIPHOLUS Thou art Dromio, thou art my man,
thou art thyself.

S. DROMIO I am an ass, I am a woman's man, and be- 77
sides myself. 78

S. ANTIPHOLUS What woman's man? And how besides 79
thyself?

S. DROMIO Marry, sir, besides myself, I am due to a
woman: one that claims me, one that haunts me, one
that will have me.

S. ANTIPHOLUS What claim lays she to thee?

S. DROMIO Marry, sir, such claim as you would lay to
your horse; and she would have me as a beast—not 86
that, I being a beast, she would have me, but that she,
being a very beastly creature, lays claim to me.

S. ANTIPHOLUS What is she?

S. DROMIO A very reverend body; ay, such a one as a
man may not speak of without he say "Sir-reverence." 91
I have but lean luck in the match, and yet is she a 92
wondrous fat marriage.

S. ANTIPHOLUS How dost thou mean, a fat marriage?

S. DROMIO Marry, sir, she's the kitchen wench, and all
grease, and I know not what use to put her to but to 96
make a lamp of her and run from her by her own light.
I warrant, her rags and the tallow in them will burn a

77–78 **besides myself** also myself (with a pun on the sense of "out of my
mind") 79 **besides** (a further quibble: "in addition to") 86 **a beast** (with a
pun on *abased*, reflecting Elizabethan pronunciation of *beast* as "baste")
91 **without** unless. **"Sir-reverence"** i.e., save your reverence, an expression
used in apology for the remark that follows it 92 **lean** poor, meager
96 **grease** (with a pun on *grace*, reflecting Elizabethan pronunciation)

Poland winter. If she lives till doomsday, she'll burn a 99
week longer than the whole world.

S. ANTIPHOLUS   What complexion is she of?

S. DROMIO   Swart, like my shoe, but her face nothing 102
like so clean kept; for why? She sweats; a man may go
over shoes in the grime of it.   104

S. ANTIPHOLUS   That's a fault that water will mend.

S. DROMIO   No, sir, 'tis in grain. Noah's flood could not 106
do it.

S. ANTIPHOLUS   What's her name?

S. DROMIO   Nell, sir; but her name and three quarters— 109
that's an ell and three quarters—will not measure her 110
from hip to hip.

S. ANTIPHOLUS   Then she bears some breadth?

S. DROMIO   No longer from head to foot than from hip
to hip; she is spherical, like a globe. I could find out
countries in her.

S. ANTIPHOLUS   In what part of her body stands Ireland?

S. DROMIO   Marry, sir, in her buttocks. I found it out by
the bogs.

S. ANTIPHOLUS   Where Scotland?

S. DROMIO   I found it by the barrenness, hard in the 120
palm of the hand.

S. ANTIPHOLUS   Where France?

S. DROMIO   In her forehead, armed and reverted, making 123
war against her heir.   124

S. ANTIPHOLUS   Where England?

S. DROMIO   I looked for the chalky cliffs, but I could find 126
no whiteness in them. But I guess it stood in her chin, 127
by the salt rheum that ran between France and it.   128

99 Poland winter i.e., a long, cold winter   **102 Swart** swarthy, dark
104 over shoes ankle-deep. (Her sweat makes mud of her face's grime,
so deep that a man would be ankle deep in it.)   **106 in grain** indelible,
fast dyed   **109 Nell** (The maidservant appearing in 3.1 is named Luce;
usually the two are assumed to be one person.)   **110 an ell** forty-five
inches (with a pun on "a Nell")   **120 barrenness** calloused hardness and
dryness (perhaps with a pun on *barren ness,* a barren promontory)
123 reverted in rebellion. (See Introduction for explanation of reference
to the French war.)   **124 heir** (with a pun on *hair* and a joke about
syphilis as causing baldness)   **126 chalky cliffs** i.e., her teeth. (In his
geographic metaphor, S. Dromio identifies white teeth with the
cliffs of Dover.)   **127 them** i.e., her teeth   **128 salt rheum** nasal discharge. (Here S. Dromio jokingly makes a comparison to the English
Channel.)

S. ANTIPHOLUS   Where Spain?

S. DROMIO   Faith, I saw it not, but I felt it hot in her
breath.

S. ANTIPHOLUS   Where America, the Indies?

S. DROMIO   O, sir, upon her nose, all o'er embellished
with rubies, carbuncles, sapphires, declining their rich   134
aspect to the hot breath of Spain, who sent whole ar-   135
madoes of carracks to be ballast at her nose.   136

S. ANTIPHOLUS   Where stood Belgia, the Netherlands?

S. DROMIO   O, sir, I did not look so low. To conclude,   138
this drudge or diviner laid claim to me, called me   139
Dromio, swore I was assured to her, told me what   140
privy marks I had about me, as the mark of my shoul-   141
der, the mole in my neck, the great wart on my left
arm, that I amazed ran from her as a witch.

And, I think, if my breast had not been made of faith and
    my heart of steel,

She had transformed me to a curtal dog and made me
    turn i' the wheel.   145

S. ANTIPHOLUS

Go hie thee presently; post to the road.   146

An if the wind blow any way from shore,   147

I will not harbor in this town tonight.

If any bark put forth, come to the mart,   149

Where I will walk till thou return to me.

If everyone knows us and we know none,

'Tis time, I think, to trudge, pack, and be gone.   152

S. DROMIO

As from a bear a man would run for life,

So fly I from her that would be my wife.   *Exit.*

S. ANTIPHOLUS

There's none but witches do inhabit here,

And therefore 'tis high time that I were hence.

---

134 carbuncles (1) precious stones (2) inflammations of the skin resembling large boils   **134–135 declining . . . aspect** looking or bending
downward   **135–136 armadoes of carracks** fleets of galleons
136 ballast ballasted, loaded   **138 so low** (A bawdy joke. The Netherlands were known as the Low Countries.)   **139 diviner** sorceress
140 assured affianced   **141 privy** secret, personal   **145 curtal dog** dog
with a docked tail (and hence not used in hunting).   **turn i' the wheel**
run in a wheel to turn the spit   **146 hie** hasten.   **presently** at once.
post hasten.   **road** harbor, roadstead   **147 An if** if   **149 bark** ship
152 pack depart

She that doth call me husband, even my soul
Doth for a wife abhor. But her fair sister,
Possessed with such a gentle sovereign grace,   159
Of such enchanting presence and discourse,
Hath almost made me traitor to myself.
But, lest myself be guilty to self-wrong,   162
I'll stop mine ears against the mermaid's song.

 Enter Angelo with the chain.

ANGELO
Master Antipholus—
S. ANTIPHOLUS   Ay, that's my name.
ANGELO
I know it well, sir. Lo, here's the chain.
I thought to have ta'en you at the Porpentine;   166
The chain unfinished made me stay thus long.
        [*He presents the chain.*]
S. ANTIPHOLUS
What is your will that I shall do with this?
ANGELO
What please yourself, sir. I have made it for you.
S. ANTIPHOLUS
Made it for me, sir? I bespoke it not.   170
ANGELO
Not once, nor twice, but twenty times you have.
Go home with it and please your wife withal,
And soon at suppertime I'll visit you
And then receive my money for the chain.
S. ANTIPHOLUS
I pray you, sir, receive the money now,
For fear you ne'er see chain nor money more.
ANGELO
You are a merry man, sir. Fare you well. *Exit.*
S. ANTIPHOLUS
What I should think of this, I cannot tell.
But this I think: there's no man is so vain   179
That would refuse so fair an offered chain.
I see a man here needs not live by shifts,   181

159 Possessed with having possession of **162 to** of **166 ta'en** over-
taken, met up with **170 bespoke** requested **179 vain** foolish
181 shifts stratagems, tricks

When in the streets he meets such golden gifts.
I'll to the mart and there for Dromio stay;
If any ship put out, then straight away.   *Exit.* 184

---

184 **straight** at once

4.1   *Enter [Second] Merchant, [Angelo the]*
goldsmith, and an Officer.

SECOND MERCHANT
You know since Pentecost the sum is due,   1
And since I have not much importuned you,   2
Nor now I had not, but that I am bound
To Persia and want guilders for my voyage.   4
Therefore make present satisfaction,   5
Or I'll attach you by this officer.   6

ANGELO
Even just the sum that I do owe to you   7
Is growing to me by Antipholus,   8
And in the instant that I met with you
He had of me a chain. At five o'clock
I shall receive the money for the same.
Pleaseth you walk with me down to his house,   12
I will discharge my bond and thank you too.

> *Enter Antipholus [and] Dromio of Ephesus from*
> *the Courtesan's.*

OFFICER
That labor may you save. See where he comes.
E. ANTIPHOLUS [*To Dromio of Ephesus*]
While I go to the goldsmith's house, go thou
And buy a rope's end; that will I bestow   16
Among my wife and her confederates
For locking me out of my doors by day.
But, soft! I see the goldsmith. Get thee gone.   19
Buy thou a rope and bring it home to me.

E. DROMIO
I buy a thousand pound a year! I buy a rope!   21
                                    Exit Dromio.

4.1. Location: The street.
1 Pentecost the commemoration of the descent of the Holy Ghost upon
the Apostles, celebrated on the seventh Sunday after Easter   **2 since** since
then.   **importuned** harassed with demands, bothered   **4 want** lack
5 present satisfaction immediate payment   **6 attach** arrest, seize   **7 Even
just** precisely   **8 growing** due, accruing   **12 Pleaseth** may it please
16 bestow employ   **19 soft** i.e., wait a minute   **21 I . . . rope** (An obscure
line. Dromio may mean that in buying a rope as he is bidden, he is pur-
chasing for himself a thousand poundings or beatings a year.)

E. ANTIPHOLUS [*To Angelo*]
A man is well holp up that trusts to you. 22
I promisèd your presence and the chain, 23
But neither chain nor goldsmith came to me.
Belike you thought our love would last too long 25
If it were chained together, and therefore came not.
ANGELO [*Showing a paper*]
Saving your merry humor, here's the note 27
How much your chain weighs to the utmost carat,
The fineness of the gold and chargeful fashion, 29
Which doth amount to three odd ducats more 30
Than I stand debted to this gentleman.
I pray you, see him presently discharged,
For he is bound to sea and stays but for it.
E. ANTIPHOLUS
I am not furnished with the present money; 34
Besides, I have some business in the town.
Good signor, take the stranger to my house,
And with you take the chain, and bid my wife
Disburse the sum on the receipt thereof.
Perchance I will be there as soon as you.
ANGELO
Then you will bring the chain to her yourself?
E. ANTIPHOLUS
No, bear it with you, lest I come not time enough. 41
ANGELO
Well, sir, I will. Have you the chain about you?
E. ANTIPHOLUS
An if I have not, sir, I hope you have,
Or else you may return without your money.
ANGELO
Nay, come, I pray you, sir, give me the chain.
Both wind and tide stays for this gentleman,
And I, too blame, have held him here too long. 47
E. ANTIPHOLUS
Good Lord! You use this dalliance to excuse 48
Your breach of promise to the Porpentine.

22 holp helped   **23 promisèd** was promised   **25 Belike** perhaps
27 Saving with respect for   **29 chargeful fashion** expensive workmanship   **30 ducats** gold coins (of several European countries)   **34 present**
available   **41 time enough** in time   **47 too blame** too blameworthy
48 dalliance idle delay

I should have chid you for not bringing it,   50
But, like a shrew, you first begin to brawl.

SECOND MERCHANT [*To Angelo*]
The hour steals on. I pray you, sir, dispatch.

ANGELO
You hear how he importunes me. The chain!   53

E. ANTIPHOLUS
Why, give it to my wife and fetch your money.

ANGELO
Come, come, you know I gave it you even now.
Either send the chain or send me by some token.   56

E. ANTIPHOLUS
Fie, now you run this humor out of breath.   57
Come, where's the chain? I pray you, let me see it.

SECOND MERCHANT
My business cannot brook this dalliance.   59
Good sir, say whe'er you'll answer me or no.   60
If not, I'll leave him to the officer.

E. ANTIPHOLUS
I answer you? What should I answer you?

ANGELO
The money that you owe me for the chain.

E. ANTIPHOLUS
I owe you none till I receive the chain.

ANGELO
You know I gave it you half an hour since.

E. ANTIPHOLUS
You gave me none. You wrong me much to say so.

ANGELO
You wrong me more, sir, in denying it.
Consider how it stands upon my credit.   68

SECOND MERCHANT
Well, officer, arrest him at my suit.   69

OFFICER
I do, and charge you in the Duke's name to obey me.

ANGELO
This touches me in reputation.   71

---

50 chid chided   **53 importunes** harasses   **56 send me . . . token** send me
with some object of yours authorizing me to receive payment   **57 run . . .**
breath i.e., carry the joke too far   **59 brook** endure   **60 whe'er** whether.
answer pay   **68 how . . . credit** how it affects my reputation for honesty
69 at my suit on my petition   **71 touches** injures, affects

Either consent to pay this sum for me,
Or I attach you by this officer.

E. ANTIPHOLUS
Consent to pay thee that I never had?
Arrest me, foolish fellow, if thou dar'st.

ANGELO
Here is thy fee. Arrest him, officer. [*He gives money.*]
I would not spare my brother in this case
If he should scorn me so apparently.   78

OFFICER
I do arrest you, sir. You hear the suit.

E. ANTIPHOLUS
I do obey thee till I give thee bail.
But, sirrah, you shall buy this sport as dear
As all the metal in your shop will answer.

ANGELO
Sir, sir, I shall have law in Ephesus,
To your notorious shame, I doubt it not.

Enter Dromio of Syracuse, from the bay.

S. DROMIO
Master, there's a bark of Epidamium
That stays but till her owner comes aboard,
And then she bears away. Our freightage, sir,
I have conveyed aboard, and I have bought
The oil, the balsamum, and aqua vitae.   89
The ship is in her trim; the merry wind   90
Blows fair from land; they stay for naught at all
But for their owner, master, and yourself.

E. ANTIPHOLUS
How now? A madman? Why, thou peevish sheep,   93
What ship of Epidamium stays for me?

S. DROMIO
A ship you sent me to, to hire waftage.   95

E. ANTIPHOLUS
Thou drunken slave, I sent thee for a rope
And told thee to what purpose and what end.

---

78 apparently openly   **89 balsamum** balm.   **aqua vitae** strong liquor
90 in her trim rigged and ready to sail   **93 peevish** silly.   **sheep** (with
play on *ship* in next line)   **95 waftage** passage

S. DROMIO
  You sent me for a rope's end as soon.   98
  You sent me to the bay, sir, for a bark.

E. ANTIPHOLUS
  I will debate this matter at more leisure
  And teach your ears to list me with more heed.   101
  To Adriana, villain, hie thee straight. [*He gives a key.*]
  Give her this key, and tell her, in the desk
  That's covered o'er with Turkish tapestry
  There is a purse of ducats; let her send it.
  Tell her I am arrested in the street,
  And that shall bail me. Hie thee, slave, begone!—
  On, officer, to prison till it come.
                Exeunt [all but Dromio of Syracuse].

S. DROMIO
  To Adriana! That is where we dined,
  Where Dowsabel did claim me for her husband.   110
  She is too big, I hope, for me to compass.   111
  Thither I must, although against my will,
  For servants must their masters' minds fulfill.   *Exit.*

❖

4.2   *Enter Adriana and Luciana.*

ADRIANA
  Ah, Luciana, did he tempt thee so?
    Mightst thou perceive austerely in his eye   2
  That he did plead in earnest, yea or no?
    Looked he or red or pale, or sad or merrily?   4
  What observation mad'st thou in this case
  Of his heart's meteors tilting in his face?   6

LUCIANA
  First he denied you had in him no right.   7

---

98 a rope's end i.e., a whipping, or perhaps a hangman's noose **101 list**
listen to **110 Dowsabel** (Used ironically for Nell or Luce; derived from
the French *douce et belle*, gentle and beautiful.) **111 compass** achieve
(with added meaning of "put my arms around")

4.2. Location: The house of Antipholus of Ephesus.
2 austerely objectively, strictly **4 or red** either red. **or sad** either
sad **6 meteors tilting** i.e., passions warring. (The next line begins a passage
of stichomythia, dialogue in which each speech consists of a single line,
much used in classical drama.) **7 no** i.e., any

ADRIANA
He meant he did me none; the more my spite.   8
LUCIANA
Then swore he that he was a stranger here.
ADRIANA
And true he swore, though yet forsworn he were.   10
LUCIANA
Then pleaded I for you.
ADRIANA   And what said he?
LUCIANA
That love I begged for you he begged of me.
ADRIANA
With what persuasion did he tempt thy love?
LUCIANA
With words that in an honest suit might move.   14
First he did praise my beauty, then my speech.
ADRIANA
Didst speak him fair?
LUCIANA   Have patience, I beseech.   16
ADRIANA
I cannot, nor I will not, hold me still;
My tongue, though not my heart, shall have his will.   18
He is deformèd, crooked, old, and sere,   19
Ill faced, worse bodied, shapeless everywhere;   20
Vicious, ungentle, foolish, blunt, unkind,
Stigmatical in making, worse in mind.   22
LUCIANA
Who would be jealous then of such a one?
No evil lost is wailed when it is gone.
ADRIANA
Ah, but I think him better than I say,
And yet would herein others' eyes were worse.   26
Far from her nest the lapwing cries away;   27
My heart prays for him, though my tongue do curse.

---

8 spite vexation, grief   **10 true . . . were** i.e., though he is not a stranger,
soon he will be one   **14 honest** honorable   **16 speak him fair** speak
engagingly to him   **18 his** its   **19 sere** withered   **20 shapeless** misshapen   **22 Stigmatical in making** deformed in body   **26 And . . . worse**
i.e., and yet I wish other women found him in a less favorable light
27 lapwing a bird that flies away from its nest to divert attention from
its young

Enter Dromio of Syracuse [with the key].

S. DROMIO
  Here, go—the desk, the purse! Sweet, now, make haste. 29
LUCIANA
  How hast thou lost thy breath?
S. DROMIO   By running fast.
ADRIANA
  Where is thy master, Dromio? Is he well?
S. DROMIO
  No, he's in Tartar limbo, worse than hell.   32
  A devil in an everlasting garment hath him,   33
  One whose hard heart is buttoned up with steel;
  A fiend, a fairy, pitiless and rough;
  A wolf, nay, worse, a fellow all in buff;
  A back friend, a shoulder clapper, one that
    countermands   37
  The passages of alleys, creeks, and narrow lands;   38
  A hound that runs counter and yet draws dry-foot well;   39
  One that before the judgment carries poor souls to hell.   40
ADRIANA   Why, man, what is the matter?
S. DROMIO
  I do not know the matter. He is 'rested on the case.   42
ADRIANA
  What, is he arrested? Tell me at whose suit.
S. DROMIO
  I know not at whose suit he is arrested well;
  But he's in a suit of buff which 'rested him, that can I
    tell.

29 Sweet (An inoffensive term of endearment; some editors emend to
Sweat.)   **32 Tartar limbo** Tartarus or pagan hell, worse than Christian
hell   **33 everlasting garment** i.e., buff leather attire of the police officer,
everlasting both because of its durability and because of the joke about
perpetual durance in limbo or jail. (*Everlasting* is itself the name of a
coarse woolen fabric sometimes used for the uniforms of petty officers
of justice.)   **37 A back friend** i.e., a false friend; here the police officer
who comes up behind and claps his victim on the back to signify arrest.   **countermands** prohibits   **38 passages** movement of people.   **of**
in.   **creeks** narrow or winding passages   **39 runs counter** follows a
trail in the direction opposite to that which the game has taken (with a
quibble on *counter*, a prison).   **draws dry-foot** follows game by mere
scent of the foot   **40 judgment** legal decision (with a pun on "Judgment
Day," continuing the joke about jail as Tartar limbo)   **42 'rested on the
case** arrested in a lawsuit (with a pun on *case* meaning "the container"
as distinguished from the *matter* contained in it. Dromio means that his
master has been arrested in his suit of clothes.)

Will you send him, mistress, redemption—the money in
  his desk?

ADRIANA

Go fetch it, sister. (*Exit Luciana.*) This I wonder at,
That he, unknown to me, should be in debt.
Tell me, was he arrested on a band?   49

S. DROMIO

Not on a band, but on a stronger thing:
A chain, a chain! Do you not hear it ring?

ADRIANA   What, the chain?

S. DROMIO

No, no, the bell. 'Tis time that I were gone.
It was two ere I left him, and now the clock strikes one.   54

ADRIANA

The hours come back! That did I never hear.

S. DROMIO

O, yes, if any hour meet a sergeant, 'a turns back for very
  fear.   56

ADRIANA

As if Time were in debt! How fondly dost thou reason!   57

S. DROMIO

Time is a very bankrupt and owes more than he's worth
  to season.   58
Nay, he's a thief too. Have you not heard men say
That Time comes stealing on by night and day?
If 'a be in debt and theft, and a sergeant in the way,   61
Hath he not reason to turn back an hour in a day?

    Enter Luciana [with the purse].

ADRIANA

Go, Dromio, there's the money. Bear it straight,   63
              [*Giving the purse*]
And bring thy master home immediately.
Come, sister. I am pressed down with conceit—   65
Conceit, my comfort and my injury.   *Exeunt.*

49 band bond. (But Dromio puns on the sense "neckband" in the next line.)
54 one (*One* and *on* were pronounced very much alike; the word here rhymes
with *gone*.)   **56 hour** (with a pun on *whore*, similarly pronounced, or perhaps
too on *ower*, one who owes).   **sergeant** arresting officer.   **'a** it, she, he
57 fondly foolishly   **58 to season** at any given time or opportunity   **61 theft**
i.e., a thief   **63 straight** straight away, immediately   **65 conceit** thought

4.3   *Enter Antipholus of Syracuse [wearing the chain].*

S. ANTIPHOLUS
There's not a man I meet but doth salute me
As if I were their well-acquainted friend,
And everyone doth call me by my name.
Some tender money to me; some invite me;   4
Some other give me thanks for kindnesses;
Some offer me commodities to buy.
Even now a tailor called me in his shop
And showed me silks that he had bought for me
And therewithal took measure of my body.
Sure, these are but imaginary wiles,   10
And Lapland sorcerers inhabit here.   11

Enter Dromio of Syracuse [with the purse].

S. DROMIO   Master, here's the gold you sent me for.
What, have you got the picture of old Adam new-ap-   13
pareled?   14

S. ANTIPHOLUS
What gold is this? What Adam dost thou mean?

S. DROMIO   Not that Adam that kept the Paradise, but
that Adam that keeps the prison; he that goes in the
calf's skin that was killed for the Prodigal; he that came   18
behind you, sir, like an evil angel, and bid you forsake
your liberty.

S. ANTIPHOLUS   I understand thee not.

S. DROMIO   No? Why, 'tis a plain case: he that went, like
a bass viol, in a case of leather; the man, sir, that,
when gentlemen are tired, gives them a sob and 'rests   24
them; he, sir, that takes pity on decayed men and gives   25

4.3. Location: The street.
4 tender offer   **10 imaginary wiles** tricks of the imagination   **11 Lapland sorcerers** (Lapland was said to surpass all nations in the practice of witchcraft and sorcery.)   **13–14 have . . . appareled** (Dromio, noting the absence of the arresting officer, asks if his master has obtained for that officer a new apparel or "suit"—with a pun on "lawsuit." The officer is likened to old Adam in that his buff leather jerkin resembles Adam's garments of beasts' skins; see Genesis 3:21.)   **18 calf's . . . Prodigal** (An allusion to the fatted calf killed for the Prodigal Son's return; see Luke 15:23.)   **24 sob** i.e., breathing space (followed by a pun on *'rests*, meaning "arrests" and "gives a rest to")   **25 decayed** financially ruined

them suits of durance; he that sets up his rest to do 26
more exploits with his mace than a morris-pike.   27

S. ANTIPHOLUS   What, thou mean'st an officer?

S. DROMIO   Ay, sir, the sergeant of the band; he that 29
brings any man to answer it that breaks his band; one 30
that thinks a man always going to bed, and says, "God
give you good rest!"   32

S. ANTIPHOLUS   Well, sir, there rest in your foolery. Is
there any ships puts forth tonight? May we be gone?

S. DROMIO   Why, sir, I brought you word an hour since
that the bark *Expedition* put forth tonight, and then   36
were you hindered by the sergeant to tarry for the hoy   37
Delay. Here are the angels that you sent for to de-   38
liver you.   [*He gives the purse.*]

S. ANTIPHOLUS
The fellow is distract, and so am I,   40
And here we wander in illusions.
Some blessèd power deliver us from hence!

        Enter a Courtesan.

COURTESAN
Well met, well met, Master Antipholus.
I see, sir, you have found the goldsmith now.
Is that the chain you promised me today?

S. ANTIPHOLUS
Satan, avoid! I charge thee, tempt me not.   46

S. DROMIO   Master, is this Mistress Satan?

S. ANTIPHOLUS   It is the devil.

S. DROMIO   Nay, she is worse, she is the devil's dam,   49
and here she comes in the habit of a light wench; and   50
thereof comes that the wenches say, "God damn me,"   51
that's as much to say, "God make me a light wench."

26 durance a kind of long-wearing cloth like buff (with a pun on "imprisonment").   **sets . . . rest** stakes his all (with a continuing pun on
'rest; the metaphor of staking all one's venture is from the game of
primero)   **27 mace** staff of office carried by a constable.   **morris-pike** a
weapon supposedly of Moorish origin   **29 band** troop   **30 band**
bond   **32 rest** (continuing the pun on *arrest*)   **36 bark** seagoing vessel
37 hoy a small coasting vessel   **38 angels** gold coins worth about 10
shillings   **40 distract** deranged, distracted   **46 avoid** begone. (See Matthew 4:10.)   **49 dam** mother   **50 habit** demeanor, manner; also, dress.
light wanton   **51 damn me** i.e., dam me, make me a mother

It is written, they appear to men like angels of light; 53
light is an effect of fire, and fire will burn; ergo, light 54
wenches will burn. Come not near her. 55

COURTESAN
Your man and you are marvelous merry, sir.
Will you go with me? We'll mend our dinner here. 57

S. DROMIO   Master, if you do, expect spoon meat, or 58
bespeak a long spoon. 59

S. ANTIPHOLUS   Why, Dromio?

S. DROMIO   Marry, he must have a long spoon that must 61
eat with the devil. 62

S. ANTIPHOLUS [*To the Courtesan*]
Avoid then, fiend! What tell'st thou me of supping? 63
Thou art, as you are all, a sorceress.
I conjure thee to leave me and be gone.

COURTESAN
Give me the ring of mine you had at dinner
Or, for my diamond, the chain you promised,
And I'll be gone, sir, and not trouble you.

S. DROMIO
Some devils ask but the parings of one's nail,
A rush, a hair, a drop of blood, a pin,
A nut, a cherrystone;
But she, more covetous, would have a chain.
Master, be wise; an if you give it her, 73
The devil will shake her chain and fright us with it.

COURTESAN
I pray you, sir, my ring, or else the chain!
I hope you do not mean to cheat me so?

S. ANTIPHOLUS
Avaunt, thou witch! Come, Dromio, let us go.

S. DROMIO
"Fly pride," says the peacock. Mistress, that you know. 78
    Exeunt [Antipholus and Dromio of Syracuse].

---

53 angels of light (See 2 Corinthians 11:14, where Satan is referred to as
transformed into an angel of light.) **54 ergo** therefore **55 will burn**
i.e., will transmit venereal disease **57 mend** supplement, complete
58 spoon meat food for infants, hence delicacies **59 bespeak** order
61–62 he ... devil (A proverbial idea.) **63 What** why **73 an if** if
78 Fly ... peacock (i.e., the accusation of dishonesty coming from this
woman, whom Dromio takes to be dishonest, seems to him as out of
place as a warning against pride given by a peacock)

COURTESAN
> Now, out of doubt Antipholus is mad,   79
> Else would he never so demean himself.   80
> A ring he hath of mine worth forty ducats,
> And for the same he promised me a chain;
> Both one and other he denies me now.
> The reason that I gather he is mad,
> Besides this present instance of his rage,
> Is a mad tale he told today at dinner
> Of his own doors being shut against his entrance.
> Belike his wife, acquainted with his fits,
> On purpose shut the doors against his way.
> My way is now to hie home to his house   90
> And tell his wife that, being lunatic,
> He rushed into my house and took perforce   92
> My ring away. This course I fittest choose,   93
> For forty ducats is too much to lose.   [*Exit.*]

❖

4.4   *Enter Antipholus of Ephesus with a Jailer [or Officer].*

E. ANTIPHOLUS
> Fear me not, man, I will not break away.
> I'll give thee, ere I leave thee, so much money,
> To warrant thee, as I am 'rested for.   3
> My wife is in a wayward mood today   4
> And will not lightly trust the messenger.   5
> That I should be attached in Ephesus,   6
> I tell you, 'twill sound harshly in her ears.

> *Enter Dromio of Ephesus with a rope's end.*

> Here comes my man; I think he brings the money.—
> How now, sir? Have you that I sent you for?

E. DROMIO [*Giving the rope*]
> Here's that, I warrant you, will pay them all.

---

79 out of doubt no doubt   **80 demean** conduct   **90 My way** my best course   **92 perforce** forcibly   **93 fittest** as most appropriate

4.4. Location: The street.
3 warrant give security to   **4 wayward** perverse, ill-tempered   **5 lightly** easily   **6 attached** arrested

E. ANTIPHOLUS   But where's the money?

E. DROMIO
Why, sir, I gave the money for the rope.

E. ANTIPHOLUS
Five hundred ducats, villain, for a rope?

E. DROMIO
I'll serve you, sir, five hundred at the rate.   14

E. ANTIPHOLUS
To what end did I bid thee hie thee home?

E. DROMIO   To a rope's end, sir; and to that end am I
returned.

E. ANTIPHOLUS
And to that end, sir, I will welcome you.
        [*He starts to beat Dromio of Ephesus.*]

OFFICER   Good sir, be patient.

E. DROMIO   Nay, 'tis for me to be patient. I am in adversity.

OFFICER   Good now, hold thy tongue.   22

E. DROMIO   Nay, rather persuade him to hold his hands.

E. ANTIPHOLUS   Thou whoreson, senseless villain!

E. DROMIO   I would I were senseless, sir, that I might
not feel your blows.

E. ANTIPHOLUS   Thou art sensible in nothing but blows, 27
and so is an ass.

E. DROMIO   I am an ass, indeed; you may prove it by
my long ears. I have served him from the hour of my 30
nativity to this instant and have nothing at his hands
for my service but blows. When I am cold, he heats
me with beating; when I am warm, he cools me with
beating. I am waked with it when I sleep, raised with
it when I sit, driven out of doors with it when I go
from home, welcomed home with it when I return.
Nay, I bear it on my shoulders, as a beggar wont her 37
brat; and I think when he hath lamed me, I shall beg
with it from door to door.

        Enter Adriana, Luciana, Courtesan, and a
        schoolmaster called Pinch.

14 at the rate for that amount   **22 Good now** pray you   **27 sensible in**
sensitive to; also, made sensible by   **30 ears** (with a pun on *years;*
Dromio says he is an ass for having served his master so long)   **37 wont**
is accustomed to (bear)

E. ANTIPHOLUS
Come, go along; my wife is coming yonder.

E. DROMIO Mistress, *respice finem,* respect your end; 41
or rather, to prophesy like the parrot, "beware the
rope's end."

E. ANTIPHOLUS Wilt thou still talk?   *Beats Dromio.*

COURTESAN [*To Adriana*]
How say you now? Is not your husband mad?

ADRIANA
His incivility confirms no less.—
Good Doctor Pinch, you are a conjurer;   47
Establish him in his true sense again,   48
And I will please you what you will demand.   49

LUCIANA
Alas, how fiery and how sharp he looks!   50

COURTESAN
Mark how he trembles in his ecstasy!   51

PINCH
Give me your hand, and let me feel your pulse.

E. ANTIPHOLUS
There is my hand, and let it feel your ear.
                              [*Striking him.*]

PINCH
I charge thee, Satan, housed within this man,
To yield possession to my holy prayers
And to thy state of darkness hie thee straight!
I conjure thee by all the saints in heaven!

E. ANTIPHOLUS
Peace, doting wizard, peace! I am not mad.

ADRIANA
O, that thou wert not, poor distressèd soul!

E. ANTIPHOLUS
You minion, you, are these your customers?   60
Did this companion with the saffron face   61
Revel and feast it at my house today,

---

41 respice finem consider your end. (A pious sentiment on the brevity of
life and the approach of death; with a play on *respice funem,* "consider
the hangman's rope." A parrot might be taught to say *"respice finem,"*
or perhaps "rope.")   **47 conjurer** (Being able to speak Latin, Pinch
could conjure spirits.)   **48 true sense** right mind   **49 please** pay
50 sharp angry   **51 ecstasy** fit, frenzy   **60 minion** hussy, i.e., Adriana
61 companion fellow, i.e., Pinch.   **saffron** yellow

Whilst upon me the guilty doors were shut
And I denied to enter in my house?

ADRIANA
O husband, God doth know you dined at home,
Where would you had remained until this time,
Free from these slanders and this open shame!

E. ANTIPHOLUS
Dined at home? [*To E. Dromio.*] Thou villain, what
  sayest thou?

E. DROMIO
Sir, sooth to say, you did not dine at home.

E. ANTIPHOLUS
Were not my doors locked up and I shut out?

E. DROMIO
Pardie, your doors were locked and you shut out.   71

E. ANTIPHOLUS
And did not she herself revile me there?

E. DROMIO
Sans fable, she herself reviled you there.   73

E. ANTIPHOLUS
Did not her kitchen maid rail, taunt, and scorn me?

E. DROMIO
Certes, she did; the kitchen vestal scorned you.   75

E. ANTIPHOLUS
And did not I in rage depart from thence?

E. DROMIO
In verity you did; my bones bears witness,
That since have felt the vigor of his rage.

ADRIANA [*To Pinch*]
Is 't good to soothe him in these contraries?   79

PINCH
It is no shame; the fellow finds his vein   80
And, yielding to him, humors well his frenzy.

E. ANTIPHOLUS [*To Adriana*]
Thou hast suborned the goldsmith to arrest me.   82

---

71 Pardie (An oath, from the French *par Dieu*, by God.)   **73 Sans** without
75 Certes certainly.   **kitchen vestal** (Ironically, her task was like that of
the vestal virgins of ancient Rome, to keep the fire burning.)   **79 soothe**
encourage, humor.   **contraries** denials   **80 finds his vein** i.e., understands his master's frame of mind   **82 suborned** induced

ADRIANA
　Alas, I sent you money to redeem you
　By Dromio here, who came in haste for it.
E. DROMIO
　Money by me? Heart and good will you might,
　But surely, master, not a rag of money.   86
E. ANTIPHOLUS
　Went'st not thou to her for a purse of ducats?
ADRIANA
　He came to me, and I delivered it.
LUCIANA
　And I am witness with her that she did.
E. DROMIO
　God and the rope maker bear me witness
　That I was sent for nothing but a rope!
PINCH
　Mistress, both man and master is possessed;
　I know it by their pale and deadly looks.   93
　They must be bound and laid in some dark room.   94
E. ANTIPHOLUS [*To Adriana*]
　Say wherefore didst thou lock me forth today?   95
　[*To E. Dromio.*] And why dost thou deny the bag of gold?
ADRIANA
　I did not, gentle husband, lock thee forth.
E. DROMIO
　And, gentle master, I received no gold.
　But I confess, sir, that we were locked out.
ADRIANA
　Dissembling villain, thou speak'st false in both.
E. ANTIPHOLUS
　Dissembling harlot, thou art false in all
　And art confederate with a damnèd pack   102
　To make a loathsome abject scorn of me!   103
　But with these nails I'll pluck out these false eyes
　That would behold in me this shameful sport.
　　　　　　　　　　　　　　[*He threatens Adriana.*]

---

86 rag scrap　**93 deadly** deathlike　**94 bound . . . room** (The regular
treatment for lunacy in Shakespeare's day.)　**95 forth** out (also in
l. 97)　**102 pack** i.e., of conspirators　**103 abject scorn** despicable object
of contempt

ADRIANA
O, bind him, bind him! Let him not come near me.   106

Enter three or four, and offer to bind him. He
strives.

PINCH
More company! The fiend is strong within him.

LUCIANA
Ay me, poor man, how pale and wan he looks!

E. ANTIPHOLUS
What, will you murder me? Thou jailer, thou,
I am thy prisoner. Wilt thou suffer them
To make a rescue?

OFFICER   Masters, let him go.   111
He is my prisoner, and you shall not have him.

PINCH
Go bind his man, for he is frantic too.
                              [*They bind Dromio of Ephesus.*]

ADRIANA
What wilt thou do, thou peevish officer?   114
Hast thou delight to see a wretched man
Do outrage and displeasure to himself?   116

OFFICER
He is my prisoner. If I let him go,
The debt he owes will be required of me.

ADRIANA
I will discharge thee ere I go from thee.   119
Bear me forthwith unto his creditor,
And, knowing how the debt grows, I will pay it.—   121
Good Master Doctor, see him safe conveyed
Home to my house. O most unhappy day!   123

E. ANTIPHOLUS   O most unhappy strumpet!

E. DROMIO
Master, I am here entered in bond for you.   125

E. ANTIPHOLUS
Out on thee, villain! Wherefore dost thou mad me?   126

106 s.d. offer attempt   **111 make a rescue** take a prisoner by force from
legal custody   **114 peevish** silly, senseless   **116 displeasure** injury,
wrong   **119 discharge** pay   **121 knowing . . . grows** when I know how
the debt accrued   **123 unhappy** fatal, miserable   **125 entered in bond**
(1) bound up, tied (2) pledged   **126 mad** exasperate

E. DROMIO Will you be bound for nothing? Be mad,
good master; cry, "The devil!"

LUCIANA
God help, poor souls, how idly do they talk!   129

ADRIANA
Go bear him hence. Sister, go you with me.   130
              Exeunt [Pinch and his assistants, carrying off
                  Antipholus and Dromio of Ephesus].
                    Manent Officer, Adriana,
                        Luciana, Courtesan.
Say now, whose suit is he arrested at?

OFFICER
One Angelo, a goldsmith. Do you know him?

ADRIANA
I know the man. What is the sum he owes?

OFFICER
Two hundred ducats.

ADRIANA   Say, how grows it due?

OFFICER
Due for a chain your husband had of him.

ADRIANA
He did bespeak a chain for me but had it not.   136

COURTESAN
Whenas your husband all in rage today   137
Came to my house and took away my ring—
The ring I saw upon his finger now—
Straight after did I meet him with a chain.

ADRIANA
It may be so, but I did never see it.
Come, jailer, bring me where the goldsmith is.
I long to know the truth hereof at large.   143

        Enter Antipholus and Dromio [of] Syracuse with
        their rapiers drawn.

LUCIANA
God, for thy mercy! They are loose again.

ADRIANA
And come with naked swords. Let's call more help   145
To have them bound again.

---

129 idly senselessly   **130 s.d. Manent** they remain onstage   **136 bespeak**
order   **137 Whenas** when   **143 at large** in full, in detail   **145 naked** drawn

OFFICER   Away! They'll kill us.
*Run all out. Exeunt omnes, as fast as may be,
frighted. [Antipholus and Dromio
of Syracuse remain.]*

S. ANTIPHOLUS
I see these witches are afraid of swords.

S. DROMIO
She that would be your wife now ran from you.

S. ANTIPHOLUS
Come to the Centaur; fetch our stuff from thence.   149
I long that we were safe and sound aboard.

S. DROMIO   Faith, stay here this night. They will surely
do us no harm. You saw they speak us fair, give us 152
gold. Methinks they are such a gentle nation that, but
for the mountain of mad flesh that claims marriage of
me, I could find in my heart to stay here still and turn 155
witch.

S. ANTIPHOLUS
I will not stay tonight for all the town;
Therefore away, to get our stuff aboard.   *Exeunt.*

---

149 stuff goods, baggage   **152 speak us fair** speak courteously to us
155 still always

5.1   *Enter [Second] Merchant and [Angelo] the*
       goldsmith.

ANGELO
  I am sorry, sir, that I have hindered you;   1
  But I protest he had the chain of me,
  Though most dishonestly he doth deny it.
SECOND MERCHANT
  How is the man esteemed here in the city?
ANGELO
  Of very reverend reputation, sir,
  Of credit infinite, highly beloved,
  Second to none that lives here in the city.
  His word might bear my wealth at any time.   8
SECOND MERCHANT
  Speak softly. Yonder, as I think, he walks.

       Enter Antipholus and Dromio [of Syracuse]
       again, [Antipholus wearing the chain].

ANGELO
  'Tis so; and that self chain about his neck   10
  Which he forswore most monstrously to have.   11
  Good sir, draw near to me; I'll speak to him.—
  Signor Antipholus, I wonder much
  That you would put me to this shame and trouble
  And, not without some scandal to yourself,
  With circumstance and oaths so to deny   16
  This chain which now you wear so openly.
  Besides the charge, the shame, imprisonment,   18
  You have done wrong to this my honest friend,   19
  Who, but for staying on our controversy,   20
  Had hoisted sail and put to sea today.
  This chain you had of me. Can you deny it?
S. ANTIPHOLUS
  I think I had. I never did deny it.
SECOND MERCHANT
  Yes, that you did, sir, and forswore it too.

5.1. Location: Before the priory and Antipholus of Ephesus' house.
1 hindered delayed   **8 might bear** is worth   **10 self** same   **11 forswore**
denied under oath   **16 circumstance** details, particulars   **18 charge**
cost   **19 honest** honorable   **20 on** as a result of

S. ANTIPHOLUS
    Who heard me to deny it or forswear it?
SECOND MERCHANT
    These ears of mine, thou know'st, did hear thee.
    Fie on thee, wretch! 'Tis pity that thou liv'st
    To walk where any honest men resort.
S. ANTIPHOLUS
    Thou art a villain to impeach me thus.   29
    I'll prove mine honor and mine honesty
    Against thee presently, if thou dar'st stand.   31
SECOND MERCHANT
    I dare, and do defy thee for a villain.   *They draw.* 32

        *Enter Adriana, Luciana, [the] Courtesan, and
        others.*

ADRIANA
    Hold, hurt him not, for God's sake! He is mad.
    Some get within him; take his sword away.   34
    Bind Dromio too, and bear them to my house.
S. DROMIO
    Run, master, run; for God's sake, take a house!   36
    This is some priory. In, or we are spoiled!   37
        *Exeunt [Antipholus and Dromio of Syracuse]
                                        to the priory.*

        Enter [Emilia, the] Lady Abbess.

ABBESS
    Be quiet, people. Wherefore throng you hither?
ADRIANA
    To fetch my poor distracted husband hence.
    Let us come in, that we may bind him fast
    And bear him home for his recovery.
ANGELO
    I knew he was not in his perfect wits.
SECOND MERCHANT
    I am sorry now that I did draw on him.
ABBESS
    How long hath this possession held the man?

29 impeach accuse **31 presently** at once. **stand** take a fighting
stance **32 defy** challenge. **villain** base person **34 within him** under
his guard **36 take** take refuge in **37 spoiled** ruined, done for

ADRIANA
This week he hath been heavy, sour, sad,
And much, much different from the man he was;
But till this afternoon his passion
Ne'er brake into extremity of rage.   48

ABBESS
Hath he not lost much wealth by wreck of sea?   49
Buried some dear friend? Hath not else his eye
Strayed his affection in unlawful love—   51
A sin prevailing much in youthful men,
Who give their eyes the liberty of gazing?
Which of these sorrows is he subject to?

ADRIANA
To none of these, except it be the last,
Namely, some love that drew him oft from home.

ABBESS
You should for that have reprehended him.   57

ADRIANA
Why, so I did.

ABBESS   Ay, but not rough enough.

ADRIANA
As roughly as my modesty would let me.

ABBESS
Haply in private.

ADRIANA   And in assemblies too.

ABBESS   Ay, but not enough.

ADRIANA
It was the copy of our conference.   62
In bed he slept not for my urging it;   63
At board he fed not for my urging it;
Alone, it was the subject of my theme;
In company I often glancèd it;   66
Still did I tell him it was vile and bad.   67

ABBESS
And thereof came it that the man was mad.
The venom clamors of a jealous woman   69
Poisons more deadly than a mad dog's tooth.
It seems his sleeps were hindered by thy railing,

48 brake broke **49 wreck of** shipwreck at **51 Strayed** led astray
57 reprehended rebuked **62 copy** topic, theme. **conference** conversation **63 for** because of **66 glancèd** alluded to **67 Still** continually
69 venom venomous

And thereof comes it that his head is light.
Thou sayst his meat was sauced with thy upbraidings.
Unquiet meals make ill digestions;
Thereof the raging fire of fever bred,
And what's a fever but a fit of madness?
Thou sayst his sports were hindered by thy brawls.
Sweet recreation barred, what doth ensue
But moody and dull melancholy,
Kinsman to grim and comfortless despair,
And at her heels a huge infectious troop
Of pale distemperatures and foes to life?   82
In food, in sport, and life-preserving rest
To be disturbed would mad or man or beast.   84
The consequence is, then, thy jealous fits
Hath scared thy husband from the use of wits.

LUCIANA
She never reprehended him but mildly,
When he demeaned himself rough, rude, and wildly.   88
[*To Adriana.*] Why bear you these rebukes and answer
    not?

ADRIANA
She did betray me to my own reproof.   90
Good people, enter and lay hold on him.

ABBESS
No, not a creature enters in my house.

ADRIANA
Then let your servants bring my husband forth.

ABBESS
Neither. He took this place for sanctuary,
And it shall privilege him from your hands
Till I have brought him to his wits again
Or lose my labor in assaying it.   97

ADRIANA
I will attend my husband, be his nurse,
Diet his sickness, for it is my office,   99
And will have no attorney but myself;   100
And therefore let me have him home with me.

---

82 distemperatures physical disorder, illness   **84 mad or** madden
either   **88 demeaned** behaved, conducted   **90 She . . . reproof** i.e., she
led me to see that for which I rebuke myself   **97 assaying** attempting
99 office duty   **100 attorney** agent, deputy

ABBESS

Be patient, for I will not let him stir
Till I have used the approvèd means I have,   103
With wholesome syrups, drugs, and holy prayers,
To make of him a formal man again.   105
It is a branch and parcel of mine oath,   106
A charitable duty of my order.
Therefore depart and leave him here with me.

ADRIANA

I will not hence and leave my husband here;
And ill it doth beseem your holiness
To separate the husband and the wife.

ABBESS

Be quiet and depart. Thou shalt not have him.   [*Exit.*]

LUCIANA [*To Adriana*]

Complain unto the Duke of this indignity.

ADRIANA

Come, go. I will fall prostrate at his feet
And never rise until my tears and prayers
Have won His Grace to come in person hither
And take perforce my husband from the Abbess.

SECOND MERCHANT

By this, I think, the dial points at five.
Anon, I'm sure, the Duke himself in person
Comes this way to the melancholy vale,
The place of death and sorry execution   121
Behind the ditches of the abbey here.

ANGELO   Upon what cause?

SECOND MERCHANT

To see a reverend Syracusian merchant,
Who put unluckily into this bay
Against the laws and statutes of this town,
Beheaded publicly for his offense.

ANGELO

See where they come. We will behold his death.

LUCIANA

Kneel to the Duke before he pass the abbey.

> *Enter the Duke of Ephesus and [Egeon] the*
> *merchant of Syracuse, barehead [and bound],*
> *with the Headsman and other officers.*

103 approvèd proved   **105 formal** normal   **106 parcel** part, portion
121 sorry sad

DUKE
　Yet once again proclaim it publicly,
　If any friend will pay the sum for him,
　He shall not die; so much we tender him.   132
ADRIANA [*Kneeling*]
　Justice, most sacred Duke, against the Abbess!
DUKE
　She is a virtuous and a reverend lady.
　It cannot be that she hath done thee wrong.
ADRIANA
　May it please Your Grace, Antipholus my husband,
　Who I made lord of me and all I had,
　At your important letters, this ill day   138
　A most outrageous fit of madness took him,
　That desperately he hurried through the street—   140
　With him his bondman, all as mad as he—   141
　Doing displeasure to the citizens   142
　By rushing in their houses, bearing thence
　Rings, jewels, anything his rage did like.   144
　Once did I get him bound and sent him home,
　Whilst to take order for the wrongs I went   146
　That here and there his fury had committed.
　Anon, I wot not by what strong escape,   148
　He broke from those that had the guard of him,
　And with his mad attendant and himself,
　Each one with ireful passion, with drawn swords,
　Met us again and, madly bent on us,   152
　Chased us away, till raising of more aid
　We came again to bind them. Then they fled
　Into this abbey, whither we pursued them;
　And here the Abbess shuts the gates on us
　And will not suffer us to fetch him out,
　Nor send him forth that we may bear him hence.
　Therefore, most gracious Duke, with thy command
　Let him be brought forth and borne hence for help.   160

---

132 so . . . him so much consideration we grant him   **138 important**
importunate, pressing.   **letters** (Adriana would seem to have been ward
to the Duke and married at his urging.)   **140 That** so that.   **desperately**
recklessly   **141 all** totally   **142 displeasure** wrong, injury   **144 rage**
madness, insanity   **146 take order** settle, make reparation   **148 wot**
know.   **strong** violent   **152 bent** turned   **160 help** cure

DUKE [*Raising Adriana*]
  Long since, thy husband served me in my wars,
  And I to thee engaged a prince's word,   162
  When thou didst make him master of thy bed,
  To do him all the grace and good I could.—
  Go, some of you, knock at the abbey gate
  And bid the Lady Abbess come to me.
  I will determine this before I stir.   167

    Enter a [Servant as] messenger.

SERVANT
  O mistress, mistress, shift and save yourself!   168
  My master and his man are both broke loose,
  Beaten the maids a-row, and bound the doctor,   170
  Whose beard they have singed off with brands of fire,
  And ever as it blazed they threw on him
  Great pails of puddled mire to quench the hair.   173
  My master preaches patience to him, and the while
  His man with scissors nicks him like a fool;   175
  And sure, unless you send some present help,
  Between them they will kill the conjurer.
ADRIANA
  Peace, fool! Thy master and his man are here,
  And that is false thou dost report to us.
SERVANT
  Mistress, upon my life, I tell you true;
  I have not breathed almost since I did see it.
  He cries for you and vows, if he can take you,
  To scorch your face and to disfigure you.   183
                         Cry within.
  Hark, hark! I hear him, mistress. Fly, begone!
DUKE
  Come, stand by me. Fear nothing. Guard with halberds! 185
ADRIANA
  Ay me, it is my husband! Witness you
  That he is borne about invisible.

162 engaged pledged   **167 determine** settle   **168 shift** escape, depart
170 a-row one after another   **173 puddled** from filthy puddles   **175 nicks**
... fool gives him a fantastic haircut in the short fashion of the court
fool   **183 scorch** slash   **185 halberds** long-handled spears with blades

Even now we housed him in the abbey here,   188
And now he's there, past thought of human reason.

Enter Antipholus and Dromio of Ephesus.

E. ANTIPHOLUS
Justice, most gracious Duke, O, grant me justice!
Even for the service that long since I did thee,
When I bestrid thee in the wars and took   192
Deep scars to save thy life; even for the blood
That then I lost for thee, now grant me justice.

EGEON
Unless the fear of death doth make me dote,
I see my son Antipholus and Dromio.

E. ANTIPHOLUS
Justice, sweet prince, against that woman there!
She whom thou gav'st to me to be my wife,
That hath abusèd and dishonored me   199
Even in the strength and height of injury!
Beyond imagination is the wrong
That she this day hath shameless thrown on me.

DUKE
Discover how, and thou shalt find me just.   203

E. ANTIPHOLUS
This day, great Duke, she shut the doors upon me,
While she with harlots feasted in my house.   205

DUKE
A grievous fault. Say, woman, didst thou so?

ADRIANA
No, my good lord. Myself, he, and my sister
Today did dine together. So befall my soul   208
As this is false he burdens me withal.   209

LUCIANA
Ne'er may I look on day nor sleep on night   210
But she tells to Your Highness simple truth.

ANGELO
O perjured woman! They are both forsworn.
In this the madman justly chargeth them.

---

188 housed him i.e., drove him into   **192 bestrid** stood over (to defend
when fallen in battle)   **199 abusèd** maltreated   **203 Discover** reveal
205 harlots rascals, vile companions   **208 So ... soul** i.e., as I hope to
be saved   **209 he ... withal** he charges me with   **210 on** at

E. ANTIPHOLUS
My liege, I am advisèd what I say,   214
Neither disturbèd with the effect of wine,
Nor heady-rash, provoked with raging ire,
Albeit my wrongs might make one wiser mad.
This woman locked me out this day from dinner.
That goldsmith there, were he not packed with her,   219
Could witness it, for he was with me then;
Who parted with me to go fetch a chain,   221
Promising to bring it to the Porpentine,
Where Balthasar and I did dine together.
Our dinner done, and he not coming thither,
I went to seek him. In the street I met him,
And in his company that gentleman.

> [*Indicating Second Merchant.*]

There did this perjured goldsmith swear me down
That I this day of him received the chain,
Which, God he knows, I saw not; for the which
He did arrest me with an officer.
I did obey, and sent my peasant home
For certain ducats; he with none returned.
Then fairly I bespoke the officer   233
To go in person with me to my house.
By the way we met
My wife, her sister, and a rabble more
Of vile confederates. Along with them
They brought one Pinch, a hungry, lean-faced villain,
A mere anatomy, a mountebank,   239
A threadbare juggler and a fortune-teller,   240
A needy, hollow-eyed, sharp-looking wretch,
A living dead man. This pernicious slave,
Forsooth, took on him as a conjurer   243
And, gazing in mine eyes, feeling my pulse,
And with no face, as 'twere, outfacing me,
Cries out I was possessed. Then all together   246
They fell upon me, bound me, bore me thence,
And in a dark and dankish vault at home
There left me and my man, both bound together,

---

214 am advisèd know very well **219 packed** in conspiracy **221 parted**
departed **233 fairly** civilly. **bespoke** requested **239 mere anatomy**
absolute skeleton. **mountebank** quack, charlatan **240 juggler** sor-
cerer **243 took . . . as** pretended to be **246 possessed** mad

Till, gnawing with my teeth my bonds in sunder,
I gained my freedom and immediately
Ran hither to Your Grace, whom I beseech
To give me ample satisfaction
For these deep shames and great indignities.

ANGELO
My lord, in truth, thus far I witness with him,
That he dined not at home but was locked out.

DUKE
But had he such a chain of thee, or no?

ANGELO
He had, my lord, and when he ran in here,
These people saw the chain about his neck.

SECOND MERCHANT [*To E. Antipholus*]
Besides, I will be sworn these ears of mine
Heard you confess you had the chain of him
After you first forswore it on the mart,
And thereupon I drew my sword on you;
And then you fled into this abbey here,
From whence, I think, you are come by miracle.

E. ANTIPHOLUS
I never came within these abbey walls,
Nor ever didst thou draw thy sword on me.
I never saw the chain, so help me Heaven!
And this is false you burden me withal.

DUKE
Why, what an intricate impeach is this!   270
I think you all have drunk of Circe's cup.   271
If here you housed him, here he would have been.
If he were mad, he would not plead so coldly.   273
You say he dined at home; the goldsmith here
Denies that saying.—Sirrah, what say you?

E. DROMIO
Sir, he dined with her there, at the Porpentine.

COURTESAN
He did, and from my finger snatched that ring.

E. ANTIPHOLUS [*Showing ring*]
'Tis true, my liege; this ring I had of her.

DUKE [*To Courtesan*]
Sawst thou him enter at the abbey here?

270 intricate impeach involved accusation **271 Circe's cup** the
charmed cup, a draft of which turned men into beasts **273 coldly**
calmly, rationally

COURTESAN

As sure, my liege, as I do see Your Grace.

DUKE

Why, this is strange. Go call the Abbess hither.
I think you are all mated or stark mad.   282

Exit one to the Abbess.

EGEON

Most mighty Duke, vouchsafe me speak a word.
Haply I see a friend will save my life
And pay the sum that may deliver me.

DUKE

Speak freely, Syracusian, what thou wilt.

EGEON

Is not your name, sir, called Antipholus?
And is not that your bondman, Dromio?

E. DROMIO

Within this hour I was his bondman, sir,
But he, I thank him, gnawed in two my cords.
Now am I Dromio and his man, unbound.

EGEON

I am sure you both of you remember me.

E. DROMIO

Ourselves we do remember, sir, by you;
For lately we were bound, as you are now.
You are not Pinch's patient, are you, sir?

EGEON

Why look you strange on me? You know me well.

E. ANTIPHOLUS

I never saw you in my life till now.

EGEON

O, grief hath changed me since you saw me last,
And careful hours with Time's deformèd hand   299
Have written strange defeatures in my face.   300
But tell me yet, dost thou not know my voice?

E. ANTIPHOLUS   Neither.

EGEON   Dromio, nor thou?

E. DROMIO   No, trust me, sir, nor I.

EGEON   I am sure thou dost.

---

282 mated stupefied   **299 careful** full of care.   **deformèd** deforming (or
perhaps referring to the withered hands of Father Time)
300 defeatures disfigurements, blemishes

E. DROMIO   Ay, sir, but I am sure I do not; and whatsoever a man denies, you are now bound to believe him.

EGEON
Not know my voice! O time's extremity,
Hast thou so cracked and splitted my poor tongue
In seven short years, that here my only son
Knows not my feeble key of untuned cares?   311
Though now this grainèd face of mine be hid   312
In sap-consuming winter's drizzled snow
And all the conduits of my blood froze up,
Yet hath my night of life some memory,
My wasting lamps some fading glimmer left,   316
My dull deaf ears a little use to hear.
All these old witnesses—I cannot err—
Tell me thou art my son Antipholus.

E. ANTIPHOLUS
I never saw my father in my life.

EGEON
But seven years since, in Syracusa, boy,   321
Thou know'st we parted. But perhaps, my son,
Thou sham'st to acknowledge me in misery.

E. ANTIPHOLUS
The Duke and all that know me in the city
Can witness with me that it is not so.
I ne'er saw Syracusa in my life.

DUKE
I tell thee, Syracusian, twenty years
Have I been patron to Antipholus,
During which time he ne'er saw Syracusa.
I see thy age and dangers make thee dote.

> *Enter the Abbess, with Antipholus and Dromio of
> Syracuse.*

ABBESS
Most mighty Duke, behold a man much wronged.
                         All gather to see them.

ADRIANA
I see two husbands, or mine eyes deceive me.

311 my . . . cares my voice enfeebled by discordant cares   312 grainèd
lined, furrowed   316 wasting lamps i.e., dimming eyes   321 But only

DUKE

One of these men is genius to the other;   333
And so of these, which is the natural man,
And which the spirit? Who deciphers them?   335

S. DROMIO

I, sir, am Dromio. Command him away.

E. DROMIO

I, sir, am Dromio. Pray, let me stay.

S. ANTIPHOLUS

Egeon art thou not? Or else his ghost?

S. DROMIO

O, my old master! Who hath bound him here?

ABBESS

Whoever bound him, I will loose his bonds
And gain a husband by his liberty.
Speak, old Egeon, if thou be'st the man
That hadst a wife once called Emilia
That bore thee at a burden two fair sons.   344
O, if thou be'st the same Egeon, speak,
And speak unto the same Emilia!

EGEON

If I dream not, thou art Emilia.
If thou art she, tell me where is that son
That floated with thee on the fatal raft?

ABBESS

By men of Epidamium he and I
And the twin Dromio all were taken up;
But by and by rude fishermen of Corinth
By force took Dromio and my son from them,
And me they left with those of Epidamium.
What then became of them I cannot tell;
I to this fortune that you see me in.

DUKE

Why, here begins his morning story right: 357
These two Antipholuses, these two so like,
And these two Dromios, one in semblance—   359
Besides her urging of her wreck at sea—   360
These are the parents to these children,

333 **genius** attendant spirit 335 **deciphers** distinguishes 344 **burden**
birth 357 **his morning story** i.e., the history he related this morning
359 **semblance** appearance 360 **urging** urgent account

Which accidentally are met together.
Antipholus, thou cam'st from Corinth first?

S. ANTIPHOLUS
No, sir, not I; I came from Syracuse.

DUKE
Stay, stand apart. I know not which is which.

E. ANTIPHOLUS
I came from Corinth, my most gracious lord—

E. DROMIO   And I with him.

E. ANTIPHOLUS
Brought to this town by that most famous warrior,
Duke Menaphon, your most renownèd uncle.

ADRIANA
Which of you two did dine with me today?

S. ANTIPHOLUS
I, gentle mistress.

ADRIANA   And are not you my husband?

E. ANTIPHOLUS   No, I say nay to that.

S. ANTIPHOLUS
And so do I. Yet did she call me so,
And this fair gentlewoman, her sister here,
Did call me brother. [*To Luciana.*] What I told you then
I hope I shall have leisure to make good,   376
If this be not a dream I see and hear.

ANGELO [*Pointing to chain Antipholus S. wears*]
That is the chain, sir, which you had of me.

S. ANTIPHOLUS
I think it be, sir. I deny it not.

E. ANTIPHOLUS
And you, sir, for this chain arrested me.

ANGELO
I think I did, sir. I deny it not.

ADRIANA [*To Antipholus of Ephesus*]
I sent you money, sir, to be your bail,
By Dromio, but I think he brought it not.

E. DROMIO   No, none by me.

S. ANTIPHOLUS [*Showing purse*]
This purse of ducats I received from you,
And Dromio my man did bring them me.
I see we still did meet each other's man,   387

376 **leisure** opportunity   387 **still** continually

And I was ta'en for him, and he for me,
And thereupon these errors are arose.

E. ANTIPHOLUS [*Offering money*]
These ducats pawn I for my father here.

DUKE
It shall not need. Thy father hath his life.

COURTESAN
Sir, I must have that diamond from you.

E. ANTIPHOLUS [*Giving ring*]
There, take it, and much thanks for my good cheer.

ABBESS
Renownèd Duke, vouchsafe to take the pains   394
To go with us into the abbey here
And hear at large discoursèd all our fortunes,   396
And all that are assembled in this place,
That by this sympathizèd one day's error   398
Have suffered wrong. Go, keep us company,
And we shall make full satisfaction.
Thirty-three years have I but gone in travail
Of you, my sons, and till this present hour
My heavy burden ne'er deliverèd.
The Duke, my husband, and my children both,
And you the calendars of their nativity,   405
Go to a gossips' feast, and joy with me;   406
After so long grief, such nativity!

DUKE
With all my heart, I'll gossip at this feast.   408
                    Exeunt omnes. Manent the two Dromios
                            and two brothers [*Antipholus*].

S. DROMIO [*To Antipholus of Ephesus*]
Master, shall I fetch your stuff from shipboard?

E. ANTIPHOLUS
Dromio, what stuff of mine hast thou embarked?

S. DROMIO
Your goods that lay at host, sir, in the Centaur. 411

S. ANTIPHOLUS
He speaks to me. I am your master, Dromio.

---

394 vouchsafe deign, agree   **396 at large** at length   **398 sympathizèd**
shared in by all equally   **405 calendars . . . nativity** i.e., the Dromios,
since the servants were born at the same time as their masters
406 gossips' feast feast of the godparents, christening feast   **408 gossip**
i.e., be a hearty companion, take part   **411 lay at host** were put up

Come, go with us, we'll look to that anon.
Embrace thy brother there; rejoice with him.

> *Exeunt [the two brothers Antipholus].*

S. DROMIO
There is a fat friend at your master's house
That kitchened me for you today at dinner.   416
She now shall be my sister, not my wife.

E. DROMIO
Methinks you are my glass, and not my brother.   418
I see by you I am a sweet-faced youth.
Will you walk in to see their gossiping?   420

S. DROMIO   Not I, sir; you are my elder.

E. DROMIO   That's a question. How shall we try it?

S. DROMIO   We'll draw cuts for the senior; till then lead   423
thou first.

E. DROMIO   Nay, then, thus:
We came into the world like brother and brother,
And now let's go hand in hand, not one before another.

> *Exeunt.*

---

416 kitchened entertained in the kitchen   **418 glass** mirror
420 gossiping merrymaking   **423 cuts** lots

Date and Text

The earliest known edition of *The Comedy of Errors* is in the First Folio of 1623. Its first-mentioned production, however, was on Innocents Day, December 28, 1594, when a "Comedy of Errors (like to *Plautus* his *Menaechmus*)" was performed by professional actors as part of the Christmas Revels at Gray's Inn (one of the Inns of Court, where young men studied law) in London. The evening's festivities are set down in *Gesta Grayorum*, a contemporary account of the revels, though not published until 1688. According to this record, the evening was marred by such tumult and disorder that the invited guests from the Inner Temple (another of the Inns of Court) refused to stay; thereafter, the night became known as "The Night of Errors." References to sorcery and enchantment in the play leave little doubt that it was Shakespeare's.

Scholars generally agree that the play was not newly written for this occasion. Internally, the play seems early: its characterization is slight, for example, and its punning wit reminds us of *Love's Labor's Lost* and *The Two Gentlemen of Verona*. Topical clues are suggestive but not conclusive. Chief of these is the joke about France being "armed and reverted, making war against her heir" (3.2.123–124). Unquestionably this refers to France's civil wars between Henry of Navarre and his Catholic opposition. Since Henry became a Catholic and the King of France in 1593, most scholars prefer a date before 1593. Peter Alexander (*Shakespeare's Life and Art*, 1961) has even argued for a date prior to 1589, since Henry III died in that year leaving Henry of Navarre as nominal king rather than heir. The sad truth is that we probably cannot attach too much weight to either conclusion. Allusions to the French civil wars during the early 1590s were common but also imprecise; the joke would have seemed relevant at almost any time up to 1595. The same is probably true of the allusion to Spain's sending "whole armadoes of carracks" (3.2.135–136). This is often taken to refer to the Spanish Armada, 1588, but may instead refer to the Portuguese *Madre de Dios* captured and brought to England in 1592 or to a similar venture. In short, it is virtually impossible to prove that *The Comedy of Errors* precedes *Love's Labor's Lost, The Two Gentlemen of Verona,* or *The Taming of the Shrew.*

A lost play called *The History of Error* was acted before the Queen by the Children of Paul's (a company of boy actors from St. Paul's School) at Hampton Court on New Year's night, 1577. About this play we know nothing other than its suggestive title, and speculation that Shakespeare may have adapted it has been generally abandoned.

The Folio text, based probably on Shakespeare's own manuscript, is generally a good text although, as is common in authorial manuscripts, the form of the characters' names frequently varies in the stage directions and speech prefixes. Perhaps a few performance-oriented annotations have been added to the authorial manuscript.

Textual Notes

These textual notes are not a historical collation, either of the early folios or of more recent editions; they are simply a record of departure in this edition from the copy text. The reading adopted in this edition appears in bold-face, followed by the rejected reading from the copy text, i.e., the First Folio. Changes in lineation are not indicated, nor are some minor and obvious typographical errors.

Abbreviations used:
F the First Folio
s.d. stage direction
s.p. speech prefix
Copy text: the First Folio.

1.1. 1 s.p. [and elsewhere] Egeon Marchant   **42 the** he   **102 upon** vp
116 bark backe   **123 hath** haue   **thee** they   **151 life** helpe

1.2. s.d. Antipholus [of Syracuse] Antipholis Erotes   **[First] Merchant** a
Marchant   **1 s.p. [and elsewhere] First Merchant** Mer [also called E. Mar]
4 arrival a riuall   **32 s.d. Exit** Exeunt   **40 unhappy** vnhappie a   **66 clock**
cooke   **94 s.d. Exit** Exeunt

2.1. s.d. Antipholus of Ephesus Antipholis Sereptus   **11 o' door** adore   **12 ill**
thus   **60 thousand** hundred   **106 alone, alone** alone, a loue   **111 Wear**
Where   **115 s.d. Exeunt** Exit

2.2. s.d. Antipholus of Syracuse Antipholus Errotis   **6 s.d. of Syracuse**
Siracusia   **12 didst** did didst   **14 s.p. S. Antipholus** E. Ant   **79 men** them
97 tiring trying   **101 e'en** in   **135 off** of   **174 stronger** stranger   **185 offered**
free'd   **189 elves** Owles   **193 drone** Dromio   **194 not I** I not

3.1. 71 there here   **75 you** your   **89 her** your   **91 her** your

3.2. s.d. Luciana Iuliana   **1 s.p. Luciana** Iulia   **4 building** buildings   **ruinous** ruinate   **16 attaint** attaine   **21 but** not   **26 wife** wise   **46 sister's** sister
49 bed bud   **them** thee   **57 where** when   **103 sweats; a** sweats a   **109 and**
is   **126 chalky** chalke   **136 carracks** Carrects

4.1. 1 s.p. [and elsewhere] Second Merchant Mar   **7 s.p. [and elsewhere]
Angelo** Gold   **17 her** their   **28 carat** charect   **87 then** then sir

4.2. 6 Of Oh   **34 One** On   **45 he's** is   **48 That** Thus   **61 'a** I   **66 s.d. Exeunt**
Exit

4.3. 1 s.p. S. Antipholus [not in F]   **58 if you** if   **78 s.d. Exeunt** Exit

4.4. 42 to prophesy the prophesie   **106 s.d. Enter . . . strives** [at l. 105 in F]
113 his this   **130 s.d.** [at l. 131 in F]   **Manent** Manet   **143 s.d. Enter . . .
drawn** Antipholus Siracusia with his Rapier drawne, and Dromio Sirac.

5.1. 46 much, much much   **121 death** depth   **168 s.p. Servant** [not in F]
175 scissors Cizers   **180 s.p. Servant** Mess   **195 s.p. Egeon** Mar. Fat
283 s.p. Egeon Fa   **330 s.d. Antipholus . . . Syracuse** Antipholus Siracusa,
and Dromio Sir   **357–362** [these lines follow l. 346 in F]   **358 Antipholuses**
Antipholus   **403 ne'er** are   **406 joy** go   **408 s.d. Manent** Manet
414 s.d. Exeunt Exit

Shakespeare's Sources

The Comedy of Errors is based chiefly on the *Menaechmi* of Plautus (c. 254–184 B.C.). Shakespeare appears to have used the Latin, which was available to him in numerous Renaissance texts. He may also have known in manuscript the translation into English by "W. W." (? William Warner), published in 1595.

A full modernized text of the "W. W." translation of the *Menaechmi* follows. A comparison of it with Shakespeare's play suggests how much he has retained and what he has changed. In Plautus, the story concerns two separated twins, one of whom (Menaechmus the Traveler of Syracuse) has come by chance, accompanied by his servant, Messenio, to the city of Epidamnum, where his long-lost brother, Menaechmus the Citizen, lives. Menaechmus the Citizen, in the company of the parasite Peniculus, quarrels with his wife and arranges to lunch with the courtesan Erotium. The confusion begins when Menaechmus the Traveler is mistaken for his twin by Erotium's cook, Cylindrus, and then by Erotium herself, who invites him to lunch and to her bed. She bids him take a cloak (which Menaechmus the Citizen had given her that morning) to the dyer's for alteration. A short time later, Peniculus too mistakes Menaechmus the Traveler for the Epidamnian twin, upbraids him for having dined while the parasite was absent, and threatens to tell Menaechmus' wife of his carryings-on. Erotium's maid brings Menaechmus the Traveler a chain or bracelet to be mended at the goldsmith's. Menaechmus the Citizen now returns home from a busy day to a furious wife and a vindictive Peniculus. Among other matters the wife demands the return of her cloak, which, as she suspects, her husband stole from her and gave to Erotium. The husband, locked out of his own house by his angry wife, must now confront Erotium, who inists that she gave her chain and the cloak to him. The Citizen goes to seek the help of his friends. Menaechmus the Traveler shows up at this point and is angrily abused by the wife and by her father, both of whom consider the supposed husband to be mad. They send for a doctor, who arrives after Menaechmus the Traveler has fled; they instead detain

Menaechmus the Citizen as a madman. Messenio the servant now returns to his supposed master and fights manfully with his master's captors. Finally the two twins confront one another and unravel the mystery.

Shakespeare creates the two Dromios in place of Messenio, plays down the role of the courtesan, dignifies the part of the wife, invents the sympathetic role of Luciana her sister, eliminates the parasite and the wife's father, and replaces the courtesan's maid and cook with comic servants such as Luce, or Nell, the kitchen-wench in the household of Antipholus of Ephesus. The conventional doctor, Medicus, becomes the zany Dr. Pinch. The setting is Ephesus rather than Epidamnum. Plautus' detached ironic tone and his matter-of-fact depiction of courtesans and parasites are replaced by a thematic emphasis on patience and loyalty in marriage. The name "Dromio" may have come from John Lyly's *Mother Bombie*.

The dual identity of the servants, and the superb confusion of Act 3 when Antipholus of Ephesus is locked out of his own house, are derived in good part from Plautus' *Amphitruo*. In the relevant portion of that play, Amphitryon's wife, Alcmena, is courted by Jupiter disguised as her husband, while Mercury guards the door in the guise of Amphitryon's slave Sosia. The real Sosia approaches, but is so bewildered by Mercury's inventive wit that he begins to doubt his own identity. Later, at Jupiter's behest, Mercury again poses as Sosia to dupe Amphitryon and deny him entrance to his own house. Ultimately, after Alcmena has given birth to twins, one by Jupiter (Hercules) and one by Amphitryon (Iphiclus), Jupiter tells Amphitryon the truth.

The "framing" action of *The Comedy of Errors,* concerning old Egeon's painful separation from his wife and their eventual reunion, is derived not from Plautus but from the story of Apollonius of Tyre. Shakespeare later used this story for *Pericles,* and for that play his sources were chiefly two: the *Confessio Amantis* by John Gower, Book 8, and Laurence Twine's *The Pattern of Painful Adventures,* translated from a French version based in turn on a popular story in the *Gesta Romanorum.* Perhaps Shakespeare was acquainted with these same versions when he wrote *The Comedy of Errors;* in 1576 Twine's account was entered in the Stationers' Register, the official record book of the London Company of Stationers (booksellers and printers), although the earliest extant edition dates from around 1594–1595. Gower's account had been printed by William Caxton (England's first printer) in 1493 and reprinted in 1532 and 1554.

In Gower's *Confessio*, Apollonius' wife Lucina gives birth to a daughter on board ship and, having apparently died in childbirth, is put into a chest and committed to the sea. Washing ashore at Ephesus, she is restored by the physician Cerimon. She becomes a priestess in the Temple of Diana. Years later, Apollonius comes to Ephesus, is first reunited with his daughter Thaisa, and then is told in a vision to go to the Temple. There he discovers the "Abbess" to be his long-lost wife. Shakespeare has added the threatened hanging from which Egeon is finally rescued.

Menaechmi
By Plautus
Translated by William Warner (?)

Any departures from the original text are noted with an asterisk and appear at the bottom of the page in boldface; original readings are in roman.

[*Dramatis personae*

MENAECHMUS THE CITIZEN, *residing in Epidamnum*
MENAECHMUS THE TRAVELER, *his twin, also called Sosicles*
MESSENIO, *bondslave of Menaechmus the Traveler*
PENICULUS, *parasite attached to Menaechmus the Citizen*
MULIER, *wife of Menaechmus the Citizen*
EROTIUM, *a courtesan*
CYLINDRUS, *her cook*
ANCILLA, *her maid*
SENEX, *Mulier's father*
MEDICUS, *a doctor*
SAILORS
SCENE: *A street in Epidamnum, on which are facing the houses of Menaechmus the Citizen and Erotium the courtesan*]

The Argument
Two twinborn sons a Sicil merchant had:
   Menaechmus one and Sosicles the other.
The first his father lost a little lad;
   The grandsire named the latter like his brother.

This, grown a man, long travel took to seek
  His brother, and to Epidamnum came
Where th' other dwelt enriched, and him so like
  That citizens there take him for the same.
Father, wife, neighbors each mistaking either,
Much pleasant error ere they meet together.

❖

1.1 *Enter Peniculus, a parasite.*

PENICULUS Peniculus was given me for my name[1] when I
was young, because like a broom I swept all clean away
wheresoe'er I be come: namely, all the victuals which are set
before me. Now, in my judgment men that clap iron bolts on
such captives as they would keep safe and tie those servants
in chains who they think will run away, they commit an
exceeding great folly. My reason is, these poor wretches
enduring one misery upon another never cease devising
how, by wrenching asunder their gyves[2] or by some subtlety
or other, they may escape such cursed bonds. If then ye
would keep a man without all suspicion of running away
from ye, the surest way is to tie him with meat, drink, and
ease; let him ever be idle, eat his bellyful, and carouse while
his skin will hold, and he shall never, I warrant ye, stir a foot.
These strings to tie one by the teeth pass all the bonds of
iron, steel, or what metal soever, for the more slack and easy
ye make them, the faster still they tie the party which is in
them. I speak this upon experience of myself, who am now
going for Menaechmus, there willingly to be tied to his good
cheer. He is commonly so exceeding bountiful and liberal in
his fare, as no marvel though such guests as myself be
drawn to his table and tied there in his dishes. Now, because
I have lately been a stranger there, I mean to visit him at
dinner, for my stomach methinks even thrusts me into the
fetters of his dainty fare. But yonder I see his door open and
himself ready to come forth.

1.1. 1 for my name (*Peniculus* in Latin means "brush for removing
dirt.") **2 gyves** fetters

1.2   *Enter Menaechmus [the Citizen, from his house],*
talking back to his wife within.

MENAECHMUS THE CITIZEN   If ye were not such a brabbling[1]
fool and madbrain scold as ye are, ye would never thus cross
your husband in all his actions! [*To himself.*] 'Tis no matter.
Let her serve me thus once more, I'll send her home to her
dad with a vengeance. I can never go forth a-doors but she
asketh me whither I go, what I do, what business, what I
fetch, what I carry, as though she were a constable or a toll-
gatherer. I have pampered her too much. She hath servants
about her, wool, flax, and all things necessary to busy her
withal,[2] yet she watcheth and wondereth whither I go. Well,
sith[3] it is so, she shall now have some cause. I mean to dine
this day abroad with a sweet friend of mine.

PENICULUS [*Aside*]   Yea, marry, now comes he to the point that
pricks me. This last speech galls me as much as it would do
his wife. If he dine not at home, I am dressed.[4]

MENAECHMUS THE CITIZEN [*To himself*]   We that have loves
abroad and wives at home are miserably hampered. Yet,
would every man could tame his shrew as well as I do mine!
I have now filched away a fine riding cloak of my wife's
which I mean to bestow upon one that I love better. Nay, if
she be so wary and watchful over me, I count it an alms
deed[5] to deceive her.

PENICULUS [*Advancing*]   Come, what share have I in that
same?

MENAECHMUS THE CITIZEN   Out, alas, I am taken.

PENICULUS   True, but by your friend.

MENAECHMUS THE CITIZEN   What, mine own Peniculus?

PENICULUS   Yours, i' faith, body and goods—if I had any.

MENAECHMUS THE CITIZEN   Why, thou hast a body.

PENICULUS   Yea, but neither goods nor good body.

MENAECHMUS THE CITIZEN   Thou couldst never come fitter in
all thy life.

PENICULUS   Tush, I ever do so to my friends. I know how to
come always in the nick. Where dine ye today?

MENAECHMUS THE CITIZEN   I'll tell thee of a notable prank.

1.2. 1 brabbling brawling (also in 4.1)   **2 withal** with   **3 sith** since
4 dressed treated with severity   **5 an alms deed** a deed of charity

PENICULUS   What, did the cook mar your meat in the dressing?[6] Would I might see the reversion.[7]

MENAECHMUS THE CITIZEN   Tell me, didst thou see a picture how Jupiter's eagle snatched away Ganymede, or how Venus stole away Adonis?[8]

PENICULUS   Often, but what care I for shadows? I want substance.

MENAECHMUS THE CITIZEN [*Showing a cloak he has concealed*] Look thee here. Look not I like such a picture?

PENICULUS   Oho, what cloak have ye got here?

MENAECHMUS THE CITIZEN   Prithee, say I am now a brave[9] fellow.

PENICULUS   But hark ye, where shall we dine?

MENAECHMUS THE CITIZEN   Tush, say as I bid thee, man.

PENICULUS   Out of doubt ye are a fine man.

MENAECHMUS THE CITIZEN   What? Canst add nothing of thine own?

PENICULUS   Ye are a most pleasant gentleman.

MENAECHMUS THE CITIZEN   On, yet.

PENICULUS   Nay, not a word more, unless ye tell me how you and your wife be fallen out.

MENAECHMUS THE CITIZEN   Nay, I have a greater secret than that to impart to thee.

PENICULUS   Say your mind.

MENAECHMUS THE CITIZEN   Come farther this way from my house.

PENICULUS [*As they move away from the house*]   So, let me hear.

MENAECHMUS THE CITIZEN   Nay, farther yet.

PENICULUS   I warrant ye, man.

MENAECHMUS THE CITIZEN   Nay, yet farther.

PENICULUS   'Tis pity ye were not made a waterman, to row in a wherry.[10]

MENAECHMUS THE CITIZEN   Why?

PENICULUS   Because ye go one way and look another still, lest your wife should follow ye. But what's the matter, is 't not almost dinnertime?

---

6 dressing preparing   **7 reversion** leftovers   **8 Jupiter's . . . Adonis** (Menaechmus the Citizen compares his stealth in stealing his wife's cloak with the stealth used by the gods in their amours with mortals.) **9 brave** fine   **10 waterman . . . wherry** boatman plying his rowboat for hire on a river

MENAECHMUS THE CITIZEN Seest thou this cloak?

PENICULUS Not yet. Well, what of it?

MENAECHMUS THE CITIZEN This same I mean to give to Erotium.

PENICULUS That's well, but what of all this?

MENAECHMUS THE CITIZEN There I mean to have a delicious dinner prepared for her and me.

PENICULUS And me?

MENAECHMUS THE CITIZEN And thee.

PENICULUS O sweet word! What, shall I knock presently at her door?

MENAECHMUS THE CITIZEN Ay, knock. But stay too, Peniculus; let's not be too rash. O, see, she is in good time coming forth.

PENICULUS Ah, he now looks against[11] the sun. How her beams dazzle his eyes!

Enter Erotium [from her house].

EROTIUM What, mine own Menaechmus? Welcome, sweet-heart.

PENICULUS And what, am I welcome too?

EROTIUM You, sir? Ye are out of the number of my welcome guests.

PENICULUS I am like a voluntary soldier—out of pay.

MENAECHMUS THE CITIZEN Erotium, I have determined that here shall be pitched a field[12] this day. We mean to drink, for the heavens,[13] and which of us performs the bravest service at his weapon—the wine bowl—yourself as captain shall pay him his wages according to his deserts.

EROTIUM Agreed.

PENICULUS I would we had the weapons, for my valor pricks me to the battle.

MENAECHMUS THE CITIZEN Shall I tell thee, sweet mouse? I never look upon thee but I am quite out of love with my wife.

EROTIUM Yet ye cannot choose but ye must still wear some-thing of hers. What's this same? [*Indicating the cloak.*]

MENAECHMUS THE CITIZEN This? Such a spoil,[14] sweetheart, as I took from her to put on thee.

EROTIUM Mine own Menaechmus, well worthy to be my dear, of all dearest!

---

11 against toward, into **12 be pitched a field** a battle be fought **13 for the heavens** i.e., by heaven. (A mild oath.) **14 spoil** booty

PENICULUS [*Aside*]   Now she shows herself in her likeness:[15] when she finds him in the giving vein, she draws close to him.

MENAECHMUS THE CITIZEN   I think Hercules got not the garter from Hippolyta so hardly[16] as I got this from my wife. Take this, and with the same take my heart.

[*He gives her the cloak.*]

PENICULUS   Thus they must do that are right[17] lovers—[*Aside*] especially if they mean to be beggars with any speed.[18]

MENAECHMUS THE CITIZEN   I bought this same of late[19] for my wife. It stood me, I think, in[20] some ten pound.

PENICULUS [*Aside*]   There's ten pound bestowed very thriftily.

MENAECHMUS THE CITIZEN   But know ye what I would have ye do?

EROTIUM   It shall be done. Your dinner shall be ready.

MENAECHMUS THE CITIZEN   Let a good dinner be made for us three. Hark ye: some oysters, a marrowbone pie or two, some artichokes, and potato roots;[21] let our other dishes be as you please.

EROTIUM   You shall, sir.

MENAECHMUS THE CITIZEN   I have a little business in this city; by that time dinner will be prepared. Farewell till then, sweet Erotium. Come, Peniculus.

PENICULUS   Nay, I mean to follow ye. I will sooner leese[22] my life than sight of you till this dinner be done.

Exeunt [*Menaechmus and Peniculus*].

EROTIUM [*Calling into her house*]   Who's there? Call me Cylindrus the cook hither.

Enter Cylindrus.

Cylindrus, take the handbasket, and here, there's ten shillings, is there not?

[*Giving a handbasket and money.*]

CYLINDRUS   'Tis so, mistress.

EROTIUM   Buy me of all the daintiest[23] meats ye can get—ye

---

15 in her likeness i.e., in her true colors   **16 so hardly** with as much difficulty. (One of Hercules' twelve labors was to defeat the Amazons in battle and to obtain the girdle—here called a *garter*—of their Queen Hippolyta.)   **17 right** true   **18 speed** success   **19 of late** lately
20 stood me . . . in cost me   **21 potato roots** potatoes   **22 leese** lose
23 daintiest choicest

know what I mean—so as three may dine passing[24] well and yet no more than enough.

CYLINDRUS   What guests have ye today, mistress?

EROTIUM   Here will be Menaechmus and his parasite, and myself.

CYLINDRUS   That's ten persons in all.

EROTIUM   How many?

CYLINDRUS   Ten, for I warrant you that parasite may stand for eight at his victuals.

EROTIUM   Go, dispatch as I bid you, and look ye return with all speed.

CYLINDRUS   I will have all ready with a trice.

Exeunt [separately].

❖

2.1   *Enter Menaechmus Sosicles [the Traveler],*
Messenio his servant, and some sailors.

MENAECHMUS THE TRAVELER   Surely, Messenio, I think seafarers never take so comfortable a joy in anything as, when they have been long tossed and turmoiled in the wide seas, they hap at last to ken land.[1]

MESSENIO   I'll be sworn, I should not be gladder to see a whole country of mine own than I have been at such a sight. But, I pray, wherefore are we now come to Epidamnum? Must we needs go to see every town that we hear of?

MENAECHMUS THE TRAVELER   Till I find my brother, all towns are alike to me. I must try in all places.

MESSENIO   Why, then, let's even as long as we live seek your brother. Six years now have we roamed about thus—Istria, Hispania, Massilia, Illyria, all the Upper Sea, all high Greece, all haven[2] towns in Italy. I think if we had sought a needle all this time we must needs have found it, had it been above ground. It cannot be that he is alive; and to seek a dead man thus among the living, what folly is it?

MENAECHMUS THE TRAVELER   Yea, could I but once find any man that could certainly inform me of his death, I were

---

24 **passing** surpassing, very

2.1. 1 **hap . . . land** happen finally to catch sight of land   2 **haven** port satisfied. Otherwise I can never desist seeking. Little knowest thou, Messenio, how near my heart it goes.

MESSENIO This is washing of a blackamoor.[3] Faith, let's go home, unless ye mean we should write a story of our travel.

MENAECHMUS THE TRAVELER Sirrah, no more of these saucy speeches. I perceive I must teach ye how to serve me, not to rule me.

MESSENIO Ay, so, now it appears what it is to be a servant. Well, yet I must speak my conscience. Do ye hear, sir? Faith, I must tell ye one thing: when I look into the lean estate of your purse and consider advisedly of your decaying stock, I hold it very needful to be drawing homeward, lest in looking your brother we quite lose ourselves. For, this assure yourself: this town Epidamnum is a place of outrageous expenses, exceeding in all riot and lasciviousness and, I hear, as full of ribalds,[4] parasites, drunkards, catchpoles, coneycatchers,[5] and sycophants as it can hold. Then, for courtesans, why, here's the currentest stamp[6] of them in the world. Ye must not think here to scape with as light cost as in other places. The very name shows the nature: no man comes here *sine damno*.[7]

MENAECHMUS THE TRAVELER Ye say very well indeed. Give me my purse into mine own keeping, because I will so be the safer, *sine damno*.

MESSENIO Why, sir?

MENAECHMUS THE TRAVELER Because I fear you will be busy among the* courtesans and so be cozened[8] of it. Then should I take great pains in belaboring your shoulders. So, to avoid both these harms, I'll keep it myself. [*He takes the purse.*]

MESSENIO I pray do so, sir. All the better.

Enter Cylindrus [with a handbasket].

CYLINDRUS [*To himself*] I have tickling gear[9] here, i' faith, for their dinners. It grieves me to the heart to think how that cormorant[10] knave Peniculus must have his share in these dainty morsels. But what? Is Menaechmus come already,

---

*the the the

3 washing of a blackamoor i.e., performing an impossible task
4 ribalds rascals **5 catchpoles, coneycatchers** petty officers of justice
and swindlers (both terms of contempt) **6 currentest stamp** most
current fashion **7 sine damno** without being condemned (with a wordplay on Epi*damn*um) **8 cozened** cheated (also in 3.1) **9 tickling gear**
delicate fare **10 cormorant** i.e., devouring (like the large seabird)

before I could come from the market?—Menaechmus, how
do ye, sir? How haps it ye come so soon?

MENAECHMUS THE TRAVELER God-a-mercy, my good friend,
dost thou know me?

CYLINDRUS Know ye? No, not I. Where's Moldychaps that
must dine with ye? A murrain[11] on his manners!

MENAECHMUS THE TRAVELER Whom meanest thou, good fellow?

CYLINDRUS Why, Peniculus, worship,[12] that whoreson lick-
trencher,[13] your parasitical attendant.

MENAECHMUS THE TRAVELER What Peniculus? What attendant? My attendant?—Surely this fellow is mad.

MESSENIO Did I not tell ye what coneycatching villains ye
should find here?

CYLINDRUS Menaechmus, hark ye, sir: ye come too soon back
again to dinner. I am but returned from the market.

MENAECHMUS THE TRAVELER Fellow, here, thou shalt have
money of me. [*He offers money.*] Go, get the priest to
sacrifice for thee. I know thou art mad, else thou wouldst
never use a stranger thus.

CYLINDRUS Alas, sir, Cylindrus was wont to be no stranger to
you. Know ye not Cylindrus?

MENAECHMUS THE TRAVELER Cylindrus or Coliendrus[14] or
what the devil thou art I know not; neither do I care to know.

CYLINDRUS I know you to be Menaechmus.

MENAECHMUS THE TRAVELER Thou shouldst be in thy wits, in
that thou namest me so right. But tell me, where hast thou
known me?

CYLINDRUS Where? Even here, where ye first fell in love with
my mistress, Erotium.

MENAECHMUS THE TRAVELER I neither have lover, neither
know I who thou art.

CYLINDRUS Know ye not who I am? Who fills your cup and
dresses your meat at our house?

MESSENIO What a slave is this? That[15] I had somewhat to
break the rascal's pate withal![16]

---

11 murrain plague **12 worship** i.e., your worship, your honor
13 whoreson lick-trencher i.e., good-for-nothing lick-platter or parasite
14 Coliendrus (Menaechmus the Traveler distorts the name so that it
sounds like a word meaning "testicle.") **15 That** would that **16 break
. . . withal** beat the rascal over the head with

MENAECHMUS THE TRAVELER At your house, whenas I never came in Epidamnum till this day?

CYLINDRUS O, that's true. Do ye not dwell in yonder house? [*Indicating the house of Menaechmus the Citizen.*]

MENAECHMUS THE TRAVELER Foul shame light upon them that dwell there, for my part!

CYLINDRUS Questionless he is mad indeed, to curse himself thus.—Hark ye, Menaechmus.

MENAECHMUS THE TRAVELER What sayst thou?

CYLINDRUS If I may advise ye, ye shall bestow this money which ye offered me upon a sacrifice for yourself, for out of doubt you are mad that curse yourself.

MESSENIO What a varlet art thou to trouble us thus?

CYLINDRUS Tush, he will many times jest with me thus. Yet, when his wife is not by, 'tis a ridiculous jest.

MENAECHMUS THE TRAVELER What's that?

CYLINDRUS This I say: think ye I have brought meat enough for three of you? If not, I'll fetch more for you and your wench, and Snatchcrust your parasite.

MENAECHMUS THE TRAVELER What wenches? What parasites?

MESSENIO Villain, I'll make thee tell me what thou meanest by all this talk!

CYLINDRUS Away, jackanapes![17] I say nothing to thee, for I know thee not. I speak to him that I know.

MENAECHMUS THE TRAVELER Out, drunken fool! Without doubt thou art out of thy wits.

CYLINDRUS That you shall see by the dressing of your meat. Go, go, ye were better to go in and find somewhat to do there whiles your dinner is making ready. I'll tell my mistress ye be here. [*Exit to the courtesan's.*]

MENAECHMUS THE TRAVELER Is he gone? Messenio, I think upon thy words already.

MESSENIO Tush, mark, I pray. I'll lay[18] forty pound here dwells some courtesan to whom this fellow belongs.*

MENAECHMUS THE TRAVELER But I wonder how he knows my name.

MESSENIO O, I'll tell ye. These courtesans, as soon as any strange ship arriveth at the haven, they send a boy or a

*belongs belong

17 jackanapes tame monkey, i.e., coxcomb, ridiculous fellow **18 lay** bet wench to inquire what they be, what their names be, whence they come, wherefore they come, etc. If they can by any means strike acquaintance with him, or allure him to their houses, he is their own. We are here in a tickle[19] place, master; 'tis best to be circumspect.

MENAECHMUS THE TRAVELER I mislike not thy counsesl, Messenio.

MESSENIO Ay, but follow it, then. Soft,[20] here comes somebody forth. [*To the sailors, giving them money.*] Here, sirs, mariners, keep this same amongst you.

Enter Erotium [from her house].

EROTIUM [*Calling within*] Let the door stand so. Away, it shall not be shut. Make haste within there, ho! Maids, look that all things be ready. Cover the board,[21] put fire under the perfuming pans, let all things be very handsome. Where is he that Cylindrus said stood without[22] here?—O, what mean you, sweetheart, that ye come not in? I trust you think yourself more welcome to this house than to your own, and great reason why you should do so. Your dinner and all things are ready as you willed. Will ye go sit down?

MENAECHMUS THE TRAVELER Whom doth this woman speak to?

EROTIUM Even to you, sir. To whom else should I speak?

MENAECHMUS THE TRAVELER Gentlewoman, ye are a stranger to me, and I marvel at your speeches.

EROTIUM Yea, sir, but such a stranger as I acknowledge ye for my best and dearest friend, and well you have deserved it.

MENAECHMUS THE TRAVELER Surely, Messenio, this woman is also mad or drunk, that useth all this kindness to me upon so small acquaintance.

MESSENIO Tush, did not I tell ye right? These be but leaves which fall upon you now in comparison of the trees that will tumble on your neck shortly. I told ye here were silver-tongued hacksters.[23] But let me talk with her a little.— Gentlewoman, what acquaintance have you with this man? Where have you seen him?

EROTIUM Where he saw me, here in Epidamnum.

---

19 tickle risky   **20 Soft** i.e., wait a moment   **21 Cover the board** set the table   **22 without** outside the door   **23 hacksters** swaggering ruffians

MESSENIO   In Epidamnum? Who never till this day set his foot within the town?

EROTIUM   Go, go, flouting jack.[24]—Menaechmus, what need all this? I pray, go in.

MENAECHMUS THE TRAVELER   She also calls me by my name.

MESSENIO   She smells your purse.

MENAECHMUS THE TRAVELER   Messenio, come hither. Here, take my purse. [*He gives him his purse.*] I'll know whether she aim at me or my purse ere I go.

EROTIUM   Will ye go in to dinner, sir?

MENAECHMUS THE TRAVELER   A good motion.[25] Yea, and thanks with all my heart.

EROTIUM   Never thank me for that which you commanded to be provided for yourself.

MENAECHMUS THE TRAVELER   That I commanded?

EROTIUM   Yea, for you and your parasite.

MENAECHMUS THE TRAVELER   My parasite?

EROTIUM   Peniculus, who came with you this morning when you brought me the cloak which you got from your wife.

MENAECHMUS THE TRAVELER   A cloak that I brought you which I got from my wife?

EROTIUM   Tush, what needeth all this jesting? Pray, leave off.

MENAECHMUS THE TRAVELER   Jest or earnest, this I tell ye for a truth: I never had wife, neither have I nor never was in this place till this instant. For only thus far am I come since I brake my fast[26] in the ship.

EROTIUM   What ship do ye tell me of?

MESSENIO   Marry, I'll tell ye: an old rotten weather-beaten ship that we have sailed up and down in this six years. Is 't not time to be going homewards, think ye?

EROTIUM   Come, come, Menaechmus, I pray, leave this sporting and go in.

MENAECHMUS THE TRAVELER   Well, gentlewoman, the truth is you mistake my person. It is some other that you look for.

EROTIUM   Why, think ye I know ye not to be Menaechmus, the son of Moschus, and have heard ye say ye were born at Syracuse,* where Agathocles did reign, then Pythia, then Liparo, and now Hiero?

*Syracuse Syracusis

24 flouting jack jeering fellow   **25 motion** proposal   **26 brake my fast** broke my fast, dined

MENAECHMUS THE TRAVELER   All this is true.

MESSENIO   Either she is a witch, or else she hath dwelt there and knew ye there.

MENAECHMUS THE TRAVELER   I'll go in with her, Messenio; I'll see further of this matter.

MESSENIO   Ye are cast away,[27] then.

MENAECHMUS THE TRAVELER   Why so? I warrant thee I can lose nothing. Somewhat I shall gain—perhaps a good lodging during my abode here. I'll dissemble with her another while.—Now, when you please, let us go in. I made strange[28] with you because of this fellow here, lest he should tell my wife of the cloak which I gave you.

EROTIUM   Will ye stay any longer for your Peniculus, your parasite?

MENAECHMUS THE TRAVELER   Not I. I'll neither stay for him nor have him let in if he do come.

EROTIUM   All the better. But sir, will ye do one thing for me?

MENAECHMUS THE TRAVELER   What is that?

EROTIUM   To bear that cloak which you gave me to the dyer's to have it new trimmed and altered.

MENAECHMUS THE TRAVELER   Yea, that will be well, so my wife shall not know it. Let me have it with me after dinner. I will but speak a word or two with this fellow and then I'll follow ye in. [*Exit Erotium into her house.*] Ho, Messenio, come aside. Go and provide for thyself and these shipboys in some inn, then look that after dinner you come hither for me.

MESSENIO   Ah, master, will ye be coneycatched thus willfully?

MENAECHMUS THE TRAVELER   Peace, foolish knave. Seest thou not what a sot she is? I shall cozen her, I warrant thee.

MESSENIO   Ay, master.

MENAECHMUS THE TRAVELER   Wilt thou be gone?

[*Exit to the courtesan's.*]

MESSENIO   See, see, she hath him safe enough now. Thus he hath escaped a hundred pirates' hands at sea, and now one land-rover hath boarded him at first encounter.—Come away, fellows.   [*Exeunt Messenio and sailors.*]

❖

27 cast away ruined   **28 made strange** acted distant

3.1   *Enter Peniculus.*

PENICULUS   Twenty years, I think, and more have I played the knave, yet never played I the foolish knave as I have done this morning. I follow Menaechmus, and he goes to the hall where now the sessions are holden. There thrusting ourselves into the press of people, when I was in the midst of all the throng he gave me the slip, that I could nevermore set eye on him, and, I dare swear, came directly to dinner. That I would he that first devised these sessions were hanged, and all that ever came of him! 'Tis such a hindrance to men that have belly business in hand. If a man be not there at his call, they amerce[1] him with a vengeance. Men that have nothing else to do, that do neither bid any man nor are themselves bidden to dinner, such should come to sessions, not we that have these matters to look to. If it were so, I had not thus lost my dinner this day, which I think in my conscience he did even purposely cozen me of.* Yet I mean to go see. If I can but light upon the reversion, I may perhaps get my pennyworth's. But how now? Is this Menaechmus coming away from thence? Dinner done, and all dispatched? What execrable luck have I!

> *Enter Menaechmus the Traveler [from the*
> *courtesan's, carrying a cloak].*

MENAECHMUS THE TRAVELER [*Calling back into the courtesan's*] Tush, I warrant ye, it shall be done as ye would wish. I'll have it so altered and trimmed new that it shall by no means be known again.

PENICULUS [*Aside*]   He carries the cloak to the dyer's, dinner done, the wine drunk up, the parasite shut out-of-doors. Well, let me live no longer but I'll revenge this injurious mockery. But first I'll hearken awhile what he saith.

MENAECHMUS THE TRAVELER   Good gods, whoever had such luck as I? Such cheer, such a dinner, such kind entertainment! And, for a farewell, this cloak, which I mean shall go with me.

PENICULUS [*Aside*]   He speaks so softly I cannot hear what he saith. I am sure he is now flouting at me for the loss of my dinner.

*of off
3.1. 1 amerce penalize, fine

MENAECHMUS THE TRAVELER She tells me how I gave it her and stole it from my wife. When I perceived she was in an error, though I know not how, I began to soothe[2] her and to say everything as she said. Meanwhile I fared well, and that a' free cost.

PENICULUS [*Aside*] Well, I'll go talk with him.

[*He comes forward.*]

MENAECHMUS THE TRAVELER Who is this same that comes to me?

PENICULUS O, well met, ficklebrain, false and treacherous dealer, crafty and unjust promise-breaker! How have I deserved you should so give me the slip, come before and dispatch the dinner, deal so badly with him that hath reverenced ye like a son?

MENAECHMUS THE TRAVELER Good fellow, what meanest thou by these speeches? Rail not on me, unless thou intend'st to receive a railer's hire.[3]

PENICULUS I have received the injury, sure I am, already.

MENAECHMUS THE TRAVELER Prithee, tell me, what is thy name?

PENICULUS Well, well, mock on, sir, mock on. Do ye not know my name?

MENAECHMUS THE TRAVELER In troth, I never saw thee in all my life, much less do I know thee.

PENICULUS Fie, awake, Menaechmus, awake! Ye oversleep yourself.

MENAECHMUS THE TRAVELER I am awake. I know what I say.

PENICULUS Know you not Peniculus?

MENAECHMUS THE TRAVELER Peniculus or Pediculus,[4] I know thee not.

PENICULUS Did ye filch a cloak from your wife this morning and bring it hither to Erotium?

MENAECHMUS THE TRAVELER Neither have I wife, neither gave I any cloak to Erotium, neither filched I any from anybody.

PENICULUS Will ye deny that which you did in my company?

MENAECHMUS THE TRAVELER* Wilt thou say I have done this in thy company?

PENICULUS Will I say it? Yea, I will stand to it.

*Menaechmus the Traveler Pen

2 **soothe** corroborate, back up, encourage, humor   3 **hire** payment, wage, reward   4 **Pediculus** pedant

MENAECHMUS THE TRAVELER   Away, filthy mad drivel,[5] away! I will talk no longer with thee.

PENICULUS [*Aside*]   Not a world of men shall stay me but I'll go tell his wife of all the whole matter, sith he is at this point[6] with me. I will make this same as unblessed a dinner as ever he ate.   [*Exit.*]

MENAECHMUS THE TRAVELER   It makes me wonder to see how everyone that meets me cavils[7] thus with me. Wherefore comes forth the maid, now?

> *Enter Ancilla, Erotium's maid [from the courtesan's].*

ANCILLA [*Offering a gold chain*]   Menaechmus, my mistress commends her heartily to you, and, seeing you go that way to the dyer's, she also desireth you to take this chain with you and put it to mending at the goldsmith's. She would have two or three ounces of gold more in it and the fashion amended.

MENAECHMUS THE TRAVELER [*Taking the chain*]   Either this or anything else within my power, tell her, I am ready to accomplish.

ANCILLA   Do ye know this chain, sir?

MENAECHMUS THE TRAVELER   Yea, I know it to be gold.

ANCILLA   This is the same you once took out of your wife's casket.

MENAECHMUS THE TRAVELER   Who, did I?

ANCILLA   Have you forgotten?

MENAECHMUS THE TRAVELER   I never did it.

ANCILLA   Give it me again, then.

MENAECHMUS THE TRAVELER   Tarry. Yes, I remember it. 'Tis it I gave[8] your mistress.

ANCILLA   O, are ye advised?[9]

MENAECHMUS THE TRAVELER   Where are the bracelets that I gave her likewise?

ANCILLA   I never knew of any.

MENAECHMUS THE TRAVELER   Faith, when I gave this, I gave them too.

ANCILLA   Well, sir, I'll tell her this shall be done?

---

5 drivel drudge, menial   **6 point** position, determination   **7 cavils** disputes, finds fault (also in 4.1)   **8 'Tis it I gave** this is the one I gave   **9 are ye advised** have you considered

MENAECHMUS THE TRAVELER Ay, ay, tell her so. She shall have the cloak and this both together.

ANCILLA I pray, Menaechmus, put a little jewel for my ear to making[10] for me. Ye know I am always ready to pleasure you.

MENAECHMUS THE TRAVELER I will. Give me the gold; I'll pay for the workmanship.

ANCILLA Lay out[11] for me. I'll pay it ye again.

MENAECHMUS THE TRAVELER Alas, I have none now.

ANCILLA When you have, will ye?

MENAECHMUS THE TRAVELER I will. Go, bid your mistress make no doubt of these. I warrant her I'll make the best hand[12] I can of them. [*Exit Ancilla.*] Is she gone? Do not all the gods conspire to load me with good luck? Well, I see 'tis high time to get me out of these coasts,[13] lest all these matters should be lewd[14] devices to draw me into some snare. There shall my garland lie, because, if they seek me, they may think I am gone that way. [*He lays down his garland.*] I will now go see if I can find my man Messenio, that I may tell him how I have sped.[15]   [*Exit.*]

4.1   *Enter Mulier, the wife of Menaechmus the Citizen, and Peniculus.*

MULIER Thinks he I will be made such a sot, and to be still his drudge, while he prowls and purloins all that I have to give his trulls?

PENICULUS Nay, hold your peace. We'll catch him in the nick.[1] This way he came, in his garland, forsooth, bearing the cloak to the dyer's. And see, I pray, where the garland lies. This way he is gone. See, see, where he comes again now without the cloak.

MULIER What shall I now do?

PENICULUS What? That which ye ever do: bait him for life.[2]

MULIER Surely I think it best so.

---

10 **put ... to making** have a little earring made   11 **Lay out** provide it
12 **hand** deal   13 **these coasts** this territory   14 **lewd** wicked   15 **sped** succeeded

4.1. 1 the nick the act   **2 bait him for life** i.e., harass him within an inch of his life

PENICULUS   Stay. We will stand aside a little; ye shall catch him unawares.   [*They stand aside.*]

Enter Menaechmus the Citizen.

MENAECHMUS THE CITIZEN   It would make a man at his wit's end to see how brabbling causes are handled yonder at the court. If a poor man, never so honest, have a matter come to be scanned,[3] there is he outfaced[4] and overlaid with countenance.[5] If a rich man, never so vile a wretch, come to speak, there they are all ready to favor his cause. What with facing out bad causes for the oppressors and patronizing some just actions for the wronged, the lawyers, they pocket up all the gains. For mine own part, I come not away empty, though I have been kept long against my will; for, taking in hand to dispatch a matter this morning for one of my acquaintance, I was no sooner entered into it but his adversaries laid so hard unto his charge and brought such matter against him that, do what I could, I could not wind myself out[6] till now. I am sore afraid Erotium thinks much unkindness in me that I stayed so long; yet she will not be angry, considering the gift I gave her today.

PENICULUS [*To Mulier*]   How think ye by that?[7]

MULIER [*To Peniculus*]   I think him a most vile wretch thus to abuse me.

MENAECHMUS THE CITIZEN   I will hie me thither.
                           [*He starts for the courtesan's.*]

MULIER [*Coming forward*]   Yea, go, pilferer, go with shame enough! Nobody sees your lewd dealings and vile thievery.

MENAECHMUS THE CITIZEN   How now, wife, what ails* thee? What is the matter?

MULIER   Ask ye me what's the matter? Fie upon thee!

PENICULUS [*To Mulier*]   Are ye not in a fit of an ague, your pulses beat so sore? To him, I say.

MENAECHMUS THE CITIZEN   Pray, wife, why are ye so angry with me?

MULIER   O, you know not?

PENICULUS   He knows, but he would dissemble it.

MENAECHMUS THE CITIZEN   What is it?

---

*ails aile

3 scanned judged   **4 outfaced** brazenly contradicted   **5 overlaid with countenance** crushed by a show of virtue   **6 wind myself out** extricate myself   **7 How . . . that** what do you think of that

MULIER My cloak.

MENAECHMUS THE CITIZEN Your cloak?

MULIER My cloak, man. Why do ye blush?

PENICULUS He cannot cloak his blushing.—Nay, I might not go to dinner with you, do ye remember?—To him, I say.

MENAECHMUS THE CITIZEN Hold thy peace, Peniculus.

PENICULUS Ha! Hold my peace? Look ye, he beckons on[8] me to hold my peace.

MENAECHMUS THE CITIZEN I neither beckon nor wink on him.

MULIER Out,[9] out, what a wretched life is this that I live!

MENAECHMUS THE CITIZEN Why, what ails ye, woman?

MULIER Are ye not ashamed to deny so confidently that which is apparent?

MENAECHMUS THE CITIZEN I protest unto you before all the gods—is not this enough?—that I beckoned not on him.

PENICULUS O, sir, this is another matter.—Touch him in[10] the former cause.

MENAECHMUS THE CITIZEN What former cause?

PENICULUS The cloak, man, the cloak! Fetch the cloak again from the dyer's.

MENAECHMUS THE CITIZEN What cloak?

MULIER Nay, I'll say no more, sith ye know nothing of your own doings.

MENAECHMUS THE CITIZEN Tell me, wife, hath any of your servants abused you? Let me know.

MULIER Tush, tush.

MENAECHMUS THE CITIZEN I would not have you to be thus disquieted.

MULIER Tush, tush.

MENAECHMUS THE CITIZEN You are fallen out with some of your friends.

MULIER Tush, tush.

MENAECHMUS THE CITIZEN Sure I am I have not offended you.

MULIER No, you have dealt very honestly.

MENAECHMUS THE CITIZEN Indeed, wife, I have deserved none of these words. Tell me, are ye not well?

PENICULUS [To Mulier] What, shall he flatter ye now?

MENAECHMUS THE CITIZEN I speak not to thee, knave.—Good wife, come hither.

8 beckons on gestures to **9 Out** (An exclamation of anger.) **10 Touch him in** ask him about

MULIER   Away, away! Keep your hands off.

PENICULUS   So, bid me to dinner with you again, then slip away from me; when you have done, come forth bravely in your garland to flout me! Alas, you knew not me even now.

MENAECHMUS THE CITIZEN   Why, ass, I neither have yet dined, nor came I there, since we were there together.

PENICULUS   Whoever heard one so impudent? Did ye not meet me here even now and would make me believe I was mad, and said ye were a stranger and ye knew me not?

MENAECHMUS THE CITIZEN   Of a truth, since we went together to the sessions hall I never returned till this very instant, as you two met me.

PENICULUS   Go to,[11] go to, I know ye well enough. Did ye think I would not cry quittance[12] with you? Yes, faith, I have told your wife all.

MENAECHMUS THE CITIZEN   What hast thou told her?

PENICULUS   I cannot tell. Ask her.

MENAECHMUS THE CITIZEN   Tell me, wife, what hath he told ye of me? Tell me, I say. What was it?

MULIER   As though you knew not. My cloak is stolen from me.

MENAECHMUS THE CITIZEN   Is your cloak stolen from ye?

MULIER   Do ye ask me?

MENAECHMUS THE CITIZEN   If I knew, I would not ask.

PENICULUS   O, crafty companion![13] How he would shift the matter.—Come, come, deny it not. I tell ye, I have bewrayed[14] all.

MENAECHMUS THE CITIZEN   What hast thou bewrayed?

MULIER   Seeing ye will yield to nothing, be it never so manifest, hear me, and ye shall know in few words both the cause of my grief and what he hath told me. I say my cloak is stolen from me.

MENAECHMUS THE CITIZEN   My cloak is stolen from me?

PENICULUS   Look how he cavils.—She saith it is stolen from her.

MENAECHMUS THE CITIZEN   I have nothing to say to thee.—I say, wife, tell me.

MULIER   I tell ye my cloak is stolen out of my house.

---

11 Go to (An expression of remonstrance.)   **12 cry quittance** declare myself even, get even   **13 companion** fellow. (A term of contempt.)   **14 bewrayed** exposed, revealed

MENAECHMUS THE CITIZEN   Who stole it?

MULIER   He knows best that carried it away.

MENAECHMUS THE CITIZEN   Who was that?

MULIER   Menaechmus.

MENAECHMUS THE CITIZEN   'Twas very ill done of him. What Menaechmus was that?

MULIER   You.

MENAECHMUS THE CITIZEN   I? Who will say so?

MULIER   I will.

PENICULUS   And I. And that you gave it to Erotium.

MENAECHMUS THE CITIZEN   I gave it?

MULIER   You.

PENICULUS   You, you, you. Shall we fetch a kennel of beagles that may cry nothing but "You, you, you, you"? For we are weary of it.

MENAECHMUS THE CITIZEN   Hear me one word, wife. I protest unto you, by all the gods, I gave it her not. Indeed, I lent it her to use a while.

MULIER   Faith, sir, I never give nor lend your apparel out-of-doors. Methinks ye might let me dispose of mine own garments as you do of yours. I pray, then, fetch it me home again.

MENAECHMUS THE CITIZEN   You shall have it again without fail.

MULIER   'Tis best for you that I have. Otherwise think not to roost within these doors again.

PENICULUS [*To Mulier*] Hark ye, what say ye to me now, for bringing these matters to your knowledge?

MULIER   I say, when thou hast anything stolen from thee, come to me and I will help thee to seek it. And so farewell.
[*Exit into her house.*]

PENICULUS   God-a-mercy for nothing! That can never be, for I have nothing in the world worth the stealing. So, now with husband and wife and all I am clean out of favor. A mischief on ye all!   *Exit.*

MENAECHMUS THE CITIZEN   My wife thinks she is notably revenged on me, now she shuts me out-of-doors, as though I had not a better place to be welcome to. If she shut me out, I know who will shut me in. Now will I entreat Erotium to let me have the cloak again to stop my wife's mouth withal, and then will I provide a better for her.—Ho, who is within there? Somebody tell Erotium I must speak with her.

Enter Erotium [from her house].

EROTIUM Who calls?

MENAECHMUS THE CITIZEN Your friend more than his own.[15]

EROTIUM O Menaechmus, why stand ye here? Pray, come in.*

MENAECHMUS THE CITIZEN Tarry. I must speak with ye here.

EROTIUM Say your mind.

MENAECHMUS THE CITIZEN Wot ye what? My wife knows all the matter now, and my coming is to request you that I may have again the cloak which I brought you that so I may appease her. And, I promise you, I'll give ye another worth two of it.

EROTIUM Why, I gave it you to carry to your dyer's, and my chain likewise, to have it altered.

MENAECHMUS THE CITIZEN Gave me the cloak and your chain? In truth, I never saw ye since I left it here with you and so went to the sessions, from whence I am but now returned.

EROTIUM Ah, then, sir, I see you wrought a device to defraud me of them both. Did I therefore put ye in trust? Well, well.

MENAECHMUS THE CITIZEN To defraud ye? No, but I say my wife hath intelligence of the matter.

EROTIUM Why, sir, I asked them not; ye brought them me of your own free motion. Now ye require them again, take them, make sops of them![16] You and your wife together, think ye I esteem them or you either? Go, come to me again when I send for you.

MENAECHMUS THE CITIZEN What, so angry with me, sweet Erotium? Stay, I pray, stay.

EROTIUM Stay? Faith, sir, no. Think ye I will stay at your request?   *[Exit into her house.]*

MENAECHMUS THE CITIZEN What, gone in chafing,[17] and clapped to[18] the doors? Now I am every way shut out for a very benchwhistler;[19] neither shall I have entertainment here nor at home. I were best to go try some other friends and ask counsel what to do.   *[Exit.]*

---

*come in come it

15 more than his own (i.e., because I am out of sorts with myself)
16 make sops of them i.e., do what you like with them. (A *sop* is a bit of bread soaked in wine.) **17 chafing** fretting, angry **18 clapped to** slammed shut **19 benchwhistler** i.e., idle person

5.1 *Enter Menaechmus the Traveler [as from the city, carrying the cloak, and] Mulier [from the house of Menaechmus the Citizen].*

MENAECHMUS THE TRAVELER *[To himself]* Most foolishly was I overseen[1] in giving my purse and money to Messenio, whom I can nowhere find. I fear he is fallen into some lewd company.

MULIER *[To herself]* I marvel that my husband comes not yet. But see where he is now, and brings my cloak with him.

MENAECHMUS THE TRAVELER *[To himself]* I muse[2] where the knave should be.

MULIER *[To herself]* I will go ring a peal through both his ears for this his dishonest behavior.—O sir, ye are welcome home, with your thievery on your shoulders. Are ye not ashamed to let all the world see and speak of your lewdness?[3]

MENAECHMUS THE TRAVELER How now? What lacks[4] this woman?

MULIER Impudent beast, stand ye to question about it? For shame, hold thy peace.

MENAECHMUS THE TRAVELER What offense have I done, woman, that I should not speak to you?

MULIER Askest thou what offense? O shameless boldness!

MENAECHMUS THE TRAVELER Good woman, did ye never hear why the Grecians termed Hecuba[5] to be a bitch?

MULIER Never.

MENAECHMUS THE TRAVELER Because she did as you do now: on whomsoever she met withal she railed, and therefore well deserved that dogged name.

MULIER These foul abuses and contumelies[6] I can never endure; nay, rather will I live a widow's life to my dying day.

MENAECHMUS THE TRAVELER What care I whether thou livest as a widow or as a wife? This passeth,[7] that I meet with none but thus they vex me with strange speeches.

MULIER What strange speeches? I say I will surely live a widow's life rather than suffer thy vile dealings.

5.1. 1 overseen imprudent **2 muse** wonder **3 lewdness** wickedness
4 lacks i.e., ails **5 Hecuba** (The widow of King Priam of Troy is portrayed as embittered in Euripides' play *Hecuba* and elsewhere.)
6 contumelies insults **7 passeth** exceeds, goes too far

MENAECHMUS THE TRAVELER Prithee, for my part, live a widow till the world's end if thou wilt.

MULIER Even now thou deniedst that thou stolest it from me, and now thou bringest it home openly in my sight. Art not ashamed?

MENAECHMUS THE TRAVELER Woman, you are greatly to blame to charge me with stealing of this cloak, which this day another gave me to carry to be trimmed.

MULIER Well, I will first complain to my father. [*Calling into her house.*] Ho, boy! Who is within there? [*Enter Boy.*] Vecio, go run quickly to my father. Desire him of all love[8] to come over quickly to my house. [*Exit Boy.*] I'll tell him first of your pranks. I hope he will not see me[9] thus handled.

MENAECHMUS THE TRAVELER What i' God's name meaneth this madwoman thus to vex me?

MULIER I am mad because I tell ye of your vile actions and lewd pilfering away my apparel and my jewels to carry to your filthy drabs.[10]

MENAECHMUS THE TRAVELER For whom this woman taketh me I know not. I know her as much as I know Hercules' wife's father.[11]

MULIER Do ye not know me? That's well. I hope ye know my father. Here he comes. Look, do ye know him?

MENAECHMUS THE TRAVELER As much as I knew Calchas of Troy.[12] Even him and thee I know both alike.

MULIER Dost know neither of us both, me nor my father?

MENAECHMUS THE TRAVELER Faith, nor thy grandfather neither.

MULIER This is like the rest of your behavior.

Enter Senex.

SENEX [*To himself*] Though bearing so great a burden as old age, I can make no great haste; yet, as I can, I will go to my daughter, who I know hath some earnest business with me that she sends in such haste, not telling the cause why I should come. But I durst lay a wager I can guess near the matter. I suppose it is some brabble between her husband

---

8 of all love for love's sake **9 see me** i.e., stand idly by and see me
10 drabs sluts **11 Hercules' wife's father** Oeneus of Calydon, father of
Deianira **12 Calchas of Troy** a Greek priest and seer, father of Cressida

and her. These young women that bring great dowries to their husbands are so masterful and obstinate that they will have their own wills in everything and make men servants to their weak affections. And young men, too, I must needs say, be naught nowadays. Well, I'll go see. But yonder methinks stands my daughter, and her husband too. Oh, 'tis even as I guessed.

MULIER   Father, ye are welcome.

> [*She and her father stand apart from
> Menaechmus the Traveler.*]

SENEX   How now, daughter? What, is all well? Why is your husband so sad? Have ye been chiding? Tell me, which of you is in the fault?

MULIER   First, Father, know that I have not any way misbehaved myself, but the truth is I can by no means endure this bad man, to die for it,[13] and therefore desire you to take me home to you again.

SENEX   What is the matter?

MULIER   He makes me a stale[14] and laughingstock to all the world.

SENEX   Who doth?

MULIER   This good husband here, to whom you married me.

SENEX   See, see, how oft have I warned you of falling out with your husband?

MULIER   I cannot avoid it, if he doth so foully abuse me.

SENEX   I always told ye you must bear with him, ye must let him alone, ye must not watch him nor dog him nor meddle with his courses in any sort.

MULIER   He haunts naughty harlots under my nose.

SENEX   He is the wiser,[15] because he cannot be quiet[16] at home.

MULIER   There he feasts and banquets and spends and spoils.[17]

SENEX   Would ye have your husband serve ye as your drudge? Ye will not let him make merry nor entertain his friends at home.

MULIER   Father, will ye take his part in these abuses and forsake me?

---

13 to die for it if I should have to die for it   **14 stale** object of ridicule
15 is the wiser i.e., chooses a sensible course   **16 be quiet** find quiet
17 spoils is extravagant

SENEX   Not so, daughter; but if I see cause, I will as well tell him of his duty.

MENAECHMUS THE TRAVELER [*Aside*]   I would I were gone from this prating father and daughter.

SENEX   Hitherto I see not but he keeps ye well. Ye want nothing—apparel, money, servants, meat, drink, all things necessary. I fear there is fault in you.

MULIER   But he filcheth away my apparel and my jewels to give to his trulls.

SENEX   If he doth so, 'tis very ill done; if not, you do ill to say so.

MULIER   You may believe me, Father, for there you may see my cloak, which now he hath fetched home again, and my chain, which he stole from me.

SENEX   Now will I go talk with him to know the truth. [*He approaches Menaechmus the Traveler.*] Tell me, Menaechmus, how is it that I hear such disorder in your life? Why are ye so sad, man? Wherein hath your wife offended you?

MENAECHMUS THE TRAVELER   Old man—what to call ye I know not—by high Jove* and by all the gods I swear unto you, whatsoever this woman here accuseth me to have stolen from her, it is utterly false and untrue, and if I ever set foot within her doors I wish the greatest misery in the world to light upon me.

SENEX   Why, fond[18] man, art thou mad to deny that thou ever sett'st foot within thine own house where thou dwellest?

MENAECHMUS THE TRAVELER   Do I dwell in that house?

SENEX   Dost thou deny it?

MENAECHMUS THE TRAVELER   I do.

SENEX   Hark ye, daughter, are ye removed[19] out of your house?

MULIER   Father, he useth you as he doth me. This life I have with him!

SENEX   Menaechmus, I pray, leave this fondness. Ye jest too perversely with your friends.

MENAECHMUS THE TRAVELER   Good old father, what, I pray, have you to do with me? Or why should this woman thus trouble me, with whom I have no dealings in the world?

MULIER   Father, mark, I pray, how his eyes sparkle. They roll

*Jove Iobe
18 fond foolish   19 removed moved

in his head; his color goes and comes; he looks wildly. See, see.

MENAECHMUS THE TRAVELER [*Aside*]   What? They say now I am mad. The best way for me is to feign myself mad indeed; so I shall be rid of them.

MULIER   Look how he stares about! Now he gapes.

SENEX   Come away, daughter. Come from him.

MENAECHMUS THE TRAVELER [*Feigning madness*]   Bacchus, Apollo, Phoebus, do ye call me to come hunt in the woods with you? I see, I hear, I come, I fly, but I cannot get out of these fields. Here is an old mastiff bitch stands barking at me, and by her stands an old goat that bears false witness against many a poor man.

SENEX   Out upon him, Bedlam fool!

MENAECHMUS THE TRAVELER   Hark! Apollo commands me that I should rend out her eyes with a burning lamp.

MULIER   O Father, he threatens to pull out mine eyes!

MENAECHMUS THE TRAVELER   Good gods, these folk say I am mad, and doubtless they are mad themselves.

SENEX   Daughter!

MULIER   Here, Father. What shall we do?

SENEX   What if I fetch my folks hither and have him carried in before he do any harm?

MENAECHMUS THE TRAVELER [*Aside*]   How now? They will carry me in if I look not to myself. I were best to scare them better yet.—Dost thou bid me, Phoebus, to tear this dog in pieces with my nails? If I lay hold on him I will do thy commandment.

SENEX   Get thee into thy house, daughter. Away, quickly!

> [*Mulier exits into her house.*]

MENAECHMUS THE TRAVELER   She is gone.—Yea, Apollo, I will sacrifice this old beast unto thee; and, if thou commandest me, I will cut his throat with that dagger that hangs at his girdle.   [*He advances threateningly toward Senex.*]

SENEX   Come not near me, sirrah.

MENAECHMUS THE TRAVELER   Yea, I will quarter[20] him and pull all the bones out of his flesh. Then will I barrel up[21] his bowles.

---

20 quarter cut in quarters, as one would a traitor or criminal
21 barrel up pack up, stow away

SENEX Sure I am sore afraid he will do some hurt.

MENAECHMUS THE TRAVELER Many things thou commandest me, Apollo. Wouldst thou have me harness up these wild horses and then climb up into the chariot and so override this old stinking toothless lion? So, now I am in the chariot, and I have hold on the reins. Here is my whip. Hait![22] Come, ye wild jades, make a hideous noise with your stamping. Hait, I say! Will ye not go?

SENEX What, doth he threaten me with his horses?

MENAECHMUS THE TRAVELER Hark, now, Apollo bids me ride over him that stands there and kill him. How now? Who pulls me down from my chariot by the hairs of my head? O, shall I not fulfill Apollo's commandment?

SENEX See, see, what a sharp disease this is, and how well he was even now! I will fetch a physician straight, before he grow too far into this rage.   *Exit.*

MENAECHMUS THE TRAVELER Are they both gone now? I'll then hie me away to my ship. 'Tis time to be gone from hence.   *Exit.*

Enter Senex and Medicus [the doctor, following].

SENEX My loins ache with sitting and mine eyes with looking while I stay for yonder lazy physician. See now where the creeping drawlatch[23] comes.

MEDICUS What disease hath he, said you? Is it a lethargy or a lunacy, or melancholy, or dropsy?

SENEX Wherefore, I pray, do I bring you, but that you should tell me what it is and cure him of it?

MEDICUS Fie, make no question of that. I'll cure him, I warrant ye. O, here he comes. Stay, let us mark what he doth.
                                                                          [They stand aside.]

Enter Menaechmus the Citizen.

MENAECHMUS THE CITIZEN Never in my life had I more overthwart[24] fortune in one day! And all by the villainy of this false knave the parasite, my Ulysses,[25] that works such mischiefs against me, his king. But let me live no longer but I'll be revenged upon the life of him. His life? Nay, 'tis my

----

22 Hait i.e., giddap **23 drawlatch** thief **24 overthwart** perverse
25 Ulysses (This hero of the Trojan War was famous for his cunning.)

life, for he lives by my meat and drink. I'll utterly withdraw
the slave's life from him. And Erotium! She showeth plainly
what she is, who, because I require the cloak again to carry
to my wife, saith I gave it her, and flatly falls out with me.
How unfortunate am I!

SENEX Do ye hear him?

MEDICUS He complains of his fortune.

SENEX Go to him.

MEDICUS [*Approaching Menaechmus the Citizen*] Menaechmus, how do ye, man? Why keep you not your cloak over
your arm? It is very hurtful to your disease. Keep ye warm, I
pray.

MENAECHMUS THE CITIZEN Why, hang thyself. What carest
thou?

MEDICUS Sir, can you smell anything?

MENAECHMUS THE CITIZEN I smell a prating dolt of thee.

MEDICUS O, I will have your head thoroughly purged.²⁶ Pray
tell me, Menaechmus, what use you to drink? White wine or
claret?

MENAECHMUS THE CITIZEN What the devil carest thou?

SENEX Look. His fit now begins.

MENAECHMUS THE CITIZEN Why dost not as well ask me
whether I eat bread, or cheese, or beef, or porridge, or birds
that bear feathers, or fishes that have fins?

SENEX See what idle talk he falleth into.

MEDICUS Tarry, I will ask him further.—Menaechmus, tell
me, be not your eyes heavy and dull sometimes?

MENAECHMUS THE CITIZEN What dost think I am, an owl?

MEDICUS Do not your guts gripe²⁷ ye and croak in your belly?

MENAECHMUS THE CITIZEN When I am hungry they do, else
not.

MEDICUS He speaks not like a madman in that.—Sleep ye
soundly all night?

MENAECHMUS THE CITIZEN When I have paid my debts, I do.
The mischief light on thee with all thy frivolous questions!

MEDICUS O, now he rageth upon those words. Take heed.

SENEX O, this is nothing to the rage he was in even now. He
called his wife bitch, and all to naught.²⁸

MENAECHMUS THE CITIZEN Did I?

---

26 have . . . purged i.e., use a purging medicine to clear your brain
27 gripe offend, distress **28 all to naught** i.e., abused her vehemently

SENEX   Thou didst, mad fellow, and threatenedst to ride over me here with a chariot and horses, and to kill me and tear me in pieces. This thou didst. I know what I say.

MENAECHMUS THE CITIZEN   I say thou stolest Jupiter's crown from his head, and thou wert whipped through the town for it, and that thou hast killed thy father and beaten thy mother. Do ye think I am so mad that I cannot devise as notable lies of you as you do of me?

SENEX   Master Doctor, pray heartily, make speed to cure him. See ye not how mad he waxeth?

MEDICUS   I'll tell ye, he shall be brought over to my house and there will I cure him.

SENEX   Is that best?

MEDICUS   What else? There I can order him as I list.²⁹

SENEX   Well, it shall be so.

MEDICUS   O, sir, I will make ye take neesing³⁰ powder this twenty days.

MENAECHMUS THE CITIZEN   I'll beat ye first with a bastinado³¹ this thirty days.

MEDICUS   Fetch men to carry him to my house.

SENEX   How many will serve the turn?

MEDICUS   Being no madder than he is now, four will serve.

SENEX   I'll fetch them. Stay you with him, Master Doctor.

MEDICUS   No, by my faith, I'll go home to make ready all things needful. Let your men bring him hither.

SENEX   I go.   *Exeunt [Medicus and Senex].*

MENAECHMUS THE CITIZEN   Are they both gone? Good gods, what meaneth this? These men say I am mad, who without doubt are mad themselves. I stir not, I fight not, I am not sick. I speak to them, I know them. Well, what were I now best to do? I would go home, but my wife shuts me forth o' doors. Erotium is as far out with me too. Even here I will rest me till the evening. [*He lies down.*] I hope by that time they will take pity on me.

Enter Messenio, the Traveler's servant.

MESSENIO   The proof of a good servant is to regard his master's business as well in his absence as in his presence, and I think him a very fool that is not careful as well for his

---

29 order . . . list provide for him as I think best   **30 neesing** sneezing
31 bastinado cudgel

ribs and shoulders as for his belly and throat. When I think upon the rewards of a sluggard, I am ever pricked[32] with a careful regard of my back and shoulders, for in truth I have no fancy to these blows, as many a one hath. Methinks it is no pleasure to a man to be basted[33] with a rope's end two or three hours together. I have provided yonder in the town for all our mariners, and safely bestowed all my master's trunks and fardels,[34] and am now coming to see if he be yet got forth of this dangerous gulf where, I fear me, he* is overplunged. Pray God he be not overwhelmed and past help ere I come!

Enter Senex, with four lorarii, porters.

SENEX [*To the porters*]   Before gods and men, I charge and command you, sirs, to execute with great care that which I appoint you. If ye love the safety of your own ribs and shoulders, then go take me up my son-in-law. Lay all hands upon him. Why stand ye still? What do ye doubt? I say, care not for his threatenings nor for any of his words. Take him up and bring him to the physician's house. I will go thither before.   *Exit.*

MENAECHMUS THE CITIZEN   [*As the porters seize and lift him*] What news?[35] How now, masters?[36] What will ye do with me? Why do ye thus beset[37] me? Whither carry ye me? Help, help! Neighbors, friends, citizens!

MESSENIO   O Jupiter, what do I see? My master abused by a company of varlets.

MENAECHMUS THE CITIZEN   Is there no good man will help me?

MESSENIO [*Coming to the rescue*]   Help ye, master? Yes, the villains shall have my life before they shall thus wrong ye. 'Tis more fit I should be killed than you thus handled. Pull out that rascal's eye that holds ye about the neck there. I'll clout these peasants. Out, ye rogue! Let go, ye varlet!

MENAECHMUS THE CITIZEN   I have hold of this villain's eye.

MESSENIO   Pull it out, and let the place appear in his head.[38] Away, ye cutthroat thieves! Ye murderers!

ALL THE PORTERS   O, O, ai, ai!   *Cry pitifully.**

---

*he [not in 1595]   *s.d. **Cry pitifully** [included as part of spoken text in 1595]
32 pricked spurred   **33 basted** beaten   **34 fardels** parcels   **35 What news** i.e., what's going on   **36 masters** i.e., sirs   **37 beset** surround with hostile intent   **38 let . . . head** i.e., leave an empty eye socket

MESSENIO   Away! Get ye hence, ye mongrels, ye dogs. [*Some flee.*] Will ye be gone? Thou rascal behind there, I'll give thee somewhat more. [*He attacks a straggler.*] Take that. [*All disappear.*] It was time to come, master; you had been in good case[39] if I had not been here now. I told you what would come of it.

MENAECHMUS THE CITIZEN   Now, as the gods love me, my good friend, I thank thee. Thou hast done that for me which I shall never be able to requite.[40]

MESSENIO   I'll tell ye how, sir: give me my freedom.

MENAECHMUS THE CITIZEN   Should I give it thee?

MESSENIO   Seeing you cannot requite my good turn.

MENAECHMUS THE CITIZEN   Thou art deceived, man.

MESSENIO   Wherein?

MENAECHMUS THE CITIZEN   On mine honesty, I am none of thy master.[41] I had never yet any servant would do so much for me.

MESSENIO   Why, then, bid me be free. Will you?

MENAECHMUS THE CITIZEN   Yea, surely. Be free, for my part.

MESSENIO   O, sweetly spoken! Thanks, my good master. [*To himself.*]*   Messenio, we are all glad of your good fortune.

MESSENIO   O master—I'll call ye master still—I pray, use me in any service as ye did before; I'll dwell with you still, and when ye go home I'll wait upon you.

MENAECHMUS THE CITIZEN   Nay, nay, it shall not need.

MESSENIO   I'll go straight to the inn and deliver up my accounts and all your stuff. Your purse is locked up safely sealed in the casket, as you gave it me. I will go fetch it to you.

MENAECHMUS THE CITIZEN   Do, fetch it.

MESSENIO   I will.   [*Exit.*]

MENAECHMUS THE CITIZEN   I was never thus perplexed. Some deny me to be him that I am and shut me out of their doors. This fellow saith he is my bondman, and of me he begs his freedom. He will fetch my purse and money. Well, if he bring it, I will receive it and set him free. I would he would, so he* go his way. My old father-in-law and the Doctor say I am mad. Whoever saw such strange demeanors? Well, though Erotium be never so angry, yet once again I'll go see if by

*[**To himself**] [1595 here has a s.p., "Seruus Alius"]   *he [not in 1595]

39 you . . . case i.e., you would have been in a fine fix   **40 requite** pay
41 none . . . master no master of yours

entreaty I can get the cloak of* her to carry to my wife.

Exit [to the courtesan's].

Enter Menaechmus the Traveler, and Messenio.

MENAECHMUS THE TRAVELER   Impudent knave, wilt thou say that I ever saw thee since I sent thee away today and bade thee come for me after dinner?

MESSENIO   Ye make me stark mad! I took ye away and rescued ye from four great big-boned villains that were carrying ye away even here in this place. Here they had ye up. You cried, "Help, help!" I came running to you. You and I together beat them away by main force. Then, for my good turn and faithful service, ye gave me my freedom. I told ye I would go fetch your casket. Now in the meantime you ran some other way to get before me, and so you deny it all again.

MENAECHMUS THE TRAVELER   I gave thee thy freedom?

MESSENIO   You did.

MENAECHMUS THE TRAVELER   When I give thee thy freedom, I'll be a bondman myself. Go thy ways.⁴²

MESSENIO   Whew! Marry, I thank ye for nothing.

Enter Menaechmus the Citizen.

MENAECHMUS THE CITIZEN [*Calling back into the courtesan's house*]   Forsworn queans,⁴³ swear till your hearts ache and your eyes fall out! Ye shall never make me believe that I carried hence either cloak or chain.

MESSENIO [*To Menaechmus the Traveler*]   O heavens, master, what do I see?

MENAECHMUS THE TRAVELER   What?

MESSENIO   Your ghost.

MENAECHMUS THE TRAVELER   What ghost?

MESSENIO   Your image, as like you as can be possible.

MENAECHMUS THE TRAVELER   Surely not much unlike me, as I think.

MENAECHMUS THE CITIZEN [*Seeing Messenio*]   O my good friend and helper, well met! Thanks for thy late good help.

MESSENIO   Sir, may I crave to know your name?

MENAECHMUS THE CITIZEN   I were too blame⁴⁴ if I should not tell thee anything. My name is Menaechmus.

*of on
42 Go thy ways get along with you   **43 Forsworn queans** lying whores
44 too blame exceedingly blameworthy

MENAECHMUS THE TRAVELER   Nay, my friend, that is my name.

MENAECHMUS THE CITIZEN   I am of Syracuse in Sicily.

MENAECHMUS THE TRAVELER   So am I.

MESSENIO [*To Menaechmus the Citizen*]   Are you a Syracusan?

MENAECHMUS THE CITIZEN   I am.

MESSENIO   Oho, I know ye! This [*Indicating the Citizen*] is my master; I thought he there had been my master, and was proffering my service to him. Pray pardon me, sir, if I said anything I should not.

MENAECHMUS THE TRAVELER   Why, doting patch,[45] didst thou not come with me this morning from the ship?

MESSENIO   My faith, he says true. This [*Indicating the Traveler*] is my master; you may go look ye a man.—God save ye, master!—You, sir, farewell. This is Menaechmus.

MENAECHMUS THE CITIZEN   I say that I am Menaechmus.

MESSENIO   What a jest is this! Are you Menaechmus?

MENAECHMUS THE CITIZEN   Even Menaechmus, the son of Moschus.

MENAECHMUS THE TRAVELER   My father's son?

MENAECHMUS THE CITIZEN   Friend, I go about neither to take your father nor your country from you.

MESSENIO   O immortal gods, let it fall out as I hope! And, for my life, these are the two twins, all things agree so jump[46] together. I will speak to my master.—Menaechmus?

BOTH   What wilt thou?

MESSENIO   I call ye not both. But which of you came with me from the ship?

MENAECHMUS THE CITIZEN   Not I.

MENAECHMUS THE TRAVELER   I did.

MESSENIO   Then I call you. Come hither.

[*He takes Menaechmus the Traveler aside.*]

MENAECHMUS THE TRAVELER   What's the matter?

MESSENIO   This same is either some notable cozening juggler or else it is your brother whom we seek. I never saw one man so like another. Water to water nor milk to milk is not liker than he is to you.

MENAECHMUS THE TRAVELER   Indeed, I think thou sayst true.

45 doting patch foolish clown   **46 jump** precisely

Find it that he is my brother, and I here promise thee thy freedom.

MESSENIO Well, let me about it. [*He takes Menaechmus the Citizen aside.*] Hear ye, sir, you say your name is Menaechmus?

MENAECHMUS THE CITIZEN I do.

MESSENIO So is this man's. You are of Syracuse?

MENAECHMUS THE CITIZEN True.

MESSENIO So is he. Moschus was your father?

MENAECHMUS THE CITIZEN He was.

MESSENIO So was he his. What will you say if I find that ye are brethren and twins?

MENAECHMUS THE CITIZEN I would think it happy news.

MESSENIO Nay, stay, masters both. I mean to have the honor of this exploit. Answer me: your name is Menaechmus?

MENAECHMUS THE CITIZEN Yea.

MESSENIO And yours?

MENAECHMUS THE TRAVELER And mine.

MESSENIO You are of Syracuse?

MENAECHMUS THE CITIZEN I am.

MENAECHMUS THE TRAVELER And I.

MESSENIO Well, this goeth right thus far. What is the farthest[47] thing that you remember there?

MENAECHMUS THE CITIZEN How I went with my father to Tarentum, to a great mart,[48] and there in the press[49] I was stolen from him.

MENAECHMUS THE TRAVELER O Jupiter!

MESSENIO Peace, what exclaiming is this?—How old were ye then?

MENAECHMUS THE CITIZEN About seven year old, for even then I shed teeth;[50] and since that time I never heard of any of my kindred.

MESSENIO Had ye never a brother?

MENAECHMUS THE CITIZEN Yes, as I remember I heard them say we were two twins.

MENAECHMUS THE TRAVELER O Fortune!

MESSENIO Tush, can ye not be quiet?—Were ye both of one name?

---

47 farthest i.e., furthest back in time **48 mart** market, fair **49 press** crowd **50 shed teeth** i.e., lost baby teeth

MENAECHMUS THE CITIZEN   Nay, as I think, they called my brother Sosicles.

MENAECHMUS THE TRAVELER   It is he. What need farther proof? O brother, brother, let me embrace thee!

MENAECHMUS THE CITIZEN   Sir, if this be true I am wonderfully glad. But how is it that ye are called Menaechmus?

MENAECHMUS THE TRAVELER   When it was told us that you and our father were both dead, our grandsire, in memory of my father's name, changed mine to Menaechmus.

MENAECHMUS THE CITIZEN   'Tis very like[51] he would do so, indeed. But let me ask ye one question more: what was our mother's name?

MENAECHMUS THE TRAVELER   Theusimarche.

MENAECHMUS THE CITIZEN   Brother, the most welcome man to me that the world holdeth!

MENAECHMUS THE TRAVELER   Ay, joy, and ten thousand joys the more, having taken so long travail and huge pains to seek you.

MESSENIO   See now how all this matter comes about. This it was [*Indicating Menaechmus the Traveler*] that the gentlewoman had ye in to dinner, thinking it had been he.

MENAECHMUS THE CITIZEN   True it is, I willed a dinner to be provided for me here this morning, and I also brought hither closely[52] a cloak of my wife's and gave it to this woman.

MENAECHMUS THE TRAVELER [*Producing the cloak*]   Is not this the same, brother?

MENAECHMUS THE CITIZEN   How came you by this?

MENAECHMUS THE TRAVELER   This woman met me, had me into dinner, entertained me most kindly, and gave me this cloak and this chain. [*He shows the chain.*]

MENAECHMUS THE CITIZEN   Indeed, she took ye for me, and I believe I have been as strangely handled by occasion of your coming.

MESSENIO   You shall have time enough to laugh at all these matters hereafter. Do ye remember, master, what ye promised me?

MENAECHMUS THE CITIZEN   Brother, I will entreat you to perform your promise to Messenio. He is worthy of it.

MENAECHMUS THE TRAVELER   I am content.

MESSENIO   Io,[53] triumph!

51 like likely   **52 closely** secretly   **53 Io** (An exclamation of joy.)

MENAECHMUS THE TRAVELER Brother, will ye now go with me to Syracuse?

MENAECHMUS THE CITIZEN So soon as I can sell away such goods as I possess here in Epidamnum, I will go with you.

MENAECHMUS THE TRAVELER Thanks, my good brother.

MENAECHMUS THE CITIZEN Messenio, play thou the crier for me and make a proclamation.

MESSENIO A fit office. Come on. Oyez! What day shall your sale be?

MENAECHMUS THE CITIZEN This day sennight.[54]

MESSENIO [*Making proclamation*] All men, women, and children in Epidamnum or elsewhere that will repair to Menaechmus' house this day sennight shall there find all manner of things to sell:[55] servants, household stuff, house, ground, and all, so they bring ready money.—Will ye sell your wife too, sir?

MENAECHMUS THE CITIZEN Yea, but I think nobody will bid money for her.

MESSENIO [*As Epilogue*] Thus, gentlemen, we take our leaves, and if we have pleased, we require a *Plaudite*.[56]

[*Exeunt.*]

Text based on *Menaechmi. A Pleasant and Fine Conceited Comedy, Taken out of the Most Excellent Witty Poet, Plautus. . . . Written in English by W. W. . . . Printed by Tho. Creede . . . 1595.*

54 This day sennight one week from now **55 to sell** on sale **56 require a Plaudite** request applause at the end of the play

Further Reading

Arthos, John. "Shakespeare's Transformation of Plautus." *Comparative Drama* 1 (1967–1968): 239–253. Rpt. and rev. in *Shakespeare: The Early Writings.* London: Bowes and Bowes, 1972. In a sustained analysis of Plautus, Arthos finds aspects in addition to farce that were resources for Shakespeare's transformation of the *Menaechmi*. In *The Comedy of Errors*, Shakespeare also exploits the "musicality" and "exuberance" of Plautus' art, heightening the Plautine emphasis on wonder and the power of love.

Baldwin, T. W. *On the Compositional Genetics of "The Comedy of Errors."* Urbana, Ill.: Univ. of Illinois Press, 1965. Baldwin offers an exhaustive study of the background of Shakespeare's play. He discusses the play's structure, sources, and date in terms of the literary, intellectual, and political activity of England in the 1580s.

Barber, C. L. "Shakespearean Comedy in *The Comedy of Errors.*" *College English* 25 (1964): 493–497. Barber argues that the play transcends the outrageousness of its Roman model, framing the "animal or natural or foolish side of man by presentation of the normal and the ideal." The totality of Shakespeare's characterization, his testing and display of the bond of marriage, and his control of the "rhythm of feeling" serve to elevate the play above the farce of its source.

Berry, Ralph. "And Here We Wander in Illusions." *Shakespeare's Comedies: Explorations in Form.* Princeton, N.J.: Princeton Univ. Press, 1972. For Berry, the tragic frame and the psychological complexity of the characters work to graft onto the farce of *The Comedy of Errors* the serious thematic concerns of the later comedies. Out of the errors of farcical action emerges a comedy that explores the problems of human identity.

Brooks, Harold F. "Themes and Structure in *The Comedy of Errors.*" In *Early Shakespeare,* ed. John Russell Brown and Bernard Harris. Stratford-upon-Avon Studies 3. London: Edward Arnold, 1961. Rpt. in *Shakespeare, the Comedies: A Collection of Critical Essays,* ed. Kenneth Muir. Englewood Cliffs, N.J.: Prentice-Hall, 1965. Brooks discovers the play's richness in its complex structure, which "by parallel, contrast, or cross-reference . . . makes us compare one passage or person of the play with another." These juxtapositions organize the play's serious concerns with time and timing, order and illusion, into a dramatic whole that has the achievement of proper relationships at its center.

Elliott, G. R. "Weirdness in *The Comedy of Errors.*" *University of Toronto Quarterly* 9 (1939): 95–106. The psychological horror of the suggestion of dual identity, the "strange" tones of romance, and the play's subtle sounding of pathos all combine to shed what Elliott describes as a "ray of weird light, romantic and comic . . . upon *The Comedy of Errors.*"

Freedman, Barbara. "Egeon's Debt: Self-Division and Self-Redemption in *The Comedy of Errors.*" *English Literary Renaissance* 10 (1980): 360–383. Freedman argues for the play's integrated structure: the frame of Egeon's redemption is filled and resolved by the activity in Ephesus, which is the site of a "carefully orchestrated psychological drama in which disassociated parts of the self are meaningfully united."

Hamilton, A. C. "The Early Comedies: *The Comedy of Errors.*" *The Early Shakespeare.* San Marino, Calif.: Huntington Library, 1967. For Hamilton, plot is the primary concern of the play: Shakespeare reshapes the mechanics of the Plautine comedy by doubling its twins, relocating its setting, and infusing a note of madness and nightmare into the simple comedy of mistaken identities. The result is a play in which the restoration of stable identities at the end is a significant assertion of the logic of the comic form.

Leggatt, Alexander. *"The Comedy of Errors." Shakespeare's Comedy of Love.* London: Methuen; New York: Barnes and Noble, 1974. Leggatt argues that underlying the play's "farcical comedy of situation" is a subtler comedy of character. The play's confusions of identity and collisions of dramatic styles permit an examination of the difficulties of fully knowing and understanding ourselves or others difficulties that are resolved in the restoration of the family unit at the end.

Nevo, Ruth. "My Glass and Not My Brother." *Comic Transformations in Shakespeare*. London and New York: Methuen, 1980. The role-playing demanded by the farce of *The Comedy of Errors* is, according to Nevo, therapeutic for the characters: "fooled, they become, to whatever degree, aware of themselves as selves and as fooled, and so have a basis for the regaining of control." In its concern with the discovery of identity, *The Comedy of Errors* reveals its strong affinities with Shakespeare's later comedies.

Salgādo, Gāmini. " 'Time's Deformed Hand': Sequence, Consequence, and Inconsequence in *The Comedy of Errors*." *Shakespeare Survey* 25 (1972): 81–91. Salgādo sees the play's preoccupation with time as a function of its concern with identity. The play's farcical duplications of identity apparently distort time and disrupt the logic of cause and effect, but the play's design "is essentially benevolent," leading to a conclusion in which "all disorders are healed and all divisions settled."

Salingar, Leo. *Shakespeare and the Traditions of Comedy*, esp. pp. 59–67. Cambridge: Cambridge Univ. Press, 1974. Salingar discusses the play in terms of its relation to classical and medieval prose romance, and offers, among others, *Apollonius of Tyre* and the legends of Saint Clement and Saint Eustace as possible influences upon the play's construction.

Shaw, Catherine M. "The Conscious Art of *The Comedy of Errors*." In *Shakespearean Comedy*, ed. Maurice Charney. New York: New York Literary Forum, 1980. Shaw demonstrates how Shakespeare "outdoes" both Plautus and Terence, adding to their comic example "both the realism and romance of the English stage and the learned and dialectical wit of Renaissance thought," thus turning a classical farce into a sophisticated comedy.

The Two Gentlemen of Verona, with (l. to r.) Dylan Baker as Lance, Roxanne as Crab, Thomas Gibson as Proteus, and Elizabeth McGovern as Julia, directed by Stuart Vaughan in 1987.

THE
TWO GENTLEMEN
OF VERONA

THE TWO
GENTLEMEN OF VERONA

Foreword

The interesting thing about *The Two Gentlemen of Verona* is its theme of male infidelity, which Shakespeare also treats elsewhere in his plays. Proteus is the male in question; first he loves Julia; then he goes away and falls for Sylvia, his best friend's girl. Of all Shakespeare's fickle and unfaithful young men—and there's a long list, which includes Angelo in *Measure for Measure*, Demetrius and Lysander in *A Midsummer Night's Dream*, and even young Romeo, who drops Rosaline for Juliet in a flash—Proteus is the most unforgivable. Yet he is also the most spectacularly forgiven, winning back the favor of his betrayed love, Julia, and his offended friend, Valentine, in less than one hundred lines.

Shakespeare is meting out to Proteus the same kind of mercy he grants to Angelo, Demetrius, and Lysander in the other plays. It's as if he's saying, "Boys will be boys," and giving Proteus another chance to prove his faithfulness to Julia. I find it intriguing that the infidelity is always in the men, never in the women. The women in Shakespeare's comedies often change their outward appearance, putting on a male disguise, but they remain unswervingly faithful to their men. As Julia observes at the end of *The Two Gentlemen of Verona*, "It is the lesser blot, modesty finds, / Women to change their shapes than men their minds." But she's as generous as Shakespeare, and promptly forgives Proteus.

Joseph Papp

Joseph Papp gratefully acknowledges the help of Elizabeth Kirkland in preparing this Foreword.

Introduction

If by "romantic comedy" we mean a love story in which the lovers overcome parental obstacles, jealousies, separations, and dangers to be united at last in married bliss, then *The Two Gentlemen of Verona* is perhaps Shakespeare's first. Although *The Comedy of Errors* may be an earlier play, it is a farce of mistaken identity with only a secondary interest in marriage, whereas *Love's Labor's Lost* is a courtly confection ending in the postponement of all marriages. No mention of *The Two Gentlemen of Verona* occurs until it is listed in Francis Meres's *Palladis Tamia: Wit's Treasury* of 1598, but the play is often dated around 1590–1594 on the basis of style: rhymed couplets, end-stopped verse, passages of excessive wit combat, and the like. *The Taming of the Shrew* (c. 1592–1594) is often dated a little later than *The Two Gentlemen*, although admittedly the two plays are much alike and perhaps ought to share the credit and the blame for Shakespeare's first experimentation with romantic comedy. In any event, this was to be the genre of Shakespeare's best-known "festive" comedies from *A Midsummer Night's Dream* to *Twelfth Night*.

The Two Gentlemen of Verona, then, is Shakespeare's apprenticeship to the romantic fiction of Italy and other southern European countries, whence he later derived so many plots of threatened love. He locates his story in Italy and gives his characters Italian names. He uses the conventional plot devices of romantic fiction: inconstancy in love and in friendship, the disguise of the heroine as a page, the overhearing of false vows, banishment, elopement, capture by outlaws, and so on. Virtually all the characters have a recognizable ancestry, not only in continental fiction but in neoclassical drama as well: Lucetta is the usual female companion, Thurio is the rich but unwelcome rival wooer (the pantaloon), Antonio and the Duke are typically strong-willed fathers opposing the romantic marriages of their children, Speed and Lance are at least supposed to be the clever servants who deliver messages and arrange rendezvous, and the four young lovers are the romantic protagonists.

Even in this early apprenticeship, to be sure, Shakespeare departs from the neoclassical norm of his continental sources. The setting remains nominally Italian, but the tone is often heartily English and Shakespeare's attitude toward his romantic models borders occasionally on the irreverent. Lucetta is a true friend of Julia and a virtuous counselor in love; the jest about her being a "broker" or a go-between (1.2.41) reminds us how unlike a bawdy duenna she really is. Thurio, Antonio, and the Duke are all portrayed with such amiable forbearance that they often seem inadequately motivated as the opponents of romantic happiness. Most of all, Speed and Lance have departed from their traditional roles as comic manipulators to become vaudeville jokesters.

Moreover, the very conventions of love and friendship are presented in such a way as to cast those conventions in an improbable light. What are we to make of the inconstant Proteus, who rejects his faithful Julia the moment he is away from her, tries instead to win the lady-fair of his dearest friend Valentine, informs the Duke of Valentine's plan to elope with Sylvia, and then attempts a violent assault on Sylvia's chastity? What sort of romantic hero is this, and why should he be rewarded by being forgiven and restored to his Julia? Most puzzling of all, is it credible that Valentine should respond to all this perfidy by offering to relinquish Sylvia to Proteus? By the same token, isn't it absurd that the outlaws in the forest near Mantua should turn out to be gentlemen in exile, and that they should offer command of their group to Valentine, whom they have just captured? Isn't the Duke's forgiveness of his eloped daughter Sylvia rather sudden and unconvincing? These problems, which have troubled many readers of the play (though they generally seem less formidable to spectators of an actual production), can perhaps best be analyzed in two ways: as a result of Shakespeare's having combined two sources with conflicting conventions, thereby subjecting those conventions to a playfully ironic perspective, and as a result of Shakespeare's conscious interest in the theme of unexpected forgiveness for his erring protagonist.

Using a device of plotting that was to become customary in his romantic comedies, Shakespeare combines two fictional sources and thereby sets up a dramatic tension between the two. His chief source appears to have been *Diana Enamorada*, a popular pastoral romance in Spanish by the Portuguese Jorge de Montemayor (1520–1561). Its heroine, Felismena (corresponding to Julia), is wooed by Don Felix (Proteus), whose father (Antonio) disapproves of the match and sends Don Felix away to court. Felismena, following after him disguised as a page, stops at an inn and is invited by the Host to listen to some music, whereupon she overhears Don Felix protesting his love to a new lady, Celia (Sylvia). At this point the resemblance between *Diana* and Shakespeare's play breaks off. Even thus far, despite several striking resemblances, the story provides no counterpart for Valentine, Proteus's best friend and the faithful lover of Sylvia. Montemayor's romance concentrates mainly on inconstancy in love.

For the motif of true friendship, Shakespeare may have turned to the story of Titus and Gisippus, as told by Sir Thomas Elyot in *The Governor* (1531). Here Gisippus, upon learning that his dear friend Titus has fallen in love with Gisippus' ladylove, not only relinquishes the lady to Titus but actually smuggles him into bed with her, all unbeknownst to the lady. The point of this story, as of other well-known treatises on friendship such as John Lyly's *Euphues* (1578) and *Endymion* (1588), or Richard Edwards's *Damon and Pythias* (1565), is that friendship is a higher form of human affection than erotic love since it is disinterested, platonically pure, and capable of teaching selflessness to others. Such a tale of perfect friendship provides, however, no counterpart for Julia, the lady abandoned by Proteus. Shakespeare has neatly dovetailed the two stories, making a quartet of lovers out of two triangular situations. The false lover of the first story becomes also the false friend of the second—only to be overwhelmed at the end by the generosity of his true friend.

The dramatic problem created by combining these two stories is that they arouse different expectations. The one is dedicated to the virtue of constancy in love, the other to friendship. Valentine's ultimate function is to demonstrate the triumph of selfless friendship over love, and yet his function in the plot of love rivalry is to demonstrate true loyalty to his Sylvia. His relinquishing of her to Proteus seems inconsistent with his vows as a lover. Conversely,

Proteus's double perfidy, toward his lover Julia and his friend Valentine, seems to render him unworthy of the generous action Valentine bestows on him. Proteus's very name is synonymous with inconstancy; his namesake in *The Odyssey* was infamous for his ability to change shapes at will. (Valentine's name, on the other hand, betokens constancy in love.) The coupling of the two plots simultaneously intensifies Proteus's guilt and Valentine's magnanimity.

Yet Shakespeare makes a virtue out of the seeming lack of credibility. First, the very implausibility of Valentine's selflessness in love and of Proteus's sudden conversion to virtue allows Shakespeare to mock gently the literary commonplaces of his sources. At the same time, Shakespeare finds serious value in his conventional topics of love and friendship, through the device of paradox. The more unlikely Valentine's actions seem, the more transcendent and wondrous they are bound to appear. Shakespeare prepares for his climactic scene of forgiveness in several ways. First, he presents Proteus as an essentially noble person who has fallen through a single fault. Proteus is wellborn, accomplished, handsome. The worthy Julia loves him for his good qualities, and he responds with sincerity and passion. He is equally ardent as a friend to Valentine. Only when he sees Sylvia does Proteus become helpless, "metamorphosed" (1.1.67). He cannot completely be blamed for being overwhelmed by passion, for the other lovers are no less obedient to love's command. According to the code of love that infuses this play, love cannot choose its object. Proteus's unhappy fate is to love Sylvia. His self-hatred increases as he turns flatterer, liar, betrayer, and finally would-be rapist. Like Angelo in *Measure for Measure*, Proteus is compulsively driven to abhorrent sin. The psychological insight of that later dark comedy is lacking—the soliloquies do not create the suffocating atmosphere of a nightmare—but the pattern of a guilty fall is still manifest.

This pattern may in turn clarify Valentine's role as the selfless friend. He should not be taken too seriously as such; Shakespeare makes no attempt to conceal the absurd aspect of Valentine's self-righteous renunciation of the woman who has been unswervingly loyal to him and who has no wish to be traded from one lover to another as

though she were the object of some kind of moralistic barter. Nonetheless, the very implausibility of Valentine's offer to relinquish Sylvia accentuates the noble intent behind
the gesture. We are surprised, even comically surprised, because we don't expect such selflessness in human nature;
but if friendship is to be seen as a supreme achievement of
the human spirit, it must transcend humanity's all-too-
common penchant for rivalry and ingratitude. Valentine's
generosity is not achieved without inner struggle. In the climactic scene of attempted rape, his first natural reaction is
angry denunciation. What changes his mind is the depth
and earnestness of Proteus's confession and desire for forgiveness: "If hearty sorrow / Be a sufficient ransom for offense, / I tender 't here" (5.4.74–76). Valentine responds in
the name of mercy and at the prompting of divine example:
"By penitence th' Eternal's wrath's appeased" (l. 81). The
more undeserved the pardon, the more selfless the act of
the one who pardons. Only by conquering his desire for Sylvia can Valentine teach his friend selflessness and thus reunite all four lovers in perfect joy. *The Two Gentlemen* is
thus in part a comedy of forgiveness, anticipating later
plays in which the romantic protagonist is equally culpable
and yet equally forgiven: *Much Ado about Nothing, Measure
for Measure, All's Well that Ends Well, Cymbeline*, and
others (see R. G. Hunter's *Shakespeare and the Comedy of
Forgiveness*, 1965).

Forgiveness of Proteus must proceed no less from Julia
than from Valentine. She too has much to pardon; as Proteus contritely observes, "O heaven! Were man / But constant, he were perfect" (5.4.110–111). Julia initiates a line of
Shakespearean heroines, including Hero, Isabella, Helena,
and Imogen in the plays already named, who must similarly cure inconstancy by their constancy. Like many
Shakespearean heroines Julia is plucky, resourceful, modest yet witty, patiently obedient in love and yet coyly flirtatious, a true friend, and long-suffering. Disguised as a page,
she overhears her lover's infidelity and yet never loses her
faith in him. She patiently delivers Proteus's messages to
her rival (like Viola in *Twelfth Night*) and gently acts as conscience to her erring master.

The repeated device of overhearing, as in later comedies,
provides a test for the protagonists' intentions. Thinking

themselves unobserved, they reveal their true natures for better or for worse. In the ingeniously devised if improbable climactic scene (5.4), Proteus as would-be ravisher is overheard by both his rejected mistress and his betrayed friend. Conversely, Sylvia proves loyal and chaste whenever she is silently observed by Julia (disguised as Sebastian) or by Valentine in the forest scenes. These overhearings suggest not only that humanity's good and evil deeds are witnessed, but that a beneficent providence will protect the virtuous. Valentine's unseen presence assures that Sylvia will be saved from rape and that Proteus will be prevented from committing an actual crime of violence. As in later comedies of this sort, forgiveness is possible because the guilt remains one of intent only.

These slightly absurd but happy resolutions of conflict take place in a forest near Mantua, the first of what Northrop Frye calls Shakespeare's "green worlds" (*English Institute Essays 1948*, pp. 58–73). Although sketchily presented, this forest does anticipate the Forest of Arden and other sylvan restorative landscapes. Its inhabitants are banished men protesting the injustice of society at court, or fugitives from unkind love. Valentine learns to prefer "unfrequented woods" to "flourishing peopled towns." His "wild faction" of outlaws desist from attacking "silly women or poor passengers," and appropriately swear "By the bare scalp of Robin Hood's fat friar" (5.4.2–3; 4.1.36–37, 72). They are charmingly suited to their role of threatening and then reuniting the lovers, providentially capturing Sylvia just as she is on her way to find Valentine. Their actions are highly improbable and poke fun at the very conventions they illustrate, but then the same can be said of Valentine's forgiveness of Proteus and the Duke's sudden reconciliation with his prospective son-in-law, Valentine. Like Arden, this forest is a strange place in which such changes of heart are expected to occur. The aura of improbability may also partly explain the play's carelessness about social distinctions and the realities of geography: the Duke is sometimes called the Emperor, and at one point Valentine sets sail from Verona to Milan (both located inland).

The buffoonish comedy of Lance and Speed performs a function similar to that of romantic improbability by undercutting the artifice and melodrama of the love story. How can we worry long over Valentine's banishment when Lance bursts out, "Sir, there is a proclamation that you are vanished" (3.1.216)? Or how can we fret about Proteus's courtship of Sylvia when the love token he sends her turns out to be Lance's odoriferous dog? This sort of absurd anticlimax occurs at every turn. Lance's first soliloquy, about the dog's refusal to mourn their departure from Verona (2.3), is a brilliant example of what we would call vaudeville or stand-up comic joking, but it also comments on the immediately preceding scene of Proteus's tearful farewell to Julia. Lance's friendship for Speed, and especially his friendship for the dog, delightfully blaspheme the play's serious interest in true friendship. In one of Lance's funniest scenes (4.4.1–38), he describes how he has selflessly taken on himself the punishment meted out to the dog for urinating on Sylvia's hooped petticoat. Similarly, the spectacle of Lance in love, cataloguing his mistress's virtues and vices, insures us against too deep an involvement in the hazards of Cupid. The play continually reminds us of the folly of love without denying its exquisite joys or its highest potential for selflessness.

The Two Gentlemen of Verona
in Performance

—What's her history?
—A blank, my lord.
Twelfth Night (2.4.109–110)

The Two Gentlemen of Verona has been, even beyond *Love's Labor's Lost,* the most neglected of Shakespeare's romantic comedies in the theater. The earliest recorded performance of any kind is of an adaptation by Benjamin Victor, treasurer of the Theatre Royal, Drury Lane, at that theater in 1762. David Garrick presented the play but took no role. Victor's avowed aim was to remove "the rankest of those weeds" in which "this comedy abounds," and to that end he not only cut and shifted a good deal but reintroduced Lance and Speed in two additional scenes. Lance, with of course his dog, Crab, turns up in the forest near Mantua in a comic fright and is captured by the outlaws. This slender plot reaches its climax in the final scene when the outlaws drag Lance before the Duke (who has just consented to the marriage of Valentine and Sylvia), Valentine, and others, including Speed, who are all in disguise. When the outlaws give Lance the option of drawing lots with Crab to see which of them must die, Lance vows that he cannot live without his dog. The assembled friends, who have been let in on the jest, enjoy a good-natured laugh at his expense. Recognition and the resolution of all difficulties bring the play to a happy close. Earlier in the play, Victor moved scenes about in order to permit all the events at Milan to be played consecutively and thereby preserve a uniformity in the scenery. Lance's famous scene with Crab and the shoe (2.3) was transferred from Verona to Milan, assisting the scenic arrangement but rather detracting from the point of Lance's sorrow in leaving, since by then he had been away from Verona for some time. During the performance on the sixth night of the production, in January of 1763, a gang taking part in the so-called "Half-Price Riots" nearly managed to set the scenery on fire.

Something closer to Shakespeare's play appeared at the Theatre Royal, Covent Garden, in 1784, in a production that had two of the leading comic actors of the late eighteenth century, John Edwin and John Quick, as Speed and Lance. John Philip Kemble similarly revived a Shakespearean version in 1790 at Drury Lane, but by 1808 at Covent Garden he had returned to something closer to Victor's adaptation, dividing the action into two continuous sequences, first at Verona and then Milan, for the convenience of the scene painters. He combined Victor's two scenes of Lance and Speed in the forest into one, and provided the outlaws with such names as Ubaldo, Luigi, Carlos, Stephano, Giacamo, Rodolfo, and Valerio. Kemble took the role of Valentine in this production, which ran for only three performances.

More successful in box office terms (twenty-nine performances) was an operatic version by Frederic Reynolds and H. R. Bishop at Covent Garden in 1821. The script of this musical is lost, but the liberties it took must have been considerable; the cast of characters included the Genius of Pleasure, someone called Philippo, and, not to be outdone by Kemble, an array of outlaws named Ubaldo, Rodolfo, Carlos, and Stephano. Wholesale rearrangement was necessary in any case to make room for a medley of songs, mostly from Shakespeare's other plays, poems, and sonnets. The sonnets formed the staple of the entertainment. Philippo led off with "When I have seen the hungry ocean gain" (Sonnet 64), followed by Julia in "That time of year thou mayst in me behold" (Sonnet 73), and then a duet between Philippo and Julia based on the text of Sonnet 92. Act 2 proceeded with Sonnets 109 ("O, never say that I was false of heart") and 29 ("When, in disgrace with fortune and men's eyes"), along with a song, "Good night, good rest," doubtfully ascribed to Shakespeare in *The Passionate Pilgrim*, 1599. The finale brought in Sonnets 97 ("How like a winter hath my absence been") and 25 ("Let those who are in favor with their stars"). Meantime, the famous song that really belongs to *The Two Gentlemen*, "Who is Sylvia?" (4.2.39–52), was sung by none other than Ubaldo, Rodolfo, Carlos, and Stephano, who had already given a rendition of "To see his face the lion walked along" from *Venus and Adonis* (l. 1093), and who also joined in a rousing chorus in Act 4 of "Now the hungry lion roars" from *A Midsummer Night's*

Dream (5.1.366). Still other songs were added. At the third performance of this opera, a pageant called "Palace of the Hours, and the Temple of Apollo" was newly introduced, but ran into such difficulty with the unperfected scenic effects that the audience was continually diverted.

Later nineteenth-century productions also tended toward splendid pictorial representation and a good deal of music. William Charles Macready revived *The Two Gentlemen* with elaborate scenery and faithful reproductions of fifteenth-century Italian costume in 1841 at Drury Lane. Macready played Valentine, according to his own estimate, "imperfectly," but the production was repeated thirteen times and was acted in January of 1842 when the King of Prussia visited the theater. Charles Kean acted the play at New York's Park Theatre in 1846 and again in Benjamin Webster's production at London's Haymarket Theatre in 1848. Kean and his wife (Ellen Tree) starred as Valentine and Julia; the new scenery was lavish and considerable music was added. In 1857 Samuel Phelps added *The Two Gentlemen* to the list of seldom-acted plays he conscientiously and courageously revived at the Sadler's Wells Theatre throughout the 1850s. Despite its unfamiliarity, the play was received enthusiastically by the critic of the *Illustrated London News,* who found it "deliciously acted and well mounted," while the production as a whole gave further testimony to "the taste with which this theatre is conducted by Mr. Phelps." Augustin Daly produced a four-act version in 1895 in New York and London, with Ada Rehan as Julia, that generally pleased the critics and delighted the public. For all the elaborateness of these handsomely pictorial productions, however, the biggest boost the play received in the nineteenth century was undoubtedly not in the theater but in Franz Schubert's setting of "Who is Sylvia?" now immortalized in the lieder repertory.

If only for financial reasons, the nineteenth-century taste for extravagant productions of Shakespeare that sacrificed text to spectacle could not be endlessly indulged, and a reaction soon set in against visual elaboration and the slow pacing that it demanded. William Poel, the innovative and influential champion of Elizabethan staging techniques, directed a reading of the play in 1892 at the St. James Banqueting Hall that was revived with costumes later that year in an outdoor performance at Kingston. He produced the play in 1896 for the Elizabethan Stage Society in the Merchant Taylors' Hall, and again in January the following year in the Great Hall of the Charterhouse, with the swift pacing and continuous simple staging for which Poel deservedly is remembered. The costume designs for Valentine and Proteus were taken from a mid-sixteenth-century fresco and those for the outlaws from some sketches for the Fishmongers' pageant in the 1609 Lord Mayor's Show. In 1910, at the invitation of Herbert Beerbohm Tree, Poel presented *The Two Gentlemen* at His Majesty's Theatre, in which an apron had to be constructed over the orchestra pit to accommodate Poel's resistance to the proscenium stage. Harley Granville-Barker, who had worked with Poel and shared his enthusiasm for the flexibility of Elizabethan stagecraft, directed the play at the Court Theatre in 1904, and appeared as Speed. A. B. Walker, *The Times*'s reviewer, was enchanted by the vitality of the production: "I came away under so strong a charm that I almost told the cabman, 'To Mantua—by sea.'"

Free of Poel's antiquarianism, Granville-Barker was able to turn Poel's commitment to swift, intimate staging into something both artistically and commercially successful, thereby extending Poel's influence over later directors. In 1916 Ben Greet, similarly committed to fast-paced action on a simple, flexible set, though for reasons as much fiscal as philosophical, directed the play at Stratford-upon-Avon. In 1925 Robert Atkins, who, like Granville-Barker and Greet, had earlier worked with Poel, produced the play at London's Apollo Theatre with a young John Gielgud as Valentine. Ben Iden Payne, perhaps the last in the Poel succession, produced the play at Stratford-upon-Avon in 1938.

In the second half of the twentieth century, revivals of *The Two Gentlemen* have been more common, in part because some theaters have undertaken to perform the whole Shakespearean canon. In 1957 the play took its place in the Old Vic's project, in the middle years of the 1950s, of presenting all of Shakespeare's plays, and it has been staged for similar reasons at festivals at Stratford, Ontario; Ashland, Oregon; Madison, New Jersey; and in the BBC television series, among others. But the play need not depend upon such acts of homage. It does work onstage, as

Granville-Barker's success at the Court Theatre proved, or indeed the Old Vic's spritely *The Two Gentlemen* of 1957, set in a world of Regency capes and curly-brimmed top hats. Five years earlier at London's Old Vic, the company of the Bristol Old Vic, directed by Denis Carey, had great success with the play "as a Renaissance masque," as critic J. C. Trewin reported, "in a mistily shining set of filigreed pillars." Stuart Vaughan directed an energetic, ebullient version for the New York Shakespeare Festival in 1957, in which the Duke of Milan was a passionate gardener whose tools and prize plants were wheeled behind him by a servant. Vaughan directed the play again for the festival in 1987. In 1975 at Stratford, Ontario, Robin Phillips and David Toguri set the play on the Italian Riviera, with the Duke of Milan and Proteus's father as Mafia dons, and Sylvia so silly and self-indulgent that Valentine's gift of her to Proteus seemed not to bother anybody. John Barton directed the play, as part of a double bill with *Titus Andronicus*, at Stratford-upon-Avon in 1981, as a comic romp burlesquing romantic literary conventions; a female outlaw waving a blunderbuss turned out to be the most serious threat to the action.

The play does not readily encourage comment on the dilemmas of modern life and so has been spared the kinds of modernizing interpretation brought to *Measure for Measure*, for example, or *Julius Caesar*. A rock musical version in New York in 1971, to be sure, did make an attempt to be topical by picturing the frosty-spirited Duke of Milan as a proponent of the Vietnam War (some added lines were necessary for this), but the idea seemed irrelevant to the play, however relevant it may have been to current history, and demonstrated in fact how wise most directors are not to strive for portentous effects. As its recent stage history demonstrates, *The Two Gentlemen* does best in Elizabethan costume or in period dress, either as cheerful burlesque or as comic fluff. The love plot cannot be taken seriously; everything from Speed's wryly comic view of lovesickness to the outlaws' improbable interventions demands a performance that is, like the text itself, tongue in cheek.

The play is in fact very actable, with a number of surefire bits of comic business. The delivering, reading, and tearing of letters provides diversion onstage; so too with the rings that change fortunes with the vicissitudes of the love plot. Hand properties and costume changes, especially disguises, play a major role in the comic intrigue. Overhearings and recognitions offer moments of surprise and reversal. The play features a number of comically stereotyped roles in which actors can be entertaining: the inconstant lover, the constant lover, the overbearing father, the unattractive rival, the bumbling though well-meaning servant, the romantic fugitive from justice. Most of all, the play gives us Lance and Speed—and Crab. The adapters in the eighteenth century may have made unnecessary and clumsy additions, but their instinct of making the most of Lance and Speed showed sound theatrical judgment. Lance's stand-up comic routine with his shoe and his dog, Crab, can be disablingly funny in the theater. Various canine thespians have proved on more than one occasion that a dumb and lovable animal is likely to steal the show.

THE
TWO GENTLEMEN
OF VERONA

The Names of All the Actors

DUKE [OF MILAN], *father to Sylvia*

VALENTINE, ⎫
PROTEUS, ⎭ *the two gentlemen*

ANTONIO, *father to Proteus*

THURIO, *a foolish rival to Valentine*

EGLAMOUR, *agent for Sylvia in her escape*

HOST [*of the inn*] *where Julia lodges*

OUTLAWS *with Valentine*

SPEED, *a clownish servant to Valentine*

LANCE, *the like to Proteus*

PANTHINO, *servant to Antonio*

JULIA, *beloved of Proteus*

SYLVIA, *beloved of Valentine*

LUCETTA, *waiting-woman to Julia*

[*Servants, Musicians*

SCENE: *Verona; Milan; the frontiers of Mantua*]

1.1 *[Enter] Valentine [and] Proteus.*

VALENTINE
Cease to persuade, my loving Proteus;
Home-keeping youth have ever homely wits.   2
Were 't not affection chains thy tender days   3
To the sweet glances of thy honored love,
I rather would entreat thy company
To see the wonders of the world abroad
Than, living dully sluggardized at home,
Wear out thy youth with shapeless idleness.   8
But since thou lov'st, love still and thrive therein,   9
Even as I would when I to love begin.

PROTEUS
Wilt thou be gone? Sweet Valentine, adieu!
Think on thy Proteus when thou haply seest   12
Some rare noteworthy object in thy travel.
Wish me partaker in thy happiness
When thou dost meet good hap; and in thy danger,   15
If ever danger do environ thee,
Commend thy grievance to my holy prayers,   17
For I will be thy beadsman, Valentine.   18

VALENTINE
And on a love book pray for my success?   19

PROTEUS
Upon some book I love I'll pray for thee.

VALENTINE
That's on some shallow story of deep love,
How young Leander crossed the Hellespont.   22

PROTEUS
That's a deep story of a deeper love,
For he was more than over shoes in love.

VALENTINE
'Tis true; for you are over boots in love,
And yet you never swam the Hellespont.

1.1. Location: Verona. A street.
2 homely dull, simple   **3 affection** passion, love.   **tender** youthful   **8 shapeless** aimless   **9 still** always, constantly   **12 haply** by chance   **15 hap** fortune   **17 Commend thy grievance** commit your distress   **18 beadsman** one
engaged to pray for others   **19 love book** manual of courtship or a love story
(rather than a prayer book)   **22 Leander** famous lover of Greek legend who
drowned as he swam the Hellespont to see his love Hero

PROTEUS
Over the boots? Nay, give me not the boots.   27
VALENTINE
No, I will not, for it boots thee not.   28
PROTEUS   What?
VALENTINE
To be in love, where scorn is bought with groans,
Coy looks with heartsore sighs, one fading moment's
      mirth
With twenty watchful, weary, tedious nights.   32
If haply won, perhaps a hapless gain;   33
If lost, why then a grievous labor won;
However, but a folly bought with wit,   35
Or else a wit by folly vanquishèd.
PROTEUS
So, by your circumstance, you call me fool.   37
VALENTINE
So, by your circumstance, I fear you'll prove.   38
PROTEUS
'Tis love you cavil at. I am not Love.   39
VALENTINE
Love is your master, for he masters you;
And he that is so yokèd by a fool
Methinks should not be chronicled for wise.   42
PROTEUS
Yet writers say, as in the sweetest bud
The eating canker dwells, so eating love   44
Inhabits in the finest wits of all.   45
VALENTINE
And writers say, as the most forward bud   46
Is eaten by the canker ere it blow,   47
Even so by love the young and tender wit
Is turned to folly, blasting in the bud,   49
Losing his verdure even in the prime,   50

27 give . . . boots i.e., don't make fun of me   28 boots profits, avails (with
play on *boots* in l. 27. This passage is full of punning, on *shallow* and *deep*,
over shoes, over boots, etc.)   32 watchful wakeful   33 hapless unlucky
35 However either way.   but nothing but.   wit intellect (also in ll. 36, 45,
and 48)   37 circumstance detailed discourse   38 circumstance situation,
condition   39 Love i.e., Cupid   42 chronicled for wise set down as being
wise   44 canker cankerworm   45 Inhabits dwells   46 forward early
47 blow bloom   49 blasting withering   50 his verdure its flourishing
vigor.   prime spring

And all the fair effects of future hopes.   51
But wherefore waste I time to counsel thee   52
That art a votary to fond desire?   53
Once more adieu! My father at the road   54
Expects my coming, there to see me shipped.   55

PROTEUS
And thither will I bring thee, Valentine.   56

VALENTINE
Sweet Proteus, no. Now let us take our leave.
To Milan let me hear from thee by letters
Of thy success in love, and what news else   59
Betideth here in absence of thy friend;   60
And I likewise will visit thee with mine.   61

PROTEUS
All happiness bechance to thee in Milan!

VALENTINE
As much to you at home! And so, farewell.   *Exit.*

PROTEUS
He after honor hunts, I after love.
He leaves his friends to dignify them more;   65
I leave myself, my friends, and all, for love.   66
Thou, Julia, thou hast metamorphosed me,
Made me neglect my studies, lose my time,   68
War with good counsel, set the world at naught;   69
Made wit with musing weak, heart sick with thought.   70

       [*Enter*] *Speed.*

SPEED
Sir Proteus, save you! Saw you my master?   71

PROTEUS
But now he parted hence, to embark for Milan.   72

---

51 fair . . . hopes bright fulfillment of future happiness   **52 wherefore**
why   **53 fond** foolish   **54 road** roadstead, harbor   **55 Expects** awaits.
shipped aboard. (Shakespeare evidently assumes that Verona and Milan
are connected by water; Proteus also travels by ship, though Julia later
makes the journey by land.)   **56 bring** accompany   **59 success** outcome   **60 Betideth** occurs   **61 visit** enrich with a similar benefit
65 friends (including family).   **dignify** i.e., honor (by increasing his own
fame)   **66 leave** neglect   **68 lose** waste   **69 War . . . counsel** reject good
advice   **70 thought** melancholy   **71 save you** God save you   **72 parted**
departed

SPEED
 Twenty to one, then, he is shipped already, 73
 And I have played the sheep in losing him.   74
PROTEUS
 Indeed, a sheep doth very often stray,
 An if the shepherd be awhile away.   76
SPEED You conclude that my master is a shepherd, then,
and I a sheep?
PROTEUS I do.
SPEED Why then, my horns are his horns, whether I 80
wake or sleep.
PROTEUS A silly answer, and fitting well a sheep.
SPEED This proves me still a sheep.
PROTEUS True; and thy master a shepherd.
SPEED Nay, that I can deny by a circumstance. 85
PROTEUS It shall go hard but I'll prove it by another. 86
SPEED The shepherd seeks the sheep, and not the sheep
the shepherd; but I seek my master, and my master
seeks not me. Therefore I am no sheep.
PROTEUS The sheep for fodder follow the shepherd; the
shepherd for food follows not the sheep. Thou for
wages followest thy master; thy master for wages fol-
lows not thee. Therefore thou art a sheep.
SPEED Such another proof will make me cry "Baa." 94
PROTEUS But dost thou hear? Gav'st thou my letter to 95
Julia?
SPEED Ay, sir. I, a lost mutton, gave your letter to her, 97
a laced mutton, and she, a laced mutton, gave me, a 98
lost mutton, nothing for my labor.
PROTEUS Here's too small a pasture for such store of
muttons.
SPEED If the ground be overcharged, you were best 102
stick her.   103

73, 74 shipped, sheep (Elizabethan pronunciation doubtless made the
pun obvious.) **76 An if** if **80 my horns . . . horns** he owns my horns;
i.e., presumably my master is a cuckold. (Traditionally, husbands whose
wives deceived them were supposed to grow horns.) **85 circumstance**
process of reasoning **86 It . . . I'll** I'll be doing pretty badly if I cannot **94 Baa** (with a pun on *bah*, as in "bah, humbug") **95 dost thou
hear** i.e., listen here **97, 98 lost, laced** (As with *shipped, sheep*, above,
the Elizabethan pronunciation of the two words was similar.) **98 laced
mutton** i.e., whore **102 overcharged** overcrowded **103 stick** stab (with
bawdy suggestion)

PROTEUS   Nay, in that you are astray; 'twere best   104
pound you.   105

SPEED   Nay, sir, less than a pound shall serve me for   106
carrying your letter.

PROTEUS   You mistake. I mean the pound—a pinfold.   108

SPEED
From a pound to a pin? Fold it over and over,   109
'Tis threefold too little for carrying a letter to your
    lover.

PROTEUS   But what said she?

SPEED [First nodding]   Ay.

PROTEUS   Nod—ay—why, that's "noddy."   113

SPEED   You mistook, sir. I say she did nod, and you ask
me if she did nod, and I say, "Ay."

PROTEUS   And that set together is "noddy."

SPEED   Now you have taken the pains to set it together,
take it for your pains.   118

PROTEUS   No, no, you shall have it for bearing the letter.

SPEED   Well, I perceive I must be fain to bear with you.   120

PROTEUS   Why, sir, how do you bear with me?

SPEED   Marry, sir, the letter, very orderly, having noth-   122
ing but the word "noddy" for my pains.

PROTEUS   Beshrew me, but you have a quick wit.   124

SPEED   And yet it cannot overtake your slow purse.

PROTEUS   Come, come, open the matter in brief. What   126
said she?

SPEED   Open your purse, that the money and the matter
may be both at once delivered.   129

PROTEUS [Giving him money]   Well, sir, here is for your
pains. What said she?

SPEED   Truly, sir, I think you'll hardly win her.   132

---

104 astray (1) wandering like a lost sheep (2) going too far   **105 pound**
(1) impound, shut up in an animal pen (2) beat   **106 pound** (1) 20 shillings (2) a beating   **108 pinfold** pen for stray animals   **109 a pin** i.e., an
object worth very little.   **Fold** (1) as in folding a letter (2) multiply
113 noddy a simpleton   **118 take . . . pains** i.e., here's your tip (playing
on *taken the pains*, taken the trouble, in l. 117)   **120 fain** content.   **bear
with** (1) put up with (2) carry for. (Speed sees he is to get no tip.)
122 Marry i.e., indeed. (Originally an oath, "by the Virgin Mary.")
124 Beshrew me (A mild oath.)   **126 open** disclose (with a pun in l. 128
on *opening* a purse)   **129 delivered** (1) handed over (said of the *money*)
(2) reported (said of the *matter* or business being discussed)   **132 hardly**
with difficulty

PROTEUS   Why, couldst thou perceive so much from her?

SPEED   Sir, I could perceive nothing at all from her, no, 134
not so much as a ducat for delivering your letter. And 135
being so hard to me that brought your mind, I fear 136
she'll prove as hard to you in telling your mind. Give 137
her no token but stones, for she's as hard as steel.   138

PROTEUS   What said she? Nothing?

SPEED   No, not so much as "Take this for thy pains." To
testify your bounty, I thank you, you have testerned 141
me; in requital whereof, henceforth carry your letters 142
yourself. And so, sir, I'll commend you to my master.   143

PROTEUS

Go, go, begone, to save your ship from wreck,
Which cannot perish having thee aboard,   145
Being destined to a drier death on shore. [Exit Speed.] 146
I must go send some better messenger.
I fear my Julia would not deign my lines,   148
Receiving them from such a worthless post.   Exit. 149

❖

1.2   Enter Julia and Lucetta.

JULIA

But say, Lucetta, now we are alone,
Wouldst thou then counsel me to fall in love?

LUCETTA

Ay, madam, so you stumble not unheedfully.   3

JULIA

Of all the fair resort of gentlemen   4
That every day with parle encounter me,   5
In thy opinion which is worthiest love?   6

134 **perceive** receive (punning on *perceive*, "understand," in the previous line)   135 **a ducat** a silver coin   136 **mind** desires, intentions
137 **in telling** when you tell her   138 **stones** jewels such as
diamonds, harder than steel and well suited to hard-hearted ladies
141–142 **testerned me** given me a testern, a sixpence   143 **commend
you** deliver your greetings   145–146 **Which . . . shore** (An allusion to
the proverb "He that is born to be hanged shall never be drowned.")
148 **deign** deign to accept   149 **post** (1) messenger (2) blockhead

1.2. Location: Verona. Julia's house.
3 **so** provided that   4 **resort** company, assemblage   5 **parle** talk
6 **worthiest love** most worthy of love

LUCETTA
  Please you repeat their names, I'll show my mind   7
  According to my shallow simple skill.
JULIA
  What think'st thou of the fair Sir Eglamour?   9
LUCETTA
  As of a knight well-spoken, neat, and fine;
  But, were I you, he never should be mine.
JULIA
  What think'st thou of the rich Mercatio?
LUCETTA
  Well of his wealth, but of himself, so-so.
JULIA
  What think'st thou of the gentle Proteus?
LUCETTA
  Lord, Lord, to see what folly reigns in us!
JULIA
  How now? What means this passion at his name?   16
LUCETTA
  Pardon, dear madam, 'tis a passing shame   17
  That I, unworthy body as I am,
  Should censure thus on lovely gentlemen.   19
JULIA
  Why not on Proteus, as of all the rest?
LUCETTA
  Then thus: of many good I think him best.
JULIA   Your reason?
LUCETTA
  I have no other but a woman's reason;
  I think him so because I think him so.
JULIA
  And wouldst thou have me cast my love on him?
LUCETTA
  Ay, if you thought your love not cast away.
JULIA
  Why, he of all the rest hath never moved me.   27
LUCETTA
  Yet he of all the rest I think best loves ye.

7 Please if it please   **9 Eglamour** (Not to be identified with Sylvia's
friend of the same name.)   **16 passion** passionate outburst   **17 passing**
surpassing   **19 censure** pass judgment   **27 moved** urged (with a suit of
love)

JULIA
His little speaking shows his love but small.
LUCETTA
Fire that's closest kept burns most of all.
JULIA
They do not love that do not show their love.
LUCETTA
O, they love least that let men know their love.
JULIA   I would I knew his mind.
LUCETTA [*Giving a letter*]   Peruse this paper, madam.
JULIA   "To Julia." Say, from whom?
LUCETTA   That the contents will show.
JULIA   Say, say, who gave it thee?
LUCETTA
Sir Valentine's page; and sent, I think, from Proteus.
He would have given it you, but I, being in the way,   39
Did in your name receive it. Pardon the fault, I pray.
JULIA
Now, by my modesty, a goodly broker!   41
Dare you presume to harbor wanton lines?
To whisper, and conspire against my youth?
Now trust me, 'tis an office of great worth,
And you an officer fit for the place.
There, take the paper. See it be returned,
Or else return no more into my sight.
                    [*Giving the letter back*.]
LUCETTA
To plead for love deserves more fee than hate.   48
JULIA
Will ye be gone?
LUCETTA   That you may ruminate.   *Exit.*
JULIA
And yet I would I had o'erlooked the letter.   50
It were a shame to call her back again
And pray her to a fault for which I chid her.   52
What 'fool is she, that knows I am a maid   53
And would not force the letter to my view!
Since maids, in modesty, say no to that

---

39 being . . . way i.e., happening to encounter him   **41 broker** intermediary   **48 more fee** better recompense   **50 o'erlooked** read   **52 to a fault** to commit a fault   **53 'fool** a fool

Which they would have the profferer construe ay.
Fie, fie, how wayward is this foolish love
That, like a testy babe, will scratch the nurse   58
And presently, all humbled, kiss the rod!   59
How churlishly I chid Lucetta hence,
When willingly I would have had her here!
How angerly I taught my brow to frown,   62
When inward joy enforced my heart to smile!
My penance is to call Lucetta back
And ask remission for my folly past.
What ho! Lucetta!

          [*Enter Lucetta.*]

LUCETTA   What would your ladyship?
JULIA
Is 't near dinnertime?
LUCETTA   I would it were,
That you might kill your stomach on your meat   68
And not upon your maid.
          [*She drops the letter, and stoops to pick it up.*]
JULIA
What is 't that you took up so gingerly?
LUCETTA   Nothing.
JULIA   Why didst thou stoop, then?
LUCETTA
To take a paper up that I let fall.
JULIA   And is that paper nothing?
LUCETTA   Nothing concerning me.
JULIA
Then let it lie for those that it concerns.
LUCETTA
Madam, it will not lie where it concerns,   77
Unless it have a false interpreter.
JULIA
Some love of yours hath writ to you in rhyme.

---

58 **testy** fretful   59 **presently** immediately afterward.   **rod** spanking
rod   62 **angerly** angrily   68 **kill your stomach** (1) satisfy your appetite
(2) appease your anger.   **meat** (Pronounced "mate," with a pun on *maid*
in the next line.)   77 **lie where it concerns** tell falsehoods in matters of
importance (punning on the meaning "be left for those whose business
it is" in the preceding line)

LUCETTA

That I might sing it, madam, to a tune,   80
Give me a note; your ladyship can set.   81

JULIA

As little by such toys as may be possible.   82
Best sing it to the tune of "Light o' Love."   83

LUCETTA

It is too heavy for so light a tune.   84

JULIA

Heavy! Belike it hath some burden then?   85

LUCETTA

Ay, and melodious were it, would you sing it.

JULIA

And why not you?

LUCETTA   I cannot reach so high.   87

JULIA

Let's see your song. How now, minion?   88

                              [*She takes the letter.*]

LUCETTA

Keep tune there still; so you will sing it out.   89
And yet methinks I do not like this tune.

JULIA   You do not?

LUCETTA   No, madam, 'tis too sharp.   92

JULIA   You, minion, are too saucy.

LUCETTA   Nay, now you are too flat,   94
And mar the concord with too harsh a descant.   95
There wanteth but a mean to fill your song.   96

---

80 That in order that   **81 note** (with a punning reference to Proteus's
letter).   **set** (1) set to music (2) write a letter. (But Julia takes the word
in the sense of setting store by something, regarding it of value.)
82 toys trifles   **83 "Light o' Love"** (A familiar tune of the time.)
84 heavy serious   **85 Belike** perhaps.   **burden** (1) bass accompaniment
to a melody (2) heavy load (with an added sexual suggestion of the
burden women must bear)   **87 reach so high** (1) sing so high (2) aspire
to a person of Proteus's rank   **88 minion** hussy (with a pun on *minim*,
half note)   **89 tune** (1) pitch (2) temper, mood.   **so . . . out** (1) if you do
so, you'll be able to sing the song completely (2) that way you'll get over
your bad mood   **92 sharp** (1) high in pitch (2) saucy, bitter. (Perhaps
Julia pinches Lucetta here.)   **94 flat** (1) low in pitch (2) blunt. (Perhaps
Julia slaps Lucetta here.)   **95 descant** (1) soprano counterpoint sung
above the melody (2) carping criticism   **96 wanteth but** is lacking
only.   **mean** (1) middle or tenor voice between the *descant* and the *bass*,
i.e., Proteus (2) opportunity

JULIA
The mean is drowned with your unruly bass.   97
LUCETTA
Indeed, I bid the base for Proteus.   98
JULIA
This babble shall not henceforth trouble me.
Here is a coil with protestation!   100
        [*She tears the letter and drops the pieces.*]
Go, get you gone, and let the papers lie.
You would be fing'ring them to anger me.
LUCETTA
She makes it strange, but she would be best pleased   103
To be so angered with another letter.   [*Exit.*]
JULIA
Nay, would I were so angered with the same!   105
        [*She picks up some fragments.*]
O hateful hands, to tear such loving words!
Injurious wasps, to feed on such sweet honey   107
And kill the bees that yield it with your stings!
I'll kiss each several paper for amends.   109
Look, here is writ "kind Julia." Unkind Julia!   110
As in revenge of thy ingratitude,   111
I throw thy name against the bruising stones,
Trampling contemptuously on thy disdain.
        [*Throwing down a fragment.*]
And here is writ "love-wounded Proteus."
Poor wounded name! My bosom as a bed
Shall lodge thee till thy wound be throughly healed;   116
And thus I search it with a sovereign kiss.   117
But twice or thrice was "Proteus" written down.

97 unruly bass (with pun on "base behavior")   **98 bid the base for** i.e., act in behalf of (referring to the game of "prisoner's base," and with a pun on *base*, "bass, low")   **100 coil with protestation** commotion or fuss about protestations of love (i.e., about Proteus's letter)   **103 makes it strange** pretends indifference. (Lucetta says this speech for the audience's benefit, but it is a catty third-person reference to Julia rather than an aside, and Julia makes it clear in l. 105 that she has heard it.) **105 Nay . . . same** i.e., indeed, I wish I had this same letter intact to pretend to be angry about   **107 wasps** i.e., her fingers   **109 several paper** separate scrap of paper   **110 Unkind** unnatural, cruel   **111 As** as if, or, thus   **116 throughly** thoroughly   **117 search** probe, cleanse (as one would a wound).   **sovereign** healing

Be calm, good wind, blow not a word away
Till I have found each letter in the letter,
Except mine own name; that some whirlwind bear
Unto a ragged, fearful, hanging rock
And throw it thence into the raging sea!
Lo, here in one line is his name twice writ,
"Poor forlorn Proteus, passionate Proteus,
To the sweet Julia." That I'll tear away;
And yet I will not, sith so prettily   127
He couples it to his complaining names.
Thus will I fold them, one upon another.
Now kiss, embrace, contend, do what you will.
            [*She puts some folded papers in her bosom.*]

        [*Enter Lucetta.*]

LUCETTA Madam,
    Dinner is ready, and your father stays.   132
JULIA Well, let us go.
LUCETTA
    What, shall these papers lie like telltales here?
JULIA
    If you respect them, best to take them up.   135
LUCETTA
    Nay, I was taken up for laying them down;   136
    Yet here they shall not lie, for catching cold.   137
            [*She gathers up the remaining fragments.*]
JULIA
    I see you have a month's mind to them.   138
LUCETTA
    Ay, madam, you may say what sights you see;
    I see things too, although you judge I wink.   140
JULIA Come, come, will 't please you go?   *Exeunt.*

                            ❖

127 sith since   **132 stays** waits   **135 respect** prize, esteem   **136 taken
up** scolded (with a play on *take them up* in the preceding line)   **137 for**
for fear of   **138 month's mind** inclination, liking   **140 wink** close the
eyes

1.3   *Enter Antonio and Panthino.*

ANTONIO
> Tell me, Panthino, what sad talk was that   1
> Wherewith my brother held you in the cloister?   2

PANTHINO
> 'Twas of his nephew Proteus, your son.

ANTONIO
> Why, what of him?

PANTHINO   He wondered that your lordship
> Would suffer him to spend his youth at home,   5
> While other men, of slender reputation,   6
> Put forth their sons to seek preferment out: 7
> Some to the wars, to try their fortune there,
> Some to discover islands far away,
> Some to the studious universities.
> For any or for all these exercises
> He said that Proteus your son was meet,   12
> And did request me to importune you   13
> To let him spend his time no more at home,
> Which would be great impeachment to his age   15
> In having known no travel in his youth.

ANTONIO
> Nor need'st thou much importune me to that
> Whereon this month I have been hammering.   18
> I have considered well his loss of time,
> And how he cannot be a perfect man,   20
> Not being tried and tutored in the world.   21
> Experience is by industry achieved
> And perfected by the swift course of time.
> Then tell me, whither were I best to send him?   24

PANTHINO
> I think your lordship is not ignorant

1.3. Location: Verona. Antonio's house.
1 sad serious   **2 the cloister** any covered arcade attached to other
buildings   **5 suffer** allow   **6 of slender reputation** i.e., of lower station
than yourself   **7 Put . . . out** send their sons away from home to seek
advancement   **12 meet** fitted   **13 importune** urge   **15 impeachment to
his age** detriment or cause for reproach to him in his mature years
18 hammering beating (an idea) into shape   **20 perfect** i.e., educated,
mature   **21 tried** tested   **24 were I best** would it be best for me

How his companion, youthful Valentine,
Attends the Emperor in his royal court.   27
ANTONIO   I know it well.
PANTHINO
'Twere good, I think, your lordship sent him thither.
There shall he practice tilts and tournaments,   30
Hear sweet discourse, converse with noblemen,   31
And be in eye of every exercise   32
Worthy his youth and nobleness of birth.   33
ANTONIO
I like thy counsel; well hast thou advised;
And that thou mayst perceive how well I like it,
The execution of it shall make known.
Even with the speediest expedition   37
I will dispatch him to the Emperor's court.
PANTHINO
Tomorrow, may it please you, Don Alphonso
With other gentlemen of good esteem
Are journeying to salute the Emperor
And to commend their service to his will.   42
ANTONIO
Good company. With them shall Proteus go—

[*Enter*] Proteus, [*reading a letter.*]

And in good time! Now will we break with him.   44
PROTEUS [*To himself*]
Sweet love, sweet lines, sweet life!
Here is her hand, the agent of her heart;
Here is her oath for love, her honor's pawn.   47
O, that our fathers would applaud our loves,
To seal our happiness with their consents!   49
O heavenly Julia!
ANTONIO
How now? What letter are you reading there?
PROTEUS
May 't please your lordship, 'tis a word or two

---

27 Emperor i.e., the Duke of Milan. (An apparent inconsistency.)
30 practice perform, take part in   **31 discourse** conversation.   **converse** associate   **32 in eye of** in a position to see   **33 Worthy** worthy
of   **37 expedition** swiftness   **42 commend** commit, dedicate   **44 in
good time** i.e., just at the right time (here he comes).   **break with** reveal,
disclose the plan to   **47 pawn** pledge   **49 seal** ratify

Of commendations sent from Valentine,   53
Delivered by a friend that came from him.

ANTONIO
Lend me the letter. Let me see what news.

PROTEUS
There is no news, my lord, but that he writes
How happily he lives, how well beloved
And daily gracèd by the Emperor,   58
Wishing me with him, partner of his fortune.

ANTONIO
And how stand you affected to his wish?   60

PROTEUS
As one relying on your lordship's will,
And not depending on his friendly wish.

ANTONIO
My will is something sorted with his wish.   63
Muse not that I thus suddenly proceed,   64
For what I will, I will, and there an end.
I am resolved that thou shalt spend some time
With Valentinus in the Emperor's court.
What maintenance he from his friends receives,   68
Like exhibition thou shalt have from me.   69
Tomorrow be in readiness to go.
Excuse it not, for I am peremptory.   71

PROTEUS
My lord, I cannot be so soon provided.   72
Please you, deliberate a day or two.

ANTONIO
Look what thou want'st shall be sent after thee.   74
No more of stay. Tomorrow thou must go.   75
Come on, Panthino. You shall be employed
To hasten on his expedition.
                          [*Exeunt Antonio and Panthino.*]

PROTEUS
Thus have I shunned the fire for fear of burning,
And drenched me in the sea, where I am drowned.

53 commendations greetings   **58 gracèd** favored   **60 stand you affected**
are you disposed, inclined   **63 something sorted** rather in accordance
64 Muse wonder   **68 maintenance** allowance.   **friends** i.e., relatives
69 exhibition allowance of money   **71 Excuse it not** offer no excuses.
peremptory resolved   **72 provided** equipped   **74 Look what** whatever
75 No more of stay no more talk of delay

I feared to show my father Julia's letter
Lest he should take exceptions to my love,
And with the vantage of mine own excuse
Hath he excepted most against my love.   83
O, how this spring of love resembleth
The uncertain glory of an April day,
Which now shows all the beauty of the sun,
And by and by a cloud takes all away!

[*Enter Panthino.*]

PANTHINO
Sir Proteus, your father calls for you.
He is in haste; therefore, I pray you, go.
PROTEUS
Why, this it is: my heart accords thereto,
And yet a thousand times it answers no.   *Exeunt.*

❖

---

83 excepted most against most effectively hindered

2.1 *Enter Valentine [and] Speed.*

SPEED
  Sir, your glove.   [*Offering a glove.*]
VALENTINE   Not mine. My gloves are on.
SPEED
  Why, then, this may be yours, for this is but one.   2
VALENTINE
  Ha! Let me see. Ay, give it me, it's mine.
  Sweet ornament that decks a thing divine!
  Ah, Sylvia, Sylvia!
SPEED [*Calling*]   Madam Sylvia! Madam Sylvia!
VALENTINE   How now, sirrah?   7
SPEED   She is not within hearing, sir.
VALENTINE   Why, sir, who bade you call her?
SPEED   Your worship, sir, or else I mistook.
VALENTINE   Well, you'll still be too forward.   11
SPEED   And yet I was last chidden for being too slow.
VALENTINE   Go to, sir. Tell me, do you know Madam   13
  Sylvia?
SPEED   She that your worship loves?
VALENTINE   Why, how know you that I am in love?
SPEED   Marry, by these special marks: first, you have
  learned, like Sir Proteus, to wreathe your arms, like a   18
  malcontent; to relish a love song, like a robin red-   19
  breast; to walk alone, like one that had the pestilence;
  to sigh, like a schoolboy that had lost his A B C; to   21
  weep, like a young wench that had buried her grandam; to fast, like one that takes diet; to watch, like one 23
  that fears robbing; to speak puling, like a beggar at Hal- 24
  lowmas. You were wont, when you laughed, to crow   25
  like a cock; when you walked, to walk like one of the
  lions; when you fasted, it was presently after dinner;   27

2.1. Location: Milan. Perhaps at the Duke's palace, or in some unspeci-
fied location.
2 one (Pronounced like *on*, thus providing a pun on the line above.)
7 sirrah fellow. (Form of address to inferiors.)   **11 still** always   **13 Go to**
(An expression of remonstrance.)   **18 wreathe** fold. (Folded arms were a
conventional gesture of melancholy, such as love melancholy.)   **19 relish**
sing, warble   **21 A B C** primer   **23 watch** lie awake, sit up at night
24 puling whiningly   **24–25 Hallowmas** All Saints' Day, November 1
(a day when beggars asked special alms)   **27 lions** (Perhaps the lions
in the Tower of London, or heraldic lions.)   **presently** immediately

when you looked sadly, it was for want of money. And
now you are metamorphosed with a mistress, that 29
when I look on you I can hardly think you my master.
VALENTINE   Are all these things perceived in me?
SPEED   They are all perceived without ye.   32
VALENTINE   Without me? They cannot.
SPEED   Without you? Nay, that's certain, for, without 34
you were so simple, none else would. But you are so 35
without these follies that these follies are within you, 36
and shine through you like the water in an urinal, that 37
not an eye that sees you but is a physician to comment
on your malady.
VALENTINE   But tell me, dost thou know my lady Sylvia?
SPEED   She that you gaze on so as she sits at supper?
VALENTINE   Hast thou observed that? Even she I mean.
SPEED   Why, sir, I know her not.
VALENTINE   Dost thou know her by my gazing on her,
and yet know'st her not?
SPEED   Is she not hard-favored, sir?   46
VALENTINE   Not so fair, boy, as well-favored.   47
SPEED   Sir, I know that well enough.
VALENTINE   What dost thou know?
SPEED   That she is not so fair as, of you, well-favored.   50
VALENTINE   I mean that her beauty is exquisite but her
favor infinite.   52
SPEED   That's because the one is painted and the other 53
out of all count.   54
VALENTINE   How painted? And how out of count?
SPEED   Marry, sir, so painted, to make her fair, that no
man counts of her beauty.   57
VALENTINE   How esteem'st thou me? I account of her 58
beauty.

29 with by.   **that** so that   **32 without ye** from your outside appearance   **34 without** unless   **35 would** i.e., would perceive them
35–36 you are . . . follies i.e., you so surround and encompass these
follies   **37 urinal** glass container for medical examination of urine
46 hard-favored ugly   **47 fair** beautiful, blond-haired.   **well-favored**
gracious, charming; also, good-looking. (But Speed takes the word in the
sense of "looked upon with approval.")   **50 of** by   **52 favor** grace,
charm   **53 painted** achieved by cosmetics   **54 out of all count** incalcu-
lable   **57 counts of** esteems   **58 How . . . me** i.e., are you impugning my
judgment.   **account of** esteem

SPEED   You never saw her since she was deformed.   60
VALENTINE   How long hath she been deformed?
SPEED   Ever since you loved her.
VALENTINE   I have loved her ever since I saw her, and
    still I see her beautiful.
SPEED   If you love her, you cannot see her.
VALENTINE   Why?
SPEED   Because Love is blind. O, that you had mine   67
    eyes, or your own eyes had the lights they were wont   68
    to have when you chid at Sir Proteus for going un-   69
    gartered!   70
VALENTINE   What should I see then?
SPEED   Your own present folly and her passing defor-   72
    mity; for he, being in love, could not see to garter his
    hose, and you, being in love, cannot see to put on   74
    your hose.   75
VALENTINE   Belike, boy, then you are in love, for last
    morning you could not see to wipe my shoes.
SPEED   True, sir. I was in love with my bed. I thank you,
    you swinged me for my love, which makes me the   79
    bolder to chide you for yours.
VALENTINE   In conclusion, I stand affected to her.   81
SPEED   I would you were set; so your affection would
    cease.
VALENTINE   Last night she enjoined me to write some
    lines to one she loves.
SPEED   And have you?
VALENTINE   I have.
SPEED   Are they not lamely writ?
VALENTINE   No, boy, but as well as I can do them.
    Peace, here she comes.

---

60 deformed i.e., transformed by the distorting perspective of Valentine's love for her   **67 Love** i.e., Cupid, traditionally represented as
blind   **68 lights** sight   **69–70 going ungartered** i.e., neglecting appearance in dress, a traditional sign of love melancholy   **72 passing** very
great   **74–75 cannot . . . hose** i.e., you are in even worse shape than
Proteus, and he was perfectly helpless   **79 swinged** thrashed   **81 I
stand affected to** I am in love with. (But Speed quibbles on a bawdy
sense of *stand*, suggesting Valentine would be better off if his desire
were *set* or caused to subside and *cease*. *Set* also means "be seated,"
as contrasted with *stand* in the usual sense.)

[*Enter*] *Sylvia.*

SPEED [*Aside*]   O, excellent motion! O, exceeding puppet!   91
Now will he interpret to her.   92
VALENTINE   Madam and mistress, a thousand good-
morrows.
SPEED [*Aside*]   O, give ye good even! Here's a million of   95
manners.
SYLVIA   Sir Valentine and servant, to you two thousand.   97
SPEED [*Aside*]   He should give her interest, and she   98
gives it him.   99
VALENTINE
As you enjoined me, I have writ your letter
Unto the secret, nameless friend of yours,
Which I was much unwilling to proceed in
But for my duty to your ladyship.   [*Giving a letter.*]   103
SYLVIA   I thank you, gentle servant. 'Tis very clerkly done.   104
VALENTINE
Now trust me, madam, it came hardly off,   105
For, being ignorant to whom it goes,
I writ at random, very doubtfully.   107
SYLVIA
Perchance you think too much of so much pains?   108
VALENTINE
No, madam. So it stead you, I will write—   109
Please you command—a thousand times as much.
And yet—
SYLVIA
A pretty period! Well, I guess the sequel;   112
And yet I will not name it—and yet I care not—

---

91 motion puppet show.   **puppet** i.e., Sylvia   **92 interpret** i.e., supply
dialogue or commentary as for a puppet show   **95 give** i.e., God give.
a million i.e., an excessive amount   **97 servant** i.e., a man devoted to
serving a lady in love   **98–99 He . . . him** i.e., he is the one who should
be showing *interest* in her, as her *servant*, and yet she gives him *interest*
by doubling what he has given her. (Playing on the financial meaning of
interest.)   **103 duty** obedience, submission   **104 clerkly** in a scholarly
manner (and perhaps with good penmanship)   **105 came hardly off** was
done with difficulty   **107 doubtfully** uncertainly   **108 Perchance
. . . pains** perhaps you think I have given you too much trouble   **109 So**
so long as.   **stead** benefit   **112 A pretty period** a fine pause (i.e., to
finish your eloquent protestation of devoted service with "And yet" is to
spoil all that came before it)

And yet take this again—and yet I thank you,   114
Meaning henceforth to trouble you no more.
                              [*She offers him the letter.*]
SPEED [*Aside*]
   And yet you will, and yet another "yet."
VALENTINE
   What means your ladyship? Do you not like it?
SYLVIA
   Yes, yes. The lines are very quaintly writ,   118
   But since unwillingly, take them again.
   Nay, take them.   [*She gives back the letter.*]
VALENTINE   Madam, they are for you.
SYLVIA
   Ay, ay. You writ them, sir, at my request,
   But I will none of them. They are for you.
   I would have had them writ more movingly.
VALENTINE
   Please you, I'll write your ladyship another.
SYLVIA
   And when it's writ, for my sake read it over.
   And if it please you, so; if not, why, so.   127
VALENTINE
   If it please me, madam, what then?
SYLVIA
   Why, if it please you, take it for your labor.
   And so good morrow, servant.   *Exit Sylvia.*
SPEED [*Aside*]
   O jest unseen, inscrutable, invisible
   As a nose on a man's face or a weathercock on a steeple!
   My master sues to her, and she hath taught her suitor,
   He being her pupil, to become her tutor.
   O excellent device! Was there ever heard a better,
   That my master, being scribe, to himself should write
      the letter?
VALENTINE   How now, sir? What, are you reasoning 137
   with yourself?
SPEED   Nay, I was rhyming. 'Tis you that have the
   reason.
VALENTINE   To do what?

114 again back   **118 quaintly** ingeniously   **127 so** well and good
137 reasoning discussing

SPEED   To be a spokesman from Madam Sylvia.

VALENTINE   To whom?

SPEED   To yourself. Why, she woos you by a figure.   144

VALENTINE   What figure?

SPEED   By a letter, I should say.

VALENTINE   Why, she hath not writ to me.

SPEED   What need she, when she hath made you write to yourself? Why, do you not perceive the jest?

VALENTINE   No, believe me.

SPEED   No believing you, indeed, sir. But did you per-   151
ceive her earnest?   152

VALENTINE   She gave me none, except an angry word.

SPEED   Why, she hath given you a letter.

VALENTINE   That's the letter I writ to her friend.

SPEED   And that letter hath she delivered, and there an   156
end.   157

VALENTINE   I would it were no worse.

SPEED   I'll warrant you, 'tis as well.
For often have you writ to her, and she, in modesty,
Or else for want of idle time, could not again reply;
Or fearing else some messenger that might her mind
    discover,
Herself hath taught her love himself to write unto her
    lover.
All this I speak in print, for in print I found it. Why muse   164
you, sir? 'Tis dinnertime.

VALENTINE   I have dined.   166

SPEED   Ay, but hearken, sir: though the chameleon Love   167
can feed on the air, I am one that am nourished by my
victuals, and would fain have meat. O, be not like your   169
mistress; be moved, be moved!   *Exeunt.*   170

144 figure device   **151 No believing you** there's no believing anything
you say (playing on *No, believe me* in the previous line)   **152 earnest** to
be serious. (But Valentine takes the word as a noun meaning "money
paid as an installment to secure a bargain.")   **156–157 there an end**
there's nothing more to be said on that score   **164 speak . . . found it**
i.e., speak precisely, as though having read the speech somewhere.
(Speed claims that what he says is as infallible as if he had read it in a
book.)   **166 dined** i.e., feasted on the sight of Sylvia   **167 chameleon** an
animal popularly thought to be able to live on air.   **Love** (Love is also a
chameleon because it is so changeable.)   **169 fain** gladly   **170 be moved**
(1) be not hard-hearted (2) be persuaded to go to dinner

2.2 *Enter Proteus [and] Julia.*

PROTEUS Have patience, gentle Julia.

JULIA I must, where is no remedy.   2

PROTEUS

When possibly I can, I will return.

JULIA

If you turn not, you will return the sooner.   4

Keep this remembrance for thy Julia's sake.

                    [*She gives him a ring.*]

PROTEUS

Why, then, we'll make exchange; here, take you this.

                    [*He gives her a ring.*]

JULIA

And seal the bargain with a holy kiss.   [*They kiss.*]

PROTEUS

Here is my hand for my true constancy;

And when that hour o'erslips me in the day   9

Wherein I sigh not, Julia, for thy sake,

The next ensuing hour some foul mischance

Torment me for my love's forgetfulness!

My father stays my coming. Answer not.   13

The tide is now—nay, not thy tide of tears;   14

That tide will stay me longer than I should.

Julia, farewell!   [*Exit Julia.*]

            What, gone without a word?

Ay, so true love should do; it cannot speak,

For truth hath better deeds than words to grace it.   18

        [*Enter*] *Panthino.*

PANTHINO

Sir Proteus, you are stayed for.

PROTEUS   Go. I come, I come.

Alas! This parting strikes poor lovers dumb.   *Exeunt.*

❧

2.2. Location: Verona. Julia's house.
2 where is where there is   **4 turn not** do not prove to be unfaithful
9 o'erslips me slips by me unnoticed   **13 stays** awaits   **14 The tide** the
high tide for departure by sail   **18 grace** adorn

2.3   *Enter Lance [leading his dog Crab].*

LANCE   Nay, 'twill be this hour ere I have done weeping. All the kind of the Lances have this very fault. I ²
have received my proportion, like the prodigious son, ³
and am going with Sir Proteus to the Imperial's court. ⁴
I think Crab, my dog, be the sourest-natured dog that
lives. My mother weeping, my father wailing, my sister crying, our maid howling, our cat wringing her
hands, and all our house in a great perplexity, yet did   .
not this cruel-hearted cur shed one tear. He is a stone,
a very pebblestone, and has no more pity in him than
a dog. A Jew would have wept to have seen our parting. Why, my grandam, having no eyes, look you,
wept herself blind at my parting. Nay, I'll show you
the manner of it. This shoe is my father. No, this left ¹⁴
shoe is my father. No, no, this left shoe is my mother.
Nay, that cannot be so neither. Yes, it is so, it is so—
it hath the worser sole. This shoe, with the hole in it, ¹⁷
is my mother, and this my father. A vengeance on 't! ¹⁸
There 'tis. Now, sir, this staff is my sister, for, look
you, she is as white as a lily and as small as a wand.
This hat is Nan, our maid. I am the dog. No, the dog is
himself, and I am the dog—O, the dog is me, and I
am myself. Ay, so, so. Now come I to my father: "Father, your blessing." Now should not the shoe speak
a word for weeping. Now should I kiss my father.
Well, he weeps on. Now come I to my mother. O, that
she could speak now like a wood woman! Well, I kiss ²⁷
her. Why, there 'tis. Here's my mother's breath up and ²⁸
down. Now come I to my sister; mark the moan she ²⁹
makes. Now the dog all this while sheds not a tear nor

2.3. Location: Verona. A street.
2 kind kindred, race   **3 proportion** (A malapropism for *portion*, "allot-
ment.")   **prodigious** (A malapropism for *prodigal*.)   **4 Imperial's** i.e.,
Emperor's   **14 This shoe** (Lance demonstrates.)   **17 sole** (with a pun on
soul. Lance refers to a common debate as to whether a woman's soul
was inferior to a man's. *The hole in it* may also suggest a bawdy joke
about the feminine anatomy.)   **18 A vengeance on 't** (A mild curse,
probably occasioned by the difficulty Lance has in pulling his shoe
off.)   **27 wood** mad, distraught (with punning allusion to a wooden
shoe)   **28–29 up and down** i.e., exactly

speaks a word; but see how I lay the dust with my
tears.

[*Enter*] *Panthino.*

PANTHINO   Lance, away, away, aboard! Thy master is
shipped, and thou art to post after with oars. What's   34
the matter? Why weep'st thou, man? Away, ass! You'll
lose the tide if you tarry any longer.

LANCE   It is no matter if the tied were lost, for it is the
unkindest tied that ever any man tied.

PANTHINO   What's the unkindest tide?

LANCE   Why, he that's tied here, Crab, my dog.

PANTHINO   Tut, man, I mean thou'lt lose the flood, and   41
in losing the flood, lose thy voyage, and in losing thy
voyage, lose thy master, and in losing thy master, lose
thy service, and in losing thy service—[*Lance puts his
hand over Panthino's mouth.*] Why dost thou stop my
mouth?

LANCE   For fear thou shouldst lose thy tongue.   47

PANTHINO   Where should I lose my tongue?

LANCE   In thy tale.

PANTHINO   In thy tail!

LANCE   Lose the tide, and the voyage, and the master,
and the service, and the tied? Why, man, if the river
were dry, I am able to fill it with my tears; if the wind
were down, I could drive the boat with my sighs.

PANTHINO   Come, come away, man. I was sent to call   55
thee.

LANCE   Sir, call me what thou dar'st.   57

PANTHINO   Wilt thou go?

LANCE   Well, I will go.   *Exeunt.*

❖

2.4   *Enter Valentine, Sylvia, Thurio, [and] Speed.*

SYLVIA   Servant!

VALENTINE   Mistress?

---

34 post hasten. **with oars,** i.e., in a rowboat, in order to reach the sailing
vessel at anchor **41 lose the flood** miss the tide **47 lose** (1) lose (2) loose
55 call summon **57 call me what** call me whatever names

2.4. Location: Milan. The Duke's palace.

SPEED   Master, Sir Thurio frowns on you.

VALENTINE   Ay, boy, it's for love.

SPEED   Not of you.

VALENTINE   Of my mistress, then.

SPEED   'Twere good you knocked him.   [*Exit.*]

SYLVIA   Servant, you are sad.

VALENTINE   Indeed, madam, I seem so.

THURIO   Seem you that you are not?   10

VALENTINE   Haply I do.   11

THURIO   So do counterfeits.

VALENTINE   So do you.

THURIO   What seem I that I am not?

VALENTINE   Wise.

THURIO   What instance of the contrary?   16

VALENTINE   Your folly.

THURIO   And how quote you my folly?   18

VALENTINE   I quote it in your jerkin.   19

THURIO   My "jerkin" is a doublet.   20

VALENTINE   Well, then, I'll double your folly.

THURIO   How?   22

SYLVIA   What, angry, Sir Thurio? Do you change color?

VALENTINE   Give him leave, madam; he is a kind of
chameleon.

THURIO   That hath more mind to feed on your blood   26
than live in your air.   27

VALENTINE   You have said, sir.   28

THURIO   Ay, sir, and done too, for this time.   29

VALENTINE   I know it well, sir; you always end ere you   30
begin.   31

---

10 that what   **11 Haply** perhaps   **16 instance** proof   **18 quote** notice,
observe. (Pronounced like *coat*, enabling Valentine to pun on that
idea.)   **19 jerkin** close-fitting jacket worn over, or in place of, the doublet   **20 My . . . doublet** i.e., what you ignorantly call my "jerkin" is
in fact a doublet.   **a doublet** (with a play on *double* in the next line)
22 How (An expression of annoyance or incredulity.)   **26 That** i.e., one
who   **27 in your air** (1) in the air you breathe, i.e., near you (2) listening
to your talk. (The phrase also plays on *chameleon* in the previous
speech, since chameleons were supposed to be able to live on air
alone.)   **28 You have said** i.e., that's a lot of fine talk   **29 done** (1) acted,
in contrast to *said* (2) finished. (Thurio hints here that he's prepared to
duel with Valentine at some future date.)   **30–31 end . . . begin** i.e., stop
before you come to actual blows

SYLVIA   A fine volley of words, gentlemen, and quickly
    shot off.
VALENTINE   'Tis indeed, madam, we thank the giver.
SYLVIA   Who is that, servant?
VALENTINE   Yourself, sweet lady, for you gave the fire.   36
    Sir Thurio borrows his wit from your ladyship's looks,
    and spends what he borrows kindly in your company.   38
THURIO   Sir, if you spend word for word with me, I shall
    make your wit bankrupt.
VALENTINE   I know it well, sir; you have an exchequer   41
    of words, and, I think, no other treasure to give your
    followers, for it appears, by their bare liveries, that   43
    they live by your bare words.   44
SYLVIA   No more, gentlemen, no more. Here comes my
    father.

    [*Enter the*] *Duke.*

DUKE
    Now, daughter Sylvia, you are hard beset.   47
    Sir Valentine, your father is in good health.
    What say you to a letter from your friends
    Of much good news?
VALENTINE   My lord, I will be thankful
    To any happy messenger from thence.   51
DUKE
    Know ye Don Antonio, your countryman?
VALENTINE
    Ay, my good lord, I know the gentleman
    To be of worth and worthy estimation,   54
    And not without desert so well reputed.   55
DUKE   Hath he not a son?
VALENTINE
    Ay, my good lord, a son that well deserves
    The honor and regard of such a father.

---

36 fire i.e., spark to set off the volley   **38 kindly** fittingly, naturally
41 exchequer treasury   **43 bare** threadbare.   **liveries** uniforms worn by
a gentleman's retainers   **44 bare** mere   **47 hard beset** strongly besieged
(with two wooers at once)   **51 happy messenger** bringer of good
tidings   **54 worthy** worthy of   **55 without desert** undeservedly

DUKE   You know him well?

VALENTINE
I know him as myself, for from our infancy
We have conversed and spent our hours together.   61
And though myself have been an idle truant,
Omitting the sweet benefit of time   63
To clothe mine age with angel-like perfection,
Yet hath Sir Proteus—for that's his name—
Made use and fair advantage of his days;
His years but young, but his experience old;
His head unmellowed, but his judgment ripe.   68
And, in a word—for far behind his worth
Comes all the praises that I now bestow—
He is complete in feature and in mind   71
With all good grace to grace a gentleman.

DUKE
Beshrew me, sir, but if he make this good,   73
He is as worthy for an empress' love
As meet to be an emperor's counselor.   75
Well, sir, this gentleman is come to me,
With commendation from great potentates,
And here he means to spend his time awhile.
I think 'tis no unwelcome news to you.

VALENTINE
Should I have wished a thing, it had been he.

DUKE
Welcome him then according to his worth.
Sylvia, I speak to you, and you, Sir Thurio;
For Valentine, I need not cite him to it.   83
I will send him hither to you presently.   [*Exit.*]   84

VALENTINE
This is the gentleman I told your ladyship
Had come along with me but that his mistress
Did hold his eyes locked in her crystal looks.

SYLVIA
Belike that now she hath enfranchised them   88

---

61 conversed associated   **63 Omitting** neglecting   **68 unmellowed** i.e.,
unmixed with gray hair   **71 complete in feature** perfect in shape of
body and personal appearance   **73 Beshrew me** (A mild oath.)   **make
this good** i.e., match your description   **75 meet** suited   **83 cite** urge
84 presently at once   **88 Belike that** perhaps.   **enfranchised** freed

Upon some other pawn for fealty.   89

VALENTINE
Nay, sure, I think she holds them prisoners still.

SYLVIA
Nay, then he should be blind, and being blind
How could he see his way to seek out you?

VALENTINE
Why, lady, Love hath twenty pair of eyes.

THURIO
They say that Love hath not an eye at all.

VALENTINE
To see such lovers, Thurio, as yourself.
Upon a homely object Love can wink.   96

SYLVIA
Have done, have done. Here comes the gentleman.

    [*Enter*] *Proteus.*

VALENTINE
Welcome, dear Proteus!—Mistress, I beseech you,
Confirm his welcome with some special favor.

SYLVIA
His worth is warrant for his welcome hither,
If this be he you oft have wished to hear from.

VALENTINE
Mistress, it is. Sweet lady, entertain him   102
To be my fellow servant to your ladyship.

SYLVIA
Too low a mistress for so high a servant.

PROTEUS
Not so, sweet lady, but too mean a servant
To have a look of such a worthy mistress.   106

VALENTINE
Leave off discourse of disability.   107
Sweet lady, entertain him for your servant.

PROTEUS
My duty will I boast of, nothing else.   109

---

89 Upon . . . fealty in return for some other pledge of fidelity, or, now
that some other lover has pledged his service to her   **96 homely**
plain. **wink** close the eyes   **102 entertain** take into service   **106 of**
from   **107 Leave . . . disability** stop talking about your unworthiness
109 duty i.e., to Sylvia

SYLVIA

   And duty never yet did want his meed.   110

   Servant, you are welcome to a worthless mistress.

PROTEUS

   I'll die on him that says so but yourself.   112

SYLVIA

   That you are welcome?

PROTEUS   That you are worthless.

     [*Enter a Servant.*]

SERVANT

   Madam, my lord your father would speak with you.

SYLVIA

   I wait upon his pleasure. [*Exit Servant.*] Come, Sir
     Thurio,

   Go with me. Once more, new servant, welcome.

   I'll leave you to confer of home affairs.

   When you have done, we look to hear from you.

PROTEUS

   We'll both attend upon your ladyship.

               [*Exeunt Sylvia and Thurio.*]

VALENTINE

   Now tell me, how do all from whence you came?

PROTEUS

   Your friends are well and have them much commended. 121

VALENTINE

   And how do yours?

PROTEUS   I left them all in health.

VALENTINE

   How does your lady, and how thrives your love?

PROTEUS

   My tales of love were wont to weary you;

   I know you joy not in a love discourse.

VALENTINE

   Ay, Proteus, but that life is altered now.

   I have done penance for contemning Love,   127

   Whose high imperious thoughts have punished me

   With bitter fasts, with penitential groans,

---

110 want his meed lack its reward   **112 die on** die fighting with
121 them much commended i.e., sent warm greetings   **127 contemning**
scorning

With nightly tears, and daily heartsore sighs;
For, in revenge of my contempt of love,
Love hath chased sleep from my enthrallèd eyes
And made them watchers of mine own heart's sorrow.   133
O gentle Proteus, Love's a mighty lord,
And hath so humbled me as I confess   135
There is no woe to his correction,   136
Nor to his service no such joy on earth.   137
Now, no discourse except it be of love;
Now can I break my fast, dine, sup, and sleep
Upon the very naked name of love.   139

PROTEUS
Enough. I read your fortune in your eye.
Was this the idol that you worship so?

VALENTINE
Even she. And is she not a heavenly saint?

PROTEUS
No, but she is an earthly paragon.

VALENTINE
Call her divine.

PROTEUS   I will not flatter her.

VALENTINE
O, flatter me, for love delights in praises.

PROTEUS
When I was sick, you gave me bitter pills,
And I must minister the like to you.

VALENTINE
Then speak the truth by her; if not divine,   148
Yet let her be a principality,   149
Sovereign to all the creatures on the earth.

PROTEUS
Except my mistress.

VALENTINE   Sweet, except not any,   151
Except thou wilt except against my love.   152

PROTEUS
Have I not reason to prefer mine own?   153

---

133 watchers of those who stay awake with   **135 as** that   **136 to his correction** compared to the woe of his punishment   **137 to his service** i.e., compared to serving Love   **139 very naked** mere   **148 by** about   **149 a
principality** a member of one of the nine orders of angels   **151 Sweet** (A
term of affection used with both men and women.)   **152 Except . . . except**
unless you want to cast aspersions   **153 prefer** like better

VALENTINE
And I will help thee to prefer her, too.   154
She shall be dignified with this high honor:
To bear my lady's train, lest the base earth
Should from her vesture chance to steal a kiss
And, of so great a favor growing proud,
Disdain to root the summer-swelling flower,   159
And make rough winter everlastingly.

PROTEUS
Why, Valentine, what braggartism is this?

VALENTINE
Pardon me, Proteus, all I can is nothing   162
To her whose worth makes other worthies nothing.   163
She is alone.

PROTEUS   Then let her alone.   164

VALENTINE
Not for the world. Why, man, she is mine own,
And I as rich in having such a jewel
As twenty seas, if all their sand were pearl,
The water nectar, and the rocks pure gold.
Forgive me that I do not dream on thee,   169
Because thou seest me dote upon my love.
My foolish rival, that her father likes
Only for his possessions are so huge,   172
Is gone with her along, and I must after,
For love, thou know'st, is full of jealousy.

PROTEUS   But she loves you?

VALENTINE
Ay, and we are betrothed. Nay, more, our marriage hour,
With all the cunning manner of our flight,
Determined of—how I must climb her window,   178
The ladder made of cords, and all the means
Plotted and 'greed on for my happiness.
Good Proteus, go with me to my chamber,
In these affairs to aid me with thy counsel.

---

154 prefer advance   **159 root** provide rooting for   **162 can** i.e., can say
of her   **163 To her** compared to her   **164 is alone** is peerless. (But
Proteus plays on the sense of "let her be.")   **169 that . . . thee** i.e., that I
seem neglectful of you   **172 for** because   **178 Determined of** is decided,
arranged

PROTEUS
   Go on before; I shall inquire you forth.   183
   I must unto the road, to disembark   184
   Some necessaries that I needs must use,
   And then I'll presently attend you.   186
VALENTINE   Will you make haste?   *Exit.*
PROTEUS   I will.
   Even as one heat another heat expels,   189
   Or as one nail by strength drives out another,
   So the remembrance of my former love
   Is by a newer object quite forgotten.
   Is it mine eye, or Valentine's praise,
   Her true perfection, or my false transgression
   That makes me, reasonless, to reason thus?   195
   She is fair; and so is Julia that I love—
   That I did love, for now my love is thawed,
   Which like a waxen image 'gainst a fire
   Bears no impression of the thing it was.
   Methinks my zeal to Valentine is cold,
   And that I love him not as I was wont.
   O, but I love his lady too, too much,
   And that's the reason I love him so little.
   How shall I dote on her with more advice,   204
   That thus without advice begin to love her!   205
   'Tis but her picture I have yet beheld,   206
   And that hath dazzlèd my reason's light;
   But when I look on her perfections,   208
   There is no reason but I shall be blind.   209
   If I can check my erring love, I will;   210
   If not, to compass her I'll use my skill.   *Exit.* 211

❖

183 forth out   **184 road** roadstead, harbor   **186 presently** immediately   **189 Even . . . expels** (It was a common saying that the application
of heat would relieve the pain of a burn.)   **195 reasonless** without
justification, wrongly   **204 advice** deliberation, reflection   **205 without
advice** unadvisedly (with a play on *with advice* in the previous line)
206 picture i.e., outer appearance   **208 perfections** true qualities, not
immediately apparent to view   **209 no reason but** no doubt but that
210 check restrain   **211 compass** obtain

2.5   *Enter, [meeting,] Speed and Lance [with his dog Crab].*

SPEED   Lance, by mine honesty, welcome to Milan!

LANCE   Forswear not thyself, sweet youth, for I am not welcome. I reckon this always, that a man is never un- ³ done till he be hanged, nor never welcome to a place ⁴ till some certain shot be paid and the hostess say, ⁵ "Welcome!"

SPEED   Come on, you madcap, I'll to the alehouse with you presently, where, for one shot of five pence, thou ⁸ shalt have five thousand welcomes. But, sirrah, how did thy master part with Madam Julia?

LANCE   Marry, after they closed in earnest, they parted ¹¹ very fairly in jest.   ¹²

SPEED   But shall she marry him?

LANCE   No.

SPEED   How then? Shall he marry her?

LANCE   No, neither.

SPEED   What, are they broken?   ¹⁷

LANCE   No, they are both as whole as a fish.   ¹⁸

SPEED   Why, then, how stands the matter with them?

LANCE   Marry, thus: when it stands well with him, it ²⁰ stands well with her.

SPEED   What an ass art thou! I understand thee not.

LANCE   What a block art thou, that thou canst not! My ²³ staff understands me.

SPEED   What thou sayst?

LANCE   Ay, and what I do too. Look thee, I'll but lean, and my staff understands me.

SPEED   It stands under thee, indeed.

LANCE   Why, stand-under and under-stand is all one.

SPEED   But tell me true, will 't be a match?

2.5. Location: Milan. A street.
3–4 undone ruined   **5 shot** fee, tavern reckoning   **8 presently** immediately   **11 closed** (1) embraced (2) came to terms   **12 fairly** kindly,
gently.   **jest** (Playing on the antithesis of *earnest* and *jest*.)   **17 broken**
no longer engaged. (But Lance plays on the word in the sense of
"smashed to pieces.")   **18 whole as a fish** (A proverbial comparison.)
20 stands well (with a bawdy pun about erection)   **23 block** blockhead

LANCE   Ask my dog. If he say ay, it will; if he say no,
it will; if he shake his tail and say nothing, it will.

SPEED   The conclusion is then that it will.

LANCE   Thou shalt never get such a secret from me but
by a parable.   35

SPEED   'Tis well that I get it so. But, Lance, how sayst   36
thou, that my master is become a notable lover?   37

LANCE   I never knew him otherwise.

SPEED   Than how?

LANCE   A notable lubber, as thou reportest him to be.   40

SPEED   Why, thou whoreson ass, thou mistak'st me.   41

LANCE   Why, fool, I meant not thee. I meant thy
master.

SPEED   I tell thee, my master is become a hot lover.

LANCE   Why, I tell thee I care not, though he burn   45
himself in love. If thou wilt, go with me to the ale-   46
house; if not, thou art an Hebrew, a Jew, and not
worth the name of a Christian.

SPEED   Why?

LANCE   Because thou hast not so much charity in thee
as to go to the ale with a Christian. Wilt thou go?   51

SPEED   At thy service.   *Exeunt.*

❖

2.6   *Enter Proteus solus.*

PROTEUS
To leave my Julia, shall I be forsworn;
To love fair Sylvia, shall I be forsworn;
To wrong my friend, I shall be much forsworn.
And ev'n that power which gave me first my oath   4
Provokes me to this threefold perjury.   5

---

35 a parable enigmatic talk   **36–37 how sayst thou** what do you say
to this   **40 lubber** big, clumsy fellow (with obvious pun on *lover*)
41 whoreson (A friendly term of abuse.)   **thou mistak'st me** you mistake my meaning. (But Lance replies to the sense of "you mistake me
[Speed] for Valentine.")   **45–46 burn himself in love** (with a punning
sense of "acquire venereal disease")   **51 go . . . Christian** i.e., go to a
church-ale, a village festival used to raise money for the church

2.6. Location: Milan. The Duke's palace.
s.d. solus alone   **4 that power** i.e., Love   **5 Provokes** incites

Love bade me swear, and Love bids me forswear.
O sweet-suggesting Love, if thou hast sinned,   7
Teach me, thy tempted subject, to excuse it!   8
At first I did adore a twinkling star,
But now I worship a celestial sun.
Unheedful vows may heedfully be broken,   11
And he wants wit that wants resolvèd will   12
To learn his wit t' exchange the bad for better.   13
Fie, fie, unreverent tongue, to call her bad
Whose sovereignty so oft thou hast preferred   15
With twenty thousand soul-confirming oaths!   16
I cannot leave to love, and yet I do;   17
But there I leave to love where I should love.
Julia I lose and Valentine I lose.
If I keep them, I needs must lose myself.
If I lose them, thus find I by their loss
For Valentine, myself; for Julia, Sylvia.
I to myself am dearer than a friend,
For love is still most precious in itself,   24
And Sylvia—witness Heaven, that made her fair!—
Shows Julia but a swarthy Ethiop.   26
I will forget that Julia is alive,
Remembering that my love to her is dead;
And Valentine I'll hold an enemy,
Aiming at Sylvia as a sweeter friend.
I cannot now prove constant to myself
Without some treachery used to Valentine.
This night he meaneth with a corded ladder
To climb celestial Sylvia's chamber window,
Myself in counsel, his competitor.   35
Now presently I'll give her father notice
Of their disguising and pretended flight,   37
Who, all enraged, will banish Valentine;
For Thurio, he intends, shall wed his daughter.

7 sweet-suggesting sweetly seductive   **7–8 if thou . . . it** i.e., if even you,
Love, have committed falsehoods or follies in love, teach frail me how to
excuse myself by your example   **11 Unheedful** ill-considered.
heedfully after careful consideration   **12 wants** lacks   **13 learn** teach
15 preferred recommended, urged   **16 soul-confirming** sworn on the
soul   **17 leave** cease   **24 still** always   **26 Shows Julia but** reveals Julia
to be by comparison no more than   **35 in counsel** taken into confidence.   **competitor** associate, partner   **37 pretended** intended

But Valentine being gone, I'll quickly cross   40
By some sly trick blunt Thurio's dull proceeding.   41
Love, lend me wings to make my purpose swift,
As thou hast lent me wit to plot this drift!   *Exit.* 43

❖

2.7   *Enter Julia and Lucetta.*

JULIA
Counsel, Lucetta. Gentle girl, assist me;
And ev'n in kind love I do conjure thee,
Who art the table wherein all my thoughts   3
Are visibly charactered and engraved,   4
To lesson me and tell me some good means   5
How, with my honor, I may undertake
A journey to my loving Proteus.

LUCETTA
Alas, the way is wearisome and long!

JULIA
A true-devoted pilgrim is not weary
To measure kingdoms with his feeble steps;   10
Much less shall she that hath Love's wings to fly,
And when the flight is made to one so dear,
Of such divine perfection, as Sir Proteus.

LUCETTA
Better forbear till Proteus make return.

JULIA
O, know'st thou not his looks are my soul's food?
Pity the dearth that I have pinèd in
By longing for that food so long a time.
Didst thou but know the inly touch of love,   18
Thou wouldst as soon go kindle fire with snow
As seek to quench the fire of love with words.

LUCETTA
I do not seek to quench your love's hot fire,
But qualify the fire's extreme rage,   22

---

40 **cross** thwart   41 **blunt** stupid   43 **drift** scheme

2.7. Location: Verona. Julia's house.
3 **table** tablet   4 **charactered** engraved, inscribed   5 **lesson** teach
10 **measure** traverse   18 **inly** inward   22 **qualify** control, moderate

Lest it should burn above the bounds of reason.

JULIA
The more thou damm'st it up, the more it burns.
The current that with gentle murmur glides,
Thou know'st, being stopped, impatiently doth rage;
But when his fair course is not hinderèd,
He makes sweet music with th' enameled stones,   28
Giving a gentle kiss to every sedge   29
He overtaketh in his pilgrimage,
And so by many winding nooks he strays
With willing sport to the wild ocean.   32
Then let me go, and hinder not my course.
I'll be as patient as a gentle stream
And make a pastime of each weary step,
Till the last step have brought me to my love,
And there I'll rest, as after much turmoil
A blessèd soul doth in Elysium.

LUCETTA
But in what habit will you go along?   39

JULIA
Not like a woman, for I would prevent   40
The loose encounters of lascivious men.
Gentle Lucetta, fit me with such weeds   42
As may beseem some well-reputed page.   43

LUCETTA
Why, then, your ladyship must cut your hair.

JULIA
No, girl, I'll knit it up in silken strings
With twenty odd-conceited true-love knots.   46
To be fantastic may become a youth   47
Of greater time than I shall show to be.   48

LUCETTA
What fashion, madam, shall I make your breeches?

JULIA
That fits as well as "Tell me, good my lord,
What compass will you wear your farthingale?"   51
Why, ev'n what fashion thou best likes, Lucetta.

---

28 enameled having shiny, polished surfaces; variegated   **29 sedge** grassy, rush-like plant   **32 wild** open   **39 habit** apparel   **40 prevent** forestall
42 weeds garments   **43 beseem** suit   **46 odd-conceited** strangely devised
47 fantastic fanciful (in appearance)   **48 Of greater time** of more years
51 compass circumference, fullness.   **farthingale** hooped petticoat

LUCETTA

   You must needs have them with a codpiece, madam.   53

JULIA

   Out, out, Lucetta! That will be ill-favored.   54

LUCETTA

   A round hose, madam, now's not worth a pin   55
   Unless you have a codpiece to stick pins on.   56

JULIA

   Lucetta, as thou lov'st me, let me have
   What thou think'st meet and is most mannerly.
   But tell me, wench, how will the world repute me
   For undertaking so unstaid a journey?   60
   I fear me it will make me scandalized.

LUCETTA

   If you think so, then stay at home and go not.

JULIA   Nay, that I will not.

LUCETTA

   Then never dream on infamy, but go.
   If Proteus like your journey when you come,
   No matter who's displeased when you are gone.
   I fear me he will scarce be pleased withal.   67

JULIA

   That is the least, Lucetta, of my fear.
   A thousand oaths, an ocean of his tears,
   And instances of infinite of love,   70
   Warrant me welcome to my Proteus.

LUCETTA

   All these are servants to deceitful men.

JULIA

   Base men, that use them to so base effect!
   But truer stars did govern Proteus' birth;
   His words are bonds, his oaths are oracles,
   His love sincere, his thoughts immaculate,
   His tears pure messengers sent from his heart,
   His heart as far from fraud as heaven from earth.

LUCETTA

   Pray heaven he prove so when you come to him!

53 codpiece bagged appendage to the front of close-fitting hose
or breeches, often conspicuous and ornamented   **54 Out** (An expression
of reproach or indignation.)   **ill-favored** unsightly   **55 round hose**
padded breeches   **56 stick pins on** (One method used to decorate the
codpiece.)   **60 unstaid** reckless, unconventional   **67 withal** with it
70 infinite infinity

JULIA
   Now, as thou lov'st me, do him not that wrong
   To bear a hard opinion of his truth.
   Only deserve my love by loving him,
   And presently go with me to my chamber
   To take a note of what I stand in need of
   To furnish me upon my longing journey.   85
   All that is mine I leave at thy dispose,   86
   My goods, my lands, my reputation;
   Only, in lieu thereof, dispatch me hence.
   Come, answer not, but to it presently!
   I am impatient of my tarriance.   *Exeunt.* 90

85 longing prompted by longing   **86 at thy dispose** in your charge
90 tarriance delaying

3.1 *Enter Duke, Thurio, [and] Proteus.*

DUKE

  Sir Thurio, give us leave, I pray, awhile.   1
  We have some secrets to confer about.   *[Exit Thurio.]*
  Now, tell me, Proteus, what's your will with me?

PROTEUS

  My gracious lord, that which I would discover   4
  The law of friendship bids me to conceal;
  But when I call to mind your gracious favors
  Done to me, undeserving as I am,
  My duty pricks me on to utter that
  Which else no worldly good should draw from me.
  Know, worthy prince, Sir Valentine, my friend,
  This night intends to steal away your daughter.
  Myself am one made privy to the plot.
  I know you have determined to bestow her
  On Thurio, whom your gentle daughter hates;
  And should she thus be stolen away from you,
  It would be much vexation to your age.
  Thus, for my duty's sake, I rather chose
  To cross my friend in his intended drift   18
  Than, by concealing it, heap on your head
  A pack of sorrows which would press you down,
  Being unprevented, to your timeless grave.   21

DUKE

  Proteus, I thank thee for thine honest care,
  Which to requite, command me while I live.   23
  This love of theirs myself have often seen,
  Haply when they have judged me fast asleep,
  And oftentimes have purposed to forbid
  Sir Valentine her company and my court.
  But, fearing lest my jealous aim might err,   28
  And so unworthily disgrace the man—
  A rashness that I ever yet have shunned—
  I gave him gentle looks, thereby to find
  That which thyself hast now disclosed to me.

3.1. Location: Milan. The Duke's palace.
1 give us leave (A polite form of dismissal.) **4 discover** reveal **18 cross**
thwart. **drift** scheme **21 timeless** untimely **23 command me** ask any
favor of me **28 jealous aim** suspicious conjecture

And, that thou mayst perceive my fear of this,
Knowing that tender youth is soon suggested,   34
I nightly lodge her in an upper tower,
The key whereof myself have ever kept;
And thence she cannot be conveyed away.

PROTEUS
Know, noble lord, they have devised a means
How he her chamber window will ascend
And with a corded ladder fetch her down;
For which the youthful lover now is gone,
And this way comes he with it presently,   42
Where, if it please you, you may intercept him.
But, good my lord, do it so cunningly
That my discovery be not aimèd at;   45
For, love of you, not hate unto my friend,   46
Hath made me publisher of this pretense.   47

DUKE
Upon mine honor, he shall never know
That I had any light from thee of this.

PROTEUS
Adieu, my lord. Sir Valentine is coming.   [Exit.]

[Enter] Valentine, [hurrying elsewhere, concealing
a rope ladder beneath his cloak].

DUKE
Sir Valentine, whither away so fast?

VALENTINE
Please it Your Grace, there is a messenger
That stays to bear my letters to my friends,
And I am going to deliver them.

DUKE   Be they of much import?

VALENTINE
The tenor of them doth but signify
My health and happy being at your court.

DUKE
Nay then, no matter. Stay with me awhile.
I am to break with thee of some affairs   58

---

34 suggested tempted   **42 presently** now   **45 discovery** disclosure.
aimèd at guessed   **46 For** because   **47 publisher** proclaimer.   **pretense**
intention   **58 break with thee of** disclose to you

That touch me near, wherein thou must be secret.   59
'Tis not unknown to thee that I have sought
To match my friend Sir Thurio to my daughter.

VALENTINE
I know it well, my lord, and sure the match
Were rich and honorable. Besides, the gentleman   63
Is full of virtue, bounty, worth, and qualities   64
Beseeming such a wife as your fair daughter.   65
Cannot Your Grace win her to fancy him?

DUKE
No, trust me. She is peevish, sullen, froward,   67
Proud, disobedient, stubborn, lacking duty,
Neither regarding that she is my child
Nor fearing me as if I were her father.
And, may I say to thee, this pride of hers,
Upon advice, hath drawn my love from her;   72
And, where I thought the remnant of mine age   73
Should have been cherished by her childlike duty,
I now am full resolved to take a wife,
And turn her out to who will take her in.   76
Then let her beauty be her wedding dower,
For me and my possessions she esteems not.

VALENTINE
What would Your Grace have me to do in this?

DUKE
There is a lady in Verona here   80
Whom I affect, but she is nice and coy,   81
And naught esteems my agèd eloquence.
Now therefore would I have thee to my tutor—   83
For long agone I have forgot to court;   84
Besides, the fashion of the time is changed—
How and which way I may bestow myself   86
To be regarded in her sun-bright eye.

---

59 touch me near are of vital concern to me   **63 Were** would be
64 virtue good accomplishments.   **qualities** attainments   **65 Beseeming**
befitting   **67 peevish** willful.   **froward** perverse   **72 Upon advice** after
some careful consideration   **73 where** whereas   **76 who** whoever
80 Verona (An error for Milan, seemingly, but *Verona* fits the line metri-
cally.)   **81 affect** am fond of.   **nice** difficult to please.   **coy** shy   **83 to**
as, for   **84 agone** ago.   **forgot** forgotten how   **86 bestow** behave,
conduct

VALENTINE

Win her with gifts, if she respect not words. 88
Dumb jewels often in their silent kind 89
More than quick words do move a woman's mind. 90

DUKE

But she did scorn a present that I sent her.

VALENTINE

A woman sometimes scorns what best contents her.
Send her another. Never give her o'er,
For scorn at first makes after-love the more.
If she do frown, 'tis not in hate of you,
But rather to beget more love in you.
If she do chide, 'tis not to have you gone,
Forwhy the fools are mad if left alone. 98
Take no repulse, whatever she doth say;
For "Get you gone," she doth not mean "Away!" 100
Flatter and praise, commend, extol their graces;
Though ne'er so black, say they have angels' faces. 102
That man that hath a tongue, I say, is no man
If with his tongue he cannot win a woman.

DUKE

But she I mean is promised by her friends 105
Unto a youthful gentleman of worth,
And kept severely from resort of men,
That no man hath access by day to her. 108

VALENTINE

Why then I would resort to her by night.

DUKE

Ay, but the doors be locked and keys kept safe,
That no man hath recourse to her by night.

VALENTINE

What lets but one may enter at her window? 112

DUKE

Her chamber is aloft, far from the ground,
And built so shelving that one cannot climb it 114
Without apparent hazard of his life. 115

88 respect heed   89 kind nature   90 quick lively (as contrasted with
Dumb, silent)   98 Forwhy because   100 For by   102 black dark of
complexion   105 friends i.e., relatives   108 That so that (also in
l. 111)   112 lets hinders   114 shelving projecting, overhanging
115 apparent plain, evident

VALENTINE
  Why then, a ladder quaintly made of cords   116
  To cast up, with a pair of anchoring hooks,
  Would serve to scale another Hero's tower,   118
  So bold Leander would adventure it.   119
DUKE
  Now, as thou art a gentleman of blood,   120
  Advise me where I may have such a ladder.
VALENTINE
  When would you use it? Pray, sir, tell me that.
DUKE
  This very night; for Love is like a child,
  That longs for everything that he can come by.
VALENTINE
  By seven o'clock I'll get you such a ladder.
DUKE
  But, hark thee, I will go to her alone.
  How shall I best convey the ladder thither?
VALENTINE
  It will be light, my lord, that you may bear it
  Under a cloak that is of any length.   129
DUKE
  A cloak as long as thine will serve the turn?   130
VALENTINE
  Ay, my good lord.
DUKE   Then let me see thy cloak.
  I'll get me one of such another length.   132
VALENTINE
  Why, any cloak will serve the turn, my lord.
DUKE
  How shall I fashion me to wear a cloak?
  I pray thee, let me feel thy cloak upon me.
                [*He pulls open Valentine's cloak.*]
  What letter is this same? What's here? "To Sylvia"?
  And here an engine fit for my proceeding.   137
  I'll be so bold to break the seal for once.   [*He reads.*]
  "My thoughts do harbor with my Sylvia nightly,   139

---

116 quaintly skillfully   **118, 119 Hero's, Leander** (See note to 1.1.22.)
119 So provided   **120 blood** good family   **129 of any length** tolerably
long   **130 turn** purpose   **132 such another** the same   **137 engine**
contrivance, i.e., the rope ladder   **139 harbor** reside

And slaves they are to me that send them flying.
O, could their master come and go as lightly,   141
  Himself would lodge where, senseless, they are lying! 142
My herald thoughts in thy pure bosom rest them,   143
  While I, their king, that thither them importune,   144
Do curse the grace that with such grace hath blessed
    them,   145
  Because myself do want my servants' fortune.   146
I curse myself, for they are sent by me,   147
That they should harbor where their lord should be."
What's here?
"Sylvia, this night I will enfranchise thee."
'Tis so; and here's the ladder for the purpose.
Why, Phaëthon, for thou art Merops' son   152
Wilt thou aspire to guide the heavenly car
And with thy daring folly burn the world?
Wilt thou reach stars because they shine on thee?   155
Go, base intruder, overweening slave!   156
Bestow thy fawning smiles on equal mates,   157
And think my patience, more than thy desert,
Is privilege for thy departure hence.   159
Thank me for this more than for all the favors
Which, all too much, I have bestowed on thee.
But if thou linger in my territories
Longer than swiftest expedition   163
Will give thee time to leave our royal court,
By heaven, my wrath shall far exceed the love
I ever bore my daughter or thyself.
Begone! I will not hear thy vain excuse,
But, as thou lov'st thy life, make speed from hence.
                                 [*Exit.*]

VALENTINE
And why not death rather than living torment?

---

141 lightly easily, quickly   **142 senseless** insensible.   **lying** dwelling
143 them themselves   **144 importune** command   **145 grace . . .
grace** good fortune . . . charm, favor   **146 want** lack   **147 for** since
152 Phaëthon, Merops (Phaëthon was the son of Helios, the sun god,
and of Clymene, lawful wife of Merops. Phaëthon aspired to guide
the sun god's *car* [l. 153] or chariot and was slain by Zeus for his
presumption after he had scorched a large portion of the earth.)
for just because   **155 reach** reach for   **156 overweening** presumptuous   **157 equal mates** i.e., women of your own social status   **159 Is
privilege for** authorizes, grants   **163 expedition** speed

To die is to be banished from myself,
And Sylvia is myself. Banished from her
Is self from self—a deadly banishment!
What light is light, if Sylvia be not seen?
What joy is joy, if Sylvia be not by?
Unless it be to think that she is by
And feed upon the shadow of perfection.   176
Except I be by Sylvia in the night,   177
There is no music in the nightingale;
Unless I look on Sylvia in the day,
There is no day for me to look upon.
She is my essence, and I leave to be   181
If I be not by her fair influence   182
Fostered, illumined, cherished, kept alive.
I fly not death, to fly his deadly doom;   184
Tarry I here, I but attend on death,   185
But, fly I hence, I fly away from life.

      [*Enter Proteus and*] *Lance.*

PROTEUS   Run, boy, run, run, and seek him out.
LANCE   So-ho, so-ho!   188
PROTEUS   What seest thou?
LANCE   Him we go to find. There's not a hair on 's   190
      head but 'tis a Valentine.   191
PROTEUS   Valentine?
VALENTINE   No.
PROTEUS   Who then? His spirit?
VALENTINE   Neither.
PROTEUS   What then?
VALENTINE   Nothing.
LANCE   Can nothing speak? Master, shall I strike?   198
PROTEUS   Who wouldst thou strike?
LANCE   Nothing.
PROTEUS   Villain, forbear.

176 shadow image   **177 Except** unless   **181 leave** cease   **182 influence**
(An astrological term for the emanations supposed to flow from the
stars and to have power over the destinies of men.)   **184 I . . . doom** I
shall not escape death by flying from the Duke's sentence of death, or,
from death's deadly sentence   **185 attend on** wait for   **188 So-ho**
(Hunting cry used when the game is sighted.)   **190 hair** (with pun on
hare)   **191 Valentine** (His name means "token of true love.")   **198 shall
I strike** (Lance wonders if he should strike at a *spirit*, l. 194, to ward off
evil effects, as in *Hamlet*, 1.1.144.)

LANCE Why, sir, I'll strike nothing. I pray you—
PROTEUS Sirrah, I say, forbear.—Friend Valentine, a
  word.
VALENTINE
  My ears are stopped and cannot hear good news,
  So much of bad already hath possessed them.
PROTEUS
  Then in dumb silence will I bury mine,   207
  For they are harsh, untuneable, and bad.
VALENTINE Is Sylvia dead?
PROTEUS No, Valentine.
VALENTINE
  No Valentine, indeed, for sacred Sylvia.   211
  Hath she forsworn me?
PROTEUS No, Valentine.
VALENTINE
  No Valentine, if Sylvia have forsworn me.
  What is your news?
LANCE Sir, there is a proclamation that you are vanished.
PROTEUS
  That thou art banished—O, that's the news!—
  From hence, from Sylvia, and from me thy friend.
VALENTINE
  O, I have fed upon this woe already,
  And now excess of it will make me surfeit.
  Doth Sylvia know that I am banished?
PROTEUS
  Ay, ay; and she hath offered to the doom—   222
  Which, unreversed, stands in effectual force—   223
  A sea of melting pearl, which some call tears.
  Those at her father's churlish feet she tendered;
  With them, upon her knees, her humble self,
  Wringing her hands, whose whiteness so became them
  As if but now they waxèd pale for woe.
  But neither bended knees, pure hands held up,
  Sad sighs, deep groans, nor silver-shedding tears

---

207 mine i.e., my news   **211 No Valentine** (Valentine jests bitterly on
the inappropriateness of his name and on the loss of his very identity,
playing on *No, Valentine* in the previous line.)   **222 to the doom** i.e., to
this news of the sentence   **223 Which . . . force** which, if not reversed,
must certainly take effect

Could penetrate her uncompassionate sire,
But Valentine, if he be ta'en, must die.   232
Besides, her intercession chafed him so,
When she for thy repeal was suppliant,   234
That to close prison he commanded her,   235
With many bitter threats of biding there.   236

VALENTINE
No more, unless the next word that thou speak'st
Have some malignant power upon my life!
If so, I pray thee, breathe it in mine ear,
As ending anthem of my endless dolor.   240

PROTEUS
Cease to lament for that thou canst not help,   241
And study help for that which thou lament'st.   242
Time is the nurse and breeder of all good.
Here if thou stay thou canst not see thy love;
Besides, thy staying will abridge thy life.
Hope is a lover's staff; walk hence with that
And manage it against despairing thoughts.   247
Thy letters may be here, though thou art hence,
Which, being writ to me, shall be delivered
Even in the milk-white bosom of thy love.
The time now serves not to expostulate.   251
Come, I'll convey thee through the city gate,
And ere I part with thee confer at large   253
Of all that may concern thy love affairs.
As thou lov'st Sylvia, though not for thyself,   255
Regard thy danger, and along with me!

VALENTINE
I pray thee, Lance, an if thou seest my boy,
Bid him make haste and meet me at the north gate.

PROTEUS
Go, sirrah, find him out.—Come, Valentine.

VALENTINE
O my dear Sylvia! Hapless Valentine!
                        [*Exeunt Valentine and Proteus.*]

---

232 But but that   **234 repeal** recall from exile   **235 close** tightly enclosed   **236 biding** permanently dwelling   **240 ending anthem** re-
quiem   **241 that** what   **242 study** devise   **247 manage** wield
251 expostulate discuss at length   **253 confer at large** discuss at
length   **255 though not for thyself** even though not for your own sake

LANCE   I am but a fool, look you, and yet I have the
wit to think my master is a kind of a knave. But that's   262
all one, if he be but one knave. He lives not now that   263
knows me to be in love, yet I am in love. But a team of
horse shall not pluck that from me, nor who 'tis I love.
And yet 'tis a woman, but what woman, I will not tell
myself. And yet 'tis a milkmaid. Yet 'tis not a maid,
for she hath had gossips. Yet 'tis a maid, for she is her   268
master's maid, and serves for wages. She hath more
qualities than a water spaniel, which is much in a bare   270
Christian. [*Pulling out a paper.*] Here is the catalog of
her condition. "Imprimis: She can fetch and carry."   272
Why, a horse can do no more. Nay, a horse cannot   273
fetch, but only carry; therefore is she better than a   274
jade. "Item: She can milk." Look you, a sweet virtue in   275
a maid with clean hands.

        [*Enter*] *Speed.*

SPEED   How now, Signor Lance, what news with your
mastership?
LANCE   With my master's ship? Why, it is at sea.   279
SPEED   Well, your old vice still: mistake the word. What   280
news, then, in your paper?
LANCE   The black'st news that ever thou heardst.
SPEED   Why, man, how black?
LANCE   Why, as black as ink.
SPEED   Let me read them.   285
LANCE   Fie on thee, jolt-head! Thou canst not read.   286
SPEED   Thou liest. I can.
LANCE   I will try thee. Tell me this: who begot thee?

262–263 **that's . . . knave** i.e., it's all right so long as he's knavish in one
thing only (that is, in love)   263 **He lives not now** there is no one alive
268 **gossips** i.e., godparents to a child of hers.   **maid** (Lance quibbles on
[1] maidservant [2] virgin. She is the first, even if no longer the second.)   270 **water spaniel** (A fawning, subservient kind of dog.)   **bare**
(1) mere (2) naked, hairless   272 **condition** qualities.   **Imprimis** in the
first place (to be followed, in a list, with each particular marked *Item*)
273–274 **cannot fetch** cannot be ordered to go and fetch something
275 **jade** (1) ill-conditioned mare (2) loose woman   279 **at sea** (1) on the
high seas (2) adrift, at loose ends   280 **vice** (with added meaning of
Vice, comic character in morality plays who speaks with double meaning)   285 **them** the news   286 **jolt-head** blockhead

SPEED   Marry, the son of my grandfather.

LANCE   O illiterate loiterer! It was the son of thy grand-   290
mother. This proves that thou canst not read.

SPEED   Come, fool, come. Try me in thy paper.

LANCE   There. [*Giving him the paper*.] And Saint Nicho-   293
las be thy speed!   294

SPEED   [*Reads*] "Imprimis: She can milk."

LANCE   Ay, that she can.

SPEED   "Item: She brews good ale."

LANCE   And thereof comes the proverb: "Blessing of
your heart, you brew good ale."

SPEED   "Item: She can sew."

LANCE   That's as much as to say, "Can she so?"

SPEED   "Item: She can knit."

LANCE   What need a man care for a stock with a   303
wench when she can knit him a stock?   304

SPEED   "Item: She can wash and scour."

LANCE   A special virtue, for then she need not be
washed and scoured.   307

SPEED   "Item: She can spin."

LANCE   Then may I set the world on wheels, when she   309
can spin for her living.   310

SPEED   "Item: She hath many nameless virtues."   311

LANCE   That's as much as to say, bastard virtues, that
indeed know not their fathers and therefore have no
names.

SPEED   Here follow her vices.

LANCE   Close at the heels of her virtues.

SPEED   "Item: She is not to be kissed fasting, in respect of   317
her breath."

LANCE   Well, that fault may be mended with a breakfast. Read on.

SPEED   "Item: She hath a sweet mouth."   321

---

290 loiterer idle person, lazy student   **293–294 Saint Nicholas** patron
saint of scholars   **294 speed** protection (with a play on Speed's name)
303 stock dowry   **304 stock** stocking   **307 scoured** (1) scrubbed
(2) beaten, drubbed. (*Washed* probably has a similar double meaning.)
309 set . . . wheels i.e., take life easy   **310 spin for her living** (Probably
with a sexual double meaning, as in *Twelfth Night*, 1.3. 100–102: "I
hope to see a huswife take thee between her legs and spin it off.")
311 nameless inexpressible   **317 in respect of** on account of   **321 sweet
mouth** sweet tooth (with a wanton sense)

LANCE   That makes amends for her sour breath.

SPEED   "Item: She doth talk in her sleep."

LANCE   It's no matter for that, so she sleep not in her 324
talk.

SPEED   "Item: She is slow in words."

LANCE   O villain, that set this down among her vices!
To be slow in words is a woman's only virtue. I pray
thee, out with 't, and place it for her chief virtue.

SPEED   "Item: She is proud."   330

LANCE   Out with that too; it was Eve's legacy, and cannot be ta'en from her.

SPEED   "Item: She hath no teeth."

LANCE   I care not for that neither, because I love crusts.

SPEED   "Item: She is curst."   335

LANCE   Well, the best is, she hath no teeth to bite.

SPEED   "Item: She will often praise her liquor."   337

LANCE   If her liquor be good, she shall. If she will not,
I will, for good things should be praised.   339

SPEED   "Item: She is too liberal."   340

LANCE   Of her tongue she cannot, for that's writ down
she is slow of; of her purse she shall not, for that I'll
keep shut. Now, of another thing she may, and that 343
cannot I help. Well, proceed.

SPEED   "Item: She hath more hair than wit, and more
faults than hairs, and more wealth than faults."

LANCE   Stop there; I'll have her. She was mine and not
mine twice or thrice in that last article. Rehearse that 348
once more.

SPEED   "Item: She hath more hair than wit—"

LANCE   More hair than wit? It may be: I'll prove it. The
cover of the salt hides the salt, and therefore it is more 352
than the salt; the hair that covers the wit is more than
the wit, for the greater hides the less. What's next?

SPEED   "And more faults than hairs—"

---

324 sleep (with a pun on *slip;* pronunciation was similar)   **330 proud** (with
additional meaning of "lascivious")   **335 curst** shrewish   **337 praise** appraise, taste   **339 praised** commended (with a play on the sense "appraise"
in l. 337)   **340 liberal** free   **343 another thing** (with bawdy suggestion,
playing on the idea of *her purse* which her husband is to *keep shut* to
strangers)   **348 Rehearse** repeat   **352 cover of the salt** lid of the salt
cellar.   **more** i.e., more visible or prominent, like hair on the head

LANCE   That's monstrous. O, that that were out!

SPEED   "And more wealth than faults."

LANCE   Why, that word makes the faults gracious. 358
Well, I'll have her; and if it be a match, as nothing is
impossible—

SPEED   What then?

LANCE   Why, then will I tell thee—that thy master
stays for thee at the north gate.   363

SPEED   For me?

LANCE   For thee? Ay, who art thou? He hath stayed for
a better man than thee.

SPEED   And must I go to him?

LANCE   Thou must run to him, for thou hast stayed so
long that going will scarce serve the turn.   369

SPEED   Why didst not tell me sooner? Pox of your love
letters!   [*Exit.*]

LANCE   Now will he be swinged for reading my 372
letter—an unmannerly slave, that will thrust himself
into secrets! I'll after, to rejoice in the boy's correction. 374

                                                     Exit.

❖

3.2   *Enter Duke [and] Thurio.*

DUKE
Sir Thurio, fear not but that she will love you,
Now Valentine is banished from her sight.

THURIO
Since his exile she hath despised me most,
Forsworn my company and railed at me,
That I am desperate of obtaining her.   5

DUKE
This weak impress of love is as a figure   6
Trenchèd in ice, which with an hour's heat   7
Dissolves to water and doth lose his form.   8
A little time will melt her frozen thoughts,

---

358 gracious acceptable   **363 stays** waits   **369 going** walking
372 swinged thrashed   **374 correction** punishment

3.2. Location: Milan. The Duke's palace.
5 That so that   **6 impress** impression   **7 Trenchèd** cut   **8 his** its

And worthless Valentine shall be forgot.

[*Enter*] *Proteus.*

How now, Sir Proteus? Is your countryman,
According to our proclamation, gone?
PROTEUS   Gone, my good lord.
DUKE
My daughter takes his going grievously.
PROTEUS
A little time, my lord, will kill that grief.
DUKE
So I believe, but Thurio thinks not so.
Proteus, the good conceit I hold of thee—   17
For thou hast shown some sign of good desert—
Makes me the better to confer with thee.   19
PROTEUS
Longer than I prove loyal to Your Grace
Let me not live to look upon Your Grace.
DUKE
Thou know'st how willingly I would effect
The match between Sir Thurio and my daughter.
PROTEUS   I do, my lord.
DUKE
And also, I think, thou art not ignorant
How she opposes her against my will.   26
PROTEUS
She did, my lord, when Valentine was here.
DUKE
Ay, and perversely she persevers so.
What might we do to make the girl forget
The love of Valentine, and love Sir Thurio?
PROTEUS
The best way is to slander Valentine
With falsehood, cowardice, and poor descent,
Three things that women highly hold in hate.
DUKE
Ay, but she'll think that it is spoke in hate.
PROTEUS
Ay, if his enemy deliver it;   35

17 conceit opinion   **19 the better** the rather, more willingly   **26 opposes her** contends   **35 deliver** speak

Therefore it must with circumstance be spoken   36
By one whom she esteemeth as his friend.

DUKE
Then you must undertake to slander him.

PROTEUS
And that, my lord, I shall be loath to do.
'Tis an ill office for a gentleman,
Especially against his very friend.   41

DUKE
Where your good word cannot advantage him,   42
Your slander never can endamage him;
Therefore the office is indifferent,   44
Being entreated to it by your friend.   45

PROTEUS
You have prevailed, my lord. If I can do it
By aught that I can speak in his dispraise,
She shall not long continue love to him.
But say this weed her love from Valentine,   49
It follows not that she will love Sir Thurio.

THURIO
Therefore, as you unwind her love from him,
Lest it should ravel and be good to none,
You must provide to bottom it on me;   53
Which must be done by praising me as much
As you in worth dispraise Sir Valentine.

DUKE
And, Proteus, we dare trust you in this kind
Because we know, on Valentine's report,
You are already Love's firm votary
And cannot soon revolt and change your mind.
Upon this warrant shall you have access
Where you with Sylvia may confer at large;
For she is lumpish, heavy, melancholy,   62
And, for your friend's sake, will be glad of you,
Where you may temper her by your persuasion   64
To hate young Valentine and love my friend.

---

36 **circumstance** confirming detail   41 **very** true   42 **advantage** profit
44 **indifferent** neither good nor bad   45 **your friend** i.e., the Duke
49 **say . . . Valentine** even supposing this should root out the love she
feels for Valentine   53 **bottom** wind, as a skein of thread   62 **lumpish**
dull, spiritless   64 **temper** mould

PROTEUS
  As much as I can do, I will effect.
  But you, Sir Thurio, are not sharp enough;
  You must lay lime to tangle her desires   68
  By wailful sonnets, whose composèd rhymes
  Should be full-fraught with serviceable vows.   70
DUKE
  Ay, much is the force of heaven-bred poesy.
PROTEUS
  Say that upon the altar of her beauty
  You sacrifice your tears, your sighs, your heart.
  Write till your ink be dry, and with your tears
  Moist it again, and frame some feeling line   75
  That may discover such integrity.   76
  For Orpheus' lute was strung with poets' sinews,   77
  Whose golden touch could soften steel and stones,
  Make tigers tame, and huge leviathans   79
  Forsake unsounded deeps to dance on sands.
  After your dire-lamenting elegies,
  Visit by night your lady's chamber window
  With some sweet consort. To their instruments   83
  Tune a deploring dump; the night's dead silence   84
  Will well become such sweet-complaining grievance.   85
  This, or else nothing, will inherit her.   86
DUKE
  This discipline shows thou hast been in love.   87
THURIO
  And thy advice this night I'll put in practice.
  Therefore, sweet Proteus, my direction-giver,
  Let us into the city presently
  To sort some gentlemen well skilled in music.   91
  I have a sonnet that will serve the turn
  To give the onset to thy good advice.   93
DUKE About it, gentlemen!

---

68 lime birdlime, a sticky substance smeared on twigs to ensnare small
birds **70 serviceable vows** vows of service **75 frame** compose
76 discover reveal. **integrity** true devotion **77 Orpheus** legendary
musician whose music had the power to move inanimate objects as well
as animals. **sinews** nerves **79 leviathans** whales **83 consort** company
of musicians **84 deploring** doleful. **dump** mournful melody
85 grievance grief **86 inherit** put you in possession of **87 discipline**
teaching **91 sort** choose **93 onset** beginning

PROTEUS
  We'll wait upon Your Grace till after supper,
  And afterward determine our proceedings.
DUKE
  Even now about it! I will pardon you.   *Exeunt.* 97

---

97 **pardon you** i.e., excuse you your *waiting upon* or attending upon me

4.1 *Enter certain Outlaws.*

FIRST OUTLAW
  Fellows, stand fast. I see a passenger.   1

SECOND OUTLAW
  If there be ten, shrink not, but down with 'em.

  [*Enter*] *Valentine* [*and*] *Speed.*

THIRD OUTLAW
  Stand, sir! And throw us that you have about ye.   3
  If not, we'll make you sit, and rifle you.

SPEED [*To Valentine*]
  Sir, we are undone. These are the villains
  That all the travelers do fear so much.

VALENTINE   My friends—

FIRST OUTLAW
  That's not so, sir. We are your enemies.

SECOND OUTLAW   Peace! We'll hear him.

THIRD OUTLAW
  Ay, by my beard will we, for he is a proper man.   10

VALENTINE
  Then know that I have little wealth to lose.
  A man I am, crossed with adversity;   12
  My riches are these poor habiliments,
  Of which if you should here disfurnish me   14
  You take the sum and substance that I have.

SECOND OUTLAW   Whither travel you?

VALENTINE   To Verona.

FIRST OUTLAW   Whence came you?

VALENTINE   From Milan.

THIRD OUTLAW   Have you long sojourned there?

VALENTINE
  Some sixteen months, and longer might have stayed
  If crooked fortune had not thwarted me.   22

FIRST OUTLAW   What, were you banished thence?

4.1. Location: The frontiers of Mantua. A forest.
1 passenger traveler   **3 Stand** halt. (But the Third Outlaw puns on
sit, l. 4, as the opposite of "stand up.")   **10 proper** good-looking
12 crossed with thwarted by   **14 disfurnish** deprive   **22 crooked** perverse, malignant

VALENTINE   I was.
SECOND OUTLAW   For what offense?
VALENTINE
  For that which now torments me to rehearse: 26
  I killed a man, whose death I much repent,   27
  But yet I slew him manfully in fight
  Without false vantage or base treachery.
FIRST OUTLAW
  Why, ne'er repent it, if it were done so.
  But were you banished for so small a fault?
VALENTINE
  I was, and held me glad of such a doom.   32
SECOND OUTLAW   Have you the tongues?   33
VALENTINE
  My youthful travel therein made me happy,   34
  Or else I often had been miserable.
THIRD OUTLAW
  By the bare scalp of Robin Hood's fat friar,   36
  This fellow were a king for our wild faction!   37
FIRST OUTLAW   We'll have him. Sirs, a word.
                    [The Outlaws confer in whispers.]
SPEED   Master, be one of them;
  It's an honorable kind of thievery.
VALENTINE   Peace, villain!   41
SECOND OUTLAW [*Returning to Valentine*]
  Tell us this: have you anything to take to?   42
VALENTINE   Nothing but my fortune.
THIRD OUTLAW
  Know, then, that some of us are gentlemen,
  Such as the fury of ungoverned youth
  Thrust from the company of awful men.   46
  Myself was from Verona banishèd
  For practicing to steal away a lady,   48

26 rehearse repeat   **27 I killed a man** (A lie presumably intended to
impress the outlaws.)   **32 held . . . doom** i.e., was pleased with such a
light sentence   **33 the tongues** ability in foreign languages   **34 travel**
(The Folio spelling, *trauaile*, may also suggest laborious study.) **happy**
proficient   **36 friar** i.e., Friar Tuck   **37 were** would be suitable as.
faction band, set of persons   **41 villain** i.e., you rogue   **42 anything to
take to** any means of subsistence   **46 awful** law-abiding   **48 practicing**
plotting

An heir, and near allied unto the Duke.

SECOND OUTLAW
 And I from Mantua, for a gentleman
 Who, in my mood, I stabbed unto the heart. 51

FIRST OUTLAW
 And I for suchlike petty crimes as these.
 But to the purpose—for we cite our faults
 That they may hold excused our lawless lives;
 And partly, seeing you are beautified
 With goodly shape, and by your own report
 A linguist, and a man of such perfection
 As we do in our quality much want— 58

SECOND OUTLAW
 Indeed, because you are a banished man,
 Therefore, above the rest, we parley to you. 60
 Are you content to be our general?
 To make a virtue of necessity
 And live, as we do, in this wilderness?

THIRD OUTLAW
 What sayst thou? Wilt thou be of our consort? 64
 Say ay, and be the captain of us all.
 We'll do thee homage and be ruled by thee,
 Love thee as our commander and our king.

FIRST OUTLAW
 But if thou scorn our courtesy, thou diest.

SECOND OUTLAW
 Thou shalt not live to brag what we have offered.

VALENTINE
 I take your offer and will live with you,
 Provided that you do no outrages
 On silly women or poor passengers. 72

THIRD OUTLAW
 No, we detest such vile base practices.
 Come, go with us. We'll bring thee to our crews 74
 And show thee all the treasure we have got,
 Which, with ourselves, all rest at thy dispose. *Exeunt.* 76

❧

51 **mood** anger, displeasure 58 **quality** profession. **want** lack
60 above the rest for this reason chiefly **64 consort** company **72 silly**
defenseless **74 crews** bands **76 dispose** disposal

4.2   *Enter Proteus.*

PROTEUS
  Already have I been false to Valentine,
  And now I must be as unjust to Thurio.
  Under the color of commending him,   3
  I have access my own love to prefer.   4
  But Sylvia is too fair, too true, too holy
  To be corrupted with my worthless gifts.
  When I protest true loyalty to her,
  She twits me with my falsehood to my friend.
  When to her beauty I commend my vows,   9
  She bids me think how I have been forsworn
  In breaking faith with Julia, whom I loved.
  And notwithstanding all her sudden quips,   12
  The least whereof would quell a lover's hope,
  Yet, spaniel-like, the more she spurns my love,
  The more it grows and fawneth on her still.
  But here comes Thurio. Now must we to her window
  And give some evening music to her ear.

        [*Enter*] *Thurio* [*and*] *Musicians.*

THURIO
  How now, Sir Proteus, are you crept before us?
PROTEUS
  Ay, gentle Thurio, for you know that love
  Will creep in service where it cannot go.   20
THURIO
  Ay, but I hope, sir, that you love not here.
PROTEUS
  Sir, but I do, or else I would be hence.
THURIO
  Who? Sylvia?
PROTEUS   Ay, Sylvia—for your sake.
THURIO
  I thank you for your own.—Now, gentlemen,
  Let's tune, and to it lustily awhile.   25

4.2. Location: Milan. Outside the Duke's palace, under Sylvia's window.
3 color pretext   **4 prefer** urge   **9 commend** offer, direct   **12 quips**
sharp, sarcastic remarks   **20 go** walk at an ordinary pace   **25 lustily**
heartily, with a will

[*Enter, at a distance,*] *Host,* [*and*] *Julia*
[*disguised as a page. They talk apart.*]

HOST Now, my young guest, methinks you're ally- 26
cholly. I pray you, why is it? 27

JULIA Marry, mine Host, because I cannot be merry.

HOST Come, we'll have you merry. I'll bring you where
you shall hear music and see the gentleman that you
asked for. 31

JULIA But shall I hear him speak?

HOST Ay, that you shall.

JULIA That will be music. [*Music plays.*]

HOST Hark, hark!

JULIA Is he among these?

HOST Ay, but peace! Let's hear 'em.

                    Song

MUSICIAN
            Who is Sylvia? What is she,
                That all our swains commend her?
            Holy, fair, and wise is she;
                The heaven such grace did lend her,
            That she might admirèd be. 42

            Is she kind as she is fair?
                For beauty lives with kindness. 44
            Love doth to her eyes repair 45
                To help him of his blindness,
            And, being helped, inhabits there.

            Then to Sylvia let us sing,
                That Sylvia is excelling.
            She excels each mortal thing
                Upon the dull earth dwelling.
            To her let us garlands bring.

HOST How now? Are you sadder than you were before?
How do you, man? The music likes you not. 54

26–27 allycholly (A colloquial form of *melancholy*.) **31 asked for**
inquired about **42 admirèd** wondered at **44 beauty lives with kindness** i.e., if she is kind also, her beauty will be true beauty and not mere
show **45 repair** hasten, visit **54 likes** pleases

JULIA   You mistake; the musician likes me not.   55
HOST   Why, my pretty youth?
JULIA   He plays false, father.   57
HOST   How? Out of tune on the strings?
JULIA   Not so, but yet so false that he grieves my very
heartstrings.
HOST   You have a quick ear.
JULIA   Ay, I would I were deaf; it makes me have a slow   62
heart.
HOST   I perceive you delight not in music.
JULIA   Not a whit, when it jars so.   65
HOST   Hark, what fine change is in the music!   66
JULIA   Ay, that change is the spite.   67
HOST   You would have them always play but one thing?   68
JULIA   I would always have one play but one thing. But,
Host, doth this Sir Proteus that we talk on often resort 70
unto this gentlewoman?
HOST   I tell you what Lance, his man, told me: he loved
her out of all nick.   73
JULIA   Where is Lance?
HOST   Gone to seek his dog, which tomorrow, by his
master's command, he must carry for a present to his
lady.
JULIA
Peace! Stand aside. The company parts.
                    [Julia and Host stand aside.]
PROTEUS
Sir Thurio, fear not you. I will so plead
That you shall say my cunning drift excels.   80
THURIO
Where meet we?
PROTEUS   At Saint Gregory's well.
THURIO   Farewell.
            [Exeunt Thurio and Musicians.]

55 likes me not (1) displeases me with his music (2) does not love me.
(The first meaning is intended for the Host; the second is hidden except
from the audience.)   **57 plays false** (1) plays out of tune (2) is unfaithful   **62 slow** heavy (playing also on *slow* as the opposite of *quick*)
65 jars is discordant   **66 change** modulation. (But Julia plays on the
sense of "fickleness.")   **67 spite** injury, annoyance   **68 play but one
thing** play only one musical piece. (But Julia plays on the sense of "play
only one role as lover" in l. 69.)   **70 talk on** talk of   **73 out of all nick**
i.e., beyond all reckoning   **80 drift** scheme

[Enter] Sylvia [above, at her window].

PROTEUS
Madam, good even to your ladyship.

SYLVIA
I thank you for your music, gentlemen.
Who is that that spake?

PROTEUS
One, lady, if you knew his pure heart's truth,
You would quickly learn to know him by his voice.

SYLVIA Sir Proteus, as I take it.

PROTEUS
Sir Proteus, gentle lady, and your servant.

SYLVIA
What's your will?

PROTEUS   That I may compass yours.   89

SYLVIA
You have your wish. My will is even this:
That presently you hie you home to bed.   91
Thou subtle, perjured, false, disloyal man!   92
Think'st thou I am so shallow, so conceitless,   93
To be seducèd by thy flattery,   94
That hast deceived so many with thy vows?
Return, return, and make thy love amends.
For me, by this pale queen of night I swear,   97
I am so far from granting thy request
That I despise thee for thy wrongful suit,
And by and by intend to chide myself
Even for this time I spend in talking to thee.

PROTEUS
I grant, sweet love, that I did love a lady,
But she is dead.

JULIA *[Aside]*   'Twere false, if I should speak it,   103
For I am sure she is not burièd.

SYLVIA
Say that she be, yet Valentine, thy friend,

---

89 will desire. **compass yours** (1) obtain your good will (2) perform
your every wish **91 presently** immediately. **hie** hasten **92 subtle**
crafty **93 conceitless** witless **94 To be** as to be **97 this pale . . . night**
i.e., the moon, Diana, goddess of chastity **103 if . . . it** i.e., even if I
should say such a thing in the sense that I am slain in my heart by
Proteus's faithlessness and thus transformed into "Sebastian"

Survives, to whom—thyself art witness—
I am betrothed. And art thou not ashamed
To wrong him with thy importunacy?   108

PROTEUS
I likewise hear that Valentine is dead.

SYLVIA
And so suppose am I, for in his grave,
Assure thyself, my love is burièd.

PROTEUS
Sweet lady, let me rake it from the earth.

SYLVIA
Go to thy lady's grave and call hers thence.
Or, at the least, in hers sepulcher thine.

JULIA [*Aside*]   He heard not that.   115

PROTEUS
Madam, if your heart be so obdurate,
Vouchsafe me yet your picture for my love,
The picture that is hanging in your chamber.
To that I'll speak, to that I'll sigh and weep;
For since the substance of your perfect self
Is else devoted, I am but a shadow,   121
And to your shadow will I make true love.   122

JULIA [*Aside*]
If 'twere a substance, you would, sure, deceive it,
And make it but a shadow, as I am.   124

SYLVIA
I am very loath to be your idol, sir.
But since your falsehood shall become you well   126
To worship shadows and adore false shapes,
Send to me in the morning, and I'll send it.   128
And so, good rest.

PROTEUS   As wretches have o'ernight
That wait for execution in the morn.

                   [*Exeunt Proteus and Sylvia separately.*]

JULIA   Host, will you go?

---

108 **importunacy** importunity   115 **He heard not that** i.e., he will turn a
deaf ear to such unwelcome talk   121 **else** elsewhere.   **shadow** i.e.,
shadow of myself, mere nothing   122 **shadow** i.e., portrait   124 **shadow**
(1) opposite of *substance*, l. 123 (2) disguised version of the true self, as I
am disguised   126 **since . . . well** i.e., since it befits your false nature
128 **Send** i.e., send a messenger

HOST By my halidom, I was fast asleep.   132
JULIA Pray you, where lies Sir Proteus?   133
HOST Marry, at my house. Trust me, I think 'tis almost 134
day.

JULIA
Not so; but it hath been the longest night
That e'er I watched, and the most heaviest. [*Exeunt.*] 137

❖

4.3   *Enter [Sir] Eglamour.*

EGLAMOUR
This is the hour that Madam Sylvia
Entreated me to call and know her mind.
There's some great matter she'd employ me in.
Madam, madam!

[*Enter*] *Sylvia* [*above, at her window*].

SYLVIA Who calls?
EGLAMOUR Your servant and your friend;
One that attends your ladyship's command.
SYLVIA
Sir Eglamour, a thousand times good morrow.
EGLAMOUR
As many, worthy lady, to yourself.
According to your ladyship's impose,   10
I am thus early come to know what service
It is your pleasure to command me in.
SYLVIA
O Eglamour, thou art a gentleman—
Think not I flatter, for I swear I do not—
Valiant, wise, remorseful, well accomplished.   15
Thou art not ignorant what dear good will   16
I bear unto the banished Valentine,

132 halidom (Originally, a holy relic; here, a mild oath.) **133 lies**
lodges **134 Marry** indeed. (Originally, an oath, "by the Virgin
Mary.") **house** inn. **Trust me** i.e., on my honor. (An asseveration.)
137 watched stayed awake through

**4.3. Location: The same, early in the morning (and perhaps only a
short time after 4.2, which ends as it is "almost day," ll. 134–135).**
10 impose command **15 remorseful** compassionate **16 dear**
affectionate

Nor how my father would enforce me marry
Vain Thurio, whom my very soul abhors.
Thyself hast loved, and I have heard thee say
No grief did ever come so near thy heart
As when thy lady and thy true love died,
Upon whose grave thou vowedst pure chastity.
Sir Eglamour, I would to Valentine,   24
To Mantua, where I hear he makes abode;
And, for the ways are dangerous to pass,   26
I do desire thy worthy company,
Upon whose faith and honor I repose.
Urge not my father's anger, Eglamour,
But think upon my grief, a lady's grief,
And on the justice of my flying hence
To keep me from a most unholy match,
Which heaven and fortune still rewards with plagues.   33
I do desire thee, even from a heart
As full of sorrows as the sea of sands,
To bear me company and go with me;
If not, to hide what I have said to thee,
That I may venture to depart alone.

EGLAMOUR
Madam, I pity much your grievances,
Which, since I know they virtuously are placed,
I give consent to go along with you,
Recking as little what betideth me   42
As much I wish all good befortune you.   43
When will you go?

SYLVIA   This evening coming.

EGLAMOUR
Where shall I meet you?

SYLVIA   At Friar Patrick's cell,
Where I intend holy confession.

EGLAMOUR
I will not fail your ladyship.
Good morrow, gentle lady.

SYLVIA
Good morrow, kind Sir Eglamour.
                                        Exeunt [*separately*].

24 would wish to go   **26 for** because   **33 still** always.   **rewards**
reward   **42 Recking** heeding   **43 befortune** befall

4.4 *Enter Lance [with his dog, Crab].*

LANCE When a man's servant shall play the cur with
him, look you, it goes hard—one that I brought up of 2
a puppy, one that I saved from drowning when three
or four of his blind brothers and sisters went to it. I 4
have taught him, even as one would say precisely,
"Thus I would teach a dog." I was sent to deliver him
as a present to Mistress Sylvia from my master, and I
came no sooner into the dining chamber but he steps
me to her trencher and steals her capon's leg. O, 'tis a 9
foul thing when a cur cannot keep himself in all com- 10
panies! I would have, as one should say, one that takes 11
upon him to be a dog indeed, to be, as it were, a dog 12
at all things. If I had not had more wit than he, to take 13
a fault upon me that he did, I think verily he had been 14
hanged for 't; sure as I live, he had suffered for 't. You
shall judge. He thrusts me himself into the company
of three or four gentlemanlike dogs, under the Duke's
table. He had not been there—bless the mark!—a 18
pissing while but all the chamber smelt him. "Out 19
with the dog!" says one. "What cur is that?" says another. "Whip him out," says the third. "Hang him up,"
says the Duke. I, having been acquainted with the
smell before, knew it was Crab, and goes me to the 23
fellow that whips the dogs. "Friend," quoth I, "you
mean to whip the dog?" "Ay, marry do I," quoth he.
"You do him the more wrong," quoth I; "'twas I did
the thing you wot of." He makes me no more ado, but 27
whips me out of the chamber. How many masters
would do this for his servant? Nay, I'll be sworn I
have sat in the stocks for puddings he hath stolen, oth- 30

4.4. Location: The same, some hours later.
2 of from   **4 to it** i.e., to drowning   **9 me** i.e., to my injury, to my
detriment. (Cf. *thrusts me*, l. 16.)   **trencher** wooden dish or plate
10 keep restrain   **11–12 one that takes upon him** such a dog as undertakes   **12–13 a dog at** adept at (but with literal meaning as well)
13–14 to take . . . did to take the blame upon myself for the fault he
did   **18 bless the mark** (A phrase used to apologize for indecorous
language.)   **18–19 a pissing while** a short while (but with literal meaning as well)   **23 goes me** i.e., I went   **27 wot of** know about.   **makes me**
makes   **30 puddings** sausages made by stuffing animal entrails with
spicy minced meat, etc.

erwise he had been executed. I have stood on the pil-
lory for geese he hath killed, otherwise he had suffered
for 't.—Thou think'st not of this now. Nay, I remember the trick you served me when I took my leave of
Madam Sylvia. Did not I bid thee still mark me and do
as I do? When didst thou see me heave up my leg and
make water against a gentlewoman's farthingale? 37
Didst thou ever see me do such a trick?

> [*Enter*] *Proteus* [*and*] *Julia* [*disguised*].

PROTEUS [*To Julia*]
Sebastian is thy name? I like thee well,
And will employ thee in some service presently.
JULIA
In what you please. I'll do what I can.
PROTEUS
I hope thou wilt. [*To Lance.*] How now, you whoreson
    peasant,   42
Where have you been these two days loitering?
LANCE   Marry, sir, I carried Mistress Sylvia the dog you
bade me.
PROTEUS   And what says she to my little jewel?   46
LANCE   Marry, she says your dog was a cur, and tells
you currish thanks is good enough for such a present. 48
PROTEUS   But she received my dog?
LANCE   No, indeed, did she not. Here have I brought
him back again.   [*He points to his dog.*]
PROTEUS   What, didst thou offer her this from me?
LANCE   Ay, sir. The other squirrel was stolen from me 53
by the hangman boys in the marketplace, and then 54
I offered her mine own, who is a dog as big as ten of
yours, and therefore the gift the greater.
PROTEUS
Go get thee hence, and find my dog again,
Or ne'er return again into my sight.
Away, I say! Stayest thou to vex me here?
                              [*Exit Lance with Crab.*]

---

37 farthingale hooped petticoat   **42 whoreson peasant** (A term of
jocular familiarity.)   **46 jewel** (Proteus is thinking of the small, elegant
dog he intended as a present to Sylvia.)   **48 currish** i.e., mean-spirited
(with a play on *cur*)   **53 squirrel** i.e., little dog   **54 hangman** i.e., fit for
the hangman

A slave, that still an end turns me to shame!—   60
Sebastian, I have entertainèd thee,   61
Partly that I have need of such a youth
That can with some discretion do my business,
For 'tis no trusting to yond foolish lout,
But chiefly for thy face and thy behavior,
Which, if my augury deceive me not,
Witness good bringing up, fortune, and truth.   67
Therefore know thou, for this I entertain thee.
Go presently and take this ring with thee.

                              [*He gives a ring.*]

Deliver it to Madam Sylvia—
She loved me well delivered it to me.   71

JULIA

It seems you loved not her, to leave her token.   72
She is dead, belike?

PROTEUS   Not so. I think she lives.   73

JULIA   Alas!

PROTEUS   Why dost thou cry "Alas"?

JULIA   I cannot choose but pity her.

PROTEUS   Wherefore shouldst thou pity her?

JULIA

Because methinks that she loved you as well
As you do love your lady Sylvia.
She dreams on him that has forgot her love;   80
You dote on her that cares not for your love.   81
'Tis pity love should be so contrary;
And thinking on it makes me cry "Alas!"

PROTEUS

Well, give her that ring and therewithal   84
This letter. [*Giving a letter.*] That's her chamber. Tell
    my lady
I claim the promise for her heavenly picture.
Your message done, hie home unto my chamber,
Where thou shalt find me, sad and solitary.   [*Exit.*]

JULIA

How many women would do such a message?

---

60 still an end continually   **61 entertainèd** taken into service
67 Witness bear witness to   **71 delivered** who gave   **72 leave** part
with   **73 belike** perhaps   **80 him that** one who (i.e., Proteus)   **81 her**
i.e., Sylvia   **84 therewithal** with it

Alas, poor Proteus! Thou hast entertained
A fox to be the shepherd of thy lambs.
Alas, poor fool, why do I pity him   92
That with his very heart despiseth me?
Because he loves her, he despiseth me;
Because I love him, I must pity him.
This ring I gave him when he parted from me,
To bind him to remember my good will;
And now am I, unhappy messenger,
To plead for that which I would not obtain,
To carry that which I would have refused,
To praise his faith which I would have dispraised.   101
I am my master's true-confirmèd love,
But cannot be true servant to my master
Unless I prove false traitor to myself.
Yet will I woo for him, but yet so coldly
As, heaven it knows, I would not have him speed.   106

    [Enter] Sylvia [attended].

Gentlewoman, good day! I pray you, be my means
To bring me where to speak with Madam Sylvia.   108
SYLVIA
What would you with her, if that I be she?
JULIA
If you be she, I do entreat your patience
To hear me speak the message I am sent on.
SYLVIA   From whom?
JULIA   From my master, Sir Proteus, madam.
SYLVIA   O, he sends you for a picture?
JULIA   Ay, madam.
SYLVIA   Ursula, bring my picture there.   116
              [A servant brings Sylvia a picture,
                    which she gives to Julia.]
Go give your master this. Tell him from me,

---

92 poor fool i.e., Julia herself   **101 would have** desire to have
106 speed succeed   **s.d. Enter Sylvia** (Perhaps the location of the scene
has shifted by now to inside the tower, near Sylvia's chamber [see l. 85];
earlier, at 4.2.81 s.d., she appeared at her window, above.)   **108 where to**
where I may   **116 s.d. A servant . . . picture** (Perhaps the servant has
brought the picture onstage anticipating its need, since Sylvia promised
at 4.2.128 to give it to a messenger from Proteus.)

One Julia, that his changing thoughts forget,
Would better fit his chamber than this shadow.

JULIA
Madam, please you peruse this letter.—
                    [*She offers a letter and withdraws it.*]
Pardon me, madam; I have unadvised   121
Delivered you a paper that I should not.
                    [*She gives another letter.*]
This is the letter to your ladyship.

SYLVIA
I pray thee, let me look on that again.

JULIA
It may not be. Good madam, pardon me.

SYLVIA   There, hold!
I will not look upon your master's lines.
I know they are stuffed with protestations
And full of newfound oaths, which he will break   129
As easily as I do tear his paper.   [*She tears the letter.*]

JULIA [*Offering the ring*]
Madam, he sends your ladyship this ring.

SYLVIA
The more shame for him that he sends it me,
For I have heard him say a thousand times
His Julia gave it him at his departure.
Though his false finger have profaned the ring,
Mine shall not do his Julia so much wrong.

JULIA   She thanks you.

SYLVIA   What sayst thou?

JULIA
I thank you, madam, that you tender her.   139
Poor gentlewoman! My master wrongs her much.

SYLVIA   Dost thou know her?

JULIA
Almost as well as I do know myself.
To think upon her woes I do protest
That I have wept a hundred several times.   144

SYLVIA
Belike she thinks that Proteus hath forsook her?

121 unadvised inadvertently   **129 newfound** recently devised
139 tender feel sympathetically toward   **144 several** different

JULIA
I think she doth, and that's her cause of sorrow.

SYLVIA   Is she not passing fair?   147

JULIA
She hath been fairer, madam, than she is.
When she did think my master loved her well,
She, in my judgment, was as fair as you;
But since she did neglect her looking glass
And threw her sun-expelling mask away,   152
The air hath starved the roses in her cheeks   153
And pinched the lily tincture of her face,
That now she is become as black as I.   155

SYLVIA   How tall was she?

JULIA
About my stature; for at Pentecost,   157
When all our pageants of delight were played,   158
Our youth got me to play the woman's part,
And I was trimmed in Madam Julia's gown,   160
Which servèd me as fit, by all men's judgments,
As if the garment had been made for me.
Therefore I know she is about my height.
And at that time I made her weep agood,   164
For I did play a lamentable part:
Madam, 'twas Ariadne passioning   166
For Theseus' perjury and unjust flight;
Which I so lively acted with my tears
That my poor mistress, movèd therewithal,
Wept bitterly; and would I might be dead
If I in thought felt not her very sorrow!

SYLVIA
She is beholding to thee, gentle youth.   172
Alas, poor lady, desolate and left!

147 passing surpassingly   **152 sun-expelling mask** mask to keep the
complexion fair (considered more beautiful than a tan)   **153 starved**
caused to die   **155 black** of a dark complexion, tanned   **157 Pentecost**
Whitsuntide (seven weeks after Easter)   **158 pageants of delight** delightful entertainments   **160 trimmed** dressed up   **164 agood** in earnest
166 Ariadne daughter of Minos, King of Crete. (Ariadne, having fallen
in love with one of her father's captives, Theseus, gave him a clue of
thread by which he was able to find his way out of the labyrinth. He
fled with her, but abandoned her on the island of Naxos.)   **passioning**
sorrowing   **172 beholding** indebted, beholden

I weep myself to think upon thy words.
Here, youth, there is my purse. [*She gives money.*] I give
  thee this
For thy sweet mistress' sake, because thou lov'st her.
Farewell.   [*Exit Sylvia, with attendants.*]

JULIA
And she shall thank you for 't, if e'er you know her.—
A virtuous gentlewoman, mild and beautiful!
I hope my master's suit will be but cold,   180
Since she respects my mistress' love so much.   181
Alas, how love can trifle with itself!
Here is her picture. [*She looks at the picture.*] Let me see,
  I think
If I had such a tire, this face of mine   184
Were full as lovely as is this of hers;
And yet the painter flattered her a little,
Unless I flatter with myself too much.   187
Her hair is auburn, mine is perfect yellow;
If that be all the difference in his love,
I'll get me such a colored periwig.
Her eyes are gray as glass, and so are mine.
Ay, but her forehead's low, and mine's as high.   192
What should it be that he respects in her
But I can make respective in myself,   194
If this fond Love were not a blinded god?   195
Come, shadow, come, and take this shadow up,   196
For 'tis thy rival. [*She picks up the picture.*] O thou
  senseless form,   197
Thou shalt be worshiped, kissed, loved, and adored!
And, were there sense in his idolatry,   199
My substance should be statue in thy stead.   200
I'll use thee kindly for thy mistress' sake,

---

180 cold vain   **181 my mistress'** (Julia ironically refers thus to herself,
as formerly beloved by her master, Proteus.)   **184 tire** headdress
187 flatter with myself (1) praise myself with flattery (2) flatter myself
with deceiving hopes   **192 as high** i.e., as high as hers is low. (High
foreheads were much admired, as was yellow hair.)   **194 But I can** that
I cannot.   **respective** worthy of regard (with a play on *respects*, l. 193)
195 fond foolish   **196 shadow . . . shadow** i.e., the mere shadow of myself
. . . the picture of Sylvia. (See also 4.2.120–124.)   **take . . . up** (1) pick up,
carry (2) oppose, accept a challenge   **197 senseless** insensible   **199 sense**
reason   **200 My . . . stead** i.e., my real person would be the object of his
veneration, his idol, instead of Sylvia's mere picture

That used me so; or else, by Jove I vow,
I should have scratched out your unseeing eyes
To make my master out of love with thee!   *Exit.*

5.1   *Enter [Sir] Eglamour.*

EGLAMOUR
The sun begins to gild the western sky,
And now it is about the very hour
That Sylvia at Friar Patrick's cell should meet me.
She will not fail, for lovers break not hours
Unless it be to come before their time,
So much they spur their expedition.   6

      [Enter] Sylvia.

See where she comes.—Lady, a happy evening!
SYLVIA
Amen, amen! Go on, good Eglamour,
Out at the postern by the abbey wall.   9
I fear I am attended by some spies.
EGLAMOUR
Fear not. The forest is not three leagues off.
If we recover that, we are sure enough.   *Exeunt.* 12

❧

5.2   *Enter Thurio, Proteus, [and] Julia [disguised in
page's attire].*

THURIO
Sir Proteus, what says Sylvia to my suit?
PROTEUS
O, sir, I find her milder than she was,
And yet she takes exceptions at your person.   3
THURIO   What, that my leg is too long?
PROTEUS   No, that it is too little.
THURIO
I'll wear a boot, to make it somewhat rounder.
JULIA [*Aside*]
But love will not be spurred to what it loathes.   7

<hr>

5.1. Location: Milan. An abbey.
6 expedition haste   **9 postern** small back or side door   **12 recover**
reach.   **sure** safe

5.2. Location: Milan. The Duke's palace.
3 takes exceptions at finds fault with   **7 spurred** incited (with a quibble
on *boot*, i.e., "riding boot," in the preceding line)

THURIO   What says she to my face?

PROTEUS   She says it is a fair one.   9

THURIO

Nay then, the wanton lies; my face is black.   10

PROTEUS

But pearls are fair, and the old saying is,

Black men are pearls in beauteous ladies' eyes.   12

JULIA [*Aside*]

'Tis true, such pearls as put out ladies' eyes,   13

For I had rather wink than look on them.   14

THURIO   How likes she my discourse?

PROTEUS   Ill, when you talk of war.   16

THURIO

But well, when I discourse of love and peace?

JULIA [*Aside*]

But better, indeed, when you hold your peace.   18

THURIO   What says she to my valor?

PROTEUS   O, sir, she makes no doubt of that.   20

JULIA [*Aside*]

She needs not, when she knows it cowardice.

THURIO   What says she to my birth?

PROTEUS   That you are well derived.   23

JULIA [*Aside*] True; from a gentleman to a fool.   24

THURIO   Considers she my possessions?

PROTEUS   O, ay, and pities them.   26

THURIO   Wherefore?

JULIA [*Aside*]   That such an ass should owe them.   28

PROTEUS   That they are out by lease.   29

[*Enter*] *Duke.*

---

9 fair i.e., pale. (Beneath the seeming compliment is a suggestion of
effeminacy or fair-faced deception.)   **10 black** dark, tanned (as contrasted with *fair,* light-skinned)   **12 pearls** i.e., rare and beautiful objects   **13 pearls** i.e., cataracts   **14 wink** close the eyes   **16 Ill . . . war**
i.e., (1) you upset her with frightening talk of war (2) your absurd talk of
war shows how ill-suited you are for manly pursuits   **18 hold your
peace** are silent (with quibble on *peace* in previous line)   **20 makes
. . . of** has no uncertainty about. (Another deliberately ambiguous
reply.)   **23 derived** descended   **24 from . . . fool** (Julia plays on *derived*
in another sense from that in l. 23: fallen away from, lowered.)
26 pities (1) shows concern for (2) despises   **28 owe** own   **29 out by
lease** rented out. (If *possessions* in l. 25 also suggests "possession by evil
spirits," then Sylvia's contemptuous pity may be for the fact of their
being *out by lease,* beyond Thurio's control.)

JULIA Here comes the Duke.

DUKE
How now, Sir Proteus? How now, Thurio?
Which of you saw Sir Eglamour of late?

THURIO Not I.

PROTEUS Nor I.

DUKE Saw you my daughter?

PROTEUS Neither.

DUKE Why then,
She's fled unto that peasant Valentine,   38
And Eglamour is in her company.
'Tis true, for Friar Laurence met them both
As he in penance wandered through the forest.
Him he knew well, and guessed that it was she,
But, being masked, he was not sure of it.   43
Besides, she did intend confession
At Patrick's cell this even, and there she was not.   45
These likelihoods confirm her flight from hence.
Therefore, I pray you, stand not to discourse,
But mount you presently, and meet with me   48
Upon the rising of the mountain foot
That leads toward Mantua, whither they are fled.
Dispatch, sweet gentlemen, and follow me.   [*Exit.*] 51

THURIO
Why, this it is to be a peevish girl,   52
That flies her fortune when it follows her.   53
I'll after, more to be revenged on Eglamour
Than for the love of reckless Sylvia.   [*Exit.*] 55

PROTEUS
And I will follow, more for Sylvia's love
Than hate of Eglamour that goes with her.   [*Exit.*]

JULIA
And I will follow, more to cross that love
Than hate for Sylvia, that is gone for love.   *Exit.*

38 **peasant** i.e., base scoundrel   43 **being masked** i.e., since Sylvia was
masked—perhaps with a *sun-expelling mask* (4.4.152) rather than a
disguise   45 **even** evening   48 **presently** immediately   51 **Dispatch**
make haste   52 **peevish** perverse   53 **flies her fortune** flees from her
good fortune   55 **reckless** uncaring

5.3   [*Enter*] *Sylvia,* [*led by*] *Outlaws.*

FIRST OUTLAW   Come, come,
  Be patient. We must bring you to our captain.
SYLVIA
  A thousand more mischances than this one   3
  Have learned me how to brook this patiently.   4
SECOND OUTLAW   Come, bring her away.
FIRST OUTLAW
  Where is the gentleman that was with her?   6
THIRD OUTLAW
  Being nimble-footed, he hath outrun us,
  But Moses and Valerius follow him.
  Go thou with her to the west end of the wood;
  There is our captain. We'll follow him that's fled.
  The thicket is beset; he cannot scape.   11
            [*Exeunt all but First Outlaw and Sylvia.*]
FIRST OUTLAW
  Come, I must bring you to our captain's cave.
  Fear not; he bears an honorable mind
  And will not use a woman lawlessly.
SYLVIA
  O Valentine, this I endure for thee!   *Exeunt.*

❖

5.4   *Enter Valentine.*

VALENTINE
  How use doth breed a habit in a man!   1
  This shadowy desert, unfrequented woods,   2
  I better brook than flourishing peopled towns.   3
  Here can I sit alone, unseen of any,
  And to the nightingale's complaining notes
  Tune my distresses and record my woes.   6
  O thou that dost inhabit in my breast,

5.3. Location: The frontiers of Mantua. The forest.
3 more greater   **4 learned** taught.   **brook** endure   **6 gentleman** i.e., Sir
Eglamour   **11 beset** surrounded

5.4. Location: The forest.
1 use custom   **2 desert** deserted region   **3 brook** endure   **6 record** sing

Leave not the mansion so long tenantless,
Lest, growing ruinous, the building fall
And leave no memory of what it was!
Repair me with thy presence, Sylvia;
Thou gentle nymph, cherish thy forlorn swain!
                              [*Shouting within.*]
What halloing and what stir is this today?
These are my mates, that make their wills their law,
Have some unhappy passenger in chase.   15
They love me well, yet I have much to do
To keep them from uncivil outrages.
Withdraw thee, Valentine. Who's this comes here?
                              [*He stands aside.*]

[*Enter*] *Proteus, Sylvia,* [*and*] *Julia* [*disguised as
   Sebastian*].

PROTEUS
Madam, this service I have done for you—
Though you respect not aught your servant doth—   20
To hazard life and rescue you from him
That would have forced your honor and your love.
Vouchsafe me, for my meed, but one fair look;   23
A smaller boon than this I cannot beg,
And less than this, I am sure, you cannot give.
VALENTINE [*Aside*]
How like a dream is this I see and hear!
Love, lend me patience to forbear awhile.
SYLVIA
O miserable, unhappy that I am!
PROTEUS
Unhappy were you, madam, ere I came;
But by my coming I have made you happy.
SYLVIA
By thy approach thou mak'st me most unhappy.   31
JULIA [*Aside*]
And me, when he approacheth to your presence.
SYLVIA
Had I been seizèd by a hungry lion,
I would have been a breakfast to the beast

15 **Have** who have. **unhappy passenger** unlucky traveler **20 respect**
heed **23 meed** reward. **fair** kind **31 approach** amorous advances

Rather than have false Proteus rescue me.
O, heaven be judge how I love Valentine,
Whose life's as tender to me as my soul!   37
And full as much—for more there cannot be—
I do detest false perjured Proteus.
Therefore begone, solicit me no more.

PROTEUS
What dangerous action, stood it next to death,
Would I not undergo for one calm look?   42
O, 'tis the curse in love, and still approved,   43
When women cannot love where they're beloved!

SYLVIA
When Proteus cannot love where he's beloved.
Read over Julia's heart, thy first, best love,
For whose dear sake thou didst then rend thy faith
Into a thousand oaths, and all those oaths
Descended into perjury, to love me.
Thou hast no faith left now, unless thou'dst two,
And that's far worse than none. Better have none
Than plural faith, which is too much by one.
Thou counterfeit to thy true friend!

PROTEUS   In love
Who respects friend?

SYLVIA   All men but Proteus.   54

PROTEUS
Nay, if the gentle spirit of moving words
Can no way change you to a milder form,
I'll woo you like a soldier, at arms' end,   57
And love you 'gainst the nature of love—force ye.

SYLVIA
O heaven!

PROTEUS [*Assailing her*]   I'll force thee yield to my desire.

VALENTINE [*Coming forward*]
Ruffian, let go that rude uncivil touch,
Thou friend of an ill fashion!

PROTEUS   Valentine!   61

---

37 tender dear   **42 undergo** undertake.   **calm** gentle, kind   **43 still
approved** continually reaffirmed by experience   **54 respects** takes into
consideration   **57 arms' end** sword's point (with bawdy suggestion)
61 fashion kind, sort

VALENTINE
Thou common friend, that's without faith or love!   62
For such is a friend now. Treacherous man,
Thou hast beguiled my hopes. Naught but mine eye
Could have persuaded me. Now I dare not say
I have one friend alive; thou wouldst disprove me.
Who should be trusted, when one's right hand
Is perjured to the bosom? Proteus,
I am sorry I must never trust thee more,
But count the world a stranger for thy sake.
The private wound is deepest. O time most accurst,
'Mongst all foes that a friend should be the worst!

PROTEUS
My shame and guilt confounds me.
Forgive me, Valentine. If hearty sorrow
Be a sufficient ransom for offense,
I tender 't here. I do as truly suffer   76
As e'er I did commit.

VALENTINE   Then I am paid,   77
And once again I do receive thee honest.   78
Who by repentance is not satisfied
Is nor of heaven nor earth, for these are pleased.   80
By penitence th' Eternal's wrath's appeased;
And, that my love may appear plain and free,   82
All that was mine in Sylvia I give thee.

JULIA O me unhappy!   [*She swoons.*]

PROTEUS Look to the boy.

VALENTINE Why, boy! Why, wag! How now? What's   86
the matter? Look up. Speak.

JULIA [*Recovering*] O good sir, my master charged me to
deliver a ring to Madam Sylvia, which, out of my
neglect, was never done.

PROTEUS
Where is that ring, boy?

JULIA [*Giving her own ring*] Here 'tis. This is it.

PROTEUS How? Let me see.
Why, this is the ring I gave to Julia.

---

62 common ordinary, superficial **76 tender** offer **77 commit** sin
78 receive believe, acknowledge **80 these** i.e., heaven and earth **82 love**
friendship **86 wag** (A term of endearment for a youth.)

JULIA

O, cry you mercy, sir, I have mistook.   94
This is the ring you sent to Sylvia.

                         [She offers another ring.]

PROTEUS

But how cam'st thou by this ring? At my depart
I gave this unto Julia.

JULIA

And Julia herself did give it me;
And Julia herself hath brought it hither.

                         [She reveals her identity.]

PROTEUS   How? Julia?

JULIA

Behold her that gave aim to all thy oaths   101
And entertained 'em deeply in her heart.
How oft hast thou with perjury cleft the root!
O Proteus, let this habit make thee blush!   104
Be thou ashamed that I have took upon me
Such an immodest raiment, if shame live   106
In a disguise of love.   107
It is the lesser blot, modesty finds,
Women to change their shapes than men their minds.

PROTEUS

Than men their minds! 'Tis true. O heaven! Were man
But constant, he were perfect. That one error
Fills him with faults, makes him run through all th' sins;
Inconstancy falls off ere it begins.   113
What is in Sylvia's face but I may spy
More fresh in Julia's with a constant eye?   115

VALENTINE

Come, come, a hand from either.
Let me be blest to make this happy close;   117
'Twere pity two such friends should be long foes.

                    [Proteus and Julia join hands.]

PROTEUS

Bear witness, heaven, I have my wish forever.

---

94 cry you mercy I beg your pardon   **101 gave aim to** was the object of
104 this habit i.e., page's costume   **106–107 if shame . . . love** if a disguise
undertaken for love can be thought shameful; or, if one who feigns love
(such as Proteus) can feel shame   **113 Inconstancy . . . begins** i.e., inconstant love falls away from loving almost before it has even begun
115 constant steady, loyal   **117 close** union, conclusion

JULIA And I mine.

[*Enter*] *Duke* [*and*] *Thurio*, [*led by*] *Outlaws*.

OUTLAWS A prize, a prize, a prize!

VALENTINE
Forbear, forbear, I say! It is my lord the Duke.
              [*The Duke and Thurio are released*.]
Your Grace is welcome to a man disgraced,
Banishèd Valentine.

DUKE   Sir Valentine!

THURIO [*Advancing*]
Yonder is Sylvia, and Sylvia's mine.

VALENTINE [*Drawing his sword*]
Thurio, give back, or else embrace thy death.   126
Come not within the measure of my wrath.   127
Do not name Sylvia thine; if once again,
Verona shall not hold thee. Here she stands.   129
Take but possession of her with a touch;
I dare thee but to breathe upon my love.

THURIO
Sir Valentine, I care not for her, I.
I hold him but a fool that will endanger
His body for a girl that loves him not.
I claim her not, and therefore she is thine.

DUKE
The more degenerate and base art thou,
To make such means for her as thou hast done   137
And leave her on such slight conditions.   138
Now, by the honor of my ancestry,
I do applaud thy spirit, Valentine,
And think thee worthy of an empress' love.
Know then, I here forget all former griefs,   142
Cancel all grudge, repeal thee home again,   143
Plead a new state in thy unrivaled merit,   144
To which I thus subscribe: Sir Valentine,

---

126 give back stand back   **127 measure** reach   **129 Verona** (Again, probably
an error for *Milan;* see 3.1.80.)   **hold thee** keep you safe   **137 means** exer-
tions   **138 on . . . conditions** on such easy terms   **142 griefs** grievances
143 repeal recall   **144 Plead . . . merit** i.e., I justify my abrupt reversal of my
former judgment by arguing that there is a new state of affairs in your
newly demonstrated superiority to Thurio

Thou art a gentleman and well derived.
Take thou thy Sylvia, for thou hast deserved her.

VALENTINE
I thank Your Grace. The gift hath made me happy.
I now beseech you, for your daughter's sake,
To grant one boon that I shall ask of you.

DUKE
I grant it, for thine own, whate'er it be.

VALENTINE
These banished men, that I have kept withal,   152
Are men endued with worthy qualities.
Forgive them what they have committed here,
And let them be recalled from their exile.
They are reformèd, civil, full of good,
And fit for great employment, worthy lord.

DUKE
Thou hast prevailed; I pardon them and thee.
Dispose of them as thou know'st their deserts.
Come, let us go. We will include all jars   160
With triumphs, mirth, and rare solemnity.   161

VALENTINE
And, as we walk along, I dare be bold
With our discourse to make Your Grace to smile.
What think you of this page, my lord?

DUKE
I think the boy hath grace in him. He blushes.

VALENTINE
I warrant you, my lord, more grace than boy.

DUKE   What mean you by that saying?

VALENTINE
Please you, I'll tell you as we pass along,
That you will wonder what hath fortunèd.—   169
Come, Proteus, 'tis your penance but to hear
The story of your loves discoverèd.   171
That done, our day of marriage shall be yours:
One feast, one house, one mutual happiness. *Exeunt.*

152 **kept withal** lived with   160 **include all jars** conclude all discords
161 **triumphs** festive celebrations.   **rare solemnity** marvelous festivity
169 **That** so that.   **wonder** marvel at.   **fortunèd** happened
171 **discoverèd** declared, disclosed

Date and Text

The Two Gentlemen of Verona was not published until the First Folio of 1623. Other than Francis Meres's listing of it in 1598 in his *Palladis Tamia: Wit's Treasury* (a slender volume on contemporary literature and art; valuable because it lists most of the plays of Shakespeare that existed at that time), evidence as to dating is scarce. No convincing allusions to contemporary events have been found. From the internal evidence of style, most scholars prefer an early date, though some believe that the play was composed in various stages. (Numerous factual inconsistencies in the text lend support to this theory.) The influence of John Lyly's romantic comedies, such as *Campaspe* (1584) and *Endymion* (1588), is still perceptible in the play's overly ingenious wit-combat.

An unusual feature of the text, its grouping of characters' names at the beginning of each scene, seems to indicate that the manuscript was copied at some point by the scrivener Ralph Crane, probably from an authorial manuscript still containing a number of inconsistencies; its speech prefixes are sufficiently regular, on the other hand, that it may have been prepared for the theater or else tidied up by Crane.

Textual Notes

These textual notes are not a historical collation, either of the early folios or of more recent editions; they are simply a record of departures in this edition from the copy text. The reading adopted in this edition appears in boldface, followed by the rejected reading from the copy text, i.e., the First Folio. Only major alterations in punctuation are noted. Changes in lineation are not indicated, nor are some minor and obvious typographical errors.

Abbreviations used:
F the First Folio
s.d. stage direction
s.p. speech prefix

Copy text: the First Folio. Characters' names are grouped at the head of each scene.

1.1. 26 swam swom   **66 leave** loue   **78 I a** I   **141 testerned** cestern'd

1.2. 97 your you

1.3. 24 [and elsewhere] whither whether   **50** [here F repeats speech prefix "Pro"]   **88 father calls** Fathers call's   **91 s.d. Exeunt** Exeunt. Finis

2.1. 109 stead steed

2.2. 18 s.d. [and elsewhere] Panthino Panthion [in F, grouped with characters' names at head of scene, as with entrance directions generally]

2.3. 27 wood would   **37 tied** tide [also at ll. 38, 40, and 52]

2.4. 60 know knew   **106 mistress** a Mistresse   **114 s.p. Servant** Thur   **161 braggartism** Bragadisme   **163 makes** make   **193 Is it mine eye** It is mine   **211 s.d. Exit** Exeunt

2.5. 1 Milan Padua   **37 that my** that that my

3.1. 279 master's ship Mastership   **317 kissed fasting** fasting   **374 s.d. Exit** Exeunt

4.1. 35 been beene often   **49 An** And   **near** Neece

4.2. 17 s.d. Musicians Musitian [grouped with characters' names at head of scene]   **38 s.p. Musician** [not in F]   **110 his** her

4.3. 19 abhors abhor'd   **42 Recking** Wreaking

4.4. 54 hangman Hangmans   **68 thou** thee   **72 to** not   **148 is.** is,   **149 well,** well;   **204 s.d. Exit** Exeunt

5.2. 7 s.p. Julia Pro   **13 s.p. Julia** Thu   **18 your** you   **32 Sir Eglamour** Eglamoure   **59 s.d. Exit** Exeunt

5.4. 26 this . . . hear! this? I see, and heare: **33 seizèd** ceazed   **49 me.** me,

Shakespeare's Sources

Shakespeare appears to have combined two kinds of stories in *The Two Gentlemen of Verona*, one of romantic love triumphing over inconstancy and one of perfect friendship triumphing over perfidy. For the story of the deserted heroine and her inconstant lover, Shakespeare's main source was evidently *Diana Enamorada*, a Spanish pastoral by Jorge de Montemayor (published c. 1559). This work was translated into French in 1578 and 1587 and was published in English in 1598 by Bartholomew Yonge. Yonge states that he began his translation some nineteen years earlier. Possibly, then, Shakespeare saw it in manuscript, or he may have relied on the Spanish original or the French translation. A play, now lost, was performed at court in 1585 called *The History of Felix & Philiomena* (i.e., Felismena). It must surely have been based on Montemayor's prose pastoral and may have provided Shakespeare with a dramatic model.

A modernized excerpt of Yonge's translation of *Diana* follows. The story of Felix and Felismena is only one of the many narratives in *Diana* that are set in contrast to the central story of Diana the shepherdess. It is told by Felismena as her own narrative, beginning in Book 2. The story contains no character corresponding to Valentine, but Proteus and Julia find their equivalents in Felix and Felismena. The latter is attended by a maid, Rosina, like Julia's Lucetta, who is hypocritically scolded by her mistress for delivering a letter from Felix that Felismena in fact longs to have. Like Proteus in Shakespeare's play, Don Felix is sent off to court (in this case, the court of Princess Augusta Caesarina) to prevent his marriage to the orphaned Felismena. She follows after, appareled as a young man named Valerius (as Julia travels under the name of Sebastian). Stopping at an inn, she is invited by the host of the inn to hear some music, whereupon she happens to overhear the faithless Felix courting a lady named Celia (Shakespeare's Sylvia). Disguised as Valerius, Felismena ingratiates herself with Felix's servant Fabius and takes service with Don Felix. She is sent on embassages to Celia, with whom she converses about Felix's first love. Celia falls in love with "Valerius," like Olivia in *Twelfth Night*, and subsequently dies of unrequited passion. Hereupon the distraught Felix disappears. Later, in Book 7, we hear how Felismena, disguised as an Amazonian shepherdess, rescues Felix from his attackers and is reconciled to him. Felix acknowledges her beauty to be superior to that of Celia. Shakespeare has changed some important matters, notably Celia's falling in love with "Valerius" and her dying of unrequited love; Sylvia's remaining faithful to Valentine and following him into banishment are essential parts of her character in Shakespeare's account. Shakespeare also adds several new characters: the Duke of Milan (Sylvia's father), Thurio, Eglamour, Lance, Speed, and the outlaws. Still, the debt to *Diana* is considerable.

In Sir Philip Sidney's *Arcadia* (1590), Zelmane follows Felismena's example by disguising herself as a page (Daiphantus) in the service of her beloved Pyrocles. When she falls ill and is on the verge of death, Zelmane's identity is revealed to Pyrocles. The *Arcadia* also offers a noble example of perfect friendship in the relation between Pyrocles and Musidorus. Shakespeare used the *Arcadia* as a source elsewhere, especially in the Gloucester plot of *King Lear*.

The story of perfect friendship has many antecedents, including the fourteenth-century *Amis and Amiloun* and Richard Edwards's play *Damon and Pythias* (1565). The falling-out of sworn friends over a woman is the central theme of Geoffrey Chaucer's "The Knight's Tale" and of John Lyly's *Euphues* (1578). Perhaps the most suggestive example of perfect friendship is the story of Titus and Gisippus as it appears in Book 2, Chapter 12, of Sir Thomas Elyot's *The Governor* (1531). Elyot derived his account from Day 10, Novel 8, of Giovanni Boccaccio's *Decameron*. Titus and Gisippus were proverbially famous friends, like Damon and Pythias, and other Renaissance versions of the story were available (including a Latin school play of 1546[?] and a children's play at court in 1577, both now lost). Perhaps Shakespeare knew the story as a commonplace rather than having to depend on one particular literary source.

Elyot's version tells of two look-alike friends dwelling in Athens of whom one, Gisippus, is persuaded by his kindred and acquaintances to marry. Despite a preference for the study of philosophy, he finds his fiancée most attractive.

When, however, his Roman-born friend Titus falls desperately in love with the same lady and confesses as much to Gisippus, the husband-to-be generously proposes that Titus take his place on the wedding night. Because the binding element of the marriage contract is the bestowing of the ring in bed and the undoing of the girdle of virginity, the lady is now Titus' legal wife and returns with him to Rome. Gisippus, accused by the Athenians of having mismanaged the affair, follows his friend to Rome and is there wrongly accused of a murder. Titus' turn has now arrived to be magnanimous, and he insists that he be punished for the murder. Eventually the real culprit, touched by this selflessness, confesses the crime, allowing Titus to return with Gisippus to Athens and forcibly to restore him to his rightful possessions.

Valentine's sojourn in the forest and his leadership of a band of outlaws would seem to be indebted to the tradition of Robin Hood, although no single source has been found. An analogue to the outlaw episode does appear in Henry Wotton's *A Courtly Controversy of Cupid's Cautels* (1578), where it is linked to a story of perfidy in friendship. Valentine's unwelcome rival Thurio may owe something to the braggart soldier, Captain Spavento, of the *commedia dell' arte* tradition. Sylvia's father, the Duke, is a similarly conventional comic stage type.

One final analogue worthy of note is a German play, *Julio und Hyppolita,* from a collection called *Englische Comedien und Tragedien* (1620). It may have been derived from performances by English players around 1600. Although some of its lines are suggestively close to those of Shakespeare's play, we cannot determine which version is prior to the other.

Diana Enamorada
By Jorge de Montemayor
Translated by Bartholomew Yonge

Book 2

[Felismena, appareled as an Amazonian shepherdess, tells her own story to three nymphs dwelling in Diana's wood whom she has rescued from three wild men.]

You shall therefore know, fair nymphs, that great Vandalia is my native country, a province not far hence, where I was born in a city called Soldina; my mother called Delia, my father Andronius, for lineage and possessions the chiefest of all that province.

It fell out that, as my mother was married many years and had no children, by reason whereof she lived so sad and malcontent that she enjoyed not one merry day, with tears and sighs she daily importuned the heavens and with a thousand vows and devout offerings besought God to grant her the sum of her desire; whose omnipotency it pleased, beholding from his imperial throne her continual orisons,[1] to make her barren body (the greater part of her age being now spent and gone) to become fruitful. What infinite joy she conceived thereof, let her judge that, after a long desire of anything, Fortune at last doth put it into her hands. Of which content my father Andronius, being no less partaker, showed such tokens of inward joy as are impossible to be expressed.

My mother Delia was so much given to reading of ancient histories[2] that if by reason of sickness or any important business she had not been hindered she would never, by her will, have passed the time away in any other delight. Who, as I said, being now with child and finding herself on a night[3] ill at ease, entreated my father to read something unto her that, her mind being occupied in contemplation thereof, she might the better pass her grief away.

My father, who studied for nothing else but to please her in all he might, began to read unto her the history of Paris, when the three ladies referred their proud contention for the golden apple to his conclusion and judgment. But as my mother held it for an infallible opinion that Paris had partially[4] given that sentence, persuaded thereunto by a blind passion of beauty, so she said that without all doubt he did not with due reason and wisdom consider the goddess of battles;[5] for as martial and heroical feats, said she, excelled all other qualities, so with equity and justice the apple should have been given to her. My father answered that since the apple was to be given to the fairest and that Venus

---

1 orisons prayers   **2 histories** stories   **3 on a night** one night   **4 partially** unfairly, in a biased manner   **5 goddess of battles** i.e., Pallas Athene

was fairer than any of the rest, Paris had rightly given his judgment, if that[6] harm had not ensued thereof, which afterwards did. To this my mother replied that, though it was written in the apple that it should be given to the fairest, it was not to be understood of corporal beauty but of the intellectual beauty of the mind. And therefore since fortitude was a thing that made one most beautiful and the exercise of arms an exterior act of this virtue, she affirmed that to the goddess of battles this apple should be given, if Paris had judged like a prudent and unappassionate[7] judge. So that, fair nymphs, they spent a great part of the night in this controversy, both of them alleging the most reasons they could to confirm their own purpose.

They persisting in this point, sleep began to overcome her whom the reasons and arguments of her husband could not once move. So that, being very deep in her disputations, she fell into as deep a sleep, to whom, my father being now gone to his chamber, appeared the goddess Venus, with as frowning a countenance as fair, and said: "I marvel, Delia, who hath moved thee to be so contrary to her that was never opposite to thee? If thou hadst but called to mind the time when thou wert so overcome in love for Andronius, thou wouldst not have paid me the debt thou owest me with so ill coin. But thou shalt not escape free from my due anger. For thou shalt bring forth a son and a daughter, whose birth shall cost thee no less than thy life and them their contentment, for uttering so much in disgrace of my honor and beauty; both which[8] shall be as infortunate in their love as any were ever in all their lives, or to the age wherein, with remediless sighs, they shall breathe forth the sum of their ceaseless sorrows."[9] And having said thus, she vanished away.

When likewise it seemed to my mother that the goddess Pallas came to her in a vision and with a merry countenance said thus unto her: "With what sufficient rewards may I be

6 if that provided that 7 unappassionate impartial 8 both which both of whom 9 or to the age . . . sorrows (The two children will be plagued all their lives with misfortune in love, or at least to the age when people fall in love and breathe forth their remediless sighs and sorrows.)

able to requite the due regard, most happy and discreet Delia, which thou hast alleged in my favor against thy husband's obstinate opinion? Except it be by making thee understand that thou shalt bring forth a son and a daughter, the most fortunate in arms that have been to their times."[10] Having thus said, she vanished out of her sight, and my mother, through exceeding fear, awaked immediately. Who, within a month after, at one birth was delivered of me and of a brother of mine, and died in childbed, leaving my father the most sorrowful man in the world for her sudden death; for grief whereof, within a little while after, he also died.

And because you may know, fair nymphs, in what great extremities love hath put me, you must understand that, being a woman of that quality and disposition as you have heard, I have been forced by my cruel destiny to leave my natural habit[11] and liberty and the due respect of mine honor to follow him who thinks, perhaps, that I do but leese[12] it by loving him so extremely. Behold how bootless[13] and unseemly it is for a woman to be so dexterous in arms, as if it were her proper[14] nature and kind; wherewith, fair nymphs, I had never been endued, but that, by means thereof, I should come to do you this little service against these villains;[15] which I account no less than if Fortune had begun to satisfy in part some of those infinite wrongs that she hath continually done me.

The nymphs were so amazed at her words that they could neither ask nor answer anything to that[16] the fair shepherdess told them, who, prosecuting her history,[17] said:

My brother and I were brought up in a nunnery where an aunt of ours was abbess until we had accomplished twelve

10 been to their times ever been in their generation or previously   **11 habit** i.e., woman's costume. (Felismena anticipates her story that she has been obliged to adopt the disguise of a young man.)   **12 leese** lose. (Felismena has been forced, in following after the man she loves, to put her *honor* or reputation for chastity at risk.)   **13 bootless** profitless   **14 proper** true, own **15 this little . . . villains** (Prior to telling the nymphs this tale, Felismena has rescued them from three wild men by means of her bow and arrows and a steel-tipped staff.)   **16 that** that which   **17 prosecuting her history** continuing her story

years of age. At what[18] time we were taken from thence again, and my brother was carried to the mighty and invincible King of Portugal his[19] court, whose noble fame and princely liberality was bruited[20] over all the world. Where, being grown to years able to manage arms, he achieved as valiant and almost incredible enterprises by them as he suffered unfortunate disgraces and foils by love. And with all this he was so highly favored of[21] that magnificent king that he would never suffer[22] him to depart from his court.

Unfortunate I, reserved by my sinister destinies to greater mishaps, was carried to a grandmother of mine, which place I would I had never seen, since it was an occasion of such a sorrowful life as never any woman suffered the like. And because there is not anything, fair nymphs, which I am not forced to tell you, as well for the great virtue and deserts which your excellent beauties do testify as also[23] for that my mind doth give me[24] that you shall be no small part and means of my comfort, know that as I was in my grandmother's house and almost seventeen years old, a certain young gentleman fell in love with me, who dwelt no further from our house than the length of a garden terrace, so that he might see me every summer's night when I walked in the garden.

Whenas[25] therefore ingrateful Felix had beheld in that place the unfortunate Felismena (for this is the name of the woeful woman that tells you her mishaps), he was extremely enamored of me, or else did cunningly dissemble it—I not knowing then whether[26] of these two I might believe, but am now assured that whosoever believes least or nothing at all in these affairs shall be most at ease. Many days Don Felix spent in endeavoring to make me know the pains which he suffered for me. And many more did I spend in making the matter strange[27] and that he did not suffer them for my sake.[28] And I know not why Love delayed the time so long by forcing[29] me to love him, but only that, when

---

18 what which **19 Portugal his** Portugal's **20 bruited** spoken of, celebrated **21 of** by **22 suffer** allow **23 as well . . . as** also both . . . and **24 for that . . . give me** because my mind tells me **25 Whenas** when **26 whether** which **27 making the matter strange** holding back, pretending not to understand **28 for my sake** (Felismena resists accepting Felix as her servant in love, one who suffers and performs deeds for her sake.) **29 delayed . . . forcing** took so long in forcing

he[30] came indeed, he might enter into my heart at once and with greater force and violence.

When he had, therefore, by sundry signs, as by tilt and tourneys and by prancing up and down upon his proud jennet[31] before my windows, made it manifest that he was in love with me (for at the first I did not so well perceive it), he determined in the end to write a letter unto me. And having practiced divers times before with a maid of mine, and at length with many gifts and fair promises gotten her good will and furtherance,[32] he gave her the letter to deliver to me. But to see the means that Rosina made unto me (for so was she called), the dutiful services and unwonted circumstances[33] before she did deliver it, the oaths that she sware unto me, and the subtle words and serious protestations she used, it was a pleasant thing and worthy the noting. To whom, nevertheless, with an angry countenance I turned again, saying: "If I had not regard of mine own estate and what hereafter might be said, I would make this shameless face of thine be known ever after for a mark of an impudent and bold minion.[34] But because it is the first time, let this suffice that I have said and give thee warning to take heed of the second."

Methinks I see now the crafty wench, how she held her peace,[35] dissembling very cunningly the sorrow that she conceived by my angry answer. For she feigned a counterfeit smiling, saying: "Jesus, mistress, I gave it you because you might laugh at it and not to move[36] your patience with it in this sort. For if I had any thought that it would have provoked you to anger, I pray God he may show his wrath as great towards me as ever he did to the daughter of any mother." And with this she added many words more, as she could do well enough, to pacify the feigned anger and ill opinion that I conceived of her. And taking her letter with her, she departed from me.

This having passed thus, I began to imagine what might ensue thereof. And love, methought, did put a certain desire into my mind to see the letter, though modesty and shame

---

30 he i.e., Felix (but also suggesting Love, Cupid) **31 jennet** a small Spanish horse **32 furtherance** aid **33 unwonted circumstances** unaccustomed formalities **34 minion** hussy **35 held her peace** i.e., held back what she felt like saying **36 because . . . move** so that . . . disturb

forbade me to ask it of my maid, especially for[37] the words that had passed between us, as you have heard. And so I continued all that day until night in variety of many thoughts.

But when Rosina came to help me to bed, God knows how desirous I was to have her entreat me again to take the letter. But she would never speak unto me about it, nor, as it seemed, did so much as once think thereof. Yet to try if by giving her some occasion I might prevail, I said unto her: "And is it so, Rosina, that Don Felix, without any regard to mine honor, dares write unto me?"

"These are things, mistress," said she demurely to me again, "that are commonly incident to love. Wherefore I beseech you pardon me. For if I had thought to have angered you with it, I would have first pulled out the balls of mine eyes."

How cold my heart was at that blow, God knows. Yet did I dissemble the matter and suffer myself to remain that night only with my desire and with occasion of little sleep. And so it was indeed, for that, methought, was the longest and most painful night that ever I passed. But when, with a slower pace than I desired, the wished day was come, the discreet and subtle Rosina came into my chamber to help me to make me ready; in doing whereof, of[38] purpose she let the letter closely[39] fall. Which when I perceived, "What is that that fell down?" said I. "Let me see it."

"It is nothing, mistress," said she.

"Come, come, let me see it," said I. "What! Move[40] me not, or else tell me what it is."

"Good Lord, mistress," said she, "why will you see it? It is the letter I would have given you yesterday."

"Nay, that it is not," said I. "Wherefore show it me, that I may see if you lie or no."

I had no sooner said so but she put it into my hands, saying: "God never give me good if it be any other thing."

And although I knew it well indeed, yet I said: "What, this is not the same, for I know that well enough. But it is one of thy lover's letters. I will read it to see in what need he standeth of thy favor."

37 for because of **38 of** on **39 closely** secretly **40 Move** anger

And, opening it, I found it contained this that followeth:

> I ever imagined, dear mistress, that your discretion and wisdom would have taken away the fear I had to write unto you, the same[41] knowing well enough, without any letter at all, how much I love you. But the very same hath so cunningly dissembled[42] that, wherein I hoped the only remedy of my griefs had been, therein consisted my greatest harm. If according to your wisdom you censure my boldness, I shall not then, I know, enjoy one hour of life. But if you do consider of[43] it according to love's accustomed effects, then will I not exchange my hope for it. Be not offended, I beseech you, good lady, with my letter; and blame me not for writing unto you until you see by experience whether I can leave off to write. And take me besides into the possession of that which is yours, since all is mine doth wholly consist[44] in your hands; the which, with all reverence and dutiful affection, a thousand times I kiss.

When I had now seen my Don Felix his[45] letter, whether it was for reading it at such a time, when by the same he showed that he loved me more than himself, or whether he had disposition and regiment[46] over part of this wearied soul to imprint that love in it whereof he wrote unto me, I began to love him too well, and alas! for my harm, since he was the cause of so much sorrow as I have passed[47] for his sake. Whereupon, asking Rosina forgiveness of what was past (as a thing needful for that which was to come) and committing the secrecy of my love to her fidelity, I read the letter once again, pausing a little at every word—and a very little[48] indeed it was, because I concluded so soon with myself to do that[49] I did, although in very truth it lay not otherwise in my power to do. Wherefore, calling for paper and ink, I answered his letter thus:

> Esteem not so slightly of mine honor, Don Felix, as with feigned words to think to inveigle[50] it or with thy vain pretenses to offend it any ways. I know well enough what manner of man thou art and how great thy desert and presumption is; from whence thy boldness doth arise, I

---

41 the same i.e., you   **42 But . . . dissembled** i.e., but you have so concealed your own feeling   **43 consider of** consider   **44 all . . . consist** all that is mine exists only   **45 Felix his** Felix's   **46 disposition and regiment** control and rule   **47 passed** suffered   **48 very little** i.e., a very short pause   **49 that** what   **50 inveigle** beguile, deceive

guess, and not from the force (which thing thou wouldst fain persuade me) of thy fervent love. And if it be so as my suspicion suggesteth, thy labor is as vain as thy imagination presumptuous by thinking to make me do anything contrary to that which I owe unto mine honor. Consider, I beseech thee, how seldom things commenced under subtlety and dissimulation have good success, and that it is not the part of a gentleman to mean them one way and speak them another. Thou prayest me, amongst other things, to admit thee into possession of that that is mine. But I am of so ill an humor in matters of this quality that I trust not things experienced; how much less, then, thy bare words. Yet, nevertheless, I make no small account of that which thou hast manifested to me in thy letter; for it is enough that I am incredulous, though not unthankful.

This letter did I send—contrary to that[51] I should have done, because it was the occasion of all my harms and griefs. For after this he began to wax more bold by unfolding his thoughts and seeking out the means to have a parley with me. In the end, fair nymphs, a few days being spent in his demands and my answers, false love did work in me after his wonted fashions, every hour seizing more strongly upon my unfortunate soul. The tourneys were now renewed; the music by night did never cease; amorous letters and verses were recontinued on both sides. And thus passed I away almost a whole year, at the end whereof I felt myself so far in his love that I had no power to retire nor stay myself from disclosing my thoughts unto him—the thing which he desired more than his own life.

But my adverse fortune afterwards would[52] that of these our mutual loves, whenas now they were most assured, his father had some intelligence.[53] And whosoever revealed them first persuaded him so cunningly that his father, fearing lest he would have married me out of hand,[54] sent him to the great Princess Augusta Caesarina's court, telling him it was not meet that a young gentleman, and of so noble a house as he was, should spend his youth idly at home, where nothing could be learned but examples of vice;

---

51 that what   **52 But ... would** but afterward, my perverse fortune willed it
53 intelligence news, information   **54 lest ... hand** lest he (Felix) would have married me at once

whereof the very same idleness, he said, was the only mistress.

He[55] went away so pensive that his great grief would not suffer him to acquaint me with his departure; which when I knew, how sorrowful I remained, she may imagine that hath been at any time tormented with like passion. To tell you now the life that I led in his absence—my sadness, sighs, and tears, which every day I poured out of these wearied eyes—my tongue is far unable. If, then, my pains were such that I cannot now express them, how could I then suffer them?

But being in the midst of my mishaps and in the depth of those woes which the absence of Don Felix caused me to feel, and it seeming to me that my grief was without remedy if he were once seen or known of the ladies in that court more beautiful and gracious than myself (by occasion whereof, as also by absence, a capital enemy to love, I might easily be forgotten), I determined to adventure that which I think never any woman imagined: which was to apparel myself in the habit of a man and to hie me to the court to see him in whose sight all my hope and content remained. Which determination I no sooner thought of than I put in practice, love blinding my eyes and mind with an inconsiderate[56] regard of mine own estate and condition. To the execution of which attempt I wanted no industry.[57] For, being furnished with the help of one of my approved[58] friends and treasuress of my secrets, who bought me such apparel as I willed her and a good horse for my journey, I went not only out of my country but out of my dear reputation, which I think I shall never recover again. And so trotted directly to the court, passing by the way many accidents which, if time would give me leave to tell them, would not make you laugh a little to hear them.

Twenty days I was in going thither, at the end of which, being come to the desired place, I took up mine inn in a street least frequented with concourse of people. And the great desire I had to see the destroyer of my joy did not suffer me to think of any other thing but how or where I might

55 He i.e., Felix   **56 inconsiderate** careless   **57 wanted no industry** lacked no industriousness   **58 approved** proven see him. To inquire of him of mine host[59] I durst not, lest my coming might perhaps have been discovered;[60] and to seek him forth I thought it not best, lest some inopinate[61] mishap might have fallen out whereby I might have been known. Wherefore I passed all that day in these perplexities while[62] night came on, each hour whereof, methought, was a whole year unto me.

But midnight being a little past, mine host called at my chamber door and told me, if I was desirous to hear some brave[63] music, I should arise quickly and open a window towards the street. The which I did by and by,[64] and making no noise at all, I heard how Don Felix his[65] page, called Fabius, whom I knew by his voice, said to others that came with him: "Now it is time, my masters, because the lady is in the gallery over her garden, taking the fresh air of the cool night."

He had no sooner said so but they began to wind[66] three cornets and a sackbut with such skill and sweetness that it seemed celestial music. And then began a voice to sing, the sweetest, in my opinion, that ever I heard. And though I was in suspense by hearing Fabius speak, whereby a thousand doubts and imaginations, repugnant to my rest, occurred in my mind, yet I neglected not to hear what was sung, because their operations[67] were not of such force that they were able to hinder the desire nor distemper the delight that I conceived by hearing it. That therefore which was sung were these verses:

[The song is the plea of a woeful lover to his reluctant mistress, begging her favor. Don Felix then sings another to the accompaniment of lute and harp. A third song is sung by four voices, and there is instrumental music as well. The host cannot tell Felismena what lady the music is intended for.]

About dawning of the day the music ended, and I did what I could to espy out my Don Felix. But the darkness of

---

59 mine host the innkeeper **60 discovered** revealed, made public **61 inopinate** unlooked-for **62 while** until **63 brave** splendid, fine **64 by and by** at once **65 Felix his** Felix's **66 wind** blow. (Cornets and the *sackbut*, a trombonelike instrument, are all wind instruments in the sense that they are blown into, though classified today as brasses.) **67 their operations** i.e., the effects of my fearful imaginings the night was mine enemy therein. And seeing now that they were gone, I went to bed again, where I bewailed my great mishap, knowing that he whom most of all I loved had so unworthily forgotten me, whereof his music was too manifest a witness.

And when it was time, I arose and, without any other consideration, went straight to the Princess her[68] palace, where I thought I might see that which I so greatly desired, determining to call myself Valerius if any perhaps did ask my name. Coming therefore to a fair broad court before the palace gate, I viewed the windows and galleries, where I saw such store of blazing beauties and gallant ladies that I am not able now to recount—nor then to do any more but wonder at—their graces, their gorgeous attire, their jewels, their brave[69] fashions of apparel, and ornaments wherewith they were so richly set out. Up and down this place, before the windows, rode many lords and brave gentlemen in rich and sumptuous habits and mounted upon proud jennets, everyone casting his eye to that part where his thoughts were secretly placed. God knows how greatly I desired to see Don Felix there, and that his injurious love[70] had been in that famous palace, because I might then have been assured that he should never have got any other guerdon[71] of his suits and services but only to see and to be seen and sometimes to speak to his mistress, whom he must serve before a thousand eyes[72] because the privilege of that place doth not give him any further leave. But it was my ill fortune that he had settled his love in that place where I might not be assured of this poor help.

Thus, as I was standing near to the palace gate, I espied Fabius, Don Felix his page, coming in great haste to the palace, where, speaking a word or two with a porter that kept the second entry, he returned the same way he came. I guessed his errand was to know whether it were fit time for Don Felix to come to dispatch certain business that his

68 Princess her Princess's   **69 brave** splendid   **70 his injurious love** his wrongful and hurtful love (Felismena wishes that, if Felix must be in love with someone, he be in love with some great lady of the court, especially the Princess herself, from whom he could expect little reciprocation.)
71 guerdon reward   **72 before a thousand eyes** i.e., only in public. (The *privilege* of the court would allow Felix to declare himself a servant in love of the Princess Augusta Caesarina, but only in a ceremonial sense.)

father had in the court, and that he could not choose but come thither out of hand.[73]

[Felix indeed appears at court, elegantly dressed and followed by servants who are also "bravely appareled." Striking up a conversation with Fabius, Felismena learns that Felix courts a lady named Celia, forgetting another lady to whom he was previously committed in his native city of Soldina who, in Fabius's view, is far more beautiful and loving than is Celia. It is the absence of that lady that has led Felix to this inconstancy. Felismena, listening to this, has difficulty suppressing her tears.]

And then the page did ask me what countryman I was, my name, and of what calling and condition I was; whom I answered that my country where I was born was Vandalia, my name Valerius, and till that time served no master.

"Then by this reckoning," said he, "we are both countrymen, and may be both fellows in one house if thou wilt. For Don Felix my master commanded me long since to seek him out a page. Therefore, if thou wilt serve him, say so. As for meat, drink, and apparel, and a couple of shillings to play away,[74] thou shalt never want; besides pretty wenches, which are not dainty[75] in our street, as fair and amorous as queens, of which there is not any that will not die for the love of so proper[76] a youth as thou art. And to tell thee in secret (because, perhaps, we may be fellows),[77] I know where an old canon's maid[78] is, a gallant fine girl, whom if thou canst but find in thy heart to love and serve as I do, thou shalt never want at her hands fine handkerchiefs, pieces of bacon, and now and then wine of Saint Martin."[79]

When I heard this, I could not choose but laugh to see how naturally the unhappy[80] page played his part by depainting forth their properties[81] in their lively colors. And

---

73 out of hand at once **74 play away** gamble with **75 dainty** standoffish
76 proper handsome **77 fellows** friends **78 canon's maid** maidservant to a
clergyman living according to the canons of the Church **79 of Saint Martin**
of Saint Martin's Day, November 11, a fine wine **80 unhappy** poor. (Said
with affectionate irony, as in "the poor fellow.") **81 depainting . . . properties** depicting the qualities of such things (as loose women, gambling, favors,
and the like)

because I thought nothing more commodious for my rest[82] and for the enjoying of my desire than to follow Fabius his counsel, I answered him thus:

"In truth, I determined to serve none. But now, since Fortune hath offered me so good a service and at such a time when I am constrained to take this course of life, I shall not do amiss if I frame[83] myself to the service of some lord or gentleman in this court, but especially of your master, because he seems to be a worthy gentleman and such an one that makes more reckoning of his servants than another."

"Ha, thou knowest him not as well as I," said Fabius. "For I promise thee by the faith of a gentleman (for I am one indeed, for my father comes of the Cachopines of Laredo) that my master Don Felix is the best-natured gentleman that ever thou knewest in thy life, and one who useth his pages better than any other. And were it not for those troublesome loves, which makes us run up and down more and sleep less than we would, there were not such a master in the whole world again."

In the end, fair nymphs, Fabius spake to his master, Don Felix, as soon as he was come forth, in my behalf, who commanded me the same night to come to him at his lodging. Thither I went, and he entertained me for[84] his page, making the most of me in the world;[85] where, being but a few days with him, I saw the messages, letters, and gifts that were brought and carried on both sides—grievous wounds, alas! and corrosives to my dying heart, which made my soul to fly sometimes out of my body and every hour in hazard to leese my forced patience before everyone.

But after one month was past, Don Felix began to like so well of me that he disclosed his whole love unto me from the beginning unto the present estate and forwardness that it was then in, committing the charge[86] thereof to my secrecy and help, telling me that he was favored of her at the beginning and that afterwards she waxed weary of her loving and accustomed entertainment,[87] the cause whereof was a secret report (whosoever it was that buzzed it into her ears) of

---

82 commodious for my rest convenient for my purposes **83 frame** shape, adapt **84 entertained me for** received me as **85 in the world** possible **86 charge** keeping, managing **87 her . . . entertainment** i.e., the loving and steady attention she got from him

the love that he did bear to a lady in his own country, and that his present love unto her was but to entertain[88] the time while his business in the court were dispatched.

"And there is no doubt," said Don Felix unto me, "but that indeed I did once commence that love that she lays to my charge.[89] But God knows if now there be anything in the world that I love and esteem more dear and precious than her."

When I heard him say so, you may imagine, fair nymphs, what a mortal dagger pierced my wounded heart. But with dissembling the matter the best I could, I answered him thus: "It were better, sir, methinks, that the gentlewoman should complain with cause and that it were so indeed.[90] For if the other lady, whom you served before, did not deserve to be forgotten of you, you do her (under correction, my lord) the greatest wrong in the world."

"The love," said Don Felix again, "which I bear to my Celia will not let me understand it so. But I have done her, methinks, the greater injury, having placed my love first in another and not in her."

"Of these wrongs," said I to myself, "I know who bears the worst away."[91]

And disloyal he, pulling a letter out of his bosom which he had received the same hour from his mistress, read it unto me, thinking that he did me a great favor thereby; the contents whereof were these:

Celia's letter to Don Felix

Never anything that I suspected, touching thy love, hath been so far from the truth that hath not given me occasion to believe more often mine own imagination than thy innocency. Wherein if I do thee any wrong, refer it but to the censure of thine own folly. For well thou mightest have denied or not declared thy past love without giving me occasion to condemn thee by thine own confession. Thou sayest I was the cause that made thee forget thy former love. Comfort thyself, for there shall not want[92] another to make thee forget thy second. And assure thyself of this, Lord Don Fe-

---

88 entertain pass, occupy   **89 charge** responsibility   **90 It were . . . indeed** i.e., if there is substance to what she complains about, it's better that she go ahead and complain   **91 who bears . . . away** who bears the heaviest wrong (i.e., Felismena herself)   **92 want** lack

lix, that there is not anything more unbeseeming a gentleman than to find an occasion in a gentlewoman to leese himself for her love.[93] I will say no more but that in an ill where there is no remedy, the best is not to seek out any.

After he had made an end of reading the letter, he said unto me: "What thinkest thou, Valerius, of these words?"

"With pardon be it spoken, my lord: that[94] your deeds are showed by them."

"Go to,"[95] said Don Felix, "and speak no more of that."

"Sir," said I, "they must like[96] me well if they like you, because none can judge better of their words that love well than they themselves. But that which I think of the letter is that this gentlewoman would have been the first, and that Fortune had entreated[97] her in such sort that all others might have envied her estate."

"But what wouldst thou counsel me?" said Don Felix.

"If thy grief doth suffer any counsel,"[98] said I, "that[99] thy thoughts be divided into this second passion,[100] since there is so much due to the first."

Don Felix answered me again, sighing and knocking[101] me gently on the shoulder, saying: "How wise art thou, Valerius, and what good counsel dost thou give me if I could follow it! Let us now go in to dinner. For when I have dined, I will have thee carry me a letter to my lady Celia. And then thou shalt see if any other love is not worthy to be forgotten in lieu of thinking only of her."

These were words that grieved Felismena[102] to the heart. But because she had him before her eyes whom she loved more than herself, the content that she had by only seeing him was a sufficient remedy of the pain that the greatest of these stings did make her feel.

After Don Felix had dined he called me unto him, and giving me a special charge what I should do—because he had imparted his grief unto me and put his hope and remedy in

---

93 than . . . love i.e., than for a gentleman to fall helplessly in love with a gentlewoman and blame her for it.   **leese** lose   **94 that** i.e., I think that   **95 Go to** (An expression of impatience or annoyance.)   **96 like** please   **97 had entreated** would have treated   **98 doth suffer any counsel** will accept any advice   **99 that** i.e., my advice is that   **100 thy thoughts . . . passion** i.e., (that) you temper the extremes of your passion for Celia   **101 knocking** tapping   **102 Felismena** (In this brief paragraph the author speaks in his own voice before returning the first-person narrative to Felismena.)

my hands—he willed me to carry a letter to Celia, which he had already written, and, reading it first unto me, it said thus:

Don Felix his letter to Celia

The thought that seeks an occasion to forget the thing which it doth love and desire suffers itself so easily to be known that, without troubling the mind much, it may be quickly discerned. And think not, fair lady, that I seek a remedy to excuse you of that wherewith it pleased you to use me, since I never came to be so much in credit with you that in lesser things I would do it. I have confessed unto you that indeed I once loved well, because that[103] true love without dissimulation doth not suffer anything to be hid; and you, dear lady, make that an occasion to forget me which should be rather a motive to love me better. I cannot persuade me that you make so small an account of yourself to think that I can forget you for anything that is or hath ever been, but rather imagine that you write clean contrary to that which you have tried by my zealous love and faith towards you. Touching all those things that, in prejudice of my good will towards you, it pleaseth you to imagine, my innocent thoughts assure me to the contrary, which shall suffice to be ill recompensed besides being so ill thought of as they are.

After Don Felix had read this letter unto me, he asked me if the answer was correspondent[104] to those words that his lady Celia had sent him in hers and if there was anything therein that might be amended. Whereunto I answered thus: "I think, sir, it is needless to amend this letter or to make the gentlewoman amends to whom it is sent, but her[105] whom you do injury so much with it. Which under your lordship's pardon I speak, because I am so much affected to the first love in all my life[106] that there is not anything that can make me alter my mind."

"Thou hast the greatest reason in the world,"[107] said Don Felix, "if I could persuade myself to leave off that which I have begun. But what wilt thou have me do, since absence hath frozen the former love and the continual presence of a

---

103 because that because   **104 correspondent** responsive   **105 but her** i.e., but rather it is needful to make amends to her, Felismena   **106 so much . . . my life** so partial to your first love with my whole being. (Said with a double meaning that Felix presumably does not understand.)   **107 Thou . . . world** you would be absolutely right

peerless beauty rekindled another more hot and fervent in me?"

"Thus may she think herself," said I again, "unjustly deceived, whom first you loved, because that love which is subject to the power of absence cannot be termed love; and none can persuade me that it hath been love."

These words did I dissemble the best I could, because I felt so sensible[108] grief to see myself forgotten of[109] him who had so great reason to love me and whom I did love so much that I did more than any would have thought[110] to make myself still unknown. But, taking the letter and mine errand with me, I went to Celia's house, imagining by the way the woeful estate whereunto my hapless love had brought me, since I was forced to make war against mine own self and to be the intercessor of a thing so contrary to mine own content. But coming to Celia's house and finding a page standing at the door, I asked him if I might speak with his lady, who, being informed of me from whence I came, told Celia how I would speak with her, commending therewithal my beauty and person unto her and telling her besides that Don Felix had but lately entertained me into his service. Which made Celia say unto him: "What, doth Don Felix so soon disclose his secret loves to a page but newly entertained? He hath, belike,[111] some great occasion that moves him to do it. Bid him come in, and let us know what he would have."

In I came, and to the place where the enemy of my life was, and with great reverence kissing her hands, I delivered Don Felix his letter unto her. Celia took it, and casting her eyes upon me, I might perceive how my sight had made a sudden alteration in her countenance. For she was so far beside herself that for a good while she was not able to speak a word.

[At this point the story begins to resemble *Twelfth Night* more than *The Two Gentlemen of Verona*, though Celia does ask Valerius about Felismena and is guardedly informed by the seeming page that Felismena is less beautiful than she ought to be because she lacks contentedness. As in *Twelfth Night*, Celia proceeds to fall in love with Valerius and, hav-

---

108 sensible acutely felt, painful   **109 of** by   **110 thought** thought possible
111 belike perhaps. (Said ironically.)

ing read Felix's letter, sends an ambiguous reply. She leaves Valerius in no uncertainty that she prefers the page to the master. Felix is happy at first with what Valerius has to report but soon falls into a decline at Celia's continued indifference. Valerius goes on many embassies to Celia, reluctantly but loyally urging the case of Felix but perceiving that Celia's warm response is only to Valerius. Celia, distraught at Valerius's indifference, at last rejects Felix entirely and refuses to see the page any more. When news arrives next day of Celia's having died during the night, Felix is stricken beyond measure and disappears without explanation. Felismena, no longer disguised as Valerius but dressed instead in Amazonian attire, has been seeking him without success for two years at the time of her telling this sad tale to the three nymphs in Diana's wood.

The nymphs are greatly moved by Felismena's tale. One of them, Doria, wishing to help Felismena, conducts her to the sage Felicia's palace where remedy can be found for her griefs. There, in Book 4, Felicia discusses the relationship of love and reason, concluding that although Love "hath Reason for his mother," he "is not therefore limited or governed by it."]

Book 7

[Later in *Diana Enoramada* we encounter Felismena again, still attired as an Amazonian shepherdess, having reunited the parted lovers Amarillis and Filemon. She listens to Duarda, a Portuguese shepherdess, who will have nothing to do with Danteus, a woeful shepherd.]

The shepherdess having made an end of her sharp answer and Felismena beginning to arbitrate the matter between them, they heard a great noise in the other side of the meadow, like to the sound of blows and smiting of swords upon harness,[1] as if some armed men had fought together, so that all of them with great haste ran to the place where they heard the noise to see what the matter was. And being come somewhat near, they saw, in a little island which the river with a round turning had made, three knights fighting

---

1 harness armor

against one. And although he defended himself valiantly, by showing his approved strength and courage, yet the three knights gave him so much to do that he was fain to help himself by all the force and policy[2] he could. They fought on foot, for their horses were tied to little trees that grew thereabouts. And now by this time the knight that fought all alone and defended himself had laid one of them at his feet with a blow of his good sword, which ended his life. But the other two, that were very strong and valiant, redoubled their force and blows so thick on him that he looked for no other thing than death.

The shepherdess Felismena, seeing the knight in so great danger, and if she did not speedily help him that he could not escape with life, was not afraid to put hers in jeopardy by doing that which in such a case she thought she was bound to perform. Wherefore, putting a sharp-headed arrow into her bow, she said unto them:[3] "Keep out, knights. For it is not beseeming men[4] that make account of this name and honor to take advantage of their enemies with so great odds."

And aiming at the sight[5] of one of their helmets, she burst it with such force that the arrow, running into his eyes, came out of the other side of his head, so that he fell down dead to the ground.

When the distressed knight saw two of his enemies dead, he ran upon the third with such force as if he had but then begun the combat. But Felismena helped him out of that trouble by putting another arrow into her bow, the which, transpiercing his armor, she left under his left pap[6] and so justly[7] smote his heart that this knight also followed his two companions.

When the shepherds and the knight beheld what Felismena had done, and how at two shoots she had killed two such valiant knights, they were all in great wonder. The knight, therefore, taking off his helmet and coming unto her, said: "How am I able, fair shepherdess, to requite so great a benefit and good turn as I have received at thy hands

---

2 policy cunning   **3 them** i.e., the two knights still alive who are fighting against one knight   **4 beseeming men** fitting for men   **5 sight** slit in the helmet through which the wearer sees   **6 she left . . . pap** she lodged under his left breast   **7 justly** precisely

this day but by acknowledging this debt forever in my grateful mind?"

When Felismena beheld the knight's face and knew him, her senses were so troubled that, being in such a trance, she could scarce speak. But coming to herself again, she answered him: "Ah, my Don Felix, this is not the first debt wherein thou art bound unto me. And I cannot believe that thou wilt acknowledge this, as thou sayest, no more than thou hast done greater than this before.[8] Behold to what a time and end my fortune and thy forgetness hath brought me: that she that was wont to be served of thee in the city with tilt and tourneys[9] and honored with many other things whereby thou didst deceive me (or I suffered myself to be deceived) doth now wander up and down, exiled from her native country and liberty, for using thus thine own.[10] If this brings thee not into the knowledge of that which thou owest me, remember how one whole year I served thee as thy page in the Princess Caesarina's Court; and how I was a solicitor[11] against myself, without discovering[12] myself or my thoughts unto thee, but only to procure thy remedy[13] and to help the grief which thine made thee feel. How many times did I get thee favors from thy mistress Celia, to the great cost of my tears and griefs! All which account but small,[14] Don Felix, in respect of those dangers (had they been unsufficient) wherein I would have spent my life[15] for redress of thy pains which thy injurious love afforded thee.[16]

"And unless thou art weary of the great love that I have borne thee, consider and weigh with thyself the strange effects which the force of love hath caused me to pass.[17] I

---

8 I cannot . . . this before i.e., I cannot believe that you will continue to acknowledge this present debt of gratitude on your part (for my having saved your life), as you say you are going to, any more than you have acknowledged your previous and greater indebtednesses to me in the past **9 that she . . . tourneys** that she (i.e., myself, Felismena), whom you used to serve as faithful lover by defending my name in tilting and tournaments **10 for using thus thine own** i.e., for having presumed to exercise my liberty and freedom of choice in choosing you **11 solicitor** pleader, agent **12 discovering** revealing **13 thy remedy** the remedy for your lovesickness, i.e., the winning of Celia **14 All . . . small** all of which you should reckon of small account **15 dangers . . . my life** dangers, which, if they had been insufficient in themselves to ensure my death, I would have given my life anyway **16 for redress . . . thee** to remedy (by trying to win Celia for you) those pains which you suffered in love— even though that love of yours was so directly injurious to me **17 pass** suffer

went out of my native country and came to serve thee, to lament the ill that thou didst suffer, to take upon me the injuries and disgraces that I received therein. And to give thee any content,[18] I cared not to lead the most bitter and painful life that ever woman lived. In the habit of a tender and dainty lady I loved thee more than thou canst imagine, and in the habit of a base page I served thee (a thing more contrary to my rest[19] and reputation than I mean now to rehearse);[20] and yet now in the habit of a poor and simple shepherdess I came to do thee this small service. What remains, then, more for me to do but to sacrifice my life to thy loveless soul, if with the same yet I could give thee more content? And if in lieu thereof thou wouldst but remember how much I have loved and do yet love thee! Here hast thou thy sword in thy hand. Let none therefore but thyself revenge the offense that I have done thee."

When the knight heard Felismena's words and knew them all to be as true as he was disloyal, his heart by this strange and sudden accident recovered some force again to see what great injury he had done her, so that the thought thereof, and the plenteous effusion of blood that issued out of his wounds, made him like a dead man fall down in a swoon at fair Felismena's feet; who with great care and no less fear, laying his head in her lap, with showers of tears that rained from her eyes upon the knight's pale visage began thus to lament:

"What means this cruel Fortune? Is the period[21] of my life come just with the last end of my Don Felix his days? Ah, my Don Felix, the cause of all my pain, if the plenteous tears which for thy sake I have shed are not sufficient, and these which I now distill upon thy lovely cheeks too few to make thee come to thyself again, what remedy shall this miserable soul have to prevent that this bitter joy, by seeing thee, turn not into occasion of utter despair? Ah, my Don Felix, awake, my love, if thou dost but sleep or beest in a trance! Although I would not wonder if thou dost not, since never anything that I could do prevailed with thee to frame[22] my least content."

And in these and other lamentations was fair Felismena

---

18 to give . . . content so long as I contented you in any way   **19 rest** peace of mind   **20 rehearse** recite, tell   **21 period** end   **22 frame** contrive, bring about

plunged, whom the Portugal shepherdesses with their tears and poor supplies endeavored to encourage, when on the sudden they saw a fair nymph coming over the stony causey[23] that led the way into the island, with a golden bottle in one hand and a silver one in the other; whom Felismena, knowing by and by, said unto her:

"Ah, Doria, could any come at this time to succor me but thou, fair nymph? Come hither, then, and thou shalt see the cause of all my troubles, the substance of my sighs and the object of my thoughts, lying in the greatest danger of death that may be."

"In like occurrents,"[24] said Doria, "virtue and a good heart must take place. Recall it then, fair Felismena, and revive thy daunted spirits. Trouble not thyself any more, for now is the end of thy sorrows and the beginning of thy contentment come."

And speaking these words, she besprinkled his face with a certain odoriferous water which she brought in the silver bottle, whereby he came to his memory again. And then said unto him: "If thou wilt recover thy life, sir knight, and give it her that hath passed such an ill one for thy sake, drink of the water in this bottle."

The which Don Felix, taking in his hand, drunk a good draft and, resting upon it a little, found himself so whole of his wounds which the three knights had given him and of that which the love of Celia had made in his breast that now he felt the pain no more which either of them had caused in him than if he had never had them. And in this sort he began to rekindle the old love that he bare to Felismena, the which he thought was never more zealous than now. Whereupon sitting down upon the green grass, he took his lady and shepherdess by the hands and, kissing them many times, said thus unto her:

"How small account would I make of my life, my dearest Felismena, for[25] canceling that great bond wherein, with more than life, I am forever bound unto thee! For since I enjoy it by thy means, I think it no more than right to restore thee that which is thine own. With what eyes can I behold thy peerless beauty, which, though unadvisedly,[26] I

---

23 causey causeway   **24 In like occurrents** in situations of this sort   **25 for** in terms of   **26 unadvisedly** rashly, thoughtlessly

knew not to be such?[27] Yet how dare I, for that which I owe thee, cast them in any other part?[28] What words are sufficient to excuse the faults that I have committed against thy faith and firmest love and loyalty? Wretched and accursed forever shall I be, if thy condition[29] and clemency be not inclined to my favor and pardon! For no satisfaction can suffice for so great an offense, nor reason to excuse me for that which thou hast to forget[30] me. Truth it is that I loved Celia well and forgot thee, but not in such sort that thy wisdom and beauty did ever slide out of my mind.

"And the best[31] is that I know not wherein to put this fault that may be so justly attributed to me. For if I will impute it to the young age that I was then in, since I had it to love thee I should not have wanted it to have been firm in the faith that I owed thee. If to Celia's beauty, it is clear that thine did far excel hers and all the world's besides. If to the change of time, this should have been the touchstone which should have showed the force and virtue of my firmness. If to injurious and traitorous absence, it serves as little for my excuse, since the desire of seeing thee should not have been absent from supporting thy image in my memory.

"Behold, then, Felismena, what assured trust I put in thy goodness that, without any other means,[32] I dare put before thee the small reason thou hast to pardon me. But what shall I do to purchase pardon at thy gracious hands? Or after thou hast pardoned me, to believe that thou art satisfied? For one thing grieves me more than anything else in the world, and this it is: that though the love which thou hast borne me and wherewith thou dost yet bless me is an occasion, perhaps, to make thee forgive me and forget so many faults, yet I shall never lift up mine eyes to behold thee but that every injury which I have done thee will be worse than a mortal incision in my guilty heart."

The shepherdess Felismena, who saw Don Felix so penitent for his past misdeeds and so affectionately returned to his first thoughts, with many tears told him that she did pardon him, because the love that she had ever borne him

---

27 such i.e., peerless **28 cast . . . part** i.e., assign them any value less than peerless **29 condition** nature, character **30 forget** (as in "forget and forgive") **31 best** most important thing **32 other means** i.e., other means of hoping for forgiveness than your goodness, your generosity in forgiving

would suffer her to do no less; which if she had not thought to do, she would never have taken so great pains and so many weary journeys to seek him out; and many other things, wherewith Don Felix was confirmed in his former love.

Whereupon the fair nymph Doria came then to the knight, and after many loving words and courteous offers in the lady Felicia's behalf passed between them, she requested him and fair Felismena to go with her to Diana's Temple, where the sage lady,[33] with great desire to see them, was attending their coming. Don Felix agreed thereunto. And taking their leave of the Portugal shepherdesses (who wondered not a little to see what had happened) and of the woeful shepherd Danteus, mounting upon the horses of the dead knights that were slain in the late combat, they went on their way.

And as they were going, Felismena told Don Felix with great joy what she had passed since she had last seen him. . . . And Don Felix wondered not a little to understand how his lady Felismena had served him so many days as his page, and that he was so far gone out of his wits and memory that he knew her not all that while. And his joy on the other side, to see that his lady loved him so well, was so great that by no means he could hide it.

Thus therefore riding on their way they came to Diana's Temple, where the sage Felicia was looking for their coming, and likewise the shepherd Arsileus, and Belisa, Sylvanus, and Selvagia, who were now come thither not many days before. They were welcomed on every side and with great joy entertained, but fair Felismena especially, who for her rare virtues and singular beauty was greatly honored of them all. There they were all married with great joy, feasts, and triumphs, which were made by all the goodly nymphs and by the sage and noble lady Felicia.

Text based on *Diana of George of Montemayor. Translated out of Spanish into English by Bartholomew Yonge of the Middle Temple, Gentleman. At London, Printed by Edm. Bollifant, Impensis G.B. 1598.*

33 the sage lady i.e., Felicia

Further Reading

Berry, Ralph. "Love and Friendship." *Shakespeare's Comedies: Explorations in Form*. Princeton, N.J.: Princeton Univ. Press, 1972. *The Two Gentlemen*, writes Berry, purposefully turns the conventions of romance into comedy, allowing the "fantastic code of conventional behavior" to reveal its "inner contradictions." Women, Berry argues, are the "center of sanity" in this play where male action too often is self-absorbed and self-deceived.

Brooks, Harold F. "Two Clowns in a Comedy (to Say Nothing of the Dog): Speed, Launce (and Crab) in *The Two Gentlemen of Verona*." *English Association Essays and Studies* n.s. 16 (1963): 91–100. Brooks focuses on Shakespeare's use of the clowns (and dog) as comic foils that extend and clarify the action of the play. Lance, in particular, in his burlesque of the themes of friendship and love, is carefully integrated into the structure of the play, enforcing our sense of *The Two Gentlemen* as a drama of education in and through love.

Champion, Larry S. *The Evolution of Shakespeare's Comedy: A Study in Dramatic Perspective*, pp. 25–38. Cambridge: Harvard Univ. Press, 1970. *The Two Gentlemen of Verona* is an experimental play focusing on plot rather than on credible actions and motivations. Champion examines the ways in which plot, character, and rhetoric control the audience's perspective, insuring that it not respond "sentimentally to what Shakespeare would have us laugh at."

Charlton, H. B. "Romanticism in Shakespearian Comedy." *Shakespearian Comedy*, 1938. Rpt. New York: Barnes and Noble, 1966. Charlton sees *The Two Gentlemen of Verona* as a failed attempt to adapt the world of courtly romance to the service of comedy: the romantic heroes are as ridiculous and foolish as clowns. Charlton's conclusion is often quoted by those who find the synthesis of romance and drama in *The Two Gentlemen* unsatisfying: "Shakespeare's first attempt to create romantic comedy had only succeeded so far that it had unexpectedly and inadvertently made romance comic."

Evans, Bertrand. *Shakespeare's Comedies*, pp. 9–19. Oxford: Clarendon Press, 1960. Evans finds the comic effects in *The Two Gentlemen of Verona* determined by a sophisticated handling of discrepancies between different characters' and the audience's understanding of the action. As in other romantic comedies, the heroines and clown occupy a privileged position of awareness, just below that of the audience itself. The scheming Proteus believes himself fully aware, but the gap between his understanding and ours renders him harmless and subject to humiliation.

Ewbank, Inga-Stina. " 'Were Man but Constant, He Were Perfect': Constancy and Consistency in *The Two Gentlemen of Verona*." In *Shakespearian Comedy*, ed. Malcolm Bradbury and David Palmer. Stratford-upon-Avon Studies 14. London: Edward Arnold; New York: Crane, Russak, 1972. Ewbank holds that though the play is not entirely successful it nonetheless represents an effort to be "truthful to troubled, complex human relationships." In the play's insistently conventionalized language and behavior she finds the source of "many of the play's inconsistencies but also much of its sense of life."

Johnson, Samuel. *"Two Gentlemen of Verona." Johnson on Shakespeare*, ed. Arthur Sherbo. *The Yale Edition of the Works of Samuel Johnson*, vol. 7. New Haven and London: Yale Univ. Press, 1968. Johnson discovers in *The Two Gentlemen* "a strange mixture of knowledge and ignorance, of care and negligence." He praises the "eminently beautiful" lines and passages the play abounds in but finds troubling its dramatic inconsistencies and confusions. Nonetheless, he deems the play unquestionably Shakespeare's, for it is more credible that Shakespeare "might sometimes sink below his highest than that any other should rise up to his lowest."

Leggatt, Alexander. *"The Two Gentlemen of Verona." Shakespeare's Comedy of Love*. New York: Barnes and Noble, 1974. Leggatt argues that *The Two Gentlemen* is "cool, reticent, and somewhat rueful," never offering an unequivocal assertion of the value of love. Through different styles and shifts of perspective, love is "distanced and exposed," though no other values are offered in its place. In the comic conclusion "there is the technical satisfaction of seeing a dance pattern completed," but something more restrained and fragile than the joyful endings of the romantic comedies.

Lindenbaum, Peter. "Education in *The Two Gentlemen of Verona.*" *Studies in English Literature* 15 (1975): 229–244. Lindenbaum sees that the comedy depends upon characters shifting their notion of true nobility from a superficial idea of courtly grace to a more profound sense of moral renewal. The education that the characters undergo serves "as the central structure" of the play and is also its "legacy to Shakespeare's later comedies."

Nevo, Ruth. *"The Two Gentlemen of Verona." Comic Transformations in Shakespeare.* London and New York: Methuen, 1980. Though Nevo finds that the play moves only to the "threshold" of the achievement of the later comedies, it does reveal their major concerns and strategies. The play "examines the remedial and beneficent power of the ladies' love, and the uncertain, image-dependent, wavering volatile nature of the gentlemen's."

Rossky, William. *"The Two Gentlemen of Verona* as Burlesque." *English Literary Renaissance* 12 (1982): 210–219. Concerned with establishing the tone of the play, Rossky examines the theme of friendship as developed in the play's sources and analogues, and in Shakespeare's other works, and shows "how ridiculous Valentine's adherence to a false code is, even in Elizabethan terms."

Slights, Camille Wells. *"The Two Gentlemen of Verona* and the Courtesy Book Tradition." *Shakespeare Studies* 16 (1983): 13–31. Slights sees the play as "a comic exploration of the nature and function of a gentleman." Valentine's and Proteus's perversion of courtly styles and ideals hints that the emulation inherent in such behavior threatens "social coherence and cohesion," but the ending reveals that happiness is possible when the desire for excellence is combined with a "realistic understanding of human imperfection . . . and respect for other people."

Weimann, Robert. "Laughing with the Audience: *The Two Gentlemen of Verona* and the Popular Tradition of Comedy." *Shakespeare Survey* 22 (1969): 35–42. Weimann examines the play's comic structure in relation to the social structure of the Elizabethan popular theater. The comic actors in *The Two Gentlemen* play *with*, not just *at*, the audience, and the resulting unity of mirth between audience and actor creates a comic perspective that permits a criticism of the play's aristocratic themes of friendship and courtly love.

From the 1970 New York Shakespeare Festival production of *Henry VI, Part One*, with (l. to r.)
Paul Sparer as Richard Plantagenet, Dan Darning as a priest, Nicholas Kepros as King
Henry VI, and (kneeling) Ronny Cox as Vernon, directed by Stuart Vaughan
at the Delacorte Theater in Central Park.

HENRY VI
PARTS ONE, TWO, AND THREE

—HENRY VI—
PARTS ONE, TWO,
AND THREE

Foreword

The three parts of *Henry VI* are interesting for their history alone; Shakespeare wrote them before he wrote the *Henry IV* plays, which precede them chronologically. And so there's an intriguing contrast between the history *in* the plays and the history *of* the plays. Once you've started reading these plays, it's hard to put them down, because you get caught up in the whole sequence of English history that leads up to Richard III and ends with the beginning of the Tudor dynasty after him.

There's a lot of historical meat in these plays, and I'd be curious to do them all, one after the other, in their proper sequence, just to follow the development of the kings and other characters, the squabblings and usurpations, and the various factions. In what other plays besides Shakespeare's can you find history treated in such an interesting way?

As I think back over these three plays in particular, what I recall are the lovely little touches scattered throughout them—specific scenes, or stage directions, or speeches, or characters. The first scene that comes to mind, one of the most moving in the trilogy, is the death of the noble English hero Talbot in Part One. Throughout the play Shakespeare has portrayed him as brave, valiant, and unstoppable against the French—such a remarkable figure that he wins praise even from his French enemies. In a sense, the whole play builds remorselessly toward his downfall in Act 4, scene 7, where, wounded in battle, he dies with his young son dead in his arms. Knowing he is dying, he bids farewell to the soldiers gathered around him, saying, "Come, come, and lay him in his father's arms. / My spirit can no longer bear these harms. / Soldiers, adieu! I have what I would have, / Now my old arms are young John Talbot's grave." It's an incredibly moving moment.

I've always found Shakespeare's treatment of Joan of Arc, or Joan la Pucelle as he calls her, to be very interesting. He completely abandons fairness in his portrait of her, unabashedly taking the English side. Though history knows her as a shining heroine who was a scourge to the English and later a saint, this play shows her to be a whore, sharp-tongued and ambitious, a shrew who doesn't inspire a jot of sympathy in the audience. Her character tells us more about Shakespeare's interest in catering to English patriotism than it does about who she actually was, but that's precisely what's fascinating about it.

There is another strong-willed Frenchwoman in the *Henry VI* plays—Margaret of Anjou, who enters the story at the end of Part One, when she becomes the wife of King Henry VI. She quickly establishes herself as a force to be reckoned with, and through the rest of the sequence we see her relentlessly building up her role as the power behind the weak-willed Henry, who is totally incapable of dealing with the infighting of the English nobles.

Margaret has a great scene in Part Three, Act 1, scene 4, where she confronts the captured Duke of York, a claimant to the throne, and utterly humiliates him. She sits him on a small mound, puts a paper crown on his head, and waves a handkerchief dipped in the blood of his slaughtered young son in his face. It's a powerful piece of writing and a heart-wrenching scene when played on the stage, as the defeated and sorrowful York suffers Margaret's cruel taunts:

> Look, York, I stained this napkin with the blood
> That valiant Clifford, with his rapier's point,
> Made issue from the bosom of the boy;
> And if thine eyes can water for his death,
> I give thee this to dry thy cheeks withal.
> Alas, poor York, but that I hate thee deadly,
> I should lament thy miserable state.

As usual, Shakespeare doesn't neglect the ordinary people, no matter how many kings and princes are in the play. This leads to a marvelous scene in Part Three (2.5) where the stage directions say *"Enter a Son that hath killed his father, at one door,"* and then *"Enter at another door a Father that hath killed his son."* What's terrible in this scene is that neither the father nor the son knows who it is he's killed—until it's too late. The father says, "But let me see. Is this our foeman's face? / Ah, no, no, no, it is mine only son! / Ah, boy, if any life be left in thee, / Throw up thine eye!" Shakespeare is illustrating the enormous price of civil war, which pits members of the same family against each other. It's an unbearably sad scene, and unforgettable.

And finally, one of the greatest characters in all of Shakespeare—in all of English history, for that matter—

makes his diabolical entrance in Part Three: Richard, Duke of Gloucester, who will take over the stage in the next play as Richard III. Very few people know that he appears at the end of the *Henry VI* sequence, but he's worth looking at. He is depicted at first as a fierce fighter, but Shakespeare also gives a few clues about what this schemer has in store for us.

Though Richard has several good speeches in the play, my favorite is the one he makes at the end of Part Three as he is stabbing King Henry VI to death: "Down, down to hell," he cries, "and say I sent thee thither, / [*Stabs him again*] I, that have neither pity, love, nor fear." He goes on to describe his monstrous birth—feet first, and with teeth—and his hunchback. He reasons, with words that are heavy with omen, "Then, since the heavens have shaped my body so, / Let hell make crook'd my mind to answer it."

And he concludes with a warning to all those who may stand between him and the crown of England, beginning with his brother Clarence, "I am myself alone. / Clarence, beware. Thou keep'st me from the light. . . . Clarence, thy turn is next, and then the rest, / Counting myself but bad till I be best." It's a marvelous speech, and looks straight ahead to the plots and schemings this hunchbacked duke will carry out in the play that bears his name.

JOSEPH PAPP

JOSEPH PAPP GRATEFULLY ACKNOWLEDGES THE HELP OF
ELIZABETH KIRKLAND IN PREPARING THIS FOREWORD.

The *Henry VI* Plays

Among Shakespeare's ten plays on English history, the best known are the four plays (c. 1595–1599) from *Richard II* through *1* and *2 Henry IV* to *Henry V*, in which Shakespeare follows the maturation and career of Prince Hal, the future Henry V. This sequence of four plays was actually Shakespeare's second such sequence, for he had begun, in the years from about 1589 to 1594, to write on English history with three plays on the reign of Henry VI and a fourth on the reign of Richard III. Together these four plays told the agonizing and eventually triumphant story of England's civil wars in the fifteenth century, concluding at last in 1485 with the victory of Henry Tudor over Richard III at Bosworth Field. Henry Tudor, thereupon King Henry VII, was to become Henry VIII's father and Queen Elizabeth I's grandfather. These four plays thus dramatized a conflict in which England's very identity as a nation, having been tested in extremity, was restored by the Tudor dynasty that was still in power when Shakespeare wrote. The political relevance of such an account to Elizabethan spectators must have added greatly to their pleasure in the spectacle of sieges, confrontations, and bloodshed. There is good evidence that Shakespeare's first historical plays, though seldom read or seen today, were very popular in his own time.

Together, the three plays about the reign of Henry VI offer a paradigm of civil conflict. (*Richard III*, though last in the series, takes place after the actual civil wars have ceased.) Shakespeare is deeply interested in the causes and evolution of civil war. His villains are, especially at first, not the lower classes but the aristocrats of England bickering among themselves. Because Henry V has died an untimely death in 1422, leaving an infant son on the throne and a disputed claim originating in Henry IV's seizure of the throne from Richard II, a struggle for power is inevitable. Shakespeare depicts Humphrey, Duke of Gloucester, one of young Henry's uncles, as virtuous in his attempts to serve as Protector, but unable to cope with Henry Beaufort, Bishop of Winchester and later Cardinal, a great-uncle of the King. Though barred by his illegitimate birth from claiming the crown for himself, Winchester is ready to foment all the strife he can in an effort to gain political control of the kingdom. The Duke of Somerset joins in a conspiracy to get rid of Gloucester so that the ambitions of the various challengers will be unchecked by the one remaining proponent of honest government. The most dangerous intriguer is Richard Plantagenet, later Duke of York, whose claim to the English throne goes back to Edward III through two grandfathers, Edmund Langley, Duke of York, and Lionel, Duke of Clarence, and is arguably stronger than that of King Henry VI. Richard is the scion of the Yorkist claim, soon to challenge that of the Lancastrian King Henry (so named for his title derived from his grandfather, John of Gaunt, Duke of Lancaster).

Faction of this sort naturally leads to divided authority on the battlefield. The English quickly begin to lose their territories in France, owing in part to the baleful rise of a (as the English see her) witch, Joan of Arc, who dons man's warlike attire and dominates the effete French aristocrats whom she seduces one by one. Still, the main cause of the English failure in France is division at home, and its chief victim is the valiant Lord Talbot, betrayed by lack of English reinforcement at Bordeaux. His death, in company with his son, signals the end of English ascendancy in France. When the Earl of Suffolk cynically negotiates an end to hostilities in terms outrageously favorable to the French and especially to Margaret of Anjou, with whom Suffolk has fallen in love, the capitulation is complete. Margaret is brought back to England, where she will dominate her new husband, King Henry, much as Joan of Arc dominated her French lovers, and where Suffolk can have his adulterous way with her. This yielding to the enervation of erotic passion is symptomatic of the decline into which England continues to plunge.

Once the aristocrats of England have succeeded in betraying their nation by their self-interested grasping, the commoners are not slow to emulate the factionalism of their social betters. *2 Henry VI* gives a significantly increased role to commoners, who turn against one another (1.3), promote themselves through sham miracles (2.1), buzz with restive anger at the suspicious death of their beloved Duke of Gloucester (3.2), and take justice into their own hands by seizing and summarily executing the hated Duke of Suffolk (4.1). These protestations and acts are at least directed against aristocratic villains, but the precedent of popular unrest is an unnerving one, and it soon erupts into a full-scale, if abortive, popular rebellion (4.2–10). Jack Cade and his cohorts ape political ambition in such a way as to render it mordantly amusing, but the Cade rebellion also dismays and threatens those who cling to a hope of public calm. Not the least threatening aspect of this rebellion is that it has been secretly fomented by Richard of York, who sees anarchy as a way to bring down established authority and thereby clear the way for his challenge. He is right, and by the end of this play the country is divided into two warring camps.

Richard of York dies in *3 Henry VI*, in a bloody and revengeful ritual slaughter on the battlefield, but he is succeeded like a many-headed Hydra by his three sons, Edward, Clarence, and Richard of Gloucester. The Yorkist side ultimately achieves victory, after much uncertain shifting back and forth in the fortunes of war, and yet victory is achieved at a terrible cost to England. The struggle has become a feud in which a Yorkist must pay for the blood of a Lancastrian, son for son, brother for brother, until there are few survivors. The conflict is all the more horrible in view of the fact that the two sides are closely bound by the ties of kinship. Emblematically, on the field of battle a father discovers he has killed his own son, while another son discovers he has killed his father. In the family of the new King Edward IV, as well, brother turns against brother: Clarence, offended by his brother's surrender to women (so reminiscent of Henry VI before him), changes sides more than once.

The only person to profit from all this division is Richard of Gloucester, the youngest of the three Yorkist brothers, whose plan is to cut his way to the throne by whatever murder and deception will prove necessary. Richard is the genius of faction and discord, the perfect embodiment and product of the long and enervating wars now drawing to a close. The final scenes of *3 Henry VI*, though offering a seeming hope of peace, are devastated by the contrary perception that Richard is only biding his time until he can seize power. His murder of Henry VI in the Tower of London (5.6) is only a promise of what will follow.

The *Henry VI* Plays
in Performance

Although Shakespeare's *Henry VI* plays are seldom read
and seldom staged, they contain individual scenes that have
struck the imaginations of theater managers over the centuries: in Part One, Lord Talbot's encounters with the
Countess of Auvergne and Joan of Arc, and the deaths of
Talbot and his son; in Part Two, the public penance of the
Duchess of Gloucester, the murder of Humphrey, Duke of
Gloucester, and the instructive end of the Cardinal of Winchester; in Part Three, the killing of the young Rutland, and
King Henry's witnessing of a son who has killed his father
and of a father who has killed his son. Artists too have
found these scenes irresistible, as seen for example in the
fifteen paintings of episodes from the plays that appear in
John Boydell's nineteenth-century collection of illustra-
tions from Shakespeare. Almost all these scenes are of
tragic high emotion.

Prior to the twentieth century especially, on those infre-
quent occasions when theater managers have deigned to
consider the *Henry VI* plays at all, they have been tempted
to put together a medley of such scenes, omitting intervening material or indulging in wholesale rewriting. More
often than not, the selection of scenes has been politically motivated as well. The earliest known revivals or,
more properly, adaptations, John Crowne's two parts of
Henry VI, acted at the Dorset Garden Theatre in 1680 and in
1681, are a case in point. Crowne's first part, "with the
murder of Humphrey, Duke of Gloucester," really centers
on the first three acts of Shakespeare's Part Two, including
the conspiracy against Duke Humphrey and his Duchess's
fatal trafficking in witchcraft. Crowne makes of this material a diatribe against the Catholic Church, with the Cardinal of Winchester as his chief villain, obviously in reference
to the then current controversy over the exclusion of the
Catholic Duke of York, Charles II's brother, from the English throne. The plotting against the good Duke Humphrey
is plainly reminiscent of the infamous Popish Plot of 1678.

At the play's end, the Cardinal dies a horrible, ranting death, visited by the ghost of his noble victim. Like many Englishmen of his time, Crowne tempered his loyalty to Charles II with a strong objection to his brother James's open Catholicism, and said so in this play. It ran into difficulties with the censor and was eventually suppressed.

The title of Crowne's second part, *The Misery of Civil War*, again suggests the kind of didactic analogy to England's current political troubles that Restoration audiences discovered in a number of Shakespeare's plays. Crowne mixes together scenes from Shakespeare's Part Two and Part Three, especially the Cade rebellion, the killing of little Rutland (preceded by a touching scene of farewell between Rutland and his father York), and Edward IV's problems with women. The King's amorous adventures (not unlike those of Charles II) are augmented by the introduction of Lady Elianor Butler, one of Edward's mistresses, and Edward's extensive wooing of Lady Elizabeth Grey. The action and even the scenery magnify the horrors of civil war: in one battle sequence, "the scene is drawn, and there appears houses and towns burning, men and women hanged upon trees, and children on the tops of pikes." King Henry VI, though a weak ruler, is made prophetically wise in his hatred of rebellion and his certain faith that God will eventually punish all those who promote anarchy. Explicit parallels to England's own civil wars of the seventeenth century constitute a warning against mob rule, extremism of the religious left as well as the religious right, and conspiracy.

Throughout the eighteenth century and much of the nineteenth, Shakespeare's *Henry VI* plays continued to be dissected in this manner and employed either as political analogy or as part of some larger theatrical enterprise. Ambrose Philips's *Humfrey, Duke of Gloucester*, acted at the Theatre Royal, Drury Lane, in 1723 and based, like Crowne's first part, on the tragic stories of Duke Humphrey and his Duchess, took even greater liberties than did Crowne. In a text that preserved few of Shakespeare's lines, Philips represented the Duchess as an innocent victim of Queen Margaret, Suffolk, and the Cardinal, thereby eliminating any ambiguity in the didactic contrast between right and wrong—that is, sturdy English national self-interest versus Catholic meddling. Humfrey (or Humphrey, played by Barton Booth) was a saintly martyr, while the Cardinal (played by Colley Cibber) was a melodramatic villain. Theophilus Cibber's adaptation of 1723 included Crowne's touching scene of the Duke of York's farewell to his young son Rutland and went on to provide new love interest, especially that of the young Prince Edward for Warwick's daughter, the Lady Anne.

The one exception to the pattern of redaction was a performance of Shakespeare's *1 Henry VI* with Dennis Delane as Talbot, Anthony Ryan as Henry, and Anne Hallam as Joan, at the Theatre Royal, Covent Garden, in 1738. The play, "not acted these fifty years," according to the playbill, was produced "at the desire of several ladies of quality," members of The Shakespeare Club that some fashionable women of Covent Garden had formed in 1737 to promote the production of Shakespeare's plays. The experiment with the restored Shakespearean text, however, was not soon repeated, and the *Henry VI* plays continued to appear only in cut and adapted form. Edmund Kean's production of *Richard Duke of York* (Drury Lane, 1817, in a version usually attributed to John Herman Merivale) blended material from all three *Henry VI* plays, all heavily cut and interspersed with passages from George Chapman, John Webster, and John Marston. Portions of Shakespeare's Part Three, especially the murder of Henry VI in the Tower by Richard of Gloucester and the coronation of Edward IV, were detached from their original to turn up in Colley Cibber's long-playing *Richard III*.

Not until 1864, at the Surrey Theatre in Lambeth, do we hear of a revival of Shakespeare's Part Two in something like its original form. The *Athenaeum* was delighted with James Anderson's decision to produce it, "particularly as it acts very well, and manifestly excites interest in the audience." Stratford-upon-Avon saw *1 Henry VI* lavishly directed by Osmond Tearle in 1889 (in what was claimed to be the first performance of the play since Shakespeare's time). The year 1899 witnessed Frank Benson's version of *2 Henry VI*. Benson played a tortured Beaufort, his wife, Constance, appeared as Margaret, and Oscar Asche was a truculent Jack Cade. This costly production was revived in 1901 as part of a cycle of six histories, popularly known as "the Week of Kings." In early May of 1906 Benson produced the three *Henry VI* plays on successive nights. Benson was praised for his boldness in mounting the trilogy, though the *Athenaeum* complained, "Many may have wished to see less scenery and more Shakespeare." Benson revived *2 Henry VI* in 1909. Thereafter the plays did not again appear at Stratford-upon-Avon until 1963 in Peter Hall's direction of an adaptation by John Barton. Barton edited Shakespeare's three plays into two, *Henry VI* and *Edward IV*, to form—along with Shakespeare's *Richard III*—a sequence called *The Wars of the Roses*. Set on a bare stage with massive metallic walls, the plays revealed with impressive clarity the grim, retributive action of fifteenth-century England's long agony of civil war.

During the hiatus at Stratford-upon-Avon between Benson's revivals and Barton's adaptation, other theaters continued to show new interest in these forgotten plays. In London, at the Old Vic in 1923, Robert Atkins used a simple set and swift pacing to present the plays in a two-part conflation. Under the management of Barry Jackson, the Birmingham Repertory Theatre produced *2 Henry VI* in 1951, and *3 Henry VI* and then *1 Henry VI* in the two subsequent years. With only minimal cuts in the text, Douglas Seale's direction revealed how "eminently actable," in Jackson's phrase, the plays are. All three productions were revived at the Old Vic in 1953, and four years later Seale was invited back to that theater to direct the plays in the final year of the Old Vic's five-year plan to produce all of the plays of the First Folio. This time Seale made more extensive cuts to reduce the material of the three plays to two, the first a conflation of *1* and *2 Henry VI* (eliminating both Talbot and Joan from Part One) and the second a virtually complete version of *3 Henry VI*. To emphasize the trilogy's links to Shakespeare's other histories, the epilogue of *Henry V* was spoken in the funeral scene that opens Part One, and at the end of Part Three, as all departed after Edward's coronation, a grimly determined Gloucester limped toward the vacant throne and began the opening soliloquy of *Richard III*, his words, however, drowned out by the exuberant celebration offstage.

Productions of the *Henry VI* plays in recent years have been undertaken almost exclusively by theaters and festivals committed to performing the entire canon, as though they were Shakespearean curiosities unworthy of consideration in their own right, and yet several of those productions have been both successful and artistically rewarding. The Oregon Shakespeare Festival at Ashland, Oregon, has thrice performed the three parts of *Henry VI* in successive years, in the 1950s, 1960s, and 1970s, in intelligent, vigorous productions. In 1970 Stuart Vaughan directed a two-part version of the *Henry VI* plays for the New York Shakespeare Festival that made excellent use of Ming Cho Lee's multilevel platform set. Terry Hands brilliantly directed the trilogy for the Royal Shakespeare Company at Stratford-upon-Avon in 1977. Alan Howard as King Henry grew increasingly aware, even though he was incapable of resisting it, of the sinister political farce playing itself out. Hands's success in presenting the three plays uncut did not, however, discourage renewed tampering with Shakespeare's texts. As directed by Pam Brighton at Stratford, Ontario, in 1980, the three plays were conflated into a single drama focusing on the political machinations of the English court; and even the 1983 BBC television productions, thoughtfully directed by Jane Howell, have suffered the ignominious fate (in parts of the United States at least) of being shown in the late evening over a six-week period, one half a play at a clip, as though they were episodes of *Poldark* or *The Pallisers*.

For all their uneven and often ignoble treatment in stage history, Shakespeare's *Henry VI* plays were among his greatest early successes. *1 Henry VI* was acted fourteen times in 1592 alone, and *2* and *3 Henry VI* were "sundry times acted" by Pembroke's men before 1600. Thomas Nashe, in his *Pierce Penniless* (1592), considers how it would have "joyed brave Talbot, the terror of the French, to think that after he had lain two hundred years in his tomb he should triumph again on the stage, and have his bones new enbalmed with the tears of ten thousand spectators at least, at several times, who in that tragedian that represents his person imagine they behold him fresh bleeding." Nashe's description suggests that the tragic fate of Talbot was the emotional high point of Part One. The titles of the early quarto of Part Two and octavo of Part Three offer similar evidence as to what interested spectators in those plays:

Part Two is called *The First Part of the Contention Betwixt the Two Famous Houses of York and Lancaster, with the Death of the Good Duke Humphrey, and the Banishment and Death of the Duke of Suffolk, and the Tragical End of the Proud Cardinal of Winchester, with the Notable Rebellion of Jack Cade, and the Duke of York's First Claim unto the Crown;* while Part Three is called *The True Tragedy of Richard Duke of York, and the Death of Good King Henry the Sixth, with the Whole Contention Between the Two Houses Lancaster and York.* Actor-managers of the eighteenth and nineteenth centuries were not misguided in their perception that the plays were structured around emotionally powerful scenes, however much they were misled by that perception to dismantle and reassemble them into new plays.

Certainly the actor-managers' mistrust of so much material contained in these plays overlooks the plays' original success and their stageworthiness. Shakespeare designed these plays for the theater. When first produced in the late 1580s and early 1590s, they must have tested to the limit the physical capabilities of the theater building or buildings in which they were staged. *1 Henry VI* makes spectacular vertical demands. Salisbury and others, entering *"on the turrets"* (some upper acting area) in Act 1, scene 4, are blown to bits by French cannon, probably fired offstage. Joan of Arc and her cohorts *"enter the town"* of Orleans in Act 1, scene 5, presumably by breaching the doors onstage leading into the tiring-house, the backstage area of the Elizabethan theater, and then are routed by the English *"with scaling ladders"* set against the back wall of the theater, allowing the English soldiers to climb up to the gallery above the stage. Moments later the French, in undignified retreat, *"leap over the walls in their shirts,"* that is, jump down half-dressed from the gallery onto the main stage. Later, at Rouen (3.2), Joan talks her way through the city gates (i.e., stage doors) disguised as a peasant and appears *"on the top,"* high in the theater, brandishing a signal of attack to her associates at the gate.

In Part Two, similarly, the Duchess of Gloucester watches from aloft, from the gallery (1.4), as the witch Margery Jourdain and two priests summon a spirit by means of a trapdoor to pronounce dire prophecies amid terrible thunder

and lightning. Part Three features appearances on the walls
of York (4.7) and the Tower of London (5.6), where Henry VI
is murdered.

It is as though the young Shakespeare wanted to try out
every physical dimension of his theater in order to dramatize the imaginative landscape of civil war on as all-
encompassing a pictorial scale as possible. His scenes are
full of emblematic effects that lend theatrical power to the
emotional high points of the story. Contending noblemen
and lawyers choose up sides in *1 Henry VI* by alternately
plucking white and red roses in the Temple Garden (2.4).
Lord Talbot, entertained by the Countess of Auvergne in
Act 2, scene 3, makes the point that he is "but shadow of
himself" and that he merely represents in a kind of image
or figure the many thousands of troops at his call; he and
the Duchess are suggestive of Mars and Venus, the warrior
and the fair lady. Talbot's confrontations with Joan of Arc
also suggest a pairing of symbolic figures, one a mighty
warrior, the other a witch dressed in man's attire. Cade's
rebellion in Part Two is an elaborate and profane parody of
the struggle for power more somberly visualized in other
parts of these plays. In Part Three the sad encounter of a
son that has killed his father and a father that has killed his
son (2.5) is witnessed by King Henry, sitting on a symbolic
molehill while he ponders the vanity of human striving and
his own longing for rustic solitude. These are potent theatrical moments, highly visual in their impact, and it may be
that the plays' eclipse over the centuries owes something to
the fact that so many theater managers (until recently, at
least) lost touch with the theatrical conventions in which
these plays were conceived.

HENRY VI
PART ONE

Introduction

Throughout much of the fifteenth century, England had suffered the ravages of civil war. From the long struggles between the Lancastrians and the Yorkists, the so-called Wars of the Roses, the country had emerged in 1485 shaken but united at last under the strong rule of the Tudors. To Elizabethans, this period of civil war was a still-recent event that had tested and almost destroyed England's nationhood. They were, moreover, still troubled by political and dynastic uncertainties of their own. Queen Elizabeth, granddaughter of the first Tudor king, Henry VII, was unmarried and aging, her successor unchosen. Her Catholic enemies at home and abroad plotted a return to the ancient faith renounced by Henry VIII in his reformation of the church. Spain had attempted an invasion of England with the great Armada in 1588, perhaps one year before Shakespeare began writing his *Henry VI* plays. It was in such an era of crisis and patriotic excitement that the *Henry VI* plays first appeared. Indeed, they helped to establish the vogue of the English history play, which was to flourish throughout the 1590s. England's civil wars could be studied and analyzed now, from a perspective of over one hundred years later, and perhaps could provide a key to the present time. At hand was a new edition of Raphael Holinshed's *Chronicles*, 1587, along with the earlier chronicle writings of Robert Fabyan, John Stow, and Richard Grafton, as well as Edward Hall's *Union of the Two Noble and Illustre Families of Lancaster and York*, John Foxe's *Acts and Monuments of Martyrs*, and *A Mirror for Magistrates*.

How had these wars begun? Elizabethan Englishmen searched for an answer not in economic or social terms, but in religious and moral ones. According to a traditional and government-sponsored explanation, reflected to a large extent (though with many contradictions) in the chronicles of Edward Hall and familiar to Shakespeare whether he accepted it fully or not, the Wars of the Roses were a manifestation of God's wrath, a divine punishment inflicted on the English people for their wayward behavior. The people and their rulers had brought civil war on themselves by self-serving ambition, arrogance, and disloyalty. King Henry VI's grandfather, Henry IV, had come to the throne in 1399 by deposing and then executing his own cousin Richard II (a momentous event to be portrayed by Shakespeare in a later history play). Henry VI was himself an infant when he succeeded to the throne in 1422, owing to the untimely death of his father Henry V. Too young at first to rule, and never blessed with his father's ability to act decisively, Henry VI was utterly unable to halt the struggle for power that developed among members of his large but discordant family. Ultimately, his very title to the throne was challenged by his kinsman Richard Plantagenet, Duke of York, who claimed to be rightful king by virtue of his descent from Henry IV's uncle Lionel, Duke of Clarence. The Yorkist faction marched to battle against Henry VI's Lancastrian faction (so named because for generations the family had been possessors of the dukedom of Lancaster), and the war was on.

This official view was never wholly endorsed by the chroniclers, and certainly not by Shakespeare. Edward Hall's overall scheme is undeniably providential, and yet as a historian he presents a multiplicity of detail that cumulatively raises difficult issues of interpretation. At the same time, the providential view served the purposes of the Tudor state, and as such it gave widespread currency to the theory of God's anger toward a rebellious people. The outcome of the war seemed to confirm this pattern: universal devastation and the deaths of those most responsible for the conflict led eventually, according to the theory, to appeasement of God's anger and a restoration of order. Richard Plantagenet died in the struggle, as did Henry VI, Henry's son Edward, and much of the English nobility. Richard's son Edward survived to become Edward IV; but his manner of obtaining the throne was so manifestly offensive to Providence that (according to the theory) he suffered a retributive death at the hands of an angry God and was succeeded by his younger brother, Richard III. This last Yorkist ruler governed only two years, 1483–1485, and it was through Richard's insane vengeance that God finally settled all his scores against the wayward English people. Having completed this purgation, God chose as his instrument of a new order Henry Tudor, Earl of Richmond,

Henry VII. Although Henry's return to England and defeat of Richard at the battle of Bosworth Field might outwardly resemble Henry IV's seizure of power from Richard II, the difference was crucial to Tudor apologists. Richard III had to be seen, from the Tudor point of view, not as a flawed legitimate monarch but as a mad usurper and tyrant; his defeat was not the disobedient act of one man but a rising up of the entire English nation at the prompting of divine command. Henry VII's accession to power was officially viewed not as a precedent for further rebellion but as a manifestation of divine will without parallel in human history.

The essence of this providential view of events was that divine retribution and eventual reconciliation revealed themselves in the history of the war. The theory of course served the interests of the Tudor state and was in part a propaganda weapon calculatedly employed by the ruling class. Shakespeare's commitment to it should not be taken for granted, and indeed a number of recent studies have expressed a profound skepticism toward the theory as the basis of Shakespeare's dramaturgy. Especially in his later tetralogy, or four-play series, from *Richard II* to *Henry V,* Shakespeare reveals considerably more interest in the clash of personalities than in patterns of divine retribution. Shakespeare does not endorse the orthodox view that Bolingbroke's seizure of the throne is a violation of divine purpose for which he and England must be humbled; instead, Shakespeare portrays the issues as many-sided and subject to varying interpretations.

Throughout his history plays, indeed, Shakespeare avoids expressing the Tudor providential view of recent history through didactic narrators or chorus figures who might seem to represent the point of view of the entire plays; instead, he puts this providential interpretation into the mouths of avowedly biased and self-interested characters whose motives and testimony the audience can then evaluate as it sees fit. In *1 Henry VI,* for example, the most detailed exposition of the providential historical view is given to Mortimer (2.5), whose interpretation, though strengthened by a dying man's last speech, is self-interestedly consistent with his own frustrated claim to the English throne. His nephew, Richard Plantagenet, who of course endorses the providential logic of Mortimer's speech, is portrayed as consumed with ambition for the crown. In Shakespeare's depiction of the Lancastrian-Yorkist conflict, neither side maintains a consistent ideological position, but instead shifts argument as required by the expediency of the moment. Although in his earlier tetralogy from *1 Henry VI* to *Richard III* Shakespeare does sometimes allow his contending characters to hearken back to the deposition of Richard II in order to explain the misfortunes of England's civil wars, those characters speak from self-interest and interpret history to their own advantage.

The individual plays of this earlier tetralogy, if seen or read separately, do not consistently comfort the spectator or reader with an assurance that all is working out according to God's plan. At the end of *1 Henry VI*, King Henry has surrendered to a disastrous marriage and has lost most of France; at the end of *2 Henry VI* the good Duke Humphrey of Gloucester is dead and his opportunistic political enemies are about to turn King Henry out of his throne. The hostilities of Lancaster and York end at the conclusion of *3 Henry VI*, to be sure, but prospects for a stable peace are doubtful in view of Richard of Gloucester's baleful presence. The reciprocity of slaughter visited on both sides appears to stem as much from humanity's insane desire for vengeance as from God's evening of the score. Only in *Richard III* do we retroactively see a pattern of divine anger, retribution, and eventual appeasement that can then be applied to the tetralogy as a continuous narrative. E.M.W. Tillyard's argument for a providential reading of these plays (in his *Shakespeare's History Plays*, 1944) is based not coincidentally on a view of the tetralogy as a cohesive whole. What about the playgoers who saw the plays one at a time? The plays, so far as we know, were written and produced singly and were never staged in a continuous series. Even though the tetralogy as a whole may harmonize in part with the chronicles of Edward Hall and others, written to glorify the Tudor state and to give thanks for its having ended the prolonged anarchy of the fifteenth century, we can see that Shakespeare is no apologist for the Tudor state. He gives expression to a widely felt distrust of political chaos. A pattern of divine wrath and appeasement, seen retrospectively in *Richard III*, provides at last a causal explanation of England's darkest hour. More immediately, in each individual play, the overriding cosmic irony stressing the gulf between foolish humanity and the inscrutable intentions of Providence offers a potentially stirring conflict of which Shakespeare makes rich use.

Shakespeare wrote his first tetralogy some time between 1589 and 1594. Just how much of this first tetralogy may have been planned out when Shakespeare began work is hard to say. In fact the very order of composition has long been in dispute. Despite the commonsense pleading of Dr. Johnson that Part Two follows from Part One as a logical consequence, some scholars argue that Part One was composed last. One piece of evidence is that a corrupt version of Part Two was published in quarto version in 1594 as *The First Part of the Contention Betwixt the Two Famous Houses of York and Lancaster*, and a corrupt version of Part Three in octavo in 1595 as *The True Tragedy of Richard Duke of York*. Part One had to await publication in the First Folio of 1623 and was registered for publication at that time as "The third part of Henry the sixth." It seems odd, moreover, that Parts Two and Three make no mention of Lord Talbot, so prominent in Part One. If, however, as seems likely, the early printed versions of Parts Two and Three were memorial reconstructions without the authority of the official promptbook, the claim of Part Two to have been written first may be unsubstantial. The very fact of prior publication of Parts Two and Three could explain why Part One was called "The third part" in 1623. Although Talbot is not mentioned in Parts Two and Three, these texts do recall important aspects of Part One. It is certainly possible that Shakespeare wrote all three parts in normal order.

Equally vexing is the question of authorship. Many Elizabethan plays were written by teams of authors, and Shakespeare might have collaborated, especially at the beginning of his career. Perhaps he rewrote older works by such writers as Thomas Nashe, Robert Greene, and Christopher Marlowe. Yet the theories of multiple authorship, once a commonplace of scholarship, are now generally in disfavor. Greene's famous resentment toward Shakespeare as the "upstart crow beautified with our feathers" seems more the envy of a lesser talent than the righteous indignation of one who has been plagiarized. The chief criteria used to "disintegrate" the plays into the hands of various supposed contributors are those of taste and style: for example, the low comic scenes of Joan of Arc were long held to be too coarse for Shakespeare's genius. Today most critics see a consistency of view throughout the *Henry VI* plays despite minor inconsistencies of fact that might be the result of simple error or of using multiple sources, and find nothing in these plays inimical to Shakespeare's budding genius. This belief confirms the judgment of Heminges and Condell, Shakespeare's fellow actors and editors of the 1623 Folio, who placed all the *Henry VI* plays among Shakespeare's collected works in their historical order.

If Shakespeare was at least chiefly responsible for the *Henry VI* series, he may also have been an important innovator in the new genre of the history play. Only the anonymous *Famous Victories of Henry V* is certainly earlier in dealing with recent English history. There were, to be sure, plays about legendary British history such as *Gorboduc* or *The Misfortunes of Arthur*, or about far-off lands such as *Cambises* or Marlowe's *Tamburlaine*. All these plays had explored by analogue political questions fascinating to Elizabethan England, and *Tamburlaine*'s immense success had certainly established a vogue for grand scenes of military conquest. Still, the English history play as a recognizable form came into being with *Henry VI*. The success was evidently tremendous and established Shakespeare as a major playwright.

1 Henry VI, like all the plays in Shakespeare's first tetralogy, comprises a large number of episodes, a sizable cast of characters, and a wide geographical range. The subject is England's loss of French territories because of political division at home. The structure of the play is one of sequential action displayed in great variety and in alternating scenes that are thematically juxtaposed and contrasted with one another. In the rapid shifting back and forth between the English and French court, for example, Shakespeare establishes a paradoxical theme: France triumphs in England's weakness, not in her own strength. The French court is merely one of debased sexual frivolity. The English are naturally superior but are torn apart by internal dissension, by a "jarring discord of nobility" and a "shouldering of each other in the court" (4.1.188–189) among those attempting to take advantage of Henry VI's weak minority rule and his vulnerable genealogical claim. Two of young Henry's kinsmen jockeying for position are Humphrey, Duke of Gloucester, and the Bishop of Winchester. Humphrey's intentions are virtuous, but he is unable to prevent the opportunistic scheming of his rival. Winchester, despite his ecclesiastical calling, is a man of evil ambition and corrupt life, wholly intent on destroying the right-minded Gloucester. Shakespeare employs derisive anticlerical humor against Winchester, and enlists the Protestant sympathies of his Elizabethan audience against the meddling Catholic church attempting to exploit England's weak kingship for its own ulterior purposes.

Even so, the menace threatening England is not seen as a Catholic conspiracy throughout; Winchester is only one opportunist seeking to exploit the political vacillation and faction at court. Of greater danger in the long term is Richard Plantagenet, scion of the Yorkist claim. From the start, Shakespeare portrays him as cunning, able to ingratiate himself and bide his time, ultimately ruthless. In these qualities he ominously foreshadows his youngest son and namesake, Richard III. In this play, Plantagenet's strategy is to allow England to wear herself down by the various conflicts at court and military losses abroad; once the situation is reduced to anarchy, Plantagenet will be able to move in. The strategy works only too well.

Chief defender of England's military might in France, and eventual victim of the bickering among the English nobility, is Lord Talbot. He is the heroic figure of this play with whom Elizabethan audiences identified. He pleads for political and military unity against the French and demonstrates that with such unity England would be invincible. Talbot is "the terror of the French" (1.4.42), able to hold off a troop of French soldiers with his bare fists, reputed to twist bars of steel. As the embodiment of chivalry, he delivers a richly deserved rebuke to Sir John Falstaff (historically "Fastolfe," but called "Falstaff" in the Folio text of this play), the cowardly soldier who foreshadows the fat knight of *1 Henry IV*. In *1 Henry VI*, cowardice and honor are rendered in black and white extremes. Talbot is a model general, illustrating all the qualities of great leadership advocated by the textbooks of the age: he is a stirring orator, fearless, witty, and concerned with a proper lasting fame. In the touching scenes with his son, Talbot rises triumphantly above death to become the immortal embodiment of brave soldiership. Yet even if *1 Henry VI* offers this one important model of rhetoric and arts of leadership put to right use, Talbot's presence nonetheless lends itself more to a profound anxiety about historical event than to a reassuring confidence in divine assistance. Talbot's unnecessary death offers a devastating critique of the weak leadership that has allowed authority in France to be divided among political rivals.

The relations between men and women in this play are also used to create thematic contrasts. Talbot's chief military rival in France is Joan of Arc; and, although many earlier scholars have wanted to deny Shakespeare's authorship of the Joan of Arc scenes, their thematic function is central. As a woman in armor, Joan is the embodiment of the domineering Amazonian woman to whom the effete and self-indulgent dauphin, Charles, weakly capitulates. The sexual roles have been reversed; Venus triumphs over Mars. Joan's role as virgin-warrior, her trafficking in demonology, and her obscenely parodic resemblance to the Virgin Mary all suggest a profound male-oriented ambivalence toward women in positions of authority—including, by implication, Queen Elizabeth. Joan's sexuality is not only demonic but obsessive in its promiscuity and seeming insatiability. The name by which she is known in France, *la Pucelle*, can mean both "virgin" and "slut." She even attempts to practice her witchcraft (with sexual overtones) on Talbot and his son, but in vain. Talbot's sense of duty never succumbs to Circean voluptuousness. In his encounter with the Countess of Auvergne, Talbot resourcefully outwits another woman who, like Joan, seeks to entrap him. The Countess finally submits to Talbot's courteous but firm authority, thereby reestablishing the traditional relationship of male and female. Talbot stands for every kind of decency and order that ought to prevail but is senselessly destroyed through England's political division.

The last woman introduced in the play, Margaret of Anjou, is another domineering female. Her adulterous relationship with the fleshly Suffolk, and her ascendancy over the weak Henry VI, are to be of fateful consequence in the ensuing plays. Her scenes, although once dismissed as an afterthought linking *1 Henry VI* with the following plays, in fact recapitulate the motifs of female dominance with great dramatic effect. Young Henry VI is no Talbot; inexperienced in love and highly impressionable, he surrenders to the mere description of a woman he has not even seen and refuses a politically advantageous match arranged by Duke Humphrey in order that he may marry a conniving French-woman without dowry. The marriage also anticipates that of Edward IV (in *3 Henry VI*) to a penniless widow who has caught his roving eye, when Edward could have obtained a handsome dowry and a favorable alliance by marrying the French King's sister-in-law. Such dismal triumphs of passion over reason are emblematic of the general decay among the English aristocracy. Despite Henry's weakness, he is the central character of this play after all, and his enervating surrender in love is a fitting anticlimax with which to end the first installment of England's decline. It is events such as these that seriously challenge any providential view of history.

HENRY VI
PART ONE

GENERAL *of the French forces at Bordeaux*
COUNTESS *of Auvergne*
PORTER *to the Countess*
MASTER GUNNER *of Orleans*
A BOY, *his son*
JOAN LA PUCELLE, *Joan of Arc*
SHEPHERD, *her father*
SERGEANT *of a French detachment*
SENTINEL *of a French detachment*
SOLDIER *with Pucelle at Rouen*
A SCOUT *in the Dauphin's army at Angiers*

English and French Heralds, Soldiers, Officers, Sentinels, Servingmen, Keepers or Jailers, Attendants, the Governor of Paris, Ambassadors, Fiends attending on La Pucelle

SCENE: *Partly in England, and partly in France*]

1.1 *Dead march. Enter the funeral of King Henry the Fifth, attended on by the Duke of Bedford, Regent of France; the Duke of Gloucester, Protector; the Duke of Exeter, [the Earl of] Warwick, the Bishop of Winchester, and the Duke of Somerset, [heralds, etc.].*

BEDFORD

Hung be the heavens with black, yield day to night! 1
Comets, importing change of times and states, 2
Brandish your crystal tresses in the sky, 3
And with them scourge the bad revolting stars 4
That have consented unto Henry's death— 5
King Henry the Fifth, too famous to live long!
England ne'er lost a king of so much worth.

GLOUCESTER

England ne'er had a king until his time.
Virtue he had, deserving to command. 9
His brandished sword did blind men with his beams; 10
His arms spread wider than a dragon's wings;
His sparkling eyes, replete with wrathful fire,
More dazzled and drove back his enemies
Than midday sun fierce bent against their faces.
What should I say? His deeds exceed all speech.
He ne'er lift up his hand but conquerèd. 16

EXETER

We mourn in black. Why mourn we not in blood?
Henry is dead and never shall revive.
Upon a wooden coffin we attend,
And death's dishonorable victory
We with our stately presence glorify,
Like captives bound to a triumphant car. 22
What? Shall we curse the planets of mishap 23

1.1. Location: Westminster Abbey.
1 Hung . . . black (A metaphor from the theatrical practice of draping the "heavens" or roof projecting over the stage in black when a tragedy was to be performed.) **2 importing** foretelling, portending **3 crystal** bright, shining. **tresses** hair, i.e., the trail of the comet **4 scourge** (as if the tresses were whips). **revolting** rebelling **5 consented unto** conspired to bring about **9 Virtue** excellence, authority **10 his beams** its beams **16 lift** lifted. **but conquerèd** without conquering **22 car** chariot **23 planets of mishap** misfortune-causing planets

That plotted thus our glory's overthrow?
Or shall we think the subtle-witted French
Conjurers and sorcerers, that, afraid of him,
By magic verses have contrived his end?   27

WINCHESTER
He was a king blest of the King of kings.
Unto the French the dreadful Judgment Day
So dreadful will not be as was his sight.   30
The battles of the Lord of hosts he fought;
The Church's prayers made him so prosperous.   32

GLOUCESTER
The Church? Where is it? Had not churchmen prayed,   33
His thread of life had not so soon decayed.   34
None do you like but an effeminate prince,
Whom like a schoolboy you may overawe.

WINCHESTER
Gloucester, whate'er we like, thou art Protector,   37
And lookest to command the Prince and realm.
Thy wife is proud. She holdeth thee in awe   39
More than God or religious churchmen may.

GLOUCESTER
Name not religion, for thou lov'st the flesh,
And ne'er throughout the year to church thou go'st
Except it be to pray against thy foes.

BEDFORD
Cease, cease these jars and rest your minds in peace!   44
Let's to the altar. Heralds, wait on us.   45
                              [*They prepare to leave.*]
Instead of gold we'll offer up our arms,
Since arms avail not now that Henry's dead.
Posterity, await for wretched years,   48

---

27 verses spells   **30 his sight** the sight of him   **32 prosperous** successful
33 prayed (with pun on *preyed;* also in l. 43)   **34 decayed** been destroyed
37 Protector head of state during the king's minority   **39 Thy wife is
proud** (A reference to Gloucester's ambitious wife, Eleanor, whose inordinate desire for greatness is depicted in *2 Henry VI.*)   **holdeth . . . awe**
overawes you   **44 jars** discords   **45 wait on us** i.e., lead the procession
s.d. They prepare to leave (Here or later in the scene, the various members of the funeral procession not specifically mentioned in the exits at ll.
166–177, including Warwick, Somerset, and the heralds, must leave the
stage.)   **48 await for** expect

When at their mothers' moistened eyes babes shall
　　suck,　　　　　　　　　　　　　　　　　　　　49
Our isle be made a nourish of salt tears,　　　　　50
And none but women left to wail the dead.
Henry the Fifth, thy ghost I invoke:　　　　　　　52
Prosper this realm, keep it from civil broils;　　　53
Combat with adverse planets in the heavens!
A far more glorious star thy soul will make
Than Julius Caesar or bright——

　　Enter a Messenger.

FIRST MESSENGER
　My honorable lords, health to you all!
　Sad tidings bring I to you out of France,
　Of loss, of slaughter, and discomfiture.
　Guyenne, Champagne, Rouen, Rheims, Orleans,　60
　Paris, Gisors, Poitiers, are all quite lost.
BEDFORD
　What sayst thou, man, before dead Henry's corpse?
　Speak softly, or the loss of those great towns
　Will make him burst his lead and rise from death.　64
GLOUCESTER
　Is Paris lost? Is Rouen yielded up?
　If Henry were recalled to life again,
　These news would cause him once more yield the ghost.
EXETER
　How were they lost? What treachery was used?
FIRST MESSENGER
　No treachery, but want of men and money.
　Amongst the soldiers this is mutterèd,
　That here you maintain several factions,　　　　71
　And whilst a field should be dispatched and fought,　72
　You are disputing of your generals.　　　　　　73
　One would have lingering wars with little cost;

---

49 When . . . suck i.e., when mothers will feed their children with tears
only　**50 nourish . . . tears** i.e., a nurse feeding with tears only　**52 invocate** invoke, as one would call on a saint　**53 Prosper** make prosperous　**60 Champagne** the city of Compiègne　**64 lead** leaden inner coffin
or wrapping, inside the wooden coffin (l. 19)　**71 several** separate (and
divisive)　**72 field** (1) battle (2) combat force　**73 of** about

Another would fly swift, but wanteth wings;   75
A third thinks, without expense at all,
By guileful fair words peace may be obtained.
Awake, awake, English nobility!
Let not sloth dim your honors new-begot.
Cropped are the flower-de-luces in your arms;   80
Of England's coat one half is cut away.   [*Exit.*]

EXETER
Were our tears wanting to this funeral,   82
These tidings would call forth her flowing tides.

BEDFORD
Me they concern; Regent I am of France.   84
Give me my steelèd coat. I'll fight for France.
Away with these disgraceful wailing robes!
Wounds will I lend the French instead of eyes,   87
To weep their intermissive miseries.   88

Enter to them another Messenger, [with letters].

SECOND MESSENGER
Lords, view these letters, full of bad mischance.
France is revolted from the English quite,
Except some petty towns of no import.
The Dauphin Charles is crownèd king in Rheims;
The Bastard of Orleans with him is joined;
Reignier, Duke of Anjou, doth take his part;   94
The Duke of Alençon flieth to his side.   *Exit.*

EXETER
The Dauphin crownèd king? All fly to him?   96
O, whither shall we fly from this reproach?   97

---

75 wanteth lacks   **80 Cropped** plucked.   **flower-de-luces** the *fleur-de-lis*, or iris, national emblem of France. (According to the Treaty of Troyes, 1420, the crown of France was ceded to England but was nominally to belong to the French king, Charles VI, as long as he lived. Henry V's title was designated "King of England and Heir of France." At his death this title passed to Henry VI; but within two months after this took place, Charles VI died and his son Charles VII was proclaimed king. The loss of the French crown would deprive the English king of the right to display the *fleur-de-lis* in his coat of arms.)   **82 wanting** lacking   **84 Regent** ruler in the king's absence   **87–88 Wounds . . . weep** i.e., I'll make the French shed blood instead of weep tears   **88 intermissive** intermittent but now to be resumed   **94 Reignier** René   **96–97 fly . . . fly** flock . . . flee

GLOUCESTER
We will not fly but to our enemies' throats!   98
Bedford, if thou be slack, I'll fight it out.

BEDFORD
Gloucester, why doubt'st thou of my forwardness?
An army have I mustered in my thoughts,
Wherewith already France is overrun.

Enter another Messenger.

THIRD MESSENGER
My gracious lords, to add to your laments,
Wherewith you now bedew King Henry's hearse,
I must inform you of a dismal fight   105
Betwixt the stout Lord Talbot and the French.   106

WINCHESTER
What? Wherein Talbot overcame, is 't so?

THIRD MESSENGER
O, no! Wherein Lord Talbot was o'erthrown.
The circumstance I'll tell you more at large.   109
The tenth of August last this dreadful lord,   110
Retiring from the siege of Orleans,
Having full scarce six thousand in his troop,   112
By three-and-twenty thousand of the French
Was round encompassèd and set upon.   114
No leisure had he to enrank his men.   115
He wanted pikes to set before his archers,   116
Instead whereof sharp stakes plucked out of hedges
They pitchèd in the ground confusedly,
To keep the horsemen off from breaking in.
More than three hours the fight continuèd,
Where valiant Talbot above human thought   121
Enacted wonders with his sword and lance.
Hundreds he sent to hell, and none durst stand him;   123

98 fly (Gloucester turns the word to mean "fly at their throats.")
105 dismal savage, terrible   **106 stout** brave   **109 circumstance** particulars.   **at large** in full detail   **110 dreadful** to be dreaded   **112 full
scarce** scarce full, barely   **114 round encompassèd** surrounded
115 enrank draw up in battle array   **116 wanted pikes** lacked iron-
bound stakes, sharpened at the ends and set in the ground in front of
archers as protection against cavalry   **121 above human thought** beyond imagining   **123 stand him** stand up against him

Here, there, and everywhere, enraged he slew.
The French exclaimed the devil was in arms;
All the whole army stood agazed on him.   126
His soldiers, spying his undaunted spirit,
"A Talbot, a Talbot!" crièd out amain   128
And rushed into the bowels of the battle.
Here had the conquest fully been sealed up   130
If Sir John Falstaff had not played the coward.   131
He, being in the vaward, placed behind   132
With purpose to relieve and follow them,
Cowardly fled, not having struck one stroke.
Hence grew the general wrack and massacre.   135
Enclosèd were they with their enemies.   136
A base Walloon, to win the Dauphin's grace,   137
Thrust Talbot with a spear into the back,
Whom all France with their chief assembled strength
Durst not presume to look once in the face.

BEDFORD
Is Talbot slain? Then I will slay myself
For living idly here in pomp and ease
Whilst such a worthy leader, wanting aid,
Unto his dastard foemen is betrayed.

THIRD MESSENGER
O no, he lives, but is took prisoner,
And Lord Scales with him, and Lord Hungerford;
Most of the rest slaughtered or took likewise.

BEDFORD
His ransom there is none but I shall pay.   148
I'll hale the Dauphin headlong from his throne;
His crown shall be the ransom of my friend.
Four of their lords I'll change for one of ours.   151
Farewell, my masters; to my task will I.
Bonfires in France forthwith I am to make,   153

---

126 agazed on astounded at **128 A Talbot** rally to Talbot. **amain** with full
force **130 sealed up** completed **131 Falstaff** ("Fastolfe" in the chronicles;
but the Shakespearean spelling used here shows us the origin of the name
used in the *Henry IV* plays.) **132 vaward** vanguard **135 wrack** wreckage,
destruction **136 with** by **137 Walloon** an inhabitant of that province,
now a part of southern Belgium and the adjoining part of France
148 His . . . pay i.e., I'll pay all the ransom there's going to be, by retaliat-
ing **151 change** i.e., kill in exchange **153 am** intend

To keep our great Saint George's feast withal.   154
Ten thousand soldiers with me I will take,
Whose bloody deeds shall make all Europe quake.

THIRD MESSENGER
So you had need, for Orleans is besieged;   157
The English army is grown weak and faint;
The Earl of Salisbury craveth supply   159
And hardly keeps his men from mutiny,
Since they, so few, watch such a multitude.   [*Exit.*]

EXETER
Remember, lords, your oaths to Henry sworn,
Either to quell the Dauphin utterly
Or bring him in obedience to your yoke.

BEDFORD
I do remember it, and here take my leave
To go about my preparation.   *Exit Bedford.*

GLOUCESTER
I'll to the Tower with all the haste I can   167
To view th' artillery and munition,
And then I will proclaim young Henry king.
                               Exit Gloucester.

EXETER
To Eltham will I, where the young King is,   170
Being ordained his special governor,
And for his safety there I'll best devise.   *Exit.*

WINCHESTER
Each hath his place and function to attend.
I am left out; for me nothing remains.
But long I will not be jack-out-of-office.   175
The King from Eltham I intend to steal
And sit at chiefest stern of public weal.   *Exit.*   177

154 **Saint George's feast** the twenty-third of April. (Saint George was the
patron saint of England. To celebrate his day in France would be to assert
England's claim to that territory.)   157 **Orleans is besieged** (At l. 60 a
messenger says that Orleans has fallen; at 1.2.8 ff. an English siege to
recover Orleans is under way. The messenger here may mean that the
besieging English army needs help.)   159 **supply** reinforcements
167 **Tower** Tower of London, ancient palace-fortress, later a prison for
persons of eminence   170 **Eltham** a royal residence southeast of London
175 **jack-out-of-office** i.e., a dismissed fellow with nothing to do   177 **at
chiefest stern** in the steersman's seat; i.e., in a position of supreme control

1.2   *Sound a flourish. Enter Charles, Alençon, and
Reignier, marching with drum and soldiers.*

CHARLES

Mars his true moving, even as in the heavens   1
So in the earth, to this day is not known.
Late did he shine upon the English side;   3
Now we are victors, upon us he smiles.
What towns of any moment but we have?   5
At pleasure here we lie near Orleans;   6
Otherwhiles the famished English, like pale ghosts,   7
Faintly besiege us one hour in a month.

ALENÇON

They want their porridge and their fat bull-beeves.
Either they must be dieted like mules   10
And have their provender tied to their mouths,
Or piteous they will look, like drownèd mice.

REIGNIER

Let's raise the siege. Why live we idly here?   13
Talbot is taken, whom we wont to fear.   14
Remaineth none but mad-brained Salisbury,
And he may well in fretting spend his gall—   16
Nor men nor money hath he to make war.   17

CHARLES

Sound, sound alarum! We will rush on them.   18
Now for the honor of the forlorn French!   19
Him I forgive my death that killeth me
When he sees me go back one foot or fly.   *Exeunt.*

*Here alarum. They are beaten back by the
English with great loss. Enter Charles, Alençon,
and Reignier.*

1.2. Location: France. Before Orleans.
s.d. flourish trumpet fanfare.   **drum** drummer   **1 Mars . . . moving** Mars's
precise orbit. (The planet's seemingly eccentric orbit was a source of
perplexity in Shakespeare's day; here, its influence on earth in human
affairs is likewise mysterious. Mars is also the god of war.)   **3 Late** lately,
recently   **5 What . . . have** what towns of any consequence do we not
possess   **6 lie** are encamped   **7 Otherwhiles** at times   **10 dieted** fed. (The
eating of beef, l. 9, was believed to confer courage.)   **13 raise the siege** i.e.,
drive off the English from their siege   **14 wont** were accustomed
16 spend expend, waste.   **gall** i.e., bitterness of spirit   **17 Nor** neither
18 alarum call to arms   **19 forlorn** in extreme risk

CHARLES
   Who ever saw the like? What men have I!
   Dogs, cowards, dastards! I would ne'er have fled
   But that they left me 'midst my enemies.

REIGNIER
   Salisbury is a desperate homicide;
   He fighteth as one weary of his life.   26
   The other lords, like lions wanting food,
   Do rush upon us as their hungry prey.   28

ALENÇON
   Froissart, a countryman of ours, records   29
   England all Olivers and Rolands bred   30
   During the time Edward the Third did reign.
   More truly now may this be verified,
   For none but Samsons and Goliases   33
   It sendeth forth to skirmish. One to ten!
   Lean raw-boned rascals! Who would e'er suppose   35
   They had such courage and audacity?

CHARLES
   Let's leave this town; for they are harebrained slaves,
   And hunger will enforce them to be more eager.   38
   Of old I know them. Rather with their teeth
   The walls they'll tear down than forsake the siege.

REIGNIER
   I think by some odd gimmers or device   41
   Their arms are set, like clocks, still to strike on;   42
   Else ne'er could they hold out so as they do.
   By my consent, we'll even let them alone.   44

ALENÇON   Be it so.

Enter the Bastard of Orleans.

BASTARD
   Where's the Prince Dauphin? I have news for him.

26 as one like one who is   **28 hungry prey** prey of their hunger
29 Froissart a fourteenth-century French chronicler who wrote of
contemporary events in Flanders, France, Spain, and England
30 Olivers and Rolands paladins in the Charlemagne legends, the most
famous of the twelve for their daring exploits   **33 Samsons, Goliases**
(i.e., Goliaths), biblical characters typifying great physical strength
35 rascals young, lean, or inferior deer of a herd   **38 eager** (1) fierce
(2) hungry   **41 gimmers** gimmals, joints or connecting parts for trans-
mitting motion   **42 still** continually   **44 consent** advice. **even** i.e., do
nothing but

CHARLES
  Bastard of Orleans, thrice welcome to us.
BASTARD
  Methinks your looks are sad, your cheer appalled.   48
  Hath the late overthrow wrought this offense?   49
  Be not dismayed, for succor is at hand.
  A holy maid hither with me I bring,
  Which, by a vision sent to her from heaven,
  Ordainèd is to raise this tedious siege
  And drive the English forth the bounds of France.   54
  The spirit of deep prophecy she hath,
  Exceeding the nine sibyls of old Rome.   56
  What's past and what's to come she can descry.
  Speak, shall I call her in? Believe my words,
  For they are certain and unfallible.
CHARLES
  Go, call her in. [*Bastard goes to the door.*] But first, to try
    her skill,
  Reignier, stand thou as Dauphin in my place.
  Question her proudly; let thy looks be stern.
  By this means shall we sound what skill she hath.   63
                              [*They exchange places.*]

    *Enter Joan [la] Pucelle, [the Bastard escorting
    her].*

REIGNIER
  Fair maid, is 't thou wilt do these wondrous feats?
PUCELLE
  Reignier, is 't thou that thinkest to beguile me?
  Where is the Dauphin?—Come, come from behind;
  I know thee well, though never seen before.
  Be not amazed. There's nothing hid from me.
  In private will I talk with thee apart.
  Stand back, you lords, and give us leave awhile.
                              [*The lords stand aside.*]

---

48 cheer appalled countenances made pale   **49 late ... offense** recent
defeat brought about this harm   **54 forth** out of   **56 nine ... Rome**
inspired women of the ancient world. (Not only of Rome, however; the
phrase here is probably owing to a confusion with the Cumaean sibyl
who came to Tarquin with nine prophetic books.)   **63 sound** test, determine   **s.d. Pucelle** virgin

REIGNIER
　She takes upon her bravely at first dash.　　　　71

PUCELLE
　Dauphin, I am by birth a shepherd's daughter,
　My wit untrained in any kind of art.　　　　73
　Heaven and our Lady gracious hath it pleased
　To shine on my contemptible estate.
　Lo, whilst I waited on my tender lambs
　And to sun's parching heat displayed my cheeks,
　God's mother deignèd to appear to me,
　And in a vision full of majesty
　Willed me to leave my base vocation
　And free my country from calamity.
　Her aid she promised, and assured success.
　In complete glory she revealed herself;
　And, whereas I was black and swart before,　　　　84
　With those clear rays which she infused on me　　　　85
　That beauty am I blest with which you may see.
　Ask me what question thou canst possible,
　And I will answer unpremeditated.
　My courage try by combat, if thou dar'st,
　And thou shalt find that I exceed my sex.
　Resolve on this: thou shalt be fortunate　　　　91
　If thou receive me for thy warlike mate.　　　　92

CHARLES
　Thou hast astonished me with thy high terms.　　　　93
　Only this proof I'll of thy valor make:　　　　94
　In single combat thou shalt buckle with me,　　　　95
　And if thou vanquishest, thy words are true.
　Otherwise I renounce all confidence.　　　　97

PUCELLE
　I am prepared. Here is my keen-edged sword,
　Decked with five flower-de-luces on each side,　　　　99
　The which at Touraine, in Saint Katharine's churchyard,
　Out of a great deal of old iron I chose forth.

---

71 takes . . . bravely plays her part well　73 wit mind, intelligence.　art
learning　84 black and swart i.e., heavily tanned　85 infused poured
91 Resolve on be sure of　92 warlike mate (with sexual suggestion, as in
the military terms throughout this interview)　93 high lofty　94 proof
trial, test　95 buckle join in close combat (with bawdy suggestion)
97 confidence (1) trust in your speech (2) intimacy　99 Decked adorned

CHARLES
>Then come, i' God's name! I fear no woman.

PUCELLE
>And while I live, I'll ne'er fly from a man.   103
>>*Here they fight, and Joan la Pucelle overcomes.*

CHARLES
>Stay, stay thy hands! Thou art an Amazon,   104
>And fightest with the sword of Deborah.   105

PUCELLE
>Christ's mother helps me, else I were too weak.

CHARLES
>Whoe'er helps thee, 'tis thou that must help me!
>Impatiently I burn with thy desire;   108
>My heart and hands thou hast at once subdued.
>Excellent Pucelle, if thy name be so,
>Let me thy servant and not sovereign be.   111
>'Tis the French Dauphin sueth to thee thus.

PUCELLE
>I must not yield to any rites of love,
>For my profession's sacred from above.
>When I have chasèd all thy foes from hence,
>Then will I think upon a recompense.

CHARLES
>Meantime, look gracious on thy prostrate thrall.

REIGNIER [*To the other lords apart*]
>My lord, methinks, is very long in talk.

ALENÇON
>Doubtless he shrives this woman to her smock;   119
>Else ne'er could he so long protract his speech.

REIGNIER
>Shall we disturb him, since he keeps no mean?   121

---

103 ne'er . . . man (with bawdy suggestion)   **104 Amazon** race of warrior women   **105 Deborah** Hebrew prophetess who "judged" Israel in the fourteenth century B.C. (She led an army against the Canaanite oppressors, whom she overcame; Judges 4, 5.)   **108 thy desire** desire for you   **111 servant** (with suggestion of a lover who will fulfill his mistress's commands)   **119 shrives** hears confession, i.e., examines. **to her smock** to her undergarment, i.e., completely (with bawdy suggestion) **121 keeps no mean** observes no middle position, is immoderate

ALENÇON
  He may mean more than we poor men do know.
  These women are shrewd tempters with their tongues. 123
REIGNIER [*To Charles*]
  My lord, where are you? What devise you on? 124
  Shall we give o'er Orleans, or no?
PUCELLE
  Why, no, I say. Distrustful recreants, 126
  Fight till the last gasp. I'll be your guard.
CHARLES
  What she says I'll confirm. We'll fight it out.
PUCELLE
  Assigned am I to be the English scourge.
  This night the siege assuredly I'll raise.
  Expect Saint Martin's summer, halcyon days, 131
  Since I have enterèd into these wars.
  Glory is like a circle in the water,
  Which never ceaseth to enlarge itself
  Till by broad spreading it disperse to naught.
  With Henry's death the English circle ends;
  Dispersèd are the glories it included.
  Now am I like that proud insulting ship 138
  Which Caesar and his fortune bare at once. 139
CHARLES
  Was Mahomet inspirèd with a dove? 140
  Thou with an eagle art inspirèd then.
  Helen, the mother of great Constantine, 142
  Nor yet Saint Philip's daughters, were like thee. 143

---

123 shrewd cunning, mischievous   **124 where are you** i.e., what are you
up to.   **devise** decide   **126 Distrustful recreants** faithless cowards
131 Saint Martin's summer i.e., Indian summer; Saint Martin's Day is
November 11.   **halcyon days** i.e., unseasonable calm. (The halcyon is
the kingfisher, which, according to fable, nested at midwinter on the
seas, which became calm for that purpose.)   **138–139 Now . . . once**
(North's translation of Plutarch relates how Caesar, encountering a
storm, said to the mariners, "Fear not, for thou hast Caesar and his
fortune with thee.")   **140 Was . . . dove** (Mohammed supposedly
claimed that he received divine inspiration from a dove whispering in
his ear.)   **142 Helen** mother of the emperor Constantine and supposed
discoverer of the holy cross and sepulcher of the Lord   **143 Saint
Philip's daughters** the four daughters of Philip the Evangelist, said in
Acts 21:9 to have the power of prophecy

Bright star of Venus, fall'n down on the earth,
How may I reverently worship thee enough?

ALENÇON

Leave off delays, and let us raise the siege.

REIGNIER

Woman, do what thou canst to save our honors.
Drive them from Orleans and be immortalized.

CHARLES

Presently we'll try. Come, let's away about it.   149
No prophet will I trust, if she prove false.   *Exeunt.*

❖

1.3   *Enter [the Duke of] Gloucester, with his
Servingmen [in blue coats].*

GLOUCESTER

I am come to survey the Tower this day.   1
Since Henry's death, I fear, there is conveyance.   2
Where be these warders, that they wait not here?
Open the gates! 'Tis Gloucester that calls.

          [They knock.]

FIRST WARDER [*Within*]

Who's there that knocks so imperiously?

FIRST SERVINGMAN

It is the noble Duke of Gloucester.

SECOND WARDER [*Within*]

Whoe'er he be, you may not be let in.

FIRST SERVINGMAN

Villains, answer you so the Lord Protector?

FIRST WARDER [*Within*]

The Lord protect him! So we answer him.
We do no otherwise than we are willed.   10

GLOUCESTER

Who willèd you? Or whose will stands but mine?   11

---

149 Presently immediately

1.3. Location: Before the Tower of London.
s.d. blue coats (Customarily worn by servingmen.)   **1 survey** inspect
2 conveyance trickery   **10 willed** commanded   **11 stands** has authority

There's none Protector of the realm but I.—
Break up the gates. I'll be your warrantize.   13
Shall I be flouted thus by dunghill grooms?   14
> *Gloucester's men rush at the Tower gates, and*
> *Woodville the Lieutenant speaks within.*

WOODVILLE [*Within*]
What noise is this? What traitors have we here?

GLOUCESTER
Lieutenant, is it you whose voice I hear?
Open the gates. Here's Gloucester that would enter.

WOODVILLE [*Within*]
Have patience, noble Duke. I may not open;
The Cardinal of Winchester forbids.   19
From him I have express commandement   20
That thou nor none of thine shall be let in.

GLOUCESTER
Fainthearted Woodville, prizest him 'fore me?
Arrogant Winchester, that haughty prelate,
Whom Henry, our late sovereign, ne'er could brook?   24
Thou art no friend to God or to the King.
Open the gates, or I'll shut thee out shortly.   26

SERVINGMEN
Open the gates unto the Lord Protector,
Or we'll burst them open, if that you come not quickly.   28

> *Enter to the Protector at the Tower gates*
> *Winchester and his men in tawny coats.*

WINCHESTER
How now, ambitious Humphrey, what means this?

GLOUCESTER
Peeled priest, dost thou command me to be shut out?   30

---

13 warrantize guarantee   **14 dunghill grooms** i.e., base fellows   **s.d. rush
. . . gates** (Gloucester's men assault the facade of the tiring-house wall
backstage, which represents the Tower gates; Woodville and the warders
are "within," or behind that wall, invisible to the audience.)   **19 Cardinal** (An inconsistency with 5.1.28 ff., where Winchester has just been
installed as cardinal.)   **20 commandement** commandment (pronounced
in four syllables)   **24 brook** endure   **26 I'll . . . shortly** i.e., I'll take
possession and shut you out   **28 if that** if   **s.d. tawny coats** (Customarily worn by attendants of a mighty churchman.)   **30 Peeled** shaven,
tonsured

WINCHESTER
> I do, thou most usurping proditor,   31
> And not Protector, of the King or realm.

GLOUCESTER
> Stand back, thou manifest conspirator,
> Thou that contrivedst to murder our dead lord,   34
> Thou that giv'st whores indulgences to sin.   35
> I'll canvass thee in thy broad cardinal's hat   36
> If thou proceed in this thy insolence.

WINCHESTER
> Nay, stand thou back. I will not budge a foot.
> This be Damascus, be thou cursèd Cain,   39
> To slay thy brother Abel, if thou wilt.   40

GLOUCESTER
> I will not slay thee, but I'll drive thee back.
> Thy scarlet robes as a child's bearing cloth   42
> I'll use to carry thee out of this place.

WINCHESTER
> Do what thou dar'st! I beard thee to thy face.   44

GLOUCESTER
> What, am I dared and bearded to my face?
> Draw, men, for all this privilegèd place—   46
> Blue coats to tawny coats. Priest, beware your beard.
> I mean to tug it and to cuff you soundly.
> Under my feet I stamp thy cardinal's hat.
> In spite of Pope or dignities of Church,   50
> Here by the cheeks I'll drag thee up and down.

WINCHESTER
> Gloucester, thou wilt answer this before the Pope.   52

---

31 proditor traitor   **34–35 Thou . . . sin** (Gloucester, in his bill of particulars against Winchester, charged that the cleric had suborned someone to attempt the murder of Henry V. Here he refers also to the fact that Winchester collected revenues from houses of prostitution on the south bank of the Thames.)   **indulgences** forgiveness of sins. (One could buy indulgences from the Church.)   **36 canvass** i.e., deal with severely. (The metaphor is that of tossing someone in a canvas or blanket as sport or punishment.)   **39 This be** let this be.   **Damascus** a city reputed to have been built on the site of Cain's slaying of Abel   **40 thy brother** (Winchester is Gloucester's half uncle.)   **42 bearing cloth** christening robe   **44 beard** openly defy   **46 for all this** in spite of this being a. **privilegèd place** (The Tower, as a royal residence, was one of the precincts where drawing of weapons was forbidden by the law of arms; cf. 2.4.86, note.)   **50 dignities** dignitaries   **52 answer** render an account of, pay for

GLOUCESTER
Winchester goose! I cry, a rope, a rope!   53
[*To his Servingmen.*] Now beat them hence. Why do you
    let them stay?—
Thee I'll chase hence, thou wolf in sheep's array.
Out, tawny coats! Out, scarlet hypocrite!

> *Here Gloucester's men beat out the Cardinal's
> men, and enter in the hurly-burly the Mayor of
> London and his Officers.*

MAYOR
Fie, lords, that you, being supreme magistrates,   57
Thus contumeliously should break the peace!   58
GLOUCESTER
Peace, Mayor! Thou know'st little of my wrongs.
Here's Beaufort, that regards nor God nor king,   60
Hath here distrained the Tower to his use.   61
WINCHESTER
Here's Gloucester, a foe to citizens,
One that still motions war and never peace,   63
O'ercharging your free purses with large fines,   64
That seeks to overthrow religion
Because he is Protector of the realm,
And would have armor here out of the Tower
To crown himself king and suppress the Prince.   68
GLOUCESTER
I will not answer thee with words, but blows.
                              Here they skirmish again.
MAYOR
Naught rests for me in this tumultuous strife   70
But to make open proclamation.
Come, officer, as loud as e'er thou canst,
Cry.
OFFICER   All manner of men assembled here in arms
    this day against God's peace and the King's, we charge

---

53 Winchester goose (Slang for a symptom of venereal disease.) **a rope**
i.e., a halter for hanging   **57 magistrates** rulers   **58 contumeliously**
arrogantly, contemptuously   **60 regards nor** has a proper respect for
neither   **61 distrained** confiscated   **63 still motions** incessantly advo-
cates   **64 O'ercharging . . . fines** overburdening you with excessive taxation   **68 Prince** i.e., Henry VI   **70 rests for me** remains for me to do

and command you, in His Highness' name, to repair
to your several dwelling places, and not to wear, han- 77
dle, or use any sword, weapon, or dagger henceforward, upon pain of death.   79

GLOUCESTER
Cardinal, I'll be no breaker of the law;
But we shall meet and break our minds at large.   81

WINCHESTER
Gloucester, we'll meet to thy cost, be sure.
Thy heart-blood I will have for this day's work.

MAYOR
I'll call for clubs, if you will not away.   84
This cardinal's more haughty than the devil.

GLOUCESTER
Mayor, farewell. Thou dost but what thou mayst.

WINCHESTER
Abominable Gloucester, guard thy head,
For I intend to have it ere long.
                    Exeunt, [*separately, Gloucester and*
                              Winchester with their
                              Servingmen].

MAYOR
See the coast cleared, and then we will depart.
Good God, these nobles should such stomachs bear!   90
I myself fight not once in forty year.   *Exeunt.*

❖

1.4   *Enter the Master Gunner of Orleans and his
          Boy.*

MASTER GUNNER
Sirrah, thou know'st how Orleans is besieged   1
And how the English have the suburbs won.

---

77 several individual   **79 pain** punishment   **81 break our minds**
(1) reveal our purposes (2) crack our heads.   **at large** at length   **84 call
for clubs** i.e., sound the rallying cry for London apprentices armed with
clubs   **90 these** that these.   **stomachs** i.e., angry tempers

1.4. Location: France. Orleans.
1 Sirrah (Customary form of address to an inferior.)

BOY

Father, I know, and oft have shot at them,
Howe'er unfortunate I missed my aim. 4

MASTER GUNNER

But now thou shalt not. Be thou ruled by me.
Chief master gunner am I of this town;
Something I must do to procure me grace. 7
The Prince's espials have informèd me 8
How the English, in the suburbs close entrenched,
Wont through a secret grate of iron bars 10
In yonder tower to overpeer the city
And thence discover how with most advantage
They may vex us with shot or with assault.
To intercept this inconvenience, 14
A piece of ordnance 'gainst it I have placed, 15
And even these three days have I watched,
If I could see them. Now do thou watch,
For I can stay no longer.
If thou spy'st any, run and bring me word,
And thou shalt find me at the governor's. *Exit.*

BOY

Father, I warrant you; take you no care. 21
I'll never trouble you, if I may spy them. *Exit.* 22

> *Enter Salisbury and Talbot on the turrets, with
> [Sir William Glansdale, Sir Thomas Gargrave,
> and] others.*

SALISBURY

Talbot, my life, my joy, again returned?
How wert thou handled, being prisoner?
Or by what means gott'st thou to be released?
Discourse, I prithee, on this turret's top.

TALBOT

The Duke of Bedford had a prisoner
Called the brave Lord Ponton de Santrailles;
For him was I exchanged and ransomèd.
But with a baser man-of-arms by far 30

4 **Howe'er unfortunate** although unfortunately 7 **grace** honor, credit
8 **espials** spies 10 **Wont** are accustomed 14 **inconvenience** mischief
15 **'gainst** directed toward 21 **take you no care** don't you worry
22 **s.d. turrets** i.e., some high point of vantage in the theater, above the
main stage 30 **baser** of lower rank

Once in contempt they would have bartered me;
Which I disdaining scorned, and cravèd death
Rather than I would be so pilled esteemed.   33
In fine, redeemed I was as I desired.   34
But O, the treacherous Falstaff wounds my heart,
Whom with my bare fists I would execute
If I now had him brought into my power.

SALISBURY
Yet tell'st thou not how thou wert entertained.   38

TALBOT
With scoffs and scorns and contumelious taunts.
In open marketplace produced they me
To be a public spectacle to all.
"Here," said they, "is the terror of the French,
The scarecrow that affrights our children so."
Then broke I from the officers that led me
And with my nails digged stones out of the ground
To hurl at the beholders of my shame.
My grisly countenance made others fly;
None durst come near for fear of sudden death.
In iron walls they deemed me not secure;
So great fear of my name 'mongst them were spread
That they supposed I could rend bars of steel
And spurn in pieces posts of adamant.   52
Wherefore a guard of chosen shot I had   53
That walked about me every minute while;   54
And if I did but stir out of my bed,
Ready they were to shoot me to the heart.   56

Enter the Boy with a linstock.

SALISBURY
I grieve to hear what torments you endured.
But we will be revenged sufficiently.
Now it is suppertime in Orleans.
Here, through this grate, I count each one

---

33 pilled peeled, i.e., despoiled of honor   **34 In fine** finally.   **redeemed**
ransomed   **38 entertained** treated   **52 spurn** kick.   **adamant** a legendary substance supposedly of incredible hardness, like diamond, or like a
magnet   **53 chosen shot** carefully selected marksmen   **54 every minute
while** i.e., constantly, at minute intervals   **56 s.d. linstock** forked stick
used to hold a lighted match for firing cannon

And view the Frenchmen how they fortify.
Let us look in; the sight will much delight thee.
Sir Thomas Gargrave and Sir William Glansdale,
Let me have your express opinions   64
Where is best place to make our battery next.   65

GARGRAVE
I think at the north gate, for there stands lords.

GLANSDALE
And I here, at the bulwark of the bridge.   67

TALBOT
For aught I see, this city must be famished   68
Or with light skirmishes enfeeblèd.   69
                    Here they shoot, and Salisbury falls down
                                    [together with Gargrave].

SALISBURY
O Lord, have mercy on us, wretched sinners!

GARGRAVE
O Lord, have mercy on me, woeful man!

TALBOT
What chance is this that suddenly hath crossed us?   72
Speak, Salisbury—at least, if thou canst, speak.
How far'st thou, mirror of all martial men?   74
One of thy eyes and thy cheek's side struck off?
Accursèd tower! Accursèd fatal hand
That hath contrived this woeful tragedy!
In thirteen battles Salisbury o'ercame;
Henry the Fifth he first trained to the wars.
Whilst any trump did sound or drum struck up,
His sword did ne'er leave striking in the field.   81
Yet liv'st thou, Salisbury? Though thy speech doth fail,
One eye thou hast to look to heaven for grace.
The sun with one eye vieweth all the world.
Heaven, be thou gracious to none alive
If Salisbury wants mercy at thy hands!   86
Sir Thomas Gargrave, hast thou any life?

---

64 express precise   **65 battery** attack   **67 bulwark** fortification (protect-
ing the bridge)   **68 must be famished** will have to be reduced to famine   **69 s.d. Here they shoot** i.e., the French. (Probably offstage, though
the Boy's appearance with the linstock at l. 56 visually symbolizes the
action of preparing to fire.)   **72 chance** misfortune.   **crossed** afflicted
74 mirror of example to   **81 leave** leave off   **86 wants** lacks

Speak unto Talbot. Nay, look up to him.—
Bear hence his body; I will help to bury it.
               [*Gargrave's body is borne off.*]
Salisbury, cheer thy spirit with this comfort;
Thou shalt not die whiles—
He beckons with his hand and smiles on me,
As who should say "When I am dead and gone,   93
Remember to avenge me on the French."
Plantagenet, I will; and Nero-like   95
Play on the lute, beholding the towns burn.
Wretched shall France be only in my name.   97
     Here an alarum, and it thunders and lightens.
What stir is this? What tumult's in the heavens?
Whence cometh this alarum and the noise?

     Enter a Messenger.

MESSENGER
My lord, my lord, the French have gathered head!   100
The Dauphin, with one Joan la Pucelle joined,
A holy prophetess new risen up,
Is come with a great power to raise the siege.   103
     Here Salisbury lifteth himself up and groans.
TALBOT
Hear, hear how dying Salisbury doth groan!
It irks his heart he cannot be revenged.
Frenchmen, I'll be a Salisbury to you.
Pucelle or pussel, Dauphin or dogfish,   107
Your hearts I'll stamp out with my horse's heels
And make a quagmire of your mingled brains.
Convey me Salisbury into his tent,   110
And then we'll try what these dastard Frenchmen dare.
     Alarum. Exeunt, [bearing out Salisbury].

---

93 As who as one who   **95 Plantagenet** (The Earl of Salisbury was
Thomas Montacute; he was descended from the Plantagenet Edward I.)   **Nero-like** (Talbot is being compared to Nero, who played
music while Rome burned.)   **97 only in** at the mere sound of
100 gathered head drawn their forces together   **103 power** army
107 pussel drab, slut. (A punning spelling variant of *pucelle*, maid.)
Dauphin (The normal Folio Elizabethan spelling of Dauphin is *Dolphin*.
The sea mammal by that name is included in the meaning and is contrasted with *dogfish*, a very low form of sealife.)   **110 me** for my benefit. (*Me* is used colloquially.)

1.5   *Here an alarum again, and Talbot pursueth the*
Dauphin and driveth him. Then enter Joan la
Pucelle, driving Englishmen before her [and
exit after them]. Then enter [again] Talbot.

TALBOT
Where is my strength, my valor, and my force?
Our English troops retire; I cannot stay them;   2
A woman clad in armor chaseth them.

   Enter [Joan la] Pucelle.

Here, here she comes.—I'll have a bout with thee;   4
Devil or devil's dam, I'll conjure thee.   5
Blood will I draw on thee—thou art a witch—   6
And straightway give thy soul to him thou serv'st.   7
PUCELLE
Come, come, 'tis only I that must disgrace thee.
   Here they fight.

TALBOT
Heavens, can you suffer hell so to prevail?
My breast I'll burst with straining of my courage
And from my shoulders crack my arms asunder,
But I will chastise this high-minded strumpet.   12
   They fight again.

PUCELLE
Talbot, farewell. Thy hour is not yet come.
I must go victual Orleans forthwith.   14
   A short alarum. Then enter the
   town with soldiers.
O'ertake me if thou canst! I scorn thy strength.
Go, go, cheer up thy hungry starvèd men;
Help Salisbury to make his testament.
This day is ours, as many more shall be.   *Exit.*
TALBOT
My thoughts are whirlèd like a potter's wheel;

1.5. Location: Scene continues at Orleans.
2 stay halt   **4 bout** encounter in the fighting (but with sexual overtones)
5 dam dame, mother   **6 Blood . . . witch** (Anyone who succeeded in
drawing blood from a witch was thought to be invulnerable to her
magic.)   **7 him** i.e., the devil   **12 But I will** if I do not.   **high-minded**
arrogant   **14 victual** supply with provisions   **s.d. enter** i.e., they, the
French, enter Orleans; Joan follows four lines later

I know not where I am nor what I do.
A witch by fear, not force, like Hannibal   21
Drives back our troops and conquers as she lists.   22
So bees with smoke and doves with noisome stench   23
Are from their hives and houses driven away.
They called us, for our fierceness, English dogs;
Now, like to whelps, we crying run away.
                                        A short alarum.
Hark, countrymen! Either renew the fight
Or tear the lions out of England's coat!   28
Renounce your soil; give sheep in lions' stead.   29
Sheep run not half so treacherous from the wolf,   30
Or horse or oxen from the leopard,
As you fly from your oft-subduèd slaves.
                            Alarum. Here another skirmish.
It will not be. Retire into your trenches.   33
You all consented unto Salisbury's death,
For none would strike a stroke in his revenge.   35
Pucelle is entered into Orleans
In spite of us or aught that we could do.
O, would I were to die with Salisbury!
The shame hereof will make me hide my head.   39
                            Exit Talbot. Alarum. Retreat.

1.6   *Flourish. Enter, on the walls, Pucelle, Dauphin*
           [Charles], Reignier, Alençon, and soldiers.

PUCELLE
Advance our waving colors on the walls;   1

21 Hannibal Carthaginian general who once repulsed a Roman army by
tying firebrands to the horns of a herd of oxen and driving the animals
toward the Romans **22 lists** pleases **23 noisome** noxious **28 lions . . .
coat** i.e., the three lions passant displayed in the English coat of arms
29 soil country (?) disgrace (?) **give** display (on coat of arms)
30 treacherous i.e., cowardly **33 It will not be** i.e., it's hopeless **35 his
revenge** revenge of him **39 s.d. Retreat** trumpet call to signal a withdrawal from the attack

1.6. Location: Scene continues at Orleans.
s.d. on the walls i.e., in the gallery backstage, above the main doors of
the tiring-house facade. (When Joan enters Orleans in 1.5, she enters the
tiring-house through one of its doors, and that tiring-house facade
remains the visual equivalent of the walls of Orleans through 2.1.)
1 Advance lift up

Rescued is Orleans from the English!
Thus Joan la Pucelle hath performed her word.
CHARLES
  Divinest creature, Astraea's daughter,   4
  How shall I honor thee for this success?
  Thy promises are like Adonis' garden,   6
  That one day bloomed and fruitful were the next.
  France, triumph in thy glorious prophetess!
  Recovered is the town of Orleans.
  More blessèd hap did ne'er befall our state.   10
REIGNIER
  Why ring not out the bells aloud throughout the town?
  Dauphin, command the citizens make bonfires
  And feast and banquet in the open streets
  To celebrate the joy that God hath given us.
ALENÇON
  All France will be replete with mirth and joy
  When they shall hear how we have played the men.
CHARLES
  'Tis Joan, not we, by whom the day is won;
  For which I will divide my crown with her,
  And all the priests and friars in my realm
  Shall in procession sing her endless praise.
  A statelier pyramid to her I'll rear
  Than Rhodope's of Memphis ever was.   22
  In memory of her when she is dead,
  Her ashes, in an urn more precious
  Than the rich-jeweled coffer of Darius,   25
  Transported shall be at high festivals
  Before the kings and queens of France.
  No longer on Saint Denis will we cry,   28
  But Joan la Pucelle shall be France's saint.
  Come in, and let us banquet royally
  After this golden day of victory.   *Flourish. Exeunt.*

4 Astraea goddess of Justice **6 Adonis' garden** mythical garden of
eternal fecundity **10 hap** event **22 Rhodope** a Greek courtesan who
became the wife of the King of Egypt. (A legend was current that she
built the third pyramid.) **Memphis** an ancient city of Egypt near which
stand the pyramids of Ramses II **25 Darius** King of Persia conquered
by Alexander the Great. Alexander, according to legend, used Darius'
rich-jeweled coffer to carry about the poems of Homer. **28 on** in the
name of. **Saint Denis** patron saint of France

2.1 *Enter [on the walls] a [French] Sergeant of a
band, with two Sentinels.*

SERGEANT
    Sirs, take your places and be vigilant.
    If any noise or soldier you perceive
    Near to the walls, by some apparent sign   3
    Let us have knowledge at the court of guard.   4
FIRST SENTINEL
    Sergeant, you shall. [*Exit Sergeant.*] Thus are poor
        servitors,   5
    When others sleep upon their quiet beds,   6
    Constrained to watch in darkness, rain, and cold.   7

        *Enter Talbot, Bedford, and Burgundy, [and
        forces,] with scaling ladders.*

TALBOT
    Lord Regent, and redoubted Burgundy,
    By whose approach the regions of Artois,   9
    Walloon, and Picardy are friends to us,
    This happy night the Frenchmen are secure,   11
    Having all day caroused and banqueted.
    Embrace we then this opportunity
    As fitting best to quittance their deceit,   14
    Contrived by art and baleful sorcery.   15
BEDFORD
    Coward of France, how much he wrongs his fame,   16
    Despairing of his own arm's fortitude,
    To join with witches and the help of hell!
BURGUNDY
    Traitors have never other company.
    But what's that Pucelle whom they term so pure?

**2.1. Location: Before Orleans, as in the previous scenes; the time is later
that night.**
s.d. band detachment of soldiers   **3 apparent** plain   **4 court of guard**
guardhouse   **5 servitors** soldiers   **6 upon their quiet beds** quietly in their
beds   **7 s.d. Burgundy** the Duke of Burgundy, allied to the English by the
Treaty of Troyes, 1420. (His support brought with it the cooperation of
territories near to Burgundy, in the Low Countries, such as Walloon and
Picardy.)   **9 By whose approach** by means of whose joining our alliance
11 secure overconfident   **14 quittance** requite   **15 art** i.e., black magic
16 Coward of France i.e., the Dauphin.   **fame** reputation

TALBOT
A maid, they say.

BEDFORD   A maid, and be so martial?

BURGUNDY
Pray God she prove not masculine ere long,   22
If underneath the standard of the French
She carry armor as she hath begun.

TALBOT
Well, let them practice and converse with spirits.
God is our fortress, in whose conquering name
Let us resolve to scale their flinty bulwarks.

BEDFORD
Ascend, brave Talbot. We will follow thee.

TALBOT
Not all together. Better far, I guess,
That we do make our entrance several ways,   30
That, if it chance the one of us do fail,   31
The other yet may rise against their force.

BEDFORD
Agreed. I'll to yond corner.

BURGUNDY   And I to this.

TALBOT
And here will Talbot mount, or make his grave.
Now, Salisbury, for thee, and for the right
Of English Henry, shall this night appear   36
How much in duty I am bound to both.

FIRST SENTINEL
Arm, arm! The enemy doth make assault!   38
          [*The English scale the walls, Talbot in the
          center, and exeunt above into the city.*]
                    Cry: "Saint George! A Talbot!"

---

22 prove not masculine i.e., (1) proves not to be so manly after all
(2) proves herself feminine by becoming pregnant. (The bawdy punning
continues in *standard*, "that which stands up," *carry armor*, "bear the
weight of a man," *practice and converse*, "engage in sexual contact,"
etc.) **30 several ways** i.e., on ladders at different points. (The three
leaders place their ladders against the tiring-house facade, one in the
middle for Talbot and one on each wing, and actually ascend to the
gallery or top of the "walls" where they surprise the French. Some of
the French, thus surprised, leap from the gallery down onto the main
stage, where the Bastard, Alençon, and others consult in a state of
disorder about their situation.) **31 That** so that **36 shall** it shall

The French leap o'er the walls in their shirts.
Enter, several ways, [the] Bastard [of Orleans],
Alençon, [and] Reignier, half ready, and half
unready.

ALENÇON
How now, my lords? What, all unready so?
BASTARD
Unready? Ay, and glad we scaped so well.
REIGNIER
'Twas time, I trow, to wake and leave our beds,   41
Hearing alarums at our chamber doors.
ALENÇON
Of all exploits since first I followed arms,
Ne'er heard I of a warlike enterprise
More venturous or desperate than this.
BASTARD
I think this Talbot be a fiend of hell.
REIGNIER
If not of hell, the heavens sure favor him.
ALENÇON
Here cometh Charles. I marvel how he sped.   48

Enter Charles and Joan [la Pucelle].

BASTARD
Tut, holy Joan was his defensive guard.
CHARLES
Is this thy cunning, thou deceitful dame?   50
Didst thou at first, to flatter us withal,   51
Make us partakers of a little gain
That now our loss might be ten times so much?
PUCELLE
Wherefore is Charles impatient with his friend?
At all times will you have my power alike?
Sleeping or waking must I still prevail,   56
Or will you blame and lay the fault on me?

---

38 s.d. unready not fully clothed. (This scene is based on an incident
occurring at Le Mans, a year prior to the siege of Orleans.)   **41 trow**
believe   **48 marvel** wonder.   **sped** fared   **50 cunning** skill   **51 flatter**
lead on with false hopes.   **withal** with it   **56 still prevail** always
succeed

Improvident soldiers! Had your watch been good,
This sudden mischief never could have fallen.

CHARLES
Duke of Alençon, this was your default,   60
That, being captain of the watch tonight,   61
Did look no better to that weighty charge.   62

ALENÇON
Had all your quarters been as safely kept
As that whereof I had the government,
We had not been thus shamefully surprised.

BASTARD
Mine was secure.

REIGNIER   And so was mine, my lord.

CHARLES
And, for myself, most part of all this night
Within her quarter and mine own precinct   68
I was employed in passing to and fro
About relieving of the sentinels.
Then how or which way should they first break in?

PUCELLE
Question, my lords, no further of the case,
How or which way. 'Tis sure they found some place
But weakly guarded, where the breach was made.
And now there rests no other shift but this: 75
To gather our soldiers, scattered and dispersed,
And lay new platforms to endamage them.   77

> *Alarum. Enter a[n English] Soldier, crying "A*
> *Talbot! A Talbot!" They fly, leaving their clothes*
> *behind.*

SOLDIER
I'll be so bold to take what they have left.
The cry of "Talbot" serves me for a sword,
For I have loaden me with many spoils,   80
Using no other weapon but his name.
                                   Exit, [bearing spoils].

❧

60 **default** failure   61 **tonight** i.e., this previous night   62 **charge** responsibility   68 **her** i.e., Joan's (with a bawdy suggestion, continued in
passing to and fro, l. 69)   75 **rests** remains.   **shift** strategy   77 **platforms** plans   80 **loaden me** laden myself

2.2 *Enter Talbot, Bedford, Burgundy, [a Captain,
and others].*

BEDFORD
 The day begins to break, and night is fled,
 Whose pitchy mantle overveiled the earth.   2
 Here sound retreat and cease our hot pursuit.
                                   Retreat [sounded].
TALBOT
 Bring forth the body of old Salisbury
 And here advance it in the marketplace,   5
 The middle center of this cursèd town.

   [*Enter a funeral procession with Salisbury's
   body,*] *their drums beating a dead march.*

 Now have I paid my vow unto his soul;
 For every drop of blood was drawn from him   8
 There hath at least five Frenchmen died tonight.
 And that hereafter ages may behold
 What ruin happened in revenge of him,
 Within their chiefest temple I'll erect
 A tomb, wherein his corpse shall be interred;
 Upon the which, that everyone may read,
 Shall be engraved the sack of Orleans,
 The treacherous manner of his mournful death,
 And what a terror he had been to France.
                              [*Exit funeral procession.*]
 But, lords, in all our bloody massacre,
 I muse we met not with the Dauphin's grace,   19
 His new-come champion, virtuous Joan of Arc,   20
 Nor any of his false confederates.
BEDFORD
 'Tis thought, Lord Talbot, when the fight began,
 Roused on the sudden from their drowsy beds,
 They did amongst the troops of armèd men
 Leap o'er the walls for refuge in the field.

2.2. Location: Orleans. Within the town.
2 pitchy i.e., pitch black   **5 advance** raise aloft (on a bier)   **8 was** that
was   **19 muse** wonder.   **the Dauphin's grace** His Grace the Dauphin
20 virtuous (Said ironically.)

BURGUNDY
  Myself, as far as I could well discern
  For smoke and dusky vapors of the night,
  Am sure I scared the Dauphin and his trull,   28
  When arm in arm they both came swiftly running,
  Like to a pair of loving turtledoves
  That could not live asunder day or night.
  After that things are set in order here,
  We'll follow them with all the power we have.

    Enter a Messenger.

MESSENGER
  All hail, my lords! Which of this princely train
  Call ye the warlike Talbot, for his acts
  So much applauded through the realm of France?
TALBOT
  Here is the Talbot. Who would speak with him?
MESSENGER
  The virtuous lady, Countess of Auvergne,
  With modesty admiring thy renown,
  By me entreats, great lord, thou wouldst vouchsafe·
  To visit her poor castle where she lies,   41
  That she may boast she hath beheld the man
  Whose glory fills the world with loud report.   43
BURGUNDY
  Is it even so? Nay, then, I see our wars
  Will turn unto a peaceful comic sport,
  When ladies crave to be encountered with.   46
  You may not, my lord, despise her gentle suit.   47
TALBOT
  Ne'er trust me, then; for when a world of men
  Could not prevail with all their oratory,
  Yet hath a woman's kindness overruled.   50
  And therefore tell her I return great thanks,
  And in submission will attend on her.
  Will not your honors bear me company?

---

28 trull strumpet (i.e., Joan)   **41 lies** dwells   **43 report** (1) acclaim
(2) noise of battle   **46 encountered with** i.e., encountered socially, as an
adversary in the battle of the sexes, and as the object of wooing
47 gentle gracious, courteous   **50 overruled** prevailed

BEDFORD

   No, truly, 'tis more than manners will;   54

   And I have heard it said unbidden guests

   Are often welcomest when they are gone.

TALBOT

   Well then, alone, since there's no remedy,

   I mean to prove this lady's courtesy.   58

   Come hither, Captain. (*Whispers*.) You perceive my

     mind?

CAPTAIN

   I do, my lord, and mean accordingly.   *Exeunt.* 60

❖

2.3   *Enter [the] Countess [and her Porter].*

COUNTESS

   Porter, remember what I gave in charge,   1

   And when you have done so, bring the keys to me.

PORTER   Madam, I will.   *Exit.*

COUNTESS

   The plot is laid. If all things fall out right,

   I shall as famous be by this exploit

   As Scythian Tomyris by Cyrus' death.   6

   Great is the rumor of this dreadful knight,   7

   And his achievements of no less account.

   Fain would mine eyes be witness with mine ears,

   To give their censure of these rare reports.   10

     Enter Messenger and Talbot.

MESSENGER   Madam,

   According as your ladyship desired,

   By message craved, so is Lord Talbot come.

COUNTESS

   And he is welcome. What? Is this the man?

54 will require, allow   **58 prove** test   **60 mean** i.e., intend to act

2.3. Location: Auvergne. The Countess's castle.
1 gave in charge commanded   **6 Scythian Tomyris** tribal queen of the
Massagetae, who slew Cyrus the Great when he invaded her territory
and, in revenge for her son's death, had the head of Cyrus placed in a
wineskin filled with blood   **7 rumor** reputation. **dreadful** inspiring
dread   **10 censure** judgment. **rare** remarkable

MESSENGER
Madam, it is.
COUNTESS   Is this the scourge of France?
Is this the Talbot, so much feared abroad   16
That with his name the mothers still their babes?   17
I see report is fabulous and false.
I thought I should have seen some Hercules,   19
A second Hector, for his grim aspect   20
And large proportion of his strong-knit limbs.   21
Alas, this is a child, a silly dwarf!   22
It cannot be this weak and writhled shrimp   23
Should strike such terror to his enemies.
TALBOT
Madam, I have been bold to trouble you;
But since your ladyship is not at leisure,
I'll sort some other time to visit you.   [*Going.*]   27
COUNTESS
What means he now? Go ask him whither he goes.
MESSENGER
Stay, my Lord Talbot, for my lady craves
To know the cause of your abrupt departure.
TALBOT
Marry, for that she's in a wrong belief,   31
I go to certify her Talbot's here.   32

Enter Porter with keys.

COUNTESS
If thou be he, then art thou prisoner.
TALBOT
Prisoner? To whom?
COUNTESS   To me, bloodthirsty lord;
And for that cause I trained thee to my house.   35
Long time thy shadow hath been thrall to me,   36
For in my gallery thy picture hangs;

---

16 abroad everywhere   **17 still** quiet   **19–20 Hercules, Hector** (Types of
great physical strength.)   **21 proportion** size   **22 silly** i.e., frail, mere
23 writhled wrinkled   **27 sort** choose   **31 Marry** (A mild interjection;
originally an oath, "by the Virgin Mary.")   **for that** because   **32 I
go . . . here** i.e., I leave as a way of informing her that I am the real
Talbot, not the legendary figure of popular report   **35 trained** lured,
enticed   **36 shadow** image, likeness.   **thrall** enslaved

But now the substance shall endure the like,
And I will chain these legs and arms of thine
That hast by tyranny these many years   40
Wasted our country, slain our citizens,
And sent our sons and husbands captive.   42

TALBOT   Ha, ha, ha!

COUNTESS
Laughest thou, wretch? Thy mirth shall turn to moan.

TALBOT
I laugh to see your ladyship so fond   45
To think that you have aught but Talbot's shadow
Whereon to practice your severity.

COUNTESS   Why, art not thou the man?

TALBOT   I am indeed.

COUNTESS   Then have I substance too.

TALBOT
No, no, I am but shadow of myself.
You are deceived. My substance is not here;
For what you see is but the smallest part
And least proportion of humanity.   54
I tell you, madam, were the whole frame here,   55
It is of such a spacious lofty pitch   56
Your roof were not sufficient to contain 't.

COUNTESS
This is a riddling merchant for the nonce!   58
He will be here, and yet he is not here.
How can these contrarieties agree?

TALBOT
That will I show you presently.   61

> *Winds his horn. Drums strike up. A peal of*
> *ordnance. Enter soldiers.*

How say you, madam? Are you now persuaded
That Talbot is but shadow of himself?
These are his substance, sinews, arms, and strength,
With which he yoketh your rebellious necks,

---

40 tyranny cruelty   **42 captive** taken captive   **45 fond** foolish
54 proportion of humanity (1) part of the whole man (2) portion of my
army   **55 frame** structure, construct, i.e., of man and of the army
56 pitch height   **58 riddling merchant** dealer in riddles.   **nonce** occasion   **61 presently** immediately   **s.d. Winds** sounds

Razeth your cities, and subverts your towns,   66
And in a moment makes them desolate.

COUNTESS
Victorious Talbot, pardon my abuse.   68
I find thou art no less than fame hath bruited,   69
And more than may be gathered by thy shape.
Let my presumption not provoke thy wrath,
For I am sorry that with reverence
I did not entertain thee as thou art.   73

TALBOT
Be not dismayed, fair lady, nor misconster   74
The mind of Talbot, as you did mistake
The outward composition of his body.
What you have done hath not offended me;
Nor other satisfaction do I crave
But only, with your patience, that we may   79
Taste of your wine and see what cates you have;   80
For soldiers' stomachs always serve them well.   81

COUNTESS
With all my heart, and think me honorèd
To feast so great a warrior in my house.   *Exeunt.*

❖

2.4   *Enter Richard Plantagenet, Warwick, Somerset,*
[William de la] Pole, [Earl of Suffolk, Vernon],
and others [including a Lawyer].

PLANTAGENET
Great lords and gentlemen, what means this silence?
Dare no man answer in a case of truth?

---

66 subverts overthrows   **68 abuse** (1) error (2) deception   **69 fame**
report.   **bruited** reported, rumored   **73 entertain** receive   **74 misconster** misconstrue   **79 patience** permission   **80 cates** delicacies, dainty
confections   **81 stomachs** (1) appetites (2) bravery

**2.4. Location: London. The Temple Garden, with rosebushes. (The
Temple was a district of London taking its name from the Knights
Templars, who owned it during the twelfth and thirteenth centuries. Its
buildings were converted into Inns of Court, housing the legal societies
of London, including the Inner Temple and the Middle Temple, in the
fourteenth century.)**

SUFFOLK

Within the Temple hall we were too loud.   3
The garden here is more convenient.

PLANTAGENET

Then say at once if I maintained the truth;
Or else was wrangling Somerset in th' error?   6

SUFFOLK

Faith, I have been a truant in the law   7
And never yet could frame my will to it,   8
And therefore frame the law unto my will.

SOMERSET

Judge you, my lord of Warwick, then, between us.

WARWICK

Between two hawks, which flies the higher pitch,   11
Between two dogs, which hath the deeper mouth,   12
Between two blades, which bears the better temper,
Between two horses, which doth bear him best,   14
Between two girls, which hath the merriest eye,
I have perhaps some shallow spirit of judgment;
But in these nice sharp quillets of the law,   17
Good faith, I am no wiser than a daw.   18

PLANTAGENET

Tut, tut, here is a mannerly forbearance.   19
The truth appears so naked on my side
That any purblind eye may find it out.   21

SOMERSET

And on my side it is so well appareled,
So clear, so shining, and so evident,
That it will glimmer through a blind man's eye.

PLANTAGENET

Since you are tongue-tied and so loath to speak,
In dumb significants proclaim your thoughts.   26
Let him that is a trueborn gentleman
And stands upon the honor of his birth,

3 were would have been **6 Or else** i.e., in other words (?) (Or Plantagenet may be saying, ll. 5–6, with intended humor, Am I right or is Somerset wrong?) **7 a truant** a neglectful student **8 frame** adapt **11 pitch** elevation in flight **12 mouth** voice **14 bear him** carry himself **17 nice** subtle, precise. **quillets** subtle distinctions **18 daw** jackdaw. (A type of foolishness.) **19 here . . . forbearance** (Plantagenet sardonically deplores this offering of polite excuses.) **21 purblind** dimsighted **26 dumb significants** silent tokens, signs

If he suppose that I have pleaded truth,   29
From off this brier pluck a white rose with me.   30
                          [*He plucks a white rose.*]

SOMERSET
Let him that is no coward nor no flatterer,
But dare maintain the party of the truth,   32
Pluck a red rose from off this thorn with me.   33
                    [*He plucks a red rose. The others similarly*
                              pluck roses as they speak.]

WARWICK
I love no colors, and without all color   34
Of base insinuating flattery
I pluck this white rose with Plantagenet.   36

SUFFOLK
I pluck this red rose with young Somerset
And say withal I think he held the right.   38

VERNON
Stay, lords and gentlemen, and pluck no more
Till you conclude that he upon whose side
The fewest roses are cropped from the tree
Shall yield the other in the right opinion.   42

SOMERSET
Good Master Vernon, it is well objected.   43
If I have fewest, I subscribe in silence.   44

PLANTAGENET   And I.

VERNON
Then, for the truth and plainness of the case,
I pluck this pale and maiden blossom here,
Giving my verdict on the white rose side.

SOMERSET
Prick not your finger as you pluck it off,

---

29 pleaded argued. (One of many legal terms occurring throughout this
scene.)   **30 white rose** badge of the Mortimers and subsequently of the
house of York   **32 party** side (in law)   **33 red rose** badge of the house of
Lancaster   **34 colors** pretexts   **36 Plantagenet** (The nickname of Geoffrey of Anjou, founder of the Angevin dynasty, which ruled England
from the reign of Geoffrey's son, Henry II, to that of Richard III. None
of Geoffrey's descendants assumed the name until Richard, Duke of
York, adopted it in order to proclaim his superior right to the crown.)
38 withal besides   **42 yield** concede. (Another legal term, like *objected*
and *subscribe* in the following two lines and *verdict* in l. 48.)
43 objected urged   **44 subscribe** submit

Lest, bleeding, you do paint the white rose red,
And fall on my side so against your will.

VERNON
If I, my lord, for my opinion bleed,
Opinion shall be surgeon to my hurt   53
And keep me on the side where still I am.

SOMERSET   Well, well, come on, who else?

LAWYER [*To Somerset*]
Unless my study and my books be false,
The argument you held was wrong in law;
In sign whereof I pluck a white rose too.

PLANTAGENET
Now, Somerset, where is your argument?

SOMERSET
Here in my scabbard, meditating that   60
Shall dye your white rose in a bloody red.

PLANTAGENET
Meantime your cheeks do counterfeit our roses;   62
For pale they look with fear, as witnessing
The truth on our side.

SOMERSET   No, Plantagenet,
'Tis not for fear, but anger, that thy cheeks
Blush for pure shame to counterfeit our roses,
And yet thy tongue will not confess thy error.

PLANTAGENET
Hath not thy rose a canker, Somerset?   68

SOMERSET
Hath not thy rose a thorn, Plantagenet?

PLANTAGENET
Ay, sharp and piercing, to maintain his truth,   70
Whiles thy consuming canker eats his falsehood.

SOMERSET
Well, I'll find friends to wear my bleeding roses
That shall maintain what I have said is true,
Where false Plantagenet dare not be seen.

53 Opinion public opinion, i.e., my reputation (punning on *opinion* in
the sense of "conviction" in the previous line)   **60 that** that which
62 counterfeit imitate   **68 canker** cankerworm (that feeds on buds)
70 his its (also in l. 71)

PLANTAGENET
　Now, by this maiden blossom in my hand,
　I scorn thee and thy fashion, peevish boy.   76
SUFFOLK
　Turn not thy scorns this way, Plantagenet.
PLANTAGENET
　Proud Pole, I will, and scorn both him and thee.   78
SUFFOLK
　I'll turn my part thereof into thy throat.   79
SOMERSET
　Away, away, good William de la Pole!
　We grace the yeoman by conversing with him.   81
WARWICK
　Now, by God's will, thou wrong'st him, Somerset.
　His grandfather was Lionel, Duke of Clarence,   83
　Third son to the third Edward, King of England.
　Spring crestless yeomen from so deep a root?   85
PLANTAGENET
　He bears him on the place's privilege,   86
　Or durst not, for his craven heart, say thus.
SOMERSET
　By him that made me, I'll maintain my words
　On any plot of ground in Christendom.
　Was not thy father, Richard, Earl of Cambridge,
　For treason executed in our late king's days?   91

76 fashion sort, or, the fashion of wearing red roses.   **peevish** silly
78 Pole family name of the Duke of Suffolk. (See also l. 80.)   **79 I'll . . .
throat** I'll throw the lies or slanders back into the throat from which
they proceeded   **81 grace** do honor to.   **yeoman** a small freeholder,
below the rank of landed gentleman. (A jibe at Plantagenet for having
lost his lands and titles when his father, Richard, Earl of Cambridge,
was executed in 1415 by Henry V for treason.)   **83 His . . . Clarence**
(Lionel was actually Richard's maternal great-great-grandfather; but
Edmund, Duke of York, fifth son of Edward III, was his paternal grandfather. Richard thus could trace his descent from Edward III through
both Lionel and Edmund.)   **85 crestless** lacking heraldic titles (with a
suggestion also of cowardice)   **86 He . . . privilege** i.e., Somerset presumes upon the safety of a privileged place (since engaging in quarrels
with drawn weapons was prohibited in certain precincts including the
official residences of the sovereign; in fact, however, the Inns of Court
were not thus privileged)   **91 late king's** i.e., Henry V's

And by his treason stand'st not thou attainted,   92
Corrupted, and exempt from ancient gentry?   93
His trespass yet lives guilty in thy blood,
And till thou be restored, thou art a yeoman.

PLANTAGENET
My father was attachèd, not attainted,   96
Condemned to die for treason, but no traitor;
And that I'll prove on better men than Somerset,
Were growing time once ripened to my will.   99
For your partaker Pole, and you yourself,   100
I'll note you in my book of memory
To scourge you for this apprehension.   102
Look to it well, and say you are well warned.

SOMERSET
Ah, thou shalt find us ready for thee still,   104
And know us by these colors for thy foes,   105
For these my friends in spite of thee shall wear.

PLANTAGENET
And, by my soul, this pale and angry rose,
As cognizance of my blood-drinking hate,   108
Will I forever, and my faction, wear
Until it wither with me to my grave
Or flourish to the height of my degree.   111

SUFFOLK
Go forward, and be choked with thy ambition!
And so farewell until I meet thee next.   *Exit.*

SOMERSET
Have with thee, Pole. Farewell, ambitious Richard.   114
       Exit.

PLANTAGENET
How I am braved and must perforce endure it!   115

---

92 attainted convicted and condemned. (According to law, the heirs of a person so attainted were deprived of all the rights and titles of their forebears; their blood was pronounced *corrupted*.)   **93 exempt** excluded.   **ancient gentry** hereditary rank   **96 attachèd, not attainted** (Historically, as Plantagenet insists, his father was *attached*, i.e., arrested, and summarily executed for treason without a bill of attainder.)   **99 Were . . . will** i.e., if the unfolding of time provides me opportunity   **100 For your partaker** as for your supporter   **102 apprehension** conception   **104 still** always   **105 know . . . foes** i.e., recognize us by these red badges as your enemies   **108 cognizance** badge   **111 degree** noble rank   **114 Have with thee** let us go   **115 braved** defied.   **perforce** necessarily

WARWICK
> This blot that they object against your house   116
> Shall be wiped out in the next parliament,
> Called for the truce of Winchester and Gloucester;   118
> And if thou be not then created York,
> I will not live to be accounted Warwick.
> Meantime, in signal of my love to thee,   121
> Against proud Somerset and William Pole,
> Will I upon thy party wear this rose.
> And here I prophesy: this brawl today,
> Grown to this faction in the Temple Garden,
> Shall send, between the red rose and the white,
> A thousand souls to death and deadly night.

PLANTAGENET
> Good Master Vernon, I am bound to you
> That you on my behalf would pluck a flower.

VERNON
> In your behalf still will I wear the same.

LAWYER   And so will I.

PLANTAGENET   Thanks, gentlemen.
> Come, let us four to dinner. I dare say
> This quarrel will drink blood another day.   *Exeunt.*

❖

2.5   *Enter Mortimer, brought in a chair, and Jailers.*

MORTIMER
> Kind keepers of my weak decaying age,
> Let dying Mortimer here rest himself.
> Even like a man new-halèd from the rack,
> So fare my limbs with long imprisonment;
> And these gray locks, the pursuivants of death,   5
> Nestor-like agèd in an age of care,   6
> Argue the end of Edmund Mortimer.   7

---

116 object urge, allege   **118 Called . . . of** assembled to make peace between   **121 signal** token

2.5. Location: The Tower of London.
5 pursuivants heralds   **6 Nestor-like** i.e., extremely old. (Nestor, the oldest of the Greek chieftains at the siege of Troy, came to represent a type of old age.)   **7 Argue** portend

These eyes, like lamps whose wasting oil is spent,
Wax dim, as drawing to their exigent;   9
Weak shoulders, overborne with burdening grief,
And pithless arms, like to a withered vine   11
That droops his sapless branches to the ground.
Yet are these feet, whose strengthless stay is numb,   13
Unable to support this lump of clay,
Swift-wingèd with desire to get a grave,
As witting I no other comfort have.   16
But tell me, keeper, will my nephew come?   17

FIRST KEEPER
Richard Plantagenet, my lord, will come.
We sent unto the Temple, unto his chamber,
And answer was returned that he will come.

MORTIMER
Enough. My soul shall then be satisfied.
Poor gentleman, his wrong doth equal mine.   22
Since Henry Monmouth first began to reign,   23
Before whose glory I was great in arms,
This loathsome sequestration have I had;   25
And even since then hath Richard been obscured,
Deprived of honor and inheritance.
But now the arbitrator of despairs,   28
Just Death, kind umpire of men's miseries,
With sweet enlargement doth dismiss me hence.   30
I would his troubles likewise were expired,   31
That so he might recover what was lost.

Enter Richard [*Plantagenet*].

9 **exigent** end   11 **pithless** marrowless, weak   13 **stay** support   16 **As
witting** as if knowing   17 **nephew** (Richard was son of the fifth Earl of
March's sister, Anne Mortimer, who married Richard, Earl of Cambridge.)   22 **his wrong** i.e., the wrong done him   23 **Henry Monmouth**
i.e., Henry V   25 **sequestration** imprisonment. (Shakespeare, following
the chroniclers, confuses Edmund Mortimer, fifth Earl of March and
great-grandson of Lionel, Duke of Clarence, hence potential heir to the
throne, with his uncle Sir Edmund Mortimer, who was imprisoned by
Glendower, and also with the Earl of March's cousin Sir John Mortimer,
who was imprisoned and finally executed for agitating in behalf of
Edmund's royal claim. The Earl of March remained loyal to Henry V.)
28 **arbitrator** bringer about of a definite issue   30 **enlargement** release
from confinement   31 **his** i.e., Richard's

FIRST KEEPER
  My lord, your loving nephew now is come.
MORTIMER
  Richard Plantagenet, my friend, is he come?
PLANTAGENET
  Ay, noble uncle, thus ignobly used,
  Your nephew, late despisèd Richard, comes.   36
MORTIMER
  Direct mine arms I may embrace his neck   37
  And in his bosom spend my latter gasp.   38
  O, tell me when my lips do touch his cheeks,
  That I may kindly give one fainting kiss.
                          [*He embraces Richard.*]
  And now declare, sweet stem from York's great stock,
  Why didst thou say of late thou wert despised?
PLANTAGENET
  First, lean thine agèd back against mine arm,
  And, in that ease, I'll tell thee my disease.   44
  This day, in argument upon a case,
  Some words there grew twixt Somerset and me;
  Among which terms he used his lavish tongue
  And did upbraid me with my father's death;
  Which obloquy set bars before my tongue,
  Else with the like I had requited him.
  Therefore, good uncle, for my father's sake,
  In honor of a true Plantagenet,
  And for alliance' sake, declare the cause   53
  My father, Earl of Cambridge, lost his head.
MORTIMER
  That cause, fair nephew, that imprisoned me
  And hath detained me all my flowering youth
  Within a loathsome dungeon, there to pine,
  Was cursèd instrument of his decease.
PLANTAGENET
  Discover more at large what cause that was,   59
  For I am ignorant and cannot guess.

---

36 late lately **37 I may** so that I may **38 latter** last **44 disease** un-
ease, trouble, grievance **53 alliance'** kinship's **59 Discover** make
known. **at large** at length

MORTIMER
  I will, if that my fading breath permit
  And death approach not ere my tale be done.
  Henry the Fourth, grandfather to this king,
  Deposed his nephew Richard, Edward's son,   64
  The first-begotten and the lawful heir
  Of Edward king, the third of that descent;
  During whose reign the Percys of the north,   67
  Finding his usurpation most unjust,
  Endeavored my advancement to the throne.
  The reason moved these warlike lords to this   70
  Was for that—young King Richard thus removed,   71
  Leaving no heir begotten of his body—
  I was the next by birth and parentage;
  For by my mother I derivèd am   74
  From Lionel, Duke of Clarence, third son
  To King Edward the Third; whereas he   76
  From John of Gaunt doth bring his pedigree,
  Being but fourth of that heroic line.
  But mark. As in this haughty great attempt   79
  They laborèd to plant the rightful heir,
  I lost my liberty and they their lives.
  Long after this, when Henry the Fifth,
  Succeeding his father Bolingbroke, did reign,
  Thy father, Earl of Cambridge, then derived
  From famous Edmund Langley, Duke of York,
  Marrying my sister that thy mother was,
  Again, in pity of my hard distress,
  Levied an army, weening to redeem   88
  And have installed me in the diadem.   89
  But, as the rest, so fell that noble earl
  And was beheaded. Thus the Mortimers,
  In whom the title rested, were suppressed.
PLANTAGENET
  Of which, my lord, your honor is the last.

---

64 nephew kinsman. (Here, cousin.)   **67 whose** i.e., Henry IV's
70 moved i.e., that moved   **71 for that** that   **74 mother** (Shakespeare
appears to confuse this Edmund with his uncle, Edmund Mortimer,
second son of Lionel's daughter Philippa.)   **76 he** i.e., Henry VI, or
perhaps Henry IV. (See l. 63.)   **79 haughty** proud   **88 weening** thinking   **89 installed . . . diadem** crowned me king

MORTIMER
  True, and thou seest that I no issue have,
  And that my fainting words do warrant death.   95
  Thou art my heir. The rest I wish thee gather;   96
  But yet be wary in thy studious care.   97

PLANTAGENET
  Thy grave admonishments prevail with me.
  But yet methinks my father's execution
  Was nothing less than bloody tyranny.

MORTIMER
  With silence, nephew, be thou politic.
  Strong-fixèd is the house of Lancaster
  And like a mountain, not to be removed.
  But now thy uncle is removing hence,   104
  As princes do their courts, when they are cloyed
  With long continuance in a settled place.

PLANTAGENET
  O uncle, would some part of my young years
  Might but redeem the passage of your age!   108

MORTIMER
  Thou dost then wrong me, as that slaughterer doth
  Which giveth many wounds when one will kill.
  Mourn not, except thou sorrow for my good;   111
  Only give order for my funeral.   112
  And so farewell, and fair be all thy hopes,
  And prosperous be thy life in peace and war!   *Dies.*

PLANTAGENET
  And peace, no war, befall thy parting soul!
  In prison hast thou spent a pilgrimage
  And like a hermit overpassed thy days.   117
  Well, I will lock his counsel in my breast,
  And what I do imagine, let that rest.   119
  Keepers, convey him hence, and I myself
  Will see his burial better than his life.
             Exeunt [*Keepers, bearing out*
                  the body of Mortimer].

---

95 warrant promise, assure   **96 gather** infer   **97 studious** diligent
104 removing hence departing from here, i.e., dying   **108 redeem the**
passage buy back the passing   **111 except** unless   **112 give order** make
arrangements   **117 overpassed** passed   **119 let that rest** leave it alone,
i.e., let that be my business

Here dies the dusky torch of Mortimer,
Choked with ambition of the meaner sort.   123
And for those wrongs, those bitter injuries,
Which Somerset hath offered to my house,
I doubt not but with honor to redress;
And therefore haste I to the parliament,
Either to be restorèd to my blood   128
Or make mine ill th' advantage of my good.   *Exit.*   129

123 with by.   **meaner sort** those whose claim to the throne was inferior
to his, i.e., the Lancastrians   **128 blood** hereditary rights   **129 Or . . .
good** or make my wrongs the means of achieving my ambition

3.1   *Flourish. Enter King, Exeter, Gloucester,*
       Winchester, Warwick, Somerset, Suffolk,
       Richard Plantagenet, [and others]. Gloucester
       offers to put up a bill; Winchester snatches it,
       [and] tears it.

WINCHESTER
  Com'st thou with deep premeditated lines,
  With written pamphlets studiously devised?
  Humphrey of Gloucester, if thou canst accuse,
  Or aught intend'st to lay unto my charge,   4
  Do it without invention, suddenly,   5
  As I with sudden and extemporal speech
  Purpose to answer what thou canst object.   7
GLOUCESTER
  Presumptuous priest, this place commands my
      patience,   8
  Or thou shouldst find thou hast dishonored me.
  Think not, although in writing I preferred   10
  The manner of thy vile outrageous crimes,
  That therefore I have forged, or am not able
  Verbatim to rehearse the method of my pen.   •   13
  No, prelate, such is thy audacious wickedness,
  Thy lewd, pestiferous, and dissentious pranks,   15
  As very infants prattle of thy pride.   16
  Thou art a most pernicious usurer,
  Froward by nature, enemy to peace,   18
  Lascivious, wanton, more than well beseems
  A man of thy profession and degree.
  And for thy treachery, what's more manifest?   21
  In that thou laidst a trap to take my life,

As well at London Bridge as at the Tower.   23
Besides, I fear me, if thy thoughts were sifted,
The King, thy sovereign, is not quite exempt
From envious malice of thy swelling heart.
WINCHESTER
   Gloucester, I do defy thee. Lords, vouchsafe
To give me hearing what I shall reply.
If I were covetous, ambitious, or perverse,
As he will have me, how am I so poor?
Or how haps it I seek not to advance   31
Or raise myself, but keep my wonted calling?   32
And for dissension, who preferreth peace
More than I do, except I be provoked?   34
No, my good lords, it is not that offends;   35
It is not that that hath incensed the Duke.
It is because no one should sway but he,   37
No one but he should be about the King;   38
And that engenders thunder in his breast
And makes him roar these accusations forth.
But he shall know I am as good—
GLOUCESTER   As good?
   Thou bastard of my grandfather!   42
WINCHESTER
   Ay, lordly sir! For what are you, I pray,
But one imperious in another's throne?   44
GLOUCESTER
   Am I not Protector, saucy priest?
WINCHESTER
   And am not I a prelate of the Church?
GLOUCESTER
   Yes, as an outlaw in a castle keeps   47
And useth it to patronage his theft.   48

23 at London Bridge (Gloucester's articles of accusation against Winchester presented to the Parliament stated that the latter had "set men-
of-arms and archers at the end of London Bridge next Southwark," to
prevent Gloucester's going to Eltham to interfere with the Bishop's
plans regarding the young King.)   **31 haps** happens   **32 wonted calling**
customary profession   **34 except** unless   **35 that** that that   **37 sway**
govern   **38 about** near to   **42 Thou bastard** (Winchester—son of John
of Gaunt and Katharine Swynford before their marriage—was, with his
two brothers and one sister, legitimatized by act of Parliament in Richard II's reign.)   **44 imperious** (1) exercising rule (2) domineering
47 keeps dwells   **48 patronage** maintain

WINCHESTER
 Unreverent Gloucester!
GLOUCESTER   Thou art reverend   49
 Touching thy spiritual function, not thy life.   50
WINCHESTER
 Rome shall remedy this.
WARWICK   Roam thither, then.
SOMERSET [*To Warwick*]
 My lord, it were your duty to forbear.   52
WARWICK
 Ay, see the Bishop be not overborne.   53
SOMERSET
 Methinks my lord should be religious   54
 And know the office that belongs to such.   55
WARWICK
 Methinks his lordship should be humbler.
 It fitteth not a prelate so to plead.
SOMERSET
 Yes, when his holy state is touched so near.   58
WARWICK
 State holy or unhallowed, what of that?
 Is not His Grace Protector to the King?   60
PLANTAGENET [*Aside*]
 Plantagenet, I see, must hold his tongue,
 Lest it be said, "Speak, sirrah, when you should;
 Must your bold verdict enter talk with lords?"   63
 Else would I have a fling at Winchester.
KING
 Uncles of Gloucester and of Winchester,
 The special watchmen of our English weal,   66
 I would prevail, if prayers might prevail,
 To join your hearts in love and amity.
 O, what a scandal is it to our crown
 That two such noble peers as ye should jar!   70

49 Unreverent . . . reverend irreverent, hostile to spiritual authority . . .
respected, revered. (The Folio spellings, *Vnreuerent* and *reuerent*, accentuate the wordplay.)   **50 Touching . . . function** i.e., in ecclesiastical title
only   **52 were** should be   **53 overborne** prevailed over   **54 my lord** i.e.,
Winchester.   **should be** i.e., should be regarded as. (But Warwick, two
lines below, uses the phrase in the sense "ought to be.")   **55 office**
duty   **58 state** degree, rank.   **touched so near** so closely concerned
60 His Grace i.e., Gloucester   **63 bold verdict** audacious opinion.   **enter
talk** hold conversation   **66 weal** common good   **70 jar** quarrel

Believe me, lords, my tender years can tell   71
Civil dissension is a viperous worm
That gnaws the bowels of the commonwealth.
          A noise within, "Down with the tawny coats!"
What tumult's this?
WARWICK   An uproar, I dare warrant,
Begun through malice of the Bishop's men.
          A noise again, "Stones! Stones!"

          Enter Mayor.

MAYOR
O my good lords, and virtuous Henry,
Pity the city of London, pity us!
The Bishop and the Duke of Gloucester's men,   80
Forbidden late to carry any weapon,   81
Have filled their pockets full of pebblestones
And, banding themselves in contrary parts,   83
Do pelt so fast at one another's pate
That many have their giddy brains knocked out.
Our windows are broke down in every street,
And we for fear compelled to shut our shops.

          Enter [Servingmen of both parties], in skirmish,
          with bloody pates.

KING
We charge you, on allegiance to ourself,
To hold your slaughtering hands and keep the peace.
Pray, uncle Gloucester, mitigate this strife.
FIRST SERVINGMAN Nay, if we be forbidden stones,
we'll fall to it with our teeth.
SECOND SERVINGMAN
Do what ye dare, we are as resolute. *Skirmish again.*
GLOUCESTER
You of my household, leave this peevish broil   94
And set this unaccustomed fight aside.   95
THIRD SERVINGMAN
My lord, we know Your Grace to be a man

---

71 my tender years (The King was actually five years old at the time of
this episode.) **80 Bishop** i.e., Bishop's **81 late** lately **83 contrary
parts** contending factions **94 peevish** petty, senseless
95 unaccustomed contrary to custom and normality

Just and upright, and for your royal birth
Inferior to none but to His Majesty;
And ere that we will suffer such a prince,   99
So kind a father of the commonweal,
To be disgracèd by an inkhorn mate,   101
We and our wives and children all will fight
And have our bodies slaughtered by thy foes.

FIRST SERVINGMAN
Ay, and the very parings of our nails
Shall pitch a field when we are dead.   *Begin again.*

GLOUCESTER   Stay, stay, I say!   105
An if you love me, as you say you do,
Let me persuade you to forbear awhile.

KING
O, how this discord doth afflict my soul!
Can you, my lord of Winchester, behold
My sighs and tears and will not once relent?
Who should be pitiful, if you be not?
Or who should study to prefer a peace   112
If holy churchmen take delight in broils?

WARWICK
Yield, my Lord Protector, yield, Winchester,
Except you mean with obstinate repulse   115
To slay your sovereign and destroy the realm.
You see what mischief, and what murder too,
Hath been enacted through your enmity.
Then be at peace, except ye thirst for blood.

WINCHESTER
He shall submit, or I will never yield.

GLOUCESTER
Compassion on the King commands me stoop,
Or I would see his heart out ere the priest
Should ever get that privilege of me.   123

WARWICK
Behold, my lord of Winchester, the Duke
Hath banished moody discontented fury,   125

---

99 ere that before   **101 inkhorn mate** scribbler. (Alludes scornfully to
Winchester as a cleric or clerk.)   **105 pitch a field** fight a battle, set in
array for fighting   **112 prefer** propose, assist in arranging   **115 Except**
unless.   **repulse** refusal   **123 privilege of** advantage over   **125 moody**
haughty

As by his smoothèd brows it doth appear.
Why look you still so stern and tragical?

GLOUCESTER
Here, Winchester, I offer thee my hand.
         [*He offers his hand, which Winchester refuses.*]

KING
Fie, uncle Beaufort! I have heard you preach
That malice was a great and grievous sin;
And will not you maintain the thing you teach,
But prove a chief offender in the same?

WARWICK
Sweet King! The Bishop hath a kindly gird.   133
For shame, my lord of Winchester, relent!
What, shall a child instruct you what to do?

WINCHESTER
Well, Duke of Gloucester, I will yield to thee;
Love for thy love and hand for hand I give.
                              [*They clasp hands.*]

GLOUCESTER [*Aside*]
Ay, but, I fear me, with a hollow heart.—   138
See here, my friends and loving countrymen,
This token serveth for a flag of truce   140
Betwixt ourselves and all our followers.
So help me God, as I dissemble not!

WINCHESTER [*Aside*]
So help me God, as I intend it not!

KING
O loving uncle, kind Duke of Gloucester,
How joyful am I made by this contract!
[*To Servingmen.*] Away, my masters. Trouble us no more,   146
But join in friendship, as your lords have done.

FIRST SERVINGMAN
Content. I'll to the surgeon's.

SECOND SERVINGMAN   And so will I.

THIRD SERVINGMAN
And I will see what physic the tavern affords.   149
                    Exeunt [*Servingmen and Mayor*].

---

133 kindly gird appropriate rebuke   **138 hollow** treacherous   **140 This
token** i.e., the handshake   **146 masters** (Condescending term of address
to social inferiors.)   **149 physic** remedy

WARWICK [*Proferring scroll*]
> Accept this scroll, most gracious sovereign,
> Which in the right of Richard Plantagenet
> We do exhibit to Your Majesty.   152

GLOUCESTER
> Well urged, my lord of Warwick. For, sweet prince,
> An if Your Grace mark every circumstance,   154
> You have great reason to do Richard right,
> Especially for those occasions   156
> At Eltham Place I told Your Majesty.

KING
> And those occasions, uncle, were of force.   158
> Therefore, my loving lords, our pleasure is
> That Richard be restorèd to his blood.   160

WARWICK
> Let Richard be restorèd to his blood;
> So shall his father's wrongs be recompensed.

WINCHESTER
> As will the rest, so willeth Winchester.

KING
> If Richard will be true, not that alone
> But all the whole inheritance I give
> That doth belong unto the house of York,
> From whence you spring by lineal descent.

PLANTAGENET
> Thy humble servant vows obedience
> And humble service till the point of death.

KING
> Stoop then and set your knee against my foot.
>   [*Richard kneels.*]
> And in reguerdon of that duty done,   171
> I gird thee with the valiant sword of York.
> Rise, Richard, like a true Plantagenet,
> And rise created princely Duke of York.

PLANTAGENET [*Rising*]
> And so thrive Richard as thy foes may fall!
> And as my duty springs, so perish they

---

152 exhibit present for official consideration   **154 An if** if   **156 occasions** reasons   **158 of force** compelling   **160 blood** hereditary right, inherited from his father   **171 reguerdon** reward

That grudge one thought against Your Majesty!   177
ALL
   Welcome, high prince, the mighty Duke of York!
SOMERSET [*Aside*]
   Perish, base prince, ignoble Duke of York!
GLOUCESTER
   Now will it best avail Your Majesty
   To cross the seas and to be crowned in France.
   The presence of a king engenders love
   Amongst his subjects and his loyal friends,
   As it disanimates his enemies.   184
KING
   When Gloucester says the word, King Henry goes,
   For friendly counsel cuts off many foes.
GLOUCESTER
   Your ships already are in readiness.   187
          Sennet. Flourish. Exeunt. Manet Exeter.
EXETER
   Ay, we may march in England or in France,
   Not seeing what is likely to ensue.
   This late dissension grown betwixt the peers   190
   Burns under feignèd ashes of forged love   191
   And will at last break out into a flame.
   As festered members rot but by degree
   Till bones and flesh and sinews fall away,
   So will this base and envious discord breed.
   And now I fear that fatal prophecy
   Which in the time of Henry named the Fifth
   Was in the mouth of every sucking babe:
   That Henry born at Monmouth should win all   199
   And Henry born at Windsor lose all;   200
   Which is so plain that Exeter doth wish
   His days may finish ere that hapless time.   *Exit.*

177 **grudge one thought** harbor one grudging thought   184 **disanimates**
discourages   187 **s.d. Sennet** set of notes played on a trumpet as a
signal for the approach or departure of processions.   **Manet** he remains
onstage   190 **late** recent   191 **forged** feigned   199 **Henry born at**
Monmouth i.e., Henry V   200 **Henry born at Windsor** i.e., Henry VI

3.2   *Enter [Joan la] Pucelle disguised, with four*
Soldiers with sacks upon their backs.

PUCELLE

These are the city gates, the gates of Rouen,   1
Through which our policy must make a breach.   2
Take heed, be wary how you place your words;
Talk like the vulgar sort of marketmen   4
That come to gather money for their corn.   5
If we have entrance, as I hope we shall,
And that we find the slothful watch but weak,   7
I'll by a sign give notice to our friends,
That Charles the Dauphin may encounter them.

FIRST SOLDIER

Our sacks shall be a mean to sack the city,   10
And we be lords and rulers over Rouen.
Therefore we'll knock.   *Knock.*

WATCH [*Within*]   *Qui là?*   13

PUCELLE

Paysans, la pauvre gens de France,
Poor market folks that come to sell their corn.

WATCH [*Opening the gates*]

Enter, go in. The market bell is rung.

PUCELLE

Now, Rouen, I'll shake thy bulwarks to the ground.
                                Exeunt [to the town].

Enter Charles, [the] Bastard [of Orleans],
Alençon, [Reignier, and forces].

CHARLES

Saint Denis bless this happy stratagem!
And once again we'll sleep secure in Rouen.

BASTARD

Here entered Pucelle and her practisants.   20

3.2. Location: France. Before Rouen.
1 Rouen (As at Orleans in 1.5 through 2.1, the city gates here are represented by doors in the tiring-house facade, the "walls" of Rouen. Appearances "on the walls," as at l. 40 s.d., take place on the gallery
backstage.)   **2 policy** stratagem   **4 vulgar** common   **5 corn** grain
7 that if   **10 mean** means   **13 Qui là** qui est là, who is there. (Rustic
French.)   **20 practisants** conspirators

Now she is there, how will she specify
Here is the best and safest passage in?   22

REIGNIER
By thrusting out a torch from yonder tower,
Which, once discerned, shows that her meaning is,
No way to that, for weakness, which she entered.   25

*Enter Pucelle on the top, thrusting out a torch
burning.*

PUCELLE
Behold, this is the happy wedding torch
That joineth Rouen unto her countrymen,
But burning fatal to the Talbonites!   28

BASTARD
See, noble Charles, the beacon of our friend!
The burning torch in yonder turret stands.

CHARLES
Now shine it like a comet of revenge,   31
A prophet to the fall of all our foes!

REIGNIER
Defer no time! Delays have dangerous ends.
Enter, and cry "The Dauphin!" presently,   34
And then do execution on the watch.   35
                    Alarum. [They storm the gates.]

*An alarum. [Enter] Talbot in an excursion [from
within].*

TALBOT
France, thou shalt rue this treason with thy tears,
If Talbot but survive thy treachery.
Pucelle, that witch, that damnèd sorceress,
Hath wrought this hellish mischief unawares,   39

22 Here . . . in i.e., that here (the same spot she entered) is the best and
safest place for us to enter as well   **25 No . . . entered** i.e., no other
place can be compared to the one where she entered for weakness; it is
the most weakly defended   **s.d. on the top** i.e., at some upper vantage
point in the theater   **28 Talbonites** followers of Talbot   **31 shine it** may
it shine   **34 presently** immediately   **35 do . . . watch** kill all the
guards   **s.d. excursion** skirmish, sortie   **39 unawares** unexpectedly

That hardly we escaped the pride of France.   *Exit.* 40

> *An alarum. Excursions. Bedford, brought in sick*
> *in a chair. Enter Talbot and Burgundy without;*
> *within, Pucelle, Charles, Bastard, [Alençon,] and*
> *Reignier, on the walls.*

PUCELLE
Good morrow, gallants, want ye corn for bread?
I think the Duke of Burgundy will fast
Before he'll buy again at such a rate.
'Twas full of darnel. Do you like the taste?   44

BURGUNDY
Scoff on, vile fiend and shameless courtesan!
I trust ere long to choke thee with thine own   46
And make thee curse the harvest of that corn.

CHARLES
Your Grace may starve, perhaps, before that time.

BEDFORD
O, let no words, but deeds, revenge this treason!

PUCELLE
What will you do, good graybeard, break a lance
And run atilt at Death within a chair?   51

TALBOT
Foul fiend of France and hag of all despite,   52
Encompassed with thy lustful paramours!
Becomes it thee to taunt his valiant age
And twit with cowardice a man half dead?
Damsel, I'll have a bout with you again,   56
Or else let Talbot perish with this shame.

PUCELLE
Are ye so hot, sir? Yet, Pucelle, hold thy peace.   58

---

40 pride princely power   **s.d. Bedford . . . sick** (Actually, Bedford out-
lived Joan of Arc by four years. The entire episode of the capture of
Rouen, as presented here, is unhistorical; the English did not relinquish
the city until 1449, some eighteen years after Joan's death.)   **without**
i.e., on the main stage.   **within** i.e., in the gallery backstage   **44 darnel**
injurious weed   **46 thine own** i.e., your own bread   **51 run atilt at** joust
with.   **within** i.e., sitting in   **52 of all despite** thoroughly despicable
56 bout encounter with weapons (with sexual overtones, as earlier at
1.5.4)   **58 hot** (1) hot-tempered (2) lustful

If Talbot do but thunder, rain will follow.   59
  They [the English] whisper together in council.
God speed the parliament! Who shall be the speaker?   60

TALBOT
Dare ye come forth and meet us in the field?

PUCELLE
Belike your lordship takes us then for fools,
To try if that our own be ours or no.

TALBOT
I speak not to that railing Hecate,   64
But unto thee, Alençon, and the rest.
Will ye, like soldiers, come and fight it out?

ALENÇON Seigneur, no.

TALBOT
Seigneur, hang! Base muleteers of France!   68
Like peasant footboys do they keep the walls   69
And dare not take up arms like gentlemen.

PUCELLE
Away, captains. Let's get us from the walls,
For Talbot means no goodness by his looks.
Good-bye, my lord. We came but to tell you
That we are here. *Exeunt from the walls.*

TALBOT
And there will we be too, ere it be long,
Or else reproach be Talbot's greatest fame!   76
Vow, Burgundy, by honor of thy house,
Pricked on by public wrongs sustained in France,   78
Either to get the town again or die.
And I, as sure as English Henry lives
And as his father here was conqueror,   81
As sure as in this late-betrayèd town   82

59 If . . . follow (A proverb, suggesting that ranting is usually followed
by grief; Talbot will soon have reason to be sorry.) **60 speaker** spokesman (playing on the sense of "parliamentary leader") **64 Hecate**
goddess of night and of black magic **68 muleteers** mule drivers
69 keep keep safely within **76 fame** reputation **78 Pricked on**
goaded **81 father . . . conqueror** (Henry V captured Rouen in 1419.)
82 late-betrayèd recently lost to the enemy through treachery

Great Coeur de Lion's heart was burièd,   83
So sure I swear to get the town or die.

BURGUNDY
My vows are equal partners with thy vows.

TALBOT
But ere we go, regard this dying prince,   86
The valiant Duke of Bedford.—Come, my lord,
We will bestow you in some better place,
Fitter for sickness and for crazy age.   89

BEDFORD
Lord Talbot, do not so dishonor me.
Here will I sit before the walls of Rouen
And will be partner of your weal or woe.   92

BURGUNDY
Courageous Bedford, let us now persuade you.

BEDFORD
Not to be gone from hence; for once I read
That stout Pendragon in his litter sick   95
Came to the field and vanquishèd his foes.
Methinks I should revive the soldiers' hearts,
Because I ever found them as myself.

TALBOT
Undaunted spirit in a dying breast!
Then be it so. Heavens keep old Bedford safe!
And now no more ado, brave Burgundy,
But gather we our forces out of hand   102
And set upon our boasting enemy.
            Exeunt [all but Bedford and attendants].

            *An alarum. Excursions. Enter Sir John Falstaff
            and a Captain.*

83 Great . . . heart (According to Holinshed, Richard Coeur de Lion, "the
lion-hearted," King of England 1189–1199, had willed that "his heart be
conveyed unto Rouen and there buried, in testimony of the love which he
had ever borne unto that city.")   **86 regard** attend to   **89 crazy** decrepit
92 weal welfare   **95 Pendragon** (According to Holinshed, it was the brother
of Uther Pendragon who, "even sick as he was, caused himself to be
carried forth in a litter; with whose presence his people were so encouraged that, encountering with the Saxons, they won the victory." Geoffrey of
Monmouth, on the other hand, credits this feat to Uther himself. Uther was
father of King Arthur.)   **102 out of hand** at once

CAPTAIN
Whither away, Sir John Falstaff, in such haste?
FALSTAFF
Whither away? To save myself by flight.
We are like to have the overthrow again.   106
CAPTAIN
What? Will you fly, and leave Lord Talbot?
FALSTAFF   Ay,
All the Talbots in the world, to save my life.   *Exit.*
CAPTAIN
Cowardly knight, ill fortune follow thee!   *Exit.*

> *Retreat. Excursions. Pucelle, Alençon, and*
> *Charles fly.*

BEDFORD
Now, quiet soul, depart when heaven please,   110
For I have seen our enemies' overthrow.   111
What is the trust or strength of foolish man?
They that of late were daring with their scoffs
Are glad and fain by flight to save themselves.   114
> *Bedford dies, and is carried in by two in his chair.*

> *An alarum. Enter Talbot, Burgundy, and the rest*
> [*of the English soldiers*].

TALBOT
Lost and recovered in a day again!
This is a double honor, Burgundy.
Yet heavens have glory for this victory!
BURGUNDY
Warlike and martial Talbot, Burgundy
Enshrines thee in his heart and there erects
Thy noble deeds as valor's monuments.
TALBOT
Thanks, gentle Duke. But where is Pucelle now?   121
I think her old familiar is asleep.   122

---

106 like to . . . overthrow likely to be overthrown   **110–111 Now . . .
overthrow** (A secular version of Luke 2:29–30, "Lord, now lettest thou
thy servant depart in peace," etc., sung as the *Nunc dimittis* in evensong
in the Book of Common Prayer.)   **114 fain** eager   **s.d. carried in** carried
offstage   **121 gentle** noble   **122 old familiar** customary attendant
demon

Now where's the Bastard's braves, and Charles his
   gleeks?   123
What, all amort? Rouen hangs her head for grief   124
That such a valiant company are fled.
Now will we take some order in the town,   126
Placing therein some expert officers,
And then depart to Paris to the King,
For there young Henry with his nobles lie.

BURGUNDY
What wills Lord Talbot pleaseth Burgundy.

TALBOT
But yet, before we go, let's not forget
The noble Duke of Bedford late deceased,
But see his exequies fulfilled in Rouen.   133
A braver soldier never couchèd lance;   134
A gentler heart did never sway in court.   135
But kings and mightiest potentates must die,
For that's the end of human misery.   *Exeunt.*

❖

3.3   *Enter Charles, [the] Bastard [of Orleans],*
      Alençon, Pucelle, [and French soldiers].

PUCELLE
Dismay not, princes, at this accident,   1
Nor grieve that Rouen is so recoverèd.
Care is no cure, but rather corrosive,   3
For things that are not to be remedied.
Let frantic Talbot triumph for a while
And like a peacock sweep along his tail;
We'll pull his plumes and take away his train,   7
If Dauphin and the rest will be but ruled.

---

123 braves boasts. **Charles his gleeks** Charles's gibes, jests **124 amort**
sick to death, dispirited **126 take some order** establish order and
government **133 exequies** funeral rites **134 couchèd lance** carried his
lance lowered, in the position of attack **135 gentler** more noble. **sway**
exercise influence

3.3. Location: Near Rouen.
1 Dismay not be not dismayed, disheartened. **accident** bad luck,
untoward event **3 Care** sorrow **7 train** (1) peacock's tail (2) army

CHARLES
We have been guided by thee hitherto,
And of thy cunning had no diffidence.   10
One sudden foil shall never breed distrust.   11

BASTARD
Search out thy wit for secret policies,   12
And we will make thee famous through the world.

ALENÇON
We'll set thy statue in some holy place
And have thee reverenced like a blessèd saint.
Employ thee, then, sweet virgin, for our good.

PUCELLE
Then thus it must be; this doth Joan devise:
By fair persuasions, mixed with sugared words,
We will entice the Duke of Burgundy
To leave the Talbot and to follow us.

CHARLES
Ay, marry, sweeting, if we could do that,
France were no place for Henry's warriors,
Nor should that nation boast it so with us,
But be extirpèd from our provinces.   24

ALENÇON
Forever should they be expulsed from France
And not have title of an earldom here.

PUCELLE
Your honors shall perceive how I will work
To bring this matter to the wishèd end.
                                Drum sounds afar off.
Hark, by the sound of drum you may perceive
Their powers are marching unto Paris-ward.   30
                        Here sound an English march.
There goes the Talbot, with his colors spread,
And all the troops of English after him.
                                    French march.
Now in the rearward comes the Duke and his.
Fortune in favor makes him lag behind.   34

10 diffidence distrust   **11 foil** repulse, defeat   **12 policies** stratagems
24 extirpèd rooted out   **30 s.d. Here . . . march** (Probably the English
are heard from offstage, and the French at l. 32, but conceivably soldiers could pass over the stage.)   **34 in favor** benevolently, i.e., in our
favor

Summon a parley. We will talk with him.   35

        Trumpets sound a parley.

[*Enter the Duke of Burgundy.*]

CHARLES
A parley with the Duke of Burgundy!

BURGUNDY
Who craves a parley with the Burgundy?

PUCELLE
The princely Charles of France, thy countryman.

BURGUNDY
What sayst thou, Charles? For I am marching hence.

CHARLES
Speak, Pucelle, and enchant him with thy words.   40

PUCELLE
Brave Burgundy, undoubted hope of France,   41
Stay. Let thy humble handmaid speak to thee.

BURGUNDY
Speak on, but be not overtedious.

PUCELLE
Look on thy country, look on fertile France,
And see the cities and the towns defaced
By wasting ruin of the cruel foe.
As looks the mother on her lowly babe   47
When death doth close his tender-dying eyes,   48
See, see the pining malady of France!   49
Behold the wounds, the most unnatural wounds,   50
Which thou thyself hast given her woeful breast.
O, turn thy edgèd sword another way!
Strike those that hurt, and hurt not those that help!
One drop of blood drawn from thy country's bosom
Should grieve thee more than streams of foreign gore.
Return thee therefore with a flood of tears
And wash away thy country's stainèd spots.   57

---

35 Summon a parley sound a trumpet signal requesting negotiations
40 enchant put spells on   **41 undoubted** i.e., whose bravery and
strength are sure bulwarks   **47 lowly** little, or humbled by misfortune,
lying low   **48 tender-dying** dying at a tender age   **49 malady of France**
(With comic double meaning; the phrase normally refers to venereal
disease.)   **50 unnatural** i.e., turned against the doer's own country
57 thy . . . spots blemishes to your country's reputation

BURGUNDY [*Aside*]
   Either she hath bewitched me with her words,
   Or nature makes me suddenly relent.

PUCELLE
   Besides, all French and France exclaims on thee,   60
   Doubting thy birth and lawful progeny.   61
   Who join'st thou with but with a lordly nation
   That will not trust thee but for profit's sake?
   When Talbot hath set footing once in France
   And fashioned thee that instrument of ill,   65
   Who then but English Henry will be lord,
   And thou be thrust out like a fugitive?   67
   Call we to mind, and mark but this for proof: 68
   Was not the Duke of Orleans thy foe?
   And was he not in England prisoner?
   But when they heard he was thine enemy,
   They set him free without his ransom paid,
   In spite of Burgundy and all his friends.
   See, then, thou fight'st against thy countrymen
   And join'st with them will be thy slaughtermen.   75
   Come, come, return. Return, thou wandering lord!
   Charles and the rest will take thee in their arms.

BURGUNDY [*Aside*]
   I am vanquished. These haughty words of hers   78
   Have battered me like roaring cannon-shot
   And made me almost yield upon my knees.—
   Forgive me, country, and sweet countrymen!
   And, lords, accept this hearty kind embrace.
   My forces and my power of men are yours.
   So farewell, Talbot. I'll no longer trust thee.

PUCELLE
   Done like a Frenchman—[*Aside*] turn and turn again!

CHARLES
   Welcome, brave Duke! Thy friendship makes us fresh.

---

60 exclaims on denounces, accuses **61 progeny** ancestry **65 fashioned
thee** turned you into **67 fugitive** renegade, deserter of your own nation **68 Call we to mind** let us remember **75 them** those who **78 I
am vanquished** (Historically, Burgundy did not desert the English
alliance until four years after Joan's death. This desertion occurred five
years before the Duke of Orleans was released by the English; see
ll. 69–73.) **haughty** lofty

BASTARD
And doth beget new courage in our breasts.

ALENÇON
Pucelle hath bravely played her part in this   88
And doth deserve a coronet of gold.

CHARLES
Now let us on, my lords, and join our powers,   90
And seek how we may prejudice the foe.   *Exeunt.* 91

❖

3.4   *Enter the King, Gloucester, Winchester,*
           [Richard, Duke of] York, Suffolk, Somerset,
           Warwick, Exeter, [Vernon, wearing a white
           rose, Basset, wearing a red rose, and others]. To
           them, with his soldiers, Talbot.

TALBOT
My gracious prince, and honorable peers,
Hearing of your arrival in this realm,
I have awhile given truce unto my wars
To do my duty to my sovereign;   4
In sign whereof, this arm, that hath reclaimed
To your obedience fifty fortresses,
Twelve cities, and seven walled towns of strength,
Besides five hundred prisoners of esteem,
Lets fall his sword before Your Highness' feet,
And with submissive loyalty of heart
Ascribes the glory of his conquest got
First to my God and next unto Your Grace. [*He kneels.*]

KING
Is this the Lord Talbot, uncle Gloucester,
That hath so long been resident in France?

GLOUCESTER
Yes, if it please Your Majesty, my liege.

KING
Welcome, brave captain and victorious lord!

---

88 bravely courageously and excellently   **90 powers** armed forces
91 prejudice harm

3.4. Location: Paris. The royal court.
4 duty homage

When I was young—as yet I am not old—
I do remember how my father said   18
A stouter champion never handled sword.   19
Long since we were resolvèd of your truth,   20
Your faithful service, and your toil in war;
Yet never have you tasted our reward
Or been reguerdoned with so much as thanks,   23
Because till now we never saw your face.
Therefore, stand up. [*Talbot rises.*] And for these good
   deserts   25
We here create you Earl of Shrewsbury;
And in our coronation take your place.   27
       Sennet. Flourish. Exeunt. Manent Vernon and
                         Basset.

VERNON
Now, sir, to you, that were so hot at sea,   28
Disgracing of these colors that I wear   29
In honor of my noble lord of York:
Dar'st thou maintain the former words thou spak'st?
BASSET
Yes, sir, as well as you dare patronage   32
The envious barking of your saucy tongue
Against my lord the Duke of Somerset.
VERNON
Sirrah, thy lord I honor as he is.   35
BASSET
Why, what is he? As good a man as York.
VERNON
Hark ye, not so. In witness, take ye that.
                           Strikes him.

BASSET
Villain, thou knowest the law of arms is such   38

---

18 I . . . said (Historically, Henry VI was an infant of nine months at his
father's death.) **19 stouter** more intrepid **20 we** i.e., I. (The royal
"we.") **resolvèd** convinced. **truth** loyalty **23 reguerdoned** rewarded
25 deserts deservings **27 s.d. Manent** they remain onstage **28 so hot
at sea** (The details of this quarrel are given below, 4.1.87–97.)
29 Disgracing of insulting. **these colors** i.e., the white rose of York
32 patronage defend **35 as he is** i.e., for what he is—a person of no
worth **38 law of arms** (This law forbade the drawing of weapons near
a royal residence; see 1.3.46 and note, and 2.4.86 and note.)

That whoso draws a sword, 'tis present death,   39
Or else this blow should broach thy dearest blood.   40
But I'll unto His Majesty and crave
I may have liberty to venge this wrong,   42
When thou shalt see I'll meet thee to thy cost.

VERNON
Well, miscreant, I'll be there as soon as you,
And after meet you, sooner than you would.   *Exeunt.* 45

4.1   *Enter King, Gloucester, Winchester, [Richard,*
          Duke of] York, Suffolk, Somerset, Warwick,
          Talbot, Exeter, Governor [of Paris, and others].

GLOUCESTER
Lord Bishop, set the crown upon his head.
WINCHESTER
God save King Henry, of that name the sixth!
                              [The King is crowned.]
GLOUCESTER
Now, Governor of Paris, take your oath,
                              [The Governor kneels]
That you elect no other king but him,   4
Esteem none friends but such as are his friends,
And none your foes but such as shall pretend   6
Malicious practices against his state.   7
This shall ye do, so help you righteous God!
                              [The Governor retires.]

          Enter [Sir John] Falstaff.

FALSTAFF
My gracious sovereign, as I rode from Calais

39 present instant   **40 broach** tap, draw.   **dearest blood** i.e., lifeblood
42 wrong insult   **45 after** i.e., once the royal permission to fight a duel
has been obtained

**4.1. Location: Paris. Scene continues. (The action appears to go on
immediately after the events of 3.4.)**
s.d. York i.e., Richard Plantagenet, created Duke of York in 3.1 and
hereafter identified by the speech prefix YORK   **4 elect** acknowledge
6 pretend purpose, intend   **7 practices** stratagems

To haste unto your coronation,
A letter was delivered to my hands,
Writ to Your Grace from th' Duke of Burgundy.

[*He presents a letter.*]

TALBOT
Shame to the Duke of Burgundy and thee!
I vowed, base knight, when I did meet thee next,
To tear the Garter from thy craven's leg,   15

[*Plucking it off*]

Which I have done, because unworthily
Thou wast installèd in that high degree.
Pardon me, princely Henry, and the rest.
This dastard, at the battle of Poitiers,   19
When but in all I was six thousand strong   20
And that the French were almost ten to one,   21
Before we met or that a stroke was given,
Like to a trusty squire did run away;   23
In which assault we lost twelve hundred men.
Myself and divers gentlemen besides
Were there surprised and taken prisoners.
Then judge, great lords, if I have done amiss,
Or whether that such cowards ought to wear
This ornament of knighthood, yea or no?

GLOUCESTER
To say the truth, this fact was infamous   30
And ill beseeming any common man,
Much more a knight, a captain, and a leader.

TALBOT
When first this order was ordained, my lords,
Knights of the Garter were of noble birth,
Valiant and virtuous, full of haughty courage,   35
Such as were grown to credit by the wars—   36
Not fearing death, nor shrinking for distress,

15 Garter badge of the Knights of the Garter, a ribbon of blue velvet
edged and buckled with gold, worn below the left knee. (Historically,
the Garter was apparently taken from Fastolfe by the Duke of Bedford;
Talbot, who was a captive of the French at the time of Henry VI's
coronation in Paris, was opposed to the restoration of the Garter to
Fastolfe.)   **19 Poitiers** (Seemingly confused with Patay.)   **20 but in all** all
told   **21 And that** and   **23 trusty squire** (Said contemptuously.)   **30 fact**
deed   **35 haughty** exalted   **36 were grown to credit** had achieved
renown

But always resolute in most extremes.   38
He then that is not furnished in this sort   39
Doth but usurp the sacred name of knight,
Profaning this most honorable order,
And should, if I were worthy to be judge,
Be quite degraded, like a hedge-born swain   43
That doth presume to boast of gentle blood.   44

KING
Stain to thy countrymen, thou hear'st thy doom.   45
Be packing, therefore, thou that wast a knight.   46
Henceforth we banish thee, on pain of death.
                                        [*Exit Falstaff.*]
And now, my Lord Protector, view the letter
Sent from our uncle, Duke of Burgundy.   49

GLOUCESTER [*Taking the letter*]
What means His Grace, that he hath changed his style?   50
No more but, plain and bluntly, "To the King"?
Hath he forgot he is his sovereign?
Or doth this churlish superscription   53
Pretend some alteration in good will?   54
What's here? [*He reads.*] "I have, upon especial cause,
Moved with compassion of my country's wrack,   56
Together with the pitiful complaints
Of such as your oppression feeds upon,
Forsaken your pernicious faction
And joined with Charles, the rightful King of France."
O monstrous treachery! Can this be so,
That in alliance, amity, and oaths
There should be found such false dissembling guile?

KING
What? Doth my uncle Burgundy revolt?   64

GLOUCESTER
He doth, my lord, and is become your foe.

---

38 most greatest   **39 furnished ... sort** endowed thus   **43 degraded**
lowered in rank.   **hedge-born swain** lowly-born rustic   **44 gentle** noble   **45 doom** sentence   **46 Be packing** be off   **49 uncle** (The Lancastrian and Burgundian houses were allied by the marriage of the Duke
of Bedford, the King's uncle, to Anne, sister of the Duke of Burgundy.)
50 style form of address   **53 churlish superscription** insolent form of
address on the outside of the letter   **54 Pretend** portend, import
56 wrack ruin   **64 revolt** fall away to the other side

KING
  Is that the worst this letter doth contain?
GLOUCESTER
  It is the worst, and all, my lord, he writes.
KING
  Why, then, Lord Talbot there shall talk with him
  And give him chastisement for this abuse.   69
  [*To Talbot.*] How say you, my lord? Are you not content?
TALBOT
  Content, my liege? Yes. But that I am prevented,   71
  I should have begged I might have been employed.
KING
  Then gather strength and march unto him straight.   73
  Let him perceive how ill we brook his treason,   74
  And what offense it is to flout his friends.
TALBOT
  I go, my lord, in heart desiring still   76
  You may behold confusion of your foes.   [*Exit.*]   77

          Enter Vernon and Basset, [*wearing a white and a
          red rose respectively, as before*].

VERNON
  Grant me the combat, gracious sovereign.   78
BASSET
  And me, my lord, grant me the combat too.
YORK
  This is my servant. Hear him, noble prince.   80
SOMERSET
  And this is mine. Sweet Henry, favor him.
KING
  Be patient, lords, and give them leave to speak.
  Say, gentlemen, what makes you thus exclaim?
  And wherefore crave you combat, or with whom?
VERNON
  With him, my lord, for he hath done me wrong.
BASSET
  And I with him, for he hath done me wrong.

---

69 abuse deception **71 prevented** anticipated **73 straight** immediately **74 brook** endure **76 still** always **77 confusion** destruction
78 the combat permission to fight a trial by duel **80 servant** i.e.,
follower

KING
  What is that wrong whereof you both complain?
  First let me know, and then I'll answer you.

BASSET
  Crossing the sea from England into France,
  This fellow here, with envious carping tongue,   90
  Upbraided me about the rose I wear,
  Saying the sanguine color of the leaves   92
  Did represent my master's blushing cheeks,
  When stubbornly he did repugn the truth   94
  About a certain question in the law
  Argued betwixt the Duke of York and him;
  With other vile and ignominious terms.
  In confutation of which rude reproach,
  And in defense of my lord's worthiness,
  I crave the benefit of law of arms.   100

VERNON
  And that is my petition, noble lord.
  For though he seem with forgèd quaint conceit   102
  To set a gloss upon his bold intent,   103
  Yet know, my lord, I was provoked by him,
  And he first took exceptions at this badge,
  Pronouncing that the paleness of this flower
  Bewrayed the faintness of my master's heart.   107

YORK
  Will not this malice, Somerset, be left?   108

SOMERSET
  Your private grudge, my lord of York, will out,   109
  Though ne'er so cunningly you smother it.

KING
  Good Lord, what madness rules in brainsick men,
  When for so slight and frivolous a cause
  Such factious emulations shall arise!   113
  Good cousins both, of York and Somerset,   114
  Quiet yourselves, I pray, and be at peace.

---

90 envious malicious   **92 sanguine** bloodred. **leaves** petals   **94 repugn**
oppose, resist   **100 benefit . . . arms** right to protect my honor in a
duel   **102 forgèd quaint conceit** false ingenious rhetoric   **103 gloss**
speciously fair appearance   **107 Bewrayed** revealed   **108 left** i.e.,
forgotten   **109 out** appear, be revealed   **113 emulations** contentions
between rivals   **114 cousins** kinsmen

YORK
Let this dissension first be tried by fight,
And then Your Highness shall command a peace.

SOMERSET
The quarrel toucheth none but us alone;   118
Betwixt ourselves let us decide it, then.

YORK
There is my pledge. Accept it, Somerset.   120
                    [*He throws down a gage.*]

VERNON [*To Somerset*]
Nay, let it rest where it began at first.   121

BASSET [*To Somerset*]
Confirm it so, mine honorable lord.   122

GLOUCESTER
Confirm it so? Confounded be your strife!
And perish ye, with your audacious prate!
Presumptuous vassals, are you not ashamed
With this immodest clamorous outrage   126
To trouble and disturb the King and us?
And you, my lords, methinks you do not well   128
To bear with their perverse objections,   129
Much less to take occasion from their mouths
To raise a mutiny betwixt yourselves.   131
Let me persuade you take a better course.

EXETER
It grieves His Highness. Good my lords, be friends.

KING
Come hither, you that would be combatants:
Henceforth I charge you, as you love our favor,
Quite to forget this quarrel and the cause.
And you, my lords: remember where we are—
In France, amongst a fickle wavering nation.
If they perceive dissension in our looks

---

118 toucheth concerns   **120 pledge** i.e., a glove or gauntlet flung down
as a gage in a duel   **121 let . . . first** i.e., let the quarrel remain with me
and Basset, who began it. Don't answer York's challenge by throwing
down your gage.   **122 Confirm . . . lord** (Basset, contradicting Vernon,
asks his lord, Somerset, to confirm York's challenge by throwing down
his glove, or perhaps asks Somerset to confirm the suggestion that
Vernon and Basset fight it out themselves.)   **126 immodest** arrogant,
impudent   **128 my lords** i.e., York and Somerset (also in l. 137)
129 objections charges, accusations   **131 mutiny** quarrel, strife

And that within ourselves we disagree, 140
How will their grudging stomachs be provoked 141
To willful disobedience, and rebel!
Besides, what infamy will there arise
When foreign princes shall be certified 144
That for a toy, a thing of no regard, 145
King Henry's peers and chief nobility
Destroyed themselves and lost the realm of France!
O, think upon the conquest of my father,
My tender years, and let us not forgo
That for a trifle that was bought with blood! 150
Let me be umpire in this doubtful strife. 151
I see no reason, if I wear this rose,
　　　　　　　　　　　[*Putting on a red rose*]
That anyone should therefore be suspicious
I more incline to Somerset than York.
Both are my kinsmen, and I love them both.
As well they may upbraid me with my crown
Because, forsooth, the King of Scots is crowned.
But your discretions better can persuade
Than I am able to instruct or teach;
And therefore, as we hither came in peace,
So let us still continue peace and love. 161
Cousin of York, we institute Your Grace
To be our regent in these parts of France.
And, good my lord of Somerset, unite
Your troops of horsemen with his bands of foot; 165
And like true subjects, sons of your progenitors,
Go cheerfully together and digest 167
Your angry choler on your enemies.
Ourself, my Lord Protector, and the rest,
After some respite, will return to Calais;
From thence to England, where I hope ere long
To be presented by your victories
With Charles, Alençon, and that traitorous rout. 173
　　　　　Flourish. Exeunt. Manent York, Warwick,
　　　　　　　　　　Exeter, [*and*] *Vernon.*

140 within among　**141 grudging stomachs** resentful tempers
144 certified informed　**145 toy** trifle　**150 That . . . that** for a trifle that
which　**151 doubtful** causing apprehension　**161 still** ever　**165 bands
of foot** troops of infantry　**167 digest** disperse, dissipate　**173 rout**
rabble　**s.d. Manent** they remain onstage

WARWICK
My lord of York, I promise you, the King   174
Prettily, methought, did play the orator.

YORK
And so he did; but yet I like it not
In that he wears the badge of Somerset.

WARWICK
Tush, that was but his fancy. Blame him not.
I dare presume, sweet prince, he thought no harm.

YORK
An if I wist he did—But let it rest.   180
Other affairs must now be managèd.

                        Exeunt. Manet Exeter.

EXETER
Well didst thou, Richard, to suppress thy voice;
For, had the passions of thy heart burst out,
I fear we should have seen deciphered there   184
More rancorous spite, more furious raging broils,
Than yet can be imagined or supposed.
But howsoe'er, no simple man that sees   187
This jarring discord of nobility,
This shouldering of each other in the court,
This factious bandying of their favorites,   190
But that it doth presage some ill event.   191
'Tis much when scepters are in children's hands,
But more when envy breeds unkind division.   193
There comes the ruin, there begins confusion.   *Exit.*

4.2   *Enter Talbot, with trump and drum [and
          forces], before Bordeaux.*

---

174 promise assure   **180 An . . . wist** if I knew for certain
184 deciphered detected, expressed   **187 simple** common
190 bandying contending.   **favorites** followers   **191 But that** i.e., but
sees that.   **event** outcome   **193 envy** malice.   **unkind** unnatural

4.2. Location: France. Before Bordeaux.
s.d. trump and drum trumpeter and drummer

TALBOT

   Go to the gates of Bordeaux, trumpeter.   1
   Summon their general unto the wall.

    [Trumpet] sounds. Enter General, aloft.

   English John Talbot, captains, calls you forth,
   Servant in arms to Harry King of England,
   And thus he would: Open your city gates,   5
   Be humble to us, call my sovereign yours,
   And do him homage as obedient subjects,
   And I'll withdraw me and my bloody power.   8
   But if you frown upon this proffered peace,
   You tempt the fury of my three attendants,
   Lean famine, quartering steel, and climbing fire,   11
   Who in a moment even with the earth   12
   Shall lay your stately and air-braving towers,   13
   If you forsake the offer of their love.   14

GENERAL

   Thou ominous and fearful owl of death,   15
   Our nation's terror and their bloody scourge,
   The period of thy tyranny approacheth.   17
   On us thou canst not enter but by death;
   For I protest we are well fortified
   And strong enough to issue out and fight.
   If thou retire, the Dauphin, well appointed,   21
   Stands with the snares of war to tangle thee.
   On either hand thee there are squadrons pitched   23
   To wall thee from the liberty of flight;
   And no way canst thou turn thee for redress
   But death doth front thee with apparent spoil   26

---

1 gates (As before at Orleans and Rouen, these city gates are represented
by a door in the tiring-house facade, which is imagined to be the walls
of Bordeaux. Occupants of Bordeaux appearing *aloft* or on the walls are
seen in the gallery backstage.) **5 would** wishes **8 bloody power** bloodthirsty army **11 quartering** dismembering **12 even** level **13 air-
braving** defying the heavens (by their height) **14 forsake** refuse. **their**
i.e., *famine, steel,* and *fire* **15 owl** i.e., portent **17 period** termination. **tyranny** cruelty **21 appointed** equipped **23 thee** i.e., of you.
pitched set in battle array **26 front** face. **apparent spoil** obvious
destruction

And pale destruction meets thee in the face.   27
Ten thousand French have ta'en the Sacrament   28
To rive their dangerous artillery   29
Upon no Christian soul but English Talbot.
Lo, there thou stand'st, a breathing valiant man
Of an invincible unconquered spirit.
This is the latest glory of thy praise   33
That I, thy enemy, due thee withal;   34
For ere the glass that now begins to run   35
Finish the process of his sandy hour,   36
These eyes, that see thee now well colorèd,   37
Shall see thee withered, bloody, pale, and dead.
                                        Drum afar off.
Hark, hark! The Dauphin's drum, a warning bell,
Sings heavy music to thy timorous soul,
And mine shall ring thy dire departure out.   41
                                        Exit [*with his men*].

TALBOT
He fables not. I hear the enemy.
Out, some light horsemen, and peruse their wings.   43
                                        [*Exeunt some.*]
O, negligent and heedless discipline!   44
How are we parked and bounded in a pale—   45
A little herd of England's timorous deer,
Mazed with a yelping kennel of French curs!   47
If we be English deer, be then in blood: 48
Not rascal-like to fall down with a pinch,   49
But rather, moody-mad and desperate stags,   50
Turn on the bloody hounds with heads of steel   51
And make the cowards stand aloof at bay.
Sell every man his life as dear as mine
And they shall find dear deer of us, my friends.

27 pale (because Death is portrayed as pale)   **28 ta'en the Sacrament**
i.e., confirmed their solemn oaths by taking the Sacrament   **29 rive**
burst, fire   **33 latest** final   **34 due** endue, invest   **35 glass** hourglass
36 sandy hour hour as measured by the running of the sand   **37 well
colorèd** i.e., in health   **41 departure** i.e., death   **43 peruse** survey,
reconnoiter.   **wings** flanks   **44 discipline** military tactics   **45 parked**
enclosed.   **pale** fenced-in space   **47 Mazed with** (1) bewildered, amazed
by (2) enclosed by, as in a labyrinth (?)   **48 in blood** in prime condition   **49 rascal-like** (1) like young or inferior deer (2) like rascals.   **pinch**
nip   **50 moody-mad** high-spirited and mad with rage   **51 heads of steel**
(1) swordlike antlers (2) helmeted heads

God and Saint George, Talbot and England's right,
Prosper our colors in this dangerous fight!   [*Exeunt.*]

❖

4.3   *Enter a Messenger that meets York. Enter York*
with trumpet and many soldiers.

YORK
    Are not the speedy scouts returned again
    That dogged the mighty army of the Dauphin?
MESSENGER
    They are returned, my lord, and give it out   3
    That he is marched to Bordeaux with his power
    To fight with Talbot. As he marched along,
    By your espials were discoverèd   6
    Two mightier troops than that the Dauphin led,
    Which joined with him and made their march for
      Bordeaux.
YORK
    A plague upon that villain Somerset,
    That thus delays my promisèd supply   10
    Of horsemen that were levied for this siege!
    Renownèd Talbot doth expect my aid,
    And I am louted by a traitor villain   13
    And cannot help the noble chevalier.
    God comfort him in this necessity!
    If he miscarry, farewell wars in France.   16

    Enter another Messenger, [*Sir William Lucy*].

LUCY
    Thou princely leader of our English strength,
    Never so needful on the earth of France,
    Spur to the rescue of the noble Talbot,
    Who now is girdled with a waist of iron
    And hemmed about with grim destruction.
    To Bordeaux, warlike Duke! To Bordeaux, York!
    Else, farewell Talbot, France, and England's honor.

4.3. Location: France. Plains in Gascony.
3 give it out report   **6 espials** spies   **10 supply** reinforcements
13 louted made a fool of, mocked   **16 miscarry** come to grief

YORK

O God, that Somerset, who in proud heart
Doth stop my cornets, were in Talbot's place!   25
So should we save a valiant gentleman
By forfeiting a traitor and a coward.
Mad ire and wrathful fury makes me weep
That thus we die while remiss traitors sleep.

LUCY

O, send some succor to the distressed lord!   30

YORK

He dies, we lose; I break my warlike word;
We mourn, France smiles; we lose, they daily get;
All 'long of this vile traitor Somerset.   33

LUCY

Then God take mercy on brave Talbot's soul,
And on his son young John, who two hours since
I met in travel toward his warlike father.
This seven years did not Talbot see his son,
And now they meet where both their lives are done.

YORK

Alas, what joy shall noble Talbot have
To bid his young son welcome to his grave?
Away! Vexation almost stops my breath,   41
That sundered friends greet in the hour of death.
Lucy, farewell. No more my fortune can   43
But curse the cause I cannot aid the man.
Maine, Blois, Poitiers, and Tours are won away,
'Long all of Somerset and his delay.

Exit [*with his soldiers*].

LUCY

Thus, while the vulture of sedition
Feeds in the bosom of such great commanders,
Sleeping neglection doth betray to loss
The conquest of our scarce-cold conqueror,
That ever-living man of memory,   51
Henry the Fifth. Whiles they each other cross,
Lives, honors, lands, and all hurry to loss.

---

25 stop hold back.   **cornets** cavalry units   **30 distressed** in difficulties   **33 'long of** on account of   **41 Vexation** anguish   **43 can** is able to
do   **51 ever-living . . . memory** man of ever-living memory

4.4   *Enter Somerset, with his army; [a Captain of
Talbot's with him].*

SOMERSET
    It is too late. I cannot send them now.
    This expedition was by York and Talbot
    Too rashly plotted. All our general force   3
    Might with a sally of the very town   4
    Be buckled with. The overdaring Talbot   5
    Hath sullied all his gloss of former honor
    By this unheedful, desperate, wild adventure.
    York set him on to fight and die in shame,
    That, Talbot dead, great York might bear the name. 9
CAPTAIN
    Here is Sir William Lucy, who with me
    Set from our o'ermatched forces forth for aid.

        [*Sir William Lucy comes forward.*]

SOMERSET
    How now, Sir William, whither were you sent?
LUCY
    Whither, my lord? From bought and sold Lord Talbot,
    Who, ringed about with bold adversity,
    Cries out for noble York and Somerset
    To beat assailing death from his weak legions;
    And whiles the honorable captain there
    Drops bloody sweat from his war-wearied limbs,
    And, in advantage lingering, looks for rescue,   19
    You, his false hopes, the trust of England's honor, 20
    Keep off aloof with worthless emulation.   21
    Let not your private discord keep away
    The levied succors that should lend him aid,   23
    While he, renownèd noble gentleman,

4.4. Location: France. Scene continues. Lucy does not leave the stage.
3–5 All . . . with i.e., our entire army might be successfully encountered
by a sortie of the mere French garrison in Bordeaux, unsupported by
the other French armies coming to the relief of Bordeaux   **9 That** so
that.   **bear the name** i.e., receive all honor as supreme commander in
France   **19 in advantage lingering** making the best he can out of delaying tactics, or finding every way he can to delay matters   **20 trust**
guardian   **21 worthless emulation** ignoble rivalry   **23 levied succors**
raised reinforcements

Yield up his life unto a world of odds.   25
Orleans the Bastard, Charles, Burgundy,
Alençon, Reignier, compass him about,
And Talbot perisheth by your default.   28

SOMERSET
York set him on. York should have sent him aid.

LUCY
And York as fast upon Your Grace exclaims,   30
Swearing that you withhold his levied horse,
Collected for this expedition.

SOMERSET
York lies. He might have sent and had the horse.   33
I owe him little duty, and less love,
And take foul scorn to fawn on him by sending.   35

LUCY
The fraud of England, not the force of France,
Hath now entrapped the noble-minded Talbot.
Never to England shall he bear his life,
But dies betrayed to fortune by your strife.

SOMERSET
Come, go. I will dispatch the horsemen straight.
Within six hours they will be at his aid.

LUCY
Too late comes rescue. He is ta'en or slain;
For fly he could not, if he would have fled;
And fly would Talbot never, though he might.

SOMERSET
If he be dead, brave Talbot, then adieu!

LUCY
His fame lives in the world, his shame in you.
                                          Exeunt [separately].

❧

4.5   *Enter Talbot and his son [John].*

TALBOT
O young John Talbot, I did send for thee

---

25 a world of huge   **28 default** failure   **30 upon . . . exclaims** accuses
Your Grace   **33 might . . . had** i.e., had and could have sent   **35 take
foul scorn** consider it humiliating

4.5. Location: France. A field of battle near Bordeaux.

To tutor thee in stratagems of war,
That Talbot's name might be in thee revived
When sapless age and weak unable limbs
Should bring thy father to his drooping chair.   5
But, O malignant and ill-boding stars!
Now thou art come unto a feast of death,
A terrible and unavoided danger.   8
Therefore, dear boy, mount on my swiftest horse,
And I'll direct thee how thou shalt escape
By sudden flight. Come, dally not, begone.

JOHN
Is my name Talbot, and am I your son,
And shall I fly? O, if you love my mother,
Dishonor not her honorable name
To make a bastard and a slave of me!   15
The world will say he is not Talbot's blood
That basely fled when noble Talbot stood.

TALBOT
Fly to revenge my death if I be slain.

JOHN
He that flies so will ne'er return again.

TALBOT
If we both stay, we both are sure to die.

JOHN
Then let me stay, and, Father, do you fly.
Your loss is great; so your regard should be.   22
My worth unknown, no loss is known in me.   23
Upon my death the French can little boast;
In yours they will, in you all hopes are lost.
Flight cannot stain the honor you have won;
But mine it will, that no exploit have done.   27
You fled for vantage, everyone will swear,   28
But if I bow they'll say it was for fear.
There is no hope that ever I will stay,
If the first hour I shrink and run away.

---

5 drooping invalid   **8 unavoided** unavoidable   **15 To . . . me** by prompting me to act the part of a bastard and contemptible low person
22 Your loss is great the loss of you would be a severe setback.   **regard**
heed for yourself   **23 no loss . . . me** the loss of me would scarcely be
noticed   **27 that** I who   **28 vantage** military advantage

Here on my knee I beg mortality,   32
Rather than life preserved with infamy.
TALBOT
Shall all thy mother's hopes lie in one tomb?
JOHN
Ay, rather than I'll shame my mother's womb.
TALBOT
Upon my blessing I command thee go.
JOHN
To fight I will, but not to fly the foe.
TALBOT
Part of thy father may be saved in thee.
JOHN
No part of him but will be shame in me.
TALBOT
Thou never hadst renown, nor canst not lose it.
JOHN
Yes, your renownèd name. Shall flight abuse it?   41
TALBOT
Thy father's charge shall clear thee from that stain.   42
JOHN
You cannot witness for me, being slain.   43
If death be so apparent, then both fly.
TALBOT
And leave my followers here to fight and die?
My age was never tainted with such shame.   46
JOHN
And shall my youth be guilty of such blame?
No more can I be severed from your side
Than can yourself yourself in twain divide.
Stay, go, do what you will—the like do I;
For live I will not, if my father die.
TALBOT
Then here I take my leave of thee, fair son,
Born to eclipse thy life this afternoon.   53
Come, side by side together live and die,
And soul with soul from France to heaven fly.
                                              Exeunt.

32 mortality death   **41 abuse** dishonor   **42 charge** giving you an order   **43 being slain** i.e., you having been slain   **46 age** lifetime
53 eclipse (suggesting a pun on *son, sun* in the previous line)

4.6   *Alarum. Excursions, wherein Talbot's son is
hemmed about, and Talbot rescues him.*

TALBOT
  Saint George and victory! Fight, soldiers, fight!
  The Regent hath with Talbot broke his word   2
  And left us to the rage of France his sword.   3
  Where is John Talbot?—Pause, and take thy breath.
  I gave thee life and rescued thee from death.
JOHN
  O, twice my father, twice am I thy son!
  The life thou gav'st me first was lost and done
  Till with thy warlike sword, despite of fate,   8
  To my determined time thou gav'st new date.   9
TALBOT
  When from the Dauphin's crest thy sword struck fire, 10
  It warmed thy father's heart with proud desire
  Of boldfaced victory. Then leaden age,
  Quickened with youthful spleen and warlike rage,   13
  Beat down Alençon, Orleans, Burgundy,
  And from the pride of Gallia rescued thee.   15
  The ireful bastard Orleans, that drew blood
  From thee, my boy, and had the maidenhood
  Of thy first fight, I soon encounterèd,
  And interchanging blows, I quickly shed
  Some of his bastard blood; and in disgrace   20
  Bespoke him thus: "Contaminated, base,
  And misbegotten blood I spill of thine,
  Mean and right poor, for that pure blood of mine   23
  Which thou didst force from Talbot, my brave boy."
  Here, purposing the Bastard to destroy,   25
  Came in strong rescue. Speak, thy father's care.
  Art thou not weary, John? How dost thou fare?

4.6. Location: The battlefield still, moments later; the scene is continuous.
2 The Regent i.e., the Duke of York. (Cf. 4.1.162–163.) **3 France his**
France's **8 despite of fate** defying what fate had seemingly decreed
9 determined having been determined to end. **date** limit, termination
10 crest i.e., helmet **13 Quickened** revived. **spleen** i.e., courage,
ardor **15 Gallia** France **20 in disgrace** by way of insult **23 Mean**
base, inferior **25 purposing** as I purposed

Wilt thou yet leave the battle, boy, and fly,
Now thou art sealed the son of chivalry?   29
Fly, to revenge my death when I am dead.
The help of one stands me in little stead.
O, too much folly is it, well I wot,   32
To hazard all our lives in one small boat!
If I today die not with Frenchmen's rage,
Tomorrow I shall die with mickle age.   35
By me they nothing gain an if I stay;
'Tis but the shortening of my life one day.
In thee thy mother dies, our household's name,
My death's revenge, thy youth, and England's fame.
All these and more we hazard by thy stay;
All these are saved if thou wilt fly away.

JOHN
The sword of Orleans hath not made me smart;   42
These words of yours draw lifeblood from my heart.
On that advantage, bought with such a shame,   44
To save a paltry life and slay bright fame,
Before young Talbot from old Talbot fly,
The coward horse that bears me fall and die!   47
And like me to the peasant boys of France,   48
To be shame's scorn and subject of mischance!
Surely, by all the glory you have won,
An if I fly, I am not Talbot's son.
Then talk no more of flight. It is no boot.   52
If son to Talbot, die at Talbot's foot.

TALBOT
Then follow thou thy desperate sire of Crete,
Thou Icarus. Thy life to me is sweet.   55
If thou wilt fight, fight by thy father's side;
And, commendable proved, let's die in pride.

                                        Exeunt.

---

29 sealed certified   **32 wot** know   **35 mickle** great   **42 smart** feel
pain   **44 On that advantage** i.e., to gain that advantage of safety
47 fall i.e., may it fall   **48 like** liken   **52 boot** profit, advantage
55 Thou Icarus (Daedalus of Crete and his son Icarus escaped from the
labyrinth by means of wings that the father's ingenuity had devised. As
they flew across the sea, Icarus mounted too high, the sun's heat melted
the wax by which his wings were attached, and he fell into the sea,
hence called the Icarian Sea, and was lost.)

4.7   *Alarum. Excursions. Enter old Talbot*
            led [by a Servant].

TALBOT
Where is my other life? Mine own is gone.
O, where's young Talbot? Where is valiant John?
Triumphant Death, smeared with captivity,   3
Young Talbot's valor makes me smile at thee.
When he perceived me shrink and on my knee,   5
His bloody sword he brandished over me,
And like a hungry lion did commence
Rough deeds of rage and stern impatience.
But when my angry guardant stood alone,   9
Tend'ring my ruin and assailed of none,   10
Dizzy-eyed fury and great rage of heart
Suddenly made him from my side to start
Into the clustering battle of the French;   13
And in that sea of blood my boy did drench   14
His overmounting spirit; and there died
My Icarus, my blossom, in his pride.   16

       Enter [soldiers], with John Talbot, borne.

SERVANT
O my dear lord, lo, where your son is borne!
TALBOT
Thou antic Death, which laugh'st us here to scorn,   18
Anon, from thy insulting tyranny,
Coupled in bonds of perpetuity,
Two Talbots, wingèd through the lither sky,   21
In thy despite shall scape mortality.   22
O thou, whose wounds become hard-favored Death,   23

4.7. Location: The battlefield still; the scene is continuous.
3 smeared with captivity i.e., stained with the blood of your captives.
(The image is of a triumphal procession.)   **5 shrink** retire in battle
9 guardant guardian   **10 Tend'ring** being concerned for.   **of** by
13 battle army   **14 drench** drown   **16 pride** glory   **18 antic** i.e., grin-
ning. (A personification probably suggested by grotesque pictorial
representations in the Middle Ages and early Renaissance such as the
Dance of Death.)   **here** here on earth   **21 lither** yielding   **22 In thy
despite** in spite of you.   **scape mortality** escape the bonds of death
(through immortality)   **23 thou** i.e., John.   **become ... Death** make
Death, otherwise hideous, beautiful

Speak to thy father ere thou yield thy breath!
Brave Death by speaking, whether he will or no;   25
Imagine him a Frenchman and thy foe.
Poor boy! He smiles, methinks, as who should say,   27
"Had Death been French, then Death had died today."
Come, come, and lay him in his father's arms.
                    [*John is laid in his father's arms.*]
My spirit can no longer bear these harms.
Soldiers, adieu! I have what I would have,
Now my old arms are young John Talbot's grave.   32
                    Dies. [*Exeunt soldiers.*]

*Enter Charles, Alençon, Burgundy, Bastard,
and Pucelle.*

CHARLES
Had York and Somerset brought rescue in,
We should have found a bloody day of this.

BASTARD
How the young whelp of Talbot's, raging wood,   35
Did flesh his puny sword in Frenchmen's blood!   36

PUCELLE
Once I encountered him, and thus I said:
"Thou maiden youth, be vanquished by a maid."   38
But with a proud, majestical high scorn
He answered thus: "Young Talbot was not born
To be the pillage of a giglot wench."   41
So, rushing in the bowels of the French,
He left me proudly, as unworthy fight.   43

BURGUNDY
Doubtless he would have made a noble knight.
See where he lies inhearsèd in the arms   45
Of the most bloody nurser of his harms!   46

---

25 Brave defy   **27 as who** as if one   **32 s.d. Dies** (Historically, Talbot did
not die until some twenty-two years after Henry VI's coronation in Paris.
Talbot's campaign in the Bordeaux region was successful, and included the
taking of the city.)   **35 whelp of Talbot's** (Talbot is the name of a species of
hound.)   **wood** mad   **36 flesh** use for the first time in battle.   **puny**
inexperienced (in bloodshed)   **38 maiden** i.e., not yet initiated in warfare
41 giglot wanton   **43 unworthy** unworthy of   **45 inhearsèd** as in a coffin
46 nurser . . . harms i.e., sire of his capacity for doing harm to his enemy

BASTARD

    Hew them to pieces, hack their bones asunder,

    Whose life was England's glory, Gallia's wonder.

CHARLES

    O, no, forbear! For that which we have fled

    During the life, let us not wrong it dead.

> *Enter [Sir William] Lucy [attended; Herald of the*
> *French preceding].*

LUCY

    Herald, conduct me to the Dauphin's tent,

    To know who hath obtained the glory of the day.

CHARLES

    On what submissive message art thou sent?

LUCY

    Submission, Dauphin? 'Tis a mere French word.

    We English warriors wot not what it means.

    I come to know what prisoners thou hast ta'en

    And to survey the bodies of the dead.

CHARLES

    For prisoners ask'st thou? Hell our prison is.   58

    But tell me whom thou seek'st.

LUCY

    But where's the great Alcides of the field,   60

    Valiant Lord Talbot, Earl of Shrewsbury,

    Created for his rare success in arms

    Great Earl of Wexford, Waterford, and Valence,

    Lord Talbot of Goodrich and Urchinfield,

    Lord Strange of Blackmere, Lord Verdun of Alton,

    Lord Cromwell of Wingfield, Lord Furnival of Sheffield,

    The thrice-victorious Lord of Falconbridge,

    Knight of the noble order of Saint George,

    Worthy Saint Michael, and the Golden Fleece,

    Great Marshal to Henry the Sixth

    Of all his wars within the realm of France?

PUCELLE

    Here's a silly stately style indeed!   72

---

58 Hell . . . is i.e., we have slain and thus sent our enemies to hell rather
than taking any prisoners   **60 Alcides** Hercules. (Literally, descendant
of Alcaeus, who was the father of Hercules' stepfather.)   **72 style** list of
titles, manner of address

The Turk, that two-and-fifty kingdoms hath,   73
Writes not so tedious a style as this.
Him that thou magnifi'st with all these titles
Stinking and flyblown lies here at our feet.

LUCY
Is Talbot slain, the Frenchmen's only scourge,   77
Your kingdom's terror and black nemesis?   78
O, were mine eyeballs into bullets turned,
That I in rage might shoot them at your faces!
O, that I could but call these dead to life!
It were enough to fright the realm of France.
Were but his picture left amongst you here,
It would amaze the proudest of you all.   84
Give me their bodies, that I may bear them hence
And give them burial as beseems their worth.   86

PUCELLE
I think this upstart is old Talbot's ghost,
He speaks with such a proud commanding spirit.
For God's sake, let him have them! To keep them here,
They would but stink and putrefy the air.

CHARLES   Go, take their bodies hence.

LUCY
I'll bear them hence; but from their ashes shall be reared
A phoenix that shall make all France afeard.   93
                  [*Exeunt Lucy, Herald, and attendants*
                                    with the bodies.]

CHARLES
So we be rid of them, do with them what thou wilt.   94
And now to Paris in this conquering vein.
All will be ours, now bloody Talbot's slain.   *Exeunt.*

❖

73 **The Turk** i.e., the Sultan of Turkey   77 **only** supreme   78 **nemesis**
agent for retribution or punishment   84 **amaze** stun, throw into confusion   86 **beseems their worth** befits their rank   93 **phoenix** fabulous
bird, the only one of its kind, which every five hundred years built itself
a funeral pile and died upon it; from the ashes a new phoenix arose
94 **So** as long as

5.1 *Sennet. Enter King, Gloucester, and Exeter.*

KING
 Have you perused the letters from the Pope,   1
 The Emperor, and the Earl of Armagnac?   2
GLOUCESTER
 I have, my lord, and their intent is this:
 They humbly sue unto your excellence
 To have a godly peace concluded of
 Between the realms of England and of France.
KING
 How doth Your Grace affect their motion?   7
GLOUCESTER
 Well, my good lord, and as the only means
 To stop effusion of our Christian blood
 And stablish quietness on every side.
KING
 Ay, marry, uncle; for I always thought
 It was both impious and unnatural
 That such immanity and bloody strife   13
 Should reign among professors of one faith.
GLOUCESTER
 Besides, my lord, the sooner to effect
 And surer bind this knot of amity,
 The Earl of Armagnac, near knit to Charles,   17
 A man of great authority in France,
 Proffers his only daughter to Your Grace
 In marriage, with a large and sumptuous dowry.
KING
 Marriage, uncle! Alas, my years are young,
 And fitter is my study and my books
 Than wanton dalliance with a paramour.
 Yet call th' ambassadors. [*Exit one or more.*] And, as
   you please,

5.1. Location: London. The royal court.
1–2 Pope . . . Armagnac (During the year 1434–1435 efforts were made
by the Emperor Sigismund and other potentates to effect a peace. The
marriage proposal of the King to the Earl of Armagnac's daughter,
however, was made eight or nine years later.) **7 affect their motion**
incline toward their proposal **13 immanity** atrocious savagery **17 knit**
i.e., by ties of kinship

So let them have their answers every one.
I shall be well content with any choice
Tends to God's glory and my country's weal.   27

> Enter Winchester [in cardinal's habit], and three
> Ambassadors, [one a Papal Legate].

EXETER [Aside]
  What? Is my lord of Winchester installed
  And called unto a cardinal's degree?   29
  Then I perceive that will be verified
  Henry the Fifth did sometime prophesy: 31
  "If once he come to be a cardinal,
  He'll make his cap coequal with the crown."   33
KING
  My Lords Ambassadors, your several suits   34
  Have been considered and debated on.
  Your purpose is both good and reasonable,
  And therefore are we certainly resolved
  To draw conditions of a friendly peace,   38
  Which by my lord of Winchester we mean
  Shall be transported presently to France.   40
GLOUCESTER [To the Ambassadors from Armagnac]
  And for the proffer of my lord your master,   41
  I have informed His Highness so at large   42
  As, liking of the lady's virtuous gifts,
  Her beauty, and the value of her dower,
  He doth intend she shall be England's queen.
KING
  In argument and proof of which contract,
  Bear her this jewel, pledge of my affection.
  ·   [A jewel is presented to the Ambassadors.]
  And so, my Lord Protector, see them guarded
  And safely brought to Dover, wherein shipped,   49
  Commit them to the fortune of the sea.
> Exeunt [all but Winchester and Legate].

---

27 Tends that tends   **29 called . . . degree** (Winchester's newly being
made a cardinal is inconsistent with l.3.19 and 36.)   **31 sometime** at one
time   **33 cap** i.e., cardinal's skullcap   **34 several** various   **38 draw**
draw up   **40 presently** immediately   **41 for** as for, regarding   **42 at
large** in full   **49 shipped** embarked

WINCHESTER
   Stay, my Lord Legate. You shall first receive
   The sum of money which I promisèd
   Should be delivered to His Holiness
   For clothing me in these grave ornaments.   54
LEGATE
   I will attend upon your lordship's leisure.
                              [He steps aside.]
WINCHESTER [*Aside*]
   Now Winchester will not submit, I trow,
   Or be inferior to the proudest peer.
   Humphrey of Gloucester, thou shalt well perceive
   That neither in birth or for authority
   The Bishop will be overborne by thee.
   I'll either make thee stoop and bend thy knee,
   Or sack this country with a mutiny.   *Exeunt.* 62

5.2   *Enter Charles, Burgundy, Alençon, Bastard,*
        Reignier, and Joan [la Pucelle].

CHARLES
   These news, my lords, may cheer our drooping spirits:
   'Tis said the stout Parisians do revolt   2
   And turn again unto the warlike French.
ALENÇON
   Then march to Paris, royal Charles of France,
   And keep not back your powers in dalliance.   5
PUCELLE
   Peace be amongst them, if they turn to us;
   Else, ruin combat with their palaces!   7

    Enter Scout.

---

54 grave ornaments i.e., solemn robes of ecclesiastical office
62 mutiny rebellion

5.2. Location: France. Fields before Angiers.
2 stout courageous **5 powers** forces **7 Else . . . palaces** otherwise, let
ruin destroy their palaces

SCOUT
　Success unto our valiant general,
　And happiness to his accomplices!   9
CHARLES
　What tidings send our scouts? I prithee, speak.
SCOUT
　The English army, that divided was
　Into two parties, is now conjoined in one
　And means to give you battle presently.
CHARLES
　Somewhat too sudden, sirs, the warning is,
　But we will presently provide for them.
BURGUNDY
　I trust the ghost of Talbot is not there.
　Now he is gone, my lord, you need not fear.
PUCELLE
　Of all base passions, fear is most accurst.
　Command the conquest, Charles, it shall be thine,
　Let Henry fret and all the world repine.
CHARLES
　Then on, my lords, and France be fortunate!
                                              Exeunt.

5.3　*Alarum. Excursions. Enter Joan la Pucelle.*

PUCELLE
　The Regent conquers and the Frenchmen fly.   1
　Now help, ye charming spells and periapts,   2
　And ye choice spirits that admonish me   3
　And give me signs of future accidents.   *Thunder.*   4
　You speedy helpers, that are substitutes   5
　Under the lordly monarch of the north,   6
　Appear and aid me in this enterprise!

　　Enter Fiends.

　This speedy and quick appearance argues proof   8

---

9 accomplices allies

5.3. Location: Before Angiers still. The scene is continuous.
1 The Regent i.e., the Duke of York   **2 charming** working by charms.
periapts amulets   **3 admonish** forewarn   **4 accidents** occurrences
5 substitutes deputies, agents   **6 north** (Evil spirits were frequently
associated with the north.)   **8 argues proof** gives evidence

Of your accustomed diligence to me.
Now, ye familiar spirits, that are culled
Out of the powerful regions under earth,
Help me this once, that France may get the field.   12
                 They walk, and speak not.
O, hold me not with silence overlong!
Where I was wont to feed you with my blood,   14
I'll lop a member off and give it you
In earnest of a further benefit,   16
So you do condescend to help me now.   17
                 They hang their heads.
No hope to have redress? My body shall
Pay recompense, if you will grant my suit.
                 They shake their heads.
Cannot my body nor blood sacrifice
Entreat you to your wonted furtherance?   21
Then take my soul—my body, soul, and all—
Before that England give the French the foil.   23
                 They depart.
See, they forsake me! Now the time is come
That France must vail her lofty-plumèd crest   25
And let her head fall into England's lap.
My ancient incantations are too weak,   27
And hell too strong for me to buckle with.   28
Now, France, thy glory droopeth to the dust.   *Exit.*

     Excursions. Burgundy and York fight hand to
     hand. French fly. [Joan la Pucelle is taken.]

YORK
Damsel of France, I think I have you fast.
Unchain your spirits now with spelling charms,   31
And try if they can gain your liberty.
A goodly prize, fit for the devil's grace!   33

---

12 get the field win the battle   **14 Where** (1) whereas (2) where
16 earnest advance payment.   **further benefit** (with sexual suggestion,
as in *member*, l. 15, and *Pay recompense*, l. 19)   **17 So** provided
21 wonted furtherance customary aid   **23 Before that** before.   **foil**
defeat   **25 vail** lower.   **lofty-plumèd crest** plume proudly waving at the
top of the helmet (in token of arrogant pride)   **27 ancient** former
28 buckle with do combat with (continuing the sexual suggestion of
ll. 15–19)   **31 spirits** i.e., the demons—"familiars"—attending on Joan.
(Cf. l. 10.)   **spelling charms** charms that cast a spell   **33 the devil's
grace** His Grace the devil. (Said sardonically.)

See how the ugly witch doth bend her brows
As if, with Circe, she would change my shape!   35
PUCELLE
Changed to a worser shape thou canst not be.
YORK
O, Charles the Dauphin is a proper man!   37
No shape but his can please your dainty eye.   38
PUCELLE
A plaguing mischief light on Charles and thee!   39
And may ye both be suddenly surprised   40
By bloody hands in sleeping on your beds!
YORK
Fell banning hag! Enchantress, hold thy tongue!   42
PUCELLE
I prithee, give me leave to curse awhile.
YORK
Curse, miscreant, when thou com'st to the stake.   44

Exeunt.

Alarum. Enter Suffolk, with Margaret in his hand.

SUFFOLK
Be what thou wilt, thou art my prisoner.

Gazes on her.

O fairest beauty, do not fear nor fly!
For I will touch thee but with reverent hands.
I kiss these fingers for eternal peace   48
And lay them gently on thy tender side.   49
Who art thou? Say, that I may honor thee.
MARGARET
Margaret my name, and daughter to a king,
The King of Naples, whosoe'er thou art.
SUFFOLK
An earl I am, and Suffolk am I called.

---

35 with like.   **Circe** sorceress celebrated for her power to change men
into swine   **37 proper** handsome. (Said sardonically.)   **38 dainty** fastidious   **39 mischief** misfortune   **40 surprised** assailed, taken   **42 Fell**
fierce, cruel.   **banning** cursing   **44 s.d. in his hand** by the hand
48–49 I kiss . . . side i.e., I kiss your hand (which I am holding) in token
of eternal peace between us, and then I release your hand to hang by
your side in token of giving you your freedom. (See l. 61, where Suffolk
speaks of freeing her hand, even though his heart tells him to keep her.)

Be not offended, nature's miracle,
Thou art allotted to be ta'en by me.   55
So doth the swan her downy cygnets save,
Keeping them prisoner underneath her wings.
Yet if this servile usage once offend,   58
Go and be free again as Suffolk's friend.   59

                               She is going.

O, stay! [*Aside.*] I have no power to let her pass;
My hand would free her, but my heart says no.
As plays the sun upon the glassy streams,   62
Twinkling another counterfeited beam,   63
So seems this gorgeous beauty to mine eyes.
Fain would I woo her, yet I dare not speak.
I'll call for pen and ink and write my mind.
Fie, de la Pole, disable not thyself!   67
Hast not a tongue? Is she not here?   68
Wilt thou be daunted at a woman's sight?   69
Ay, beauty's princely majesty is such
Confounds the tongue and makes the senses rough.   71

MARGARET
Say, Earl of Suffolk—if thy name be so—
What ransom must I pay before I pass?
For I perceive I am thy prisoner.

SUFFOLK [*Aside*]
How canst thou tell she will deny thy suit
Before thou make a trial of her love?

MARGARET
Why speak'st thou not? What ransom must I pay?

SUFFOLK [*Aside*]
She's beautiful, and therefore to be wooed;
She is a woman, therefore to be won.

MARGARET
Wilt thou accept of ransom, yea or no?

SUFFOLK [*Aside*]
Fond man, remember that thou hast a wife.   81
Then how can Margaret be thy paramour?

---

55 allotted destined   **58 servile usage** being treated as a captive
59 friend (with suggestion of "lover")   **62 As . . . streams** just as the sun
plays upon the glassy surface of a stream   **63 Twinkling** causing to
twinkle. **counterfeited** i.e., reflected   **67 disable** disparage   **68 here**
i.e., here with me, ready to be wooed   **69 a woman's sight** the sight of a
woman   **71 Confounds** that it confounds   **81 Fond** foolish

MARGARET
I were best to leave him, for he will not hear.

SUFFOLK [*Aside*]
There all is marred; there lies a cooling card.   84

MARGARET
He talks at random. Sure the man is mad.

SUFFOLK [*Aside*]
And yet a dispensation may be had.   86

MARGARET
And yet I would that you would answer me.

SUFFOLK [*Aside*]
I'll win this Lady Margaret. For whom?
Why, for my king. Tush, that's a wooden thing!   89

MARGARET
He talks of wood. It is some carpenter.

SUFFOLK [*Aside*]
Yet so my fancy may be satisfied,   91
And peace established between these realms.
But there remains a scruple in that too;
For though her father be the King of Naples,
Duke of Anjou and Maine, yet is he poor,
And our nobility will scorn the match.

MARGARET
Hear ye, Captain, are you not at leisure?

SUFFOLK [*Aside*]
It shall be so, disdain they ne'er so much.
Henry is youthful and will quickly yield.—
Madam, I have a secret to reveal.

MARGARET [*Aside*]
What though I be enthralled? He seems a knight,   101
And will not any way dishonor me.

SUFFOLK
Lady, vouchsafe to listen what I say.

MARGARET [*Aside*]
Perhaps I shall be rescued by the French,
And then I need not crave his courtesy.

---

84 cooling card something that cools one's ardor or dashes one's hopes.
(A metaphor from card playing.) **86 dispensation** papal permission (to
divorce a wife) **89 wooden** stupid (i.e., either King Henry, or Suffolk's
plan) **91 fancy** desire in love **101 enthralled** captured

SUFFOLK
　Sweet madam, give me hearing in a cause—
MARGARET [*Aside*]
　Tush, women have been captivate ere now.　　　　107
SUFFOLK
　Lady, wherefore talk you so?
MARGARET
　I cry you mercy, 'tis but quid for quo.　　　　109
SUFFOLK
　Say, gentle Princess, would you not suppose
　Your bondage happy, to be made a queen?　　　　111
MARGARET
　To be a queen in bondage is more vile
　Than is a slave in base servility,
　For princes should be free.
SUFFOLK　　　　　　　　　　　　And so shall you,　　　　114
　If happy England's royal king be free.　　　　115
MARGARET
　Why, what concerns his freedom unto me?
SUFFOLK
　I'll undertake to make thee Henry's queen,
　To put a golden scepter in thy hand,
　And set a precious crown upon thy head,
　If thou wilt condescend to be my—
MARGARET　　　　　　　　　　　　　　What?　　　　120
SUFFOLK　　His love.
MARGARET
　I am unworthy to be Henry's wife.
SUFFOLK
　No, gentle madam. I unworthy am
　To woo so fair a dame to be his wife
　And have no portion in the choice myself.　　　　125
　How say you, madam, are ye so content?

---

107 captivate taken captive　**109 cry you mercy** beg your pardon.　**quid for quo** tit for tat　**111 to be** i.e., if you were to be　**114 princes** i.e., men or women of royal birth　**115 happy** fortunate　**120 condescend** consent　**125 And have . . . myself** (Suffolk seems to say to Margaret that he is only the unworthy agent, not deserving to have any other role, but his double meaning points to his having a "piece" out of this for himself.)　**choice** (1) choosing (2) person chosen

MARGARET
  An if my father please, I am content.   127
SUFFOLK
  Then call our captains and our colors forth.   128
  And, madam, at your father's castle walls
  We'll crave a parley, to confer with him.   130

     Sound [a parley]. Enter Reignier on the walls.

  See, Reignier, see thy daughter prisoner!
REIGNIER
  To whom?
SUFFOLK   To me.
REIGNIER   Suffolk, what remedy?
  I am a soldier, and unapt to weep
  Or to exclaim on fortune's fickleness.   134
SUFFOLK
  Yes, there is remedy enough, my lord.
  Consent, and for thy honor give consent,   136
  Thy daughter shall be wedded to my king,
  Whom I with pain have wooed and won thereto;   138
  And this her easy-held imprisonment   139
  Hath gained thy daughter princely liberty.
REIGNIER
  Speaks Suffolk as he thinks?
SUFFOLK   Fair Margaret knows
  That Suffolk doth not flatter, face, or feign.   142
REIGNIER
  Upon thy princely warrant, I descend
  To give thee answer of thy just demand.
                   [Exit from the walls.]
SUFFOLK
  And here I will expect thy coming.   145

     Trumpets sound. Enter Reignier [below].

---

127 An if if **128 Then . . . forth** (Suffolk probably calls offstage to
attendants.) **130 s.d. on the walls** (As in previous sieges, the "walls" of
Angiers are here represented by the tiring-house facade, with Reignier
appearing above, in the gallery backstage.) **134 exclaim on** complain
against **136 Consent . . . consent** consent, and do so for the sake of
your honor **138 Whom** i.e., Margaret **139 easy-held** easily endured
142 face show a false face, deceive **145 expect** await

REIGNIER
  Welcome, brave earl, into our territories.
  Command in Anjou what your honor pleases.
SUFFOLK
  Thanks, Reignier, happy for so sweet a child,   148
  Fit to be made companion with a king.
  What answer makes Your Grace unto my suit?
REIGNIER
  Since thou dost deign to woo her little worth   151
  To be the princely bride of such a lord,
  Upon condition I may quietly
  Enjoy mine own, the country Maine and Anjou,   154
  Free from oppression or the stroke of war,
  My daughter shall be Henry's, if he please.
SUFFOLK
  That is her ransom. I deliver her,   157
  And those two counties I will undertake
  Your Grace shall well and quietly enjoy.
REIGNIER
  And I again, in Henry's royal name,   160
  As deputy unto that gracious king,   161
  Give thee her hand for sign of plighted faith.
SUFFOLK
  Reignier of France, I give thee kingly thanks,
  Because this is in traffic of a king.   164
  [Aside.] And yet methinks I could be well content
  To be mine own attorney in this case.—
  I'll over then to England with this news
  And make this marriage to be solemnized.
  So farewell, Reignier. Set this diamond safe
  In golden palaces, as it becomes.   170
REIGNIER
  I do embrace thee, as I would embrace
  The Christian prince, King Henry, were he here.
                              [He embraces Suffolk.]

---

148 happy for fortunate in having   **151 her little worth** her, little worthy as
she is   **154 country** i.e., district or region including   **157 deliver** free. (*Her
ransom* having been agreed upon, Suffolk releases her.)   **160 again** in
return. (In return for promises made in the name of King Henry, Reignier
gives back his daughter into the hands of Suffolk, who released her to her
father three lines earlier.)   **161 As deputy** i.e., to you, Suffolk, as deputy
164 traffic business   **170 as it becomes** as befits such a jewel

MARGARET

Farewell, my lord. Good wishes, praise, and prayers

Shall Suffolk ever have of Margaret.   *She is going.*

SUFFOLK

Farewell, sweet madam. But hark you, Margaret—

No princely commendations to my king?

MARGARET

Such commendations as becomes a maid,

A virgin, and his servant, say to him.

SUFFOLK

Words sweetly placed and modestly directed.   179

But, madam, I must trouble you again—

No loving token to His Majesty?

MARGARET

Yes, my good lord: a pure unspotted heart,

Never yet taint with love, I send the King.   183

SUFFOLK   And this withal.   *Kiss her.* 184

MARGARET

That for thyself. I will not so presume

To send such peevish tokens to a king.   186

[*Exeunt Reignier and Margaret.*]

SUFFOLK

O, wert thou for myself! But, Suffolk, stay.

Thou mayest not wander in that labyrinth;   188

There Minotaurs and ugly treasons lurk.

Solicit Henry with her wondrous praise;   190

Bethink thee on her virtues that surmount

And natural graces that extinguish art;   192

Repeat their semblance often on the seas,   193

That, when thou com'st to kneel at Henry's feet,

Thou mayest bereave him of his wits with wonder.

Exit.

❖

179 **placed** arranged   183 **taint** tainted   184 **withal** in addition
186 **peevish** trivial   188 **labyrinth** a structure built by Daedalus consisting of intricate passageways where the Minotaur—a monster born from the union of the Cretan king's wife with a bull—was confined   190 **her wondrous praise** praise of her wondrous beauty   192 **extinguish** eclipse
193 **Repeat their semblance** rehearse mentally the image of her virtues

5.4   *Enter York, Warwick, Shepherd, [and] Pucelle [guarded].*

YORK
Bring forth that sorceress condemned to burn.

SHEPHERD
Ah, Joan, this kills thy father's heart outright!
Have I sought every country far and near,   3
And, now it is my chance to find thee out,   4
Must I behold thy timeless cruel death?   5
Ah, Joan, sweet daughter Joan, I'll die with thee!

PUCELLE
Decrepit miser, base ignoble wretch!   7
I am descended of a gentler blood.   8
Thou art no father nor no friend of mine.   9

SHEPHERD
Out, out! My lords, an please you, 'tis not so.
I did beget her, all the parish knows.
Her mother liveth yet, can testify
She was the first fruit of my bach'lorship.   13

WARWICK
Graceless, wilt thou deny thy parentage?

YORK
This argues what her kind of life hath been,
Wicked and vile; and so her death concludes.   16

SHEPHERD
Fie, Joan, that thou wilt be so obstacle!   17
God knows thou art a collop of my flesh,   18
And for thy sake have I shed many a tear.
Deny me not, I prithee, gentle Joan.

PUCELLE
Peasant, avaunt!—You have suborned this man   21
Of purpose to obscure my noble birth.   22

5.4. Location: France. Camp of the Duke of York in Anjou.
3 country district   **4 chance** fortune.   **find thee out** discover you
5 timeless premature   **7 miser** wretch   **8 gentler** more noble   **9 friend**
kinsman   **13 was . . . bach'lorship** i.e., was conceived out of wedlock,
was the first product of my endeavor as a young man   **16 concludes**
(1) confirms (2) ends   **17 obstacle** (For *obstinate*.)   **18 collop** slice
21 suborned induced to commit perjury   **22 Of** on

SHEPHERD

    'Tis true, I gave a noble to the priest   23
    The morn that I was wedded to her mother.
    Kneel down and take my blessing, good my girl.
    Wilt thou not stoop? Now cursèd be the time
    Of thy nativity! I would the milk
    Thy mother gave thee when thou suckedst her breast
    Had been a little ratsbane for thy sake!   29
    Or else, when thou didst keep my lambs afield,   30
    I wish some ravenous wolf had eaten thee!
    Dost thou deny thy father, cursèd drab?   32
    O, burn her, burn her! Hanging is too good.   *Exit.*

YORK [*To guards*]

    Take her away, for she hath lived too long,
    To fill the world with vicious qualities.

PUCELLE

    First, let me tell you whom you have condemned:
    Not me begotten of a shepherd swain,
    But issued from the progeny of kings,
    Virtuous and holy, chosen from above
    By inspiration of celestial grace
    To work exceeding miracles on earth.   41
    I never had to do with wicked spirits.
    But you, that are polluted with your lusts,
    Stained with the guiltless blood of innocents,
    Corrupt and tainted with a thousand vices—
    Because you want the grace that others have,   46
    You judge it straight a thing impossible   47
    To compass wonders but by help of devils.   48
    No, misconceivèd! Joan of Arc hath been   49
    A virgin from her tender infancy,
    Chaste and immaculate in very thought,
    Whose maiden blood, thus rigorously effused,   52
    Will cry for vengeance at the gates of heaven.

YORK

    Ay, ay. Away with her to execution.

---

23 noble coin worth 6 shillings 8 pence   **29 ratsbane** rat poison
30 keep tend   **32 drab** whore   **41 exceeding** exceptional   **46 want**
lack   **47 straight** straightway, at once   **48 compass** encompass, bring
about   **49 misconceivèd** you who have a wrong idea. (The word has an
ironic application to Joan.)   **52 rigorously effused** mercilessly shed

WARWICK
And hark ye, sirs: because she is a maid,
Spare for no faggots. Let there be enough.
Place barrels of pitch upon the fatal stake,   57
That so her torture may be shortenèd.

PUCELLE
Will nothing turn your unrelenting hearts?
Then, Joan, discover thine infirmity,   60
That warranteth by law to be thy privilege: 61
I am with child, ye bloody homicides.
Murder not then the fruit within my womb,
Although ye hale me to a violent death.

YORK
Now heaven forfend! The holy maid with child?   65

WARWICK
The greatest miracle that e'er ye wrought.
Is all your strict preciseness come to this?   67

YORK
She and the Dauphin have been juggling.   68
I did imagine what would be her refuge.

WARWICK
Well, go to. We'll have no bastards live,
Especially since Charles must father it.   71

PUCELLE
You are deceived. My child is none of his.
It was Alençon that enjoyed my love.

YORK
Alençon, that notorious Machiavel?   74
It dies an if it had a thousand lives.

PUCELLE
O, give me leave, I have deluded you.

---

57 pitch (Pitch would produce heavy smoke, asphyxiating the person
being burned and thereby shortening the suffering. Warwick may be
speaking sardonically, however: we're going to give you a nice quick
death.)   **60 discover** reveal   **61 warranteth** guarantees.   **privilege** i.e., to
be spared until the birth of her supposed child   **65 forfend** forbid. (Said
sardonically.)   **67 preciseness** propriety, modesty   **68 juggling** playing
conjuring tricks (with sexual suggestion)   **71 must father it** is evidently
the father   **74 Machiavel** (In the popular Elizabethan conception,
Niccolò Machiavelli, Italian political philosopher, symbolized political
immorality and ruthless ambition.)

'Twas neither Charles nor yet the Duke I named,
But Reignier, King of Naples, that prevailed.

WARWICK

A married man! That's most intolerable.

YORK

Why, here's a girl! I think she knows not well,
There were so many, whom she may accuse.

WARWICK

It's sign she hath been liberal and free.   82

YORK

And yet, forsooth, she is a virgin pure!
Strumpet, thy words condemn thy brat and thee.
Use no entreaty, for it is in vain.

PUCELLE

Then lead me hence; with whom I leave my curse.
May never glorious sun reflex his beams   87
Upon the country where you make abode,
But darkness and the gloomy shade of death
Environ you, till mischief and despair   90
Drive you to break your necks or hang yourselves!

                                                  Exit [guarded].

*Enter [Winchester, now] Cardinal [Beaufort, with
letters, attended].*

YORK [*To Joan as she exits*]
Break thou in pieces and consume to ashes,   92
Thou foul accursèd minister of hell!   93

CARDINAL

Lord Regent, I do greet your excellence
With letters of commission from the King.
For know, my lords, the states of Christendom,
Moved with remorse of these outrageous broils,   97
Have earnestly implored a general peace
Betwixt our nation and the aspiring French;
And here at hand the Dauphin and his train   100
Approacheth, to confer about some matter.

---

82 liberal unrestrained, licentious (with a mocking glance at a more innocent meaning, "generous")   **87 reflex** reflect, shed   **90 mischief** misfortune   **92–93 Break . . . hell** (Winchester's entrance in time to hear these
lines seemingly directed at Joan provides added irony, since Winchester is
also a villain.)   **97 remorse of** pity for   **100 train** entourage

YORK

Is all our travail turned to this effect?   102
After the slaughter of so many peers,
So many captains, gentlemen, and soldiers,
That in this quarrel have been overthrown
And sold their bodies for their country's benefit,
Shall we at last conclude effeminate peace?
Have we not lost most part of all the towns,
By treason, falsehood, and by treachery,
Our great progenitors had conquerèd?
O Warwick, Warwick! I foresee with grief
The utter loss of all the realm of France.

WARWICK

Be patient, York. If we conclude a peace,
It shall be with such strict and severe covenants   114
As little shall the Frenchmen gain thereby.

Enter Charles, Alençon, Bastard, Reignier.

CHARLES

Since, lords of England, it is thus agreed
That peaceful truce shall be proclaimed in France,
We come to be informèd by yourselves
What the conditions of that league must be.

YORK

Speak, Winchester, for boiling choler chokes   120
The hollow passage of my poisoned voice
By sight of these our baleful enemies.   122

CARDINAL

Charles, and the rest, it is enacted thus:
That, in regard King Henry gives consent,   124
Of mere compassion and of lenity,   125
To ease your country of distressful war
And suffer you to breathe in fruitful peace,
You shall become true liegemen to his crown.   128
And, Charles, upon condition thou wilt swear
To pay him tribute and submit thyself,
Thou shalt be placed as viceroy under him,
And still enjoy thy regal dignity.

102 travail labor   **114 covenants** articles of agreement   **120 choler** i.e.,
anger   **122 By** at the   **124 in regard** inasmuch as   **125 Of mere** out of
pure   **128 true liegemen** loyal subjects

ALENÇON
    Must he be then as shadow of himself?
    Adorn his temples with a coronet,
    And yet in substance and authority   135
    Retain but privilege of a private man?
    This proffer is absurd and reasonless.
CHARLES
    'Tis known already that I am possessed
    With more than half the Gallian territories   139
    And therein reverenced for their lawful king.
    Shall I, for lucre of the rest unvanquished,   141
    Detract so much from that prerogative   142
    As to be called but viceroy of the whole?   143
    No, Lord Ambassador, I'll rather keep
    That which I have than, coveting for more,
    Be cast from possibility of all.   146
YORK
    Insulting Charles, hast thou by secret means
    Used intercession to obtain a league,
    And, now the matter grows to compromise,   149
    Stand'st thou aloof upon comparison?   150
    Either accept the title thou usurp'st,
    Of benefit proceeding from our king   152
    And not of any challenge of desert,   153
    Or we will plague thee with incessant wars.
REIGNIER [Aside to Charles]
    My lord, you do not well in obstinacy
    To cavil in the course of this contract.   156
    If once it be neglected, ten to one
    We shall not find like opportunity.
ALENÇON [Aside to Charles]
    To say the truth, it is your policy   159
    To save your subjects from such massacre
    And ruthless slaughters as are daily seen

135 in . . . authority in actual power 139 Gallian French 141 for lucre
of in order to gain 142 Detract . . . prerogative i.e., yield up my right to
be called king in the territories I already possess 143 As so as, in order
to 146 cast excluded 149 grows to compromise moves toward a
peaceful settlement 150 upon comparison i.e., quibbling about the
proposed articles 152 Of benefit as a feudal bestowal 153 challenge
of desert claim of inherent right 156 cavil raise frivolous or faultfinding objections 159 policy politic course

By our proceeding in hostility;
And therefore take this compact of a truce,
Although you break it when your pleasure serves.

WARWICK
How sayst thou, Charles? Shall our condition stand?   165
CHARLES   It shall;
Only reserved, you claim no interest   167
In any of our towns of garrison.   168

YORK
Then swear allegiance to His Majesty,
As thou art knight, never to disobey
Nor be rebellious to the crown of England,
Thou nor thy nobles, to the crown of England.
       [*Charles and his nobles give tokens of fealty.*]
So, now dismiss your army when ye please.
Hang up your ensigns, let your drums be still,
For here we entertain a solemn peace.   *Exeunt.*   175

❖

5.5   *Enter Suffolk in conference with the King,
            Gloucester, and Exeter.*

KING
Your wondrous rare description, noble earl,
Of beauteous Margaret hath astonished me.
Her virtues, gracèd with external gifts,
Do breed love's settled passions in my heart;   4
And like as rigor of tempestuous gusts   5
Provokes the mightiest hulk against the tide,   6
So am I driven by breath of her renown   7
Either to suffer shipwreck or arrive
Where I may have fruition of her love.

SUFFOLK
Tush, my good lord, this superficial tale

---

165 condition treaty, contract   **167 Only reserved** with this single
proviso, that   **168 towns of garrison** fortified towns   **175 entertain**
accept

5.5. Location: London. The royal court.
4 settled fixed, rooted   **5 like as rigor** just as the severity   **6 Provokes**
drives.   **hulk** vessel   **7 breath** (1) report (2) wind in the sails

Is but a preface of her worthy praise.   11
The chief perfections of that lovely dame,
Had I sufficient skill to utter them,
Would make a volume of enticing lines
Able to ravish any dull conceit;   15
And, which is more, she is not so divine,
So full replete with choice of all delights,   17
But with as humble lowliness of mind
She is content to be at your command—
Command, I mean, of virtuous chaste intents,
To love and honor Henry as her lord.

KING
And otherwise will Henry ne'er presume.
Therefore, my Lord Protector, give consent
That Margaret may be England's royal queen.

GLOUCESTER
So should I give consent to flatter sin.   25
You know, my lord, Your Highness is betrothed
Unto another lady of esteem.   27
How shall we then dispense with that contract
And not deface your honor with reproach?

SUFFOLK
As doth a ruler with unlawful oaths;
Or one that, at a triumph having vowed   31
To try his strength, forsaketh yet the lists   32
By reason of his adversary's odds.
A poor earl's daughter is unequal odds,
And therefore may be broke without offense.   35

GLOUCESTER
Why, what, I pray, is Margaret more than that?
Her father is no better than an earl,
Although in glorious titles he excel.

SUFFOLK
Yes, my lord, her father is a king,
The King of Naples and Jerusalem,
And of such great authority in France

---

11 her worthy praise the praise she is truly worth   **15 conceit** imagination   **17 full** fully   **25 flatter** countenance, excuse   **27 another lady** i.e., the Earl of Armagnac's daughter. (See 5.1.17ff.)   **31 triumph** tournament   **32 lists** place of combat in a tournament   **35 may be broke** i.e., the contract with her may be broken

As his alliance will confirm our peace   42
And keep the Frenchmen in allegiance.

GLOUCESTER

And so the Earl of Armagnac may do,
Because he is near kinsman unto Charles.

EXETER

Besides, his wealth doth warrant a liberal dower,   46
Where Reignier sooner will receive than give.   47

SUFFOLK

A dower, my lords? Disgrace not so your king
That he should be so abject, base, and poor
To choose for wealth and not for perfect love.
Henry is able to enrich his queen,
And not to seek a queen to make him rich.
So worthless peasants bargain for their wives,   53
As marketmen for oxen, sheep, or horse.
Marriage is a matter of more worth
Than to be dealt in by attorneyship.   56
Not whom we will, but whom His Grace affects, 57
Must be companion of his nuptial bed.
And therefore, lords, since he affects her most,
That most of all these reasons bindeth us
In our opinions she should be preferred.
For what is wedlock forcèd but a hell,
An age of discord and continual strife?   63
Whereas the contrary bringeth bliss,
And is a pattern of celestial peace.   65
Whom should we match with Henry, being a king,
But Margaret, that is daughter to a king?
Her peerless feature, joinèd with her birth,   68
Approves her fit for none but for a king.
Her valiant courage and undaunted spirit,
More than in women commonly is seen,
Will answer our hope in issue of a king;   72
For Henry, son unto a conqueror,
Is likely to beget more conquerors,

---

42 As that. **confirm** strengthen **46 warrant** guarantee **47 Where**
whereas **53 So** thus do **56 attorneyship** haggling proxies **57 affects**
desires **63 age** lifetime **65 pattern** image. **peace** harmony
68 feature figure **72 Will . . . king** i.e., will fulfill our hopes of royal
progeny

If with a lady of so high resolve
As is fair Margaret he be linked in love.
Then yield, my lords, and here conclude with me
That Margaret shall be queen, and none but she.

KING
Whether it be through force of your report,
My noble lord of Suffolk, or for that   80
My tender youth was never yet attaint   81
With any passion of inflaming love,
I cannot tell; but this I am assured,
I feel such sharp dissension in my breast,
Such fierce alarums both of hope and fear,
As I am sick with working of my thoughts.
Take therefore shipping; post, my lord, to France.   87
Agree to any covenants, and procure   88
That Lady Margaret do vouchsafe to come
To cross the seas to England and be crowned
King Henry's faithful and anointed queen.
For your expenses and sufficient charge,   92
Among the people gather up a tenth.   93
Begone, I say, for till you do return
I rest perplexèd with a thousand cares.   95
And you, good uncle, banish all offense.   96
If you do censure me by what you were,   97
Not what you are, I know it will excuse   98
This sudden execution of my will.
And so, conduct me where, from company.   100
I may revolve and ruminate my grief.   *Exit.*   101

GLOUCESTER
Ay, grief, I fear me, both at first and last.   102
                              Exit Gloucester [with Exeter].

SUFFOLK
Thus Suffolk hath prevailed; and thus he goes,
As did the youthful Paris once to Greece,   104

80 for that because **81 attaint** infected **87 post** hasten **88 procure**
bring it about **92 charge** money **93 gather up a tenth** levy a tax of ten
percent of the produce of lands and industry **95 rest** remain
96 offense feeling of resentment and disapproval **97–98 censure . . . are**
i.e., judge me (in my lovesickness) in comparison to your own youthful
ways, not to your present wisdom **100 from company** i.e., alone
101–102 grief . . . grief love melancholy . . . remorse **104 Paris** Trojan
prince whose abduction of Helen of Sparta instigated the Trojan war

With hope to find the like event in love,   105
But prosper better than the Trojan did.
Margaret shall now be Queen and rule the King;
But I will rule both her, the King, and realm.   *Exit.*

105 the like event a similar outcome

Date and Text

The date and textual situation for *1 Henry VI* needs to be discussed in the context of all three *Henry VI* plays. *1 Henry VI* was not the first to be published. Shortened versions of *2* and *3 Henry VI* appeared in 1594 and 1595. One was titled as follows:

> THE First part of the Contention betwixt the two famous Houses of Yorke and Lancaster, with the death of the good Duke Humphrey: And the banishment and death of the Duke of *Suffolke*, and the Tragicall end of the proud Cardinall of *VVinchester*, vvith the notable Rebellion of *Iacke Cade: And the Duke of Yorkes first claime vnto the Crowne*. LONDON Printed by Thomas Creed, for Thomas Millington, and are to be sold at his shop vnder Saint Peters Church in Cornwall. 1594.

Its sequel was titled as follows:

> The true Tragedie of Richard *Duke of Yorke, and the death of* good King Henrie the Sixt, *with the whole contention betweene* the two Houses Lancaster and Yorke, as it was sundrie times acted by the Right Honourable the Earle of Pembrooke his seruants. Printed at London by P. S. [Peter Short] for Thomas Milling*ton, and are to be sold at his shoppe vnder Saint Peters Church in Cornwal*. 1595.

Once thought to be source plays for Shakespeare's *2* and *3 Henry VI*, these texts, the first a quarto and the second an octavo, have been independently demonstrated by Peter Alexander and Madeleine Doran to be "bad quartos" or memorial reconstructions of Shakespeare's texts, put together by actors for sale to a printer or for acting in the provinces. As such, they have little textual authority but may be of significance in those occasional passages where the Folio compositors seem to have had recourse to a later reprint (the third quarto) of these texts. In 1619 they were combined in a reprint by the printer William Jaggard called *The Whole Contention betweene the two Famous Houses, Lancaster and Yorke*. These texts are considerably shorter than the Folio versions of 1623, which appeared there under the titles "The second Part of Henry the Sixt, with the death of the Good Duke HVMFREY," and "The third Part of Henry the Sixt, with the death of the Duke of YORKE." Since, as memorially reconstructed texts, they are ultimately derived from the promptbook, these texts may contain some materials that were revised as the plays were put into performance, but the likelihood of contamination through reporting, actors' interpolations, and transmission are so great that the textual authority here must be regarded with great caution. The Folio texts seem to have been based on authorial manuscripts, although there is evidence too that both plays or portions thereof were printed from pages of the third quartos of each play or at least with some consultation of the respective third quartos by the Folio compositors. The third quarto of *2 Henry VI* may embody some independent authority, although not necessarily the author's; the third quarto of *3 Henry VI* seems to have no such independent authority.

The text of *1 Henry VI*, based seemingly on an authorial manuscript that had been annotated in the theater and possibly recopied, was first published in the Folio of 1623. It alone of the three parts was registered for publication at this time. The Stationers' Register entry refers to this play as "The thirde parte of Henry the sixt." These circumstances once led to the assumption that *1 Henry VI* was written after the other two plays, especially since those two plays do not often recall events of *1 Henry VI*—for example, they make no mention of its hero, Lord Talbot. The seeming fact that the 1594 and 1595 quartos were pirated editions would, however, explain their publication before *1 Henry VI* and the necessity of registering Part One later. In other ways, *1 Henry VI* has shown itself to be no hasty afterthought, but a play with thematic unity throughout and a sense of direction anticipating the remainder of the series. Hence, scholars now tend to support Dr. Johnson's commonsense hunch that the three plays in this historical tetralogy were written in order.

With the notable exception of the editors of the recent Oxford Shakespeare, scholars also generally agree now that the entire series is Shakespeare's own work, or at the very least dominated by his artistic conception of the whole. The once-prevailing and recently reasserted hypotheses of multiple authorship rest on questionable internal evidence such as vocabulary or versification. What sounds like Robert Greene or George Peele in these very early plays may simply be the result of those men's undoubted influence on Shakespeare during his apprenticeship. Greene's famous outburst at Shakespeare (see below) suggests that he was keenly aware of Shakespeare's facility for learning quickly from his contemporaries. The inconsistencies in these early plays, especially in Part One—mislineation, defective verse, inaccuracy in speech prefixes, confusion about time, discrepancy in facts—may be the result not of multiple authorship but of reliance on various sources, hasty composition, and problems of transcription.

Several contemporary allusions to the *Henry VI* plays help considerably with dating the series. Thomas Nashe wrote in his *Pierce Penniless* (registered August 1592) that it would "have joyed brave Talbot (the terror of the French) to think that after he had lain two hundred years in his tomb, he should triumph again on the stage." Probably he was referring to Shakespeare's play. The reference in Henslowe's diary to a "ne" (new?) performance of *Harey the vi* in March of 1592 may or may not refer to Shakespeare's work, however, for this performance was by Lord Strange's men whereas Shakespeare's *Henry VI* series is associated elsewhere with Pembroke's men. In any event, *3 Henry VI* must have been completed by the time of Robert Greene's death in September of 1592, when Greene (or his literary executor, Chettle) alludes plainly to it (1.4.137) in his angry remark about "an upstart crow, beautified with our feathers, that with his *tiger's heart wrapped in a player's hide* supposes he is as well able to bombast out a blank verse as the best of you." These contemporary references are confirmed by allusions in the texts themselves, for all the *Henry VI* plays seem to contain echoes of Books 1–3 of Edmund Spenser's *Faerie Queene* (printed 1590), whereas *3 Henry VI* seems to have influenced parts of *The Troublesome Reign of King John* (printed 1591). An inclusive date of 1589–1591 or 1592 ought to account for the entire series.

Textual Notes

These textual notes are not a historical collation, either of the early folios or of more recent editions; they are simply a record of departures in this edition from the copy text. The reading adopted in this edition appears in boldface, followed by the rejected reading from the copy text, i.e., the First Folio. Only major alterations in punctuation are noted. Changes in lineation are not indicated, nor are some minor and obvious typographical errors.

Abbreviations used:
F the First Folio
s.d. stage direction
s.p. speech prefix

Copy text: the First Folio.

1.1. 57 s.p. First Messenger Mess [also at l. 69]   **60 Rouen** [not in F]
65 [and elsewhere] Rouen Roan   **89 s.p. Second Messenger** Mess
94 Reignier Reynold   **103 s.p. Third Messenger** Mes   **176 steal** send

1.2. 30 bred breed   **47 s.p. [and elsewhere] Charles** Dolph   **63 s.d. [and elsewhere] Pucelle** Puzel   **76 whilst** whilest   **99 five** fine   **103 s.d. [and elsewhere] la** de   **113 rites** rights   **131 halcyon** Halcyons

1.3. 6 s.p. First Servingman Glost. 1. Man [at l. 8, 1. Man]   **29 Humphrey** Vmpheir   **30 Peeled** Piel'd   **74 s.p. Officer** [not in F]

1.4. 10 Wont Went   **25 gott'st** got's   **27 Duke** Earle   **69 s.d. shoot** shot   **89 Bear . . . bury it** [before l. 87 in F]   **95 Nero-like** like thee   **107 [and elsewhere] Dauphin** Dolphin

1.5. 16 hungry starvèd hungry-starued

1.6. 21 pyramid Pyramis   **22 of** or

2.1. 5 s.p. First Sentinel Sent [also at l. 38]   **7 s.d. ladders** [F adds "Their Drummes beating a Dead March"; see textual note at 2.2.s.d.]
54 s.p. Pucelle Ioane [also at l. 72]   **77 s.d.** [F has Exeunt preceding this s.d.]

2.2. 6 s.d. their . . . march [appears at 2.1.7 in F]   **20 Arc** Acre   **38 Auvergne** Ouergne

2.4. 1 s.p. Plantagenet Yorke [and thus through Act 3]   **57 law** you   **117 wiped** whipt   **132 gentlemen** gentle

2.5. 18 s.p. First Keeper Keeper [and at l. 33]   **35 s.p. [and elsewhere] Plantagenet** Rich   **71 King Richard** Richard   **121 s.d. Exeunt** Exit   **129 mine ill** my will

3.1. 52 s.p. Somerset [not in F]   **53 s.p. Warwick** Som   **54 s.p. Somerset** [not in F]   **74** [F provides an s.p. here, "King"]   **164 that** that all

3.2. 10 s.p. First Soldier Souldier   **13 Qui là** Che la   **21–22 specify . . . in?** specifie? . . . in.   **40 s.d. Burgundy** Burgonie [also at l. 42]   **41 Good** God   **103 s.d. Exeunt** Exit

3.4. 27 s.d. Manent Manet

4.1. s.d. Exeter, Governor and Gouernor Exeter   **14 thee** the   **48 my Lord**
Lord   **151 umpire** Vmper   **173 s.d. Flourish** [at l. 181 in F]   **Manent**
Manet   **180 wist** wish

4.2. 3 calls call   **15 s.p. General** Cap

4.3. 5 Talbot . . . along, Talbot as he march'd along.   **17 s.p. [and throughout
scene] Lucy** 2 Mes [or *Mes*]   **20 waist** waste   **36 travel** trauaile   **53 lands**
Lauds

4.4. 13 Whither Whether   **16 legions** Regions   **27 Reignier** Reignard
31 horse hoast

4.5. 55 s.d. Exeunt Exit

4.6. 57 s.d. Exeunt Exit

4.7. 18 antic antique   **25 whether** whither   **63 Wexford** Washford
64 Goodrich Goodrig   **89 have them** haue him   **94 with them** with him
96 s.d. Exeunt Exit

5.1. 0 [F here reads "Scena secunda"]

5.2. 0 [F here reads "Scœna Tertia"]

5.3. 57 her his   **65 [and elsewhere in scene] woo** woe   **85 random** randon
179 modestly modestie   **192 And** Mad

5.4. 28 suckedst suck'st   **49 Arc** Aire   **74 Machiavel** Macheuile   **102 travail**
trauell   **123 s.p. Cardinal** Win   **127 breathe** breath   **149 compromise**
compremize

5.5. 0 [F here reads "Actus Quintus"]   **60 That most** Most   **82 love** Ioue

HENRY VI
PART TWO

Introduction

Henry VI, Part Two is at once a continuation of the historical narrative begun in *1 Henry VI* (based indeed on the same chronicle sources) and an independent play that must have been staged on a separate occasion in Shakespeare's theater. As a middle play of a four-play series it is open-ended, commencing in a state of political flux and concluding as the civil war is in its early phase. Providential consolation seems far away, even if there are signs of divine wrath at work in human affairs. At the same time, this play has its own integrity of theme and dramatic form.

2 Henry VI picks up where the first play ends (in the year 1445) and continues down to the start of actual civil war at the Battle of St. Albans (1455). The major events portrayed are the downfall of Humphrey, Duke of Gloucester, and the angry stirrings of the commoners leading finally to Jack Cade's rebellion. Popular agitation brings about the death of the Duke of Suffolk, thereby claiming the life of one of those most cynically responsible for England's troubles. The villainous Cardinal of Winchester also dies a horrible and edifying death, suggesting that divine retribution is beginning to reveal its inexorable force. Yet throughout this declining action we witness in countermovement the ominous rise of Richard Plantagenet, Duke of York.

Richard's strategy, like that of his namesake in *Richard III*, is to exploit antagonisms at the English court, turning feuding nobles against one another until his potential rivals for power have destroyed themselves. In particular, he takes advantage of the animosity between the new Queen Margaret and Duke Humphrey. Margaret, daughter of a foreign prince, is a consort in the autocratic European style. She haughtily insists on the privileges of her exalted rank and spurns those who govern in the name of justice. "Is this the guise, / Is this the fashions in the court of England?" she incredulously inquires of Suffolk, her lover and political ally (1.3.42–43). Suffolk is an apt mate for Margaret, since he too oppresses the commoners. A petition "against the Duke of Suffolk, for enclosing the commons of Melford" (ll. 23–24) is one of many heartfelt grievances brought to the attention of the throne by the common people. Margaret naturally resents the moderate and fair-minded counsel of Duke Humphrey, who urges King Henry to remedy the distress of the commoners.

Richard of York has no inherent admiration for Suffolk and Margaret but cynically backs them as a way of destroying the good Duke of Gloucester. He advises his partners Salisbury and Warwick, "Wink at the Duke of Suffolk's insolence, / At Beaufort's pride, at Somerset's ambition, / At Buckingham, and all the crew of them, / Till they have snared the shepherd of the flock, / That virtuous prince, the good Duke Humphrey" (2.2.70–74). And Humphrey has in fact a fatal weakness through which he can be pulled down: the ambition of his wife, Eleanor. Intent on being first lady of the land, Eleanor comes into inevitable conflict with the remorseless Queen Margaret. Winchester and Suffolk, knowing Eleanor's self-blinding pride, find it pathetically easy to plant spies in her household who will encourage her penchant for witchcraft. Humphrey is never contaminated personally by his wife's pride but is doomed nonetheless. King Henry knows of Humphrey's goodness but cannot save him. This fall of a courageous moderate, highlighted in the title of the 1594 quarto text ("with the death of the good Duke Humphrey"), singles Humphrey out as the most prominent victim of the second play, like Talbot in Part One. He is cut down by an insincere and temporary alliance of extremists from both sides: those such as Margaret and Suffolk who cling to despotic privilege, and those such as York who wish to stir up the commoners for their own ulterior purposes. In times of confrontation the middle position is inherently vulnerable, and its destruction leads to escalating polarization.

As York both foresees and desires, the commoners are indeed unruly when deprived of Humphrey's moderating leadership. Shakespeare has already shown that they tend to ape the quarrels of their elders (as in the ludicrous duels between Horner the Armorer and his man Peter Thump), and are superstitiously gullible (as in the episode of Simpcox the fraudulent blind man). Now, no longer able to petition through channels, their voice becomes importunate. "The commons, like an angry hive of bees / That want their leader, scatter up and down / And care not who they sting in his revenge" (3.2.125–127). At first their grievances are plausible and their wrath directed at guilty objects. They suspect rightly that their hero, Humphrey, has been destroyed by Suffolk and the Cardinal, and they demand Suffolk's banishment. The request is laudable, but the peremptory tone suggests that the people are beginning to feel their own political power. Unless Suffolk is banished, they warn, they will take him by force from the palace. Poor King Henry, lamenting the lost conciliatory authority of Humphrey, aptly points up the central issue of royal prerogative: "And had I not been cited so by them, / Yet did I purpose as they do entreat" (3.2.281–282). In the perspective of this play, Henry's yielding to popular force is regrettable, but he has no alternative. Equally lamentable is the execution of Suffolk by private citizens taking justice into their own hands. However much this despot deserved to be condemned, his murder is an affront to justice. Servant has turned against master; the commoners have begun to feel their own power.

The popular rebellion itself, Cade's uprising, is a travesty of popular longings for social justice, and suggests that any movement of this sort is bound to end in absurdity. Shakespeare, for all his appreciative depiction of individual commoners, never credits them with collective political sagacity once they are demonstrating for their rights. In fact Shakespeare unhistorically brings together the worst excesses of the Cade rebellion itself (1450) and the famous Peasants' Revolt of 1381 in order to exaggerate the dangers of popular agitation. The Cade scenes abound in degrading comedy in the shape of lower-class self-assertion. We laugh at the contrast between Cade's professed utopian notions of abundance for all and his petty ambition to be king. He kills those who refer to him as Jack Cade rather than by his pretended title of Lord Mortimer. His movement is fiercely anti-intellectual. Yet the sour joke does not indict the commoners alone. Cade's insolent pretentions and his claptrap genealogical claims are an exaggerated but recognizable parody of aristocratic behavior. More important, we remember that Cade was whetted on to his rebellion by the demagogic York. That schemer has "seduced" Cade to make commotion while York himself raises a huge personal army and advances his fortunes in Ireland. "This devil here shall be my substitute" (3.1.371). The commoners can indeed prove irresponsible when goaded, but throughout *2 Henry VI* feuding aristocrats must bear the chief blame for causing popular discontent.

In view of the need for some kind of coherence amid this universal decline into anarchy and strife, prophecy assumes a structural importance in *2 Henry VI* that is to be accentuated in later plays of the tetralogy. As in ancient Greek drama, prophecies are always eventually fulfilled. They reveal divine necessity, but in such ambiguous and riddling language that the persons affected by the prophecy do not comprehend the true nature of the utterance until the event itself is upon them. In this play, for example, the spirit conjured to appear before the Duchess of Gloucester (1.4) predicts that Suffolk will die "by water" and that Somerset should "shun castles." What sorts of warnings are these? When his time comes, Suffolk dies at the hands of a man named Walter (pronounced "water," though Suffolk tries desperately to insist on the French "Gualtier"), whereas Somerset dies at the Castle Inn near St. Albans, at the play's end. Through such paltry quibbles, as in *Macbeth*, great men are misled into a false security. No less riddling is the prophecy about King Henry and his political antagonist: "The duke yet lives that Henry shall depose, / But him outlive, and die a violent death" (1.4.31–32). The first phrase of this oracle is perfectly ambiguous: it can mean that a still-living duke will depose Henry, or that Henry will depose this duke. Both interpretations turn out to be valid; during the wars of Lancaster and York shown in *3 Henry VI*, King Henry and his Yorkist opponent will by turns take the throne from one another. Eventually, too, in *3 Henry VI* and *Richard III*, Edward of York will outlive Henry only to die a retributive death. In such prophecy there is already the concept of an eye for an eye, a Lancastrian for a Yorkist, through which Providence will finally impose its penalty on a rebellious people. Prophecy then serves not to allow human beings to escape their destiny, which is unavoidable, but to give them the opportunity to perceive at last the pattern of divine justice. The audience realizes that prophecy is a divine warning too often unheeded by foolish human beings, and acknowledges the necessity of a fulfillment that is tragic and dispiriting but also comforting to the extent that it shows the heavens to be just.

The role of prophecy is thus central in *2 Henry VI*, in that it gives to the play a dominant pattern of prediction and eventual fulfillment. Yet the experience of *2 Henry VI* is one of turbulence. Events increasingly take on their own unstoppable momentum. Ceremonies and institutions attempt to control the flux without success. Abstract ideas conflict with stern realities; the idea of kingship is appealed to as a rallying cry for authority and stability, but the fact of King Henry's inept leadership and the self-serving ambitions of his antagonists invite continual disarray. As a work of art, *2 Henry VI* thus grapples with the problem of making something artistically coherent out of chaos. It does so, as does *3 Henry VI*, by containing the instability within the recurring pattern of an eye for an eye.

Any sense of comfort is slow to arrive in this play. England's political and moral decline remains unchecked. The commoner's rebellion, cynically fomented by Richard, Duke of York, has established the precedent for further rebellion. Knowing his enemies to be weak and divided, Richard no longer conceals the ambition that has led him to accept an assignment in Ireland and thereby raise an army. His excuse for returning to England in arms, to rid King Henry of the hated adviser Somerset, is similarly shown to be no more than a pretext for declaring open civil war. His final justification for challenging King Henry, despite all the fine talk about genealogies, is that Richard has the ambition and the raw power to carry out his plan. Henry's assertions of right are no less governed by expediency, for he privately confesses the weakness of his claim. The admirable example, shown late in this play, of a Kentish gentleman named Iden who is content to live peaceably on his estate, serves as a contrast to the dismaying ambitions that have seized not only Richard of York and his allies but also the remorseless Queen Margaret and those loyal to her. If, as A. P. Rossiter has cogently argued, *2 Henry VI* is a "morality of state" in which forces of good and evil struggle for the soul of that beleaguered heroine, Respublica, the commonwealth, then the play must ultimately be viewed as one in which the forces of good do not fare well. To be sure, the haughty Suffolk meets his dire fate, though by a means that encourages further private revenge; Somerset falls as predicted at St. Albans; and Winchester suffers a death of edifying horror. Still, Richard of York and Queen Margaret, having profited from the victimization of the virtuous Duke Humphrey, are more powerful than ever, and Richard's son and namesake is only beginning to make his presence felt. Many scores remain to be settled at the close of *2 Henry VI*.

HENRY VI
PART TWO

[*Dramatis Personae*

KING HENRY THE SIXTH
QUEEN MARGARET
Humphrey, DUKE OF GLOUCESTER, *King Henry's uncle,
  and Lord Protector*
DUCHESS OF GLOUCESTER, *Dame Eleanor Cobham*
CARDINAL BEAUFORT, *Bishop of Winchester, the King's great-uncle*
DUKE OF SOMERSET
DUKE OF SUFFOLK, *William de la Pole, earlier Marquess
  of Suffolk*
DUKE OF BUCKINGHAM
LORD CLIFFORD
YOUNG CLIFFORD, *his son*

RICHARD PLANTAGENET, DUKE OF YORK, *leader of the York faction*
EDWARD, *Earl of March, his eldest son*
RICHARD, *his son*
EARL OF SALISBURY,
EARL OF WARWICK, *his son,* } *supporters of the Yorkist claim*

LORD SCALES,
LORD SAYE,   } *supporters of King Henry*
SIR HUMPHREY STAFFORD,   } *against Cade's rebellion*
WILLIAM STAFFORD, *his* BROTHER,

SIR JOHN STANLEY, *custodian of the Duchess of Gloucester*
SHERIFF *of London, custodian of the Duchess of Gloucester*

SIR JOHN HUME, *a priest*
JOHN SOUTHWELL, *a priest*
MARGERY JOURDAIN, *a witch*
ROGER BOLINGBROKE, *a conjurer*
A SPIRIT *named* ASNATH

Two or Three PETITIONERS
THOMAS HORNER, *the Armorer*
PETER THUMP, *the Armorer's man*
Three NEIGHBORS *of Horner*
Three Fellow PRENTICES *of Peter*

A TOWNSMAN *of St. Albans*
SIMPCOX *or Simon, supposedly restored to sight*
His WIFE
MAYOR *of St. Albans*
A BEADLE *of St. Albans*

LIEUTENANT *or Captain of a ship*
MASTER *of the ship*
WALTER WHITMORE
Two GENTLEMEN *prisoners*

JACK CADE, *rebel leader from Kent*
GEORGE BEVIS,
JOHN HOLLAND,
DICK, *the butcher,* } *followers of Cade*
SMITH, *the weaver,*
MICHAEL,

MESSENGERS
Two SERVINGMEN, *of Gloucester and York*
A HERALD
POST *or Messenger to Parliament*
Two MURDERERS *of Gloucester*
VAUX, *a messenger*
A CLERK *of Chartham*
ALEXANDER IDEN, *a gentleman of Kent*

*Falconers, Townsmen and Aldermen, Commons, Rebels, a
   Sawyer, Soldiers, Servingmen, Attendants, Guards, Officers,
   Matthew Gough*

SCENE: *England*]

1.1 *Flourish of trumpets, then hautboys. Enter [the] King, Duke Humphrey [of Gloucester], Salisbury, Warwick, and [Cardinal] Beaufort, on the one side; the Queen, Suffolk, York, Somerset, and Buckingham, on the other.*

SUFFOLK
As by Your High Imperial Majesty
I had in charge at my depart for France,   2
As procurator to Your Excellence,   3
To marry Princess Margaret for Your Grace,
So, in the famous ancient city Tours,
In presence of the Kings of France and Sicil,   6
The Dukes of Orleans, Calaber, Brittaine, and Alençon,   7
Seven earls, twelve barons, and twenty reverend
   bishops,
I have performed my task and was espoused;
And humbly now upon my bended knee, [*Kneeling*]
In sight of England and her lordly peers,
Deliver up my title in the Queen
To your most gracious hands, that are the substance
Of that great shadow I did represent: 14
The happiest gift that ever marquess gave,   15
The fairest queen that ever king received.
KING
Suffolk, arise. Welcome, Queen Margaret.
                     [*Suffolk rises.*]
I can express no kinder sign of love   18
Than this kind kiss. [*He kisses her.*] O Lord, that lends
   me life,   19
Lend me a heart replete with thankfulness!
For thou hast given me in this beauteous face
A world of earthly blessings to my soul,
If sympathy of love unite our thoughts.

1.1. Location: London. The royal court.
s.d. Flourish fanfare.   **hautboys** oboelike instruments   **2 had in charge**
was commissioned.   **depart** departure   **3 procurator** agent, proxy
6 Sicil Sicily. (Titularly ruled by Margaret's father, the Duke of Anjou.)   **7 Caraber** Calabria, in southern Italy   **14 shadow** image, i.e., of
royalty   **15 happiest** most fortunate   **18 kinder** more natural   **19 kind**
loving

QUEEN
Great King of England and my gracious lord,
The mutual conference that my mind hath had   25
By day, by night, waking and in my dreams,
In courtly company or at my beads,   27
With you, mine alderliefest sovereign,   28
Makes me the bolder to salute my king
With ruder terms, such as my wit affords   30
And overjoy of heart doth minister.   31

KING
Her sight did ravish, but her grace in speech,   32
Her words yclad with wisdom's majesty,   33
Makes me from wondering fall to weeping joys,   34
Such is the fullness of my heart's content.
Lords, with one cheerful voice welcome my love.

ALL (*Kneeling*)
Long live Queen Margaret, England's happiness!

QUEEN   We thank you all.   *Flourish. [They all rise.]*

SUFFOLK
My Lord Protector, so it please Your Grace,
Here are the articles of contracted peace
Between our sovereign and the French king Charles,
For eighteen months concluded by consent.

GLOUCESTER (*Reads*) "Imprimis, it is agreed between 43
the French king Charles and William de la Pole, Mar- 44
quess of Suffolk, ambassador for Henry, King of En-   45
gland, that the said Henry shall espouse the Lady Margaret, daughter unto Reignier, King of Naples, Sicilia,
and Jerusalem, and crown her Queen of England ere
the thirtieth of May next ensuing. Item, that the duchy 49
of Anjou and the county of Maine shall be released and
delivered to the King her father—"
                              [He lets the paper fall.]

---

25 mutual conference intimate communication (of the mind with itself)   **27 In . . . beads** in courtly society or at my prayers (with the
rosary)   **28 alderliefest** most loved   **30 ruder** less polished.   **wit** intelligence   **31 minister** supply   **32 Her sight** the sight of her   **33 yclad**
clad, clothed   **34 wondering** admiring   **43 Imprimis** in the first place
44–45 Marquess (William de la Pole was fourth Earl and then first Duke
of Suffolk. Edward Hall writes that he was elevated from earl to marquess "when the marriage contract was agreed.")   **49 Item** also

KING
  Uncle, how now?
GLOUCESTER   Pardon me, gracious lord.
  Some sudden qualm hath struck me at the heart
  And dimmed mine eyes, that I can read no further.   54
KING
  Uncle of Winchester, I pray, read on.   55
CARDINAL [*Reads*] "Item, it is further agreed between
  them that the duchies of Anjou and Maine shall be   57
  released and delivered over to the King her father, and
  she sent over of the King of England's own proper cost 59
  and charges, without having any dowry."
KING
  They please us well. Lord Marquess, kneel down.
                            [*Suffolk kneels.*]
  We here create thee the first Duke of Suffolk,
  And gird thee with the sword. [*Suffolk rises.*] Cousin
      of York,   63
  We here discharge Your Grace from being regent
  I' the parts of France, till term of eighteen months   65
  Be full expired. Thanks, uncle Winchester,
  Gloucester, York, Buckingham, Somerset,
  Salisbury, and Warwick;
  We thank you all for this great favor done
  In entertainment to my princely queen.   70
  Come, let us in, and with all speed provide
  To see her coronation be performed.   72
                  Exeunt King, Queen, and Suffolk.
                            Manent the rest.
GLOUCESTER
  Brave peers of England, pillars of the state,
  To you Duke Humphrey must unload his grief,
  Your grief, the common grief of all the land.
  What? Did my brother Henry spend his youth,   76

---

54 that so that   **55 Uncle** (Actually, great-uncle.)   **57 duchies . . . Maine**
i.e., the duchy of Anjou and the county of Maine, as in ll. 49–50 above.
(Perhaps the text is in error.)   **59 of** at.   **proper** personal   **63 Cousin**
(An appropriate title for the King to use toward any peer, but York is
also his distant cousin.)   **65 parts** territories.   **term . . . months** i.e., the
period of the truce between England and France   **70 entertainment to**
gracious reception of   **72 s.d. Manent** they remain onstage   **76 Henry**
i.e., Henry V

His valor, coin, and people in the wars?
Did he so often lodge in open field,
In winter's cold and summer's parching heat,
To conquer France, his true inheritance?
And did my brother Bedford toil his wits   81
To keep by policy what Henry got?   82
Have you yourselves, Somerset, Buckingham,
Brave York, Salisbury, and victorious Warwick,
Received deep scars in France and Normandy?
Or hath mine uncle Beaufort and myself,
With all the learnèd Council of the realm,
Studied so long, sat in the Council House
Early and late, debating to and fro
How France and Frenchmen might be kept in awe,   90
And had His Highness in his infancy
Crowned in Paris in despite of foes?
And shall these labors and these honors die?
Shall Henry's conquest, Bedford's vigilance,
Your deeds of war, and all our counsel die?
O peers of England, shameful is this league!
Fatal this marriage, canceling your fame,
Blotting your names from books of memory,   98
Rasing the characters of your renown,   99
Defacing monuments of conquered France,
Undoing all, as all had never been!   101

CARDINAL
Nephew, what means this passionate discourse,
This peroration with such circumstance?   103
For France, 'tis ours; and we will keep it still.   104

GLOUCESTER
Ay, uncle, we will keep it if we can,
But now it is impossible we should.
Suffolk, the new-made duke that rules the roast,   107
Hath given the duchy of Anjou, and Maine,

81 Bedford (as portrayed in *1 Henry VI*)   **82 policy** prudent management   **90 awe** subjection   **98 books of memory** i.e., chronicles   **99 Rasing the characters** erasing the records, or *razing*, scraping away   **101 as**
as if   **103 circumstance** detail   **104 For** as for.   **still** always   **107 rules
the roast** i.e., domineers. (The Folio spelling, "rost," may also suggest
"roost," but the etymology is uncertain.)

Unto the poor King Reignier, whose large style   109
Agrees not with the leanness of his purse.

SALISBURY

Now, by the death of Him that died for all,
These counties were the keys of Normandy.
But wherefore weeps Warwick, my valiant son?

WARWICK

For grief that they are past recovery;
For, were there hope to conquer them again,
My sword should shed hot blood, mine eyes no tears.
Anjou and Maine? Myself did win them both!
Those provinces these arms of mine did conquer.
And are the cities that I got with wounds
Delivered up again with peaceful words?
Mort Dieu!   121

YORK

For Suffolk's duke, may he be suffocate,   122
That dims the honor of this warlike isle!
France should have torn and rent my very heart
Before I would have yielded to this league.   125
I never read but England's kings have had
Large sums of gold and dowries with their wives;
And our King Henry gives away his own
To match with her that brings no vantages.   129

GLOUCESTER

A proper jest, and never heard before,
That Suffolk should demand a whole fifteenth   131
For costs and charges in transporting her!
She should have stayed in France and starved in France
Before—

CARDINAL

My lord of Gloucester, now ye grow too hot.
It was the pleasure of my lord the King.

GLOUCESTER

My lord of Winchester, I know your mind.

---

109 large style lavish title   **121 Mort Dieu** by God's (Christ's) death
122 For as for.   **suffocate** (punning on *Suffolk*)   **125 yielded** consented   **129 vantages** benefits, profits   **131 whole fifteenth** i.e., tax levy
consisting of one-fifteenth of the produce of lands and industry.
(Cf. *1 Henry VI*, 5.5.92–93, where the figure is put at one tenth.)

'Tis not my speeches that you do mislike,
But 'tis my presence that doth trouble ye.
Rancor will out. Proud prelate, in thy face
I see thy fury. If I longer stay,
We shall begin our ancient bickerings.
Lordings, farewell; and say, when I am gone,   143
I prophesied France will be lost ere long.

                                         Exit Humphrey.

CARDINAL
So, there goes our Protector in a rage.
'Tis known to you he is mine enemy,
Nay, more, an enemy unto you all,
And no great friend, I fear me, to the King.
Consider, lords, he is the next of blood   149
And heir apparent to the English crown.
Had Henry got an empire by his marriage,
And all the wealthy kingdoms of the west,   152
There's reason he should be displeased at it.   153
Look to it, lords; let not his smoothing words   154
Bewitch your hearts. Be wise and circumspect.
What though the common people favor him,
Calling him "Humphrey, the good Duke of Gloucester,"
Clapping their hands and crying with loud voice,
"Jesu maintain Your Royal Excellence!"
With "God preserve the good Duke Humphrey!"
I fear me, lords, for all this flattering gloss,   161
He will be found a dangerous Protector.

BUCKINGHAM
Why should he, then, protect our sovereign,
He being of age to govern of himself?   164
Cousin of Somerset, join you with me,   165
And all together, with the Duke of Suffolk,
We'll quickly hoist Duke Humphrey from his seat.

CARDINAL
This weighty business will not brook delay.   168

---

143 Lordings my lords, gentlemen   **149 next of blood** i.e., in line to
succeed to the throne, as Henry's eldest uncle. (Henry was as yet child-
less.)   **152 the wealthy . . . west** (Seemingly an anachronistic reference
to New World possessions.)   **153 he** i.e., Gloucester   **154 smoothing**
flattering   **161 flattering gloss** i.e., attractive appearance   **164 He** i.e.,
King Henry   **165 join you** if you join   **168 brook** endure, permit

I'll to the Duke of Suffolk presently.   *Exit Cardinal.* 169

SOMERSET
Cousin of Buckingham, though Humphrey's pride   170
And greatness of his place be grief to us,   171
Yet let us watch the haughty Cardinal.
His insolence is more intolerable
Than all the princes in the land besides.   174
If Gloucester be displaced, he'll be Protector.

BUCKINGHAM
Or thou or I, Somerset, will be Protector,   176
Despite Duke Humphrey or the Cardinal.
          Exeunt Buckingham and Somerset.

SALISBURY
Pride went before, Ambition follows him.   178
While these do labor for their own preferment,   179
Behooves it us to labor for the realm.
I never saw but Humphrey, Duke of Gloucester,
Did bear him like a noble gentleman.   182
Oft have I seen the haughty Cardinal,
More like a soldier than a man o' the Church,
As stout and proud as he were lord of all,   185
Swear like a ruffian and demean himself   186
Unlike the ruler of a commonweal.
Warwick, my son, the comfort of my age,
Thy deeds, thy plainness, and thy housekeeping   189
Hath won the greatest favor of the commons,
Excepting none but good Duke Humphrey.   191
And, brother York, thy acts in Ireland,   192
In bringing them to civil discipline,
Thy late exploits done in the heart of France,
When thou wert regent for our sovereign,
Have made thee feared and honored of the people.
Join we together for the public good,
In what we can, to bridle and suppress
The pride of Suffolk and the Cardinal,

---

169 presently immediately   **170 Cousin** kinsman, fellow peer   **171 grief** grievance   **174 Than** i.e., than that of.   **princes** peers   **176 Or** either **178 Pride** i.e., Winchester.   **Ambition** i.e., Buckingham and Somerset **179 preferment** advancement   **182 him** himself   **185 stout** haughty.   **as** as if   **186 demean** conduct   **189 housekeeping** hospitality   **191 Excepting none but** second only to   **192 brother** i.e., brother-in-law; see note to l. 238 below

With Somerset's and Buckingham's ambition;
And, as we may, cherish Duke Humphrey's deeds,   201
While they do tend the profit of the land.   202

WARWICK

So God help Warwick, as he loves the land
And common profit of his country!

YORK

And so says York—[*Aside*] for he hath greatest cause.   205

SALISBURY

Then let's away and look unto the main.   206

WARWICK

Unto the main? O Father, Maine is lost!
That Maine which by main force Warwick did win,
And would have kept so long as breath did last!
Main chance, Father, you meant; but I meant Maine,
Which I will win from France, or else be slain.   211

                    Exeunt Warwick and Salisbury.
                              Manet York.

YORK

Anjou and Maine are given to the French;
Paris is lost; the state of Normandy
Stands on a tickle point now they are gone.   214
Suffolk concluded on the articles,   215
The peers agreed, and Henry was well pleased
To change two dukedoms for a duke's fair daughter.
I cannot blame them all. What is 't to them?
'Tis thine they give away, and not their own.   219
Pirates may make cheap pennyworths of their pillage,   220
And purchase friends, and give to courtesans,   221
Still reveling like lords till all be gone;   222
Whileas the silly owner of the goods   223

---

201 cherish support   **202 tend** tend to, serve   **205 greatest cause** i.e., as
hopeful claimant to the throne   **206 unto the main** to the most important business (with several puns in the following lines: [1] *Maine*, a
French province lost in the treaty [2] *main force*, brute force [3] *Main
chance*, a gambling term from the dice game called hazard)   **211 s.d.
Manet** he remains onstage   **214 tickle** unstable, insecure   **215 concluded on the articles** negotiated the exact terms (of the marriage
agreement)   **219 thine** (York speaks to himself.)   **220 make cheap
pennyworths of** i.e., practically give away   **221 purchase friends** i.e.,
win friends through reckless generosity   **222 Still** continually
223 Whileas while.   **silly** wretched, helpless

Weeps over them, and wrings his hapless hands,
And shakes his head, and trembling stands aloof,   225
While all is shared and all is borne away,
Ready to starve and dare not touch his own.   227
So York must sit and fret and bite his tongue,
While his own lands are bargained for and sold.
Methinks the realms of England, France, and Ireland
Bear that proportion to my flesh and blood   231
As did the fatal brand Althaea burnt   232
Unto the Prince's heart of Calydon.   233
Anjou and Maine both given unto the French!
Cold news for me, for I had hope of France,
Even as I have of fertile England's soil.
A day will come when York shall claim his own;
And therefore I will take the Nevilles' parts   238
And make a show of love to proud Duke Humphrey,
And, when I spy advantage, claim the crown,   240
For that's the golden mark I seek to hit.   241
Nor shall proud Lancaster usurp my right,   242
Nor hold the scepter in his childish fist,
Nor wear the diadem upon his head,
Whose churchlike humors fits not for a crown.   245
Then, York, be still awhile, till time do serve.
Watch thou and wake when others be asleep,
To pry into the secrets of the state,
Till Henry, surfeiting in joys of love
With his new bride and England's dear-bought queen,
And Humphrey with the peers be fall'n at jars.   251
Then will I raise aloft the milk-white rose,   252

---

225 **stands aloof** stands to one side (unable to intervene)   227 **Ready . . . and** he being on the point of starvation and yet   231 **proportion** relationship   232 **Althaea** mother of Meleager, prince of Calydon. (At his birth she was told that her son would live only as long as a brand of wood remained unconsumed. She snatched the brand from the fire; but years later, when Meleager quarreled with Althaea's brothers and slew them, she resentfully threw the fatal brand into the fire, thus causing his death.)   233 **Unto . . . Calydon** unto the heart of the Prince of Calydon   238 **the Nevilles'** i.e., Salisbury's and his son Warwick's (to whom Richard of York was allied by marriage, having married Cecille or Cicely Neville, Salisbury's sister)   240 **advantage** opportunity   241 **mark** archery target   242 **Lancaster** i.e., Henry VI, here demoted to his title of duke   245 **humors** temperament   251 **at jars** in discords, quarreling   252 **milk-white rose** (Emblem of the Yorkist dynasty.)

With whose sweet smell the air shall be perfumed,
And in my standard bear the arms of York,   254
To grapple with the house of Lancaster;
And force perforce I'll make him yield the crown,   256
Whose bookish rule hath pulled fair England down.   257

Exit York.

❖

1.2   *Enter Duke Humphrey and his wife Eleanor.*

DUCHESS
Why droops my lord, like overripened corn,   1
Hanging the head at Ceres' plenteous load?   2
Why doth the great Duke Humphrey knit his brows,
As frowning at the favors of the world?   4
Why are thine eyes fixed to the sullen earth,
Gazing on that which seems to dim thy sight?
What seest thou there? King Henry's diadem,
Enchased with all the honors of the world?   8
If so, gaze on, and grovel on thy face,
Until thy head be circled with the same.
Put forth thy hand; reach at the glorious gold.
What, is 't too short? I'll lengthen it with mine;   12
And having both together heaved it up,   13
We'll both together lift our heads to heaven
And nevermore abase our sight so low
As to vouchsafe one glance unto the ground.
GLOUCESTER
O Nell, sweet Nell, if thou dost love thy lord,
Banish the canker of ambitious thoughts!   18
And may that hour when I imagine ill
Against my king and nephew, virtuous Henry,

---

254 standard battle standard, ensign.   **arms** coat of arms   **256 force
perforce** by violent compulsion   **257 bookish** scholarly and ineffectual

1.2. Location: The Duke of Gloucester's house.
1 corn grain   **2 Ceres** goddess of the harvest and agriculture   **4 As**
as if   **8 Enchased** adorned as with gems   **12 is 't** i.e., is your arm
13 heaved it i.e., lifted the crown   **18 canker** ulcer

Be my last breathing in this mortal world!
My troublous dream this night doth make me sad.   22
DUCHESS
What dreamed my lord? Tell me, and I'll requite it
With sweet rehearsal of my morning's dream.   24
GLOUCESTER
Methought this staff, mine office badge in court,   25
Was broke in twain—by whom, I have forgot,
But, as I think, it was by the Cardinal—
And on the pieces of the broken wand
Were placed the heads of Edmund, Duke of Somerset,
And William de la Pole, first Duke of Suffolk.
This was my dream. What it doth bode, God knows.
DUCHESS
Tut, this was nothing but an argument   32
That he that breaks a stick of Gloucester's grove
Shall lose his head for his presumption.
But list to me, my Humphrey, my sweet duke: 35
Methought I sat in seat of majesty
In the cathedral church of Westminster,
And in that chair where kings and queens are crowned,
Where Henry and Dame Margaret kneeled to me
And on my head did set the diadem.
GLOUCESTER
Nay, Eleanor, then must I chide outright.
Presumptuous dame, ill-nurtured Eleanor,   42
Art thou not second woman in the realm,
And the Protector's wife, beloved of him?
Hast thou not worldly pleasure at command
Above the reach or compass of thy thought?   46
And wilt thou still be hammering treachery,   47
To tumble down thy husband and thyself
From top of honor to disgrace's feet?
Away from me, and let me hear no more!

---

22 this night this past night   **24 rehearsal** recounting.   **morning's
dream** (Morning dreams were, in folklore, regarded as foretelling true
things.)   **25 mine office badge** the symbol of my office of Protector
32 argument proof, evidence   **35 list** listen   **42 ill-nurtured** ill-bred
46 compass encompassing   **47 hammering** i.e., devising

DUCHESS
What, what, my lord? Are you so choleric
With Eleanor for telling but her dream?
Next time I'll keep my dreams unto myself,
And not be checked.   54
GLOUCESTER
Nay, be not angry. I am pleased again.

Enter Messenger.

MESSENGER
My Lord Protector, 'tis His Highness' pleasure
You do prepare to ride unto Saint Albans,
Whereas the King and Queen do mean to hawk.   58
GLOUCESTER
I go. Come, Nell, thou wilt ride with us?
DUCHESS
Yes, my good lord, I'll follow presently.   60
                    Exit Humphrey [with Messenger].
Follow I must; I cannot go before   61
While Gloucester bears this base and humble mind.
Were I a man, a duke, and next of blood,
I would remove these tedious stumbling blocks
And smooth my way upon their headless necks;
And, being a woman, I will not be slack
To play my part in Fortune's pageant.—   67
Where are you there? Sir John! Nay, fear not, man,   68
We are alone; here's none but thee and I.

Enter Hume.

HUME
Jesus preserve Your Royal Majesty!
DUCHESS
What sayst thou? "Majesty"? I am but "Grace."   71
HUME
But by the grace of God and Hume's advice
Your Grace's title shall be multiplied.

---

54 checked rebuked **58 Whereas** where. **hawk** hunt with hawks
60 presently at once **61 go before** i.e., advance my own ambitions to be
second to none **67 pageant** spectacular entertainment **68 Sir John**
(Conventional form of addressing a priest.) **71 Grace** (Appropriate
address to a duchess.)

DUCHESS

   What sayst thou, man? Hast thou as yet conferred
   With Margery Jourdain, the cunning witch,
   With Roger Bolingbroke, the conjurer?
   And will they undertake to do me good?

HUME

   This they have promisèd: to show Your Highness
   A spirit raised from depth of underground
   That shall make answer to such questions
   As by Your Grace shall be propounded him.

DUCHESS

   It is enough. I'll think upon the questions.
   When from Saint Albans we do make return,
   We'll see these things effected to the full.
   Here, Hume, take this reward. [*She gives money.*]
     Make merry, man,
   With thy confederates in this weighty cause.

                             Exit Eleanor.

HUME

   Hume must make merry with the Duchess' gold.
   Marry, and shall! But, how now, Sir John Hume?   88
   Seal up your lips, and give no words but mum;
   The business asketh silent secrecy.
   Dame Eleanor gives gold to bring the witch;
   Gold cannot come amiss, were she a devil.
   Yet have I gold flies from another coast—   93
   I dare not say, from the rich Cardinal
   And from the great and new-made Duke of Suffolk,
   Yet I do find it so; for, to be plain,
   They, knowing Dame Eleanor's aspiring humor,   97
   Have hirèd me to undermine the Duchess
   And buzz these conjurations in her brain.
   They say "A crafty knave does need no broker,"   100
   Yet am I Suffolk and the Cardinal's broker.
   Hume, if you take not heed, you shall go near   102
   To call them both a pair of crafty knaves.   103
   Well, so it stands; and thus, I fear, at last

---

88 Marry, and shall i.e., indeed he will. (*Marry* was originally an oath,
"by the Virgin Mary.") **93 flies** i.e., that flies, approaches. **coast**
quarter, source **97 humor** temperament, fancy **100 They say** people
say. **broker** agent **102–103 go near To call** come close to calling

Hume's knavery will be the Duchess' wrack,   105
And her attainture will be Humphrey's fall.   106
Sort how it will, I shall have gold for all.   *Exit.* 107

❖

1.3   *Enter three or four Petitioners, [Peter,] the*
           Armorer's man, being one.

FIRST PETITIONER My masters, let's stand close. My 1
Lord Protector will come this way by and by, and then
we may deliver our supplications in the quill.   3
SECOND PETITIONER Marry, the Lord protect him, for
he's a good man! Jesu bless him!

     Enter Suffolk and Queen.

FIRST PETITIONER Here 'a comes, methinks, and the Queen 6
with him. I'll be the first, sure.   [*He starts forward.*]
SECOND PETITIONER Come back, fool. This is the Duke
of Suffolk, and not my Lord Protector.
SUFFOLK How now, fellow? Wouldst anything with
me?
FIRST PETITIONER I pray, my lord, pardon me. I took ye
for my Lord Protector.
QUEEN [*Reads*] "To my Lord Protector"? Are your sup- 14
plications to his lordship? Let me see them. What is
thine? [*She takes the petition.*]
FIRST PETITIONER Mine is, an 't please Your Grace, 17
against John Goodman, my Lord Cardinal's man, for
keeping my house, and lands, and wife and all,
from me.
SUFFOLK Thy wife too? That's some wrong, indeed.—
What's yours? What's here? [*He takes the petition.*]

---

105 wrack destruction, ruin **106 attainture** conviction and disgrace
107 Sort . . . will turn out which way it will. **for all** i.e., in any case

1.3. Location: London. The royal court.
1 close near together **3 in the quill** i.e., simultaneously, in a body **6 'a**
he **14 s.d. Reads** (The Queen evidently reads the superscription while
the First Petitioner is holding his petition.) **17 an 't** if it

"Against the Duke of Suffolk, for enclosing the 23
commons of Melford." How now, sir knave?   24
SECOND PETITIONER   Alas, sir, I am but a poor petitioner
of our whole township.   26
PETER [*Giving his petition*]   Against my master, Thomas
Horner, for saying that the Duke of York was rightful
heir to the crown.
QUEEN   What sayst thou? Did the Duke of York say he
was rightful heir to the crown?
PETER   That my master was? No, forsooth; my master
said that he was, and that the King was an usurper.
SUFFOLK   Who is there? (*Enter Servant.*) Take this fellow
in, and send for his master with a pursuivant pres- 35
ently.—We'll hear more of your matter before the King. 36
                              Exit [Servant with Peter].

QUEEN [*To the Petitioners*]
And as for you, that love to be protected
Under the wings of our Protector's grace,
Begin your suits anew and sue to him.
                              Tear the supplication.
Away, base cullions! Suffolk, let them go.   40
ALL   Come, let's be gone.   *Exeunt [Petitioners].*
QUEEN
My lord of Suffolk, say, is this the guise,   42
Is this the fashions in the court of England?
Is this the government of Britain's isle,
And this the royalty of Albion's king?   45
What, shall King Henry be a pupil still
Under the surly Gloucester's governance?
Am I a queen in title and in style,
And must be made a subject to a duke?
I tell thee, Pole, when in the city Tours   50
Thou rann'st atilt in honor of my love   51

23–24 **enclosing the commons** the action of a lord of a manor in enclosing or converting into private property lands formerly undivided and
used by the community as a whole   26 **of** on behalf of   35 **pursuivant**
minor messenger or officer with authority to execute warrants
35–36 **presently** at once   40 **cullions** base fellows. (Originally, *cullion*
meant "testicle.")   42 **guise** custom, manner   45 **Albion's** England's
50 **Pole** i.e., Suffolk   51 **rann'st atilt** jousted in a tournament

And stol'st away the ladies' hearts of France,
I thought King Henry had resembled thee
In courage, courtship, and proportion.   54
But all his mind is bent to holiness,
To number Ave Marys on his beads.
His champions are the prophets and apostles,
His weapons holy saws of sacred writ,   58
His study is his tiltyard, and his loves   59
Are brazen images of canonized saints.   60
I would the College of the Cardinals
Would choose him Pope and carry him to Rome
And set the triple crown upon his head;   63
That were a state fit for his holiness.   64

SUFFOLK
Madam, be patient. As I was cause
Your Highness came to England, so will I
In England work Your Grace's full content.

QUEEN
Besides the haughty Protector, have we Beaufort
The imperious churchman, Somerset, Buckingham,
And grumbling York; and not the least of these
But can do more in England than the King.

SUFFOLK
And he of these that can do most of all
Cannot do more in England than the Nevilles.
Salisbury and Warwick are no simple peers.

QUEEN
Not all these lords do vex me half so much
As that proud dame, the Lord Protector's wife.
She sweeps it through the court with troops of ladies,   77
More like an empress than Duke Humphrey's wife.
Strangers in court do take her for the Queen.   79

---

54 courtship courtly manners.   **proportion** carriage, build   **58 saws**
sayings   **59 tiltyard** enclosed space for tilts or tournaments   **60 brazen**
images bronze statues   **63 the triple crown** i.e., the diadem of the
papacy—a large hat enriched by three gold crowns symbolizing perhaps
the Church militant, suffering, and triumphant   **64 state** status.   **his**
holiness Henry's piety (but playing on the Pope's title, "His Holiness")   **77 sweeps it** moves majestically, with trailing garments
79 Strangers visiting foreigners

She bears a duke's revenues on her back,   80
And in her heart she scorns our poverty.
Shall I not live to be avenged on her?
Contemptuous baseborn callet as she is,   83
She vaunted 'mongst her minions t' other day   84
The very train of her worst wearing gown   85
Was better worth than all my father's lands,   86
Till Suffolk gave two dukedoms for his daughter.   87

SUFFOLK
Madam, myself have limed a bush for her,   88
And placed a choir of such enticing birds   89
That she will light to listen to the lays   90
And never mount to trouble you again.   91
So let her rest. And, madam, list to me,   92
For I am bold to counsel you in this:
Although we fancy not the Cardinal,   94
Yet must we join with him and with the lords
Till we have brought Duke Humphrey in disgrace.
As for the Duke of York, this late complaint   97
Will make but little for his benefit.
So one by one we'll weed them all at last,
And you yourself shall steer the happy helm.   100

> *Sound a sennet. Enter the King, Duke Humphrey*
> *[of Gloucester], Cardinal [Beaufort], Buckingham,*
> *York, [Somerset,] Salisbury, Warwick, and the*
> *Duchess [of Gloucester].*

---

80 on her back i.e., in her garments   **83 Contemptuous** (1) contemptible
(2) full of contempt.   **callet** lewd woman   **84 vaunted** boasted.   **minions** followers, attendants (with overtones of "saucy women")
85–87 The very . . . daughter i.e., (Eleanor boasted that) the mere trailing part of her least expensive gown was worth more than all the lands
possessed by the Duke of Anjou until Suffolk arranged a dowry whereby
the Duke received two rich dukedoms (Anjou and Maine) in return for
the marriage of me, his daughter, to King Henry   **88 limed a bush** set a
trap. (A metaphor from the practice of catching birds by putting sticky
birdlime on twigs of trees.)   **89 enticing birds** i.e., decoys   **90 light**
alight.   **lays** songs   **91 mount** (1) fly off, fly aloft (2) aspire   **92 let her
rest** i.e., forget about her   **94 fancy not** do not like   **97 late complaint**
i.e., recent allegation made by Peter that his master, the armorer, had
spoken of York as the proper King of England   **100 s.d. sennet** trumpet
signal for the approach or departure of processions

KING

    For my part, noble lords, I care not which;   101

    Or Somerset or York, all's one to me.   102

YORK

    If York have ill demeaned himself in France,   103

    Then let him be denied the regentship.

SOMERSET

    If Somerset be unworthy of the place,

    Let York be regent. I will yield to him.

WARWICK

    Whether Your Grace be worthy, yea or no,

    Dispute not that. York is the worthier.

CARDINAL

    Ambitious Warwick, let thy betters speak.

WARWICK

    The Cardinal's not my better in the field.   110

BUCKINGHAM

    All in this presence are thy betters, Warwick.

WARWICK

    Warwick may live to be the best of all.

SALISBURY

    Peace, son!—And show some reason, Buckingham,

    Why Somerset should be preferred in this.

QUEEN

    Because the King, forsooth, will have it so.

GLOUCESTER

    Madam, the King is old enough himself

    To give his censure. These are no women's matters.   117

QUEEN

    If he be old enough, what needs Your Grace

    To be Protector of His Excellence?

GLOUCESTER

    Madam, I am Protector of the realm,

    And at his pleasure will resign my place.

SUFFOLK

    Resign it then, and leave thine insolence.

    Since thou wert king—as who is king but thou?—

---

101 For my part (The quarto stage direction makes it clear that York and Somerset enter "on both sides of the King, whispering with him." The King is thus answering their requests.)   **102 Or** either   **103 have . . . himself** has conducted himself badly   **110 field** field of combat   **117 censure** opinion

The commonwealth hath daily run to wrack,
The Dauphin hath prevailed beyond the seas,   125
And all the peers and nobles of the realm
Have been as bondmen to thy sovereignty.   127

CARDINAL
The commons hast thou racked; the clergy's bags   128
Are lank and lean with thy extortions.

SOMERSET
Thy sumptuous buildings and thy wife's attire
Have cost a mass of public treasury.

BUCKINGHAM
Thy cruelty in execution
Upon offenders hath exceeded law,
And left thee to the mercy of the law.

QUEEN
Thy sale of offices and towns in France—
If they were known, as the suspect is great—   136
Would make thee quickly hop without thy head.
            Exit Humphrey. [The Queen drops her fan.]
Give me my fan. What, minion, can ye not?
                She gives the Duchess a box on the ear.
I cry you mercy, madam. Was it you?   139

DUCHESS
Was 't I? Yea, I it was, proud Frenchwoman.
Could I come near your beauty with my nails,
I'd set my ten commandments in your face.   142

KING
Sweet aunt, be quiet. 'Twas against her will.   143

DUCHESS
Against her will, good King? Look to 't in time.
She'll hamper thee and dandle thee like a baby.   145

---

125 Dauphin (Suffolk here uses the title of the heir apparent of France
to refer to King Charles VII because Suffolk, like all Englishmen,
considers Henry the rightful King of France.)   **127 bondmen** slaves
128 racked (Literally, tortured; here, strained beyond endurance in
matters of taxation.)   **bags** moneybags   **136 suspect** suspicion   **139 cry
you mercy** beg your pardon. (The Queen pretends that she thought she
was merely slapping one of her ladies in attendance for being slow to
obey.)   **142 ten commandments** i.e., ten fingernails (like the fingernails
Moses is proverbially thought to have used in inscribing the ten commandments)   **143 against her will** unintentional   **145 hamper** (1) fetter
(2) cradle

Though in this place most master wear no breeches,   146
She shall not strike Dame Eleanor unrevenged.
                                        Exit Eleanor.
BUCKINGHAM [*Aside to Cardinal*]
Lord Cardinal, I will follow Eleanor,
And listen after Humphrey, how he proceeds.   149
She's tickled now; her fume needs no spurs.   150
She'll gallop far enough to her destruction.
                                      Exit Buckingham.

    Enter Humphrey.

GLOUCESTER
Now, lords, my choler being overblown   152
With walking once about the quadrangle,
I come to talk of commonwealth affairs.
As for your spiteful false objections,
Prove them, and I lie open to the law;
But God in mercy so deal with my soul
As I in duty love my king and country!
But, to the matter that we have in hand:
I say, my sovereign, York is meetest man   160
To be your regent in the realm of France.
SUFFOLK
Before we make election, give me leave   162
To show some reason, of no little force,
That York is most unmeet of any man.
YORK
I'll tell thee, Suffolk, why I am unmeet:
First, for I cannot flatter thee in pride;   166
Next, if I be appointed for the place,
My lord of Somerset will keep me here
Without discharge, money, or furniture   169
Till France be won into the Dauphin's hands.
Last time I danced attendance on his will   171
Till Paris was besieged, famished, and lost.

---

146 most master the one most in command (i.e., the Queen)   **149 listen**
inquire   **150 tickled** (1) vexed, irritated (2) like a fish about to be caught
by tickling.   **fume** smoke, i.e., rage   **152 choler . . . overblown** anger
being dissipated   **160 meetest** fittest   **162 election** choice   **166 for**
because   **169 discharge** payment of what is owed.   **furniture** military
equipment   **171 Last time** (See *1 Henry VI*, 4.3.)

WARWICK
  That can I witness, and a fouler fact   173
  Did never traitor in the land commit.
SUFFOLK Peace, headstrong Warwick!
WARWICK
  Image of pride, why should I hold my peace?   176

    Enter [Horner, the] Armorer, and his man
    [Peter, guarded].

SUFFOLK
  Because here is a man accused of treason.
  Pray God the Duke of York excuse himself!
YORK
  Doth anyone accuse York for a traitor?   179
KING
  What mean'st thou, Suffolk? Tell me, what are these?   180
SUFFOLK
  Please it Your Majesty, this is the man
  That doth accuse his master of high treason.
  His words were these: that Richard, Duke of York,
  Was rightful heir unto the English crown,
  And that Your Majesty was an usurper.
KING Say, man, were these thy words?
HORNER An 't shall please Your Majesty, I never said   187
  nor thought any such matter. God is my witness, I am
  falsely accused by the villain.
PETER By these ten bones, my lords, he did speak them   190
  to me in the garret one night as we were scouring my
  lord of York's armor.
YORK
  Base dunghill villain and mechanical,   193
  I'll have thy head for this thy traitor's speech!
  [To the King.] I do beseech Your Royal Majesty,
  Let him have all the rigor of the law.
HORNER Alas, my lord, hang me if ever I spake the
  words. My accuser is my prentice; and when I did
  correct him for his fault the other day, he did vow   199
  upon his knees he would be even with me. I have

---

173 fact deed   **176 Image** i.e., symbol   **179 for** of being   **180 what**
who   **187 An 't** if it   **190 bones** i.e., fingers   **193 mechanical** common
workman   **199 correct** punish. **fault** mistake

good witness of this. Therefore I beseech Your Majesty,
do not cast away an honest man for a villain's accusa-   202
tion.

KING [*To Gloucester*]
Uncle, what shall we say to this in law?

GLOUCESTER
This doom, my lord, if I may judge: 205
Let Somerset be regent o'er the French,
Because in York this breeds suspicion;   207
And let these have a day appointed them   208
For single combat in convenient place,   209
For he hath witness of his servant's malice.
This is the law, and this Duke Humphrey's doom.

KING
Then be it so. My lord of Somerset,
We make Your Grace regent over the French.

SOMERSET
I humbly thank Your Royal Majesty.

HORNER   And I accept the combat willingly.

PETER   Alas, my lord, I cannot fight. For God's sake, pity
my case. The spite of man prevaileth against me. O
Lord, have mercy upon me! I shall never be able to
fight a blow. O Lord, my heart!

GLOUCESTER
Sirrah, or you must fight or else be hanged.   220

KING   Away with them to prison; and the day of combat
shall be the last of the next month. Come, Somerset,
we'll see thee sent away.   *Flourish. Exeunt.*

❧

202 **for** because of   205 **doom** judgment   207 **in York . . . breeds** i.e.,
this arouses suspicions about York's loyalty   208 **these** i.e., Peter and
Horner   209 **single combat** combat one-on-one   220 **Sirrah** (Customary
form of address to servants.)

1.4 *Enter [Margery Jourdain] the Witch,*
the two priests [Hume and Southwell],
and Bolingbroke.

HUME Come, my masters. The Duchess, I tell you, ex- 1
pects performance of your promises.
BOLINGBROKE Master Hume, we are therefore pro- 3
vided. Will her ladyship behold and hear our exor- 4
cisms? 5
HUME Ay, what else? Fear you not her courage. 6
BOLINGBROKE I have heard her reported to be a woman
of an invincible spirit. But it shall be convenient, Master Hume, that you be by her aloft, while we be busy
below; and so, I pray you, go in God's name and
leave us. (*Exit Hume.*) Mother Jourdain, be you prostrate and grovel on the earth. John Southwell, read 12
you; and let us to our work. 13
           [Margery Jourdain lies face downward.]

Enter [Duchess] Eleanor aloft, [Hume following].

DUCHESS Well said, my masters, and welcome all. To 14
this gear, the sooner the better. 15
BOLINGBROKE
Patience, good lady. Wizards know their times.
Deep night, dark night, the silent of the night,
The time of night when Troy was set on fire, 18
The time when screech owls cry and bandogs howl, 19
And spirits walk, and ghosts break up their graves—
That time best fits the work we have in hand.

1.4. **Location: Gloucester's house.**
1 my masters sirs   **3 therefore** for that very purpose   **4–5 exorcisms**
conjurations   **6 Fear** doubt   **12–13 read you** (In the stage direction at
l. 23, Southwell or Bolingbroke *reads* or recites a black magic spell.)
13 s.d. aloft (The quarto specifies that the Duchess "goes up to the
tower," i.e., some elevated place in the theater.)   **14 Well said** well done
14–15 To this gear get on with this business   **18 set on fire** (i.e., by the
Greeks concealed in the Trojan horse; described in Virgil, *Aeneid*,
Book 2)   **19 bandogs** leashed watchdogs

Madam, sit you and fear not. Whom we raise
We will make fast within a hallowed verge.   23

> *Here [they] do the ceremonies belonging, and*
> *make the circle. Bolingbroke or Southwell reads*
> Conjuro te, *etc. It thunders and lightens terribly;*
> *then the Spirit riseth.*

SPIRIT   *Adsum.*   24

MARGERY JOURDAIN   Asnath,   25
   By the eternal God, whose name and power
   Thou tremblest at, answer that I shall ask,   27
   For till thou speak thou shalt not pass from hence.
SPIRIT
   Ask what thou wilt. That I had said and done!   29
BOLINGBROKE [*Reading out of a paper*]
   "First, of the King: what shall of him become?"
SPIRIT
   The duke yet lives that Henry shall depose,   31
   But him outlive, and die a violent death.   32

> [*As the Spirit speaks, Southwell writes the answer.*]

BOLINGBROKE
   "What fates await the Duke of Suffolk?"
SPIRIT
   By water shall he die and take his end.
BOLINGBROKE
   "What shall befall the Duke of Somerset?"
SPIRIT   Let him shun castles;   36
   Safer shall he be upon the sandy plains
   Than where castles mounted stand.   38
   Have done, for more I hardly can endure.   39

---

23 hallowed verge magic circle   **s.d. the ceremonies belonging** i.e., the
"hocus-pocus" necessary to conjure spirits, such as drawing a magic
circle and reciting a formula.   **Conjuro te** I conjure you.   **riseth** (Presumably a trapdoor is used on the main stage.)   **24 Adsum** I am here
25 Asnath (An anagram for *Sathan*.)   **27 that** that which   **29 That** would
that. (The Spirit is reluctant to answer questions.)   **31–32 The duke . . .
death** (The first line of the prophecy, as is characteristic of such utter-
ances, is capable of a double construction: "whom Henry will depose,"
or "who will depose Henry." The second line is fulfilled in *3 Henry VI*
in the deaths of Henry VI and Edward IV.)   **36 Let him shun castles**
(The warning is fulfilled in 5.2.65 ff.)   **38 mounted** on a mount
39 Have done finish up

BOLINGBROKE
Descend to darkness and the burning lake!
False fiend, avoid!   41
                Thunder and lightning. Exit Spirit,
                           [sinking down again].

    Enter the Duke of York and the Duke of
    Buckingham with their guard and break in.
    [They seize Jourdain and her cohorts, with their
    papers.]

YORK
Lay hands upon these traitors and their trash.
[*To Jourdain.*] Beldam, I think we watched you at an
   inch.   43
[*To the Duchess.*] What, madam, are you there? The King
   and commonweal
Are deeply indebted for this piece of pains.   45
My Lord Protector will, I doubt it not,
See you well guerdoned for these good deserts.   47
DUCHESS
Not half so bad as thine to England's king,
Injurious Duke, that threatest where's no cause.   49
BUCKINGHAM
True, madam, none at all. What call you this?
             [He shows her the papers he has seized.]
Away with them! Let them be clapped up close   51
And kept asunder. You, madam, shall with us.
Stafford, take her to thee.   53
          [Exeunt above Duchess and Hume, guarded.]
We'll see your trinkets here all forthcoming.   54
All away!   *Exit [guard with Jourdain, Southwell,*
                        and Bolingbroke].

YORK
Lord Buckingham, methinks you watched her well.   56

---

41 False treacherous. **avoid** begone **43 Beldam** witch, hag. **at an
inch** i.e., closely **45 piece of pains** trouble undergone. (Said ironically.) **47 guerdoned** rewarded. **deserts** deserving acts. (Said ironically.) **49 Injurious** insulting **51 clapped up close** imprisoned
securely **53 Stafford** (Presumably one of Buckingham's kinsmen,
perhaps Sir Humphrey Stafford, acting as an officer of the arresting
guard.) **54 trinkets** trifles, rubbish (used in performing magical acts,
and now confiscated to be *forthcoming,* used as legal evidence)
56 watched kept surveillance over

A pretty plot, well chosen to build upon!   57
Now, pray, my lord, let's see the devil's writ.
What have we here?   *Reads.*
"The duke yet lives that Henry shall depose;
But him outlive, and die a violent death."
Why, this is just *"Aio te, Aeacida,*   62
Romanos vincere posse." Well, to the rest: 63
"Tell me what fate awaits the Duke of Suffolk?"
"By water shall he die and take his end."
"What shall betide the Duke of Somerset?"
"Let him shun castles;
Safer shall he be upon the sandy plains
Than where castles mounted stand."
Come, come, my lords, these oracles
Are hardly attained and hardly understood.   71
The King is now in progress towards Saint Albans;   72
With him the husband of this lovely lady.
Thither goes these news, as fast as horse can carry
    them—
A sorry breakfast for my Lord Protector.

BUCKINGHAM
Your Grace shall give me leave, my lord of York,
To be the post, in hope of his reward.   77

YORK
At your pleasure, my good lord.   [*Exit Buckingham.*]
Who's within there, ho!

        Enter a Servingman.

Invite my lords of Salisbury and Warwick
To sup with me tomorrow night. Away!   *Exeunt.*

❧

57 plot clever plan (with pun on the sense of "plot of ground"). **build upon** erect a scheme on (continuing the architectural pun) **62 just** precisely **62–63 Aio . . . posse** I say that you, Aeacides, the Romans can conquer. (This prophecy, given by the Delphic oracle to Pyrrhus, descendant of Aeacus, is grammatically ambiguous in just the same fashion as the English oracle about Henry and the Yorkists, ll. 31–32.) **71 hardly attained** with difficulty obtained, or comprehended **72 in progress** on a state journey **77 post** messenger

2.1 *Enter the King, Queen [with her hawk on her fist], Protector [Gloucester], Cardinal, and Suffolk, with falconers halloing.*

QUEEN
Believe me, lords, for flying at the brook   1
I saw not better sport these seven years' day.   2
Yet, by your leave, the wind was very high,
And ten to one old Joan had not gone out.   4
KING [*To Gloucester*]
But what a point, my lord, your falcon made,   5
And what a pitch she flew above the rest!   6
To see how God in all his creatures works!
Yea, man and birds are fain of climbing high.   8
SUFFOLK
No marvel, an it like Your Majesty,   9
My Lord Protector's hawks do tower so well;   10
They know their master loves to be aloft
And bears his thoughts above his falcon's pitch.
GLOUCESTER
My lord, 'tis but a base ignoble mind
That mounts no higher than a bird can soar.
CARDINAL
I thought as much. He would be above the clouds.
GLOUCESTER
Ay, my Lord Cardinal, how think you by that?
Were it not good Your Grace could fly to heaven?
KING
The treasury of everlasting joy.
CARDINAL [*To Gloucester*]
Thy heaven is on earth; thine eyes and thoughts

2.1. Location: St. Albans.
1 flying . . . brook i.e., hawking for waterfowl   **2 these . . . day** in seven years' time   **4 old . . . out** i.e., the hawk named old Joan would not have flown in such a high wind   **5 point** advantageous position from which the hawk attacks the bird   **6 pitch** height to which a hawk soars before descending on its prey   **8 fain** fond   **9 an it like** if it please (also in ll. 30 and 78)   **10 hawks** (Refers not only to the hawks flown by Gloucester in this hunt, but also to the falcon with a maiden's head portrayed on his heraldic badge.)   **tower** rise wheeling up to the *point* from which the hawk swoops down

Beat on a crown, the treasure of thy heart.   20
Pernicious Protector, dangerous peer,
That smooth'st it so with King and commonweal!   22
GLOUCESTER
What, Cardinal, is your priesthood grown peremptory?
Tantaene animis caelestibus irae?   24
Churchmen so hot? Good uncle, hide such malice.
With such holiness, can you do it?
SUFFOLK
No malice, sir, no more than well becomes
So good a quarrel and so bad a peer.
GLOUCESTER
As who, my lord?
SUFFOLK   Why, as you, my lord,
An 't like your lordly Lord-Protectorship.
GLOUCESTER
Why, Suffolk, England knows thine insolence.
QUEEN
And thy ambition, Gloucester.
KING   I prithee, peace,
Good Queen, and whet not on these furious peers;   33
For blessèd are the peacemakers on earth.   34
CARDINAL
Let me be blessèd for the peace I make
Against this proud Protector with my sword!
GLOUCESTER [*Aside to Cardinal*]
Faith, holy uncle, would 'twere come to that!
CARDINAL [*Aside to Gloucester*]   Marry, when thou dar'st.
GLOUCESTER [*Aside to Cardinal*]
Make up no factious numbers for the matter;   39
In thine own person answer thy abuse.   40
CARDINAL [*Aside to Gloucester*]
Ay, where thou dar'st not peep. An if thou dar'st,   41
This evening, on the east side of the grove.

20 Beat on dwell on, think about constantly   **22 smooth'st it** flatters
24 Tantaene . . . irae can there be such resentment in heavenly minds.
(Virgil, *Aeneid*, 1.11.)   **33 whet not on** do not encourage   **34 blessèd . . .**
earth (King Henry cites the Sermon on the Mount, Matthew 5:9.)
39 Make . . . numbers i.e., do not bring a party of your quarrelsome
supporters into the quarrel   **40 abuse** offense, insult   **41 peep** i.e., show
your face.   **An if** if

KING
  How now, my lords?
CARDINAL [*Aloud*]   Believe me, cousin Gloucester,
  Had not your man put up the fowl so suddenly,   44
  We had had more sport. [*Aside to Gloucester.*] Come
    with thy two-hand sword.
GLOUCESTER [*Aloud*]   True, uncle.
  [*Aside to Cardinal.*] Are ye advised? The east side of
    the grove.   47
CARDINAL [*Aside to Gloucester*]
  I am with you.
KING   Why, how now, uncle Gloucester?
GLOUCESTER
  Talking of hawking; nothing else, my lord.
  [*Aside to Cardinal.*] Now by God's mother, priest,
    I'll shave your crown for this,   50
  Or all my fence shall fail.
CARDINAL [*Aside to Gloucester*]   *Medice, teipsum*—   51
  Protector, see to 't well. Protect yourself.   52
KING
  The winds grow high; so do your stomachs, lords.   53
  How irksome is this music to my heart!
  When such strings jar, what hope of harmony?
  I pray, my lords, let me compound this strife.   56

        Enter one [*a Townsman of Saint Albans*] *crying*
        "A miracle!"

GLOUCESTER   What means this noise?
  Fellow, what miracle dost thou proclaim?
TOWNSMAN   A miracle! A miracle!
SUFFOLK
  Come to the King and tell him what miracle.

44 man i.e., falconer.   **put . . . fowl** startled the game into flight
47 advised agreed   **50 I'll shave your crown** (Since a priest is already
tonsured, this would be to give him a close shave indeed.)   **51 fence**
skill in fighting with a sword.   **Medice, teipsum** physician, [heal] thyself. (Luke 4:23.)   **52 Protect** (with a pun on *Protector*)   **53 stomachs**
tempers   **56 compound** settle   **s.d. Saint Albans** a shrine and a town
named for Saint Alban, supposedly the first Christian martyr in Britain,
executed under the edicts of Diocletian in 304 B.C. for sheltering a
Christian priest

TOWNSMAN

    Forsooth, a blind man at Saint Alban's shrine
    Within this half hour hath received his sight—
    A man that ne'er saw in his life before.

KING

    Now, God be praised, that to believing souls
    Gives light in darkness, comfort in despair!   65

       Enter the Mayor of Saint Albans and his
       brethren, bearing the man [Simpcox]
       between two in a chair, [Simpcox's Wife
       and others following].

CARDINAL

    Here comes the townsmen on procession,   66
    To present Your Highness with the man.

KING

    Great is his comfort in this earthly vale,
    Although by his sight his sin be multiplied.   69

GLOUCESTER

    Stand by, my masters. Bring him near the King;
    His Highness' pleasure is to talk with him.

KING

    Good fellow, tell us here the circumstance,
    That we for thee may glorify the Lord.
    What, hast thou been long blind and now restored?

SIMPCOX   Born blind, an 't please Your Grace.

WIFE   Ay, indeed, was he.

SUFFOLK   What woman is this?

WIFE   His wife, an 't like your worship.

GLOUCESTER   Hadst thou been his mother, thou couldst
    have better told.

KING   Where wert thou born?

SIMPCOX

    At Berwick in the north, an 't like Your Grace.

KING

    Poor soul, God's goodness hath been great to thee.
    Let never day nor night unhallowed pass,   84
    But still remember what the Lord hath done.   85

---

65 s.d. brethren aldermen, fellow members of the corporation or guild
66 on in   **69 by his sight . . . multiplied** i.e., he may now be subject to
more temptations, being able to see   **84 unhallowed** unblessed   **85 still**
continually

QUEEN
  Tell me, good fellow, cam'st thou here by chance,
  Or of devotion, to this holy shrine?
SIMPCOX
  God knows, of pure devotion, being called
  A hundred times and oftener in my sleep
  By good Saint Alban, who said, "Simon, come,   90
  Come offer at my shrine and I will help thee."   91
WIFE
  Most true, forsooth; and many time and oft
  Myself have heard a voice to call him so.
CARDINAL   What, art thou lame?
SIMPCOX   Ay, God Almighty help me!
SUFFOLK   How cam'st thou so?
SIMPCOX   A fall off of a tree.
WIFE   A plum tree, master.   98
GLOUCESTER   How long hast thou been blind?
SIMPCOX   O, born so, master.
GLOUCESTER   What, and wouldst climb a tree?
SIMPCOX   But that in all my life, when I was a youth.   102
WIFE
  Too true, and bought his climbing very dear.
GLOUCESTER   Mass, thou lov'dst plums well, that wouldst 104
  venture so.
SIMPCOX   Alas, good master, my wife desired some
  damsons and made me climb, with danger of my life. 107
GLOUCESTER
  A subtle knave! But yet it shall not serve.   108
  Let me see thine eyes. Wink now. Now open them.   109
  In my opinion yet thou seest not well.
SIMPCOX   Yes, master, clear as day, I thank God and Saint
  Alban.
GLOUCESTER
  Sayst thou me so? What color is this cloak of?
SIMPCOX   Red, master, red as blood.

---

90 Simon (His proper name; *Simpcox* is a variant.)   **91 offer** make an
offering   **98 plum tree** (A slang phrase for the female pudenda that sets
up an elaborate ribald joke here about a husband risking his life to try
to satisfy his wife's craving.)   **102 But that** only that once   **104 Mass** by
the Mass. (An oath.)   **107 damsons** a variety of plum (commonly used as
a slang phrase for testicles)   **108 shall not serve** won't serve to fool
me   **109 Wink** close your eyes

GLOUCESTER
  Why, that's well said. What color is my gown of?
SIMPCOX Black, forsooth, coal black as jet.
KING
  Why, then, thou know'st what color jet is of?
SUFFOLK
  And yet, I think, jet did he never see.
GLOUCESTER
  But cloaks and gowns, before this day, a many.   119
WIFE
  Never, before this day, in all his life.
GLOUCESTER Tell me, sirrah, what's my name?
SIMPCOX Alas, master, I know not.
GLOUCESTER [*Pointing*] What's his name?
SIMPCOX I know not.
GLOUCESTER [*Pointing to another*] Nor his?
SIMPCOX No, indeed, master.
GLOUCESTER What's thine own name?
SIMPCOX Sander Simpcox, an if it please you, master.
GLOUCESTER Then, Sander, sit there, the lying'st
  knave in Christendom. If thou hadst been born
  blind, thou mightst as well have known all our names
  as thus to name the several colors we do wear. Sight
  may distinguish of colors, but suddenly to nominate   133
  them all, it is impossible. My lords, Saint Alban here
  hath done a miracle; and would ye not think his cun-
  ning to be great that could restore this cripple to his
  legs again?
SIMPCOX O master, that you could!
GLOUCESTER My masters of Saint Albans, have you not
  beadles in your town, and things called whips?   140
MAYOR Yes, my lord, if it please Your Grace.
GLOUCESTER Then send for one presently.   142
MAYOR Sirrah, go fetch the beadle hither straight.   143
                          Exit [*an Attendant*].
GLOUCESTER Now fetch me a stool hither by and by. [*A*   144
  stool is brought.] Now, sirrah, if you mean to save

119 **many** multitude   133 **nominate** call by name   140 **beadles** minor
parish officers who might punish petty offenses   142 **presently** immediately   143 **straight** immediately   144 **by and by** at once

yourself from whipping, leap me over this stool and   146
run away.

SIMPCOX   Alas, master, I am not able to stand alone. You
go about to torture me in vain.

  Enter a Beadle with whips.

GLOUCESTER   Well, sir, we must have you find your legs.
Sirrah beadle, whip him till he leap over that same
stool.

BEADLE   I will, my lord. Come on, sirrah, off with your
doublet quickly.   154

SIMPCOX   Alas, master, what shall I do? I am not able to
stand.

  After the Beadle hath hit him once, he leaps over
  the stool and runs away; and they follow and cry,
  "A miracle!"

KING
O God, seest Thou this, and bearest so long?

QUEEN
It made me laugh to see the villain run.

GLOUCESTER [*To the Beadle*]
Follow the knave, and take this drab away.   159

WIFE   Alas, sir, we did it for pure need.

GLOUCESTER   Let them be whipped through every market town till they come to Berwick, from whence they
came.
                  Exit [Wife, with Beadle, Mayor, etc.].

CARDINAL
Duke Humphrey has done a miracle today.

SUFFOLK
True; made the lame to leap and fly away.

GLOUCESTER
But you have done more miracles than I;
You made in a day, my lord, whole towns to fly.   167

  Enter Buckingham.

---

146 me for me   154 doublet close-fitting jacket   159 drab slut
167 You . . . fly i.e., you gave away French towns in a day, as part of
Queen Margaret's dowry

KING
> What tidings with our cousin Buckingham?

BUCKINGHAM
> Such as my heart doth tremble to unfold:
> A sort of naughty persons, lewdly bent,   170
> Under the countenance and confederacy   171
> Of Lady Eleanor, the Protector's wife,
> The ringleader and head of all this rout,   173
> Have practiced dangerously against your state,   174
> Dealing with witches and with conjurers,
> Whom we have apprehended in the fact,   176
> Raising up wicked spirits from under ground,
> Demanding of King Henry's life and death   178
> And other of Your Highness' Privy Council,
> As more at large Your Grace shall understand.   180

CARDINAL
> And so, my Lord Protector, by this means
> Your lady is forthcoming yet at London.   182
> [*Aside to Gloucester.*] This news, I think, hath turned
>   your weapon's edge;
> 'Tis like, my lord, you will not keep your hour.   184

GLOUCESTER
> Ambitious churchman, leave to afflict my heart.   185
> Sorrow and grief have vanquished all my powers;
> And, vanquished as I am, I yield to thee
> Or to the meanest groom.   188

KING
> O God, what mischiefs work the wicked ones,
> Heaping confusion on their own heads thereby!   190

QUEEN
> Gloucester, see here the tainture of thy nest,   191
> And look thyself be faultless, thou wert best.   192

---

170 sort lot, gang. **naughty** wicked. **lewdly** evilly **171 Under . . . confederacy** with the authorization and even complicity **173 rout** crew **174 practiced** conspired **176 fact** deed **178 Demanding of** inquiring about **180 at large** in detail **182 forthcoming** ready to appear (in court) **184 like** likely. **hour** appointment (for the duel between Gloucester and the Cardinal) **185 leave to afflict** cease afflicting **188 meanest** of lowest degree **190 confusion** destruction **191 tainture** defilement **192 look** take care, see to it. **thou wert best** you'd be well advised

GLOUCESTER
Madam, for myself, to heaven I do appeal   193
How I have loved my king and commonweal;
And, for my wife, I know not how it stands.   195
Sorry I am to hear what I have heard.
Noble she is; but if she have forgot
Honor and virtue, and conversed with such   198
As, like to pitch, defile nobility,
I banish her my bed and company
And give her as a prey to law and shame
That hath dishonored Gloucester's honest name.
KING
Well, for this night we will repose us here;
Tomorrow toward London back again,
To look into this business thoroughly,
And call these foul offenders to their answers,
And poise the cause in Justice' equal scales,   207
Whose beam stands sure, whose rightful cause
    prevails.   *Flourish. Exeunt.* 208

♣

2.2   *Enter York, Salisbury, and Warwick.*

YORK
Now, my good lords of Salisbury and Warwick,
Our simple supper ended, give me leave,
In this close walk, to satisfy myself   3
In craving your opinion of my title,
Which is infallible, to England's crown.
SALISBURY   My lord, I long to hear it at full.
WARWICK
Sweet York, begin; and if thy claim be good,
The Nevilles are thy subjects to command.
YORK   Then thus:

193, 195 **for** as for   **198 conversed** had to do with   **207 poise** weigh
208 beam bar on which the scales are suspended.   **stands sure** is
perfectly level

2.2. Location: London. The Duke of York's garden.
3 close private

Edward the Third, my lords, had seven sons:
The first, Edward the Black Prince, Prince of Wales;
The second, William of Hatfield, and the third,
Lionel, Duke of Clarence; next to whom
Was John of Gaunt, the Duke of Lancaster;
The fifth was Edmund Langley, Duke of York;
The sixth was Thomas of Woodstock, Duke of
  Gloucester;
William of Windsor was the seventh and last.
Edward the Black Prince died before his father
And left behind him Richard, his only son,   19
Who after Edward the Third's death reigned as king
Till Henry Bolingbroke, Duke of Lancaster,
The eldest son and heir of John of Gaunt,
Crowned by the name of Henry the Fourth,
Seized on the realm, deposed the rightful king,
Sent his poor queen to France, from whence she came,
And him to Pomfret; where, as all you know,
Harmless Richard was murdered traitorously.

WARWICK
Father, the Duke hath told the truth.
Thus got the house of Lancaster the crown.

YORK
Which now they hold by force and not by right;
For Richard, the first son's heir, being dead,
The issue of the next son should have reigned.   32

SALISBURY
But William of Hatfield died without an heir.

YORK
The third son, Duke of Clarence, from whose line
I claim the crown, had issue, Philippe, a daughter,
Who married Edmund Mortimer, Earl of March.
Edmund had issue, Roger, Earl of March;
Roger had issue, Edmund, Anne, and Eleanor.

SALISBURY
This Edmund, in the reign of Bolingbroke,   39

---

19 Richard i.e., Richard II   **32 issue** offspring   **39 This Edmund** (A
historical error, found also in the chronicles, of confusing Edmund
Mortimer, fifth Earl of March, who was named heir to the throne by
Richard II, with his uncle Edmund, brother of Roger, who married
Glendower's daughter. See *1 Henry VI*, 2.5, and *1 Henry IV*, 1.3.)

As I have read, laid claim unto the crown,
And, but for Owen Glendower, had been king,
Who kept him in captivity till he died.   42
But to the rest.
YORK   His eldest sister, Anne,
My mother, being heir unto the crown,
Married Richard, Earl of Cambridge, who was son
To Edmund Langley, Edward the Third's fifth son.
By her I claim the kingdom. She was heir
To Roger, Earl of March, who was the son
Of Edmund Mortimer, who married Philippe,
Sole daughter unto Lionel, Duke of Clarence.
So, if the issue of the elder son
Succeed before the younger, I am king.
WARWICK
What plain proceeding is more plain than this?
Henry doth claim the crown from John of Gaunt,
The fourth son; York claims it from the third.
Till Lionel's issue fails, his should not reign.   56
It fails not yet, but flourishes in thee   57
And in thy sons, fair slips of such a stock.   58
Then, father Salisbury, kneel we together,
And in this private plot be we the first   60
That shall salute our rightful sovereign
With honor of his birthright to the crown.
BOTH [*Kneeling*]
Long live our sovereign Richard, England's king!
YORK
We thank you, lords. [*They rise*.] But I am not your king   64
Till I be crowned, and that my sword be stained   65
With heart-blood of the house of Lancaster;
And that's not suddenly to be performed,
But with advice and silent secrecy.   68
Do you as I do in these dangerous days:
Wink at the Duke of Suffolk's insolence,   70
At Beaufort's pride, at Somerset's ambition,
At Buckingham, and all the crew of them,

---

42 Who i.e., Glendower   **56 his** i.e., John of Gaunt's   **57 It fails not** i.e.,
Lionel's line of descent has not died out   **58 slips** cuttings   **60 plot** plot
of ground   **64 We** (The royal "we"!)   **65 and that** and until the time
that   **68 advice** careful reflection   **70 Wink at** shut your eyes to

Till they have snared the shepherd of the flock,
That virtuous prince, the good Duke Humphrey.
'Tis that they seek, and they in seeking that
Shall find their deaths, if York can prophesy.

SALISBURY
My lord, break we off. We know your mind at full.

WARWICK
My heart assures me that the Earl of Warwick
Shall one day make the Duke of York a king.

YORK
And, Neville, this I do assure myself:
Richard shall live to make the Earl of Warwick
The greatest man in England but the King.   *Exeunt.*

❖

2.3   *Sound trumpets. Enter the King and state, [the
Queen, Gloucester, York, Suffolk, Salisbury,
and others,] with guard, to banish the Duchess
[of Gloucester, who is brought on under guard
with Margery Jourdain, Southwell, Hume, and
Bolingbroke].*

KING
Stand forth, Dame Eleanor Cobham, Gloucester's wife.
In sight of God and us, your guilt is great.
Receive the sentence of the law for sins
Such as by God's book are adjudged to death.   4
[*To Margery and the others.*] You four, from hence to
    prison back again;
From thence unto the place of execution.
The witch in Smithfield shall be burnt to ashes,
And you three shall be strangled on the gallows.
[*To the Duchess.*] You, madam, for you are more
    nobly born,   9

2.3. Location: London. A hall of justice.
s.d. and others (In the quarto, the Cardinal, Buckingham, and Warwick
are also named. Warwick, York, and Salisbury enter "to them," i.e.,
meeting the royal party.)   **4 by God's book** i.e., according to the commandments in the Bible against witches, Exodus 22:18, and enchant-
ments, Leviticus 19:26, among other passages   **9 for** because

Despoilèd of your honor in your life,   10
Shall, after three days' open penance done,
Live in your country here in banishment
With Sir John Stanley in the Isle of Man.   13

DUCHESS
Welcome is banishment. Welcome were my death.   14

GLOUCESTER
Eleanor, the law, thou seest, hath judged thee.
I cannot justify whom the law condemns.
        [*Exeunt Duchess and other prisoners, guarded.*]
Mine eyes are full of tears, my heart of grief.
Ah, Humphrey, this dishonor in thine age
Will bring thy head with sorrow to the grave!
I beseech Your Majesty, give me leave to go;
Sorrow would solace and mine age would ease.   21

KING
Stay, Humphrey, Duke of Gloucester. Ere thou go,
Give up thy staff. Henry will to himself   23
Protector be; and God shall be my hope,
My stay, my guide, and lantern to my feet.
And go in peace, Humphrey, no less beloved
Than when thou wert Protector to thy king.

QUEEN
I see no reason why a king of years   28
Should be to be protected like a child.   29
God and King Henry govern England's realm!
Give up your staff, sir, and the King his realm.   31

GLOUCESTER
My staff? Here, noble Henry, is my staff.
                        [*He surrenders his staff.*]
As willingly do I the same resign
As ere thy father Henry made it mine;   34
And even as willingly at thy feet I leave it
As others would ambitiously receive it.

---

10 Despoilèd deprived.   **in your life** during the remainder of your life
13 With . . . Stanley (An error for Sir Thomas Stanley, the Duchess's
custodian and the Lord Stanley of *Richard III*.)   **14 were** would be
21 would wishes to have   **23 staff** staff of office   **28 of years** who is of
age   **29 be to be** need to be   **31 King his** King's   **34 ere** at an earlier
time. (The quarto reading, "erst," conveys the same meaning.)

Farewell, good King. When I am dead and gone,
May honorable peace attend thy throne!

Exit Gloucester.

QUEEN
Why, now is Henry king and Margaret queen,
And Humphrey, Duke of Gloucester, scarce himself,
That bears so shrewd a maim. Two pulls at once: 41
His lady banished, and a limb lopped off.   42
This staff of honor raught, there let it stand   43
Where it best fits to be, in Henry's hand.

SUFFOLK
Thus droops this lofty pine and hangs his sprays;   45
Thus Eleanor's pride dies in her youngest days.   46

YORK
Lords, let him go. Please it Your Majesty,
This is the day appointed for the combat,
And ready are the appellant and defendant—   49
The armorer and his man—to enter the lists,
So please Your Highness to behold the fight.

QUEEN
Ay, good my lord, for purposely therefor
Left I the court, to see this quarrel tried.

KING
I' God's name, see the lists and all things fit.
Here let them end it, and God defend the right!

YORK
I never saw a fellow worse bestead,   56
Or more afraid to fight, than is the appellant,
The servant of this armorer, my lords.   58

*Enter at one door, the Armorer [Horner] and his
Neighbors, drinking to him so much that he is
drunk; and he enters with a drum before him
and his staff with a sandbag fastened to it; and*

41 **bears . . . maim** endures so grievous a mutilation. **pulls** pluckings
42 **a limb lopped off** i.e., his staff of office taken away, so much a part
of him that the severing was like an amputation   43 **raught** attained,
seized   45 **lofty pine** (An emblem adopted by Henry IV, Gloucester's
father.) **sprays** branches 46 **her youngest days** i.e., when her ambition
and pride are at their height 49 **appellant** challenger 56 **bestead**
prepared 58 **s.d. drinking to him** offering toasts to him (to which he is
obliged to drink in return, drink for drink). **drum** drummer

*at the other door his man [Peter], with a drum
and sandbag, and Prentices drinking to him.*

FIRST NEIGHBOR   Here, neighbor Horner, I drink to you
in a cup of sack; and fear not, neighbor, you shall do   60
well enough.

SECOND NEIGHBOR   And here, neighbor, here's a cup of
charneco.   63

THIRD NEIGHBOR   And here's a pot of good double beer,   64
neighbor. Drink, and fear not your man.

HORNER   Let it come, i' faith, and I'll pledge you all; and   66
a fig for Peter!   67

FIRST PRENTICE   Here, Peter, I drink to thee, and be not
afraid.

SECOND PRENTICE   Be merry, Peter, and fear not thy
master. Fight for credit of the prentices.   71

PETER   I thank you all. Drink, and pray for me, I pray
you, for I think I have taken my last draft in this
world. Here, Robin, an if I die, I give thee my apron;
and Will, thou shalt have my hammer; and here,
Tom, take all the money that I have. [*He gives away his
things.*] O Lord bless me, I pray God, for I am never
able to deal with my master, he hath learned so much
fence already.   79

SALISBURY   Come, leave your drinking and fall to
blows. Sirrah, what's thy name?

PETER   Peter, forsooth.

SALISBURY   Peter? What more?

PETER   Thump.

SALISBURY   Thump? Then see thou thump thy master
well.

HORNER   Masters, I am come hither, as it were, upon
my man's instigation, to prove him a knave and myself an honest man; and touching the Duke of York, I
will take my death, I never meant him any ill, nor the   90

---

60 sack a dry Spanish or Canary wine   **63 charneco** a sweet Portuguese
wine   **64 double** strong   **66 Let it come** i.e., let the drink be passed
around.   **pledge you** drink your health   **67 a fig** (An obscene insult,
accompanied by the gesture of putting the thumb between the first and
second fingers.)   **71 credit** reputation, good name   **79 fence** skill in
fencing   **90 take my death** i.e., take an oath on pain of death

King, nor the Queen. And therefore, Peter, have at 91
thee with a downright blow!   92
YORK
Dispatch. This knave's tongue begins to double.   93
Sound, trumpets, alarum to the combatants!   94
    [*Alarum.*] *They fight, and Peter strikes him down.*
HORNER   Hold, Peter, hold! I confess, I confess treason.
                                    [*He dies.*]
YORK   Take away his weapon. Fellow, thank God and
the good wine in thy master's way.   97
PETER   O God, have I overcome mine enemies in this
presence? O Peter, thou hast prevailed in right!
KING
Go, take hence that traitor from our sight;   100
For by his death we do perceive his guilt,
And God in justice hath revealed to us
The truth and innocence of this poor fellow,
Which he had thought to have murdered wrongfully.   104
[*To Peter.*] Come, fellow, follow us for thy reward.
                Sound a flourish. Exeunt
                  [*with Horner's body*].

❖

2.4   *Enter Duke Humphrey [of Gloucester] and his
Men in mourning cloaks.*

GLOUCESTER
Thus sometimes hath the brightest day a cloud,
And after summer evermore succeeds
Barren winter, with his wrathful nipping cold;
So cares and joys abound, as seasons fleet.   4
Sirs, what's o'clock?
SERVANT   Ten, my lord.
GLOUCESTER
Ten is the hour that was appointed me

91–92 have at thee here I come at you   **93 double** thicken and slur (with
intoxication)   **94 alarum** call to arms   **97 in thy master's way** i.e., that
marred your master's fighting ability   **100 that traitor** i.e., Horner
104 Which he i.e., whom Horner

2.4. Location: London. A street.
4 fleet flow by

To watch the coming of my punished duchess.
Uneath may she endure the flinty streets,   9
To tread them with her tender-feeling feet.
Sweet Nell, ill can thy noble mind abrook   11
The abject people gazing on thy face,   12
With envious looks laughing at thy shame,   13
That erst did follow thy proud chariot wheels   14
When thou didst ride in triumph through the streets.
But soft! I think she comes, and I'll prepare   16
My tearstained eyes to see her miseries.   17

> *Enter the Duchess [of Gloucester, barefoot], in a*
> *white sheet, [with verses pinned upon her back,]*
> *and a taper burning in her hand; with [Sir John*
> *Stanley,] the Sheriff, and officers [with bills and*
> *halberds].*

SERVANT
So please Your Grace, we'll take her from the sheriff.   18
GLOUCESTER
No, stir not for your lives. Let her pass by.
DUCHESS
Come you, my lord, to see my open shame?
Now thou dost penance too. Look how they gaze!   21
See how the giddy multitude do point
And nod their heads and throw their eyes on thee!
Ah, Gloucester, hide thee from their hateful looks   24
And, in thy closet pent up, rue my shame   25
And ban thine enemies, both mine and thine!   26
GLOUCESTER
Be patient, gentle Nell. Forget this grief.
DUCHESS
Ah, Gloucester, teach me to forget myself!
For whilst I think I am thy married wife
And thou a prince, Protector of this land,
Methinks I should not thus be led along,

9 **Uneath** with difficulty, scarcely   11 **abrook** endure   12 **abject** lowly
born   13 **envious** full of malice   14 **erst** formerly   16 **soft** wait a
minute   17 **s.d. with bills and halberds** with long-handled axlike weapons. (The bracketed stage directions are derived from the quarto.)
18 **take her** rescue her by force   21 **Look how they gaze** (The crowd of
commoners may be represented onstage, or the Duchess may gesture
offstage.)   24 **hateful** full of hate   25 **closet** private room   26 **ban** curse

Mailed up in shame, with papers on my back,   32
And followed with a rabble that rejoice   33
To see my tears and hear my deep-fet groans.   34
The ruthless flint doth cut my tender feet,
And when I start, the envious people laugh   36
And bid me be advisèd how I tread.   37
Ah, Humphrey, can I bear this shameful yoke?
Trowest thou that e'er I'll look upon the world,   39
Or count them happy that enjoy the sun?
No, dark shall be my light and night my day;
To think upon my pomp shall be my hell.
Sometimes I'll say I am Duke Humphrey's wife,
And he a prince and ruler of the land;
Yet so he ruled, and such a prince he was,
As he stood by whilst I, his forlorn duchess,   46
Was made a wonder and a pointing-stock   47
To every idle rascal follower.
But be thou mild and blush not at my shame,
Nor stir at nothing till the ax of death
Hang over thee, as, sure, it shortly will.
For Suffolk, he that can do all in all
With her that hateth thee and hates us all,   53
And York, and impious Beaufort, that false priest,
Have all limed bushes to betray thy wings,   55
And fly thou how thou canst, they'll tangle thee.   56
But fear not thou until thy foot be snared,   57
Nor never seek prevention of thy foes.   58
GLOUCESTER
Ah, Nell, forbear! Thou aimest all awry.
I must offend before I be attainted;   60
And had I twenty times so many foes,

---

32 Mailed up enveloped. (Used in hawking to prevent the hawk from
struggling, just as Eleanor is wrapped in a white sheet.) **papers on my
back** (The verses pinned upon her back describe the sin for which she is
doing penance.) **33 with** by **34 deep-fet** fetched from the depths
36 start flinch, wince. **envious** malicious **37 advisèd** careful
39 Trowest thou do you believe **46 As** that **47 pointing-stock** one
pointed at in scorn **53 her** i.e., Queen Margaret **55 limed** put out
sticky birdlime as a trap on **56 fly . . . thee** no matter how you try to
fly away, they will ensnare you **57 fear not thou** i.e., you are not properly wary. (Or the Duchess may be ironically urging him to wait until it
is too late.) **58 prevention** forestalling **60 attainted** condemned for
treason or other serious wrongdoing

And each of them had twenty times their power,
All these could not procure me any scathe   63
So long as I am loyal, true, and crimeless.
Wouldst have me rescue thee from this reproach?
Why, yet thy scandal were not wiped away,   66
But I in danger for the breach of law.
Thy greatest help is quiet, gentle Nell.   68
I pray thee, sort thy heart to patience;   69
These few days' wonder will be quickly worn.   70

    Enter a Herald.

HERALD
I summon Your Grace to His Majesty's Parliament,
Holden at Bury the first of this next month.   72
GLOUCESTER
And my consent ne'er asked herein before?
This is close dealing. Well, I will be there.   74
                        [Exit Herald.]
My Nell, I take my leave. And, Master Sheriff,
Let not her penance exceed the King's commission.
SHERIFF
An 't please Your Grace, here my commission stays,   77
And Sir John Stanley is appointed now
To take her with him to the Isle of Man.
GLOUCESTER
Must you, Sir John, protect my lady here?
STANLEY
So am I given in charge, may 't please Your Grace.   81
GLOUCESTER
Entreat her not the worse in that I pray   82
You use her well. The world may laugh again,   83
And I may live to do you kindness if
You do it her. And so, Sir John, farewell.
DUCHESS
What, gone, my lord, and bid me not farewell?

---

63 **scathe** injury   66 **were not** would not be   68 **quiet** i.e., patient
endurance   69 **sort** adapt   70 **These . . . wonder** i.e., this passing
notoriety (as in the phrase "a nine-days' wonder").   **worn** worn out, i.e.,
forgotten   72 **Holden at Bury** to be held at Bury St. Edmunds (in
Suffolk)   74 **close** secret, underhand   77 **stays** stops, ends   81 **given in
charge** commanded   82 **Entreat** treat.   **in that** merely because   83 **The
world . . . again** i.e., we may see happier times. (Proverbial.)

GLOUCESTER

Witness my tears, I cannot stay to speak.

Exit Gloucester [with his Men].

DUCHESS

Art thou gone too? All comfort go with thee!
For none abides with me. My joy is death—
Death, at whose name I oft have been afeard,
Because I wished this world's eternity.   91
Stanley, I prithee, go, and take me hence.
I care not whither, for I beg no favor;
Only convey me where thou art commanded.

STANLEY

Why, madam, that is to the Isle of Man,
There to be used according to your state.   96

DUCHESS

That's bad enough, for I am but reproach;   97
And shall I then be used reproachfully?

STANLEY

Like to a duchess and Duke Humphrey's lady,
According to that state you shall be used.

DUCHESS

Sheriff, farewell, and better than I fare,   101
Although thou hast been conduct of my shame.   102

SHERIFF

It is my office; and, madam, pardon me.

DUCHESS

Ay, ay, farewell. Thy office is discharged.
Come, Stanley, shall we go?

STANLEY

Madam, your penance done, throw off this sheet,
And go we to attire you for our journey.

DUCHESS

My shame will not be shifted with my sheet.   108
No, it will hang upon my richest robes
And show itself, attire me how I can.
Go, lead the way. I long to see my prison.   *Exeunt.*

❧

91 this world's eternity endless worldly success **96 state** noble rank.
(But Eleanor plays on *state* in the sense of "condition.") **97 I . . .
reproach** I am the embodiment of reproach or disgrace, deserve only
my shame **101 better . . . fare** may you fare better than I **102 conduct**
conductor **108 shifted** changed (with a pun on *shift,* a chemise)

3.1 *Sound a sennet. Enter King, Queen, Cardinal*
[Beaufort], Suffolk, York, Buckingham,
Salisbury, and Warwick to the Parliament.

KING

I muse my lord of Gloucester is not come.   1
'Tis not his wont to be the hindmost man,   2
Whate'er occasion keeps him from us now.

QUEEN

Can you not see, or will ye not observe,
The strangeness of his altered countenance?   5
With what a majesty he bears himself,
How insolent of late he is become,
How proud, how peremptory, and unlike himself?
We know the time since he was mild and affable,   9
And if we did but glance a far-off look,
Immediately he was upon his knee,
That all the court admired him for submission;   12
But meet him now, and, be it in the morn,
When everyone will give the time of day,   14
He knits his brow and shows an angry eye
And passeth by with stiff unbowèd knee,
Disdaining duty that to us belongs.   17
Small curs are not regarded when they grin,   18
But great men tremble when the lion roars—
And Humphrey is no little man in England.
First note that he is near you in descent,
And should you fall, he is the next will mount.   22
Me seemeth then it is no policy,   23
Respecting what a rancorous mind he bears   24
And his advantage following your decease,
That he should come about your royal person

**3.1. Location: A hall for a session of Parliament at Bury St. Edmunds
(historically, the Abbey).**
s.d. Sound a sennet (The quarto stage direction specifies that two
heralds enter first, leading a formal procession.)   **1 muse** wonder
2 wont custom   **5 strangeness** aloofness   **9 know** remember.   **since**
when   **12 admired** wondered at   **14 give . . . day** say good morning
17 Disdaining . . . belongs disdaining to show the ceremonial respect
that is our (or my) due   **18 grin** bare their teeth   **22 will mount** who
will mount the throne   **23 Me seemeth** it seems to me.   **policy** prudent
course   **24 Respecting** considering

Or be admitted to Your Highness' Council.
By flattery hath he won the commons' hearts;
And when he please to make commotion,   29
'Tis to be feared they all will follow him.
Now 'tis the spring, and weeds are shallow-rooted;
Suffer them now, and they'll o'ergrow the garden
And choke the herbs for want of husbandry.   33
The reverent care I bear unto my lord
Made me collect these dangers in the Duke.   35
If it be fond, call it a woman's fear—   36
Which fear, if better reasons can supplant,   37
I will subscribe and say I wronged the Duke.   38
My lord of Suffolk, Buckingham, and York,
Reprove my allegation if you can,   40
Or else conclude my words effectual.   41

SUFFOLK
Well hath Your Highness seen into this duke,
And, had I first been put to speak my mind,
I think I should have told Your Grace's tale.
The Duchess by his subornation,   45
Upon my life, began her devilish practices;   46
Or if he were not privy to those faults,   47
Yet, by reputing of his high descent—   48
As next the King he was successive heir,
And such high vaunts of his nobility—   50
Did instigate the bedlam brainsick Duchess   51
By wicked means to frame our sovereign's fall.   52
Smooth runs the water where the brook is deep,
And in his simple show he harbors treason.   54
The fox barks not when he would steal the lamb.
No, no, my sovereign, Gloucester is a man
Unsounded yet and full of deep deceit.   57

---

29 make commotion foment unrest   **33 husbandry** proper cultivation
35 collect gather, infer   **36 fond** foolish   **37 Which . . . supplant** if
better reasons can supplant which fear   **38 subscribe** agree. (Literally,
"undersign.")   **40 Reprove** disprove   **41 effectual** decisive
45 subornation instigation   **46 Upon my life** i.e., I swear this on pain of
death.   **practices** intrigues   **47 privy to those faults** informed as to
those crimes   **48 reputing** boasting, overvaluing   **50 vaunts** boasts
51 bedlam crazy   **52 frame** devise   **54 simple show** innocent outward
appearance   **57 Unsounded** with depths still undiscovered

CARDINAL
  Did he not, contrary to form of law,
  Devise strange deaths for small offenses done?

YORK
  And did he not, in his protectorship,
  Levy great sums of money through the realm
  For soldiers' pay in France, and never sent it,
  By means whereof the towns each day revolted?   63

BUCKINGHAM
  Tut, these are petty faults to faults unknown,   64
  Which time will bring to light in smooth Duke
    Humphrey.

KING
  My lords, at once: the care you have of us   66
  To mow down thorns that would annoy our foot   67
  Is worthy praise; but, shall I speak my conscience,   68
  Our kinsman Gloucester is as innocent
  From meaning treason to our royal person
  As is the sucking lamb or harmless dove.
  The Duke is virtuous, mild, and too well given   72
  To dream on evil or to work my downfall.

QUEEN
  Ah, what's more dangerous than this fond affiance?   74
  Seems he a dove? His feathers are but borrowed,
  For he's disposèd as the hateful raven.   76
  Is he a lamb? His skin is surely lent him,
  For he's inclined as is the ravenous wolves.
  Who cannot steal a shape that means deceit?   79
  Take heed, my lord. The welfare of us all
  Hangs on the cutting short that fraudful man.   81

    Enter Somerset.

SOMERSET
  All health unto my gracious sovereign!

---

63 By means whereof on which account   **64 to** compared to   **66 at
once** answering all of you; or, without more ado; or, once and for all
67 annoy injure   **68 shall I speak** if I may speak in accordance with
72 well given kindly disposed   **74 fond affiance** foolish confidence
76 disposèd as has the disposition of   **79 Who . . . deceit** who is there,
intending to deceive, that cannot assume an appropriate disguise
81 cutting short (with a grisly suggestion of beheading)

KING

Welcome, Lord Somerset. What news from France?

SOMERSET

That all your interest in those territories

Is utterly bereft you. All is lost.

KING

Cold news, Lord Somerset; but God's will be done!

YORK [*Aside*]

Cold news for me, for I had hope of France

As firmly as I hope for fertile England.

Thus are my blossoms blasted in the bud,

And caterpillars eat my leaves away;

But I will remedy this gear ere long,   91

Or sell my title for a glorious grave.

Enter Gloucester.

GLOUCESTER

All happiness unto my lord the King!

Pardon, my liege, that I have stayed so long.   94

SUFFOLK

Nay, Gloucester, know that thou art come too soon,

Unless thou wert more loyal than thou art.

I do arrest thee of high treason here.

GLOUCESTER

Well, Suffolk, thou shalt not see me blush

Nor change my countenance for this arrest.

A heart unspotted is not easily daunted.

The purest spring is not so free from mud

As I am clear from treason to my sovereign.

Who can accuse me? Wherein am I guilty?

YORK

'Tis thought, my lord, that you took bribes of France

And, being Protector, stayed the soldiers' pay,   105

By means whereof His Highness hath lost France.

GLOUCESTER

Is it but thought so? What are they that think it?   107

I never robbed the soldiers of their pay,

Nor ever had one penny bribe from France.

So help me God as I have watched the night,   110

91 gear business   **94 stayed** delayed   **105 stayed** held back   **107 What**
who   **110 watched the night** remained awake all night

Ay, night by night, in studying good for England!
That doit that e'er I wrested from the King,   112
Or any groat I hoarded to my use,   113
Be brought against me at my trial day!   114
No, many a pound of mine own proper store,   115
Because I would not tax the needy commons,
Have I dispursèd to the garrisons   117
And never asked for restitution.

CARDINAL
It serves you well, my lord, to say so much.

GLOUCESTER
I say no more than truth, so help me God!

YORK
In your protectorship you did devise
Strange tortures for offenders, never heard of,
That England was defamed by tyranny.   123

GLOUCESTER
Why, 'tis well known that, whiles I was Protector,
Pity was all the fault that was in me;
For I should melt at an offender's tears,   126
And lowly words were ransom for their fault.   127
Unless it were a bloody murderer,
Or foul felonious thief that fleeced poor passengers,   129
I never gave them condign punishment.   130
Murder indeed, that bloody sin, I tortured
Above the felon or what trespass else.   132

SUFFOLK
My lord, these faults are easy, quickly answered;   133
But mightier crimes are laid unto your charge
Whereof you cannot easily purge yourself.
I do arrest you in His Highness' name,
And here commit you to my Lord Cardinal
To keep until your further time of trial.   138

KING
My lord of Gloucester, 'tis my special hope

112, 113 doit, groat coins of small value   114 Be may it be.   trial day
i.e., Day of Judgment before God   115 proper personal   117 dispursèd
disbursed   123 That so that.   was defamed by became notorious for
126 should would   127 lowly humble.   their fault the offenders'
crimes   129 fleeced poor passengers robbed unfortunate travelers
130 condign worthily deserved   132 Above . . . else beyond any other
kind of felony or misdemeanor   133 easy slight   138 further future

That you will clear yourself from all suspense.   140
My conscience tells me you are innocent.
GLOUCESTER
Ah, gracious lord, these days are dangerous!
Virtue is choked with foul ambition
And charity chased hence by rancor's hand;
Foul subornation is predominant,   145
And equity exiled Your Highness' land.   146
I know their complot is to have my life,   147
And if my death might make this island happy
And prove the period of their tyranny,   149
I would expend it with all willingness.
But mine is made the prologue to their play;   151
For thousands more, that yet suspect no peril,
Will not conclude their plotted tragedy.   153
Beaufort's red sparkling eyes blab his heart's malice,
And Suffolk's cloudy brow his stormy hate;   155
Sharp Buckingham unburdens with his tongue
The envious load that lies upon his heart;
And dogged York, that reaches at the moon,   158
Whose overweening arm I have plucked back,
By false accuse doth level at my life.   160
[*To the Queen.*] And you, my sovereign lady, with the rest,
Causeless have laid disgraces on my head,
And with your best endeavor have stirred up
My liefest liege to be mine enemy.   164
Ay, all of you have laid your heads together—
Myself had notice of your conventicles—   166
And all to make away my guiltless life.
I shall not want false witness to condemn me   168
Nor store of treasons to augment my guilt.
The ancient proverb will be well effected: 170
"A staff is quickly found to beat a dog."

---

140 suspense i.e., doubt as to your innocence   **145 subornation** instigating others to commit crimes, including perjury   **146 exiled** exiled from   **147 complot** plot, conspiracy   **149 prove the period** turn out to be the end   **151 mine** i.e., my death   **153 Will . . . tragedy** i.e., will not suffice to bring to an end this tragedy they have devised (with a suggestion of plotting a play)   **155 cloudy** threatening   **158 dogged** (1) relentless (2) currish   **160 accuse** accusation.   **level** aim   **164 liefest liege** dearest sovereign   **166 conventicles** private or secret meetings   **168 want** lack   **170 effected** fulfilled, realized

CARDINAL
My liege, his railing is intolerable.
If those that care to keep your royal person   173
From treason's secret knife and traitors' rage
Be thus upbraided, chid, and rated at,   175
And the offender granted scope of speech,   176
'Twill make them cool in zeal unto Your Grace.

SUFFOLK
Hath he not twit our sovereign lady here   178
With ignominious words, though clerkly couched,   179
As if she had subornèd some to swear
False allegations to o'erthrow his state?

QUEEN
But I can give the loser leave to chide.   182

GLOUCESTER
Far truer spoke than meant. I lose, indeed;
Beshrew the winners, for they played me false!   184
And well such losers may have leave to speak.

BUCKINGHAM
He'll wrest the sense and hold us here all day.   186
Lord Cardinal, he is your prisoner.

CARDINAL [*To his attendants*]
Sirs, take away the Duke and guard him sure.

GLOUCESTER
Ah, thus King Henry throws away his crutch
Before his legs be firm to bear his body.
Thus is the shepherd beaten from thy side,
And wolves are gnarling who shall gnaw thee first.   192
Ah, that my fear were false; ah, that it were!
For, good King Henry, thy decay I fear.   194
                    Exit Gloucester [guarded].

KING [*Rising*]
My lords, what to your wisdoms seemeth best,
Do or undo, as if ourself were here.

QUEEN
What, will Your Highness leave the Parliament?

---

173 care take care   **175 rated** scolded   **176 scope** freedom   **178 twit**
twitted   **179 clerkly couched** learnedly and cleverly phrased   **182 leave**
permission   **184 Beshrew** curse   **186 wrest the sense** twist the meaning   **192 gnarling** snarling over   **194 decay** downfall

KING
>   Ay, Margaret. My heart is drowned with grief,
>   Whose flood begins to flow within mine eyes,
>   My body round engirt with misery;
>   For what's more miserable than discontent?
>   Ah, uncle Humphrey, in thy face I see
>   The map of honor, truth, and loyalty;
>   And yet, good Humphrey, is the hour to come
>   That e'er I proved thee false or feared thy faith.   205
>   What louring star now envies thy estate,
>   That these great lords and Margaret our queen
>   Do seek subversion of thy harmless life?
>   Thou never didst them wrong nor no man wrong.
>   And as the butcher takes away the calf
>   And binds the wretch and beats it when it strains,   211
>   Bearing it to the bloody slaughterhouse,
>   Even so remorseless have they borne him hence;
>   And as the dam runs lowing up and down,   214
>   Looking the way her harmless young one went,
>   And can do naught but wail her darling's loss,
>   Even so myself bewails good Gloucester's case
>   With sad unhelpful tears, and with dimmed eyes
>   Look after him and cannot do him good,
>   So mighty are his vowèd enemies.
>   His fortunes I will weep, and twixt each groan
>   Say "Who's a traitor? Gloucester he is none."   222

Exeunt [_King, Buckingham, Salisbury,_
and Warwick with attendants;
Somerset remains apart].

QUEEN
>   Free lords, cold snow melts with the sun's hot beams.   223
>   Henry my lord is cold in great affairs,   224
>   Too full of foolish pity; and Gloucester's show   225

---

205 feared thy faith doubted your loyalty   **211 strains** strives. (The
Folio reading, _strays_, is perhaps possible if _binds_ means "pens in.")
214 dam mother   **222 s.d. Exeunt** (The quarto version has Salisbury
and Warwick exit here with the King. Buckingham, with no further role
in the scene, possibly leaves too. But the Folio reads _Exit_, and it is
possible the King departs alone, leaving the others in little groups,
trying to conduct a parliament without a king.)   **223 Free** noble
224 cold i.e., faint, neglectful, and ready to melt or give way   **225 show**
false appearance

Beguiles him, as the mournful crocodile   226
With sorrow snares relenting passengers,   227
Or as the snake, rolled in a flowering bank,   228
With shining checkered slough, doth sting a child   229
That for the beauty thinks it excellent.
Believe me, lords, were none more wise than I—   231
And yet herein I judge mine own wit good—   232
This Gloucester should be quickly rid the world,
To rid us from the fear we have of him.

CARDINAL
That he should die is worthy policy,   235
But yet we want a color for his death.   236
'Tis meet he be condemned by course of law.

SUFFOLK
But, in my mind, that were no policy.   238
The King will labor still to save his life,   239
The commons haply rise to save his life;   240
And yet we have but trivial argument,   241
More than mistrust, that shows him worthy death.   242

YORK
So that, by this, you would not have him die.   243

SUFFOLK
Ah, York, no man alive so fain as I!   244

YORK
'Tis York that hath more reason for his death.
But, my Lord Cardinal, and you, my lord of Suffolk,
Say as you think, and speak it from your souls:
Were 't not all one an empty eagle were set   248
To guard the chicken from a hungry kite   249
As place Duke Humphrey for the King's Protector?

QUEEN
So the poor chicken should be sure of death.

---

226 mournful crocodile i.e., the animal famous for its "crocodile
tears"   **227 relenting passengers** i.e., gullible passersby   **228 rolled**
coiled   **229 slough** skin   **231 were . . . than I** i.e., I would venture my
opinion, were there not wiser heads than I   **232 wit** intelligence   **235 is
worthy policy** is a sound scheme   **236 color** pretext   **238 were no
policy** would be a poor stratagem   **239 still** continually   **240 haply**
perhaps   **241 argument** evidence   **242 More than mistrust** other than
suspicion   **243 by this** i.e., by this reasoning   **244 fain** glad, eager
248 all one all the same, the same thing that.   **empty** hungry   **249 kite**
scavenger bird, a kind of hawk

SUFFOLK

Madam, 'tis true; and were 't not madness then
To make the fox surveyor of the fold?   253
Who, being accused a crafty murderer,
His guilt should be but idly posted over   255
Because his purpose is not executed.
No, let him die in that he is a fox,
By nature proved an enemy to the flock,
Before his chaps be stained with crimson blood,   259
As Humphrey, proved by reasons, to my liege.   260
And do not stand on quillets how to slay him—   261
Be it by gins, by snares, by subtlety,   262
Sleeping or waking, 'tis no matter how,
So he be dead. For that is good deceit   264
Which mates him first that first intends deceit.   265

QUEEN

Thrice-noble Suffolk, 'tis resolutely spoke.

SUFFOLK

Not resolute, except so much were done,   267
For things are often spoke and seldom meant;
But that my heart accordeth with my tongue,   269
Seeing the deed is meritorious,
And to preserve my sovereign from his foe,
Say but the word and I will be his priest.   272

CARDINAL

But I would have him dead, my lord of Suffolk,
Ere you can take due orders for a priest.   274
Say you consent and censure well the deed,   275
And I'll provide his executioner,
I tender so the safety of my liege.   277

---

253 surveyor guardian   **255 idly posted over** foolishly ignored or has-
tened over. (Suffolk argues that it would be foolish to place a fox in
charge of a chicken coop and then exonerate him of being a killer
simply because he hasn't yet killed the chickens.)   **259 chaps** jaws
260 proved i.e., proved to be an enemy.   **by reasons** by arguments
261 quillets subtle distinctions or disputes   **262 gins** engines, traps
264 So so long as   **265 mates** checkmates, foils (i.e., strikes quickly
before the enemy can move first)   **267 except . . . done** unless what I've
spoken is converted into action   **269 that** i.e., to prove that   **272 be his
priest** i.e., perform the last rites for him, preside over his death
274 take . . . priest (1) make arrangements to have a priest there (2) prepare yourself for the priesthood   **275 censure well** approve   **277 tender**
am concerned for, care for

SUFFOLK
Here is my hand. The deed is worthy doing.
QUEEN   And so say I.
YORK
And I. And now we three have spoke it,
It skills not greatly who impugns our doom.   281

    Enter a Post.

POST
Great lords, from Ireland am I come amain   282
To signify that rebels there are up   283
And put the Englishmen unto the sword.
Send succors, lords, and stop the rage betimes,   285
Before the wound do grow uncurable;
For, being green, there is great hope of help.   [*Exit.*] 287
CARDINAL
A breach that craves a quick expedient stop!
What counsel give you in this weighty cause?
YORK
That Somerset be sent as regent thither.
'Tis meet that lucky ruler be employed—   291
Witness the fortune he hath had in France.
SOMERSET [*Coming forward*]
If York, with all his far-fet policy,   293
Had been the regent there instead of me,
He never would have stayed in France so long.
YORK
No, not to lose it all, as thou hast done.
I rather would have lost my life betimes   297
Than bring a burden of dishonor home
By staying there so long till all were lost.   299
Show me one scar charactered on thy skin.   300
Men's flesh preserved so whole do seldom win.   301

281 skills not makes no great difference.   **impugns our doom** questions
our decision   **s.d. Post** messenger   **282 amain** with full speed
283 signify report.   **up** up in arms   **285 betimes** early, swiftly
287 green fresh   **291 meet** fitting. (Said ironically; York is hostile
toward Somerset.)   **293 far-fet** farfetched, artful, deep. (Said ironically;
Somerset comes forward to defend himself against York's insulting way
of speaking as though Somerset were not there.)   **297 betimes** forthwith, sooner   **299 staying ... long** temporizing   **300 charactered**
inscribed   **301 Men's ... win** men who can show no wounds are seldom victors

QUEEN
  Nay, then, this spark will prove a raging fire
  If wind and fuel be brought to feed it with.
  No more, good York; sweet Somerset, be still.
  Thy fortune, York, hadst thou been regent there,
  Might happily have proved far worse than his.   306
YORK
  What, worse than naught? Nay, then a shame take all!
SOMERSET
  And, in the number, thee that wishest shame!   308
CARDINAL
  My lord of York, try what your fortune is.
  Th' uncivil kerns of Ireland are in arms   310
  And temper clay with blood of Englishmen.   311
  To Ireland will you lead a band of men,
  Collected choicely, from each county some,
  And try your hap against the Irishmen?   314
YORK
  I will, my lord, so please His Majesty.
SUFFOLK
  Why, our authority is his consent,
  And what we do establish he confirms.
  Then, noble York, take thou this task in hand.
YORK
  I am content. Provide me soldiers, lords,
  Whiles I take order for mine own affairs.   320
SUFFOLK
  A charge, Lord York, that I will see performed.
  But now return we to the false Duke Humphrey.
CARDINAL
  No more of him; for I will deal with him
  That henceforth he shall trouble us no more.
  And so, break off. The day is almost spent.   325
  Lord Suffolk, you and I must talk of that event.   326
YORK
  My lord of Suffolk, within fourteen days

---

306 happily haply, perhaps   **308 in . . . shame** i.e., among the "all" to
whom you wish shame, may you be included   **310 uncivil kerns** disorderly and irregular light-armed Irish soldiers   **311 temper clay** moisten
the soil   **314 hap** fortune   **320 take order for** arrange   **325 break off**
cease conversation   **326 event** affair, business

At Bristol I expect my soldiers,
For there I'll ship them all for Ireland.

SUFFOLK
I'll see it truly done, my lord of York.   330

Exeunt. Manet York.

YORK
Now, York, or never, steel thy fearful thoughts   331
And change misdoubt to resolution.   332
Be that thou hop'st to be, or what thou art   333
Resign to death; it is not worth th' enjoying.
Let pale-faced fear keep with the mean-born man   335
And find no harbor in a royal heart.
Faster than springtime showers comes thought on
   thought,
And not a thought but thinks on dignity.   338
My brain, more busy than the laboring spider,
Weaves tedious snares to trap mine enemies.   340
Well, nobles, well, 'tis politicly done,   341
To send me packing with an host of men.   342
I fear me you but warm the starvèd snake,   343
Who, cherished in your breasts, will sting your hearts.
'Twas men I lacked, and you will give them me;
I take it kindly. Yet be well assured
You put sharp weapons in a madman's hands.
Whiles I in Ireland nourish a mighty band,
I will stir up in England some black storm
Shall blow ten thousand souls to heaven or hell;   350
And this fell tempest shall not cease to rage   351
Until the golden circuit on my head,   352
Like to the glorious sun's transparent beams,
Do calm the fury of this mad-bred flaw.   354
And, for a minister of my intent,   355
I have seduced a headstrong Kentishman,

---

330 s.d. Manet he remains onstage   **331 fearful** timid   **332 misdoubt**
suspicion, fear   **333 that** that which   **335 keep** dwell.   **mean-born**
lowly-born   **338 dignity** i.e., the dignity of high office—kingship
340 tedious intricate   **341 politicly** shrewdly. (Said ironically.)
342 packing away, a-journeying   **343 starvèd** i.e., deathlike with cold.
(One of Aesop's fables is about a man who puts a snake next to his
chest to warm it and is stung by it.)   **350 Shall** that shall   **351 fell**
fierce   **352 circuit** circlet, crown   **354 mad-bred** produced by madness.   **flaw** squall, tempest   **355 minister** agent

John Cade of Ashford,
To make commotion, as full well he can,
Under the title of John Mortimer.   359
In Ireland have I seen this stubborn Cade
Oppose himself against a troop of kerns,
And fought so long till that his thighs with darts   362
Were almost like a sharp-quilled porpentine;   363
And in the end being rescued, I have seen
Him caper upright like a wild Morisco,   365
Shaking the bloody darts as he his bells.   366
Full often, like a shag-haired crafty kern,
Hath he conversèd with the enemy,
And undiscovered come to me again
And given me notice of their villainies.
This devil here shall be my substitute,
For that John Mortimer, which now is dead,   372
In face, in gait, in speech, he doth resemble.
By this I shall perceive the commons' mind,
How they affect the house and claim of York.   375
Say he be taken, racked, and torturèd,
I know no pain they can inflict upon him
Will make him say I moved him to those arms.   378
Say that he thrive, as 'tis great like he will,   379
Why then from Ireland come I with my strength
And reap the harvest which that rascal sowed.
For Humphrey being dead, as he shall be,
And Henry put apart, the next for me.   *Exit.*

❧

359 Mortimer (The name of a powerful family claiming descent from
Lionel, Duke of Clarence, and hence entitled to the crown. See
1 Henry VI, 2.5.)   **362 till that** until.   **darts** light spears or arrows
363 porpentine porcupine   **365 Morisco** morris dancer, always fancily
or grotesquely dressed; or the dance itself   **366 he** i.e., the morris
dancer   **372 For that** because   **375 affect** incline toward   **378 Will**
that will.   **moved** incited, prompted   **379 great like** very likely

3.2 *Enter two or three running over the stage, from the murder of Duke Humphrey.*

FIRST MURDERER
　Run to my lord of Suffolk. Let him know
　We have dispatched the Duke, as he commanded.
SECOND MURDERER
　O, that it were to do! What have we done?　　　3
　Didst ever hear a man so penitent?

　　Enter Suffolk.

FIRST MURDERER　Here comes my lord.
SUFFOLK
　Now, sirs, have you dispatched this thing?
FIRST MURDERER　Ay, my good lord, he's dead.
SUFFOLK
　Why, that's well said. Go get you to my house.　　8
　I will reward you for this venturous deed.
　The King and all the peers are here at hand.
　Have you laid fair the bed? Is all things well,　　11
　According as I gave directions?
FIRST MURDERER　'Tis, my good lord.
SUFFOLK　Away! Begone.　　　　*Exeunt [Murderers].*

　　*Sound trumpets. Enter the King, the Queen,
　　Cardinal [Beaufort], Somerset, with attendants.*

KING
　Go call our uncle to our presence straight.　　15
　Say we intend to try His Grace today,
　If he be guilty, as 'tis publishèd.　　　　17
SUFFOLK
　I'll call him presently, my noble lord.　　　*Exit.* 18

3.2. Location: Bury St. Edmunds, in a room of state adjoining the place of imprisonment where Gloucester has been murdered. Seats are prepared, as for his trial.
s.d. from the murder (In the quarto version, "the curtains being drawn, Duke Humphrey is discovered in his bed, and two men lying on his breast and smothering him in his bed." Suffolk enters to them. The curtains are closed as the Murderers exit at l. 14.)　**3 that . . . do** i.e., that it were not yet done and thus could be avoided　**8 well said** well done　**11 laid fair the bed** i.e., straightened the bed linen to conceal the signs of struggle　**15 straight** straightway　**17 If** whether.　**publishèd** publicly proclaimed　**18 presently** at once

KING
  Lords, take your places; and, I pray you all,
  Proceed no straiter 'gainst our uncle Gloucester   20
  Than from true evidence of good esteem   21
  He be approved in practice culpable.   22
                            [*They take their places.*]
QUEEN
  God forbid any malice should prevail
  That faultless may condemn a nobleman!   24
  Pray God he may acquit him of suspicion!   25
KING
  I thank thee, Meg. These words content me much.

      Enter Suffolk.

  How now? Why look'st thou pale? Why tremblest thou?
  Where is our uncle? What's the matter, Suffolk?
SUFFOLK
  Dead in his bed, my lord. Gloucester is dead.
QUEEN Marry, God forfend!   30
CARDINAL
  God's secret judgment. I did dream tonight   31
  The Duke was dumb and could not speak a word.
                            King swoons.
QUEEN
  How fares my lord? Help, lords, the King is dead!
SOMERSET
  Rear up his body. Wring him by the nose.   34
QUEEN
  Run, go, help, help! O Henry, ope thine eyes!
                            [*They revive the King.*]
SUFFOLK
  He doth revive again. Madam, be patient.
KING
  O heavenly God!
QUEEN   How fares my gracious lord?
SUFFOLK
  Comfort, my sovereign! Gracious Henry, comfort!

---

20 straiter more severely   **21 of good esteem** worthy of belief   **22 approved in** proved guilty of   **24 faultless** (Modifies *nobleman*.)   **25 acquit him** exonerate himself   **30 forfend** forbid   **31 tonight** this past night **34 Wring . . . nose** (Evidently a common first-aid remedy for restoring consciousness; cf. *Venus and Adonis*, l. 475.)

KING
What, doth my lord of Suffolk comfort me?
Came he right now to sing a raven's note,   40
Whose dismal tune bereft my vital powers,
And thinks he that the chirping of a wren,
By crying comfort from a hollow breast,   43
Can chase away the first-conceivèd sound?   44
Hide not thy poison with such sugared words.
Lay not thy hands on me. Forbear, I say!
Their touch affrights me as a serpent's sting.
Thou baleful messenger, out of my sight!
Upon thy eyeballs murderous Tyranny
Sits in grim majesty to fright the world.
Look not upon me, for thine eyes are wounding.
Yet do not go away. Come, basilisk,   52
And kill the innocent gazer with thy sight;
For in the shade of death I shall find joy,
In life but double death, now Gloucester's dead.
QUEEN
Why do you rate my lord of Suffolk thus?   56
Although the Duke was enemy to him,
Yet he most Christian-like laments his death.
And for myself, foe as he was to me,   59
Might liquid tears or heart-offending groans   60
Or blood-consuming sighs recall his life,   61
I would be blind with weeping, sick with groans,
Look pale as primrose with blood-drinking sighs,   63
And all to have the noble Duke alive.
What know I how the world may deem of me?   65
For it is known we were but hollow friends.
It may be judged I made the Duke away;
So shall my name with slander's tongue be wounded,
And princes' courts be filled with my reproach.
This get I by his death. Ay me, unhappy,
To be a queen, and crowned with infamy!

---

40 right now just now.   **raven's note** a supposed omen of death
43 hollow deceitful   **44 first-conceivèd sound** sound that was perceived
first   **52 basilisk** fabulous reptile, said to kill by its look   **56 rate**
berate   **59 for** as for   **60, 61, 63 heart-offending, blood-consuming,
blood-drinking** (It was commonly believed that groans and sighs cost
the heart a drop of blood.)   **65 deem** judge

KING
> Ah, woe is me for Gloucester, wretched man!

QUEEN
> Be woe for me, more wretched than he is.   73
> What, dost thou turn away and hide thy face?
> I am no loathsome leper. Look on me.
> What? Art thou, like the adder, waxen deaf?   76
> Be poisonous too and kill thy forlorn queen.
> Is all thy comfort shut in Gloucester's tomb?
> Why, then, Dame Margaret was ne'er thy joy.
> Erect his statue and worship it,
> And make my image but an alehouse sign.
> Was I for this nigh wrecked upon the sea,
> And twice by awkward wind from England's bank   83
> Drove back again unto my native clime?   84
> What boded this, but well forewarning wind   85
> Did seem to say, "Seek not a scorpion's nest,
> Nor set no footing on this unkind shore"?
> What did I then but cursed the gentle gusts
> And he that loosed them forth their brazen caves,   89
> And bid them blow towards England's blessèd shore
> Or turn our stern upon a dreadful rock?
> Yet Aeolus would not be a murderer,
> But left that hateful office unto thee.
> The pretty-vaulting sea refused to drown me,   94
> Knowing that thou wouldst have me drowned on shore
> With tears as salt as sea, through thy unkindness.
> The splitting rocks cow'red in the sinking sands   97
> And would not dash me with their ragged sides,
> Because thy flinty heart, more hard than they,   99
> Might in thy palace perish Margaret.   100
> As far as I could ken thy chalky cliffs,   101
> When from thy shore the tempest beat us back,

73 woe sorry   **76 waxen deaf** grown deaf. (Snakes were popularly
supposed to be deaf.)   **83 awkward** adverse.   **bank** shore   **84 Drove**
driven.   **clime** country   **85 but** but that   **89 he** i.e., Aeolus, god of the
winds.   **forth** forth from.   **brazen** (In Homer's *Odyssey,* 10.3–4,
the floating island of Aeolus is enclosed by a rampart of bronze.)
94 pretty-vaulting handsomely rising and falling   **97 splitting rocks**
rocks on which ships split.   **sinking sands** sandbars on which ships
founder and sink   **99 Because** so that   **100 perish** cause to perish
101 ken discern

I stood upon the hatches in the storm,
And when the dusky sky began to rob
My earnest-gaping sight of thy land's view,   105
I took a costly jewel from my neck—
A heart it was, bound in with diamonds—
And threw it towards thy land. The sea received it,
And so I wished thy body might my heart.
And even with this I lost fair England's view,
And bid mine eyes be packing with my heart,   111
And called them blind and dusky spectacles   112
For losing ken of Albion's wishèd coast.   113
How often have I tempted Suffolk's tongue,   114
The agent of thy foul inconstancy,   115
To sit and witch me, as Ascanius did   116
When he to madding Dido would unfold   117
His father's acts commenced in burning Troy!
Am I not witched like her, or thou not false like him? 119
Ay me, I can no more. Die, Margaret!
For Henry weeps that thou dost live so long.

> *Noise within. Enter Warwick, [Salisbury,] and*
> *many Commons.*

WARWICK
It is reported, mighty sovereign,
That good Duke Humphrey traitorously is murdered
By Suffolk and the Cardinal Beaufort's means.
The commons, like an angry hive of bees
That want their leader, scatter up and down   126
And care not who they sting in his revenge.   127

---

105 My earnest-gaping . . . view my ardently peering eyesight of the
view of your land   **111 be packing** begone.   **my heart** (1) my affection,
left behind in England (2) my heart-shaped jewel   **112 spectacles** instruments of sight   **113 Albion's** England's.   **wishèd** longed-for
114 tempted (Queen Margaret's point is that, by her beauty, she has
innocently induced Suffolk to practice witchcraft on her in behalf of
King Henry.)   **115 agent** i.e., arranger of the marriage agreement
between Henry and Margaret   **116 witch** bewitch.   **Ascanius** young son
of Aeneas. (In Virgil's *Aeneid*, Book 1, during Aeneas' narration of his
adventures and misfortunes to Queen Dido, Aeneas' mother Venus sends
Cupid disguised as Ascanius to afflict the Queen with love for
Aeneas.)   **117 madding** becoming frantic (with love).   **unfold** disclose,
narrate   **119 witched** bewitched.   **him** i.e., Aeneas   **126 want** lack
127 his revenge revenge of him

Myself have calmed their spleenful mutiny,   128
Until they hear the order of his death.   129

KING

That he is dead, good Warwick, 'tis too true;
But how he died God knows, not Henry.
Enter his chamber, view his breathless corpse,
And comment then upon his sudden death.   133

WARWICK

That shall I do, my liege.—Stay, Salisbury,
With the rude multitude till I return.   [*Exit.*] 135
                    [*Exit Salisbury with the Commons.*]

KING

O Thou that judgest all things, stay my thoughts,   136
My thoughts that labor to persuade my soul
Some violent hands were laid on Humphrey's life!
If my suspect be false, forgive me, God,   139
For judgment only doth belong to Thee.
Fain would I go to chafe his paly lips   141
With twenty thousand kisses, and to drain
Upon his face an ocean of salt tears,
To tell my love unto his dumb deaf trunk
And with my fingers feel his hand unfeeling.
But all in vain are these mean obsequies.   146

        Bed put forth [*bearing Gloucester's body. Enter
        Warwick*].

And to survey his dead and earthy image,
What were it but to make my sorrow greater?

WARWICK

Come hither, gracious sovereign. View this body.

KING

That is to see how deep my grave is made.
For with his soul fled all my worldly solace;
For seeing him I see my life in death.   152

---

128 spleenful mutiny wrathful uprising   **129 order** manner
133 comment . . . upon explain   **135 rude** turbulent, unpolished
136 stay hold back   **139 suspect** suspicion   **141 Fain** gladly.   **chafe**
rub, warm.   **paly** pale   **146 mean obsequies** deficient funeral rites
s.d. Bed put forth (In the quarto version, Warwick need not leave the
stage [see l. 135] to view Gloucester's dead body; he simply "draws the
curtain and shows Duke Humphrey in his bed." In the present Folio
version the bed must be thrust forth onto the stage with Humphrey in
it.)   **152 For . . . death** i.e., for in his death I see an image of my own

WARWICK
  As surely as my soul intends to live
  With that dread King that took our state upon Him   154
  To free us from His Father's wrathful curse,
  I do believe that violent hands were laid
  Upon the life of this thrice-faméd duke.   157
SUFFOLK
  A dreadful oath, sworn with a solemn tongue!
  What instance gives Lord Warwick for his vow?   159
WARWICK
  See how the blood is settled in his face.
  Oft have I seen a timely-parted ghost,   161
  Of ashy semblance, meager, pale, and bloodless,
  Being all descended to the laboring heart,   163
  Who, in the conflict that it holds with death,   164
  Attracts the same for aidance 'gainst the enemy,   165
  Which with the heart there cools and ne'er returneth   166
  To blush and beautify the cheek again.   167
  But see, his face is black and full of blood;
  His eyeballs further out than when he lived,
  Staring full ghastly, like a strangled man;
  His hair upreared, his nostrils stretched with
    struggling;   171
  His hands abroad displayed, as one that grasped   172
  And tugged for life and was by strength subdued.
  Look, on the sheets his hair, you see, is sticking;
  His well-proportioned beard made rough and rugged,
  Like to the summer's corn by tempest lodged.   176
  It cannot be but he was murdered here.
  The least of all these signs were probable.   178
SUFFOLK
  Why, Warwick, who should do the Duke to death?
  Myself and Beaufort had him in protection,
  And we, I hope, sir, are no murderers.

154 King i.e., Christ.   **state** i.e., human nature   **157 thrice-faméd** very famous   **159 instance** proof   **161 a timely-parted ghost** the remains of one having died in the natural course of events   **163 Being all descended** i.e., the blood having all descended   **164 Who** i.e., the heart **165 the same** i.e., the blood.   **aidance** aid.   **the enemy** i.e., death **166 Which** i.e., the blood   **167 blush** cause to blush, take on sanguine color   **171 upreared** standing on end   **172 abroad displayed** i.e., spread out   **176 corn** grain.   **lodged** beaten down   **178 were probable** would be sufficient confirmation

WARWICK

But both of you were vowed Duke Humphrey's foes,
[*To Cardinal*] And you, forsooth, had the good Duke
   to keep.   183
'Tis like you would not feast him like a friend,   184
And 'tis well seen he found an enemy.   185

QUEEN

Then you, belike, suspect these noblemen   186
As guilty of Duke Humphrey's timeless death.   187

WARWICK

Who finds the heifer dead and bleeding fresh
And sees fast by a butcher with an ax,   189
But will suspect 'twas he that made the slaughter?
Who finds the partridge in the puttock's nest   191
But may imagine how the bird was dead,
Although the kite soar with unbloodied beak?
Even so suspicious is this tragedy.

QUEEN

Are you the butcher, Suffolk? Where's your knife?
Is Beaufort termed a kite? Where are his talons?

SUFFOLK

I wear no knife to slaughter sleeping men;
But here's a vengeful sword, rusted with ease,   198
That shall be scourèd in his rancorous heart
That slanders me with murder's crimson badge.
Say, if thou dar'st, proud lord of Warwickshire,
That I am faulty in Duke Humphrey's death.   202
        [*Exeunt Cardinal, Somerset, and others.*]

WARWICK

What dares not Warwick, if false Suffolk dare him?

QUEEN

He dares not calm his contumelious spirit,   204

---

183 to keep in your custody   **184 like** likely   **185 well seen** obvious
186 belike perchance   **187 timeless** untimely   **189 fast by** close by
191 puttock's kite's   **198 ease** i.e., disuse   **202 faulty in** guilty of
s.d. Exeunt . . . others (The Cardinal's exit is marked in the quarto, not
in the Folio. Somerset's exit here is even more uncertain, but he is not
needed for the ensuing quarrel and may help the ailing and guilt-ridden
Cardinal offstage. Also, at some point the bed and its dead occupant
must be withdrawn or concealed by curtains.)   **204 contumelious**
contemptuous, contentious

Nor cease to be an arrogant controller,   205
Though Suffolk dare him twenty thousand times.

WARWICK
Madam, be still—with reverence may I say—
For every word you speak in his behalf
Is slander to your royal dignity.

SUFFOLK
Blunt-witted lord, ignoble in demeanor!
If ever lady wronged her lord so much,
Thy mother took into her blameful bed
Some stern untutored churl, and noble stock   213
Was graft with crab-tree slip—whose fruit thou art   214
And never of the Nevilles' noble race.

WARWICK
But that the guilt of murder bucklers thee   216
And I should rob the deathsman of his fee,   217
Quitting thee thereby of ten thousand shames,   218
And that my sovereign's presence makes me mild,   219
I would, false murderous coward, on thy knee
Make thee beg pardon for thy passèd speech   221
And say it was thy mother that thou meant'st,   222
That thou thyself wast born in bastardy;
And after all this fearful homage done,   224
Give thee thy hire and send thy soul to hell,   225
Pernicious bloodsucker of sleeping men!   226

SUFFOLK
Thou shalt be waking while I shed thy blood,   227
If from this presence thou dar'st go with me.   228

WARWICK
Away even now, or I will drag thee hence!

205 controller critic, detractor   **213 stern** rough   **214 graft** grafted.
slip cutting (with a possible play on the sense of "moral lapse")
216 But that were it not that.   **bucklers** shields   **217 deathsman** executioner   **218 Quitting** ridding   **219 that** were it not that   **221 passèd** just
spoken   **222 And . . . thy mother** i.e., and force you to admit it was your
own mother. (The emphasis is on *thy*.)   **224 fearful homage** craven
submission   **225 Give** i.e., I would give.   **hire** reward (i.e., death)
226 bloodsucker . . . men (Warwick accuses Suffolk of killing Gloucester in his sleep, suggesting further that he is a sort of vampire.)
227 waking (Suffolk responds sarcastically to the accusation of killing
sleeping men.)   **228 this presence** (Drawing swords is not allowed in the
King's presence, as also at ll. 237–238.)

Unworthy though thou art, I'll cope with thee   230
And do some service to Duke Humphrey's ghost.
                    Exeunt [Suffolk and Warwick].

KING
What stronger breastplate than a heart untainted!
Thrice is he armed that hath his quarrel just,
And he but naked, though locked up in steel,   234
Whose conscience with injustice is corrupted.
                    A noise within.

QUEEN   What noise is this?

     *Enter Suffolk and Warwick with their weapons
     drawn.*

KING
· Why, how now, lords? Your wrathful weapons drawn
Here in our presence? Dare you be so bold?
Why, what tumultuous clamor have we here?

SUFFOLK
The traitorous Warwick, with the men of Bury,
Set all upon me, mighty sovereign.

     Enter Salisbury.

SALISBURY [*To the Commons, within*]
Sirs, stand apart. The King shall know your mind.—
Dread lord, the commons send you word by me,
Unless Lord Suffolk straight be done to death   244
Or banishèd fair England's territories,
They will by violence tear him from your palace
And torture him with grievous lingering death.
They say, by him the good Duke Humphrey died;
They say, in him they fear Your Highness' death;
And mere instinct of love and loyalty,   250
Free from a stubborn opposite intent,   251
As being thought to contradict your liking,   252
Makes them thus forward in his banishment.   253
They say, in care of your most royal person,
That if Your Highness should intend to sleep,

---

230 cope with encounter   **234 naked** i.e., unarmed   **244 straight** at
once   **250 mere instinct** pure impulse   **251–252 Free ... liking** innocent of any stubborn willfulness that might be interpreted as crossing
your wishes   **253 forward in** bold, insistent upon

And charge that no man should disturb your rest
In pain of your dislike or pain of death,
Yet, notwithstanding such a strait edict,   258
Were there a serpent seen with forkèd tongue
That slyly glided towards Your Majesty,
It were but necessary you were waked,
Lest, being suffered in that harmful slumber,   262
The mortal worm might make the sleep eternal.   263
And therefore do they cry, though you forbid,
That they will guard you, whe'er you will or no,   265
From such fell serpents as false Suffolk is—   266
With whose envenomèd and fatal sting   267
Your loving uncle, twenty times his worth,   268
They say, is shamefully bereft of life.   269

COMMONS (*Within*)
  An answer from the King, my lord of Salisbury!

SUFFOLK
  'Tis like the commons, rude unpolished hinds,   271
Could send such message to their sovereign!
[*To Salisbury.*] But you, my lord, were glad to be
  employed,
To show how quaint an orator you are.   274
But all the honor Salisbury hath won
Is that he was the lord ambassador
Sent from a sort of tinkers to the King.   277

COMMONS (*Within*)
  An answer from the King, or we will all break in!

KING
  Go, Salisbury, and tell them all from me,
I thank them for their tender loving care;
And had I not been cited so by them,   281
Yet did I purpose as they do entreat.
For, sure, my thoughts do hourly prophesy
Mischance unto my state by Suffolk's means.   284
And therefore, by His majesty I swear,   285

---

258 strait strict   262 being suffered you being permitted to remain
263 mortal worm deadly serpent   265 whe'er whether   266 fell cruel
267–269 With . . . life with whose venomous and fatal sting, they say,
your uncle (who is twenty times more worthy than Suffolk) is deprived
of life   271 like likely. (Said ironically.)   hinds boors, rustics
274 quaint skilled, clever   277 sort gang   281 cited incited, urged
284 Mischance disaster   285 His i.e., God's

Whose far unworthy deputy I am,
He shall not breathe infection in this air   287
But three days longer, on the pain of death.

                            [Exit Salisbury.]

QUEEN

O Henry, let me plead for gentle Suffolk!   289

KING

Ungentle queen, to call him gentle Suffolk!
No more, I say! If thou dost plead for him,
Thou wilt but add increase unto my wrath.
Had I but said, I would have kept my word,   293
But when I swear, it is irrevocable.
[*To Suffolk.*] If, after three days' space, thou here
   be'st found
On any ground that I am ruler of,
The world shall not be ransom for thy life.
Come, Warwick, come, good Warwick, go with me.
I have great matters to impart to thee.   299

            Exit [with all but Queen and Suffolk].

QUEEN

Mischance and sorrow go along with you!
Heart's discontent and sour affliction
Be playfellows to keep you company!
There's two of you; the devil make a third,   303
And threefold vengeance tend upon your steps!   304

SUFFOLK

Cease, gentle Queen, these execrations,
And let thy Suffolk take his heavy leave.   306

QUEEN

Fie, coward woman and softhearted wretch!
Hast thou not spirit to curse thine enemy?

SUFFOLK

A plague upon them, wherefore should I curse them?
Would curses kill, as doth the mandrake's groan,   310

---

287 breathe breathe out, spread   **289 gentle** noble   **293 but said** merely
spoken, without an oath   **299 s.d. Exit** (Possibly the bed and Gloucester's body are concealed or withdrawn at this point; see l. 202 s.d., note.)
303 two i.e., the King and Warwick   **304 tend upon** follow   **306 heavy**
sorrowful   **310 mandrake's groan** (Folk belief held that when the
forked and man-shaped mandrake root was pulled from the ground, it
uttered a shriek that was fatal to the hearer or would drive him mad; cf.
Romeo and Juliet, 4.3.47–48.)

I would invent as bitter searching terms,   311
As curst, as harsh, and horrible to hear,   312
Delivered strongly through my fixèd teeth,
With full as many signs of deadly hate,
As lean-faced Envy in her loathsome cave.
My tongue should stumble in mine earnest words,
Mine eyes should sparkle like the beaten flint,
Mine hair be fixed on end, as one distract;   318
Ay, every joint should seem to curse and ban;   319
And even now my burdened heart would break,
Should I not curse them. Poison be their drink!
Gall, worse than gall, the daintiest that they taste!
Their sweetest shade a grove of cypress trees!   323
Their chiefest prospect murdering basilisks!   324
Their softest touch as smart as lizards' stings!   325
Their music frightful as the serpent's hiss,
And boding screech owls make the consort full!   327
All the foul terrors in dark-seated hell—

QUEEN
  Enough, sweet Suffolk. Thou torment'st thyself,
And these dread curses, like the sun 'gainst glass,
Or like an overchargèd gun, recoil,   331
And turns the force of them upon thyself.

SUFFOLK
  You bade me ban, and will you bid me leave?   333
Now, by the ground that I am banished from,
Well could I curse away a winter's night,
Though standing naked on a mountain top,
Where biting cold would never let grass grow,
And think it but a minute spent in sport.

QUEEN
  O, let me entreat thee cease! Give me thy hand,
That I may dew it with my mournful tears;
Nor let the rain of heaven wet this place
To wash away my woeful monuments.   342
                    [*She kisses his hand.*]

311 **searching** probing, cutting   312 **curst** malignant   318 **distract**
mad   319 **ban** curse   323 **cypress trees** (Associated with death because
they were often planted near graveyards.)   324 **prospect** view.   **basilisks**
(See l. 52 above.)   325 **smart** stinging   327 **boding** portending evil.
consort ensemble of musicians   331 **overchargèd** overloaded   333 **leave**
leave off   342 **monuments** i.e., traces of her tears

O, could this kiss be printed in thy hand,
That thou mightst think upon these by the seal,   344
Through whom a thousand sighs are breathed for thee!   345
So, get thee gone, that I may know my grief;   346
'Tis but surmised whiles thou art standing by,
As one that surfeits thinking on a want.   348
I will repeal thee, or, be well assured,   349
Adventure to be banishèd myself;   350
And banishèd I am, if but from thee.
Go, speak not to me. Even now, begone!
O, go not yet! Even thus two friends condemned
Embrace and kiss and take ten thousand leaves,
Loather a hundred times to part than die.
                              [*They embrace.*]
Yet now farewell, and farewell life with thee!

SUFFOLK
Thus is poor Suffolk ten times banishèd,
Once by the King, and three times thrice by thee.
'Tis not the land I care for, wert thou thence.
A wilderness is populous enough,
So Suffolk had thy heavenly company;   361
For where thou art, there is the world itself,
With every several pleasure in the world,   363
And where thou art not, desolation.
I can no more. Live thou to joy thy life;   365
Myself no joy in naught but that thou liv'st.

          Enter Vaux.

QUEEN
Whither goes Vaux so fast? What news, I prithee?

VAUX
To signify unto His Majesty   368
That Cardinal Beaufort is at point of death;
For suddenly a grievous sickness took him,
That makes him gasp and stare and catch the air,
Blaspheming God and cursing men on earth.

---

344 these i.e., my lips.   **seal** imprint   **345 Through whom** i.e., through
which lips   **346 know** fully comprehend   **348 As . . . want** like a person
(such as myself) who, enjoying plenty, anticipates a time of depriva-
tion   **349 repeal thee** bring about your recall   **350 Adventure** risk
361 So so long as   **363 several** distinct   **365 joy** enjoy   **368 signify**
report

Sometimes he talks as if Duke Humphrey's ghost
Were by his side; sometimes he calls the King,
And whispers to his pillow as to him
The secrets of his overchargèd soul;   376
And I am sent to tell His Majesty
That even now he cries aloud for him.

QUEEN
Go tell this heavy message to the King.   *Exit [Vaux]*.
Ay me, what is this world? What news are these!
But wherefore grieve I at an hour's poor loss,   381
Omitting Suffolk's exile, my soul's treasure?   382
Why only, Suffolk, mourn I not for thee,
And with the southern clouds contend in tears—   384
Theirs for the earth's increase, mine for my sorrows?
Now get thee hence. The King, thou know'st, is coming.
If thou be found by me, thou art but dead.   387

SUFFOLK
If I depart from thee, I cannot live,
And in thy sight to die, what were it else
But like a pleasant slumber in thy lap?
Here could I breathe my soul into the air,
As mild and gentle as the cradle babe
Dying with mother's dug between its lips—   393
Where, from thy sight, I should be raging mad   394
And cry out for thee to close up mine eyes,
To have thee with thy lips to stop my mouth.
So shouldst thou either turn my flying soul,   397
Or I should breathe it so into thy body,
And then it lived in sweet Elysium.   399
To die by thee were but to die in jest;   400
From thee to die were torture more than death.   401
O, let me stay, befall what may befall!

376 overchargèd overburdened with guilt   **381 an hour's** (i.e., the
Cardinal has figuratively but an hour left to live in any case)
382 Omitting neglecting   **384 southern** i.e., especially moist   **387 by me**
near me   **393 dug** breast   **394 from** out of   **397 turn** turn back, i.e.,
prevent the soul's escape, preserve my life. (The soul was thought to
leave the body through the mouth.)   **399 lived** would live.   **Elysium**
classical abode after death of those favored by the gods   **400 in jest** i.e.,
not truly to die at all. (*To die* carries the suggestion of experiencing
orgasm.)   **401 From** away from

QUEEN
　Away! Though parting be a fretful corrosive,　　403
　It is applièd to a deathful wound.　　404
　To France, sweet Suffolk. Let me hear from thee,
　For wheresoe'er thou art in this world's globe,
　I'll have an Iris that shall find thee out.　　407

SUFFOLK　I go.

QUEEN　And take my heart with thee.　[*She kisses him.*]

SUFFOLK
　A jewel, locked into the woefull'st cask　　410
　That ever did contain a thing of worth.
　Even as a splitted bark, so sunder we;　　412
　This way fall I to death.

QUEEN　　　　　　　This way for me.　　413

　　　　　　　　　Exeunt [separately].

❖

3.3　*Enter the King, Salisbury, and Warwick,*
　　　　to the Cardinal in bed, [raving and staring
　　　　as if he were mad].

KING
　How fares my lord? Speak, Beaufort, to thy sovereign.

CARDINAL
　If thou be'st Death, I'll give thee England's treasure,
　Enough to purchase such another island,
　So thou wilt let me live and feel no pain.　　4

KING
　Ah, what a sign it is of evil life,
　Where death's approach is seen so terrible!

WARWICK
　Beaufort, it is thy sovereign speaks to thee.

---

403 fretful corrosive painful and caustic course of treatment
404 deathful fatal (since Suffolk's remaining would prove fatal)
407 Iris Juno's messenger　**410 cask** casket　**412 splitted bark** sailing
vessel split in two　**413 s.d. Exeunt** (Gloucester's body in its bed is
probably concealed or removed earlier, perhaps at l. 202 or l. 299; since
the bed is needed immediately in the next scene, it almost certainly
does not remain onstage until the end of this scene.)

3.3. Location: The Cardinal's bedchamber.
s.d. in bed (In the quarto version, the curtains are drawn and the Cardinal "is discovered in his bed," raving and staring. Cf. 3.2.0 s.d.)　**4 So**
provided

CARDINAL
   Bring me unto my trial when you will.
   Died he not in his bed? Where should he die?   9
   Can I make men live, whe'er they will or no?   10
   O, torture me no more! I will confess.
   Alive again? Then show me where he is.
   I'll give a thousand pound to look upon him.
   He hath no eyes! The dust hath blinded them.
   Comb down his hair. Look, look! It stands upright,
   Like lime-twigs set to catch my wingèd soul.   16
   Give me some drink, and bid the apothecary
   Bring the strong poison that I bought of him.   18

KING
   O thou eternal mover of the heavens,
   Look with a gentle eye upon this wretch!
   O, beat away the busy meddling fiend
   That lays strong siege unto this wretch's soul
   And from his bosom purge this black despair!

WARWICK
   See how the pangs of death do make him grin!

SALISBURY
   Disturb him not. Let him pass peaceably.

KING
   Peace to his soul, if God's good pleasure be!
   Lord Cardinal, if thou think'st on heaven's bliss,
   Hold up thy hand. Make signal of thy hope.
                   [*The Cardinal dies.*]
   He dies and makes no sign. O God, forgive him!

WARWICK
   So bad a death argues a monstrous life.

KING
   Forbear to judge, for we are sinners all.
   Close up his eyes and draw the curtain close,   32
   And let us all to meditation. [*The curtains are closed.*]
                             Exeunt.

❖

9 he i.e., Gloucester **10 whe'er** whether **16 lime-twigs** twigs smeared
with sticky lime to trap birds **18 of** from **32 curtain** (The bed itself,
presumably "thrust out" onstage for this brief scene, would have to be
removed at this point; the curtains here are presumably bed curtains,
although in the quarto version they are drawn open at l. 1 in such a way
as to discover the Cardinal to view without having to bring on a bed,
i.e., using a curtained area backstage.)

4.1 *Alarum [within]. Fight at sea. Ordnance goes*
off. Enter Lieutenant, [a Master, a Master's
Mate, Walter Whitmore, and others; with them]
Suffolk [disguised], and others, [prisoners].

LIEUTENANT
   The gaudy, blabbing, and remorseful day   1
   Is crept into the bosom of the sea,
   And now loud-howling wolves arouse the jades   3
   That drag the tragic melancholy night,
   Who, with their drowsy, slow, and flagging wings
   Clip dead men's graves, and from their misty jaws   6
   Breathe foul contagious darkness in the air.
   Therefore bring forth the soldiers of our prize;   8
   For, whilst our pinnace anchors in the Downs,   9
   Here shall they make their ransom on the sand,
   Or with their blood stain this discolored shore.   11
   Master, this prisoner freely give I thee;   12
   And thou that art his mate, make boot of this;   13
   The other, Walter Whitmore, is thy share.   14
      [Three gentlemen prisoners, one of them Suffolk,
              are apportioned and handed over.]
FIRST GENTLEMAN
   What is my ransom, Master? Let me know.
MASTER
   A thousand crowns, or else lay down your head.
MATE *[To the Second Gentleman]*
   And so much shall you give, or off goes yours.
LIEUTENANT
   What, think you much to pay two thousand crowns,

4.1. Location: The coast of Kent.
1 s.p. Lieutenant i.e., captain in charge of the fighting; see ll. 65 and
107. (He is called "Captain of the ship" in the quarto stage direction,
but the Master is the mariner in charge of sailing the vessel.)
1 blabbing telltale, revealing.   **remorseful** causing remorse   **3 the jades**
i.e., the dragons of Hecate that draw the chariot of the night   **6 Clip**
embrace   **8 soldiers . . . prize** i.e., those we have captured   **9 pinnace**
one-masted vessel.   **Downs** anchorage off the Kentish coast
11 discolored i.e., to be discolored by blood   **12 this prisoner** i.e., the
First Gentleman   **13 his** i.e., the ship master's.   **make . . . this** i.e.,
make a profit by ransoming this Second Gentleman   **14 The other** i.e.,
Suffolk

And bear the name and port of gentlemen?   19
Cut both the villains' throats, for die you shall.
The lives of those which we have lost in fight   21
Be counterpoised with such a petty sum?   22
FIRST GENTLEMAN
I'll give it, sir, and therefore spare my life.
SECOND GENTLEMAN
And so will I, and write home for it straight.
WHITMORE [*To Suffolk*]
I lost mine eye in laying the prize aboard,   25
And therefore to revenge it shalt thou die;
And so should these, if I might have my will.
LIEUTENANT
Be not so rash. Take ransom, let him live.   28
SUFFOLK
Look on my George; I am a gentleman.   29
Rate me at what thou wilt, thou shalt be paid.   30
WHITMORE
And so am I. My name is Walter Whitmore.   31
                              [*Suffolk starts.*]
How now, why starts thou? What, doth death affright?
SUFFOLK
Thy name affrights me, in whose sound is death.   33
A cunning man did calculate my birth   34
And told me that by water I should die.
Yet let not this make thee be bloody-minded;
Thy name is Gualtier, being rightly sounded.

19 port demeanor   **21–22 The lives . . . sum** (An indignant question,
and one that should perhaps be spoken by Whitmore rather than the
Lieutenant; see ll. 25–28.)   **25 laying . . . aboard** boarding the captured
ship   **28 Be . . . live** (The Lieutenant's caution about killing the prisoners
seems to contradict his threatening speech at ll. 20–22. Perhaps those
lines should be assigned to Whitmore, but it's also possible that the
Lieutenant is simply being pragmatic in l. 28, advising against killing
the goose with the golden egg.)   **29 George** the gold or jeweled figure of
Saint George, worn as the insignium of the Order of the Knights of the
Garter   **30 Rate** value, assess   **31 am I** i.e., am I a gentleman. (Whitmore
denies Suffolk's assertion of distinction in rank.)   **33 Thy name** (i.e.,
Walter, pronounced like "water." In l. 37 below, Suffolk tries to avert the
prophecy referred to in ll. 34–35 [cf. 1.4.33–34] by urging the French
form of the name, *Gualtier* or *Gaultier*.)   **34 A . . . birth** a fortune-teller
cast my horoscope

WHITMORE

  Gualtier or Walter, which it is, I care not.
Never yet did base dishonor blur our name
But with our sword we wiped away the blot.
Therefore, when merchantlike I sell revenge,   41
Broke be my sword, my arms torn and defaced,   42
And I proclaimed a coward through the world!

SUFFOLK [*Revealing his face*]

  Stay, Whitmore, for thy prisoner is a prince,
The Duke of Suffolk, William de la Pole.

WHITMORE

The Duke of Suffolk muffled up in rags?

SUFFOLK

Ay, but these rags are no part of the Duke.
Jove sometime went disguised, and why not I?

LIEUTENANT

But Jove was never slain, as thou shalt be.

SUFFOLK

  Obscure and lousy swain, King Henry's blood,   50
The honorable blood of Lancaster,
Must not be shed by such a jaded groom.   52
Hast thou not kissed thy hand and held my stirrup?
Bareheaded plodded by my footcloth mule   54
And thought thee happy when I shook my head?   55
How often hast thou waited at my cup,
Fed from my trencher, kneeled down at the board, 57
When I have feasted with Queen Margaret?
Remember it and let it make thee crestfall'n,   59
Ay, and allay this thy abortive pride,   60
How in our voiding lobby hast thou stood   61
And duly waited for my coming forth.   62

---

41 sell revenge i.e., give up revenge (for my lost eye) in return for ransom money **42 arms** coat of arms **50 lousy** louse-infested. **King
Henry's blood** (Suffolk's claim to be connected to the house of Lancaster is a dubious one.) **52 jaded** ignoble (with a play in the next line on
one who deals with *jades*, or horses) **54 footcloth** with a large, richly
ornamented cloth laid over the back of a horse or mule, hanging down
to the ground on each side **55 happy** fortunate. **shook** i.e., nodded
57 trencher wooden dish or plate. **board** dining table **59 it** all this.
crestfall'n (1) downcast, abashed (2) deprived of the coat of arms
boasted of in l. 42 **60 abortive** monstrous **61 our voiding lobby** my
anteroom **62 duly** dutifully

This hand of mine hath writ in thy behalf,   63
And therefore shall it charm thy riotous tongue.   64

WHITMORE
Speak, Captain, shall I stab the forlorn swain?   65

LIEUTENANT
First let my words stab him, as he hath me.

SUFFOLK
Base slave, thy words are blunt and so art thou.   67

LIEUTENANT
Convey him hence, and on our longboat's side
Strike off his head.

SUFFOLK   Thou dar'st not, for thy own.   69

LIEUTENANT
Yes, Pole.

SUFFOLK   Pole?

LIEUTENANT   Pool! Sir Pool! Lord!   70
Ay, kennel, puddle, sink, whose filth and dirt   71
Troubles the silver spring where England drinks.
Now will I dam up this thy yawning mouth
For swallowing the treasure of the realm.   74
Thy lips that kissed the Queen shall sweep the ground,
And thou that smiledst at good Duke Humphrey's death
Against the senseless winds shalt grin in vain,   77
Who in contempt shall hiss at thee again.   78
And wedded be thou to the hags of hell   79
For daring to affy a mighty lord   80
Unto the daughter of a worthless king,
Having neither subject, wealth, nor diadem.   82
By devilish policy art thou grown great,   83
And, like ambitious Sylla, overgorged   84

63 writ . . . behalf i.e., written to recommend you, or because you
cannot write   **64 charm** put a spell on, silence   **65 Captain** (Appropriate courtesy title for the Lieutenant, since he is the military commander.)   **forlorn swain** desolate, wretched fellow   **67 blunt** blunted like an
arrow with no point, harmless   **69 for thy own** i.e., for fear of losing
your own head   **70 Pole, Pool** (with verbal play on *poll*, head, *Pole*,
Suffolk's family name, and *pool*, a pool of water, all similar in pronunciation)   **71 kennel** gutter.   **sink** cesspool   **74 For swallowing** lest it
swallow   **77 senseless** insensible. (Suffolk's head is to be put up on
display.)   **78 Who** which, i.e., the winds.   **again** in return   **79 the hags
of hell** i.e., the Furies   **80 affy** betroth.   **lord** i.e., King Henry
82 Having i.e., he, Reignier, having   **83 policy** political cunning
84 ambitious Sylla i.e., Sulla, Roman dictator of the second century
B.C., notorious for his cruel proceedings against his adversaries

With gobbets of thy mother's bleeding heart.   85
By thee Anjou and Maine were sold to France.
The false revolting Normans thorough thee   87
Disdain to call us lord, and Picardy
Hath slain their governors, surprised our forts,
And sent the ragged soldiers wounded home.
The princely Warwick, and the Nevilles all,
Whose dreadful swords were never drawn in vain,
As hating thee, are rising up in arms;
And now the house of York, thrust from the crown
By shameful murder of a guiltless king   95
And lofty, proud, encroaching tyranny,
Burns with revenging fire, whose hopeful colors
Advance our half-faced sun, striving to shine,   98
Under the which is writ *"Invitis nubibus."*   99
The commons here in Kent are up in arms,
And, to conclude, reproach and beggary
Is crept into the palace of our King,
And all by thee.—Away! Convey him hence.

SUFFOLK
O, that I were a god, to shoot forth thunder
Upon these paltry, servile, abject drudges!
Small things make base men proud. This villain here,
Being captain of a pinnace, threatens more
Than Bargulus, the strong Illyrian pirate.   108
Drones suck not eagles' blood, but rob beehives.   109
It is impossible that I should die
By such a lowly vassal as thyself.
Thy words move rage and not remorse in me.
I go of message from the Queen to France;   113
I charge thee waft me safely cross the Channel.   114

85 gobbets pieces of raw flesh.   **mother's** i.e., England's   **87 thorough**
through, because of   **95 shameful . . . king** i.e., the murder of Richard
II by Bolingbroke, who thereupon sidestepped the Yorkist claim and
became King Henry IV   **98 Advance** raise, display.   **half-faced sun** (Edward III's and Richard II's banner displayed the rays of the sun dispers-
ing themselves out of a cloud.)   **99 Invitis nubibus** in spite of the
clouds   **108 Bargulus** (A pirate, Bardulis, mentioned in Cicero's *De
Officiis*, 2.11.)   **109 Drones** beetles, worthless parasites. (The legends
referred to here, that beetles suck the blood of eagles and rob beehives
of honey, are typical of much imaginary natural history in the
Renaissance.)   **113 of message** as messenger   **114 waft** transport,
convey

LIEUTENANT   Walter—
WHITMORE
  Come, Suffolk, I must waft thee to thy death.
SUFFOLK
  Paene gelidus timor occupat artus.   117
  It is thee I fear.
WHITMORE
  Thou shalt have cause to fear before I leave thee.
  What, are ye daunted now? Now will ye stoop.
FIRST GENTLEMAN [*To Suffolk*]
  My gracious lord, entreat him, speak him fair.   121
SUFFOLK
  Suffolk's imperial tongue is stern and rough,
  Used to command, untaught to plead for favor.
  Far be it we should honor such as these
  With humble suit. No, rather let my head
  Stoop to the block than these knees bow to any
  Save to the God of heaven and to my king;
  And sooner dance upon a bloody pole   128
  Than stand uncovered to the vulgar groom.   129
  True nobility is exempt from fear.
  More can I bear than you dare execute.
LIEUTENANT
  Hale him away, and let him talk no more.   132
SUFFOLK
  Come, soldiers, show what cruelty ye can,
  That this my death may never be forgot!
  Great men oft die by vile bezonians: 135
  A Roman sworder and banditto slave   136
  Murdered sweet Tully; Brutus' bastard hand   137
  Stabbed Julius Caesar; savage islanders   138
  Pompey the Great; and Suffolk dies by pirates.

---

117 Paene . . . artus cold fear takes hold of my limbs almost entirely
121 fair courteously   **128 And . . . pole** i.e., and rather have my head
stuck on a bloodstained pole on London Bridge for treason
129 uncovered bareheaded   **132 Hale** haul   **135 bezonians** needy
beggars, rascals   **136 sworder** gladiator. **banditto** bandit   **137 Tully**
Cicero. **bastard** (According to an unreliable tradition, Brutus was
thought to be Caesar's bastard son.)   **138 savage islanders** i.e., inhabitants of Lesbos. (But Plutarch reports, quite to the contrary, that Pompey
the Great was stabbed by his former officers at the instigation of Ptol-
emy, in Egypt after his defeat by Caesar at Pharsalus.)

Exit Walter [Whitmore and others] with Suffolk.

LIEUTENANT
And as for these whose ransom we have set,
It is our pleasure one of them depart;
Therefore [*To the Second Gentleman*] come you with us
    and let him go.   142

> *Exeunt Lieutenant and the rest.*
> *Manet the First Gentleman.*

> *Enter Walter [Whitmore] with the body*
> *[and severed head of Suffolk].*

WHITMORE
There let his head and lifeless body lie,
Until the Queen his mistress bury it.   *Exit Walter.*

FIRST GENTLEMAN
O barbarous and bloody spectacle!
His body will I bear unto the King.
If he revenge it not, yet will his friends;   147
So will the Queen, that living held him dear.   148

> [*Exit with the body and head.*]

❖

4.2   *Enter [George] Bevis and John Holland, [with*
            long staves].

BEVIS   Come, and get thee a sword, though made of a
    lath. They have been up these two days.   2
HOLLAND   They have the more need to sleep now, then.   3
BEVIS   I tell thee, Jack Cade the clothier means to dress 4
    the commonwealth, and turn it, and set a new nap   5
    upon it.

---

142 him i.e., the First Gentleman   **s.d. Manet** he remains onstage
147 his i.e., Suffolk's   **148 living** while he was living

4.2. Location: Blackheath, a heath in Kent near London.
s.d. John Holland (The name of the actor assigned to a bit part in this
scene; probably *George Bevis* is similarly a hired man in the company.)   **2 lath** wood strip (often used by the comic Vice character in
morality plays).   **up** i.e., up in arms   **3 They . . . then** (Holland's joke is
that if they've been *up*, awake, for two days, they must be sleepy.)
4 dress (1) clothe, array (2) remedy   **5 turn** (1) turn inside out (as a way
of refurbishing old cloth) (2) turn upside down socially.   **nap** (1) fuzz
or down on the surface of cloth (2) surface of the social structure

HOLLAND So he had need, for 'tis threadbare. Well, I ⁷
say it was never merry world in England since gentlemen came up.   9

BEVIS O miserable age! Virtue is not regarded in handi- ¹⁰
craftsmen.

HOLLAND The nobility think scorn to go in leather ¹²
aprons.

BEVIS Nay, more, the King's Council are no good work- ¹⁴
men.   15

HOLLAND True. And yet it is said, "Labor in thy vocation,"
which is as much to say as, "Let the magistrates be laboring men." And therefore should we be magistrates.

BEVIS Thou hast hit it, for there's no better sign of a ¹⁹
brave mind than a hard hand.   20

HOLLAND I see them, I see them! There's Best's son, the
tanner of Wingham—   22

BEVIS He shall have the skins of our enemies to make
dog's leather of.   24

HOLLAND And Dick the butcher—

BEVIS Then is sin struck down like an ox, and iniquity's
throat cut like a calf.

HOLLAND And Smith the weaver—

BEVIS Argo, their thread of life is spun.   29

HOLLAND Come, come, let's fall in with them.   30

> *Drum. Enter Cade, Dick [the] butcher, Smith the*
> *weaver, and a Sawyer, with infinite numbers,*
> *[bearing long staves].*

CADE We, John Cade, so termed of our supposed ³¹
father—

DICK [*Aside*] Or rather, of stealing a cade of herrings.   33

CADE For our enemies shall fall before us, inspired with ³⁴

---

7 threadbare (1) shabby (2) down-at-heels **9 came up** came into fashion,
rose to prominence **10 regarded** esteemed **12 think scorn** disdain
14–15 workmen (1) laborers (2) masters of their calling **19 hit it** hit
the nail on the head **20 brave** noble. **hard** callused **22 Wingham** a
village near Canterbury **24 dog's leather** (Used in the manufacture of
gloves.) **29 Argo** i.e., ergo, therefore **30 s.d. infinite numbers** i.e., as
many supers as the theater can provide **31 We** (The royal "we," fatu-
ously misappropriated.) **so termed of** named after **33 of** on account
of. **cade** barrel, cask **34 For** because. **fall** (with a pun on the Latin
cado, I fall)

the spirit of putting down kings and princes—command silence.

DICK Silence!

CADE My father was a Mortimer—   38

DICK [*Aside*] He was an honest man and a good brick-   39
layer.   40

CADE My mother a Plantagenet—

DICK [*Aside*] I knew her well. She was a midwife.

CADE My wife descended of the Lacys—   43

DICK [*Aside*] She was, indeed, a peddler's daughter, and
sold many laces.

SMITH [*Aside*] But now of late, not able to travel with   46
her furred pack, she washes bucks here at home.   47

CADE Therefore am I of an honorable house.

DICK [*Aside*] Ay, by my faith, the field is honorable;   49
and there was he born, under a hedge, for his father
had never a house but the cage.   51

CADE Valiant I am.

SMITH [*Aside*] 'A must needs, for beggary is valiant.   53

CADE I am able to endure much.

DICK [*Aside*] No question of that; for I have seen him
whipped three market days together.   56

CADE I fear neither sword nor fire.

SMITH [*Aside*] He need not fear the sword, for his coat
is of proof.   59

DICK [*Aside*] But methinks he should stand in fear of
fire, being burnt i' the hand for stealing of sheep.   61

CADE Be brave, then, for your captain is brave, and
vows reformation. There shall be in England seven

---

38 Mortimer (See 3.1.359 and note.)   **39–40 bricklayer** (with a play on
mortarer, Mortimer)   **43 Lacys** the family name of the Earls of Lincoln.
(But Dick makes an obvious pun on *laces*.)   **46 travel** (suggesting also
travail, work)   **47 furred pack** peddler's pack made of hides turned hair
outward (with a pun on "herd of deer").   **bucks** soiled clothes treated
with *buck* or lye. (There is a bawdy suggestion of a loose woman, a
vagabond's daughter, who has given up streetwalking with her *furred
pack*, her genital organs, to service men [*bucks*] at home.)   **49 field**
(1) field in a coat of arms (2) out in the fields   **51 cage** prison for petty
malefactors   **53 'A must needs** he must be.   **valiant** sturdy, able to
work. (Ordnances forbade those who were sturdy to beg.)   **56 whipped**
i.e., for vagabondage   **59 of proof** (1) impenetrable, tried by experience
and hence reliable (2) well-worn   **61 burnt i' the hand** branded

halfpenny loaves sold for a penny, the three-hooped 64
pot shall have ten hoops, and I will make it felony to 65
drink small beer. All the realm shall be in common, 66
and in Cheapside shall my palfry go to grass. And 67
when I am king, as king I will be—

ALL   God save Your Majesty!

CADE   I thank you, good people—there shall be no
money; all shall eat and drink on my score; and I will 71
apparel them all in one livery, that they may agree like
brothers and worship me their lord.

DICK   The first thing we do, let's kill all the lawyers.

CADE   Nay, that I mean to do. Is not this a lamentable
thing, that of the skin of an innocent lamb should be
made parchment? That parchment, being scribbled
o'er, should undo a man? Some say the bee stings, but
I say 'tis the bee's wax; for I did but seal once to a 79
thing, and I was never mine own man since. How
now? Who's there?

> *Enter [some, bringing forward] a Clerk [of*
> *Chartham].*

SMITH   The clerk of Chartham. He can write and read 82
and cast account. 83

CADE   O, monstrous!

SMITH   We took him setting of boys' copies. 85

CADE   Here's a villain!

SMITH   H'as a book in his pocket with red letters in 't. 87

CADE   Nay, then, he is a conjurer.

DICK   Nay, he can make obligations and write court 89
hand. 90

64–65 three-hooped pot wooden quart-pot made with three metal bands
or staves. (A ten-hooped pot would presumably hold a lot more.)
66 small weak. (Cade intends that everyone shall drink strong beer.) **be
in common** belong to everyone, be free from enclosure. (See 1.3.23–24
and note.)   **67 Cheapside** chief location for markets in London (which
Cade wishes to abolish)   **71 on my score** at my expense   **79 seal** i.e.,
sign and seal (with sealing wax) a legal agreement   **82 Chartham** a
town near Canterbury   **83 cast account** i.e., do arithmetic
85 setting . . . copies writing out words, etc., as models to be repro-
duced by schoolboys   **87 H'as** he has.   **book . . . in 't** a schoolbook,
probably a primer, with "rubricated" or red-lettered capitals   **89 make
obligations** draw up bonds   **89–90 court hand** professional hand, used
in preparing legal documents

CADE I am sorry for 't. The man is a proper man, of ⟨91⟩
mine honor; unless I find him guilty, he shall not die.
Come hither, sirrah, I must examine thee. What is thy
name?

CLERK Emmanuel.   ⟨95⟩

DICK They use to write it on the top of letters. 'Twill go
hard with you.

CADE Let me alone.—Dost thou use to write thy name?
Or hast thou a mark to thyself, like an honest, plain-
dealing man?

CLERK Sir, I thank God, I have been so well brought up
that I can write my name.

ALL He hath confessed. Away with him! He's a villain
and a traitor.

CADE Away with him, I say! Hang him with his pen
and inkhorn about his neck. *Exit one with the Clerk.*

     Enter Michael.

MICHAEL Where's our general?

CADE Here I am, thou particular fellow.   ⟨108⟩

MICHAEL Fly, fly, fly! Sir Humphrey Stafford and his
brother are hard by, with the King's forces.

CADE Stand, villain, stand, or I'll fell thee down. He
shall be encountered with a man as good as himself.
He is but a knight, is 'a?

MICHAEL No.   ⟨114⟩

CADE To equal him, I will make myself a knight pres- ⟨115⟩
ently. [*He kneels.*] Rise up Sir John Mortimer. [*He rises.*] ⟨116⟩
Now have at him!   ⟨117⟩

     Enter Sir Humphrey Stafford and his Brother,
     with drum and soldiers.

STAFFORD
Rebellious hinds, the filth and scum of Kent,   ⟨118⟩
Marked for the gallows, lay your weapons down!

---

91 proper handsome-looking. **of** upon **95 Emmanuel** i.e., God with us.
(Used frequently as heading for letters and documents.) **108 particular**
private (as opposed to *general* in the previous line) **114 No** i.e., he is
only a knight **115–116 presently** immediately **117 have at him** let me
at him **s.d. drum** drummer **118 hinds** peasants

Home to your cottages; forsake this groom.   120
The King is merciful, if you revolt.   121
BROTHER
But angry, wrathful, and inclined to blood
If you go forward. Therefore yield, or die.
CADE
As for these silken-coated slaves, I pass not.   124
It is to you, good people, that I speak,
Over whom, in time to come, I hope to reign;
For I am rightful heir unto the crown.
STAFFORD
Villain, thy father was a plasterer,
And thou thyself a shearman, art thou not?   129
CADE   And Adam was a gardener.
BROTHER   And what of that?
CADE
Marry, this: Edmund Mortimer, Earl of March,
Married the Duke of Clarence' daughter, did he not?
STAFFORD   Ay, sir.
CADE
By her he had two children at one birth.
BROTHER   That's false.
CADE
Ay, there's the question. But I say 'tis true.
The elder of them, being put to nurse,
Was by a beggar-woman stolen away,
And, ignorant of his birth and parentage,
Became a bricklayer when he came to age.
His son am I. Deny it if you can.
DICK
Nay, 'tis too true. Therefore he shall be king.   142
SMITH   Sir, he made a chimney in my father's house,   143
and the bricks are alive at this day to testify it. There-
fore deny it not.
STAFFORD
And will you credit this base drudge's words,
That speaks he knows not what?

---

120 groom i.e., low wretch   **121 revolt** turn back   **124 pass** care
129 shearman one who shears the excess nap (see l. 5) from woolen
cloth during its manufacture   **142 too** very   **143 he** i.e., Cade's father

ALL
Ay, marry, will we. Therefore get ye gone.

BROTHER
Jack Cade, the Duke of York hath taught you this.

CADE [*Aside*] He lies, for I invented it myself.—Go to,
sirrah, tell the King from me that for his father's sake,
Henry the Fifth, in whose time boys went to span- 152
counter for French crowns, I am content he shall reign; 153
but I'll be Protector over him.

DICK   And furthermore, we'll have the Lord Saye's head 155
for selling the dukedom of Maine.

CADE   And good reason; for thereby is England mained 157
and fain to go with a staff, but that my puissance holds 158
it up. Fellow kings, I tell you that that Lord Saye hath
gelded the commonwealth and made it an eunuch;
and more than that, he can speak French, and therefore he is a traitor.

STAFFORD
O gross and miserable ignorance!

CADE   Nay, answer, if you can. The Frenchmen are our
enemies. Go to, then, I ask but this: can he that speaks
with the tongue of an enemy be a good counselor,
or no?

ALL   No, no! And therefore we'll have his head.

BROTHER [*To Stafford*]
Well, seeing gentle words will not prevail,
Assail them with the army of the King.

STAFFORD
Herald, away, and throughout every town
Proclaim them traitors that are up with Cade,
That those which fly before the battle ends   173
May, even in their wives' and children's sight,
Be hanged up for example at their doors.
And you that be the King's friends, follow me.
           Exeunt [the two Staffords, and soldiers].

152–153 span-counter a boys' game in which one throws a counter or
piece of money that the other wins if he can throw another that hits it
or falls within a span (nine inches) of it   **153 crowns** (1) coins (2) kingdoms   **155 Lord Saye** (A peer implicated with Suffolk in the loss of
Anjou and Maine.)   **157 mained** maimed (with a pun on *Maine*)
158 fain obliged.   **go** walk   **173 That . . . fly** i.e., so that those cowardly
traitors who will surely flee

CADE
  And you that love the commons, follow me.
  Now show yourselves men; 'tis for liberty!
  We will not leave one lord, one gentleman;
  Spare none but such as go in clouted shoon,   180
  For they are thrifty honest men and such
  As would, but that they dare not, take our parts.
DICK   They are all in order and march toward us.
CADE   But then are we in order when we are most out
  of order. Come, march forward.   [*Exeunt.*]

4.3   *Alarums to the fight, wherein both the*
        Staffords are slain. Enter Cade and the rest.

CADE   Where's Dick, the butcher of Ashford?
DICK   Here, sir.
CADE   They fell before thee like sheep and oxen, and
  thou behavedst thyself as if thou hadst been in thine
  own slaughterhouse. Therefore thus will I reward
  thee: the Lent shall be as long again as it is, and thou 6
  shalt have a license to kill for a hundred lacking one.   7
DICK   I desire no more.
CADE   And, to speak truth, thou deserv'st no less. This
  monument of the victory will I bear [*Putting on Sir* 10
  Humphrey's armor]; and the bodies shall be dragged at
  my horse heels till I do come to London, where we
  will have the Mayor's sword borne before us.
DICK   If we mean to thrive and do good, break open the 14
  jails and let out the prisoners.
CADE   Fear not that, I warrant thee. Come, let's march 16
  towards London.   *Exeunt* [*with the Staffords' bodies*].

❖

180 clouted shoon hobnailed or patched shoes
4.3. Location: Scene continues at Blackheath.
s.d. (The bodies of the slain Staffords must be removed at some
point.) **6–7 Lent . . . one** (For Dick the butcher's benefit, Cade proposes to double the length of Lent, during which animals could be
butchered only by special license in order to supply the sick and others
with particular needs; and during this period, Dick is to have license to
kill 99 animals a week, or to supply 99 persons, or for 99 years
10 monument memorial   **14 do good** succeed   **16 Fear** doubt

4.4   *Enter the King with a supplication, and
the Queen with Suffolk's head, the Duke
of Buckingham, and the Lord Saye.*

QUEEN [*To herself*]
Oft have I heard that grief softens the mind
And makes it fearful and degenerate.
Think therefore on revenge and cease to weep.
But who can cease to weep and look on this?
Here may his head lie on my throbbing breast,
But where's the body that I should embrace?

BUCKINGHAM   What answer makes Your Grace to the
rebels' supplication?

KING
I'll send some holy bishop to entreat,
For God forbid so many simple souls
Should perish by the sword! And I myself,
Rather than bloody war shall cut them short,
Will parley with Jack Cade their general.
But stay, I'll read it over once again.

QUEEN [*To herself*]
Ah, barbarous villains! Hath this lovely face
Ruled, like a wandering planet, over me,   16
And could it not enforce them to relent
That were unworthy to behold the same?

KING
Lord Saye, Jack Cade hath sworn to have thy head.

SAYE
Ay, but I hope Your Highness shall have his.

KING   How now, madam?
Still lamenting and mourning for Suffolk's death?
I fear me, love, if that I had been dead,
Thou wouldst not have mourned so much for me.

QUEEN
No, my love, I should not mourn, but die for thee.

     Enter a Messenger.

KING
How now, what news? Why com'st thou in such haste?

4.4. **Location: London. The royal court.**
16 wandering i.e., not fixed, like the stars

FIRST MESSENGER

The rebels are in Southwark. Fly, my lord!   27
Jack Cade proclaims himself Lord Mortimer,
Descended from the Duke of Clarence' house,
And calls Your Grace usurper, openly,
And vows to crown himself in Westminster.
His army is a ragged multitude
Of hinds and peasants, rude and merciless.
Sir Humphrey Stafford and his brother's death
Hath given them heart and courage to proceed.
All scholars, lawyers, courtiers, gentlemen,
They call false caterpillars and intend their death.

KING

O graceless men! They know not what they do.

BUCKINGHAM

My gracious lord, retire to Killingworth   39
Until a power be raised to put them down.   40

QUEEN

Ah, were the Duke of Suffolk now alive,
These Kentish rebels would be soon appeased!   42

KING

Lord Saye, the traitors hateth thee;
Therefore away with us to Killingworth.

SAYE

So might Your Grace's person be in danger.
The sight of me is odious in their eyes;
And therefore in this city will I stay
And live alone as secret as I may.

Enter another Messenger.

SECOND MESSENGER

Jack Cade hath gotten London Bridge!
The citizens fly and forsake their houses.
The rascal people, thirsting after prey,
Join with the traitor, and they jointly swear
To spoil the city and your royal court.   53

BUCKINGHAM

Then linger not, my lord. Away, take horse!

27 Southwark suburb on the south bank of the Thames, just across the
river from London   **39 Killingworth** Kenilworth (in Warwickshire)
40 power army   **42 appeased** pacified   **53 spoil** despoil, sack

KING
  Come, Margaret. God, our hope, will succor us.
QUEEN
  My hope is gone, now Suffolk is deceased.
KING [*To Saye*]
  Farewell, my lord. Trust not the Kentish rebels.
BUCKINGHAM
  Trust nobody, for fear you be betrayed.
SAYE
  The trust I have is in mine innocence,
  And therefore am I bold and resolute.   *Exeunt.*

❖

4.5 *Enter Lord Scales upon the Tower, walking.*
      Then enter two or three Citizens below.

SCALES How now, is Jack Cade slain?
FIRST CITIZEN No, my lord, nor likely to be slain; for
  they have won the bridge, killing all those that with-
  stand them. The Lord Mayor craves aid of your honor
  from the Tower to defend the city from the rebels.
SCALES
  Such aid as I can spare you shall command.
  But I am troubled here with them myself;
  The rebels have assayed to win the Tower.
  But get you to Smithfield and gather head,   9
  And thither I will send you Matthew Gough.
  Fight for your king, your country, and your lives.
  And so, farewell, for I must hence again.   *Exeunt.*

❖

4.5. Location: The Tower of London.
s.d. upon the Tower i.e., probably in the rear gallery above the main
stage 9 Smithfield area of open fields to the northwest, just outside
London's walls. head an armed force

4.6 *Enter Jack Cade and the rest, and strikes his staff on London Stone.*

CADE Now is Mortimer lord of this city. And here, sitting upon London Stone, I charge and command that, of the city's cost, the Pissing Conduit run nothing but 3 claret wine this first year of our reign. And now henceforward it shall be treason for any that calls me other than Lord Mortimer.

    Enter a Soldier, running.

SOLDIER Jack Cade! Jack Cade!
CADE Knock him down there.   *They kill him.*
SMITH If this fellow be wise, he'll never call ye Jack Cade more. I think he hath a very fair warning.
DICK My lord, there's an army gathered together in Smithfield.
CADE Zounds, then, let's go fight with them. But first go and set London Bridge on fire, and, if you can, burn down the Tower too. Come, let's away. *Exeunt omnes.*

4.7 *Alarums. Matthew Gough is slain, and all the rest. Then enter Jack Cade, with his company.*

CADE So, sirs. Now go some and pull down the Savoy; 1 others to th' Inns of Court. Down with them all.   2
DICK I have a suit unto your lordship.

4.6. Location: London.
s.d. London Stone ancient landmark, located in Cannon Street **3 of at. Pissing Conduit** popular name of a conduit, or common fountain, near the Royal Exchange

4.7. Location: London. The rebellion continues. (The historical location moves from Cannon Street to Smithfield, but onstage the action is continuous.)
s.d. all the rest i.e., the King's forces. (The bodies of Gough and other slain must be removed at some point.) **1 the Savoy** (This palace, residence of the Duke of Lancaster, was actually destroyed during Wat Tyler's rebellion in 1381 and not rebuilt until the sixteenth century.)
2 Inns of Court sets of buildings in London belonging to legal societies training persons in the law

CADE Be it a lordship, thou shalt have it for that word. 4
DICK Only that the laws of England may come out of
your mouth.
HOLLAND [*Aside*] Mass, 'twill be sore law then, for he
was thrust in the mouth with a spear, and 'tis not
whole yet.
SMITH [*Aside*] Nay, John, it will be stinking law, for his
breath stinks with eating toasted cheese.
CADE I have thought upon it. It shall be so. Away! Burn
all the records of the realm. My mouth shall be the
Parliament of England.
HOLLAND [*Aside*] Then we are like to have biting stat-
utes, unless his teeth be pulled out.
CADE And henceforward all things shall be in common.

Enter a Messenger.

MESSENGER My lord, a prize, a prize! Here's the Lord
Saye, which sold the towns in France; he that made us
pay one-and-twenty fifteens, and one shilling to the 20
pound, the last subsidy. 21

Enter George [Bevis], with the Lord Saye.

CADE Well, he shall be beheaded for it ten times. Ah,
thou say, thou serge, nay, thou buckram lord! Now art 23
thou within point-blank of our jurisdiction regal. 24
What canst thou answer to My Majesty for giving up
of Normandy unto Monsieur Basimecu, the Dau- 26
phin of France? Be it known unto thee by these 27
presence, even the presence of Lord Mortimer, that I 28
am the besom that must sweep the court clean of such 29
filth as thou art. Thou hast most traitorously corrupted
the youth of the realm in erecting a grammar school;
and whereas, before, our forefathers had no other

---

4 lordship title and estates of a noble lord (playing on the honorific *your
lordship* in l. 3, by which Cade is flattered) **20–21 one . . . pound** (An
exaggeratedly inflated estimate of personal property.) **21 subsidy** tax
levied on special occasions; see 1.1.131–134.) **23 say, serge, buckram**
kinds of cloth, respectively of silk, wool, and coarse linen (with a pun on
say/Saye) **24 point-blank** so close that a missile will travel straight to
the target **26 Basimecu** *baise mon cul* (French), kiss my ass
27–28 these presence i.e., Cade's error, or joke, for "these presents, this
present document." (A legal phrase.) **29 besom** broom

books but the score and the tally, thou hast caused 33
printing to be used, and, contrary to the King his crown 34
and dignity, thou hast built a paper mill. It will be
proved to thy face that thou hast men about thee that
usually talk of a noun and a verb and such abomina- 37
ble words as no Christian ear can endure to hear. Thou
hast appointed justices of peace to call poor men before them about matters they were not able to answer.
Moreover, thou hast put them in prison, and because
they could not read thou hast hanged them, when in- 42
deed only for that cause they have been most worthy to 43
live. Thou dost ride in a footcloth, dost thou not?   44
SAYE   What of that?
CADE   Marry, thou oughtst not to let thy horse wear a
cloak, when honester men than thou go in their hose 47
and doublets. 48
DICK   And work in their shirt too—as myself, for exam-
ple, that am a butcher.
SAYE   You men of Kent—
DICK   What say you of Kent?
SAYE   Nothing but this: 'tis *bona terra, mala gens.* 53
CADE   Away with him, away with him! He speaks
Latin.
SAYE

Hear me but speak, and bear me where you will.
Kent, in the *Commentaries* Caesar writ,
Is termed the civil'st place of all this isle.
Sweet is the country, because full of riches,
The people liberal, valiant, active, wealthy, 60
Which makes me hope you are not void of pity.
I sold not Maine, I lost not Normandy,

---

33 score . . . tally means of reckoning accounts or keeping score, in
which a stick was notched and then split lengthwise, thereby giving
both debtor and creditor a record of what was owed   **34 printing** (An
anachronism; the first printing press was set up in England twenty-
seven years after Cade's rebellion, and the first paper mill in 1495.)
King his King's   **37 usually** habitually   **42 could not read** i.e., could
not demonstrate their literacy in Latin and thereby claim exemption
from civil prosecution through "benefit of clergy"   **43 only . . . cause**
for that reason alone   **44 footcloth** richly ornamented horse covering;
see 4.1.54 note   **47–48 hose and doublets** breeches and jacket (without
a cloak)   **53 bona . . . gens** good land, bad people   **60 liberal** generous,
free, refined

Yet to recover them would lose my life.
Justice with favor have I always done;   64
Prayers and tears have moved me, gifts could never.
When have I aught exacted at your hands   66
But to maintain the King, the realm, and you?
Large gifts have I bestowed on learnèd clerks,   68
Because my book preferred me to the King;   69
And, seeing ignorance is the curse of God,
Knowledge the wing wherewith we fly to heaven,
Unless you be possessed with devilish spirits
You cannot but forbear to murder me.
This tongue hath parleyed unto foreign kings   74
For your behoof—   75

CADE Tut, when struck'st thou one blow in the field?

SAYE
Great men have reaching hands. Oft have I struck   77
Those that I never saw, and struck them dead.

BEVIS O monstrous coward! What, to come behind folks?

SAYE
These cheeks are pale for watching for your good.   81

CADE Give him a box o' the ear and that will make 'em red again.

SAYE
Long sitting to determine poor men's causes   84
Hath made me full of sickness and diseases.

CADE Ye shall have a hempen caudle, then, and the help 86
of hatchet.   87

DICK Why dost thou quiver, man?

SAYE
The palsy, and not fear, provokes me.

CADE Nay, he nods at us, as who should say, "I'll be 90

---

64 favor compassion **66 aught . . . hands** taken any taxes from you (in
my capacity as Lord Treasurer) **68 clerks** scholars **69 book** learning. **preferred . . . King** gave me advancement at court **74 parleyed
unto** entered into negotiations with **75 behoof** benefit **77 reaching**
far-reaching **81 for watching** from remaining awake, on watch
84 sitting i.e., on the judge's bench. **determine** settle, decide
86 caudle warm gruel, given to sick people. (*Hempen caudle* means that
his restorative is to be a hanging.) **86–87 the help of hatchet** i.e., the
assistance of the executioner's ax. (Possibly a variant of or error for
"pap with a hatchet," the administering of punishment under the
ironical guise of kindly correction.) **90 as who should** as one might

even with you." I'll see if his head will stand steadier
on a pole, or no. Take him away and behead him.

SAYE
Tell me wherein have I offended most?
Have I affected wealth or honor? Speak.   94
Are my chests filled up with extorted gold?
Is my apparel sumptuous to behold?
Whom have I injured, that ye seek my death?
These hands are free from guiltless blood-shedding,   98
This breast from harboring foul deceitful thoughts.
O, let me live!

CADE [Aside]   I feel remorse in myself with his words,
but I'll bridle it. He shall die, an it be but for pleading 102
so well for his life.—Away with him! He has a familiar   103
under his tongue; he speaks not i' God's name. Go,
take him away, I say, and strike off his head presently;   105
and then break into his son-in-law's house, Sir James
Cromer, and strike off his head, and bring them both
upon two poles hither.

ALL   It shall be done.

SAYE
Ah, countrymen! If when you make your prayers,
God should be so obdurate as yourselves,
How would it fare with your departed souls?   112
And therefore yet relent, and save my life.

CADE
Away with him! And do as I command ye.
                        [Exeunt some with Lord Saye.]
The proudest peer in the realm shall not wear a head
on his shoulders, unless he pay me tribute. There shall
not a maid be married but she shall pay to me her
maidenhead ere they have it. Men shall hold of me *in*   118
capite; and we charge and command that their wives   119
be as free as heart can wish or tongue can tell.   120

---

94 affected preferred, striven for   **98 guiltless blood-shedding** shedding
of guiltless blood   **102 an it be but** if only   **103 familiar** familiar spirit,
attendant demon   **105 presently** immediately   **112 your departed souls**
your souls when you die   **118 maidenhead** (Cade claims the *droit de
seigneur,* presumed customary right of a feudal lord to be the first to
enjoy a bride sexually on her marriage night.)   **118–119 in capite** as
tenant in chief, i.e., directly from the crown. The Latin *caput,* head, also
puns on *maidenhead.*)   **120 free** (1) legally unencumbered (2) licentious

DICK   My lord, when shall we go to Cheapside and take 121
   up commodities upon our bills?   122
CADE   Marry, presently.
ALL   O, brave!   124

   *Enter one with the heads [of Lord Saye and Sir
   John Cromer upon two poles].*

CADE   But is not this braver? Let them kiss one another,
   for they loved well when they were alive. [*The heads
   are made to touch one another.*] Now part them again,
   lest they consult about the giving up of some more
   towns in France. Soldiers, defer the spoil of the city 129
   until night, for with these borne before us, instead of
   maces, will we ride through the streets, and at every   131
   corner have them kiss. Away!   *Exeunt.*

4.8   *Alarum and retreat. Enter again Cade and all
   his rabblement.*

CADE   Up Fish Street! Down Saint Magnus' Corner! Kill 1
   and knock down! Throw them into Thames! (*Sound a
   parley.*) What noise is this I hear? Dare any be so bold 3
   to sound retreat or parley when I command them kill?

   Enter Buckingham and old Clifford [attended].

BUCKINGHAM
   Ay, here they be that dare and will disturb thee.
   Know, Cade, we come ambassadors from the King

121–122 take . . . bills obtain goods on credit (with a pun on *bills*,
military weapons having wooden handles and a blade or ax-shaped
head)   **124 brave** fine, splendid   **129 spoil** plundering   **131 maces**
staves of office carried by sergeants

**4.8. Location: Southwark. The rebellion continues. (The historical
location moves from Smithfield to Southwark, but the onstage action
is uninterrupted.)**
s.d. retreat signal to cease attack   **1 Fish Street, Saint Magnus' Corner**
locations in London near London Bridge, directly across from Southwark   **3 s.d. parley** trumpet signal requesting a conference between the
contending forces (also in l. 4)

Unto the commons whom thou hast misled,
And here pronounce free pardon to them all   8
That will forsake thee and go home in peace.
CLIFFORD
What say ye, countrymen? Will ye relent,
And yield to mercy whilst 'tis offered you,
Or let a rebel lead you to your deaths?
Who loves the King and will embrace his pardon,   13
Fling up his cap and say "God save His Majesty!"
Who hateth him and honors not his father,
Henry the Fifth, that made all France to quake,
Shake he his weapon at us and pass by.   17
ALL   God save the King! God save the King!
                     [*They fling up their caps.*]
CADE   What, Buckingham and Clifford, are ye so brave?   19
And you, base peasants, do ye believe him? Will you
needs be hanged with your pardons about your necks?   21
Hath my sword therefore broke through London
gates, that you should leave me at the White Hart in   23
Southwark? I thought ye would never have given out   24
these arms till you had recovered your ancient free-
dom. But you are all recreants and dastards, and de-   26
light to live in slavery to the nobility. Let them break
your backs with burdens, take your houses over your
heads, ravish your wives and daughters before your
faces. For me, I will make shift for one, and so God's   30
curse light upon you all!
ALL   We'll follow Cade, we'll follow Cade!
CLIFFORD
Is Cade the son of Henry the Fifth,
That thus you do exclaim you'll go with him?
Will he conduct you through the heart of France
And make the meanest of you earls and dukes?   36
Alas, he hath no home, no place to fly to,
Nor knows he how to live but by the spoil,   38

8 **pronounce** proclaim   13 **Who** anyone who (also in l. 15)   17 **Shake he**
let him shake (in a gesture of defiance)   19 **brave** haughty
21 **pardons . . . necks** (because the pardons would be not only worthless
but also the very means of their hanging)   23 **that** to the end that.
White Hart a famous inn in Southwark   24 **out** up   26 **recreants** those
who break faith, cowards   30 **make shift for one** manage for myself
36 **meanest** lowest born   38 **the spoil** pillaging

Unless by robbing of your friends and us.
Were 't not a shame that, whilst you live at jar,   40
The fearful French, whom you late vanquishèd,   41
Should make a start o'er seas and vanquish you?   42
Methinks already in this civil broil
I see them lording it in London streets,
Crying *"Villiago!"* unto all they meet.   45
Better ten thousand baseborn Cades miscarry   46
Than you should stoop unto a Frenchman's mercy.
To France, to France, and get what you have lost!
Spare England, for it is your native coast.
Henry hath money; you are strong and manly;
God on our side, doubt not of victory.

ALL   A Clifford! A Clifford! We'll follow the King and   52
Clifford!

CADE *[Aside]*   Was ever feather so lightly blown to and
fro as this multitude? The name of Henry the Fifth
hales them to an hundred mischiefs and makes them   56
leave me desolate. I see them lay their heads together
to surprise me. My sword make way for me, for here   58
is no staying.—In despite of the devils and hell, have   59
through the very middest of you! And heavens and   60
honor be witness that no want of resolution in me, but
only my followers' base and ignominious treasons,
makes me betake me to my heels.   63

                    Exit [Cade, running through the crowd
                              with drawn sword].

BUCKINGHAM
What, is he fled? Go some, and follow him,
And he that brings his head unto the King
Shall have a thousand crowns for his reward.

                              Exeunt some of them.
Follow me, soldiers. We'll devise a means
To reconcile you all unto the King.   *Exeunt omnes.*

40 at jar in discord   **41 fearful** timid.   **late** lately   **42 make a start**
suddenly arouse themselves   **45 Villiago** rascal, villain. (Italian.)
46 miscarry encounter misfortune   **52 A Clifford** rally to Clifford
56 hales draws   **58 surprise** capture   **59 despite** spite   **59–60 have**
through i.e., here I come through   **63 s.d. Exit** (In the quarto version,
Cade "runs through them with his staff and flies away.")

4.9   *Sound trumpets. Enter King, Queen, and*
            Somerset, on the terrace [aloft].

KING
   Was ever king that joyed an earthly throne   1
   And could command no more content than I?
   No sooner was I crept out of my cradle
   But I was made a king at nine months old.
   Was never subject longed to be a king
   As I do long and wish to be a subject.

     Enter Buckingham and [old] Clifford.

BUCKINGHAM
   Health and glad tidings to Your Majesty!
KING
   Why, Buckingham, is the traitor Cade surprised?   8
   Or is he but retired to make him strong?

     Enter [below] multitudes, with halters about
     their necks.

CLIFFORD
   He is fled, my lord, and all his powers do yield,   10
   And humbly thus, with halters on their necks,
   Expect Your Highness' doom, of life or death.   12
KING
   Then, heaven, set ope thy everlasting gates
   To entertain my vows of thanks and praise!   14
   Soldiers, this day have you redeemed your lives
   And showed how well you love your prince and country.
   Continue still in this so good a mind,
   And Henry, though he be infortunate,
   Assure yourselves, will never be unkind.
   And so, with thanks and pardon to you all,
   I do dismiss you to your several countries.   21

4.9. Location: A castle, historically identified as **Kenilworth Castle**
in Warwickshire, though in the theater we only know that the King
receives the submission of the rebels shortly after the fighting in
London.
s.d. terrace i.e., probably in the gallery to the rear above the main
stage **1 joyed** enjoyed **8 surprised** captured **10 powers** troops (also
in l. 25) **12 Expect** await. **doom** judgment **14 entertain** receive
21 several countries various localities

ALL   God save the King! God save the King!
                    [*Exeunt the multitudes.*]
          Enter a Messenger.

MESSENGER
    Please it Your Grace to be advertisèd   23
    The Duke of York is newly come from Ireland,
    And with a puissant and a mighty power
    Of gallowglasses and stout kerns   26
    Is marching hitherward in proud array,
    And still proclaimeth, as he comes along,   28
    His arms are only to remove from thee
    The Duke of Somerset, whom he terms a traitor.
KING
    Thus stands my state, twixt Cade and York distressed,
    Like to a ship that, having scaped a tempest,
    Is straightway calmed and boarded with a pirate.   33
    But now is Cade driven back, his men dispersed,   34
    And now is York in arms to second him.
    I pray thee, Buckingham, go and meet him,
    And ask him what's the reason of these arms.
    Tell him I'll send Duke Edmund to the Tower;   38
    And, Somerset, we will commit thee thither,
    Until his army be dismissed from him.
SOMERSET   My lord,
    I'll yield myself to prison willingly,
    Or unto death, to do my country good.
KING [*To Buckingham*]
    In any case, be not too rough in terms,
    For he is fierce and cannot brook hard language.   45
BUCKINGHAM
    I will, my lord, and doubt not so to deal
    As all things shall redound unto your good.
KING
    Come, wife, let's in, and learn to govern better,
    For yet may England curse my wretched reign.   49
                              Flourish. Exeunt.

                              ❖

23 **advertisèd** informed   26 **gallowglasses, kerns** Irish horsemen and foot-
soldiers, armed with heavy and light weapons respectively   28 **still** continually   33 **calmed** becalmed.   **with** by   34 **But now** even now, just now
38 **Duke Edmund** i.e., Edmund Beaufort, the Duke of Somerset   45 **brook**
endure   49 **yet** until now

4.10   *Enter Cade.*

CADE Fie on ambitions! Fie on myself, that have a
sword and yet am ready to famish! These five days
have I hid me in these woods and durst not peep out,
for all the country is laid for me. But now am I so hun- 4
gry that, if I might have a lease of my life for a thousand years, I could stay no longer. Wherefore, o'er a 6
brick wall have I climbed into this garden, to see if I
can eat grass, or pick a sallet another while, which is 8
not amiss to cool a man's stomach this hot weather.
And I think this word "sallet" was born to do me
good; for many a time, but for a sallet, my brainpan
had been cleft with a brown bill; and many a time, 12
when I have been dry and bravely marching, it hath
served me instead of a quart pot to drink in; and now
the word "sallet" must serve me to feed on. 15

Enter Iden [and his men].

IDEN
Lord, who would live turmoilèd in the court,
And may enjoy such quiet walks as these?
This small inheritance my father left me
Contenteth me, and worth a monarchy.
I seek not to wax great by others' waning,
Or gather wealth, I care not with what envy.
Sufficeth that I have maintains my state 22
And sends the poor well pleasèd from my gate. 23
CADE [*Aside*] Zounds, here's the lord of the soil come to
seize me for a stray, for entering his fee simple without 25
leave.—Ah, villain, thou wilt betray me and get a

4.10. Location: Kent. Iden's garden.
4 is laid is lying in wait   **6 stay** wait   **8 sallet** salad greens (with a pun
in the following lines on *sallet*, light helmet)   **12 brown bill** brown-
handled weapon with a blade or ax-shaped head   **15 s.d. and his men**
(The quarto reads, "Enter Jack Cade at me door, and at the other Master Alexander Eyden and his men," and at ll. 38–39 Cade refers to
Iden's "five men.")   **22 Sufficeth . . . state** it suffices that what I have
supports my manner of life   **23 And . . . gate** i.e., and also provides
enough to feed the poor who come to my gate   **25 stray** trespasser.   **fee
simple** estate belonging to an owner and his heirs forever

thousand crowns of the King by carrying my head to
him; but I'll make thee eat iron like an ostrich and
swallow my sword like a great pin, ere thou and I part.

IDEN

Why, rude companion, whatsoe'er thou be,   30
I know thee not. Why then should I betray thee?
Is 't not enough to break into my garden,
And like a thief to come to rob my grounds,
Climbing my walls in spite of me the owner,
But thou wilt brave me with these saucy terms?   35

CADE   Brave thee? Ay, by the best blood that ever was   36
broached, and beard thee too. Look on me well. I have   37
eat no meat these five days, yet come thou and thy   38
five men, and if I do not leave you all as dead as a
doornail, I pray God I may never eat grass more.

IDEN

Nay, it shall ne'er be said, while England stands,
That Alexander Iden, an esquire of Kent,
Took odds to combat a poor famished man.   43
Oppose thy steadfast-gazing eyes to mine;
See if thou canst outface me with thy looks.
Set limb to limb, and thou art far the lesser;   46
Thy hand is but a finger to my fist,
Thy leg a stick comparèd with this truncheon;   48
My foot shall fight with all the strength thou hast;
And if mine arm be heavèd in the air,   50
Thy grave is digged already in the earth.   51
As for words, whose greatness answers words,   52
Let this my sword report what speech forbears.   53

CADE   By my valor, the most complete champion that   54
ever I heard! Steel, if thou turn the edge, or cut not out 55
the burly-boned clown in chines of beef ere thou sleep   56

---

30 rude companion base fellow   **35 brave** defy, taunt.   **saucy** insolent
36 best blood i.e., Christ's blood   **37 broached** tapped, shed.   **beard**
defy **38 eat** eaten. (Pronounced "et.")   **43 odds** advantage   **46 Set**
compare   **48 truncheon** heavy staff (i.e., Iden's leg)   **50–51 And . . .**
earth i.e., if I but lift my arm, you're as good as dead already
52 whose . . . words i.e., I whose might is more than a match for your
words   **53 report . . . forbears** i.e., speak through actions in place of
words   **54 complete** accomplished   **55 turn the edge** fail to cut
56 chines roasts

in thy sheath, I beseech God on my knees thou mayst
be turned to hobnails.   *Here they fight. [Cade falls.]*   58
O, I am slain! Famine and no other hath slain me. Let
ten thousand devils come against me, and give me but
the ten meals I have lost, and I'd defy them all. Wither,
garden, and be henceforth a burying place to all that
do dwell in this house, because the unconquered soul
of Cade is fled.

IDEN
Is 't Cade that I have slain, that monstrous traitor?
Sword, I will hallow thee for this thy deed
And hang thee o'er my tomb when I am dead.
Ne'er shall this blood be wipèd from thy point
But thou shalt wear it as a herald's coat
To emblaze the honor that thy master got.   70

CADE Iden, farewell, and be proud of thy victory. Tell
Kent from me she hath lost her best man, and exhort
all the world to be cowards; for I, that never feared any,
am vanquished by famine, not by valor.   *Dies.*

IDEN
How much thou wrong'st me, heaven be my judge.
Die, damnèd wretch, the curse of her that bare thee!   76
And as I thrust thy body in with my sword,
                    [Stabbing Cade's body]
So wish I, I might thrust thy soul to hell.
Hence will I drag thee headlong by the heels   79
Unto a dunghill, which shall be thy grave,
And there cut off thy most ungracious head,
Which I will bear in triumph to the King,
Leaving thy trunk for crows to feed upon.
                    Exeunt, [dragging out the body].

❖

58 turned to hobnails i.e., melted down and recast as nails   **70 emblaze**
proclaim as by a heraldic device   **76 bare** bore, gave birth to
79 headlong at full length

5.1   *Enter York and his army of Irish, with drum and colors.*

YORK
From Ireland thus comes York to claim his right
And pluck the crown from feeble Henry's head.
Ring, bells, aloud! Burn, bonfires, clear and bright
To entertain great England's lawful king!   4
Ah, *sancta maiestas,* who would not buy thee dear?   5
Let them obey that knows not how to rule;
This hand was made to handle naught but gold.
I cannot give due action to my words
Except a sword or scepter balance it.   9
A scepter shall it have, have I a soul,   10
On which I'll toss the flower-de-luce of France.   11

  Enter Buckingham.

Whom have we here? Buckingham, to disturb me?
The King hath sent him, sure. I must dissemble.
BUCKINGHAM
York, if thou meanest well, I greet thee well.
YORK
Humphrey of Buckingham, I accept thy greeting.
Art thou a messenger, or come of pleasure?
BUCKINGHAM
A messenger from Henry, our dread liege,
To know the reason of these arms in peace;
Or why thou, being a subject as I am,
Against thy oath and true allegiance sworn
Should raise so great a power without his leave,   21
Or dare to bring thy force so near the court.

5.1. Location: In the theater, Act 5 appears to take place in one continuous sweep, though historically the action begins between Dartford and Blackheath just southeast of London in 1452–1453 (see l. 46) and then shifts to a battlefield between London and St. Albans, near the Castle Inn, in 1455.
s.d. **drum and colors** drummer and flagbearer   **4 entertain** welcome
5 sancta maiestas sacred majesty   **9 Except** unless.   **balance it** i.e., give due weight to my action   **10 have I** i.e., just as sure as I have   **11 On which** i.e., my sword-holding hand, my action. (The *it* of l. 10.)   **toss** carry aloft on the point of a sword.   **flower-de-luce** France's national emblem   **21 power** armed force

YORK [*Aside*]
    Scarce can I speak, my choler is so great.
    O, I could hew up rocks and fight with flint,
    I am so angry at these abject terms!   25
    And now, like Ajax Telamonius,   26
    On sheep or oxen could I spend my fury.
    I am far better born than is the King,
    More like a king, more kingly in my thoughts.
    But I must make fair weather yet awhile,   30
    Till Henry be more weak and I more strong.—
    Buckingham, I prithee, pardon me,
    That I have given no answer all this while;
    My mind was troubled with deep melancholy.
    The cause why I have brought this army hither
    Is to remove proud Somerset from the King,
    Seditious to His Grace and to the state.

BUCKINGHAM
    That is too much presumption on thy part.
    But if thy arms be to no other end,
    The King hath yielded unto thy demand;
    The Duke of Somerset is in the Tower.

YORK
    Upon thine honor, is he prisoner?

BUCKINGHAM
    Upon mine honor, he is prisoner.

YORK
    Then, Buckingham, I do dismiss my powers.
    Soldiers, I thank you all. Disperse yourselves.
    Meet me tomorrow in Saint George's field;   46
    You shall have pay and everything you wish.
                              [*Exeunt soldiers.*]
    And let my sovereign, virtuous Henry,
    Command my eldest son, nay, all my sons,   49
    As pledges of my fealty and love;   50

---

25 abject terms degrading, insulting words   **26 Ajax Telamonius** Ajax
the son of Telamon, one of the Greek heroes of the Trojan War who,
when the weapons of Achilles were allotted to Odysseus, slaughtered in
his fury a flock of sheep, mistaking them for the enemy   **30 make fair
weather** i.e., dissemble   **46 Saint George's field** an open area south of
the Thames River near Southwark   **49 Command** hold under his
authority   **50 pledges** hostages

I'll send them all as willing as I live.
Lands, goods, horse, armor, anything I have,
Is his to use, so Somerset may die.   53
BUCKINGHAM
York, I commend this kind submission.
We twain will go into His Highness' tent.

                  [*They walk arm in arm.*]

    Enter King and Attendants.

KING
Buckingham, doth York intend no harm to us,
That thus he marcheth with thee arm in arm?
YORK
In all submission and humility
York doth present himself unto Your Highness.
KING
Then what intends these forces thou dost bring?
YORK
To heave the traitor Somerset from hence
And fight against that monstrous rebel Cade,
Who since I heard to be discomfited.   63

    Enter Iden, with Cade's head.

IDEN
If one so rude and of so mean condition   64
May pass into the presence of a king,
Lo, I present Your Grace a traitor's head,
The head of Cade, whom I in combat slew.
KING
The head of Cade? Great God, how just art Thou!
O, let me view his visage, being dead,
That living wrought me such exceeding trouble.
Tell me, my friend, art thou the man that slew him?
IDEN   I was, an 't like Your Majesty.   72
KING
How art thou called, and what is thy degree?   73
IDEN
Alexander Iden, that's my name,
A poor esquire of Kent that loves his king.

---

53 so as long as   **63 discomfited** routed   **64 rude** uncultivated.   **mean
condition** low rank   **72 an 't like** if it please   **73 degree** social rank

BUCKINGHAM [*To the King*]
    So please it you, my lord, 'twere not amiss
    He were created knight for his good service.
KING
    Iden, kneel down. [*He kneels.*] Rise up a knight.
                                        [*Iden rises.*]
    We give thee for reward a thousand marks,   79
    And will that thou henceforth attend on us.   80
IDEN
    May Iden live to merit such a bounty,
    And never live but true unto his liege!

        Enter Queen and Somerset.

KING
    See, Buckingham, Somerset comes with the Queen.
    Go bid her hide him quickly from the Duke.   84
QUEEN
    For thousand Yorks he shall not hide his head,
    But boldly stand and front him to his face.   86
YORK
    How now? Is Somerset at liberty?
    Then, York, unloose thy long-imprisoned thoughts
    And let thy tongue be equal with thy heart.
    Shall I endure the sight of Somerset?
    False king, why hast thou broken faith with me,
    Knowing how hardly I can brook abuse?   92
    "King" did I call thee? No, thou art not king,
    Not fit to govern and rule multitudes,
    Which dar'st not—no, nor canst not—rule a traitor. 95
    That head of thine doth not become a crown;
    Thy hand is made to grasp a palmer's staff,   97
    And not to grace an awful princely scepter.   98
    That gold must round engirt these brows of mine,
    Whose smile and frown, like to Achilles' spear,   100
    Is able with the change to kill and cure.

---

79 marks (Valued at two thirds of a pound.)   **80 will** command   **84 the
Duke** i.e., of York   **86 front** confront   **92 brook abuse** tolerate deception   **95 Which** who   **97 palmer's** pilgrim's   **98 awful** awe-inspiring
100 Achilles' spear (Telephus, wounded by Achilles' spear, learned from
an oracle that he could be cured only by the wounder. He was eventually cured by an application of rust from the point of the spear.)

Here is a hand to hold a scepter up
And with the same to act controlling laws.   103
Give place. By heaven, thou shalt rule no more
O'er him whom heaven created for thy ruler.

SOMERSET

O monstrous traitor! I arrest thee, York,
Of capital treason 'gainst the King and crown.
Obey, audacious traitor. Kneel for grace.

YORK

Wouldst have me kneel? First let me ask of these,   109
If they can brook I bow a knee to man.   110
[*To an Attendant.*] Sirrah, call in my sons to be my bail.
                                        [*Exit Attendant.*]
I know, ere they will have me go to ward,   112
They'll pawn their swords for my enfranchisement.   113

QUEEN [*To Buckingham*]

Call hither Clifford. Bid him come amain,   114
To say if that the bastard boys of York
Shall be the surety for their traitor father.   116
                                        [*Exit Buckingham.*]

YORK [*To the Queen*]

O blood-bespotted Neapolitan,   117
Outcast of Naples, England's bloody scourge!
The sons of York, thy betters in their birth,
Shall be their father's bail, and bane to those   120
That for my surety will refuse the boys!   121

> *Enter Edward and Richard [Plantagenet, with
> drum and soldiers, at one door].*

See where they come. I'll warrant they'll make it good.

> *Enter [old] Clifford [and his Son, with drum and
> soldiers, at the other door].*

103 act enact   **109 these** i.e., his sons, who are waiting outside, or
attendants, or possibly his hands or weapons   **110 brook . . . man**
tolerate that I should bow my knee in submission to anyone   **112 to
ward** into custody   **113 pawn** pledge.   **enfranchisement** freedom
114 amain swiftly   **116 s.d. Exit Buckingham** (Buckingham must exit
somewhere before an attendant is sent to find him at l. 192, and here
seems a likely place.)   **117 Neapolitan** (Margaret's father Reignier or
René was titular King of Naples.)   **120 bane** destruction   **121 s.d. drum**
drummer.   **at one door** (The quarto version is explicit that Plantagenet's sons enter "at one door" and Clifford with his son and forces "at
the other.")

QUEEN
　And here comes Clifford to deny their bail.
CLIFFORD [*Kneeling before King Henry*]
　Health and all happiness to my lord the King!
　　　　　　　　　　　　　　　　　　[*He rises.*]

YORK
　I thank thee, Clifford. Say, what news with thee?
　Nay, do not fright us with an angry look.
　We are thy sovereign, Clifford, kneel again.
　For thy mistaking so, we pardon thee.
CLIFFORD
　This is my king, York. I do not mistake,
　But thou mistakes me much to think I do.—
　To Bedlam with him! Is the man grown mad?   131
KING
　Ay, Clifford, a bedlam and ambitious humor   132
　Makes him oppose himself against his king.
CLIFFORD
　He is a traitor. Let him to the Tower,
　And chop away that factious pate of his.   135
QUEEN
　He is arrested, but will not obey.
　His sons, he says, shall give their words for him.
YORK　Will you not, sons?
EDWARD
　Ay, noble Father, if our words will serve.
RICHARD
　And if words will not, then our weapons shall.
CLIFFORD
　Why, what a brood of traitors have we here!
YORK
　Look in a glass, and call thy image so.   142
　I am thy king, and thou a false-heart traitor.
　Call hither to the stake my two brave bears,   144

---

131 Bedlam hospital of St. Mary of Bethlehem in London, used as an
asylum for the mentally deranged　**132 bedlam** mad.　**humor** disposition　**135 factious pate** rebellious head　**142 glass** looking glass
144 brave bears i.e., Salisbury and his son Warwick. (Cf. ll. 202–203
below, where Warwick describes the badge of his house as a *rampant
bear chained to the ragged staff.* The image is from bearbaiting, in
which bears were chained to a stake and attacked by *fell-lurking curs,*
cruelly waiting dogs, l. 146.)

That with the very shaking of their chains
They may astonish these fell-lurking curs.—
Bid Salisbury and Warwick come to me.
                    [*An Attendant goes to summon them.*]

Enter the Earls of Warwick and Salisbury, [*with
drum and soldiers*].

CLIFFORD
Are these thy bears? We'll bait thy bears to death
And manacle the bearherd in their chains,   149
If thou dar'st bring them to the baiting place.   150
RICHARD
Oft have I seen a hot o'erweening cur   151
Run back and bite, because he was withheld,   152
Who, being suffered with the bear's fell paw,   153
Hath clapped his tail between his legs and cried;
And such a piece of service will you do,
If you oppose yourselves to match Lord Warwick.   156
CLIFFORD
Hence, heap of wrath, foul indigested lump,   157
As crooked in thy manners as thy shape!
YORK
Nay, we shall heat you thoroughly anon.   159
CLIFFORD
Take heed, lest by your heat you burn yourselves.
KING
Why, Warwick, hath thy knee forgot to bow?
Old Salisbury, shame to thy silver hair,
Thou mad misleader of thy brainsick son!
What, wilt thou on thy deathbed play the ruffian,
And seek for sorrow with thy spectacles?   165

---

149 bearherd bear handler, keeper (i.e., York)   **150 baiting place** bearbaiting pit   **151 hot o'erweening** hot-tempered and overconfident
152 bite i.e., at his trainer, who is restraining him   **153 suffered with**
permitted to do battle with, or, injured by.   **fell** fierce, terrible
156 oppose yourselves set yourselves up as opponents   **157 indigested**
ill-formed.   **lump** (Bear cubs were supposedly born unformed and had
to be licked into shape by their mother. See *3 Henry VI*, 3.2.161, where
Richard's hunched back and other deformities are compared with those
of *an unlicked bear whelp*.)   **159 heat you** i.e., warm you in the fighting   **165 spectacles** (A sign of advanced age, like *silver hair*, l. 162, and
frosty, white-haired, l. 167.)

O, where is faith? O, where is loyalty?
If it be banished from the frosty head,
Where shall it find a harbor in the earth?
Wilt thou go dig a grave to find out war,
And shame thine honorable age with blood?
Why art thou old and want'st experience?   171
Or wherefore dost abuse it if thou hast it?   172
For shame! In duty bend thy knee to me
That bows unto the grave with mickle age.   174

SALISBURY
My lord, I have considered with myself
The title of this most renownèd duke,
And in my conscience do repute His Grace
The rightful heir to England's royal seat.

KING
Hast thou not sworn allegiance unto me?

SALISBURY   I have.

KING
Canst thou dispense with heaven for such an oath?   181

SALISBURY
It is great sin to swear unto a sin,
But greater sin to keep a sinful oath.
Who can be bound by any solemn vow
To do a murderous deed, to rob a man,
To force a spotless virgin's chastity,
To reave the orphan of his patrimony,   187
To wring the widow from her customed right,   188
And have no other reason for this wrong
But that he was bound by a solemn oath?

QUEEN
A subtle traitor needs no sophister.   191

KING [*To an Attendant*]
Call Buckingham, and bid him arm himself.
                                        [*Exit Attendant.*]

---

171 want'st lack. (Why are you old before you are wise?) **172 Or . . . it**
or why do you put wisdom and experience to such bad use if you have
them **174 That bows** you that bow or your knee that bows. **mickle**
great **181 dispense with heaven for** expect or obtain dispensation from
heaven for breaking **187 reave** bereave **188 customed right** i.e., right
to inherit a portion of her husband's estate **191 sophister** equivocator,
expert in casuistry

YORK [*To King Henry*]
Call Buckingham and all the friends thou hast,   193
I am resolved for death or dignity.   194

CLIFFORD
The first, I warrant thee, if dreams prove true.

WARWICK
You were best to go to bed and dream again,   196
To keep thee from the tempest of the field.

CLIFFORD
I am resolved to bear a greater storm
Than any thou canst conjure up today;
And that I'll write upon thy burgonet,   200
Might I but know thee by thy household badge.

WARWICK
Now, by my father's badge, old Neville's crest,   202
The rampant bear chained to the ragged staff,
This day I'll wear aloft my burgonet,   204
As on a mountaintop the cedar shows
That keeps his leaves in spite of any storm,
Even to affright thee with the view thereof.

CLIFFORD
And from thy burgonet I'll rend thy bear
And tread it underfoot with all contempt,
Despite the bearherd that protects the bear.

YOUNG CLIFFORD
And so to arms, victorious Father,
To quell the rebels and their complices.   212

RICHARD
Fie! Charity, for shame! Speak not in spite,
For you shall sup with Jesu Christ tonight.

YOUNG CLIFFORD
Foul stigmatic, that's more than thou canst tell.   215

RICHARD
If not in heaven, you'll surely sup in hell.

    Exeunt [*separately*].

193 Call even if you call   **194 dignity** exalted rank   **196 You were best**
you had better   **200 burgonet** light helmet or steel cap (upon which the
wearer's heraldic device was often mounted)   **202 old Neville's crest**
(The Nevilles' crest was in fact a bull; Warwick inherited his badge of a
chained bear from his wife's family, the Beauchamps.)   **204 aloft** on top
of   **212 complices** accomplices   **215 stigmatic** one branded with the
mark of his crime (just as Richard is marked by his deformities)

5.2   [*Alarums to the battle.*] *Enter Warwick.*

WARWICK
Clifford of Cumberland, 'tis Warwick calls!
And if thou dost not hide thee from the bear,
Now, when the angry trumpet sounds alarum
And dead men's cries do fill the empty air,   4
Clifford, I say, come forth and fight with me!
Proud northern lord, Clifford of Cumberland,
Warwick is hoarse with calling thee to arms.

     Enter York.

How now, my noble lord? What, all afoot?
YORK
The deadly-handed Clifford slew my steed,
But match to match I have encountered him
And made a prey for carrion kites and crows
Even of the bonny beast he loved so well.

     Enter [old] Clifford.

WARWICK
Of one or both of us the time is come.
YORK
Hold, Warwick, seek thee out some other chase,   14
For I myself must hunt this deer to death.
WARWICK
Then, nobly, York! 'Tis for a crown thou fight'st.—
As I intend, Clifford, to thrive today,
It grieves my soul to leave thee unassailed.
                           Exit Warwick.

CLIFFORD
What seest thou in me, York? Why dost thou pause?
YORK
With thy brave bearing should I be in love,   20
But that thou art so fast mine enemy.   21
CLIFFORD
Nor should thy prowess want praise and esteem,   22
But that 'tis shown ignobly and in treason.

5.2. Location: Scene continues at the battlefield near the Castle Inn.
4 dead dying   **14 chase** game, prey   **20 bearing** demeanor   **21 fast**
completely   **22 want** lack

YORK

So let it help me now against thy sword
As I in justice and true right express it.

CLIFFORD

My soul and body on the action both!   26

YORK

A dreadful lay! Address thee instantly.   27

                    [*They fight, and Clifford falls.*]

CLIFFORD

La fin couronne les oeuvres.   [*He dies.*] 28

YORK

Thus war hath given thee peace, for thou art still.
Peace with his soul, heaven, if it be thy will!   [*Exit.*]

      Enter young Clifford.

YOUNG CLIFFORD

Shame and confusion! All is on the rout.   31
Fear frames disorder, and disorder wounds   32
Where it should guard. O war, thou son of hell,
Whom angry heavens do make their minister,
Throw in the frozen bosoms of our part   35
Hot coals of vengeance! Let no soldier fly.
He that is truly dedicate to war   37
Hath no self-love, nor he that loves himself   38
Hath not essentially but by circumstance   39
The name of valor. [*Seeing his dead father.*] O, let the
   vile world end
And the premisèd flames of the last day   41
Knit earth and heaven together!
Now let the general trumpet blow his blast,
Particularities and petty sounds   44
To cease! Wast thou ordained, dear Father,   45
To lose thy youth in peace, and to achieve   46

---

26 action outcome of action **27 lay** wager, oath. **Address thee** prepare
yourself **28 La . . . oeuvres** the end crowns the work **31 confusion**
destruction. **on the rout** in disorderly retreat **32 frames** causes
35 frozen i.e., unwarmed by wrathful courage. **part** party, faction
37 dedicate dedicated **38 nor** conversely **39 not . . . circumstance** not
by any virtue of his own, but only outwardly and by happenstance
41 premisèd foreordained. **last day** Day of Judgment **44 Particularities**
individual affairs **45 cease** bring to an end. **ordained** chosen, fated
46 lose expend

The silver livery of advisèd age,   47
And, in thy reverence and thy chair days, thus   48
To die in ruffian battle? Even at this sight
My heart is turned to stone, and while 'tis mine
It shall be stony. York not our old men spares;
No more will I their babes. Tears virginal   52
Shall be to me even as the dew to fire,   53
And beauty, that the tyrant oft reclaims,   54
Shall to my flaming wrath be oil and flax.
Henceforth I will not have to do with pity.
Meet I an infant of the house of York,   57
Into as many gobbets will I cut it   58
As wild Medea young Absyrtus did.   59
In cruelty will I seek out my fame.
Come, thou new ruin of old Clifford's house.
As did Aeneas old Anchises bear,   62
So bear I thee upon my manly shoulders;
But then Aeneas bare a living load,   64
Nothing so heavy as these woes of mine.   65
                    [*Exit, bearing off his father.*]

*Enter Richard and Somerset to fight. [Somerset
is killed under the sign of the Castle Inn.]*

RICHARD   So, lie thou there;
For underneath an alehouse' paltry sign,
The Castle in Saint Albans, Somerset
Hath made the wizard famous in his death.   69
Sword, hold thy temper; heart, be wrathful still.   70
Priests pray for enemies, but princes kill.   [*Exit.*] 71

---

47 silvery livery i.e., white hair, worn as though part of a uniform.
advisèd wise, prudent   **48 reverence** revered old age.   **chair days** i.e.,
inactive years of old age   **52 virginal** of young maidens   **53 dew to fire**
(Water finely sprayed on a fire was thought to cause it to burn hotter.)
54 that . . . reclaims which often softens the temper of the tyrant   **57 Meet
I** if I should meet   **58 gobbets** pieces, lumps of flesh   **59 Medea** daughter
of Aeetes, King of Colchis, who helped Jason recover the Golden Fleece
and fled with him. (To delay her father's pursuit, she killed her brother
Absyrtus and left pieces of his dismembered body in the father's path.)
62 Aeneas, Anchises (In Virgil's *Aeneid*, Aeneas, fleeing from Troy, carried
his aged father on his shoulders.)   **64 bare** bore   **65 Nothing** not at all.
heavy (1) weighty (2) sorrowful   **69 Hath . . . death** i.e., has confirmed by
his death the prophecy that he would die *where castles mounted stand*.
(See 1.4.36–38.)   **70 still** always   **71 s.d. Exit** (The body of the slain Somerset must be removed at some point.)

Fight. Excursions. Enter King, Queen, and others.

QUEEN
Away, my lord! You are slow. For shame, away!

KING
Can we outrun the heavens? Good Margaret, stay.

QUEEN
What are you made of? You'll nor fight nor fly.   74
Now is it manhood, wisdom, and defense
To give the enemy way, and to secure us   76
By what we can, which can no more but fly.   77
                              Alarum afar off.
If you be ta'en, we then should see the bottom
Of all our fortunes; but if we haply scape,
As well we may, if not through your neglect,   80
We shall to London get, where you are loved
And where this breach now in our fortunes made
May readily be stopped.

          Enter [young] Clifford.

YOUNG CLIFFORD
But that my heart's on future mischief set,
I would speak blasphemy ere bid you fly;
But fly you must. Uncurable discomfit   86
Reigns in the hearts of all our present parts.   87
Away, for your relief! And we will live
To see their day and them our fortune give.   89
Away, my lord, away!   *Exeunt.*

5.3   *Alarum. Retreat. Enter York, Richard,*
          Warwick, and soldiers, with drum
          and colors.

YORK
Of Salisbury, who can report of him,

---

71 s.d. Excursions sorties   **74 nor . . . nor** neither . . . nor   **76 secure us**
save ourselves   **77 what** whatever means.   **which** (we) who   **80 if not**
unless   **86 Uncurable discomfit** hopeless discouragement   **87 our present**
parts those forces still remaining to us   **89 To . . . give** to see a day of
success like theirs and let them experience our misfortune

5.3. Location: Scene continues at the battlefield.

That winter lion, who in rage forgets   2
Agèd contusions and all brush of time,   3
And like a gallant in the brow of youth   4
Repairs him with occasion? This happy day   5
Is not itself, nor have we won one foot,
If Salisbury be lost.
RICHARD   My noble Father,
Three times today I holp him to his horse,   8
Three times bestrid him; thrice I led him off,   9
Persuaded him from any further act.
But still, where danger was, still there I met him,   11
And like rich hangings in a homely house,   12
So was his will in his old feeble body.
But, noble as he is, look where he comes.

   Enter Salisbury.

SALISBURY
Now, by my sword, well hast thou fought today!
By th' Mass, so did we all. I thank you, Richard.
God knows how long it is I have to live,
And it hath pleased Him that three times today
You have defended me from imminent death.
Well, lords, we have not got that which we have;   20
'Tis not enough our foes are this time fled,
Being opposites of such repairing nature.   22
YORK
I know our safety is to follow them;
For, as I hear, the King is fled to London
To call a present court of Parliament.
Let us pursue him ere the writs go forth.   26
What says Lord Warwick? Shall we after them?
WARWICK
After them? Nay, before them, if we can.

---

2 winter i.e., aged   **3 brush** assault, collision   **4 gallant** young man of
fashion.   **brow** i.e., crown, height   **5 Repairs . . . occasion** i.e., renews
his strength with the opportunity of further military action   **8 holp**
helped   **9 bestrid him** i.e., stood over him to defend him when he was
down   **11 still** continually   **12 hangings** tapestries.   **homely** modest
20 not . . . have i.e., not decisively overwhelmed the forces we today
defeated in order to secure the whole country   **22 Being . . . nature**
they being adversaries with such ability to recover quickly   **26 writs**
official summonses issued by the King to members of Parliament

Now, by my faith, lords, 'twas a glorious day.
Saint Albans battle won by famous York
Shall be eternized in all age to come.   31
Sound drum and trumpets, and to London all,
And more such days as these to us befall!
                              [*Flourish.*] *Exeunt.*

31 eternized immortalized

Date and Text

A shortened and memorially reconstructed text of *Henry VI, Part Two* was published in quarto in 1594 with the title, *The First Part of the Contention Betwixt the Two Famous Houses of York and Lancaster*. The play appears to have been written about 1590–1591. The First Folio text seems to have been based on an authorial manuscript with some reference to the third quarto, which in turn may have been corrected by reference to a theatrical manuscript. For a more extensive discussion of date and textual situation in all three *Henry VI* plays, see "Date and Text" to *Henry VI, Part One* in this volume.

Textual Notes

These textual notes are not a historical collation, either of the early quartos and folios or of more recent editions; they are simply a record of departures in this edition from the copy text. The reading adopted in this edition appears in boldface, followed by the rejected reading from the copy text, i.e., the First Folio. Only major alterations in punctuation are noted. Changes in lineation are not indicated, nor are some minor and obvious typographical errors.

Abbreviations used:
F the First Folio
Q the quarto of 1594
s.d. stage direction
s.p. speech prefix

Copy text: the First Folio.

1.1. 4 Princess Princes   **37 s.d. Kneeling** kneel   **56 s.p. Cardinal** [Q] Win
57 duchies Dutchesse   **72 s.d. Exeunt** Exit   **Manent** Manet   **91 had** hath
99 Rasing Racing   **107 roast** rost   **130 s.d. [and elsewhere] Gloucester** Hum
167 hoist hoyse   **176 Protector** [Q] Protectors   **177 s.d. Exeunt** Exit   **206 let's
away** lets make hast away   **211 s.d. Exeunt** Exit   **254 in** [Q1] in in

1.2. 1 s.p. [and elsewhere] Duchess Elia   **19 hour** thought   **22 dream**
dreames   **38 are** wer   **60 s.d. Exit Humphrey** [at l. 59 in F]

1.3. 6 s.p. First Petitioner Peter   **32 master** Mistresse   **41 s.d. Exeunt** Exit
100 [F has "Exit" here]   **104 denied** denay'd   **142 I'd** I could   **187 s.p. [and
throughout scene] Horner** Armorer   **212–213 King. Then . . . French** [Q; not
in F]

1.4. 25 s.p. Margery Jourdain Witch   **25 Asnath** Asmath   **62 Aio te** Aio
63 posse posso

2.1. 30 Lord-Protectorship Lords Protectorship   **48 Cardinal [Aside to
Gloucester] I am with you** Cardinall, I am with you [as part of Gloucester's
speech]   **59 s.p. Townsman** One [also at l. 61]   **111 Alban** Albones   **135 his**
[Q] it

2.2. 45 was son was   **46 son** Sonnes Sonne

2.3. 3 sins sinne   **19 grave** ground   **74 apron** Aporne

2.4. 88 too to

3.1. 211 strains strayes   **218–219 eyes . . . good,** eyes; . . . good:
222 s.d. Exeunt Exit   **333–334 art . . . death; it** art; . . . death, it

3.2. 14 s.d. Somerset Suffolke, Somerset   **26 Meg** Nell   **79 Margaret** Elianor
[also at ll. 100 and 120]   **113 losing** loosing   **116 witch** watch
278 s.p. Commons [not in F]   **391 breathe** breath

3.3. 8 s.p. Cardinal [Q] Beau   **10 whe'er** where

4.1. 6 Clip Cleape   **7 Breathe** Breath   **48 Jove . . . I** [Q; not in F]

50 s.p. Suffolk [Q; at l. 51 in F]   **70 Lieutenant. Yes, Pole. Suffolk. Pole?**
[Q; not in F]   **85 mother's bleeding** Mother-bleeding   **93 are** and
115–116 Lieutenant. Walter– / Whitmore Lieu. Water: W.   **117 Paene** Pine
119 s.p. Whitmore Wal [also at l. 143]   **133 s.p. Suffolk** [at l. 134 in F]
142 s.d. Exeunt Exit

4.2. 33 s.p. [and elsewhere] Dick [Q] But [or "Butch"]   **34 fall** faile
46 s.p. [and elsewhere] Smith Weauer [or "Wea"]   **99 an** a   **131 this:** this
176 s.d. Exeunt Exit

4.4. 19 have huae   **27 s.p. First Messenger** Mess   **49 s.p. Second Messenger**
Mess   **58 you be** you

4.5 s.d. enter enters

4.6. 9 s.p. Smith But   **13 Zounds** Come

4.7. 7 s.p. Holland Iohn [also at l. 15]   **63 lose** loose   **66 hands** hands?
67 But Kent   **you?** you,   **79 s.p. Bevis** Geo   **86 caudle** Candle
132 s.d. Exeunt Exit

4.8. 12 rebel rabble

4.9. 0 s.d. terrace Tarras   **33 calmed** calme

4.10. 6 o'er on   **20 waning** warning   **24 Zounds** [Q; not in F]   **28 I'll** He
57 God Ioue

5.1. 109 these thee   **111 sons** [Q] sonne   **113 for** of   **149 bearherd** Berard
[also at l. 210]   **194 or** and   **195 s.p. Clifford** Old Clif [and at ll. 198 and 208]
201 household [Q] housed

5.2. 8 [F repeats s.p. "War"]   **28 oeuvres** eumenes   **31 s.p. Young Clifford**
Clif [also at l. 84]   **46 lose** loose

5.3. 29 faith [Q] hand

HENRY VI
PART THREE

Introduction

Henry VI, Part Three must be seen not only as a part of Shakespeare's first historical four-play series but as a play in its own right, presumably seen on its first showing by an Elizabethan audience who, though aware of a larger context, witnessed this dramatic action as a self-contained event. Because *3 Henry VI* represents nearly the entire military phase of the civil war, it is the most crowded and bustling play of the series. Historically it covers the period from the battles of Wakefield and second St. Albans (1460–1461) to the decisive Yorkist victories at Barnet and Tewkesbury (1471). These and other battles are actually represented onstage. The conventional method of representing armed conflict is by means of alarums and excursions (i.e., sudden assaults and forays by armed soldiers in response to a signal to attack), employing as many soldiers as the acting company could muster, with martial music and numerous entrances and exits in rapid succession. Battles are usually preceded by florid boastful rhetorical exchanges, or *flytings*, between the combatants. The military contests focus on heroic confrontations between individual leaders. Staging of battles often uses the Elizabethan playhouse to its physical capacity, with appearances "on the walls" of some town (i.e., from the upper gallery), scaling operations, sieges, and the like. *3 Henry VI* abounds in spectacular deaths, often performed as gruesome rituals. Young Rutland is dragged from his tutor by the implacable Clifford, and Richard of York is mocked with a paper crown by Queen Margaret; Clifford dies with an arrow in his neck, and Warwick the kingmaker dies lamenting the vanity of all earthly achievement; King Henry dies in the Tower, a defenseless prisoner in the hands of Richard of Gloucester. The play is perhaps confusing to the reader, but it breathes with violent energy onstage.

Symbolic of the chaos is the lack of a single central character. The title of the 1595 octavo edition pairs the deaths of Richard of York and of King Henry as the play's most memorable episodes; and in this dual focus we see the dominant motif of reciprocity, a Yorkist death for a Lancastrian death.

This pattern will continue into *Richard III*, for *3 Henry VI* ends with an ominous amount of unfinished business; Clarence, for example, later sees that he must die in atonement for his part in the slaughter of Edward, the Lancastrian Prince of Wales. Just as the deaths are balanced and contrasted with one another, the military action also seesaws back and forth. Both Henry VI and Edward IV are at times imprisoned. The wheel of fortune elevates one side and then the other. Political alliances shift the balance of power one way and then the other. The action is painfully indecisive, the carnage leading pointlessly only to further violence. The spectacle is made infinitely more agonizing by the realization that all this is a family quarrel. The commoners suffer accordingly: we witness the grief of a father who has mistakenly killed his son in battle, and a son who has killed his father (2.5). The people, seldom seen, are no longer political troublemakers but mere victims, waiting patiently for an end. A recurrent emblem used to convey the utter futility of this war is the molehill. York is mockingly crowned before his execution on a molehill, and King Henry retires from a battle to a molehill in order to meditate on the happy contemplative life he has been denied. The molehill suggests the ironic perversity of the quest for worldly power, whereby those who possess power are incapable of exercising it wisely, and those who burn with ambition are denied legitimate opportunity.

One sure sign of moral chaos throughout this play is the phenomenon of oath breaking. In the opening scene, Richard of York accepts under oath an obligation to honor Henry VI as his king in return for being named king after Henry's death, but is soon talked out of his promise by his son Richard on the specious grounds that the oath was not made before "a true and lawful magistrate" (1.2.23). This masterful equivocation prepares us for Richard's later perfidies. (In Shakespeare's sources, Hall and Holinshed Parliament plays a major role in working out the compromise between York and Henry; Shakespeare shows us instead a personal agreement made between two contending leaders on the basis of private will and assertion of military power, and easily broken on the same pragmatic grounds.) King Henry is no less forsworn in denying to his own son the crown bestowed on him as birthright by sacred law and custom. Lewis the French King excuses his shifting of alliance from King Henry to the Yorkists on the grounds of simple expediency. Clarence forswears his oaths made to his brother Edward and changes sides in the wars, offended at Edward's perfidy in having renounced his intent to marry the French King's sister-in-law. Soon Clarence is back again in the Yorkist camp, having now betrayed the promises he made to the Lancastrians. Warwick the king-maker forswears his oaths to Edward because Edward has undermined Warwick's embassy to France. Where in fact do truth and justice reside, now that England is governed by two kings who are both forsworn? The common people sense this dilemma, as revealed in the attitudes of two game-keepers: they capture Henry to whom they were once loyal because they are now "sworn in all allegiance" to Edward, but would be true subjects again to Henry "If he were seated as King Edward is" (3.1.70, 95). Political and military reality governs political ethics; the ruler to be acknowledged is he who can establish control.

Another sign of moral decay in this play is the dominance of vengeful purpose. *3 Henry VI* indeed can be viewed as a kind of revenge play in which Richard of Gloucester finally emerges as the consummate avenger in a society of avengers. In the opening confrontation between the Yorkists and Lancastrians, Warwick taunts the Lancastrians with having lost many of their fathers in the recent military action at St. Albans; the fathers of Northumberland, Westmorland, and Clifford have all fallen in that one battle. The sons of course vow vengeance. Clifford, renowned as "the butcher" for his cruelty, exacts a terrible price for his father's death through the slaughter of the defenseless young Rutland and the mocking execution of Rutland's father, the Duke of York. York's surviving sons take vengeance not only on Clifford but on King Henry, his son Edward, and many others. Warwick turns against Edward of York more to avenge an insult than to aid Henry, and is himself cut down by the Yorkists at Barnet (4.2). The implacable pattern of an eye for an eye eventually takes on a providential meaning, especially as seen from the hindsight of *Richard III*, but as we experience this play in the theater the reality is chiefly one of brutality and horror.

As in earlier plays of the series, the relationships between men and women echo the discord of the English nation, and contribute in turn to further discord. Margaret of Anjou, the remorseless defender of her son Edward's claim, acts with increasingly masculine authority, while her ineffectual husband abdicates responsibility. She is the Lancastrian general, resourceful in battle and often victorious, implacable in vengeance. This inversion of male and female roles is reflected on the Yorkist side by Edward IV's disastrous marriage with Lady Elizabeth Grey. She is the widow of a Lancastrian soldier with no family position or political power to bring to the marriage—nothing, in fact, but her ambition on behalf of her kinsmen. Edward's attraction to her is fleshly and imprudent. To make matters worse, Warwick is at that very moment negotiating a highly favorable marriage treaty for Edward with the King of France. Edward IV thus unconsciously apes the earlier willfulness of his counterpart, Henry VI. Edward IV's snubbing of Warwick leads to the defection of that powerful leader, and through him the defection of Edward's brother Clarence, who has succumbed to the charms of Warwick's daughter Isabel. And whereas *1 Henry VI* at least counterbalances the uxoriousness of Henry with the positive example of Lord Talbot, *3 Henry VI* fails to discover any such central noble character. (To be sure, we are briefly introduced to the young Earl of Richmond, who is to be Henry VII, but only as a glimpse of a hopeful future.) The almost total lack of any distinctly virtuous character gives to *3 Henry VI* its predominantly dismaying and helpless mood. The heroes have been destroyed.

Richard of Gloucester alone seems to profit from England's decline. Like his father, York, his strategy has been to let England flay herself into anarchic vulnerability. Once the father York has disappeared from the scene, young Richard's malevolent character becomes increasingly apparent. No longer merely one of York's brave sons, Richard is the new genius of discord. His bravura soliloquy in scene 2 of Act 3 is often included in performances of *Richard III*, for it yields rich clues to his emerging character: he is ambitious, ruthless, deformed from birth, and above all a consummate deceiver. To the audience he boasts of his ability, claiming that as a hypocrite he will excel the combined talents of Nestor, Ulysses, Sinon, Proteus, and Machiavelli.

The superb self-assurance is arresting, the heartless consistency admirable even though despicable. In a second soliloquy, virtually at the end of the play, having already dispatched Henry VI and his son Edward, Richard confides to the audience that Clarence is to be his next victim. And although Richard pledges fealty to his young nephew Edward, the Yorkist crown prince, at the Yorkist victory celebration with which the play ends, we know that Richard's kiss of peace is no more trustworthy than Judas' kiss given to Christ. All those standing between Richard and the throne are to be eliminated. Clearly, the pious longings for peace expressed by King Edward IV are to be cruelly violated.

HENRY VI
PART THREE

[*Dramatis Personae*

KING HENRY THE SIXTH
QUEEN MARGARET
PRINCE EDWARD, *their son*
DUKE OF EXETER,
EARL OF NORTHUMBERLAND,
EARL OF WESTMORLAND,
EARL OF OXFORD,   *supporters of the house of Lancaster*
LORD CLIFFORD,
SIR JOHN SOMERVILLE,
A HUNTSMAN *guarding Edward*

DUKE OF YORK, *Richard Plantagenet*
EDWARD, *Earl of March, later Duke*
   of York and KING EDWARD IV,
GEORGE, *later Duke of Clarence,*   *York's sons*
RICHARD, *later Duke of Gloucester,*
EARL OF RUTLAND,
LADY GREY, *later Edward IV's queen*
PRINCE EDWARD, *her infant son*
EARL RIVERS, *her brother*
SIR JOHN MORTIMER,   *York's uncles*
SIR HUGH MORTIMER,
DUKE OF NORFOLK,
EARL OF PEMBROKE,
LORD HASTINGS,
LORD STAFFORD,   *supporters of the house of York*
SIR WILLIAM STANLEY,
SIR JOHN MONTGOMERY,
A NOBLEMAN,
TUTOR *of the Earl of Rutland*
Two KEEPERS *or gamekeepers*
Three WATCHMEN *guarding Edward's tent*
A SOLDIER *in the Yorkist army*

EARL OF WARWICK,
MARQUESS MONTAGUE,   *supporters of York and then of Lancaster*
DUKE OF SOMERSET,
HENRY, EARL OF RICHMOND
LIEUTENANT *of the Tower of London*
MAYOR OF YORK

MAYOR OF COVENTRY
A SON *that has killed his father*
A FATHER *that has killed his son*
MESSENGERS
POSTS

KING LEWIS *of France*
LADY BONA, *his sister-in-law*
LORD BOURBON, *French Admiral*

English and French Soldiers, Attendants, Aldermen, a Nurse to Prince Edward

SCENE: *England and France*]

1.1   *Alarum. Enter [Richard] Plantagenet, [Duke of York,] Edward, Richard, Norfolk, Montague, Warwick, [with drum] and soldiers, [wearing white roses in their hats].*

WARWICK
   I wonder how the King escaped our hands.

YORK
   While we pursued the horsemen of the north,
   He slyly stole away and left his men;
   Whereat the great lord of Northumberland,
   Whose warlike ears could never brook retreat,   5
   Cheered up the drooping army, and himself,
   Lord Clifford, and Lord Stafford, all abreast,
   Charged our main battle's front and, breaking in,   8
   Were by the swords of common soldiers slain.   9

EDWARD
   Lord Stafford's father, Duke of Buckingham,
   Is either slain or wounded dangerous;   11
   I cleft his beaver with a downright blow.   12
   That this is true, Father, behold his blood.
                    [He shows his bloody sword.]

MONTAGUE *[To York]*
   And, brother, here's the Earl of Wiltshire's blood,   14
   Whom I encountered as the battles joined.   15
                    [He shows his sword.]

RICHARD *[Showing the Duke of Somerset's head]*
   Speak thou for me and tell them what I did.

1.1. Location: London. The Parliament House (see ll. 35–39, 71, etc.),
but also referred to as King Henry VI's palace; see l. 25. The throne
is onstage, seemingly on a raised platform.
s.d. Alarum trumpet call to arms. (York and his followers, in hot pursuit
of King Henry, have just arrived from St. Albans.)   **drum** drummer.
white roses (The badge of the house of York.)   **5 brook** endure.   **retreat**
the call sounding withdrawal from the attack   **8 battle's** army's
9 Were . . . slain (In *2 Henry VI*, 5.2, it is York who kills old Clifford.)
11 dangerous dangerously   **12 beaver** face guard of a helmet, i.e., here
the helmet itself   **14 brother** (Montague was actually brother to
Warwick, but his father, Salisbury of *2 Henry VI*, was brother-in-law of
York.)   **15 battles joined** battalions joined in combat

YORK

Richard hath best deserved of all my sons.
But is Your Grace dead, my lord of Somerset?   18

NORFOLK

Such hap have all the line of John of Gaunt!   19

RICHARD

Thus do I hope to shake King Henry's head.

WARWICK

And so do I. Victorious prince of York,
Before I see thee seated in that throne   22
Which now the house of Lancaster usurps,
I vow by heaven these eyes shall never close.
This is the palace of the fearful King,   25
And this the regal seat. Possess it, York,
For this is thine and not King Henry's heirs'.

YORK

Assist me, then, sweet Warwick, and I will,
For hither we have broken in by force.

NORFOLK

We'll all assist you. He that flies shall die.

YORK

Thanks, gentle Norfolk. Stay by me, my lords;
And soldiers, stay and lodge by me this night.   32
                    They go up [to the chair of state].

WARWICK

And when the King comes, offer him no violence,
Unless he seek to thrust you out perforce.   34

YORK

The Queen this day here holds her Parliament,
But little thinks we shall be of her council.   36
By words or blows here let us win our right.

---

18 But . . . Somerset i.e., are you really dead, my lord. (Like his son,
York contemptuously addresses his slain enemy.)   **19 Such . . . Gaunt**
(The descendants of John of Gaunt, to whom Norfolk wishes ill luck,
include King Henry VI as well as Somerset who is already dead.)
22 Before i.e., until   **25 fearful** timid   **32 s.d. They go up** i.e., Plantagenet, his sons, Norfolk, Montague, and Warwick, all seemingly go up
onto the dais or raised platform supporting the throne. (The soldiers
may withdraw at this point; they must reenter later at l. 169.)   **34 perforce** by force   **36 of her council** (1) taking part in the Privy Council
meeting (2) serving as confidential advisers

RICHARD
  Armed as we are, let's stay within this house.
WARWICK
  "The Bloody Parliament" shall this be called,
  Unless Plantagenet, Duke of York, be king   40
  And bashful Henry deposed, whose cowardice
  Hath made us bywords to our enemies.   42
YORK
  Then leave me not, my lords. Be resolute.
  I mean to take possession of my right.
WARWICK
  Neither the King, nor he that loves him best,
  The proudest he that holds up Lancaster,   46
  Dares stir a wing if Warwick shake his bells.   47
  I'll plant Plantagenet, root him up who dares.
  Resolve thee, Richard; claim the English crown.   49
                    [*York seats himself in the throne.*]

           Flourish. Enter King Henry, Clifford,
           Northumberland, Westmorland, Exeter,
           and the rest. [*All wear red roses.*]

KING HENRY
  My lords, look where the sturdy rebel sits,
  Even in the chair of state! Belike he means,   51
  Backed by the power of Warwick, that false peer,
  To aspire unto the crown and reign as king.
  Earl of Northumberland, he slew thy father,
  And thine, Lord Clifford, and you both have vowed
    revenge
  On him, his sons, his favorites, and his friends.
NORTHUMBERLAND
  If I be not, heavens be revenged on me!   57
CLIFFORD
  The hope thereof makes Clifford mourn in steel.   58

---

40 be become   **42 bywords** i.e., objects of scorn.   **our enemies** i.e., the
French   **46 he . . . up** person that supports   **47 shake his bells** (Bells
were sometimes fastened to the legs of a falcon to incite it to greater
ferocity.)   **49 Resolve thee** be resolute   **s.d. Flourish** trumpet fanfare.
red roses (The badge of the house of Lancaster.)   **51 chair of state**
throne.   **Belike** evidently   **57 be not** i.e., be not avenged   **58 in steel**
i.e., in armor, not in mourning attire

WESTMORLAND
  What, shall we suffer this? Let's pluck him down.
  My heart for anger burns. I cannot brook it.
KING HENRY
  Be patient, gentle Earl of Westmorland.
CLIFFORD
  Patience is for poltroons, such as he.   62
  He durst not sit there, had your father lived.
  My gracious lord, here in the Parliament
  Let us assail the family of York.
NORTHUMBERLAND
  Well hast thou spoken, cousin. Be it so.   66
KING HENRY
  Ah, know you not the city favors them,   67
  And they have troops of soldiers at their beck?
EXETER
  But when the Duke is slain, they'll quickly fly.
KING HENRY
  Far be the thought of this from Henry's heart,
  To make a shambles of the Parliament House!   71
  Cousin of Exeter, frowns, words, and threats
  Shall be the war that Henry means to use.—
  Thou factious Duke of York, descend my throne
  And kneel for grace and mercy at my feet!
  I am thy sovereign.
YORK   I am thine.
EXETER
  For shame, come down. He made thee Duke of York. 77
YORK
  It was my inheritance, as the earldom was.   78
EXETER
  Thy father was a traitor to the crown.   79

62 poltroons arrant cowards. **he** i.e., York, who must not be impatient
for the throne, in Clifford's view **66 cousin** kinsman (also in l. 72)
67 the city i.e., London **71 shambles** slaughterhouse **77–78 He ...
was** (Cf. *1 Henry VI*, 3.1.161–174, where the King restored to Richard
the whole inheritance of the house of York, which included the earldom
of March.) **79 Thy ... crown** (On the execution of Richard, Earl of
Cambridge, for treason by Henry V, see *Henry V*, 2.2, and *1 Henry VI*,
2.4.90–94, 2.5.84–91.)

WARWICK
　Exeter, thou art a traitor to the crown
　In following this usurping Henry.

CLIFFORD
　Whom should he follow but his natural king?

WARWICK
　True, Clifford. That's Richard, Duke of York.

KING HENRY [*To York*]
　And shall I stand, and thou sit in my throne?

YORK
　It must and shall be so. Content thyself.

WARWICK [*To King Henry*]
　Be Duke of Lancaster. Let him be King.

WESTMORLAND
　He is both King and Duke of Lancaster,
　And that the lord of Westmorland shall maintain.

WARWICK
　And Warwick shall disprove it. You forget
　That we are those which chased you from the field
　And slew your fathers, and with colors spread　　91
　Marched through the city to the palace gates.

NORTHUMBERLAND
　Yes, Warwick, I remember it to my grief;
　And, by his soul, thou and thy house shall rue it.　94

WESTMORLAND
　Plantagenet, of thee and these thy sons,
　Thy kinsmen and thy friends, I'll have more lives
　Than drops of blood were in my father's veins.　　97

CLIFFORD
　Urge it no more, lest that, instead of words,
　I send thee, Warwick, such a messenger
　As shall revenge his death before I stir.　　　100

91 colors battle flags　**94 his** i.e., the second Earl of Northumberland's, who fell at St. Albans on the Lancastrian side. (This event is not shown in *2 Henry VI*.) The speaker is the third earl.　**97 my father's** (Three noble fathers died on the Lancastrian side at St. Albans, according to Hall: Northumberland, old Clifford, and Somerset. Westmorland's father was not a casualty in that battle, but Shakespeare may be replacing Somerset here to keep the symmetry of three.)　**100 his** i.e., old Clifford's; see previous note

WARWICK
>Poor Clifford, how I scorn his worthless threats!

YORK
>Will you we show our title to the crown?   102
>If not, our swords shall plead it in the field.

KING HENRY
>What title hast thou, traitor, to the crown?
>Thy father was, as thou art, Duke of York,   105
>Thy grandfather, Roger Mortimer, Earl of March.
>I am the son of Henry the Fifth,
>Who made the Dauphin and the French to stoop
>And seized upon their towns and provinces.

WARWICK
>Talk not of France, sith thou hast lost it all.   110

KING HENRY
>The Lord Protector lost it, and not I.   111
>When I was crowned I was but nine months old.

RICHARD
>You are old enough now, and yet, methinks, you lose.
>Father, tear the crown from the usurper's head.

EDWARD
>Sweet father, do so. Set it on your head.

MONTAGUE [To York]
>Good brother, as thou lov'st and honorest arms,
>Let's fight it out and not stand caviling thus.

RICHARD
>Sound drums and trumpets, and the King will fly.

YORK   Sons, peace!

NORTHUMBERLAND
>Peace, thou! And give King Henry leave to speak.

WARWICK
>Plantagenet shall speak first. Hear him, lords,
>And be you silent and attentive too,
>For he that interrupts him shall not live.

KING HENRY
>Think'st thou that I will leave my kingly throne,

---

102 Will you do you desire   **105 Thy . . . York** (Shakespeare's historical
inaccuracy; Richard's father was never Duke of York. That title belonged to his oldest brother, Edward, who died at Agincourt; it was
given by Henry VI to Richard.)   **110 sith** since   **111 Lord Protector** i.e.,
Humphrey, Duke of Gloucester

Wherein my grandsire and my father sat?
No! First shall war unpeople this my realm;
Ay, and their colors, often borne in France,
And now in England to our heart's great sorrow,
Shall be my winding-sheet. Why faint you, lords?   129
My title's good, and better far than his.

WARWICK
Prove it, Henry, and thou shalt be king.

KING HENRY
Henry the Fourth by conquest got the crown.

YORK
'Twas by rebellion against his king.

KING HENRY [*Aside*]
I know not what to say; my title's weak.—
Tell me, may not a king adopt an heir?

YORK   What then?

KING HENRY
An if he may, then am I lawful king;   137
For Richard, in the view of many lords,
Resigned the crown to Henry the Fourth,
Whose heir my father was, and I am his.

YORK
He rose against him, being his sovereign,   141
And made him to resign his crown perforce.

WARWICK
Suppose, my lords, he did it unconstrained,
Think you 'twere prejudicial to his crown?   144

EXETER
No, for he could not so resign his crown
But that the next heir should succeed and reign.

KING HENRY
Art thou against us, Duke of Exeter?

EXETER
His is the right, and therefore pardon me.   148

YORK
Why whisper you, my lords, and answer not?

---

129 **winding-sheet** sheet in which a corpse was wrapped.   **faint** lose
heart   **137 An if** if   **141 him, being** i.e., Richard, who was
144 'twere . . . crown it would invalidate his, Richard's, entitlement to
the throne   **148 His** i.e., York's

EXETER
My conscience tells me he is lawful king.

KING HENRY [*Aside*]
All will revolt from me and turn to him.

NORTHUMBERLAND
Plantagenet, for all the claim thou lay'st,
Think not that Henry shall be so deposed.

WARWICK
Deposed he shall be, in despite of all.   154

NORTHUMBERLAND
Thou art deceived. 'Tis not thy southern power   155
Of Essex, Norfolk, Suffolk, nor of Kent,
Which makes thee thus presumptuous and proud,
Can set the Duke up in despite of me.

CLIFFORD
King Henry, be thy title right or wrong,
Lord Clifford vows to fight in thy defense.
May that ground gape and swallow me alive
Where I shall kneel to him that slew my father!

KING HENRY
O Clifford, how thy words revive my heart!

YORK
Henry of Lancaster, resign thy crown.
What mutter you, or what conspire you, lords?

WARWICK
Do right unto this princely Duke of York,   166
Or I will fill the house with armèd men,
And over the chair of state, where now he sits,
Write up his title with usurping blood.   169
He stamps with his foot, and the
soldiers show themselves.

KING HENRY
My lord of Warwick, hear but one word:
Let me for this my lifetime reign as king.

YORK
Confirm the crown to me and to mine heirs,
And thou shalt reign in quiet while thou liv'st.   173

---

154 despite spite (also in l. 158)   **155 deceived** mistaken   **166 Do right
unto** deal justly with   **169 usurping blood** i.e., the blood of usurping
Henry VI   **173 while** as long as

KING HENRY
  I am content. Richard Plantagenet,
  Enjoy the kingdom after my decease.
CLIFFORD
  What wrong is this unto the Prince your son!
WARWICK
  What good is this to England and himself!   177
WESTMORLAND
  Base, fearful, and despairing Henry!
CLIFFORD
  How hast thou injured both thyself and us!
WESTMORLAND
  I cannot stay to hear these articles.   180
NORTHUMBERLAND   Nor I.
CLIFFORD
  Come, cousin, let us tell the Queen these news.
WESTMORLAND
  Farewell, fainthearted and degenerate King,
  In whose cold blood no spark of honor bides.   184
                              [*Exit with his men.*]

NORTHUMBERLAND
  Be thou a prey unto the house of York
  And die in bonds for this unmanly deed!   186
                              [*Exit with his men.*]

CLIFFORD
  In dreadful war mayst thou be overcome,
  Or live in peace abandoned and despised!
                              [*Exit with his men.*]

WARWICK
  Turn this way, Henry, and regard them not.
EXETER
  They seek revenge and therefore will not yield.   190
KING HENRY
  Ah, Exeter!
WARWICK   Why should you sigh, my lord?
KING HENRY
  Not for myself, Lord Warwick, but my son,

---

177 What . . . to i.e., what a good thing for. (Warwick welcomes Henry's
decision.) **180 articles** terms of agreement **184 cold** listless, cowardly
186 bonds fetters **190 revenge** i.e., for their fathers' deaths

Whom I unnaturally shall disinherit.
But be it as it may: [*To York*] I here entail   194
The crown to thee and to thine heirs forever,
Conditionally, that here thou take an oath
To cease this civil war, and whilst I live
To honor me as thy king and sovereign,
And neither by treason nor hostility
To seek to put me down and reign thyself.

YORK
This oath I willingly take and will perform.

WARWICK
Long live King Henry! Plantagenet, embrace him.
                    [*York descends and embraces Henry.*]

KING HENRY
And long live thou and these thy forward sons!   203

YORK
Now York and Lancaster are reconciled.

EXETER
Accurst be he that seeks to make them foes!   205
                    Sennet. Here they come down.

YORK
Farewell, my gracious lord. I'll to my castle.   206
              [*Exeunt York and his sons with their men.*]

WARWICK
And I'll keep London with my soldiers.
                    [*Exit Warwick with his men.*]

NORFOLK
And I to Norfolk with my followers.
                    [*Exit Norfolk with his men.*]

MONTAGUE
And I unto the sea, from whence I came.   209
                    [*Exit Montague with his men.*]

---

194 entail bequeath irrevocably   **203 forward** precocious, zealous,
promising   **205 s.d. Sennet** trumpet notes signaling a procession. **Here
they come down** (York and his sons, together with Norfolk, Montague,
and Warwick, have evidently been on the dais around the throne since
l. 32. Once York has descended and embraced Henry, formalizing their
agreement, the rest of the York faction can descend and prepare to
depart.)   **206 castle** i.e., Sandal Castle in Yorkshire. (See next scene.)
209 unto the sea (Actually, Montague appears in scene 2 at Sandal
Castle, not at the sea; possibly he is confused here with his uncle,
William Neville, Baron Falconbridge. See l. 239 below.)

KING HENRY
  And I, with grief and sorrow, to the court.

  Enter the Queen [*Margaret and Edward,*
  Prince of Wales].

EXETER
  Here comes the Queen, whose looks bewray her anger.   211
  I'll steal away.
KING HENRY   Exeter, so will I.   [*They start to leave.*]
QUEEN MARGARET
  Nay, go not from me. I will follow thee.
KING HENRY
  Be patient, gentle Queen, and I will stay.
QUEEN MARGARET
  Who can be patient in such extremes?
  Ah, wretched man! Would I had died a maid
  And never seen thee, never borne thee son,
  Seeing thou hast proved so unnatural a father!   218
  Hath he deserved to lose his birthright thus?
  Hadst thou but loved him half so well as I,
  Or felt that pain which I did for him once,
  Or nourished him as I did with my blood,
  Thou wouldst have left thy dearest heart-blood there,
  Rather than have made that savage duke thine heir
  And disinherited thine only son.
PRINCE
  Father, you cannot disinherit me.
  If you be king, why should not I succeed?
KING HENRY
  Pardon me, Margaret. Pardon me, sweet son.
  The Earl of Warwick and the Duke enforced me.
QUEEN MARGARET
  Enforced thee? Art thou king, and wilt be forced?
  I shame to hear thee speak. Ah, timorous wretch!
  Thou hast undone thyself, thy son, and me,
  And given unto the house of York such head   233
  As thou shalt reign but by their sufferance.   234
  To entail him and his heirs unto the crown,
  What is it but to make thy sepulcher

211 bewray betray, reveal   **218 unnatural** i.e., showing no feeling for a
son   **233 head** i.e., free rein   **234 As** that

And creep into it far before thy time?
Warwick is Chancellor and the lord of Calais;
Stern Falconbridge commands the narrow seas,   239
The Duke is made Protector of the realm,   240
And yet shalt thou be safe? Such safety finds
The trembling lamb environèd with wolves.   242
Had I been there, which am a silly woman,   243
The soldiers should have tossed me on their pikes   244
Before I would have granted to that act.   245
But thou preferr'st thy life before thine honor;
And seeing thou dost, I here divorce myself
Both from thy table, Henry, and thy bed,
Until that act of Parliament be repealed
Whereby my son is disinherited.
The northern lords that have forsworn thy colors   251
Will follow mine, if once they see them spread;
And spread they shall be, to thy foul disgrace
And utter ruin of the house of York.
Thus do I leave thee. Come, son, let's away.
Our army is ready. Come, we'll after them.

KING HENRY
Stay, gentle Margaret, and hear me speak.

QUEEN MARGARET
Thou hast spoke too much already. Get thee gone.

KING HENRY
Gentle son Edward, thou wilt stay with me?

QUEEN MARGARET
Ay, to be murdered by his enemies!

PRINCE
When I return with victory from the field,
I'll see Your Grace. Till then I'll follow her.

QUEEN MARGARET
Come, son, away. We may not linger thus.
          [*Exeunt Queen Margaret and the Prince.*]

KING HENRY
Poor Queen! How love to me and to her son

---

239 Falconbridge i.e., William Neville or his son Thomas. (See l. 209
above, and note.)   **narrow seas** i.e., English Channel   **240 Duke** i.e.,
Duke of York   **242 environèd** surrounded   **243 silly** helpless
244 tossed impaled.   **pikes** long steel-pointed or axlike weapons
245 granted yielded   **251 The northern lords** i.e., Northumberland,
Westmorland, and Clifford (as also in the *three lords* of l. 270)

Hath made her break out into terms of rage!   265
Revenged may she be on that hateful duke,
Whose haughty spirit, wingèd with desire,
Will cost my crown, and like an empty eagle   268
Tire on the flesh of me and of my son!   269
The loss of those three lords torments my heart.
I'll write unto them and entreat them fair.   271
Come, cousin, you shall be the messenger.

EXETER
And I, I hope, shall reconcile them all.

                              Flourish. Exeunt.

❖

1.2   *Enter Richard, Edward, and Montague.*

RICHARD
Brother, though I be youngest, give me leave.   1

EDWARD
No, I can better play the orator.

MONTAGUE
But I have reasons strong and forcible.

        Enter the Duke of York.

YORK
Why, how now, sons and brother, at a strife?   4
What is your quarrel? How began it first?

EDWARD
No quarrel, but a slight contention.

YORK   About what?

RICHARD
About that which concerns Your Grace and us:
The crown of England, Father, which is yours.

YORK
Mine, boy? Not till King Henry be dead.

---

265 terms words   **268 cost** i.e., deprive me of (with a pun on *coast*, attack, fly from the straight course, a metaphor that generates the image of the eagle).   **empty** hungry   **269 Tire** feed ravenously   **271 fair** civilly, kindly

1.2. Location: Sandal Castle (the Duke of York's castle) in Yorkshire.
1 give me leave permit me (to speak first)   **4 brother** (See 1.1.14, note.)

RICHARD

Your right depends not on his life or death.

EDWARD

Now you are heir; therefore enjoy it now.

By giving the house of Lancaster leave to breathe,   13

It will outrun you, Father, in the end.

YORK

I took an oath that he should quietly reign.

EDWARD

But for a kingdom any oath may be broken.

I would break a thousand oaths to reign one year.

RICHARD

No. God forbid Your Grace should be forsworn.

YORK

I shall be, if I claim by open war.

RICHARD

I'll prove the contrary, if you'll hear me speak.

YORK

Thou canst not, son. It is impossible.

RICHARD

An oath is of no moment, being not took   22

Before a true and lawful magistrate

That hath authority over him that swears.

Henry had none, but did usurp the place.

Then, seeing 'twas he that made you to depose,   26

Your oath, my lord, is vain and frivolous.

Therefore, to arms! And, Father, do but think

How sweet a thing it is to wear a crown,

Within whose circuit is Elysium   30

And all that poets feign of bliss and joy.   31

Why do we linger thus? I cannot rest

Until the white rose that I wear be dyed

Even in the lukewarm blood of Henry's heart.

YORK

Richard, enough. I will be king, or die.

[*To Montague.*] Brother, thou shalt to London presently 36

And whet on Warwick to this enterprise.

---

13 to breathe i.e., to enjoy a respite   **22 moment** significance
26 depose take an oath   **30 Elysium** the classical abode after life of
those beloved of the gods   **31 feign** portray imaginatively   **36 presently**
immediately

Thou, Richard, shalt to the Duke of Norfolk
And tell him privily of our intent.   39
You, Edward, shall unto my Lord Cobham,
With whom the Kentishmen will willingly rise.
In them I trust, for they are soldiers,
Witty, courteous, liberal, full of spirit.   43
While you are thus employed, what resteth more   44
But that I seek occasion how to rise,
And yet the King not privy to my drift,   46
Nor any of the house of Lancaster?

     Enter a Messenger.

But stay, what news? Why com'st thou in such post?   48
MESSENGER
The Queen, with all the northern earls and lords,
Intend here to besiege you in your castle.
She is hard by with twenty thousand men,
And therefore fortify your hold, my lord.   52
YORK
Ay, with my sword. What, think'st thou that we
   fear them?
Edward and Richard, you shall stay with me;
My brother Montague shall post to London.
Let noble Warwick, Cobham, and the rest,
Whom we have left protectors of the King,
With powerful policy strengthen themselves   58
And trust not simple Henry nor his oaths.
MONTAGUE
Brother, I go. I'll win them, fear it not.
And thus most humbly I do take my leave.
                   Exit Montague.

     Enter [Sir John] Mortimer and [Sir Hugh,]
     his brother.

YORK
Sir John and Sir Hugh Mortimer, mine uncles,

---

39 privily secretly   **43 Witty** intelligent.   **liberal** large-minded   **44 what
resteth more** what else remains   **46 privy to** aware of   **48 post** haste
52 hold stronghold, castle   **58 policy** stratagem, cunning

You are come to Sandal in a happy hour.   63
The army of the Queen mean to besiege us.

SIR JOHN
She shall not need. We'll meet her in the field.

YORK   What, with five thousand men?

RICHARD
Ay, with five hundred, Father, for a need.   67
A woman's general. What should we fear?

A march afar off.

EDWARD
I hear their drums. Let's set our men in order,
And issue forth and bid them battle straight.   70

YORK
Five men to twenty! Though the odds be great,
I doubt not, uncle, of our victory.
Many a battle have I won in France
Whenas the enemy hath been ten to one.   74
Why should I not now have the like success?   75

Alarum. Exeunt.

1.3   [*Alarums.*] *Enter Rutland and his Tutor.*

RUTLAND
Ah, whither shall I fly to scape their hands?
Ah, tutor, look where bloody Clifford comes!

Enter Clifford [and soldiers].

CLIFFORD
Chaplain, away! Thy priesthood saves thy life.
As for the brat of this accursèd duke,   4
Whose father slew my father, he shall die.

TUTOR
And I, my lord, will bear him company.

___

63 in a happy hour opportunely   **67 for a need** if necessary
70 straight immediately   **74 Whenas** when   **75 the like** a similar

**1.3. Location: Field of battle between Sandal Castle and Wakefield. The
action follows continuously from the previous scene.**
s.d. Alarums calls to arms (signaling by sound effects a battle fought
offstage)   **4 duke** i.e., Duke of York, who killed old Clifford in
2 Henry VI, 5.2

CLIFFORD   Soldiers, away with him!

TUTOR
  Ah, Clifford, murder not this innocent child,
  Lest thou be hated both of God and man!
                              Exit [dragged off by soldiers].

CLIFFORD
  How now, is he dead already? Or is it fear
  That makes him close his eyes? I'll open them.

RUTLAND
  So looks the pent-up lion o'er the wretch   12
  That trembles under his devouring paws;
  And so he walks, insulting o'er his prey,   14
  And so he comes, to rend his limbs asunder.
  Ah, gentle Clifford, kill me with thy sword   16
  And not with such a cruel threatening look!
  Sweet Clifford, hear me speak before I die!
  I am too mean a subject for thy wrath.   19
  Be thou revenged on men, and let me live.

CLIFFORD
  In vain thou speak'st, poor boy. My father's blood
  Hath stopped the passage where thy words should enter.

RUTLAND
  Then let my father's blood open it again.
  He is a man, and, Clifford, cope with him.   24

CLIFFORD
  Had I thy brethren here, their lives and thine
  Were not revenge sufficient for me;
  No, if I digged up thy forefathers' graves
  And hung their rotten coffins up in chains,
  It could not slake mine ire nor ease my heart.   29
  The sight of any of the house of York
  Is as a fury to torment my soul;
  And till I root out their accursèd line
  And leave not one alive, I live in hell.
  Therefore—   *[Lifting his sword.]*

12 **pent-up** caged, hence fierce and hungry   14 **insulting** gloating,
exulting   16 **gentle** noble (with ironic suggestion of "free from harsh-
ness")   19 **mean** lowly. (Rutland appeals to the popular notion that
because the lion was a royal beast it would show compassion to women
and children. See 2.2.11–12.)   24 **cope with** engage in combat with
29 **slake** lessen

RUTLAND
  O, let me pray before I take my death!
  To thee I pray. Sweet Clifford, pity me!
CLIFFORD
  Such pity as my rapier's point affords.
RUTLAND
  I never did thee harm. Why wilt thou slay me?
CLIFFORD
  Thy father hath.
RUTLAND   But 'twas ere I was born.
  Thou hast one son. For his sake pity me,
  Lest in revenge thereof, sith God is just,   41
  He be as miserably slain as I.
  Ah, let me live in prison all my days,
  And when I give occasion of offense,
  Then let me die, for now thou hast no cause.
CLIFFORD   No cause?
  Thy father slew my father. Therefore, die.
                                    [*He stabs him.*]
RUTLAND
  Di faciant laudis summa sit ista tuae!   [*He dies.*] 48
CLIFFORD
  Plantagenet, I come, Plantagenet!
  And this thy son's blood cleaving to my blade
  Shall rust upon my weapon, till thy blood,
  Congealed with this, do make me wipe off both.
                          Exit [*with soldiers, bearing
                                off Rutland's body*].

1.4   *Alarum. Enter Richard, Duke of York.*

YORK
  The army of the Queen hath got the field.   1
  My uncles both are slain in rescuing me,   2
  And all my followers to the eager foe   3
  Turn back and fly, like ships before the wind   4

---

41 sith since   **48 Di . . . tuae** The gods grant that this may be the height
of your glory. (Ovid, *Heroides*, 2.66.)

1.4. Location: The battle of Wakefield continues.
1 got the field won the battle   **2 uncles** i.e., Sir John and Sir Hugh
Mortimer   **3 eager** fierce, zealous   **4 Turn back** turn their backs

Or lambs pursued by hunger-starvèd wolves.
My sons—God knows what hath bechancèd them;
But this I know, they have demeaned themselves   7
Like men born to renown by life or death.
Three times did Richard make a lane to me,
And thrice cried "Courage, Father, fight it out!"
And full as oft came Edward to my side,
With purple falchion painted to the hilt   12
In blood of those that had encountered him.
And when the hardiest warriors did retire,
Richard cried "Charge, and give no foot of ground!"
And cried "A crown, or else a glorious tomb!   16
A scepter, or an earthly sepulcher!"
With this, we charged again, but out, alas!   18
We budged again, as I have seen a swan   19
With bootless labor swim against the tide   20
And spend her strength with overmatching waves.   21

> *A short alarum within.*

Ah, hark! The fatal followers do pursue,   22
And I am faint and cannot fly their fury;
And, were I strong, I would not shun their fury.
The sands are numbered that makes up my life.   25
Here must I stay, and here my life must end.

> *Enter the Queen [Margaret], Clifford,*
> *Northumberland, the young Prince,*
> *and soldiers.*

Come, bloody Clifford, rough Northumberland,
I dare your quenchless fury to more rage.   28
I am your butt, and I abide your shot.   29

NORTHUMBERLAND
　Yield to our mercy, proud Plantagenet.   30
CLIFFORD
　Ay, to such mercy as his ruthless arm,
　With downright payment, showed unto my father.

---

7 demeaned conducted　**12 purple** purple with blood.　**falchion** curved
sword　**16 And cried** (Some text may be missing here; the parallelism of
ll. 9–13 suggests that Edward is quoted as speaking after Richard.)
18 out (An expression of reproach.)　**19 budged** gave way　**20 bootless**
fruitless　**21 with** against　**22 followers** pursuing troops　**25 sands** (of
the hourglass)　**28 dare** defy.　**more** even more　**29 butt** target
30 Yield . . . mercy put yourself at our mercy

Now Phaëthon hath tumbled from his car   33
And made an evening at the noontide prick.   34

YORK
My ashes, as the phoenix, may bring forth   35
A bird that will revenge upon you all;
And in that hope I throw mine eyes to heaven,
Scorning whate'er you can afflict me with.
Why come you not? What? Multitudes, and fear?

CLIFFORD
So cowards fight when they can fly no further;
So doves do peck the falcon's piercing talons;
So desperate thieves, all hopeless of their lives,
Breathe out invectives 'gainst the officers.

YORK
O Clifford, but bethink thee once again,   44
And in thy thought o'errun my former time;   45
And, if thou canst for blushing, view this face,   46
And bite thy tongue, that slanders him with cowardice
Whose frown hath made thee faint and fly ere this!

CLIFFORD
I will not bandy with thee word for word,   49
But buckler with thee blows, twice two for one.   50
                    [*He threatens with his sword.*]

QUEEN MARGARET
Hold, valiant Clifford! For a thousand causes
I would prolong awhile the traitor's life.—
Wrath makes him deaf. Speak thou, Northumberland. 53

NORTHUMBERLAND
Hold, Clifford! Do not honor him so much
To prick thy finger, though to wound his heart.
What valor were it, when a cur doth grin,   56
For one to thrust his hand between his teeth,
When he might spurn him with his foot away?   58

---

33 Phaëthon son of the sun god, who begged his father to allow him to
drive the chariot of the sun; he drove it so near the earth that Zeus
destroyed him with a thunderbolt   **34 noontide prick** exact point of
noon on a sundial   **35 phoenix** fabulous bird that was consumed
through spontaneous combustion and was reborn from its own ashes
44 but bethink thee only call to mind   **45 o'errun** review   **46 for**
despite   **49 bandy** exchange   **50 buckler** join in close combat, grapple
53 him i.e., Clifford   **56 grin** show its teeth   **58 spurn** kick

It is war's prize to take all vantages,   59
And ten to one is no impeach of valor.   60
              [They capture York, who struggles.]

CLIFFORD
Ay, ay, so strives the woodcock with the gin.   61

NORTHUMBERLAND
So doth the coney struggle in the net.   62

YORK
So triumph thieves upon their conquered booty;
So true men yield, with robbers so o'ermatched.   64

NORTHUMBERLAND [*To the Queen*]
What would Your Grace have done unto him now?

QUEEN MARGARET
Brave warriors, Clifford and Northumberland,
Come, make him stand upon this molehill here,
That raught at mountains with outstretchèd arms   68
Yet parted but the shadow with his hand.   69
What, was it you that would be England's king?
Was 't you that reveled in our Parliament   71
And made a preachment of your high descent?
Where are your mess of sons to back you now,   73
The wanton Edward and the lusty George?
And where's that valiant crookback prodigy,   75
Dicky, your boy, that with his grumbling voice
Was wont to cheer his dad in mutinies?
Or, with the rest, where is your darling Rutland?
Look, York, I stained this napkin with the blood   79
That valiant Clifford, with his rapier's point,
Made issue from the bosom of the boy;
And if thine eyes can water for his death,
I give thee this to dry thy cheeks withal.   83
              [She gives him the bloodstained cloth.]
Alas, poor York, but that I hate thee deadly,   84
I should lament thy miserable state.
I prithee, grieve, to make me merry, York.

---

59 prize reward, benefit   **60 impeach** calling in question   **61 woodcock**
(A proverbially stupid bird.)   **gin** snare, trap   **62 coney** rabbit   **64 true**
honest   **68 That raught** he that reached   **69 parted but** only divided.
(The prize York reached for turned out to be illusory.)   **71 reveled** rioted
73 mess group of four   **75 prodigy** monster   **79 napkin** handkerchief
83 withal with   **84 but** were it not

What, hath thy fiery heart so parched thine entrails
That not a tear can fall for Rutland's death?
Why art thou patient, man? Thou shouldst be mad;
And I, to make thee mad, do mock thee thus.
Stamp, rave, and fret, that I may sing and dance.
Thou wouldst be fee'd, I see, to make me sport.   92
York cannot speak, unless he wear a crown.—
A crown for York! And, lords, bow low to him.
Hold you his hands, whilst I do set it on.
          [*She puts a paper crown on his head.*]
Ay, marry, sir, now looks he like a king!   96
Ay, this is he that took King Henry's chair,   97
And this is he was his adopted heir.
But how is it that great Plantagenet
Is crowned so soon, and broke his solemn oath?
As I bethink me, you should not be king
Till our King Henry had shook hands with death.
And will you pale your head in Henry's glory,   103
And rob his temples of the diadem,
Now, in his life, against your holy oath?   105
O, 'tis a fault too-too unpardonable!
Off with the crown, and, with the crown, his head!
And whilst we breathe, take time to do him dead.   108

CLIFFORD
That is my office, for my father's sake.

QUEEN MARGARET
Nay, stay. Let's hear the orisons he makes.   110

YORK
She-wolf of France, but worse than wolves of France,
Whose tongue more poisons than the adder's tooth!
How ill-beseeming is it in thy sex
To triumph, like an Amazonian trull,   114
Upon their woes whom fortune captivates!   115
But that thy face is, vizardlike, unchanging,   116
Made impudent with use of evil deeds,

92 fee'd paid   **96 marry** i.e., indeed. (Originally an oath, "by the Virgin
Mary.")   **97 chair** throne   **103 pale** encircle   **105 life** lifetime
108 breathe rest.   **do him dead** kill him   **110 orisons** prayers   **114 triumph** exult.   **Amazonian** from the race of legendary female warriors.
trull wench, whore   **115 Upon . . . captivates** upon the woes of those
whom fortune takes captive   **116 But that** were it not that.   **vizardlike**
masklike

I would essay, proud Queen, to make thee blush.   118
To tell thee whence thou cam'st, of whom derived,
Were shame enough to shame thee, wert thou not
    shameless.
Thy father bears the type of King of Naples,   121
Of both the Sicils and Jerusalem,   122
Yet not so wealthy as an English yeoman.   123
Hath that poor monarch taught thee to insult?
It needs not, nor it boots thee not, proud Queen,   125
Unless the adage must be verified
That beggars mounted run their horse to death.
'Tis beauty that doth oft make women proud;
But, God he knows, thy share thereof is small.
'Tis virtue that doth make them most admired;
The contrary doth make thee wondered at.
'Tis government that makes them seem divine;   132
The want thereof makes thee abominable.   133
Thou art as opposite to every good
As the Antipodes are unto us,   135
Or as the south to the Septentrion.   136
O tiger's heart wrapped in a woman's hide!
How couldst thou drain the lifeblood of the child,
To bid the father wipe his eyes withal,
And yet be seen to bear a woman's face?
Women are soft, mild, pitiful, and flexible;   141
Thou stern, obdurate, flinty, rough, remorseless.
Bidd'st thou me rage? Why, now thou hast thy wish.
Wouldst have me weep? Why, now thou hast thy will.
For raging wind blows up incessant showers,
And, when the rage allays, the rain begins.[*He weeps.*] 146
These tears are my sweet Rutland's obsequies,   147
And every drop cries vengeance for his death
'Gainst thee, fell Clifford, and thee, false Frenchwoman. 149

---

118 essay attempt   **121 type** title   **122 both the Sicils** i.e., Sicily and
Naples (known as the Kingdom of the Two Sicilies)   **123 yeoman** land-
owner below rank of gentleman   **125 needs not** is unnecessary.   **boots**
profits   **132 government** self-government   **133 want** lack   **135 Antipodes** people dwelling on the opposite side of the world   **136 Septentrion** the seven stars, i.e., the Big Dipper, representing the north
141 pitiful capable of pity   **146 allays** abates   **147 obsequies** funeral
observances   **149 fell** cruel

NORTHUMBERLAND
   Beshrew me, but his passions moves me so   150
   That hardly can I check my eyes from tears.   151
YORK
   That face of his the hungry cannibals
   Would not have touched, would not have stained with
      blood.
   But you are more inhuman, more inexorable,
   O, ten times more, than tigers of Hyrcania.   155
   See, ruthless Queen, a hapless father's tears!
   This cloth thou dippedst in blood of my sweet boy,
   And I with tears do wash the blood away.
   Keep thou the napkin, and go boast of this;
   And if thou tell'st the heavy story right,   160
   Upon my soul, the hearers will shed tears.
   Yea, even my foes will shed fast-falling tears
   And say, "Alas, it was a piteous deed!"
   There, take the crown, and with the crown my curse;   164
   And in thy need such comfort come to thee
   As now I reap at thy too cruel hand!
   Hardhearted Clifford, take me from the world.
   My soul to heaven, my blood upon your heads!
NORTHUMBERLAND
   Had he been slaughterman to all my kin,
   I should not for my life but weep with him,
   To see how inly sorrow gripes his soul.   171
QUEEN MARGARET
   What, weeping-ripe, my Lord Northumberland?   172
   Think but upon the wrong he did us all,
   And that will quickly dry thy melting tears.
CLIFFORD [*Stabbing him*]
   Here's for my oath. Here's for my father's death.
QUEEN MARGARET [*Stabbing him*]
   And here's to right our gentlehearted king.

---

150 Beshrew curse   **151 check** restrain   **155 Hyrcania** region of the
ancient Persian empire, reputed to abound in wild beasts. (See *Aeneid*,
4.366–367.)   **160 heavy** sorrowful   **164 There . . . crown** (Unless his
hands are restrained, as at l. 95, York probably removes his paper
crown and throws it to them, as with the handkerchief at l. 159.)
171 inly inward.   **gripes** grieves (with suggestion also of *grips*, seizes)
172 weeping-ripe ready to weep

YORK
    Open Thy gate of mercy, gracious God!
    My soul flies through these wounds to seek out Thee.
                                        [*He dies.*]

QUEEN MARGARET
    Off with his head and set it on York gates,
    So York may overlook the town of York.
                        Flourish. Exeunt [*with the body*].

❖

2.1 *A march. Enter Edward, Richard,
and their power.*

EDWARD
  I wonder how our princely father scaped,
  Or whether he be scaped away or no
  From Clifford's and Northumberland's pursuit.
  Had he been ta'en, we should have heard the news;
  Had he been slain, we should have heard the news;
  Or had he scaped, methinks we should have heard
  The happy tidings of his good escape.
  How fares my brother? Why is he so sad?
RICHARD
  I cannot joy until I be resolved   9
  Where our right valiant father is become.   10
  I saw him in the battle range about
  And watched him how he singled Clifford forth.
  Methought he bore him in the thickest troop   13
  As doth a lion in a herd of neat,   14
  Or as a bear encompassed round with dogs,
  Who having pinched a few and made them cry,   16
  The rest stand all aloof and bark at him.
  So fared our father with his enemies;
  So fled his enemies my warlike father.   19
  Methinks 'tis prize enough to be his son.
  See how the morning opes her golden gates
  And takes her farewell of the glorious sun!   22
  How well resembles it the prime of youth,
  Trimmed like a younker prancing to his love!   24
EDWARD
  Dazzle mine eyes, or do I see three suns?   25

2.1. Location: Fields near the Welsh border or marches (l. 140), historically identified as near Mortimer's Cross in Herefordshire, several days after the battle of Wakefield.
s.d. power army **9 resolved** informed **10 Where . . . become** what is become of our very valiant father **13 bore him** conducted himself
14 neat cattle **16 pinched** bit **19 fled his enemies** his enemies fled from **22 farewell** (The dawn is pictured as remaining behind while the sun ascends the sky.) **24 Trimmed** dressed up. **younker** young man
25 three suns (According to the chronicles, it was because Edward saw three suns as a favorable omen before the battle of Mortimer's Cross, in which he triumphed, that he chose the bright sun as his badge.)

RICHARD

Three glorious suns, each one a perfect sun,
Not separated with the racking clouds,   27
But severed in a pale clear-shining sky.
See, see! They join, embrace, and seem to kiss,
As if they vowed some league inviolable.
Now are they but one lamp, one light, one sun.
In this the heaven figures some event.   32

EDWARD

'Tis wondrous strange, the like yet never heard of.
I think it cites us, brother, to the field,   34
That we, the sons of brave Plantagenet,
Each one already blazing by our meeds,   36
Should notwithstanding join our lights together
And overshine the earth as this the world.   38
Whate'er it bodes, henceforward will I bear
Upon my target three fair-shining suns.   40

RICHARD

Nay, bear three daughters. By your leave I speak it,   41
You love the breeder better than the male.   42

Enter one [a Messenger] blowing [a horn].

But what art thou, whose heavy looks foretell   43
Some dreadful story hanging on thy tongue?

MESSENGER

Ah, one that was a woeful looker-on
Whenas the noble Duke of York was slain,   46
Your princely father and my loving lord!

EDWARD

O, speak no more, for I have heard too much.

RICHARD

Say how he died, for I will hear it all.

MESSENGER

Environèd he was with many foes,   50

---

27 with by. **racking** driving, scudding **32 figures** prefigures **34 cites** incites, impels **36 meeds** worth, deserts **38 overshine** (1) shine upon (2) surpass in shining. **this** i.e., this phenomenon **40 target** shield **41 daughters** i.e., instead of sons or *suns* **42 breeder** female. (Richard jokes about Edward's weakness for women, to be demonstrated in 3.2 and following.) **s.d. blowing a horn** (Express riders thus announced themselves.) **43 heavy** sorrowful **46 Whenas** when **50 Environèd** surrounded

And stood against them, as the hope of Troy   51
Against the Greeks that would have entered Troy.
But Hercules himself must yield to odds;
And many strokes, though with a little ax,
Hews down and fells the hardest-timbered oak.
By many hands your father was subdued,
But only slaughtered by the ireful arm   57
Of unrelenting Clifford and the Queen,
Who crowned the gracious Duke in high despite,
Laughed in his face; and when with grief he wept,
The ruthless Queen gave him to dry his cheeks
A napkin steepèd in the harmless blood
Of sweet young Rutland, by rough Clifford slain.
And after many scorns, many foul taunts,
They took his head, and on the gates of York
They set the same; and there it doth remain,
The saddest spectacle that e'er I viewed.

EDWARD
Sweet Duke of York, our prop to lean upon,
Now thou art gone, we have no staff, no stay.   69
O Clifford, boisterous Clifford! Thou hast slain   70
The flower of Europe for his chivalry;
And treacherously hast thou vanquished him,
For hand to hand he would have vanquished thee.
Now my soul's palace is become a prison.   74
Ah, would she break from hence, that this my body
Might in the ground be closèd up in rest!
For never henceforth shall I joy again.
Never, O, never, shall I see more joy!   78

RICHARD
I cannot weep, for all my body's moisture
Scarce serves to quench my furnace-burning heart;
Nor can my tongue unload my heart's great burden,
For selfsame wind that I should speak withal   82
Is kindling coals that fires all my breast,
And burns me up with flames that tears would quench.
To weep is to make less the depth of grief.

51 the hope of Troy i.e., Hector   **57 ireful** angry   **69 stay** support
70 boisterous savage   **74 soul's palace** i.e., body   **78 see more joy** see
joy any more   **82 For . . . withal** for that very breath that I should use
in speaking

Tears, then, for babes; blows and revenge for me!
Richard, I bear thy name. I'll venge thy death,
Or die renownèd by attempting it.

EDWARD
His name that valiant duke hath left with thee;
His dukedom and his chair with me is left.   90

RICHARD
Nay, if thou be that princely eagle's bird,   91
Show thy descent by gazing 'gainst the sun;   92
For "chair" and "dukedom," "throne" and "kingdom"
  say;
Either that is thine, or else thou wert not his.   94

March. Enter Warwick, Marquess Montague,
and their army.

WARWICK
How now, fair lords? What fare? What news abroad?   95

RICHARD
Great lord of Warwick, if we should recount
Our baleful news, and at each word's deliverance
Stab poniards in our flesh till all were told,   98
The words would add more anguish than the wounds.
O valiant lord, the Duke of York is slain!

EDWARD
O Warwick, Warwick! That Plantagenet,
Which held thee dearly as his soul's redemption,
Is by the stern Lord Clifford done to death.

WARWICK
Ten days ago I drowned these news in tears;
And now, to add more measure to your woes,   105
I come to tell you things sith then befallen.   106
After the bloody fray at Wakefield fought,
Where your brave father breathed his latest gasp,   108
Tidings, as swiftly as the posts could run,   109

---

90 his chair i.e., his ducal seat, but also the claim to the throne   **91 bird**
i.e., offspring   **92 gazing . . . sun** (According to Pliny and other writers,
eagles could gaze unblinkingly at the sun and would test their young by
forcing them to do so.)   **94 that** i.e., the throne, symbolized by the sun.
his i.e., Plantagenet's son   **s.d. army** (The octavo text specifies drum,
i.e., drummer, and ensign along with soldiers.)   **95 What fare** how are
things faring   **98 poniards** daggers   **105 measure** quantity   **106 sith**
since   **108 latest** last   **109 posts** messengers

Were brought me of your loss and his depart.   110
I, then in London, keeper of the King,   111
Mustered my soldiers, gathered flocks of friends,
And very well appointed, as I thought,   113
Marched toward Saint Albans to intercept the Queen,
Bearing the King in my behalf along;   115
For by my scouts I was advertisèd   116
That she was coming with a full intent
To dash our late decree in Parliament   118
Touching King Henry's oath and your succession.   119
Short tale to make, we at Saint Albans met,
Our battles joined, and both sides fiercely fought.   121
But whether 'twas the coldness of the King,
Who looked full gently on his warlike queen,
That robbed my soldiers of their heated spleen,   124
Or whether 'twas report of her success,
Or more than common fear of Clifford's rigor,   126
Who thunders to his captives blood and death,
I cannot judge; but, to conclude with truth,
Their weapons like to lightning came and went;
Our soldiers', like the night owl's lazy flight,
Or like an idle thresher with a flail,   131
Fell gently down, as if they struck their friends.
I cheered them up with justice of our cause,
With promise of high pay and great rewards,
But all in vain. They had no heart to fight,
And we in them no hope to win the day,
So that we fled: the King unto the Queen;
Lord George your brother, Norfolk, and myself   138
In haste, posthaste, are come to join with you.
For in the marches here we heard you were,   140
Making another head to fight again.   141

---

110 depart departure, i.e., death   **111 keeper** jailer   **113 appointed** equipped   **115 in my behalf** for my advantage   **116 advertisèd** informed   **118 dash** overthrow.   **late** recent   **119 Touching** regarding   **121 battles** armies   **124 heated spleen** i.e., courage roused to a high pitch   **126 rigor** fierceness   **131 flail** threshing tool   **138 Lord George** i.e., George, later Duke of Clarence, brother to Edward and Richard   **140 marches** borders (of Wales)   **141 Making another head** raising another armed force

EDWARD

Where is the Duke of Norfolk, gentle Warwick?   142
And when came George from Burgundy to England?

WARWICK

Some six miles off the Duke is with the soldiers;
And for your brother, he was lately sent   145
From your kind aunt, Duchess of Burgundy,   146
With aid of soldiers to this needful war.

RICHARD

'Twas odds, belike, when valiant Warwick fled.   148
Oft have I heard his praises in pursuit,   149
But ne'er till now his scandal of retire.   150

WARWICK

Nor now my scandal, Richard, dost thou hear;
For thou shalt know this strong right hand of mine
Can pluck the diadem from faint Henry's head
And wring the awful scepter from his fist,   154
Were he as famous and as bold in war
As he is famed for mildness, peace, and prayer.

RICHARD

I know it well, Lord Warwick. Blame me not.
'Tis love I bear thy glories make me speak.   158
But in this troublous time what's to be done?
Shall we go throw away our coats of steel
And wrap our bodies in black mourning gowns,
Numb'ring our Ave Marys with our beads?   162
Or shall we on the helmets of our foes
Tell our devotion with revengeful arms?   164
If for the last, say ay, and to it, lords.

WARWICK

Why, therefore Warwick came to seek you out,

---

142 gentle noble   **145 for** as for   **146 Duchess of Burgundy** (A granddaughter of John of Gaunt and distant relative of Richard of York, to
whom, according to the chroniclers, both George and Richard were sent
for protection after York's execution.)   **148 'Twas odds, belike** i.e., no
doubt the odds were very heavy   **149 in pursuit** i.e., for pursuing the
enemy   **150 his . . . retire** i.e., condemnation of him for retreating
154 awful awe-inspiring   **158 make** that makes   **162 beads** rosary
beads (used in reciting *Ave Marys*, i.e., Ave Marias or Hail Marys)
164 Tell our devotion (1) count off our prayers (2) proclaim our love.
(Said ironically.)

And therefore comes my brother Montague.
Attend me, lords. The proud insulting Queen,
With Clifford and the haught Northumberland,   169
And of their feather many more proud birds,
Have wrought the easy-melting King like wax.   171
He swore consent to your succession,
His oath enrollèd in the Parliament,   173
And now to London all the crew are gone
To frustrate both his oath and what besides   175
May make against the house of Lancaster.   176
Their power, I think, is thirty thousand strong.
Now, if the help of Norfolk and myself,
With all the friends that thou, brave Earl of March,   179
Amongst the loving Welshmen canst procure,   180
Will but amount to five-and-twenty thousand,
Why, *via*! To London will we march,   182
And once again bestride our foaming steeds,
And once again cry "Charge!" upon our foes,
But never once again turn back and fly.   185

RICHARD
Ay, now methinks I hear great Warwick speak.
Ne'er may he live to see a sunshine day   187
That cries "Retire!" if Warwick bid him stay.   188

EDWARD
Lord Warwick, on thy shoulder will I lean;
And when thou fail'st—as God forbid the hour!—
Must Edward fall, which peril heaven forfend!   191

WARWICK
No longer Earl of March, but Duke of York;
The next degree is England's royal throne.   193
For King of England shalt thou be proclaimed
In every borough as we pass along;
And he that throws not up his cap for joy
Shall for the fault make forfeit of his head.
King Edward, valiant Richard, Montague,

---

169 haught haughty   **171 wrought** worked on, manipulated
173 enrollèd recorded on official rolls   **175 frustrate** annul.   **what
besides** anything else   **176 make** be effective   **179 Earl of March** i.e.,
Edward, who at his father's death inherited this with other titles
180 loving loyal, friendly   **182 via** forward   **185 turn back** turn our
backs   **187 he** i.e., anyone   **188 stay** stand firm   **191 forfend** forbid
193 degree step, rank

Stay we no longer, dreaming of renown,   199
But sound the trumpets and about our task.

RICHARD
    Then, Clifford, were thy heart as hard as steel,
    As thou hast shown it flinty by thy deeds,
    I come to pierce it or to give thee mine.

EDWARD
    Then strike up drums. God and Saint George for us!   204

    Enter a Messenger.

WARWICK   How now? What news?

MESSENGER
    The Duke of Norfolk sends you word by me
    The Queen is coming with a puissant host;   207
    And craves your company for speedy counsel.

WARWICK
    Why then it sorts, brave warriors. Let's away.   209
                                        Exeunt omnes.

                            ❖

2.2   *Flourish. Enter the King [Henry], the Queen
           [Margaret], Clifford, Northumberland, and
           young Prince, with drum and trumpets.
           [York's head is set above the gates.]*

QUEEN MARGARET
    Welcome, my lord, to this brave town of York.   1
    Yonder's the head of that archenemy
    That sought to be encompassed with your crown.
    Doth not the object cheer your heart, my lord?

KING HENRY
    Ay, as the rocks cheer them that fear their wreck.   5
    To see this sight, it irks my very soul.
    Withhold revenge, dear God! 'Tis not my fault,
    Nor wittingly have I infringed my vow.

---

199 Stay we let us remain   **204 Saint George** patron saint of England
207 puissant powerful   **209 sorts** is fitting, is working out

2.2. Location: Before the walls of York.
s.d. drum drummer.   **trumpets** trumpeters   **1 brave** fine   **5 wreck**
shipwreck, destruction

CLIFFORD
    My gracious liege, this too much lenity
    And harmful pity must be laid aside.
    To whom do lions cast their gentle looks?
    Not to the beast that would usurp their den.
    Whose hand is that the forest bear doth lick?
    Not his that spoils her young before her face.   14
    Who scapes the lurking serpent's mortal sting?
    Not he that sets his foot upon her back.
    The smallest worm will turn, being trodden on,
    And doves will peck in safeguard of their brood.   18
    Ambitious York did level at thy crown,   19
    Thou smiling while he knit his angry brows.
    He, but a duke, would have his son a king
    And raise his issue, like a loving sire;   22
    Thou, being a king, blest with a goodly son,
    Didst yield consent to disinherit him,
    Which argued thee a most unloving father.   25
    Unreasonable creatures feed their young;   26
    And though man's face be fearful to their eyes,   27
    Yet, in protection of their tender ones,
    Who hath not seen them, even with those wings
    Which sometimes they have used with fearful flight,
    Make war with him that climbed unto their nest,
    Offering their own lives in their young's defense?
    For shame, my liege, make them your precedent!
    Were it not pity that this goodly boy
    Should lose his birthright by his father's fault,
    And long hereafter say unto his child,
    "What my great-grandfather and grandsire got,
    My careless father fondly gave away"?   38
    Ah, what a shame were this! Look on the boy,
    And let his manly face, which promiseth
    Successful fortune, steel thy melting heart
    To hold thine own and leave thine own with him.
KING HENRY
    Full well hath Clifford played the orator,

---

14 spoils destroys, seizes as prey   **18 safeguard of** safeguarding
19 level aim   **22 raise** raise in dignity   **25 argued thee** showed you to
be   **26 Unreasonable** not endowed with reason   **27 fearful** causing fear
38 fondly foolishly

Proclaims him king, and many fly to him.
Darraign your battle, for they are at hand.   72

CLIFFORD
I would Your Highness would depart the field.
The Queen hath best success when you are absent.

QUEEN MARGARET
Ay, good my lord, and leave us to our fortune.

KING HENRY
Why, that's my fortune too. Therefore I'll stay.

NORTHUMBERLAND
Be it with resolution then to fight.

PRINCE
My royal Father, cheer these noble lords
And hearten those that fight in your defense.
Unsheathe your sword, good Father; cry "Saint
    George!"   80

> *March. Enter Edward, Warwick, Richard, [George*
> *of] Clarence, Norfolk, Montague, and soldiers.*

EDWARD
Now, perjured Henry, wilt thou kneel for grace   81
And set thy diadem upon my head,
Or bide the mortal fortune of the field?   83

QUEEN MARGARET
Go rate thy minions, proud insulting boy!   84
Becomes it thee to be thus bold in terms   85
Before thy sovereign and thy lawful king?

EDWARD
I am his king, and he should bow his knee.
I was adopted heir by his consent.
Since when, his oath is broke; for, as I hear,
You, that are king, though he do wear the crown,   90
Have caused him, by new act of Parliament,
To blot out me and put his own son in.

CLIFFORD   And reason too.
Who should succeed the father but the son?

_____

Darraign your battle set your army in battle array   **80 s.d. George of**
Clarence (Actually, George is not made Duke of Clarence until 2.6.104.)
grace mercy, pardon   **83 bide** wait for.   **mortal** fatal   **84 rate thy**
minions chide your followers or favorites   **85 terms** language   **90 You,**
that are king i.e., you, Margaret, who in fact rule

Inferring arguments of mighty force.   44
But, Clifford, tell me, didst thou never hear
That things ill got had ever bad success?   46
And happy always was it for that son   47
Whose father for his hoarding went to hell?   48
I'll leave my son my virtuous deeds behind;
And would my father had left me no more!
For all the rest is held at such a rate   51
As brings a thousandfold more care to keep
Than in possession any jot of pleasure.
Ah, cousin York, would thy best friends did know
How it doth grieve me that thy head is here!

QUEEN MARGARET
  My lord, cheer up your spirits. Our foes are nigh,
  And this soft courage makes your followers faint.   57
  You promised knighthood to our forward son.   5
  Unsheathe your sword and dub him presently.
  Edward, kneel down.   [*The Prince kneels.*]

KING HENRY
  Edward Plantagenet, arise a knight,
  And learn this lesson: Draw thy sword in right.

PRINCE [*Rising*]
  My gracious Father, by your kingly leave,
  I'll draw it as apparent to the crown,
  And in that quarrel use it to the death.

CLIFFORD
  Why, that is spoken like a toward prince.

        Enter a Messenger.

MESSENGER
  Royal commanders, be in readiness,
  For with a band of thirty thousand men
  Comes Warwick, backing of the Duke of York,
  And in the towns, as they do march along,

                                                          CL

44 **Inferring** alleging, adducing   **46 success** outcome   **47–**
hell i.e., the son may be fortunate in inheriting wealth, bu
who obtained that wealth by hoarding and miserly grasp
hell   **51 rate** cost   **57 faint** fainthearted   **58 forward** pr
59 presently at once   **64 apparent** heir   **66 toward** read
ing   **69 Duke of York** i.e., Edward

RICHARD
Are you there, butcher? O, I cannot speak!   95
CLIFFORD
Ay, crookback, here I stand to answer thee,
Or any he the proudest of thy sort.   97
RICHARD
'Twas you that killed young Rutland, was it not?
CLIFFORD
Ay, and old York, and yet not satisfied.
RICHARD
For God's sake, lords, give signal to the fight.
WARWICK
What sayst thou, Henry, wilt thou yield the crown?
QUEEN MARGARET
Why, how now, long-tongued Warwick, dare you speak?
When you and I met at Saint Albans last,
Your legs did better service than your hands.
WARWICK
Then 'twas my turn to fly, and now 'tis thine.
CLIFFORD
You said so much before, and yet you fled.
WARWICK
'Twas not your valor, Clifford, drove me thence.
NORTHUMBERLAND
No, nor your manhood that durst make you stay.
RICHARD
Northumberland, I hold thee reverently.   109
Break off the parley, for scarce I can refrain   110
The execution of my big-swollen heart   111
Upon that Clifford, that cruel child-killer.
CLIFFORD
I slew thy father. Call'st thou him a child?
RICHARD
Ay, like a dastard and a treacherous coward,
As thou didst kill our tender brother Rutland;
But ere sunset I'll make thee curse the deed.

---

95 butcher (Clifford was nicknamed "the butcher" for his cruelty.)
97 any he any man.   **sort** gang   **109 hold thee reverently** hold you in
the greatest respect   **110 refrain** give up, hold back   **111 execution** i.e.,
giving practical effect to my passion

KING HENRY
  Have done with words, my lords, and hear me speak.
QUEEN MARGARET
  Defy them, then, or else hold close thy lips.
KING HENRY
  I prithee, give no limits to my tongue.
  I am a king, and privileged to speak.
CLIFFORD
  My liege, the wound that bred this meeting here
  Cannot be cured by words. Therefore be still.
RICHARD
  Then, executioner, unsheathe thy sword.
  By Him that made us all, I am resolved   124
  That Clifford's manhood lies upon his tongue.   125
EDWARD
  Say, Henry, shall I have my right or no?
  A thousand men have broke their fasts today   127
  That ne'er shall dine unless thou yield the crown.
WARWICK
  If thou deny, their blood upon thy head,   129
  For York in justice puts his armor on.
PRINCE
  If that be right which Warwick says is right,
  There is no wrong, but everything is right.
RICHARD
  Whoever got thee, there thy mother stands;   133
  For, well I wot, thou hast thy mother's tongue.   134
QUEEN MARGARET
  But thou art neither like thy sire nor dam,
  But like a foul misshapen stigmatic,   136
  Marked by the destinies to be avoided,
  As venom toads or lizards' dreadful stings.   138
RICHARD
  Iron of Naples hid with English gilt,   139
  Whose father bears the title of a king—

---

124 resolved convinced **125 lies . . . tongue** i.e., consists only in words
127 broke their fasts i.e., had breakfast **129 deny** refuse. **upon** be
upon **133 got** begot, sired **134 wot** know **136 stigmatic** one branded
with the mark of his crime or deformity. (See *2 Henry VI*, 5.1.215.)
138 venom venomous **139 Iron . . . gilt** i.e., you cheap product of
Naples (being daughter of the titular King of Naples), being gilded over
by an English marriage

As if a channel should be called the sea—   141
Sham'st thou not, knowing whence thou art extraught,   142
To let thy tongue detect thy baseborn heart?   143

EDWARD

A wisp of straw were worth a thousand crowns   144
To make this shameless callet know herself.   145
Helen of Greece was fairer far than thou,
Although thy husband may be Menelaus;   147
And ne'er was Agamemnon's brother wronged   148
By that false woman, as this king by thee.
His father reveled in the heart of France,   150
And tamed the King, and made the Dauphin stoop;
And had he matched according to his state,   152
He might have kept that glory to this day.
But when he took a beggar to his bed
And graced thy poor sire with his bridal day,   155
Even then that sunshine brewed a shower for him
That washed his father's fortunes forth of France   157
And heaped sedition on his crown at home.
For what hath broached this tumult but thy pride?   159
Hadst thou been meek, our title still had slept,   160
And we, in pity of the gentle King,
Had slipped our claim until another age.   162

GEORGE

But when we saw our sunshine made thy spring,   163
And that thy summer bred us no increase,   164
We set the ax to thy usurping root;
And though the edge hath something hit ourselves,   166
Yet know thou, since we have begun to strike,

---

141 As ... sea i.e., comparing your father to a king is like comparing
a gutter (*channel*) to the sea   **142 extraught** descended, extracted
143 detect expose   **144 wisp of straw** (A traditional way of marking or
branding a scolding woman.)   **145 callet** lewd woman   **147 Menelaus**
husband of Helen of Greece, whose abduction led to the Trojan War. (By
implication, King Henry is the cuckolded husband just as Menelaus
was.)   **148 Agamemnon** brother of Menelaus and leader of the Greeks
in the Trojan War   **150 His father** i.e., Henry V   **152 had ... state** i.e.,
if Henry VI had married someone equal to him in social position
155 graced honored.   **thy poor sire** i.e., Reignier, King of Naples.   **his**
i.e., Henry VI's   **157 of** out of   **159 broached** set flowing, started
160 title claim to the throne   **162 Had slipped** would have postponed
163 But ... spring i.e., but when we saw you reaping all the benefit of
what should be ours   **164 increase** harvest   **166 something** somewhat

We'll never leave till we have hewn thee down　　168
Or bathed thy growing with our heated bloods.　　169

EDWARD
And in this resolution I defy thee,
Not willing any longer conference,
Since thou deniedst the gentle King to speak.
Sound trumpets! Let our bloody colors wave!
And either victory, or else a grave.

QUEEN MARGARET　　Stay, Edward.

EDWARD
No, wrangling woman, we'll no longer stay.
These words will cost ten thousand lives this day.　　177

Exeunt omnes.

2.3　　*Alarum. Excursions. Enter Warwick.*

WARWICK
Forspent with toil, as runners with a race,　　1
I lay me down a little while to breathe;　　2
For strokes received and many blows repaid
Have robbed my strong-knit sinews of their strength,
And, spite of spite, needs must I rest awhile.　　5

Enter Edward, running.

EDWARD
Smile, gentle heaven, or strike, ungentle death!　　6
For this world frowns, and Edward's sun is clouded.

WARWICK
How now, my lord, what hap? What hope of good?

Enter [George of] Clarence.

GEORGE
Our hap is loss, our hope but sad despair;

---

168 leave leave off　　**169 bathed thy growing** watered your growth
177 s.d. omnes all

**2.3. Location: The field of battle near York, immediately following the
preceding scene. (Historically, the field of battle was between Towton
and Saxton in Yorkshire.)**
s.d. Excursions sorties, forays of armed soldiers　　**1 Forspent** exhausted
2 breathe rest　　**5 spite of spite** i.e., come what may.　　**needs must I** I
must　　**6 ungentle** ignoble

Our ranks are broke, and ruin follows us.
What counsel give you? Whither shall we fly?

EDWARD
    Bootless is flight. They follow us with wings,   12
    And weak we are and cannot shun pursuit.

    Enter Richard.

RICHARD
    Ah, Warwick, why hast thou withdrawn thyself?
    Thy brother's blood the thirsty earth hath drunk,   15
    Broached with the steely point of Clifford's lance;   16
    And in the very pangs of death he cried,
    Like to a dismal clangor heard from far,
    "Warwick, revenge! Brother, revenge my death!"
    So, underneath the belly of their steeds,
    That stained their fetlocks in his smoking blood,
    The noble gentleman gave up the ghost.

WARWICK
    Then let the earth be drunken with our blood!
    I'll kill my horse, because I will not fly.
    Why stand we like softhearted women here,
    Wailing our losses, whiles the foe doth rage,
    And look upon, as if the tragedy   27
    Were played in jest by counterfeiting actors?   28
    Here on my knee I vow to God above   [*Kneeling*]
    I'll never pause again, never stand still,
    Till either death hath closed these eyes of mine
    Or fortune given me measure of revenge.   32

EDWARD [*Kneeling*]
    O Warwick, I do bend my knee with thine,
    And in this vow do chain my soul to thine!
    And, ere my knee rise from the earth's cold face,
    I throw my hands, mine eyes, my heart to Thee,   36
    Thou setter-up and plucker-down of kings,
    Beseeching Thee, if with Thy will it stands   38

12 Bootless useless   **15 Thy brother's blood** (Warwick's half brother,
the Bastard of Salisbury, not among the *Dramatis Personae* of this play,
was killed at Ferrybridge shortly before the battle of Towton.)
16 Broached with set flowing by   **27 upon** on   **28 counterfeiting actors**
actors performing roles   **32 measure** full quantity   **36 Thee** i.e., God
38 stands agrees

That to my foes this body must be prey,
Yet that Thy brazen gates of heaven may ope
And give sweet passage to my sinful soul!

                              [*They rise.*]

Now, lords, take leave until we meet again,
Where'er it be, in heaven or in earth.

RICHARD

Brother, give me thy hand; and, gentle Warwick,   44
Let me embrace thee in my weary arms.

                         [*They embrace.*]

I, that did never weep, now melt with woe
That winter should cut off our springtime so.

WARWICK

Away, away! Once more, sweet lords, farewell.

GEORGE

Yet let us all together to our troops,
And give them leave to fly that will not stay,
And call them pillars that will stand to us;   51
And, if we thrive, promise them such rewards
As victors wear at the Olympian games.
This may plant courage in their quailing breasts,
For yet is hope of life and victory.
Forslow no longer! Make we hence amain.   *Exeunt.* 56

2.4   *Excursions. Enter Richard and Clifford*
         [*meeting*].

RICHARD

Now, Clifford, I have singled thee alone.   1
Suppose this arm is for the Duke of York,
And this for Rutland—both bound to revenge,
Wert thou environed with a brazen wall.   4

CLIFFORD

Now, Richard, I am with thee here alone.
This is the hand that stabbed thy father York,
And this the hand that slew thy brother Rutland,
And here's the heart that triumphs in their death

---

44 gentle noble **51 stand to** support **56 Forslow** delay. **amain**
with full speed

2.4. Location: Scene continues at the battlefield.
1 singled singled out, chosen **4 environed** surrounded

And cheers these hands that slew thy sire and brother 9
To execute the like upon thyself.
And so, have at thee!   11

> *They fight. Warwick comes; Clifford flies.*

RICHARD
Nay, Warwick, single out some other chase,   12
For I myself will hunt this wolf to death.

> *Exeunt.*

2.5   *Alarum. Enter King Henry alone.*

KING HENRY
This battle fares like to the morning's war,
When dying clouds contend with growing light,
What time the shepherd, blowing of his nails,   3
Can neither call it perfect day nor night.
Now sways it this way, like a mighty sea
Forced by the tide to combat with the wind;
Now sways it that way, like the selfsame sea
Forced to retire by fury of the wind.
Sometimes the flood prevails, and then the wind;
Now one the better, then another best;
Both tugging to be victors, breast to breast,
Yet neither conqueror nor conquerèd.
So is the equal poise of this fell war.   13
Here on this molehill will I sit me down.   [*He sits.*]
To whom God will, there be the victory!
For Margaret my queen, and Clifford too,
Have chid me from the battle, swearing both
They prosper best of all when I am thence.
Would I were dead, if God's good will were so!
For what is in this world but grief and woe?
O God! Methinks it were a happy life
To be no better than a homely swain,   22
To sit upon a hill, as I do now,
To carve out dials quaintly, point by point,   24

9 **cheers** urges on   11 **have at thee** i.e., on guard, here I come   12 **chase**
prey

2.5. Location: The battlefield, as before.
3 **What time** when.   **of** on (to warm them)   13 **poise** balance.   **fell** cruel
22 **homely** simple   24 **dials** sundials.   **quaintly** artfully, intricately

Thereby to see the minutes how they run:
How many makes the hour full complete,
How many hours brings about the day,
How many days will finish up the year,
How many years a mortal man may live.
When this is known, then to divide the times:
So many hours must I tend my flock,
So many hours must I take my rest,
So many hours must I contemplate,
So many hours must I sport myself,   34
So many days my ewes have been with young,
So many weeks ere the poor fools will ean,   36
So many years ere I shall shear the fleece.
So minutes, hours, days, months, and years,
Passed over to the end they were created,   39
Would bring white hairs unto a quiet grave.
Ah, what a life were this, how sweet, how lovely!
Gives not the hawthorn bush a sweeter shade
To shepherds looking on their silly sheep   43
Than doth a rich embroidered canopy
To kings that fear their subjects' treachery?
O, yes, it doth, a thousandfold it doth.
And to conclude, the shepherd's homely curds,
His cold thin drink out of his leather bottle,
His wonted sleep under a fresh tree's shade,   49
All which secure and sweetly he enjoys,
Is far beyond a prince's delicates—   51
His viands sparkling in a golden cup,
His body couchèd in a curious bed—   53
When care, mistrust, and treason waits on him.

> *Alarum. Enter a Son that hath killed his father,*
> *at one door [bearing in the dead body].*

SON
Ill blows the wind that profits nobody.
This man, whom hand to hand I slew in fight,
May be possessèd with some store of crowns;   57

---

34 sport amuse   **36 ean** bring forth (lambs)   **39 end they** end for which
they   **43 silly** innocent, helpless   **49 wonted** accustomed   **51 delicates**
luxuries   **53 curious** skillfully and daintily made, decorated   **57 crowns**
i.e., coins, money

And I, that haply take them from him now,   58
May yet ere night yield both my life and them
To some man else, as this dead man doth me.—
Who's this? O God! It is my father's face,
Whom in this conflict I unwares have killed.
O, heavy times, begetting such events!   63
From London by the King was I pressed forth;   64
My father, being the Earl of Warwick's man,   65
Came on the part of York, pressed by his master;   66
And I, who at his hands received my life,
Have by my hands of life bereavèd him.
Pardon me, God, I knew not what I did!   69
And pardon, Father, for I knew not thee!
My tears shall wipe away these bloody marks;
And no more words till they have flowed their fill.

           [*He weeps.*]

KING HENRY
O piteous spectacle! O bloody times!
Whiles lions war and battle for their dens,
Poor harmless lambs abide their enmity.   75
Weep, wretched man. I'll aid thee tear for tear;
And let our hearts and eyes, like civil war,
Be blind with tears, and break o'ercharged with
 grief.   [*He weeps.*] 78

  Enter at another door a Father that hath killed
  his son, bearing of his son.

FATHER
Thou that so stoutly hast resisted me,
Give me thy gold, if thou hast any gold;
For I have bought it with an hundred blows.
But let me see. Is this our foeman's face?
Ah, no, no, no, it is mine only son!
Ah, boy, if any life be left in thee,
Throw up thine eye! See, see what showers arise,
Blown with the windy tempest of my heart,

---

58 haply by chance **63 heavy** sorrowful **64 pressed forth** impressed
into military service **65 man** retainer, servant **66 part** party, side
69 Pardon . . . did (An echo of Luke 23:34, "Father, forgive them,
for they know not what they do.") **75 abide** endure, pay for
78 o'ercharged overfilled

Upon thy wounds, that kills mine eye and heart!

[*He weeps.*]

O, pity, God, this miserable age!
What stratagems, how fell, how butcherly,   89
Erroneous, mutinous, and unnatural,   90
This deadly quarrel daily doth beget!
O boy, thy father gave thee life too soon,
And hath bereft thee of thy life too late!   93

KING HENRY
Woe above woe, grief more than common grief!   94
O, that my death would stay these ruthful deeds!   95
O, pity, pity, gentle heaven, pity!
The red rose and the white are on his face,
The fatal colors of our striving houses.
The one his purple blood right well resembles;
The other his pale cheeks, methinks, presenteth.   100
Wither one rose, and let the other flourish;
If you contend, a thousand lives must wither.

SON
How will my mother for a father's death
Take on with me and ne'er be satisfied!   104

FATHER
How will my wife for slaughter of my son
Shed seas of tears and ne'er be satisfied!

KING HENRY
How will the country for these woeful chances   107
Misthink the King and not be satisfied!   108

SON
Was ever son so rued a father's death?

FATHER
Was ever father so bemoaned his son?

KING HENRY
Was ever king so grieved for subjects' woe?
Much is your sorrow; mine ten times so much.

SON
I'll bear thee hence, where I may weep my fill.

[*Exit with the body.*]

---

89 stratagems deeds of violence. **fell** cruel   **90 Erroneous** criminal
93 late lately   **94 above** piled on   **95 stay** put a halt to. **ruthful** pitiful
100 presenteth represents   **104 Take on with** cry out against. **satisfied**
comforted   **107 chances** happenings   **108 Misthink** think ill of

FATHER
　　These arms of mine shall be thy winding-sheet;　　　　114
　　My heart, sweet boy, shall be thy sepulcher,
　　For from my heart thine image ne'er shall go.
　　My sighing breast shall be thy funeral bell;
　　And so obsequious will thy father be,　　　　　　　　118
　　E'en for the loss of thee, having no more,
　　As Priam was for all his valiant sons.　　　　　　　　120
　　I'll bear thee hence, and let them fight that will,
　　For I have murdered where I should not kill.
　　　　　　　　　　　　　　　Exit [with the body].

KING HENRY
　　Sad-hearted men, much overgone with care,　　　　　123
　　Here sits a king more woeful than you are.

　　　　Alarums. Excursions. Enter the Queen
　　　　[*Margaret*], *the Prince, and Exeter.*

PRINCE
　　Fly, Father, fly! For all your friends are fled,
　　And Warwick rages like a chafèd bull.　　　　　　　126
　　Away! For death doth hold us in pursuit.

QUEEN MARGARET
　　Mount you, my lord. Towards Berwick post amain.　　128
　　Edward and Richard, like a brace of greyhounds　　129
　　Having the fearful flying hare in sight,
　　With fiery eyes sparkling for very wrath,
　　And bloody steel grasped in their ireful hands,
　　Are at our backs; and therefore hence amain.

EXETER
　　Away! For vengeance comes along with them.
　　Nay, stay not to expostulate, make speed!
　　Or else come after. I'll away before.

KING HENRY
　　Nay, take me with thee, good sweet Exeter.
　　Not that I fear to stay, but love to go
　　Whither the Queen intends. Forward! Away!　　*Exeunt.*

---

114 winding-sheet shroud, burial cloth　**118 obsequious** dutiful in mani-
festing regard for the dead　**120 Priam** King of Troy, whose fifty sons fell
in the war against the Greeks　**123 overgone** overcome　**126 chafèd** enraged　**128 Berwick** Berwick-on-Tweed, on the Scottish border at the
North Sea shore.　**post amain** hasten with full speed　**129 brace** pair

2.6   *A loud alarum. Enter Clifford, wounded, [with an arrow in his neck].*

CLIFFORD
Here burns my candle out; ay, here it dies,
Which, whiles it lasted, gave King Henry light.
O Lancaster, I fear thy overthrow
More than my body's parting with my soul!
My love and fear glued many friends to thee;   5
And, now I fall, thy tough commixture melts,   6
Impairing Henry, strengthening misproud York.   7
The common people swarm like summer flies;
And whither fly the gnats but to the sun?   9
And who shines now but Henry's enemies?
O Phoebus, hadst thou never given consent
That Phaëthon should check thy fiery steeds,   12
Thy burning car never had scorched the earth!   13
And, Henry, hadst thou swayed as kings should do,   14
Or as thy father and his father did,
Giving no ground unto the house of York,
They never then had sprung like summer flies;
I and ten thousand in this luckless realm
Had left no mourning widows for our death,   19
And thou this day hadst kept thy chair in peace.   20
For what doth cherish weeds but gentle air?   21
And what makes robbers bold but too much lenity?
Bootless are plaints, and cureless are my wounds;   23
No way to fly, nor strength to hold out flight.   24
The foe is merciless, and will not pity,
For at their hands I have deserved no pity.
The air hath got into my deadly wounds,
And much effuse of blood doth make me faint.   28
Come, York and Richard, Warwick and the rest;

2.6. Location: The battlefield, as before.
5 My love and fear love and fear of me   **6 now** now that.   **commixture** compound (i.e., the *glue* that held many friends)   **7 Impairing** weakening.   **misproud** falsely proud   **9 the sun** (Refers to Edward's emblem.)   **12 Phaëthon** (See 1.4.33, note.)   **check** control, manage   **13 car** chariot   **14 swayed** reigned   **19 mourning widows** widows mourning   **20 chair** throne   **21 cherish** foster, encourage   **23 Bootless** fruitless.   **plaints** lamentations   **24 hold out** sustain   **28 effuse** effusion

I stabbed your fathers' bosoms. Split my breast.   30
                              [*He faints.*]

Alarum and retreat. Enter Edward, Warwick,
Richard, and soldiers, Montague, and [George of]
Clarence.

EDWARD
Now breathe we, lords. Good fortune bids us pause   31
And smooth the frowns of war with peaceful looks.
Some troops pursue the bloody-minded Queen,
That led calm Henry, though he were a king,
As doth a sail, filled with a fretting gust,   35
Command an argosy to stem the waves.   36
But think you, lords, that Clifford fled with them?
WARWICK
No, 'tis impossible he should escape;
For, though before his face I speak the words,   39
Your brother Richard marked him for the grave,
And wheresoe'er he is, he's surely dead.
                    Clifford groans [and dies].
EDWARD
Whose soul is that which takes her heavy leave?
RICHARD
A deadly groan, like life and death's departing.   43
EDWARD
See who it is. And, now the battle's ended,
If friend or foe, let him be gently used.   45
RICHARD
Revoke that doom of mercy, for 'tis Clifford,   46
Who not contented that he lopped the branch   47
In hewing Rutland when his leaves put forth,
But set his murdering knife unto the root
From whence that tender spray did sweetly spring—   50
I mean our princely father, Duke of York.

---

30 s.d. retreat signal to cease the attack   **31 breathe we** let us pause for
breath   **35 fretting** blowing in gusts (with a suggestion also of "nag-
ging")   **36 Command** compel forward.   **argosy** large merchant vessel.
stem make headway against, cut through   **39 his** i.e., Richard's
43 departing parting   **45 If** whether.   **gently used** treated in death with
dignity   **46 doom** judgment   **47 Who not contented** who did not rest
contented   **50 spray** small and tender twig

WARWICK
  From off the gates of York fetch down the head,
  Your father's head, which Clifford placèd there;
  Instead whereof let this supply the room.   54
  Measure for measure must be answerèd.   55

EDWARD
  Bring forth that fatal screech owl to our house,   56
  That nothing sung but death to us and ours.

              [*Soldiers drag Clifford's body
                    in front of York gates.*]

  Now death shall stop his dismal threatening sound,
  And his ill-boding tongue no more shall speak.

WARWICK
  I think his understanding is bereft.   60
  Speak, Clifford, dost thou know who speaks to thee?—
  Dark cloudy death o'ershades his beams of life,
  And he nor sees nor hears us what we say.   63

RICHARD
  O, would he did! And so perhaps he doth.
  'Tis but his policy to counterfeit,   65
  Because he would avoid such bitter taunts
  Which in the time of death he gave our father.

GEORGE
  If so thou think'st, vex him with eager words.   68

RICHARD
  Clifford, ask mercy and obtain no grace.

EDWARD
  Clifford, repent in bootless penitence.

WARWICK
  Clifford, devise excuses for thy faults.

GEORGE
  While we devise fell tortures for thy faults.   72

RICHARD
  Thou didst love York, and I am son to York.

EDWARD
  Thou pitiedst Rutland. I will pity thee.

---

54 this i.e., Clifford's head.   **supply the room** take the place
55 answerèd given in return   **56 screech owl** (A conventional omen of
death, here likened to Clifford.)   **house** family   **60 bereft** taken from
him   **63 nor . . . nor** neither . . . nor   **65 policy** stratagem   **68 eager**
biting, bitter   **72 fell** cruel

GEORGE
Where's Captain Margaret to fence you now?   75
WARWICK
They mock thee, Clifford. Swear as thou wast wont.   76
RICHARD
What, not an oath? Nay, then the world goes hard
When Clifford cannot spare his friends an oath.
I know by that he's dead; and, by my soul,
If this right hand would buy two hours' life,
That I in all despite might rail at him,   81
This hand should chop it off, and with the issuing blood   82
Stifle the villain whose unstanchèd thirst   83
York and young Rutland could not satisfy.
WARWICK
Ay, but he's dead. Off with the traitor's head,
And rear it in the place your father's stands.
And now to London with triumphant march,
There to be crownèd England's royal king;
From whence shall Warwick cut the sea to France
And ask the Lady Bona for thy queen.   90
So shalt thou sinew both these lands together,   91
And, having France thy friend, thou shalt not dread   92
The scattered foe that hopes to rise again;
For though they cannot greatly sting to hurt,
Yet look to have them buzz to offend thine ears.
First will I see the coronation,
And then to Brittany I'll cross the sea
To effect this marriage, so it please my lord.
EDWARD
Even as thou wilt, sweet Warwick, let it be;
For in thy shoulder do I build my seat,   100
And never will I undertake the thing
Wherein thy counsel and consent is wanting.
Richard, I will create thee Duke of Gloucester,
And George, of Clarence. Warwick, as ourself,
Shall do and undo as him pleaseth best.

---

75 fence defend   **76 wont** accustomed   **81 despite** spite, contempt
82 This hand i.e., this left hand   **83 unstanchèd** unquenchable   **90 Lady
Bona** daughter of the Duke of Savoy and sister to the Queen of France
91 sinew join (as with sinew)   **92 France** the King of France   **100 in thy
shoulder** i.e., with your support.   **seat** throne

RICHARD
   Let me be Duke of Clarence, George of Gloucester;
   For Gloucester's dukedom is too ominous.   107
WARWICK
   Tut, that's a foolish observation.
   Richard, be Duke of Gloucester. Now to London,
   To see these honors in possession.   *Exeunt.* 110

❖

107 Gloucester's . . . ominous (Three dukes of Gloucester had met with
violent deaths: Hugh Spenser, a favorite of Edward II, Thomas of Woodstock, youngest son of Edward III [see *Richard II*, 1.1], and Humphrey,
uncle of Henry VI [see *2 Henry VI*, 3.2].)   **110 in possession** i.e., in our
possession

3.1 *Enter two Keepers with crossbows in their hands.*

FIRST KEEPER
  Under this thick-grown brake we'll shroud ourselves,   1
  For through this laund anon the deer will come;   2
  And in this covert will we make our stand,
  Culling the principal of all the deer.   4

SECOND KEEPER
  I'll stay above the hill, so both may shoot.

FIRST KEEPER
  That cannot be. The noise of thy crossbow
  Will scare the herd, and so my shoot is lost.
  Here stand we both, and aim we at the best;   8
  And, for the time shall not seem tedious,   9
  I'll tell thee what befell me on a day
  In this self place where now we mean to stand.   11

SECOND KEEPER
  Here comes a man. Let's stay till he be past.
                          [They remain concealed.]

    Enter the King [Henry, disguised,] with
    a prayer book.

KING HENRY
  From Scotland am I stol'n, even of pure love,   13
  To greet mine own land with my wishful sight.   14
  No, Harry, Harry, 'tis no land of thine!
  Thy place is filled, thy scepter wrung from thee,
  Thy balm washed off wherewith thou wast anointed.
  No bending knee will call thee Caesar now,
  No humble suitors press to speak for right,   19
  No, not a man comes for redress of thee;   20
  For how can I help them, and not myself?

3.1. Location: A forest in the north of England, near the Scottish border.
s.d. Keepers gamekeepers **1 brake** thicket **2 laund** glade **4 Culling
. . . deer** selecting the best deer **8 at the best** as best we can **9 for**
so that **11 self** same, very **13 of** out of **14 wishful** longing **19 speak
for right** plead for justice **20 of** from

FIRST KEEPER [*Aside to Second Keeper*]
    Ay, here's a deer whose skin's a keeper's fee: 22
    This is the quondam king. Let's seize upon him.   23
KING HENRY
    Let me embrace thee, sour adversity,
    For wise men say it is the wisest course.
SECOND KEEPER [*Aside*]
    Why linger we? Let us lay hands upon him.
FIRST KEEPER [*Aside*]
    Forbear awhile. We'll hear a little more.
KING HENRY
    My queen and son are gone to France for aid;
    And, as I hear, the great commanding Warwick
    Is thither gone, to crave the French King's sister
    To wife for Edward. If this news be true,   31
    Poor Queen and son, your labor is but lost,
    For Warwick is a subtle orator,
    And Lewis a prince soon won with moving words.
    By this account, then, Margaret may win him,
    For she's a woman to be pitied much.
    Her sighs will make a battery in his breast;   37
    Her tears will pierce into a marble heart.
    The tiger will be mild whiles she doth mourn,
    And Nero will be tainted with remorse   40
    To hear and see her plaints, her brinish tears.   41
    Ay, but she's come to beg, Warwick to give;
    She, on his left side, craving aid for Henry,
    He, on his right, asking a wife for Edward.
    She weeps, and says her Henry is deposed;
    He smiles, and says his Edward is installed;
    That she, poor wretch, for grief can speak no more,   47
    Whiles Warwick tells his title, smooths the wrong,   48
    Inferreth arguments of mighty strength,   49
    And in conclusion wins the King from her

22 fee perquisite. (The gamekeeper will get a reward for capturing the King, just as gamekeepers were customarily awarded the horn and skins of a slain deer.)   **23 quondam** onetime, former   **31 To** as a **37 battery** breach   **40 Nero** Roman emperor famed for his cruelty. **tainted** touched, affected   **41 brinish** salty   **47 That** so that   **48 his title** i.e., Edward's royal claim.   **smooths** explains away   **49 Inferreth** adduces

With promise of his sister, and what else,   51
To strengthen and support King Edward's place.
O Margaret, thus 'twill be, and thou, poor soul,
Art then forsaken, as thou went'st forlorn!
                    [*The Keepers come forward.*]

SECOND KEEPER
Say, what art thou that talk'st of kings and queens?   55

KING HENRY
More than I seem, and less than I was born to.
A man at least, for less I should not be;
And men may talk of kings, and why not I?

SECOND KEEPER
Ay, but thou talk'st as if thou wert a king.

KING HENRY
Why, so I am, in mind, and that's enough.

SECOND KEEPER
But, if thou be a king, where is thy crown?

KING HENRY
My crown is in my heart, not on my head;
Not decked with diamonds and Indian stones,   63
Nor to be seen. My crown is called content;
A crown it is that seldom kings enjoy.

SECOND KEEPER
Well, if you be a king crowned with content,
Your crown content and you must be contented
To go along with us. For, as we think,
You are the king King Edward hath deposed;
And we his subjects sworn in all allegiance
Will apprehend you as his enemy.   71

KING HENRY
But did you never swear, and break an oath?

SECOND KEEPER
No, never such an oath, nor will not now.

KING HENRY
Where did you dwell when I was King of England?

SECOND KEEPER
Here in this country where we now remain.   75

51 what else other things also   **55 what** who   **63 Indian stones** gems
71 apprehend arrest   **75 country** region

KING HENRY
> I was anointed king at nine months old;
> My father and my grandfather were kings,
> And you were sworn true subjects unto me.
> And tell me, then, have you not broke your oaths?

FIRST KEEPER
> No, for we were subjects but while you were king.   80

KING HENRY
> Why, am I dead? Do I not breathe a man?
> Ah, simple men, you know not what you swear!   82
> Look as I blow this feather from my face,   83
> And as the air blows it to me again,
> Obeying with my wind when I do blow,   85
> And yielding to another when it blows,
> Commanded always by the greater gust—
> Such is the lightness of you common men.
> But do not break your oaths, for of that sin
> My mild entreaty shall not make you guilty.
> Go where you will, the King shall be commanded;
> And be you kings, command, and I'll obey.

FIRST KEEPER
> We are true subjects to the King, King Edward.

KING HENRY
> So would you be again to Henry,
> If he were seated as King Edward is.

FIRST KEEPER
> We charge you, in God's name and the King's,
> To go with us unto the officers.

KING HENRY
> In God's name, lead. Your king's name be obeyed,
> And what God will, that let your king perform;
> And what he will, I humbly yield unto.   *Exeunt.*

❧

---

80 but only   **82 simple** foolish   **83 Look as** just as.   **this feather**
(Henry may take a feather from his hat.)   **85 wind** breath

3.2 *Enter King Edward, Gloucester, Clarence, [and] Lady Grey.*

KING EDWARD

  Brother of Gloucester, at Saint Albans field
  This lady's husband, Sir Richard Grey, was slain,   2
  His land then seized on by the conqueror.
  Her suit is now to repossess those lands,
  Which we in justice cannot well deny,
  Because in quarrel of the house of York
  The worthy gentleman did lose his life.

GLOUCESTER

  Your Highness shall do well to grant her suit.
  It were dishonor to deny it her.

KING EDWARD

  It were no less, but yet I'll make a pause.

GLOUCESTER [*Aside to Clarence*]   Yea, is it so?

  I see the lady hath a thing to grant   12
  Before the King will grant her humble suit.

CLARENCE [*Aside to Gloucester*]

  He knows the game. How true he keeps the wind!   14

GLOUCESTER [*Aside to Clarence*]   Silence!

KING EDWARD

  Widow, we will consider of your suit;
  And come some other time to know our mind.

LADY GREY

  Right gracious lord, I cannot brook delay.   18
  May it please Your Highness to resolve me now,   19
  And what your pleasure is shall satisfy me.   20

GLOUCESTER [*Aside to Clarence*]

  Ay, widow? Then I'll warrant you all your lands,   21

3.2. Location: London. The royal court.
s.d. Gloucester, Clarence i.e., Richard and George, King Edward's brothers, made dukes in 2.6.103–104   **2 Sir Richard Grey** (An error for Sir John Grey, who fell at the second battle of St. Albans fighting on the Lancastrian side; cf. *Richard III*, 1.3.127–130.)   **12 a thing** (with a sexual double entendre that runs through much of this scene)   **14 game** (1) quarry in hunting (2) game of seduction.   **keeps the wind** hunts downwind (to prevent the game from catching the scent)   **18 brook** tolerate   **19 resolve me** answer me, end my uncertainty   **20 And . . . me** and whatever you please to grant will content me. (But Richard, in the next speech, plays on sexual meanings of *pleasure* and *satisfy*.)   **21 warrant** guarantee

An if what pleases him shall pleasure you.   22
Fight closer or, good faith, you'll catch a blow.   23
CLARENCE [*Aside to Gloucester*]
I fear her not, unless she chance to fall.   24
GLOUCESTER [*Aside to Clarence*]
God forbid that, for he'll take vantages.
KING EDWARD
How many children hast thou, widow? Tell me.
CLARENCE [*Aside to Gloucester*]
I think he means to beg a child of her.   27
GLOUCESTER [*Aside to Clarence*]
Nay, whip me, then; he'll rather give her two.   28
LADY GREY   Three, my most gracious lord.
GLOUCESTER [*Aside to Clarence*]
You shall have four, if you'll be ruled by him.   30
KING EDWARD
'Twere pity they should lose their father's lands.
LADY GREY
Be pitiful, dread lord, and grant it then.
KING EDWARD
Lords, give us leave. I'll try this widow's wit.   33
GLOUCESTER [*Aside to Clarence*]
Ay, good leave have you; for you will have leave   34
Till youth take leave and leave you to the crutch.   35
          [*Gloucester and Clarence stand apart.*]
KING EDWARD
Now tell me, madam, do you love your children?
LADY GREY
Ay, full as dearly as I love myself.

22 An if if. **pleasure** please   **23 Fight closer ... catch a blow** (The
dueling terms here are used with sexual double meaning, as also in *fall*
and *vantages*, ll. 24, 25. See also *a thing*, l. 12, *beg a child*, l. 27, *crutch*,
i.e., crotch, l. 35, *service*, l. 43, *do*, l. 48, and *shift*, i.e., a woman's smock,
l. 108, for other sexual double entendres.)   **24 fear** i.e., fear for   **27 beg
a child** i.e., seek to be appointed guardian of her child, or to be guardian of some rich young ward—a lucrative sinecure (with sexual double
meaning)   **28 whip me** i.e., I'll bet a whipping the King has other
designs.   **give her two** make her pregnant twice   **30 have four** (Her
fourth child would be sired by Edward.)   **33 give us leave** pardon us,
i.e., leave us to confer alone.   **wit** intelligence   **34–35 Ay ... crutch** yes,
may you be pardoned, for you will take liberties, until your youth bids
you farewell and leaves you hobbling on a crutch, too old for lovemak-
ing (with a pun on *crutch*, *crotch*, the loins)

KING EDWARD
    And would you not do much to do them good?
LADY GREY
    To do them good I would sustain some harm.
KING EDWARD
    Then get your husband's lands, to do them good.
LADY GREY
    Therefore I came unto Your Majesty.
KING EDWARD
    I'll tell you how these lands are to be got.
LADY GREY
    So shall you bind me to Your Highness' service.
KING EDWARD
    What service wilt thou do me if I give them?
LADY GREY
    What you command that rests in me to do.   45
KING EDWARD
    But you will take exceptions to my boon.   46
LADY GREY
    No, gracious lord, except I cannot do it.   47
KING EDWARD
    Ay, but thou canst do what I mean to ask.
LADY GREY
    Why, then I will do what Your Grace commands.
GLOUCESTER [*Aside to Clarence*]
    He plies her hard; and much rain wears the marble.
CLARENCE [*Aside to Gloucester*]
    As red as fire? Nay, then, her wax must melt.   51
LADY GREY
    Why stops my lord? Shall I not hear my task?
KING EDWARD
    An easy task. 'Tis but to love a king.
LADY GREY
    That's soon performed, because I am a subject.
KING EDWARD
    Why, then, thy husband's lands I freely give thee.
LADY GREY
    I take my leave with many thousand thanks.
                        [*She curtsies, preparing to go.*]

45 rests in me lies in my power   **46 take . . . boon** object to the request I
ask   **47 except** unless   **51 As red as fire** i.e., Edward is hotly importunate

GLOUCESTER [*Aside to Clarence*]
    The match is made; she seals it with a curtsy.   57
KING EDWARD
    But stay thee. 'Tis the fruits of love I mean.
LADY GREY
    The fruits of love I mean, my loving liege.   59
KING EDWARD
    Ay, but, I fear me, in another sense.
    What love, think'st thou, I sue so much to get?
LADY GREY
    My love till death, my humble thanks, my prayers—
    That love which virtue begs and virtue grants.
KING EDWARD
    No, by my troth, I did not mean such love.   64
LADY GREY
    Why then you mean not as I thought you did.
KING EDWARD
    But now you partly may perceive my mind.
LADY GREY
    My mind will never grant what I perceive
    Your Highness aims at, if I aim aright.   68
KING EDWARD
    To tell thee plain, I aim to lie with thee.
LADY GREY
    To tell you plain, I had rather lie in prison.   70
KING EDWARD
    Why, then, thou shalt not have thy husband's lands.
LADY GREY
    Why, then, mine honesty shall be my dower,   72
    For by that loss I will not purchase them.   73
KING EDWARD
    Therein thou wrong'st thy children mightily.
LADY GREY
    Herein Your Highness wrongs both them and me.
    But, mighty lord, this merry inclination

---

57 seals confirms (as in affixing a seal to a document)   **59 fruits of love**
(Lady Grey interprets the King's sexual phrase in the innocent sense of
"loyal feelings of affection toward the monarch.")   **64 troth** faith
68 aim guess   **70 lie** be confined (with a play on King Edward's *lie* in
sexual embrace)   **72 honesty** chastity, virtue   **73 that loss** loss of that

Accords not with the sadness of my suit.   77
Please you dismiss me, either with ay or no.

KING EDWARD
Ay, if thou wilt say ay to my request;
No, if thou dost say no to my demand.

LADY GREY
Then, no, my lord. My suit is at an end.

GLOUCESTER [*Aside to Clarence*]
The widow likes him not. She knits her brows.

CLARENCE [*Aside to Gloucester*]
He is the bluntest wooer in Christendom.

KING EDWARD [*Aside*]
Her looks doth argue her replete with modesty;   84
Her words doth show her wit incomparable;
All her perfections challenge sovereignty.   86
One way or other, she is for a king,
And she shall be my love, or else my queen.—
Say that King Edward take thee for his queen?

LADY GREY
'Tis better said than done, my gracious lord.
I am a subject fit to jest withal,
But far unfit to be a sovereign.

KING EDWARD
Sweet widow, by my state I swear to thee   93
I speak no more than what my soul intends,
And that is, to enjoy thee for my love.

LADY GREY
And that is more than I will yield unto.
I know I am too mean to be your queen,   97
And yet too good to be your concubine.

KING EDWARD
You cavil, widow. I did mean my queen.

LADY GREY
'Twill grieve Your Grace my sons should call you father.

KING EDWARD
No more than when my daughters call thee mother.
Thou art a widow, and thou hast some children;
And, by God's mother, I, being but a bachelor,

77 sadness seriousness   **84 argue her** show her to be   **86 challenge** lay
claim to   **93 state** i.e., kingship   **97 mean** low in social rank

Have other some. Why, 'tis a happy thing   104
To be the father unto many sons.
Answer no more, for thou shalt be my queen.

GLOUCESTER [*Aside to Clarence*]
The ghostly father now hath done his shrift.   107

CLARENCE [*Aside to Gloucester*]
When he was made a shriver, 'twas for shift.   108

KING EDWARD
Brothers, you muse what chat we two have had.   109
                    [*Gloucester and Clarence come forward.*]

GLOUCESTER
The widow likes it not, for she looks very sad.   110

KING EDWARD
You'd think it strange if I should marry her.

CLARENCE
To who, my lord?

KING EDWARD   Why, Clarence, to myself.   112

GLOUCESTER
That would be ten days' wonder at the least.   113

CLARENCE
That's a day longer than a wonder lasts.

GLOUCESTER
By so much is the wonder in extremes.   115

KING EDWARD
Well, jest on, brothers. I can tell you both
Her suit is granted for her husband's lands.

         Enter a Nobleman.

NOBLEMAN
My gracious lord, Henry your foe is taken
And brought your prisoner to your palace gate.

KING EDWARD
See that he be conveyed unto the Tower.

---

104 other some some others. **happy** fortunate **107 ghostly father**
spiritual father, confessor. **done his shrift** finished hearing confession
108 for shift (1) to serve a devious purpose (2) for a woman's smock or
chemise **109 muse** wonder **110 sad** serious **112 To who** (Edward
might *marry her* in the sense of giving her in marriage to a wealthy
subject; he might then take her as his mistress.) **113 ten days' wonder**
(One day longer than the proverbial "nine days' wonder," i.e., an event
of sudden notoriety. Clarence points out the exaggeration in the next
line.) **115 in extremes** an unusual wonder indeed

And go we, brothers, to the man that took him,
To question of his apprehension.   122
Widow, go you along. Lords, use her honorably.
                    Exeunt. Manet Richard [of Gloucester].

GLOUCESTER
Ay, Edward will use women honorably.
Would he were wasted, marrow, bones, and all,   125
That from his loins no hopeful branch may spring
To cross me from the golden time I look for!   127
And yet, between my soul's desire and me—
The lustful Edward's title burièd—   129
Is Clarence, Henry, and his son young Edward,
And all the unlooked-for issue of their bodies,   131
To take their rooms ere I can place myself.   132
A cold premeditation for my purpose!   133
Why, then, I do but dream on sovereignty,
Like one that stands upon a promontory
And spies a far-off shore where he would tread,
Wishing his foot were equal with his eye,   137
And chides the sea that sunders him from thence,
Saying he'll lade it dry to have his way.   139
So do I wish the crown, being so far off,
And so I chide the means that keeps me from it,   141
And so I say I'll cut the causes off,   142
Flattering me with impossibilities.   143
My eye's too quick, my heart o'erweens too much,   144
Unless my hand and strength could equal them.
Well, say there is no kingdom then for Richard;
What other pleasure can the world afford?
I'll make my heaven in a lady's lap,
And deck my body in gay ornaments,
And witch sweet ladies with my words and looks.   150
O miserable thought, and more unlikely

---

122 of his apprehension about his being taken   **125 wasted** wasted with
disease—syphilis in particular   **127 cross** thwart, frustrate
129 The . . . burièd i.e., even after lustful Edward's title to the throne is
eliminated by his death   **131 unlooked-for** unforeseeable and undesir-
able   **132 rooms** places   **133 cold premeditation** discouraging prospect
137 equal with his eye i.e., able to achieve what he views   **139 lade**
empty (by ladling, scooping)   **141 means** obstacles   **142 causes** i.e., of
my impatience   **143 Flattering . . . impossibilities** i.e., deceiving myself
with vain hopes   **144 o'erweens** presumes   **150 witch** bewitch

Than to accomplish twenty golden crowns!   152
Why, love forswore me in my mother's womb;
And, for I should not deal in her soft laws,   154
She did corrupt frail nature with some bribe
To shrink mine arm up like a withered shrub;
To make an envious mountain on my back,   157
Where sits deformity to mock my body;
To shape my legs of an unequal size;
To disproportion me in every part,
Like to a chaos, or an unlicked bear whelp   161
That carries no impression like the dam.   162
And am I then a man to be beloved?
O monstrous fault, to harbor such a thought!
Then, since this earth affords no joy to me
But to command, to check, to o'erbear such   166
As are of better person than myself,
I'll make my heaven to dream upon the crown,
And, whiles I live, t' account this world but hell,
Until my misshaped trunk that bears this head
Be round impalèd with a glorious crown.   171
And yet I know not how to get the crown,
For many lives stand between me and home;   173
And I—like one lost in a thorny wood,
That rends the thorns and is rent with the thorns,
Seeking a way and straying from the way,
Not knowing how to find the open air,
But toiling desperately to find it out—
Torment myself to catch the English crown;
And from that torment I will free myself
Or hew my way out with a bloody ax.
Why, I can smile, and murder whiles I smile,
And cry "Content" to that which grieves my heart,
And wet my cheeks with artificial tears,
And frame my face to all occasions.
I'll drown more sailors than the mermaid shall;   186

---

152 accomplish get possession of   **154 for** so that   **157 envious** spiteful, detested   **161 unlicked bear whelp** (It was a popular notion that bears licked their shapeless newly born cubs into a proper shape.)
162 impression shape   **166 check** control, rebuke.   **o'erbear** dominate
171 impalèd enclosed   **173 home** i.e., the goal   **186 mermaid** (Mermaids allegedly had the power to lure sailors to destruction by their singing or weeping.)

I'll slay more gazers than the basilisk;   187
I'll play the orator as well as Nestor,   188
Deceive more slyly than Ulysses could,   189
And, like a Sinon, take another Troy.   190
I can add colors to the chameleon,
Change shapes with Proteus for advantages,   192
And set the murderous Machiavel to school.   193
Can I do this, and cannot get a crown?
Tut, were it farther off, I'll pluck it down.   *Exit.*

❖

3.3   *Flourish. Enter Lewis the French King, his
            sister Bona, his Admiral, called Bourbon,
            Prince Edward, Queen Margaret, and the Earl
            of Oxford. Lewis sits, and riseth up again.*

KING LEWIS
    Fair Queen of England, worthy Margaret,
    Sit down with us. It ill befits thy state   2
    And birth that thou shouldst stand while Lewis doth sit.
QUEEN MARGARET
    No, mighty King of France. Now Margaret
    Must strike her sail and learn awhile to serve   5
    Where kings command. I was, I must confess,
    Great Albion's queen in former golden days.   7
    But now mischance hath trod my title down   8
    And with dishonor laid me on the ground,

---

187 basilisk fabulous reptile said to kill by its gaze   **188–189 Nestor,
Ulysses** Greek leaders in the Trojan War, noted respectively for aged
wisdom and cunning   **190 Sinon** Greek warrior who allowed himself to
be taken captive by the Trojans, and then, feigning resentment toward
his Greek companions, persuaded Priam to bring the wooden horse
within the city walls by which Troy was taken   **192 Proteus** old man of
the sea, able to assume different shapes.   **for advantages** to suit my
purpose   **193 set . . . school** teach Machiavelli how to be ruthless. (In
the popular imagination, Machiavelli was the archetype of ruthless
political cunning and atheism.)

**3.3. Location: France. The royal court. A throne and a seat or seats are
provided.**
2 state rank   **5 strike her sail** lower her sail, i.e., act deferentially, as
the captain of a sea vessel does to one of higher rank   **7 Albion's**
England's   **8 mischance** misfortune

Where I must take like seat unto my fortune   10
And to my humble seat conform myself.

KING LEWIS

Why, say, fair Queen, whence springs this deep despair?

QUEEN MARGARET

From such a cause as fills mine eyes with tears
And stops my tongue, while heart is drowned in cares.

KING LEWIS

Whate'er it be, be thou still like thyself,   15
And sit thee by our side. (*Seats her by him.*) Yield not
     thy neck
To fortune's yoke, but let thy dauntless mind
Still ride in triumph over all mischance.
Be plain, Queen Margaret, and tell thy grief.   19
It shall be eased, if France can yield relief.   20

QUEEN MARGARET

Those gracious words revive my drooping thoughts
And give my tongue-tied sorrows leave to speak.
Now, therefore, be it known to noble Lewis
That Henry, sole possessor of my love,
Is, of a king, become a banished man   25
And forced to live in Scotland a forlorn,   26
While proud, ambitious Edward, Duke of York,
Usurps the regal title and the seat
Of England's true-anointed lawful king.
This is the cause that I, poor Margaret,
With this my son, Prince Edward, Henry's heir,
Am come to crave thy just and lawful aid;
And if thou fail us, all our hope is done.
Scotland hath will to help, but cannot help;
Our people and our peers are both misled,
Our treasure seized, our soldiers put to flight,
And, as thou seest, ourselves in heavy plight.

KING LEWIS

Renownèd Queen, with patience calm the storm,
While we bethink a means to break it off.   39

---

10 like seat unto a place befitting   **15 like thyself** i.e., as befits your
title   **19 grief** grievances   **20 France** i.e., the King of France   **25 of**
instead of   **26 forlorn** outcast   **39 break it off** i.e., cease the storm
of grief

QUEEN MARGARET
  The more we stay, the stronger grows our foe.   40
KING LEWIS
  The more I stay, the more I'll succor thee.   41
QUEEN MARGARET
  O, but impatience waiteth on true sorrow.   42
  And see where comes the breeder of my sorrow!

    Enter Warwick.

KING LEWIS
  What's he approacheth boldly to our presence?   44
QUEEN MARGARET
  Our Earl of Warwick, Edward's greatest friend.
KING LEWIS
  Welcome, brave Warwick! What brings thee to
    France?   *He descends. She ariseth.*
QUEEN MARGARET
  Ay, now begins a second storm to rise,
  For this is he that moves both wind and tide.
WARWICK
  From worthy Edward, King of Albion,
  My lord and sovereign, and thy vowèd friend,
  I come in kindness and unfeignèd love,
  First, to do greetings to thy royal person,
  And then to crave a league of amity;
  And lastly, to confirm that amity
  With nuptial knot, if thou vouchsafe to grant
  That virtuous Lady Bona, thy fair sister,   56
  To England's king in lawful marriage.
QUEEN MARGARET [*Aside*]
  If that go forward, Henry's hope is done.
WARWICK (*Speaking to Bona*)
  And, gracious madam, in our king's behalf
  I am commanded, with your leave and favor,   60
  Humbly to kiss your hand, and with my tongue
  To tell the passion of my sovereign's heart—

---

40 stay delay **41 The . . . thee** i.e., the longer preparation I make, the greater help I can give you **42 waiteth on** attends, accompanies **44 he** he who **56 sister** i.e., sister-in-law **60 leave and favor** kind permission

Where fame, late entering at his heedful ears,   63
Hath placed thy beauty's image and thy virtue.
QUEEN MARGARET
  King Lewis and Lady Bona, hear me speak
  Before you answer Warwick. His demand
  Springs not from Edward's well-meant honest love,
  But from deceit bred by necessity.
  For how can tyrants safely govern home
  Unless abroad they purchase great alliance?
  To prove him tyrant this reason may suffice,
  That Henry liveth still; but were he dead,
  Yet here Prince Edward stands, King Henry's son.
  Look, therefore, Lewis, that by this league and marriage
  Thou draw not on thy danger and dishonor.   75
  For though usurpers sway the rule awhile,   76
  Yet heavens are just, and time suppresseth wrongs.
WARWICK
  Injurious Margaret!
PRINCE   And why not "Queen"?   78
WARWICK
  Because thy father Henry did usurp,
  And thou no more art prince than she is queen.
OXFORD
  Then Warwick disannuls great John of Gaunt,   81
  Which did subdue the greatest part of Spain;   82
  And after John of Gaunt, Henry the Fourth,
  Whose wisdom was a mirror to the wisest;   84
  And after that wise prince, Henry the Fifth,
  Who by his prowess conquerèd all France.
  From these our Henry lineally descends.
WARWICK
  Oxford, how haps it in this smooth discourse   88
  You told not how Henry the Sixth hath lost
  All that which Henry the Fifth had gotten?
  Methinks these peers of France should smile at that.
  But for the rest: you tell a pedigree

---

63 fame report. **late** lately **75 draw not on** do not bring about
76 sway exercise **78 Injurious** insulting **81 disannuls** cancels, takes
no account of **82 Which** who **84 a mirror** a model for emulation
88 haps it does it happen that

Of threescore-and-two years—a silly time   93
To make prescription for a kingdom's worth.   94

OXFORD
Why, Warwick, canst thou speak against thy liege,
Whom thou obeyèd'st thirty-and-six years,
And not bewray thy treason with a blush?   97

WARWICK
Can Oxford, that did ever fence the right,   98
Now buckler falsehood with a pedigree?   99
For shame! Leave Henry, and call Edward king.

OXFORD
Call him my king by whose injurious doom   101
My elder brother, the Lord Aubrey Vere,   102
Was done to death? And more than so, my father,   103
Even in the downfall of his mellowed years,
When nature brought him to the door of death?
No, Warwick, no! While life upholds this arm,
This arm upholds the house of Lancaster.

WARWICK   And I the house of York.

KING LEWIS
Queen Margaret, Prince Edward, and Oxford,
Vouchsafe, at our request, to stand aside
While I use further conference with Warwick.   111
                                        They stand aloof.

QUEEN MARGARET
Heavens grant that Warwick's words bewitch him not!

KING LEWIS
Now, Warwick, tell me, even upon thy conscience,
Is Edward your true king? For I were loath
To link with him that were not lawful chosen.

WARWICK
Thereon I pawn my credit and mine honor.   116

---

93 threescore-and-two i.e., from 1399, the date of Henry IV's accession,
to 1461, that of Edward's.   **silly** i.e., ridiculously short   **94 prescription**
claim founded upon long use and de facto possession   **97 bewray** reveal
98 fence defend   **99 buckler** shield, protect   **101 doom** judgment
102 Lord Aubrey Vere the eldest son of the twelfth Earl of Oxford, John
de Vere. (Both he and his father were attainted and executed for treason
by the Yorkists in 1462.)   **103 more than so** even more than that
111 use further conference hold further conversation   **s.d. aloof** to one
side   **116 pawn my credit** stake my reputation

KING LEWIS
  But is he gracious in the people's eye?
WARWICK
  The more that Henry was unfortunate.
KING LEWIS
  Then further, all dissembling set aside,
  Tell me for truth the measure of his love   120
  Unto our sister Bona.
WARWICK   Such it seems
  As may beseem a monarch like himself.   122
  Myself have often heard him say and swear
  That this his love was an eternal plant,
  Whereof the root was fixed in virtue's ground,
  The leaves and fruit maintained with beauty's sun,
  Exempt from envy, but not from disdain,   127
  Unless the Lady Bona quit his pain.   128
KING LEWIS
  Now, sister, let us hear your firm resolve.
BONA
  Your grant, or your denial, shall be mine.   130
  (*Speaks to Warwick.*) Yet I confess that often ere this day,
  When I have heard your king's desert recounted,   132
  Mine ear hath tempted judgment to desire.   133
KING LEWIS
  Then, Warwick, thus: our sister shall be Edward's.
  And now forthwith shall articles be drawn   135
  Touching the jointure that your king must make, 136
  Which with her dowry shall be counterpoised.— 137
  Draw near, Queen Margaret, and be a witness
  That Bona shall be wife to the English King.
      [*Margaret, Edward, and Oxford come forward.*]
PRINCE
  To Edward, but not to the English King.

---

120 for truth truly **122 beseem** befit **127 envy** ill will, malice. **but . . .
disdain** i.e., his love will wither if the lady disdains him. (Warwick uses
the stock hyperbole of Petrarchan devotion.) **128 quit** requite, allevi-
ate **130 grant** granting, agreeing **132 desert** deserving **133 Mine . . .
desire** what I have heard has prompted my judgment to desire him
135 articles i.e., articles of a marriage contract **136 Touching** concerning. **jointure** marriage settlement made by the groom in behalf of the
bride **137 counterpoised** matched, balanced in amount

QUEEN MARGARET
   Deceitful Warwick! It was thy device   141
   By this alliance to make void my suit.
   Before thy coming, Lewis was Henry's friend.
KING LEWIS
   And still is friend to him and Margaret.
   But if your title to the crown be weak,
   As may appear by Edward's good success,
   Then 'tis but reason that I be released
   From giving aid which late I promisèd.
   Yet shall you have all kindness at my hand
   That your estate requires and mine can yield.   150
WARWICK [*To Queen Margaret*]
   Henry now lives in Scotland at his ease,
   Where, having nothing, nothing can he lose.
   And as for you yourself, our quondam queen,   153
   You have a father able to maintain you,
   And better 'twere you troubled him than France.
QUEEN MARGARET
   Peace, impudent and shameless Warwick,
   Proud setter-up and puller-down of kings!
   I will not hence till, with my talk and tears,
   Both full of truth, I make King Lewis behold
   Thy sly conveyance and thy lord's false love;   160
   For both of you are birds of selfsame feather.   161
                    Post blowing a horn within.
KING LEWIS
   Warwick, this is some post to us or thee.

   Enter the Post.

POST (*Speaks to Warwick*)
   My Lord Ambassador, these letters are for you,
   Sent from your brother, Marquess Montague.
   (*To Lewis.*) These from our king unto Your Majesty.
   (*To Margaret.*) And, madam, these for you; from whom I
     know not.   *They all read their letters.*
OXFORD [*To Edward*]
   I like it well that our fair queen and mistress
   Smiles at her news, while Warwick frowns at his.

---

141 device stratagem   **150 estate** rank, condition   **153 quondam** former
160 conveyance underhand dealing   **161 s.d. Post** messenger

PRINCE [*To Oxford*]
Nay, mark how Lewis stamps, as he were nettled.   169
I hope all's for the best.
KING LEWIS
Warwick, what are thy news? And yours, fair Queen?
QUEEN MARGARET
Mine, such as fill my heart with unhoped joys.
WARWICK
Mine, full of sorrow and heart's discontent.
KING LEWIS
What, has your king married the Lady Grey?
And now, to soothe your forgery and his,   175
Sends me a paper to persuade me patience?   176
Is this th' alliance that he seeks with France?
Dare he presume to scorn us in this manner?
QUEEN MARGARET
I told Your Majesty as much before.
This proveth Edward's love and Warwick's honesty.
WARWICK
King Lewis, I here protest, in sight of heaven
And by the hope I have of heavenly bliss,
That I am clear from this misdeed of Edward's—   183
No more my king, for he dishonors me,
But most himself, if he could see his shame.
Did I forget that by the house of York
My father came untimely to his death?   187
Did I let pass th' abuse done to my niece?   188
Did I impale him with the regal crown?   189
Did I put Henry from his native right?
And am I guerdoned at the last with shame?   191
Shame on himself! For my desert is honor;   192
And to repair my honor lost for him,
I here renounce him and return to Henry.
My noble Queen, let former grudges pass,
And henceforth I am thy true servitor.   196

169 as as if   **175 soothe** gloss over.   **forgery** deceit   **176 persuade**
advise   **183 clear from** innocent of   **187 My father** i.e., Salisbury (who,
according to the chronicles, was captured at Wakefield and beheaded by
the Lancastrians)   **188 abuse . . . niece** (The chronicles report that
Edward attempted to "deflower" Warwick's niece while a guest in his
house.)   **189 impale him** i.e., encircle his head   **191 guerdoned** rewarded   **192 my desert** what I deserve   **196 true servitor** loyal servant

I will revenge his wrong to Lady Bona
And replant Henry in his former state.

QUEEN MARGARET
    Warwick, these words have turned my hate to love;
    And I forgive and quite forget old faults,
    And joy that thou becom'st King Henry's friend.

WARWICK
    So much his friend, ay, his unfeignèd friend,
    That, if King Lewis vouchsafe to furnish us
    With some few bands of chosen soldiers,
    I'll undertake to land them on our coast
    And force the tyrant from his seat by war.   206
    'Tis not his new-made bride shall succor him.   207
    And as for Clarence, as my letters tell me,
    He's very likely now to fall from him,   209
    For matching more for wanton lust than honor,   210
    Or than for strength and safety of our country.

BONA
    Dear brother, how shall Bona be revenged
    But by thy help to this distressèd queen?

QUEEN MARGARET
    Renownèd prince, how shall poor Henry live,
    Unless thou rescue him from foul despair?

BONA
    My quarrel and this English queen's are one.

WARWICK
    And mine, fair Lady Bona, joins with yours.

KING LEWIS
    And mine with hers, and thine, and Margaret's.
    Therefore at last I firmly am resolved
    You shall have aid.

QUEEN MARGARET
    Let me give humble thanks for all at once.

KING LEWIS
    Then, England's messenger, return in post   222
    And tell false Edward, thy supposèd king,
    That Lewis of France is sending over maskers   224

---

206 tyrant usurper   **207 'Tis . . . him** i.e., no newly chosen bride like
Lady Grey is going to be enough to save him   **209 fall from** desert
210 matching marrying   **222 in post** in haste   **224 maskers** dancers in
a masque or court revels. (Said ironically.)

To revel it with him and his new bride.
Thou seest what's passed. Go fear thy king withal.   226

BONA
Tell him, in hope he'll prove a widower shortly,
I'll wear the willow garland for his sake.   228

QUEEN MARGARET
Tell him my mourning weeds are laid aside   229
And I am ready to put armor on.

WARWICK
Tell him from me that he hath done me wrong,
And therefore I'll uncrown him ere 't be long.
There's thy reward. [*He gives money.*] Begone.
                                    Exit Post.
KING LEWIS   But, Warwick,
Thou and Oxford, with five thousand men,
Shall cross the seas and bid false Edward battle;
And, as occasion serves, this noble queen
And prince shall follow with a fresh supply.   237
Yet, ere thou go, but answer me one doubt: 238
What pledge have we of thy firm loyalty?

WARWICK
This shall assure my constant loyalty,
That, if our queen and this young prince agree,
I'll join mine eldest daughter and my joy   242
To him forthwith in holy wedlock bands.

QUEEN MARGARET
Yes, I agree, and thank you for your motion.   244
Son Edward, she is fair and virtuous;
Therefore delay not. Give thy hand to Warwick,
And, with thy hand, thy faith irrevocable
That only Warwick's daughter shall be thine.

PRINCE
Yes, I accept her, for she well deserves it;

---

226 fear frighten.   **withal** with this   **228 willow garland** (Symbol of a
forsaken lover; said here contemptuously. The leaves are from the great
willow herb, or loosestrife, not from the willow tree.)   **229 weeds**
garments   **237 supply** reinforcements   **238 but** only   **242 eldest daughter** (A historical inaccuracy; Prince Edward was betrothed to a younger
daughter of Warwick, Anne, who later married Richard of Gloucester;
the eldest daughter, Isabella, was already the wife of the Duke of Clarence.)   **244 motion** proposal

And here, to pledge my vow, I give my hand.
He gives his hand to Warwick.

KING LEWIS

Why stay we now? These soldiers shall be levied,   251
And thou, Lord Bourbon, our high admiral,
Shall waft them over with our royal fleet.   253
I long till Edward fall by war's mischance
For mocking marriage with a dame of France.   255
Exeunt. Manet Warwick.

WARWICK

I came from Edward as ambassador,
But I return his sworn and mortal foe.
Matter of marriage was the charge he gave me,
But dreadful war shall answer his demand.
Had he none else to make a stale but me?   260
Then none but I shall turn his jest to sorrow.
I was the chief that raised him to the crown,
And I'll be chief to bring him down again—
Not that I pity Henry's misery,
But seek revenge on Edward's mockery.   *Exit.*

❖

---

251 stay delay   **253 waft** convey by water   **255 s.d. Manet** he remains
onstage   **260 stale** dupe, laughingstock

4.1 *Enter Richard, [Duke of Gloucester,] Clarence,*
       Somerset, and Montague.

GLOUCESTER
   Now tell me, brother Clarence, what think you
   Of this new marriage with the Lady Grey?
   Hath not our brother made a worthy choice?
CLARENCE
   Alas, you know, 'tis far from hence to France.
   How could he stay till Warwick made return?   5
SOMERSET
   My lords, forbear this talk. Here comes the King.   6

       Flourish. Enter King Edward, Lady Grey [as
       Queen Elizabeth], Pembroke, Stafford, Hastings.
       Four stand on one side and four on the other.

GLOUCESTER   And his well-chosen bride.
CLARENCE
   I mind to tell him plainly what I think.   8
KING EDWARD
   Now, brother of Clarence, how like you our choice,
   That you stand pensive, as half malcontent?   10
CLARENCE
   As well as Lewis of France, or the Earl of Warwick,
   Which are so weak of courage and in judgment   12
   That they'll take no offense at our abuse.   13
KING EDWARD
   Suppose they take offense without a cause;
   They are but Lewis and Warwick. I am Edward,
   Your king and Warwick's, and must have my will.   16
GLOUCESTER
   And shall have your will, because our king.
   Yet hasty marriage seldom proveth well.
KING EDWARD
   Yea, brother Richard, are you offended too?

4.1. Location: London. The royal court.
5 stay wait. (Clarence speaks ironically.)   **6 s.d. Four stand** i.e., the four
already onstage. Edward is seemingly in the middle.   **8 mind** intend
10 malcontent discontented   **12 Which** who   **13 abuse** insult. (Clarence
speaks scornfully, as does Gloucester in ll. 21–23.)   **16 have my will**
(1) have my way (2) fulfill my lust

GLOUCESTER   Not I.
No, God forbid that I should wish them severed
Whom God hath joined together! Ay, and 'twere pity
To sunder them that yoke so well together.   23

KING EDWARD
Setting your scorns and your mislike aside,   24
Tell me some reason why the Lady Grey
Should not become my wife and England's queen.
And you too, Somerset and Montague,
Speak freely what you think.

CLARENCE
Then this is mine opinion: that King Lewis
Becomes your enemy for mocking him
About the marriage of the Lady Bona.

GLOUCESTER
And Warwick, doing what you gave in charge,   32
Is now dishonorèd by this new marriage.

KING EDWARD
What if both Lewis and Warwick be appeased
By such invention as I can devise?   35

MONTAGUE
Yet, to have joined with France in such alliance
Would more have strengthened this our commonwealth
'Gainst foreign storms than any homebred marriage.

HASTINGS
Why, knows not Montague that of itself
England is safe, if true within itself?

MONTAGUE
But the safer when 'tis backed with France.

HASTINGS
'Tis better using France than trusting France.
Let us be backed with God and with the seas
Which He hath given for fence impregnable,
And with their helps only defend ourselves;   45
In them and in ourselves our safety lies.

23 yoke are bound in marriage. (But Gloucester parodies the language
of the marriage service in such a way as to suggest sexual coupling and
the yoking of oxen.)   **24 mislike** displeasure   **32 gave in charge** commissioned   **35 invention** scheme, plan   **45 only** alone

CLARENCE
  For this one speech Lord Hastings well deserves
  To have the heir of the Lord Hungerford.   48
KING EDWARD
  Ay, what of that? It was my will and grant,
  And for this once my will shall stand for law.
GLOUCESTER
  And yet methinks Your Grace hath not done well
  To give the heir and daughter of Lord Scales
  Unto the brother of your loving bride.   53
  She better would have fitted me or Clarence.
  But in your bride you bury brotherhood.
CLARENCE
  Or else you would not have bestowed the heir
  Of the Lord Bonville on your new wife's son,   57
  And leave your brothers to go speed elsewhere.   58
KING EDWARD
  Alas, poor Clarence! Is it for a wife
  That thou art malcontent? I will provide thee.
CLARENCE
  In choosing for yourself you showed your judgment,
  Which being shallow, you shall give me leave
  To play the broker in mine own behalf;   63
  And to that end I shortly mind to leave you.   64
KING EDWARD
  Leave me or tarry, Edward will be king,   65
  And not be tied unto his brother's will.
QUEEN ELIZABETH
  My lords, before it pleased His Majesty
  To raise my state to title of a queen,
  Do me but right, and you must all confess
  That I was not ignoble of descent;
  And meaner than myself have had like fortune.   71

---

48 To . . . Hungerford (Clarence objects to the marriage of Lord Hastings to the daughter of Lord Hungerford.) **53 brother** i.e., Lord Anthony Rivers (whose marriage to the daughter of Lord Scales was one of the advancements of Queen Elizabeth's kindred so much resented by Edward's brothers and other noble supporters) **57 son** i.e., Sir Thomas Grey, Marquess Dorset, another of the Queen's upstart relatives advanced by Edward **58 speed** prosper **63 broker** agent, go-between **64 mind** intend **65 Leave** whether you leave **71 meaner** more lowly

But as this title honors me and mine,
So your dislikes, to whom I would be pleasing,   73
Doth cloud my joys with danger and with sorrow.   74

KING EDWARD
My love, forbear to fawn upon their frowns.   75
What danger or what sorrow can befall thee
So long as Edward is thy constant friend
And their true sovereign, whom they must obey?
Nay, whom they shall obey, and love thee too,
Unless they seek for hatred at my hands;
Which if they do, yet will I keep thee safe,
And they shall feel the vengeance of my wrath.

GLOUCESTER [*Aside*]
I hear, yet say not much, but think the more.

Enter a Post.

KING EDWARD
Now, messenger, what letters or what news
From France?

POST
My sovereign liege, no letters, and few words,
But such as I, without your special pardon,   87
Dare not relate.

KING EDWARD
Go to, we pardon thee. Therefore, in brief,   89
Tell me their words as near as thou canst guess them.   90
What answer makes King Lewis unto our letters?

POST
At my depart, these were his very words: 92
"Go tell false Edward, the supposèd king,
That Lewis of France is sending over maskers
To revel it with him and his new bride."

KING EDWARD
Is Lewis so brave? Belike he thinks me Henry.   96
But what said Lady Bona to my marriage?

POST
These were her words, uttered with mild disdain:

---

73 would wish to   **74 danger** apprehension   **75 forbear . . . frowns** stop
trying to overcome their disapproval by ingratiating yourself   **87 pardon**
i.e., permission   **89 Go to** (An expression of remonstrance.)   **90 guess** i.e.,
reproduce from memory   **92 depart** departure   **96 Belike** perhaps

"Tell him, in hope he'll prove a widower shortly,
I'll wear the willow garland for his sake."

KING EDWARD
I blame not her, she could say little less;
She had the wrong. But what said Henry's queen?
For I have heard that she was there in place.

POST
"Tell him," quoth she, "my mourning weeds are done,   104
And I am ready to put armor on."

KING EDWARD
Belike she minds to play the Amazon.   106
But what said Warwick to these injuries?   107

POST
He, more incensed against Your Majesty
Than all the rest, discharged me with these words: 109
"Tell him from me that he hath done me wrong,
And therefore I'll uncrown him ere 't be long."

KING EDWARD
Ha? Durst the traitor breathe out so proud words?
Well, I will arm me, being thus forewarned.
They shall have wars and pay for their presumption.
But say, is Warwick friends with Margaret?

POST
Ay, gracious sovereign, they are so linked in friendship
That young Prince Edward marries Warwick's
   daughter.

CLARENCE
Belike the elder; Clarence will have the younger.   118
Now, brother king, farewell, and sit you fast,   119
For I will hence to Warwick's other daughter,
That, though I want a kingdom, yet in marriage   121
I may not prove inferior to yourself.
You that love me and Warwick, follow me.
                    Exit Clarence, and Somerset follows.
GLOUCESTER [*Aside*]   Not I.
My thoughts aim at a further matter. I
Stay not for the love of Edward, but the crown.

---

104 done i.e., no longer needed   **106 Amazon** mythical female warrior
107 injuries insults   **109 discharged** dismissed   **118 the elder** (Cf.
3.3.242, note.)   **119 sit you fast** i.e., hold on tight to your throne
121 want lack

KING EDWARD

  Clarence and Somerset both gone to Warwick?

  Yet am I armed against the worst can happen;   128

  And haste is needful in this desperate case.

  Pembroke and Stafford, you in our behalf

  Go levy men and make prepare for war.   131

  They are already, or quickly will be, landed.

  Myself in person will straight follow you.   133

                  Exeunt Pembroke and Stafford.

  But ere I go, Hastings and Montague,

  Resolve my doubt. You twain, of all the rest,

  Are near to Warwick by blood and by alliance.

  Tell me if you love Warwick more than me.

  If it be so, then both depart to him;

  I rather wish you foes than hollow friends.

  But if you mind to hold your true obedience,   140

  Give me assurance with some friendly vow,

  That I may never have you in suspect.   142

MONTAGUE

  So God help Montague as he proves true!

HASTINGS

  And Hastings as he favors Edward's cause!

KING EDWARD

  Now, brother Richard, will you stand by us?

GLOUCESTER

  Ay, in despite of all that shall withstand you.   146

KING EDWARD

  Why, so. Then am I sure of victory.

  Now therefore let us hence, and lose no hour

  Till we meet Warwick with his foreign power.

                          Exeunt.

❖

128 can that can   **131 prepare** preparation   **133 straight** immediately
140 mind intend   **142 suspect** suspicion   **146 despite** spite

4.2 *Enter Warwick and Oxford in England, with French soldiers.*

WARWICK
Trust me, my lord, all hitherto goes well.
The common people by numbers swarm to us.

Enter Clarence and Somerset.

But see where Somerset and Clarence comes!
Speak suddenly, my lords, are we all friends?
CLARENCE   Fear not that, my lord.
WARWICK
Then, gentle Clarence, welcome unto Warwick;   6
And welcome, Somerset! I hold it cowardice
To rest mistrustful where a noble heart   8
Hath pawned an open hand in sign of love;   9
Else might I think that Clarence, Edward's brother,
Were but a feignèd friend to our proceedings.
But welcome, sweet Clarence. My daughter shall be
    thine.
And now what rests but, in night's coverture,   13
Thy brother being carelessly encamped,
His soldiers lurking in the towns about,   15
And but attended by a simple guard,   16
We may surprise and take him at our pleasure?   17
Our scouts have found the adventure very easy;   18
That as Ulysses and stout Diomed   19
With sleight and manhood stole to Rhesus' tents   20
And brought from thence the Thracian fatal steeds,   21
So we, well covered with the night's black mantle,
At unawares may beat down Edward's guard   23

4.2. Location: Fields in Warwickshire.
6 gentle noble **8 rest** remain **9 pawned** pledged **13 rests** remains.
in night's coverture under cover of night **15 lurking** idling, lodging
16 simple mere **17 at our pleasure** whenever we wish **18 adventure**
venturing (into Edward's camp) **19–21 Ulysses . . . steeds** (In Book 10
of the *Iliad*, Ulysses and Diomedes under cover of night stealthily enter
the camp of the Thracian leader Rhesus, slay him and twelve of his
men, and lead away his horses. The horses are called *fatal steeds* because of a prophecy foretelling that Troy would not fall if once these
horses drank from the River Xanthus and grazed on the Trojan plain.)
19 stout brave **20 sleight** cunning **23 At unawares** unexpectedly,
suddenly

And seize himself. I say not "slaughter him,"
For I intend but only to surprise him.   25
You that will follow me to this attempt,
Applaud the name of Henry with your leader.
                        They all cry "Henry!"
Why, then, let's on our way in silent sort.   28
For Warwick and his friends, God and Saint George!
                                Exeunt.

❖

4.3   *Enter three Watchmen to guard*
         the King's tent.

FIRST WATCH
  Come on, my masters, each man take his stand.
  The King by this is set him down to sleep.   2
SECOND WATCH   What, will he not to bed?
FIRST WATCH
  Why, no, for he hath made a solemn vow
  Never to lie and take his natural rest
  Till Warwick or himself be quite suppressed.
SECOND WATCH
  Tomorrow then belike shall be the day,
  If Warwick be so near as men report.
THIRD WATCH
  But say, I pray, what nobleman is that
  That with the King here resteth in his tent?
FIRST WATCH
  'Tis the Lord Hastings, the King's chiefest friend.
THIRD WATCH
  O, is it so? But why commands the King
  That his chief followers lodge in towns about him,   13
  While he himself keeps in the cold field?   14
SECOND WATCH
  'Tis the more honor, because more dangerous.

---

25 surprise capture   **28 sort** fashion

4.3. Location: Edward's camp near Warwick.
2 by this by this time.   **set him** settled himself   **13 about** round about
14 keeps lodges

THIRD WATCH
  Ay, but give me worship and quietness;   16
  I like it better than a dangerous honor.
  If Warwick knew in what estate he stands,   18
  'Tis to be doubted he would waken him.   19
FIRST WATCH
  Unless our halberds did shut up his passage.   20
SECOND WATCH
  Ay, wherefore else guard we his royal tent
  But to defend his person from night foes?

  Enter Warwick, Clarence, Oxford, Somerset,
  and French soldiers, silent all.

WARWICK
  This is his tent, and see where stand his guard.
  Courage, my masters! Honor now or never!
  But follow me, and Edward shall be ours.   25
FIRST WATCH   Who goes there?
SECOND WATCH   Stay, or thou diest!
            Warwick and the rest cry all "Warwick!
            Warwick!" and set upon the guard, who
            fly, crying "Arm! Arm!" Warwick and
                   the rest following them.

  The drum playing and trumpet sounding, enter
  Warwick, Somerset, and the rest, bringing the
  King [Edward] out in his gown, sitting in a chair.
  Richard [of Gloucester] and Hastings fly over the
  stage.

SOMERSET   What are they that fly there?
WARWICK
  Richard and Hastings. Let them go. Here is
  The Duke.
KING EDWARD   "The Duke"? Why, Warwick, when we
    parted
  Thou calledst me King.

---

16 worship ease and dignity   **18 estate** situation.   **he** i.e., King Edward
19 doubted feared   **20 halberds** long-handled weapons bearing axlike
heads.   **shut up his passage** prevent Warwick's getting through
25 But only

WARWICK   Ay, but the case is altered.
  When you disgraced me in my ambassade,   32
  Then I degraded you from being king,
  And come now to create you Duke of York.
  Alas, how should you govern any kingdom,
  That know not how to use ambassadors,
  Nor how to be contented with one wife,
  Nor how to use your brothers brotherly,
  Nor how to study for the people's welfare,
  Nor how to shroud yourself from enemies?   40

KING EDWARD
  Yea, brother of Clarence, art thou here too?
  Nay, then I see that Edward needs must down.   42
  Yet, Warwick, in despite of all mischance,
  Of thee thyself and all thy complices,   44
  Edward will always bear himself as king.
  Though Fortune's malice overthrow my state,
  My mind exceeds the compass of her wheel.   47

WARWICK
  Then, for his mind, be Edward England's king.   48
                              Takes off his crown.
  But Henry now shall wear the English crown
  And be true king indeed, thou but the shadow.
  My lord of Somerset, at my request
  See that forthwith Duke Edward be conveyed
  Unto my brother, Archbishop of York.   53
  When I have fought with Pembroke and his fellows,
  I'll follow you, and tell what answer
  Lewis and the Lady Bona send to him.
  Now, for a while farewell, good Duke of York.
                    They [begin to] lead him out forcibly.

KING EDWARD
  What fates impose, that men must needs abide.
  It boots not to resist both wind and tide.   59
                    Exeunt [Edward, Somerset, and soldiers].

---

32 ambassade ambassadorial mission   **40 shroud** conceal, shield
42 needs must down must fall of necessity   **44 complices** accomplices
47 My . . . wheel i.e., my spirit rises above the misery of Fortune and her
wheel.   **compass** range, circumference   **48 for his mind** i.e., in his own
thoughts   **53 Archbishop of York** i.e., George Neville   **59 boots** avails

OXFORD
> What now remains, my lords, for us to do
> But march to London with our soldiers?

WARWICK
> Ay, that's the first thing that we have to do,
> To free King Henry from imprisonment
> And see him seated in the regal throne.   *Exeunt.*

❖

4.4   *Enter Rivers and Lady Grey [Queen Elizabeth].*

RIVERS
> Madam, what makes you in this sudden change?   1

QUEEN ELIZABETH
> Why, brother Rivers, are you yet to learn
> What late misfortune is befall'n King Edward?   3

RIVERS
> What? Loss of some pitched battle against Warwick?

QUEEN ELIZABETH
> No, but the loss of his own royal person.

RIVERS   Then is my sovereign slain?

QUEEN ELIZABETH
> Ay, almost slain, for he is taken prisoner,
> Either betrayed by falsehood of his guard
> Or by his foe surprised at unawares;
> And, as I further have to understand,   10
> Is new committed to the Bishop of York,   11
> Fell Warwick's brother, and by that our foe.   12

RIVERS
> These news I must confess are full of grief,
> Yet, gracious madam, bear it as you may.
> Warwick may lose, that now hath won the day.

QUEEN ELIZABETH
> Till then fair hope must hinder life's decay.   16
> And I the rather wean me from despair

4.4. Location: London. The royal court.
1 makes ... change causes this sudden change (of mood) in you   **3 late**
recent   **10 have to** am given to   **11 new** newly.   **Bishop** i.e., Archbishop
12 Fell cruel.   **by that** i.e., by that token   **16 hope ... decay** i.e., only
hope can hold off my downfall and death

For love of Edward's offspring in my womb.
This is it that makes me bridle passion   19
And bear with mildness my misfortune's cross.
Ay, ay, for this I draw in many a tear   21
And stop the rising of bloodsucking sighs,   22
Lest with my sighs or tears I blast or drown   23
King Edward's fruit, true heir to th' English crown.

RIVERS
But, madam, where is Warwick then become?

QUEEN ELIZABETH
I am informed that he comes towards London
To set the crown once more on Henry's head.
Guess thou the rest. King Edward's friends must down. 28
But, to prevent the tyrant's violence—   29
For trust not him that hath once broken faith—
I'll hence forthwith unto the sanctuary,   31
To save at least the heir of Edward's right.   32
There shall I rest secure from force and fraud.
Come, therefore, let us fly while we may fly.
If Warwick take us we are sure to die.   *Exeunt.*

❖

4.5   *Enter Richard, [Duke of Gloucester,] Lord
Hastings, and Sir William Stanley.*

GLOUCESTER
Now, my Lord Hastings and Sir William Stanley,
Leave off to wonder why I drew you hither   2
Into this chiefest thicket of the park.   3
Thus stands the case: you know our king, my brother,
Is prisoner to the Bishop here, at whose hands
He hath good usage and great liberty,

---

19 bridle passion control my grief   **21 draw in** hold back   **22 bloodsucking sighs** (Sighs were thought to cost the heart a drop of blood.)
23 blast wither, blight   **28 must down** are destined to fall   **29 prevent**
forestall   **31 the sanctuary** residence inside a church building, providing immunity from law   **32 right** royal claim

**4.5. Location: A park belonging to the Archbishop of York, historically
identified as Middleham Castle in Yorkshire.**
2 Leave off cease   **3 chiefest thicket** thickest copse

And, often but attended with weak guard,   7
Comes hunting this way to disport himself.   8
I have advertised him by secret means   9
That if about this hour he make this way   10
Under the color of his usual game,   11
He shall here find his friends with horse and men
To set him free from his captivity.

Enter King Edward and a Huntsman with him.

HUNTSMAN
This way, my lord, for this way lies the game.   14
KING EDWARD
Nay, this way, man. See where the huntsmen stand.
Now, brother of Gloucester, Lord Hastings, and the rest,
Stand you thus close to steal the Bishop's deer?   17
GLOUCESTER
Brother, the time and case requireth haste.   18
Your horse stands ready at the park corner.
KING EDWARD
But whither shall we then?
HASTINGS   To Lynn, my lord—   20
And shipped from thence to Flanders?
GLOUCESTER
Well guessed, believe me, for that was my meaning.
KING EDWARD
Stanley, I will requite thy forwardness.   23
GLOUCESTER
But wherefore stay we? 'Tis no time to talk.
KING EDWARD
Huntsman, what sayst thou? Wilt thou go along?   25
HUNTSMAN
Better do so than tarry and be hanged.
GLOUCESTER
Come then, away. Let's ha' no more ado.

7 but attended with attended only by   **8 disport** amuse   **9 advertised**
notified   **10 make** come   **11 color** pretext.   **his usual game** his usual
custom of the hunt   **14 game** quarry   **17 close** concealed   **18 case**
circumstance   **20 Lynn** King's Lynn, a seaport in Norfolk   **23 requite**
repay.   **forwardness** zeal   **25 go along** come along with us

KING EDWARD
  Bishop, farewell! Shield thee from Warwick's frown,
  And pray that I may repossess the crown.   *Exeunt.*

❖

4.6   *Flourish. Enter King Henry the Sixth,*
          Clarence, Warwick, Somerset, young Henry
          [Earl of Richmond], Oxford, Montague, and
          Lieutenant [of the Tower].

KING HENRY
  Master Lieutenant, now that God and friends
  Have shaken Edward from the regal seat
  And turned my captive state to liberty,
  My fear to hope, my sorrows unto joys,
  At our enlargement what are thy due fees?   5
LIEUTENANT
  Subjects may challenge nothing of their sovereigns;   6
  But if an humble prayer may prevail,
  I then crave pardon of Your Majesty.
KING HENRY
  For what, Lieutenant? For well using me?
  Nay, be thou sure I'll well requite thy kindness,
  For that it made my imprisonment a pleasure—   11
  Ay, such a pleasure as encagèd birds
  Conceive when, after many moody thoughts,
  At last by notes of household harmony   14
  They quite forget their loss of liberty.
  But, Warwick, after God, thou sett'st me free,
  And chiefly therefore I thank God and thee.
  He was the author, thou the instrument.
  Therefore, that I may conquer fortune's spite
  By living low, where fortune cannot hurt me,   20

4.6. Location: The Tower of London.
s.d. Enter . . . Tower (In the octavo stage direction, Warwick and Clarence enter first "with the crown," then Henry, Oxford, Somerset, and
"the young Earl of Richmond.")   **5 enlargement** release from confinement   **6 challenge** claim as a right   **11 For that** because   **14 household
harmony** harmonious song suited to a domestic life   **20 low** humbly

And that the people of this blessèd land
May not be punished with my thwarting stars,   22
Warwick, although my head still wear the crown,
I here resign my government to thee,
For thou art fortunate in all thy deeds.

WARWICK
Your Grace hath still been famed for virtuous,   26
And now may seem as wise as virtuous
By spying and avoiding fortune's malice,   28
For few men rightly temper with the stars.   29
Yet in this one thing let me blame Your Grace:
For choosing me when Clarence is in place.   31

CLARENCE
No, Warwick, thou art worthy of the sway,   32
To whom the heavens in thy nativity
Adjudged an olive branch and laurel crown,   34
As likely to be blest in peace and war;
And therefore I yield thee my free consent.   36

WARWICK
And I choose Clarence only for Protector.   37

KING HENRY
Warwick and Clarence, give me both your hands.
                    [*The King joins their hands.*]
Now join your hands, and with your hands your hearts,
That no dissension hinder government.
I make you both Protectors of this land,
While I myself will lead a private life
And in devotion spend my latter days,   43
To sin's rebuke and my Creator's praise.

WARWICK
What answers Clarence to his sovereign's will?

CLARENCE
That he consents, if Warwick yield consent;
For on thy fortune I repose myself.   47

---

22 thwarting crossing (in their astrological influence)   **26 still** always.
famed for virtuous reputed to be virtuous   **28 spying** spying out,
foreseeing   **29 temper . . . stars** i.e., blend or accord with their destiny
31 in place present   **32 sway** rule   **34 olive branch** (Symbol of peace.)
laurel crown (Symbol of honor in war.)   **36 free** freely given   **37 only
for** as sole   **43 latter** last   **47 repose myself** rely

WARWICK
  Why, then, though loath, yet must I be content.
  We'll yoke together, like a double shadow
  To Henry's body, and supply his place—
  I mean, in bearing weight of government
  While he enjoys the honor and his ease.
  And, Clarence, now then it is more than needful
  Forthwith that Edward be pronounced a traitor,
  And all his lands and goods be confiscate.

CLARENCE
  What else? And that succession be determined.   56

WARWICK
  Ay, therein Clarence shall not want his part.   57

KING HENRY
  But with the first of all your chief affairs,
  Let me entreat—for I command no more—
  That Margaret your queen and my son Edward
  Be sent for, to return from France with speed;
  For till I see them here, by doubtful fear
  My joy of liberty is half eclipsed.

CLARENCE
  It shall be done, my sovereign, with all speed.

KING HENRY
  My lord of Somerset, what youth is that
  Of whom you seem to have so tender care?

SOMERSET
  My liege, it is young Henry, Earl of Richmond.   67

KING HENRY
  Come hither, England's hope. (*Lays his hand on
     his head.*) If secret powers
  Suggest but truth to my divining thoughts,   69
  This pretty lad will prove our country's bliss.
  His looks are full of peaceful majesty,
  His head by nature framed to wear a crown,
  His hand to wield a scepter, and himself

56 **What else** i.e., yes, certainly. **succession be determined** the order of
succession to the throne (in view of Edward's removal) be definitely
established 57 **want** lack. (Clarence would have an interest in the
crown previously claimed by his brother and willed to him after Henry's death.) 67 **Henry . . . Richmond** Henry Tudor, later Henry VII and
founder of the Tudor dynasty 69 **divining** foreseeing the future

Likely in time to bless a regal throne.
Make much of him, my lords, for this is he
Must help you more than you are hurt by me.

 Enter a Post.

WARWICK What news, my friend?
POST
 That Edward is escapèd from your brother   78
 And fled, as he hears since, to Burgundy.   79
WARWICK
 Unsavory news! But how made he escape?
POST
 He was conveyed by Richard, Duke of Gloucester, 81
 And the Lord Hastings, who attended him   82
 In secret ambush on the forest side
 And from the Bishop's huntsmen rescued him;
 For hunting was his daily exercise.
WARWICK
 My brother was too careless of his charge.
 But let us hence, my sovereign, to provide
 A salve for any sore that may betide.   88
      Exeunt. Manent Somerset,
       Richmond, and Oxford.
SOMERSET [*To Oxford*]
 My lord, I like not of this flight of Edward's; 89
 For doubtless Burgundy will yield him help,
 And we shall have more wars before 't be long.
 As Henry's late presaging prophecy
 Did glad my heart with hope of this young Richmond,
 So doth my heart misgive me, in these conflicts
 What may befall him, to his harm and ours.
 Therefore, Lord Oxford, to prevent the worst,
 Forthwith we'll send him hence to Brittany,
 Till storms be past of civil enmity.
OXFORD
 Ay, for if Edward repossess the crown,

---

78 your brother i.e., the Archbishop of York **79 he** i.e., your brother
81 conveyed spirited away **82 attended** awaited **88 betide** occur,
develop **s.d. Manent** they remain onstage **89 like not of** am displeased by

'Tis like that Richmond with the rest shall down.   100
SOMERSET
It shall be so. He shall to Brittany.
Come, therefore, let's about it speedily.   *Exeunt.*

❖

4.7   *Flourish. Enter [King] Edward, Richard, [Duke*
          of Gloucester,] Hastings, and soldiers, [a troop
          of Hollanders].

KING EDWARD
Now, brother Richard, Lord Hastings, and the rest,
Yet thus far fortune maketh us amends
And says that once more I shall interchange
My wanèd state for Henry's regal crown.
Well have we passed and now repassed the seas,
And brought desirèd help from Burgundy.
What then remains, we being thus arrived
From Ravenspurgh haven before the gates of York,   8
But that we enter, as into our dukedom?
GLOUCESTER
The gates made fast? Brother, I like not this;
For many men that stumble at the threshold
Are well foretold that danger lurks within.
KING EDWARD
Tush, man, abodements must not now affright us.   13
By fair or foul means we must enter in,
For hither will our friends repair to us.
HASTINGS
My liege, I'll knock once more to summon them.   16

          Enter, on the walls, the Mayor of York and his
          brethren [the aldermen].

100 like likely.   **down** fall

4.7. Location: Before the walls of York.
8 Ravenspurgh former seaport on the Yorkshire coast, at the mouth of
the River Humber   **13 abodements** omens (such as stumbling at the
threshold, a conventional sign of bad luck)   **16 s.d. on the walls** (In this
scene, the back wall of the stage, or tiring-house facade, is imagined
to be the walls of York; a door in the facade represents the gates; and
persons in the rear gallery above the stage are *on the walls.*)

MAYOR

My lords, we were forewarnèd of your coming
And shut the gates for safety of ourselves;
For now we owe allegiance unto Henry.

KING EDWARD

But, Master Mayor, if Henry be your king,
Yet Edward at the least is Duke of York.

MAYOR

True, my good lord, I know you for no less.

KING EDWARD

Why, and I challenge nothing but my dukedom,   23
As being well content with that alone.

GLOUCESTER [Aside]

But when the fox hath once got in his nose,
He'll soon find means to make the body follow.

HASTINGS

Why, Master Mayor, why stand you in a doubt?
Open the gates. We are King Henry's friends.

MAYOR

Ay, say you so? The gates shall then be opened.   29
                    He descends [with the aldermen].

GLOUCESTER

A wise stout captain, and soon persuaded!   30

HASTINGS

The good old man would fain that all were well,   31
So 'twere not long of him; but being entered,   32
I doubt not, I, but we shall soon persuade
Both him and all his brothers unto reason.

Enter [below] the Mayor and two aldermen.

KING EDWARD

So, Master Mayor, these gates must not be shut
But in the night or in the time of war.
What, fear not, man, but yield me up the keys,
                    Takes his keys

23 **challenge** claim   29 **s.d. descends** (The Mayor and aldermen descend
from the rear gallery behind the scenes, and then enter below through
the door representing the gates of York.)   30 **stout** brave   31 **fain** be
glad   32 **So . . . him** as long as he does not bear the responsibility

For Edward will defend the town and thee,
And all those friends that deign to follow me.   39

*March. Enter Montgomery, with drum
and Soldiers.*

GLOUCESTER
Brother, this is Sir John Montgomery,   40
Our trusty friend, unless I be deceived.
KING EDWARD
Welcome, Sir John! But why come you in arms?
MONTGOMERY
To help King Edward in his time of storm,
As every loyal subject ought to do.
KING EDWARD
Thanks, good Montgomery; but we now forget
Our title to the crown, and only claim
Our dukedom till God please to send the rest.
MONTGOMERY
Then fare you well, for I will hence again.
I came to serve a king and not a duke.
Drummer, strike up, and let us march away.   50
                    The drum begins to march.
KING EDWARD
Nay, stay, Sir John, awhile, and we'll debate
By what safe means the crown may be recovered.
MONTGOMERY
What talk you of debating? In few words,
If you'll not here proclaim yourself our king,
I'll leave you to your fortune and be gone
To keep them back that come to succor you.
Why shall we fight, if you pretend no title?   57
GLOUCESTER
Why, brother, wherefore stand you on nice points?   58
KING EDWARD
When we grow stronger, then we'll make our claim;
Till then, 'tis wisdom to conceal our meaning.   60

39 deign are willing   **s.d. drum** drummer   **40 Sir John Montgomery**
(Called "Sir Thomas" in the chronicles.)   **50 s.d. drum . . . march**
drummer strikes up a marching beat   **57 pretend** claim   **58 nice points**
overscrupulous details   **60 meaning** intentions

HASTINGS
Away with scrupulous wit! Now arms must rule.   61
GLOUCESTER
And fearless minds climb soonest unto crowns.
Brother, we will proclaim you out of hand;   63
The bruit thereof will bring you many friends.   64
KING EDWARD
Then be it as you will. For 'tis my right,
And Henry but usurps the diadem.
MONTGOMERY
Ay, now my sovereign speaketh like himself,
And now will I be Edward's champion.
HASTINGS
Sound trumpet! Edward shall be here proclaimed.
Come, fellow soldier, make thou proclamation.
                    [He gives a Soldier a paper.]
                         Flourish. Sound.
SOLDIER [*Reads*] "Edward the Fourth, by the grace of
God, King of England and France, and lord of Ireland,
etc."
MONTGOMERY
And whosoe'er gainsays King Edward's right,   74
By this I challenge him to single fight.
                    Throws down his gauntlet.
ALL   Long live Edward the Fourth!
KING EDWARD
Thanks, brave Montgomery, and thanks unto you all.
If fortune serve me, I'll requite this kindness.
Now, for this night, let's harbor here in York;
And when the morning sun shall raise his car   80
Above the border of this horizon,
We'll forward towards Warwick and his mates;
For well I wot that Henry is no soldier.   83
Ah, froward Clarence, how evil it beseems thee   84
To flatter Henry and forsake thy brother!
Yet, as we may, we'll meet both thee and Warwick.

---

61 scrupulous wit cautious or prudent reasoning   **63 out of hand** at
once   **64 bruit** rumor, report   **74 gainsays** denies   **80 his car** i.e.,
Phoebus' chariot   **83 wot** know   **84 froward** perverse.   **evil** ill

Come on, brave soldiers. Doubt not of the day,   87
And that once gotten, doubt not of large pay.

Exeunt.

❖

4.8   *Flourish. Enter the King [Henry], Warwick,*
Montague, Clarence, Oxford, and Exeter.

WARWICK
  What counsel, lords? Edward from Belgia,   1
  With hasty Germans and blunt Hollanders,   2
  Hath passed in safety through the narrow seas   3
  And with his troops doth march amain to London,   4
  And many giddy people flock to him.   5
KING HENRY
  Let's levy men and beat him back again.
CLARENCE
  A little fire is quickly trodden out
  Which, being suffered, rivers cannot quench.   8
WARWICK
  In Warwickshire I have truehearted friends,
  Not mutinous in peace, yet bold in war.
  Those will I muster up. And thou, son Clarence,   11
  Shalt stir up in Suffolk, Norfolk, and in Kent
  The knights and gentlemen to come with thee.
  Thou, brother Montague, in Buckingham,
  Northampton, and in Leicestershire, shalt find
  Men well inclined to hear what thou command'st.
  And thou, brave Oxford, wondrous well beloved,
  In Oxfordshire shalt muster up thy friends.
  My sovereign, with the loving citizens,
  Like to his island girt in with the ocean,
  Or modest Dian circled with her nymphs,   21

---

87 the day the day's outcome

4.8. Location: The Bishop of London's palace.
1 Belgia i.e., the Low Countries   **2 hasty** quick-tempered.   **blunt** harsh,
merciless   **3 narrow seas** English Channel   **4 amain** with full speed
5 giddy fickle   **8 suffered** allowed   **11 son** i.e., son-in-law   **21 modest
Dian** chaste Diana, goddess of the moon and of chastity

Shall rest in London till we come to him.   22
Fair lords, take leave and stand not to reply.   23
Farewell, my sovereign.

KING HENRY
Farewell, my Hector and my Troy's true hope.   25

CLARENCE [*Kissing the King's hand*]
In sign of truth, I kiss Your Highness' hand.

KING HENRY
Well-minded Clarence, be thou fortunate!   27

MONTAGUE [*Kissing the King's hand*]
Comfort, my lord; and so I take my leave.

OXFORD [*Kissing the King's hand*]
And thus I seal my truth, and bid adieu.   29

KING HENRY
Sweet Oxford, and my loving Montague,
And all at once, once more a happy farewell.   31

WARWICK
Farewell, sweet lords. Let's meet at Coventry.
        Exeunt [*all but King Henry and Exeter*].

KING HENRY
Here at the palace will I rest awhile.   33
Cousin of Exeter, what thinks your lordship?   34
Methinks the power that Edward hath in field
Should not be able to encounter mine.

EXETER
The doubt is that he will seduce the rest.   37

KING HENRY
That's not my fear. My meed hath got me fame.   38
I have not stopped mine ears to their demands,
Nor posted off their suits with slow delays.   40
My pity hath been balm to heal their wounds,
My mildness hath allayed their swelling griefs,

---

22 rest remain   **23 stand** wait   **25 Hector** i.e., chief protector of Troy. (England derived its legendary descent from Troy, through Brutus, great-grandson of Aeneas, supposed founder of the English nation.) **27 Well-minded** virtuously inclined   **29 seal my truth** confirm my loyalty (as though putting a seal to a document)   **31 at once** together **33 palace** i.e., Bishop's palace   **34 Cousin** (Form of address from the King to his peers.)   **37 doubt** fear, danger   **38 My . . . fame** my merits (for dealing generously and justly) have established my reputation **40 posted off** put off

My mercy dried their water-flowing tears.   43
I have not been desirous of their wealth,
Nor much oppressed them with great subsidies,   45
Nor forward of revenge, though they much erred.   46
Then why should they love Edward more than me?
No, Exeter, these graces challenge grace;   48
And when the lion fawns upon the lamb,
The lamb will never cease to follow him.   50

> *Shout within,* "A Lancaster!" "A York!"

EXETER
Hark, hark, my lord! What shouts are these?

> *Enter [King] Edward and his soldiers [with*
> *Gloucester].*

KING EDWARD
Seize on the shamefaced Henry. Bear him hence,   52
And once again proclaim us king of England!
You are the fount that makes small brooks to flow.
Now stops thy spring; my sea shall suck them dry   55
And swell so much the higher by their ebb.
Hence with him to the Tower. Let him not speak.

> *Exit [guard] with King Henry.*

And, lords, towards Coventry bend we our course,
Where peremptory Warwick now remains.   59
The sun shines hot, and, if we use delay,   60
Cold biting winter mars our hoped-for hay.   61

GLOUCESTER
Away betimes, before his forces join,   62
And take the great-grown traitor unawares.
Brave warriors, march amain towards Coventry.

> *Exeunt.*

❖

43 **water-flowing tears** tears flowing like water   45 **subsidies** taxes
46 **forward of** eager for   48 **challenge grace** claim favor   50 **s.d. A
Lancaster! A York** (Conflicting rallying cries for both sides.)   52 **shamefaced** shy, shamefast   55 **thy spring** i.e., the source of your power
59 **peremptory** overbearing   60–61 **The sun . . . hay** i.e., make hay while
the sun shines   62 **betimes** quickly.   **join** unite

5.1   *Enter Warwick, the Mayor of Coventry, two*
Messengers, and others upon the walls.

WARWICK
　Where is the post that came from valiant Oxford?—   1
　How far hence is thy lord, mine honest fellow?
FIRST MESSENGER
　By this at Dunsmore, marching hitherward.   3
WARWICK
　How far off is our brother Montague?
　Where is the post that came from Montague?
SECOND MESSENGER
　By this at Daintry, with a puissant troop.   6

　　Enter [Sir John] Somerville [to them, aloft].

WARWICK
　Say, Somerville, what says my loving son?   7
　And, by thy guess, how nigh is Clarence now?
SOMERVILLE
　At Southam I did leave him with his forces,   9
　And do expect him here some two hours hence.
　　　　　　　　　　　　　　[A march afar off.]
WARWICK
　Then Clarence is at hand. I hear his drum.
SOMERVILLE
　It is not his, my lord. Here Southam lies.   *[He points.]*
　The drum your honor hears marcheth from Warwick.   13
WARWICK
　Who should that be? Belike unlooked-for friends.
SOMERVILLE
　They are at hand, and you shall quickly know.

　　March. Flourish. Enter [King] Edward, Richard,
　　[Duke of Gloucester,] and soldiers [below].

5.1. Location: Before the walls of Coventry.
s.d. upon the walls (As in 4.7, the *walls* of this town are the tiring-house
facade backstage, and those appearing *on the walls* are in the rear
gallery above the stage.)   **1 post** messenger (also in l. 5)   **3 By this** by
this time   **3, 6, 9, 13 Dunsmore, Daintry** (i.e., Daventry), **Southam,**
Warwick (Towns within a day's march of Coventry.)   **6 puissant** powerful   **7 son** i.e., son-in-law

KING EDWARD
  Go, trumpet, to the walls and sound a parle.   16
                      [*A parley is sounded.*]

GLOUCESTER
  See how the surly Warwick mans the wall!

WARWICK
  O unbid spite! Is sportful Edward come?   18
  Where slept our scouts, or how are they seduced,
  That we could hear no news of his repair?   20

KING EDWARD
  Now, Warwick, wilt thou ope the city gates,
  Speak gentle words, and humbly bend thy knee,
  Call Edward king, and at his hands beg mercy?
  And he shall pardon thee these outrages.

WARWICK
  Nay, rather, wilt thou draw thy forces hence,   25
  Confess who set thee up and plucked thee down,
  Call Warwick patron, and be penitent?
  And thou shalt still remain the Duke of York.

GLOUCESTER
  I thought at least he would have said "the King";
  Or did he make the jest against his will?

WARWICK
  Is not a dukedom, sir, a goodly gift?

GLOUCESTER
  Ay, by my faith, for a poor earl to give.
  I'll do thee service for so good a gift.   33

WARWICK
  'Twas I that gave the kingdom to thy brother.

KING EDWARD
  Why then, 'tis mine, if but by Warwick's gift.

WARWICK
  Thou art no Atlas for so great a weight;   36
  And, weakling, Warwick takes his gift again,
  And Henry is my king, Warwick his subject.

---

16 trumpet trumpeter. **parle** trumpet call for a parley **18 unbid**
unwelcome. **spite** vexatious circumstance. **sportful** lascivious
20 repair approach **25 draw** withdraw **33 do thee service** i.e., pay
feudal homage. (Said ironically.) **36 Atlas** the Titan's son in classical
myth who carried the world on his shoulders

KING EDWARD

But Warwick's king is Edward's prisoner.
And, gallant Warwick, do but answer this:
What is the body when the head is off?

GLOUCESTER

Alas, that Warwick had no more forecast,   42
But, whiles he thought to steal the single ten,   43
The King was slyly fingered from the deck!
You left poor Henry at the Bishop's palace,
And ten to one you'll meet him in the Tower.

KING EDWARD

'Tis even so. Yet you are Warwick still.   47

GLOUCESTER

Come, Warwick, take the time. Kneel down, kneel down.   48
Nay, when? Strike now, or else the iron cools.   49

WARWICK

I had rather chop this hand off at a blow,
And with the other fling it at thy face,
Than bear so low a sail to strike to thee.

KING EDWARD

Sail how thou canst, have wind and tide thy friend,
This hand, fast wound about thy coal black hair,
Shall, whiles thy head is warm and new cut off,
Write in the dust this sentence with thy blood:
"Wind-changing Warwick now can change no more."   57

Enter Oxford, with drum and colors.

WARWICK

O cheerful colors! See where Oxford comes!

OXFORD

Oxford, Oxford, for Lancaster!
                    [*He and his forces enter the city.*]

---

42 forecast forethought   **43 single ten** mere ten-card. (Less valuable
than the king-card.)   **47 Yet . . . still** i.e., you are still the Duke of
Warwick and still have time to change before disaster strikes   **48 time**
opportunity   **49 when** i.e., when are you going to act. (An expression of
impatience.)   **Strike . . . cools** i.e., strike while the iron is hot. (But
strike also means to lower sail, yield; hence Warwick's refusal to *bear so
low a sail,* i.e., offer tokens of submission, in l. 52. Cf. 3.3.5, note.)
57 Wind-changing i.e., shifting, like a weathervane   **s.d. drum** drummer.
colors flags borne by flag carriers

GLOUCESTER
  The gates are open. Let us enter too.

KING EDWARD
  So other foes may set upon our backs.   61
  Stand we in good array, for they no doubt
  Will issue out again and bid us battle.
  If not, the city being but of small defense,
  We'll quickly rouse the traitors in the same.   65
            [*Oxford appears above, on the walls.*]

WARWICK
  O, welcome, Oxford, for we want thy help.

     Enter Montague, with drum and colors.

MONTAGUE
  Montague, Montague, for Lancaster!
          [*He and his forces enter the city.*]

GLOUCESTER
  Thou and thy brother both shall buy this treason   68
  Even with the dearest blood your bodies bear.

KING EDWARD
  The harder matched, the greater victory.   70
  My mind presageth happy gain and conquest.   71

     Enter Somerset, with drum and colors.

SOMERSET
  Somerset, Somerset, for Lancaster!
          [*He and his forces enter the city.*]

GLOUCESTER
  Two of thy name, both Dukes of Somerset,   73
  Have sold their lives unto the house of York,
  And thou shalt be the third, if this sword hold.

     Enter Clarence, with drum and colors.

---

61 So in that case. **set . . . backs** attack us from the rear **65 rouse**
cause (an animal) to rise from its lair **68 buy** pay dearly for **70 The
harder . . . victory** the more powerful the enemy, the greater the victory.
(Proverbial.) **71 happy** fortunate **73 Two of thy name** i.e., Edmund
Beaufort, second Duke of Somerset, killed at St. Albans in 1455, and his
son Henry (not a character in this play), beheaded in 1464 for his Lancastrian sympathies. (The duke addressed here is Henry's brother
Edmund, fourth duke.)

WARWICK
And lo, where George of Clarence sweeps along,
Of force enough to bid his brother battle;   77
With whom an upright zeal to right prevails   78
More than the nature of a brother's love!   79
          [*Gloucester and Clarence whisper together.*]
Come, Clarence, come. Thou wilt, if Warwick call.

CLARENCE
Father of Warwick, know you what this means?   81
          [*He takes his red rose out of his hat and
                              throws it at Warwick.*]
Look here, I throw my infamy at thee.
I will not ruinate my father's house,   83
Who gave his blood to lime the stones together,   84
And set up Lancaster. Why, trowest thou, Warwick,   85
That Clarence is so harsh, so blunt, unnatural,
To bend the fatal instruments of war   87
Against his brother and his lawful king?
Perhaps thou wilt object my holy oath.   89
To keep that oath were more impiety
Than Jephthah when he sacrificed his daughter.   91
I am so sorry for my trespass made
That, to deserve well at my brother's hands,
I here proclaim myself thy mortal foe,
With resolution, wheresoe'er I meet thee—
As I will meet thee, if thou stir abroad—   96
To plague thee for thy foul misleading me.
And so, proudhearted Warwick, I defy thee,
And to my brother turn my blushing cheeks.
Pardon me, Edward, I will make amends;
And, Richard, do not frown upon my faults,
For I will henceforth be no more unconstant.

77 **Of force enough** with a powerful enough army   **78 to right** on behalf
of justice   **79 nature** natural feeling   **s.d. Gloucester . . . together** (This
stage direction, and that at l. 81, are basically from the octavo text.)
81 Father i.e., father-in-law   **83 ruinate** bring into ruin   **84 lime** cement
85 trowest thou do you think   **87 bend** direct   **89 object** urge   **91 Jephthah** (See Judges 11:30 ff. for the account of Jephthah's vow to sacrifice,
if victorious, the first living creature that came to meet him on his
return. His daughter was the victim.)   **96 abroad** from home, i.e.,
outside the city walls

KING EDWARD
Now welcome more, and ten times more beloved,
Than if thou never hadst deserved our hate!
GLOUCESTER
Welcome, good Clarence. This is brotherlike.
WARWICK
O passing traitor, perjured and unjust!   106
KING EDWARD
What, Warwick, wilt thou leave the town and fight?
Or shall we beat the stones about thine ears?
WARWICK
Alas, I am not cooped here for defense!
I will away towards Barnet presently,   110
And bid thee battle, Edward, if thou dar'st.
KING EDWARD
Yes, Warwick, Edward dares, and leads the way.
Lords, to the field! Saint George and victory!
                    Exeunt [King Edward and his company].
                        March. Warwick and his company
                            follows [out of the city].

5.2   *Alarum and excursions. Enter [King] Edward,*
           bringing forth Warwick wounded.

KING EDWARD
So, lie thou there. Die thou, and die our fear,
For Warwick was a bug that feared us all.   2
Now, Montague, sit fast. I seek for thee,   3
That Warwick's bones may keep thine company. *Exit.*
WARWICK
Ah, who is nigh? Come to me, friend or foe,
And tell me who is victor, York or Warwick?

106 passing surpassing   **110 Barnet** a town in Hertfordshire, about ten
miles north of London. (Warwick's illogical proposal that the armies
meet at Barnet, some seventy-five miles from Coventry, is a result of
Shakespeare's telescoping and rearranging of historical events.)   **presently** immediately

**5.2. Location: A field of battle near Barnet. (Despite the distance from
Coventry to Barnet, the sense here is of virtually continuous action.)
2 bug** bugbear, goblin.   **feared** frightened   **3 sit fast** position yourself
as securely as you can

Why ask I that? My mangled body shows,
My blood, my want of strength, my sick heart shows,
That I must yield my body to the earth
And, by my fall, the conquest to my foe.
Thus yields the cedar to the ax's edge,
Whose arms gave shelter to the princely eagle,   12
Under whose shade the ramping lion slept,   13
Whose top branch overpeered Jove's spreading tree   14
And kept low shrubs from winter's powerful wind.
These eyes, that now are dimmed with death's black veil,
Have been as piercing as the midday sun
To search the secret treasons of the world.
The wrinkles in my brows, now filled with blood,
Were likened oft to kingly sepulchers;
For who lived king, but I could dig his grave?
And who durst smile when Warwick bent his brow?   22
Lo, now my glory smeared in dust and blood!
My parks, my walks, my manors that I had,
Even now forsake me, and of all my lands
Is nothing left me but my body's length.
Why, what is pomp, rule, reign, but earth and dust?
And, live we how we can, yet die we must.

> *Enter Oxford and Somerset.*

SOMERSET
Ah, Warwick, Warwick! Wert thou as we are,
We might recover all our loss again.
The Queen from France hath brought a puissant power;   31
Even now we heard the news. Ah, couldst thou fly!
WARWICK
Why, then I would not fly. Ah, Montague,
If thou be there, sweet brother, take my hand,
And with thy lips keep in my soul awhile!   35
Thou lov'st me not, for, brother, if thou didst,
Thy tears would wash this cold congealèd blood

12, 13 eagle, lion (Royal emblems; Warwick, the lofty *cedar* in this
metaphor, has at times given his protection to both Edward and Henry.)
13 ramping rampant, upreared. (A heraldic term.)   **14 Jove's spreading
tree** i.e., the oak   **22 bent his brow** frowned   **31 puissant** powerful
35 with thy lips i.e., with a kiss. (The soul was thought to leave the body
through the mouth.)

That glues my lips and will not let me speak.
Come quickly, Montague, or I am dead.

SOMERSET
Ah, Warwick, Montague hath breathed his last,
And to the latest gasp cried out for Warwick   41
And said "Commend me to my valiant brother."
And more he would have said, and more he spoke,
Which sounded like a cannon in a vault,
That mought not be distinguished; but at last   45
I well might hear, delivered with a groan,
"O, farewell, Warwick!"

WARWICK
Sweet rest his soul! Fly, lords, and save yourselves,
For Warwick bids you all farewell, to meet in heaven.
                                        [*He dies.*]

OXFORD
Away, away, to meet the Queen's great power!
                Here they bear away his body. Exeunt.

5.3   *Flourish. Enter King Edward in triumph, with
           Richard, [Duke of Gloucester,] Clarence, and
           the rest.*

KING EDWARD
Thus far our fortune keeps an upward course,
And we are graced with wreaths of victory.
But in the midst of this bright-shining day
I spy a black, suspicious, threatening cloud
That will encounter with our glorious sun   5
Ere he attain his easeful western bed:
I mean, my lords, those powers that the Queen
Hath raised in Gallia have arrived our coast   8
And, as we hear, march on to fight with us.

CLARENCE
A little gale will soon disperse that cloud
And blow it to the source from whence it came.

41 **latest** last   45 **mought** might

5.3. Location: The field of battle near Barnet, as before.
5 **sun** i.e., the heraldic sun on the Yorkist coat of arms   8 **Gallia** France.
arrived reached

The very beams will dry those vapors up,   12
For every cloud engenders not a storm.

GLOUCESTER
The Queen is valued thirty thousand strong,
And Somerset, with Oxford, fled to her.
If she have time to breathe, be well assured   16
Her faction will be full as strong as ours.

KING EDWARD
We are advertised by our loving friends   18
That they do hold their course toward Tewkesbury.   19
We, having now the best at Barnet field,
Will thither straight, for willingness rids way;   21
And, as we march, our strength will be augmented
In every county as we go along.
Strike up the drum, cry "Courage!" and away.

Exeunt.

❖

5.4   *Flourish. March. Enter the Queen [Margaret],
young [Prince] Edward, Somerset, Oxford,
and soldiers.*

QUEEN MARGARET
Great lords, wise men ne'er sit and wail their loss,
But cheerly seek how to redress their harms.   2
What though the mast be now blown overboard,
The cable broke, the holding anchor lost,
And half our sailors swallowed in the flood?
Yet lives our pilot still. Is 't meet that he   6
Should leave the helm and, like a fearful lad,
With tearful eyes add water to the sea
And give more strength to that which hath too much,
Whiles, in his moan, the ship splits on the rock,   10

---

12 **very** mere   16 **breathe** i.e., pause and muster her strength   18 **advertised** notified   19 **Tewkesbury** a town in Gloucestershire   21 **straight**
immediately.   **rids way** annihilates distance, makes the way seem short

5.4. Location: Near Tewkesbury.
2 **cheerly** cheerfully   6 **our pilot** i.e., King Henry   10 **in his moan** as he
makes lamentation

Which industry and courage might have saved?
Ah, what a shame, ah, what a fault were this!
Say Warwick was our anchor. What of that?
And Montague our topmast. What of him?
Our slaughtered friends the tackles. What of these?   15
Why, is not Oxford here another anchor?
And Somerset another goodly mast?
The friends of France our shrouds and tacklings?   18
And, though unskillful, why not Ned and I
For once allowed the skillful pilot's charge?   20
We will not from the helm to sit and weep,   21
But keep our course, though the rough wind say no,
From shelves and rocks that threaten us with wreck.   23
As good to chide the waves as speak them fair.   24
And what is Edward but a ruthless sea?
What Clarence but a quicksand of deceit?
And Richard but a ragged fatal rock?
All these the enemies to our poor bark.
Say you can swim, alas, 'tis but a while;
Tread on the sand, why, there you quickly sink;
Bestride the rock, the tide will wash you off,
Or else you famish—that's a threefold death.
This speak I, lords, to let you understand,
If case some one of you would fly from us,   34
That there's no hoped-for mercy with the brothers
More than with ruthless waves, with sands and rocks.
Why, courage then! What cannot be avoided
'Twere childish weakness to lament or fear.
PRINCE
Methinks a woman of this valiant spirit
Should, if a coward heard her speak these words,
Infuse his breast with magnanimity
And make him, naked, foil a man at arms.   42
I speak not this as doubting any here;
For did I but suspect a fearful man,
He should have leave to go away betimes,   45

15 **tackles** rigging   18 **shrouds** ropes or cables supporting the mast
20 **charge** responsibility   21 **from** go away from   23 **shelves** sandbanks,
shoals   24 **As good to** i.e., one might as well.   **speak them fair** address
them courteously   34 **If** in   42 **naked** unarmed.   **foil** defeat.   **man at
arms** armed soldier   45 **betimes** at once

Lest in our need he might infect another
And make him of like spirit to himself.
If any such be here—as God forbid!—
Let him depart before we need his help.

OXFORD
Women and children of so high a courage,
And warriors faint! Why, 'twere perpetual shame.
O brave young Prince! Thy famous grandfather   52
Doth live again in thee. Long mayst thou live
To bear his image and renew his glories!   54

SOMERSET
And he that will not fight for such a hope,
Go home to bed, and, like the owl by day,
If he arise, be mocked and wondered at.

QUEEN MARGARET
Thanks, gentle Somerset; sweet Oxford, thanks.

PRINCE
And take his thanks that yet hath nothing else.   59

        Enter a Messenger.

MESSENGER
Prepare you, lords, for Edward is at hand,
Ready to fight. Therefore be resolute.

OXFORD
I thought no less. It is his policy   62
To haste thus fast, to find us unprovided.   63

SOMERSET
But he's deceived. We are in readiness.

QUEEN MARGARET
This cheers my heart, to see your forwardness.   65

OXFORD
Here pitch our battle. Hence we will not budge.   66

        Flourish and march. Enter [King] Edward,
        Richard, [Duke of Gloucester,] Clarence,
        and soldiers.

---

52 grandfather i.e., Henry V   **54 image** likeness   **59 his . . . else** i.e., my
thanks, I who as yet have nothing else to give   **62 policy** stratagem
63 unprovided unprepared   **65 forwardness** eagerness   **66 pitch our**
battle draw up our armies

KING EDWARD
  Brave followers, yonder stands the thorny wood
  Which, by the heavens' assistance and your strength,
  Must by the roots be hewn up yet ere night.
  I need not add more fuel to your fire,
  For well I wot ye blaze to burn them out.   71
  Give signal to the fight, and to it, lords!
QUEEN MARGARET
  Lords, knights, and gentlemen, what I should say
  My tears gainsay; for every word I speak,   74
  Ye see, I drink the water of mine eye.
  Therefore, no more but this: Henry, your sovereign,
  Is prisoner to the foe, his state usurped,   77
  His realm a slaughterhouse, his subjects slain,
  His statutes canceled, and his treasure spent;
  And yonder is the wolf that makes this spoil.   80
  You fight in justice. Then, in God's name, lords,
  Be valiant, and give signal to the fight.   82
              Alarum. Retreat. Excursions [in which
                Queen Margaret, Prince Edward, Oxford,
                and Somerset are taken]. Exeunt.

5.5   *Flourish. Enter [King] Edward, Richard, [Duke*
          of Gloucester,] Queen [Margaret, as prisoner],
          Clarence; Oxford, Somerset [as prisoners].

KING EDWARD
  Now here a period of tumultuous broils.   1
  Away with Oxford to Hames Castle straight.   2
  For Somerset, off with his guilty head.   3
  Go, bear them hence. I will not hear them speak.

---

71 **wot** know   74 **gainsay** forbid   77 **state** royal status as king   80 **spoil**
plunder, destruction   82 **s.d. Alarum** (The octavo version provides that
chambers or short cannon are "discharged," after which King Edward
and his brothers and allies enter with "a great shout," and cry "For
York! For York!" and take the Queen and her son.)

5.5. Location: Scene continues at the battlefield near Tewkesbury.
1 **period** termination   2 **Hames Castle** i.e., Hammes Castle near Calais
(where Oxford was indeed confined, but not until his capture some
three years after Tewkesbury).   **straight** at once   3 **For** as for

OXFORD
    For my part, I'll not trouble thee with words.
SOMERSET
    Nor I, but stoop with patience to my fortune.
                    Exeunt [Oxford and Somerset, guarded].
QUEEN MARGARET
    So part we sadly in this troublous world,
    To meet with joy in sweet Jerusalem.   8
KING EDWARD
    Is proclamation made that who finds Edward   9
    Shall have a high reward, and he his life?
GLOUCESTER
    It is. And lo, where youthful Edward comes!

            Enter [soldiers, with] the Prince [Edward].

KING EDWARD
    Bring forth the gallant. Let us hear him speak.
    What, can so young a thorn begin to prick?
    Edward, what satisfaction canst thou make   14
    For bearing arms, for stirring up my subjects,
    And all the trouble thou hast turned me to?
PRINCE
    Speak like a subject, proud ambitious York!
    Suppose that I am now my father's mouth;
    Resign thy chair, and where I stand kneel thou,   19
    Whilst I propose the selfsame words to thee,
    Which, traitor, thou wouldst have me answer to.
QUEEN MARGARET
    Ah, that thy father had been so resolved!
GLOUCESTER
    That you might still have worn the petticoat
    And ne'er have stol'n the breech from Lancaster.   24
PRINCE
    Let Aesop fable in a winter's night;   25
    His currish riddles sorts not with this place.   26

---

8 sweet Jerusalem i.e., the heavenly Jerusalem   **9 who** anyone who
14 satisfaction recompense   **19 chair** throne   **24 breech** breeches,
symbol of male authority   **25 Aesop** Greek teller of fables (who, like
Gloucester, was reputed to have been deformed). **in . . . night** i.e., in a
setting fitted for such childish tales   **26 His . . . place** his mean riddles
are inappropriate to this place. (Prince Edward is retorting to Gloucester's jibe, denying the allegation that his father was henpecked.)

GLOUCESTER
By heaven, brat, I'll plague ye for that word.

QUEEN MARGARET
Ay, thou wast born to be a plague to men.

GLOUCESTER
For God's sake, take away this captive scold.

PRINCE
Nay, take away this scolding crookback rather.

KING EDWARD
Peace, willful boy, or I will charm your tongue.   31

CLARENCE
Untutored lad, thou art too malapert.   32

PRINCE
I know my duty. You are all undutiful.
Lascivious Edward, and thou perjured George,
And thou misshapen Dick, I tell ye all
I am your better, traitors as ye are,
And thou usurp'st my father's right and mine.

KING EDWARD
Take that, thou likeness of this railer here!   38
                              Stabs him.

GLOUCESTER
Sprawl'st thou? Take that, to end thy agony.   39
                          Richard stabs him.

CLARENCE
And there's for twitting me with perjury.
              Clarence stabs him. [*Prince Edward dies.*]

QUEEN MARGARET   O, kill me too!

GLOUCESTER   Marry, and shall.   *Offers to kill her.* 42

KING EDWARD
Hold, Richard, hold, for we have done too much.

GLOUCESTER
Why should she live, to fill the world with words?
                              [*Margaret swoons.*]

KING EDWARD
What, doth she swoon? Use means for her recovery.

---

31 charm cast a spell upon, i.e., silence **32 malapert** saucy **38 this railer here** i.e., Queen Margaret **39 Sprawl'st thou** i.e., are you twitching in the throes of death **42 Marry, and shall** i.e., indeed, I will **s.d. Offers to** is about to

GLOUCESTER [*Aside to Clarence*]
  Clarence, excuse me to the King my brother;
  I'll hence to London on a serious matter.
  Ere ye come there, be sure to hear some news.   48
CLARENCE [*Aside to Gloucester*]   What? What?
GLOUCESTER [*Aside to Clarence*]   The Tower, the Tower.
                                   Exit.

QUEEN MARGARET [*Reviving*]
  O Ned, sweet Ned, speak to thy mother, boy!
  Canst thou not speak? O traitors, murderers!
  They that stabbed Caesar shed no blood at all,
  Did not offend, nor were not worthy blame,
  If this foul deed were by to equal it.   55
  He was a man; this, in respect, a child,   56
  And men ne'er spend their fury on a child.
  What's worse than murderer, that I may name it?
  No, no, my heart will burst, an if I speak;
  And I will speak, that so my heart may burst.
  Butchers and villains, bloody cannibals!
  How sweet a plant have you untimely cropped!
  You have no children, butchers; if you had,
  The thought of them would have stirred up remorse.
  But if you ever chance to have a child,
  Look in his youth to have him so cut off
  As, deathsmen, you have rid this sweet young prince! 67
KING EDWARD
  Away with her. Go, bear her hence perforce.   68
QUEEN MARGARET
  Nay, never bear me hence. Dispatch me here!
  Here sheathe thy sword. I'll pardon thee my death.
  What, wilt thou not? Then, Clarence, do it thou.
CLARENCE
  By heaven, I will not do thee so much ease.   72
QUEEN MARGARET
  Good Clarence, do. Sweet Clarence, do thou do it.
CLARENCE
  Didst thou not hear me swear I would not do it?

---

48 be sure expect   **55 equal** compare with   **56 respect** comparison
67 rid removed, killed   **68 perforce** by force   **72 ease** i.e., easing of
your grief in death

QUEEN MARGARET
Ay, but thou usest to forswear thyself.   75
'Twas sin before, but now 'tis charity.
What, wilt thou not? Where is that devil's butcher,
Hard-favored Richard? Richard, where art thou?   78
Thou art not here. Murder is thy almsdeed;   79
Petitioners for blood thou ne'er putt'st back.   80
KING EDWARD
Away, I say! I charge ye, bear her hence.
QUEEN MARGARET
So come to you and yours as to this prince!   82
                              Exit Queen, [guarded].
KING EDWARD   Where's Richard gone?
CLARENCE
To London, all in post—[*Aside*] and, as I guess,   84
To make a bloody supper in the Tower.
KING EDWARD
He's sudden, if a thing comes in his head.
Now march we hence. Discharge the common sort   87
With pay and thanks, and let's away to London
And see our gentle queen how well she fares.
By this, I hope, she hath a son for me.   *Exeunt.* 90

❖

5.6   *Enter Henry the Sixth and Richard, [Duke of*
           Gloucester,] with the Lieutenant [of the Tower],
           on the walls.

GLOUCESTER
Good day, my lord. What, at your book so hard?   1
KING HENRY
Ay, my good lord—"my lord," I should say rather.
'Tis sin to flatter. "Good" was little better.   3

---

75 thou usest you are accustomed   **78 Hard-favored** ugly   **79 almsdeed**
act of charity   **80 Petitioners . . . back** you never turn away men asking
for blood   **82 So come** may it happen   **84 post** haste   **87 common sort**
ordinary soldiers   **90 this** this time

5.6. Location: The Tower of London.
1 book i.e., book of devotion   **3 little better** i.e., little more than flattery

"Good Gloucester" and "good devil" were alike,   4
And both preposterous; therefore, not "good lord."   5

GLOUCESTER [*To the Lieutenant*]
Sirrah, leave us to ourselves. We must confer.   6

[*Exit Lieutenant.*]

KING HENRY
So flies the reckless shepherd from the wolf;   7
So first the harmless sheep doth yield his fleece
And next his throat unto the butcher's knife.
What scene of death hath Roscius now to act?   10

GLOUCESTER
Suspicion always haunts the guilty mind;
The thief doth fear each bush an officer.   12

KING HENRY
The bird that hath been limèd in a bush,   13
With trembling wings misdoubteth every bush;   14
And I, the hapless male to one sweet bird,   15
Have now the fatal object in my eye
Where my poor young was limed, was caught, and
    killed.

GLOUCESTER
Why, what a peevish fool was that of Crete,   18
That taught his son the office of a fowl!
And yet, for all his wings, the fool was drowned.

KING HENRY
I, Daedalus; my poor boy, Icarus;
Thy father, Minos, that denied our course;   22
The sun that seared the wings of my sweet boy,   23
Thy brother Edward; and thyself, the sea
Whose envious gulf did swallow up his life.   25

---

4 were would be   **5 preposterous** unnatural   **6 Sirrah** (Customary form
of address to inferiors.)   **7 reckless** heedless   **10 Roscius** celebrated
Roman actor much admired by Cicero and regarded by the Elizabethans
as a model of tragic acting   **12 an officer** to be an arresting officer
13 limèd snared with birdlime, a sticky substance smeared on branches
14 misdoubteth is mistrustful of   **15 male** father, begetter.   **bird** chick,
offspring   **18 peevish** silly.   **that of Crete** (Daedalus escaped from
Crete, where he had fashioned for King Minos a labyrinth to contain the
Minotaur, by devising wings for himself and his son Icarus, but Icarus
flew too near the sun, which melted the wax in his wings, thus causing
him to fall into the sea.)   **22 course** i.e., departure   **23 sun** (with reference to the Yorkist heraldic badge, as at 2.1.25)   **25 envious gulf** malicious whirlpool

Ah, kill me with thy weapon, not with words!
My breast can better brook thy dagger's point   27
Than can my ears that tragic history.   28
But wherefore dost thou come? Is 't for my life?

KING HENRY
GLOUCESTER
Think'st thou I am an executioner?

KING HENRY
A persecutor I am sure thou art.
If murdering innocents be executing,
Why, then thou art an executioner.

GLOUCESTER
Thy son I killed for his presumption.

KING HENRY
Hadst thou been killed when first thou didst presume,
Thou hadst not lived to kill a son of mine.
And thus I prophesy, that many a thousand,
Which now mistrust no parcel of my fear,   38
And many an old man's sigh and many a widow's,
And many an orphan's water-standing eye—   40
Men for their sons', wives for their husbands',
Orphans for their parents' timeless death—   42
Shall rue the hour that ever thou wast born.
The owl shrieked at thy birth—an evil sign;
The night crow cried, aboding luckless time;   45
Dogs howled, and hideous tempest shook down trees;
The raven rooked her on the chimney's top,   47
And chattering pies in dismal discords sung.   48
Thy mother felt more than a mother's pain,
And yet brought forth less than a mother's hope,
To wit, an indigested and deformèd lump,   51
Not like the fruit of such a goodly tree.
Teeth hadst thou in thy head when thou wast born,
To signify thou cam'st to bite the world;
And if the rest be true which I have heard,
Thou cam'st—

---

27 brook endure   **28 history** story   **38 mistrust . . . fear** i.e., feel none
of the suspicion that I feel   **40 water-standing** i.e., filled with tears
42 timeless untimely   **45 night crow** nightjar or owl.   **aboding** foreboding
ing   **47 rooked her** alighted, roosted   **48 pies** magpies   **51 indigested**
shapeless, chaotic

GLOUCESTER
I'll hear no more. Die, prophet, in thy speech.
                        Stabs him.

For this, amongst the rest, was I ordained.
KING HENRY
Ay, and for much more slaughter after this.
O, God forgive my sins, and pardon thee!   *Dies.*
GLOUCESTER
What, will the aspiring blood of Lancaster
Sink in the ground? I thought it would have mounted.
See how my sword weeps for the poor King's death!
O, may such purple tears be always shed   64
From those that wish the downfall of our house!
If any spark of life be yet remaining,
Down, down to hell, and say I sent thee thither,
                    Stabs him again
I, that have neither pity, love, nor fear.
Indeed, 'tis true that Henry told me of;   69
For I have often heard my mother say
I came into the world with my legs forward.
Had I not reason, think ye, to make haste
And seek their ruin that usurped our right?
The midwife wondered and the women cried
"O, Jesus bless us, he is born with teeth!"
And so I was, which plainly signified
That I should snarl and bite and play the dog.
Then, since the heavens have shaped my body so,
Let hell make crook'd my mind to answer it.   79
I have no brother, I am like no brother;
And this word "love," which graybeards call divine,
Be resident in men like one another
And not in me. I am myself alone.
Clarence, beware. Thou keep'st me from the light;
But I will sort a pitchy day for thee;   85
For I will buzz abroad such prophecies
That Edward shall be fearful of his life,   87
And then, to purge his fear, I'll be thy death.
King Henry and the Prince his son are gone;

64 purple bloodred   **69 that** what   **79 answer** match   **85 sort** select.
pitchy black   **87 of** for

Clarence, thy turn is next, and then the rest,
Counting myself but bad till I be best.   91
I'll throw thy body in another room
And triumph, Henry, in thy day of doom.

Exit [with the body].

❧

5.7   *Flourish. Enter King [Edward], Queen
[Elizabeth], Clarence, Richard, [Duke of
Gloucester,] Hastings, Nurse [with the
young Prince], and attendants.*

KING EDWARD
Once more we sit in England's royal throne,
Repurchased with the blood of enemies.
What valiant foemen, like to autumn's corn,   3
Have we mowed down in tops of all their pride!   4
Three Dukes of Somerset, threefold renowned
For hardy and undoubted champions;   6
Two Cliffords, as the father and the son;   7
And two Northumberlands—two braver men
Ne'er spurred their coursers at the trumpet's sound; 9
With them, the two brave bears, Warwick and
     Montague,   10
That in their chains fettered the kingly lion
And made the forest tremble when they roared.
Thus have we swept suspicion from our seat   13
And made our footstool of security.
Come hither, Bess, and let me kiss my boy.
                              [He kisses his son.]
Young Ned, for thee, thine uncles and myself
Have in our armors watched the winter's night,   17
Went all afoot in summer's scalding heat,

---

91 bad unfortunate

5.7. Location: London. The royal court. A throne is provided onstage.
3 corn grain   **4 in tops** at the height   **6 undoubted** fearless   **7 as** to wit
9 coursers horses   **10 bears** (Refers to the Neville family emblem.)
13 seat throne   **17 watched** stayed awake throughout

That thou mightst repossess the crown in peace;
And of our labors thou shalt reap the gain.
GLOUCESTER [*Aside*]
I'll blast his harvest, if your head were laid;   21
For yet I am not looked on in the world.   22
This shoulder was ordained so thick to heave,
And heave it shall some weight, or break my back.
Work thou the way, and thou shalt execute.   25
KING EDWARD
Clarence and Gloucester, love my lovely queen,
And kiss your princely nephew, brothers both.
CLARENCE
The duty that I owe unto Your Majesty
I seal upon the lips of this sweet babe.
                    [*He kisses the Prince.*]
QUEEN ELIZABETH
Thanks, noble Clarence; worthy brother, thanks.   30
GLOUCESTER
And, that I love the tree from whence thou sprang'st,
Witness the loving kiss I give the fruit.
                    [*He kisses the Prince.*]
[*Aside.*] To say the truth, so Judas kissed his master,
And cried "All hail!" whenas he meant all harm.
KING EDWARD
Now am I seated as my soul delights,
Having my country's peace and brothers' loves.
CLARENCE
What will Your Grace have done with Margaret?
Reignier, her father, to the King of France
Hath pawned the Sicils and Jerusalem,   39
And hither have they sent it for her ransom.   40
KING EDWARD
Away with her, and waft her hence to France.   41
And now what rests but that we spend the time   42
With stately triumphs, mirthful comic shows,   43

---

21 **blast** blight. **if . . . laid** i.e., once you are laid out on the bier in
death (with a suggestion also of grain flattened by a storm) **22 looked
on** heeded, respected **25 Work thou** (Addressed to himself, indicating
his head.) **thou shalt** (Addressed to his shoulder and arm.) **30 brother**
i.e., brother-in-law **39 the Sicils** (See note to 1.4.122.) **40 it** i.e., the
money raised by "pawn" **41 waft** convey by water **42 rests** remains
43 triumphs festivities

Such as befits the pleasure of the court?
Sound drums and trumpets! Farewell sour annoy!
For here, I hope, begins our lasting joy.   46
                    [*Flourish.*] *Exeunt omnes.*

46 s.d. **omnes** all

Date and Text

A shortened and memorially reconstructed text of *Henry VI, Part Three* was published in octavo in 1595 with the title, *The True Tragedy of Richard, Duke of York, and the Death of Good King Henry the Sixth, with the Whole Contention Between the Two Houses Lancaster and York*. The play appears to have been written in about 1590–1592. The First Folio text seems to have been based on an authorial manuscript with some consultation of the third quarto, which seems to have been without independent textual authority. For a more extensive discussion of date and textual situation in all three *Henry VI* plays, see "Date and Text" to *Henry VI, Part One* in this volume.

Textual Notes

These textual notes are not a historical collation, either of the early texts or of more recent editions; they are simply a record of departures in this edition from the copy text. The reading adopted in this edition appears in boldface, followed by the rejected reading from the copy text, i.e., the First Folio. Only major alterations in punctuation are noted. Changes in lineation are not indicated, nor are some minor and obvious typographical errors.

Abbreviations used:
F the First Folio
O the octavo of 1595
s.d. stage direction
s.p. speech prefix

Copy text: the First Folio.

1.1. 2 s.p. York Pl [and elsewhere referred to in the s.p. as Plan and Plant as well as Yorke]   **19 hap** hope   **69 s.p. Exeter** [O] Westm   **105 Thy** [O] My
120 s.p. Northumberland [O] Henry   **259 with me** [O] me   **261 from** [O] to
273 s.d. Flourish [at beginning of 1.2 in F]   Exeunt Exit

1.2. 47 s.d. a Messenger [O] Gabriel   **49 s.p. Messenger** [O] Gabriel
75 s.d. Exeunt Exit

1.4. 180 s.d. Exeunt [O] Exit

2.1. 94 s.d. Montague Mountacute   **113 And . . . thought** [O; not in F]
124 spleen, Spleene   **131 an idle** [O] a lazie

2.2. 89 Since Cla. Since   **130 puts** put's   **133 s.p. Richard** [O] War
163 s.p. [and elsewhere until 3.2] George [O] Cla

2.5. 54 s.d. [followed in F by "and a Father that hath kill'd his Sonne at another doore"]   **78 s.d.** [F reads: "Enter Father, bearing of his Sonne"]
89 stratagems Stragems   **119 E'en** Men   **139 Whither** Whether [also at 2.6.9]

2.6. 6 fall, thy fall. Thy   **commixture** [O] Commixtures   **8 The common . . . flies** [O; not in F]   **19 Had** [O] Hed   **42–45 Edward. Whose . . . used** [The speech assignments here follow O; F assigns 42–44, "Whose . . . is," to Richard, and the rest to Edward.]   **60 his** [O] is

3.1 s.d. two Keepers [O] Sinklo, and Humfrey [and throughout scene, in s.p.]
7 scare scarre   **12 s.p. Second Keeper** Sink   **17 wast** was   **24 thee, sour adversity** the sower Aduersaries   **30 Is** I: **55 thou that** [O] thou

3.2. 1 s.p. [and elsewhere] King Edward King   **8 s.p. [and throughout] Gloucester** Rich   **18 s.p. [and throughout] Lady Grey** Wid   **28 whip me, then** [O] then whip me   **123 honorably** [O] honourable   **175 rends** rents

3.3. 78 s.p. Prince Edw   **124 eternal** [O] externall   **161 s.d.** [at l. 160 in F]
228 I'll [O] I

4.1. 67 s.p. Queen Elizabeth [O: Queen] Lady Grey

4.2. 15 towns Towne

4.3. 27 s.d. Hastings fly Hastings flyes   **64 s.d. Exeunt** exit

4.4. 2 s.p. [and throughout scene] Queen Elizabeth [O: Queen] Gray   **17 wean** waine

4.5. 4 stands stand   **8 Comes** Come

4.6. 55 goods be Goods   **88 s.d. Manent** Manet

4.8. 0 s.d. Exeter Somerset   **50 s.d. A Lancaster! A York!** A Lancaster, A Lancaster

5.1. 78 an in

5.3. 22–23 augmented . . . along. augmented: . . . along,

5.4. 27 ragged raged   **46 Lest** Least

5.5. 38 thou the   **50 The Tower** [O] Tower   **77 butcher** [O] butcher Richard **90 s.d. Exeunt** [O] Exit

5.6. 43 wast was't

5.7. 5 renowned [O] Renowne   **25 thou shalt** [O] that shalt   **30 s.p. Queen Elizabeth** [O] Cla   **Thanks** [O] Thanke   **38 Reignier** Reynard

Shakespeare's Sources

The chief source for Shakespeare's conception of the entire *Henry VI* trilogy is Edward Hall's *The Union of the Two Noble and Illustre Families of Lancaster and York* (1548), a work written to glorify the Tudor monarchs by demonstrating how their lineage reconciled the fatally warring factions of Lancaster and York. Shakespeare may actually have done much of his reading for historical particulars in the second edition of Raphael Holinshed's *The Chronicles of England, Scotland, and Ireland* (1587), which included much of Hall's material. (A selection from Volume 3 of Holinshed's *Chronicles* is presented in the pages that follow.) He may also have used John Foxe's *Acts and Monuments of Martyrs* (1583 edition), and still other sources. Richard Grafton's *Chronicle* (1568) plagiarized so heavily from Hall that one cannot always be sure which of the two Shakespeare may have consulted. In any event, Hall's interpretation provided the guiding spirit.

To intensify Hall's theme of the horrors of civil dissension, Shakespeare takes considerable liberties with the chronicles. He frequently disregards chronology, telescopes events of many years into a single sequence, invents scenes and characters, and transfers details from one historical scene to another. The artistic unity of each play is his overriding consideration, not historical accuracy.

In *1 Henry VI*, for example, Shakespeare shows the English losing Orleans to the French and then retaking the city (1.5–2.1). In fact, Orleans was never retaken once it had fallen. Shakespeare has transferred events from the recapture of Le Mans to his partly invented account of Orleans. Talbot's visit to the Countess of Auvergne (2.3) is fictitious. The scene in the Temple Garden when the leaders of Lancaster and York pluck red and white roses (2.4) is fictitious in a different sense: antagonisms between the two factions certainly did exist, but not in the allegorically schematized fashion here pictured. In Act 3, scene 2, Shakespeare shows us Rouen lost and recaptured in a day, whereas in fact the city was (like Orleans) never recovered. Shakespeare's intention is to suggest that France is lost through England's political divisions at home, not through any failure on the part of Lord Talbot. Shakespeare exalts Talbot's might and chivalry (hence the scene with the Countess of Auvergne), and contrastingly overstates the cowardice of Falstaff (called Falstolfe in Holinshed, Fastolfe in some other historical sources). Joan la Pucelle is another exaggeratedly evil foil to Talbot; Shakespeare combines her worst traits in Hall and Holinshed. The play covers the events of about three decades. When Henry V died in 1422, his son was less than a year old; by the time of Talbot's fall in 1453 the King was over thirty.

In *2 Henry VI* Shakespeare accentuates the threat of popular unrest in a number of ways. He conflates reports of the Jack Cade rebellion in 1450 with those of the Peasants' Revolt in 1381, using the most unattractive features of each. Shakespeare ridicules the peasants' utopian aims and omits a list of sympathetic demands. Similarly, the dispute between the Armorer and his apprentice (1.3) is put into a context of courtly politics that we do not find in the chronicles. Simpcox's name and his lameness (2.1) are added to stress the farcical nature of this "miracle." (Shakespeare could have found this account in Thomas More's *Dialogue . . . of the Veneration and Worship of Images*, 1529, or in Foxe's *Acts and Monuments*.) Although the indictment of Suffolk (3.2) was historically an act of the House of Commons, Shakespeare portrays it as a near riot in which the people hammer at the King's very door with their strident demands. In every way, *2 Henry VI* stresses the fickleness, inhumanity, and ignorance of men caught up in a mob. Despite all this, however, the play alters its sources less than does *1 Henry VI*. And for all its disapproval of mob unrest, Shakespeare's play is considerably less hostile toward the populace than an anonymous contemporary play, *The Life and Death of Jack Straw* (1590–1593).

3 Henry VI similarly alters its sources less than does *1 Henry VI*. The alterations are chiefly those of telescoping and highlighting for emphasis. The ritual killings, which form an integral part of the spectacle in *3 Henry VI*, are cleverly adapted or rearranged from chronicle accounts. Concerning the death of the Duke of York (1.4), for example, Hall reports merely that York died fighting manfully, whereas Holinshed tells us that the remorseless Clifford caused the dead York's head to be struck off, "and set on it a crown of paper, fixed it on a pole, and presented it to the Queen." Shakespeare's version goes still further: Queen Margaret mocks York while he is still alive by putting a paper crown on his head. The ritual killing of the Lancastrian Prince Edward (5.5) is similarly enhanced. Throughout, Shakespeare's purpose is to intensify the scourgelike role of the Yorkist Edward IV and his brethren. Among the three, Richard of Gloucester is the most ominous. Shakespeare introduces crookbacked Richard into the fighting (2.1) when historically this man was abroad.

According to Andrew Cairncross's Arden edition, *3 Henry VI* contains occasional allusions to Edmund Spenser's *The Faerie Queene* (see 2.1.9 ff. and *FQ* 1.5.2), to *A Mirror for Magistrates* (especially in the sections "Richard, Duke of York" and "King Henry the Sixth"), and to Arthur Brooke's *The Tragical History of Romeus and Juliet* (see 5.4.1–33 and *Romeus* 2.1359–1377). David Riggs argues (*Shakespeare's Heroical Histories: "Henry VI" and Its Literary Tradition*, 1971) that Christopher Marlowe's *Tamburlaine* (1587–1588) was an important source for Shakespeare's *Henry VI* plays, and that behind *Tamburlaine* lay a classical rhetorical tradition of praise for heroism. Shakespeare would have thoroughly absorbed this tradition through the Tudor grammar-school curriculum.

[For *Henry VI, Part One*]

The Third Volume of Chronicles (1587 edition)
Compiled by Raphael Holinshed

HENRY THE SIXTH

Any departures from the original text are noted with an asterisk and appear at the bottom of the page in boldface; original readings are in roman.

After that[1] death had bereft the world of that noble prince King Henry the Fifth, his only son Prince Henry, being of the age of nine months or thereabouts, with the sound of trumpets was openly proclaimed King of England and France the thirtieth day of August, by the name of Henry the Sixth, in the year of the world 5389, after the birth of our Savior 1422, about the twelfth year of the Emperor Frederick the Third,[2] the fortieth and two (and last) of Charles the Sixth,[3] and the third year of Mordake's regiment[4] after his father Robert, Governor of Scotland. The custody of this young prince was appointed to Thomas, Duke of Exeter, and to Henry Beaufort, Bishop of Winchester. The Duke of Bedford was deputed Regent of France, and the Duke of Gloucester was ordained Protector of England, who, taking upon him that office, called to him wise and grave councillors by whose advice he provided and took order as well for the good government of the realm and subjects of the same at home as also for the maintenance of the wars abroad and further conquest to be made in France.

[Later, in October of that same year, Charles VI of France dies.]

And surely the death of this King Charles caused alterations in France. For a great many of the nobility, which before—either for fear of the English puissance or for the love of this King Charles, whose authority they followed, held on the English part[5]—did now revolt to the Dauphin with all endeavor to drive the English nation out of the French territories. Whereto they were the more earnestly bent, and thought it a thing of greater facility, because of

1 After that after   **2 Frederick the Third** Emperor of Germany
3 Charles the Sixth King of France   **4 regiment** rule   **5 held . . . part** remained loyal to the English side

King Henry's young years; whom, because he was a child, they esteemed not but, with one consent, revolted from their sworn fealty. . . .

The Dauphin, which lay the same time[6] in the city of Poitiers, after his father's decease caused himself to be proclaimed King of France by the name of Charles the Seventh; and, in good hope to recover his patrimony, with an haughty courage preparing war, assembled a great army.

[The fighting in France begins with "light skirmishes" but soon intensifies. Back in England, "Edmund Mortimer, the last Earl of March of that name" (conflated by Holinshed with his cousin, Sir John Mortimer), dies without issue, leaving his inheritance to Richard Plantagenet, son and heir to Richard, Earl of Cambridge, who was beheaded by Henry V at Southampton. Conflict erupts in 1425 around the time of a Parliament called by the King.]

Somewhat before this season fell a great division in the realm of England, which of a sparkle was like to have grown to a great flame. For whether the Bishop of Winchester, called Henry Beaufort (son to John, Duke of Lancaster,[7] by his third wife), envied the authority of Humphrey, Duke of Gloucester, Protector of the realm, or whether the Duke disdained at[8] the riches and pompous estate of the Bishop, sure it is that the whole realm was troubled with them and their partakers;[9] so that the citizens of London were fain[10] to keep daily and nightly watches and to shut up their shops for fear of that which was doubted[11] to have ensued of their assembling of people about them.

[The quarrel is continued in a Parliament held at Leicester in March, 1426.]

In this Parliament the Duke of Gloucester laid certain articles to the Bishop of Winchester his[12] charge, the which with the answers hereafter do ensue as followeth: . . .

---

6 **which . . . time** who dwelt at that same time   7 **John, Duke of Lancaster** i.e., John of Gaunt, father of Henry IV   8 **disdained at** held in disdain   9 **partakers** supporters, followers   10 **fain** obliged
11 **doubted** feared   12 **Winchester his** Winchester's

"1. First, whereas he,[13] being Protector and defender of this land, desired the Tower[14] to be opened to him and to lodge him therein, Richard Woodville, esquire, having at that time the charge of the keeping of the Tower refused his desire and kept the same Tower against him unduly and against reason, by the commandment of my said lord of Winchester. . . .

"2. Item, my said lord of Winchester, without the advice and assent of my said lord of Gloucester or of the King's Council, purposed and disposed him[15] to set hand on the King's person and to have removed him from Eltham, the place that he was in, to Windsor, to the intent to put him in governance as him list.[16]

"3. Item, that where my said lord of Gloucester (to whom of all persons that should be in the land, by the way of nature and birth, it belongeth to see the governance of the King's person), informed of the said undue purpose of my said lord of Winchester declared in the article next abovesaid, and, in letting[17] thereof, determining to have gone to Eltham unto the King to have provided as the cause required, my said lord of Winchester, untruly and against the King's peace, to the intent to trouble my said lord of Gloucester going to the King, purposing his death, in case that he had gone that way, set men-of-arms and archers at the end of London Bridge next[18] Southwark; and, in forbarring of the King's highway, let draw the chain of the stoops[19] there, and set up pipes and hurdles in manner and form of bulwarks; and set men in chambers, cellars, and windows, with bows and arrows and other weapons, to the intent to bring final destruction to my said lord of Gloucester's person as well as of those that then should come with him.

"4. Item, my said lord of Gloucester saith and affirmeth that our sovereign lord his brother, that was King Henry the Fifth, told him, on a time when our sovereign lord, being Prince,[20] was lodged in the palace of Westminster in the great chamber, by the noise of a spaniel there was on a night

---

13 he i.e., the Duke of Gloucester   **14 Tower** Tower of London
15 disposed him made himself ready   **16 as him list** i.e., as it should please the Bishop of Winchester   **17 letting** hindering, preventing
18 next nearest   **19 let draw . . . stoops** caused to be drawn tight the chain posts.   **stoops** posts   **20 told him . . . Prince** told him (Gloucester) that once when young Henry, then Prince of Wales

a man spied and taken behind a tapet*[21] of the said chamber, the which man was delivered to the Earl of Arundel to be examined upon the cause of his being there at that time; the which, so examined, at that time confessed that he was there by the stirring and procuring of my said lord of Winchester, ordained to have slain the said Prince there in his bed. Wherefore the said Earl of Arundel let sack him[22] forthwith and drowned him in the Thames.

"5. Item, our sovereign lord that was, King Henry the Fifth, said unto my said lord of Gloucester that, his father King Henry the Fourth living and visited then greatly with sickness by the hand of God, my said lord of Winchester said unto the King (Henry the Fifth, then being Prince) that the King his father so visited with sickness was not personable,[23] and therefore not disposed to come in conversation and governance of the people; and, forsomuch, counseled him to take the governance and crown of this land upon him."

[The Bishop replies, and the matter is put to the "arbitrement" of the King's Council.]

After the which words thus said, as before is declared, it was decreed also by the said lords arbitrators that the said lord of Winchester should have these words that follow unto my said lord of Gloucester: "My lord of Gloucester, I have conceived, to my great heaviness,[24] that ye should have received by divers reports that I should have purposed and imagined[25] against your person, honor, and estate in divers manners, for the which ye have taken against me great displeasure. Sir, I take God to my witness that what reports soever have been to you of me—peradventure of such as have had no great affection to me, God forgive it them—I never imagined ne purposed anything that might be hindering or prejudice to your person, honor, or estate; and therefore I pray you that ye be unto me good lord from this time forth, for, by my will, I gave never other occasion, nor pur-

*tapet [Holinshed adds a marginal gloss: "Or hanging."]

21 on a night . . . tapet one night, by night . . . tapestry **22 let sack him** caused him to be put in a sack **23 personable** having the status of a legal person, legally competent **24 conceived . . . heaviness** understood, to my great sorrow **25 imagined** meditated, plotted

pose not to do hereafter, by the grace of God." The which words so by him said, it was decreed by the same arbitrators that my lord of Gloucester should answer and say: "Fair uncle, sith ye declare you such a man as ye say, I am right glad that it is so, and for such a man I take you." And when this was done, it was decreed by the same arbitrators that every each of my lord[26] of Gloucester and Winchester should take either other by the hand, in the presence of the King and all the Parliament, in sign and token of good love and accord; the which was done, and the Parliament adjourned till after Easter. . . .

But when the great fire of this dissension between these two noble personages was thus by the arbitrators, to their knowledge and judgment, utterly quenched out and laid underboard,[27] all other controversies between other lords, taking part with the one party or the other, were appeased and brought to concord; so that, for joy, the King caused a solemn feast to be kept on Whitsunday, on which day he created Richard Plantagenet, son and heir to the Earl of Cambridge (whom his father at Southampton had put to death, as before ye have heard), Duke of York—not foreseeing that this preferment should be his destruction, nor that his seed should of his generation be the extreme end and final conclusion.

[In 1427 the Bishop of Winchester is made cardinal. In France, meanwhile, Lord Talbot is made governor of Anjou and Maine, and gains a dreaded reputation for fierceness and courage among the French. Sir John Falstolf is assigned to another place. Under the Duke of Alençon, the French resolve to recover the city of Le Mans from the English; he is joined at the city's walls by the Dauphin, Lord Delabreth, and others. The fighting begins.]

The Earl of Suffolk, which was governor of the town, having perfect knowledge by such as scaped from the walls how the matter went, withdrew without any tarriance into the castle which standeth at the gate of Saint Vincent, whereof was Constable Thomas Gower, esquire; whither

26 every each of my lord both lords **27 to . . . laid underboard** to the best of . . . put under the table, i.e., put to rest

also fled many Englishmen; so as for urging of the enemy, press of the number, and lack of victuals, they could not have endured long. Wherefore they privily sent a messenger to the Lord Talbot, which then lay[28] at Alençon, certifying him in how hard a case they were. The Lord Talbot, hearing these news, like a careful captain[29] in all haste assembled together about seven hundred men, and in the evening departed from Alençon so as in the morning he came to a castle called Guierche, two miles from Mans, and there stayed awhile till he had sent out Matthew Goffe,* as an espial,[30] to understand how the Frenchmen demeaned[31] themselves.

Matthew Goffe so well sped his business that privily in the night he came into the castle, where he learned that the Frenchmen very negligently used themselves, without taking heed to their watch, as though they had been out of all danger. Which well understood, he returned again and within a mile of the city met the Lord Talbot and the Lord Scales, and opened[32] unto them all things according to his credence.[33] The lords then, to make haste in the matter, because the day approached, with all speed possible came to the postern gate, and, alighting from their horses, about six of the clock in the morning they issued out of the castle, crying, "Saint George! Talbot!"

The Frenchmen, being thus suddenly taken,[34] were sore amazed, insomuch that some of them, being not out of their beds, got up in their shirts[35] and leapt over the walls. Other ran naked out of the gates to save their lives, leaving all their apparel, horses, armor, and riches behind them. None was hurt but such as resisted.

[Lord Talbot returns to Alençon. In the next year, 1428, Lord Thomas Montague, Earl of Salisbury, joins the Duke of Bedford at Paris, where they resolve on a plan to win Orleans. The siege begins in September.]

After the siege had continued full three weeks, the Bas-

---

*Goffe Gough. [Holinshed adds a marginal note here and elsewhere for this name: "Or rather Goche."]

28 lay resided, was headquartered   29 careful captain attentive and thoughtful general   30 an espial a spy   31 demeaned managed, behaved, conducted. (Used in the next sentence has the same meaning.)
32 opened disclosed   33 credence belief, understanding   34 taken i.e., surprised   35 shirts i.e., nightshirts

tard of Orleans issued out of the gate of the bridge and fought with the Englishmen; but they received him with so fierce and terrible strokes that he was with all his company compelled to retire and flee back into the city. But the Englishmen followed so fast, in killing and taking of their enemies, that they entered with them. The bulwark of the bridge, with a great tower standing at the end of the same, was taken incontinently[36] by the Englishmen, who behaved themselves right valiantly under the conduct of their courageous captain, as at this assault so in divers skirmishes against the French; partly to keep possession of that which Henry the Fifth had by his magnanimity and puissance[37] achieved, as also to enlarge the same. But all helped not, for who can hold that which will away? Insomuch that some cities by fraudulent practices, other some by martial prowess, were recovered by the French. . . .

The Bastard of Orleans and the Hire[38] were appointed to see the walls and watches kept, and the Bishop saw that the inhabitants within the city were put in good order and that victuals were not vainly spent. In the tower that was taken at the bridge end, as before you have heard, there was an high chamber having a grate full of bars of iron by the which a man might look all the length of the bridge into the city; at which grate many of the chief captains stood many times, viewing the city and devising in what place it was best to give the assault. They within the city well perceived this tooting-hole[39] and laid a piece of ordnance directly against[40] the window.

It so chanced that, the nine and fiftieth day after the siege was laid, the Earl of Salisbury, Sir Thomas Gargrave, and William Glansdale,* with divers other, went into the said tower and so into the high chamber, and looked out at the grate; and within a short space the son of the Master Gunner, perceiving men looking out at the window, took his match (as his father had taught him, who was gone down to dinner) and fired the gun, the shot whereof brake and shivered the iron bars of the grate so that one of the same bars

---

*Glansdale** Glasdale

36 incontinently immediately   **37 magnanimity and puissance** lofty courage and might   **38 the Hire** "Steven de Vignoilles, surnamed la Hire" (Holinshed)   **39 tooting-hole** peephole   **40 against** pointing toward

strake the Earl so violently on the head that it struck away one of his eyes and the side of his cheek. Sir Thomas Gargrave was likewise stricken and died within two days.

The Earl was conveyed to Meun-on-Loire, where after eight days he likewise departed this world. . . . The damage that the realm of England received by the loss of this nobleman manifestly appeared in that, immediately after his death, the prosperous good luck which had followed the English nation began to decline, and the glory of their victories gotten in the parties[41] beyond the sea fell in decay.

Though all men were sorrowful for his death, yet the Duke of Bedford was most stricken with heaviness, as he that had lost his only right hand and chief aid in time of necessity. But sith that[42] dead men cannot help the chances of men that be living, he like a prudent governor appointed the Earl of Suffolk to be his lieutenant and captain of the siege, and joined with him the Lord Scales, the Lord Talbot, Sir John Falstolf,[43] and divers other right valiant captains.

[The siege of Orleans continues on into 1429.]

In time of this siege at Orleans, French stories say, the first week of March 1428,[44] unto Charles the Dauphin at Chinon, as he was in very great care and study how to wrestle against the English nation, by one Peter Baudricourt, Captain of Vaucouleurs (made after Marshal of France by the Dauphin's creation), was carried a young wench of an eighteen years old, called Joan Arc,* by name of her father, a sorry[45] shepherd, James of Arc, and Isabel her mother; brought up poorly in their trade of keeping cattle; born at Domremy* (therefore reported by Bale, Joan Domremy) upon Meuse in Lorraine, within the diocese of Toul. Of favor[46] was she counted likesome,[47] of person strongly made and manly, of courage great, hardy and stout[48] withal; an understander of councils though she were not at them; great semblance of chastity both of body and behavior; the

*Arc Are [and similarly throughout text]
*Domremy Domprin [and later again in this sentence]

41 **parties** parts, regions   42 **sith that** since   43 **Falstolf** (The name, usually spelled Falstolfe in Holinshed, sometimes appears also in the chronicles as Fastolfe and in similar forms.)   44 **stories ... 1428** histories ... i.e., 1429   45 **sorry** wretched, poor   46 **favor** appearance, feature   47 **likesome** agreeable, attractive   48 **stout** brave

name of Jesus in her mouth about all her businesses; humble, obedient, and fasting divers days in the week. A person, as their books make her, raised up by power divine only for succor to the French estate[49] then deeply in distress; in whom, for planting a credit the rather,[50] first the company that toward the Dauphin did conduct her, through places all dangerous as holden[51] by the English, where she never was afore, all the way and by nightertale[52] safely did she lead. Then, at the Dauphin's sending by her assignment,[53] from Saint Catherine's Church of Fierbois in Touraine, where she never had been and knew not, in a secret place there among old iron, appointed she her sword to be sought out[54] and brought her that with five fleurs-de-lis was graven on both sides, wherewith she fought and did many slaughters by her own hands. On warfare rode she in armor cap-a-pie*[55] and mustered[56] as a man, before her an ensign[57] all white wherein was Jesus Christ painted with a fleur-de-lis in his hand.

Unto the Dauphin into his gallery when first she was brought, and he, shadowing[58] himself behind, setting other gay lords before him to try her cunning, from all the company, with a salutation that indeed marred all the matter, she picked him out alone; who thereupon had her to the end of the gallery where she held him an hour in secret and private talk, that of his privy chamber was thought very long and therefore would have broken it off, but he made them a sign to let her say on. In which, among other, as likely it was,[59] she set out unto him the singular feats (forsooth) given her to understand by revelation divine that in virtue of that sword she should achieve; which were, how with

---

*cap-a-pie [Holinshed adds a marginal gloss: "From head to foot"]

49 estate kingdom   50 for planting . . . rather the sooner to establish her credit (as a performer of miracles)   51 holden held, occupied
52 by nightertale through the night. (Joan led those who were escorting her straight to the Dauphin, through places occupied by the English and that she had never seen before.)   53 at the . . . assignment i.e., when the Dauphin sent her off to relieve Orleans   54 appointed . . . sought out she ordered a sword to be sought out for her   55 On warfare . . . cap-a-pie she rode into battle armed from head to foot   56 mustered come forward ready for battle   57 ensign banner   58 shadowing hiding
59 as likely it was as probably was said. (The conversation, being private, cannot be vouched for by the chronicler.)

honor and victory she would raise the siege at Orleans, set him in state of the crown of France, and drive the English out of the country, thereby he to enjoy the kingdom alone. Hereupon he heartened at full,[60] appointed her a sufficient army with absolute power to lead them, and they obediently to do as she bade them. Then fell she to work and first defeated, indeed, the siege at Orleans; by and by[61] encouraged him to crown himself King of France at Rheims, that a little before from the English she had won. Thus, after, pursued she many bold enterprises, to our great displeasure a two year together;[62] for the time she kept in state[63] until she were taken and for heresy and witchery burned, as in particularities hereafter followeth. But in her prime time she armed at all points like a jolly captain, rode from Poitiers to Blois, and there found men-of-war, victuals, and munition ready to be conveyed to Orleans.

Here was it known that the Englishmen kept not so diligent watch as they had been accustomed to do, and therefore this maid, with other French captains coming forward in the dead time of the night and in a great rain and thunder, entered into the city with all their victuals, artillery, and other necessary provisions. The next day the Englishmen boldly assaulted the town, but the Frenchmen defended the walls so as no great feat worthy of memory chanced that day betwixt them, though the Frenchmen were amazed at the valiant attempt of the Englishmen. Whereupon the Bastard of Orleans gave knowledge to the Duke of Alençon in what danger the town stood without his present help; who, coming within two leagues of the city, gave knowledge to them within that they should be ready the next day to receive him.

This accordingly was accomplished, for the Englishmen willingly suffered him and his army also to enter, supposing that it should be for their advantage to have so great a multitude to enter the city, whereby their victuals (whereof they within had great scarcity) might the sooner be consumed.

---

60 heartened at full rallied, cheered up completely   **61 by and by** at once   **62 a two year together** for a period of two years   **63 for the . . . state** for that length of time she remained in power

[The English abandon the siege of Orleans, hoping to encounter the French instead in open battle. The French reinforce to the number of 20,000 or 23,000 men.]

All which being once joined in one army, shortly after fought with the Lord Talbot, who had with him not past six thousand men, near unto a village in Beauce called Patay; at which battle the charge was given by the French so upon a sudden that the Englishmen had not leisure to put themselves in array after they had put up their stakes before their archers; so that there was no remedy but to fight at adventure.[64] This battle continued by the space of three long hours, for the Englishmen, though they were overpressed with multitude of their enemies, yet they never fled back one foot till their captain, the Lord Talbot, was sore wounded at the back, and so taken.

Then their hearts began to faint, and they fled, in which flight were slain above twelve hundred, and forty taken, of whom the Lord Talbot, the Lord Scales, the Lord Hungerford, and Sir Thomas Rampston were chief. . . . From this battle departed, without any stroke stricken, Sir John Falstolf, the same year for his valiantness elected into the Order of the Garter. But for doubt[65] of misdealing at this brunt[66] the Duke of Bedford took from him the image of Saint George and his garter, though afterward, by means of friends and apparent causes of good excuse, the same were to him again delivered, against the mind of the Lord Talbot.

Charles the Dauphin, that called himself French king, perceiving Fortune to smile thus upon him, assembled a great power and determined to conquer the city of Rheims, that he might be there sacred,[67] crowned, and anointed according to the custom of his progenitors, that all men might judge that he was by all laws and decrees a just and lawful king. . . . When Rheims was thus become French, the foresaid Charles the Dauphin, in the presence of the Dukes of Lorraine and Bar and of all the noblemen of his faction, was sacred there King of France by the name of Charles the Seventh, with all rites and ceremonies thereto belonging.

---

64 at adventure pell mell, recklessly   **65 doubt** suspicion   **66 brunt** assault   **67 sacred** consecrated to office. (The passive infinitive of the verb *sacre*.)

["Joan the Pucelle" is captured in 1430 at Compiègne, and, for the large sum of 10,000 pounds in money and 300 pounds rent, is "sold into the English hands."]

In which, for her pranks so uncouth and suspicious, the Lord Regent, by Peter Cauchon, Bishop of Beauvais (in whose diocese she was taken), caused her life and belief, after order of law, to be inquired upon and examined. Wherein found, though a virgin, yet first, shamefully rejecting her sex abominably in acts and apparel, to have counterfeit mankind,[68] and then, all damnably faithless, to be a pernicious instrument to hostility and bloodshed in devilish witchcraft and sorcery, sentence accordingly was pronounced against her. Howbeit, upon humble confession of her iniquities, with a counterfeit contrition pretending a careful sorrow for the same, execution was spared* and all mollified into this: that from thenceforth she should cast off her unnatural wearing of man's habiliments and keep her to garments of her own kind,[69] abjure her pernicious practices of sorcery and witchery, and have life and leisure in perpetual prison to bewail her misdeeds. Which to perform, according to the manner of abjuration, a solemn oath very gladly she took.

But herein (God help us!) she, fully afore possessed of the fiend, not able to hold her in any towardness of[70] grace, falling straightway into her former abominations, and yet seeking to eke out life as long as she might, stake not,[71] though the shift were shameful, to confess herself a strumpet and, unmarried as she was, to be with child. For trial, the Lord Regent's lenity gave her nine months' stay,[72] at the end whereof she (found herein[73] as false as wicked in the rest), an eight days after, upon a further definitive sentence declared against her to be relapse[74] and a renouncer of her oath and repentance, was she thereupon delivered over to secular power and so executed by consumption of fire in the old marketplace at Rouen, in the selfsame stead[75] where now Saint Michael's Church stands—her ashes afterward

---

*was spared spared

68 counterfeit mankind counterfeited the male sex **69 kind** sex
70 towardness of inclination toward, readiness for **71 stake not** did not stick or scruple **72 stay** respite **73 found herein** found in this to be
74 relapse a relapsed sinner **75 stead** place

without[76] the town walls shaken[77] into the wind. Now, recounting altogether her pastoral bringing up, rude, without any virtuous instruction, her campestral[78] conversation with wicked spirits, whom, in her first salutation to Charles the Dauphin, she uttered[79] to be Our Lady, Saint Catherine, and Saint Anne,* that in this behalf came and gave her commandments from God her maker as she kept her father's lambs in the fields . . . [all these outward shows of divine inspiration not to be trusted,] sith Satan (after[80] Saint Paul) can change himself into an angel of light, the deeplier to deceive.

[The English conclude that their cause would be best served by King Henry VI himself coming into France. He sets sail in 1431, going first to Calais and then Rouen.]

But to return to the affairs of King Henry, who in the month of November removed from Rouen to Pontoise, and so to Saint Denis, to the intent to make his entry into Paris and there to be sacred[81] King of France. There were in his company, of his own nation, his uncle the Cardinal of Winchester, the Cardinal and Archbishop of York, the Dukes of Bedford, York, and Norfolk, the Earls of Warwick, Salisbury, Oxenford, Huntington, Ormonde, Mortain, and Suffolk. . . .

To speak with what honor he was received into the city of Paris, what pageants were prepared, and how richly the gates, streets, and bridges on every side were hanged with costly cloths of arras and tapestry, it would be too long a process and therefore I do here pass it over with silence. On the seventeenth day of December he was crowned King of France, in Our Lady Church of Paris, by the Cardinal of Winchester, the Bishop of Paris not being contented that the Cardinal should do such an high ceremony in his church and jurisdiction. After all the ceremonies were finished, the King returned toward the palace, having one crown on his head and another borne before him, and one scepter in his hand and the second borne before him.

---

*Anne Annes

76 without outside of   **77 shaken** scattered. (She was denied burial.)
78 campestral in the fields   **79 uttered** declared   **80 sith Satan (after** since Satan (in the words of   **81 sacred** consecrated to office

[Lord Talbot, captured at the Battle of Patay, is exchanged for the French prisoner Ponton de Santrailles. King Henry returns triumphantly to London in February 1432, a six-years' truce having been signed. Violations of the truce occur not infrequently, and so in 1435 the Emperor Sigismund and other kings of Europe urge a new attempt at mediation. French and English demands are far apart. The Duke of Burgundy, though pretending friendship to England, sends a letter to King Henry alleging that he, Burgundy, has been constrained to enter into league with King Charles of France. The letter, addressed "To the high and mighty Prince Henry, by the grace of God King of England, his well-beloved cousin," distresses the King's Council, who regard Burgundy as a traitor. The Duke of Bedford dies in this same year, 1435, and is buried at Rouen. But the most serious worry in 1435 is the outbreak of dissension between Richard, Duke of York, and Edmund, Duke of Somerset.]

After the death of that noble prince the Duke of Bedford, the bright sun in France toward Englishmen began to be cloudy and daily to darken. The Frenchmen began not only to withdraw their obedience by oath to the King of England but also took sword in hand and openly rebelled. Howbeit, all these mishaps could not anything[82] abash the valiant courages of the English people, for they, having no mistrust in God and good fortune, set up a new sail, began the war afresh, and appointed for Regent in France Richard, Duke of York, son to Richard, Earl of Cambridge.

Although the Duke of York was worthy, both for birth and courage, of this honor and preferment, yet so disdained of Edmund, Duke of Somerset, being cousin to the King, that by all means possible he sought his hindrance,[83] as one glad of his loss and sorry of his well doing; by reason whereof, ere the Duke of York could get his dispatch,[84] Paris and divers other of the chiefest places in France were gotten by the French King. The Duke of York, perceiving his[85] evil

---

82 anything in any way   **83 he sought his hindrance** i.e., Somerset sought to hinder York   **84 get his dispatch** obtain permission to leave on his assignment   **85 his** i.e., Somerset's

will, openly dissembled that which he inwardly minded,[86] either[87] of them working things to the other's displeasure; till, through malice and division between them, at length by mortal war they were both consumed, with almost all their whole lines and offspring.

[York as regent is faced with other losses as a result, including Dieppe, Bois, and Vincennes.]

So that here partly was accomplished the prophecy of Henry the Fifth, given out in the ninth year of his reign when he lay at siege before Meaux, that Henry of Windsor[88] should lose all that Henry of Monmouth[89] had gotten—for so they are named according to the place of their nativity; and this prediction was complete and full by that time the years of his regiment[90] were expired.

But here is one chief point to be noted, that either the disdain amongst the chief peers of the realm of England (as ye have heard), or the negligence of the King's Council, which did not foresee dangers to come, was the loss of the whole dominion of France between the rivers of Somme and Marne and, in especial, of the noble city of Paris. For where before there were sent over thousands for defense of the holds and fortresses, now were sent hundreds, yea, and scores; some rascals, and some not able to draw a bow or carry a bill.[91]

[The war drags on, and the English are faced with new losses. Paris falls to the possession of King Charles. York and Somerset carry the attack to Anjou. In England, Winchester and Gloucester continue to quarrel. John Talbot is created Earl of Shrewsbury in 1442.]

In this year [1443] died in Guînes the Countess of Comminges, to whom the French King and also the Earl of Armagnac pretended[92] to be heir, insomuch that the Earl entered into all the lands of the said lady. And because he

---

86 minded intended   **87 either** both   **88 Henry of Windsor** Henry VI
89 Henry of Monmouth Henry V   **90 his regiment** i.e., Henry VI's rule
91 a bill a long-handled infantry weapon, a halberd   **92 pretended** claimed

knew the French King would not take the matter well to have a Roland for an Oliver,[93] he sent solemn ambassadors to the King of England, offering him his daughter in marriage, with promise to be bound (beside great sums of money which he would give with her) to deliver into the King of England's hands all such castles and towns as he or his ancestors detained from him within any part of the duchy of Aquitaine, either by conquest of his progenitors or by gift and delivery of any French king, and further to aid the same King with money for the recovery of other cities within the same duchy from the French King or from any other person that against King Henry unjustly kept[94] and wrongfully withholden[95] them.

This offer seemed so profitable and also honorable to King Henry and the realm that the ambassadors were well heard, honorably received, and with rewards sent home into their country. After whom were sent for the conclusion of the marriage into Guienne Sir Edward Hull, Sir Robert Ros, and John Grafton,* Dean of Saint Severinus, the which, as all the chronographers agree, both concluded the marriage and by proxy affied[96] the young lady.

[The French King is "not a little offended" at this treaty. William de la Pole, Earl of Suffolk, is sent to represent King Henry at the Diet (i.e., Assembly) of Tours, where peace between England and France is discussed.]

Many meetings were had, and many things moved for a final peace, but in conclusion, by reason of many doubts which rose on both parties, no full concord could be agreed upon; but in hope to come to a peace, a certain truce as well by sea as by land was concluded by the commissioners for eighteen months, which afterward again was prolonged to the year of our Lord 1449.

*Grafton Gralton

93 not take . . . Oliver i.e., not be well pleased to be thus foiled by an equal match. (Roland, the nephew of Charlemagne and the most famous of his paladins in medieval romance, is said once to have fought for five days with Oliver, or Olivier, son of Regnier, Duke of Genoa (another of Charlemagne's paladins). Hence to give a Roland for an Oliver is to match or trade blow for blow.)   94 unjustly kept had unjustly kept
95 withholden withheld   96 affied espoused

In treating of this truce, the Earl of Suffolk, adventuring somewhat upon his commission,[97] without the assent of his associates, imagined that the next[98] way to come to a perfect peace was to contrive a marriage between the French King's kinswoman the Lady Margaret, daughter to Reiner,[99] Duke of Anjou, and his sovereign lord King Henry. This Reiner, Duke of Anjou, named himself King of Sicily, Naples, and Jerusalem, having only the name and style of those realms, without any penny profit or foot of possession. This marriage was made strange to[100] the Earl at the first, and one thing seemed to be a great hindrance to it: which was because the King of England occupied a great part of the duchy of Anjou and the whole county of Maine, appertaining,[101] as was alleged, to King Reiner.

The Earl of Suffolk (I cannot say either corrupted with bribes or too much affectioned to[102] this unprofitable marriage) condescended[103] that the duchy of Anjou and the county of Maine should be delivered to the King, the bride's father, demanding for her marriage[104] neither penny nor farthing, as who would say[105] that this new affinity[106] passed all riches and excelled both gold and precious stones. And to the intent that of this truce might ensue a final concord, a day of interview was appointed between the two Kings in a place convenient between Chartres and Rouen. When these things were concluded, the Earl of Suffolk with his company returned into England, where he forgat not to declare what an honorable truce he had taken, out of the which there was a great hope that a final peace might grow the sooner for that honorable marriage which he had concluded, omitting nothing that might extol and set forth the personage of the lady or the nobility of her kindred.

But, although this marriage pleased the King and divers of his Council, yet Humphrey, Duke of Gloucester, Protector of the realm, was much against it, alleging that it should be

---

97 adventuring . . . commission somewhat overstepping his authority
98 next nearest   **99 Reiner** i.e., René   **100 marriage was made strange to** i.e., marriage proposal was regarded with some coolness by Reiner, or René, in response to   **101 appertaining** belonging   **102 affectioned to** committed to, desirous of   **103 condescended** agreed, conceded
104 demanding for her marriage i.e., Suffolk for his part stipulating as dowry to be brought by her in marriage   **105 who would say** one might say   **106 affinity** relationship by marriage

both contrary to the laws of God and dishonorable to the Prince if he should break that promise and contract of marriage, made by ambassadors sufficiently thereto instructed, with the daughter of the Earl of Armagnac, upon conditions both to him and his realm as much profitable as honorable. But the Duke's words could not be heard, for the Earl's doings were only liked and allowed.

[This success of Suffolk's occurs in 1444. Somerset is made Regent of Normandy in 1446 and York is discharged but then reappointed. Suffolk becomes marquess. At this point the story of *2 Henry VI* begins, but Shakespeare borrows from the events of 1453 an account of Talbot's death at Bordeaux. Talbot, the Earl of Shrewsbury, is joined there by his son, Sir John Talbot, Lord Lisle.]

In the meantime, the French King, being advertised[107] of all these doings, raised an army to resist this invasion made by the Earl of Shrewsbury. And first he appointed his captains to besiege the town of Castillon, to the rescue whereof the Earl hasted forward. . . .

The Frenchmen that lay at the siege, perceiving by those good runners-away that the Earl approached, left the siege and retired in good order into the place which they had trenched, ditched, and fortified with ordnance. The Earl, advertised how the siege was removed, hasted forward towards his enemies, doubting[108] most lest they would have been quite fled and gone before his coming. But they, fearing the displeasure of the French King (who was not far off) if they should have fled, abode[109] the Earl's coming and so received him; who, though he first with manful courage and sore fighting wan the entry of their camp, yet at length they compassed him about and, shooting him through the thigh with an handgun, slew his horse and finally killed him lying on the ground whom they durst never look in the face while he stood on his feet.

It was said that after he perceived there was no remedy but present loss of the battle, he counseled his son the Lord Lisle to save himself by flight, sith[110] the same could not re-

107 **advertised** informed, warned   108 **doubting** fearing   109 **abode** awaited   110 **sith** since

dound to any great reproach in him, this being the first journey[111] in which he had been present. Many words he used to persuade him to have saved his life; but nature so wrought in the son that neither desire of life nor fear of death could either cause him to shrink or convey himself out of the danger, and so there manfully ended his life with his said father.

The second edition of Raphael Holinshed's *Chronicles* was published in 1587. This selection is based on that edition, Volume 3, folios 585–640.

111 journey battle, day's performance in fighting

[For *Henry VI, Part Two*]
The Third Volume of Chronicles (1587 edition)
Compiled by Raphael Holinshed

HENRY THE SIXTH

Any departures from the original text are noted with an asterisk and appear at the bottom of the page in boldface; original readings are in roman.

[The quarreling between King Henry's uncles, the Cardinal of Winchester and the Duke of Gloucester, never long absent during his reign, breaks out anew in 1441.]

When the King had heard the accusations thus laid by the Duke of Gloucester against the Cardinal, he committed the examination thereof to his Council, whereof the more part were spiritual persons; so that, what for fear and what for favor, the matter was winked at and nothing said to it; only fair countenance was made to the Duke, as though no malice had been conceived against him. But venom will break out and inward grudge will soon appear, which was this year to all men apparent, for divers secret attempts were advanced forward this season against this nobleman Humphrey, Duke of Gloucester, afar off, which, in conclusion, came so near that they bereft him both of life and land, as shall hereafter more plainly appear.

For, first, this year Dame Eleanor Cobham, wife to the said Duke, was accused of treason, for that she by sorcery and enchantment intended to destroy the King, to the intent to advance her husband unto the crown. Upon this, she was examined in Saint Stephen's Chapel before the Bishop of Canterbury, and there by examination convict and judged[1] to do open penance in three open places within the city of London (*Polychronicon*[2] saith she was enjoined to go through Cheapside with a taper in her hand), and after that adjudged to perpetual imprisonment in the Isle of Man, under the keeping of Sir John Stanley, knight. At the same season were arrested, arraigned, and adjudged guilty, as aiders to the Duchess, Thomas Southwell, priest and canon of Saint Stephen's at Westminster; John Hume,* priest; Roger

---

*Hume** Hun

1 convict and judged convicted and sentenced   **2 Polychronicon** a chronicle of universal history, by Ranulf Higden, written c. 1324 and subsequently continued to the year 1413; one of Holinshed's sources

Bolingbroke, a cunning necromancer, as it was said; and Margery Jourdain, surnamed the Witch of Eye.

The matter laid against them was for that they, at the request of the said Duchess, had devised an image of wax representing the King, which by their sorcery by little and little consumed, intending thereby in conclusion to waste and destroy the King's person. Margery Jourdain was burnt in Smithfield, and Roger Bolingbroke was drawn to Tyburn and hanged and quartered, taking[3] upon his death that there was never any such thing by them imagined.[4] John Hume had his pardon, and Southwell died in the Tower the night before his execution, for (saith *Polychronicon*) he did prophesy of himself that he should die in his bed and not by justice. The Duke of Gloucester bare[5] all these things patiently and said little. Edward, son to the Duke of York, was born this year, the nine and twentieth of April, at Rouen, his father being the King's lieutenant in Normandy.

[The Earl of Suffolk enjoys his daring success of having arranged a marriage between King Henry and Margaret of Anjou. He journeys into France to bring her to England in 1444–1445.]

The Earl of Suffolk was made Marquess of Suffolk; which Marquess, with his wife and many honorable personages of men and women, richly adorned both with apparel and jewels, having with them many costly chariots and gorgeous horse litters, sailed into France for the conveyance of the nominated Queen into the realm of England. For King Reiner her father, for all his long style,[6] had too short a purse to send his daughter honorably to the King her spouse.

This noble company came to the city of Tours in Touraine, where they were honorably received both of the French King and of the King of Sicily. The Marquess of Suffolk, as procurator to King Henry, espoused the said lady in the church of Saint Martin's. At the which marriage were present the father and mother of the bride, the French King

---

3 taking swearing, taking an oath   **4 imagined** contrived, plotted
5 bare bore   **6 his long style** (Reiner, or René, Duke of Anjou, styled himself King of Sicily and Jerusalem, though he enjoyed no revenues or power in those titles.)

himself, which was uncle to the husband, and the French Queen also, which was aunt to the wife. There were also the Dukes of Orleans, of Calabria, of Alençon, and of Brittany, seven earls, twelve barons, twenty bishops, besides knights and gentlemen. When the feast, triumph, banquets, and jousts were ended, the lady was delivered to the Marquess, who in great estate conveyed her through Normandy unto Dieppe and so transported her into England, where she landed at Portsmouth in the month of April. This lady excelled all other as well in beauty and favor[7] as in wit and policy,[8] and was of stomach and courage[9] more like to a man than a woman.

Shortly after her arrival she was conveyed to the town of Southwick in Hampshire, where she with all nuptial ceremonies was coupled in matrimony to King Henry, the sixth of that name. On the eighteenth of May she came to London, all the lords of England in most sumptuous sort meeting and receiving her upon the way, and specially the Duke of Gloucester, with such honor as stood with the dignity of his person.... Upon the thirtieth of May next following she was crowned queen of this realm of England at Westminster, with all the solemnity thereto appertaining.

This marriage seemed to many both infortunate and unprofitable to the realm of England, and that for many causes. First, the King had not one penny with her, and for the fetching of her the Marquess of Suffolk demanded a whole fifteenth[10] in open Parliament. And also there was delivered for her the duchy of Anjou, the city of Mans, and the whole county of Maine, which countries were the very stays and backstands to the duchy of Normandy. And furthermore, the Earl of Armagnac took such displeasure with the King of England for this marriage that he became utter enemy to the crown of England and was the chief cause that the Englishmen were expelled out of the whole duchy of Aquitaine.

But most of all it should seem that God was displeased with this marriage, for after the confirmation thereof the King's friends fell from him, both in England and in France,

---

7 favor appearance, countenance. (The date is 1445.) **8 wit and policy** intelligence and cunning **9 stomach and courage** courage and spirit **10 fifteenth** a tax of one fifteenth imposed on personal property

the lords of his realm fell at division, and the commons rebelled in such sort that finally, after many fields foughten[11]
and many thousands of men slain, the King at length was
deposed and his son killed and this queen sent home again
with as much misery and sorrow as she was received with
pomp and triumph. Such is the instability of worldly felicity and so wavering is false flattering Fortune.

[The Duke of Somerset is appointed Regent of Normandy in
1446 and the Duke of York is discharged but is then reappointed as Regent of France. The Marquess of Suffolk
gains in favor and influence.]

Whilst the wars between the two nations of England and
France ceased, by occasion of the truce, the minds of men
were not so quiet but that such as were bent to malicious
revenge sought to compass their prepensed[12] purpose, not
against foreign foes and enemies of their country, but
against their own countrymen and those that had deserved
very well of the commonwealth. And this specially for over-
much mildness in the King,[13] who by his authority might
have ruled both parts and ordered all differences betwixt
them, but that, indeed, he was thought too soft for governor
of a kingdom. The Queen, contrariwise, a lady of great wit
and no less courage, desirous of honor and furnished with
the gifts of reason, policy,[14] and wisdom, but yet sometimes,
according to her kind,[15] when she had been fully bent on a
matter, suddenly like a weathercock mutable and turning.
This lady, disdaining that her husband should be ruled
rather than rule, could not abide that the Duke of Gloucester should do all things concerning the order of weighty affairs, lest it might be said that she had neither wit nor
stomach which[16] would permit and suffer her husband, being of most perfect age,[17] like a young pupil to be governed
by the direction of another man. Although this toy[18] entered

---

11 **fell at division . . . fields foughten** fell into conflict . . . battles fought
12 **compass their prepensed** bring about their premeditated 13 **And
this . . . King** i.e., and this factionalism was especially encouraged by
the overly great mildness of King Henry 14 **policy** cunning 15 **kind**
sex 16 **stomach which** courage who 17 **being . . . age** having reached
full maturity, no longer a minor 18 **toy** whim

first into her brain through her own imagination, yet was she pricked[19] forward to the matter both by such of her husband's counsel, as of long time had[20] borne malice to the Duke for his plainness used in declaring their untruth[21] (as partly ye have heard), and also by counsel from King Reiner her father, advising that she and the King should take upon them the rule of the realm and not to be kept under as wards and mastered orphans.

What needeth many words?[22] The Queen, persuaded by these means, first of all excluded the Duke of Gloucester from all rule and governance, not prohibiting such as she knew to be his mortal foes to invent and imagine causes and griefs against him and his, insomuch that by her procurement divers noblemen conspired against him. Of the which, divers writers affirm the Marquess of Suffolk and the Duke of Buckingham to be the chief, not unprocured by the Cardinal of Winchester and the Archbishop of York. Divers articles were laid against him in open Council, and in especial one: That he had caused men adjudged to die to be put to other execution than the law of the land assigned. Surely the Duke, very well learned in the law civil, detesting malefactors and punishing offenses in severity of justice, gat him hatred of such as feared condign reward[23] for their wicked doings. And although the Duke sufficiently answered to all things against him objected, yet because his death was determined, his wisdom and innocency nothing availed.

But to avoid danger of tumult that might be raised if a prince so well beloved of the people should be openly executed, his enemies determined to work their feats in his destruction ere he should have any warning. For effecting whereof, a Parliament was summoned to be kept at Bury, whither resorted all the peers of the realm, and amongst them the Duke of Gloucester, which, on the second day of the session, was by the Lord Beaumont, then High Constable of England, accompanied with the Duke of Buckingham

---

19 pricked spurred   **20 by such . . . long time had** by those close advisers of her husband who had long   **21 declaring their untruth** i.e., denouncing the self-serving perfidies of Winchester and York   **22 What needeth many words** what more need be said   **23 condign reward** merited and appropriate punishment

and others, arrested, apprehended, and put in ward,[24] and all his servants sequestered from him; and thirty-two of the chief of his retinue were sent to divers prisons, to the great admiration[25] of the people. The Duke, the night after he was thus committed to prison, being the four and twentieth of February, was found dead in his bed, and his body showed to the lords and commons as though he had died of a palsy or of an impostume.[26]

But all indifferent[27] persons (as saith Hall)[28] might well understand that he died of some violent death. Some judged him to be strangled, some affirm that an hot spit was put in at his fundament,[29] other write that he was smoldered[30] between two featherbeds, and some have affirmed that he died of very grief for that he might not come openly to his answer. His dead corpse was conveyed to Saint Albans and there buried. . . .

Some think that the name and title of Gloucester hath been unlucky to divers which for their honors have been erected by creation of princes to that style and dignity, as Hugh Spenser,[31] Thomas of Woodstock,[32] son to King Edward the Third, and this Duke Humphrey, which three persons by miserable death finished their days; and after them King Richard the Third, also Duke of Gloucester, in civil war slain. So that this name "Duke of Gloucester" is taken for an unhappy style. . . . But surely by the pitiful death of this noble duke and politic[33] governor the public wealth of the realm came to great decay, as by sequel here may more at large appear.

Ofttimes it happeneth that a man, in quenching of smoke, burneth his fingers in the fire. So the Queen, in casting how to keep her husband in honor and herself in authority, in making away of this nobleman brought that to pass which she had most cause to have feared, which was the deposing

24 **ward** prison   25 **admiration** amazement   26 **impostume** abscess. (The date is 1447.)   27 **indifferent** impartial   28 **Hall** Edward Hall, chronicler, author and compiler of *The Union of the Noble and Illustre Families of Lancaster and York* (1548)   29 **fundament** anus
30 **smoldered** smothered   31 **Hugh Spenser** i.e., Hugh le Despenser, created Earl of Gloucester in 1397, executed for treason in 1400
32 **Thomas of Woodstock** created Earl of Gloucester in 1385, murdered in 1397 at Calais perhaps at the instigation of his nephew, King Richard II, whom he had opposed   33 **politic** judicious in public affairs

of her husband and the decay of the house of Lancaster, which of likelihood had not chanced if this Duke had lived; for then durst not the Duke of York have attempted to set forth his title to the crown, as he afterwards did, to the great trouble of the realm and destruction of King Henry and of many other noblemen besides. This is the opinion of men, but God's judgments are unsearchable, against whose decree and ordinance prevaileth no human counsel.

But to conclude of this noble duke: he was an upright and politic governor, bending all his endeavors to the advancement of the commonwealth, very loving to the poor commons, and so[34] beloved of them again; learned, wise, full of courtesy, void of pride and ambition (a virtue rare in personages of such high estate but, where it is, most commendable).

[Holinshed refers the reader to John Foxe's *Acts and Monuments* for further praise of Duke Humphrey.]

In this six and twentieth year of the reign of this king, but in the first of the rule of the Queen, I find nothing done worthy of rehearsal within the realm of England but that the Marquess of Suffolk, by great favor of the King and more desire of the Queen, was erected to the title and dignity of Duke of Suffolk, which he a short time enjoyed. For Richard, Duke of York (being greatly allied by his wife to the chief peers and potentates of the realm, besides his own progeny),[35] perceiving the King to be no ruler, but the whole burden of the realm to rest in direction of the Queen and the Duke of Suffolk, began secretly to allure his friends of the nobility, and privily declared unto them his title and right to the crown, and likewise did he to certain wise governors of divers cities and towns. Which attempt was so politicly[36] handled and so secretly kept that provision to his purpose[37] was ready before his purpose was openly published,[38] and his friends opened[39] themselves ere the contrary part could them espy; for in conclusion, all shortly in mischief burst out, as ye may hereafter hear.

---

34 so accordingly　**35 progeny** lineage　**36 politicly** cunningly, artfully
37 provision to his purpose furnishings and supply necessary to his
purpose　**38 published** revealed　**39 opened** declared

During these doings Henry Beaufort, Bishop of Winchester, and called the Rich Cardinal, departed out of this world and buried at Westminster. He was son to John,[40] Duke of Lancaster.

[Holinshed gives an account of Winchester's "insatiable covetousness," his forgetfulness of God, and some charitable acts. When a rebellion erupts in Ireland in 1447, Richard, Duke of York, is sent to put it down. In France, Normandy is lost to the English. Popular opinion begins to turn against the Duke of Suffolk as the author of many surrenders to the French. The commoners bring formal complaint against him in a Parliament of 1450.]

The Queen, which entirely loved the Duke, doubting[41] some commotion and trouble to arise if he were let go unpunished, caused him for a color[42] to be committed to the Tower, where he remained not past a month but was again delivered and restored to the King's favor, as much as ever he was before. This doing so much displeased the people that, if politic provision had not been, great mischief had immediately ensued.

[The commoners assemble in various places and elect a chief, whom they call Bluebeard, but he and other leaders are apprehended before the situation gets out of hand. Parliament is adjourned to Leicester, where Suffolk appears with the King and Queen as chief counsellor. The commoners once again insist that Suffolk be punished.]

When the King perceived that there was no remedy to appease the people's fury by any colorable ways,[43] shortly to pacify so long an hatred, he first sequestered the Lord Saye (being Treasurer of England) and other the Duke's[44] adherents from their offices and rooms, and after banished the Duke of Suffolk, as the abhorred toad and common noyance of the whole realm, for term of five years, meaning by this

---

40 John i.e., John of Gaunt, father also of Henry IV. (Beaufort was an illegitimate son.) **41 doubting** fearing **42 color** pretext **43 colorable ways** plausible pretexts **44 other the Duke's** other of the Duke of Suffolk's

exile to appease the malice of the people for the time and after, when the matter should be forgotten, to revoke him home again.

But God's justice would not that so ungracious a person should so escape; for when he shipped[45] in Suffolk, intending to transport himself over into France, he was encountered with a ship-of-war appertaining to[46] the Duke of Exeter, constable of the Tower of London, called *The Nicholas of the Tower.* The captain of that bark with small fight entered into the Duke's ship and, perceiving his person present, brought him to Dover Road and there, on the one side of a cockboat,[47] caused his head to be stricken off and left his body with the head lying there on the sands. Which corpse, being there found by a chaplain of his, was conveyed to Wingfield College in Suffolk and there buried. This end had William de la Pole, Duke of Suffolk, as men judge by God's providence for that he had procured the death of that good Duke of Gloucester, as before is partly touched.[48]

Soon after, another disquiet befell here. Those that favored the Duke of York and wished the crown upon his head for that,[49] as they judged, he had more right thereto than he that ware it, procured[50] a commotion in Kent on this manner. A certain young man, of a goodly stature and right pregnant[51] of wit, was enticed to take upon him the name of John Mortimer, cousin to the Duke of York (although his name was John Cade or, of some, John Mend-all, an Irishman, as *Polychronicon* saith), and not for a small policy,[52] thinking by that surname that those which favored the house of the Earl of March would be assistant to him. . . .

This captain,[53] assembling a great company of tall personages, assured them that the enterprise which he took in hand was both honorable to God and the King and profitable to the whole realm. For if either by force or policy they might get the King and Queen into their hands, he would cause them to be honorably used and take such order for the punishing and reforming of the misdemeanors of their

---

45 shipped took ship   **46 appertaining to** belonging to the right or privilege of   **47 cockboat** small ship's boat   **48 touched** touched upon, discussed   **49 for that** because   **50 ware it, procured** wore it, caused **51 pregnant** fertile   **52 policy** stratagem   **53 This captain** this leader or general, John Cade. (Said ironically; *tall* or "brave" in the same sentence is also ironic.)

bad counselors that neither fifteens[54] should hereafter be demanded nor once any impositions or taxes be spoken of. The Kentish people, moved at these persuasions and other fair promises of reformation, in good order of battle (though not in great number) came with their captain unto the plain of Blackheath, between Eltham and Greenwich, and there kept the field[55] more than a month, pilling[56] the country about; to whom the city of London at that time was very favorable. . . .

And to the intent the cause of this glorious captain's coming thither might be shadowed under a cloak of good meaning (though his intent nothing so), he sent unto the King an humble supplication affirming that his coming was not against His Grace but against such of his counselors as were lovers of themselves and oppressors of the poor commonalty, flatterers of the King and enemies to his honor, suckers of his purse and robbers of his subjects, partial to their friends and extreme to their enemies, through bribes corrupted and for indifferency[57] doing nothing.

[Holinshed presents in full the complaint of the commoners of Kent and the requests of their "captain," John Cade. The King's Council advises him to refuse these demands and to "suppress those rebels by force" rather than by "fair promises." But the soldiers sent by the King to conquer the rebels refuse to fight against those who are laboring "to amend the commonweal," so that their commanding officers are obliged to leave off the attempt.]

And because the Kentishmen cried out against the Lord Saye, the King's chamberlain, he was by the King committed to the Tower of London. Then went the King again to London, and within two days after went against the Kentishmen with fifteen thousand men well prepared for the war; but the said Kentishmen fled the night before his coming into the wood country near unto Sevenoaks.* Whereupon the King returned again to London.

*Sevenoaks Senocke

54 fifteens fifteenths, property taxes   **55 kept the field** held the battlefield against opposition, maintained a military posture   **56 pilling** pillaging   **57 indifferency** apathy

The Queen, that bare rule,[58] being of his retreat advertised,[59] sent Sir Humphrey Stafford, knight, and William, his brother, with many other gentlemen, to follow the Kentishmen, thinking that they had fled; but they were deceived, for at the first skirmish both the Staffords were slain and all their company discomfited. The King's army by this time commen to[60] Blackheath, hearing of this discomfiture, began to murmur amongst themselves, some wishing the Duke of York at home to aid the captain, his cousin,[61] some undutifully coveting the overthrow of the King and his Council, other[62] openly crying out on the Queen and her complices.

This rumor, published abroad,[63] caused the King and certain of his Council, for the appeasing thereof, to commit the Lord Saye, Treasurer of England, to the Tower of London, and if other against whom like displeasure was borne had been present they had been likewise committed. Jack Cade, upon victory against the Staffords, appareled himself in Sir Humphrey's brigandine[64] set full of gilt nails, and so in some glory returned again toward London, divers idle and vagrant persons out of Sussex, Surrey, and other places still increasing his number. Thus this glorious captain, guarded with a multitude of rustical people, came again to the plain of Blackheath and there strongly encamped himself; to whom were sent from the King the Archbishop of Canterbury and Humphrey, Duke of Buckingham, to commune with him of his griefs[65] and requests.

These lords found him sober in talk, wise in reasoning, arrogant in heart, and stiff in opinion, as who that by no means would grant to dissolve his army except the King in person would come to him and assent to the things he would require.[66] The King, upon the presumptuous answers and requests of this villainous rebel, beginning as much to doubt his own menial servants as his unknown subjects

---

58 bare rule held the real power **59 advertised** informed **60 discomfited . . . commen to** defeated . . . come to, arrived at **61 the captain, his cousin** i.e., Cade, masquerading as Mortimer, York's cousin **62 other** others **63 published abroad** spread around **64 brigandine** body armor composed of iron rings or small, thin iron plates sewed on heavy cloth material **65 commune . . . griefs** confer with him of his grievances **66 require** request (which spared not[67] to speak that the captain's cause was profitable for the commonwealth), departed in all haste to the castle of Kenilworth* in Warwickshire, leaving only behind him the Lord Scales to keep the Tower of London. The Kentish captain, being advertised[68] of the King's absence, came first into Southwark and there lodged at the White Hart, prohibiting to all his retinue murder, rape, and robbery, by which color[69] of well meaning he the more allured to him the hearts of the common people.

After that, he entered into London, cut the ropes of the drawbridge, and struck his sword on London stone, saying, "Now is Mortimer lord of this city!" And after a glozing[70] declaration made to the Mayor touching[71] the cause of his thither coming, he departed again into Southwark; and upon the third day of July he caused Sir James Fiennes, Lord Saye and Treasurer of England, to be brought to the Guildhall and there to be arraigned; who, being before the King's justices put to answer, desired to be tried by his peers for the longer delay of his life. The captain, perceiving his dilatory plea, by force took him from the officers and brought him to the standard[72] in Cheap, and there, before his confession ended, caused his head to be stricken off, and pitched it upon an high pole which was openly borne before him through the streets.

And not content herewith, he went to Mile End and there apprehended Sir James Cromer, then Sheriff of Kent and son-in-law to the said Lord Saye, causing him likewise, without confession or excuse heard, to be beheaded and his head to be fixed on a pole; and with these two heads this bloody wretch entered into the city again and, as it were in a spite, caused them in every street to kiss together, to the great detestation of all the beholders. . . . He also put to execution in Southwark divers persons, some for breaking his ordinance and other being of his old acquaintance, lest

*Kenilworth Killingworth

67 which spared not who did not scruple or hesitate. (The King fears that the humbly-born members of his own household are as sympathetic to Cade as are the anonymous Kentishmen assembled in arms.) 68 The Kentish . . . advertised i.e., Cade, being informed 69 color appearance, pretext 70 London stone . . . glozing a block of stone on the south side of Canwick (now Cannon) Street which was a well-known London landmark . . . cajoling, deceptive 71 touching concerning 72 standard conduit. (The date is 1450.)

they should bewray[73] his base lineage, disparaging him for his usurped surname of Mortimer.

The Mayor and other the magistrates of London, perceiving themselves neither to be sure of goods nor of life well warranted, determined to repel and keep out of their city such a mischievous caitiff[74] and his wicked company. And to be the better able so to do, they made the Lord Scales and that renowned captain Matthew Goffe* privy[75] both of their intent and enterprise, beseeching them of their help and furtherance[76] therein. The Lord Scales promised them his aid with shooting off the artillery in the Tower,[77] and Matthew Goffe was by him appointed to assist the Mayor and Londoners in all that he might; and so he and other captains appointed for defense of the city took upon them in the night to keep the bridge,[78] and would not suffer the Kentishmen once to approach. The rebels, who never soundly slept for fear of sudden assaults, hearing that the bridge was thus kept, ran with great haste to open that passage, where between both parties was a fierce and cruel fight.

Matthew Goffe, perceiving the rebels to stand to their tackling[79] more manfully than he thought they would have done, advised his company not to advance any further toward Southwark till the day appeared, that they might see where the place of jeopardy rested,[80] and so to provide for the same; but this little availed. For the rebels with their multitude drave back the citizens from the stoops[81] at the bridge foot to the drawbridge and began to set fire in divers houses. Great ruth[82] it was to behold the miserable state wherein some, desiring to eschew[83] the fire, died upon their enemies' weapon; women with children in their arms leapt for fear into the river; other, in a deadly care[84] how to save themselves between fire, water, and sword, were in their houses choked and smothered. Yet the captains, not sparing, fought on the bridge all the night valiantly; but in con-

---

*Goffe Gough. (Holinshed marginally corrects to *Goche;* also elsewhere in the text.)

73 bewray divulge, reveal   74 caitiff despicable wretch   75 privy aware, in on the secret   76 furtherance aid   77 promised . . . Tower i.e., promised them use of the artillery stored in the Tower   78 the bridge i.e., London Bridge   79 tackling arms, weapons   80 where . . . rested what area was in jeopardy   81 stoops posts, pillars   82 ruth pity   83 eschew avoid   84 other . . . care others, frightened to death

clusion, the rebels gat the drawbridge and drowned many, and slew John Sutton, alderman, and Robert Heisand, a hardy citizen, with many other, besides Matthew Goffe—a man of great wit and much experience in feats of chivalry, the which in continual wars had spent his time in service of the King and his father.

This sore conflict endured in doubtful wise[85] on the bridge till nine of the clock in the morning, for sometimes the Londoners were beaten back to Saint Magnus's corner, and suddenly again the rebels were repelled to the stoops in Southwark, so that both parts, being faint and weary, agreed to leave off from fighting till the next day, upon condition that neither Londoners should pass into Southwark nor Kentishmen into London. Upon this abstinence, this rakehell captain, for making him[86] more friends, brake up the jails of the King's Bench and Marshalsea, and so were many mates[87] set at liberty very meet[88] for his matters in hand.

The Archbishop of Canterbury, being Chancellor of England and as then for his surety lying[89] within the Tower, called to him the Bishop of Winchester, who for some safeguard lay[90] then at Holywell. These two prelates, seeing the fury of the Kentish people, by their late repulse, to be somewhat assuaged,[91] passed by the river of Thames from the Tower into Southwark, bringing with them, under the King's Great Seal, a general pardon unto all the offenders, and caused the same to be openly published. The poor people were so glad of this pardon and so ready to receive it that, without bidding farewell to their captain, they withdrew themselves the same night every man towards his home.

But Jack Cade, despairing of succors[92] and fearing the reward of his lewd[93] dealings, put all his pillage and goods that he had robbed into a barge and sent it to Rochester by

---

85 in doubtful wise uncertain as to outcome   **86 Upon . . . making him** during this truce, this dissolute leader, i.e., Cade, in order to make him   **87 mates** fellows. (Used contemptuously.)   **88 meet** fit, useful   **89 for his surety lying** for his own safety residing   **90 for some safeguard lay** for reasons of security resided   **91 by their late . . . assuaged** to be somewhat abated by their recently being driven back   **92 succors** relief, assistance   **93 lewd** base

water, and himself went by land, and would have entered into the castle of Queenborough with a few men that were left about him, but he was there let[94] of his purpose; wherefore he, disguised in strange attire, privily[95] fled into the wood country beside Lewes in Sussex, hoping so to scape. The captain and his people being thus departed,[96] not long after proclamations were made in divers places of Kent, Sussex, and Surrey,* that whosoever could take the foresaid captain alive or dead should have a thousand marks for his travail.[97]

[Holinshed reprints the proclamation.]

After which proclamation thus published, a gentleman of Kent named Alexander Iden awaited so his time that he took the said Cade in a garden in Sussex, so that there he was slain at Hothfield and brought to London in a cart, where he was quartered, his head set on London Bridge, and his quarters sent to divers places to be set up in the shire of Kent. After this, the King himself came into Kent and there sat in judgment upon the offenders; and if he had not mingled his justice with mercy, more than five hundred by rigor of law had been justly put to execution. Yet he, punishing only the stubborn heads and disordered ringleaders, pardoned the ignorant and simple persons, to the great rejoicing of all his subjects.

[Other uprisings occur in 1450, contributing to the decline of English rule in France. In 1451, Richard, Duke of York, poses anew his threat to the house of Lancaster.]

The Duke of York, pretending,[98] as ye have heard, a right to the crown as heir to Lionel, Duke of Clarence, came this year out of Ireland unto London, in the Parliament time, there to consult with his special friends: as John, Duke of Norfolk, Richard, Earl of Salisbury, and the Lord Richard his son (which after was Earl of Warwick), Thomas Courtenay, Earl of Devonshire, and Edward Brooke, Lord Cobham.

---

*Surrey Southerie

94 let prevented, hindered   **95 strange attire, privily** foreign or unusual attire, stealthily   **96 departed** separated   **97 travail** labor, effort
98 pretending claiming

After long deliberation and advice taken, it was thought expedient to keep their chief purpose secret; and that the Duke should raise an army of men under a pretext to remove divers counselors about the King and to revenge the manifest injuries done to the commonwealth by the same rulers. Of the which, as principal, the Duke of Somerset was namely[99] accused, both for that he was greatly hated of the commons for the loss of Normandy and for that it was well known that he would be altogether against the Duke of York in his challenge to be made, when time served, to the crown; insomuch that his goods by the commons were foully despoiled and borne away from the Blackfriars. After which riot, on the next morrow, proclamation was made through the city that no man should spoil[100] or rob, on pain of death. But on the same day at the standard[101] in Cheap was a man beheaded for doing contrary to the proclamation.

Therefore, when the Duke of York had thus, by advice of his special friends, framed the foundation of his long-intended enterprise, he assembled a great host, to the number of ten thousand able men, in the marches[102] of Wales, publishing openly that the cause of this his gathering of people was for the public wealth[103] of the realm. The King, much astonied at the matter, by advice of his Council raised a great power and marched forward toward the Duke. But he, being thereof advertised, turned out of that way which by espials[104] he understood that the King held, and made straight toward London; and having knowledge that he might not be suffered to pass through the city, he crossed over the Thames at Kingston Bridge and so kept on towards Kent, where he knew that he had both friends and well-willers. And there, on Burnt Heath, a mile from Dartford and twelve miles from London, he embattled[105] and encamped himself very strongly, environing his field with artillery and trenches. The King, hereof advertised, brought his army with all diligence unto Blackheath and there pight[106] his tents.

Whilst both these armies lay thus embattled, the King

---

99 namely especially   **100 spoil** pillage   **101 standard** conduit, fountain
102 marches border   **103 public wealth** prosperity   **104 espials** scouts, spies   **105 embattled** prepared for battle   **106 pight** pitched

sent the Bishop of Winchester and Thomas Bourchier, Bishop of Ely, Richard Woodville, Lord Rivers, and Richard Andrew, the Keeper of his Privy Seal, to the Duke, both to know the cause of so great a commotion and also to make a concord[107] if the requests of the Duke and his company seemed consonant to reason. The Duke, hearing the message of the bishops, answered that his coming was neither to damnify[108] the King in honor nor in person, neither yet any good man; but his intent was to remove from him certain evil-disposed persons of his Council, bloodsuckers of the nobility, pollers[109] of the clergy, and oppressors of the poor people.

Amongst these he chiefly named Edmund, Duke of Somerset, whom if the King would commit to ward[110] to answer such articles as against him in open Parliament should be both proponed[111] and proved, he promised not only to dissolve his army but also offered himself like an obedient subject to come to the King's presence and to do him true and faithful service according to his loyal and bounden duty.

[Holinshed here prints certain letters written by the Duke of York to the King, setting forth his claims, and the King's replies. It is agreed that the Duke of Somerset be committed to prison in order to pacify the Duke of York and his people, whereupon York is reconciled to the King and takes a public oath of loyalty.]

Howsoever the matter went, truth it is that the Duke of York, the first of March [1452], dissolved his army, brake up his camp, and came to the King's tent, where, contrary to his expectation and against promise made by the King (as other write), he found the Duke of Somerset going at large and set at liberty, whom the Duke of York boldly accused of treason, bribery, oppression, and many other crimes. The Duke of Somerset not only made answer to the Duke's objections but also accused him of high treason, affirming that he with his fautors[112] and complices had consulted to-

107 **concord** treaty of peace 108 **damnify** injure 109 **pollers** plunderers 110 **ward** prison 111 **proponed** proposed, put before a tribunal 112 **his fautors** i.e., York's followers

gether how to come by the scepter and regal crown of this realm. By means of which words the King removed straight[113] to London, and the Duke of York as prisoner rode before him, and so was kept awhile.

The King assembled together a great Council at Westminster to hear the accusations of the two Dukes, the one objecting to the other many heinous and grievous crimes.

[Somerset demands that York be executed, "because he knew perfectly that the Duke of York daily imagined with himself[114] how to get the crown and to depose and destroy both the King and him." But York's rising fortunes cannot be stopped now, and the case is made for York's innocence. Meantime, a rumor arises that Edward, Earl of March, son of the Duke of York, is marching toward London. An expedition to Gascony being urgently called for, the Council decides to free the Duke of York and permit him to go to his castle of Wigmore in the marches, or borders, of Wales after York has once again sworn obedience to King Henry. In York's absence from court, Somerset's influence continues to be very strong. Aquitaine is lost to English authority in 1453. In that same year, in October, the Queen gives birth to a son, Edward, though the event does not put a halt to talk that Henry is incapable of fathering a son and that the Queen is all too ready to present him with some other man's child.]

After the wars foully ended in foreign parties,[115] civil dissension began again at home, divided specially into two factions. As King Henry, descended of the house of Lancaster, possessed the crown from his grandfather, King Henry the Fourth, first author of that title, so Richard, Duke of York, as heir to Lionel, Duke of Clarence, third son to King Edward the Third, enforced.[116] By reason whereof, the nobles as well as the common people were into parts divided, to the utter destruction of many a man and to the great ruin and decay of this region; for while the one party sought to

113 removed straight moved immediately **114 imagined with himself** contrived in his imagination **115 parties** parts **116 enforced** i.e., laid claim

destroy the other, all care of the commonwealth was set aside, and justice and equity clearly exiled.

The Duke of York above all things first sought means how to stir up the malice of the people against the Duke of Somerset, imagining that, he being made away, his purpose should the sooner take effect. He also practiced[117] to bring the King into the hatred of the people, as that he should not be a man apt to[118] the government of a realm, wanting both wit and stomach sufficient to supply such a room.[119] Many of the high estates,[120] not liking the world and disallowing the doings both of the King and his Council, were fain[121] enough of some alteration. Which thing the Duke well understanding, chiefly sought the favor of the two Nevilles, both named Richard, one Earl of Salisbury, the other Earl of Warwick, the first being the father and the second the son.

[Holinshed describes the lineage and family of the Nevilles, who assist York in insisting that Somerset be imprisoned in the Tower, from which incarceration he is, however, released once the King has recovered from an illness. York and his adherents, seeing that they cannot prevail against Somerset, assemble for war in the marches of Wales. King Henry resolves to fight rather than give in to demands for the imprisonment of Somerset. The first battle of the civil wars occurs at Saint Albans in 1455.]

The fight for a time was right sharp and cruel, for the Duke of Somerset, with the other lords, coming to the succors of their companions that were put to the worse, did what they could to beat back the enemies; but the Duke of York sent ever fresh men to succor the weary and to supply the places of them that were hurt, whereby the King's army was finally brought low and all the chieftains of the field slain and beaten down.

For there died, under the sign of the Castle, Edmund,

---

117 practiced plotted   **118 as that . . . apt to** i.e., representing King Henry as being a man unskilled in   **119 wanting . . . room** lacking sufficient intelligence and courage to fill such an office   **120 estates** noble classes   **121 fain** glad

Duke of Somerset, who, as hath been reported, was warned long before to avoid all castles. And beside him lay Henry, the second of that name, Earl of Northumberland; Humphrey, Earl of Stafford, son to the Duke of Buckingham; John, Lord Clifford, [and others].

The second edition of Raphael Holinshed's *Chronicles* was published in 1587. This selection is based on that edition, Volume 3, folios 622–643.

[For *Henry VI, Part Three*]

The Third Volume of Chronicles (1587 edition)
Compiled by Raphael Holinshed
HENRY THE SIXTH

Any departures from the original text are noted with an asterisk and appear at the bottom of the page in boldface; original readings are in roman.

[The Duke of York, victorious at Saint Albans in 1455, courteously refuses to use any violence toward King Henry. York and his son Edward and several allies are convicted of high treason by Henry's Parliament in 1460. At the Battle of Northampton, in 1460, York's allies gain the victory and convey the King under guard to London, while the Duke of Somerset, son of the Duke of Somerset who died at the end of *2 Henry VI*, narrowly escapes with the Queen and her son Edward. York, not present at the battle, returns from Dublin to England at this good news and travels to London.]

From Chester by long journeys[1] he came to the city of London, which he entered the Friday before the feast of Saint Edward the Confessor, with a sword borne naked before him, with trumpets also sounding, and accompanied with a great train of men-of-arms and other of his friends and servants. At his coming to Westminster he entered the palace and, passing forth directly through the great hall, stayed not till he came to the chamber where the King and lords used to sit in the parliament time, commonly called the upper house or chamber of the peers, and, being there entered, stepped up unto the throne royal, and there, laying his hand upon the cloth of estate,[2] seemed as if he meant to take possession of that which was his right.

[York avails himself of the King's own apartments in the palace while Henry occupies the Queen's chambers. The Archbishop of Canterbury, Thomas Bourchier, carries messages between them. York addresses the lords of the Parliament on the subject of his claim, sitting in the regal seat as he does so. The matter of the Yorkist claim is negotiated.]

1 journeys daily stints of travel   **2 cloth of estate** cloth spread over a throne, canopy

After long debating of the matter and deliberate consultation amongst the peers, prelates, and commons, upon the vigil of All Saints it was condescended:[3] forsomuch as King Henry had been taken as King by the space of thirty-and-eight years and more, that he should enjoy the name and title of king and have possession of the realm during his natural life. And if he either died or resigned or forfeited the same by breaking or going against any point of this concord, then the said crown and authority royal should immediately be devoluted[4] and come to the Duke of York, if he then lived, or else to the next heir of his lineage. And that the Duke of York from thenceforth should be Protector and Regent of the land. This was the determination of the Parliament to and fro,[5] tending to peace between the King and the Duke, which was ratified accordingly, as by the articles ensuing doth appear.

[Holinshed prints the articles of agreement between King Henry and the Duke of York. The latter is solemnly proclaimed heir apparent to the crown and Protector of the realm in return for his taking an oath of fealty to Henry.]

The Duke of York, well knowing that the Queen would spurn against all this, caused both her and her son to be sent for by the King. But she, as wont rather to rule than to be ruled, and thereto counseled by the Dukes of Exeter and Somerset, not only denied to come but also assembled a great army, intending to take the King by fine force out of the lords' hands. The Protector in London, having knowledge of all these doings, assigned the Duke of Norfolk and Earl of Warwick, his trusty friends, to be about the King, while he, with the Earls of Salisbury and Rutland and a convenient number departed out of London the second day of December northward, and appointed the Earl of March, his eldest son, to follow him with all his power. The Duke came to his castle of Sandal beside Wakefield on Christmas Even and there began to make muster of his tenants and friends. The Queen, thereof ascertained, determined to cope with him ere his succor[6] were come.

---

3 condescended agreed upon **4 devoluted** devolved, passed on **5 to and fro** for and against the question, pro and con **6 succor** reinforcements

Now she, having in her company the Prince her son, the Dukes of Exeter and Somerset, the Earl of Devonshire, the Lord Clifford, the Lord Ros, and in effect all the lords of the north parts, with eighteen thousand men or (as some write) two-and-twenty thousand, marched from York to Wakefield, and bade base to[7] the Duke even before his castle gates. He, having with him not fully five thousand persons, contrary to the minds of his faithful counselors would needs issue forth to fight with his enemies. The Duke of Somerset and the Queen's part, casting upon their most advantage, appointed the Lord Clifford to lie in one stale[9] and the Earl of Wiltshire in another, and the Duke with other to keep the main battle.[10] The Duke of York with his people descended down the hill in good order and array and was suffered to pass on towards the main battle.

But when he was in the plain field between his castle and the town of Wakefield, he was environed on every side like fish in a net, so that though he fought manfully, yet was he within half an hour slain and dead, and his whole army discomfited.[11] With him died, of his trusty friends, his two bastard uncles, Sir John and Sir Hugh Mortimer,* Sir Davy Hall, Sir Hugh Hastings, Sir Thomas Neville, William and Thomas Aparre, both brethren; and two thousand and eight hundred others, whereof many were young gentlemen and heirs of great parentage in the south parts, whose kin revenged their deaths within four months next, as after shall appear.

In this conflict was wounded and taken prisoner Richard, Earl of Salisbury, Sir Richard Limbrick, Ralph Stanley, John Harrow, Captain Hanson, and divers others. The Lord Clifford, perceiving where the Earl of Rutland was conveyed out of the field (by one of his father's chaplains and schoolmaster to the same Earl) and overtaking him, stabbed him to the heart with a dagger as he kneeled afore him. This Earl was but a child at that time of twelve years of age, whom neither his tender years nor dolorous countenance, with holding up both his hands for mercy (for his

*__Mortimer__ Mortimers
__7 bade base to__ challenged. (Literally, challenged to a chase in the game of prisoner's base.) __8 casting__ calculating __9 stale__ battle position, sometimes one that is detached for reconnoitring; here a wing, flank
__10 other . . . main battle__ others . . . main body of the army
__11 discomfited__ routed, defeated

speech was gone for fear), could move the cruel heart of the Lord Clifford to take pity upon him, so that he[12] was noted of great infamy for that his unmerciful murder upon that young gentleman.

But the same Lord Clifford, not satisfied herewith, came to the place where the dead corpse of the Duke of York lay, caused his head to be stricken off and set on it a crown of paper, fixed it on a pole, and presented it to the Queen, not lying far from the field, in great despite,[13] at which great rejoicing was showed. But they laughed then that shortly after lamented, and were glad then of other men's deaths that knew not their own to be so near at hand. Some write that the Duke was taken alive and in derision caused to stand upon a molehill, on whose head they put a garland instead of a crown, which they had fashioned and made of sedges or bulrushes; and having so crowned him with that garland, they kneeled down afore him (as the Jews did unto Christ) in scorn, saying to him: "Hail, King without rule! Hail, King without heritage! Hail, Duke and prince without people or possessions!" And at length, having thus scorned him with these and divers other the like[14] despiteful words, they struck off his head, which, as ye have heard, they presented to the Queen.

Many deemed that this miserable end chanced to the Duke of York as a due punishment for breaking his oath of allegiance unto his sovereign lord King Henry; but others held him discharged thereof[15] because he obtained a dispensation from the Pope, by such suggestion as his procurators[16] made unto him, whereby the same oath was adjudged void, as that which was received unadvisedly,[17] to the prejudice of himself and disheriting of all his posterity. After this victory by the Queen, the Earl of Salisbury and all the prisoners were sent to Pomfret and there beheaded, whose heads, together with the Duke of York's head, were conveyed to York and there set on poles over the gate of the city, in despite[18] of them and their lineage. The Earl of March,

---

12 **he** i.e., Clifford 13 **despite** scorn 14 **the like** similar
15 **discharged thereof** relieved of his obligation to remain true to his oath 16 **procurators** supporters 17 **as that ... unadvisedly** as having been taken without adequate awareness of all the circumstances
18 **despite** scorn

now after the death of his father very[19] Duke of York, lying[20] at Gloucester, was wonderfully amazed[21] when the sorrowful news of these mishaps came unto him; but after comfort given to him by his faithful lovers[22] and assured allies, he removed[23] to Shrewsbury, declaring to the inhabitants of that town, and to them of the other towns in those parties, the murder of his father, the jeopardy of himself, and the present ruin of the commonwealth.

The people on the marches[24] of Wales, for the favor which they bare to the Mortimers' lineage, more gladly offered him their aid and assistance than he could desire the same, so that he had incontinently[25] a puissant army to the number of three-and-twenty thousand ready to go against the Queen and the murderers of his father. But when he was setting forward, news was brought to him that Jasper, Earl of Pembroke, half brother to King Henry, and James Butler, Earl of Ormonde and Wiltshire, had assembled a great number of Welsh and Irish people to take him. He, herewith quickened,[26] retired back and met with his enemies in a fair plain near to Mortimer's Cross, not far from Hereford East, on Candlemas Day in the morning [1461]. At which time the sun (as some write) appeared to the Earl of March like three suns and suddenly joined all together in one. Upon which sight he took such courage that he, fiercely setting on his enemies, put them to flight; and for this cause men imagined that he gave[27] the sun in his full brightness for his badge or cognizance. Of his enemies were left dead on the ground three thousand and eight hundred.

[The Queen, encouraged by her recent victory at Wakefield, marches with a northern army toward London and approaches Saint Albans where, she has learned, King Henry is under the guard of the Duke of Norfolk and the Earl of Warwick. The Second Battle of Saint Albans is fought on Shrove Tuesday, the seventeenth of February, 1461. The Queen's forces are victorious.]

19 very veritably, indeed   **20 lying** residing, headquartered
21 wonderfully amazed thunderstruck, shocked   **22 lovers** friends
23 removed moved, went   **24 marches** borders   **25 incontinently** immediately   **26 quickened** forced to move quickly, animated   **27 gave**
displayed on his coat of arms

When the day was closed, those that were about the King (in number a twenty thousand), hearing how evil their fellows had sped,[28] began utterly to despair of the victory and so fell without any long tarriance to running away. By reason whereof the nobles that were about the King, perceiving how the game went, and withal saw no comfort in the King[29] but rather a good will and affection towards the contrary part, they withdrew also, leaving the King accompanied with the Lord Bonneville and Sir Thomas Kiriell of Kent, which,[30] upon assurance of the King's promise, tarried still with him and fled not. But their trust[31] deceived them, for at the Queen's departing from Saint Albans they were both beheaded. . . .

Such was the success[32] of this second battle fought at Saint Albans, upon Shrove Tuesday, the seventeenth of February, in which were slain three-and-twenty hundred men, of whom no nobleman is remembered save Sir John Grey, which the same day was made knight, with twelve other, at the village of Colney. Now after that the noblemen and other were fled, and the King left in manner alone without any power of men to guard his person, he was counseled by an esquire called Thomas Hoo, a man well languaged and well seen[33] in the laws, to send some convenient messenger to the northern lords, advertising[34] them that he would now gladly come unto them, whom he knew to be his very friends and had assembled themselves together for his service, to the end he might remain with them, as before he had remained under the government of the southern lords.

According to the advice and counsel of this esquire, the King thought it good to send unto them, and withal[35] appointed the same esquire to bear the message, who first went and declared the same unto the Earl of Northumberland and, returning back to the King, brought certain lords with him who conveyed the King first unto the Lord Clifford's tent, that stood next to the place where the King's

---

28 how evil . . . sped how disastrously their companions had fared
29 withal . . . King i.e., thereupon saw no advantage in supporting the King   **30 which** who   **31 trust** i.e., in those promises   **32 success** outcome   **33 well languaged and well seen** well spoken and well versed **34 advertising** informing   **35 unto them, and withal** i.e., to the northern lords, and thereupon

people had encamped. This done, they went and brought the Queen and her son Prince Edward unto his presence, whom he joyfully received, embracing and kissing them in most loving wise and yielding hearty thanks to almighty God, whom it had pleased thus to strengthen the forces of the northern men, to restore his dearly beloved and only son again into his possession. Thus was the Queen fortunate in her two battles,[36] but unfortunate was the King in all his enterprises, for where his person was present the victory still fled from him to the contrary part. The Queen caused the King to dub her son Prince Edward knight, with thirty other persons which the day before fought on her side against his part.

[The Queen's northern soldiers pillage the town of Saint Albans. Upon hearing that the Earl of March has vanquished the Earls of Pembroke and Wiltshire at Chipping Norton and is now approaching London, and not trusting her own welcome in Essex and Kent, the Queen retreats northward with King Henry and their son.]

The Duchess of York, seeing her husband and son[37] slain, and not knowing what should succeed of her eldest son's chance,[38] sent her two younger sons, George and Richard, over the sea to the city of Utrecht in Almaine,[39] where they were of Philip, Duke of Burgundy, well received, and so remained there till their brother Edward had got the crown and government of the realm. The Earls of March and Warwick, having perfect knowledge that the King and Queen, with their adherents, were departed from Saint Albans, rode straight to London, entering there with a great number of men-of-war the first week of Lent. Whose coming thither was no sooner known but that the people resorted[40] out of Kent, Essex, and other the counties adjoining in great numbers, to see, aid, and comfort this lusty[41] prince and flower of chivalry, in whom the hope of their joy and trust of their quietness only consisted.

36 two battles i.e., Wakefield and the Second Battle of Saint Albans
37 son i.e., the young Earl of Rutland   **38 chance** fortune   **39 Almaine**
Germany and the Netherlands; Utrecht is in the latter   **40 resorted**
traveled, went   **41 lusty** vigorous, handsome

This prudent young prince, minding[42] to take time when time served, called a great Council both of the lords spiritual and temporal and to them repeated the title and right that he had to the crown, rehearsing also the articles concluded between King Henry and his father, by their writings signed and sealed and also confirmed by act of Parliament, the breaches whereof he neither forgat nor left undeclared. After the lords had considered of this matter, they determined by authority of the said Council that because King Henry had done contrary to the ordinances in the last Parliament concluded, and was insufficient of himself to rule the realm, he was therefore to be deprived of all kingly estate; and incontinently[43] was Edward, Earl of March, son and heir to Richard, Duke of York, by the lords in the said Council assembled, named, elected, and admitted for king and governor of the realm.

On which day, the people of the Earl's part being in their muster in Saint John's Field, and a great number of the substantial citizens there assembled to behold their order,[44] the Lord Falconbridge, who took the musters, wisely anon declared to the people the offenses and breaches of the late agreement committed by King Henry the Sixth, and demanded of the people whether they would have him to rule and reign any longer over them. To whom they with whole voice answered, "Nay, nay!" Then he asked them if they would serve, love, honor, and obey the Earl of March as their only King and sovereign lord. To which question they answered, "Yea, yea!" crying "King Edward!" with many great shouts and clapping of hands in assent and gladness of the same.

The lords were shortly advertised[45] of the loving consent which the commons frankly[46] and freely had given. Whereupon incontinently they all, with a convenient number of the most substantial commons, repaired[47] to the Earl at Baynard's Castle, making just and true report of their election and admission, and the loving assent of the commons.

[Holinshed briefly reports Edward's graceful acceptance speech.]

---

42 minding of a mind, intending   **43 incontinently** immediately
44 order formation, array   **45 advertised** informed   **46 frankly** willingly   **47 repaired** went

Thus far touching[48] the tragical state of this land under the rent regiment[49] of King Henry, who, besides the bare title of royalty and naked name of king, had little appertaining to the port[50] of a prince. For whereas the dignity of princedom standeth in sovereignty,[51] there were of his nobles that imbeciled[52] his prerogative by sundry practices, specially by main force, as seeking either to suppress or to exile or to obscure or to make him away. Otherwise what should be the meaning of all those foughten fields[53] from time to time, most miserably falling out both to prince,[54] peer, and people?

[Holinshed, before going on to Edward IV's reign, pauses to review the names and careers of the learned men that lived in Henry VI's time, such as the antiquary John Leland and the poet monk John Lydgate.]

EDWARD THE FOURTH, EARL OF MARCH, SON AND HEIR TO RICHARD, DUKE OF YORK

After that this prince, Edward, Earl of March, had taken upon him the government of this realm of England, as before ye have heard, the morrow next ensuing, being the fourth of March, he rode to the church of Saint Paul and there offered;[55] and after Te Deum sung,[56] with great solemnity he was conveyed to Westminster and there set in the hall with the scepter royal in his hand, whereto people in great numbers assembled. His claim to the crown was declared to be by two manner of ways: the first, as son and heir to Duke Richard, his father, right inheritor to the same; the second, by authority of Parliament and forfeiture committed by King Henry. Whereupon it was again demanded[57] of the commons if they would admit and take the said Earl

---

48 Thus far touching so much, then, regarding   **49 rent regiment** rule torn apart (by factionalism)   **50 appertaining to the port** belonging to the bearing and conduct   **51 standeth in sovereignty** is based upon supremacy of power   **52 there were . . . imbeciled** there were those among his nobles who enfeebled   **53 foughten fields** hardfought battles **54 prince** monarch   **55 offered** made a devotional offering   **56 after Te Deum sung** after the anthem "We praise you, O God" was sung **57 demanded** asked

as their prince and sovereign lord, which all with one voice cried, "Yea, yea!"

This part thus played, he entered into Westminster Church under a canopy with solemn procession, and there as king offered; and herewith taking the homages of all the nobles there present, he returned by water to London and was lodged in the Bishop's palace; and, on the morrow after, he was proclaimed King by the name of Edward the Fourth throughout the city. This was in the year of the world 5427, and after the birth of our Savior 1461 after our account, beginning the year at Christmas, but after the usual account of the Church of England 1460, the twentieth of Emperor Frederick the Third, the nine and thirtieth and last of Charles the Seventh, French King, and first year of the reign of James the Third, King of Scots.

Whilst these things were a-doing in the south parts, King Henry, being in the north country, assembled a great army, trusting for all this to subdue his enemies, namely sith[58] their chief ringleader, the Duke of York, was dispatched out of the way. But he was deceived, for out of the dead stock sprang a branch more mighty than the stem: this Edward the Fourth, a prince so highly favored of the people for his great liberality, clemency, upright dealing, and courage, that above all other he with them stood in grace alone, by reason whereof men of all ages and degrees to him daily repaired,[59] some offering themselves and their men to jeopard[60] their lives with him, and other plenteously gave money to support his charges[61] and to maintain his right.

By which means he gathered together a puissant army, to the intent by battle, sithence[62] none other ways would serve, at once to make an end of all. So, his army and all things prepared, he departed out of London the twelfth day of March, and by easy journeys came to the castle of Pomfret, where he rested, appointing the Lord Fitzwater to keep the passage at Ferrybridge with a good number of tall[63] men. King Henry, on the other part, having his army in readiness, committed the governance thereof to the Duke of Somerset, the Earl of Northumberland, and the Lord Clifford, as men desiring to revenge the death of their parents,

---

58 namely sith especially since   **59 repaired** went   **60 jeopard** risk
61 charges expenses   **62 sithence** since   **63 tall** brave

slain at the First Battle at Saint Albans. These captains, leaving King Henry, his wife, and son for the most safeguard within the city of York, passed the river of Wharfe with all their power,[64] intending to stop King Edward of his passage over the river of Aire.

And the better to bring that to pass, the Lord Clifford determined to make a charge upon them that kept the passage of Ferrybridge.

[In the fighting, Lord Fitzwater and the Bastard of Salisbury, brother of the Earl of Warwick, are slain.]

When the Earl of Warwick was informed hereof, like a man desperate he mounted on his hackney[65] and hasted puffing and blowing to King Edward, saying: "Sir, I pray God have mercy of their souls which in the beginning of your enterprise have lost their lives! And because I see no succors of the world but in God, I remit[66] the vengeance to Him, our Creator and Redeemer." With that he alighted down and slew his horse with his sword, saying: "Let him flee that will, for surely I will tarry with him that will tarry with me"; and kissed the cross of his sword as it were for a vow to the promise. King Edward, perceiving the courage of his trusty friend the Earl of Warwick, made proclamation that all men which were afraid to fight should depart; and to all those that tarried the battle he promised great rewards, with addition that any soldier which voluntarily would abide and afterwards, either in or before the fight, should seem to flee or turn his back, then he that could kill him should have a great reward and double wages.

After this proclamation ended, the Lord Falconbridge, Sir Walter Blunt, Robert Horne, with the foreward,[67] passed the river at Castleford, three miles from Ferrybridge, intending to have environed[68] the Lord Clifford and his company. But they, being thereof advertised, departed in great haste toward King Henry's army; yet they met with some

---

64 power army   **65 hackney** horse   **66 remit** resign, give over. (Warwick insists that God is our only hope in the world, and only He can revenge our wrongs. Warwick thereupon resolves to continue fighting those who have slain his brother, presumably in the hope that God will use him as an agent of revenge.)   **67 foreward** vanguard   **68 environed** surrounded

that they looked not for, and were so trapped ere they were aware. For the Lord Clifford, either for heat or pain putting off his gorget,[69] suddenly with an arrow (as some say, without an head) was stricken into the throat and immediately rendered his spirit; and the Earl of Westmorland's brother and all his company almost were there slain at a place called Dintingdale, not far from Towton.

[King Edward's army is ordered to take no prisoners alive. They are victorious in this Battle of Towton, driving the forces of King Henry into headlong retreat.]

After this great victory, King Edward rode to York, where he was with all solemnity received. And first he caused the heads of his father, the Earl of Salisbury, and other his friends to be taken from the gates and to be buried with their bodies; and there he caused the Earl of Devonshire and three other to be beheaded, and set their heads in the same place. King Henry, after he heard of the irrecoverable loss of his army, departed incontinently with his wife and son to the town of Berwick and, leaving the Duke of Somerset there, went into Scotland and, coming to the King of Scots, required[70] of him and his Council aid and comfort.

[King Henry is hospitably received, in return for which he delivers the town of Berwick to the King of Scotland.]

When King Henry was somewhat settled in the realm of Scotland, he sent his wife and his son into France to King Reiner her father, trusting by his aid and succor to assemble an army and once again to recover his right and dignity; but he in the meantime made his abode in Scotland, to see what way his friends in England would study[71] for his restitution.

The Queen, being in France, did obtain of[72] the young French King, then Lewis the Eleventh, that all her husband's friends and those of the Lancastrial[73] band might safely and surely have resort into any part of the realm of

---

69 gorget throat armor   **70 required** asked   **71 study** strive, employ thought and effort   **72 obtain of** obtain assurance from   **73 Lancastrial** Lancastrian, of the house of Lancaster

France, prohibiting all other of the contrary faction any access or repair into that country. Thus ye have heard how King Henry the Sixth, after he had reigned eight-and-thirty years and odd months, was driven out of this realm. But now, leaving him with the princes of his part[74] consulting together in Scotland, and Queen Margaret his wife gathering of men in France, I will return where I left, to proceed with the doings of King Edward.

This young prince, having with prosperous success obtained so glorious a victory in the mortal[75] battle at Towton, and chased all his adversaries out of the realm or at the leastways put them to silence, returned after the manner and fashion of a triumphant conqueror, with great pomp, unto London; where, according to the old custom of the realm, he called a great assembly of persons of all degrees; and the nine-and-twentieth day of June [1461] was at Westminster with solemnity crowned and anointed King. In which year this King Edward called his high court of Parliament at Westminster, in the which the state of the realm was greatly reformed and all the statutes made in Henry the Sixth his time which touched either his title or profit were revoked.

In the same Parliament the Earl of Oxford, far stricken in age, and his son and heir, the Lord Aubrey Vere, either through malice of their enemies or for that they had offended the King, were both, with divers of their counselors, attainted[76] and put to execution; which caused John, Earl of Oxford, ever after to rebel. There were also beheaded the same time Sir Thomas Tudenham, knight, William Tyrell, and John Montgomery, esquires, and after them divers others. Also, after this, he created his two younger brethren dukes; that is to say, Lord George, Duke of Clarence, Lord Richard, Duke of Gloucester; and the Lord John Neville, brother to Richard, Earl of Warwick, he first made Lord Montague* and afterwards created him Marquess Montague.

[Matters go well for King Edward in 1462 and 1463. The Duke of Somerset and other lords submit to him. When

---

*Montague Montacute [and also later in the same sentence]

74 part side, party   75 mortal deadly   76 attainted convicted

Somerset soon afterward revolts and joins Henry, he is captured by Edward's forces and executed. Queen Margaret attempts a return to England with French assistance, but without success. In 1464–1465, King Henry returns to England in disguise and is taken and brought to the Tower of London. Edward wins much popular favor by offering a pardon to all those who will submit to him.]

When his realm was thus brought into a good and quiet estate, it was thought meet[77] by him and those of his Council that a marriage were provided for him in some convenient place;[78] and therefore was the Earl of Warwick sent over into France to demand[79] the Lady Bona, daughter to Lewis, Duke of Savoy, and sister to the Lady Carlot, then Queen of France; which Bona was at that time in the French court.

The Earl of Warwick, coming to the French King then lying[80] at Tours, was of him honorably received and right courteously entertained. His message was so well liked and his request thought so honorable for the advancement of the Lady Bona that her sister Queen Carlot obtained both the good will of the King her husband and also of her sister the foresaid lady; so that the matrimony on that side was clearly assented to, and the Earl of Dammartin appointed with others to sail into England for the full finishing of the same. But here consider the old proverb to be true which saith that marriage goeth by destiny. For during the time that the Earl of Warwick was thus in France and according to his instructions brought the effect of his commission to pass, the King, being on hunting[81] in the Forest of Wichwood beside Stony Stratford, came for his recreation to the manor of Grafton where the Duchess of Bedford then sojourned, wife to Sir Richard Woodville, Lord Rivers, on whom was then attendant a daughter of hers called the Lady Elizabeth Grey, widow of Sir John Grey, knight, slain at the last Battle of Saint Albans, as before ye have heard.

This widow, having a suit to the King for such lands as

---

77 meet fitting   **78 in some convenient place** i.e., in a suitably royal family, one providing a powerful alliance   **79 demand** ask (in marriage)
80 lying residing   **81 on hunting** a-hunting

her husband had given her in jointure,[82] so kindled the King's affection towards her that he not only favored her suit but more her person; for she was a woman of a more formal countenance than of excellent beauty, and yet both of such beauty and favor that, with her sober demeanor, sweet looks, and comely smiling (neither too wanton nor too bashful), besides her pleasant tongue and trim wit,[83] she so allured and made subject unto her the heart of that great prince that, after she had denied him to be his paramour with so good manner and words so well set as better could not be devised, he finally resolved with himself to marry her, not asking counsel of any man till they might perceive it was no booty[84] to advise him to the contrary of that his concluded purpose, sith[85] he was so far gone that he was not revocable,[86] and therefore had fixed his heart upon the last resolution, namely, to apply an wholesome, honest, and honorable remedy to his affections fired with the flames of love, and not to permit his heart to the thralldom of unlawful lust; which purpose was both princely and profitable, as the poet saith:

> Utile propositum est saevas extinguere flammas,
> Nec servum vitii pectus habere sui.*[87]

But yet the Duchess of York his mother letted[88] this match as much as in her lay;[89] and when all would not serve, she caused a precontract to be alleged, made by him with the Lady Elizabeth Lucy.[90] But, all doubts resolved, all things made clear, and all cavillations avoided, privily[91] in a morning he married the said Lady Elizabeth Grey at Grafton beforesaid where he first began to fancy her. And in the next year after, she was with great solemnity crowned queen at Westminster. Her father also was created Earl Rivers and made High Constable of England; her brother, Lord Anthony, was married to the sole heir of Thomas, Lord Scales;

*vitii . . . sui vitiis . . . suum

82 in jointure i.e., in the event of widowhood   **83 trim wit** sharp intelligence   **84 no booty** no use   **85 sith** since   **86 was not revocable** could not be called back   **87 Utile . . . sui** A useful goal it is to extinguish a cruel flame and free the heart from shameful bondage. (Ovid, *Remedia Amoris*, ll. 53–54.)   **88 letted** hindered   **89 as in her lay** as she was able   **90 Elizabeth Lucy** (One of Edward's mistresses.)   **91 all cavillations avoided, privily** all cavilling or faultfinding refuted or set aside, privately

Sir Thomas Grey, son to Sir John Grey, the Queen's first husband, was created Marquess Dorset and married to Cecily, heir to the Lord Bonville. The French King was not well pleased to be thus dallied with, but he shortly, to appease the grief of his wife and her sister the Lady Bona, married the said Lady Bona to the Duke of Milan.

Now when the Earl of Warwick had knowledge, by letters sent to him out of England from his trusty friends, that King Edward had gotten him a new wife, he was not a little troubled in his mind, for that he took it his credence[92] thereby was greatly minished and his honor much stained, namely[93] in the court of France, for that it might be judged he came rather like an espial[94] to move a thing never minded[95] and to treat[96] a marriage determined before not to take effect. Surely he thought himself evil used that, when he had brought the matter to his purposed intent and wished conclusion, then to have it quaill on his part,[97] so as all men might think at the least wise[98] that his prince made small account of him to send him on such a sleeveless[99] errand.

All men for the most part agree that this marriage was the only cause why the Earl of Warwick conceived an hatred against King Edward, whom he so much before favored. Other affirm other causes, and one specially: for that King Edward did attempt a thing once in the Earl's house which was much against the Earl's honesty[100]—whether he would have deflowered his daughter or his niece, the certainty was not, for both their honors, openly revealed—for surely such a thing was attempted by King Edward, which loved well both to behold and also to feel fair damsels.

[Warwick's grudge against Edward deepens in 1467–1468.]

In this meantime the Earl of Warwick, bearing a continual grudge in his heart toward King Edward since his last return out of France, persuaded so with his two brethren

---

92 credence reputation   **93 namely** especially   **94 espial** spy   **95 move a thing never minded** set in motion a thing never intended   **96 treat** negotiate   **97 quail on his part** fail when matters were in his hands   **98 at the least wise** at the very least   **99 sleeveless** futile   **100 honesty** honor

the Archbishop and the Marquess[101] that they agreed to join with him in any attempt which he should take in hand against the said King. The Archbishop was easily allured to the Earl's purpose, but the Marquess could by no means be reduced to take any part against King Edward of a long time, till the Earl had both promised him great rewards and promotions[102] and also assured him of the aid and power of the greatest princes of the realm. And even as the Marquess was loath to consent to his unhappy conspiracy, so with a faint heart he showed himself an enemy unto King Edward; which double dissimulation was both the destruction of him and his brethren.

[Holinshed prints the persuasions used by the Earl of Warwick with his two brothers against King Edward.]

Beside all this, the Earl of Warwick, being a far-casting[103] prince, perceived somewhat[104] in the Duke of Clarence whereby he judged that he bare no great good will towards the King his brother; and thereupon, feeling his mind by such talk as he of purpose ministered,[105] understood how he was bent[106] and so wan[107] him to his purpose; and, for better assurance of his faithful friendship, he offered him his eldest daughter in marriage, with the whole half deal[108] of his wife's inheritance.

[Clarence marries Isabel, Warwick's eldest daughter. A rebellion breaks out in Yorkshire in 1469 on Warwick's behalf, and the rebels move toward London. They are met by Edward's forces near Warwick.]

The King in this meantime had assembled his power and was coming toward the Earl, who, being advertised thereof, sent to the Duke of Clarence, requiring him to come and join with him. The Duke, being not far off, with all speed repaired to the Earl, and so they joined their powers[109] to-

---

101 the Archbishop and the Marquess the Archbishop of York and the Marquess Montague   **102 promotions** preferments   **103 far-casting** forward looking, cunning   **104 somewhat** something   **105 feeling . . . ministered** i.e., feeling out the Duke of Clarence's mind by various things that Warwick said to that purpose   **106 bent** inclined   **107 wan** won   **108 deal** share   **109 powers** armies

gether, and upon secret knowledge had that the King (because they were entered into terms by way of communication to have a peace) took small heed to himself, nothing doubting any outward attempt of his enemies.[110]

The Earl of Warwick, intending not to leese[111] such opportunity of advantage, in the dead of the night, with an elect company of men-of-war, as secretly as was possible, set on the King's field,[112] killing them that kept the watch; and, ere the King was ware (for he thought of nothing less than of that which then happened), at a place called Wolney, four miles from Warwick, he was taken prisoner and brought to the castle of Warwick. And to the intent his friends should not know what was become of him, the Earl caused him by secret journeys in the night to be conveyed to Middleham Castle in Yorkshire and there to be kept under the custody of the Archbishop of York and other his friends in those parties.[113]

[King Edward, though captive, is given the freedom to hunt and exercise.]

Now, on a day, upon a plain when he was thus abroad,[114] there met with him Sir William Stanley, Sir Thomas a Borough,[115] and divers other of his friends, with such a great band of men that neither his keepers would, nor once durst, move[116] him to return unto prison again. Some have thought that his keepers were corrupted with money or fair promises and therefore suffered him thus to scape out of danger.

[Edward, thus freed, comes to York. Attempts are made to reconcile the King with his brother and with Warwick. But Warwick travels to France in 1470.]

When Queen Margaret, that sojourned with Duke Reiner her father, heard tell that the Earl of Warwick was come to

---

110 and upon secret knowledge had . . . attempt of his enemies i.e., and joined in the secret information they had obtained that King Edward, trusting in the fact that the two sides were conducting peace talks under terms of a truce, took small heed of his personal safety, not in the least fearing any overt attempt on the part of his enemies   **111 leese** lose   **112 field** camp   **113 parties** parts, regions   **114 abroad** out of doors   **115 Thomas a Borough** Thomas Burgh   **116 move** urge, compel

the French court, with all diligence she came to Amboise to see him with her only son Prince Edward.

With her also came Jasper, Earl of Pembroke, and John, Earl of Oxford, which, after divers imprisonments lately escaped, fled out of England into France and came by fortune to this assembly. These persons, after entreaty[117] had of their affairs, determined by means of the French King to conclude a league and amity between them. And first to begin withal, for the sure foundation of their new entreaty, Edward, Prince of Wales, wedded[118] Anne, second daughter to the Earl of Warwick, which lady came with her mother into France. After which marriage, the Duke[119] and the Earls took a solemn oath that they should never leave the war till either King Henry the Sixth or his son Prince Edward were restored to the crown; and that the Queen and the Prince should depute and appoint the Duke and the Earl[120] to be governors and conservators of the commonwealth, till time the Prince were come to estate. . . .

The French King lent both ships, men, and money unto Queen Margaret and to her partakers,[121] and appointed the Bastard of Bourbon, Admiral of France, with a great navy, to defend them against the navy of the Duke of Burgundy which he laid at the mouth of the river Seine ready to encounter them, being of greater force than both the French navy and the English fleet. And yet King Reiner did also help his daughter with men and munition of war.

[Many Englishmen eagerly await the arrival of Warwick and promise him support.]

When the Earl had taken land, he made proclamation in the name of King Henry the Sixth, upon high pains commanding and charging all men able to bear armor to prepare themselves to fight against Edward, Duke of York, which contrary to right had usurped the crown. It is almost not to be believed how many thousands men-of-war at the first tidings of the Earl's landing resorted unto him.

King Edward, wakened with the news of the Earl's land-

---

117 entreaty investigation, discussion   **118 wedded** i.e., was betrothed to   **119 Duke** i.e., Duke of Clarence   **120 Earl** i.e., Earl of Warwick **121 partakers** supporters

ing and the great repair[122] of people that came flocking in unto him, sent forth letters into all parts of his realm to raise an army; but of them that were sent for few came, and yet of those few the more part came with no great good wills. Which when he perceived, he began to doubt[123] the matter, and therefore, being accompanied with the Duke of Gloucester, his brother, the Lord Hastings, his Chamberlain (which had married the Earl's sister and yet was ever true to the King his master), and the Lord Scales, brother to the Queen, he departed into Lincolnshire. And because he understood that all the realm was up against him, and some part of the Earl of Warwick's power was within half a day's journey of him, following the advice of his Council, with all haste possible he passed the Washes in great jeopardy and, coming to Lynn, found there an English ship and two hulks of Holland ready (as Fortune would) to make sail.

Whereupon he, with his brother the Duke of Gloucester, the Lord Scales, and divers other his trusty friends, entered into the ship. The Lord Hastings tarried awhile after, exhorting all his acquaintance that of necessity should tarry behind to show themselves openly as friends to King Henry for their own safeguard, but heartily required them in secret to continue faithful to King Edward. This persuasion declared, he entered the ship with the other,[124] and so they departed, being in number, in that one ship and two hulks, about seven or eight hundred persons, having no furniture[125] of apparel or other necessary things with them saving apparel for war.

[King Edward and his party sail for Burgundy, narrowly avoiding being taken by some ships of Hanse citizens enroute. His friends continue to fight in his behalf, and he returns to England briefly in 1470, but, when Henry VI is proclaimed king by the Duke of Clarence and the Earl of Warwick, Edward flees once again to Burgundy. His friends take refuge in various sanctuaries, and his Queen, Elizabeth, at Westminster, gives birth to a son, Edward. Warwick heads for London.]

---

122 repair assemblage   **123 doubt** fear, suspect   **124 other** others
125 furniture provisions

When he had settled all things at his pleasure, upon the twelfth day of October he rode to the Tower of London and there delivered King Henry out of the ward[126] where he before was kept, and brought him to the King's lodging, where he was served according to his degree.[127]

On the five-and-twentieth day of the said month, the Duke of Clarence, accompanied with the Earls of Warwick and Shrewsbury, the Lord Strange, and other lords and gentlemen, some for fear and some for love and some only to gaze at the wavering world, went to the Tower; and from thence brought King Henry, appareled in a long gown of blue velvet, through London to the church of Saint Paul; the people on every side the streets rejoicing and crying "God save the King!" as though each thing had succeeded as they would have had it; and when he had offered,[128] as kings use to do, he was conveyed to the Bishop's palace, where he kept his household like a king. Thus was the principality posted over[129] sometimes to Henry, sometimes to Edward, according to the sway of the party prevailing, ambition and disdain still casting faggots on the fire whereby the heat of hatred gathered the greater force to the consumption of the peers and the destruction of the people. . . .

When King Henry had thus readepted[130] and eftsoons[131] gotten his regal power and authority, he called his high court of Parliament to begin the six-and-twentieth day of November at Westminster; in the which King Edward was adjudged a traitor to the country and an usurper of the realm. His goods were confiscate and forfeited.

[Edward's statutes are revoked and King Henry's heir, Prince Edward, is reinstated, next in succession being the Duke of Clarence and his male heirs. Warwick is appointed governor of the realm in partnership with Clarence.]

When Queen Margaret understood by her husband's letters that the victory was gotten by their friends, she with her son Prince Edward and her train entered their ships to

---

126 ward prison   **127 degree** rank, status   **128 offered** made devotional offering   **129 posted over** handed over   **130 readepted** recovered **131 eftsoons** again

take their voyage into England; but the winter was so sharp, the weather so stormy, and the wind so contrary that she was fain[132] to take land again and to defer her journey till another season.

About the same season, Jasper, Earl of Pembroke, went into Wales to visit his lands in Pembrokeshire, where he found Lord Henry, son to his brother Edmund, Earl of Richmond, having not full ten[133] years of age, he being kept in manner like a captive, but honorably brought up by the Lady Herbert, late wife to William, Earl of Pembroke.

[Holinshed gives the lineage of this young person who is to be King Henry VII.]

The Earl of Pembroke took this child, being his nephew, out of the custody of the Lady Herbert and, at his return, brought the child with him to London to King Henry the Sixth; whom when the King had a good while beheld, he said to such princes as were with him: "Lo, surely this is he to whom both we and our adversaries, leaving[134] the possession of all things, shall hereafter give room and place." So this holy man showed, before the chance that should happen, that this Earl Henry, so ordained by God, should in time to come (as he did indeed) have and enjoy the kingdom and whole rule of this realm of England; so that it might seem probable, by the coherence of holy Henry's predictions with the issue falling out in truth with the same, that for the time he was endued with a prophetical spirit. And surely the epithet or title of "holy" is not for naught attributed unto him, for it is to be read in writers that he was by nature given to peaceableness, abhorring blood and slaughter, detesting civil tumults, addicted to devotion, very frequent in prayer, and not esteeming so highly of courtly gallantness as stood with the dignity of a prince. In consideration whereof he procured against himself an apostasy of his people both native and foreign, who revolted and fell from fealty.

---

132 fain obliged   **133 ten** (Actually, fourteen; Henry Tudor was born in 1457, and the event is described in 1471.)   **134 leaving** losing (through ill fortune and death)

[Warwick is concerned about the Duke of Burgundy's having offered hospitality to Edward. Burgundy declines to provide open support for the Yorkist cause, but he does give secret aid. Edward sails for England in March 1471, encounters difficulties with storms, but lands at Ravenspurgh on the Humber (where Henry Bolingbroke had earlier landed to challenge Richard II and become King Henry IV). Edward, receiving little support, talks cautiously as though he has come back solely for his dukedom of York. He heads for York.]

When King Edward had thus gotten into the city of York, he made such means[135] among the citizens that he got of them a certain sum of money; and leaving a garrison within the city, contrary to his oath, for fear lest the citizens after his departure might haply move some rebellion against him, he set forward the next day toward Tadcaster, a town ten miles from thence belonging to the Earl of Northumberland. The next day he took his way toward Wakefield and Sandal, a castle and lordship belonging to the inheritance of the Dukes of York, leaving the castle of Pomfret upon his left hand where the Marquess Montague with his army lay and did not once offer to stop him.

[Edward is joined by some supporters, including Sir Thomas Burgh and Sir Thomas Montgomery. Toward the end of March 1471 he appears before the walls of Coventry and dares the Earl of Warwick to come forth and fight. Warwick, hoping to be reinforced by the Duke of Clarence and his forces, begins to suspect that Clarence's loyalty to Warwick is wavering. And indeed Clarence has begun "to weigh with himself the great inconvenience into the which as well his brother King Edward as himself and his younger brother the Duke of Gloucester were fallen through the dissension betwixt them." A reconciliation between Clarence and Edward takes place between their two armies at Warwick, to the great satisfaction of all beholders. Clarence tries unsuccessfully to reconcile the Earl of Warwick to King Edward. In April, the King is warmly received into

135 made such means took such steps

London, is reconciled with the Archbishop of York, and receives custody of King Henry VI from the Archbishop.

Warwick, perceiving Edward's great success in London, resolves to try his fortunes in battle, and, accompanied by the Dukes of Exeter and Somerset, the Earl of Oxford, Marquess Montague, and others, moves toward Barnet, midway between Saint Albans and London. Warwick and his brother Montague are slain in the fighting.

Also in April 1471, Queen Margaret and her son return from France to England with an army, landing in Dorsetshire. She is joined by the Duke of Somerset and other supporters. King Edward marches to do battle, meeting the Queen's forces at Tewkesbury. The Queen's forces are routed, partly by the bravery of Richard, Duke of Gloucester. "This," says Holinshed, "was the last fought field or pight[136] battle tried between the potentates of this land in King Edward the Fourth's days." The date is May 4, 1471.]

In the winning of the camp,[137] such as stood to it were slain out of hand. Prince Edward was taken, as he fled towards the town, by Sir Richard Crofts and kept close.[138] In the field and chase were slain the Lord John of Somerset, called Marquess Dorset; Thomas Courtenay, Earl of Devonshire; Sir John Delves; Sir Edward Hampden; Sir Robert Whittingham; and Sir John Leukener, with three thousand others. After the field[139] was ended, proclamation was made that whosoever could bring forth Prince Edward alive or dead should have an annuity of a hundred pounds during his life, and the Prince's life to be saved if he were brought forth alive. Sir Richard Crofts, nothing mistrusting the King's promise, brought forth his prisoner, Prince Edward, being a fair and well-proportioned young gentleman; whom when King Edward had well advised,[140] he demanded of him how he durst so presumptuously enter into his realm with banner displayed.

Whereunto the Prince boldly answered, saying: "To recover my father's kingdom and heritage, from his father and grandfather to him, and from him after him to me, lin-

---

136 pight pitched   **137 camp** battlefield   **138 close** in confinement
139 field battle   **140 advised** looked at

eally descended." At which words King Edward said nothing, but with his hand thrust him from him or (as some say) struck him with his gauntlet; whom incontinently George, Duke of Clarence, Richard, Duke of Gloucester, Thomas Grey, Marquess Dorset, and William, Lord Hastings, that stood by, suddenly murdered; for the which cruel act the more part of the doers in their latter days drank of the like cup, by the righteous justice and due punishment of God. His body was homely[141] interred with the other simple[142] corpses in the church of the monastery of Black Monks[143] in Tewkesbury.

[Edward gives thanks at the Abbey Church for his victory, and orders the beheading of Somerset and other of his captured enemies.]

The same Tuesday, the King departed from Tewkesbury towards Worcester, and by the way had knowledge that Queen Margaret was found in a poor house of religion not far from thence, into the which she was withdrawn for safeguard of herself on Saturday in the morning, being the day of the battle. She was after brought to London as prisoner, and so kept till her father ransomed her with great sums of money which he borrowed of Lewis the Eleventh, King of France.

[Edward returns triumphantly to London in May 1471. A different fate lies in store for his hapless Lancastrian counterpart.]

Moreover, here is to be remembered that poor King Henry the Sixth, a little before deprived (as ye have heard) of his realm and imperial crown, was now in the Tower spoiled of his life by Richard, Duke of Gloucester (as the constant fame[144] ran), who, to the intent that his brother King Edward might reign in more surety, murdered the said King Henry with a dagger.

141 **homely** simply   142 **simple** of ordinary subjects, common
143 **Black Monks** Benedictines   144 **constant fame** consistent rumor

[Holinshed speaks generously of the spiritual qualities of both kings, saying of Henry VI that "of his own natural inclination he abhorred all the vices as well of the body as of the soul," and of Edward IV that he was "religiously affected," wearing a sackcloth next to the skin on holy days and avoiding all oaths stronger than "forsooth and forsooth."]

The second edition of Raphael Holinshed's *Chronicles* was published in 1587. This selection is based on that edition, Volume 3, folios 655–691.

Further Reading

Berry, Edward I. *Patterns of Decay: Shakespeare's Early Histories.* Charlottesville, Va.: Univ. Press of Virginia, 1975. Berry's book explores how Shakespeare's earliest history plays dramatize a process of social and political disintegration. Character in the *Henry VI* plays is generally subordinated to larger thematic concerns: *1 Henry VI* depicts the disintegration of chivalric values and of ceremony; *2 Henry VI* the collapse of justice and law; and *3 Henry VI*, looking forward to *Richard III*, the dissolution of family bonds.

Bevington, David. "The Domineering Female in *1 Henry VI.*" *Shakespeare Studies* 2 (1966): 51–58. Bevington traces a thematic pattern in *1 Henry VI* in which domineering women, possessing enchanting powers, seek mastery over men. The reversal of sexual roles, he suggests, is both source and symbol of the cosmic and political disorder that threatens England.

Blanpied, John W. "Breaking Ground: The *Henry VI* Plays." *Time and the Artist in Shakespeare's English Histories.* Newark, Del.: Univ. of Delaware Press, 1983. For Blanpied, the disordered, confused world of the plays is not the result of immature craftsmanship but a deliberate effect of Shakespeare's artistic confrontation with history. The unstable rhythms and sympathies of the plays result from his discovery of the underlying chaos of history that ceremony (and art) would attempt to control and contain.

Brockbank, J. Philip. "The Frame of Disorder—*Henry VI.*" In *Early Shakespeare,* ed. John Russell Brown and Bernard Harris. Stratford-upon-Avon Studies 3. London: Edward Arnold; New York: St. Martin's Press, 1961. Focusing on the plays' persistent efforts to control the turbulence of history in ceremony and spectacle, Brockbank discovers the plays' center in the conflict between personal responsibility and historical process. The three parts of *Henry VI*, according to Brockbank, expose the optimistic theology of Raphael Holinshed's providential history (in his *Chronicles*) to the brutal political ideology that history reveals, releasing the tragic potential of that history.

Burckhardt, Sigurd. " 'I Am But Shadow of Myself': Ceremony and Design in *1 Henry VI*." *Modern Language Quarterly* 28 (1967): 139–158. Rpt. in *Shakespearean Meanings*. Princeton, N.J.: Princeton Univ. Press, 1968. Burckhardt suggestively moves from a consideration of the formal discontinuities of the play to Shakespeare's awareness of the inadequacy of the idealized Elizabethan world picture. In seeking an artistic design to order the apparent chaos of history, Shakespeare discovers contradictions at the heart of the Tudor orthodoxy.

Clemen, Wolfgang. "Some Aspects of Style in the *Henry VI* Plays." In *Shakespeare's Styles: Essays in Honour of Kenneth Muir*, ed. Philip Edwards, Inga-Stina Ewbank, and G. K. Hunter. Cambridge and New York: Cambridge Univ. Press, 1980. The style of the *Henry VI* plays, Clemen finds, is formal and highly patterned, designed to reveal not subtleties of character but motives and the significance of events. Paradoxically, the effect of this unsettles an audience, for the plays' eloquence and explicitness conflict sharply with the absurd nightmare of the brutal and bloody history that is enacted.

Cox, John D. "*3 Henry VI:* Dramatic Convention and the Shakespearean History Play." *Comparative Drama* 12 (1978): 42–60. Cox discovers the provocatively ambivalent historical vision of *3 Henry VI* in its relation to its literary forebears. The play mediates between the claims of salvation history in the medieval drama and the "radical assault on traditional dramaturgy in Christopher Marlowe's *Tamburlaine*." In its contrasts between sacred and secular ordering, *3 Henry VI* reveals the particular nature of the Shakespearean history play.

Dean, Paul. "Shakespeare's *Henry VI* Trilogy and Elizabethan 'Romance' Histories: The Origins of a Genre." *Shakespeare Quarterly* 33 (1982): 34–48. Dean proposes a new source for Shakespeare's *Henry VI* plays: the popular "romance" histories, such as Robert Greene's *James IV* and his *Friar Bacon and Friar Bungay*. These, more than the few pre-Shakespearean chronicle plays, inform Shakespeare's dramatic practice. Their stylizations of plot, character, and language and their major thematic concerns anticipate the interests and techniques of Shakespeare's earliest histories.

Hibbard, G. R. "Formalization in the Early History Plays." *The Making of Shakespeare's Dramatic Poetry.* Toronto: Univ. of Toronto Press, 1981. Confronted in the *Henry VI* plays with the challenge of imposing structure and logic upon a mass of historical material, Shakespeare, Hibbard argues, not only organizes each play around a dominant political theme but also weaves the three parts together into a complex whole through recurring poetic devices and patterns.

Jones, Emrys. *The Origins of Shakespeare,* pp. 142–192. Oxford: Oxford Univ. Press, 1977. Jones examines the *Henry VI* plays within the context of a broader literary response to the threat of civil war stimulated by the dangerous political climate of the 1580s. The thematic concerns of the three plays—which Jones insists were designed as a self-contained trilogy, not part of a tetralogy—are fame (*1 Henry VI,*) government (*2 Henry VI*), and disorder (*3 Henry VI*).

Kahn, Coppélia. *Man's Estate: Masculine Identity in Shakespeare,* pp. 51–62. Berkeley, Calif.: Univ. of California Press, 1981. The dominant relationship Kahn sees in the *Henry VI* plays is that between fathers and sons. Patriarchy proves a source of both order and chaos, as sons (including King Henry VI, who must follow in his heroic father's footsteps) discover and affirm their manhood through aggression. Kahn traces in the three plays a decline in the strength of the father-son bonds, from sons emulating fathers to sons avenging fathers to the total dissolution of filial bonds in Richard's anarchic villainy.

Manheim, Michael. "The Meek King." *The Weak King Dilemma in the Shakespearean History Play.* Syracuse, N.Y.: Syracuse Univ. Press, 1973. Finding in the *Henry VI* plays evidence of Shakespeare's frustration with political realities, Manheim examines the plays' polarized presentation of the claims of a weak Christian king and a strong Machiavellian aristocracy. In the disturbing world the plays dramatize, Henry's virtue disables him in the face of the ambition and greed of his nobles.

Ornstein, Robert. "The *Henry VI* Plays." *A Kingdom for a Stage: The Achievement of Shakespeare's History Plays.*

Cambridge: Harvard Univ. Press, 1972. Ornstein challenges the notion of the early histories as orthodox expressions of authorized Elizabethan political thought (e.g., Ribner, below). His analysis focuses on the aesthetic experience of the plays as well as on Shakespeare's emerging conceptions of dramatic form and the theatrical possibilities of English history.

Ribner, Irving. *The English History Play in the Age of Shakespeare*, pp. 92–112. 1957. Rev. and enl., New York: Barnes and Noble, 1965. Shakespeare's purpose in the *Henry VI* plays, Ribner argues, was to warn England of the dangers of civil war and to affirm a providential view of history in accord with the "Tudor myth." To this end, he drew upon various literary traditions—the medieval miracle and morality plays, Senecan tragedy, and poetic accounts of the falls of princes—enforcing a sense of England as a morality hero who, having sinned, must suffer before attaining salvation.

Riggs, David. *Shakespeare's Heroical Histories: "Henry VI" and Its Literary Tradition*. Cambridge: Harvard Univ. Press, 1971. Tracing the complex intellectual and literary legacy of the *Henry VI* plays, Riggs examines how Shakespeare's art draws on popular historical drama, humanist training in classical rhetoric, and Elizabethan theories of history and heroic poetry. The plays themselves, he finds, explore the relationship of heroic ideals and political realities, and dramatize the gradual deterioration of heroic idealism under the pressure of history.

Saccio, Peter. "Henry VI: The Loss of Empire." *Shakespeare's English Kings: History, Chronicle, and Drama*. New York: Oxford Univ. Press, 1977. Saccio considers the events of Henry VI's reign as they are understood by modern and Tudor historians, and examines Shakespeare's often radical reshaping of his source material as he transforms history into drama.

Tillyard, E. M. W. "The First Tetralogy." *Shakespeare's History Plays*, 1944. Rpt., New York: Barnes and Noble, 1964. For Tillyard, the *Henry VI* plays celebrate and elaborate the Tudor myth of history: the plays are governed by a providential design in which a sinful England is the tragic protagonist brought to the brink of ruin and chaos before being restored (at the end of *Richard III*, with the ascension of the Tudor line) to grace.

Wilson, F. P. "Marlowe and Shakespeare." *Marlowe and the Early Shakespeare*. Oxford: Clarendon Press, 1953. Wilson finds no certain evidence for the existence of popular plays on English history before 1588. Shakespeare's *Henry VI* plays, Wilson suggests, are not simply an improvement upon an undistinguished popular form, but perhaps the first English history plays to have been written.

From the 1983 New York Shakespeare Festival production of *Richard III* with Kevin Kline as Richard III, directed by Jane Howell at the Delacorte Theater in Central Park.

RICHARD
III

RICHARD III

Foreword

Richard III is the best advertisement I know of for a life devoted to villainy. Of course, villains are always attractive—witness the popularity of gangster movies in this country for so many years. We want to see them done in, but we also love watching them along the way as they plan and execute their dastardly crimes. This is what's so much fun about Richard III—he is so full of action and energy, as he darts from one scheme to another with diabolical glee, that it's impossible not to enjoy him.

There are two scenes in particular where Richard establishes himself as one of the greatest stage personalities of all time. The first is that incredible scene in Act 1 where he woos Anne (whose husband, the Prince of Wales, was killed by Richard) as she mourns her dead father-in-law, Henry VI, also slain by Richard. It's a powerfully dramatic scene, one which can easily be read aloud by two people. The cross fire of Richard's and Anne's language is fast and furious, as they play off one another's words:

ANNE
> O, wonderful, when devils tell the truth!

RICHARD
> More wonderful, when angels are so angry.
> Vouchsafe, divine perfection of a woman.
> Of these supposèd crimes to give me leave
> By circumstance but to acquit myself.

ANNE
> Vouchsafe, defused infection of a man,
> Of these known evils but to give me leave
> By circumstance t' accuse thy cursèd self.

Though Anne is bitter and unyielding at first, by the end of the scene Richard has out-talked her, and he gets what he wants—her favor. We watch, spellbound and amazed as his glib tongue and smooth persuasiveness completely turn this woman around until she promises him her love, even as she stands in front of the corpse of the father-in-law whom Richard has recently killed. He is a lover indeed.

If you think that *this* is enough to establish Richard as a master of manipulation, wait until you get to the scene where he approaches Queen Elizabeth, immediately after he has had her two young sons, the innocent little princes, murdered in the Tower—a deed that the murderer Tyrrel calls "the tyrannous and bloody act.... The most arch deed of piteous massacre / That ever yet this land was guilty of."

Richard insinuates himself right into the midst of their mother's grief and mourning, hellbent on gaining a political objective he considers absolutely essential to his retention of the crown—namely, the hand of her daughter in marriage. The long scene between the embittered, grief-stricken mother and the fiendishly logical King makes Richard's previous debate with Anne look like the first effort of an amateur.

His inexorable and terrifying logic becomes perfectly normal within the context of the world he has created, a world where murder is the most effective—and acceptable—means of dealing with a political problem:

> Look what is done cannot be now amended.
> Men shall deal unadvisedly sometimes,
> Which after-hours gives leisure to repent.
> If I did take the kingdom from your sons,
> To make amends I'll give it to your daughter.

In the psychologically charged atmosphere in which their encounter takes place, Richard's appeal to Elizabeth appears less irrational than it would in another setting.

This scene reveals the power of Richard's mind and the formidable intellect that endows him with the extraordinary ability to be clear and decisive; he zeroes in on the immediate problem, decides what has to be done, and then does it. Morality aside, these skills would propel him to the top of the modern corporate world today; he has raised acuity to the level of an art. If it weren't for his utter wickedness, one might almost be tempted to eulogize him at this death with the words Ophelia speaks about Hamlet: "O, what a noble mind is here o'erthrown!"

But in the end we can't really set those questions of morality aside. For Elizabeth sees past all of his well-argued rationales for this outrageous alliance to the blood-stained dagger grasped in Richard's hand. And that changes everything.

As Shakespeare pays homage to Richard's mental prowess and potential for great leadership in parts of this scene, he's also telling us to remember that Richard *is* evil. This is important because as a stage character, Richard is so attractive, so delightfully mischievous in his wicked revelry, so irrepressibly and irresistibly murderous, that we in the audience are inclined not to take his actions seriously. And unless we take him seriously, we will miss the complexity of Shakespeare's treatment of the man and the milieu in which he operated.

Richard is such an amazing, vital character—no wonder he is a coveted role for actors. He is a superbly theatrical being, really playing the stage for all it's worth, from the moment he opens the play with, "Now is the winter of our discontent / Made glorious summer by this sun of York," to his final dramatic cry, "A horse! A horse! My kingdom for a horse!" In the midst of wiping out people as if they were mere dolls, Richard is in charge—controlling the action, directing the plot, and upstaging every other character in the play with his unforgettable theatrics.

JOSEPH PAPP

JOSEPH PAPP GRATEFULLY ACKNOWLEDGES THE HELP OF ELIZABETH KIRKLAND IN PREPARING THIS FOREWORD.

Introduction

Richard III begins where *3 Henry VI* left off, and completes the action of the four-play series begun with *1 Henry VI*. On the basis of its Senecan style, the play appears to have been written soon after its predecessors, some time between 1591 and 1594. Richard's evil character, which had already begun to emerge in the last of the *Henry VI* plays, now stands fully revealed. His opening soliloquy depends for its ironically mocking effect on our familiarity with recent events. An end to the Yorkist-Lancastrian hostilities has come at last; but with his genius for evil, Richard looks upon a time of peace with only envy and contempt. His intense self-assertion and his aggressive energy must find new employment. No peace can withstand the machinations of this consummate deceiver, who gave his nephew Edward the kiss of Judas during the Yorkist triumph concluding *3 Henry VI*.

Richard dominates the play of *Richard III* to an extraordinary extent. He is the central character that the earlier plays, especially *3 Henry VI*, lacked. He is onstage almost continuously and, until the end, completely manipulates the actions of others. As chief actor and stage manager in his own drama, Richard chortlingly takes the audience into his confidence. His revelation of his plotting serves as a structural device for the play even as it manipulates and directs the audience's attention; we know in advance that Clarence's turn is next, that Richard will then attempt to woo the Lady Anne, and so forth. The dramatic excitement we experience in watching the action is not that of wondering what will happen next but that of seeing how cleverly the preannounced plans will be executed. Not until the rise of Richmond near the end of the play does Richard meet effective opposition, though quite early the voice of the deposed Queen Margaret is raised against him (1.3.117–143, 215–293). Margaret's curses upon the enemies of the Lancastrian House and her warning to Buckingham also serve as a structural device preparing us for what will happen, and they complement Richard's gloating and sardonic tone by striking a bitter and ominous note. Again the dramatic interest lies in the way the fates of the characters come upon them; these persons fall victim to Richard's machinations, and yet their downfalls also fulfill a larger, seemingly providential scheme of retribution for injustice and wickedness.

Richard's ability as an actor is seemingly limitless. He has already boasted, in *3 Henry VI*, that he can deceive more slyly than Ulysses, Sinon, or Machiavelli, and put on more false shapes than Proteus. To us as audience he is cynically candid and boastful, setting us up in advance to watch his unbelievable performances. In an instant, before our eyes, he is the concerned younger brother of Clarence, sharing a hatred of Queen Elizabeth and her kindred; or he is the jocular uncle of the little princes; or he is the pious recluse studying divinity with his clerical teachers, reluctant to accept the responsibilities of state that are thrust upon him by his importunate subjects (that is to say, by Catesby and Buckingham, who are also actors in this staged scene). Yet none of these bravura performances can match the wooing of the Lady Anne.

Is the wooing of the Lady Anne credible? One key to credibility must lie in superb acting. The actor who plays Richard must transform himself from the gloating villain we know in soliloquy to the grief-stricken lover. Richard's argument is, after all, speciously plausible: that he has killed Anne's husband and father-in-law out of desperate love for her. The argument appeals to vanity, that most fatal of human weaknesses. What power Anne suddenly appears to have over Richard! She can spare his life, or kill him. Richard shrewdly judges her as one not able to kill, and so risks offering her his sword. As stage manager, he has altered her role from that of sincere mourner to the stereotype of the proud woman worshiped by her groveling servant in love. With superb irony, Richard has inverted the appearance and the reality of control in this struggle between man and woman. He wins mastery by flattering her that only she can spare his miserable life. The implausibility of what Richard has achieved merely illustrates his thesis that ordinary men and women can be made to believe anything, and betray their own best instincts, by "the plain devil and dissembling looks" (1.2.239). Richard is of course devillike; his role as actor stems from that of the Vice in the morality play, brilliantly comic and sinister. Yet even the devil can prevail over his victims only when they acquiesce in evil. The devil can deceive the senses, but acceptance of evil is still an act of the perverted will. Anne is guilty, however much we can appreciate the mesmerizing power of Richard's personality. By the end of the scene she has violated everything she had held sacred.

The image of Richard as devil or Vice raises questions of motivation and of symbolic meaning. Is Richard a human character propelled toward the throne by his insatiable ambition, like Macbeth? Is there a clue to his behavior in his ugliness and misanthropy? Modern psychological criticism might well be tempted to examine Richard's childhood: by his own admission, he was born feet forward, hunchbacked, withered in one arm, and already toothed ("which plainly signified / That I should snarl and bite and play the dog," *3 Henry VI*, 5.6.76–77). One might argue that he compensates for his ugliness and unlovability by resolving to domineer. Feeling unwanted, he despises all men and undertakes to prove them weak and corrupt. This reading is not without merit; indeed, no matter how extraordinary Richard's behavior, he does seem plausible. He expresses a universal human penchant for cruelty and senseless domination. Yet the proposition that Richard is evil *because* he was born ugly can be logically reversed as well: he was born ugly *because* he is evil.

This concept, owing much to Renaissance notions of Platonic correspondence between outer appearances and inner qualities, is grounded on the idea of a vast struggle in the cosmos between the forces of absolute good and the forces of absolute evil, one in which every event in human life has divine meaning and cause. Richard's birth is a physical manifestation of that divine meaning. Providential destiny, having determined the need for a genius of evil at this point in English history, decrees that Richard shall be born. The teeth and hunched back merely give evidence of what is already predetermined. In the apt words of the choric Queen Margaret, Richard was "sealed in thy nativity / The slave of nature and the son of hell" (1.3.228–229). Although Richard is also plausible as a man, he is in part an emissary of the devil, and ultimately serves the righteous purpose of divine Providence in human affairs. Such a symbolic reading clarifies our impression that Richard is fundamentally unlike many of Shakespeare's human villains, such as Macbeth or King Claudius. Richard belongs instead to a special group of villains including Iago in *Othello* and Edmund in *King Lear*. Like them, Richard is driven both by human motivation and by his preexistent evil genius; he displays the "motiveless malignity" ascribed by Coleridge to Iago.

Such a reading helps explain not only Richard's delight in evil but also the necessity for so much evil and suffering in England's civil wars. This theory of history owes much to Edward Hall's *Union of the Two Noble and Illustre Families of Lancaster and York* (1542), Shakespeare's immediate source, along with Raphael Holinshed's *Chronicles* (1578), for his *Henry VI* plays. Shakespeare's treatment of Richard is ultimately indebted to Polydore Vergil's *Anglica Historia* (1534) and especially to *The History of King Richard the Third* attributed to Sir Thomas More (published 1557). This latter work, adopted in turn by Edward Hall, Richard Grafton, and Raphael Holinshed, purposefully blackens Richard's character. He becomes a study in the nature of tyranny, an object lesson to future rulers and their subjects. He is, moreover, a result of the curse placed by God on the English people for their sinful disobedience. Richard III functions as the scourge of God, destroying God's enemies until he too is destroyed for his own colossal evil.

Henry VII, in this Tudor explanation, becomes God's minister chosen to destroy the scourge and thereafter to fulfill a new and happy covenant between God and man. Although modern historians more impartially regard the defeat of Richard III at Bosworth Field in 1485 as a political overthrow not unlike Henry IV's overthrow of Richard II, and stress that Richard III was a talented administrator guilty of no worse political crimes than those of his more fortunate successor, Tudor Englishmen could not have found meaning in such a neutral interpretation. History had to reveal God's intention. Henry VII's accession could not be viewed as parallel to the rebellion of Henry IV against Richard II, but was seen as a divinely sanctioned deliverance of the English nation, a blessing continued in the reign of Elizabeth I. Accordingly, the Tudor myth stressed the tyrannical nature of Richard III's seizure of power and conversely minimized the political element in

Henry VII's takeover. Bosworth Field was seen as an act of God, a rising up of some irresistible force, and under no circumstances as a precedent for future rebellion.

In the *Henry VI* plays, Shakespeare puts considerable distance between himself and the Tudor orthodox reading of history, allowing the grim realities of civil war to speak for themselves. In *Richard III*, however, the pattern shown in the chronicles provides Shakespeare with an essential structural device. Viewing the civil wars in retrospect, *Richard III* perhaps discovers a cohesive sense in which England's suffering has fulfilled a necessary plan of fall from innocence leading through sin and penitence to regeneration. Evil is seen at last as something through which good triumphs, in English history as in the story of man's fall from grace.

This providential scheme imposes a double irony on *Richard III*. In the short run, Richard appears to be complete master over his victims. "Your imprisonment shall not be long," Richard assures his brother Clarence. "I will deliver you, or else lie for you" (1.1.114–115). The audience, already let in on the secret, can shiver at the grisly humor of these double entendres. Clarence will indeed soon be delivered—to his death. Richard's henchmen are fond of such jokes too. When Lord Hastings is on his way to the Tower, from which he will never return, and announces his intention of staying for dinner in the Tower, Buckingham observes aside, "And supper too, although thou know'st it not" (3.2.122). Shortly before, Catesby has assured Hastings of Richard's and Buckingham's favor toward him: "The princes both make high account of you— / [*Aside*.] For they account his head upon the Bridge" (3.2.69–70). Richard has a phrase for such wit: "Thus, like the formal Vice, Iniquity, / I moralize two meanings in one word" (3.1.82–83). The point of such ironies is always the same: the devil is cleverer than his victims, deceiving them through equivocation, triumphing in their spiritual blindness.

The delayed irony of the play, however, ultimately offers another possible explanation for the seemingly nihilistic conclusions of the early scenes. That is, there may be a larger plan at work, one of which Richard is unconscious and in which he plays a role quite unlike the one he creates for himself. Perhaps Shakespeare's Richard is, as he was regarded in the chronicles of Edward Hall and others, the scourge of God, fulfilling a divine plan even in the process of what he gloatingly regards as his own self-aggrandizement. Divine plans are always complex, inscrutable to the minds of mortals, understood least by those who unwittingly execute them. In attempting to prove his own contention that human nature is bestial and that a Machiavellian man of utter self-confidence can force his way to the top, flouting all conventions of morality, Richard may have succeeded in demonstrating exactly the opposite. His role in this case becomes sardonically comic: that of the proverbial beguiler beguiled.

Certainly the play offers for our consideration a theory of divine causality in which virtually all of Richard's victims deserve their fate because they have offended God. Prophecies and dreams give structure to the sequence of retributive actions and keep grim score. As the choric Margaret observes, a York must pay for a Lancaster, eye for an eye: Edward IV for Henry VI, young Edward V for Henry VI's son Edward. Thus the Yorkist princes, though guiltless, die for their family's sins. The Yorkist Queen Elizabeth, like the Lancastrian Margaret, must outlive her husband into impotent old age, bewailing her children's cruel deaths. Clarence sees his death as punishment for breaking his oath at the battle of Tewkesbury and for his part in murdering Henry VI's son, Prince Edward. The Queen's kindred have been guilty of ambition, and Lord Hastings in turn is vulnerable because he has been willing to plot with Richard against the Queen's kindred. Margaret's curses serve both to warn the characters of their fates (a warning they blindly ignore) and to invite each person to curse himself unwittingly but with ironic appropriateness. The Lady Anne wishes unhappiness on any woman so insane as to marry Richard. Buckingham protests in a most sacred oath that whenever he turns again on the Queen's kindred, he will deserve to be punished by the treachery of his dearest friend (i.e., Richard). Dreams serve the same purpose of divine warning, giving Clarence a grotesque intimation of his death by drowning (in a butt of malmsey wine), and warning Hastings (through Stanley's dream) that the boar, Richard, will cut off his head. Thus the English court punishes itself through Richard. He is the essence of the courtiers' factionalism, able to succeed as he does only because they forswear their most holy vows and conspire to destroy one another. They deserve to be outwitted at their own dismal game. Yet their falls are curative as well; again and again, Richard's victims acknowledge the justice of their undoings and penitently implore divine forgiveness. Richard alone finds conscience a torment rather than a voice of comfort and wisdom.

Richard III is not without its ironies and historical anxieties. Richard's own successful career of evil through much of the play demonstrates how rhetoric and theater itself can be used to dupe and corrupt. The political process seems endlessly prone to cynical manipulation, and triumph comes chiefly to those who know how to use rhetoric to calculated effect. The Lord Mayor and his London associates are as pliable as the aristocracy. For all the belated assurances of providential meaning in Richard's rise to power and overthrow, we are allowed to speculate uncomfortably about the pragmatic action of history and its seeming ability to thrust forward into prominence an evil king or a good one as individual temperament happens to dictate. Finally, there is the question of how Richard is supplanted. Whatever the reasons for Richard's baleful emergence, the process of his overthrow requires human agency and a rebellion against established (even if tyrannical) royal authority. To thoughtful observers in the sixteenth century, including Queen Elizabeth, any such rebellion, no matter how seemingly necessary, established a disturbing precedent and a threat to Tudor monarchical stability. If *Richard III* finds reassuring answers in a concept of providential design, it does so in the face of pressing and troublesome circumstances.

Still, providential wisdom is at last affirmed, if only because some Englishmen have the patience and common sense to endure a presumably deserved punishment and wait for deliverance. As in *3 Henry VI*, the common people have little to do with the action of the play. They are choric spokesmen and bystanders, virtuous in their attitude (except for the two suborned murderers of Clarence). In their plain folk wisdom they see the folly and evil their betters ignore: "O, full of danger is the Duke of Gloucester, / And the Queen's sons and brothers haught and proud" (2.3.28–29). And although they accept Richard as ruler, they do so most reluctantly; Buckingham's first attempt to persuade the people to this course meets with apathy and silence. Their wisdom is to "leave it all to God" (l. 46). In the fullness of time, this passive obedience brings its just reward.

Richard III
in Performance

Richard III provides a star role that few leading actors, given the choice, have been able to resist. In a long play with an unusually large cast, Richard has a remarkably large percentage of the lines (comparable in this to Hamlet) and is onstage almost continuously. Richard Burbage, the leading player of Shakespeare's acting company (perhaps a combined company of the Lord Admiral's and Lord Strange's men when this play was first performed, c. 1593–1594), became famous in the part. As the dominating figure in the play, Richard is also acutely aware of his own theatricality. He is, as the Introduction has pointed out, a versatile actor, able to change at a moment's notice from gloating schemer (taking the audience into his confidence), to staunch protector of his brother Clarence, and thence to passionate wooer of the Lady Anne.

Because of this protean shifting of roles, dramatic irony is an essential part of our response to Richard. We know that he is only "acting" when he woos the Lady Anne, but actors after all are supposed to be able to transform themselves into the part they play, and so we admire Richard's skill as we might admire a professional coolly accomplishing his task. The more impossible the assignment—in this case, undertaking to convince a widow to marry her husband's murderer—the more credit belongs to the actor capable of sounding truly persuasive. Richard steps before us in soliloquy after he has won the Lady Anne to his will, incredulous at his own success, amused, proud of his ability as an actor. If the player in the theater has managed meantime to convince us for a moment that Richard really is in love with Anne after all, our admiration will be all the greater and our complicity in his role-playing will perhaps trouble us. Richard's triumphs as an actor subvert the moral claims of the theater, demonstrating with devastating effect that acting can be used to promote evil. The more believable the actor, the greater his potential for doing harm.

Richard not only acts in but directs and stage manages

his play. He disposes of his characters one after the other, ordering the execution of Clarence and the Queen's kindred, sending his nephews to the Tower, discarding Anne so that he can make a still more politically advantageous marriage. He presides over scenes and arranges them to suit his own penchant for highly theatrical entrances and exits, as when he bursts in upon the Council meeting in the Tower and angrily bares his arm, exclaiming, "Look how I am bewitched!" (3.4.68), in order to accuse Hastings of conspiring with Queen Elizabeth and Jane Shore. He is a master of costuming effects, as when he enters with Buckingham *"in rotten armor, marvelous ill-favored"* (3.5.0). His conversation makes extensive use of theatrical metaphor, as when he queries Buckingham about his skill in deceiving appearances: "Come, cousin, canst thou quake and change thy color, / Murder thy breath in middle of a word, / And then again begin, and stop again, / As if thou wert distraught and mad with terror?" Buckingham is ready with a reply in kind: "Tut, I can counterfeit the deep tragedian, / Speak and look back, and pry on every side, / Tremble and start at wagging of a straw; / Intending deep suspicion, ghastly looks / Are at my service, like enforcèd smiles" (3.5.1–9).

Together, as an acting team, Richard and Buckingham exploit the Elizabethan theater with the practiced versatility of their trade. When the Mayor and citizens arrive at Baynard's Castle at Buckingham's invitation, Richard is coached by his acting partner to pretend reluctance to accept the crown: "And look you get a prayer book in your hand, / And stand between two churchmen, good my lord, / For on that ground I'll make a holy descant; / And be not easily won to our requests. / Play the maid's part: still answer nay and take it" (3.7.47–51). Buckingham and Catesby, on the main stage, receive the Mayor's delegation and undertake to intercede with Richard, though pretending to fear a refusal from so unworldly a man. His entrance thus prepared for, Richard enters *"aloft,"* that is, on the gallery at the rear of the stage, between two bishops, in a tableau designed to be emblematic of piety. The bishops and the book of prayer are his properties, the Lord Mayor's party his audience. The Elizabethan theater, without scenery, has been transformed into the courtyard of Richard's residence, with the Mayor and his followers staring up in wonder at an apparition of holiness speaking to them from an upper vantage point in the house.

For all the histrionic skill he displays in attaining the English throne, Richard is unable to carry off the role he has supremely coveted, that of king. Ceremonies of royal authority, when invested in him, become travesties of themselves, exposing Richard as no more than a poor player, woefully miscast. Attired in all the trappings of kingship, entering *"in pomp"* with seeming majesty, Richard ascends the throne with Buckingham at his side: "Thus high, by thy advice, / And thy assistance, is King Richard seated" (4.2.3–4). Yet the first acts of this usurping monarch are all secret and murderous. He consults privately about the killing of his nephews or about the spreading of a rumor that Anne is sick and likely to die. He threatens Lord Stanley with dire reprisals if Stanley is caught conspiring with Richmond. His courtiers stand apart, whispering among themselves, wondering what will happen next. Throne, crown, and ceremonial occasion all reinforce by contrast the unworthiness of the present king.

At Bosworth Field, too, the play's staging effects turn decisively against this erstwhile genius of theatrical illusion. Two tents, symmetrically balanced and opposite one another, represent the camps of the usurping king and his virtuous challenger. In the Elizabethan theater, these tents' must have actually been pitched onstage. The ghosts of Richard's many victims enter presumably center stage between the tents to offer curses for Richard, on the one hand, and blessings for Richmond, on the other. The antithetically balanced staging contrasts Richard and Richmond at every turn: in their relations with their subordinates, as orators to their armies, as generals. Richard is still very much the protagonist of his play, but he can no longer control its stage action. He is instead cast in the role of the villain, the scourge, whose usurped crown is offered to Richmond in a final stage gesture of restoration.

Leading actors have coveted Richard's part to such an extent that they have often enlarged it while reducing other parts of the play. Colley Cibber, at the Theatre Royal, Drury

Lane, in 1700, incorporated the ending of *3 Henry VI* (in later revivals, his version of the play opened with Richard's murder of King Henry VI in the Tower), along with parts of *Richard II* and *2 Henry IV* and *Henry V*, while excising Clarence's dream and Margaret's curse along with other matters. The roles of Clarence, Edward IV, Margaret, and Hastings were, in fact, omitted entirely, and the play's overall length was reduced from the original total of 3887 (in the Folio through-line numbering system) to some 2050 lines. Cibber wrote into the play a scene in which Richard informs his queen—the Lady Anne—that he has grown tired of her and wishes to marry someone else, and another scene of tearful farewell between Queen Elizabeth and her sons. This version, with its vividly melodramatic portrayal of Richard as villain, has had extraordinary staying power in the theater. It was the acting version of *Richard III* into the nineteenth century, and even today, many admirers of Shakespeare are not likely to know that Cibber wrote the lines "Off with his head; so much for Buckingham" and "Richard's himself again."

Shakespeare's play was taken even further afield in Nicholas Rowe's popular tragedy, *Jane Shore* (1714), but it was Cibber's version that held the stage. David Garrick made his debut on the English stage in a production of Cibber's *Richard III* at Henry Giffard's theater in Goodman's Fields, London, on October 19, 1741. Garrick kept Cibber's version in repertory during most of his years at Drury Lane in the mid-eighteenth century and was considerably more successful in the role of Richard than Cibber himself. In spite of Cibber's disdain for Garrick's performance ("all fuss and bustle"), Garrick's Richard propelled him to immediate stardom. John Philip Kemble also kept Cibber's version (albeit with minor Shakespearean restorations) in his productions at Drury Lane beginning in 1783. Edmund Kean successfully acted the part in Kemble's text at the same theater in 1814, eliciting critic William Hazlitt's enthusiastic praise for his "smooth, smiling villainy." William Charles Macready, in 1821 at the Theatre Royal, Covent Garden, hesitantly cleared away more of Cibber's interpolations and reintroduced at least a truncated role for Margaret. The production, despite its clear conception of restoring "alacrity and mirth of mind" to the character of Richard, was not successful and was withdrawn after only two performances.

Samuel Phelps was the first, at the Sadler's Wells Theatre in 1845, to restore the play to something like its original text, and in his revival of 1849 he came even closer to Shakespeare's original. Both productions were critically praised and succeeded at the box office. Phelps acted Richard "with sort of jovial *abandon*," the *Athenaeum* reviewer said; and the restored text also received favorable comment, especially for the unity brought to the play by the reintroduction of the prophetic role of Margaret, though the loss of some of Cibber's familiar phrases was lamented. Nonetheless, Shakespeare's text posed problems for the producer, as a review in *Punch* (March 15, 1845) made clear: "as for the getting up, it's twenty times as expensive as the original piece—I mean Colley Cibber's." In part for that reason, but more because he had no actress capable of playing Margaret, Phelps revived the Cibber version in 1861, as did Charles Kean at the Princess's Theatre in 1854 in an elaborate production with a cast of 121.

In America, Edwin Booth had decided to abandon Cibber's *Richard* sometime around 1868, although he was unable to mount a production of the play before Henry Jarrett and Henry Palmer claimed the honor of the first American production of Shakespeare's text in 1871 at Niblo's Garden in New York. Booth did act Shakespeare's play for several seasons after 1878 before he was persuaded to return to Cibber's version in 1886. Shakespeare "*reads* well enough," one of Booth's contemporaries said; "but Cibber's Richard *acts*." In England, meanwhile, Shakespeare's play had reclaimed the stage, though not always in responsible texts. Henry Irving's productions at London's Lyceum Theatre, in 1877 and 1896, while free of Cibber's improvements, made draconian cuts curtailing both Clarence's and Margaret's roles. The *Athenaeum* approved neither of the cuts nor of Irving's acting, in which the reviewer lamented the absence of tragic power. Irving's Richard seemed trivial, merely amusing, no more than "what is conventionally called 'a character-part.'" Other reviewers, pleased to find Cibber banished and Shakespeare restored, were more kind. Clement Scott in the *Daily Telegraph* found his pleasure in the production heightened by "the unexpected discovery of a new source of dramatic delight."

Twentieth-century directors and audiences have generally insisted on a return to something close to Shakespeare's complete play. Frank Benson acted a virtually intact Shakespearean text in his various productions of the play between 1886 and 1915 at Stratford-upon-Avon. Benson was an energetic and athletic Richard, with the capacity to "frighten as well as fascinate," in Robert Speaight's words. It was at the Old Vic that *Richard III* fully came into its own, mainly because of a group of directors at the theater before World War II who were deeply committed to simple, fast-paced staging and fidelity to Shakespeare's text. Ben Greet directed the play in 1915 with Robert Atkins as Richard and Sybil Thorndike as Anne. A program note ingenuously remarked: "we have endeavoured to arrange thirteen scenes as simple settings to avoid as many delays as possible, but our appliances are 100 years old, and our friends are asked to be forbearing." Atkins himself directed a virtually uncut *Richard III* in a four-hour production at the Old Vic in 1921. In 1925 Andrew Leigh directed Baliol Holloway as Richard and Edith Evans as Margaret in a production that emphatically showed once and for all that the play could be performed successfully much as Shakespeare wrote it and with stagecraft closer to Shakespeare's own than the elaborate scenic display of the Victorian stage.

Yet the Old Vic company's greatest triumph with the play was one that made use of some older rearrangements of the text and thus established an important precedent for more recent years, that of respect for Shakespeare's whole play combined with a pragmatic view that the play is long and that Richard's role is, after all, primary. John Burrell's production at the New Theatre in 1944, starring Laurence Olivier as Richard, used a cut text that eliminated all but one scene of Sybil Thorndike's Margaret. On a brightly lit stage ringed with darkness, Olivier played a sinuous Richard, at once menacing and mocking—"the true double Gloucester," as critic J. C. Trewin has written, "thinker and doer, mind and mask." Everything centered around the inventive villain, and audiences were invited to share in his gloating conspiracy. Revived in 1949, with Vivien Leigh as Anne, the production again was a great success, even if to one critic the "irony and glitter" of Olivier's original performance now seemed "mannered."

Olivier's Richard influenced a generation of actors. One could imitate or react against his sardonic villainy, but one could hardly ignore it. George C. Scott as Richard, in Stuart Vaughan's production for the New York Shakespeare Festival in 1957, adopted a similar mix of calculation and improvisational brilliance. When, on the other hand, Robert Helpmann consciously chose to play against Olivier's Richard in Douglas Seale's version at the Old Vic that same year, the critics were generally unhappy. One critic did call it a "fine and louring production," and audiences came in large numbers, but other reviewers missed the Olivier magic. Helpmann was no engaging villain but a nasty, brutish monster. In 1961 at Stratford-upon-Avon, Christopher Plummer's Richard was a cool, dispassionate villain, as one critic wrote, "the more frightening for his matter-of-fact, almost reasonable evil." Donald Madden's Richard at New York's Delacorte Theater in 1970 returned to something more like Olivier's Richard's grisly pleasure in his wickedness.

Terry Hands's *Richard III* in 1970 at Stratford-upon-Avon was perhaps the first significant production of the play since Olivier's triumph to focus on something other than the psychology of its fascinating hero. Successful at the box office, though not always with the critics, this often symbolic production, in which Norman Rodway's Richard was killed by Death, used other fine actors (including Ian Richardson as Buckingham and Patrick Stewart as Edward) to populate a world with characters who were more than merely available victims for Richard's evil. Two modern-dress productions marked an even sharper break with the Olivier tradition: Barry Kyle's *Richard III* at The Other Place in Stratford-upon-Avon in 1975, suggesting to critic Eric Shorter a "medieval nightmare in some royal asylum," and Michael Bogdanov's production at London's Young Vic Theatre in 1978 in which Richard was a thug, differing from the corrupt world around him only in his daring. Robin Phillips directed a stylized, Senecan version of the play at Stratford, Ontario, in 1977, featuring Brian Bedford's desperate and histrionic Richard together with Maggie Smith's fierce Elizabeth. In 1979 Al Pacino played a clowning, contemptuous Richard in a much derided production directed by David Wheeler at New York's Cort Theater. More successfully, Jane Howell, using a nearly full text, directed Kevin Kline in a production for the New York Shakespeare Festival in 1983. Kline's Richard was comically inventive, juggling a crucifix and a prayer book, for example, as he made what *The New York Times* called "farcical art out of outrageous wickedness." Certainly the most remarkable of the recent productions was Bill Alexander's *Richard III* at Stratford-upon-Avon in 1984. Antony Sher starred as a charismatic, energetic Richard trapped in a crippled body. Propped by metal crutches that served to emphasize his spidery quality as he pulled himself furiously across stage with his legs dangling beneath him, Sher's Richard could both repel and draw laughs, as with his deadpan response to Elizabeth's charge of murdering his family: "men shall deal unadvisedly sometimes."

Still, it is Olivier's Richard that remains in the modern imagination, partly because it has been seen by so many people in its film version (1955). Olivier's film uses an adapted text, beginning with the coronation of Edward IV in *3 Henry VI*, cutting the role of Margaret, and rearranging scenes with vigor; the wooing of the Lady Anne is divided in two, with intervening material, as though to allow Anne time to think over what Richard is proposing. For all its cavalier treatment of the text, Olivier's film captures the extraordinary sense of theatrical dominance that has generated such success in performance ever since the play first appeared. Olivier uses camera closeups to show us the evil glint in Richard's eye. Visual juxtapositions, well attuned to the requirements of Shakespeare's text, accentuate the contrasts among Richard's various roles. Olivier focuses his camera on key objects like the throne and the crown in order to exploit their visual symbolism. When Richard, informed of Richmond's return to England to claim the kingdom, exclaims, "Is the chair empty? Is the sword unswayed?" (4.4.469), the camera lingers on the chair of state, showing it left empty when Richard departs for battle. In the film's last minutes, the crown, formerly on Richard's head, tumbles around the battlefield and ends up in a bush until picked up by Lord Stanley and placed on the victor's brow. The language of theatrical gesture, violently usurped by the superb but unnerving histrionic ability of the protagonist, is at last reclaimed in a true ceremony of coronation.

RICHARD
——III——

[*Dramatis Personae*

KING EDWARD THE FOURTH
QUEEN ELIZABETH, *wife of King Edward*
EDWARD, PRINCE OF WALES,} *sons of Edward*
RICHARD, DUKE OF YORK, } *and Elizabeth*
GEORGE, DUKE OF CLARENCE, } *brothers of*
RICHARD, DUKE OF GLOUCESTER, *later King Richard III,*} *the King*
DUCHESS OF YORK, *mother of Edward IV, Clarence, and Richard,*
  Duke of Gloucester
LADY ANNE, *widow of Edward, Prince of Wales (son of*
Henry VI); later wife of Richard, Duke of Gloucester
MARGARET, *widow of King Henry VI*
BOY, *son of Clarence (Edward Plantagenet, Earl of Warwick)*
GIRL, *daughter of Clarence (Margaret Plantagenet, Countess of*
  Salisbury)

ANTHONY WOODVILLE, EARL RIVERS, *brother of Queen Elizabeth*
MARQUESS OF DORSET,} *sons of Queen*
LORD GREY, } *Elizabeth*
SIR THOMAS VAUGHAN, *executed with Rivers and Grey*

WILLIAM, LORD HASTINGS, *the Lord Chamberlain*
DUKE OF BUCKINGHAM, *Richard's supporter, later in opposition*
SIR WILLIAM CATESBY,
SIR RICHARD RATCLIFFE, } *Richard's supporters*
LORD LOVELL, } *and henchmen*
SIR JAMES TYRREL,
DUKE OF NORFOLK,} *Richard's*
EARL OF SURREY, } *generals*

HENRY, EARL OF RICHMOND, *later King Henry VII*
LORD STANLEY, EARL OF DERBY,
EARL OF OXFORD,
SIR JAMES BLUNT, } *supporters of*
SIR WALTER HERBERT, } *Richmond*
SIR WILLIAM BRANDON,
CHRISTOPHER URSWICK, *a priest,*

CARDINAL BOURCHIER, *Archbishop of Canterbury*
ARCHBISHOP OF YORK (*Thomas Rotherham*)
BISHOP OF ELY (*John Morton*)

GHOSTS *of King Henry VI, Edward Prince of Wales, and others murdered by Richard (Clarence, Rivers, Grey, Vaughan, Hastings, the two young princes, Anne, and Buckingham)*

SIR ROBERT BRACKENBURY, *Lieutenant of the Tower*
TRESSEL,
BERKELEY, } *attending the*
HALBERDIER, *Lady Anne*
GENTLEMAN,
Two MURDERERS
KEEPER *in the Tower*
Three CITIZENS
MESSENGER *to Queen Elizabeth*
LORD MAYOR OF LONDON
MESSENGER *to Lord Hastings*
PURSUIVANT
PRIEST
SCRIVENER
Two BISHOPS
PAGE *to Richard III*
Four MESSENGERS *to Richard III*
SHERIFF OF WILTSHIRE

Lords, Attendants, Aldermen, Citizens, Councilors, Soldiers

SCENE: *England.*]

1.1   *Enter Richard, Duke of Gloucester, solus.*

RICHARD
Now is the winter of our discontent
Made glorious summer by this sun of York,   2
And all the clouds that loured upon our house   3
In the deep bosom of the ocean buried.
Now are our brows bound with victorious wreaths,   5
Our bruisèd arms hung up for monuments,   6
Our stern alarums changed to merry meetings,   7
Our dreadful marches to delightful measures.   8
Grim-visaged War hath smoothed his wrinkled front;   9
And now, instead of mounting barbèd steeds   10
To fright the souls of fearful adversaries,   11
He capers nimbly in a lady's chamber
To the lascivious pleasing of a lute.
But I, that am not shaped for sportive tricks,   14
Nor made to court an amorous looking glass;
I, that am rudely stamped, and want love's majesty   16
To strut before a wanton ambling nymph;   17
I, that am curtailed of this fair proportion,   18
Cheated of feature by dissembling Nature,   19
Deformed, unfinished, sent before my time
Into this breathing world scarce half made up,
And that so lamely and unfashionable   22
That dogs bark at me as I halt by them—   23
Why, I, in this weak piping time of peace,   24
Have no delight to pass away the time,
Unless to see my shadow in the sun
And descant on mine own deformity.   27
And therefore, since I cannot prove a lover

1.1. Location: London. Near the Tower.
s.d. solus alone   **2 sun** (Edward IV's badge displayed three suns; with a
pun on *son*.)   **3 loured** looked threateningly   **5 brows** foreheads
6 arms armor.   **monuments** trophies   **7 alarums** calls to arms
8 dreadful formidable, awe-inspiring.   **measures** stately dances
9 wrinkled front furrowed forehead   **10 barbèd** armored   **11 fearful**
frightened   **14 sportive** amorous   **16 rudely** roughly.   **want** lack
17 ambling walking affectedly, i.e., wantonly   **18 curtailed** cut short,
denied.   **proportion** shape   **19 feature** shapeliness of body
22 unfashionable badly fashioned   **23 halt** limp   **24 piping time** i.e., a
time when the music heard is that of pipes and not fifes and drums
27 descant compose variations, warble, comment on

To entertain these fair well-spoken days,   29
I am determinèd to prove a villain
And hate the idle pleasures of these days.
Plots have I laid, inductions dangerous,   32
By drunken prophecies, libels, and dreams,
To set my brother Clarence and the King
In deadly hate the one against the other;
And if King Edward be as true and just
As I am subtle, false, and treacherous,
This day should Clarence closely be mewed up   38
About a prophecy, which says that G   39
Of Edward's heirs the murderer shall be.
Dive, thoughts, down to my soul; here Clarence comes.

> *Enter Clarence, guarded, and Brackenbury,*
> *[Lieutenant of the Tower].*

Brother, good day. What means this armèd guard
That waits upon Your Grace?
CLARENCE   His Majesty,
Tend'ring my person's safety, hath appointed   44
This conduct to convey me to the Tower.   45
RICHARD
Upon what cause?
CLARENCE   Because my name is George.
RICHARD
Alack, my lord, that fault is none of yours.
He should, for that, commit your godfathers.
O, belike His Majesty hath some intent   49
That you should be new christened in the Tower.   50
But what's the matter, Clarence, may I know?   51
CLARENCE
Yea, Richard, when I know; for I protest
As yet I do not. But, as I can learn,
He hearkens after prophecies and dreams,

29 **entertain** pass away pleasurably.   **well-spoken** refined, elegant
32 **inductions** preparations   38 **mewed up** confined (like a hawk)
39 **prophecy . . . G** (The prophecy is mentioned in the chronicles; the
quibble is that *G* stands for *Gloucester* and not for *George,* the given name
of the Duke of Clarence.)   44 **Tend'ring** having care for   45 **conduct**
escort   49 **belike** probably   50 **new christened** (Anticipates, ironically,
Clarence's death by drowning in 1.4.)   51 **matter** reason, cause

And from the crossrow plucks the letter G,   55
And says a wizard told him that by G
His issue disinherited should be;   57
And, for my name of George begins with G,   58
It follows in his thought that I am he.
These, as I learn, and suchlike toys as these   60
Hath moved His Highness to commit me now.   61

RICHARD
Why, this it is when men are ruled by women.
'Tis not the King that sends you to the Tower;
My Lady Grey his wife, Clarence, 'tis she   64
That tempers him to this extremity.   65
Was it not she, and that good man of worship,
Anthony Woodville, her brother there,   67
That made him send Lord Hastings to the Tower,
From whence this present day he is delivered?
We are not safe, Clarence, we are not safe.

CLARENCE
By heaven, I think there is no man secure
But the Queen's kindred and night-walking heralds   72
That trudge betwixt the King and Mistress Shore.   73
Heard you not what an humble suppliant
Lord Hastings was to her for his delivery?   75

RICHARD
Humbly complaining to Her Deity   76
Got my Lord Chamberlain his liberty.   77
I'll tell you what: I think it is our way,   78
If we will keep in favor with the King,

55 **crossrow** Christ-crossrow, or alphabet (so called from the cross
printed before the alphabet in the hornbook)   57 **issue** offspring
58 **for** because   60 **toys** trifles   61 **commit** arrest   64 **My Lady Grey** (A
disrespectful reference to the Queen, whose maiden name was Elizabeth
Woodville and who, when the King married her, was the widow of Sir
John Grey.)   65 **tempers** governs, directs   67 **Woodville** i.e., Earl Rivers
(whom Richard also disrespectfully refers to by his family name rather
than by his recently acquired title)   72 **night-walking heralds** i.e., secret
messengers for an assignation   73 **Mistress Shore** Jane Shore, the
King's mistress, and wife of a goldsmith in Lombard Street. (The title
Mistress is a respectful form of address for any woman, married or
unmarried.)   75 **her** i.e., Jane Shore   76 **Her Deity** (A mock title for
Jane Shore, suggesting she is even more elevated than "Her Grace" or
"Her Majesty.")   77 **Lord Chamberlain** i.e., Lord Hastings   78 **our way**
i.e., our only way (to succeed)

To be her men and wear her livery.   80
The jealous o'erworn widow and herself,   81
Since that our brother dubbed them gentlewomen,   82
Are mighty gossips in our monarchy.   83

BRACKENBURY
I beseech Your Graces both to pardon me:
His Majesty hath straitly given in charge   85
That no man shall have private conference,
Of what degree soever, with your brother.   87

RICHARD
Even so? An 't please your worship, Brackenbury,   88
You may partake of anything we say.
We speak no treason, man. We say the King
Is wise and virtuous, and his noble queen
Well struck in years, fair, and not jealous.   92
We say that Shore's wife hath a pretty foot,
A cherry lip, a bonny eye, a passing pleasing tongue;   94
And that the Queen's kindred are made gentlefolks.
How say you, sir? Can you deny all this?

BRACKENBURY
With this, my lord, myself have naught to do.

RICHARD
Naught to do with Mistress Shore? I tell thee, fellow,   98
He that doth naught with her, excepting one,
Were best to do it secretly, alone.

BRACKENBURY   What one, my lord?

RICHARD
Her husband, knave. Wouldst thou betray me?   102

BRACKENBURY
I beseech Your Grace to pardon me, and withal   103
Forbear your conference with the noble Duke.

CLARENCE
We know thy charge, Brackenbury, and will obey.

80 men servants   **81 widow** i.e., Queen Elizabeth. (See l. 64, note.)   **herself**
i.e., Jane Shore   **82 gentlewomen** (A sneer at the Queen's family, which
was gentle but not noble until after her marriage with the King; Jane
Shore was, of course, neither gentle nor noble.)   **83 mighty gossips** i.e.,
influential busybodies   **85 straitly . . . charge** strictly ordered   **87 degree**
rank   **88 An 't** if it   **92 Well struck** i.e., well along.   **not jealous** (Implies
there are things she might be jealous about.)   **94 passing** surpassingly
98 Naught (Richard quibbles on the meanings "nothing" and "the sexual
act.")   **102 betray me** i.e., into naming the King as a person who does
"naught" with Mistress Shore   **103 withal** at the same time

RICHARD
We are the Queen's abjects, and must obey.   106
Brother, farewell. I will unto the King;
And whatsoe'er you will employ me in,
Were it to call King Edward's widow sister,   109
I will perform it to enfranchise you.   110
Meantime, this deep disgrace in brotherhood
Touches me deeper than you can imagine.   112

CLARENCE
I know it pleaseth neither of us well.

RICHARD
Well, your imprisonment shall not be long;
I will deliver you, or else lie for you.   115
Meantime, have patience.

CLARENCE   I must perforce. Farewell.   116
          Exit Clarence [with Brackenbury and guard].

RICHARD
Go tread the path that thou shalt ne'er return.
Simple, plain Clarence, I do love thee so
That I will shortly send thy soul to heaven,
If heaven will take the present at our hands.
But who comes here? The new-delivered Hastings?   121

          Enter Lord Hastings.

HASTINGS
Good time of day unto my gracious lord.

RICHARD
As much unto my good Lord Chamberlain.
Well are you welcome to the open air.
How hath your lordship brooked imprisonment?   125

HASTINGS
With patience, noble lord, as prisoners must.
But I shall live, my lord, to give them thanks   127
That were the cause of my imprisonment.

---

106 abjects abjectly servile subjects   **109 King Edward's widow** i.e., the widow whom Edward has made queen   **110 enfranchise** release from imprisonment   **112 Touches . . . imagine** (1) distresses me more than can be imagined (2) concerns me (in my personal ambition) more than you could possibly guess   **115 lie for you** (1) take your place in prison (2) tell lies about you   **116 perforce** necessarily   **121 new-delivered** recently released   **125 brooked** endured   **127 give them thanks** i.e., pay them back. (Said ironically.)

RICHARD
> No doubt, no doubt; and so shall Clarence too,
> For they that were your enemies are his,
> And have prevailed as much on him as you.

HASTINGS
> More pity that the eagles should be mewed,
> Whiles kites and buzzards prey at liberty. 133

RICHARD What news abroad? 134

HASTINGS
> No news so bad abroad as this at home:
> The King is sickly, weak, and melancholy,
> And his physicians fear him mightily. 137

RICHARD
> Now, by Saint John, that news is bad indeed!
> O, he hath kept an evil diet long 139
> And overmuch consumed his royal person.
> 'Tis very grievous to be thought upon.
> Where is he, in his bed?

HASTINGS He is.

RICHARD
> Go you before, and I will follow you.   *Exit Hastings.*
> He cannot live, I hope, and must not die
> Till George be packed with post-horse up to heaven. 146
> I'll in, to urge his hatred more to Clarence
> With lies well steeled with weighty arguments; 148
> And, if I fail not in my deep intent,
> Clarence hath not another day to live.
> Which done, God take King Edward to his mercy,
> And leave the world for me to bustle in!
> For then I'll marry Warwick's youngest daughter. 153
> What though I killed her husband and her father? 154
> The readiest way to make the wench amends
> Is to become her husband and her father,
> The which will I; not all so much for love

133 kites scavengers of the hawk family   **134 abroad** at large, circulating   **137 fear** fear for   **139 diet** course of life, regimen   **146 with post-horse** by post-horses, i.e., by swiftest possible means   **148 steeled** reinforced   **153 Warwick's youngest daughter** the Lady Anne Neville (regarded by Shakespeare, following the chronicles, as widow of Edward, Prince of Wales, son of King Henry VI, though in fact they were only betrothed)   **154 father** i.e., father-in-law (Henry VI)

As for another secret close intent   158
By marrying her which I must reach unto.
But yet I run before my horse to market.
Clarence still breathes, Edward still lives and reigns;
When they are gone, then must I count my gains.

Exit.

❖

1.2   *Enter the corpse of [King] Henry the Sixth,*
         with Halberds to guard it; Lady Anne being the
         mourner [attended by Tressel and Berkeley].

ANNE
   Set down, set down your honorable load—
   If honor may be shrouded in a hearse—   2
   Whilst I awhile obsequiously lament   3
   Th' untimely fall of virtuous Lancaster.
              [*The bearers set down the coffin.*]
   Poor key-cold figure of a holy king,   5
   Pale ashes of the house of Lancaster,
   Thou bloodless remnant of that royal blood,
   Be it lawful that I invocate thy ghost   8
   To hear the lamentations of poor Anne,
   Wife to thy Edward, to thy slaughtered son,
   Stabbed by the selfsame hand that made these wounds!
   Lo, in these windows that let forth thy life   12
   I pour the helpless balm of my poor eyes.   13
   O, cursèd be the hand that made these holes!
   Cursèd the heart that had the heart to do it!
   Cursèd the blood that let this blood from hence!
   More direful hap betide that hated wretch   17
   That makes us wretched by the death of thee

---

158 intent design (i.e., Richard hopes to ally himself with the house of
Lancaster to bolster his claim to the throne)

1.2. Location: London. A street.
s.d. Halberds halberdiers, guards with halberds, or long poleaxes
2 hearse (probably here an open coffin on a bier)   **3 obsequiously** as
befits a funeral, mournfully   **5 key-cold** extremely cold, cold as a metal
key. (Proverbial.)   **8 invocate** invoke   **12 windows** i.e., wounds
13 helpless useless, unavailing   **17 hap betide** fortune befall

Than I can wish to wolves, to spiders, toads,
Or any creeping venomed thing that lives!
If ever he have child, abortive be it,   21
Prodigious, and untimely brought to light,   22
Whose ugly and unnatural aspect   23
May fright the hopeful mother at the view,
And that be heir to his unhappiness!   25
If ever he have wife, let her be made
More miserable by the life of him
Than I am made by my young lord and thee!   28
Come, now towards Chertsey with your holy load,   29
Taken from Paul's to be interrèd there.   30
            [*The bearers take up the hearse.*]
And still as you are weary of this weight,   31
Rest you, whiles I lament King Henry's corpse.

        Enter Richard, Duke of Gloucester.

RICHARD
Stay, you that bear the corpse, and set it down.
ANNE
What black magician conjures up this fiend
To stop devoted charitable deeds?   35
RICHARD
Villains, set down the corpse, or, by Saint Paul,
I'll make a corpse of him that disobeys.
HALBERDIER [*Advancing with his halberd lowered*]
My lord, stand back and let the coffin pass.
RICHARD
Unmannered dog, stand thou when I command!   39
Advance thy halberd higher than my breast,   40
Or, by Saint Paul, I'll strike thee to my foot
And spurn upon thee, beggar, for thy boldness.   42
            [*The bearers set down the hearse.*]
ANNE
What do you tremble? Are you all afraid?   43

21 **abortive** misshapen, monstrous   22 **Prodigious** monstrous, unnatural   23 **aspect** appearance   25 **unhappiness** evil nature   28 **by . . . thee** i.e., by the deaths of Prince Edward and King Henry VI   29 **Chertsey** monastery in Surrey, near London, where King Henry's body is to be buried   30 **Paul's** Saint Paul's Cathedral in London   31 **still as** as often as   35 **devoted** holy   39 **stand** halt   40 **Advance . . . breast** raise your halberd upright   42 **spurn** trample   43 **What** why

Alas, I blame you not, for you are mortal,
And mortal eyes cannot endure the devil.
Avaunt, thou dreadful minister of hell!   46
Thou hadst but power over his mortal body;
His soul thou canst not have. Therefore, begone.

RICHARD
Sweet saint, for charity, be not so curst.   49

ANNE
Foul devil, for God's sake hence and trouble us not,   50
For thou hast made the happy earth thy hell,
Filled it with cursing cries and deep exclaims.   52
If thou delight to view thy heinous deeds,
Behold this pattern of thy butcheries.   54

            [*She uncovers the corpse.*]

O, gentlemen, see, see dead Henry's wounds
Open their congealed mouths and bleed afresh!   56
Blush, blush, thou lump of foul deformity;
For 'tis thy presence that exhales this blood   58
From cold and empty veins where no blood dwells.
Thy deeds inhuman and unnatural
Provokes this deluge most unnatural.
O God, which this blood mad'st, revenge his death!
O earth, which this blood drink'st, revenge his death!
Either heaven with lightning strike the murderer dead,
Or earth gape open wide and eat him quick,   65
As thou dost swallow up this good king's blood,
Which his hell-governed arm hath butcherèd!

RICHARD
Lady, you know no rules of charity,
Which renders good for bad, blessings for curses.

ANNE
Villain, thou know'st nor law of God nor man.   70
No beast so fierce but knows some touch of pity.   71

RICHARD
But I know none, and therefore am no beast.

ANNE
O, wonderful, when devils tell the truth!

46 Avaunt begone   **49 curst** spiteful, shrewish   **50 hence** go hence,
depart   **52 exclaims** exclamations   **54 pattern** example   **56 bleed afresh**
(A phenomenon popularly supposed to occur in the presence of the
murderer.)   **58 exhales** draws out   **65 quick** alive   **70 nor . . . nor** neither . . . nor   **71 so fierce but knows** is so savage that it has not

RICHARD
More wonderful, when angels are so angry.
Vouchsafe, divine perfection of a woman, 75
Of these supposèd crimes to give me leave
By circumstance but to acquit myself. 77

ANNE
Vouchsafe, defusèd infection of a man, 78
Of these known evils but to give me leave
By circumstance t' accuse thy cursèd self.

RICHARD
Fairer than tongue can name thee, let me have
Some patient leisure to excuse myself.

ANNE
Fouler than heart can think thee, thou canst make
No excuse current but to hang thyself. 84

RICHARD
By such despair I should accuse myself.

ANNE
And by despairing shalt thou stand excused
For doing worthy vengeance on thyself
That didst unworthy slaughter upon others.

RICHARD   Say that I slew them not?

ANNE   Then say they were not slain.
But dead they are, and, devilish slave, by thee.

RICHARD   I did not kill your husband.

ANNE   Why, then he is alive.

RICHARD
Nay, he is dead, and slain by Edward's hand.

ANNE
In thy foul throat thou liest! Queen Margaret saw
Thy murderous falchion smoking in his blood, 96
The which thou once didst bend against her breast, 97
But that thy brothers beat aside the point.

RICHARD
I was provokèd by her slanderous tongue,
That laid their guilt upon my guiltless shoulders.

---

75 Vouchsafe deign, consent   **77 circumstance** detailed argument
78 defused diffused, disordered, shapeless; *defused infection* means
"spreading plague"   **84 current** genuine, acceptable (as in coinage)
96 falchion curved sword   **97 bend** direct, aim

ANNE

    Thou wast provokèd by thy bloody mind,

    That never dream'st on aught but butcheries.   102

    Didst thou not kill this king?

RICHARD   I grant ye.

ANNE

    Dost grant me, hedgehog? Then God grant me too   104

    Thou mayst be damnèd for that wicked deed!

    O, he was gentle, mild, and virtuous!

RICHARD

    The better for the King of Heaven that hath him.

ANNE

    He is in heaven, where thou shalt never come.

RICHARD

    Let him thank me that holp to send him thither;   109

    For he was fitter for that place than earth.

ANNE

    And thou unfit for any place but hell.

RICHARD

    Yes, one place else, if you will hear me name it.

ANNE   Some dungeon.

RICHARD   Your bedchamber.

ANNE

    Ill rest betide the chamber where thou liest!   115

RICHARD

    So will it, madam, till I lie with you.

ANNE

    I hope so.

RICHARD   I know so. But, gentle Lady Anne,

    To leave this keen encounter of our wits

    And fall something into a slower method,

    Is not the causer of the timeless deaths   120

    Of these Plantagenets, Henry and Edward,

    As blameful as the executioner?

ANNE

    Thou wast the cause and most accurst effect.   123

RICHARD

    Your beauty was the cause of that effect—   124

---

102 aught anything   **104 hedgehog** (Richard's heraldic emblem featured
a boar or wild hog.)   **109 holp** helped   **115 betide** befall   **120 timeless**
untimely   **123 effect** agent   **124 effect** result

Your beauty, that did haunt me in my sleep
To undertake the death of all the world,
So I might live one hour in your sweet bosom.

ANNE

If I thought that, I tell thee, homicide,   128
These nails should rend that beauty from my cheeks.   129

RICHARD

These eyes could not endure that beauty's wrack;   130
You should not blemish it, if I stood by.
As all the world is cheerèd by the sun,
So I by that. It is my day, my life.

ANNE

Black night o'ershade thy day, and death thy life!

RICHARD

Curse not thyself, fair creature—thou art both.

ANNE

I would I were, to be revenged on thee.

RICHARD

It is a quarrel most unnatural
To be revenged on him that loveth thee.

ANNE

It is a quarrel just and reasonable
To be revenged on him that killed my husband.

RICHARD

He that bereft thee, lady, of thy husband
Did it to help thee to a better husband.

ANNE

His better doth not breathe upon the earth.

RICHARD

He lives that loves thee better than he could.   144

ANNE

Name him.

RICHARD   Plantagenet.

ANNE   Why, that was he.

RICHARD

The selfsame name, but one of better nature.

ANNE

Where is he?

128 homicide murderer   **129 rend** tear   **130 wrack** destruction
144 He lives i.e., there is a man.   **he** i.e., Prince Edward

RICHARD   Here.   [*She*] *spits at him.*
     Why dost thou spit at me?

ANNE
     Would it were mortal poison for thy sake!

RICHARD
     Never came poison from so sweet a place.

ANNE
     Never hung poison on a fouler toad.   150
     Out of my sight! Thou dost infect mine eyes.

RICHARD
     Thine eyes, sweet lady, have infected mine.   152

ANNE
     Would they were basilisks, to strike thee dead!   153

RICHARD
     I would they were, that I might die at once;
     For now they kill me with a living death.
     Those eyes of thine from mine have drawn salt tears,
     Shamed their aspects with store of childish drops;   157
     These eyes, which never shed remorseful tear—
     No, when my father York and Edward wept
     To hear the piteous moan that Rutland made   160
     When black-faced Clifford shook his sword at him;   161
     Nor when thy warlike father, like a child,   162
     Told the sad story of my father's death
     And twenty times made pause to sob and weep,
     That all the standers-by had wet their cheeks   165
     Like trees bedashed with rain—in that sad time
     My manly eyes did scorn an humble tear;
     And what these sorrows could not thence exhale,   168
     Thy beauty hath, and made them blind with weeping.
     I never sued to friend nor enemy;   170
     My tongue could never learn sweet smoothing words;   171
     But, now thy beauty is proposed my fee,   172

---

150 poison . . . toad (Toads were popularly regarded as poisonous.)
152 infected i.e., with love (since love was thought to enter through the
eyes)   **153 basilisks** mythical reptiles reputed to kill by their looks
157 aspects appearance   **160 Rutland** second son of Richard, Duke of
York. (See *3 Henry VI*, 1.3, for his death scene.)   **161 black-faced** i.e.,
foreboding in appearance   **162 thy warlike father** i.e., the Earl of
Warwick   **165 That** so that   **168 exhale** draw out   **170 sued** suppli-
cated, appealed   **171 smoothing** flattering   **172 proposed my fee** offered as my reward

My proud heart sues and prompts my tongue to speak.
                    She looks scornfully at him.
Teach not thy lip such scorn, for it was made
For kissing, lady, not for such contempt.
If thy revengeful heart cannot forgive,
Lo, here I lend thee this sharp-pointed sword,
Which if thou please to hide in this true breast
And let the soul forth that adoreth thee,
I lay it naked to the deadly stroke
And humbly beg the death upon my knee.   181
                    He [kneels and] lays his breast open;
                    she offers at [it] with his sword.
Nay, do not pause; for I did kill King Henry—
But 'twas thy beauty that provokèd me.
Nay, now dispatch; 'twas I that stabbed young Edward—
But 'twas thy heavenly face that set me on.   185
                    She falls the sword.
Take up the sword again, or take up me.

ANNE
    Arise, dissembler. Though I wish thy death,
    I will not be thy executioner.

RICHARD [*rising*]
    Then bid me kill myself, and I will do it.

ANNE
    I have already.

RICHARD   That was in thy rage.
    Speak it again, and even with the word
    This hand, which for thy love did kill thy love,
    Shall for thy love kill a far truer love.
    To both their deaths shalt thou be accessory.

ANNE   I would I knew thy heart.   195

RICHARD   'Tis figured in my tongue.   196

ANNE   I fear me both are false.

RICHARD   Then never was man true.

ANNE   Well, well, put up your sword.

RICHARD   Say, then, my peace is made.

ANNE   That shalt thou know hereafter.

RICHARD   But shall I live in hope?

ANNE   All men, I hope, live so.

181 s.d. offers aims   **185 s.d. falls** lets fall   **195 would** wish
196 figured portrayed

RICHARD   Vouchsafe to wear this ring.   204
ANNE   To take is not to give.
               [*He slips the ring on her finger.*]
RICHARD
  Look how my ring encompasseth thy finger,
  Even so thy breast encloseth my poor heart;
  Wear both of them, for both of them are thine.
  And if thy poor devoted servant may   209
  But beg one favor at thy gracious hand,
  Thou dost confirm his happiness forever.
ANNE   What is it?
RICHARD
  That it may please you leave these sad designs
  To him that hath most cause to be a mourner,
  And presently repair to Crosby House,   215
  Where, after I have solemnly interred
  At Chertsey monast'ry this noble king
  And wet his grave with my repentant tears,
  I will with all expedient duty see you.   219
  For divers unknown reasons, I beseech you, 220
  Grant me this boon.
ANNE
  With all my heart, and much it joys me too
  To see you are become so penitent.
  Tressel and Berkeley, go along with me.
RICHARD
  Bid me farewell.
ANNE   'Tis more than you deserve;
  But since you teach me how to flatter you,
  Imagine I have said farewell already.
          Exeunt two [Tressel and Berkeley] with Anne.
RICHARD
  Sirs, take up the corpse.
GENTLEMAN   Towards Chertsey, noble lord?
RICHARD
  No, to Whitefriars. There attend my coming. 229
            Exeunt [bearers with] corpse.

---

204 Vouchsafe consent **209 servant** i.e., lover, one whom she may
command **215 presently** at once. **Crosby House** (One of Richard's
London dwellings; built originally by Sir John Crosby.) **219 expedient**
expeditious **220 unknown** secret **229 Whitefriars** the Carmelite
priory in London. **attend** await

Was ever woman in this humor wooed?
Was ever woman in this humor won?
I'll have her, but I will not keep her long.
What? I, that killed her husband and his father,
To take her in her heart's extremest hate,
With curses in her mouth, tears in her eyes,
The bleeding witness of my hatred by,
Having God, her conscience, and these bars against me, 237
And I no friends to back my suit at all
But the plain devil and dissembling looks?
And yet to win her! All the world to nothing!   240
Ha!
Hath she forgot already that brave prince,
Edward, her lord, whom I, some three months since,
Stabbed in my angry mood at Tewkesbury?
A sweeter and a lovelier gentleman,
Framed in the prodigality of nature,   246
Young, valiant, wise, and, no doubt, right royal,
The spacious world cannot again afford.
And will she yet abase her eyes on me,   249
That cropped the golden prime of this sweet prince   250
And made her widow to a woeful bed?
On me, whose all not equals Edward's moiety?   252
On me, that halts and am misshapen thus?   253
My dukedom to a beggarly denier,   254
I do mistake my person all this while.
Upon my life, she finds, although I cannot,
Myself to be a marvelous proper man.   257
I'll be at charges for a looking glass   258
And entertain a score or two of tailors   259
To study fashions to adorn my body.
Since I am crept in favor with myself,
I will maintain it with some little cost.
But first I'll turn yon fellow in his grave,   263
And then return lamenting to my love.

237 bars obstacles   **240 All . . . nothing** i.e., against infinite odds
246 Framed . . . nature i.e., formed in nature's most lavish mood
249 abase lower, devalue   **250 cropped** cut short   **252 moiety** half of
(Edward's virtues)   **253 halts** limps   **254 denier** small copper coin, the
twelfth part of a sou   **257 proper** handsome   **258 be . . . for** undertake
the expense of   **259 entertain** retain, employ   **263 in** into

Shine out, fair sun, till I have bought a glass,   265
That I may see my shadow as I pass.   *Exit.*

❖

1.3   *Enter the Queen Mother [Elizabeth], Lord*
Rivers, [Marquess of Dorset,] and Lord Grey.

RIVERS
Have patience, madam. There's no doubt His Majesty
Will soon recover his accustomed health.

GREY
In that you brook it ill, it makes him worse.   3
Therefore, for God's sake, entertain good comfort   4
And cheer His Grace with quick and merry eyes.

QUEEN ELIZABETH
If he were dead, what would betide on me?   6

GREY
No other harm but loss of such a lord.

QUEEN ELIZABETH
The loss of such a lord includes all harms.

GREY
The heavens have blessed you with a goodly son
To be your comforter when he is gone.

QUEEN ELIZABETH
Ah, he is young, and his minority
Is put unto the trust of Richard Gloucester,
A man that loves not me, nor none of you.

RIVERS
Is it concluded he shall be Protector?

QUEEN ELIZABETH
It is determined, not concluded yet;   15
But so it must be, if the King miscarry.   16

Enter Buckingham and [Lord Stanley, Earl of]
Derby.

---

265 glass mirror

1.3. Location: London. The royal court.
3 brook endure   **4 comfort** cheer   **6 betide on** become of
15 determined, not concluded i.e., decided though not officially
announced   **16 miscarry** perish

GREY
  Here come the lords of Buckingham and Derby.
BUCKINGHAM
  Good time of day unto Your Royal Grace!
STANLEY
  God make Your Majesty joyful, as you have been!
QUEEN ELIZABETH
  The Countess Richmond, good my lord of Derby,   20
  To your good prayer will scarcely say amen.
  Yet, Derby, notwithstanding she's your wife
  And loves not me, be you, good lord, assured
  I hate not you for her proud arrogance.   24
STANLEY
  I do beseech you, either not believe
  The envious slanders of her false accusers,   26
  Or, if she be accused on true report,
  Bear with her weakness, which I think proceeds
  From wayward sickness and no grounded malice.   29
QUEEN ELIZABETH
  Saw you the King today, my lord of Derby?
STANLEY
  But now the Duke of Buckingham and I   31
  Are come from visiting His Majesty.
QUEEN ELIZABETH
  What likelihood of his amendment, lords?   33
BUCKINGHAM
  Madam, good hope; His Grace speaks cheerfully.
QUEEN ELIZABETH
  God grant him health! Did you confer with him?
BUCKINGHAM
  Ay, madam. He desires to make atonement   36
  Between the Duke of Gloucester and your brothers,   37
  And between them and my Lord Chamberlain,

20 **Countess Richmond** i.e., Margaret Beaufort (1443–1509), who married
successively Edmund Tudor (Earl of Richmond), Lord Henry Stafford, and
Thomas Lord Stanley (here called the Earl of Derby), to whom she is
currently married. By the Earl of Richmond she was mother of the future
Henry VII.   24 **arrogance** i.e., ambition for her son   26 **envious** malicious   29 **wayward** erratic.   **grounded** firmly fixed   31 **But now** just
now   33 **amendment** recovery   36 **atonement** reconciliation   37 **brothers**
(Only one brother, Earl Rivers, is mentioned in the play, though historically Elizabeth had others; Shakespeare may be thinking of other kinsmen, including her sons, whom she helped to advance.)

And sent to warn them to his royal presence.   39
QUEEN ELIZABETH
Would all were well! But that will never be.
I fear our happiness is at the height.

> Enter Richard, [Duke of Gloucester, and Lord
> Hastings].

RICHARD
They do me wrong, and I will not endure it!
Who is it that complains unto the King
That I, forsooth, am stern and love them not?
By holy Paul, they love His Grace but lightly
That fill his ears with such dissentious rumors.   46
Because I cannot flatter and look fair,   47
Smile in men's faces, smooth, deceive, and cog,   48
Duck with French nods and apish courtesy,   49
I must be held a rancorous enemy.
Cannot a plain man live and think no harm,
But thus his simple truth must be abused
With silken, sly, insinuating Jacks?   53
GREY
To whom in all this presence speaks Your Grace?   54
RICHARD
To thee, that hast nor honesty nor grace.   55
When have I injured thee? When done thee wrong?
Or thee? Or thee? Or any of your faction?
A plague upon you all! His Royal Grace—
Whom God preserve better than you would wish!—
Cannot be quiet scarce a breathing while   60
But you must trouble him with lewd complaints.   61
QUEEN ELIZABETH
Brother of Gloucester, you mistake the matter.
The King, of his own royal disposition,   63
And not provoked by any suitor else,
Aiming, belike, at your interior hatred,   65

39 warn summon   **46 dissentious** quarrelsome, discordant   **47 fair** courteously   **48 smooth** flatter.   **cog** employ deceit   **49 Duck . . . nods** i.e., bow affectedly   **53 With** by.   **Jacks** lowbred persons   **54 presence** company   **55 grace** sense of duty or propriety (playing upon *Your Grace* in the preceding line)   **60 breathing while** i.e., brief time   **61 lewd** vile, base   **63 disposition** inclination   **65 Aiming** guessing.   **belike** probably

That in your outward action shows itself
Against my children, brothers, and myself,
Makes him to send, that he may learn the ground   68
Of your ill will, and thereby to remove it.

RICHARD
I cannot tell. The world is grown so bad
That wrens make prey where eagles dare not perch.
Since every Jack became a gentleman,
There's many a gentle person made a Jack.

QUEEN ELIZABETH
Come, come, we know your meaning, brother
    Gloucester;
You envy my advancement and my friends'.   75
God grant we never may have need of you!

RICHARD
Meantime, God grants that I have need of you.
Our brother is imprisoned by your means,   78
Myself disgraced, and the nobility
Held in contempt, while great promotions
Are daily given to ennoble those
That scarce some two days since were worth a noble.   82

QUEEN ELIZABETH
By Him that raised me to this careful height   83
From that contented hap which I enjoyed,   84
I never did incense His Majesty
Against the Duke of Clarence, but have been
An earnest advocate to plead for him.
My lord, you do me shameful injury
Falsely to draw me in these vile suspects.   89

RICHARD
You may deny that you were not the means
Of my Lord Hastings' late imprisonment.

RIVERS   She may, my lord, for—

RICHARD
She may, Lord Rivers! Why, who knows not so?
She may do more, sir, than denying that:

68 Makes him causes him. (The implied subject is "The king's own
disposition.")   **ground** cause (of your ill will)   **75 friends'** i.e., kinsmen's   **78 Our brother** i.e., Clarence.   **means** efforts   **82 noble** (1) gold
coin worth 6 shillings 8 pence (2) nobleman   **83 careful** full of cares
84 hap fortune   **89 in** into.   **suspects** suspicions

She may help you to many fair preferments,   95
And then deny her aiding hand therein,
And lay those honors on your high desert.   97
What may she not? She may, ay, marry, may she—   98
RIVERS   What, marry, may she?
RICHARD
What, marry, may she? Marry with a king,
A bachelor, and a handsome stripling too!   101
Iwis your grandam had a worser match.   102
QUEEN ELIZABETH
My lord of Gloucester, I have too long borne
Your blunt upbraidings and your bitter scoffs.
By heaven, I will acquaint His Majesty
Of those gross taunts that oft I have endured.
I had rather be a country servant maid
Than a great queen with this condition,
To be so baited, scorned, and stormèd at.   109

      Enter old Queen Margaret [behind].

Small joy have I in being England's queen.
QUEEN MARGARET [*Aside*]
And lessened be that small, God I beseech him!
Thy honor, state, and seat is due to me.   112
RICHARD
What? Threat you me with telling of the King?   113
Tell him, and spare not. Look what I have said   114
I will avouch 't in presence of the King.
I dare adventure to be sent to the Tower.   116
'Tis time to speak; my pains are quite forgot.   117
QUEEN MARGARET [*Aside*]
Out, devil! I do remember them too well: 118
Thou killedst my husband Henry in the Tower,
And Edward, my poor son, at Tewkesbury.

---

95 preferments advantages, promotions   **97 lay . . . on** attribute these
high honors to   **98 marry** i.e., indeed (followed by a pun on "wed")
101 stripling young man   **102 Iwis** certainly   **109 baited** harassed
s.d. Queen Margaret (Historically, Queen Margaret was held prisoner in England for five years following Tewkesbury and then was sent
to France; see note to l. 167 below.)   **112 state** degree, high rank.   **seat**
throne   **113 Threat** threaten   **114 Look what** whatever   **116 adventure
to be** risk being   **117 pains** efforts (in King Edward's behalf)   **118 Out**
(An exclamation of anger.)

RICHARD

    Ere you were queen, ay, or your husband king,
    I was a packhorse in his great affairs,   122
    A weeder-out of his proud adversaries,
    A liberal rewarder of his friends.
    To royalize his blood I spent mine own.

QUEEN MARGARET [*Aside*]

    Ay, and much better blood than his or thine.

RICHARD

    In all which time you and your husband Grey
    Were factious for the house of Lancaster;   128
    And, Rivers, so were you. Was not your husband 129
    In Margaret's battle at Saint Albans slain?
    Let me put in your minds, if you forget,
    What you have been ere this, and what you are;
    Withal, what I have been, and what I am.   133

QUEEN MARGARET [*Aside*]

    A murderous villain, and so still thou art.

RICHARD

    Poor Clarence did forsake his father, Warwick, 135
    Ay, and forswore himself—which Jesu pardon!—

QUEEN MARGARET [*Aside*]   Which God revenge!

RICHARD

    To fight on Edward's party for the crown;
    And for his meed, poor lord, he is mewed up.   139
    I would to God my heart were flint, like Edward's,
    Or Edward's soft and pitiful, like mine.
    I am too childish-foolish for this world.

QUEEN MARGARET [*Aside*]

    Hie thee to hell for shame, and leave this world, 143
    Thou cacodemon! There thy kingdom is.   144

RIVERS

    My lord of Gloucester, in those busy days
    Which here you urge to prove us enemies,   146

122 packhorse workhorse, beast of burden **128 factious** promoting
dissension. **for** on the side of **129 husband** (Queen Elizabeth's first
husband, Sir John Grey, fell fighting on the Lancastrian side at Saint
Albans.) **133 Withal** in addition **135 father** i.e., father-in-law. (See *3
Henry VI*, 4.1, when Clarence deserted his brothers to marry Warwick's
daughter Isabella and supported the Lancastrian cause for a time;
thereafter he forswore his oath to Warwick by returning to fight on
Edward's *party* [l. 138] or side.) **139 meed** reward. **mewed** caged (like a
hawk) **143 Hie** hasten **144 cacodemon** evil spirit **146 urge** cite

We followed then our lord, our sovereign king.
So should we you, if you should be our king.

RICHARD
If I should be? I had rather be a peddler.
Far be it from my heart, the thought thereof!

QUEEN ELIZABETH
As little joy, my lord, as you suppose
You should enjoy were you this country's king,
As little joy you may suppose in me
That I enjoy, being the queen thereof.

QUEEN MARGARET [*Aside*]
Ah, little joy enjoys the queen thereof,
For I am she, and altogether joyless.
I can no longer hold me patient.   [*Advancing.*]
Hear me, you wrangling pirates, that fall out
In sharing that which you have pilled from me!   159
Which of you trembles not that looks on me?
If not, that I am queen, you bow like subjects,   161
Yet that, by you deposed, you quake like rebels?   162
[*To Richard.*] Ah, gentle villain, do not turn away!   163

RICHARD
Foul wrinkled witch, what mak'st thou in my sight?   164

QUEEN MARGARET
But repetition of what thou hast marred;   165
That will I make before I let thee go.

RICHARD
Wert thou not banishèd on pain of death?   167

QUEEN MARGARET
I was; but I do find more pain in banishment
Than death can yield me here by my abode.
A husband and a son thou ow'st to me,   170
And thou a kingdom; all of you allegiance.   171
This sorrow that I have by right is yours,
And all the pleasures you usurp are mine.

---

159 pilled pillaged, robbed   **161–162 If . . . rebels** i.e., even if you do not
bow low to me as your queen, you quake as rebels who have deposed
me   **163 gentle** nobly born   **164 mak'st thou** are you doing   **165 But
. . . marred** only reciting your crimes   **167 banishèd** (Margaret was
banished in 1464, returned to England in 1471, and after the Battle of
Tewkesbury was confined in the Tower until 1476 when she returned to
France, dying there in 1482, one year before the historical time of this
scene.)   **170 thou** i.e., Richard   **171 thou** i.e., Elizabeth

RICHARD

The curse my noble father laid on thee   174
When thou didst crown his warlike brows with paper
And with thy scorns drew'st rivers from his eyes,
And then, to dry them, gav'st the Duke a clout   177
Steeped in the faultless blood of pretty Rutland—
His curses then, from bitterness of soul
Denounced against thee, are all fall'n upon thee;
And God, not we, hath plagued thy bloody deed.

QUEEN ELIZABETH

So just is God, to right the innocent.

HASTINGS

O, 'twas the foulest deed to slay that babe,   183
And the most merciless, that e'er was heard of!

RIVERS

Tyrants themselves wept when it was reported.

DORSET

No man but prophesied revenge for it.   186

BUCKINGHAM

Northumberland, then present, wept to see it.

QUEEN MARGARET

What? Were you snarling all before I came,
Ready to catch each other by the throat,
And turn you all your hatred now on me?
Did York's dread curse prevail so much with heaven
That Henry's death, my lovely Edward's death,
Their kingdom's loss, my woeful banishment,
Should all but answer for that peevish brat?   194
Can curses pierce the clouds and enter heaven?
Why then give way, dull clouds, to my quick curses!   196
Though not by war, by surfeit die your king,   197
As ours by murder, to make him a king!
Edward thy son, that now is Prince of Wales,
For Edward our son, that was Prince of Wales,
Die in his youth by like untimely violence!
Thyself a queen, for me that was a queen,
Outlive thy glory, like my wretched self!

174 The curse (See *3 Henry VI*, 1.4.164–166.)   **177 clout** cloth, handkerchief   **183 that babe** i.e., Rutland   **186 No . . . prophesied** there was
one who did not prophesy   **194 but answer for** merely atone for,
equal.   **peevish** silly, senseless   **196 quick** lively, piercing   **197 surfeit**
dissipated living

Long mayst thou live to wail thy children's death
And see another, as I see thee now,
Decked in thy rights, as thou art stalled in mine!   206
Long die thy happy days before thy death,
And, after many lengthened hours of grief,
Die neither mother, wife, nor England's queen!
Rivers and Dorset, you were standers-by,   210
And so wast thou, Lord Hastings, when my son   211
Was stabbed with bloody daggers: God, I pray him,
That none of you may live his natural age,   213
But by some unlooked accident cut off!   214

RICHARD
Have done thy charm, thou hateful withered hag!   215

QUEEN MARGARET
And leave out thee? Stay, dog, for thou shalt hear me.
If heaven have any grievous plague in store
Exceeding those that I can wish upon thee,
O, let them keep it till thy sins be ripe,   219
And then hurl down their indignation
On thee, the troubler of the poor world's peace!
The worm of conscience still begnaw thy soul!   222
Thy friends suspect for traitors while thou liv'st,
And take deep traitors for thy dearest friends!
No sleep close up that deadly eye of thine,
Unless it be while some tormenting dream
Affrights thee with a hell of ugly devils!
Thou elvish-marked, abortive, rooting hog,   228
Thou that wast sealed in thy nativity   229
The slave of nature and the son of hell!   230
Thou slander of thy heavy mother's womb,   231
Thou loathèd issue of thy father's loins,
Thou rag of honor, thou detested—

RICHARD
Margaret.

---

206 Decked dressed. **stalled** installed **210–211 Rivers, Dorset, Hastings** (Not present in Shakespeare's dramatization of the event in *3 Henry VI*, 5.5, but named in the chronicles as having been present.)
213 natural age full course of life **214 unlooked** unanticipated
215 charm magic curse, pronounced by a witch **219 them** i.e., the heavens, heaven **222 still begnaw** continually gnaw **228 elvish-marked** marked by elves at birth. **hog** (Alludes to Richard's badge, the wild boar.) **229 sealed** stamped **230 slave of nature** i.e., by the malignancy of nature (as seen in his deformity) **231 heavy** sorrowful

QUEEN MARGARET   Richard!

RICHARD   Ha?

QUEEN MARGARET   I call thee not.

RICHARD
I cry thee mercy then, for I did think   235
That thou hadst called me all these bitter names.

QUEEN MARGARET
Why, so I did, but looked for no reply.
O, let me make the period to my curse!   238

RICHARD
'Tis done by me, and ends in "Margaret."

QUEEN ELIZABETH
Thus have you breathed your curse against yourself.

QUEEN MARGARET
Poor painted queen, vain flourish of my fortune!   241
Why strew'st thou sugar on that bottled spider,   242
Whose deadly web ensnareth thee about?
Fool, fool, thou whet'st a knife to kill thyself.
The day will come that thou shalt wish for me
To help thee curse this poisonous bunch-backed toad.   246

HASTINGS
False-boding woman, end thy frantic curse,   247
Lest to thy harm thou move our patience.

QUEEN MARGARET
Foul shame upon you! You have all moved mine.

RIVERS
Were you well served, you would be taught your duty.   250

QUEEN MARGARET
To serve me well, you all should do me duty,   251
Teach me to be your queen, and you my subjects.
O, serve me well, and teach yourselves that duty!

DORSET
Dispute not with her; she is lunatic.

---

235 cry thee mercy beg your pardon. (Said sarcastically.)   **238 period**
conclusion   **241 painted** counterfeit.   **vain . . . fortune** i.e., mere
ornament of a position that is mine by right   **242 bottled** bottle-shaped,
swollen   **246 bunch-backed** hunchbacked   **247 False-boding** falsely
prophesying   **250 well served** treated as you deserve. (But Margaret
turns the phrase around to mean "served as befitting one of royal
rank.")   **your duty** your place (i.e., to be obedient)   **251 duty**
reverence

QUEEN MARGARET
    Peace, Master Marquess, you are malapert.   255
    Your fire-new stamp of honor is scarce current.   256
    O, that your young nobility could judge
    What 'twere to lose it and be miserable!
    They that stand high have many blasts to shake them,
    And if they fall, they dash themselves to pieces.

RICHARD
    Good counsel, marry! Learn it, learn it, Marquess.

DORSET
    It touches you, my lord, as much as me.

RICHARD
    Ay, and much more; but I was born so high.
    Our aerie buildeth in the cedar's top,   264
    And dallies with the wind and scorns the sun.

QUEEN MARGARET
    And turns the sun to shade; alas, alas!   266
    Witness my son, now in the shade of death,
    Whose bright outshining beams thy cloudy wrath
    Hath in eternal darkness folded up.
    Your aerie buildeth in our aerie's nest.
    O God, that seest it, do not suffer it!
    As it is won with blood, lost be it so!

BUCKINGHAM
    Peace, peace, for shame, if not for charity!

QUEEN MARGARET
    Urge neither charity nor shame to me.
                      [*Turning to the others.*]
    Uncharitably with me have you dealt,
    And shamefully my hopes by you are butchered.
    My charity is outrage, life my shame,   277
    And in that shame still live my sorrow's rage!

BUCKINGHAM   Have done, have done.

QUEEN MARGARET
    O princely Buckingham, I'll kiss thy hand
    In sign of league and amity with thee.
    Now fair befall thee and thy noble house!   282

---

255 malapert impudent **256 fire-new** newly coined. **current** genuine
as legal tender **264 aerie** eagle's brood **266 sun** (with a play on *son* in
the next line) **277 My . . . outrage** i.e., instead of charity I receive
outrage **282 fair befall** good luck to

Thy garments are not spotted with our blood,
Nor thou within the compass of my curse. 284
BUCKINGHAM
Nor no one here; for curses never pass 285
The lips of those that breathe them in the air. 286
QUEEN MARGARET
I will not think but they ascend the sky 287
And there awake God's gentle-sleeping peace.
O Buckingham, take heed of yonder dog!
Look when he fawns, he bites; and when he bites, 290
His venom tooth will rankle to the death. 291
Have not to do with him, beware of him;
Sin, death, and hell have set their marks on him,
And all their ministers attend on him.
RICHARD
What doth she say, my lord of Buckingham?
BUCKINGHAM
Nothing that I respect, my gracious lord. 296
QUEEN MARGARET
What, dost thou scorn me for my gentle counsel?
And soothe the devil that I warn thee from? 298
O, but remember this another day,
When he shall split thy very heart with sorrow,
And say poor Margaret was a prophetess!
Live each of you the subjects to his hate,
And he to yours, and all of you to God's!   *Exit.*
BUCKINGHAM
My hair doth stand on end to hear her curses.
RIVERS
And so doth mine. I muse why she's at liberty. 305
RICHARD
I cannot blame her. By God's holy mother,
She hath had too much wrong, and I repent
My part thereof that I have done to her.
QUEEN ELIZABETH
I never did her any, to my knowledge.

---

284 compass scope, boundary   **285–286 curses . . . air** i.e., curses have
no effect, are mere speech   **287 I . . . but** I must believe that   **290 Look
when** whenever   **291 venom** envenomed.   **rankle** cause a festering
wound   **296 respect** heed   **298 soothe** flatter   **305 muse** wonder

RICHARD

Yet you have all the vantage of her wrong.   310

I was too hot to do somebody good   311

That is too cold in thinking of it now.   312

Marry, as for Clarence, he is well repaid;

He is franked up to fatting for his pains—   314

God pardon them that are the cause thereof!

RIVERS

A virtuous and a Christian-like conclusion,

To pray for them that have done scathe to us.   317

RICHARD

So do I ever—(*Speaks to himself*) being well advised.

For had I cursed now, I had cursed myself.

    Enter Catesby.

CATESBY

Madam, His Majesty doth call for you,

And for Your Grace, and yours, my gracious lord.

QUEEN ELIZABETH

Catesby, I come. Lords, will you go with me?

RIVERS   We wait upon Your Grace.   323

    Exeunt all but [*Richard, Duke of*] *Gloucester.*

RICHARD

I do the wrong, and first begin to brawl.

The secret mischiefs that I set abroach   325

I lay unto the grievous charge of others.   326

Clarence, who I indeed have cast in darkness,

I do beweep to many simple gulls—   328

Namely, to Derby, Hastings, Buckingham—

And tell them 'tis the Queen and her allies

That stir the King against the Duke my brother.

Now they believe it, and withal whet me   332

To be revenged on Rivers, Dorset, Grey.

But then I sigh and, with a piece of Scripture,

Tell them that God bids us do good for evil.   335

310 vantage of advantage derived from   **311 hot** eager (in helping
Edward to the throne)   **312 That . . . cold** who is too ungrateful
314 franked up shut up in a frank or sty.   **to fatting** to be fattened (for
slaughter)   **317 scathe** harm   **323 wait upon** attend   **325 set abroach**
set flowing, begin   **326 lay . . . of** impute as a serious accusation
against   **328 gulls** credulous persons   **332 whet** urge, incite   **335 for** in
return for

And thus I clothe my naked villainy
With odd old ends stol'n forth of Holy Writ,   337
And seem a saint when most I play the devil.

Enter two Murderers.

But, soft! Here come my executioners.
How now, my hardy, stout, resolvèd mates,   340
Are you now going to dispatch this thing?

FIRST MURDERER
We are, my lord, and come to have the warrant
That we may be admitted where he is.

RICHARD
Well thought upon. I have it here about me.
                              [*He gives the warrant.*]
When you have done, repair to Crosby Place.   345
But, sirs, be sudden in the execution,
Withal obdurate; do not hear him plead;   347
For Clarence is well-spoken, and perhaps
May move your hearts to pity if you mark him.   349

FIRST MURDERER
Tut, tut, my lord, we will not stand to prate;
Talkers are no good doers. Be assured
We go to use our hands and not our tongues.

RICHARD
Your eyes drop millstones when fools' eyes fall tears.   353
I like you, lads; about your business straight.
Go, go, dispatch.

FIRST MURDERER   We will, my noble lord.   [*Exeunt.*]

❖

1.4   *Enter Clarence and Keeper.*

KEEPER
Why looks Your Grace so heavily today?   1

---

337 ends fragments, tags   **340 resolvèd** resolute   **345 repair** betake
yourselves   **347 Withal** at the same time   **349 mark** pay attention to
353 millstones heavy stone disks used for grinding. (To *drop millstones*
was proverbially to show signs of hardheartedness.)   **353 fall** let fall

1.4. Location: London. The Tower.
1 heavily sad

CLARENCE
O, I have passed a miserable night,
So full of fearful dreams, of ugly sights,
That, as I am a Christian faithful man,
I would not spend another such a night
Though 'twere to buy a world of happy days,
So full of dismal terror was the time!

KEEPER
What was your dream, my lord? I pray you, tell me.

CLARENCE
Methought that I had broken from the Tower   9
And was embarked to cross to Burgundy,   10
And in my company my brother Gloucester,
Who from my cabin tempted me to walk
Upon the hatches. Thence we looked toward England   13
And cited up a thousand heavy times,   14
During the wars of York and Lancaster,
That had befall'n us. As we paced along
Upon the giddy footing of the hatches,   17
Methought that Gloucester stumbled, and in falling
Struck me, that thought to stay him, overboard   19
Into the tumbling billows of the main.   20
O Lord, methought what pain it was to drown!
What dreadful noise of waters in my ears!
What sights of ugly death within my eyes!
Methought I saw a thousand fearful wracks;   24
Ten thousand men that fishes gnawed upon;
Wedges of gold, great anchors, heaps of pearl,
Inestimable stones, unvalued jewels,   27
All scattered in the bottom of the sea.
Some lay in dead men's skulls, and in the holes
Where eyes did once inhabit there were crept,
As 'twere in scorn of eyes, reflecting gems,
That wooed the slimy bottom of the deep
And mocked the dead bones that lay scattered by.

---

9 Methought it seemed to me   **10 Burgundy** (Clarence and Richard,
according to the chronicles, had been sent to Burgundy for protection
following their father's death.)   **13 hatches** movable planks forming a
deck   **14 cited up** recalled   **17 giddy** dizzying   **19 stay** hold, steady
20 main ocean   **24 wracks** shipwrecked vessels   **27 Inestimable** precious and innumerable.   **unvalued** priceless

KEEPER

Had you such leisure in the time of death
To gaze upon these secrets of the deep?

CLARENCE

Methought I had, and often did I strive
To yield the ghost; but still the envious flood   37
Stopped in my soul, and would not let it forth   38
To seek the empty, vast, and wandering air,
But smothered it within my panting bulk,   40
Which almost burst to belch it in the sea.

KEEPER

Awaked you not in this sore agony?

CLARENCE

No, no, my dream was lengthened after life.
O, then began the tempest to my soul!
I passed, methought, the melancholy flood,   45
With that sour ferryman which poets write of,   46
Unto the kingdom of perpetual night.
The first that there did greet my stranger soul   48
Was my great father-in-law, renownèd Warwick,
Who spake aloud, "What scourge for perjury
Can this dark monarchy afford false Clarence?"
And so he vanished. Then came wandering by
A shadow like an angel, with bright hair   53
Dabbled in blood, and he shrieked out aloud,
"Clarence is come—false, fleeting, perjured Clarence,   55
That stabbed me in the field by Tewkesbury.
Seize on him, Furies, take him unto torment!"
With that, methought, a legion of foul fiends
Environed me, and howlèd in mine ears
Such hideous cries that with the very noise
I trembling waked, and for a season after   61
Could not believe but that I was in hell,
Such terrible impression made my dream.

KEEPER

No marvel, my lord, though it affrighted you.
I am afraid, methinks, to hear you tell it.

37 **envious** malicious   38 **Stopped** held   40 **bulk** body   45 **melancholy flood** i.e., River Styx   46 **ferryman** i.e., Charon, who ferried souls to Hades, *the kingdom of perpetual night* (l. 47)   48 **stranger** i.e., newly arrived   53 **shadow** i.e., ghost of Edward, Prince of Wales, son of Henry VI   55 **fleeting** fickle, deceitful   61 **season** time

CLARENCE
  Ah, keeper, keeper, I have done these things,
  That now give evidence against my soul,
  For Edward's sake, and see how he requites me!   68
  O God! If my deep prayers cannot appease thee,
  But thou wilt be avenged on my misdeeds,
  Yet execute thy wrath in me alone!
  O, spare my guiltless wife and my poor children!
  Keeper, I prithee, sit by me awhile.
  My soul is heavy, and I fain would sleep.   74
KEEPER
  I will, my lord. God give Your Grace good rest!
                                [*Clarence sleeps.*]

      Enter Brackenbury, the Lieutenant.

BRACKENBURY
  Sorrow breaks seasons and reposing hours,   76
  Makes the night morning and the noontide night.
  Princes have but their titles for their glories,
  An outward honor for an inward toil,
  And, for unfelt imaginations,   80
  They often feel a world of restless cares;
  So that between their titles and low name   82
  There's nothing differs but the outward fame.   83

      Enter two Murderers.

FIRST MURDERER   Ho! Who's here?
BRACKENBURY
  What would'st thou, fellow, and how cam'st thou
     hither?
FIRST MURDERER I would speak with Clarence, and I
  came hither on my legs.
BRACKENBURY What, so brief?
SECOND MURDERER   'Tis better, sir, than to be tedious.
  Let him see our commission, and talk no more.
                          [*Brackenbury*] *reads* [*it*].

68 requites repays   **74 fain** willingly   **76 breaks seasons** i.e., disrupts
the normal rhythms of life.   **reposing hours** i.e., hours properly devoted
to sleep   **80 for unfelt imaginations** in return for glories that are only
imagined   **82 low name** i.e., the lowly position of ordinary men
83 fame reputation

BRACKENBURY
  I am in this commanded to deliver
  The noble Duke of Clarence to your hands.
  I will not reason what is meant hereby,
  Because I will be guiltless from the meaning.   94
  There lies the Duke asleep, and there the keys.
                              [*He gives keys.*]
  I'll to the King and signify to him
  That thus I have resigned to you my charge.
FIRST MURDERER You may, sir; 'tis a point of wisdom.
  Fare you well.   *Exit* [*Brackenbury with Keeper*].
SECOND MURDERER What, shall I stab him as he
  sleeps?
FIRST MURDERER No. He'll say 'twas done cowardly,
  when he wakes.
SECOND MURDERER Why, he shall never wake until the
  great Judgment Day.
FIRST MURDERER Why, then he'll say we stabbed him
  sleeping.
SECOND MURDERER The urging of that word "judg-
  ment" hath bred a kind of remorse in me.
FIRST MURDERER What, art thou afraid?
SECOND MURDERER Not to kill him, having a warrant,
  but to be damned for killing him, from the which no
  warrant can defend me.
FIRST MURDERER I thought thou hadst been resolute.
SECOND MURDERER So I am—to let him live.
FIRST MURDERER I'll back to the Duke of Gloucester and
  tell him so.
SECOND MURDERER Nay, I prithee, stay a little. I hope
  this passionate humor of mine will change. It was   119
  wont to hold me but while one tells twenty.   120
FIRST MURDERER How dost thou feel thyself now?
SECOND MURDERER Faith, some certain dregs of con-
  science are yet within me.
FIRST MURDERER Remember our reward when the deed's
  done.
SECOND MURDERER Zounds, he dies! I had forgot the   126
  reward.

94 will be wish to be   **119 passionate humor** compassionate mood
120 tells counts   **126 Zounds** i.e., by God's (Christ's) wounds

FIRST MURDERER Where's thy conscience now?

SECOND MURDERER O, in the Duke of Gloucester's purse.

FIRST MURDERER When he opens his purse to give us our reward, thy conscience flies out.

SECOND MURDERER 'Tis no matter; let it go. There's few or none will entertain it.   134

FIRST MURDERER What if it come to thee again?

SECOND MURDERER I'll not meddle with it; it makes a man a coward. A man cannot steal but it accuseth him; a man cannot swear but it checks him; a man 138 cannot lie with his neighbor's wife but it detects him. 'Tis a blushing shamefaced spirit that mutinies in a man's bosom. It fills a man full of obstacles. It made me once restore a purse of gold that by chance I found. It beggars any man that keeps it. It is turned out of towns and cities for a dangerous thing, and every man that means to live well endeavors to trust to himself and live without it.

FIRST MURDERER Zounds, 'tis even now at my elbow, persuading me not to kill the Duke.

SECOND MURDERER Take the devil in thy mind, and be- 149 lieve him not. He would insinuate with thee but to 150 make thee sigh.

FIRST MURDERER Tut, I am strong-framed; he cannot prevail with me.

SECOND MURDERER Spoke like a tall man that respects 154 thy reputation. Come, shall we fall to work?

FIRST MURDERER Take him on the costard with the hilts 156 of thy sword, and then throw him into the malmsey 157 butt in the next room.   158

SECOND MURDERER O, excellent device! And make a sop 159 of him.

FIRST MURDERER Soft, he wakes.

SECOND MURDERER Strike!

---

134 entertain it receive it, give it welcome   **138 checks** reproves
149–150 Take . . . not i.e., listen to the devil and don't heed the devil
conscience   **150 insinuate** ingratiate himself   **154 tall** brave   **156 Take**
strike.   **costard** head. (Literally, a kind of apple.)   **157–158 malmsey**
butt wine barrel. (Malmsey is a sweet wine.)   **159 sop** bread or cake
soaked in wine

FIRST MURDERER   No, we'll reason with him.   163

[*Clarence wakes.*]

CLARENCE
Where art thou, keeper? Give me a cup of wine.

SECOND MURDERER
You shall have wine enough, my lord, anon.

CLARENCE   In God's name, what art thou?

FIRST MURDERER   A man, as you are.

CLARENCE   But not, as I am, royal.

FIRST MURDERER   Nor you, as we are, loyal.

CLARENCE
Thy voice is thunder, but thy looks are humble.

FIRST MURDERER
My voice is now the King's, my looks mine own.

CLARENCE
How darkly and how deadly dost thou speak!
Your eyes do menace me. Why look you pale?
Who sent you hither? Wherefore do you come?

SECOND MURDERER   To, to, to—

CLARENCE   To murder me?

BOTH   Ay, ay.

CLARENCE
You scarcely have the hearts to tell me so,
And therefore cannot have the hearts to do it.
Wherein, my friends, have I offended you?

FIRST MURDERER
Offended us you have not, but the King.

CLARENCE
I shall be reconciled to him again.

SECOND MURDERER
Never, my lord; therefore prepare to die.

CLARENCE
Are you drawn forth among a world of men   184
To slay the innocent? What is my offense?
Where is the evidence that doth accuse me?
What lawful quest have given their verdict up   187
Unto the frowning judge? Or who pronounced
The bitter sentence of poor Clarence' death
Before I be convict by course of law?   190

163 reason talk   **184 drawn . . . men** especially selected from the whole human race   **187 quest** inquest, i.e., jury   **190 convict** convicted

To threaten me with death is most unlawful.
I charge you, as you hope to have redemption
By Christ's dear blood shed for our grievous sins,
That you depart and lay no hands on me.
The deed you undertake is damnable.

FIRST MURDERER
What we will do, we do upon command.

SECOND MURDERER
And he that hath commanded is our king.

CLARENCE
Erroneous vassals! The great King of kings   198
Hath in the table of his law commanded   199
That thou shalt do no murder. Will you then
Spurn at his edict, and fulfill a man's?
Take heed; for he holds vengeance in his hand
To hurl upon their heads that break his law.

SECOND MURDERER
And that same vengeance doth he hurl on thee
For false forswearing and for murder too.
Thou didst receive the Sacrament to fight   206
In quarrel of the house of Lancaster.

FIRST MURDERER
And, like a traitor to the name of God,
Didst break that vow, and with thy treacherous blade
Unrippedst the bowels of thy sovereign's son.   210

SECOND MURDERER
Whom thou wast sworn to cherish and defend.

FIRST MURDERER
How canst thou urge God's dreadful law to us
When thou hast broke it in such dear degree?   213

CLARENCE
Alas! For whose sake did I that ill deed?
For Edward, for my brother, for his sake.
He sends you not to murder me for this,
For in that sin he is as deep as I.
If God will be avengèd for the deed,
O, know you yet he doth it publicly!
Take not the quarrel from his powerful arm.

198 **Erroneous vassals** sinful and mistaken wretches   199 **table** tablet
206 **receive the Sacrament** i.e., swear upon the Sacrament   210 **sovereign's son** i.e., Prince Edward, son of Henry VI   213 **dear** grievous

He needs no indirect or lawless course
To cut off those that have offended him.

FIRST MURDERER
Who made thee, then, a bloody minister   223
When gallant-springing brave Plantagenet,   224
That princely novice, was struck dead by thee?   225

CLARENCE
My brother's love, the devil, and my rage.   226

FIRST MURDERER
Thy brother's love, our duty, and thy faults
Provoke us hither now to slaughter thee.

CLARENCE
If you do love my brother, hate not me!
I am his brother, and I love him well.
If you are hired for meed, go back again,   231
And I will send you to my brother Gloucester,
Who shall reward you better for my life
Than Edward will for tidings of my death.   234

SECOND MURDERER
You are deceived. Your brother Gloucester hates you.

CLARENCE
O, no, he loves me, and he holds me dear.
Go you to him from me.

FIRST MURDERER   Ay, so we will.

CLARENCE
Tell him, when that our princely father York
Blessed his three sons with his victorious arm
And charged us from his soul to love each other,
He little thought of this divided friendship.
Bid Gloucester think of this, and he will weep.

FIRST MURDERER
Ay, millstones, as he lessoned us to weep.   243

CLARENCE
O, do not slander him, for he is kind.

---

223 **minister** agent of God   224 **gallant-springing** i.e., gallant and
sprightly, aspiring.   **Plantagenet** (Originally, a nickname for Geoffrey of
Anjou, father of Henry II and founder of the dynasty that ruled England until 1485; the name is thus appropriate to the Lancastrian Prince
Edward, though the Yorkist Richard Plantagenet had attempted to take
the name for his own.)   225 **novice** youth   226 **My brother's love** i.e.,
my love for my brother   231 **meed** financial reward   234 **tidings**
news   243 **lessoned** taught

FIRST MURDERER
　　Right, as snow in harvest. Come, you deceive yourself. 245
　　'Tis he that sends us to destroy you here.

CLARENCE
　　It cannot be, for he bewept my fortune,
　　And hugged me in his arms, and swore with sobs
　　That he would labor my delivery.   249

FIRST MURDERER
　　Why, so he doth, when he delivers you
　　From this earth's thralldom to the joys of heaven.   251

SECOND MURDERER
　　Make peace with God, for you must die, my lord.

CLARENCE
　　Have you that holy feeling in your souls
　　To counsel me to make my peace with God,
　　And are you yet to your own souls so blind
　　That you will war with God by murdering me?
　　O, sirs, consider, they that set you on
　　To do this deed will hate you for the deed.

SECOND MURDERER [*To First Murderer*]
　　What shall we do?

CLARENCE   Relent, and save your souls.
　　Which of you, if you were a prince's son,
　　Being pent from liberty, as I am now,   261
　　If two such murderers as yourselves came to you,
　　Would not entreat for life?   263

FIRST MURDERER
　　Relent? No. 'Tis cowardly and womanish.

CLARENCE
　　Not to relent is beastly, savage, devilish.
　　My friend [*To Second Murderer*], I spy some pity in
　　　thy looks.
　　O, if thine eye be not a flatterer,
　　Come thou on my side, and entreat for me,
　　As you would beg, were you in my distress.
　　A begging prince what beggar pities not?

SECOND MURDERER Look behind you, my lord.

---

245 Right ... harvest i.e., he's just as kind and natural—that is, both
affectionate and with the natural feelings of a brother—as is snow at
harvest time **249 labor my delivery** work for my release **251 thralldom**
bondage, captivity **261 pent** shut up **263 entreat** beseech, beg

FIRST MURDERER

Take that, and that! (*Stabs him.*) If all this will not do,
I'll drown you in the malmsey butt within.

Exit [*with the body*].

SECOND MURDERER

A bloody deed, and desperately dispatched!
How fain, like Pilate, would I wash my hands   275
Of this most grievous murder!

Enter First Murderer.

FIRST MURDERER

How now? What mean'st thou that thou help'st me not?
By heaven, the Duke shall know how slack you have
   been.

SECOND MURDERER

I would he knew that I had saved his brother!
Take thou the fee, and tell him what I say,
For I repent me that the Duke is slain.   *Exit.*

FIRST MURDERER

So do not I. Go, coward as thou art.
Well, I'll go hide his body in some hole
Till that the Duke give order for his burial;
And when I have my meed, I will away,
For this will out, and then I must not stay.   *Exit.* 286

❖

275 fain gladly   **286 this** i.e., this murder

2.1 *Flourish. Enter the King [Edward], sick, the*
Queen [Elizabeth], Lord Marquess Dorset,
[Grey,] Rivers, Hastings, Catesby, Buckingham,
[and others].

KING EDWARD
   Why, so. Now have I done a good day's work.
   You peers, continue this united league.
   I every day expect an embassage
   From my Redeemer to redeem me hence;
   And more in peace my soul shall part to heaven,
   Since I have made my friends at peace on earth.
   Rivers and Hastings, take each other's hand;
   Dissemble not your hatred, swear your love.   8
RIVERS [*Taking Hastings' hand*]
   By heaven, my soul is purged from grudging hate,
   And with my hand I seal my true heart's love.
HASTINGS
   So thrive I, as I truly swear the like!
KING EDWARD
   Take heed you dally not before your king,   12
   Lest he that is the supreme King of kings
   Confound your hidden falsehood, and award   14
   Either of you to be the other's end.   15
HASTINGS
   So prosper I, as I swear perfect love!
RIVERS
   And I, as I love Hastings with my heart!
KING EDWARD
   Madam, yourself is not exempt from this,
   Nor you, son Dorset, Buckingham, nor you;   19
   You have been factious one against the other.   20
   Wife, love Lord Hastings; let him kiss your hand;
   And what you do, do it unfeignedly.
QUEEN ELIZABETH
   There, Hastings, I will nevermore remember

2.1. **Location: London. The royal court.**
s.d. Flourish trumpet call to announce the arrival of a distinguished
person **8 Dissemble** conceal, disguise (under a false appearance of
love) **12 dally** trifle **14 Confound** defeat **15 Either . . . end** i.e., each
of you to be the agent of death of the other **19 son** i.e., stepson
20 factious quarrelsome

Our former hatred, so thrive I and mine!

[Hastings kisses her hand.]

KING EDWARD

Dorset, embrace him. Hastings, love Lord Marquess.

DORSET

This interchange of love, I here protest,
Upon my part shall be inviolable.

HASTINGS   And so swear I.   *[They embrace.]*

KING EDWARD

Now, princely Buckingham, seal thou this league
With thy embracements to my wife's allies,
And make me happy in your unity.

BUCKINGHAM [*To the Queen*]

Whenever Buckingham doth turn his hate
Upon Your Grace, but with all duteous love   33
Doth cherish you and yours, God punish me
With hate in those where I expect most love!
When I have most need to employ a friend,
And most assurèd that he is a friend,
Deep, hollow, treacherous, and full of guile   38
Be he unto me! This do I beg of God,
When I am cold in love to you or yours.

[They] embrace.

KING EDWARD

A pleasing cordial, princely Buckingham,   41
Is this thy vow unto my sickly heart.
There wanteth now our brother Gloucester here   43
To make the blessèd period of this peace.   44

BUCKINGHAM   And, in good time,
Here comes Sir Richard Ratcliffe and the Duke.

*Enter Ratcliffe and [Richard, Duke of]
Gloucester.*

RICHARD

Good morrow to my sovereign king and queen;
And, princely peers, a happy time of day!

KING EDWARD

Happy, indeed, as we have spent the day.
Gloucester, we have done deeds of charity,

33 but i.e., nor   **38 Deep** subtle, crafty   **41 cordial** restorative
43 wanteth is lacking   **44 period** conclusion

Made peace of enmity, fair love of hate,
Between these swelling wrong-incensèd peers. 52

RICHARD
A blessèd labor, my most sovereign lord.
Among this princely heap, if any here, 54
By false intelligence, or wrong surmise, 55
Hold me a foe;
If I unwittingly, or in my rage,
Have aught committed that is hardly borne 58
By any in this presence, I desire
To reconcile me to his friendly peace.
'Tis death to me to be at enmity;
I hate it, and desire all good men's love.
First, madam, I entreat true peace of you,
Which I will purchase with my duteous service;
Of you, my noble cousin Buckingham,
If ever any grudge were lodged between us;
Of you and you, Lord Rivers, and of Dorset,
That all without desert have frowned on me; 68
Dukes, earls, lords, gentlemen—indeed, of all.
I do not know that Englishman alive
With whom my soul is any jot at odds
More than the infant that is born tonight. 72
I thank my God for my humility.

QUEEN ELIZABETH
A holy day shall this be kept hereafter.
I would to God all strifes were well compounded. 75
My sovereign lord, I do beseech Your Highness
To take our brother Clarence to your grace.

RICHARD
Why, madam, have I offered love for this,
To be so flouted in this royal presence? 79
Who knows not that the gentle Duke is dead?
                         They all start.
You do him injury to scorn his corpse.

KING EDWARD
Who knows not he is dead? Who knows he is?

---

52 swelling i.e., with anger or rivalry   **54 heap** assembly   **55 false intelligence** being misinformed   **58 hardly borne** taken amiss, deeply resented   **68 all without desert** wholly without my having deserved it   **72 More than the infant** i.e., more than is that infant's soul   **75 compounded** settled   **79 flouted** mocked

QUEEN ELIZABETH
  All-seeing heaven, what a world is this!
BUCKINGHAM
  Look I so pale, Lord Dorset, as the rest?
DORSET
  Ay, my good lord, and no man in the presence   85
  But his red color hath forsook his cheeks.
KING EDWARD
  Is Clarence dead? The order was reversed.
RICHARD
  But he, poor man, by your first order died,
  And that a wingèd Mercury did bear;
  Some tardy cripple bare the countermand,   90
  That came too lag to see him buried.   91
  God grant that some, less noble and less loyal,   92
  Nearer in bloody thoughts but not in blood,   93
  Deserve not worse than wretched Clarence did,   94
  And yet go current from suspicion!   95

  Enter [Lord Stanley,] Earl of Derby.

STANLEY [*Kneeling*]
  A boon, my sovereign, for my service done!   96
KING EDWARD
  I prithee, peace. My soul is full of sorrow.
STANLEY
  I will not rise unless Your Highness hear me.
KING EDWARD
  Then say at once what is it thou requests.
STANLEY
  The forfeit, sovereign, of my servant's life,   100
  Who slew today a riotous gentleman   101
  Lately attendant on the Duke of Norfolk.
KING EDWARD
  Have I a tongue to doom my brother's death,   103

---

85 presence i.e., royal presence   **90 bare** bore   **91 lag** late   **92–95 God . . .
suspicion** i.e., (ironically) pray God there be not persons who deserve
worse than Clarence got, persons less noble or related by blood to the
King than he although closely involved in bloody plots, who yet go unde-
tected. (Richard means the Queen and her kindred.)   **go current** are
accepted at face value (like legal currency).   **from** free from   **96 A boon** (I
crave) a favor   **100 the forfeit** i.e., the remission of the forfeit
101 riotous disorderly, wild   **103 doom** decree

And shall that tongue give pardon to a slave?   104
My brother killed no man; his fault was thought,
And yet his punishment was bitter death.
Who sued to me for him? Who, in my wrath,
Kneeled at my feet and bid me be advised?   108
Who spoke of brotherhood? Who spoke of love?
Who told me how the poor soul did forsake
The mighty Warwick and did fight for me?
Who told me, in the field at Tewkesbury,
When Oxford had me down, he rescued me   113
And said, "Dear brother, live, and be a king"?
Who told me, when we both lay in the field
Frozen almost to death, how he did lap me   116
Even in his garments, and did give himself,
All thin and naked, to the numb-cold night?
All this from my remembrance brutish wrath
Sinfully plucked, and not a man of you
Had so much grace to put it in my mind.
But when your carters or your waiting vassals   122
Have done a drunken slaughter and defaced
The precious image of our dear Redeemer,
You straight are on your knees for pardon, pardon;
And I, unjustly too, must grant it you.

                                   [*Stanley rises.*]

But for my brother not a man would speak,
Nor I, ungracious, speak unto myself
For him, poor soul. The proudest of you all
Have been beholding to him in his life;   130
Yet none of you would once beg for his life.
O God, I fear thy justice will take hold
On me and you, and mine and yours, for this!
Come, Hastings, help me to my closet. Ah, poor
    Clarence!   *Exeunt some with King and Queen.* 134
RICHARD
    This is the fruits of rashness! Marked you not
    How that the guilty kindred of the Queen
    Looked pale when they did hear of Clarence' death?
    O, they did urge it still unto the King!

104 slave wretch   **108 advised** cautious   **113 Oxford** (See *3 Henry VI*,
5.5.2; this episode has no historical basis.)   **116 lap** wrap   **122 carters**
cart drivers   **130 beholding** beholden   **134 closet** private chambers

God will revenge it. Come, lords, will you go
To comfort Edward with our company?
BUCKINGHAM   We wait upon Your Grace.   *Exeunt.*

❖

2.2   *Enter the old Duchess of York, with the two*
         children of Clarence, [Edward and Margaret
         Plantagenet].

BOY
   Good grandam, tell us, is our father dead?
DUCHESS   No, boy.
GIRL
   Why do you weep so oft, and beat your breast,
   And cry, "O Clarence, my unhappy son"?
BOY
   Why do you look on us, and shake your head,
   And call us orphans, wretches, castaways,
   If that our noble father were alive?
DUCHESS
   My pretty cousins, you mistake me both.   8
   I do lament the sickness of the King,
   As loath to lose him, not your father's death;
   It were lost sorrow to wail one that's lost.
BOY
   Then, you conclude, my grandam, he is dead.
   The King mine uncle is to blame for it.
   God will revenge it, whom I will importune   14
   With earnest prayers all to that effect.
GIRL   And so will I.
DUCHESS
   Peace, children, peace! The King doth love you well.
   Incapable and shallow innocents,   18
   You cannot guess who caused your father's death.
BOY
   Grandam, we can; for my good uncle Gloucester
   Told me the King, provoked to it by the Queen,
   Devised impeachments to imprison him;   22

2.2. Location: London. The royal court.
8 cousins kinsmen   **14 importune** solicit, beg   **18 Incapable** unable to
understand   **22 impeachments** accusations

And when my uncle told me so, he wept,
And pitied me, and kindly kissed my cheek;
Bade me rely on him as on my father,
And he would love me dearly as a child.

DUCHESS
Ah, that deceit should steal such gentle shape,
And with a virtuous visor hide deep vice!   28
He is my son—ay, and therein my shame;
Yet from my dugs he drew not this deceit.   30

BOY
Think you my uncle did dissemble, grandam?

DUCHESS   Ay, boy.

BOY
I cannot think it. Hark, what noise is this?

*Enter the Queen [Elizabeth], with her hair about
her ears; Rivers and Dorset after her.*

QUEEN ELIZABETH
Ah, who shall hinder me to wail and weep,
To chide my fortune and torment myself?
I'll join with black despair against my soul,
And to myself become an enemy.

DUCHESS
What means this scene of rude impatience?   38

QUEEN ELIZABETH
To make an act of tragic violence.   39
Edward, my lord, thy son, our king, is dead!   40
Why grow the branches when the root is gone?
Why wither not the leaves that want their sap?
If you will live, lament; if die, be brief,   43
That our swift-wingèd souls may catch the King's
Or, like obedient subjects, follow him
To his new kingdom of ne'er-changing night.

DUCHESS
Ah, so much interest have I in thy sorrow
As I had title in thy noble husband!   48
I have bewept a worthy husband's death

---

28 visor mask   **30 dugs** breasts   **38 rude** violent   **39 make** perform.
(Continues the theatrical metaphor in the previous line.)   **40 Edward
... dead** (Clarence's death, February 1478, and Edward IV's death, April
1483, are treated as if they had occurred near together.)   **43 brief**
quick   **48 title** i.e., as mother of the King

And lived with looking on his images;   50
But now two mirrors of his princely semblance   51
Are cracked in pieces by malignant death,
And I for comfort have but one false glass,   53
That grieves me when I see my shame in him.
Thou art a widow; yet thou art a mother,
And hast the comfort of thy children left;
But death hath snatched my husband from mine arms
And plucked two crutches from my feeble hands,
Clarence and Edward. O, what cause have I,   59
Thine being but a moiety of my moan,   60
To overgo thy woes and drown thy cries!   61

BOY

Ah, aunt! You wept not for our father's death.
How can we aid you with our kindred tears?   63

GIRL

Our fatherless distress was left unmoaned;
Your widow-dolor likewise be unwept!   65

QUEEN ELIZABETH

Give me no help in lamentation;
I am not barren to bring forth complaints.   67
All springs reduce their currents to mine eyes,   68
That I, being governed by the watery moon,
May send forth plenteous tears to drown the world!
Ah for my husband, for my dear lord Edward!

CHILDREN

Ah for our father, for our dear lord Clarence!

DUCHESS

Alas for both, both mine, Edward and Clarence!

QUEEN ELIZABETH

What stay had I but Edward? And he's gone.   74

CHILDREN

What stay had we but Clarence? And he's gone.

DUCHESS

What stays had I but they? And they are gone.

---

50 images likenesses; here, children   **51 two mirrors** i.e., Edward and Clarence. (She does not count Rutland.)   **53 false glass** i.e., Richard **59 what . . . I** what a cause I have   **60 moiety of my moan** half (the cause) of my grief   **61 overgo** exceed   **63 kindred tears** i.e., tears of kinsmen   **65 widow-dolor** widow's grief   **67 barren to** unable to **68 All springs reduce** let all springs bring   **74 stay** support

QUEEN ELIZABETH
Was never widow had so dear a loss!   77
CHILDREN
Were never orphans had so dear a loss!
DUCHESS
Was never mother had so dear a loss!
Alas, I am the mother of these griefs;
Their woes are parceled, mine is general.   81
She for an Edward weeps, and so do I;
I for a Clarence weep, so doth not she.
These babes for Clarence weep, and so do I;
I for an Edward weep, so do not they.
Alas, you three, on me, threefold distressed,
Pour all your tears! I am your sorrow's nurse,
And I will pamper it with lamentation.   88
DORSET [*To Queen Elizabeth*]
Comfort, dear Mother. God is much displeased
That you take with unthankfulness his doing.
In common worldly things 'tis called ungrateful
With dull unwillingness to repay a debt
Which with a bounteous hand was kindly lent;
Much more to be thus opposite with heaven   94
For it requires the royal debt it lent you.   95
RIVERS
Madam, bethink you like a careful mother
Of the young Prince your son. Send straight for him;
Let him be crowned. In him your comfort lives.
Drown desperate sorrow in dead Edward's grave
And plant your joys in living Edward's throne.

> *Enter Richard, [Duke of Gloucester,] Buckingham,
> [Lord Stanley, Earl of] Derby, Hastings, and
> Ratcliffe.*

RICHARD
Sister, have comfort. All of us have cause
To wail the dimming of our shining star,
But none can help our harms by wailing them.—

---

77 dear grievous   **81 Their . . . parceled** i.e., the woes of Queen Elizabeth and these children are single   **88 pamper** i.e., sustain   **94 opposite with** hostile toward   **95 For it requires** because it calls back

Madam, my mother, I do cry you mercy;   104
I did not see Your Grace. Humbly on my knee
I crave your blessing.   [*He kneels.*]

DUCHESS

God bless thee, and put meekness in thy breast,
Love, charity, obedience, and true duty!

RICHARD

Amen! [*Aside.*] And make me die a good old man!
That is the butt end of a mother's blessing;
I marvel that Her Grace did leave it out.

BUCKINGHAM

You cloudy princes and heart-sorrowing peers,   112
That bear this heavy mutual load of moan,   113
Now cheer each other in each other's love.
Though we have spent our harvest of this king,
We are to reap the harvest of his son.
The broken rancor of your high-swoll'n hates,
But lately splintered, knit, and joined together,   118
Must gently be preserved, cherished, and kept.   119
Meseemeth good that with some little train   120
Forthwith from Ludlow the young Prince be fet   121
Hither to London, to be crowned our king.

RIVERS

Why with some little train, my lord of Buckingham?

BUCKINGHAM

Marry, my lord, lest by a multitude   124
The new-healed wound of malice should break out,
Which would be so much the more dangerous
By how much the estate is green and yet ungoverned.   127
Where every horse bears his commanding rein   128
And may direct his course as please himself,   129
As well the fear of harm, as harm apparent,   130
In my opinion, ought to be prevented.

---

104 cry you mercy beg your pardon   **112 cloudy** clouded with grief
113 moan lamentation   **118 But lately splintered** only recently bound
together (as with a splint)   **119 Must . . . preserved** i.e., the recent mending of differences must be preserved   **120 Meseemeth** it seems to me.
train entourage   **121 Ludlow** royal castle in Shropshire, near the Welsh
border.   **fet** fetched   **124 multitude** i.e., large train or entourage
127 estate state, government.   **green** i.e., newly established   **128 bears**
. . . rein controls the reins that ought to control him   **129 as please** as it
pleases   **130 As well . . . as** both . . . and.   **apparent** evident, real

RICHARD
   I hope the King made peace with all of us;
   And the compact is firm and true in me.
RIVERS
   And so in me, and so, I think, in all.
   Yet since it is but green, it should be put
   To no apparent likelihood of breach,
   Which haply by much company might be urged.   137
   Therefore I say with noble Buckingham
   That it is meet so few should fetch the Prince.   139
HASTINGS   And so say I.
RICHARD
   Then be it so; and go we to determine
   Who they shall be that straight shall post to Ludlow.   142
   Madam, and you, my sister, will you go
   To give your censures in this business?   144
QUEEN ELIZABETH, DUCHESS   With all our hearts.   145
        Exeunt. Manent Buckingham and Richard.

BUCKINGHAM
   My lord, whoever journeys to the Prince,
   For God's sake let not us two stay at home;
   For by the way I'll sort occasion,   148
   As index to the story we late talked of,   149
   To part the Queen's proud kindred from the Prince.
RICHARD
   My other self, my counsel's consistory,   151
   My oracle, my prophet! My dear cousin,
   I, as a child, will go by thy direction.
   Toward Ludlow then, for we'll not stay behind.
                     Exeunt.

❖

2.3   *Enter one Citizen at one door, and another at*
       the other.

FIRST CITIZEN
   Good morrow, neighbor. Whither away so fast?

---

137 haply perhaps. **urged** encouraged, provoked **139 meet** fitting
142 post hasten **144 censures** judgments **145 s.d. Manent** they remain
onstage **148 by** on. **sort** find, contrive **149 index** prologue. **late**
lately **151 consistory** council chamber

2.3. Location: London. A street.

SECOND CITIZEN
 I promise you, I scarcely know myself.   2
 Hear you the news abroad?
FIRST CITIZEN   Yes, that the King is dead.
SECOND CITIZEN
 Ill news, by 'r Lady; seldom comes the better.   5
 I fear, I fear 'twill prove a giddy world.   6

Enter another Citizen.

THIRD CITIZEN
 Neighbors, God speed!
FIRST CITIZEN   Give you good morrow, sir.
THIRD CITIZEN
 Doth the news hold of good King Edward's death?   8
SECOND CITIZEN
 Ay, sir, it is too true, God help the while!
THIRD CITIZEN
 Then, masters, look to see a troublous world.   10
FIRST CITIZEN
 No, no; by God's good grace his son shall reign.
THIRD CITIZEN
 Woe to that land that's governed by a child!   12
SECOND CITIZEN
 In him there is a hope of government,
 Which in his nonage, council under him,   14
 And in his full and ripened years, himself,
 No doubt shall then, and till then, govern well.
FIRST CITIZEN
 So stood the state when Henry the Sixth
 Was crowned in Paris but at nine months old.
THIRD CITIZEN
 Stood the state so? No, no, good friends, God wot,   19
 For then this land was famously enriched
 With politic grave counsel; then the King   21
 Had virtuous uncles to protect His Grace.

2 promise assure   **5 by 'r Lady** by Our Lady.   **seldom comes the better**
i.e., rarely is the news good   **6 giddy** mad   **8 Doth the news hold** is the
news true   **10 troublous** troubled, disorderly   **12 Woe . . . child** (Compare Ecclesiastes 10:16: "Woe to thee, O land, when thy king is a
child.")   **14 nonage** minority.   **council under him** i.e., aided by wise
counsel   **19 wot** knows   **21 politic** sagacious

FIRST CITIZEN
  Why, so hath this, both by his father and mother.
THIRD CITIZEN
  Better it were they all came by his father,
  Or by his father there were none at all;
  For emulation who shall now be nearest   26
  Will touch us all too near, if God prevent not.
  O, full of danger is the Duke of Gloucester,
  And the Queen's sons and brothers haught and proud! 29
  And were they to be ruled, and not to rule,
  This sickly land might solace as before.   31
FIRST CITIZEN
  Come, come, we fear the worst. All will be well.
THIRD CITIZEN
  When clouds are seen, wise men put on their cloaks;
  When great leaves fall, then winter is at hand;
  When the sun sets, who doth not look for night?
  Untimely storms make men expect a dearth.
  All may be well; but if God sort it so,   37
  'Tis more than we deserve or I expect.
SECOND CITIZEN
  Truly, the hearts of men are full of fear.
  You cannot reason almost with a man   40
  That looks not heavily and full of dread.   41
THIRD CITIZEN
  Before the days of change, still is it so.   42
  By a divine instinct men's minds mistrust   43
  Ensuing danger; as, by proof, we see   44
  The water swell before a boisterous storm.
  But leave it all to God. Whither away?
SECOND CITIZEN
  Marry, we were sent for to the justices.
THIRD CITIZEN
  And so was I. I'll bear you company.   *Exeunt.*

❖

26 **emulation** ambitious rivalry   **29 haught** haughty   **31 solace** be
happy, have comfort   **37 sort** dispose   **40 You . . . man** there is scarcely
anyone with whom you can talk   **41 heavily** sad   **42 still** ever
43 mistrust suspect, fear   **44 proof** experience

2.4   *Enter [the] Archbishop [of York], [the] young*
         [Duke of] York, the Queen [Elizabeth], and the
         Duchess [of York].

ARCHBISHOP
    Last night, I hear, they lay at Stony Stratford,   1
    And at Northampton they do rest tonight.   2
    Tomorrow, or next day, they will be here.
DUCHESS
    I long with all my heart to see the Prince.
    I hope he is much grown since last I saw him.
QUEEN ELIZABETH
    But I hear, no; they say my son of York
    Has almost overta'en him in his growth.
YORK
    Ay, Mother, but I would not have it so.
DUCHESS
    Why, my young cousin? It is good to grow.
YORK
    Grandam, one night as we did sit at supper,
    My uncle Rivers talked how I did grow
    More than my brother. "Ay," quoth my uncle
        Gloucester,
    "Small herbs have grace; great weeds do grow apace."   13
    And since, methinks, I would not grow so fast,   14
    Because sweet flowers are slow and weeds make haste.
DUCHESS
    Good faith, good faith, the saying did not hold   16
    In him that did object the same to thee.   17
    He was the wretched'st thing when he was young,
    So long a-growing and so leisurely,
    That, if his rule were true, he should be gracious.
ARCHBISHOP
    And so no doubt he is, my gracious madam.

2.4. Location: London. The royal court.
1 Stony Stratford town in Buckinghamshire **2 Northampton** town in
Northamptonshire, and hence farther from London than Stony Stratford. The Prince was taken back to Northampton after the arrest of
Rivers, Grey, and Vaughan; but since the Archbishop does not yet know
of that arrest, his speech doesn't make sense dramatically. The quartos
reverse the order in which the two towns are named. **13 grace** virtuous
qualities. **apace** rapidly **14 since** ever since **16 hold** pertain **17 In
him** i.e., in Richard. **object . . . to** i.e., apply this saying to

DUCHESS
  I hope he is, but yet let mothers doubt.
YORK
  Now, by my troth, if I had been remembered,   23
  I could have given my uncle's Grace a flout   24
  To touch his growth nearer than he touched mine.   25
DUCHESS
  How, my young York? I prithee, let me hear it.
YORK
  Marry, they say my uncle grew so fast
  That he could gnaw a crust at two hours old;
  'Twas full two years ere I could get a tooth.
  Grandam, this would have been a biting jest.   30
DUCHESS
  I prithee, pretty York, who told thee this?
YORK Grandam, his nurse.
DUCHESS
  His nurse? Why, she was dead ere thou wast born.
YORK
  If 'twere not she, I cannot tell who told me.
QUEEN ELIZABETH
  A parlous boy! Go to, you are too shrewd.   35
DUCHESS
  Good madam, be not angry with the child.
QUEEN ELIZABETH Pitchers have ears.   37

Enter a Messenger.

ARCHBISHOP
  Here comes a messenger. What news?
MESSENGER
  Such news, my lord, as grieves me to report.
QUEEN ELIZABETH
  How doth the Prince?
MESSENGER   Well, madam, and in health.
DUCHESS What is thy news?

---

23 troth truth, faith.   **been remembered** considered, recollected   **24 my
. . . flout** His Grace, my uncle, a mocking gibe   **25 touch . . . nearer** i.e.,
taunt him about his growth more tellingly   **30 biting** (with a play on the
idea of teething)   **35 parlous** cunning, precocious.   **Go to** (An expression of remonstrance.)   **shrewd** sharp-tongued   **37 Pitchers have ears**
i.e., little pitchers have large ears. (Proverbial.)

MESSENGER
Lord Rivers and Lord Grey are sent to Pomfret,   42
And with them Sir Thomas Vaughan, prisoners.

DUCHESS
Who hath committed them?

MESSENGER   The mighty dukes
Gloucester and Buckingham.

ARCHBISHOP   For what offense?

MESSENGER
The sum of all I can, I have disclosed.   46
Why or for what the nobles were committed
Is all unknown to me, my gracious lord.

QUEEN ELIZABETH
Ay me, I see the ruin of my house!
The tiger now hath seized the gentle hind;   50
Insulting tyranny begins to jut   51
Upon the innocent and aweless throne.   52
Welcome, destruction, blood, and massacre!
I see, as in a map, the end of all.   54

DUCHESS
Accursèd and unquiet wrangling days,
How many of you have mine eyes beheld!
My husband lost his life to get the crown,
And often up and down my sons were tossed
For me to joy and weep their gain and loss;
And being seated, and domestic broils   60
Clean overblown, themselves the conquerors
Make war upon themselves, brother to brother,
Blood to blood, self against self. O, preposterous   63
And frantic outrage, end thy damnèd spleen,   64
Or let me die, to look on death no more!

QUEEN ELIZABETH
Come, come, my boy, we will to sanctuary.   66
Madam, farewell.

DUCHESS   Stay, I will go with you.

---

42 Pomfret the castle at Pontefract in Yorkshire   **46 can** know   **50 hind**
doe   **51 jut** encroach   **52 aweless** inspiring no awe (because of the youth
of the King)   **54 map** i.e., of future events   **60 seated** i.e., on the
throne   **63 preposterous** monstrous, perverse   **64 spleen** i.e., malice,
hatred   **66 sanctuary** (Queen Elizabeth, with her son, daughters, and
kinsmen, lodged in the precincts of Westminster Abbey, which served as
a legal refuge for criminals and persons in danger of their lives.)

QUEEN ELIZABETH
  You have no cause.
ARCHBISHOP [*To the Queen*]   My gracious lady, go,
  And thither bear your treasure and your goods.
  For my part, I'll resign unto Your Grace
  The seal I keep; and so betide to me   71
  As well I tender you and all of yours!   72
  Go, I'll conduct you to the sanctuary.   *Exeunt.*

❖

71 seal seal of office   **71–72 so . . . you** may my fortunes be measured
by the care I take of you

3.1 *The trumpets sound. Enter [the] young Prince [Edward], the Dukes of Gloucester and Buckingham, [Lord] Cardinal [Bourchier, Catesby], etc.*

BUCKINGHAM
    Welcome, sweet Prince, to London, to your chamber.   1
RICHARD
    Welcome, dear cousin, my thoughts' sovereign!
    The weary way hath made you melancholy.
PRINCE EDWARD
    No, uncle, but our crosses on the way   4
    Have made it tedious, wearisome, and heavy.
    I want more uncles here to welcome me.   6
RICHARD
    Sweet Prince, the untainted virtue of your years
    Hath not yet dived into the world's deceit.
    Nor more can you distinguish of a man
    Than of his outward show—which, God he knows,
    Seldom or never jumpeth with the heart.   11
    Those uncles which you want were dangerous.
    Your Grace attended to their sugared words
    But looked not on the poison of their hearts.
    God keep you from them, and from such false friends!
PRINCE EDWARD
    God keep me from false friends! But they were none.
RICHARD
    My lord, the Mayor of London comes to greet you.

        Enter [the] Lord Mayor [and his train].

MAYOR
    God bless Your Grace with health and happy days!
PRINCE EDWARD
    I thank you, good my lord, and thank you all.
            [*The Mayor and his train stand aside.*]
    I thought my mother and my brother York
    Would long ere this have met us on the way.
    Fie, what a slug is Hastings, that he comes not   22

3.1. Location: London. A street.
1 chamber (London was called the *camera regis,* or King's chamber.)
4 crosses vexations (i.e., the arrests of the Queen's kindred)   **6 want**
(1) lack (2) wish   **11 jumpeth** agrees   **22 slug** sluggard

To tell us whether they will come or no!

Enter Lord Hastings.

BUCKINGHAM
And, in good time, here comes the sweating lord.

PRINCE EDWARD
Welcome, my lord. What, will our mother come?

HASTINGS
On what occasion God he knows, not I,   26
The Queen your mother and your brother York
Have taken sanctuary. The tender Prince
Would fain have come with me to meet Your Grace
But by his mother was perforce withheld.   30

BUCKINGHAM
Fie, what an indirect and peevish course   31
Is this of hers! Lord Cardinal, will Your Grace
Persuade the Queen to send the Duke of York
Unto his princely brother presently?   34
If she deny, Lord Hastings, go with him,
And from her jealous arms pluck him perforce.   36

CARDINAL
My lord of Buckingham, if my weak oratory
Can from his mother win the Duke of York,
Anon expect him here; but if she be obdurate   39
To mild entreaties, God in heaven forbid
We should infringe the holy privilege
Of blessèd sanctuary! Not for all this land
Would I be guilty of so deep a sin.

BUCKINGHAM
You are too senseless-obstinate, my lord,
Too ceremonious and traditional.   45
Weigh it but with the grossness of this age,   46
You break not sanctuary in seizing him.
The benefit thereof is always granted
To those whose dealings have deserved the place
And those who have the wit to claim the place.
This Prince hath neither claimed it nor deserved it,
And therefore, in mine opinion, cannot have it.

26 On what occasion for what reason   **30 perforce** by force   **31 peevish** perverse   **34 presently** at once   **36 jealous** suspicious   **39 Anon** shortly   **45 ceremonious** bound by formalities   **46 grossness** lack of moral refinement

Then, taking him from thence that is not there,
You break no privilege nor charter there.
Oft have I heard of sanctuary men,
But sanctuary children never till now.

CARDINAL
My lord, you shall o'errule my mind for once.
Come on, Lord Hastings, will you go with me?

HASTINGS   I go, my lord.

PRINCE EDWARD
Good lords, make all the speedy haste you may.
                    [*Exeunt Cardinal and Hastings.*]
Say, uncle Gloucester, if our brother come,
Where shall we sojourn till our coronation?   62

RICHARD
Where it seems best unto your royal self.
If I may counsel you, some day or two
Your Highness shall repose you at the Tower;   65
Then where you please and shall be thought most fit
For your best health and recreation.

PRINCE EDWARD
I do not like the Tower of any place.   68
Did Julius Caesar build that place, my lord?

BUCKINGHAM
He did, my gracious lord, begin that place,
Which, since, succeeding ages have re-edified.   71

PRINCE EDWARD
Is it upon record, or else reported   72
Successively from age to age, he built it?

BUCKINGHAM   Upon record, my gracious lord.

PRINCE EDWARD
But say, my lord, it were not registered,   75
Methinks the truth should live from age to age,
As 'twere retailed to all posterity,   77
Even to the general all-ending day.   78

---

62 sojourn reside   **65 Tower** (Although in the fifteenth century, the
historical time this play represents, the Tower of London was a royal
palace, by Shakespeare's day it had acquired a sinister reputation.)
68 of any place of all places   **71 re-edified** rebuilt   **72 upon record** in
the written record.   **reported** i.e., by oral tradition   **75 say** suppose.
registered written down   **77 retailed** handed down from one to another   **78 general . . . day** Day of Judgment

RICHARD [*Aside*]
  So wise so young, they say, do never live long.
PRINCE EDWARD   What say you, uncle?
RICHARD
  I say, without characters fame lives long.   81
  [*Aside*.] Thus, like the formal Vice, Iniquity,   82
  I moralize two meanings in one word.   83
PRINCE EDWARD
  That Julius Caesar was a famous man;
  With what his valor did enrich his wit,   85
  His wit set down to make his valor live.   86
  Death makes no conquest of this conqueror,
  For now he lives in fame, though not in life.
  I'll tell you what, my cousin Buckingham—
BUCKINGHAM   What, my gracious lord?
PRINCE EDWARD
  An if I live until I be a man,   91
  I'll win our ancient right in France again
  Or die a soldier, as I lived a king.
RICHARD [*Aside*]
  Short summers lightly have a forward spring.   94

Enter young York, Hastings, [and the] Cardinal.

BUCKINGHAM
  Now, in good time, here comes the Duke of York.
PRINCE EDWARD
  Richard of York, how fares our loving brother?   96
YORK
  Well, my dread lord—so must I call you now.   97

---

81 without characters (1) even lacking written records (2) even in the absence of moral character   **82 formal Vice** i.e., the conventional Vice figure of the morality play, a comic tempter to evil who would habitually *moralize two meanings in one word*, that is, play on double meanings in a single phrase as Richard does in the phrase *live long*
83 moralize interpret, discover   **85–86 With . . . live** i.e., taking his military achievements, whereby his bravery as a soldier added stature to his understanding, he used his understanding to set down in writing an account (the *Gallic Wars*) that would make his valor immortal.
With what with that with which   **91 An if** if   **94 lightly** commonly, often   **forward** early. (Alludes to Edward's precociousness.)   **96 our** i.e., my. (The royal "we.")   **97 dread** inspiring reverential fear (as King)

PRINCE EDWARD

   Ay, brother, to our grief, as it is yours.

   Too late he died that might have kept that title,   99

   Which by his death hath lost much majesty.

RICHARD

   How fares our cousin, noble lord of York?

YORK

   I thank you, gentle uncle. O my lord,

   You said that idle weeds are fast in growth;   103

   The Prince my brother hath outgrown me far.

RICHARD

   He hath, my lord.

YORK   And therefore is he idle?

RICHARD

   O my fair cousin, I must not say so.

YORK

   Then he is more beholding to you than I.   107

RICHARD

   He may command me as my sovereign,

   But you have power in me as in a kinsman.

YORK

   I pray you, uncle, give me this dagger.

RICHARD

   My dagger, little cousin? With all my heart.

PRINCE EDWARD   A beggar, brother?

YORK

   Of my kind uncle, that I know will give;   112

   And being but a toy, which is no grief to give.   113

RICHARD

   A greater gift than that I'll give my cousin.

YORK

   A greater gift? O, that's the sword to it.

RICHARD

   Ay, gentle cousin, were it light enough.

YORK

   O, then I see you will part but with light gifts;   118

   In weightier things you'll say a beggar nay.

RICHARD

   It is too heavy for Your Grace to wear.

99 late lately   **103 idle** useless   **107 beholding** beholden   **112 that** who   **113 toy** trifle   **118 light** trivial

YORK
    I weigh it lightly, were it heavier.   121
RICHARD
    What, would you have my weapon, little lord?
YORK
    I would, that I might thank you as you call me.
RICHARD   How?
YORK   Little.
PRINCE EDWARD
    My lord of York will still be cross in talk.   126
    Uncle, Your Grace knows how to bear with him.
YORK
    You mean, to bear me, not to bear with me.
    Uncle, my brother mocks both you and me:
    Because that I am little, like an ape,
    He thinks that you should bear me on your shoulders. 131
BUCKINGHAM [*Aside to Hastings*]
    With what a sharp-provided wit he reasons!   132
    To mitigate the scorn he gives his uncle,
    He prettily and aptly taunts himself.
    So cunning and so young is wonderful.
RICHARD
    My lord, will 't please you pass along?
    Myself and my good cousin Buckingham
    Will to your mother, to entreat of her
    To meet you at the Tower and welcome you.
YORK
    What, will you go unto the Tower, my lord?
PRINCE EDWARD
    My Lord Protector needs will have it so.
YORK
    I shall not sleep in quiet at the Tower.
RICHARD   Why, what should you fear?
YORK
    Marry, my uncle Clarence' angry ghost.
    My grandam told me he was murdered there.

---

121 weigh it lightly consider it a trifle (playing on the literal meanings
of "light" and "heavy")   **126 still** always.   **cross in talk** perverse in
twisting words   **131 bear me . . . shoulders** (At fairs, the bear commonly carried an ape on his back. The speech is doubtless an allusion
to Richard's hump, and puns triply on *bear with*, put up with, *bear*,
carry, and *bear*, an animal.)   **132 sharp-provided** keenly thought out

PRINCE EDWARD   I fear no uncles dead.

RICHARD   Nor none that live, I hope.

PRINCE EDWARD

An if they live, I hope I need not fear.   148
But come, my lord; with a heavy heart,
Thinking on them, go I unto the Tower.   150
            [*A sennet.*] *Exeunt Prince, York, Hastings,*
                [*Cardinal, and others*]. *Manent Richard,*
                    Buckingham, [*and Catesby*].

BUCKINGHAM

Think you, my lord, this little prating York   151
Was not incensèd by his subtle mother   152
To taunt and scorn you thus opprobriously?

RICHARD

No doubt, no doubt. O, 'tis a parlous boy,   154
Bold, quick, ingenious, forward, capable.
He is all the mother's, from the top to toe.

BUCKINGHAM

Well, let them rest. Come hither, Catesby.   157
Thou art sworn as deeply to effect what we intend
As closely to conceal what we impart.
Thou know'st our reasons urged upon the way.   160
What think'st thou? Is it not an easy matter
To make William, Lord Hastings, of our mind
For the installment of this noble duke   163
In the seat royal of this famous isle?

CATESBY

He for his father's sake so loves the Prince   165
That he will not be won to aught against him.

BUCKINGHAM

What think'st thou, then, of Stanley? Will not he?

CATESBY

He will do all in all as Hastings doth.

BUCKINGHAM

Well, then, no more but this: go, gentle Catesby,

---

148 An if if.   **they** i.e., Rivers and Grey. (Grey was in fact Edward's stepbrother, not his uncle.)   **150 s.d. sennet** trumpet call to announce the
approach or departure of processions.   **Manent** they remain onstage
151 prating babbling   **152 incensèd** incited   **154 parlous** clever, but also
dangerous   **157 let them rest** leave them for the moment   **160 the way**
i.e., the journey to London from Ludlow   **163 installment** installation
165 He . . . sake i.e., Hastings for King Edward IV's sake

And, as it were far off, sound thou Lord Hastings   170
How he doth stand affected to our purpose,   171
And summon him tomorrow to the Tower
To sit about the coronation.   173
If thou dost find him tractable to us,
Encourage him, and tell him all our reasons.
If he be leaden, icy, cold, unwilling,
Be thou so too; and so break off the talk,
And give us notice of his inclination.
For we tomorrow hold divided councils,   179
Wherein thyself shalt highly be employed.

RICHARD
Commend me to Lord William. Tell him, Catesby,   181
His ancient knot of dangerous adversaries   182
Tomorrow are let blood at Pomfret Castle;   183
And bid my lord, for joy of this good news,
Give Mistress Shore one gentle kiss the more.   185

BUCKINGHAM
Good Catesby, go, effect this business soundly.   186

CATESBY
My good lords both, with all the heed I can.   187

RICHARD
Shall we hear from you, Catesby, ere we sleep?

CATESBY   You shall, my lord.

RICHARD
At Crosby House, there shall you find us both.
                                        Exit Catesby.

BUCKINGHAM
Now, my lord, what shall we do if we perceive
Lord Hastings will not yield to our complots?   192

RICHARD
Chop off his head. Something we will determine.
And look when I am king, claim thou of me   194

---

170 sound sound out   **171 doth stand affected** is disposed   **173 sit** sit
in council   **179 divided councils** (While the regular Council meets
about the coronation, Richard plans also to have his own private consultation at Crosby House.)   **181 Lord William** i.e., Hastings   **182 knot**
group, company   **183 are let blood** i.e., will be executed   **185 Mistress
Shore** (According to Thomas More, Jane Shore had become the mistress
of Hastings after the death of Edward IV.)   **186 soundly** thoroughly
187 heed attention, care   **192 complots** conspiracies   **194 look when** as
soon as

The earldom of Hereford, and all the movables   195
Whereof the King my brother was possessed.

BUCKINGHAM
I'll claim that promise at Your Grace's hand.

RICHARD
And look to have it yielded with all kindness.
Come, let us sup betimes, that afterwards   199
We may digest our complots in some form.   *Exeunt.* 200

❖

3.2   *Enter a Messenger to the door of Hastings.*

MESSENGER   My lord! My lord!
HASTINGS [*Within*]   Who knocks?
MESSENGER   One from the Lord Stanley.
HASTINGS [*Within*]   What is 't o'clock?   4
MESSENGER   Upon the stroke of four.

Enter Lord Hastings.

HASTINGS
Cannot my Lord Stanley sleep these tedious nights?

MESSENGER
So it appears by that I have to say.
First, he commends him to your noble self.

HASTINGS   What then?

MESSENGER
Then certifies your lordship that this night   10
He dreamt the boar had razèd off his helm.   11
Besides, he says there are two councils kept,
And that may be determined at the one
Which may make you and him to rue at th' other.   14
Therefore he sends to know your lordship's pleasure,
If you will presently take horse with him   16

195 **movables** personal property, other than real estate   **199 betimes**
soon   **200 digest** arrange, perfect.   **form** good order

3.2. Location: Before Lord Hastings's house.
4 What is 't o'clock what time is it   **10 certifies** informs   **11 boar** i.e.,
Richard.   **razèd** torn, slashed   **14 at th' other** i.e., the regular Council
meeting in the Tower, in which Hastings and Stanley will participate
16 presently immediately

And with all speed post with him toward the north,
To shun the danger that his soul divines.

HASTINGS
Go, fellow, go, return unto thy lord.
Bid him not fear the separated council.
His honor and myself are at the one,
And at the other is my good friend Catesby,
Where nothing can proceed that toucheth us
Whereof I shall not have intelligence.   24
Tell him his fears are shallow, without instance.   25
And for his dreams, I wonder he's so simple
To trust the mockery of unquiet slumbers.   27
To fly the boar before the boar pursues   28
Were to incense the boar to follow us,
And make pursuit where he did mean no chase.
Go, bid thy master rise and come to me,
And we will both together to the Tower,
Where he shall see the boar will use us kindly.

MESSENGER
I'll go, my lord, and tell him what you say.   *Exit.*

    Enter Catesby.

CATESBY
Many good morrows to my noble lord!

HASTINGS
Good morrow, Catesby. You are early stirring.
What news, what news, in this our tottering state?

CATESBY
It is a reeling world, indeed, my lord,
And I believe will never stand upright
Till Richard wear the garland of the realm.

HASTINGS
How? Wear the garland? Dost thou mean the crown?

CATESBY Ay, my good lord.

HASTINGS
I'll have this crown of mine cut from my shoulders   43
Before I'll see the crown so foul misplaced.
But canst thou guess that he doth aim at it?

---

24 intelligence information   **25 without instance** lacking evidence
27 To as to   **28 fly** flee   **43 crown** i.e., head. (Recalls Stanley's dream in
l. 11 and anticipates Hastings's execution by beheading.)

CATESBY

Ay, on my life, and hopes to find you forward   46
Upon his party for the gain thereof;   47
And thereupon he sends you this good news,
That this same very day your enemies,
The kindred of the Queen, must die at Pomfret.

HASTINGS

Indeed, I am no mourner for that news,
Because they have been still my adversaries.   52
But that I'll give my voice on Richard's side
To bar my master's heirs in true descent,
God knows I will not do it, to the death.   55

CATESBY

God keep your lordship in that gracious mind!

HASTINGS

But I shall laugh at this a twelvemonth hence,
That they which brought me in my master's hate,   58
I live to look upon their tragedy.   59
Well, Catesby, ere a fortnight make me older,
I'll send some packing that yet think not on 't.

CATESBY

'Tis a vile thing to die, my gracious lord,
When men are unprepared and look not for it.

HASTINGS

O, monstrous, monstrous! And so falls it out
With Rivers, Vaughan, Grey; and so 'twill do
With some men else, that think themselves as safe
As thou and I—who, as thou know'st, are dear
To princely Richard and to Buckingham.

CATESBY

The princes both make high account of you—   69
[*Aside.*] For they account his head upon the Bridge.   70

HASTINGS

I know they do, and I have well deserved it.

Enter Lord Stanley, [Earl of Derby].

46 forward inclined   **47 Upon his party** on his side   **52 still** always
55 to the death i.e., though I lose my life   **58 they which** i.e., regarding those who   **59 I live** i.e., I shall live   **69 high account** great
estimation. (The quibble on *high* appears in the next line.)   **70 account**
expect, reckon (punning on *account* in the previous line).   **the Bridge**
London Bridge, on a tower of which the heads of traitors were
exposed

Come on, come on, where is your boar spear, man?
Fear you the boar, and go so unprovided?

STANLEY
My lord, good morrow. Good morrow, Catesby.
You may jest on, but, by the Holy Rood,   75
I do not like these several councils, I.   76 .

HASTINGS   My lord,
I hold my life as dear as you do yours,
And never in my days, I do protest,
Was it so precious to me as 'tis now.
Think you, but that I know our state secure,
I would be so triumphant as I am?

STANLEY
The lords at Pomfret, when they rode from London,   83
Were jocund and supposed their states were sure,   84
And they indeed had no cause to mistrust;
But yet you see how soon the day o'ercast.   86
This sudden stab of rancor I misdoubt.   87
Pray God, I say, I prove a needless coward!
What, shall we toward the Tower? The day is spent.   89

HASTINGS
Come, come, have with you. Wot you what, my lord?   90
Today the lords you talk of are beheaded.

STANLEY
They, for their truth, might better wear their heads   92
Than some that have accused them wear their hats.   93
But come, my lord, let's away.   94

          Enter a Pursuivant.

HASTINGS
Go on before. I'll talk with this good fellow.
          Exit Lord Stanley, [Earl of Derby,] and Catesby.
How now, sirrah? How goes the world with thee?   96

PURSUIVANT
The better that your lordship please to ask.

75 the Holy Rood i.e., the cross of Christ   **76 several** separate
83 London (An error for "Ludlow"?)   **84 jocund** merry   **86 o'ercast**
became overcast   **87 misdoubt** fear (i.e., I fear more such sudden
attacks)   **89 spent** i.e., well advanced (although the scene began at 4:00
A.M.)   **90 have with you** I'll go with you.   **Wot** know   **92 for their truth**
as far as their honesty is concerned   **93 wear their hats** i.e., hold their
offices   **94 s.d. Pursuivant** attendant on a herald with authority to serve
warrants   **96 sirrah** (Form of address to inferiors.)

HASTINGS
  I tell thee, man, 'tis better with me now
  Than when thou mett'st me last where now we meet.
  Then was I going prisoner to the Tower,
  By the suggestion of the Queen's allies;   101
  But now, I tell thee—keep it to thyself—
  This day those enemies are put to death,
  And I in better state than e'er I was.
PURSUIVANT
  God hold it, to your honor's good content!   105
HASTINGS
  Gramercy, fellow. There, drink that for me.   106
                      Throws him his purse.
PURSUIVANT   I thank your honor.   *Exit Pursuivant.*

    Enter a Priest.

PRIEST
  Well met, my lord. I am glad to see your honor.
HASTINGS
  I thank thee, good Sir John, with all my heart.   109
  I am in your debt for your last exercise;   110
  Come the next Sabbath, and I will content you.   111
                  [He whispers in his ear.]
PRIEST   I'll wait upon your lordship.

    Enter Buckingham.

BUCKINGHAM
  What, talking with a priest, Lord Chamberlain?
  Your friends at Pomfret, they do need the priest;
  Your honor hath no shriving work in hand.   115
HASTINGS
  Good faith, and when I met this holy man,
  The men you talk of came into my mind.
  What, go you toward the Tower?
BUCKINGHAM
  I do, my lord, but long I cannot stay there.
  I shall return before your lordship thence.

---

101 suggestion instigation **105 hold it** continue it (i.e., the better state) **106 Gramercy** much thanks **109 Sir** (Common title for addressing any priest.) **110 exercise** sermon or religious service **111 content** compensate **115 shriving work** confession and absolution

HASTINGS
    Nay, like enough, for I stay dinner there.   121
BUCKINGHAM [*Aside*]
    And supper too, although thou know'st it not.—
    Come, will you go?
HASTINGS   I'll wait upon your lordship.

                                                Exeunt.

                              ❧

3.3   *Enter Sir Richard Ratcliffe, with Halberds,
           carrying the nobles [Rivers, Grey, and Vaughan]
           to death at Pomfret.*

RATCLIFFE   Come, bring forth the prisoners.
RIVERS
    Sir Richard Ratcliffe, let me tell thee this:
    Today shalt thou behold a subject die
    For truth, for duty, and for loyalty.
GREY
    God bless the Prince from all the pack of you!   5
    A knot you are of damnèd bloodsuckers.   6
VAUGHAN
    You live that shall cry woe for this hereafter.
RATCLIFFE
    Dispatch. The limit of your lives is out.   8
RIVERS
    O Pomfret, Pomfret! O thou bloody prison,
    Fatal and ominous to noble peers!
    Within the guilty closure of thy walls   11
    Richard the Second here was hacked to death;
    And, for more slander to thy dismal seat,   13
    We give to thee our guiltless blood to drink.
GREY
    Now Margaret's curse is fall'n upon our heads,
    When she exclaimed on Hastings, you, and I,
    For standing by when Richard stabbed her son.

---

121 stay stay for

3.3. Location: Pomfret (Pontefract) Castle.
5 pack gang   **6 knot** group   **8 Dispatch** hurry.   **is out** has been
reached   **11 closure** enclosure   **13 for . . . seat** i.e., to add further to the
evil reputation of this place

RIVERS

    Then cursed she Richard, then cursed she Buckingham,
    Then cursed she Hastings. O, remember, God,
    To hear her prayer for them, as now for us!
    And for my sister and her princely sons,
    Be satisfied, dear God, with our true blood,
    Which, as thou know'st, unjustly must be spilt.

RATCLIFFE

    Make haste. The hour of death is expiate.   24

RIVERS

    Come, Grey, come, Vaughan, let us here embrace.

                                 [They embrace.]
    Farewell, until we meet again in heaven.   *Exeunt.*

❖

3.4   *Enter Buckingham, [Lord Stanley, Earl of]*
        Derby, Hastings, Bishop of Ely, Norfolk,
        Ratcliffe, Lovell, with others, at a table.

HASTINGS

    Now, noble peers, the cause why we are met
    Is to determine of the coronation.   2
    In God's name, speak. When is the royal day?

BUCKINGHAM

    Is all things ready for the royal time?

STANLEY

    It is, and wants but nomination.   5

ELY

    Tomorrow, then, I judge a happy day.   6

BUCKINGHAM

    Who knows the Lord Protector's mind herein?
    Who is most inward with the noble Duke?   8

ELY

    Your Grace, we think, should soonest know his mind.

BUCKINGHAM

    We know each other's faces; for our hearts,   10

24 expiate fully come

3.4. Location: London. The Tower.
2 determine of decide upon **5 nomination** naming of a date **6 happy**
favorable **8 inward** intimate **10 for** as for

He knows no more of mine than I of yours,
Or I of his, my lord, than you of mine.
Lord Hastings, you and he are near in love.
HASTINGS
I thank His Grace, I know he loves me well;
But, for his purpose in the coronation,
I have not sounded him, nor he delivered
His gracious pleasure any way therein.
But you, my honorable lords, may name the time,
And in the Duke's behalf I'll give my voice,   19
Which I presume he'll take in gentle part.

  Enter [Richard, Duke of] Gloucester.

ELY
In happy time, here comes the Duke himself.
RICHARD
My noble lords and cousins all, good morrow.
I have been long a sleeper; but I trust
My absence doth neglect no great design   24
Which by my presence might have been concluded.
BUCKINGHAM
Had you not come upon your cue, my lord,
William, Lord Hastings, had pronounced your part,
I mean your voice for crowning of the King.
RICHARD
Than my Lord Hastings no man might be bolder.
His lordship knows me well, and loves me well.—
My lord of Ely, when I was last in Holborn,
I saw good strawberries in your garden there.
I do beseech you send for some of them.
ELY
Marry, and will, my lord, with all my heart.
        Exit Bishop.
RICHARD
Cousin of Buckingham, a word with you.
        [Drawing him aside.]
Catesby hath sounded Hastings in our business,
And finds the testy gentleman so hot
That he will lose his head ere give consent

19 voice vote **24 neglect** cause the neglect of

His master's child, as worshipfully he terms it,   39
Shall lose the royalty of England's throne.

BUCKINGHAM
Withdraw yourself awhile. I'll go with you.
                    Exeunt [Richard and Buckingham].

STANLEY
We have not yet set down this day of triumph.
Tomorrow, in my judgment, is too sudden,
For I myself am not so well provided   44
As else I would be, were the day prolonged.   45

        Enter the Bishop of Ely.

ELY
Where is my lord the Duke of Gloucester?
I have sent for these strawberries.

HASTINGS
His Grace looks cheerfully and smooth this morning;   48
There's some conceit or other likes him well   49
When that he bids good morrow with such spirit.
I think there's never a man in Christendom
Can lesser hide his love or hate than he,
For by his face straight shall you know his heart.

STANLEY
What of his heart perceive you in his face
By any livelihood he showed today?   55

HASTINGS
Marry, that with no man here he is offended;
For, were he, he had shown it in his looks.

STANLEY   I pray God he be not, I say.

        Enter Richard and Buckingham.

RICHARD
I pray you all, tell me what they deserve
That do conspire my death with devilish plots
Of damnèd witchcraft, and that have prevailed
Upon my body with their hellish charms?

HASTINGS
The tender love I bear Your Grace, my lord,   63

---

39 worshipfully reverently. (Said contemptuously.)   **44 provided**
equipped   **45 prolonged** postponed   **48 smooth** pleasant   **49 conceit**
fancy, idea.   **likes** pleases   **55 livelihood** liveliness   **63 tender** dear

Makes me most forward in this princely presence   64
To doom th' offenders, whosoe'er they be:
I say, my lord, they have deservèd death.

RICHARD
Then be your eyes the witness of their evil.
                        [*He bares his arm.*]
Look how I am bewitched! Behold, mine arm
Is like a blasted sapling withered up.   69
And this is Edward's wife, that monstrous witch,
Consorted with that harlot strumpet Shore,   71
That by their witchcraft thus have markèd me.

HASTINGS
If they have done this deed, my noble lord—

RICHARD
If? Thou protector of this damnèd strumpet,
Talk'st thou to me of "ifs"? Thou art a traitor.
Off with his head! Now, by Saint Paul I swear,
I will not dine until I see the same.
Lovell and Ratcliffe, look that it be done.   78
The rest that love me, rise and follow me.   79
                Exeunt. Manent Lovell and Ratcliffe,
                        with the Lord Hastings.

HASTINGS
Woe, woe for England! Not a whit for me,
For I, too fond, might have prevented this.   81
Stanley did dream the boar did raze our helms,
And I did scorn it and disdain to fly.
Three times today my footcloth horse did stumble,   84
And started, when he looked upon the Tower,
As loath to bear me to the slaughterhouse.
O, now I need the priest that spake to me!
I now repent I told the pursuivant,
As too triumphing, how mine enemies
Today at Pomfret bloodily were butchered,
And I myself secure in grace and favor.
O Margaret, Margaret, now thy heavy curse
Is lighted on poor Hastings' wretched head!

---

64 forward eager **69 blasted** shriveled **71 Consorted** associated **78 look**
see to it **79 s.d. Manent** they remain onstage **81 fond** foolish **84 footcloth** large, richly ornamented cloth laid over the back of a horse and
hanging to the ground on each side. **stumble** (An omen of misfortune.)

RATCLIFFE

Come, come, dispatch. The Duke would be at dinner.
Make a short shrift. He longs to see your head.   95

HASTINGS

O momentary grace of mortal men,   96
Which we more hunt for than the grace of God!
Who builds his hope in air of your good looks   98
Lives like a drunken sailor on a mast,
Ready with every nod to tumble down
Into the fatal bowels of the deep.

LOVELL

Come, come, dispatch. 'Tis bootless to exclaim.   102

HASTINGS

O bloody Richard! Miserable England!
I prophesy the fearfull'st time to thee
That ever wretched age hath looked upon.
Come, lead me to the block; bear him my head.
They smile at me who shortly shall be dead.

Exeunt.

❖

3.5   *Enter Richard [Duke of Gloucester] and*
Buckingham in rotten armor, marvelous
ill-favored.

RICHARD

Come, cousin, canst thou quake and change thy color,
Murder thy breath in middle of a word,   2
And then again begin, and stop again,
As if thou wert distraught and mad with terror?

BUCKINGHAM

Tut, I can counterfeit the deep tragedian,
Speak and look back, and pry on every side,   6
Tremble and start at wagging of a straw;
Intending deep suspicion, ghastly looks   8

---

95 shrift confession   **96 grace** favor, fortune   **98 Who** he who.   **in . . .
looks** on the insubstantial foundation of your favor   **102 bootless**
unavailing

3.5. Location: London. The Tower.
s.d. rotten rusty.   **marvelous ill-favored** remarkably unattractive
2 Murder i.e., stop, catch   **6 pry** peer   **8 Intending** pretending

Are at my service, like enforcèd smiles;
And both are ready in their offices,   10
At any time, to grace my stratagems.
But what, is Catesby gone?
RICHARD
He is; and, see, he brings the Mayor along.

Enter the Mayor and Catesby.

BUCKINGHAM   Lord Mayor—
RICHARD   Look to the drawbridge there!
BUCKINGHAM   Hark, a drum!
RICHARD   Catesby, o'erlook the walls.   [*Exit Catesby.*] 17
BUCKINGHAM
Lord Mayor, the reason we have sent—
RICHARD
Look back, defend thee, here are enemies!
BUCKINGHAM
God and our innocence defend and guard us!

Enter Lovell and Ratcliffe, with Hastings' head.

RICHARD
Be patient. They are friends, Ratcliffe and Lovell.
LOVELL
Here is the head of that ignoble traitor,
The dangerous and unsuspected Hastings.
RICHARD
So dear I loved the man that I must weep.
I took him for the plainest harmless creature
That breathed upon the earth a Christian;
Made him my book wherein my soul recorded   27
The history of all her secret thoughts.
So smooth he daubed his vice with show of virtue
That, his apparent open guilt omitted—   30
I mean, his conversation with Shore's wife—   31
He lived from all attainder of suspects.   32
BUCKINGHAM
Well, well, he was the covert'st sheltered traitor 33

---

10 offices uses, functions   **17 o'erlook** inspect   **27 book** i.e., table book
or diary   **30 his . . . omitted** apart from his manifest open guilt   **31 conversation** sexual intimacy   **32 from** free from.   **attainder of suspects**
stain of suspicion   **33 covert'st** most secret.   **sheltered** most hidden

That ever lived. Look ye, my Lord Mayor,
Would you imagine, or almost believe,   35
Were 't not that, by great preservation   36
We live to tell it, that the subtle traitor
This day had plotted, in the Council House,
To murder me and my good lord of Gloucester?

MAYOR   Had he done so?   39

RICHARD

What, think you we are Turks or infidels?
Or that we would, against the form of law,
Proceed thus rashly in the villain's death,
But that the extreme peril of the case,
The peace of England, and our persons' safety,
Enforced us to this execution?

MAYOR

Now fair befall you! He deserved his death,   47
And your good graces both have well proceeded   48
To warn false traitors from the like attempts.

BUCKINGHAM

I never looked for better at his hands
After he once fell in with Mistress Shore.
Yet had we not determined he should die
Until your lordship came to see his end,
Which now the loving haste of these our friends,
Something against our meaning, have prevented;   55
Because, my lord, we would have had you heard   56
The traitor speak and timorously confess
The manner and the purpose of his treasons,
That you might well have signified the same
Unto the citizens, who haply may   60
Misconster us in him and wail his death.   61

MAYOR

But, my good lord, Your Grace's words shall serve
As well as I had seen and heard him speak.   63
And do not doubt, right noble princes both,

---

35 almost even   **36 great preservation** i.e., fortunate escape through
forestalling evil   **39 Had he** would he have   **47 fair** good fortune
48 proceeded done   **55 Something . . . meaning** somewhat contrary to our
intent.   **have prevented** has anticipated   **56 we . . . heard** we would have
wished you to have heard   **60 haply** perhaps   **61 Misconster . . . him** i.e.,
misconstrue our intentions regarding him   **63 as** as if

But I'll acquaint our duteous citizens   65
With all your just proceedings in this cause.
RICHARD
And to that end we wished your lordship here,
T' avoid the censures of the carping world.
BUCKINGHAM
Which since you come too late of our intent,   69
Yet witness what you hear we did intend.   70
And so, my good Lord Mayor, we bid farewell.

                                              Exit Mayor.

RICHARD
Go, after, after, cousin Buckingham.
The Mayor towards Guildhall hies him in all post.   73
There, at your meet'st advantage of the time,   74
Infer the bastardy of Edward's children.   75
Tell them how Edward put to death a citizen
Only for saying he would make his son
Heir to the Crown—meaning indeed his house,   78
Which, by the sign thereof, was termèd so.
Moreover, urge his hateful luxury   80
And bestial appetite in change of lust,   81
Which stretched unto their servants, daughters, wives,
Even where his raging eye or savage heart,
Without control, lusted to make a prey.
Nay, for a need, thus far come near my person: 85
Tell them, when that my mother went with child   86
Of that insatiate Edward, noble York   87
My princely father then had wars in France,
And by true computation of the time
Found that the issue was not his begot—
Which well appearèd in his lineaments,   91

---

65 duteous obedient **69 of** regarding **70 witness** bear witness to
73 Guildhall central hall for municipal affairs. **hies** hastens. **post**
haste **74 meet'st advantage** most suitable opportunity **75 Infer** allege,
adduce **78 the Crown** i.e., a tavern in Cheapside identified by the sign
of the Crown. (King Edward is portrayed as having been so sensitive to
possible rivals that he put to death a man merely for naming his son
heir to "the Crown," even though the poor fellow innocently meant
nothing more than his own tavern. The story is from Sir Thomas More's
History of King Richard III.) **80 luxury** lechery **81 in . . . lust** i.e.,
constantly desiring new mistresses **85 for a need** if necessary
86–87 went . . . Of was pregnant with **91 lineaments** features

Being nothing like the noble Duke my father.
Yet touch this sparingly, as 'twere far off,
Because, my lord, you know my mother lives.

BUCKINGHAM
Doubt not, my lord, I'll play the orator   95
As if the golden fee for which I plead   96
Were for myself. And so, my lord, adieu.

RICHARD
If you thrive well, bring them to Baynard's Castle, 98
Where you shall find me well accompanied
With reverend fathers and well-learnèd bishops.

BUCKINGHAM
I go; and towards three or four o'clock
Look for the news that the Guildhall affords.
                              Exit Buckingham.

RICHARD
Go, Lovell, with all speed to Doctor Shaw.   103
[*To Ratcliffe.*] Go thou to Friar Penker. Bid them both   104
Meet me within this hour at Baynard's Castle.
                    Exeunt [all but Richard].
Now will I go to take some privy order   106
To draw the brats of Clarence out of sight,
And to give order that no manner person   108
Have any time recourse unto the princes.   *Exit.* 109

♣

3.6   *Enter a Scrivener [with a paper in his hand].*

SCRIVENER
Here is the indictment of the good Lord Hastings,
Which in a set hand fairly is engrossed   2
That it may be today read o'er in Paul's.   3

95 Doubt fear   **96 golden fee** i.e., the crown   **98 Baynard's Castle**
residence on the north bank of the Thames. It was founded by Baynard,
a nobleman in the time of the Conquest, and belonged to Richard's
father.   **103, 104 Doctor Shaw, Friar Penker** (Well-known divines who
delivered sermons in Richard's favor.)   **106 take . . . order** make some
secret disposition   **108 no manner person** no one at all   **109 any time**
at any time.   **recourse** access, admittance

3.6. Location: London. A street.
2 in . . . engrossed is written out in a style of script used for legal
documents   **3 Paul's** i.e., Saint Paul's Cathedral

And mark how well the sequel hangs together: 4
Eleven hours I have spent to write it over,
For yesternight by Catesby was it sent me;
The precedent was full as long a-doing.   7
And yet within these five hours Hastings lived,
Untainted, unexamined, free, at liberty.   9
Here's a good world the while! Who is so gross   10
That cannot see this palpable device?
Yet who's so bold but says he sees it not?
Bad is the world, and all will come to naught
When such ill dealing must be seen in thought.   14

                                            Exit.

❖

3.7   *Enter Richard [Duke of Gloucester] and*
            Buckingham, at several doors.

RICHARD
How now, how now, what say the citizens?
BUCKINGHAM
Now, by the holy mother of our Lord,
The citizens are mum, say not a word.
RICHARD
Touched you the bastardy of Edward's children?   4
BUCKINGHAM
I did; with his contract with Lady Lucy   5
And his contract by deputy in France;   6
Th' unsatiate greediness of his desire   7
And his enforcement of the city wives;   8
His tyranny for trifles; his own bastardy,   9

---

4 the sequel what follows   **7 precedent** prepared indictment serving as
a first draft   **9 Untainted** unaccused   **10 the while** meanwhile.   **gross**
dull, stupid   **14 seen in thought** i.e., perceived in silence

3.7. Location: The courtyard of Baynard's Castle.
s.d. several separate   **4 Touched you** did you deal with, touch upon,
discuss   **5 contract** betrothal.   **Lady Lucy** Elizabeth Lucy (by whom
Edward had a child, though there was no formal contract of betrothal)   **6 deputy** (See *3 Henry VI*, 3.3.49 ff., where Warwick, as deputy,
contracts with Louis XI of France for the marriage of King Edward to
Lady Bona, sister of the French queen.)   **7 unsatiate** insatiable
8 enforcement forcible seduction   **9 tyranny for trifles** harsh punishment of minor offenses

As being got, your father then in France,   10
And his resemblance, being not like the Duke.
Withal I did infer your lineaments,   12
Being the right idea of your father   13
Both in your form and nobleness of mind;
Laid open all your victories in Scotland,   15
Your discipline in war, wisdom in peace,   16
Your bounty, virtue, fair humility;
Indeed, left nothing fitting for your purpose
Untouched or slightly handled in discourse.
And when mine oratory drew toward end,
I bid them that did love their country's good
Cry, "God save Richard, England's royal king!"
RICHARD   And did they so?
BUCKINGHAM
No, so God help me, they spake not a word,
But, like dumb statues or breathing stones,
Stared each on other and looked deadly pale.
Which when I saw, I reprehended them,
And asked the Mayor what meant this willful silence.
His answer was, the people were not used
To be spoke to but by the Recorder.   30
Then he was urged to tell my tale again:
"Thus saith the Duke, thus hath the Duke inferred"—   32
But nothing spake in warrant from himself.   33
When he had done, some followers of mine own,
At lower end of the hall, hurled up their caps,
And some ten voices cried, "God save King Richard!"
And thus I took the vantage of those few: 37
"Thanks, gentle citizens and friends," quoth I,
"This general applause and cheerful shout
Argues your wisdoms and your love to Richard"—
And even here brake off and came away.   41
RICHARD
What tongueless blocks were they! Would they not
    speak?

10 got begot   12 Withal in addition. infer mention, relate. **lineaments** features   13 **right idea** exact image   15 **victories in Scotland**
(Richard had commanded the English forces in the Scottish expedition
of 1482.)   16 **discipline** skill, training   30 **the Recorder** a city official
32 **inferred** alleged, asserted   33 **in . . . himself** on his own authority
37 **vantage of** opportunity from   41 **brake** broke

BUCKINGHAM   No, by my troth, my lord.

RICHARD
Will not the Mayor then and his brethren come?

BUCKINGHAM
The Mayor is here at hand. Intend some fear;   45
Be not you spoke with but by mighty suit.   46
And look you get a prayer book in your hand,
And stand between two churchmen, good my lord,
For on that ground I'll make a holy descant;   49
And be not easily won to our requests.
Play the maid's part: still answer nay and take it.

RICHARD
I go; and if you plead as well for them
As I can say nay to thee for myself,
No doubt we'll bring it to a happy issue.   54

BUCKINGHAM
Go, go, up to the leads. The Lord Mayor knocks.   55

                          [*Exit Richard.*]

   Enter the Mayor, [aldermen,] and citizens.

Welcome, my lord. I dance attendance here;   56
I think the Duke will not be spoke withal.   57

        Enter Catesby.

Now, Catesby, what says your lord to my request?

CATESBY
He doth entreat Your Grace, my noble lord,
To visit him tomorrow or next day.
He is within, with two right reverend fathers,
Divinely bent to meditation,
And in no worldly suits would he be moved
To draw him from his holy exercise.

BUCKINGHAM
Return, good Catesby, to the gracious Duke.
Tell him myself, the Mayor and aldermen,
In deep designs, in matter of great moment,
No less importing than our general good,   68

---

45 Intend pretend   **46 mighty suit** importunate entreaty   **49 descant**
variation composed on a theme (called a *ground*)   **54 issue** outcome
55 leads flat lead coverings for roof; hence, the roof itself   **56 dance**
attendance i.e., am kept waiting   **57 withal** with   **68 No less importing**
concerned with nothing less

Are come to have some conference with His Grace.

CATESBY
I'll signify so much unto him straight.   *Exit.*

BUCKINGHAM
Aha, my lord, this prince is not an Edward!
He is not lolling on a lewd love bed
But on his knees at meditation;
Not dallying with a brace of courtesans
But meditating with two deep divines;   75
Not sleeping, to engross his idle body,   76
But praying, to enrich his watchful soul.
Happy were England, would this virtuous prince
Take on His Grace the sovereignty thereof;
But sure I fear we shall not win him to it.

MAYOR
Marry, God defend His Grace should say us nay!   81

BUCKINGHAM
I fear he will.—Here Catesby comes again.

> *Enter Catesby.*

Now, Catesby, what says His Grace?

CATESBY   My lord,
He wonders to what end you have assembled
Such troops of citizens to come to him,
His Grace not being warned thereof before.
He fears, my lord, you mean no good to him.

BUCKINGHAM
Sorry I am my noble cousin should
Suspect me that I mean no good to him.
By heaven, we come to him in perfect love,
And so once more return and tell His Grace.
                    Exit [Catesby].
When holy and devout religious men
Are at their beads, 'tis much to draw them thence,   93
So sweet is zealous contemplation.   94

> *Enter Richard aloft, between two bishops.*
> *[Catesby returns to the main stage.]*

---

75 deep learned   **76 engross** fatten   **81 defend** forbid   **93 beads** i.e., prayers   **94 s.d. aloft** i.e., on the gallery above the stage, rear. (The tiring-house facade in this scene is imagined to be the facade of Baynard's Castle.)

MAYOR
  See where His Grace stands, 'tween two clergymen!
BUCKINGHAM
  Two props of virtue for a Christian prince,
  To stay him from the fall of vanity.   97
  And, see, a book of prayer in his hand,
  True ornaments to know a holy man.—   99
  Famous Plantagenet, most gracious prince,
  Lend favorable ear to our requests,
  And pardon us the interruption
  Of thy devotion and right Christian zeal.
RICHARD
  My lord, there needs no such apology.
  I do beseech Your Grace to pardon me,
  Who, earnest in the service of my God,
  Deferred the visitation of my friends.
  But, leaving this, what is Your Grace's pleasure?
BUCKINGHAM
  Even that, I hope, which pleaseth God above
  And all good men of this ungoverned isle.
RICHARD
  I do suspect I have done some offense
  That seems disgracious in the city's eye,   112
  And that you come to reprehend my ignorance.
BUCKINGHAM
  You have, my lord. Would it might please Your Grace,
  On our entreaties, to amend your fault!
RICHARD
  Else wherefore breathe I in a Christian land?   116
BUCKINGHAM
  Know then, it is your fault that you resign
  The supreme seat, the throne majestical,
  The sceptered office of your ancestors,   119
  Your state of fortune and your due of birth,   120
  The lineal glory of your royal house,
  To the corruption of a blemished stock;
  Whiles, in the mildness of your sleepy thoughts,   123
  Which here we waken to our country's good,

97 stay prevent. **of** caused by   **99 ornaments** i.e., the bishops as well
as the prayer book   **112 disgracious** unbecoming, displeasing   **116 Else**
otherwise   **119 office** duty   **120 state of fortune** position to which
fortune entitles you   **123 sleepy** reposeful

The noble isle doth want her proper limbs;   125
Her face defaced with scars of infamy,
Her royal stock graft with ignoble plants,   127
And almost shouldered in the swallowing gulf   128
Of dark forgetfulness and deep oblivion.
Which to recure, we heartily solicit   130
Your gracious self to take on you the charge
And kingly government of this your land—
Not as protector, steward, substitute,
Or lowly factor for another's gain,   134
But as successively from blood to blood,   135
Your right of birth, your empery, your own.   136
For this, consorted with the citizens,   137
Your very worshipful and loving friends,
And by their vehement instigation,
In this just cause come I to move Your Grace.

RICHARD
I cannot tell if to depart in silence
Or bitterly to speak in your reproof
Best fitteth my degree or your condition.   143
If not to answer, you might haply think   144
Tongue-tied ambition, not replying, yielded   145
To bear the golden yoke of sovereignty,
Which fondly you would here impose on me.   147
If to reprove you for this suit of yours,
So seasoned with your faithful love to me,   149
Then on the other side I checked my friends.   150
Therefore, to speak, and to avoid the first,
And then, in speaking, not to incur the last,
Definitively thus I answer you.   153
Your love deserves my thanks, but my desert
Unmeritable shuns your high request.   155
First, if all obstacles were cut away,
And that my path were even to the crown   157

125 **want her proper** lack its own   127 **graft** engrafted   128 **shouldered in** jostled into, or immersed up to the shoulders in   130 **recure** restore, make whole   134 **factor** agent   135 **successively** in order of succession   136 **empery** realm of your sole rule   137 **consorted** associated, leagued   143 **degree** rank. **condition** social status   144 **haply** perhaps   145 **Tongue-tied** silent (i.e., silence gives consent. **yielded** consented   147 **fondly** foolishly   149 **seasoned** i.e., made agreeable or palatable   150 **checked** rebuked, i.e., would rebuke   153 **Definitively** once and for all   155 **Unmeritable** undeserving   157 **even** smooth

As the ripe revenue and due of birth,   158
Yet so much is my poverty of spirit,
So mighty and so many my defects,
That I would rather hide me from my greatness—   161
Being a bark to brook no mighty sea—   162
Than in my greatness covet to be hid   163
And in the vapor of my glory smothered.
But, God be thanked, there is no need of me,
And much I need to help you, were there need.   166
The royal tree hath left us royal fruit,
Which, mellowed by the stealing hours of time,
Will well become the seat of majesty,
And make, no doubt, us happy by his reign.
On him I lay that you would lay on me,
The right and fortune of his happy stars,
Which God defend that I should wring from him!   173

BUCKINGHAM
My lord, this argues conscience in Your Grace;
But the respects thereof are nice and trivial,   175
All circumstances well considerèd.
You say that Edward is your brother's son.
So say we too, but not by Edward's wife;
For first was he contract to Lady Lucy—   179
Your mother lives a witness to his vow—   180
And afterward by substitute betrothed   181
To Bona, sister to the King of France.   182
These both put off, a poor petitioner,
A care-crazed mother to a many sons,
A beauty-waning and distressèd widow,
Even in the afternoon of her best days,
Made prize and purchase of his wanton eye,   187

---

158 ripe revenue possession ready to be inherited **161 my greatness**
i.e., my claim to the throne **162 bark** ship. **brook** endure **163 Than
. . . hid** than wish to be enveloped in and protected by my greatness, i.e.,
the throne **166 I need** I lack the ability requisite **173 defend** forbid
175 respects thereof considerations by which you support your argument. **nice** overscrupulous **179 contract** contracted **180 Your . . .
vow** (According to the chronicles, Richard's mother, in opposing
Edward's intention of marrying Lady Grey because it was interfering
with the negotiations for his marriage to Lady Bona of Savoy, asserted
that Lady Elizabeth Lucy was already Edward's trothplight wife.
Cf. 3.5.75 and 3.7.6.) **181 substitute** proxy **182 sister** i.e., sister-in-law,
the Queen's sister **187 purchase** booty

Seduced the pitch and height of his degree   188
To base declension and loathed bigamy.   189
By her, in his unlawful bed, he got
This Edward, whom our manners call the Prince.   191
More bitterly could I expostulate,   192
Save that, for reverence to some alive,   193
I give a sparing limit to my tongue.
Then, good my lord, take to your royal self   195
This proffered benefit of dignity;
If not to bless us and the land withal,
Yet to draw forth your noble ancestry   198
From the corruption of abusing times
Unto a lineal true-derivèd course.

MAYOR
Do, good my lord; your citizens entreat you.

BUCKINGHAM
Refuse not, mighty lord, this proffered love.

CATESBY
O, make them joyful, grant their lawful suit!

RICHARD
Alas, why would you heap this care on me?
I am unfit for state and majesty.
I do beseech you, take it not amiss;
I cannot nor I will not yield to you.

BUCKINGHAM
If you refuse it—as, in love and zeal,   208
Loath to depose the child, your brother's son;
As well we know your tenderness of heart   210
And gentle, kind, effeminate remorse,   211
Which we have noted in you to your kindred
And equally indeed to all estates—   213
Yet know, whe'er you accept our suit or no,   214

---

188 Seduced debased. **pitch** height, highest point (as in falconry).
degree rank **189 declension** falling away from a high standard.
bigamy (Edward was not only bound by previous contracts as indicated
in lines 178–182 above, but, by marrying a widow, entered into a union
that canon law regarded as bigamous.) **191 manners** sense of polite-
ness **192 expostulate** discuss, dilate **193 some alive** i.e., the Duchess
of York. (See 3.5.93–94.) **195 good my lord** my good lord **198 draw
forth** rescue **208 as** from being **210 As . . . know** since we know
well **211 kind, effeminate remorse** natural, tender pity **213 estates**
ranks (i.e., this virtue is found in Richard's treatment of everyone)
214 whe'er whether

Your brother's son shall never reign our king,
But we will plant some other in the throne
To the disgrace and downfall of your house.
And in this resolution here we leave you.—
Come, citizens. Zounds! I'll entreat no more.

RICHARD

O, do not swear, my lord of Buckingham.

Exeunt [*Buckingham, Mayor, aldermen,
and the citizens*].

CATESBY

Call him again, sweet prince. Accept their suit.
If you deny them, all the land will rue it.

RICHARD

Will you enforce me to a world of cares?
Call them again. I am not made of stones,
But penetrable to your kind entreaties,
Albeit against my conscience and my soul.

Enter Buckingham and the rest.

Cousin of Buckingham, and sage, grave men,
Since you will buckle fortune on my back,
To bear her burden, whe'er I will or no,
I must have patience to endure the load.
But if black scandal or foul-faced reproach
Attend the sequel of your imposition,   232
Your mere enforcement shall acquittance me   233
From all the impure blots and stains thereof;
For God doth know, and you may partly see,
How far I am from the desire of this.

MAYOR

God bless Your Grace! We see it and will say it.

RICHARD

In saying so, you shall but say the truth.

BUCKINGHAM

Then I salute you with this royal title:
Long live Richard, England's worthy king!

MAYOR AND CITIZENS   Amen.

BUCKINGHAM

Tomorrow may it please you to be crowned?

232 your imposition the duty that you lay upon me   **233 mere** absolute,
downright.   **acquittance** acquit

RICHARD
  Even when you please, for you will have it so.
BUCKINGHAM
  Tomorrow, then, we will attend Your Grace.
  And so most joyfully we take our leave.
RICHARD [*To the Bishops*]
  Come, let us to our holy work again.—
  Farewell, my cousin; farewell, gentle friends.   *Exeunt*.

♣

4.1   *Enter [at one door] the Queen [Elizabeth,] the*
         Duchess of York, and Marquess [of] Dorset; [at
         another door] Anne, Duchess of Gloucester,
         [leading Lady Margaret Plantagenet, Clarence's
         young daughter].

DUCHESS
  Who meets us here? My niece Plantagenet   1
  Led in the hand of her kind aunt of Gloucester?
  Now, for my life, she's wandering to the Tower,   3
  On pure heart's love to greet the tender Prince.   4
  Daughter, well met.
ANNE   God give Your Graces both   5
  A happy and a joyful time of day!
QUEEN ELIZABETH
  As much to you, good sister. Whither away?   7
ANNE
  No farther than the Tower, and, as I guess,
  Upon the like devotion as yourselves,   9
  To gratulate the gentle princes there.   10
QUEEN ELIZABETH
  Kind sister, thanks. We'll enter all together.

     Enter [Brackenbury] the Lieutenant.

  And, in good time, here the Lieutenant comes.
  Master Lieutenant, pray you, by your leave,
  How doth the Prince and my young son of York?
BRACKENBURY
  Right well, dear madam. By your patience,
  I may not suffer you to visit them;   16
  The King hath strictly charged the contrary.
QUEEN ELIZABETH
  The King? Who's that?
BRACKENBURY   I mean the Lord Protector.
QUEEN ELIZABETH
  The Lord protect him from that kingly title!

4.1. Location: London. Before the Tower.
1 niece i.e., granddaughter   **3 for my life** i.e., I'd bet my life   **4 On** out
of.   **tender** young   **5 Daughter** i.e., daughter-in-law   **7 sister** i.e., sister-
in-law   **9 like devotion** same devout errand   **10 gratulate** greet, salute
16 suffer permit

Hath he set bounds between their love and me?   20
I am their mother; who shall bar me from them?

DUCHESS
I am their father's mother; I will see them.

ANNE
Their aunt I am in law, in love their mother;
Then bring me to their sights. I'll bear thy blame
And take thy office from thee, on my peril.   25

BRACKENBURY
No, madam, no; I may not leave it so.   26
I am bound by oath, and therefore pardon me.

Exit Lieutenant.

Enter [Lord] Stanley, [Earl of Derby].

STANLEY
Let me but meet you, ladies, one hour hence,
And I'll salute Your Grace of York as mother,   29
And reverend looker-on, of two fair queens.   30
[*To Anne.*] Come, madam, you must straight to
   Westminster,
There to be crownèd Richard's royal queen.

QUEEN ELIZABETH   Ah, cut my lace asunder,   33
That my pent heart may have some scope to beat,
Or else I swoon with this dead-killing news!

ANNE
Despiteful tidings! O unpleasing news!   36

DORSET
Be of good cheer. Mother, how fares Your Grace?

QUEEN ELIZABETH
O Dorset, speak not to me, get thee gone!
Death and destruction dogs thee at thy heels;
Thy mother's name is ominous to children.
If thou wilt outstrip death, go cross the seas
And live with Richmond, from the reach of hell.   42
Go, hie thee, hie thee from this slaughterhouse,   43

20 bounds barriers   **25 take . . . thee** i.e., relieve you of the responsibility   **26 leave it** i.e., fail to perform my office   **29 mother** i.e., mother-in-law (of Elizabeth as widow of Edward, and of Anne as wife of King Richard)   **30 looker-on** beholder.   **two fair queens** i.e., Elizabeth and Anne, since Anne's husband, Richard, is about to be crowned)   **33 cut my lace** i.e., of my bodice   **36 Despiteful** cruel   **42 with Richmond** i.e., with Henry Tudor, Earl of Richmond, at this time in Brittany   **43 hie** hasten

Lest thou increase the number of the dead
And make me die the thrall of Margaret's curse,   45
Nor mother, wife, nor England's counted queen.   46

STANLEY
Full of wise care is this your counsel, madam.
[*To Dorset.*] Take all the swift advantage of the hours.
You shall have letters from me to my son   49
In your behalf, to meet you on the way.   50
Be not ta'en tardy by unwise delay.   51

DUCHESS
O ill-dispersing wind of misery!   52
O my accursèd womb, the bed of death!
A cockatrice hast thou hatched to the world,   54
Whose unavoided eye is murderous.

STANLEY
Come, madam, come. I in all haste was sent.

ANNE
And I with all unwillingness will go.
O, would to God that the inclusive verge   58
Of golden metal that must round my brow
Were red-hot steel, to sear me to the brains!
Anointed let me be with deadly venom   61
And die ere men can say, "God save the Queen!"

QUEEN ELIZABETH
Go, go, poor soul, I envy not thy glory,
To feed my humor wish thyself no harm.   64

ANNE
No? Why? When he that is my husband now
Came to me, as I followed Henry's corpse,
When scarce the blood was well washed from his hands
Which issued from my other angel husband
And that dear saint which then I weeping followed—
O, when, I say, I looked on Richard's face,
This was my wish: "Be thou," quoth I, "accurst

45 **thrall** subject, victim   46 **Nor** neither.   **counted** accepted, esteemed
49 **You . . . from me** i.e., I'll dispatch letters in your behalf.   **son** i.e.,
stepson   50 **meet . . . way** i.e., catch up with you   51 **ta'en** taken, caught
52 **ill-dispersing** scattering ill fortune   54 **cockatrice** basilisk. (See 1.2.153,
note.)   58 **inclusive verge** enclosing circle, i.e., the crown, here likened to
an instrument of torture used to punish regicides or other criminals
61 **Anointed** (Anne desires to be anointed with poison rather than with
holy oil, as in the ceremony of coronation.)   64 **To . . . harm** I do not wish
you harm just to satisfy my vengeful mood

For making me, so young, so old a widow!   72
And, when thou wedd'st, let sorrow haunt thy bed;
And be thy wife—if any be so mad—
More miserable by the life of thee
Than thou hast made me by my dear lord's death!''
Lo, ere I can repeat this curse again,
Within so small a time, my woman's heart
Grossly grew captive to his honey words   79
And proved the subject of mine own soul's curse,
Which hitherto hath held mine eyes from rest;
For never yet one hour in his bed
Did I enjoy the golden dew of sleep,
But with his timorous dreams was still awaked.   84
Besides, he hates me for my father Warwick,   85
And will, no doubt, shortly be rid of me.

QUEEN ELIZABETH
Poor heart, adieu! I pity thy complaining.

ANNE
No more than with my soul I mourn for yours.

DORSET
Farewell, thou woeful welcomer of glory!

ANNE
Adieu, poor soul, that tak'st thy leave of it!

DUCHESS [*To Dorset*]
Go thou to Richmond, and good fortune guide thee!
[*To Anne.*] Go thou to Richard, and good angels
    tend thee!
[*To Queen Elizabeth.*] Go thou to sanctuary, and
    good thoughts possess thee!
I to my grave, where peace and rest lie with me!
Eighty-odd years of sorrow have I seen,
And each hour's joy wracked with a week of teen.   96
                              [*They start to go.*]

QUEEN ELIZABETH
Stay, yet look back with me unto the Tower.
Pity, you ancient stones, those tender babes
Whom envy hath immured within your walls—   99
Rough cradle for such little pretty ones!
Rude ragged nurse, old sullen playfellow   101

72 so old a widow i.e., destined to live so long as a widow   **79 Grossly**
stupidly   **84 timorous** full of fears.   **still** continually   **85 for** on account
of   **96 wracked** destroyed.   **teen** woe   **99 envy** malice   **101 Rude** rough

For tender princes, use my babies well!
So foolish sorrows bids your stones farewell. *Exeunt.*

❖

4.2   *Sound a sennet. Enter Richard, in pomp;*
             Buckingham, Catesby, Ratcliffe, Lovell, [a Page,
             and others].

KING RICHARD
   Stand all apart. Cousin of Buckingham!   1
              [The others stand aside, out of earshot.]
BUCKINGHAM   My gracious sovereign?
KING RICHARD
   Give me thy hand.
        Sound [trumpets. Here he ascends the throne.]
          Thus high, by thy advice
   And thy assistance, is King Richard seated.
   But shall we wear these glories for a day?
   Or shall they last, and we rejoice in them?
BUCKINGHAM
   Still live they, and forever let them last!
KING RICHARD
   Ah, Buckingham, now do I play the touch,   8
   To try if thou be current gold indeed: 9
   Young Edward lives. Think now what I would speak.
BUCKINGHAM   Say on, my loving lord.
KING RICHARD
   Why, Buckingham, I say I would be king.
BUCKINGHAM
   Why, so you are, my thrice-renownèd lord.
KING RICHARD
   Ha! Am I king? 'Tis so. But Edward lives.
BUCKINGHAM
   True, noble prince.
KING RICHARD   O bitter consequence,   15

4.2. Location: London. The royal court.
1 apart aside   **8 play the touch** play the part of a touchstone (to test the
quality of gold)   **9 current** sterling, genuine   **15 bitter consequence** i.e.,
intolerable answer to my words, and an intolerable fact

That Edward still should live "true, noble prince"!   16
Cousin, thou wast not wont to be so dull.   17
Shall I be plain? I wish the bastards dead,
And I would have it suddenly performed.   19
What sayst thou now? Speak suddenly; be brief.
BUCKINGHAM   Your Grace may do your pleasure.
KING RICHARD
Tut, tut, thou art all ice; thy kindness freezes.
Say, have I thy consent that they shall die?
BUCKINGHAM
Give me some little breath, some pause, dear lord,
Before I positively speak in this.
I will resolve you herein presently. *Exit Buckingham.* 26
CATESBY [*To those standing aside*]
The King is angry. See, he gnaws his lip.
KING RICHARD
I will converse with iron-witted fools   28
And unrespective boys. None are for me   29
That look into me with considerate eyes.   30
High-reaching Buckingham grows circumspect.   31
Boy!
PAGE [*Approaching*]   My lord?
KING RICHARD
Know'st thou not any whom corrupting gold
Will tempt unto a close exploit of death?   35
PAGE
My lord, I know a discontented gentleman
Whose humble means match not his haughty spirit.
Gold were as good as twenty orators,
And will, no doubt, tempt him to anything.
KING RICHARD
What is his name?
PAGE   His name, my lord, is Tyrrel.
KING RICHARD
I partly know the man. Go call him hither, boy.
                                        Exit [Page].

16 **"true, noble prince"** (Richard mockingly repeats Buckingham's evasive
reply in l. 15 and applies it to the irritating fact that young Edward still lives
and is a noble prince.)   17 **wast not wont** used not   19 **suddenly** swiftly
26 **resolve** answer   28 **converse** associate.   **iron-witted** unfeeling, stupid
29 **unrespective** thoughtless   30 **considerate** deliberate, reflective
31 **High-reaching** ambitious.   **circumspect** cautious   35 **close** secret

The deep-revolving witty Buckingham   42
No more shall be the neighbor to my counsels.
Hath he so long held out with me untired,
And stops he now for breath? Well, be it so.

Enter [Lord] Stanley, [Earl of Derby].

How now, Lord Stanley? What's the news?
STANLEY   Know, my loving lord,
    The Marquess Dorset, as I hear, is fled
    To Richmond, in the parts where he abides.
                                        [He stands apart.]
KING RICHARD
    Come hither, Catesby. Rumor it abroad
    That Anne my wife is very grievous sick;
    I will take order for her keeping close.   52
    Inquire me out some mean poor gentleman,   53
    Whom I will marry straight to Clarence' daughter.
    The boy is foolish, and I fear not him.   55
    Look how thou dream'st! I say again, give out
    That Anne my queen is sick and like to die.   57
    About it, for it stands me much upon   58
    To stop all hopes whose growth may damage me.
                                        [Exit Catesby.]
    I must be married to my brother's daughter,   60
    Or else my kingdom stands on brittle glass.
    Murder her brothers, and then marry her—
    Uncertain way of gain! But I am in
    So far in blood that sin will pluck on sin.   64
    Tear-falling pity dwells not in this eye.

Enter [Page, with] Tyrrel.

Is thy name Tyrrel?
TYRREL
    James Tyrrel, and your most obedient subject.

42 deep-revolving deeply scheming. **witty** cunning   **52 take** give.
close imprisoned, confined   **53 mean poor** of low degree   **55 boy** i.e.,
Clarence's eldest son, Edward Plantagenet, Earl of Warwick   **57 like**
likely   **58 stands . . . upon** is a matter of the utmost importance to
me   **60 brother's daughter** i.e., Elizabeth of York, daughter to Edward
IV, who will in fact later become the queen of Henry VII; see 4.5.7–9 and
5.5.29–31   **64 pluck on** draw on

KING RICHARD
　Art thou, indeed?
TYRREL　　　　　　　Prove me, my gracious lord.　　68
KING RICHARD
　Dar'st thou resolve to kill a friend of mine?
TYRREL　Please you;　　　　　　　　　　　　70
　But I had rather kill two enemies.
KING RICHARD
　Why, there thou hast it: two deep enemies,
　Foes to my rest and my sweet sleep's disturbers
　Are they that I would have thee deal upon—　　74
　Tyrrel, I mean those bastards in the Tower.
TYRREL
　Let me have open means to come to them,　　76
　And soon I'll rid you from the fear of them.
KING RICHARD
　Thou sing'st sweet music. Hark, come hither, Tyrrel.
　Go, by this token. [*He gives him a token.*] Rise, and
　　lend thine ear.　　　　　　　　　*Whispers.*
　There is no more but so. Say it is done,
　And I will love thee and prefer thee for it.　　81
TYRREL　I will dispatch it straight.　　　　*Exit.*

　　　　Enter Buckingham.

BUCKINGHAM
　My lord, I have considered in my mind
　The late request that you did sound me in.　　84
KING RICHARD
　Well, let that rest. Dorset is fled to Richmond.
BUCKINGHAM　I hear the news, my lord.
KING RICHARD
　Stanley, he is your wife's son. Well, look unto it.　　87
BUCKINGHAM
　My lord, I claim the gift, my due by promise,
　For which your honor and your faith is pawned:　　89
　Th' earldom of Hereford and the movables

68 Prove test　**70 Please** if it please　**74 deal upon** proceed against
76 open unhampered　**81 prefer** promote, advance　**84 late** recent.
sound me in ask me about　**87 he** i.e., Richmond　**89 pawned** pledged

Which you have promisèd I shall possess.

KING RICHARD
    Stanley, look to your wife. If she convey
    Letters to Richmond, you shall answer it.   93

BUCKINGHAM
    What says Your Highness to my just request?

KING RICHARD
    I do remember me, Henry the Sixth
    Did prophesy that Richmond should be king,
    When Richmond was a little peevish boy.
    A king! Perhaps, perhaps—

BUCKINGHAM My lord!

KING RICHARD
    How chance the prophet could not at that time
    Have told me, I being by, that I should kill him?   101

BUCKINGHAM
    My lord, your promise for the earldom!

KING RICHARD
    Richmond! When last I was at Exeter,
    The Mayor in courtesy showed me the castle
    And called it Rougemont, at which name I started,   105
    Because a bard of Ireland told me once
    I should not live long after I saw Richmond.

BUCKINGHAM My lord!

KING RICHARD Ay, what's o'clock?   109

BUCKINGHAM
    I am thus bold to put Your Grace in mind
    Of what you promised me.

KING RICHARD Well, but what's o'clock?

BUCKINGHAM Upon the stroke of ten.

KING RICHARD Well, let it strike.

BUCKINGHAM Why let it strike?

KING RICHARD
    Because that, like a jack, thou keep'st the stroke   116

---

93 it i.e., for it   **101 by** nearby   **105 Rougemont** i.e., Red Hill (with a
play on "Richmond")   **109 what's o'clock** what time is it   **116 jack** the
figure of a man that strikes the bell on the outside of a clock (with a
play on the meaning "lowbred fellow." Richard's complaint is that
Buckingham, like the jack of a clock, being on the point of striking the
hour—i.e., speaking his request—breaks the continuity of Richard's
reflections.)

Betwixt thy begging and my meditation.
I am not in the giving vein today.   118

BUCKINGHAM
May it please you to resolve me in my suit.   119

KING RICHARD
Thou troublest me. I am not in the vein.
                    Exit [*with all but Buckingham*].

BUCKINGHAM
And is it thus? Repays he my deep service
With such contempt? Made I him king for this?
O, let me think on Hastings, and be gone
To Brecknock, while my fearful head is on!   *Exit.* 124

❖

4.3 *Enter Tyrrel.*

TYRREL
The tyrannous and bloody act is done,
The most arch deed of piteous massacre   2
That ever yet this land was guilty of.
Dighton and Forrest, whom I did suborn   4
To do this piece of ruthless butchery,
Albeit they were fleshed villains, bloody dogs,   6
Melted with tenderness and mild compassion,
Wept like to children in their deaths' sad story.
"O, thus," quoth Dighton, "lay the gentle babes."
"Thus, thus," quoth Forrest, "girdling one another
Within their alabaster innocent arms.
Their lips were four red roses on a stalk,
Which in their summer beauty kissed each other.
A book of prayers on their pillow lay,
Which once," quoth Forrest, "almost changed my mind;
But O! the devil"—there the villain stopped;
When Dighton thus told on: "We smotherèd
The most replenishèd sweet work of Nature   18
That from the prime creation e'er she framed."   19

118 vein mood   **119 resolve me** give me a final answer   **124 Brecknock**
i.e., Brecon, Buckingham's family seat in Wales.   **fearful** full of fears

4.3. Location: London. The royal court.
2 arch deed i.e., chief or notorious act   **4 suborn** bribe   **6 fleshed** experienced in bloodshed   **18 replenishèd** complete, perfect   **19 prime** first

Hence both are gone; with conscience and remorse
They could not speak; and so I left them both,
To bear this tidings to the bloody king.

    Enter [King] Richard.

And here he comes.—All health, my sovereign lord!

KING RICHARD
Kind Tyrrel, am I happy in thy news?

TYRREL
If to have done the thing you gave in charge   25
Beget your happiness, be happy then,
For it is done.

KING RICHARD   But didst thou see them dead?

TYRREL
I did, my lord.

KING RICHARD   And buried, gentle Tyrrel?

TYRREL
The chaplain of the Tower hath buried them;
But where, to say the truth, I do not know.

KING RICHARD
Come to me, Tyrrel, soon at after-supper,   31
When thou shalt tell the process of their death.   32
Meantime, but think how I may do thee good,
And be inheritor of thy desire.
Farewell till then.

TYRREL   I humbly take my leave.   *[Exit.]*

KING RICHARD
The son of Clarence have I pent up close,   36
His daughter meanly have I matched in marriage,   37
The sons of Edward sleep in Abraham's bosom,   38
And Anne my wife hath bid this world good night.
Now, for I know the Breton Richmond aims   40
At young Elizabeth, my brother's daughter,   41
And by that knot looks proudly on the crown,   42
To her go I, a jolly thriving wooer.

25 gave in charge ordered, commanded   **31 after-supper** dessert after
supper   **32 process** story   **36 pent up close** strictly confined   **37 His . . .
marriage** (Margaret Plantagenet was about twelve years old when Richard
died. Shakespeare may have confused her with Lady Cicely, a daughter of
Edward IV, whom Richard, according to Holinshed, intended to marry to
"a man found in a cloud, and of an unknown lineage and family.")
38 Abraham's bosom (See Luke 16:22.)   **40 for** because   **41 my brother's**
Edward's   **42 by that knot** by virtue of that alliance

Enter Ratcliffe.

RATCLIFFE   My lord!

KING RICHARD
Good or bad news, that thou com'st in so bluntly?

RATCLIFFE
Bad news, my lord. Morton is fled to Richmond,   46
And Buckingham, backed with the hardy Welshmen,
Is in the field, and still his power increaseth.   48

KING RICHARD
Ely with Richmond troubles me more near   49
Than Buckingham and his rash-levied strength.   50
Come, I have learned that fearful commenting   51
Is leaden servitor to dull delay;   52
Delay leads impotent and snail-paced beggary.   53
Then fiery expedition be my wing,   54
Jove's Mercury, and herald for a king!   55
Go muster men. My counsel is my shield;   56
We must be brief when traitors brave the field.   57

Exeunt.

✤

4.4   *Enter old Queen Margaret.*

QUEEN MARGARET
So now prosperity begins to mellow   1
And drop into the rotten mouth of death.
Here in these confines slyly have I lurked
To watch the waning of mine enemies.
A dire induction am I witness to,   5
And will to France, hoping the consequence   6
Will prove as bitter, black, and tragical.

46 Morton i.e., John Morton, Bishop of Ely, who had been kept prisoner
at Brecknock (or Brecon) Castle; he is the Ely of 3.4   **48 power** army
49 near deeply   **50 rash-levied** hastily recruited   **51 fearful commenting** timorous talk   **52 leaden servitor** sluggish attendant   **53 leads**
leads to.   **beggary** ruin   **54 expedition** speed   **55 Mercury** messenger
of the gods   **56 counsel** sagacity   **57 brave** challenge

4.4. Location: London. Near the royal court.
1 mellow mature   **5 induction** beginning (as of a play)   **6 will** will go.
consequence what follows, the sequel and conclusion (as in a play)

Withdraw thee, wretched Margaret. Who comes here?
                                    [*She steps aside.*]

Enter Duchess [of York] and Queen [Elizabeth].

QUEEN ELIZABETH
  Ah, my poor princes! Ah, my tender babes!
  My unblown flowers, new-appearing sweets!   10
  If yet your gentle souls fly in the air
  And be not fixed in doom perpetual,   12
  Hover about me with your airy wings
  And hear your mother's lamentation!
QUEEN MARGARET [*Aside*]
  Hover about her; say that right for right   15
  Hath dimmed your infant morn to agèd night.   16
DUCHESS
  So many miseries have crazed my voice   17
  That my woe-wearied tongue is still and mute.
  Edward Plantagenet, why art thou dead?
QUEEN MARGARET [*Aside*]
  Plantagenet doth quit Plantagenet.   20
  Edward for Edward pays a dying debt.   21
QUEEN ELIZABETH
  Wilt thou, O God, fly from such gentle lambs   22
  And throw them in the entrails of the wolf?
  When didst thou sleep when such a deed was done?   24
QUEEN MARGARET [*Aside*]
  When holy Harry died, and my sweet son.   25
DUCHESS
  Dead life, blind sight, poor mortal-living ghost,   26
  Woe's scene, world's shame, grave's due by life usurped, 27
  Brief abstract and record of tedious days,   28

---

10 unblown unopened. **sweets** flowers **12 doom perpetual** i.e., eternal
punishment or reward **15 right for right** i.e., a just punishment for an
offense against justice **16 dimmed . . . night** i.e., brought the youthful
promise of your children to ruin and death **17 crazed** cracked **20 quit**
requite **21 Edward for Edward** i.e., Edward V, the Yorkist Prince, for
Edward, the son of Margaret and Henry VI. **dying debt** debt paid
through death **22 fly from** abandon **24 When** i.e., whenever till now
25 Harry i.e., Henry VI **26 mortal-living ghost** i.e., a dead person still
among the living **27 grave's . . . usurped** i.e., one who, by living too
long, deprives the grave of its due **28 abstract** epitome

Rest thy unrest on England's lawful earth,
                                        [*Sitting down*]
Unlawfully made drunk with innocent blood!

QUEEN ELIZABETH
Ah, that thou wouldst as soon afford a grave   31
As thou canst yield a melancholy seat!
Then would I hide my bones, not rest them here.
Ah, who hath any cause to mourn but we?
                                        [*Sitting down by her.*]

QUEEN MARGARET [*Coming forward*]
If ancient sorrow be most reverend,   35
Give mine the benefit of seniory   36
And let my griefs frown on the upper hand.   37
If sorrow can admit society, [*Sitting down with them*]
Tell o'er your woes again by viewing mine:
I had an Edward, till a Richard killed him;   40
I had a Harry, till a Richard killed him: 41
Thou hadst an Edward, till a Richard killed him;   42
Thou hadst a Richard, till a Richard killed him.   43

DUCHESS
I had a Richard too, and thou didst kill him;   44
I had a Rutland too, thou holp'st to kill him.   45

QUEEN MARGARET
Thou hadst a Clarence too, and Richard killed him.
From forth the kennel of thy womb hath crept
A hellhound that doth hunt us all to death.
That dog, that had his teeth before his eyes   49
To worry lambs and lap their gentle blood,   50
That foul defacer of God's handiwork,
That excellent grand tyrant of the earth   52
That reigns in gallèd eyes of weeping souls,   53
Thy womb let loose, to chase us to our graves.
O upright, just, and true-disposing God,

31 that would that.   **thou** i.e., the earth   **35 reverend** worthy of respect
36 seniory seniority of claim   **37 on . . . hand** i.e., from a place of precedence   **40 Edward** i.e., my son, the former Prince of Wales   **41 Harry** i.e.,
my husband, King Henry VI   **42 Thou** i.e., Queen Elizabeth.   **Edward**
i.e., Edward V   **43 Richard** i.e., the young Duke of York   **44 Richard** i.e.,
Duke of York, the Duchess's husband and father of Richard III, killed by
Margaret's army at the Battle of Wakefield in 1460   **45 Rutland** i.e.,
Edmund, son of the Duke of York, also killed at Wakefield   **49 teeth**
(Richard was supposedly born with teeth.)   **50 worry** tear to pieces
52 excellent unparalleled   **53 gallèd** sore with weeping

How do I thank thee that this carnal cur 56
Preys on the issue of his mother's body 57
And makes her pew-fellow with others' moan! 58

DUCHESS
O Harry's wife, triumph not in my woes!
God witness with me, I have wept for thine.

QUEEN MARGARET
Bear with me. I am hungry for revenge,
And now I cloy me with beholding it. 62
Thy Edward he is dead that killed my Edward; 63
Thy other Edward dead, to quit my Edward; 64
Young York he is but boot, because both they 65
Matched not the high perfection of my loss.
Thy Clarence he is dead that stabbed my Edward;
And the beholders of this frantic play, 68
Th' adulterate Hastings, Rivers, Vaughan, Grey, 69
Untimely smothered in their dusky graves.
Richard yet lives, hell's black intelligencer, 71
Only reserved their factor to buy souls 72
And send them thither; but at hand, at hand
Ensues his piteous and unpitied end. 74
Earth gapes, hell burns, fiends roar, saints pray,
To have him suddenly conveyed from hence.
Cancel his bond of life, dear God, I pray,
That I may live and say, "The dog is dead!"

QUEEN ELIZABETH
O, thou didst prophesy the time would come
That I should wish for thee to help me curse
That bottled spider, that foul bunch-backed toad! 81

QUEEN MARGARET
I called thee then vain flourish of my fortune; 82
I called thee then poor shadow, painted queen,
The presentation of but what I was, 84

56 carnal flesh-eating **57 issue** offspring **58 pew-fellow** i.e., intimate
associate **62 cloy me** satiate myself **63 Thy Edward** Edward IV. **my
Edward** the son of Henry VI **64 other Edward** Edward V. **quit** requite **65 Young York** Richard, Duke of York, the younger of the princes
murdered in the Tower. **but boot** merely into the bargain **68 frantic**
insane **69 adulterate** adulterous **71 intelligencer** agent, go-between,
spy **72 Only . . . factor** chosen above all others as their (hell's) agent
74 piteous deplorable **81 bottled** bottle-shaped, swollen (as at
1.3.242). **bunch-backed** hunchbacked **82 flourish** ornament, embellishment **84 presentation** representation

The flattering index of a direful pageant,   85
One heaved a-high to be hurled down below,
A mother only mocked with two fair babes,
A dream of what thou wast, a garish flag   88
To be the aim of every dangerous shot;   89
A sign of dignity, a breath, a bubble,   90
A queen in jest, only to fill the scene.
Where is thy husband now? Where be thy brothers?
Where be thy two sons? Wherein dost thou joy?
Who sues and kneels and says, "God save the Queen"?
Where be the bending peers that flattered thee?   95
Where be the thronging troops that followed thee?   96
Decline all this, and see what now thou art: 97
For happy wife, a most distressèd widow;
For joyful mother, one that wails the name;
For one being sued to, one that humbly sues;
For queen, a very caitiff crowned with care;   101
For she that scorned at me, now scorned of me;   102
For she being feared of all, now fearing one;   103
For she commanding all, obeyed of none.   104
Thus hath the course of justice whirled about
And left thee but a very prey to time,
Having no more but thought of what thou wast
To torture thee the more, being what thou art.
Thou didst usurp my place, and dost thou not
Usurp the just proportion of my sorrow?
Now thy proud neck bears half my burdened yoke,   111
From which even here I slip my weary head
And leave the burden of it all on thee.
Farewell, York's wife, and queen of sad mischance!
These English woes shall make me smile in France.
                              [*She starts to leave.*]
QUEEN ELIZABETH
O thou well skilled in curses, stay awhile,
And teach me how to curse mine enemies!

85 index argument, preface, prologue.   **pageant** spectacular entertainment   **88–89 garish . . . shot** i.e., standard-bearer, conspicuous in appearance, and thus the target of enemy fire   **90 sign** mere token
95 bending bowing   **96 troops** supporters   **97 Decline** go through in
order. (A grammatical metaphor.)   **101 caitiff** wretch, slave   **102, 103,
104 of** by   **111 burdened** burdensome

QUEEN MARGARET
    Forbear to sleep the nights, and fast the days;
    Compare dead happiness with living woe;
    Think that thy babes were sweeter than they were
    And he that slew them fouler than he is.
    Bett'ring thy loss makes the bad causer worse;   122
    Revolving this will teach thee how to curse.   123
QUEEN ELIZABETH
    My words are dull. O, quicken them with thine!   124
QUEEN MARGARET
    Thy woes will make them sharp, and pierce like mine.
                                        Exit Margaret.
DUCHESS
    Why should calamity be full of words?
QUEEN ELIZABETH
    Windy attorneys to their client's woes,   127
    Airy succeeders of intestate joys,   128
    Poor breathing orators of miseries,   129
    Let them have scope! Though what they will impart
    Help nothing else, yet do they ease the heart.
DUCHESS
    If so, then be not tongue-tied. Go with me,
    And in the breath of bitter words let's smother
    My damnèd son that thy two sweet sons smothered.
                                    [*Sound trumpet.*]
    The trumpet sounds. Be copious in exclaims.   135

        Enter King Richard and his train [marching,
        with drums and trumpets].

KING RICHARD
    Who intercepts me in my expedition?   136
DUCHESS
    O, she that might have intercepted thee,
    By strangling thee in her accursèd womb,
    From all the slaughters, wretch, that thou hast done!

---

122 Bett'ring magnifying   **123 Revolving** meditating on   **124 quicken**
put life into   **127 Windy . . . woes** i.e., words, which are airy pleaders
on behalf of one who is suffering   **128 succeeders** heirs.   **intestate**
having died without anything to bequeath   **129 breathing** speaking
135 exclaims exclamations   **136 expedition** (1) haste (2) military undertaking

QUEEN ELIZABETH
  Hid'st thou that forehead with a golden crown
  Where should be branded, if that right were right,
  The slaughter of the prince that owed that crown   142
  And the dire death of my poor sons and brothers?
  Tell me, thou villain slave, where are my children?
DUCHESS
  Thou toad, thou toad, where is thy brother Clarence?
  And little Ned Plantagenet, his son?   146
QUEEN ELIZABETH
  Where is the gentle Rivers, Vaughan, Grey?
DUCHESS   Where is kind Hastings?
KING RICHARD
  A flourish, trumpets! Strike alarum, drums!   149
  Let not the heavens hear these telltale women   150
  Rail on the Lord's anointed. Strike, I say!
                              Flourish. Alarums.
  Either be patient and entreat me fair,   152
  Or with the clamorous report of war   153
  Thus will I drown your exclamations.
DUCHESS   Art thou my son?
KING RICHARD
  Ay, I thank God, my father, and yourself.
DUCHESS
  Then patiently hear my impatience.
KING RICHARD
  Madam, I have a touch of your condition,   158
  That cannot brook the accent of reproof.
DUCHESS
  O, let me speak!
KING RICHARD   Do then, but I'll not hear.
DUCHESS
  I will be mild and gentle in my words.
KING RICHARD
  And brief, good Mother, for I am in haste.

142 owed owned   **146 Ned Plantagenet** (See 4.3.36.)   **149 alarum** the
cry or signal "allarme" (to arms)   **150 telltale** tattling, gabbling
152 entreat me fair treat me with courtesy   **153 report** noise
158 condition disposition

DUCHESS

Art thou so hasty? I have stayed for thee,   163
God knows, in torment and in agony.

KING RICHARD

And came I not at last to comfort you?

DUCHESS

No, by the Holy Rood, thou know'st it well,   166
Thou cam'st on earth to make the earth my hell.
A grievous burden was thy birth to me;
Tetchy and wayward was thy infancy;   169
Thy schooldays frightful, desperate, wild, and furious;   170
Thy prime of manhood daring, bold, and venturous;
Thy age confirmed, proud, subtle, sly, and bloody,   172
More mild, but yet more harmful—kind in hatred.   173
What comfortable hour canst thou name
That ever graced me with thy company?

KING RICHARD

Faith, none, but Humphrey Hour, that called Your Grace 176
To breakfast once forth of my company.   177
If I be so disgracious in your eye,   178
Let me march on and not offend you madam.—
Strike up the drum.

DUCHESS   I prithee, hear me speak.

KING RICHARD

You speak too bitterly.

DUCHESS   Hear me a word,
For I shall never speak to thee again.

KING RICHARD   So.

DUCHESS

Either thou wilt die by God's just ordinance
Ere from this war thou turn a conqueror,   185
Or I with grief and extreme age shall perish
And nevermore behold thy face again.
Therefore take with thee my most grievous curse,
Which in the day of battle tire thee more

---

163 **stayed** waited   166 **Holy Rood** Christ's cross   169 **Tetchy** fretful,
peevish   170 **frightful** frightening   172 **age confirmed** riper manhood
173 **kind in hatred** concealing hatred under pretense of kindness
176 **Humphrey Hour** (To "dine with Duke Humphrey" was to go hungry.
The passage is obscure.)   177 **forth of** away from   178 **disgracious**
unpleasing, disliked   185 **turn** return

Than all the complete armor that thou wear'st!
My prayers on the adverse party fight,   191
And there the little souls of Edward's children
Whisper the spirits of thine enemies   193
And promise them success and victory!
Bloody thou art, bloody will be thy end;
Shame serves thy life and doth thy death attend. *Exit.* 196
QUEEN ELIZABETH
  Though far more cause, yet much less spirit to curse
  Abides in me; I say amen to her.
KING RICHARD
  Stay, madam, I must talk a word with you.
QUEEN ELIZABETH
  I have no more sons of the royal blood
  For thee to slaughter. For my daughters, Richard,
  They shall be praying nuns, not weeping queens,
  And therefore level not to hit their lives.   203
KING RICHARD
  You have a daughter called Elizabeth,
  Virtuous and fair, royal and gracious.
QUEEN ELIZABETH
  And must she die for this? O, let her live,
  And I'll corrupt her manners, stain her beauty,   207
  Slander myself as false to Edward's bed,
  Throw over her the veil of infamy;
  So she may live unscarred of bleeding slaughter,   210
  I will confess she was not Edward's daughter.
KING RICHARD
  Wrong not her birth; she is a royal princess.
QUEEN ELIZABETH
  To save her life, I'll say she is not so.
KING RICHARD
  Her life is safest only in her birth.
QUEEN ELIZABETH
  And only in that safety died her brothers.
KING RICHARD
  Lo, at their birth good stars were opposite.   216

191 party side   **193 Whisper** whisper to   **196 serves** accompanies
203 level aim   **207 manners** morals   **210 So** provided   **216 opposite**
hostile, antagonistic

QUEEN ELIZABETH
No, to their lives ill friends were contrary.   217
KING RICHARD
All unavoided is the doom of destiny.   218
QUEEN ELIZABETH
True, when avoided grace makes destiny.   219
My babes were destined to a fairer death,
If grace had blessed thee with a fairer life.
KING RICHARD
You speak as if that I had slain my cousins.
QUEEN ELIZABETH
Cousins, indeed, and by their uncle cozened   223
Of comfort, kingdom, kindred, freedom, life.
Whose hand soever lanced their tender hearts,   225
Thy head, all indirectly, gave direction.   226
No doubt the murderous knife was dull and blunt
Till it was whetted on thy stone-hard heart,   228
To revel in the entrails of my lambs.
But that still use of grief makes wild grief tame,   230
My tongue should to thy ears not name my boys
Till that my nails were anchored in thine eyes;
And I, in such a desperate bay of death,   233
Like a poor bark of sails and tackling reft,   234
Rush all to pieces on thy rocky bosom.
KING RICHARD
Madam, so thrive I in my enterprise   236
And dangerous success of bloody wars   237
As I intend more good to you and yours
Than ever you or yours by me were harmed!
QUEEN ELIZABETH
What good is covered with the face of heaven,   240
To be discovered, that can do me good?
KING RICHARD
Th' advancement of your children, gentle lady.

217 **contrary** opposed   218 **unavoided** unavoidable   219 **avoided grace**
i.e., Richard, in whom grace is void or lacking   223 **cozened** cheated
225 **Whose hand soever** whoever it was whose hand   226 **all indirectly**
even if by indirect means   228 **whetted** sharpened   230 **But** except.
still continual   233 **bay** (1) inlet (2) position of a hunted animal turning
to face the hounds   234 **reft** bereft   236 **so thrive I** may I so thrive
237 **success** sequel, result   240 **covered with** hidden by (and therefore
not yet revealed to humanity)

QUEEN ELIZABETH
Up to some scaffold, there to lose their heads.
KING RICHARD
Unto the dignity and height of fortune,
The high imperial type of this earth's glory.   245
QUEEN ELIZABETH
Flatter my sorrow with report of it;
Tell me what state, what dignity, what honor,
Canst thou demise to any child of mine?   248
KING RICHARD
Even all I have—ay, and myself and all—
Will I withal endow a child of thine,
So in the Lethe of thy angry soul   251
Thou drown the sad remembrance of those wrongs
Which thou supposest I have done to thee.
QUEEN ELIZABETH
Be brief, lest that the process of thy kindness   254
Last longer telling than thy kindness' date.   255
KING RICHARD
Then know that from my soul I love thy daughter.   256
QUEEN ELIZABETH
My daughter's mother thinks it with her soul.
KING RICHARD   What do you think?
QUEEN ELIZABETH
That thou dost love my daughter from thy soul.
So from thy soul's love didst thou love her brothers,   260
And from my heart's love I do thank thee for it.
KING RICHARD
Be not so hasty to confound my meaning.
I mean that with my soul I love thy daughter
And do intend to make her Queen of England.
QUEEN ELIZABETH
Well then, who dost thou mean shall be her king?
KING RICHARD
Even he that makes her queen. Who else should be?

---

245 imperial type symbol of rule   **248 demise** convey, transmit, lease
251 So provided that.   **Lethe** river in the underworld, the waters of
which produce forgetfulness   **254 process** story   **255 date** term of
existence   **256 from** with. (But Queen Elizabeth, in the next lines,
sarcastically uses the word in the sense "apart from.")   **260 So** just so.
(Said ironically.)

QUEEN ELIZABETH
  What, thou?
KING RICHARD Even so. How think you of it?
QUEEN ELIZABETH
  How canst thou woo her?
KING RICHARD   That would I learn of you,
  As one being best acquainted with her humor.   269
QUEEN ELIZABETH
  And wilt thou learn of me?
KING RICHARD   Madam, with all my heart.
QUEEN ELIZABETH
  Send to her, by the man that slew her brothers,
  A pair of bleeding hearts; thereon engrave
  "Edward" and "York"; then haply will she weep.   273
  Therefore present to her—as sometime Margaret   274
  Did to thy father, steeped in Rutland's blood—   275
  A handkerchief, which, say to her, did drain
  The purple sap from her sweet brothers' body;
  And bid her wipe her weeping eyes withal.
  If this inducement move her not to love,
  Send her a letter of thy noble deeds.
  Tell her thou mad'st away her uncle Clarence,
  Her uncle Rivers, ay, and for her sake
  Mad'st quick conveyance with her good aunt Anne.   283
KING RICHARD
  You mock me, madam. This is not the way
  To win your daughter.
QUEEN ELIZABETH   There is no other way,
  Unless thou couldst put on some other shape
  And not be Richard that hath done all this.
KING RICHARD
  Say that I did all this for love of her.
QUEEN ELIZABETH
  Nay, then indeed she cannot choose but hate thee,
  Having bought love with such a bloody spoil.   290
KING RICHARD
  Look what is done cannot be now amended.   291

269 humor mood   **273 haply** perhaps   **274 sometime** once
275 Rutland's (See *3 Henry VI*, 1.4.79–83.)   **283 conveyance with** riddance
of   **290 spoil** slaughter. (A hunting term.)   **291 Look what** whatever

Men shall deal unadvisedly sometimes,   292
Which after-hours gives leisure to repent.
If I did take the kingdom from your sons,
To make amends I'll give it to your daughter.
If I have killed the issue of your womb,
To quicken your increase I will beget   297
Mine issue of your blood upon your daughter.
A grandam's name is little less in love
Than is the doting title of a mother;
They are as children but one step below,
Even of your metal, of your very blood,   302
Of all one pain, save for a night of groans
Endured of her for whom you bid like sorrow.   304
Your children were vexation to your youth,
But mine shall be a comfort to your age.
The loss you have is but a son being king,
And by that loss your daughter is made queen.
I cannot make you what amends I would;
Therefore accept such kindness as I can.   310
Dorset your son, that with a fearful soul
Leads discontented steps in foreign soil,
This fair alliance quickly shall call home
To high promotions and great dignity.
The king that calls your beauteous daughter wife
Familiarly shall call thy Dorset brother;   316
Again shall you be mother to a king,
And all the ruins of distressful times
Repaired with double riches of content.
What? We have many goodly days to see.
The liquid drops of tears that you have shed
Shall come again, transformed to orient pearl,   322
Advantaging their love with interest   323
Of ten times double gain of happiness.
Go then, my mother, to thy daughter go.
Make bold her bashful years with your experience;
Prepare her ears to hear a wooer's tale;

292 **deal** act   297 **quicken your increase** give new life to your (dead)
progeny   302 **metal** substance (with a suggestion also of *mettle*, spirit.
The Folio reads *mettall*.)   304 **of** by.   **bid** endured, bided   310 **can** am
able (to give)   316 **Familiarly** familially   322 **orient** bright, shining
323 **Advantaging** augmenting.   **their love** i.e., the love that prompted
tears

Put in her tender heart th' aspiring flame
Of golden sovereignty; acquaint the Princess
With the sweet silent hours of marriage joys.
And when this arm of mine hath chastisèd
The petty rebel, dull-brained Buckingham,
Bound with triumphant garlands will I come
And lead thy daughter to a conqueror's bed;
To whom I will retail my conquest won,   335
And she shall be sole victoress, Caesar's Caesar.

QUEEN ELIZABETH
What were I best to say? Her father's brother
Would be her lord? Or shall I say her uncle?
Or he that slew her brothers and her uncles?
Under what title shall I woo for thee
That God, the law, my honor, and her love
Can make seem pleasing to her tender years?

KING RICHARD
Infer fair England's peace by this alliance.   343

QUEEN ELIZABETH
Which she shall purchase with still lasting war.

KING RICHARD
Tell her the King, that may command, entreats.

QUEEN ELIZABETH
That at her hands which the King's King forbids.   346

KING RICHARD
Say she shall be a high and mighty queen.

QUEEN ELIZABETH
To vail the title, as her mother doth.   348

KING RICHARD
Say I will love her everlastingly.

QUEEN ELIZABETH
But how long shall that title "ever" last?

KING RICHARD
Sweetly in force unto her fair life's end.

QUEEN ELIZABETH
But how long fairly shall her sweet life last?

KING RICHARD
As long as heaven and nature lengthens it.

---

335 retail relate   **343 Infer** allege, adduce (as a reason)   **346 forbids**
(*The Book of Common Prayer*, echoing the injunctions of Leviticus 18,
prohibits the marriage of a man with his brother's daughter.)   **348 vail**
lower, abase as a sign of submission

QUEEN ELIZABETH
  As long as hell and Richard likes of it.
KING RICHARD
  Say I, her sovereign, am her subject low.
QUEEN ELIZABETH
  But she, your subject, loathes such sovereignty.
KING RICHARD
  Be eloquent in my behalf to her.
QUEEN ELIZABETH
  An honest tale speeds best being plainly told.   358
KING RICHARD
  Then plainly to her tell my loving tale.
QUEEN ELIZABETH
  Plain and not honest is too harsh a style.   360
KING RICHARD
  Your reasons are too shallow and too quick.   361
QUEEN ELIZABETH
  O, no, my reasons are too deep and dead—
  Too deep and dead, poor infants, in their graves.
KING RICHARD
  Harp not on that string, madam; that is past.
QUEEN ELIZABETH
  Harp on it still shall I till heartstrings break.
KING RICHARD
  Now, by my George, my Garter, and my crown—   366
QUEEN ELIZABETH
  Profaned, dishonored, and the third usurped.
KING RICHARD
  I swear—
QUEEN ELIZABETH   By nothing, for this is no oath.
  Thy George, profaned, hath lost his lordly honor;   369
  Thy Garter, blemished, pawned his knightly virtue;
  Thy crown, usurped, disgraced his kingly glory.
  If something thou wouldst swear to be believed,
  Swear then by something that thou hast not wronged.

358 speeds succeeds   **360 too . . . style** i.e., a discordant combination
361 quick hasty (with a pun on the meaning "alive," contrasted with
dead in the next line, just as *shallow* is punningly contrasted with
deep)   **366 George . . . Garter** (The George, a badge showing Saint
George slaying the dragon, was not added to the insignia of the Order
of the Garter until the reign of Henry VII or Henry VIII.)   **369 his** its
(as also in ll. 370, 371)

KING RICHARD
  Then, by myself—
QUEEN ELIZABETH   Thyself is self-misused.
KING RICHARD
  Now, by the world—
QUEEN ELIZABETH   'Tis full of thy foul wrongs.
KING RICHARD
  My father's death—
QUEEN ELIZABETH   Thy life hath it dishonored.
KING RICHARD
  Why then, by God—
QUEEN ELIZABETH   God's wrong is most of all.
  If thou didst fear to break an oath with Him,
  The unity the King my husband made   379
  Thou hadst not broken, nor my brothers died.
  If thou hadst feared to break an oath by Him,
  Th' imperial metal circling now thy head
  Had graced the tender temples of my child,
  And both the princes had been breathing here,
  Which now, two tender bedfellows for dust,
  Thy broken faith hath made the prey for worms.
  What canst thou swear by now?
KING RICHARD   The time to come.
QUEEN ELIZABETH
  That thou hast wrongèd in the time o'erpast;
  For I myself have many tears to wash
  Hereafter time, for time past wronged by thee.   390
  The children live whose fathers thou hast slaughtered,
  Ungoverned youth, to wail it in their age;   392
  The parents live whose children thou hast butchered,
  Old barren plants, to wail it with their age.
  Swear not by time to come, for that thou hast
  Misused ere used, by times ill-used o'erpast.
KING RICHARD
  As I intend to prosper and repent,   397
  So thrive I in my dangerous affairs
  Of hostile arms! Myself myself confound!   399

---

379 unity i.e., the reconciliation between Queen Elizabeth and her enemies
390 Hereafter time the future   **392 Ungoverned** i.e., without a father's
guidance or rule   **397 As . . . repent** i.e., I swear that as I hope to thrive
and intend to repent   **399 Myself . . . confound** may I destroy myself

Heaven and fortune bar me happy hours!
Day, yield me not thy light, nor, night, thy rest!
Be opposite all planets of good luck   402
To my proceeding if, with dear heart's love,
Immaculate devotion, holy thoughts,
I tender not thy beauteous princely daughter!   405
In her consists my happiness and thine;
Without her, follows to myself and thee,
Herself, the land, and many a Christian soul,
Death, desolation, ruin, and decay.
It cannot be avoided but by this;
It will not be avoided but by this.
Therefore, dear Mother—I must call you so—
Be the attorney of my love to her.
Plead what I will be, not what I have been,
Not my deserts, but what I will deserve.
Urge the necessity and state of times,
And be not peevish-fond in great designs.   417

QUEEN ELIZABETH
Shall I be tempted of the devil thus?

KING RICHARD
Ay, if the devil tempt you to do good.

QUEEN ELIZABETH
Shall I forget myself to be myself?   420

KING RICHARD
Ay, if yourself's remembrance wrong yourself.   421

QUEEN ELIZABETH   Yet thou didst kill my children.

KING RICHARD
But in your daughter's womb I bury them,
Where in that nest of spicery they will breed   424
Selves of themselves, to your recomforture.   425

QUEEN ELIZABETH
Shall I go win my daughter to thy will?

KING RICHARD
And be a happy mother by the deed.

---

402 opposite opposed, adverse   **405 tender** have a tender regard for
417 peevish-fond childishly foolish   **420 Shall . . . myself** i.e., shall I
forget who I am, the person wronged by Richard   **421 wrong yourself**
i.e., interfere with what is to your advantage   **424 nest of spicery** (The
fabled phoenix arose anew from the nest of spices, its funeral pyre.)
425 recomforture comfort, consolation

QUEEN ELIZABETH
  I go. Write to me very shortly,
  And you shall understand from me her mind.
KING RICHARD
  Bear her my true love's kiss; and so, farewell.
                    Exit Queen [Elizabeth].
  Relenting fool, and shallow, changing woman!

    Enter Ratcliffe; [Catesby following].

  How now, what news?
RATCLIFFE
  Most mighty sovereign, on the western coast
  Rideth a puissant navy; to our shores   434
  Throng many doubtful hollow-hearted friends,   435
  Unarmed, and unresolved to beat them back.
  'Tis thought that Richmond is their admiral;   437
  And there they hull, expecting but the aid   438
  Of Buckingham to welcome them ashore.
KING RICHARD
  Some light-foot friend post to the Duke of Norfolk: 440
  Ratcliffe, thyself, or Catesby. Where is he?
CATESBY
  Here, my good lord.
KING RICHARD   Catesby, fly to the Duke.
CATESBY
  I will, my lord, with all convenient haste.   443
KING RICHARD
  Ratcliffe, come hither. Post to Salisbury.
  When thou com'st thither—[*To Catesby.*] Dull,
      unmindful villain,
  Why stay'st thou here, and go'st not to the Duke?
CATESBY
  First, mighty liege, tell me Your Highness' pleasure,
  What from Your Grace I shall deliver to him.
KING RICHARD
  O, true, good Catesby. Bid him levy straight

---

434 puissant powerful   **435 doubtful** apprehensive   **437 their admiral**
i.e., of the *puissant navy* named three lines earlier   **438 hull** drift with
the sails furled   **440 light-foot** swift-footed   **443 convenient** appropriate, suitable

The greatest strength and power that he can make,   450
And meet me suddenly at Salisbury.   451
CATESBY   I go.   *Exit.*
RATCLIFFE
What, may it please you, shall I do at Salisbury?
KING RICHARD
Why, what wouldst thou do there before I go?
RATCLIFFE
Your Highness told me I should post before.   455
KING RICHARD
My mind is changed.

Enter Lord Stanley, [Earl of Derby].

                        Stanley, what news with you?
STANLEY
None good, my liege, to please you with the hearing,
Nor none so bad but well may be reported.
KING RICHARD
Heyday, a riddle! Neither good nor bad!
What need'st thou run so many miles about,
When thou mayst tell thy tale the nearest way?   461
Once more, what news?
STANLEY   Richmond is on the seas.
KING RICHARD
There let him sink, and be the seas on him!
White-livered runagate, what doth he there?   464
STANLEY
I know not, mighty sovereign, but by guess.
KING RICHARD   Well, as you guess?
STANLEY
Stirred up by Dorset, Buckingham, and Morton,
He makes for England, here to claim the crown.
KING RICHARD
Is the chair empty? Is the sword unswayed?   469
Is the King dead? The empire unpossessed?   470
What heir of York is there alive but we?
And who is England's king but great York's heir?
Then tell me, what makes he upon the seas?   473

450 make raise   **451 suddenly** swiftly   **455 post** hasten   **461 the nearest way** directly, simply   **464 White-livered runagate** cowardly renegade, fugitive   **469 chair** throne   **470 empire** kingdom   **473 makes he**
is he doing

STANLEY
Unless for that, my liege, I cannot guess.

KING RICHARD
Unless for that he comes to be your liege,
You cannot guess wherefore the Welshman comes.   476
Thou wilt revolt and fly to him, I fear.

STANLEY
No, my good lord; therefore mistrust me not.

KING RICHARD
Where is thy power, then, to beat him back?   479
Where be thy tenants and thy followers?
Are they not now upon the western shore,
Safe-conducting the rebels from their ships?

STANLEY
No, my good lord, my friends are in the north.

KING RICHARD
Cold friends to me! What do they in the north
When they should serve their sovereign in the west?

STANLEY
They have not been commanded, mighty King.
Pleaseth Your Majesty to give me leave,   487
I'll muster up my friends and meet Your Grace
Where and what time Your Majesty shall please.

KING RICHARD
Ay, thou wouldst be gone to join with Richmond.
But I'll not trust thee.

STANLEY   Most mighty sovereign,
You have no cause to hold my friendship doubtful.
I never was nor never will be false.

KING RICHARD
Go then and muster men, but leave behind
Your son, George Stanley. Look your heart be firm,
Or else his head's assurance is but frail.   496

STANLEY
So deal with him as I prove true to you.
                    Exit Stanley, [Earl of Derby].

    Enter a Messenger.

---

476 Welshman (Richmond was the grandson of Owen Tudor, a
Welshman of Anglesea, who fathered three sons and a daughter by
Katharine of Valois, widow of Henry V.)   **479 power** army
487 Pleaseth may it please   **496 assurance** safety

FIRST MESSENGER
My gracious sovereign, now in Devonshire,
As I by friends am well advisèd,   499
Sir Edward Courtney and the haughty prelate,
Bishop of Exeter, his elder brother,
With many more confederates, are in arms.

Enter another Messenger.

SECOND MESSENGER
In Kent, my liege, the Guildfords are in arms,
And every hour more competitors   504
Flock to the rebels, and their power grows strong.

Enter another Messenger.

THIRD MESSENGER
My lord, the army of great Buckingham—
KING RICHARD
Out on you, owls! Nothing but songs of death?   507
                                        He striketh him.
There, take thou that, till thou bring better news.
THIRD MESSENGER
The news I have to tell Your Majesty
Is that by sudden floods and fall of waters
Buckingham's army is dispersed and scattered,
And he himself wandered away alone,
No man knows whither.
KING RICHARD   I cry thee mercy.
There is my purse to cure that blow of thine.
                                        [*He gives money.*]
Hath any well-advisèd friend proclaimed   515
Reward to him that brings the traitor in?
THIRD MESSENGER
Such proclamation hath been made, my lord.

Enter another Messenger.

FOURTH MESSENGER
Sir Thomas Lovell and Lord Marquess Dorset,   518

---

499 advertisèd informed   **504 competitors** confederates   **507 owls** (The
cry of the owl was thought to portend death.)   **515 well-advisèd** prudent   **518 Sir Thomas Lovell** (Not the Lovell of 3.4 and 3.5, who was
historically Sir Francis Lovell, Richard's Lord Chamberlain, but perhaps related to him.)

'Tis said, my liege, in Yorkshire are in arms.
But this good comfort bring I to Your Highness:
The Breton navy is dispersed by tempest.
Richmond, in Dorsetshire, sent out a boat
Unto the shore, to ask those on the banks
If they were his assistants, yea or no,
Who answered him they came from Buckingham
Upon his party. He, mistrusting them,
Hoised sail and made his course again for Brittany.   527

KING RICHARD
March on, march on, since we are up in arms,
If not to fight with foreign enemies,
Yet to beat down these rebels here at home.

          Enter Catesby.

CATESBY
My liege, the Duke of Buckingham is taken!
That is the best news. That the Earl of Richmond
Is with a mighty power landed at Milford   533
Is colder tidings, yet they must be told.

KING RICHARD
Away towards Salisbury! While we reason here,
A royal battle might be won and lost.
Someone take order Buckingham be brought
To Salisbury. The rest march on with me.
                                        Flourish. Exeunt.

4.5   *Enter [Lord Stanley, Earl of] Derby and Sir
          Christopher [Urswick, a priest].*

STANLEY
Sir Christopher, tell Richmond this from me:

---

527 Hoised hoisted   **533 Milford** i.e., Milford Haven on the coast of
Wales in the county of Pembroke. (A gap of two years is bridged here.
Richmond's first fruitless expedition was in October 1483; his landing
at Milford was in August 1485.)

**4.5. Location: London. The house of Lord Stanley, Earl of Derby.
s.d. Sir** (Honorific title for a clergyman.)

That in the sty of the most deadly boar
My son George Stanley is franked up in hold.   3
If I revolt, off goes young George's head;
The fear of that holds off my present aid.
So get thee gone; commend me to thy lord.
Withal say that the Queen hath heartily consented   7
He should espouse Elizabeth her daughter.   8
But tell me, where is princely Richmond now?

CHRISTOPHER
At Pembroke, or at Ha'rfordwest, in Wales.   10

STANLEY   What men of name resort to him?   11

CHRISTOPHER
Sir Walter Herbert, a renownèd soldier,
Sir Gilbert Talbot, Sir William Stanley,
Oxford, redoubted Pembroke, Sir James Blunt,   14
And Rice ap Thomas, with a valiant crew,
And many other of great name and worth;
And towards London do they bend their power,   17
If by the way they be not fought withal.

STANLEY
Well, hie thee to thy lord; I kiss his hand.   19
My letter will resolve him of my mind. [*He gives a letter.*]   20
Farewell.   *Exeunt.*

❧

3 **franked up in hold** shut up in custody, as in a pigpen   7 **Withal** in
addition   8 **espouse** marry   10 **Ha'rfordwest** Haverfordwest, in Wales
11 **name** rank   14 **redoubted** dreaded.   **Pembroke** i.e., Jasper Tudor,
Earl of Pembroke, uncle to Richmond   17 **bend their power** direct their
forces   19 **hie** hasten   20 **resolve him of** inform him concerning

5.1   *Enter Buckingham, with [Sheriff and]*
halberds, led to execution.

BUCKINGHAM
  Will not King Richard let me speak with him?
SHERIFF
  No, my good lord; therefore be patient.
BUCKINGHAM
  Hastings, and Edward's children, Grey, and Rivers,
  Holy King Henry, and thy fair son Edward,   4
  Vaughan, and all that have miscarrièd   5
  By underhand corrupted foul injustice,
  If that your moody discontented souls   7
  Do through the clouds behold this present hour,
  Even for revenge mock my destruction!
  This is All Souls' Day, fellow, is it not?   10
SHERIFF   It is, my lord.
BUCKINGHAM
  Why, then All Souls' Day is my body's doomsday.
  This is the day which, in King Edward's time,
  I wished might fall on me when I was found
  False to his children and his wife's allies;
  This is the day wherein I wished to fall
  By the false faith of him whom most I trusted;
  This, this All Souls' Day to my fearful soul
  Is the determined respite of my wrongs.   19
  That high All-Seer which I dallied with
  Hath turned my feignèd prayer on my head
  And given in earnest what I begged in jest.
  Thus doth he force the swords of wicked men
  To turn their own points in their masters' bosoms.
  Thus Margaret's curse falls heavy on my neck:
  "When he," quoth she, "shall split thy heart with
      sorrow,
  Remember Margaret was a prophetess."

5.1. Location: Salisbury. An open place.
4 thy i.e., Henry's   **5 miscarrièd** perished   **7 moody** angry.   **discontented** i.e., still seeking vengeance   **10 All Souls' Day** November 2, the day on which the Roman Catholic Church intercedes for all Christian souls   **19 determined . . . wrongs** i.e., the preordained date to which the punishment of my evil practices was respited or postponed

Come lead me, officers, to the block of shame.
Wrong hath but wrong, and blame the due of blame.
                    Exeunt Buckingham with officers.

❖

5.2   *Enter Richmond, Oxford, [Sir James] Blunt,*
          [Sir Walter] Herbert, and others, with drum
          and colors.

RICHMOND
  Fellows in arms, and my most loving friends
  Bruised underneath the yoke of tyranny,
  Thus far into the bowels of the land   3
  Have we marched on without impediment;
  And here receive we from our father Stanley   5
  Lines of fair comfort and encouragement.
  The wretched, bloody, and usurping boar,
  That spoiled your summer fields and fruitful vines,   8
  Swills your warm blood like wash, and makes his trough   9
  In your emboweled bosoms, this foul swine   10
  Is now even in the center of this isle,
  Near to the town of Leicester, as we learn.
  From Tamworth thither is but one day's march.
  In God's name, cheerly on, courageous friends,   14
  To reap the harvest of perpetual peace
  By this one bloody trial of sharp war.
OXFORD
  Every man's conscience is a thousand men,
  To fight against this guilty homicide.
HERBERT
  I doubt not but his friends will turn to us.
BLUNT
  He hath no friends but what are friends for fear,   20
  Which in his dearest need will fly from him.   21
RICHMOND
  All for our vantage. Then, in God's name, march!

5.2. Location: A camp near Tamworth.
3 bowels i.e., center   **5 father** i.e., stepfather, Lord Stanley, Earl of
Derby   **8 spoiled** despoiled   **9 Swills** gulps.   **wash** hog's wash, swill
10 emboweled disemboweled   **14 cheerly** cheerily, heartily   **20 for fear**
i.e., out of fearing Richard   **21 dearest** direst

True hope is swift and flies with swallow's wings;
Kings it makes gods and meaner creatures kings.   24

                                  Exeunt omnes.

❖

5.3   *Enter King Richard in arms, with Norfolk,*
Ratcliffe, and the Earl of Surrey [and others].

KING RICHARD
Here pitch our tent, even here in Bosworth Field.
My lord of Surrey, why look you so sad?
SURREY
My heart is ten times lighter than my looks.
KING RICHARD
My lord of Norfolk—
NORFOLK   Here, most gracious liege.
KING RICHARD
Norfolk, we must have knocks; ha! Must we not?   5
NORFOLK
We must both give and take, my loving lord.
KING RICHARD
Up with my tent! Here will I lie tonight.
        [*Soldiers begin to set up King Richard's tent.*]
But where tomorrow? Well, all's one for that.   8
Who hath descried the number of the traitors?   9
NORFOLK
Six or seven thousand is their utmost power.
KING RICHARD
Why, our battalia trebles that account.   11
Besides, the King's name is a tower of strength,
Which they upon the adverse faction want.   13
Up with the tent! Come, noble gentlemen,
Let us survey the vantage of the ground.   15
Call for some men of sound direction.   16
Let's lack no discipline, make no delay,

---

24 meaner of lower degree   **s.d. omnes** all

5.3. Location: Bosworth Field.
5 knocks blows   **8 all's . . . that** be that as it may   **9 descried** discovered   **11 battalia** army   **13 want** lack   **15 vantage of the ground** i.e.,
way in which the field can best be used for tactical advantage
16 direction judgment, military skill

For, lords, tomorrow is a busy day.   *Exeunt.*

*Enter [on the other side of the stage] Richmond,
Sir William Brandon, Oxford, and Dorset, [Blunt,
Herbert, and others. Some of the soldiers pitch
Richmond's tent.]*

RICHMOND
The weary sun hath made a golden set,
And, by the bright track of his fiery car,   20
Gives token of a goodly day tomorrow.
Sir William Brandon, you shall bear my standard.
Give me some ink and paper in my tent.
I'll draw the form and model of our battle,   24
Limit each leader to his several charge,   25
And part in just proportion our small power.   26
My lord of Oxford, you, Sir William Brandon,
And you, Sir Walter Herbert, stay with me.
The Earl of Pembroke keeps his regiment;   29
Good Captain Blunt, bear my good-night to him,
And by the second hour in the morning
Desire the Earl to see me in my tent.
Yet one thing more, good Captain, do for me:
Where is Lord Stanley quartered, do you know?
BLUNT
Unless I have mista'en his colors much,
Which well I am assured I have not done,
His regiment lies half a mile at least
South from the mighty power of the King.
RICHMOND
If without peril it be possible,
Sweet Blunt, make some good means to speak with him,
And give him from me this most needful note.   41
                              [He gives a letter.]
BLUNT
Upon my life, my lord, I'll undertake it.
And so, God give you quiet rest tonight!
RICHMOND
Good night, good Captain Blunt. *[Exit Blunt.]* Come,
    gentlemen,

20 car chariot (of Phoebus)   **24 form and model** formation and plan
25 Limit appoint.   **several charge** individual command   **26 power**
army   **29 keeps** i.e., is with   **41 needful** essential

Let us consult upon tomorrow's business.
Into my tent; the dew is raw and cold.
                         They withdraw into the tent.

Enter [to his tent, King] Richard, Ratcliffe,
Norfolk, and Catesby.

KING RICHARD
  What is 't o'clock?
CATESBY   It's suppertime, my lord;
  It's nine o'clock.
KING RICHARD   I will not sup tonight.
  Give me some ink and paper.
  What, is my beaver easier than it was,   50
  And all my armor laid into my tent?
CATESBY
  It is, my liege, and all things are in readiness.
KING RICHARD
  Good Norfolk, hie thee to thy charge.
  Use careful watch, choose trusty sentinels.
NORFOLK   I go, my lord.
KING RICHARD
  Stir with the lark tomorrow, gentle Norfolk.
NORFOLK   I warrant you, my lord.   *[Exit.]* 57
KING RICHARD   Catesby!
CATESBY
  My lord?
KING RICHARD   Send out a pursuivant at arms   59
  To Stanley's regiment. Bid him bring his power   60
  Before sunrising, lest his son George fall
  Into the blind cave of eternal night.   *[Exit Catesby.]*
  Fill me a bowl of wine. Give me a watch.   63
  Saddle white Surrey for the field tomorrow.   64
  Look that my staves be sound and not too heavy.   65
  Ratcliffe!

---

50 beaver face-guard or visor of helmet.   **easier** more loosely fitting
57 warrant guarantee   **59 pursuivant at arms** junior officer attendant
on a herald   **60 power** forces   **63 watch** watch light, candle marked
into equal divisions to show time; or, perhaps, sentinel   **64 white**
Surrey (The name seems to be Shakespeare's invention. The chroniclers
say that Richard was mounted on a "great white courser.")   **65 staves**
lance shafts

RATCLIFFE   My lord?
KING RICHARD
  Sawst thou the melancholy Lord Northumberland?
RATCLIFFE
  Thomas the Earl of Surrey and himself,
  Much about cockshut time, from troop to troop   70
  Went through the army, cheering up the soldiers.
KING RICHARD
  So, I am satisfied. Give me a bowl of wine.
  I have not that alacrity of spirit,
  Nor cheer of mind, that I was wont to have.   74
                                    [*Wine is brought.*]
  Set it down. Is ink and paper ready?
RATCLIFFE
  It is, my lord.
KING RICHARD   Bid my guard watch. Leave me.
  Ratcliffe, about the mid of night come to my tent
  And help to arm me. Leave me, I say.
                          Exit Ratcliffe. [Richard sleeps.]

        *Enter [Lord Stanley, Earl of] Derby, to Richmond
        in his tent, [lords and others attending].*

STANLEY
  Fortune and victory sit on thy helm!   79
RICHMOND
  All comfort that the dark night can afford
  Be to thy person, noble father-in-law!   81
  Tell me, how fares our loving mother?
STANLEY
  I, by attorney, bless thee from thy mother,   83
  Who prays continually for Richmond's good.
  So much for that. The silent hours steal on,
  And flaky darkness breaks within the east.   86
  In brief—for so the season bids us be—   87
  Prepare thy battle early in the morning,   88
  And put thy fortune to the arbitrament   89
  Of bloody strokes and mortal-staring war.   90

70 cockshut time evening twilight; possibly, the time at which the
poultry are shut up   **74 was wont** used   **79 helm** helmet   **81 father-in-
law** i.e., stepfather   **83 attorney** deputy   **86 flaky** streaked with light
87 season time of day   **88 battle** troops   **89 arbitrament** arbitration
90 mortal-staring fatal-visaged

I, as I may—that which I would I cannot—   91
With best advantage will deceive the time   92
And aid thee in this doubtful shock of arms.   93
But on thy side I may not be too forward,   94
Lest, being seen, thy brother, tender George,   95
Be executed in his father's sight.
Farewell. The leisure and the fearful time   97
Cuts off the ceremonious vows of love
And ample interchange of sweet discourse
Which so long sundered friends should dwell upon.
God give us leisure for these rites of love!
Once more, adieu. Be valiant, and speed well!   102

RICHMOND
Good lords, conduct him to his regiment.
I'll strive with troubled thoughts to take a nap,   104
Lest leaden slumber peise me down tomorrow,   105
When I should mount with wings of victory.
Once more, good night, kind lords and gentlemen.
                 Exeunt. [Richmond remains.]
O Thou, whose captain I account myself,
Look on my forces with a gracious eye;
Put in their hands thy bruising irons of wrath,
That they may crush down with a heavy fall
The usurping helmets of our adversaries!
Make us thy ministers of chastisement,
That we may praise thee in the victory!
To thee I do commend my watchful soul
Ere I let fall the windows of mine eyes.   116
Sleeping and waking, O, defend me still!   *[He sleeps.]*

     Enter the Ghost of young Prince Edward, son [of]
     Harry the Sixth, to Richard.

GHOST (*To Richard*)
Let me sit heavy on thy soul tomorrow!   118
Think how thou stabbedst me in my prime of youth

---

91 that . . . cannot i.e., I cannot fight openly on your side, though I want to   **92 With . . . time** i.e., as best I can will work for our side without seeming to do so   **93 shock** encounter   **94 forward** zealous   **95 brother** i.e., stepbrother.   **tender** young, of tender years   **97 leisure** i.e., brief time allowed   **102 speed well** may you succeed   **104 with** i.e., in spite of   **105 peise** weigh   **116 windows** i.e., eyelids   **118 sit heavy on** be oppressive to

At Tewkesbury. Despair therefore and die!
(*To Richmond.*) Be cheerful, Richmond, for the wrongèd
    souls
Of butchered princes fight in thy behalf.
King Henry's issue, Richmond, comforts thee.   [*Exit.*]

> *Enter the Ghost of Henry the Sixth.*

GHOST (*To Richard*)
   When I was mortal, my anointed body
   By thee was punchèd full of deadly holes.
   Think on the Tower and me. Despair and die!   126
   Harry the Sixth bids thee despair and die!
   (*To Richmond.*) Virtuous and holy, be thou conqueror!
   Harry, that prophesied thou shouldst be king,   129
   Doth comfort thee in thy sleep. Live and flourish!
                                            [*Exit.*]

> *Enter the Ghost of Clarence.*

GHOST [*To Richard*]
   Let me sit heavy in thy soul tomorrow,
   I, that was washed to death with fulsome wine,   132
   Poor Clarence, by thy guile betrayed to death!
   Tomorrow in the battle think on me,
   And fall thy edgeless sword. Despair and die!   135
   (*To Richmond.*) Thou offspring of the house of
       Lancaster,
   The wrongèd heirs of York do pray for thee.
   Good angels guard thy battle! Live and flourish!   138
                                            [*Exit.*]

> *Enter the Ghosts of Rivers, Grey, [and] Vaughan.*

GHOST OF RIVERS [*To Richard*]
   Let me sit heavy in thy soul tomorrow,
   Rivers that died at Pomfret! Despair and die!
GHOST OF GREY [*To Richard*]
   Think upon Grey, and let thy soul despair!

---

126 Tower (Where Henry VI was supposed to have been murdered.)
129 prophesied (See *3 Henry VI*, 4.6.68 ff.)   **132 washed to death** i.e.,
drowned in a butt of malmsey.   **fulsome** cloying   **135 fall** may it fall.
edgeless blunt, useless   **138 battle** troops

GHOST OF VAUGHAN [*To Richard*]
Think upon Vaughan, and, with guilty fear,
Let fall thy lance. Despair and die!
ALL (*To Richmond*)
Awake, and think our wrongs in Richard's bosom
Will conquer him! Awake, and win the day!
[*Exeunt Ghosts.*]

Enter the Ghost of Hastings.

GHOST [*To Richard*]
Bloody and guilty, guiltily awake
And in a bloody battle end thy days!
Think on Lord Hastings. Despair and die!
(*To Richmond.*) Quiet untroubled soul, awake, awake!
Arm, fight, and conquer for fair England's sake!
[*Exit.*]

Enter the Ghosts of the two young Princes.

GHOSTS (*To Richard*)
Dream on thy cousins smothered in the Tower.   151
Let us be lead within thy bosom, Richard,
And weigh thee down to ruin, shame, and death!
Thy nephews' souls bid thee despair and die!
(*To Richmond.*) Sleep, Richmond, sleep in peace and
   wake in joy.
Good angels guard thee from the boar's annoy!   156
Live, and beget a happy race of kings!
Edward's unhappy sons do bid thee flourish.
[*Exeunt Ghosts.*]

Enter the Ghost of Lady Anne, his wife.

GHOST [*To Richard*]
Richard, thy wife, that wretched Anne thy wife,
That never slept a quiet hour with thee,
Now fills thy sleep with perturbations.
Tomorrow in the battle think on me,
And fall thy edgeless sword. Despair and die!
(*To Richmond.*) Thou quiet soul, sleep thou a quiet sleep;
Dream of success and happy victory!
Thy adversary's wife doth pray for thee.   [*Exit.*]

---

151 cousins i.e., nephews   **156 the boar's annoy** i.e., Richard's attack

Enter the Ghost of Buckingham.

GHOST [*To Richard*]
  The first was I that helped thee to the crown;
  The last was I that felt thy tyranny.
  O, in the battle think on Buckingham,
  And die in terror of thy guiltiness!
  Dream on, dream on of bloody deeds and death;
  Fainting, despair; despairing, yield thy breath!   172
  (*To Richmond.*) I died for hope ere I could lend thee aid; 173
  But cheer thy heart and be thou not dismayed.
  God and good angels fight on Richmond's side,
  And Richard fall in height of all his pride!   [*Exit.*] 176
            Richard starteth up out of a dream.

KING RICHARD
  Give me another horse! Bind up my wounds!
  Have mercy, Jesu!—Soft, I did but dream.
  O coward conscience, how dost thou afflict me!
  The lights burn blue. It is now dead midnight.   180
  Cold fearful drops stand on my trembling flesh.
  What do I fear? Myself? There's none else by.
  Richard loves Richard; that is, I am I.
  Is there a murderer here? No. Yes, I am.
  Then fly. What, from myself? Great reason why: 185
  Lest I revenge. What, myself upon myself?
  Alack, I love myself. Wherefore? For any good   187
  That I myself have done unto myself?
  O, no! Alas, I rather hate myself
  For hateful deeds committed by myself!
  I am a villain. Yet I lie, I am not.
  Fool, of thyself speak well. Fool, do not flatter.
  My conscience hath a thousand several tongues,   193
  And every tongue brings in a several tale,
  And every tale condemns me for a villain.
  Perjury, perjury, in the highest degree,
  Murder, stern murder, in the direst degree,
  All several sins, all used in each degree,   198

172 **Fainting** losing heart   173 **for hope** i.e., for want of hope, hoping in
vain to help   176 **Richard fall** may Richard fall   180 **lights burn blue**
(Superstitiously regarded as evidence of the presence of ghosts.)
185 **fly** flee   187 **Wherefore** why   193 **several** different, separate
198 **used** committed.   **degree** i.e., of infamy, from bad to worst

Throng to the bar, crying all, "Guilty! Guilty!"   199
I shall despair. There is no creature loves me,
And if I die no soul will pity me.
And wherefore should they, since that I myself
Find in myself no pity to myself?
Methought the souls of all that I had murdered
Came to my tent, and every one did threat
Tomorrow's vengeance on the head of Richard.

     Enter Ratcliffe.

RATCLIFFE My lord!
KING RICHARD Zounds! Who is there?
RATCLIFFE
  Ratcliffe, my lord, 'tis I. The early village cock
  Hath twice done salutation to the morn.
  Your friends are up and buckle on their armor.
KING RICHARD
  O Ratcliffe, I have dreamed a fearful dream!
  What think'st thou, will our friends prove all true?
RATCLIFFE
  No doubt, my lord.
KING RICHARD   O Ratcliffe, I fear, I fear!
RATCLIFFE
  Nay, good my lord, be not afraid of shadows.
KING RICHARD
  By the apostle Paul, shadows tonight
  Have struck more terror to the soul of Richard
  Than can the substance of ten thousand soldiers
  Armèd in proof and led by shallow Richmond.   219
  'Tis not yet near day. Come, go with me;
  Under our tents I'll play the eavesdropper,
  To see if any mean to shrink from me.
               Exeunt [Richard and Ratcliffe].

    Enter the Lords to Richmond, [sitting in his tent].

LORDS Good morrow, Richmond!
RICHMOND
  Cry mercy, lords and watchful gentlemen,   224
  That you have ta'en a tardy sluggard here.

---

199 bar i.e., bar of justice **219 proof** armor that is proof against weapons **224 Cry mercy** I beg your pardon

A LORD   How have you slept, my lord?

RICHMOND
The sweetest sleep and fairest-boding dreams
That ever entered in a drowsy head
Have I since your departure had, my lords.
Methought their souls whose bodies Richard murdered
Came to my tent and cried on victory.   231
I promise you, my soul is very jocund   232
In the remembrance of so fair a dream.
How far into the morning is it, lords?

A LORD   Upon the stroke of four.

RICHMOND
Why, then 'tis time to arm and give direction.

His oration to his soldiers.

More than I have said, loving countrymen,
The leisure and enforcement of the time   238
Forbids to dwell upon. Yet remember this:
God and our good cause fight upon our side.
The prayers of holy saints and wrongèd souls,
Like high-reared bulwarks, stand before our faces.
Richard except, those whom we fight against   243
Had rather have us win than him they follow.
For what is he they follow? Truly, gentlemen,
A bloody tyrant and a homicide;
One raised in blood, and one in blood established;   247
One that made means to come by what he hath,   248
And slaughtered those that were the means to help him;
A base foul stone, made precious by the foil   250
Of England's chair, where he is falsely set;   251
One that hath ever been God's enemy.
Then if you fight against God's enemy,
God will in justice ward you as his soldiers;   254
If you do sweat to put a tyrant down,
You sleep in peace, the tyrant being slain;
If you do fight against your country's foes,

___

231 cried on uttered the cry of. (A hunting term; i.e., "urged on to.")
232 jocund cheerful   **238 leisure** i.e., brief time allowed   **243 except**
excepted   **247 in blood** by bloodshed   **248 made means** i.e., has taken
advantage, created opportunity   **250 foil** a thin leaf of metal placed under
a gem to set it off to advantage   **251 chair** throne   **254 ward** protect

Your country's fat shall pay your pains the hire;   258
If you do fight in safeguard of your wives,
Your wives shall welcome home the conquerors;
If you do free your children from the sword,
Your children's children quits it in your age.   262
Then, in the name of God and all these rights,
Advance your standards, draw your willing swords.   264
For me, the ransom of my bold attempt   265
Shall be this cold corpse on the earth's cold face;   266
But if I thrive, the gain of my attempt
The least of you shall share his part thereof.
Sound drums and trumpets boldly and cheerfully;
God and Saint George! Richmond and victory!

                                              [*Exeunt.*]

*Enter King Richard, Ratcliffe, [attendants and
forces].*

KING RICHARD
   What said Northumberland as touching Richmond?
RATCLIFFE
   That he was never trainèd up in arms.
KING RICHARD
   He said the truth. And what said Surrey then?
RATCLIFFE
   He smiled and said, "The better for our purpose."
KING RICHARD
   He was in the right, and so indeed it is.
                                   The clock striketh.
   Tell the clock there. Give me a calendar.   276
   Who saw the sun today?   [*He takes an almanac.*]
RATCLIFFE   Not I, my lord.
KING RICHARD
   Then he disdains to shine, for by the book   278
   He should have braved the east an hour ago.   279
   A black day will it be to somebody.
   Ratcliffe!

258 fat prosperity, wealth. **pains** efforts. **hire** reward **262 quits**
requites **264 Advance** raise **265–266 the ransom . . . face** i.e., if I fail,
there will be no question of ransom, but only death **276 Tell** count the
strokes of. **calendar** almanac **278 the book** i.e., the almanac
279 braved made splendid

RATCLIFFE
  My lord?
KING RICHARD   The sun will not be seen today;
  The sky doth frown and lour upon our army.   283
  I would these dewy tears were from the ground.
  Not shine today? Why, what is that to me
  More than to Richmond? For the selfsame heaven
  That frowns on me looks sadly upon him.

     Enter Norfolk.

NORFOLK
  Arm, arm, my lord, the foe vaunts in the field!   288
KING RICHARD
  Come, bustle, bustle! Caparison my horse.   289
  Call up Lord Stanley; bid him bring his power.
  I will lead forth my soldiers to the plain,
  And thus my battle shall be ordered: 292
  My foreward shall be drawn out all in length,   293
  Consisting equally of horse and foot;
  Our archers shall be placèd in the midst.
  John, Duke of Norfolk, Thomas, Earl of Surrey,
  Shall have the leading of this foot and horse.
  They thus directed, we will follow   298
  In the main battle, whose puissance on either side   299
  Shall be well wingèd with our chiefest horse.   300
  This, and Saint George to boot! What think'st thou,
    Norfolk?   301
NORFOLK
  A good direction, warlike sovereign.
  This found I on my tent this morning.
                He showeth him a paper.
KING RICHARD [*Reads*]
  "Jockey of Norfolk, be not so bold,   304
  For Dickon thy master is bought and sold."   305
  A thing devisèd by the enemy.
  Go, gentlemen, every man unto his charge.

---

283 lour look threateningly   **288 vaunts** boasts his strength
289 Caparison put on the battle trappings of   **292 battle** troops
293 foreward vanguard   **298 directed** deployed   **299 main battle** main
body of troops   **300 wingèd** flanked. **horse** cavalry   **301 to boot** i.e., to
give us aid in addition   **304 Jockey** i.e., Jack, John   **305 Dickon** i.e., Dick,
Richard. **bought and sold** i.e., betrayed for a bribe, brought to confusion

Let not our babbling dreams affright our souls;
Conscience is but a word that cowards use,
Devised at first to keep the strong in awe.
Our strong arms be our conscience, swords our law!
March on, join bravely, let us to it pell-mell;　　　312
If not to heaven, then hand in hand to hell.

His oration to his army.

What shall I say more than I have inferred?　　　314
Remember whom you are to cope withal:
A sort of vagabonds, rascals, and runaways,　　　316
A scum of Bretons and base lackey peasants,　　　317
Whom their o'ercloyèd country vomits forth　　　318
To desperate adventures and assured destruction.
You sleeping safe, they bring to you unrest;
You having lands, and blessed with beauteous wives,
They would restrain the one, distain the other.　　　322
And who doth lead them but a paltry fellow,
Long kept in Brittany at our mother's cost?　　　324
A milksop, one that never in his life
Felt so much cold as over shoes in snow?　　　326
Let's whip these stragglers o'er the seas again.
Lash hence these overweening rags of France,
These famished beggars, weary of their lives,
Who, but for dreaming on this fond exploit,　　　330
For want of means, poor rats, had hanged themselves.　331
If we be conquered, let men conquer us,
And not these bastard Bretons, whom our fathers
Have in their own land beaten, bobbed, and thumped,　334
And in record left them the heirs of shame.　　　335
Shall these enjoy our lands? Lie with our wives?
Ravish our daughters? [*Drum afar off.*] Hark! I hear
　　their drum.

---

312 pell-mell in confused haste　**314 inferred** stated　**316 sort** gang
317 lackey servile　**318 o'ercloyèd** satiated, glutted　**322 restrain** deprive you of.　**distain** defile, sully　**324 our mother's** (Richmond's
mother was not Richard's. This error occurs in the second edition of
Holinshed's *Chronicles*. The first edition reads "brothers," the reference being to the fact that Richmond had been supported at the court
of the Duke of Brittany at the cost of Charles, Duke of Burgundy,
Richard's brother-in-law.)　**326 over shoes** i.e., over his shoe-tops
330 fond foolish　**331 want of means** poverty　**334 bobbed** thrashed
335 record history

Fight, gentlemen of England! Fight, bold yeomen!
Draw, archers, draw your arrows to the head!
Spur your proud horses hard, and ride in blood;
Amaze the welkin with your broken staves!   341

    [*Enter a Messenger.*]

What says Lord Stanley? Will he bring his power?
MESSENGER   My lord, he doth deny to come.   343
KING RICHARD   Off with his son George's head!
NORFOLK
My lord, the enemy is past the marsh.
After the battle let George Stanley die.
KING RICHARD
A thousand hearts are great within my bosom.
Advance our standards, set upon our foes;
Our ancient word of courage, fair Saint George,   349
Inspire us with the spleen of fiery dragons!
Upon them! Victory sits on our helms.   *Exeunt.*

5.4   *Alarum. Excursions. Enter [Norfolk and forces
    fighting; to him] Catesby.*

CATESBY
Rescue, my lord of Norfolk, rescue, rescue!
The King enacts more wonders than a man,   2
Daring an opposite to every danger.   3
His horse is slain, and all on foot he fights,
Seeking for Richmond in the throat of death.
Rescue, fair lord, or else the day is lost!

    [*Alarums.*] *Enter [King] Richard.*

KING RICHARD
A horse! A horse! My kingdom for a horse!
CATESBY
Withdraw, my lord. I'll help you to a horse.

---

341 **Amaze the welkin** fright the skies   343 **deny** refuse   349 **word of
courage** battle cry

5.4. Location: Bosworth Field, as before; the action is continuous.
s.d. **Excursions** sorties **2 than a man** than seems possible for a human
being **3 Daring . . . danger** boldly facing every danger in battle

KING RICHARD
    Slave, I have set my life upon a cast,   9
    And I will stand the hazard of the die.   10
    I think there be six Richmonds in the field;   11
    Five have I slain today instead of him.
    A horse! A horse! My kingdom for a horse!   [*Exeunt.*]

5.5   *Alarum. Enter Richard and Richmond; they*
        fight. Richard is slain. Then, retreat being
        sounded, [flourish, and] enter Richmond, [Lord
        Stanley, Earl of] Derby bearing the crown, with
        other lords, etc.

RICHMOND
    God and your arms be praised, victorious friends!
    The day is ours; the bloody dog is dead.
STANLEY [*Offering him the crown*]
    Courageous Richmond, well hast thou acquit thee.
    Lo, here this long-usurpèd royalty
    From the dead temples of this bloody wretch
    Have I plucked off, to grace thy brows withal.   6
    Wear it, enjoy it, and make much of it.
RICHMOND
    Great God of heaven, say amen to all!
    But, tell me, is young George Stanley living?
STANLEY
    He is, my lord, and safe in Leicester town,
    Whither, if it please you, we may now withdraw us.
RICHMOND
    What men of name are slain on either side?
STANLEY
    John, Duke of Norfolk, Walter, Lord Ferrers,
    Sir Robert Brackenbury, and Sir William Brandon.
RICHMOND
    Inter their bodies as becomes their births.
    Proclaim a pardon to the soldiers fled

---

9 cast throw of the dice   **10 die** (Singular of *dice*.)   **11 six Richmonds** i.e.,
Richmond himself and five men dressed like him as a safety precaution

5.5. Location: Action continues at Bosworth Field.
s.d. retreat trumpet signal to withdraw, cease the attack   **6 withal** with

That in submission will return to us,
And then, as we have ta'en the Sacrament,   18
We will unite the white rose and the red.
Smile heaven upon this fair conjunction,   20
That long have frowned upon their enmity!
What traitor hears me and says not amen?
England hath long been mad, and scarred herself;
The brother blindly shed the brother's blood,
The father rashly slaughtered his own son,
The son, compelled, been butcher to the sire.
All this divided York and Lancaster,
Divided in their dire division.
O, now let Richmond and Elizabeth,
The true succeeders of each royal house,
By God's fair ordinance conjoin together!   31
And let their heirs, God, if thy will be so,
Enrich the time to come with smooth-faced peace,
With smiling plenty, and fair prosperous days!
Abate the edge of traitors, gracious Lord,   35
That would reduce these bloody days again   36
And make poor England weep in streams of blood!
Let them not live to taste this land's increase
That would with treason wound this fair land's peace!
Now civil wounds are stopped, peace lives again.   40
That she may long live here, God say amen!   *Exeunt.*

18 ta'en the Sacrament sworn a sacred oath on the Sacrament (to marry
Princess Elizabeth, daughter of Edward IV, thereby uniting the houses
of York and of Lancaster, white rose and red) 20 conjunction union.
(An astrological metaphor.) 31 ordinance decree 35 Abate blunt,
render ineffective 36 reduce bring back 40 stopped closed up

Date and Text

A quarto edition of *Richard III*, registered by Andrew Wise on October 20, 1597, appeared later that same year with the following title:

> THE TRAGEDY OF King Richard the third. Containing, His treacherous Plots against his brother Clarence: the pittiefull murther of his iunocent nephewes: his tyrannicall vsurpation: with the whole course of his detested life, and most deserued death. As it hath beene lately Acted by the Right honourable the Lord Chamberlaine his seruants. AT LONDON Printed by Valentine Sims, for Andrew Wise, dwelling in Paules Chu[r]ch-yard, at the Signe of the Angell. 1597.

This text, one of the most perplexing in all Shakespeare, is generally regarded as a memorial reconstruction of a peculiar kind, one in which the acting company banded together to reconstruct a play of which the copy was missing. The reconstructed version may later have been cut, perhaps for provincial performance. This defective text was the basis of the 1597 quarto, which was reprinted in 1598, 1602, 1605, 1612, 1622, 1629, and 1634, each reprint successively more error-laden than the previous one. The First Folio text of 1623 seems to have been set mainly from copies of the third and sixth quartos (1602, 1622) which had been sporadically but heavily corrected against an independent manuscript—possibly Shakespeare's own manuscript or a copy of it. Parts of the Folio text, however, were set from an uncorrected copy of the third quarto (1602), and for those passages (3.1.1–158 and 5.3.48 to end of play) the first quarto, from which the third was derived, must serve as copy text. Otherwise, the Folio text is the most authoritative, though it must be approached with caution.

The situation is indeed fraught with unusual uncertainty, since there are many opportunities for F to have perpetuated errors of the earlier quartos; moreover, its "improvements" over the readings of those quartos could in some instances be editorial sophistications. Q1, because it may sometimes be closer to Shakespeare's original, offers some readings that demand serious attention. Especially when

F's reading differs from Q1 and is instead derived from Q2-6, Q1 should be preferred unless it is manifestly wrong. At the same time, however, since Q1 may reflect adaptation of the original acting text, its changes may not represent Shakespeare's artistic intention either. For these reasons, one must be wary of Q1's assignment of speeches when they vary from F's assignments, and also of Q1's cuts, some of them substantial.

The play is mentioned by Francis Meres in 1598 in his *Palladis Tamia: Wit's Treasury* (a slender volume on contemporary literature and art; valuable because it lists most of the plays of Shakespeare that existed at that time). John Weever names a *"Richard"* in his *Epigrams*, published in 1599. Most scholars date *Richard III* 1592–1594, on the basis of its style and its close affinity to the *Henry VI* series (completed probably in 1591). The play may have been influenced by the anonymous *The True Tragedy of Richard III*, registered in June 1594, but probably written in 1590–1592 or even earlier. Shakespeare's play may also have been influenced by Thomas Kyd's *The Spanish Tragedy* (c. 1587) and by Christopher Marlowe's dramas (he died in 1593).

Textual Notes

These textual notes are not a historical collation, either of the early quartos and folios or of more recent editions; they are simply a record of departures in this edition from the copy text. The reading adopted in this edition appears in boldface, followed by the rejected reading from the copy text, i.e., the First Folio. Only major alterations in punctuation are noted. Changes in lineation are not indicated, nor are some minor and obvious typographical errors.

Abbreviations used:
F the First Folio
Q quarto
s.d. stage direction
s.p. speech prefix

Copy text: the First Folio, except for two passages, 3.1.1–158 and 5.3.48 to end of play, for which Q1 is copy text. Unless otherwise indicated, the adopted readings are from the first quarto of 1597 [Q1].

1.1. 1 s.p. Richard [not in F] **41 s.d. Enter . . . Brackenbury** [eds.] Enter Clarence, and Brakenbury guarded **45 the** th' **52 for** but **65 tempers him to this** tempts him to this harsh **75 to her for his** for her **103 I** I do **124 the** this **133 prey** play

1.2. 27 life [eds.] death **38 s.p. Halberdier** [eds.] Gen **39 stand** Stand'st **78 of a** of **80 t' accuse** [eds.] to curse **94 hand** hands **141 thee** the **171 words** word **198 was man** Man was **204 s.p. Richard** [not in F] **205** [not in F] **227 s.d. Exeunt** [eds.] Exit [also at l. 229] **228 Richard Sirs . . . corpse** [not in F] **238 at all** withall

1.3. 17 come comes **lords** Lord **19 s.p. [and elsewhere] Stanley** Der **54 whom** who **63 of** on **70** [not in F] **109 s.d.** [at l. 110 in F] **114** [not in F] **155 Ah, little** A little **160 of** off **309 s.p. Queen Elizabeth** Mar **342 s.p. First Murderer** Vil [also at ll. 350 and 355]

1.4. 9 Methought [Q4] Me thoughts **13 Thence** There **22 waters** water **22, 23 my** mine **25 Ten** A **39 seek** find **41 Which** Who **64 my lord** Lord **86 s.p. First Murderer** [eds.] 2. Mur **89 s.p. Second Murderer** [eds.] 1 **99 s.d. Exit** [at l. 97 in F] **100 I** we **122 Faith** [not in F] **126 Zounds** come **147 Zounds** [not in F] **152 Tut** [not in F] **192 to have redemption** for any goodnesse **193** [not in F] **240** [not in F] **242 of** on **269** [in F, printed after l. 263]

2.1. s.d. Buckingham [eds.] Buckingham, Wooduill **5 in** to **7 Rivers and Hastings** Dorset and Riuers **39 God** heauen **57 unwittingly** vnwillingly **59 By** To **68** [F follows with a line: "Of you Lord *Wooduill,* and Lord *Scales* of you"] **93 but** and **108 at** and

2.2. 1 s.p. Boy Edw **3 s.p. [and throughout scene] Girl** [eds.] Daugh **3 do you** do **47 have I** haue **83 weep** weepes **84–85 Clarence . . . they** Clarence weep, so do not they **87 Pour** Power **142 Ludlow** London [also at l. 154] **145** [not in F] **145 s.d. Manent** [eds.] Manet

2.3. 44 Ensuing Pursuing [but the catchword on p. 184 in F is "Ensuing"]

2.4. 1 hear heard   **21 s.p. Archbishop** Car [Q1] Yor [F]   **65 death** earth

3.1. 1–158 [based on Q1 as copy text]   **2 s.p. [and elsewhere] Richard** Glo **60** [bracketed s.d. from F]   **150 s.d. [A sennet]** [from F]   **Hastings** Hast. Dors   **Manent** [F2] Manet

3.2. 78 as you do as

3.3. 1 [not in F]

3.4. 58 [not in F]   **79 s.d. Manent** manet   **82 raze** rowse

3.5. 4 wert were   **20 innocence** innocencie   **34 Look . . . Mayor** [not in F; after l. 26 in Q1]   **66 cause** case   **74 meet'st advantage** meetest vantage **104 Penker** [eds.] Peuker   **105 s.d. Exeunt** [eds.] Exit   **109 s.d. Exit** Exeunt

3.6. 12 who's who

3.7. 20 mine my   **33 spake** spoke   **40 wisdoms** wisdome [not in F] **44 s.p. Richard** [not in F]   **54 we'll** we   **83 My lord** [not in F]   **125 her** his [also in ll. 126 and 127]   **219 Zounds! I'll** we will   **220** [not in F] **240 Richard** King Richard   **241 s.p. Mayor and Citizens** All   **247 cousin** Cousins

4.1. s.d. [F: Enter the Queene, Anne Duchesse of Gloucester, the Duchesse of Yorke, and Marquesse Dorset]   **15 s.p. Brackenbury** Lieu [and at ll. 18 and 26]

4.2. 36 My lord [not in F]   **72 there** then   **90 Hereford** Hertford **99–118** [not in F]

4.3. 5 ruthless ruthfull   **13 Which** And   **15 once** one   **31 at** and   **33 thee** the   **53 leads** leds

4.4. 10 unblown vnblowed   **39** [not in F]   **o'er** over [Q1]   **41 Harry** [eds.] Husband   **45 holp'st** hop'st   **52–53** [lines reversed in F]   **64 Thy** The **112 weary** wearied   **118 nights . . . days** night . . . day   **128 intestate** intestine   **141 Where** Where't   **225 lanced** [eds.] lanch'd   **239 or** and **268 would I** I would   **284 This is** this   **324 Of ten** [eds.] Often **364–365** [lines reversed in F, and the s.p. Queen Elizabeth is missing] **366 s.p. King Richard** [not in F]   **377 God** Heauen   **God's** Heanens   **392 in** with   **396 o'erpast** repast   **417 fond** found   **430 s.d. Exit Queen** [at l. 429 in F]   **431 s.d. Enter Ratcliffe** [at l. 432 in F]   **444 Ratcliffe** [eds.] Catesby **498 s.p. First Messenger** Mess   **503 s.p. Second Messenger** Mess **506 s.p. Third Messenger** Mess [also at ll. 509 and 517]   **507 you** ye **518 s.p. Fourth Messenger** Mess   **534 tidings** Newes, but

5.1. 11 is, my lord is

5.2. 11 center Centry   **12 Near** Ne're

5.3. 20 track tract   **28 you** [eds.] your   **48 ff. [to the end of the play]** [copy text is Q1]   **54 sentinels** [F] centinell [Q1]   **59 s.p. Catesby** [eds.] Rat   **79 sit** [F] set [Q1; also at l. 131]   **85 that. The** that the [Q1]   **100 sundered** sundried [Q1]   **107 s.d. [Richmond remains]** [substantially from F] **139 s.p. Ghost of Rivers** King [Q1]   **141 s.p. Ghost of Grey** Gray **142 s.p. Ghost of Vaughan** Vaugh   **145 Will** Wel [Q1]   **146–150** [after line

158 in Q1]   **151 s.p. Ghosts** [F] Ghost [Q1]   **159 s.p. Ghost** [not in Q1]
167 s.p. Ghost [not in Q1]   **176 fall** [F] falls [Q1]   **183 am** and [Q1]
223 s.p. Lords Lo [Q1]   **226, 235 s.p. A Lord** Lo [Q1]   **270 s.d. Ratcliffe** Rat.
& c.   **299 main** [F] matne [Q1]   **301 boot** bootes [Q1]   **304 s.p. King Richard**
[at l. 306 ("King") in Q1]   **351 them! Victory** them victorie [Q1]

5.5. 13 s.p. Stanley [not in Q1]   **13 Ferrers** Ferri [Q1]   **15 becomes** become
[Q1]   **41 s.d. Exeunt** [F; not in Q1]

Shakespeare's Sources

Any departures from the original text are noted with an asterisk and appear at the bottom of the page in boldface; original readings are in roman.

Richard III, like the *Henry VI* series, is based on Edward Hall's *The Union of the Noble and Illustre Families of Lancaster and York* (1548) and on the 1587 edition of Raphael Holinshed's *The Chronicles of England, Scotland, and Ireland*. (A selection from the third volume of Holinshed follows.) Both of these historical compilations were deeply indebted for their hostile view of Richard III to Polydore Vergil and Thomas More. Vergil, a papal tax collector who came to England in 1501, spent many years under the patronage of Henry VII writing in Latin his *Anglica Historia* (first published in Basel, 1534). This work portrayed Richard negatively in order to glorify the claim of the Tudor monarch who had deposed Richard in 1485. Vergil argued that England's suffering was a divinely sent scourge, intended to cleanse England of rebelliousness and prepare the English people for the providential reward of Tudor rule.

Thomas More's *The History of King Richard III*, left unfinished in 1513, was published in two slightly differing versions, one in English (1557) and one in Latin (1566). Thomas More obtained much information and possibly an early draft of his narrative from Cardinal Morton, in whose household More lived as a youth. Morton had figured in the struggles of Richard III's reign—he was the Bishop of Ely from whom Richard requested the strawberries (3.4.32–33)—and had become a bitter enemy of the Yorkist king. Thomas More's own purpose in writing the life of Richard III was surely not to glorify Henry VII, with whom More had a strained relationship, but to characterize the evil of political opportunism. His portrait of Richard becomes that of the generic tyrant, behaving as such tyrants behaved in the various literary models from Renaissance Italy with which More was doubtless familiar. The result was, in any case, one-sided. The historical Richard seems to have been no worse than many another late medieval ruler and had indeed some admirable ideas on efficiency in government. More's blackened portrait, because it served the purposes of the Tudor state, became part of the legend and was available to Shakespeare in many versions. Holinshed incorporated verbatim a good deal of More's account.

Apart from Hall's and Holinshed's chronicles, those of Robert Fabyan (first published in 1516) and the *Annals* of John Stow (1580, 1592) may have provided Shakespeare with further details. Another possible source is *A Mirror for Magistrates* (first published in 1559), where, for example, in "The Complaint of George, Duke of Clarence," we find the riddling prophecy about the letter G (see 1.1.39). A second edition of the *Mirror* (1563) contains the Complaints of Edward IV, Anthony Woodville (Lord Rivers), Hastings, Buckingham, Shore's wife, and others. Shakespeare's particular indebtedness to the *Mirror* is not great, though he certainly was familiar with it. The same is probably true of the Latin tragedy *Richardus Tertius* by Thomas Legge (1579) at Cambridge, which contains an interesting scene of Richard's wooing of the Lady Anne not reported in the chronicles. The anonymous *The True Tragedy of Richard III* (published 1594, written c. 1590–1592) may have been useful in its fusing of Senecan revenge motifs with English history, and in its focus on the single figure of Richard. The Richard of this anonymous play is an overreacher, a worshiper of Fortune who meets his nemesis in the devoutly Christian Earl of Richmond. Opinion is divided as to whether Shakespeare actually used the play, chiefly because by 1590 he could have found the legend of Richard III set forth in so many works.

The Third Volume of Chronicles (1587 edition)
Compiled by Raphael Holinshed

EDWARD THE FOURTH

[Holinshed describes the funeral of King Henry VI (1471) in which the dead King, carried in an open coffin, bleeds in the presence of beholders. It is carried to Blackfriars and thence to the monastery at Chertsey.

Dissension between King Edward and his younger brother Clarence continues to be the subject of talk, especially about a prophecy that King Edward should be succeeded by a ruler whose name begins with G. Clarence is imprisoned and secretly drowned in a butt (a large cask) of malmsey in 1478. King Edward, although consenting to his death, publicly laments his loss. Edward dies in April 1483, leaving the throne nominally occupied by Prince Edward, aged thirteen. The Duke of York, his younger brother, is eleven.]

[THE REIGN OF] EDWARD THE FIFTH

Richard, the third son [of Richard, Duke of York], of whom we now entreat,[1] was in wit[1] and courage equal with either of them, in body and prowess far under them both; little of stature, ill-featured of limbs, crookbacked, his left shoulder much higher than his right; hard-favored of visage, and such as is in states called warly,[2] in other men otherwise. He was malicious, wrathful, envious, and from afore his birth ever froward.[3] It is for truth reported that the Duchess his mother had so much ado in her travail[4] that she could not be delivered of him uncut, and that he came into the world with the feet forward, as men be borne outward,[5] and (as the fame runneth[6] also) not untoothed—whether men of hatred report above the truth or else that Nature changed her course in his beginning which in the course of his life many things unnaturally committed. So that the full confluence of these qualities, with the defects of favor and amiable proportion, gave proof to this rule of physiognomy:

> *Distortum vultum*
> *sequitur distorsio morum.*[7]

None evil captain was he[8] in the war, as to which his disposition was more meetly[9] than for peace. Sundry victories had he, and sometimes overthrows; but never on default as for his own person, either of hardiness or politic order.[10] Free was he called of dispense,[11] and somewhat above his

---

1 entreat . . . wit treat, was in intelligence   **2 in states called warly** in noblemen called warlike, bellicose   **3 froward** evilly-disposed, refractory   **4 travail** labor   **5 be borne outward** i.e., are carried away on the funeral bier when they die   **6 as the fame runneth** as rumor has it
7 Distortum . . . morum a warped visage follows from a warped moral sense   **8 None evil captain was he** he was by no means a bad military commander   **9 meetly** suited   **10 and sometimes . . . politic order** and sometimes he suffered defeat, though never through his own fault either in bravery or in skillful ordering of his troops   **11 Free . . . dispense** he was reputed generous

power liberal;[12] with large gifts he gat him unsteadfast friendship for which he was fain to pill and spoil[13] in other places, and got him steadfast hatred. He was close and secret, a deep dissembler, lowly of countenance,[14] arrogant of heart, outwardly companionable where he inwardly hated, not letting[15] to kiss whom he thought to kill; despiteous[16] and cruel, not for evil will alway, but ofter for ambition, and either for the surety or increase of his estate.

Friend and foe was much what indifferent[17] where his advantage grew; he spared no man's death whose life withstood his purpose. He slew with his own hands King Henry the Sixth, being prisoner in the Tower, as men constantly said, and that without commandment or knowledge of the King, which[18] would undoubtedly, if he had intended that thing, have appointed that butcherly office to some other than his own born brother. Some wise men also ween that his drift,[19] covertly conveyed, lacked not in helping forth his brother of Clarence to his death, which he resisted[20] openly, howbeit somewhat (as men deemed) more faintly than he that were heartily minded to his wealth.[21]

And they that thus deem think that he long time in King Edward's life forethought[22] to be king in case that the King his brother (whose life he looked that evil diet should shorten) should happen to decease (as indeed he did) while his children were young. And they deem that for this intent he was glad of his brother's death the Duke of Clarence, whose life must needs have hindered him so intending, whether the same Duke of Clarence had kept him[23] true to his nephew the young King or enterprised to be king himself. But of all this point is there no certainty, and whoso divineth[24] upon conjectures may as well shoot too far as too short. . . .

But now to return to the course of this history. Were it

---

12 **above his power liberal** generous above his ability to pay for it
13 **fain to pill and spoil** obliged to plunder and despoil   14 **lowly of countenance** outwardly humble of expression   15 **letting** hesitating, scrupling   16 **despiteous** full of despite, haughty, contemptuous
17 **was much what indifferent** was a matter of indifference   18 **which** who   19 **ween that his drift** conjecture that Richard's plotting
20 **resisted** denied   21 **than he that . . . wealth** than one thinking wholeheartedly of his (Clarence's) well-being   22 **forethought** planned, intended   23 **him** himself   24 **divineth** speculates

that the Duke of Gloucester had of old foreminded this conclusion or was now at erst[25] thereunto moved and put in hope by the occasion of the tender age of the young princes his nephews, as opportunity and likelihood of speed[26] putteth a man in courage of that[27] he never intended, certain it is that he contrived their destruction, with the usurpation of the regal dignity upon himself. And forsomuch as he well wist and holp[28] to maintain a long-continued grudge and heartburning between the Queen's kindred and the King's blood,[29] either party envying other's[30] authority, he now thought that their division should be (as it was indeed) a furtherly[31] beginning to the pursuit of his intent.

Nay, he was resolved that the same was a sure ground for the foundation of all his building, if he might first, under the pretext of revenging of old displeasure, abuse the anger and ignorance of the t'one party to the destruction of the tother, and then win to his purpose as many as he could; and those that could not be won might be lost ere they looked therefor. For of one thing was he certain, that if his intent were perceived he should soon have made peace between both the parties with his own blood.[32] King Edward in his life,[33] albeit that this dissension between his friends somewhat irked him, yet in his good health he somewhat the less regarded it[34] because he thought, whatsoever business[35] should fall between them, himself should alway be able to rule both the parties.

But in his last sickness, when he perceived his natural strength so sore enfeebled that he despaired all recovery, then he, considering the youth of his children, albeit he nothing less mistrusted than that that happened,[36] yet well foreseeing that many harms might grow by their debate while the youth of his children should lack discretion of themselves and good counsel of their friends (of which either party should counsel for their own commodity,[37] and

---

25 **at erst** at first 26 **speed** success 27 **that** what 28 **wist and holp** knew about and helped 29 **blood** kindred 30 **other's** the other's 31 **furtherly** favorable 32 **he should . . . blood** i.e., his enemies would have joined together to destroy him 33 **in his life** as long as he continued to live 34 **he somewhat . . . it** he did not worry about it too much 35 **business** i.e., quarrel 36 **albeit . . . happened** i.e., although he could not imagine anything so bad as what actually happened 37 **commodity** benefit, self-interest

rather by pleasant[38] advice to win themselves favor than by profitable advertisement[39] to do the children good), he called some of them before him that were at variance, and in especial the Lord Marquess Dorset, the Queen's son by her first husband.

So did he also William, the Lord Hastings, a nobleman, then Lord Chamberlain, against whom the Queen specially grudged for the great favor the King bare[40] him, and also for that[41] she thought him secretly familiar with the King in wanton company. Her kindred also bare him sore,[42] as well for that the King had made him Captain of Calais (which office the Lord Rivers, brother to the Queen, claimed of the King's former promise) as for divers other great gifts which he received that they looked for. When these lords, with divers other of both the parties, were come in presence,[43] the King, lifting up himself, and underset with pillows, as it is reported, on[44] this wise said unto them:

[Holinshed reports the oration of King Edward on his deathbed.]

But the lords, recomforting[45] him with as good words as they could, and answering for the time as they thought to stand with his pleasure, there in his presence, as by their words appeared, each forgave other and joined their hands together, when, as it after appeared by their deeds, their hearts were far asunder. As soon as the King was departed the noble Prince his son drew toward London, which at the time of his decease kept his household at Ludlow in Wales. . . .

To the governance and ordering of this young prince, at his sending thither, was there appointed Sir Anthony Woodville, Lord Rivers and brother unto the Queen, a right honorable man, as valiant of hand as politic in counsel. Adjoined were there unto him other of the same party; and in effect, everyone, as he was nearest of kin unto the Queen, so was he planted next about[46] the Prince. That drift by the Queen not unwisely devised, whereby her blood might of

---

38 pleasant flattering   **39 advertisement** instruction, admonition
40 bare bore   **41 for that** because   **42 bare him sore** bore him a
grudge   **43 in presence** into the royal presence   **44 on** in   **45 recomforting** comforting   **46 next about** nearest to

youth be rooted into the Prince's favor, the Duke of Gloucester turned unto their destruction, and upon that ground set
the foundation of all his unhappy building.

[Richard soon wins the support of Lord Hastings and the
Duke of Buckingham by exploiting their resentment of the
Queen and her powerful kindred. Together they resolve to
remove those persons from their positions of influence
around the young Prince. Richard does so by tricking the
Queen into believing it necessary that the Prince be es-
corted to London by a large force—one so large that it
causes alarm for the Prince's safety and gives Richard excuse to order the arrests of Lord Richard Grey, Sir Thomas
Vaughan, and Lord Rivers. (These three are later beheaded
at Pomfret.) The Queen, dismayed at these arrests and separated from her son Edward, takes refuge in sanctuary at
Westminster, bringing her youngest son Richard with her.
Thomas Rotherham, the Archbishop of York and Lord
Chancellor, brings the Great Seal to her there and offers
what comfort he can.
     Prince Edward is thereupon escorted from Stony Strat-
ford to London by those who are loyal to Richard of
Gloucester.]

When the King approached near to the city, Edmund
Shaw, goldsmith, then mayor, with William White and John
Matthew, sheriffs, and all the other aldermen, in scarlet,
with five hundred horse of the citizens, in violet, received
him reverently at Hornsea and, riding from thence, accompanied him into the city, which he entered the fourth day of
May, the first and last year of his reign. But the Duke of
Gloucester bare him[47] in open sight so reverently to the
Prince, with all semblance of lowliness, that, from the great
obloquy in which he was so late[48] before, he was suddenly
fallen in so great trust that at the Council next assembled
he was made the only man chosen and thought most meet to
be Protector of the King and his realm; so that, were it destiny or were it folly, the lamb was betaken to the wolf to
keep.

---

47 bare him bore himself, conducted himself   **48 obloquy . . . late**
disgrace in which he was so recently

[Other appointments to the Privy Council are made.]

Now, all were it so[49] that the Protector so sore thirsted for the finishing of that he had begun that thought every day a year till it were achieved, yet durst he no further attempt as long as he had but half his prey in his hand.[50]

And why? Well did he wit[51] that if he deposed the one brother, all the realm would fall to the other, if he either remained in sanctuary or should haply be shortly conveyed to his father's liberty.[52] Wherefore incontinent[53] at the next meeting of the lords at the Council he proposed to them that it was a heinous deed of the Queen, and proceeding of great malice toward the King's councillors, that she should keep in sanctuary the King's brother from him, whose special pleasure and comfort were to have his brother with him.

[Holinshed reports Richard's subtle oration to the Council, urging that the Archbishop of York be sent to the Queen with the request that she surrender custody of her younger son; if she refuse, young Richard ought to be brought against her will. The Council agrees, and when the Archbishop expresses reservations about violating sanctuary, Buckingham argues that sanctuary is not available to children: "And verily, I have often heard of sanctuary men, but I never heard erst of sanctuary children." At length the Archbishop prevails upon the Queen by offering his own guarantees of protection, and brings young Richard to his uncle of Gloucester at the Council meeting.]

When the Lord Cardinal, and these other lords with him, had received this young duke,[54] they brought him into the Star Chamber,[55] where the Protector took him in his arms

---

49 all were it so albeit   **50 but half . . . hand** i.e., Prince Edward in his custody but not Edward's younger brother Richard   **51 wit** know
52 his father's liberty i.e., his father's domain or property, where Richard of Gloucester would not be able to touch him   **53 incontinent** immediately   **54 this young duke** i.e., Richard, Duke of York   **55 the Star Chamber** (In the fourteenth and fifteenth centuries, this room in the royal palace at Westminster was used by the King's Council as it sat to exercise jurisdiction; by the end of the fifteenth century it had become a court of criminal jurisdiction, and was infamous under the Stuart kings as the place from which they exercised their arbitrary use of royal power.)

and kissed him with these words: "Now welcome, my lord, even with all my very heart!" And he said in that of likelihood as he thought.[56] Thereupon, forthwith they brought him unto the King his brother into the Bishop's palace at Paul's, and from thence through the city honorably into the Tower, out of the which after that day they never came abroad.[57] When the Protector had both the children in his hands, he opened himself[58] more boldly, both to certain other men and also chiefly to the Duke of Buckingham—although I know that many thought that this Duke was privy to all the Protector's counsel even from the beginning; and some of the Protector's friends said that the Duke was the first mover of the Protector to this matter, sending a privy messenger unto him straight after King Edward's death.

But others again, which knew better the subtle wit of the Protector, deny that he ever opened his enterprise to the Duke until he had brought to pass the things before rehearsed.[59] But when he had imprisoned the Queen's kinsfolks and gotten both her sons into his own hands, then he opened the rest of his purpose with less fear to them whom he thought meet for the matter, and specially to the Duke, who, being won to his purpose, he thought his strength more than half increased.

[Buckingham is persuaded to join Richard's wicked enterprise only when he sees that it cannot be avoided in any case and that it can be turned to Buckingham's own advantage.]

Then it was agreed that the Protector should have the Duke's aid to make him king, and that the Protector's only lawful son should marry the Duke's daughter, and that the Protector should grant him the quiet possession of the earldom of Hereford, which he claimed as his inheritance and could never obtain it in King Edward's time.

Besides these requests of the Duke, the Protector, of his own mind, promised him a great quantity of the King's trea-

---

56 And he . . . thought i.e., he probably meant what he said; he *was* glad to see the young Prince **57 abroad** out in the open air **58 opened himself** revealed his intention **59 rehearsed** recited, recounted

sure and of his household stuff. And when they were thus at a point[60] between themselves, they went about to prepare for the coronation of the young King, as they would have it seem. And that they might turn both the eyes and minds of men from perceiving of their drifts otherwhere, the lords, being sent for from all parts of the realm, came thick to that solemnity. But the Protector and the Duke, after that they had sent the Lord Cardinal, the Archbishop of York (then Lord Chancellor), the Bishop of Ely, the Lord Stanley, and the Lord Hastings (then Lord Chamberlain), with many other noblemen, to commune[61] and devise about the coronation in one place, as fast were they in another place contriving the contrary, and to make the Protector king.

To which Council, albeit there were adhibited[62] very few, and they were secret,[63] yet began there, here and thereabouts, some manner of muttering among the people, as though all should not long be well, though they neither wist[64] what they feared nor wherefore—were it that before such great things, men's hearts of a secret instinct of nature misgive them, as the sea without wind swelleth of himself[65] sometimes before a tempest, or were it that some one man, haply somewhat perceiving,[66] filled many men with suspicion, though he showed few men what he knew. Howbeit, somewhat[67] the dealing itself made men to muse on the matter, though the Council were close.[68] For little by little all folk withdrew from the Tower and drew unto Crosby's in Bishopsgate's Street where the Protector kept his household. The Protector had the resort, the King in manner desolate.[69]

While some, for their business, made suit to them that had the doing,[70] some were by their friends secretly warned that it might haply turn them to no good to be too much attendant about the King without the Protector's appointment,[71] which removed also divers of the Prince's old ser-

---

60 **at a point** agreed upon terms   61 **commune** confer   62 **adhibited** admitted   63 **secret** closemouthed   64 **wist** knew   65 **himself** itself 66 **haply somewhat perceiving** perhaps perceiving something   67 **somewhat** to some extent   68 **close** reticent, secretive   69 **The Protector . . . desolate** i.e., everyone flocked to the Protector Richard, leaving the young King friendless   70 **made suit . . . doing** brought their petitions to those persons constitutionally authorized to deal with them, i.e., the young King's representatives   71 **appointment** agreement

good semblance unto the Lord Hastings, and kept him much in company.[86] And undoubtedly the Protector loved him well and loath was to have lost him, saving for fear lest his life should have quailed[87] their purpose.

For which cause he moved Catesby to prove with some words cast out afar off[88] whether he could think it possible to win the Lord Hastings unto their part. But Catesby, whether he assayed[89] him or assayed him not, reported unto them that he found him so fast,[90] and heard him speak so terrible words,[91] that he durst no further break.[92] And of truth the Lord Chamberlain of very trust[93] showed unto Catesby the distrust that others began to have in the matter. And therefore he, fearing lest their motion might with the Lord Hastings minish his credence,[94] whereunto only all the matter leaned, procured[95] the Protector hastily to rid him. And much the rather for that[96] he trusted by his death to obtain much of the rule that the Lord Hastings bare in his country, the only desire whereof was the allective[97] that induced him to be partner and one special contriver of all this horrible treason.

Whereupon soon after, that is to wit[98] on the Friday being the thirteenth of June, many lords assembled in the Tower and there sat in Council, devising the honorable solemnity of the King's coronation, of which the time appointed then so near approached that the pageants and subtleties were in making[99] day and night at Westminster, and much victuals killed therefor that afterward was cast away. These lords so sitting together communing[100] of this matter, the Protector came in amongst them first about nine of the clock, saluting them courteously and excusing himself that

86 made . . . company looked with favor on the Lord Hastings and saw a good deal of him   87 saving . . . quailed were it not for fear that he (Hastings), if he remained alive, would have spoiled   88 he moved . . . off he induced Catesby to ascertain by indirect questioning   89 assayed examined   90 fast i.e., loyal to young King Edward   91 so terrible words i.e., words so threatening to Richard's cause   92 break disclose his purpose   93 of very trust trustingly   94 lest their . . . credence i.e., lest what others were muttering cause Catesby to lose his credit with the Lord Hastings   95 procured induced, caused   96 the rather for that the sooner because   97 the only desire . . . allective the desire of which was the sole allure   98 to wit i.e., to say   99 subtleties were in making ingenious contrivances were being made   100 communing consulting

vants from him and set new about him. Thus many things coming together, partly by chance, partly of purpose, caused at length not common people only, that wonde[72] with the wind, but wise men also, and some lords eke,[73] to mark the matter and muse thereon, so far forth that the Lord Stanley (that was after[74] Earl of Derby) wisely mistrusted it and said unto the Lord Hastings that he much misliked these two several councils. "For while we," quoth he, "talk of one matter in the t'one place, little wot[75] we whereof they talk in the tother place."

"My lord," quoth the Lord Hastings, "on my life, never doubt you,[76] for while one man is there which is never thence, never can there be thing once moved[77] that should sound amiss toward me but it should be in mine ears ere it were well out of their mouths." This meant he by Catesby,[78] which was of his near secret counsel and whom he very familiarly used,[79] and in his most weighty matters put no man in so special trust, reckoning himself to no man so lief, sith[80] he well wist there was no man so much to him beholden as was this Catesby, which was a man well learned in the laws of this land and, by the special favor of the Lord Chamberlain, in good authority; and much rule bare[81] in all the county of Leicester, where the Lord Chamberlain's power chiefly lay.

But surely great pity was it that he had not had either more truth or less wit,[82] for his dissimulation only[83] kept all that mischief up. In whom if the Lord Hastings had not put so special trust, the Lord Stanley and he had departed with divers other lords and broken all the dance[84] for[85] many ill signs that he saw which he now construes all to the best. So surely thought he that there could be none harm toward him in that Council intended where Catesby was. And of truth the Protector and the Duke of Buckingham made very

---

72 wonde flinch, wind, turn   **73 eke** also   **74 that was after** who was afterward   **75 wot** know   **76 doubt you** fear   **77 moved** proposed, urged   **78 This meant . . . Catesby** by this he meant (William) Catesby   **79 which was . . . used** who was in his confidence and with whom he was on very familiar terms   **80 lief, sith** beloved, since   **81 much rule bare** bore much authority   **82 that he . . . wit** i.e., that Catesby was not either more truthful or less clever   **83 for his dissimulation only** for it was his (Catesby's) dissimulation alone that   **84 broken all the dance** i.e., would have broken up Richard's carefully orchestrated plan   **85 for** on account of

he had been from them so long, saying merrily that he had been a sleeper that day.

After a little talking with them, he said unto the Bishop of Ely: "My lord, you have very good strawberries at your garden in Holborn. I require[101] you let us have a mess[102] of them." "Gladly, my lord," quoth he, "would God I had some better thing as ready to your pleasure as that!" And therewithal in all the haste he sent his servant for a mess of strawberries. The Protector set the lords fast in communing and, thereupon praying them to spare him for a little while, departed thence. And soon after one hour, between ten and eleven, he returned into the chamber amongst them, all changed, with a wonderful sour angry countenance, knitting the brows, frowning, and fretting and gnawing on his lips, and so sat him down in his place.

All the lords were much dismayed and sore marveled at this manner of sudden change and what thing should him ail. Then, when he had sitten still awhile, thus he began: "What were they worthy to have that compass and imagine[103] the destruction of me, being so near of blood unto the King and Protector of his royal person and his realm?" At this question all the lords sat sore astonied,[104] musing much by whom this question should be meant,[105] of which every man wist himself clear. Then the Lord Chamberlain, as he that for the love between them[106] thought he might be boldest with him, answered and said that they were worthy to be punished as heinous traitors, whatsoever they were. And all the other[107] affirmed the same. "That is," quoth he,[108] "yonder sorceress my brother's wife and other with her" (meaning the Queen).

At these words many of the other lords were greatly abashed that favored her. But the Lord Hastings was in his mind better content that it was moved by her[109] than by any other whom he loved better; albeit his heart somewhat grudged that he was not afore made of counsel in this mat-

---

101 require beg **102 mess** portion, serving **103 that compass and imagine** who contrive and plot **104 sore astonied** greatly astonished **105 musing much . . . meant** wondering a good deal whom the question was directed against **106 them** i.e., Hastings and Richard **107 other** others **108 he** i.e., Richard **109 moved by her** i.e., urged against the Queen

ter, as he was of the taking of her kindred[110] and of their putting to death, which were by his assent before devised to be beheaded at Pomfret this selfsame day; in which he was not ware that it was by other devised that he himself should be beheaded the same day at London. Then said the Protector: "Ye shall all see in what wise that sorceress, and that other witch of her counsel, Shore's wife, with their affinity,[111] have by their sorcery and witchcraft wasted my body." And therewith he plucked up his doublet sleeve to his elbow, upon his left arm, where he showed a wearish withered arm and small, as it was never other.[112]

Hereupon every man's mind sore misgave them, well perceiving that this matter was but a quarrel.[113] For they well wist that the Queen was too wise to go about any such folly. And also, if she would,[114] yet would she, of all folk least, make Shore's wife of her counsel whom of all women she most hated as that concubine whom the King her husband had most loved. And also no man was there present but well knew that his arm was ever such since his birth. Natheless,[115] the Lord Chamberlain (which from the death of King Edward kept Shore's wife, on whom he somewhat doted in the King's life, saving as it is said he that while forbare her of reverence toward the King or else of a certain kind of fidelity to his friend)[116] answered and said: "Certainly, my lord, if they have so heinously done, they be worthy heinous punishment."

"What?" quoth the Protector. "Thou servest me, I ween, with if's and with and's. I tell thee they have so done, and that I will make good on thy body, traitor!" And therewith, as in a great anger, he clapped his fist upon the board a great rap. At which token one cried "Treason!" without[117]

---

110 **taking of her kindred** arresting of her, the Queen's, kindred
111 **affinity** family ties through marriage   112 **a wearish . . . other** a small, shriveled, withered arm, no different from what it had always been   113 **quarrel** ground for complaint, excuse for quarreling   114 **if she would** even if she wanted to   115 **Natheless** nevertheless   116 **in the King's life . . . to his friend** i.e., while King Edward was still alive, except that it is said he did not keep her as his mistress during that time out of a sense of reverent duty toward the King or else out of a sense of personal loyalty to the King, who was his friend. (Hastings had too much delicacy to take Shore's wife away from King Edward.)
117 **without** outside of

the chamber. Therewith a door clapped,[118] and in come[119] there rushing men in harness,[120] as many as the chamber might hold. And anon the Protector said to the Lord Hastings: "I arrest thee, traitor!" "What, me, my lord?" quoth he. "Yea, thee, traitor!" quoth the Protector. And another let fly at the Lord Stanley, which shrunk at the stroke and fell under the table or else his head had been cleft to the teeth, for as shortly as he shrank yet ran the blood about his ears.

Then were they all quickly bestowed in divers chambers, except the Lord Chamberlain, whom the Protector bade speed and shrive him apace.[121] "For, by Saint Paul," quoth he, "I will not to dinner till I see thy head off!" It booted him[122] not to ask why, but heavily took a priest at adventure[123] and made a short shrift,[124] for a longer would not be suffered, the Protector made so much haste to dinner, which he might not go to until this were done for saving of his oath. So was he brought forth to the green beside the chapel within the Tower, and his head laid down upon a long log of timber and there stricken off. . . .

A marvelous case is it to hear either the warnings of that he should have voided or the tokens[125] of that he could not void. For the self[126] night next before his death, the Lord Stanley sent a trusty messenger unto him at midnight in all the haste, requiring him to rise and ride away with him, for he was disposed utterly no longer to bide, he had so fearful a dream; in which him thought that a boar with his tusks so razed[127] them both by the heads that the blood ran about both their shoulders. And forsomuch as the Protector gave the boar for his cognizance,[128] this dream made so fearful an impression in his heart that he was throughly determined no longer to tarry, but had his horse ready, if the Lord Hastings would go with him, to ride yet so far the same night that they should be out of danger ere day.

"Ha, good lord," quoth the Lord Hastings to this messen-

---

118 clapped briskly opened with a bang **119 come** came **120 harness** armor **121 speed and shrive him apace** hurry up and make his confession quickly **122 booted him** availed him **123 heavily . . . at adventure** sadly he chose a priest at random **124 shrift** confession **125 tokens** signs, prophecies **126 self** very **127 razed** cut, wounded **128 gave the boar for his cognizance** displayed the boar as his badge on his coat of arms

ger, "leaneth my lord thy master so much to such trifles and hath such faith in dreams, which either his own fear fantasieth or do rise in the night's rest by reason of his day's thought? Tell him it is plain witchcraft to believe in such dreams, which if they were tokens of things to come, why thinketh he not that we might be as likely to make them true by our going, if we were caught and brought back, as friends fail fliers;[129] for then had the boar a cause likely to raze us with his tusks, as folk that fled for some falsehood. Wherefore, either is there peril, or none there is indeed; or, if any be, it is rather in going than biding.[130] And in case we should needs fall in peril one way or other, yet had I rather that men should see that it were by other men's falsehood than think it were either by our own fault or faint heart. And therefore go to thy master, man, and commend me to him, and pray him be merry and have no fear, for I ensure him I am as sure of the man that he wotteth of as I am of mine own hand." "God send grace, sir," quoth the messenger, and went his way.

Certain is it also that, in riding towards the Tower the same morning in which he was beheaded, his horse twice or thrice stumbled with him, almost to the falling. Which thing, albeit each man wot well daily happeneth to them to whom no such mischance is toward,[131] yet hath it been of an old rite and custom observed as a token oftentimes notably foregoing some great misfortune. Now this that followeth was no warning but an envious scorn.[132] The same morning, ere he was up, came a knight unto him, as it were of courtesy, to accompany him to the Council, but of truth sent by the Protector to haste him thitherwards, with whom he was of secret confederacy in that purpose—a mean[133] man at that time, and now of great authority.

This knight, I say, when it happened the Lord Chamberlain by the way to stay[134] his horse and commune awhile with a priest whom he met in the Tower Street, brake his tale[135] and said merrily to him: "What, my lord, I pray you, come on. Whereto talk you so long with that priest? You

---

129 **friends fail fliers** friends desert those who flee   130 **biding** staying   131 **toward** impending   132 **envious scorn** malicious mockery   133 **mean** of low station   134 **stay** stop   135 **brake his tale** interrupted

have no need of a priest yet." And therewith he laughed upon him, as though he would say, "Ye shall have soon." But so little wist the tother what he meant, and so little mistrusted, that he was never merrier nor never so full of good hope in his life. . . .

Upon the very Tower Wharf, so near the place where his head was off soon after, there met he with one Hastings, a pursuivant[136] of his own name. And at their meeting in that place, he was put in remembrance of another time in which it had happened them before to meet in like manner together in the same place. At which other time the Lord Chamberlain had been accused unto King Edward by the Lord Rivers, the Queen's brother, in such wise as he was for the while (but it lasted not long) far fallen into the King's indignation[137] and stood in great fear of himself.[138] And forsomuch as he now met this pursuivant in the same place, that jeopardy so well passed, it gave him great pleasure to talk with him thereof, with whom he had before talked thereof in the same place, while he was therein.[139]

And therefore he said: "Ha, Hastings, art thou remembered when I met thee here once with an heavy heart?" "Yea, my lord," quoth he, "that remember I well, and thanked be God they gat no good nor you no harm thereby." "Thou wouldst say so," quoth he, "if thou knewest as much as I know, which few know else as yet, and more shall shortly." That meant he by[140] the lords of the Queen's kindred, that were taken before and should that day be beheaded at Pomfret, which he well wist but nothing ware[141] that the ax hung over his own head. "In faith, man," quoth he, "I was never so sorry, nor never stood in so great dread in my life, as I did when thou and I met here. And lo, how the world is turned! Now stand mine enemies in the danger, as thou mayst hap to hear more hereafter, and I never in my life so merry nor never in so great surety."

O good God, the blindness of our mortal nature! When he most feared, he was in good surety; when he reckoned himself surest, he lost his life, and that within two hours after.

---

136 pursuivant royal messenger with power to serve summonses
137 indignation displeasure   **138 of himself** for his life   **139 therein** i.e.,
in that jeopardy   **140 That meant he by** by that he meant   **141 nothing**
ware was not at all aware

Thus ended this honorable man, a good knight and a gentle, of great authority with his prince, of living somewhat dissolute, plain and open to his enemy and secret to his friend, easy to beguile, as he that of good heart and courage forestudied no perils, a loving man and passing well[142] beloved, very faithful and trusty enough, trusting too much. Now flew the fame[143] of this lord's death swiftly through the city, and so forth further about, like a wind in every man's ear. But the Protector, immediately after dinner, intending to set some color[144] upon the matter, sent in all the haste for many substantial men[145] out of the city into the Tower.

Now, at their coming, himself with the Duke of Buckingham stood harnessed in old ill-faring briganders,[146] such as no man should ween that they would vouchsafe[147] to have put upon their backs except that some sudden necessity had constrained them. And then the Protector showed them that the Lord Chamberlain, and other of his conspiracy,[148] had contrived to have suddenly destroyed him and the Duke, there the same day in the Council. And what they intended further was as yet not well known. Of which their treason he never had knowledge before ten of the clock the same forenoon, which sudden fear drave them to put on for their defense such harness[149] as came next to hand. And so had God holpen them that the mischief turned upon them that would have done it. And this he required[150] them to report.

Every man answered him fair, as though no man mistrusted the matter, which of truth no man believed. Yet for the further appeasing of the people's minds, he sent immediately after dinner in all the haste one herald-of-arms with a proclamation to be made through the city in the King's name containing that the Lord Hastings, with divers other of his traitorous purpose, had before conspired the same day to have slain the Lord Protector and the Duke of Buckingham sitting in the Council and after to have taken upon them to rule the King and the realm at their pleasure. . . .

---

142 **passing well** surpassingly   143 **fame** rumor   144 **color** excuse, pretense of legitimacy   145 **substantial men** men of property   146 **ill-faring briganders** armor in bad condition   147 **vouchsafe** consent, deign   148 **other of his conspiracy** others in conspiracy with him   149 **harness** armor   150 **required** asked, urged

The means whereby: namely, his evil company, sinister procuring, and ungracious example, as well in many other things as in the vicious living and inordinate abusion of his body, both with many other and also specially with Shore's wife, which was one also of his most secret counsel in this most heinous treason, with whom he lay nightly and namely[151] the night last past next before his death. So that it was the less marvel if ungracious living brought him to an unhappy ending. . . .

Now was this proclamation made within two hours after that he was beheaded, and it was so curiously indited[152] and so fair written in parchment, in so well a set hand and therewith of itself so long a process,[153] that every child might well perceive that it was prepared before. For all the time between his death and the proclaiming could scant have sufficed unto the bare writing alone, all had it been but in paper[154] and scribbled forth in haste at adventure.[155]

[Shore's wife is forced to do public penance. The Queen's kindred are beheaded at Pomfret by order of Sir Richard Ratcliffe, declaring their innocence before dying. Richard's next project is to cast doubt on the legitimacy of the young King and his brother.]

But certain it is that Doctor Shaw was of counsel in the beginning, so far forth that they determined that he should first break[156] the matter in a sermon at Paul's Cross in which he should, by the authority of his preaching, incline the people to the Protector's ghostly[157] purpose. But now was all the labor and study in the device of some convenient pretext for which the people should be content to depose the Prince and accept the Protector for King. In which, divers things they devised. But the chief thing and the weightiest of all that invention rested in this: that they should allege bastardy, either in King Edward[158] himself or in his children or both, so that he[159] should seem disabled to

---

151 **namely** specifically   152 **curiously indited** skillfully inscribed
153 **process** narrative, discourse   154 **all had it been but in paper** even if it had been written on paper (rather than parchment)   155 **at adventure** at random, recklessly   156 **break** divulge   157 **ghostly** spiritual, i.e., diabolical   158 **Edward** i.e., Edward IV   159 **he** i.e., Edward IV

inherit the crown by[160] the Duke of York, and the Prince by him.

To lay[161] bastardy in King Edward sounded openly to the rebuke of the Protector's own mother, which was mother to them both, for in that point could be no other color but to pretend[162] that his own mother was an adulteress; which notwithstanding, to further this purpose he letted not.[163] But nevertheless he would that point should be less and more favorably handled,[164] not even fully plain and directly, but that the matter should be touched aslope,[165] craftily, as though men spared in that point to speak all the truth for fear of his displeasure. But the other point, concerning the bastardy that they devised to surmise[166] in King Edward's children, that would he should be openly declared and enforced to the uttermost.

[Holinshed provides some background on Edward IV's marriage relating to this issue of legitimacy, especially about his contract with Elizabeth Lucy. Doctor Shaw declares Edward's marriage with the Queen to have been unlawful because of this precontract. Besides, neither Edward IV nor Clarence is thought to bear any family resemblance to their father, the Duke of York, unlike Richard, who resembles his father closely.

At the Guildhall, on the following Tuesday, Buckingham addresses the Mayor, aldermen, and commoners on the subject of Edward IV's insatiable lust.]

"For no woman was there anywhere, young or old, rich or poor, whom he set his eye upon, in whom he anything liked, either person or favor, speech, pace, or countenance, but, without any fear of God or respect of his honor, murmur or grudge of the world, he would importunely pursue his appetite and have her, to the great destruction of many a good woman and great dolor to their husbands and their other friends, which, being honest people of themselves, so much regard the cleanness of their house, the chastity of their

---

160 **by** from 161 **lay** allege 162 **could be . . . pretend** there was nothing else for it but to allege 163 **letted not** did not hesitate 164 **he would . . . handled** wished that that point should be less plainly and more discreetly handled 165 **aslope** i.e., indirectly, gingerly 166 **devised to surmise** undertook to allege

wives and their children, that them were liefer to leese[167] all that they had besides than to have such a villainy done them. And all were it that,[168] with this and other importable[169] dealing, the realm was in every part annoyed, yet specially ye here, the citizens of this noble city, as well for that amongst you is most plenty of all such things as minister matter to such injuries, as for that you were nearest at hand, sith that near hereabouts was commonly his most abiding."[170]

[Buckingham dwells on the precontract to Elizabeth Lucy and on Richard's reluctance to have the matter of Edward IV's bastardy discussed openly because of Richard's "filial reverence to the Duchess his mother."]

When the Duke had said,[171] and looked[172] that the people, whom he hoped that the Mayor had framed[173] before, should, after this proposition made, have cried "King Richard, King Richard!" all was hushed and mute and not one word answered thereunto.

[By way of explanation, the Mayor offers the excuse that the people "had not been accustomed there to be spoken unto but by the Recorder." When the Recorder speaks to them, showing "everything as the Duke's words and no part his own," the people remain silent still.]

At these words the people began to whisper among themselves secretly, that the voice was neither loud nor distinct but, as it were, the sound of a swarm of bees; till, at the last, in the nether end of the hall, an ambushment[174] of the Duke's servants and Nesfield's,* and other belonging to the Protector, with some prentices and lads that thrust into the hall amongst the press,[175] began suddenly at men's

---

*Nesfield's Nathfields
167 them were liefer to leese they would rather lose   168 all were it that while it is certainly true that   169 importable unbearable, intolerable   170 as well for . . . abiding as much because among you are plentiful means to redress such injuries as because you have been especially vulnerable, living as you do in this area where he was usually dwelling close at hand   171 said finished talking   172 looked expected
173 framed prepared, fashioned to his purpose   174 ambushment surprise party, concealed group   175 press crowd, throng

backs to cry out as loud as their throats would give, "King Richard, King Richard!" and threw up their caps in token of joy. And they that stood before cast back their heads,[176] marveling thereof, but nothing they said. Now when the Duke and the Mayor saw this manner, they wisely turned it to their purpose and said it was a goodly cry and a joyful to hear every man with one voice, no man saying nay.

"Wherefore, friends," quoth the Duke, "sith we perceive it is all your whole minds to have this noble man for your king (whereof we shall make His Grace so effectual report that we doubt not but it shall redound unto your great weal and commodity),[177] we require ye that ye tomorrow go with us, and we with you, unto His Noble Grace to make our humble request unto him in manner before remembered." And therewith the lords came down,[178] and the company dissolved and departed, the more part all sad—some with glad semblance that were not very merry; and some of those that came thither with the Duke, not able to dissemble their sorrow, were fain[179] at his back to turn their face to the wall while the dolor of their hearts burst out of their eyes.

Then, on the morrow after, the Mayor, with all the aldermen and chief commoners of the city, in their best manner appareled, assembling themselves together, resorted unto Baynard's Castle, where the Protector lay.[180] To which place repaired also, according to their appointment,[181] the Duke of Buckingham and divers noblemen with him, besides many knights and other gentlemen. And thereupon the Duke sent word unto the Lord Protector of the being there of a great and honorable company to move[182] a great matter unto His Grace. Whereupon the Protector made difficulty[183] to come out unto them but if[184] he first knew some part of their errand, as though he doubted[185] and partly mistrusted the coming of such a number unto him so suddenly without any warning or knowledge whether they came for good or harm.

Then the Duke, when he had showed[186] this to the Mayor

---

176 cast back their heads turned their heads around   **177 weal and commodity** welfare and benefit   **178 came down** i.e., descended from the dais   **179 fain** obliged   **180 lay** resided   **181 appointment** agreement, purpose   **182 move** urge   **183 made difficulty** appeared to be reluctant, played hard to get   **184 but if** unless   **185 doubted** feared   **186 showed** revealed

and other that they might thereby see how little the Protector looked for this matter, they sent unto him by the messenger such loving message again and therewith so humbly besought him to vouchsafe that they might resort to his presence to propose[187] their intent, of which they would unto none other person any part disclose; that at the last he came forth of his chamber, and yet not down unto them, but stood above in a gallery over them, where they might see him and speak to him, as though he would not yet come too near them till he wist what they meant. And thereupon the Duke of Buckingham first made humble petition unto him, on the behalf of them all, that His Grace would pardon them and license them to propose unto His Grace the intent of their coming, without his displeasure, without which pardon obtained they durst not be bold to move him of that matter.[188]

In which, albeit they meant as much honor to His Grace as wealth to all the realm besides, yet were they not sure how His Grace would take it, whom they would in no wise offend. Then the Protector, as he was very gentle of himself,[189] and also longed sore to wit[190] what they meant, gave him leave to propose what him liked, verily trusting, for the good mind that he bare them all, none of them anything would intend unto himward wherewith[191] he ought to be grieved. When the Duke had this leave and pardon to speak, then waxed he bold to show him their intent and purpose, with all the causes moving them thereunto (as ye before have heard), and finally to beseech His Grace that it would like him, of his[192] accustomed goodness and zeal unto the realm, now with his eye of pity to behold the long-continued distress and decay of the same, and to set his gracious hands to redress and amendment thereof.

All which he might well do by taking upon him the crown and governance of this realm according to his right and title lawfully descended unto him; and, to the laud[193] of God,

---

187 propose put forward, propound   **188 move . . . matter** urge that matter to him   **189 very gentle of himself** i.e., graceful and yielding by nature. (This is, in indirect quotation, what Richard says of himself to Buckingham and the others.)   **190 longed sore to wit** longed greatly to know   **191 none . . . wherewith** none of them would have any intentions toward him with which   **192 that it . . . of his** that he would be pleased, out of his   **193 laud** praise

profit of the land, and unto His Noble Grace so much the more honor and less pain, in that never prince reigned upon any people that were so glad to live under his obeisance[194] as the people of this realm under his. When the Protector had heard the proposition he looked very strangely[195] thereat, and answered that all were it[196] that he partly knew the things by them alleged to be true, yet such entire love he bare unto King Edward and his children, and* so much more regarded his honor in other realms about[197] than the crown of any one (of which he was never desirous), that he could not find in his heart in this point to incline to their desire. For in all other nations, where the truth were not well known, it should peradventure be thought that it were his own ambitious mind and device to depose the Prince and take himself the crown. . . .

Upon this answer given, the Duke, by the Protector's license, a little round[198] as well with other noblemen about him as with the Mayor and Recorder of London. And after that, upon like pardon desired and obtained, he showed[199] aloud unto the Protector,* for a final conclusion, that the realm was appointed[200] King Edward's line should not any longer reign upon them, both for that[201] they had so far gone that it was now no surety to retreat as for that[202] they thought it for the weal universal to take that way, although[203] they had not yet begun it. Wherefore, if it would like His Grace to take the crown upon him, they would humbly beseech him thereunto. If he would give them a resolute answer to the contrary, which they would be loath to hear, then must they needs seek and should not fail to find some other nobleman that would. These words much moved the Protector, which else (as every man may wit)[204] would never of likelihood have inclined thereunto.

But when he saw there was none other way but that either

---

*and that that   *Protector protector, that

194 obeisance command, authority   195 looked very strangely i.e., acted coy, standoffish   196 all were it granted   197 regarded . . . about was concerned for his reputation in other neighboring countries   198 a little round whispered a little   199 showed demonstrated in speech   200 appointed resolved, determined (that)   201 for that because   202 as for that and also because   203 for the weal . . . although i.e., for the benefit of all to take the alternative of naming Richard, even if   204 wit know. (Said as indirect quotation of what Richard says about himself.)

he must take it or else he and his both go from it, he said unto the lords and commons: "Sith we perceive well that all the realm is so set . . . we be content and agree favorably to incline to your petition and request, and according to the same, here we take upon us the royal estate, preeminence, and kingdom of the two noble realms, England and France. . . ."

With this there was a great shout, crying "King Richard, King Richard!" And then the lords went up to the King (for so he was from that time called) and the people departed.

[THE REIGN OF] RICHARD THE THIRD

[Richard comes to the Great Hall at Westminster on July 6, 1483, with his wife, Queen Anne, whom he married in 1472, and is crowned.]

King Richard, after his coronation, taking his way to Gloucester to visit in his new honor the town of which he bare the name of old,* devised as he rode to fulfill the thing which he before had intended. And forsomuch as his mind gave him[205] that, his nephews living, men would not reckon that he could have right to the realm, he thought therefore without delay to rid them, as though the killing of his kinsmen could amend his cause and make him a kindly[206] king. Whereupon he sent one John Greene, whom he specially trusted, unto Sir Robert Brackenbury, constable of the Tower, with a letter and credence[207] also that the same Sir Robert should in any wise put the two children to death.

This John Greene did his errand unto Brackenbury, kneeling before[208] Our Lady in the Tower, who plainly answered that he would never put them to death to die therefor. With which answer John Greene, returning, recounted the same to King Richard at Warwick, yet in his way.[209] Wherewith he took such displeasure and thought[210] that the

---

*of old of his old
205 forsomuch . . . gave him forasmuch as he feared 206 kindly rightful 207 letter and credence letter of authorization 208 kneeling before i.e., kneeling before and praying to an image of 209 yet in his way still on his journey 210 thought vexation

same night he said unto a secret page of his: "Ah, whom shall a man trust? Those that I have brought up myself, those that I had weened would most surely serve me, even those fail me and at my commandment will do nothing for me." "Sir," quoth his page, "there lieth one on your pallet without[211] that, I dare well say, to do Your Grace pleasure the thing were right hard that he would refuse." Meaning this by[212] Sir James Tyrrel, which was a man of right goodly personage, and for nature's gifts worthy to have served a much better prince if he had well served God and by grace obtained as much truth and good will as he had strength and wit.

The man had an high heart[213] and sore longed upward,[214] not rising yet so fast as he had hoped, being hindered and kept under by the means of Sir Richard Ratcliffe and Sir William Catesby, which, longing for no more partners of the prince's favor and namely[215] not for him whose pride they wist would bear no peer,[216] kept him by secret drifts[217] out of all secret trust; which thing this page well had marked and known. Wherefore, this occasion offered, of very special friendship he took his time to put him forward[218] and by such wise do him good that all the enemies he had (except the devil) could never have done him so much hurt. For upon this page's words King Richard arose (for this communication had he sitting at the draft,[219] a convenient carpet for such a counsel) and came out into the pallet chamber,[220] on which he found in bed Sir James and Sir Thomas Tyrrel,* of person like and brethren of blood but nothing of kin in conditions.[221]

Then said the King merrily to them: "What, sirs, be ye in bed so soon?" And calling up Sir James brake to him secretly his mind in this mischievous matter, in which he found him nothing strange.[222] Wherefore on the morrow he

*Tyrrel Tirrels

211 there lieth . . . without there is one of your followers lying outside the room on his straw bed   212 this by by this   213 an high heart an ambitious spirit   214 sore longed upward longed greatly for promotion   215 namely especially   216 bear no peer tolerate no equal   217 drifts devices, schemes   218 of very . . . forward out of special friendship (for Tyrrel) the page took the opportunity to put forward Tyrrel's name   219 draft privy   220 pallet chamber anteroom in which attendants slept on straw beds, keeping guard   221 conditions personal qualities   222 nothing strange not at all reluctant

sent him to Brackenbury with a letter by which he was commanded to deliver Sir James all the keys of the Tower for one night, to the end he might there accomplish the King's pleasure in such things as he had given him commandment. After which letter delivered and the keys received, Sir James appointed the night next ensuing to destroy them,[223] devising before and preparing the means. The Prince, as soon as the Protector left that name and took himself as King, had it showed unto him that he should not reign but his uncle should have the crown. At which word the Prince, sore abashed, began to sigh, and said, "Alas, I would my uncle would let me have my life yet, though I leese my kingdom."

Then he that told him the tale[224] used him with good words and put him in the best comfort he could. But forthwith was the Prince and his brother both shut up and all other removed from them, only one (called Black Will or William Slaughter) excepted, set to serve them and see them sure.[225] After which time the Prince never tied his points[226] nor aught raught of[227] himself; but, with that young babe his brother, lingered with thought[228] and heaviness until this traitorous death delivered them of that wretchedness. For Sir James Tyrrel devised that they should be murdered in their beds, to the execution whereof he appointed Miles Forrest, one of the four that kept[229] them, a fellow fleshed in murder before time.[230] To him he joined one John Dighton, his own horsekeeper, a big, broad, square, and strong knave.

Then, all the other being removed from them, this Miles Forrest and John Dighton, about midnight, the silly[231] children lying in their beds, came into the chamber and, suddenly lapping them up among the clothes,[232] so to-bewrapped them[233] and entangled them, keeping down by force the featherbed and pillows hard unto their mouths, that, within

---

223 **them** i.e., the two young princes 224 **the tale** i.e., the news that Richard had assumed the kingship 225 **see them sure** make sure they didn't escape 226 **points** laces for fastening clothing. (The Prince neglected his appearance.) 227 **aught raught of** took any care of 228 **thought** grief 229 **kept** guarded 230 **fleshed . . . time** initiated into murder already 231 **silly** innocent 232 **clothes** bedclothes 233 **to-bewrapped them** wrapped them entirely

a while, smothered and stifled, their breath failing, they gave up to God their innocent souls into the joys of heaven, leaving to the tormentors[234] their bodies dead in the bed. Which after that the wretches perceived, first by the struggling with the pains of death and after long lying still, to be thoroughly dead, they laid their bodies naked out upon the bed and fetched Sir James to see them; which, upon the sight of them, caused those murderers to bury them at the stair foot, meetly[235] deep in the ground under a great heap of stones.

Then rode Sir James in great haste to King Richard and showed him all the manner of the murder; who gave him great thanks and (as some say) there made him knight. But he allowed not[236] (as I have heard) the burying in so vile a corner, saying that he would have them buried in a better place because they were a king's sons. Lo, the honorable courage[237] of a king! Whereupon they say that a priest of Sir Robert Brackenbury's took up the bodies again and secretly interred them in such place as, by the occasion of his death which only knew it, could never since come to light. Very truth is it, and well known, that at such time as Sir James Tyrrel was in the Tower, for treason committed against the most famous prince King Henry the Seventh, both Dighton and he were examined and confessed the murder in manner above written; but whither the bodies were removed they could nothing tell.

[Richard never has a quiet moment, haunted by his nephews' murder, suspecting enemies everywhere. He is troubled by fearful dreams. And indeed the Duke of Buckingham conspires against him, having been disappointed of his hopes of receiving the Earl of Hereford's lands and now repenting his part in Richard's evil schemes.

The Bishop of Ely, John Morton, goes to join the Earl of Richmond in Flanders. The Countess of Richmond, the Earl's mother, and Queen Elizabeth, widow of Edward IV, are urged to endorse a plan to unite the houses of Lancaster and York by marrying the young Earl to Elizabeth's daughter (also named Elizabeth). The Countess com-

---

234 tormentors executioners **235 meetly** suitably **236 allowed not** did not approve **237 courage** spirit. (Said ironically.)

missions Sir Christopher Urswick, a priest, to go to the Earl of Richmond (now in Brittany) with this same proposal. Richmond, thus fortified by alliance, prepares for war against Richard. Forces loyal to him gather strength in England. Richard meanwhile marches against Buckingham, who is taken and beheaded on All Souls' Day, 1483. Richmond sails in October, landing in Dorset, but returns to Brittany. Richard is troubled by a prophecy that he will not live long once he has seen Rougemont (punning on Richmond), and by Lord Stanley's presumed loyalty to Richmond since his wife is Richmond's mother. Richard takes vengeance on the deviser of a rhyme: "The Cat, the Rat, and Lovell our dog / Rule all England under an hog." Richard makes an attempt to be reconciled to Queen Elizabeth so that he may marry her daughter (his niece) if his present queen, Anne, were to die. Queen Elizabeth accedes to his messengers' persuasions and urges her son the Marquess to leave Richmond—such is "the inconstancy of this woman." Richard spreads a rumor that Anne his queen is dead, and she does in fact die in 1485.

Richmond returns to England again in August 1485 from Harfleur, landing at Milford Haven in Wales and marching toward Shrewsbury. Richard takes Lord Stanley's son George into custody as a pledge of his father's loyalty. The climactic battle takes place at Bosworth Field. The night before the battle is a terrifying one for Richard.]

The fame[238] went that he had the same night a dreadful and terrible dream, for it seemed to him, being asleep, that he did see divers images like terrible devils which pulled and haled[239] him, not suffering him to take any quiet or rest. The which strange vision not so suddenly strake[240] his heart with a sudden fear but it stuffed his head and troubled his mind with many busy and dreadful imaginations. For incontinent[241] after, his heart being almost damped, he prognosticated before the doubtful chance[242] of the battle to come, not using the alacrity and mirth of mind and countenance as he

---

238 fame rumor **239 haled** tugged **240 strake** struck **241 incontinent** immediately **242 prognosticated . . . chance** predicted the uncertain outcome

was accustomed to do before he came toward the battle. And lest that it might be suspected that he was abashed for fear of his enemies, and for that cause looked so piteously, he recited and declared to his familiar friends in the morning his wonderful vision and fearful dream.

But I think this was no dream but a punction[243] and prick of his sinful conscience; for the conscience is so much more charged and aggrieved as the offense is greater and more heinous in degree.

[Richard, on the day of battle itself, orders the disposition of his troops. His army is more than twice the size of Richmond's. In his oration to his troops, Richard confesses his wickedness in obtaining the throne but stresses his penitence therefor. The enemy, he says, are "a company of traitors, thieves, outlaws, and runagates"[244] who will "destroy us, our wives, and children," and who are led by a "Welsh milksop." Richard's followers profess to be encouraged, but in fact their loyalty is only superficial. The Earl of Richmond, meanwhile, comforts his men with his graciousness and courage. His yellow hair is "like the burnished gold," his eyes, "gray, shining, and quick," his answers to questions ready and prompt. He bids his men to fight in God's cause against soldiers who obey only out of fear.

The climax of the battle itself centers on the fight between the two leaders.]

While the two forewards[245] thus mortally fought, each intending to vanquish and convince[246] the other, King Richard was admonished by his explorators and espials[247] that the Earl of Richmond, accompanied with a small number of men-of-arms, was not far off. And as he approached and marched toward him, he perfectly knew his personage by certain demonstrations and tokens which he had learned and known of others that were able to give him full information. Now, being inflamed with ire and vexed with outrageous malice, he put his spurs to his horse and rode out

---

243 **punction** puncturing   244 **runagates** fugitives   245 **forewards** vanguards   246 **convince** overthrow   247 **admonished . . . espials** warned by his scouts

of the side of the range of his battle,[248] leaving the vanguard fighting, and like a hungry lion ran with spear in rest[249] toward him. The Earl of Richmond perceived well the King furiously coming toward him, and because the whole hope of his wealth and purpose was to be determined by battle, he gladly proffered to encounter with him body to body and man to man.

King Richard set on so sharply at the first brunt[250] that he overthrew the Earl's standard and slew Sir William Brandon, his standard-bearer (which was father to Sir Charles Brandon, by King Henry the Eighth created Duke of Suffolk), and matched hand to hand with Sir John Cheyney, a man of great force and strength, which would have resisted him, but the said John was by him manfully overthrown. And so, he making open passage by dint of sword as he went forward, the Earl of Richmond withstood his violence and kept him at the sword's point, without advantage, longer than his companions either thought or judged;[251] which,[252] being almost in despair of victory, were suddenly recomforted by Sir William Stanley, which came to his succors with three thousand tall[253] men. At which very instant, King Richard's men were driven back and fled, and he himself, manfully fighting in the middle of his enemies, was slain; and, as he worthily had deserved, came to a bloody death as he had led a bloody life.

[The casualties in the battle include John, Duke of Norfolk, who had been warned from taking Richard's side in the battle by this rhyme written upon his gate: "Jack of Norfolk, be not too bold, / For Diccon thy master is bought and sold." Also dead are Walter, Lord Ferrers of Chartley, Sir Richard Ratcliffe, and Robert Brackenbury. Sir William Catesby is beheaded afterward. The story goes about that Richard might have escaped the battle, being provided with a swift horse, as the battle started to turn against him, but that he chose instead to stake everything on his chance of success.

Richmond gives thanks to God for a great victory and is

---

248 battle battalion   **249 with spear in rest** with his spear's base resting in its support, in the attack position   **250 brunt** attack   **251 judged** i.e., judged possible   **252 which** who, i.e., Richmond's troops   **253 tall** valiant

crowned by Lord Stanley with the crown that is found "amongst the spoil in the field." On January 18, 1486, Richmond, now King Henry VII, marries Elizabeth of York.]

The second edition of Raphael Holinshed's *Chronicles* was published in 1587. This selection is based on that edition, Volume 3, folios 712–760.

Further Reading

Brooke, Nicholas. *"Richard III." Shakespeare's Early Trag-edies.* London: Methuen, 1968. Brooke argues that Shake-speare explores the contradiction between Richard's tragic assertion of his individual will and history's provi-dential pattern. For Brooke, Richard becomes a character of some sympathy: less a monster than an emblem, how-ever distorted, of human limitation and desire.

Campbell, Lily B. "The Tragical Doings of King Richard III." *Shakespeare's "Histories": Mirrors of Elizabethan Policy.* San Marino, Calif.: Huntington Library, 1947. Campbell argues that *Richard III* blurs conventional distinctions between tragedy and the history play, emphasizing both Richard's moral sins and his "offenses against the com-mon weal." Richard III was used in Elizabethan political controversy as "the archetype of Machiavellianism, his activities being made the pattern by which to interpret the doings of political aspirants," and this becomes for Campbell the key to the play's meaning.

Clemen, Wolfgang. *A Commentary on Shakespeare's "Rich-ard III,"* trans., Jean Bonheim. London: Methuen, 1968. Clemen provides a detailed scene-by-scene commentary on *Richard III*, integrating studies of style, character, conventions, staging, and influence in explicating the play.

Heilman, Robert B. "Satiety and Conscience: Aspects of *Richard III." Antioch Review* 24 (1964): 57–73. Rpt. in *Es-says in Shakespearean Criticism*, ed. James L. Calder-wood and Harold E. Toliver. Englewood Cliffs, N.J.: Prentice-Hall, 1970. Richard, according to Heilman, is an individual suffering from "a distemper of success," a "singular malaise of the summit." Richard is quickly sated with his successes, a satiety that "begets con-tempt" for his victims. While Shakespeare in his por-trayal of Richard falls short of the complex psychological realism of the later tragedies, he nonetheless succeeds in "giving a new hue to melodrama."

Hunter, Robert Grams. *"Richard III." Shakespeare and the Mystery of God's Judgments.* Athens, Ga.: Univ. of Georgia

Press, 1976. In *Richard III* Hunter finds Shakespeare first exploring "the tragic implications of a belief in providence." Is Richard's evil the result of divine permission? Is Richard, like Richmond, God's agent? Is there for Richard the possibility of attaining grace? Shakespeare does not attempt to resolve the theological issues he raises; indeed, Hunter argues, the play's power derives from the sustained mystery of God's judgment.

Jones, Emrys. "*Richard III:* A Tudor Climax." *The Origins of Shakespeare.* Oxford: Oxford Univ. Press, 1977. Jones explores Shakespeare's "inventiveness" in absorbing and combining classical, historical, and native literary models. The play, which begins as a conventional tragedy of fortune, gives way to an ending that prefigures and celebrates Elizabeth's reign, as Shakespeare "creates an occasion for national thanksgiving and communal prayer."

Krieger, Murray. "The Dark Generations of *Richard III.*" *The Play and Place of Criticism.* Baltimore: The Johns Hopkins Press, 1967. Krieger finds *Richard III* to be a world of "unrelieved ugliness." Richard is but "a fox among foxes," pretending to be a hypocrite as the others pretend to be decent. Richmond's triumph, however, transforms the world, purging it of the "spirit of usurpation and chaos" that Richard represents.

Miner, Madonne M. " 'Neither Mother, Wife, nor England's Queen.': The Roles of Women in *Richard III.*" In *The Woman's Part: Feminist Criticism of Shakespeare,* ed. Carolyn Ruth Swift Lenz, Gayle Greene, and Carol Thomas Neely. Urbana, Ill.: Univ. of Illinois Press, 1980. Though the women's roles in *Richard III* have generally not been considered by critics, Miner finds the importance of women to be signaled by the play's frequent metaphors of birth and pregnancy. The women, she finds, are not allowed to play effective, autonomous roles but function as a "currency of exchange between men." Nonetheless, she sees that the play traces the women's understanding of their situation as they move from strife to solidarity.

Neill, Michael. "Shakespeare's Halle of Mirrors: Play, Politics, and Psychology in *Richard III.*" *Shakespeare Studies* 8 (1975): 99–129. In the "ostentatious theatricality" of the play, Neill finds a political and psychological complexity that denies the neat providential design of Shakespeare's sources. England is seen as a "kingdom of mirror-plays and actor-shadows," and Richard's psyche as "at best a hall of mirrors, reflecting endlessly the insubstantial shadows of the lost self."

Ornstein, Robert. "*Richard III.*" *A Kingdom for a Stage: The Achievement of Shakespeare's History Plays.* Cambridge: Harvard Univ. Press, 1972. Ornstein focuses on an audience's pleasure in Richard's confident plotting. Though the play finally balances Richard's consummate control in gaining the throne with his subsequent loss of nerve, it does not dramatize the providential victory of virtue over vice because the play is concerned with Richard's failure rather than Richmond's success.

Ribner, Irving. *The English History Play in the Age of Shakespeare*, 1957. Rev. ed., enl., New York: Barnes and Noble, 1965, pp. 112–119. Ribner finds in *Richard III*'s structural indebtedness to the morality play evidence of Shakespeare's insistence on the role of providence in history. England becomes itself a morality hero torn between the forces of good and evil, and it ultimately "wins salvation" as Richmond achieves the throne.

Rossiter, A. P. "Angel with Horns: The Unity of *Richard III.*" *Angel with Horns and Other Shakespeare Lectures*, ed. Graham Storey. London: Longmans, Green; New York: Theatre Arts Books, 1961. Denying that the play is an orthodox demonstration of providential history, Rossiter argues that Shakespeare adopted a dialectical method of presentation, emphasizing ambiguity, irony, and above all, paradox. The play, he finds, is not a "moral history" presenting the certainties of the Tudor myth but a "comic history" reveling in the ambivalence and contradictions of history as it is lived.

Saccio, Peter. "Richard III: The Last Plantagenet." *Shakespeare's English Kings: History, Chronicle, and Drama.* New York: Oxford Univ. Press, 1977. Saccio examines the largely self-serving Tudor accounts of Richard's personality and reign that served as Shakespeare's sources as well as the evidence of modern historical research to provide a fascinating account both of the King and of the process of writing history.

Sher, Antony. *Year of the King: An Actor's Diary and Sketch-*

book. London: Chatto and Windus, 1985. Sher, who played the title role in the acclaimed Royal Shakespeare Company's production of 1984, provides an engaging account of an actor's struggle to come to terms with the part of Richard. The diary also provides insight into the process of creative interchange between director, designers, and actors as the production took shape.

Spivack, Bernard. *Shakespeare and the Allegory of Evil*, pp. 386–407. New York: Columbia Univ. Press, 1958. Richard's character is, for Spivack, a hybrid of naturalistic and allegorical elements. When Richard invokes his similarity to "the formal Vice, Iniquity," he signals his relation to the popular villain of the morality drama and establishes the moral universe of the play.

Wheeler, Richard. "History, Character, and Conscience in *Richard III*." *Comparative Drama* 5 (1971–1972): 302–321. Wheeler argues that Shakespeare presents Richard both as a scourge of God serving a divine purpose and as a highly self-conscious actor "who imposes the conditions of the stage on the real world." The providential structure of the play becomes an effort to contain the terror and fascination of the self-assertive Richard within a historical model that Shakespeare "can no longer quite believe and not yet afford to abandon."

WILLIAM SHAKESPEARE was born in Stratford-upon-Avon in April, 1564, and his birth is traditionally celebrated on April 23. The facts of his life, known from surviving documents, are sparse. He was one of eight children born to John Shakespeare, a merchant of some standing in his community. William probably went to the King's New School in Stratford, but he had no university education. In November 1582, at the age of eighteen, he married Anne Hathaway, eight years his senior, who was pregnant with their first child, Susanna. She was born on May 26, 1583. Twins, a boy, Hamnet (who would die at age eleven), and a girl, Judith, were born in 1585. By 1592 Shakespeare had gone to London, working as an actor and already known as a playwright. A rival dramatist, Robert Greene, referred to him as "an upstart crow, beautified with our feathers." Shakespeare became a principal shareholder and playwright of the successful acting troupe the Lord Chamberlain's men (later, under James I, called the King's men). In 1599 the Lord Chamberlain's men built and occupied the Globe Theatre in Southwark near the Thames River. Here many of Shakespeare's plays were performed by the most famous actors of his time, including Richard Burbage, Will Kempe, and Robert Armin. In addition to his 37 plays, Shakespeare had a hand in others, including *Sir Thomas More* and *The Two Noble Kinsmen*, and he wrote poems, including *Venus and Adonis* and *The Rape of Lucrece*. His 154 sonnets were published, probably without his authorization, in 1609. In 1611 or 1612 he gave up his lodgings in London and devoted more and more of his time to retirement in Stratford, though he continued writing such plays as *The Tempest* and *Henry VIII* until about 1613. He died on April 23, 1616, and was buried in Holy Trinity Church, Stratford. No collected edition of his plays was published during his lifetime, but in 1623 two members of his acting company, John Heminges and Henry Condell, published the great collection now called the First Folio.

Contributors

DAVID BEVINGTON, Phyllis Fay Horton Professor of Humanities at the University of Chicago, is editor of *The Complete Works of Shakespeare* (Scott, Foresman, 1980) and of *Medieval Drama* (Houghton Mifflin, 1975). His latest critical study is *Action Is Eloquence: Shakespeare's Language of Gesture* (Harvard University Press, 1984).

DAVID SCOTT KASTAN, Professor of English and Comparative Literature at Columbia University, is the author of *Shakespeare and the Shapes of Time* (University Press of New England, 1982).

JAMES HAMMERSMITH, Associate Professor of English at Auburn University, has published essays on various facets of Renaissance drama, including literary criticism, textual criticism, and printing history.

ROBERT KEAN TURNER, Professor of English at the University of Wisconsin–Milwaukee, is a general editor of the New Variorum Shakespeare (Modern Language Association of America) and a contributing editor to *The Dramatic Works in the Beaumont and Fletcher Canon* (Cambridge University Press, 1966–).

JAMES SHAPIRO, who coedited the bibliographies with David Scott Kastan, is Assistant Professor of English at Columbia University.

❖

JOSEPH PAPP, one of the most important forces in theater today, is the founder and producer of the New York Shakespeare Festival, America's largest and most prolific theatrical institution. Since 1954 Mr. Papp has produced or directed all but one of Shakespeare's plays—in Central Park, in schools, off and on Broadway, and at the Festival's permanent home, The Public Theater. He has also produced such award-winning plays and musical works as *Hair, A Chorus Line, Plenty,* and *The Mystery of Edwin Drood,* among many others.

THE COMPLETE WORKS OF WILLIAM SHAKESPEARE

Volume I

Love's Labor's Lost
The Comedy of Errors
The Two Gentlemen
of Verona
Henry VI, Parts One,
Two, and Three
Richard III

Volume II

The Taming of the Shrew
The Merchant of Venice
Romeo and Juliet
King John
A Midsummer Night's
Dream
Richard II
Much Ado about
Nothing

Volume III

Henry IV, Part One
Henry IV, Part Two
The Merry Wives of Windsor
Hamlet
As You Like It
Henry V

Volume IV

Julius Caesar
Twelfth Night
Troilus and Cressida
All's Well that
Ends Well
Measure for Measure
Othello

Volume V

King Lear
Macbeth
Antony and Cleopatra
Pericles
Cymbeline
Coriolanus

Volume VI

Timon of Athens
Titus Andronicus
The Tempest
The Winter's Tale
Henry VIII
The Complete Poems
and Sonnets